BUS 180 Business Information Tools

Indiana State University

Scott College of Business

| PEARSON COLLECTIONS |

PEARSON

Attention bookstores: For permission to return any unsold stock, contact us at pe-uscustomreturns@pearson.com

Pearson Learning Solutions, 501 Boylston Street, Suite 900, Boston, MA 02116

A Pearson Education Company
www.pearsoned.com

PEARSON

ISBN 10: 1323557717
ISBN 13: 9781323557716

Printed in the USA

Table of Contents

Working with an Operating System

Working with an Operating System

LEARNING OUTCOMES:

- You will manage the Windows 10 environment through the desktop and other components.
- You will organize files and folders using Windows 10 features and tools.

OBJECTIVES & SKILLS: After you read this chapter, you will be able to:

Windows 10 Fundamentals

OBJECTIVE 1: UNDERSTAND THE WINDOWS 10 INTERFACE
Pin an App to Start Menu, Create Start Menu Group, Rename Start Menu Group, Move Tile, Resize Tile, Pin an App to the Taskbar

OBJECTIVE 2: MANAGE AND USE THE DESKTOP AND COMPONENTS
Create Virtual Desktop; Minimize, Close, Restore Down, Maximize; Snap Windows

OBJECTIVE 3: USE WINDOWS 10 SEARCH FEATURES
Search Using Cortana, Manage Cortana Settings, Get Help

HANDS-ON EXERCISE 1:
Windows 10 Fundamentals

File Management

OBJECTIVE 4: USE FILE EXPLORER
Create Folders, Pin a Folder to Quick Access, Work with Files and Folders, Rename a Folder, Delete a Folder

OBJECTIVE 5: SELECT, COPY, AND MOVE MULTIPLE FILES AND FOLDERS
Copy a File, Move a Folder

OBJECTIVE 6: COMPRESS FILES AND FOLDERS
Compress a Folder, Extract Files from a Compressed Folder

HANDS-ON EXERCISE 2:
File Management

Windows System and Security Features

OBJECTIVE 7: WORK WITH SECURITY SETTINGS AND SOFTWARE
Use the Action Center, Modify Windows Defender Settings, Review File History Settings, Modify Windows Update Settings, Modify Firewall Settings

OBJECTIVE 8: WORK WITH ADMINISTRATIVE TOOLS
Use Systems Monitor, Use Disk Cleanup

HANDS-ON EXERCISE 3:
Windows System and Security Features

CASE STUDY | Cedar Grove Elementary School

Your good friend recently graduated with a degree in elementary education and now is excited to begin her first job as a fifth-grade teacher at Cedar Grove Elementary School. The school has a computer lab for all students as well as a computer system in each classroom. The school acquired the computers through a state technology grant so they are new models running Windows 10. Your friend's lesson plans must include a unit on operating system basics and an introduction to application software. Because you have a degree in computer information systems, she has called on you for assistance with the lesson plans.

You cannot assume that all students are exposed to computers at home, especially to those configured with Windows 10. Your material will need to include very basic instruction on Windows 10, along with a general overview of file management. Your friend must complete her lesson plans right away, so you are on a short timeline but are excited about helping students learn!

Getting Started with Microsoft®
Windows® 10

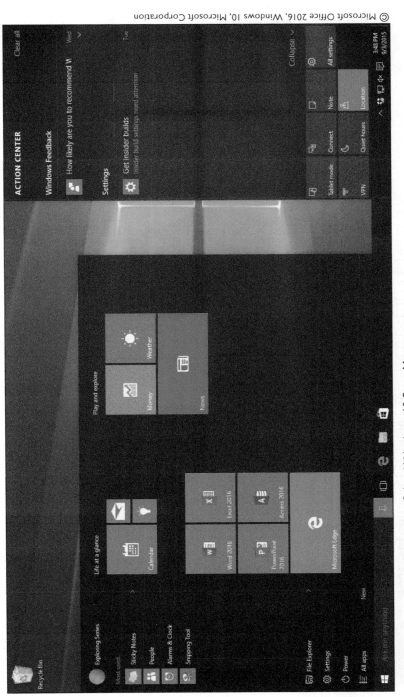

FIGURE 1 Cedar Grove Elementary School Windows 10 Start Menu

CASE STUDY | Cedar Grove Elementary School

Starting File	File to be Submitted
Blank Word document	**win01h3Windows10_LastFirst**

Working with an Operating System • Windows 10

3

Windows 10 Fundamentals

There are two types of software on your computer: application software and system software. Application software are programs you use for email, gaming, social networking, and digital photo management. Application software also includes productivity software such as word processing, spreadsheet, and presentation applications. As essential as these application programs may be to you for entertainment or for accomplishing a specific task, system software is the essential software that the computer needs. Without system software, your computer could not function. System software includes the operating system and utility programs, and helps to run application software, manage your files, and manage system resources and other computer activities.

In this section, you will learn how to work with the features of the Windows 10 operating system. In particular, you will learn how to set up a Microsoft account if you do not have one established already, and start and shut down Windows. You will also learn how to configure the Start menu and taskbar to manage programs and apps.

Understanding the Windows 10 Interface

Windows 10 is the latest version of Microsoft's operating system and is available for desktops, laptops, cell phones, and tablet computers. Windows 10 has made changes that facilitate computer use, both on touch and non-touch devices. Because you are likely to encounter Windows 10 on computers and mobile devices at school, work, and home, it is well worth your time to explore and learn how to use it, as well as its computer management and security features.

Sign In to a Microsoft Account

When you start your computer, Windows 10 opens to the Lock screen that displays an image (which you can personalize with your own image) and the date and time. Clicking on the Lock screen brings you to the sign in page where you log in using your Microsoft account username (email address) and password. To use any Microsoft services such as Outlook.com, Xbox Live®, OneDrive®, and Office Online, you need to create a free Microsoft account.

If you already have a OneDrive, Xbox Live, or Outlook.com account, use that account to sign in. If you do not have a Microsoft account, you will need to create one to use Windows 10. A Microsoft account gives you a consistent experience across any device you sign into with your Microsoft account. In addition, you get access to Office Online and OneDrive (with free cloud storage), and all your information syncs across all your devices.

To sign up for a Microsoft account, complete the following steps:

1. Open any Web browser, type signup.live.com as the URL, and then click Sign up now.
2. Fill out the form by typing your first and last name. Your user name will be an email address. You can use an existing email address, or you can get a new email address by clicking *Or get a new email address.*
3. Create a password that has at least 8 characters. To create a strong password, use a combination of upper and lowercase letters, at least one number and one other character (such as an asterisk or exclamation point).
4. Fill out the rest of the form, and then click Create account.

Access Sleep and Power Settings

To save battery life on your laptop, tablet, or smartphone, or for more energy efficiency, Windows will go to *sleep* after a pre-determined period of inactivity. Sleep is a power-saving state that puts your work and settings in memory and draws a small amount of power that allows your computer to resume full-power operation quickly.

To manage the Sleep settings, complete the following steps:

1. Click the Start icon or press the Windows key to open the Start menu.
2. Click Settings on the Start menu, click System, and then click Power & sleep.
3. Select the desired level of inactivity from either of the following options:
   - Screen: to determine when the Screen turns off on battery power or when plugged in
   - Sleep: to determine when the PC goes to sleep on battery power or when plugged in

Eventually, you will want to shut down Windows and turn off your computer. To do so, from the Start menu, click Power. Selecting Restart will turn off and immediately restart Windows. This is a "warm boot." To power down completely, click Power and then select Shut down.

Explore the Windows 10 Start Menu

After signing in, you should see the same screen configuration no matter what Windows 10 device you are using, because your Microsoft account stores your preferences and settings for your Start menu on the Internet. For instance, your laptop computer, your home computer, and even your Windows smartphone should look the same.

Initially, your computer displays the primary working area: the *desktop*. If you were used to working on a system running Windows 8, you will notice that there is not a Start screen and a desktop. Instead, the desktop is the primary working area of Windows 10, and the Windows 10 *Start menu* provides the main access to all programs and features on your computer.

There are three different ways to accomplish tasks in Windows 10:

- Use a mouse
- Touch the screen (on touch-enabled devices)
- Use keystrokes

The method you use depends on the type of device you are using and, largely, on your personal preferences. In this text, we will focus mainly on mouse and keystroke commands. If you are using a touch-screen device, you should refer to the new touch gestures shown in Figure 2. For instance, when an instruction in this text says to click a screen element, you would tap the screen element with your finger on a touch-screen device.

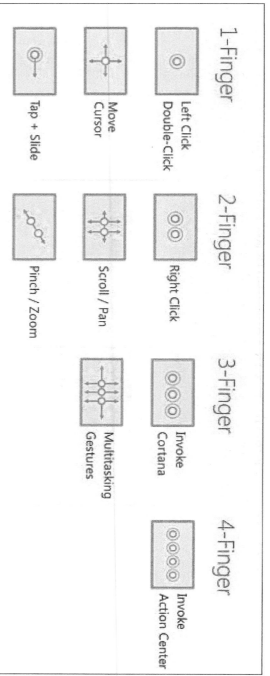

FIGURE 2 Touch Gestures in Windows 10

Precision Touchpad Overview, Windows 10 Overview Slideshow,
PowerPoint Online

Open the Start menu by clicking the Start icon in the bottom left corner of the desktop or by pressing the Windows key on the keyboard. The Start menu, as shown in Figure 3, has two areas. The right side has the same look as the metro (or modern) view first introduced in Windows 8 with block icons, called *tiles*. Tiles represent installed programs and Windows apps (such as Weather, Skype, and Money). Tiles can also represent files, folders, or other items related to your computer. If there are more tiles on the Start menu than displayed, use the scroll bar on the right. You can launch Windows 10 apps and programs by clicking or tapping a tile on the Start menu.

TIP: STICKY NOTE APP

Sticky Notes is a useful Windows accessory application. Use Sticky Notes as you would a paper sticky note, recording to-do lists, phone numbers, or anything else. Your notes display on the desktop. Sticky Notes is found in the Windows Accessories folder in All apps. Click New Note to add another note, click Delete Note to delete a note, and right-click a note to change the color.

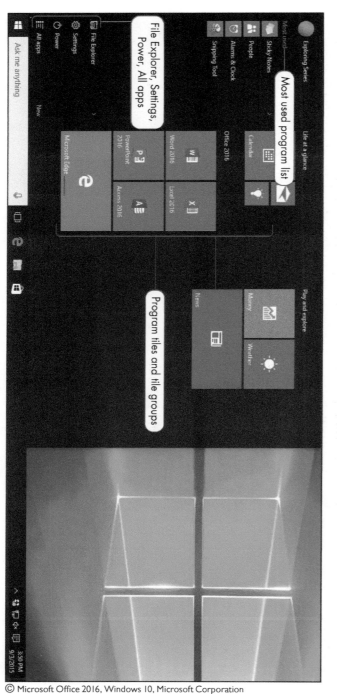

FIGURE 3 Windows 10 Start Menu

© Microsoft Office 2016, Windows 10, Microsoft Corporation

The left side of the Start menu provides access to File Explorer, Settings, and Power. These features are discussed later in this chapter. There is also a separate *Most used* section that contains a list of apps and programs you use every day. However, you can remove a program from the Most used list by right-clicking the icon and selecting *Don't show in this list*. Click *All apps* at the bottom of the left pane, and the left pane changes to display a list of all installed apps and programs on your computer, in alphabetical order.

Configure the Start Menu

STEP 1 ▶▶ You may want to customize the Start menu so you can use it most efficiently. It is easy to add and remove, resize, and move application tiles on the Start menu, as well as to group tiles, and name the groups. You can also display tiles to access folders or other areas of the computer that you use frequently. You **pin**, or add, a tile to the Start menu to make it easier to access the application.

To pin an application to the Start menu, complete the following steps:

1. Display the Start menu by clicking the Start icon or by pressing the Windows key on your keyboard.
2. Click All apps and find the application that you want to pin to the Start menu.
3. Right-click the app name and select Pin to Start. (You may also choose Pin to taskbar. The taskbar is discussed later in this chapter.)

A tile for the app displays on the Start menu. The new tile is added to the very end of your app tiles, so you may have to scroll down to find the tile you added. Once on the Start menu, the size of a tile can be modified.

To resize a tile on the Start menu, complete the following steps:

1. Right-click the tile and point to Resize.
2. Select from the list of available sizes: Small, Medium, Wide, or Large.

You may also have some tiles that you do not want on the Start menu. These might be programs or applications that appear on the Start menu by default, or tiles you added but now want to remove. Removing (or unpinning) an application is just as easy as adding one.

To unpin an application from the Start menu, complete the following steps:

1. Right-click the tile you want to remove from the Start menu.
2. Click Unpin from Start.

Tiles on the Start menu are organized in groups separated by a small amount of dividing space, as shown in Figure 3. You can easily move tiles from one group to another by clicking a tile and dragging it into another group. You can reorder groups by clicking the group name and dragging the group to its new location. You can also give any group of tiles a meaningful name.

To create a new group of tiles, complete the following steps:

1. Click and drag the first tile for the new group to the space above or below an existing tile group. An empty bar displays, indicating where the new group will be located.
2. Release the mouse button, and the tile will now be in its own new group.

To assign a new name to a group of tiles, complete the following steps:

1. Point near the top of the tile or group of tiles you want to name.
2. Click in the box that displays.
3. Type a new group name. Note, if a name exists, you can delete the existing name and then type a new name.

Explore the Taskbar

At the bottom of the Windows desktop is the *taskbar*. The taskbar is the horizontal bar that displays open application icons, the *Notification area*, the *search box*, and any pinned apps or programs. The Notification area, at the far right of the taskbar, includes the clock and a group of icons that relate to a status of a setting or program. The search box, located on the left side of the taskbar, can be used to search your computer for programs, folders and files saved on your computer, as well as to get results from the Web. The search box is also home to Cortana, the personal digital assistant. Cortana is discussed later in this chapter.

Every open program has a corresponding icon on the taskbar. You can move from one program to another by clicking the program's icon on the taskbar. Figure 4 shows two windows open on the desktop, with corresponding taskbar program icons. A blue line displays under the open program icons. Although several windows can be open at one time, only one is active. The active program icon is shaded with a lighter blue background. When you right-click a program icon, you open the *Jump List* (see Figure 4). A Jump List is a list of program-specific shortcuts to recently opened files, the program name, an option to pin or unpin an item, and a Close windows option.

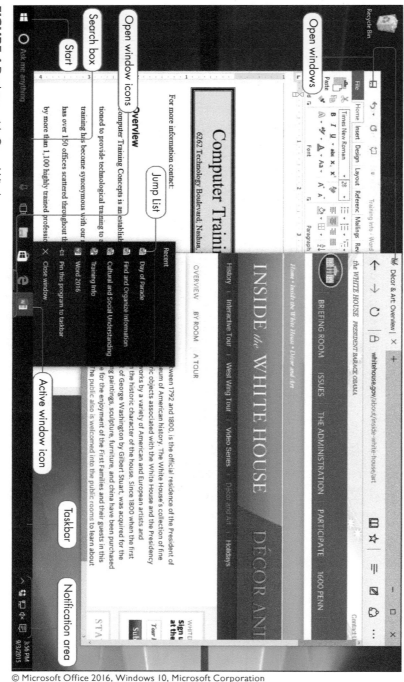

FIGURE 4 Desktop with Open Windows

© Microsoft Office 2016, Windows 10, Microsoft Corporation

Similar to pinning an app or program to the Start menu, you can place, or pin, icons of frequently used programs or websites on the taskbar for faster access. When you pin a program or website to the taskbar, its associated icon becomes a permanent part of the taskbar. You can then open the program or website by clicking its icon.

To pin to the taskbar a program that is not already open, complete the following steps:

1. Locate the program in All apps.
2. Right-click the program name.
3. Click Pin to taskbar.

To pin to the taskbar a program that is already open, complete the following steps:

1. Right-click the program icon on the taskbar.
2. Click Pin this program to taskbar.

You will find the Notification area (refer to Figure 4) on the right side of the taskbar. This area contains system icons, including Clock, Volume, OneDrive, and Action Center. The Notification area and what icons display in the Notification area are discussed later in this chapter.

Identify Desktop Components

The desktop in Windows 10 looks very much like the desktop in previous versions of Windows. On the desktop, *icons* represent links to programs, files, folders, or other items related to your computer (see Figure 5). Although the Start menu is meant to provide quick access to programs, files and folders you use most often, you can easily add and remove icons so that the desktop includes items that are important to you or that you access often.

The Recycle Bin icon displays by default on the Windows 10 desktop. The *Recycle Bin* is temporary storage for deleted files from the computer's hard drive or OneDrive. Files in the Recycle Bin are not permanently erased from the system until you right-click the Recycle Bin icon and select Empty Recycle Bin. Therefore, if you delete a file by mistake, it can be restored. The exception is if the file was from an external storage device such as a flash drive. When you delete files from an external storage device, they are permanently deleted.

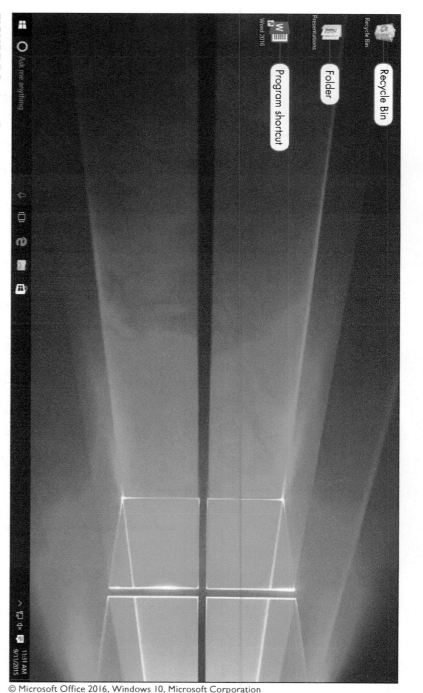

FIGURE 5 Desktop Components

© Microsoft Office 2016, Windows 10, Microsoft Corporation

Some icons that have a small arrow in the bottom-left corner are ***shortcuts*** that provide a link to programs. All other icons on the desktop are added when you save a file to the desktop. If you save files to the desktop, you should organize them in desktop folders so you can easily find related files.

To add a program or folder shortcut icon to the desktop, complete the following steps:

1. Right-click an empty area of the desktop, point to New, and then click Shortcut.
2. Click Browse and navigate to the folder that contains the program for which you wish to create a shortcut.
3. Click the program file and click OK.
4. Click Next. Type a name for the shortcut in the box
5. Click Finish to place the shortcut icon on your desktop.

You can also add a folder directly to the desktop by right-clicking an empty area of the desktop, pointing to New, and then selecting Folder. Or, if there is an existing folder you want to add to the desktop, open File Explorer, right-click the folder, choose Send to, and then select Desktop (create shortcut) from the menu.

To delete or rename icons on the desktop, complete one of the following steps:

- Right-click the icon you want to delete, and click Delete. Deleting a program shortcut icon does not remove or uninstall the program. You just remove the desktop shortcut to the program.
- Right-click the icon you want to rename, and click Rename. Type the new name and press Enter.

Customize the Desktop

For a little variety, you can customize the desktop with a different background color or theme. You can even include a slide show of favorite photos to display when your computer is idle. Customizing the desktop can be fun and creative. Windows 10 provides a wide selection of background and color choices.

The Personalization category in Settings gives you options to change the desktop background, lock screen image, or to select a different theme.

Managing and Using the Desktop and Components

The main purpose of the Start menu is to provide access to programs and apps. To launch an app or program from the Start menu, click the app tile. *Windows apps*, such as Weather, Sports, or Money, are programs that are displayed full screen without borders or many controls. This simpler design provides a viewing advantage on devices with smaller screens such as smartphones and tablets. Controls and settings are contained on app bars, such as the Address bar, which appear at the top or bottom of the opened app. Installed programs such as Microsoft Word or Google Chrome are applications that are more complex. They generally have multiple features and can perform multiple tasks.

Using the taskbar, you can move among open windows with ease, but Windows provides additional methods to switch easily between open programs and files. Windows makes it easy to move, resize, and close windows, as well as to arrange windows automatically, even snapping them quickly to the desktop borders.

Use Task View

STEP 2 It is quite possible that you will have more than one application or program window open at any time, and may need to quickly switch between the various open windows or want to see two or more open windows at the same time. *Task View* allows you to view all the tasks you are working on in one glance (see Figure 6). For example, you might have Microsoft Word, PowerPoint, and Edge all open because you are creating a presentation from your latest research paper and are doing some extra Internet research. To see all three windows at once, click the Task View icon next to the search box in the taskbar, and thumbnail previews of all open applications display. Click on any of the thumbnails to switch to that application.

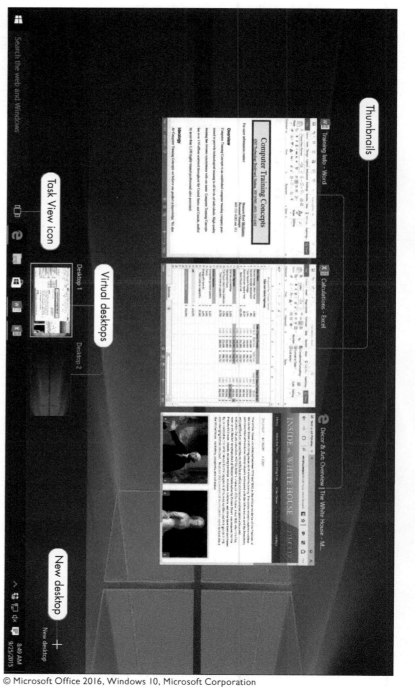

FIGURE 6 Task View

Thumbnails

Task View icon

Virtual desktops

Desktop 1

Desktop 2

New desktop

New desktop

Search the web and Windows

Training Info - Word

Calculations - Excel

Décor & Art Overview | The White House - M...

8:49 AM
9/25/2015

© Microsoft Office 2016, Windows 10, Microsoft Corporation

TIP: ALT+TAB

You can use the keyboard to cycle through all open windows. Press and hold Alt on the keyboard and repeatedly press Tab. Release Alt when the window that you want to display is selected.

Create a Virtual Desktop

Task View also enables you to create *virtual desktops* (refer to Figure 6). A virtual desktop is a way to organize and access groups of windows for different purposes. For example, when you do your schoolwork, you might have your school's learning management system (such as Blackboard or Desire to Learn), your school's email account, and MyITLab open. When you are not working on schoolwork, you might have several social media accounts open, perhaps a video game, and maybe Netflix or YouTube running. Using Task View, you can group these applications into virtual desktops, so that you can quickly switch between your "school" desktop and your "entertainment" desktop.

To create a new virtual desktop and move applications between desktops, complete the following steps:

1. Click Task View on the taskbar, and click New desktop in the lower right corner of your screen. You will then see a thumbnail preview of the new desktop (Desktop 2) alongside the current desktop (in this case, Desktop 1). Once the new desktop is created, you will need to populate it with applications by moving applications from one desktop to another.

2. Click Desktop 1, and then click Task View.

3. Drag a thumbnail of the application you want to move from Desktop 1 to Desktop 2. Alternatively, right-click a thumbnail preview of any open application in Desktop 1, point to Move to, and either select an existing virtual desktop or create a new desktop.

4. Repeat as needed to create a new virtual desktop.

To delete a virtual desktop, click Task View, point to the top right corner of the desktop thumbnail you want to delete, and click the Close button.

Identify Window Components

When you launch a folder, file, or application, the results are displayed in a window. All windows share common elements, including a title bar and controls, as shown in Figure 7. Although each window's contents vary, those common elements make it easy for you to manage windows so that you make the best use of your time and computer resources.

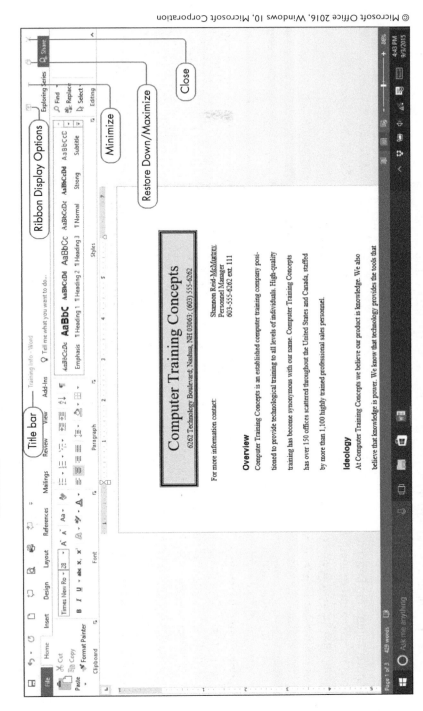

FIGURE 7 Common Window Components

The **title bar** is the long bar at the top of each window. The title bar always displays the name of the file and program displayed in the open window. Controls are found on the right side of the title bar. These controls enable you to manage the Ribbon display as well as to minimize, maximize (or restore down), or close any open window.

The Ribbon Display Options control enables you to hide the Ribbon, show only the Ribbon tabs, or to show the Ribbon tabs and commands all the time.

The Minimize control, represented by a horizontal line, when clicked hides a window from view, but does not close it. You can click on the taskbar icon to view the window again.

The next control shares two functions, depending on the current size of the window. When a window is full size, Restore Down, represented by two overlapping boxes, displays. When a window is open, but less than full size, Maximize, represented by a small box, displays. Clicking Restore Down returns a window to the size it was before the window was maximized; clicking Maximize brings a window to full size. You can also maximize or restore down a window by double-clicking the title bar of the open window.

The Close control, represented by an X, when clicked closes a window. When you close a window, you remove the file or program from the computer's random access memory (RAM). RAM is temporary (or volatile) storage, meaning files stored in RAM are not permanently saved. To save a file so you can access it later, the file must be saved to a permanent storage device such as the computer's hard drive or a flash drive, or to

OneDrive or other Web-based storage. If you have not saved a file, or any changes that you have made to a saved file that you are closing, Windows 10 will prompt you to save it.

Snap, Move, and Resize Windows

Multitasking involves working with multiple open windows at the same time, and this often requires moving or resizing windows so you can see each window. If multiple windows are open, you will need to know how to switch between windows and how to rearrange them. Windows 7 introduced "snapping" windows—displaying two windows side by side by snapping them to the left and right sides of the screen.

Windows 10 goes a bit further with Snap Assist, giving you more snapping options. For example, once you snap one window to either side of the display, thumbnails of all other open windows display (Figure 8) giving you the option of easily selecting which window(s) to snap alongside it.

To use Snap Assist, complete the following steps:

1. Snap one window to either side of the screen.
   Thumbnails of all other open windows display on the open portion of the screen.

2. Click the thumbnail you want to snap, or click in a blank area if you do not want to snap any of the choices. The selected window will snap into place, filling the open screen area.

3. Press the Windows key plus an arrow key once windows are snapped to either side of the screen to snap windows into corners. You can snap two, three, or four windows using this technique. Alternatively, you can drag a window to the corner of the screen.

Instead of snapping, there might be occasions when you want to work with multiple files that are more freely positioned, without snapping them to the edges. In these instances, you can restore down a window, modify the size, and drag the smaller window to any location on the screen.

To move or resize a window, you must first click Restore Down and then complete one of the following steps:

- Click and drag the title bar to move a window.

- Point to the border of a window you want to resize, until the pointer becomes a double-headed arrow. Click and drag the edge of a window to make the window larger or smaller. If the pointer is on a corner of the window, forming a diagonal double-headed arrow, the height and width of the window will resize at the same time.

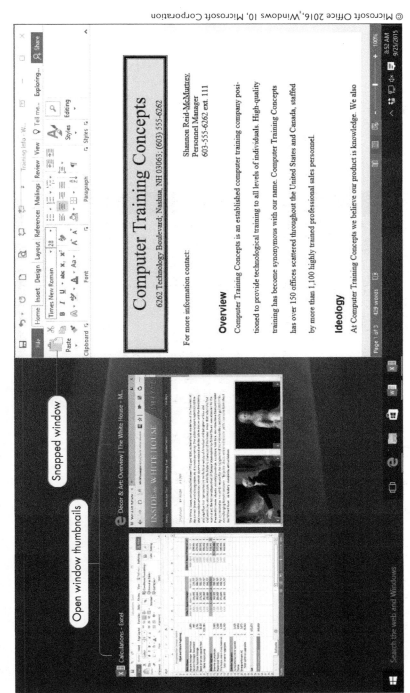

FIGURE 8 Snap Assist

You might prefer to arrange your windows automatically in a cascading fashion, vertically stacked, or next to each other. In that case, right-click an empty part of the taskbar. Then, click Cascade windows, Show windows stacked, or Show windows side by side.

Using Windows 10 Search Features

The new design of Windows 10 makes it easy to organize and find the most used programs, files and folders on either the Start menu, taskbar, or desktop. However, there will always be situations that require you to find a feature or file that you do not often use, and are not certain of its location, or you may need to find information on the Web. In those cases, you will need to use Windows 10 search features.

Use the Search Box

STEP 4 ≫ To the right of the Start button is the search box. You can use this search feature to search the Web and to search your "stuff" in Windows. When you begin typing into the search box, suggested results begin to display with a list of applications, folders, and documents, as well as Web resources that relate to the search terms you have entered (see Figure 9).

FIGURE 9 The Search Box

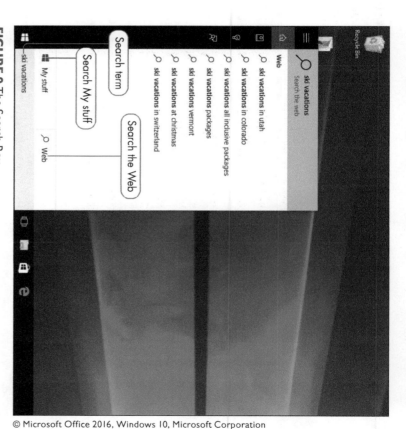

© Microsoft Office 2016, Windows 10, Microsoft Corporation

Use Cortana

If you have logged into Windows with your Microsoft account, you can use **Cortana**, Microsoft's personal assistant. Cortana is integrated into the search box and can assist you with reminders, calendar tasks, and can even tell jokes. You must initiate Cortana first, by giving her your name, and allowing her access to your information. Then, if your PC is equipped with a microphone, you begin talking to Cortana by saying, "Hey, Cortana." If no microphone is available, you can type all your questions.

Get Help

STEP 5

No longer do you have to go to a separate location on your computer, or use a different app, to get help. Cortana and the search box are your primary resources for help and support for Windows and other Microsoft related questions. Just type into the search box, or ask Cortana, and whether the answer is found in a file, an app, on the Web, or somewhere else, a list of possible results will display. Search results may also display how-to information and videos from Microsoft. You can even type the name of an app to open it right away. Finally, Cortana can help you with routine tasks such as turning on Airplane mode, just ask her!

Manage the Cortana Notebook and Settings

The more you use Cortana, the more she adapts to your personal needs and routines. When you initiate Cortana, you agree to let her collect and use some personal information that she has obtained from data on your PC (such as your location, contacts, info from email, browser history, search history, and calendar details). Once you set up Cortana, your data and information is managed in the Notebook. You can modify what Cortana remembers (or turn Cortana off altogether) in the Notebook. The Notebook contains categories that have been added by default, such as Eat & Drink, Events, Finance, and Getting around (see Figure 10).

To view or modify what is in the Notebook, complete the following steps:

1. Click the search box, and then click Notebook from the menu on the left.
2. Click any category to change a setting or add more information to the Notebook.

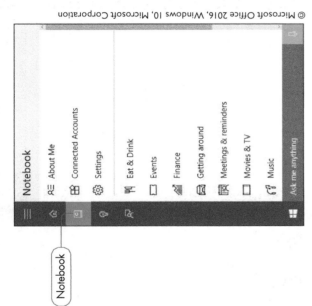

© Microsoft Office 2016, Windows 10, Microsoft Corporation

FIGURE 10 Modifying the Cortana Notebook

Once you have modified the settings, and you launch Cortana, the Home page shows a daily glance that reflects your personal settings such as the weather in your location, the scores of your favorite sports teams, your calendar events, and even how much time it will take to get to work or school based on current traffic.

You can modify other items such as Reminders, Places, and Music directly from the Cortana menu (see Figure 11).

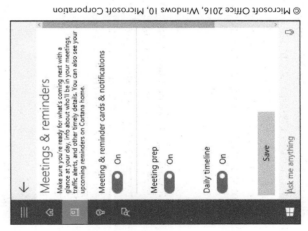

© Microsoft Office 2016, Windows 10, Microsoft Corporation

FIGURE 11 Cortana Notebook Menu Item

Quick Concepts

1. Describe the features on the Start menu, and explain the various ways in which the Start menu can be customized.

2. Explain what a virtual desktop is, and give an example of how you would use virtual desktops for school, work, or entertainment.

3. Review some of the features Cortana offers, and give some specific examples of modifications you would make in the Cortana Notebook to reflect your personal needs.

4. What features can you use to get help and support on Windows 10?

Hands-On Exercise

1 Windows 10 Fundamentals

Skills covered: Pin an App to Start Menu • Create Start Menu Group • Rename Start Menu Group • Move Tile • Resize Tile • Pin an App to the Taskbar • Create Virtual Desktop • Minimize, Close, Restore Down, Maximize • Snap Windows • Search Using Cortana • Manage Cortana Settings • Get Help

Tomorrow, you will meet with the Cedar Grove class to present an introduction to Windows 10. You plan to lead the students through a few basics of working with the operating system, including managing the Start menu and navigating among different open windows. Above all, you want to keep it simple so that you encourage class enthusiasm.

STEP 1 » CONFIGURE THE START MENU AND EXPLORE THE TASKBAR

You want to emphasize the importance of the Start menu as the location starting point for all Windows 10 apps and programs. Students will practice launching, managing, and closing Windows 10 apps and programs. Students will modify the Start menu by creating a new group and moving a tile into the group. Lastly, students will add program icons to the taskbar. Refer to Figure 12 as you complete Step 1.

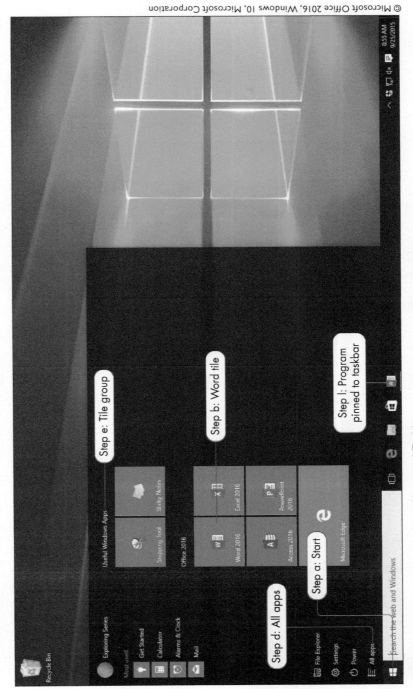

© Microsoft Office 2016, Windows 10, Microsoft Corporation

FIGURE 12 Customizing the Start Menu and Taskbar

a. Click **Start** on the taskbar (or alternatively, press the Windows key on the keyboard).

The Start menu displays.

b. Click **Word 2016** on the Start menu, and click **Blank document**.

Hands-On Exercise 1

19

c. Click **File**, select **Save As**, and then click **Browse**. Navigate to the location of your homework files. Click in the **File name box** and type **win01h1Windows10_LastFirst**, replacing LastFirst with your own last name and first name in the File name box. Click **Save** to save the document.

When you save files, use your last and first names. For example, as the Windows 10 author, I would name my document "win01h1Windows10_PoatsyMaryAnne."

You will capture screenshots of your progress in this exercise and paste them into this document to submit to your instructor.

d. Click the **Start menu**, click **All apps**, and then scroll down to locate the Windows Accessories folder. Click the **arrow** to display the contents of the Windows Accessories folder, and then locate Snipping Tool. Right-click **Snipping Tool**, and select **Pin to Start**.

The Snipping Tool tile displays on the Start menu. You will use the Snipping Tool in a later exercise.

e. Point in the blank space just above the Snipping Tool tile and click to open a name box. Type **Useful Windows Apps**, and press **Enter**.

You have created a new group on the Start menu that includes the Snipping Tool.

f. Click **All apps**, open the Windows Accessories folder, right-click **Sticky Notes** and select **Pin to Start**.

The Sticky Notes tile is added to the Start menu.

g. Drag the Sticky Notes tile into the Useful Windows Apps group you just created.

The new group has two tiles.

h. Drag the **title bar** of the Useful Windows Apps group so that the new group is at the top left corner of the Start menu tiles section.

You have repositioned the Useful Windows Apps group to a place that is more easily accessible on the Start menu.

i. Right-click the **Snipping Tool tile**, point to **Resize**, and then click **Small**.

You have resized the Snipping Tool tile so that it is smaller.

j. Right-click the **Snipping Tool tile** again, point to **Resize**, and then click **Medium**.

You realize that you like the larger tile, so you resized it back to the larger size.

k. Keep the Start menu open, press **PrtSc** on your keyboard, click **Word** on the taskbar, and then press **Ctrl+V** on your keyboard. Click **Save** on the Quick Access Toolbar in the upper left corner of the Word window.

You have captured an image of your screen and pasted it into a Word document.

TROUBLESHOOTING: If you have minimized the Word window, you will need to click the thumbnail to first maximize the Word window before pasting the Print Screen image.

l. Right-click **Word** on the taskbar, and click **Pin this program to taskbar.**

Right-clicking an icon on the taskbar opens the Jump List and the option to pin the program to the taskbar.

m. Display the Word Jump List again, press **PrtSc**, click the **Word window**, press **Enter** twice, and then press **Ctrl+V**.

n. Save the document.

STEP 2 » USE TASK VIEW AND CREATE A VIRTUAL DESKTOP

Not only do you want students to understand the basics of managing apps and windows, but also you know they will enjoy customizing the Start menu. Refer to Figure 13 as you complete Step 2.

© Microsoft Office 2016, Windows 10, Microsoft Corporation

FIGURE 13 Task View and Virtual Desktops

a. Click **Minimize** (the horizontal line button) in the top right corner of the Word window. Click **Task View** on the taskbar.

A large thumbnail of the Word window displays.

b. Click the **Word thumbnail** to activate the Word window.

c. Open the **Start menu**, and click **Microsoft Edge** in the Most used section of the Start menu, type **usa.gov** in the Address bar, and then press **Enter.**

You have opened the Microsoft Edge browser application and navigated to usa.gov, the United States government's official Web portal.

TROUBLESHOOTING: Microsoft Edge may not be in the Most used section of the Start menu. It may be on the Start menu or click All apps, and then scroll to locate Microsoft Edge. Alternatively, type Microsoft Edge in Cortana.

d. Click **Start** to return to the Start menu.

e. Click the **Calendar tile** on the Start menu.

You have now launched the Calendar app. The calendar may not have any data in it, unless you have previously entered items in the Calendar app.

TROUBLESHOOTING: If the Calendar app is not on the Start menu, click another Windows 10 app such as Sports, Money, or Weather.

f. Click **Task View**.

The Calendar, Microsoft Edge, and Word thumbnails display on the desktop.

g. Click **New desktop** on the bottom right corner of the desktop.

Two desktop thumbnails display at the bottom of the desktop. Desktop 1 thumbnail displays the three open apps. The Desktop 2 thumbnail is blank.

h. Point to the **Desktop 1 thumbnail** to display thumbnails of the three open apps on Desktop 1. Drag the Calendar thumbnail to Desktop 2.

i. Press **PrtSc**, click the **Word thumbnail**, press **Enter** twice, and then press **Ctrl+V**. Save the document.

STEP 3 ▶▶ SNAP, MOVE, AND RESIZE WINDOWS

Because there will be occasions when several windows are open simultaneously on the desktop, students should know how to arrange them. You will show them various ways that Windows 10 can help arrange open windows. Refer to Figure 14 as you complete Step 3.

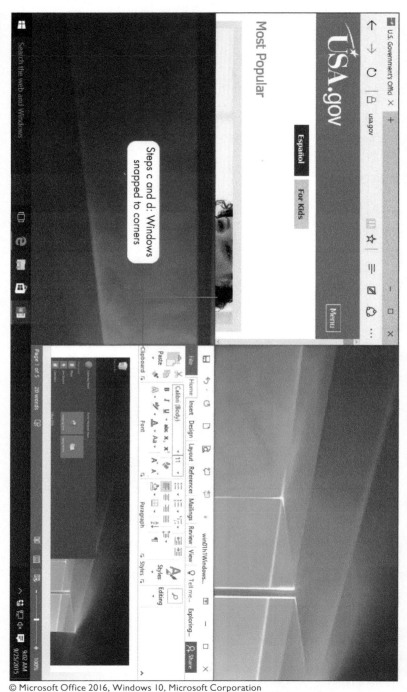

Steps c and d: Windows snapped to corners

FIGURE 14 Arrange Windows Using Snap

a. Click and hold the left mouse button on the **title bar** of the Word window. Drag the window to the far right of the screen until you see an outline of the window display. Release the mouse button.

The Word window snaps to the right side of the display, and a thumbnail of the Microsoft Edge window is in the left side of the display.

b. Click the **Microsoft Edge thumbnail.**

The Microsoft Edge window automatically snaps to the left side of the display.

c. Press and hold the **Windows key**, and then press ⬆ to snap the Microsoft Edge window to the top left corner.

d. Click the **Word window**, press and hold the **Windows key**, and then press ➡.

The Word window snaps to the bottom right corner.

e. Press **PrtSc**, click **Maximize** on the Word window, press **Enter** twice, and then press **Ctrl+V**. Right-click **Microsoft Edge** on the taskbar, click **Close window.**

f. Save and close the Word file.

Since Cortana is a cool feature of Windows 10, you want students to learn how to use it. You will show the students how to use Cortana to search for a file, schedule a reminder, and even how to tell a joke. Refer to Figure 15 as you complete Step 4.

STEP 4 》》 USE THE SEARCH BOX AND CORTANA, AND MANAGE CORTANA SETTINGS

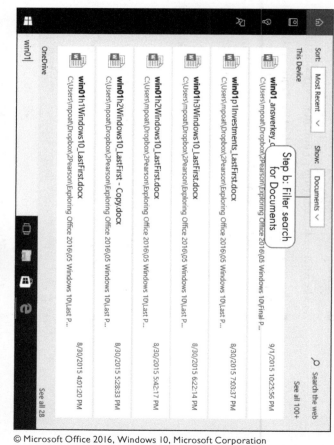

© Microsoft Office 2016, Windows 10, Microsoft Corporation

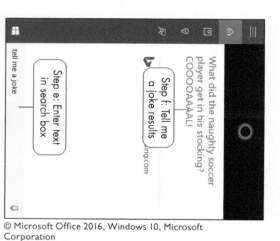

© Microsoft Office 2016, Windows 10, Microsoft Corporation

FIGURE 15 Cortana

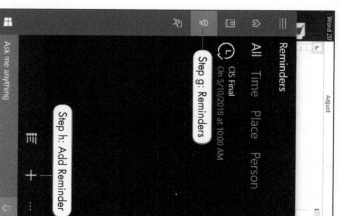

© Microsoft Office 2016, Windows 10, Microsoft Corporation

a. Click the **search box**, and type **win01**. Click **My stuff**.

A list of settings, applications, files, and folders that are stored on your PC that contain "win01" in the name displays.

b. Click the **Sort arrow**, select **Most Recent**, click the **Show arrow**, and then select **Documents**.

Filter enables you to narrow the search results to items in a specific category. In this case, you only want to display results that are documents.

c. Press **PrtSc**, and click **win01h1Windows10_LastFirst** (it will show your own last and first names) that displays in the search results to open the document you have created with this Hands-On Exercise.

d. Press **Ctrl+End**, press **Enter** twice, and then press **Ctrl+V**. Save the file and minimize Word.

e. Click the **search box**, type **tell me a joke**, and then press **Enter**.

Cortana will display a response.

TROUBLESHOOTING: You may need to initiate Cortana prior to completing Step e.

f. Press **PrtSc**, click **Word** on the taskbar, press **Enter** twice, and then press **Ctrl+V**. Save the file and minimize Word.

g. Click the **search box**, and then click **Reminders** in the Cortana menu.

Reminders display, listing any reminders you might already have.

h. Click the **plus sign**, click **Remember to** and type **CIS Final**, click **Time** and select **10:00 AM**, click the **check mark**, click **Today** (or it might say Tomorrow depending on the time of day you are completing this exercise), and then select **May 10, 2018**. (Alternatively, you can type the actual date and time of your class final.) Click the **check mark** again. Click **Remind**.

i. Press **PrtSc**, click **Word** on the taskbar, press **Enter** twice, and then press **Ctrl+V**. Save the document and minimize Word.

STEP 5 ›› EXPLORE WINDOWS HELP

As students in your class progress to middle and high school, they may have opportunities to use laptops for class work. They also are likely to find themselves in locations where they can connect to the Internet wirelessly. Using that example, you will help the class understand how to search for information on finding and safely connecting to an available wireless network. Refer to Figure 16 as you complete Step 5.

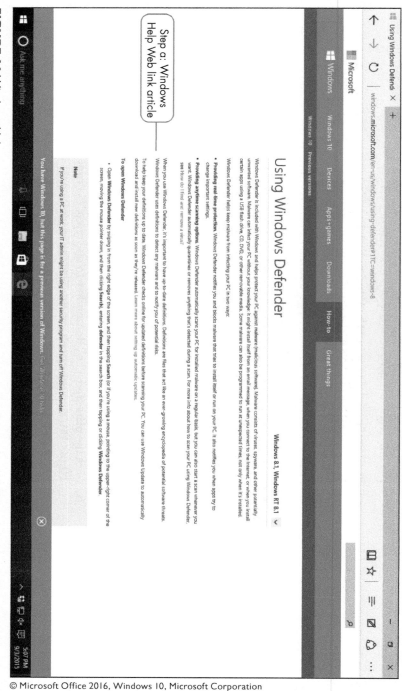

FIGURE 16 Windows Help

© Microsoft Office 2016, Windows 10, Microsoft Corporation

a. Click the **search box**, and type **Why use Windows Defender?** Press **Enter**. Select the Using Windows Defender – Windows Help Web link, and read the topic.

> **TROUBLESHOOTING:** If the webpage displays with a message, "Hi there – you're looking for Windows 10 info! We put that stuff in a new spot." Find new content for the new Windows by browsing our top categories and trending topics. Click the link, and then click Protect your PC and read the information.

b. Click the **Start menu**, click the **Snipping Tool tile**, click the **New arrow**, and then select **Full-screen Snip**.

The Snipping Tool window displays with an image of your screen.

c. Click **Word** on the taskbar, press **Enter** twice, and then press **Ctrl+V**.

d. Press **Enter**, then, in your own words, type why you should use Windows Defender, and the two ways it helps protect your PC. Save the file. Minimize the Word and Snipping Tool windows.

e. Click the **search box** and type **File History help**. Press **Enter**. At the top of the Bing results, click **Videos**, and click **Restore files or folders using File History – Windows Help** link. Watch the video.

f. Take a full-screen snip of your screen with the video information still displayed, click **Word** on the taskbar, press **Enter** twice, and then press **Ctrl+V**. Save the file.

g. Type **restore files** in the search box, and then click **Restore your files with File History – Control Panel**. Click **Snipping Tool**. Click **New**, click the **New arrow**, and then click **Full-screen Snip**. Click **Word** on the taskbar, press **Enter** twice, and then press **Ctrl+V**.

h. Save the document. Keep the document open if you plan to continue with the next Hands-On Exercise. If not, close the document, and exit Word. Close all other windows.

File Management

One of the main functions of Windows is *file management*, which provides an organizational structure to your computer's contents. Windows organizes the drives, folders, and files of your computer in a hierarchical structure. The hard drive is represented as the C: drive and is where most programs and files are permanently stored. A unique letter (D, E, F, and so on) identifies other storage devices, such as a DVD drive, external hard drive, or flash drive, when they are connected to the computer.

In this section, you will learn how to use File Explorer to manage your files and folders. You will also learn how to create a folder; then open, rename, and delete folders, so that you can better organize your files; and how to move or copy files between different folders. Lastly, you will learn how to compress and extract files and folders.

Using File Explorer

File Explorer is an app that you can use to create folders and manage folders and files across various storage locations: your PC, online storage, and external storage devices such as a flash drive or backup drive. File Explorer displays the organizational hierarchy of storage locations, folders, and files so you can locate files more easily. Often, related files are organized together into folders. A folder structure can occur across several levels, so you can create folders within other folders—called subfolders—arranged according to purpose. The most common analogy for File Explorer is that of a filing cabinet in which common documents and files are located within a single drawer (in this case a storage location), and then further grouped and organized by folders, often multiple layers of folders.

Figure 17 shows and Table 1 further describes the various functional areas of the File Explorer interface.

Understand the File Explorer Interface

Windows 10 has made it very easy to access File Explorer by incorporating an icon on the taskbar and in the Start menu. If you use File Explorer a lot, an icon may also display in the Most used section of the Start menu.

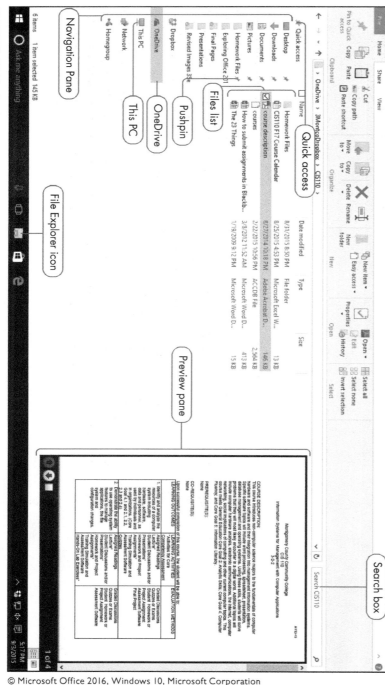

FIGURE 17 File Explorer

TABLE 1 File Explorer Interface

Ribbon	The Ribbon includes tabs and commands that are relevant to the currently selected item. If you are working with a music file, the Ribbon commands might include one for burning to a CD, whereas if you have selected a document, the Ribbon would enable you to open or share the file.
Back, Forward, and Up navigation arrows	Use these commands to visit previously opened folders. Use the Up command to open the parent folder for the current location.
Address bar	The Address bar enables you to navigate to other folders within File Explorer.
Search box	Find files and folders by typing descriptive text in the search box. Windows immediately begins a search after you type the first character, further narrowing results as you type. You can search the entire contents of File Explorer, or conduct a more directed search by first selecting a folder or drive.
Navigation Pane	The Navigation Pane contains Quick access, OneDrive, This PC, and Network. Click the arrow next to any of these content groups in the Navigation Pane to display contents and to manage files housed within a selected folder. Click any folder in the Navigation Pane to display the contained files.
Quick access	Quick access, as its name implies, provides immediate access to those files and folders that you use most often.
File list	The File list shows the contents of the currently selected folder or storage location. Files and folders can display in a variety of layouts that either show detailed information about the specific file or folder, or just file or folder names with small-, medium-, or large-sized icons. The icon is associated with the type of file or folder. For example, all Word documents will bear the W in a blue box icon.
Details pane	Displays the properties of the file or folder. Common properties include information such as the author name and the date the file was last modified. Details pane does not display by default, but displays after clicking the View tab and then clicking Details pane in the Panes group.
Preview pane	The Preview pane provides a snapshot of a selected file's contents (but not the contents of a selected folder). You can see file contents before actually opening the file. This pane can be displayed by clicking the View tab and then clicking Preview pane in the Panes group.

Use the View Tab on the Ribbon

File Explorer has a Ribbon, like all the Office applications. Use the View tab to customize what displays on File Explorer. For example, you might want to modify the size of the file and folder icons, or you might want additional details about displayed files and folders. Using the settings in the Layout group on the View tab, you can determine the size of icons by selecting Small, Medium, Large, or Extra Large icons. The Details layout will list the files and folder with other relevant information such as Date modified, Type, and Size. The List layout shows the file names without added detail, whereas Tiles and Content layouts are useful to show file thumbnails and varying levels of file details. If you want additional detail, such as who the file or folder is shared with and its availability, click Details pane on the View tab. To show a preview of a file, click Preview pane on the View tab. You can change the width of a pane by positioning the pointer on the border that separates the panes to display a double-headed arrow, and then dragging the border left or right.

TIP: ADD TAGS TO FILES

When you create a file, properties such as author, creation date, and size are automatically assigned to the file. Although these properties may be useful in some situations, you might want to create a tag to further identify a file, and make it faster and easier to locate the file in the future. You can assign a tag to a file in the Details pane. To add more than one tag, separate each entry with a semicolon.

Use and Modify Quick Access

When you launch File Explorer, it opens to the *Quick access* section on the Navigation Pane by default. Quick access contains shortcuts to the folders you use most often. Although certain folders such as Downloads, Desktop, Documents, and Pictures are pinned to Quick access by default, you can unpin any of those, and pin others, to meet your particular needs. A pushpin icon identifies a pinned folder (refer to Figure 17). If you have upgraded your system from Windows 7 or 8, all the folders in your Favorites list are added to Quick access automatically.

To pin (or unpin) a folder to Quick access, complete one of the following steps:

- Right-click the folder, and select Pin to (or Unpin from) Quick access.
- Select the folder to pin and then click Pin to Quick access on the Home tab. Clicking this button with a selected pinned folder does not unpin the folder, however.

Also displayed in Quick access is a list of Recent files. These files are the most frequently used files. As files are added, the less used files on the list are removed to make room for the new files, but you can remove any file from the Recent files list by right-clicking the file and selecting Remove from Quick access.

Use the Search Box in File Explorer

Occasionally, even the most organized person will need to search for a file or folder. While Cortana may be a convenient way to search for files and folders, you can only filter the results by type of file. When you use the search box in File Explorer, you can search only the contents of a specific folder, thus limiting the results; or you can Search an entire drive for a broader search. You can then further sort the results by file type or date modified to continue to locate the specific file or folder.

To search for a file or folder, complete the following steps:

1. Click the drive or folder in the Navigation Pane you want to search.
2. Type the search term in the search box.

Once you click in the File Explorer search box, the Search Tools tab displays. The Search Tools tab enables you to do the following:

- refine your search results by Date, Kind, Size, or Other properties
- revise the search location to include subfolders, the entire PC or another location
- save a search if you tend to conduct the same search repeatedly

TIP: USING THE ASTERISK (*) TO SEARCH

To search for all files of a particular file type in the search box, type *. and the file extension. For example, to search for all mp3 files on your computer, type *.mp3 in the search box.

Navigate File Explorer

The Navigation Pane is an easy way to move between folders and storage locations in File Explorer. As mentioned above, the Navigation Pane consists of four main areas: Quick access, OneDrive, This PC, and Network. **OneDrive** is Microsoft's cloud storage system.

Saving files to OneDrive, saves them to a Web-based location (OneDrive.com) and syncs them across all Windows devices. Sign in with your Microsoft account to access your files from any Internet-connected computer or mobile device. Changes you make will sync with the cloud, keeping your files up-to-date everywhere. Use File Explorer to access your OneDrive and to create new folders and organize existing folders.

Files stored to This PC are saved onto the hard drive, and are accessible only when working on that particular device. Documents, Music, Pictures, Videos, and Downloads are standard library folders in the This PC area of File Explorer. Clicking on Network in the Navigation Pane displays all networked devices such as gaming and entertainment systems, printers, and other networked computers.

Clicking the arrow on the left side of these main storage areas in the Navigation Pane expands or collapses the folder to show or hide the folders and documents within each group. When you select a file or folder, the location of that file or folder is displayed in the Address bar (see Figure 18).

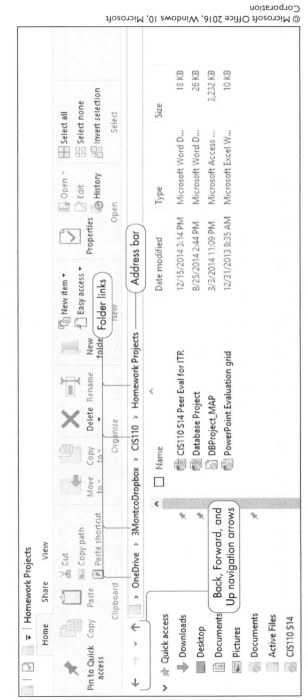

© Microsoft Office 2016, Windows 10, Microsoft Corporation

FIGURE 18 The Address Bar in File Explorer

The Address bar is located under the Ribbon, and displays the current location of a selected file or folder as a series of links and arrows. Next to the Address bar are the Back, Forward, and Up navigation arrows. These arrows help to move up or down the links in the location shown in the Address bar. Alternatively, you can click on any of the links in the Address bar to jump directly to the location. You can use the Address bar to navigate to a particular location (i.e., to Documents or Quick access), or you can click in any of the arrows between the folder links to view any subfolders. You can also use the Address bar to move files and folders to different locations. This and other ways to work with files and folders are covered in the next section.

Working with Files and Folders

STEP 1

As you work with software to create a file, such as when you type a report using Word, your primary concern will be saving the file so that you can retrieve it later. Grouping related files into folders helps to keep files organized. If you have created an appropriate and well-named folder structure, you can save the file in a location that is easy to find.

You can use File Explorer to create a folder structure, providing descriptive names and placing the folders in a well-organized hierarchy.

To create a folder in File Explorer, complete the following steps:

1. Open File Explorer, and then click OneDrive or any other location such as the hard drive or flash drive, in the Navigation Pane.
2. Click the Home tab on the Ribbon, and then click New folder in the New group.
3. Type the new folder name and press Enter. Repeat the process to create additional folders.

Undoubtedly, you will occasionally find that you have just created a file but have no appropriate folder in which to save the file. For example, you might have just finished the slide show for your speech class but have forgotten first to create a speech folder for your assignments. For those occasions, you can create a folder from within the software application at the time you are saving a file.

To create a folder as you save a file, complete the following steps:

1. Click Save As in Backstage view and click Browse, to display the Save As dialog box.
2. Navigate to the location where you want to store your file.
3. Click New folder, type the new folder name, press Enter, and then click Open to save the name and open the new folder. After typing the file name, click Save.

Open, Rename, and Delete Folders and Files

STEP 2

Once files are saved to locations such as OneDrive or Documents on This PC, you can use File Explorer to open, rename, and delete files.

Using the Navigation Pane or search box, you can locate and select a file that you want to open. For example, you might want to open the speech slide show so that you can practice before giving a presentation to the class. The program that is associated with the file will open the file. For example, Microsoft PowerPoint will launch and a presentation will display when you open a file associated with PowerPoint.

To open a file using File Explorer, complete the following steps:

1. Open File Explorer, and then navigate to the folder that contains the desired file. The file will display in the File list.
2. Enable the Preview pane from the View tab, and click the file name in the File list to preview the contents of a file before opening it.
3. Double-click the file.

At times, you may want to give a different name to a file or folder than the one that you originally gave it. Or perhaps you made a typographical mistake when you entered the name as you saved the file. In these situations, you can rename the file or folder.

To rename a file or folder, complete one of the following steps:

- Right-click the file or folder and select Rename. Type the new name and press Enter.
- Click the name twice—but much more slowly than a double-click. Type the new name and press Enter.
- Click a file or folder once to select it, click the Home tab, and then select Rename in the Organize group. Type the new name and press Enter.

It is much easier to delete a folder or file than it is to recover it if you remove it by mistake. Therefore, be very careful when deleting items so that you are sure of your intentions before proceeding. When you delete a folder, all subfolders and all files within the folder are also removed. If you are certain you want to remove a folder or file, the process is simple.

To delete a file or folder, complete one of the following steps:

- Right-click the item, click Delete, and then click Yes if asked to confirm removal to the Recycle Bin.
- Click to select the item, click the Home tab, and then click Delete in the Organize group.

Recall that items are placed in the Recycle Bin only if you are deleting them from a hard drive. Files and folders deleted from a removable storage medium, such as a flash drive, are immediately and permanently deleted, with no easy method of retrieval.

Selecting, Copying, and Moving Multiple Files and Folders

STEP 3 You will select folders and files when you need to rename, delete, copy, or paste them, or open files and folders so that you can view the contents. Click a file or folder to select it; double-click a file or folder (in the File list) to open it.

Select Multiple Files and Folders

To apply an operation to several files at once, such as deleting or moving them, you will select all of them. You can select several files and folders, regardless of whether they are adjacent to each other in the File list. Suppose that your digital pictures are contained in the Pictures folder. You might want to delete some of the pictures because you want to clear up some hard drive space.

To select multiple files or folders, complete the following steps:

1. Open File Explorer and click the desired folder or storage location.
2. Locate the desired files in the File list, and do one of the following:

   - Select the first file, press and hold Shift, and then click the last file to select adjacent files. All consecutive files will be highlighted, indicating that they are selected. At that point, you can delete, copy, or move the selected files at the same time.
   - Click the first file or folder, and press and hold Ctrl while you click all desired non-adjacent files or folders, releasing Ctrl only when you have finished selecting all the necessary files or folders. At that point, you can delete, copy, or move the selected files at the same time.
   - Open the folder, press and hold Ctrl, and then press A on the keyboard to select all items in a folder or disk drive. You can also click the Home tab, and in the Select group, click Select all to select all items. At that point, you can delete, copy, or move the selected files at the same time.

Copy and Move Files and Folders

When you copy or move a folder, you affect both the folder and any files that it contains. You can move or copy a folder or file to another location on the same drive or to another drive. If your purpose is to make a backup, or copy, of an important file or folder, you will probably want to copy it to an external drive or to OneDrive.

To move or copy an item in File Explorer, complete the following steps:

1. Right-click the item(s) and select either Cut (to move) or Copy on the shortcut menu.
2. Locate the destination drive or folder in the Navigation Pane, right-click the destination drive or folder, and then click Paste.

STEP 4

Compressing Files and Folders

Sometimes you have an extremely large file, such as a video file that you want to email or upload to the Internet. Or, you might have a group of files, such as a bunch of pictures that you want to share with friends or family, but you do not want to send them as individual attachments. You can compress a file or zip multiple files together into a single compressed folder. A **compressed (zipped) folder** or file, takes up less space, is easier to email or to upload to OneDrive or another online storage site, and facilitates sharing a group of files.

Create a Compressed Folder

Using the Zip tool in File Explorer makes it easy to create a compressed folder. When compressing a file or folder, the compressed folder is created in the same location and takes on the same name as the file or folder. However, if you are compressing a group of files, it may be best to first put them in a folder and give that folder a meaningful name. Otherwise, the zipped folder will take the name of one of the documents in the folder. Of course, you can always rename a zipped folder, using the same methods described above for renaming a file or folder. The zipped file or folder does not replace the original files.

To compress a file or folder, complete the following series of steps:

1. Open File Explorer, and select the file, group of files, or folder in the File list that you want to compress.
2. Click the Share tab, and then click Zip in the Send group. A compressed folder is created and placed in the same folder location along with the original files or folder. Alternatively, right-click the selected files or folder, select Send to, and click Compressed (zipped) folder.

Once a compressed folder is created, you can add additional files to the folder without having to undo and redo the zipping process. Just drag new files into the compressed folder.

Extract Files from a Compressed Folder

You might have received or downloaded a compressed file or folder, such as the data files from this text, and need to unzip the folder and extract the files.

To unzip (extract) files or folders from a compressed folder, complete the following steps:

1. Open File Explorer, and select the compressed folder.

2. Click the Extract tab, click Extract all, and if necessary, click Browse to select a destination where you want the individual files to be located. The individual files, by default, are saved to the same location as the zipped folder. Click Extract.

TIP: EXTRACTING FILES FROM A DOWNLOADED ZIP FOLDER

If you are extracting files from a folder you have downloaded from the Web, you should ensure your files are saved in a meaningful location. Otherwise, they may end up in the Downloads folder.

Extracting files does not remove the compressed folder from your computer. The compressed folder will remain until you decide to delete it.

Quick Concepts

5. The File Explorer interface has several functional areas. Name them and identify their characteristics.

6. Describe why it might be more efficient to use the search box in File Explorer than the search box on the taskbar to look for a file.

7. You want to delete several files, but the files are not consecutively listed in File Explorer. Describe two different methods you could use to select and delete them.

8. Explain at least two circumstances in which file compression would be useful.

Hands-On Exercises

2 File Management

You have discussed with the students the importance of good file management, now you want to show them how easy it is to use File Explorer to organize and manage their files. You first have them create and pin a folder to Quick access, then you have them modify some folder names so they are more meaningful. Lastly, you show the students how to extract files from a compressed folder and move them to one of the previously created folders.

Skills covered: Create Folders •
Pin a Folder to Quick Access •
Rename a Folder • Delete a Folder •
Copy a File • Move a Folder •
Compress a Folder • Extract Files
from a Compressed Folder

STEP 1 >> CREATE FOLDERS AND PIN A FOLDER TO QUICK ACCESS

Your friend tells you that she would like to have all the files the students are working on saved in one folder so it is easy for everyone to access in the future. Refer to Figure 19 as you complete Step 1.

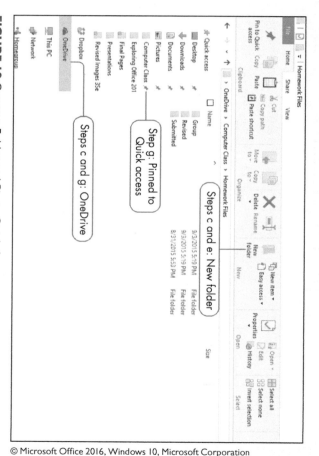

Steps c and e: New folder

Step g: Pinned to
Quick access

Steps c and g: OneDrive

FIGURE 19 Create a Folder and Pin to Quick Access

a. Open *win01h1Windows10_LastFirst* if you closed it at the end of Hands-On Exercise 1 and save it as **win01h2Windows10_LastFirst**, changing h1 to h2. Keep the document open and maximized.

> **TROUBLESHOOTING:** If you make any major mistakes in this exercise, you can close the file, open *win01h1Windows10_LastFirst* again, and then start this exercise over.

b. Click **File Explorer** on the taskbar and maximize the window.

c. Click **OneDrive** in the Navigation Pane. Click **New folder** in the New group, type **Computer Class**, and then press **Enter**.

You create a folder where you can organize subfolders and files for the students and your friend, and all the learning materials they generate for their computer class.

> **TROUBLESHOOTING:** If OneDrive does not display in the Navigation Pane, click This PC and create a new folder in Documents.

TROUBLESHOOTING: If the folder you create is called *New folder* instead of *Computer Class*, you probably clicked away from the folder before typing the name, so that it received the default name. To rename it, right-click the folder, click Rename, type the correct name, and then press Enter.

d. Double-click the **Computer Class folder** in the File list. The Address bar at the top of the File Explorer window should show that it is the currently selected folder.

e. Click **New folder** in the New group on the Home tab, type **Data Files**, and then press **Enter**. Repeat the process to create another folder, and name it **Homework Files.**

You create two subfolders of the Computer Class folder. One to contain the data files the students will need to begin some of their computer work, and another to keep track of homework files they have completed.

f. Check the Address bar to make sure Computer Class is still the current folder. Navigate to and then double-click the **Homework Files folder** in the Navigation Pane. Right-click in a blank area of the File list, point to **New**, and then click **Folder**. Type **Submitted** and press **Enter**. Using either technique in this step, create two more folders named **Group** and **Revised**.

To subdivide the Homework Files folder further, you create three subfolders, one to hold homework files that have been submitted, one for revised homework files, and one for homework files from group projects.

g. Click **OneDrive** in the Navigation Pane, and locate the Computer Class folder in the File list. Right-click the **Computer Class folder**, and select **Pin to Quick access.**

The Computer Class folder displays in the Quick access area of File Explorer.

h. Double-click the **Computer Class folder** in Quick access, and double-click the **Homework Files folder** in the Files list.

i. Click **Snipping Tool** on the taskbar, click the **New arrow**, and click **Full-screen Snip.** Click **Word** on the taskbar, press **Ctrl+End**, press **Enter** twice, and then press **Ctrl+V**.

j. Save the document. Minimize the Word and Snipping Tool windows.

TROUBLESHOOTING: If the Snipping Tool does not display on the taskbar, open the Start menu, and click the Snipping Tool tile to launch the app.

STEP 2 » RENAME AND DELETE A FOLDER

As often happens, you find that the folder structure you created is not exactly what you need. You will remove the Revised folder and will rename the Data Files folder to better describe the contents. Refer to Figure 20 as you complete Step 2.

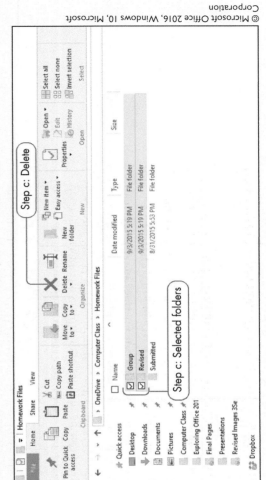

FIGURE 20 Rename and Delete a Folder

Hands-On Exercise 2

You want to show students how to copy a file, so in anticipation of completing the next assignment, you have them copy and rename the current homework file on which they are working. Refer to Figure 21 as you complete Step 3.

STEP 3 ›› SELECT AND COPY FILES

a. Double-click the **Computer Class folder** in Quick access.

b. Right-click the **Data Files folder**, click **Rename**, type **Starting Files**, and then press **Enter**.

   Your friend thinks that her students will understand the term Starting Files better than Data Files, so you rename the folder.

c. Double-click the **Homework Files folder**. Click the check box next to **Revised** and **Group**. Both folders are selected. Click **Delete** in the Organize group. If asked to confirm the deletion, click **Yes**. Click **Computer Class** in the Address bar.

> **TROUBLESHOOTING:** If check boxes do not display next to the folder name, click the View tab, and click to select item check boxes in the Show/hide group.

   You decide that dividing the homework folder into revised and group subfolders is not necessary, so you deleted both folders.

d. Take a full-screen snip of your screen, click **Word** on the taskbar, press **Enter** twice, and then press **Ctrl+V**.

e. Save the document. Minimize the Word and Snipping Tool windows.

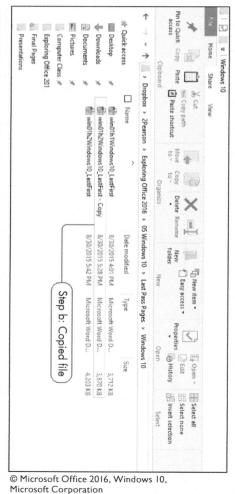

Step b: Copied file

FIGURE 21 Select and Copy Files

© Microsoft Office 2016, Windows 10,
Microsoft Corporation

a. Navigate to the location where you saved win01h2Windows10_LastFirst. Right-click the file and select **Copy**.

b. Right-click in a **blank area** of the File list and select **Paste**.

   A new document named win01h2Windows10_LastFirst - Copy displays. Two documents with the same name cannot be saved in the same location, so Windows automatically adds "- Copy" to the end of the file name to differentiate the two files.

c. Take a full-screen snip of your screen, click **Word** on the taskbar, press **Enter** twice, and then press **Ctrl+V**. Save the file. Minimize the Word and Snipping Tool windows.

d. Click **win01h2Windows10_LastFirst - Copy**, click **Rename** on the Home tab, and then rename the file as **Homework_Images**. Press **Enter**.

> **TROUBLESHOOTING:** Be sure the file you are renaming has - Copy in the file name.

e. Take a full-screen snip of your screen, click **Word** on the taskbar, press **Enter** twice, and then press **Ctrl+V**.

f. Save the document. Minimize the Word and Snipping Tool windows.

Hands-On Exercise 2

You want to show the students how to compress a group of files into a zipped folder and then move the zipped folder to a new location. You will then have the students extract the files from the zipped folder. Refer to Figure 22 as you complete Step 4.

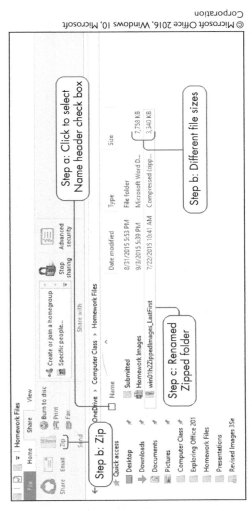

© Microsoft Office 2016, Windows 10, Microsoft
Corporation

FIGURE 22 Compress and Extract Files

a. Click the **check box** next to the Name header in the File list in File Explorer to select both documents.

> **TROUBLESHOOTING:** If more than the two documents display in the File list, click the check box to select each individual file.

b. Click the **Share tab**, click **Zip**, and then press **Enter**.

   A new zipped folder is created. Because the files were not in a separate folder, the zipped folder is named after one of the files. You will to rename the zipped folder.

c. Right-click the **zipped folder**, and click **Rename**. Type **Windows 10 Homework**, and press **Enter**.

d. Click the **Windows 10 Homework zipped folder**, press **Ctrl**, and then drag the folder to the Computer Class folder in Quick access.

   A ScreenTip will display Copy to Computer Class. Note: If you wanted to move the zipped folder, you would just drag the folder to the new location.

e. Double-click the **Computer Class folder** in Quick access, and then double-click the **Windows 10 Homework zipped folder**.

   The Compressed Folder Tools tab displays on the Ribbon, and the two files contained in the zipped folder display in the File list.

f. Take a full-screen snip of your screen, click **Word** on the taskbar, press **Enter** twice, and then press **Ctrl+V**. Save the file. Minimize the Word and Snipping Tool windows.

g. Click **Extract all**, and then click **Extract**.

   You do not need to browse, as you want the new files to stay in the Computer Class folder.

h. Click **Computer Class** on the Address bar and note that the Windows 10 Homework zipped folder and the Windows 10 Homework folder are both in the Computer Class folder.

i. Take a full-screen snip of your screen, click **Word** on the taskbar, press **Enter** twice, and then press **Ctrl+V**. Close the Snipping Tool and close File Explorer. Click **No** if asked to save changes to the snip.

j. Save the document. Keep the document open if you plan to continue with the next Hands-On Exercise. If not, close the document, and exit Word. Close all other windows.

Windows System and Security Features

Windows 10 is a full-featured operating system. As such, it includes utilities that help to monitor, maintain, and secure your devices. Windows 10 contains software that protects your system against spyware and hacking, as well as utilities that help to keep your system up-to-date or recover files should something go awry. It also includes some maintenance utilities to ensure your computer and operating system continue to run in good form.

In this section, you will learn about some maintenance and security features in Windows 10.

Working with Security Settings and Software

Windows 10 monitors your security status, providing recommendations for security settings and software updates as needed. The Action Center provides a central location where you can access any status notifications and alerts. Windows 10 includes basic security features such as Window Defender and firewall software.

Understand the Action Center

STEP 1

Windows 10 checks your system for various maintenance and security settings, providing notifications and recommending action through the *Action Center* when necessary. A major purpose of the Action Center is to provide important status information. Status information could include the detection of new devices, the availability of software updates, or recommended maintenance and security tasks. When the status of a monitored item changes, a pop-up message in an alert box displays near the Notification area. You can click the message to perform the recommended task. If you are not working on your computer at the time the pop-up message appears, the Action Center icon, located in the Notification area of the taskbar, will turn opaque indicating that there are new notifications waiting for you. Click the Action Center icon in the Notification area (see Figure 23) to display the Action Center alerts box. Once clicked, the Action Center icon will become clear or "empty."

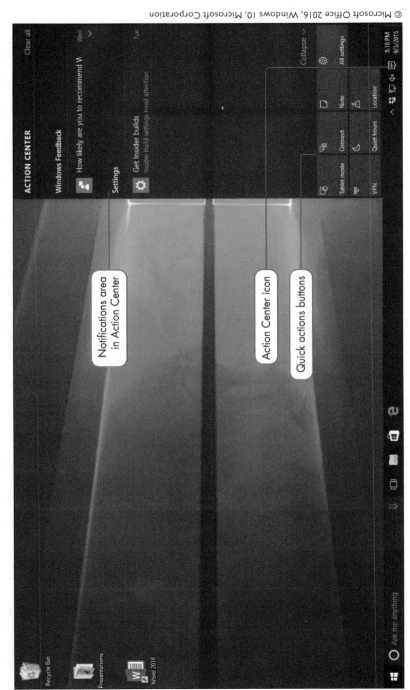

FIGURE 23 Action Center

The Action Center consists of two parts: the Notifications area at the top and Quick actions buttons at the bottom (refer to Figure 23). The Action Center runs across all your Windows devices. Therefore, in the Notifications area, you will see notifications from various apps, including Facebook, Twitter, and your email account, as well as from apps that might only be on your Windows phone or tablet. You can delete notifications by group (i.e. all your Twitter notifications) or you can delete individual notifications by pointing to the group or individual notification name and then clicking the "X" that displays. Lastly, you can click Clear All at the top of the Notifications area. Be mindful that Clear All will delete all notifications on all your Windows devices, not just the device on which you are currently working.

In the bottom of the Action Center are quick action buttons such as a Tablet mode toggle button, a button to connect your media devices, a link to All settings, a link to the Display settings, and toggle buttons for Location and Wi-Fi. Click Expand to see more quick actions such as toggle buttons for VPN and Rotation lock. Note that some buttons, such as Airplane mode or Rotation lock, will only display on mobile devices.

To change the Quick action buttons in the Action Center, complete the following steps:

1. Click the All settings button in the Action Center (or click Settings from the Start menu).
2. Click System, and then Notifications & actions. In the Quick actions area (see Figure 24), four icons display, indicating the quick actions that will display in the Action Center.
3. Click any of the icons to change any or all of the actions, and then select another action from the displayed menu.

Also from the Notifications & actions menu, you can choose which icons will always display in the Notification area on the taskbar by clicking *Select which icons appear on the taskbar.*

Windows System and Security Features • Windows 10

41

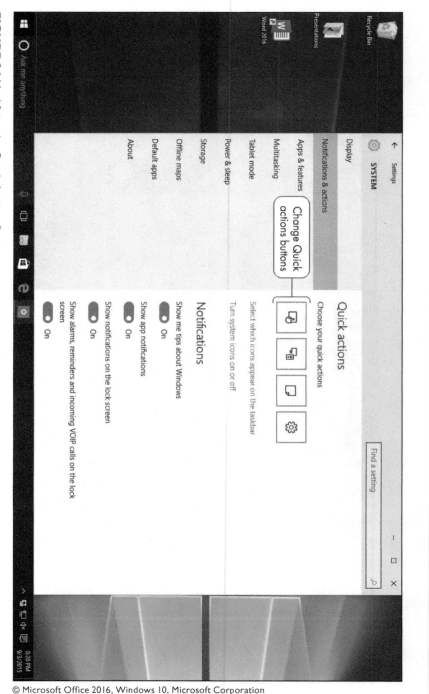

FIGURE 24 Modifying the Quick Actions Buttons

© Microsoft Office 2016, Windows 10, Microsoft Corporation

Use File History

Many things can accidentally happen to your files. You might mistakenly delete a file or a file might become corrupted, meaning it is damaged and therefore unusable by your software programs. Windows *File History* is a utility that will continuously make copies of your important files so that you can recover them if you ever encounter a file problem. In order for you to take advantage of the File History feature, you need to ensure that File History is turned on and that a storage area, such as a separate partition of your hard drive, an external drive, or cloud storage such as OneDrive, has been selected as the back-up location.

To access File History, complete the following steps:

1. Right-click Start, and select Control Panel.
2. Select System and Security, and then click File History.

File History will save files to a drive that you designate, such as an external hard drive or a separate partition (section) of your computer's internal hard drive. To set up File History for the first time, you must first designate the drive where File History will store the file backups. Click *Select drive* in the File History window to see a list of drives connected to your computer. If you need to set up a drive, click *Add network location*. Once you have selected a drive, click the *Run now* link to back up your files. As long as File History is on, it will automatically back up your personal files on your PC. If there are some folders that you do not feel need backing up, such as the Downloads folder, you can exclude them by clicking Exclude folders. Click Advanced settings to choose how often you want the backup to run and how long your saved versions are kept.

If you want to restore files after one or more have been lost, you can use the Restore feature in File History. Unlike many other restore applications, once you begin the restore process, you can browse to a specific file or folder and see all versions of the selected folder or individual file. You can then navigate to the desired version by clicking on Previous or Next and click Restore to bring it back to its original location.

Access Windows Update

Microsoft constantly identifies ways to enhance Windows security or fix problems that occur. There is no need to download or purchase an updated operating system each time changes are necessary; instead, you can simply make sure that your computer is set to download automatically any updates (fixes). *Windows Update* provides a means to initiating such modifications to the operating system.

Microsoft strongly recommends that you configure your computer to automatically download and install updates. That way, you do not have to remember to check for updates or manually download them. This is the default setting for Windows Update in Windows 10.

To check your settings for updates, complete the following steps:

1. Select Settings on the Start menu, and click Update & security.
2. Click Windows Update.
3. Click Check for updates.

You can have Windows both download and install updates automatically (strongly recommended), only download updates but let you install them, or never check for updates.

If you want to check for updates for other Microsoft products, such as Microsoft Office, open Windows Update and click the *Change settings* link. Then in the Change settings dialog box, under Microsoft Update, check *Give me updates for other Microsoft products when I update Windows.*

Use Windows Defender

Viruses and spyware can be installed on your computer without your knowledge when you connect to the Internet, open an email message, or when you install certain apps using a flash drive or other removable media. Spyware and viruses can do many unpleasant things such as:

- Keep track of websites you visit
- Change browser settings to direct you to dangerous websites
- Record keystrokes for stealing sensitive information
- Erase or corrupt files on your hard drive

Obviously, viruses and spyware are unwelcome and potential security risks. *Windows Defender* is antispyware and antivirus software. It identifies and removes malware such as viruses and spyware. Windows Defender can be set to run with real-time protection, which means that it is always on to guard against threats, alerting you when malicious programs attempt to install themselves or change your computer settings. You can also schedule routine scans so that Windows Defender checks your system for malicious software.

To open Windows Defender, complete the following steps:

1. Open the Start menu, and click All apps.
2. Click Windows System, and then click Windows Defender.

Alternatively, type Defender in the search box, and then click the corresponding link at the top of the Results list. This opens up the Windows Defender dialog box, and from there you can determine the type of Scan (Quick, Full, Custom) you want to perform.

Use Windows Firewall

STEP 2 Windows 10 also includes a *firewall*, a software program that helps to protect against unauthorized access (hacking) to your computer. Although Windows Defender and Windows Firewall provide basic protection, many computer users opt for the purchase of third-party software, such as Norton Internet Security, to provide an even greater level of protection.

When you work with the Internet, there is always a possibility that a hacker could disable your computer or view its contents. To keep that from occurring, it is imperative that you use firewall software. Windows 10 includes firewall software that is turned on by default when the operating system is installed. It protects against unauthorized traffic, both incoming and outgoing. That means that other people, computers, or programs do not have authorization to communicate with your computer unless you give permission. In addition, programs on your system are unable to communicate online unless you approve them.

Periodically, you might want to check to make sure your firewall has not been turned off accidentally. If you have another security program installed, such as Norton Internet Security, it has its own firewall software and therefore may recommend that Windows Firewall be turned off. This is because two active firewall programs can sometimes interfere with each other. But you should ensure that one firewall program is turned on at all times.

To access Windows Firewall, complete the following steps:

1. Open the Start menu, and then click Settings.
2. Type Firewall in Settings search box, and then click Windows Firewall. Alternatively, type Firewall in the search box, and select the top box in the search results.
3. Click Turn Windows Firewall on or off. You can then adjust other Firewall settings. Table 2 describes the Firewall settings that can be customized.

TABLE 2 Microsoft Firewall Settings

Setting	Description
Turn on Windows Firewall	Selected to be on by default to block most apps from receiving information through the firewall. You can add an app to a list of allowable apps.
Block all incoming connections	This setting, when turned on, blocks all unsolicited attempts to connect to your PC, even from those allowed apps. Consider turning this on when you are working in public places such as the airport or hotel. Turning this on does not affect your ability to use email and view most webpages.
Notify me when Windows Firewall blocks a new app	Selecting this option will allow you to unblock an app the Firewall has blocked.
Turn off Windows Firewall (not recommended)	Turn off Windows Firewall only if you have a separate security program, such as Norton or McAfee, running on your PC.

© Microsoft Office 2016, Windows 10, Microsoft Corporation

Working with Administrative Tools

One of the functions of the operating system is to manage computer resources such as the central processing unit (CPU) and random access memory (RAM). It is useful to have a good understanding of how well the CPU, RAM, and other computer resources are working so you can take preventative actions, such as upgrading the amount of RAM in your system, or freeing up or acquiring more hard drive capacity, if necessary. Windows 10 provides some tools that can help you monitor computer resources.

Use Task Manager

Task Manager displays the programs and processes that are running on your computer. When a program is not responding, you can use Task Manager to close it.

To close a program that is not responding, complete the following steps:

1. Right-click the taskbar, right-click the Start button, or use the search box to find Task Manager.
2. Click More details, click the Processes tab, and then click the application that is not responding in the Apps section.
3. Click End task.

To view how the computer is performing, click the Performance tab. Leave this box open as you work, so you can see how your actions affect computer resources.

Monitor System Resources

The **Resource Monitor** displays how the computer is using its key components, including the CPU and RAM. Use the search box to access the Resource Monitor, or click the Windows Administrative Tools folder in All apps. By clicking on each tab in the Resource Monitor window, you can view in real-time the system resources as they are being used. For example, click the Memory tab to view how RAM is being used (see Figure 25). The chart at the bottom displays the total amount of memory installed, what is currently being used, what is on reserve (cached), and what is currently available. Click between CPU and Memory to view how your actions affect the utilization of these components. For example, as you work, if the CPU performance nears or exceeds 50% utilization, that means you are using most or all of the CPU's capabilities. At maximum, or near maximum utilization, your computer might not run as efficiently. Unfortunately, there is not an easy way to upgrade your CPU, so if you want greater performance, it might be time to get a new computer with a faster CPU. You can also monitor memory (RAM) utilization. If you find you are using most of your memory resources, it might be possible to add additional RAM to your computer. If you cannot add additional RAM, then again, it might be time for a computer that offers greater RAM capacity.

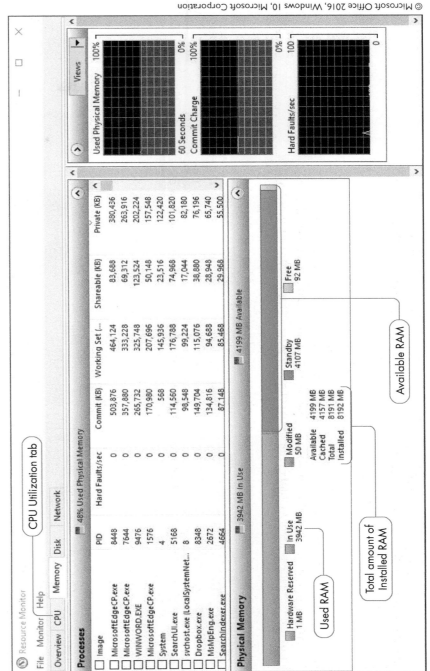

© Microsoft Office 2016, Windows 10, Microsoft Corporation

FIGURE 25 Resource Monitor

STEP 3

Use Disk Cleanup

Every now and then it is a good idea to do some internal "spring cleaning" on your computer. Over time, your computer system can accumulate many unnecessary files and program fragments that ultimately end up affecting computer performance. Some of these files accumulate in the Recycle Bin but are not completely deleted from the hard disk from the computer. Recall that deleted files go to the Recycle Bin but are not completely deleted from the system until the Recycle Bin is emptied. Windows often creates temporary files that temporarily store data. Usually Windows deletes these files automatically, but some remain. There are also files in Downloads that are not necessary anymore, such as small plug-ins and applets; or there are temporary files created when you use the Internet. The *Disk Cleanup* tool helps to free up space on your hard drive by searching for, and removing, any or all of these unnecessary files (see Figure 26). You can choose which types of files to delete. Read the description of the selected items if you do not understand what the files are. For additional information, you can click View Files to see a list of files that will be deleted. The total amount of disk space gained is displayed below the Files to delete box.

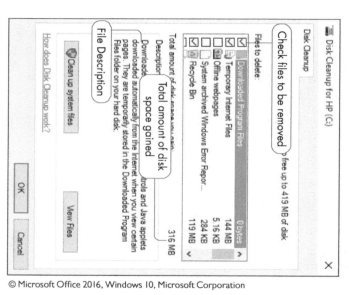

FIGURE 26 Disk Cleanup

© Microsoft Office 2016, Windows 10, Microsoft Corporation

To run Disk Cleanup, complete the following steps:

1. Click All apps from the Start menu, and click Windows Administrative Tools.
2. Click Disk Cleanup, and then select the drive you want to clean up by clicking the arrow in the Drives box. To clean the hard disk, choose the (C:) drive. Click OK. Note: If you only have one drive, the scan will start immediately without the need to select a drive.
3. Click the check boxes by all of the items you want to remove to select them.
4. Click OK after selecting all the file categories that you want to delete, and then click Delete Files to confirm that you want to delete the selected file categories.

Get Remote Assistance

Undoubtedly, you will have trouble with your computer at some time and need some assistance. You might consider getting someone to help you by letting him or her connect to your computer remotely to determine the problem. Of course, you will only want to ask someone that you trust because that person will temporarily have access to your files.

To allow Remote Assistance in Windows 10, complete the following steps:

1. Type Remote Access in the search box, and press Enter. The System Properties dialog box displays with the Remote tab selected.

2. Ensure that the Allow Remote Assistance connections to this computer check box is selected.

If the person who is helping you is also using Windows 10, you can use a method called Easy Connect. The first time you use Easy Connect to request assistance, you will receive a password that you then give to the person offering assistance. Using that password, the helper can remotely connect to your computer and exchange information. Thereafter, a password is not necessary—you simply click the contact information for the helper to initiate a session. If the person providing assistance is using an earlier Windows operating system (such as Windows 8.1), you can use an invitation file, which is a file that you create that is sent (usually by email) to the person offering assistance. The invitation file includes a password that is used to connect the two computers.

Quick Concepts

9. Describe the Action Center and the function it serves.

10. Describe why you might use File History, and how it differs from other restore applications.

11. Describe the utilities you would use to monitor and manage computer resources, such as the CPU and RAM.

12. Describe the types of files that can be removed with Disk Cleanup.

Hands-On Exercise

3 Windows System and Security Features

Skills covered: Use the Action Center • Modify Firewall Settings • Use Disk Cleanup

Windows is a gateway to using application software. You know that the fifth-grade students are most interested in the fun things that can be done with software. You want to excite them about having fun with a computer, but you also want them to understand that along with the fun comes some need to maintain the computer. They also want them to understand the concerns about security and privacy. You also want the students to be confident in their ability but well aware that help is available when they need it. In this section of your demonstration, you will encourage them to understand how they can perform some basic maintenance tasks. You will also show them features in Windows that can help address security concerns. Lastly, you will show them how easy it is to get help should they need assistance or reminders of how to work with Windows.

STEP 1 ▶ USE THE ACTION CENTER

The Action Center will occasionally display messages regarding security and privacy settings. You want the Cedar Grove students to be aware of how important those messages are, so you will show them how to use the Action Center. Refer to Figure 27 as you complete Step 1.

> **TROUBLESHOOTING:** If you are working in a campus lab, you might not have access to the Action Center or Windows Update. In that case, you should skip this Hands-On Exercise.

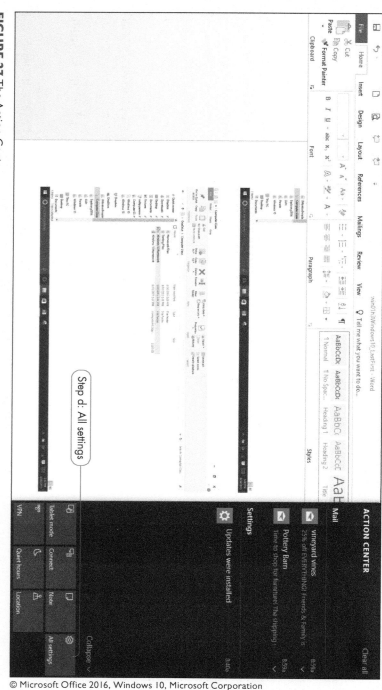

Step d: All settings

FIGURE 27 The Action Center

a. Open *win01h2Windows10_LastFirst* if you closed it at the end of Hands-On Exercise 2 and save it as **win01h3Windows10_LastFirst**, changing h2 to h3. Keep the document open and maximized.

b. Click **Action Center** in the Notification area on the taskbar.

Although any alerts displayed on your computer may vary from those shown in Figure 27, the general appearance should be similar.

c. Press **PtrSc**, click **Word** on the taskbar, press **Ctrl+End**, press **Enter** twice, and then press **Ctrl+V**. Save the file. Minimize Word.

d. Click **Action Center**, click **All settings**, click **System**, and then click **Notifications & actions**. Press **PtrSc**, click **Word** on the taskbar, press **Enter** twice, and then press **Ctrl+V**. Save the file. Minimize Word.

e. Click the **Back arrow** in the upper left of the Settings window, and then click **Update & security**.

Windows Update displays.

f. Click **Check for updates**.

g. Press **PtrSc**, click **Word** on the taskbar, press **Enter** twice, and then press **Ctrl+V**. Save the document. Minimize Word and close the Settings window.

STEP 2 >> MODIFY FIREWALL SETTINGS

Although you do not expect the students to understand completely how firewalls work, you do want them to know that Windows includes a firewall and that they can manage firewall settings. Refer to Figure 28 as you complete Step 2.

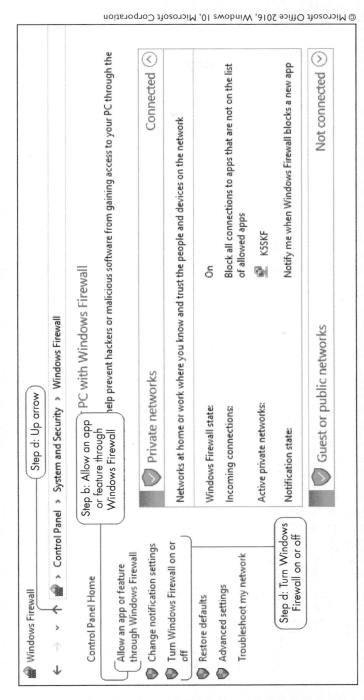

FIGURE 28 Modify Firewall Settings

a. Type **Firewall** in the search box, and then select **Windows Firewall - Control Panel**.

b. Click **Allow an App or feature through Windows Firewall**.

c. Take a full-screen snip of your screen, click **Word** on the taskbar, press **Enter** twice, and then press **Ctrl+V**. Minimize Word and the Snipping Tool windows.

d. Click the **up arrow** to return to main screen of Windows Firewall, and click **Turn Windows Firewall on or off**. Note the checkmarks.

e. Take a full-screen snip of your screen, click **Word** on the taskbar, press **Enter** twice, and then press **Ctrl+V**. Save the document. Minimize the Word and the Snipping Tool windows.

f. Click **Cancel**, and then close the Windows Firewall window.

Hands-On Exercise 3

STEP 3 >> USE DISK CLEANUP

You want to stress how important it is to run routine maintenance tasks on the computer. In addition to periodically wiping down the keyboard and monitor, you tell the students they should run the Disk Cleanup utility to remove unnecessary files that have accumulated. Refer to Figure 29 as you complete Step 3.

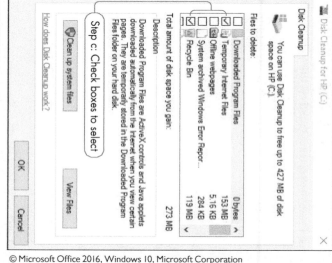

© Microsoft Office 2016, Windows 10, Microsoft Corporation

FIGURE 29 Disk Cleanup

a. Open the **Start** menu, click **All apps**, and then click **Windows Administrative Tools.** Click **Disk Cleanup.**

b. Ensure drive C: displays in the Disk cleanup: Drive Selection dialog box, and click **OK**.

Disk Cleanup scans the hard disk drive for any unnecessary files that can be removed.

c. Click the check boxes to select **Recycle Bin** and **Temporary Internet Files** in the Files to delete section. Click to deselect any other check marks.

d. Take a full-screen snip of your screen, click **Word** on the taskbar, press **Enter** twice, and then press **Ctrl+V**. Save the file.

e. Click **Disk Cleanup** on the taskbar, and then click **OK**. Click **Delete Files** when asked are you sure you want to permanently delete these files. Right-click **Snipping Tool** on the taskbar, and click **Close window**. Do not save changes.

f. Save and close the file. Based on your instructor's directions, submit win01h3Windows10_LastFirst.

Chapter Objectives Review

After reading this chapter, you have accomplished the following objectives:

1. Understand the Windows 10 Interface

- Sign in to a Microsoft account: A Microsoft account is necessary to use any Microsoft Services, including logging into Windows 10.
- Access sleep and power settings: Windows will go to sleep, a power-saving state, after a pre-determined period of inactivity. Restarting the computer is a warm boot. To power down the computer completely, choose Shut down.
- Explore the Windows 10 Start menu: The desktop is the primary working area that displays when you log into Windows. The Start menu is accessed by clicking the Start button on the taskbar. The Start menu has program tiles that can be arranged in groups, a Most used list of frequently used programs, and access to File Explorer, Documents, Settings, and Power. Clicking All apps changes the left panel of the Start menu to a list of all programs installed on the device.
- Configure the Start menu: You can easily add and remove tiles from the Windows 10 Start menu. Adding a tile to the Start menu or an icon to the taskbar is known as pinning. You can organize the tiles into groups by dragging them around the screen. You can also assign appropriate names for each group of tiles. Tiles can be resized and removed from the Start menu.
- Explore the taskbar: The taskbar displays icons of open programs, as well as Start, the search box, and the Notification area. A Task View enables you to view all current tasks in one glance. Frequently used programs can be pinned to the taskbar. Right-clicking an open program icon on the taskbar opens a Jump List.
- Identify desktop components: On the desktop, icons represent links to programs, files, folder, or other items related to your computer. The Recycle Bin is temporary storage for deleted files. Shortcuts are icons to program files.
- Customize the desktop: You can customize the desktop with a different background color or theme.

2. Manage and Use the Desktop and Components

- Use Task View: Task View enables you to see all open windows, and to organize them into separate workspaces.
- Create a virtual desktop: Virtual desktops help to organize and access groups of windows for different purposes.
- Identify windows components: Windows can be moved, resized, stacked, or snapped into position so that multiple windows are easier to work with and identify.
- Snap, move, and resize windows: You can display up to four Windows 10 apps at a time using Snap and Snap Assist. Dialog boxes are windows that display when a program requires user interaction.

3. Use Windows 10 Search Features

- Use the search box: A search box, incorporated into the taskbar for easy access, is used to search the Web and the device. If you are looking for help or specific answers, you can type search keyword(s) in the search box and then click any resulting links.
- Use Cortana: When enabled, Cortana, Microsoft's personal assistant, can assist with tasks such as reminders and directions, provide a news feed, as well as search the Web and the device. Cortana's settings are managed through the Cortana Notebook.
- Get help: Cortana and the search box are the primary resources for help and support for Windows and other Microsoft-related questions.
- Manage the Cortana Notebook and settings: You can add or modify your preferences in Cortana Notebook. As you use Cortana, she will adapt to your preferences and be able to better predict your needs.

4. Use File Explorer

- File Explorer is an app used to create and manage folders and files across various storage locations on your PC, online storage, external storage, and networks.
- Understand the File Explorer interface: File Explorer displays the organizational hierarchy of storage locations, folders, and files.
- Use the View tab on the Ribbon: The View tab contains controls that manage how files and folders are displayed in File Explorer.
- Use and modify Quick access: Quick access is a new feature of File Explorer that contains shortcuts to folders you use most often. Folders can be pinned and removed from Quick access.
- Use the search box in File Explorer: Use the search box in File Explorer to search for specific files and folders. Results can be filtered by type, date modified, or other properties for further search refinement.
- Navigate File Explorer: The Navigation Pane is used to move between folders and storage locations. Clicking next to each main area in the Navigation Pane expands or collapses the folder to show or hide contents.
- Working with files and folders: Grouping related files into folders helps keep them organized and easier to locate.
- Open, rename, and delete folders and files: Click on a file or folder to open it, right-click and select Rename to give the folder or file a different name, right-click and select Delete to remove the file or folder from File Explorer.

5. Select, Copy, and Move Multiple Files and Folders

- Select multiple files and folders: Select adjacent files while pressing the Shift key. Select non-adjacent files while pressing the Ctrl key. Alternatively, click the check box next to each item to select.

- Copy and move file and folders: Files and folders can be copied and moved by dragging to a new location, as needed.

6. Compress Files and Folders

- Create a compressed folder: Compress a folder or a group of files using the Zip tool to facilitate sending a large file or a group of files using email or uploading to the Web.

- Extract files from a compressed folder: To unzip, use the the Extract all feature on the Extract tab.

7. Work with Security Settings and Software

- Understand the Action Center: The Action Center monitors the status of your security and maintenance settings, alerting you when maintenance tasks (such as backing up your system) are overlooked or when your security is at risk (for example, when antivirus software is out of date).

- Use File History: The File History utility can be configured to automatically make backups of your important files while you work.

- Access Windows Update: Windows Update provides a means to push modifications and fixes made to the operating system to the computer.

- Use Windows Defender: Windows Defender, an antivirus and antispyware program, is included with Windows and works to identify and remove malicious software.

- Use Windows firewall: A Windows firewall protects against unauthorized access to your computer from outside entities and prohibits unauthorized programs from accessing your computer without your permission.

8. Work with Administrative Tools

- Use Task Manager: Task Manager displays programs and processes that are running on your computer. Task Manager can be used to close a program when it is not responding.

- Monitor system resources: Resource Monitor displays how the computer is using its key components, including the CPU and RAM.

- Use Disk Cleanup: Disk Cleanup is used to remove unnecessary files from the computer that can slow down system performance.

- Get remote assistance: Remote assistance allows a third party to take control of your device.

Key Terms Matching

Match the key terms with their definitions. Write the key term letter by the appropriate numbered definition.

a. Action Center
b. Compressed (zipped) folder
c. Cortana
d. Desktop
e. Disk Cleanup
f. File Explorer
g. File History
h. File management
i. Notification area
j. OneDrive

k. Pin
l. Quick access
m. Search box
n. Start menu
o. Task Manager
p. Task View
q. Taskbar
r. Tile
s. Virtual desktop
t. Windows Defender

1. _____ An administrative tool in Windows that is used to remove unnecessary files from the computer.

2. _____ Primary working area of Windows 10.

3. _____ A utility in Windows that continuously makes copies of your important files so that you can recover them if you encounter a file problem.

4. _____ Microsoft's cloud storage system.

5. _____ A folder that uses less drive space and can be transferred or shared with other users more quickly.

6. _____ A component of File Explorer that contains shortcuts to the most frequently used folders.

7. _____ The main access to all programs and features on your computer.

8. _____ The Windows 10 personal assistant that helps search the Web and your PC, and can also assist with reminders, tasks, and other activities.

9. _____ The means of providing an organizational structure to file and folders.

10. _____ Detects and removes viruses and spyware.

11. _____ Displays the programs and processes that are running on your computer. It is also used to close a non-responding program.

12. _____ Located on the taskbar, provides a convenient way to search your computer or the Web.

13. _____ Provides status information, notifications, and recommended actions for various maintenance and security settings.

14. _____ Horizontal bar at the bottom of the desktop that displays open applications, the Notification area, the search box, and pinned apps or programs.

15. _____ Provides system status alerts in pop-up boxes.

16. _____ A process to add a tile to the Start menu or an icon to the taskbar.

17. _____ A block icon on the Start menu that represents a program or app.

18. _____ A way to organize and access groups of windows for different purposes.

19. _____ The Windows app that is used to create folders and manage files and folders across various storage locations.

20. _____ Feature on the taskbar that enables the user to view thumbnail previews of all open tasks in one glance.

Multiple Choice

1. The Windows 10 feature that alerts you to any maintenance or security concerns is the:

   (a) Action Center.
   (b) Security Center.
   (c) Windows Defender.
   (d) Control Panel.

2. Snapping apps means that you:

   (a) Minimize all open apps simultaneously so that the Start menu displays.
   (b) Auto arrange all open apps so that they are of uniform size.
   (c) Manually reposition all open apps so that you can see the content of each.
   (d) Fix an app window(s) to either side or the corners of the screen.

3. What phrase is spoken to use Cortana?

   (a) Hey, Cortana
   (b) Wake up, Cortana
   (c) No specific phrase is necessary.
   (d) You cannot speak to Cortana.

4. Apps or programs on the Start menu are represented by rectangular icons known as:

   (a) Gadgets.
   (b) Tiles.
   (c) Thumbnails.
   (d) Boxes.

5. What feature is used to organize and access groups of open windows for different purposes, such as Schoolwork and Entertainment?

   (a) Windows Defender
   (b) Windows desktop
   (c) Virtual desktop
   (d) Task Manager

6. Which of the following best describes the Action Center?

   (a) Removes unnecessary files from the computer
   (b) Includes the clock and other icons that relate to the status or setting of a program
   (c) Contains shortcuts to the most frequently used folders
   (d) Provides status information, notifications, and recommended actions

7. Adding a tile to the Start menu or an icon to the taskbar is known as:

   (a) Snapping.
   (b) Snipping.
   (c) Pinning.
   (d) Tacking.

8. Which of the following is a method of switching between open windows?

   (a) Alt+Tab
   (b) Task View
   (c) Both A and B
   (d) Neither A nor B

9. When you restore down a window, you:

   (a) Keep it open, but remove it from view.
   (b) Make the window smaller, but keep it displayed on the desktop.
   (c) Minimize the window's height but leave its width unchanged.
   (d) Minimize the window's width but leave its height unchanged.

10. When you enter search keywords in the search box of File Explorer and the OneDrive option is selected:

    (a) The search is limited to that specific location.
    (b) The search cannot be further narrowed.
    (c) The search is automatically expanded to include every folder on the hard drive.
    (d) The search is limited to the selected location but can be expanded if you like.

Practice Exercises

Investments

FROM SCRATCH

You have some extra funds accumulating in your savings account. You want to begin investing, but before you take the plunge, you decide to watch a few stocks and learn more about them. You also want to take advantage of some Microsoft apps to read more about the stock market and investing, in general. You create and add tiles to a new group on your Start menu and also create a separate desktop for your investment activities, so you can easily come back to all the material. Refer to Figure 30 as you complete the exercise.

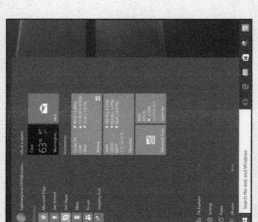

© Microsoft Office 2016, Windows 10, Microsoft Corporation

FIGURE 30 Investments Start Menu and Virtual Desktops

a. Open a Blank Word document, and save it as **win01p1Investments_LastFirst**. Minimize the window.

b. Click the **search box**, type **Money**, right-click **Money Trusted Windows Store app** that displays at the top of the results list, and then click **Pin to Start**.

> **TROUBLESHOOTING:** If the Money app is already pinned to start, skip to the next step.

c. Click **Start**, and move the Money tile to a blank area on the Start menu.

d. Point above the Money tile to display the Name group box, click inside the box, type **Investments**, and then press **Enter**.
   You have created a new group.

e. Click **Money**, and then click **Watchlist** from the top menu. Click **Add to Watchlist** (the plus sign), and then type **MSFT**, and press **Enter**. (Note: MSFT might already be added to the Watchlist.) Repeat this step to add **GOOG** and **AAPL**.

> **TROUBLESHOOTING:** If MSFT is the first stock begin added to the Watchlist, click Add a favorite in the middle of the screen. .

f. Click **Pin to Start** 📌 to pin the Watchlist to the Start menu. Click **Close**.

g. Click **MSFT** on the Watchlist, and click **Pin to Start**. Click the **Back arrow**. Repeat for **AAPL**. Minimize Money.

h. Click **Start**, and notice the three new tiles you have added. Drag the three new tiles into the Investments group.

i. Right-click the **Money tile**, and click **Resize**, and then select **Wide**. Resize the Watchlist tile to **Wide**.

j. Drag to arrange the tiles within the Investments group to match the arrangement in Figure 30.

k. Press **PrtSc**, click **Word** on the taskbar, and then press **Ctrl+V**. Save the document and minimize Word.

l. Click **Start**, and click the **Watchlist** tile.

m. Open Cortana, click the **Notebook icon**, and click **Finance**. In the Stocks you're tracking section, click **GOOG**, and click the **trashcan icon** to remove GOOG from the Watchlist.

n. Click **Excel** in the Start menu, type **Portfolio Analysis** in the Search for online templates box. Select the template that results, and click **Create**.

o. Click **File**, click **Save As**, click **Browse**, and then click **Documents** in the This PC folder. Check that This PC>Documents displays in the Address bar.

p. Type **win01p1Portfolio_LastFirst** in the File name box, click **New folder**, and name the folder **Portfolio**, click **Open**, and then click **Save**. Minimize Excel.

q. Open **Task View**, click the **plus sign** to create a new desktop, and then drag the Excel and Money thumbnails to Desktop 2.

r. Point to **Desktop 2** to display two thumbnails. Click **PrtSc**, point to **Desktop 1**, click **Word**, press **Enter** twice, and then press **Ctrl+V**. Save the document.

s. Click **Close** to delete Desktop 2, and close Excel. Open File Explorer, click **Documents** in the Quick access or This PC section, right-click the **Portfolio folder**, and then click **Pin to Quick access**.

t. Right-click **Portfolio** in the Documents folder and rename it as **Investments**. Notice that the folder name also changes in Quick access.

u. Press **PrtSc**, click **Word**, press **Enter** twice, and then press **Ctrl+V**. Save the document.

v. Click **Start**, click **Settings**, type **Firewall** in the Find a setting search box, and then click **Windows Firewall**. Click **Turn Windows Firewall on or off**, and then in the Public network settings, click to select **Block all incoming connections, including those in the list of allowed apps.**

w. Press **PrtSc**, click **Word**, press **Enter** twice, and then press **Ctrl+V**. Save the document and minimize Word.

x. Click **Cancel**, close the Windows Firewall window, and then close the Settings window.

y. Save and close the file. Based on your instructor's directions, submit win01p1Investments_ LastFirst. Close any other open windows.

2 Planning a Trip

FROM SCRATCH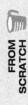

You and your family want to take a road trip through some National Parks. You volunteer to begin planning. You start by opening the Calendar app to block out the desired week, and then open the Map app to help with the navigation. You pin both apps to the Start menu, and place them in a new group. You also create a new desktop in which to display them. You create a folder and pin it to Quick access, so everyone in the family can easily find the folder and save their ideas. Your friend visited some National Parks last year and sent you her photos in a zipped folder. You move them to the new folder, and then extract the pictures so your family can better access them. You use Disk Cleanup to make sure your computer remains in tip-top shape. Refer to Figure 31 as you complete the exercise.

© Microsoft Office 2016, Windows 10, Microsoft Corporation

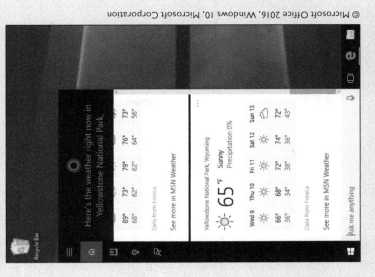

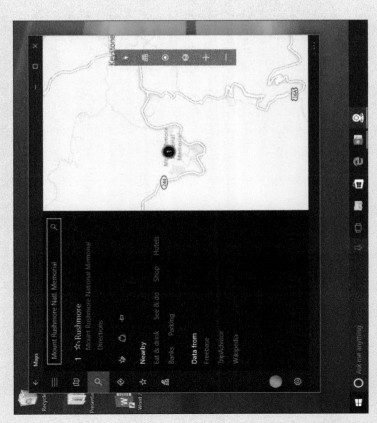

FIGURE 31 Planning a Trip

a. Start **Word**, create a **Blank document**, and then save the document as **win01p2Vacation_ LastFirst**. Keep the document open.

b. Click **Start**, click **All apps**, and scroll to find **Calendar**. Right-click and select **Pin to Start**. Note: If Calendar app is already on the Start menu, skip to the next step.

c. Click **Start**, click the **Calendar app**, click **New event**, click in the Event name box, and type **Family Vacation**. Click **Start**, and type **June 01, 2018**. Click **End**, and type **June 14, 2018**. Click to select the **All day box**, click the **Show As: box**, select **Tentative**, click the **Reminder box**, and then select **None**.

> **TROUBLESHOOTING:** If you have never worked with the Calendar app before, you might need to click Welcome, and confirm an email account before working with the application.

d. Press **PrtSc**, click **Word** on the taskbar, and then click inside a blank area of the document. Press **Ctrl+V**, click **Save**, and then minimize Word. Click **Save & Close** on the Calendar app. Close Calendar.

e. Click **Start**, click **All apps**, and scroll to find **Maps**, if it is not already on the Start menu. Right-click and select **Pin to Start**.

f. Open **Maps**, type **Yellowstone National Park**, select the entry in the resulting list, click the **Star** (Add to Favorites), type **Yellowstone** in the Nickname box, and then click **Save**. Repeat for **Grand Teton National Park**, using **Teton** as the Nickname, and **Mount Rushmore National Memorial**, using **Rushmore** as the Nickname.

g. Press **PrtSc**, click **Word**, press **Enter** twice, press **Ctrl+V**, click **Save**, and then minimize the Word document. Close Maps.

h. Open **File Explorer**, click **Documents** (in either This PC or Quick access), and then click **New folder** on the Home tab in the New group. Name the folder **Vacation**. Press **Enter**. Click **Pin to Quick access** in the Clipboard group.

i. Navigate to your student data files, and locate the *win01p2Pictures* zipped folder. Click the zipped folder, press and hold **Ctrl**, and drag it to the Vacation folder you pinned to Quick access.

j. Click **Vacation** in Quick access, click the **win01p2Pictures zipped folder**, click the **Extract tab**, and then click **Extract all**. Click **Extract**.

k. Click **Vacation** in the Address bar, click the **zipped win01p2Pictures folder** in the File list, and then click **Delete**.

l. Double-click to open the **win01p2Pictures folder** so the thumbnail images display in the File list.

m. Press **PrtSc**, click **Word** on the taskbar, press **Enter** twice, press **Ctrl+V**, and then save the Word document. Close all open File Explorer windows.

n. Click the **search box**, type **Disk Cleanup**, and then click **Disk Cleanup Desktop app.**

o. Click **OK** to run Disk Cleanup on the C: drive, and then in the results, click to select **Recycle Bin** and deselect all other check boxes.

p. Press **PrtSc**, click **Word**, press **Enter** twice, press **Ctrl+V**.

q. Save and close the file. Based on your instructor's directions submit win01p2Vacation_LastFirst.

Mid-Level Exercises

1 5K Pound Run

FROM SCRATCH

To satisfy your community outreach graduation requirement, you and a friend have decided to organize a 5K run to benefit the regional animal rescue society. You are responsible for organizing the paperwork and pulling together the details. To start, you use Windows 10 to organize the various apps and files so you can easily find and work with all that you need at any time.

a. Start **Word**, create a **Blank document**, and it save as **win01m1Race_LastFirst**.

b. Type **5K Pound Run**, and press **Enter** twice. Save the file.

c. Pin Word to the taskbar.

d. Locate the Calendar app and Map app in All apps.

e. Put the Maps and Calendar apps in a new group on the Start menu, and name the group **5K Race**.

f. Pin the Sticky Notes app to the Start menu, and add it to the 5K Race group.

g. Use PrtSc to capture a screenshot of the Start menu, and paste it in the win01m1Race_LastFirst document.

h. Use the search box to find information on the Web about 5K races in your area in April. Click any link that displays a list of races. Take a screenshot of the Web results, copy and paste to the Word document.

i. Open File Explorer, create a new folder where you save your student files named **5KPoundRun**, and then pin the folder to Quick access.

j. Create subfolders in the 5KPoundRun folder, and name them: **Sponsors, Permissions, Promotions, Registration,** and **Follow-Up.** Rename the Registration folder to **Participants.**

k. Click **Word** on the taskbar, click **File**, and then click **New**. Type **Seasonal Event Flyer (Spring)** in the templates search box. Click **Create**, and then save to the Promotions folder as **win01m1Flyer_LastFirst.**

l. Add the tag **5KPound Run** to win01m1Flyer_LastFirst. Take a screenshot to show the tag, copy and paste to the win01m1Race_LastFirst document. Save the flyer.

m. Create a new virtual desktop (Desktop 2), and drag the flyer into Desktop 2 in Task View. Display the contents of Desktop 2, and then take a screenshot and paste the screenshot into win01m1Race_LastFirst.

n. Compress the 5KPoundRun folder and rename it **win01m1PoundRun_LastFirst.**

o. Open the Action Center. Take a screenshot of the Action Center. Paste the screenshot into win01m1Race_LastFirst.

p. Save and close the file. Based on your instructor's directions, submit win01m1Race_LastFirst and win01m1PoundRun_LastFirst.

DISCOVER **H**

2 Junk Business

FROM SCRATCH

You and a college friend were asked to reconfigure some old computers for an inner city after school club. Because you had a few spare parts and some hardware expertise, you rebuilt several computers and installed Windows 10. Now you will check the system of each computer to verify that it is workable and configured correctly. Assume the computer you are working on to complete this exercise is the computer you rebuilt.

a. Open Word, create a Blank document, and save the file as **win01m2Junk_LastFirst**. Snap Word to the left side of your screen.

b. Open the Action Center. Press **PrtSc** to capture a screen image of the Action Center. In Word, type **Step b:**. Press **Enter**, and press **Ctrl+V** to paste the screen. Underneath the image, describe any Notifications that display. Save the document. Close the Action Center.

c. Type **Resource Monitor** in the search box. Pin Resource Monitor to the Start menu. Open Resource Monitor, and click the **Memory tab**. Snap the Resource Monitor window to the right side of your screen. Click **Word** on the taskbar, press **Enter** twice, type **Step c:**, press **Enter**, and then list the amount of memory *In Use, Standby, Free,* and *Installed.* Add a sentence that comments on whether the amount of memory in the system seems sufficient. Close the Resource Monitor. Save the Word document.

d. Pin Disk Cleanup to the Start menu. Type **Windows Accessories** as a new group name, in the Start menu, and drag **Disk Cleanup** and **Resource Monitor** to the group. Take a screenshot of the Start menu, open Word, type **Step d:**, and then paste the screenshot.

e. Open File Explorer, and create a new folder in Documents named **Client Invoices.** Pin the Client Invoices folder to Quick access, and then open the Client Invoices folder. Take a screenshot of File Explorer, open Word, type **Step e:**, and then paste the screenshot.

f. Save and close the file. Based on your instructor's directions, submit win01m2Junk_LastFirst.

Beyond the Classroom

Speech Class Notes

For your speech class, you must develop a speech that teaches how to do something. Because Windows 10 is a relatively new operating system, you decide to demonstrate some of its features. You will use Word to record a few notes that will help you make your presentation. After completing your notes, save the document as **win01b1Speech_ LastFirst**. Listing your points in numerical order, provide directions to the class on the following:

- Customize the Start menu.
- Pin programs to the taskbar and the Start menu.
- Use the search box to find and open a program that you think is installed on your computer and to get help on an item related to Windows 10.
- Use Cortana.
- Use the Action Center.

Based on your instructor's directions, submit win01b1Speech_LastFirst.

Computer Security Report

You depend on a laptop computer for most of what you do and you would be lost should you lose your laptop or the data and programs on it. A recent scare, when you temporarily misplaced the laptop, has led you to consider precautions you can take to make sure your computer and its data are protected. You will use the search box and Cortana to explore some suggestions for protecting your laptop. Create a report that describes how you would secure your laptop and the data, programs, and personal information on your laptop against harm. Consider virus protection software, cloud storage options, backup and recovery software and hardware, and ways to protect and secure your hardware. Use Word to record the report, save the report as **win01b2Protection_LastFirst**, and submit as directed by your instructor.

For your Entrepreneurial class, BUS401, you are planning a new business as the ongoing project. Since you will be working with many of the same apps and documents throughout the semester, you decide to use many of the new Windows 10 features to help you stay organized and be as efficient as possible.

Work with the Start Menu

To start things off, you want to pin a few apps to the Start menu that you know you will be working with consistently throughout the semester. You will put them in a group and give the group a meaningful name.

a. Open a new Word document and save it as **win01c1Business_LastFirst.**

b. Locate and pin to the Start menu, the Calculator app, the Snipping Tool, Word 2016, and Excel 2016.

c. Pin Word 2016 and the Snipping Tool to the taskbar.

d. Create a new group on the Start menu, name it **Business Apps,** and move the apps you added to the Start menu in Step b to this group.

e. Resize the Calculator app and the Snipping Tool tiles to Small. Keep Word 2016 and Excel 2016 tiles to Medium. Arrange the tiles so the Word and Excel tiles are next to each other, and the Calculator and Snipping Tool tiles are below the Word and Excel tiles.

f. Take a screenshot of the Start menu. Paste the screenshot to win01c1Business_LastFirst.

Use Task View and Virtual Desktops

There are a few Excel and Word files that you will be using for this project. So that you can get to them easily, you put them onto a separate desktop.

a. Open Word and search for a Business Plan template. Select the first template, named Business plan. Create and save the document as **win01c1BusinessPlan_ LastFirst.**

b. Open Excel and search for a Profit and Loss template. Select the first template, named Profit and Loss Statement. Save the workbook as **win01c1ProfitLoss_LastFirst.**

c. Create a new virtual desktop (Desktop 2) and drag the Excel and Word files created in Steps a and b above to Desktop 2. Keep win01c1Business_LastFirst in Desktop 1.

d. Display Desktop 2, and snap the Word document to the left and the Excel workbook to the right of the screen and take a screenshot.

e. Display Desktop 1, and paste the screenshot to win01c1Business_LastFirst.

Use Cortana and the Search Box

One of the first things you need to do for your business is to write a Mission Statement. You use the search box to find information on Mission Statements, and then use Cortana to set up a reminder for you to talk to your professor about this, as well.

a. Type **how to write a mission statement** in the search box. Open the Entrepreneur.com link (or a similar link). Drag the browser window to Desktop 2.

b. Display Desktop 2, and then using the Windows and arrow keys, snap the browser window to the lower left corner, and the Word window to the upper left corner.

c. Use Cortana in Desktop 2 to add a reminder to meet with your professor. Choose a day and time next week.

d. Take a screenshot of Desktop 2 and Cortana Reminders. Display Desktop 1, and paste the screenshot to win01c1Business_LastFirst.

e. Close all windows in Desktop 2.

Use File Explorer

Although using virtual desktops helps to organize your active documents, you want to create a good file management structure so all your Entrepreneurial class documents are in one place and easy to access throughout the semester. You use File Explorer to create folders and pin one folder to Quick access.

a. Open File Explorer, and open the Documents folder in This PC. Create a new folder named **BUS401.** Pin this folder to Quick access.

b. Open the BUS401 folder, and create three new folders named **Business Plan Documents, Financial Statements,** and **Marketing Info.**

c. Take a screenshot of File Explorer and paste the screenshot to win01c1Business_LastFirst.

Work with Files and Folders

With the new folder structure set up, you reorganize your existing files. You then compress the BUS401 folder so you can more easily share it with your professor and others.

a. Save the win01c1ProfitLoss_LastFirst workbook to the Financial Statements folder, and move win01c1BusinessPlan_LastFirst to the Business Plan Documents folder.

b. Compress the BUS401 folder, and rename the folder **win01c1BUS401_LastFirst.**

Use the Action Center and Administrative Tools

One of the other components of the BUS401 project is to create a marketing video. You know creating and editing a video uses lots of computer processing and memory, so you check the status of your system resources to see if this will be the best computer to use going forward. You also want to check the Action Center for any new notifications.

a. Open Resource Monitor. Click the **Memory tab**, use the Snipping Tool to take a Rectangular Snip of the Resource Monitor window, and then paste it into win01c1Business_LastFirst.

b. Click the **CPU tab**, and then use the Snipping Tool to take a Rectangular Snip of the Resource Monitor window and paste it into win01c1Business_LastFirst. Close the Resource Monitor.

c. Open the Action Center. Take a screenshot, and paste the screenshot in to win01c1Business_LastFirst.

d. Save and close the document. Based on your instructor's directions, submit win01c1Business_LastFirst and win01c1BUS401_LastFirst.

Action Center A location in Windows 10, accessed by an icon in the Notifications area on the taskbar, that provides status information, notifications, and recommended actions for various maintenance and security settings.

Compressed (zipped) folder A folder created with the Zip feature, contains a file or group of files. A compressed folder uses less drive space and can be transferred or shared with other users more quickly.

Cortana Microsoft 10's personal assistant that helps search the Web and your PC, and can also assist with reminders, tasks, and other activities.

Desktop The primary working area of Windows 10 that contains objects such as windows and icons.

Disk Cleanup An administrative tool in Windows that is used to remove unnecessary files from the computer.

File Explorer The Windows app that is used to create folders and manage files and folders across various storage locations.

File History A utility in Windows that continuously makes copies of your important files so that you can recover them if you encounter a file problem.

File management The means of providing an organizational structure to file and folders.

Firewall A software program included in Windows 10 that helps to product against unauthorized access, or hacking, to your computer.

Icon A graphical link to a program, file, folder, or other item related to your computer.

Jump List List of program-specific shortcuts to recently opened files, the program name, an option to pin or unpin the program, and a close window option.

Notification area An area on the far right of the taskbar, that includes the clock and a group of icons that relate to the status of a setting or program.

OneDrive Microsoft's cloud storage system. Saving files to OneDrive enables them to sync across all Windows devices and to be accessible from any Internet-connected device.

Pin A process to add a tile to the Start menu or icon to the taskbar.

Quick access A component of File Explorer that contains shortcuts to the most frequently used folders. Folders can be pinned and removed from Quick access.

Recycle Bin Temporary storage for files deleted from the computer's hard drive or OneDrive.

Resource Monitor A feature that displays how the computer is using its key resources such as the CPU and RAM.

Search box A feature located on the taskbar. Combined with Cortana, or used alone, it provides a convenient way to search your computer or the Web.

Shortcut An icon on the desktop designated with a small arrow in the bottom-left corner, that provides a link a program.

Sleep A power saving state that puts work and settings in memory and draws a small amount of power to allow the computer to resume full-power operation quickly.

Snip A screenshot taken with the Snipping Tool accessory application in Windows.

Start menu A feature that provides the main access to all programs on your computer.

Task Manager A tool that displays the programs and processes that are running on your computer. It is also used to close a non-responding program.

Task view A button on the taskbar that enables the user to view thumbnail previews of all open tasks in one glance.

Taskbar The horizontal bar at the bottom of the desktop that displays open applications, the Notification area, the Search box, and pinned apps or programs.

Tile A rectangular icon on the Start menu that allow you to access programs and apps.

Title bar The long bar at the top of each window that displays the name of the folder, file, or program displayed in the open window and the application in which you are working.

Virtual desktop A way to organize and access groups of windows for different purposes.

Windows app A program that displays full screen without any borders or many controls. It is designed to be best viewed and used on smaller screens such as those on smartphone and tablets.

Windows Defender Antispyware and antivirus software included in Windows 10.

Windows Update A utility in Windows that provides a means to initiate updates and modifications pushed to the user that enhances Windows security or fixes problems.

Office 2016
Common Features

Common Features

LEARNING OUTCOME

You will apply skills common across the Microsoft Office suite to create and format documents and edit content in Office 2016 applications.

OBJECTIVES & SKILLS: After you read this chapter, you will be able to:

CASE STUDY | Spotted Begonia Art Gallery

You are an administrative assistant for Spotted Begonia, a local art gallery. The gallery does a lot of community outreach and tries to help local artists develop a network of clients and supporters. Local schools are invited to bring students to the gallery for enrichment programs.

As the administrative assistant for Spotted Begonia, you are responsible for overseeing the production of documents, spreadsheets, newspaper articles, and presentations that will be used to increase public awareness of the gallery. Other clerical assistants who are familiar with Microsoft Office will prepare the promotional materials, and you will proofread, make necessary corrections, adjust page layouts, save and print documents, and identify appropriate templates to simplify tasks. Your experience with Microsoft Office 2016 is limited, but you know that certain fundamental tasks that are common to Word, Excel, and PowerPoint will help you accomplish your oversight task. You are excited to get started with your work!

Taking the First Step

FIGURE 1 Spotted Begonia Art Gallery Memo and Flyer

CASE STUDY | Spotted Begonia Art Gallery

Starting Files

f01h1Letter
f01h2Flyer
Blank document

Files to be Submitted

f01h2Flyer_LastFirst
f01h3Letter_LastFirst

Getting Started with Office Applications

Organizations around the world rely heavily on Microsoft Office software to produce documents, spreadsheets, presentations, and databases. *Microsoft Office* is a productivity software suite including a set of software applications, each one specializing in a particular type of output. You can use *Word* to produce all sorts of documents, including memos, newsletters, forms, tables, and brochures. *Excel* makes it easy to organize records, financial transactions, and business information in the form of worksheets. With *PowerPoint*, you can create dynamic presentations to inform and persuade audiences. *Access* is a relational database software application that enables you to record and link data, query databases, and create forms and reports.

You will sometimes find that you need to use two or more Office applications to produce your intended output. You might, for example, find that an annual report document you are preparing in Word for an art gallery should also include a chart of recent sales stored in Excel. You can use Excel to prepare the summary and then incorporate the worksheet in the Word document. Similarly, you can integrate Word tables and Excel charts into a PowerPoint presentation. The choice of which software applications to use really depends on what type of output you are producing. Table 1 describes the major tasks of the four primary applications in Microsoft Office.

TABLE 1 Microsoft Office Software

Office 2016 Product	Application Characteristics
Word	Word processing software used with text to create, edit, and format documents such as letters, memos, reports, brochures, resumes, and flyers.
Excel	Spreadsheet software used to store quantitative data and to perform accurate and rapid calculations with results ranging from simple budgets to financial and statistical analyses.
PowerPoint	Presentation graphics software used to create slide shows for presentation by a speaker, to be published as part of a website, or to run as a stand-alone application on a computer kiosk.
Access	Relational database software used to store data and convert it into information. Database software is used primarily for decision making by businesses that compile data from multiple records stored in tables to produce informative reports.

Pearson Education, Inc.

Starting an Office Application

STEP 1

Microsoft Office applications are launched from the Start menu. Click the Start button, and then click the app tile for the application in which you want to work. If the application tile is not on the Start menu, you can open the program from All apps, or alternatively, you can click in the search box on the task bar, type the name of the program, and press Enter. The program will open automatically.

As you become familiar with Microsoft Office, you will find that although each software application produces a specific type of output, all applications share common features. Such commonality gives a similar feel to each software application so that learning and working with Office software products is easy.

In this section, you will learn how to open an application, log in with your Microsoft account, and open and save a file. You will also learn to identify features common to Office software applications, including interface components such as the Ribbon, Backstage view, and the Quick Access Toolbar. You will experience Live Preview. You will learn how to get help with an application. You will also learn how to search for and install Office add-ins.

Change Your Microsoft Account

Although you can log in to Windows as a local network user, you can also log in using a Microsoft account. When you have a Microsoft account, you can sign in to any Windows computer and you will be able to access the saved settings associated with your Microsoft account. That means the computer will have the same familiar look that you are used to seeing on other computers and devices. Your Microsoft account will automatically sign in to all of the apps and services that use a Microsoft account as the authentication. You can also save your sign-in credentials for other websites that you frequently visit. If you share your computer with another user, each user can have access to his own Microsoft account; you can easily switch between accounts so you can access your own files.

To switch between accounts in an application such as Word, complete the following steps:

1. Click the profile name at the top-right of the application.
2. Select Switch account. Select an account from the list, if the account has already been added to the computer, or add a new account.

Logging in with your Microsoft account also provides additional benefits such as being connected to all of Microsoft's resources on the Internet. These resources include a free Outlook email account and access to OneDrive cloud storage. *Cloud storage* is a technology used to store files and to work with programs that are stored in a central location on the Internet. *OneDrive* is an app used to store, access, and share files and folders. It is accessible using an installed desktop app or as cloud storage using a Web address. For Office applications, OneDrive is the default location for saving files. Documents saved in OneDrive are accessible from any computer that has an Internet connection. As long as the document has been saved in OneDrive, the most recent version of the document will be accessible when you log in from any computer connected to the Internet. Moreover, files and folders stored on the computer's hard drive or saved on a portable storage device can be synced with those on the OneDrive account.

OneDrive enables you to collaborate with others. You can easily share your documents with others or edit a document on which you are collaborating. You can even work with others simultaneously on the same document.

Working with Files

When working with an Office application, you can begin by opening an existing file that has already been saved to a storage medium, or you can begin work on a new file. When you open an application within Office, you can select a template to use as you begin working on a new file.

Create a New File

After opening an Office application, such as Word, Excel, or PowerPoint, you will be presented with template choices. Click Blank document (workbook, presentation, etc.) to start a new blank file. Perhaps you are already working with a document in an Office application but want to create a new file.

To create a new Office file, complete the following steps:

1. Click the File tab and click New.
2. Click Blank.

Open a File

You will often work with a file, save it, and then continue the project at a later time. To open an existing file, you can click a location such as This PC or OneDrive and navigate to the folder or drive where your document is stored. Once you make your way to the file to be opened, double-click the file name to open the file (see Figure 2).

To open a file, complete the following steps:

1. Open the application.
2. Click Open Other Documents (Workbooks, etc.).
3. Click the location for your file (such as This PC or OneDrive).
4. Navigate to the folder or drive and double-click the file to open it.

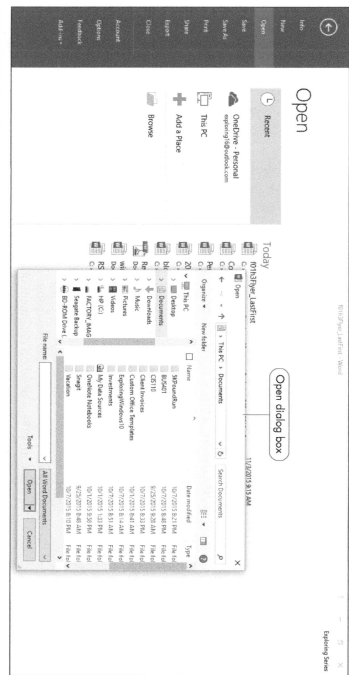

FIGURE 2 The Open Dialog Box

Word 2016, Windows 10, Microsoft Corporation

Office simplifies the task of reopening the file by providing a Recent documents list with links to your most recently opened files. Previously saved files, such as the data files for this text, are available in the Recent documents list, shown in Figure 3. If you just opened the application, the recent list displays at the left. If you do not see your file listed, you can click the link to Open Other Documents (or Workbooks, Presentations, etc.)

To access the Recent documents list, complete the following steps:

1. Open the application.
2. Click any file listed in the Recent documents list to open that document.

The list constantly changes to reflect only the most recently opened files, so if it has been quite some time since you worked with a particular file, you might have to browse for your file instead of using the Recent documents list to open the file.

TIP: KEEPING FILES ON THE RECENT DOCUMENTS LIST

The Recent documents list displays a limited list of only the most recently opened files. You might, however, want to keep a particular file in the list regardless of how recently it was opened. In Figure 3, note that the *Pin this item to the list* icon displays to the right of each file. Click the icon to pin the file to the list. At that point, you will always have access to the file by clicking the File tab and selecting the file from the Recent documents list. The pushpin of the "permanent" file will change direction so that it appears to be inserted, indicating that it is a pinned item. If later you want to remove the file from the list, click the inserted pushpin, changing its direction and allowing the file to be bumped off the list when other, more recently opened, files take its place.

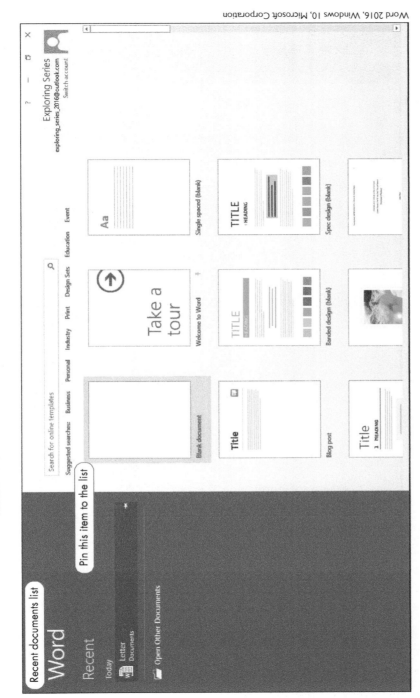

FIGURE 3 Recent Documents List

Save a File

STEP 3 ≫ Saving a file enables you to later open it for additional updates or reference. Files are saved to a storage medium such as a hard drive, CD, flash drive, or to the cloud on OneDrive.

The first time that you save a file, you should indicate where the file will be saved and assign a file name. Of course, you will want to save the file in an appropriately named folder so that you can find it easily later. Thereafter, you can quickly save the file with the same settings, or you can change one or more of those settings, perhaps saving the file to a different storage device as a backup copy. Figure 4 shows a typical Save As pane for Office that enables you to select a location before saving the file.

It is easy to save a previously saved file with its current name and file location; click the Save icon on Quick Access Toolbar. There are instances where you may want to rename the file or save it to a different location. For example, you might reuse an event flyer for another event and simply update some of the details for the new event.

To save a file with a different name and/or file location, complete the following steps:

1. Click the File tab.
2. Click Save As.
3. Select a location or click Browse to navigate to the desired file storage location.
4. Type the file name.
5. Click Save.

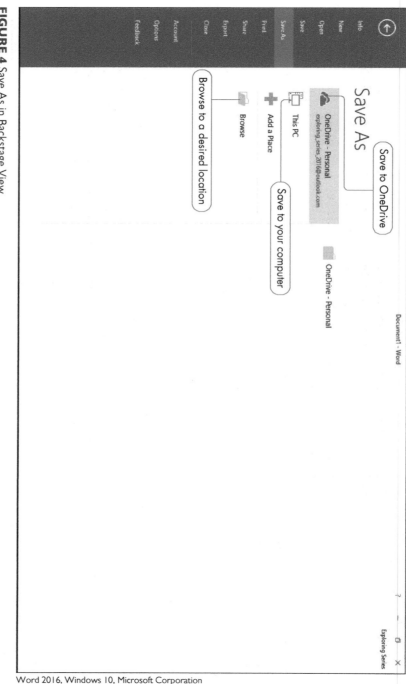

Word 2016, Windows 10, Microsoft Corporation

FIGURE 4 Save As in Backstage View

As previously mentioned, signing in to your Microsoft account enables you to save files to OneDrive and access them from virtually anywhere. To save a file to your OneDrive account follow the same steps as saving a file to your hard drive but select OneDrive and then the desired storage location on your OneDrive. You must be connected to the Internet in order to complete this action.

Using Common Interface Components

When you open any Office application you will first notice the title bar and Ribbon. The *title bar* identifies the current file name and the application in which you are working. It also includes Ribbon display options and control buttons that enable you to minimize, restore down, or close the application window (see Figure 5). The Quick Access Toolbar, on the left side of the title bar, enables you to save the file, and undo or redo editing. Located just below the title bar is the Ribbon. The **Ribbon** is the command center of Office applications. It is the long bar located just beneath the title bar, containing tabs, groups, and commands.

FIGURE 5 The Title Bar and Quick Access Toolbar

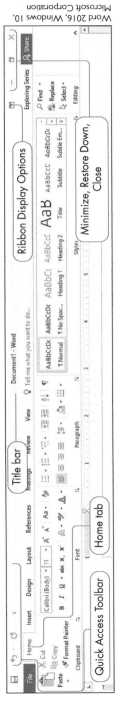

Use the Ribbon

The Ribbon is composed of tabs. Each *tab* is designed to appear much like a tab on a file folder, with the active tab highlighted. The File tab is located at the far left of the Ribbon. The File tab provides access to Backstage view which contains Save and Print, as well as additional functions. Other tabs on the Ribbon enable you to modify a file. The active tab in Figure 6 is the Home tab.

FIGURE 6 The Ribbon

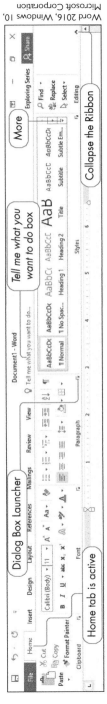

Office applications enable you to work with objects such as images, shapes, charts, and tables. When you include such objects in a project, they are considered separate components that you can manage independently. To work with an object, you must select it. When you select an object, the Ribbon is modified to include one or more *contextual tabs* that contain groups of commands related to the selected object. Figure 7 shows a contextual tab related to a selected picture in a Word document. When you click away from the selected object, the contextual tab disappears.

FIGURE 7 A Contextual Tab

On each tab, the Ribbon displays several task-oriented groups, with each group containing related commands. A **group** is a subset of a tab that organizes similar tasks together. A **command** is a button or area within a group that you click to perform tasks. Office is designed to provide the most functionality possible with the fewest clicks. For that reason, the Home tab, displayed when you first open a document in an Office software application, contains groups and commands that are most commonly used. For example, because you often want to change the way text is displayed, the Home tab in each Office application includes a Font group with commands related to modifying text. Similarly, other tabs contain groups of related actions, or commands, many of which are unique to the particular Office application.

Word, PowerPoint, Excel, and Access all share a similar Ribbon structure. Although the specific tabs, groups, and commands vary among the Office programs, the way in which you use the Ribbon and the descriptive nature of tab titles is the same regardless of which program you are using. For example, if you want to insert a chart in Excel, a header in Word, or a shape in PowerPoint, you will click the Insert tab in any of those programs. The first thing that you should do as you begin to work with an Office application is to study the Ribbon. Take a look at all tabs and their contents. That way, you will have a good idea of where to find specific commands and how the Ribbon with which you are currently working differs from one that you might have used in another application.

If you are working with a large project, you can maximize your workspace by temporarily hiding the Ribbon.

To hide the Ribbon, complete one of the following steps:

- Double-click the active tab to hide the Ribbon.
- Click Collapse the Ribbon (refer to Figure 6), located at the right side of the Ribbon.

To unhide the Ribbon, double-click any tab to redisplay the Ribbon.

Some actions do not display on the Ribbon because they are not as commonly used, but are related to commands displayed on the Ribbon. For example, you might want to change the background of a PowerPoint slide to include a picture. In that case, you will work with a **dialog box** that provides access to more precise, but less frequently used, commands. Figure 8 shows the Font dialog box in Word. Some commands display a dialog box when they are clicked. Other Ribbon groups include a **Dialog Box Launcher** ▢ that, when clicked, opens a corresponding dialog box (see Figure 8).

TIP: GETTING HELP WITH DIALOG BOXES

Getting help while you are working with a dialog box is easy. Click the Help button that displays as a question mark in the top-right corner of the dialog box. The subsequent Help window will offer suggestions relevant to your task.

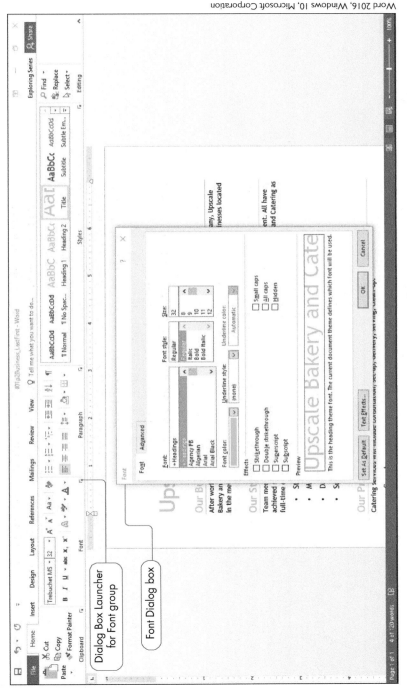

FIGURE 8 The Font Dialog Box

The Ribbon contains many selections and commands, but some selections are too numerous to include in the Ribbon's limited space. For example, Word provides far more text styles than it can easily display at once, so additional styles are available in a *gallery*. A gallery also provides a choice of Excel chart styles and PowerPoint transitions. Figure 9 shows an example of a PowerPoint Themes gallery. Most often, you can display a gallery of additional choices by clicking the More button ⊡ (refer to Figure 6) that is found in some Ribbon selections.

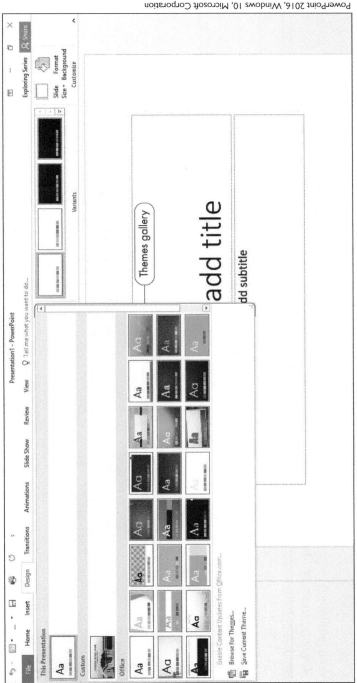

FIGURE 9 The Themes Gallery in PowerPoint

Getting Started with Office Applications • Common Features 2016

When editing a document, worksheet, or presentation, it is helpful to see the results of formatting changes before you make final selections. The feature that displays a preview of the results of a selection is called **Live Preview**. You might, for example, be considering modifying the color of an image in a document or worksheet. As you place the pointer over a color selection in a Ribbon gallery or group, the selected image will temporarily display the color to which you are pointing. Similarly, you can get a preview of how color designs would display on PowerPoint slides by pointing to specific themes in the PowerPoint Themes group and noting the effect on a displayed slide. When you click the item, such as the font color, the selection is applied. Live Preview is available in various Ribbon selections among the Office applications.

STEP 4

Use a Shortcut Menu

In Office, you can usually accomplish the same task in several ways. Although the Ribbon provides ample access to formatting and Clipboard commands (such as Cut, Copy, and Paste), you might find it convenient to access the same commands on a shortcut menu. A *shortcut menu* provides choices related to the object, selection, or area of the document at which you right-click, such as the one shown in Figure 10. A shortcut menu is also called a *context menu* because the contents of the menu vary depending on the location at which you right-clicked.

Use Keyboard Shortcuts

You might find that you prefer to use keyboard shortcuts, which are keyboard equivalents for software commands, when they are available. Universal keyboard shortcuts in Office include Ctrl+C (Copy), Ctrl+X (Cut), Ctrl+V (Paste), and Ctrl+Z (Undo). To move to the beginning of a Word document, to cell A1 in Excel, or to the first PowerPoint slide, press Ctrl+Home. To move to the end of those items, press Ctrl+End. There are many other keyboard shortcuts. To discover a keyboard shortcut for a commonly used command, press

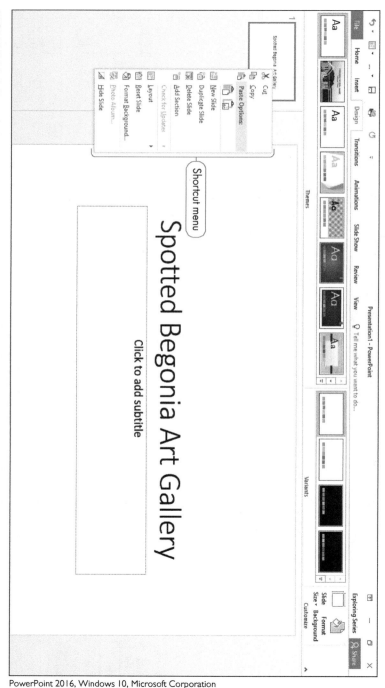

FIGURE 10 A Shortcut Menu in PowerPoint

PowerPoint 2016, Windows 10, Microsoft Corporation

Alt to display Key Tips for commands available on the Ribbon and Quick Access Toolbar. You can press the letter or number corresponding to Ribbon commands to invoke the action from the keyboard. Press Alt again to remove the Key Tips.

Customize the Ribbon

The Ribbon provides access to commands to develop, edit, save, share, and print documents. Office applications enable users to personalize the Ribbon, giving them easier access to a frequently used set of commands that are unique to them or their business. You can create and name custom tabs on the Ribbon, add groups of commands to custom or existing tabs, and alter the positioning of tabs on the Ribbon (see Figure 11). By default, the command list displays popular commands associated with other tabs (e.g. Paste, Delete, Save As), but all available commands can be displayed in the list's respective menu. The custom tabs are unique to the Office program in which they are created. You can add and remove Ribbon tabs, as well as rename them.

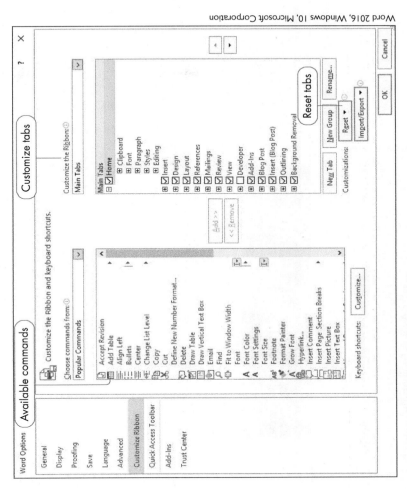

Word 2016, Windows 10, Microsoft Corporation

FIGURE 11 Customize the Ribbon in Word

To customize the Ribbon, complete the following steps:

1. Click the File tab and click Options.
2. Click Customize Ribbon. By deselecting a tab name, you can remove it from the Ribbon. Later, you can select it again to redisplay it.
3. Click a tab name and click Rename to change the name of the tab.
4. Type a new name and press Enter.

To return to showing all of the original tabs, click Reset and click Reset all customizations (refer to Figure 11).

Use the Quick Access Toolbar

The **Quick Access Toolbar**, located at the top-left corner of any Office application window (refer to Figure 5), provides one-click access to commonly executed tasks such as saving a file or undoing recent actions. By default, the Quick Access Toolbar includes buttons for saving a file and for undoing or redoing recent actions. You can recover from a mistake by clicking Undo on the Quick Access Toolbar. If you click the arrow beside Undo—known as the Undo arrow—you can select from a list of previous actions in order of occurrence. The Undo list is not maintained when you close a file or exit the application, so you can only erase an action that took place during the current Office session. Similar to Undo, you can also Redo (or Replace) an action that you have just undone. You can also customize the Quick Access Toolbar to include buttons you frequently use for commands such as printing or opening files. Because the Quick Access Toolbar is onscreen at all times, the most commonly accessed tasks are just a click away.

Customize the Quick Access Toolbar

There are certain actions in an Office application that you use often, and for more convenient access, you can add a button for each action to the Quick Access Toolbar (see Figure 12). One such action you may want to add is a Quick Print button. Rather than clicking the File tab and selecting print options, you can add a Quick Print icon to the Quick Access Toolbar, and one click will print your document with the default settings of the Print area. Other buttons can also be added such as Spelling & Grammar to quickly check the spelling of the document.

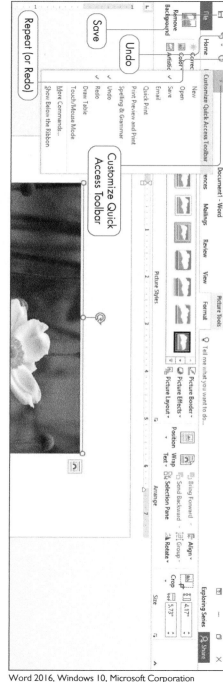

FIGURE 12 Customize the Quick Access Toolbar

Word 2016, Windows 10, Microsoft Corporation

To add a command to the Quick Access Toolbar, complete one of the following steps:

- Click Customize Quick Access Toolbar and then click More Commands near the bottom of the menu options. Then, select commands from a list and click Add.
- Right-click the command on the Ribbon and click Add to Quick Access Toolbar.

Similarly, remove a command from the Quick Access Toolbar by right-clicking the icon on the Quick Access Toolbar and clicking *Remove from Quick Access Toolbar*. If you want to display the Quick Access Toolbar beneath the Ribbon, click *Customize Quick Access Toolbar* and click *Show Below the Ribbon*.

Getting Help

One of the most frustrating things about learning new software is determining how to complete a task. Microsoft includes comprehensive help with Office so that you are less likely to feel such frustration. As you work with any Office application, you can access help online as well as within the current software installation.

Use the *Tell me what you want to do* Box

STEP 5 » New to Office 2016 is the *Tell me what you want to do* box. The **Tell me what you want to do box**, located to the right of the last tab (see Figure 13), not only enables you to search for help and information about a command or task you want to perform, but it will also present you with a shortcut directly to that command and in some instances (like Bold) it will complete the action for you. Perhaps you want to find an instance of a word in your document and replace it with another word but cannot locate the command on the Ribbon. You can type *find and replace* in the *Tell me what you want to do* box and a list of commands related to the skill will display. For example, in Figure 13, you see that Replace displays as an option in the list. If you click this option, the Find and Replace dialog box opens without you having to locate the button to do so.

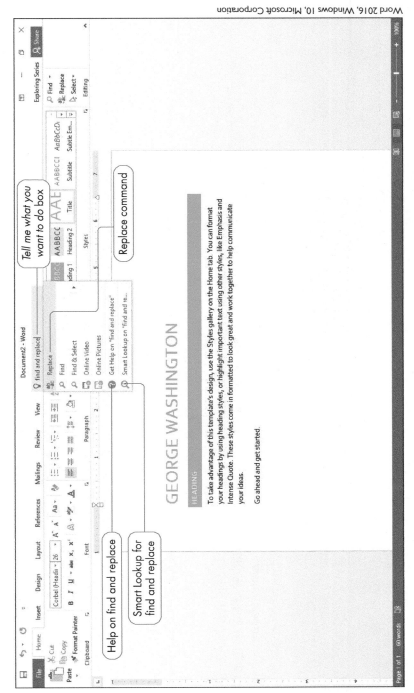

FIGURE 13 The Tell me what you want to do Box

Should you want to read about the feature instead of apply it, you can click *Get Help on "find and replace"* option, which will open Office Help for the feature. Another new feature is Smart Lookup. This feature opens the Insights pane that shows results from a Bing search on the task description typed in the box (see Figure 14). **Smart Lookup** provides information about tasks or commands in Office, and can also be used to search for general information on a topic such as *President George Washington*. Smart Lookup is also available on the shortcut menu when you right-click text.

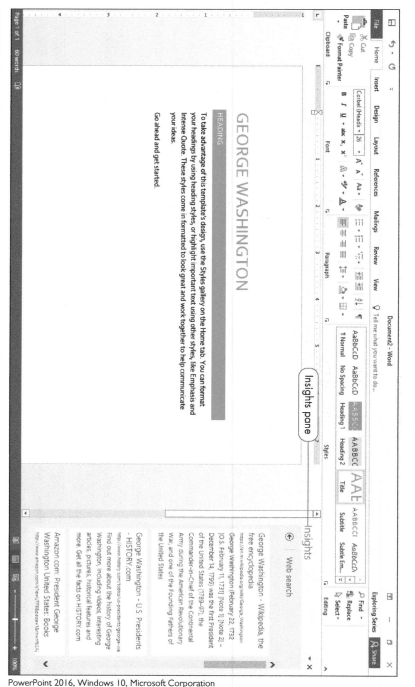

FIGURE 14 Smart Lookup

PowerPoint 2016, Windows 10, Microsoft Corporation

Use Enhanced ScreenTips

As you work on your projects you may wonder about the purpose of a specific icon on the Ribbon. For quick summary information on the purpose of a command button, place the pointer over the button. An *Enhanced ScreenTip* displays, describing the command, and providing a keyboard shortcut, if applicable. Some ScreenTips include a *Tell me more* option for additional help. The Enhanced ScreenTip, shown for the Format Painter in Figure 15, provides context-sensitive assistance. A short description of the feature is shown in addition to the steps that discuss how to use the Format Painter feature.

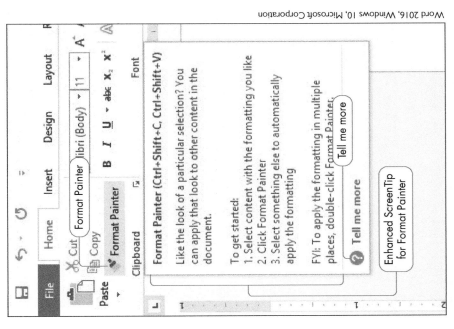

Word 2016, Windows 10, Microsoft Corporation

FIGURE 15 Enhanced ScreenTip

Installing Add-ins

Sometimes it is helpful to extend the functionality of Office programs by adding a Microsoft or third-party add-in to the program. An ***add-in*** is a custom program or additional command that extends the functionality of a Microsoft Office program (see Figure 16). Some add-ins are available for free while others may have a cost associated with them. For example, in PowerPoint you could add a Poll Everywhere poll that enables you to interact with your audience by having them respond to a question you have asked. The audience's electronic responses will appear on a slide as a real-time graph or word cloud. In Excel, add-ins provide additional functionality that can help with statistics and data mining.

FIGURE 16 Add-Ins for Excel

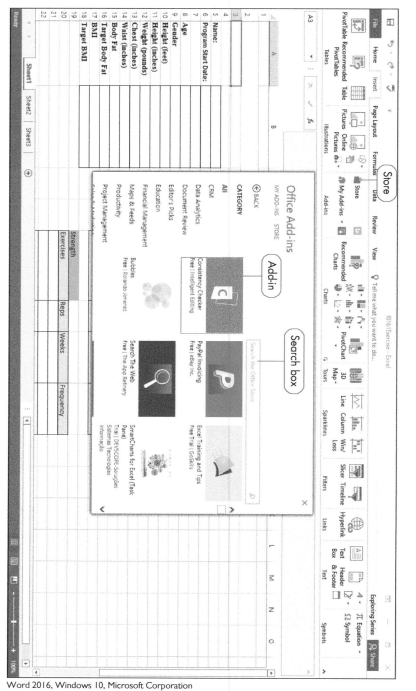

Word 2016, Windows 10, Microsoft Corporation

To search for and install an add-in from the Microsoft Store, complete the following steps:

1. Click the Insert tab.
2. Click Store (refer to Figure 16). Browse the list of add-ins or use the search box.
3. Click the add-in. A box will display with information about the add-in such as its purpose, the cost (if any), and information it may access.
4. Click Trust It to add the add-in to your application. The newly added add-in will be available for future use in the My Add-ins list located on the Insert tab.

Quick Concepts

1. What are the benefits of logging in with your Microsoft account?
2. What is the purpose of the Quick Access Toolbar?
3. You are having trouble completing a task in Microsoft Word. What are some of the Office application features you could use to assist you in getting help with that task?

Watch the Video
for this Hands-On
Exercise!

Hands-On Exercises

1 Getting Started with Office Applications

Skills covered: Open a Microsoft Office Application • Open a File • Save a File • Use a Shortcut Menu • Use the *Tell me what you want to do* Box

The Spotted Begonia Art Gallery just hired several new clerical assistants to help you develop materials for the various activities coming up throughout the year. A coworker sent you a letter and asked for your assistance in making a few minor formatting changes. The letter is to thank the ABC Arts Foundation for its generous donation to the *Discover the Artist in You!* program and to invite them to the program's kickoff party. To begin, you will open Word and then open an existing document. You will use the Shortcut menu to make simple changes to the document. Finally, you will use the *Tell me what you want to do* box to apply a style to the first line of text.

STEP 1 ≫ OPEN A MICROSOFT OFFICE APPLICATION

You start Microsoft Word from the Windows Start menu. Refer to Figure 17 as you complete Step 1.

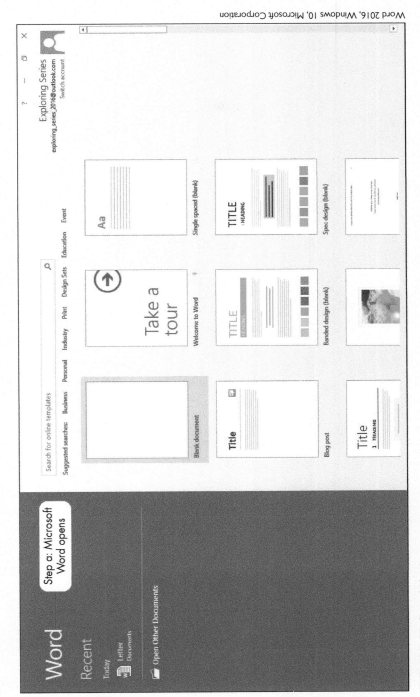

FIGURE 17 Open Word

a. Start your computer and log into your Microsoft account. On the Start menu, click **All apps** and click **Word 2016**.

Microsoft Word displays.

You open a thank-you letter that you will later modify. Refer to Figure 18 as you complete Step 2.

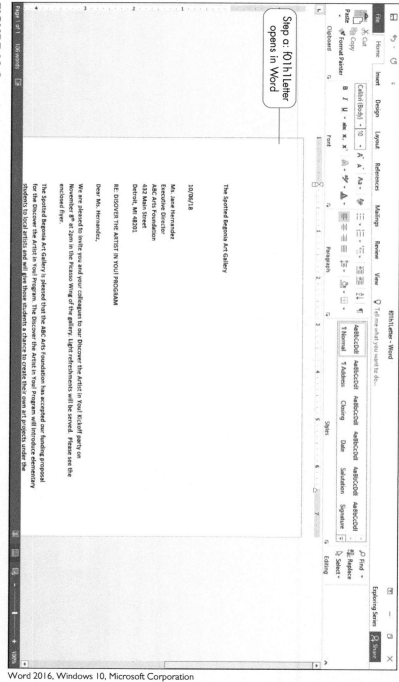

Step a: f01h1Letter opens in Word

FIGURE 18 Open the Letter

Word 2016, Windows 10, Microsoft Corporation

a. Click **Open Other Documents** and click **Browse**. Navigate to the location of your student files. Double-click *f01h1Letter* to open the file shown in Figure 18. Click Enable Content.

The thank-you letter opens.

> **TROUBLESHOOTING:** When you open a file from the student files associated with this text, you will need to enable the content. You may be confident of the trustworthiness of the files for this text.

You save the document with a different name, to preserve the original file. Refer to Figure 19 as you complete Step 3.

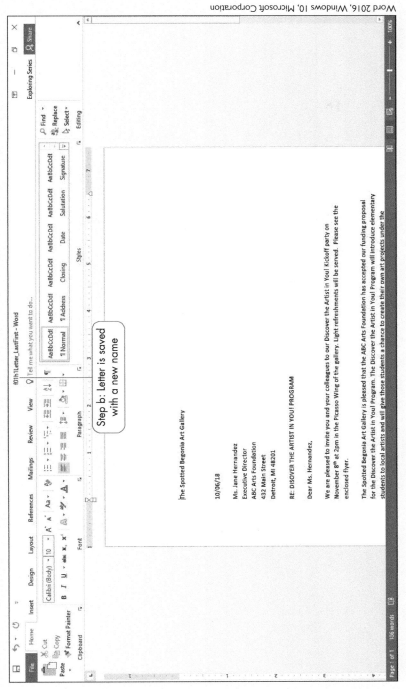

FIGURE 19 Save the Letter with a New Name

a. Click the **File tab**, click **Save As**, and then click **Browse** to display the Save As dialog box. Click **This PC** or click the location where you are saving your files.

b. Click in the **File name box** and type **f01h1Letter_LastFirst**.

When you save files, use your last and first names. For example, as the Common Features author, I would name my document "f01h1Letter_RutledgeAmy".

TROUBLESHOOTING: If you make any major mistakes in this exercise, you can close the file, open *f01h1Letter* again, and then start this exercise over.

c. Click **Save**.

The file is now saved as f01h1Letter_LastFirst. You can check the title bar of the workbook to confirm that the file has been saved with the correct name.

You would like to apply italics to the *Discover the Artist in You!* text in the first sentence of the letter. You will select the text and use the shortcut menu to apply italics to the text. Refer to Figure 20 as you complete Step 4.

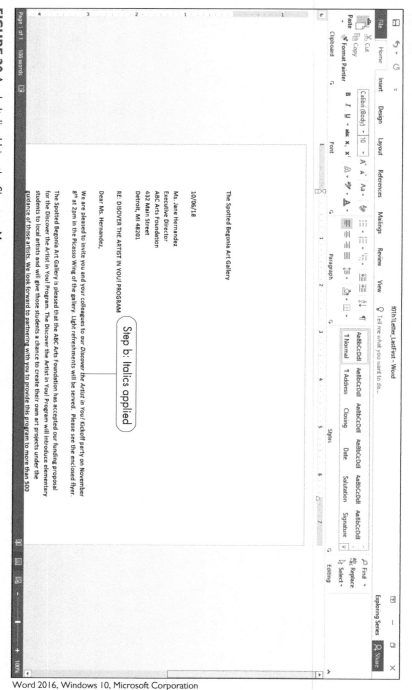

FIGURE 20 Apply Italics Using the Shortcut Menu

a. Select the text **Discover the Artist in You!** in the first sentence of the letter that starts with *We are pleased.*

The text is selected.

b. Right-click the selected text. Click **Font** on the Shortcut menu. Click **Italic** under Font style, and click **OK**.

Italics is applied to the text.

c. Click **Save** on the Quick Access Toolbar.

Word 2016, Windows 10, Microsoft Corporation

STEP 5 >> USE THE TELL ME WHAT YOU WANT TO DO BOX

You would like to apply a style to the first line in the letter. Since you do not know how to complete the task, you use the *Tell me what you want to do box* to search for and apply the change. Refer to Figure 21 as you complete Step 5.

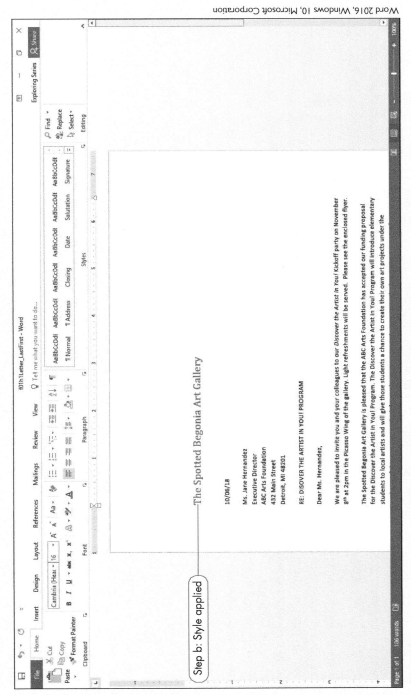

Step b: Style applied

FIGURE 21 Change the Text Style Using the *Tell me what you want to do* Box

a. Triple-click the entire first line of the letter that starts with *The Spotted Begonia Art Gallery* to select it. Click the *Tell me what you want to do box*, and type **heading 1**.

A list of options appears below the box.

b. Click **Promote to Heading1** to apply the style to the selected text.

The Heading 1 style is applied to the text.

c. Save the document. Keep the document open if you plan to continue with the next Hands-On Exercise. If not, save and close the workbook, and exit Word.

Hands-On Exercise 1

Format Document Content

After creating a document, worksheet, or presentation, you will probably want to make some formatting changes. You might prefer to center a title, or maybe you think that certain budget worksheet totals should be formatted as currency. You can change the font so that typed characters are larger or in a different style. You might even want to bold text to add emphasis. In all Office applications, the Home tab provides tools for selecting and editing text. You can also use the Mini toolbar for making quick changes to selected text.

In this section you will explore themes and templates. You will learn to use the Mini toolbar to quickly make formatting changes. You will learn how to select and edit text, as well as check your grammar and spelling. You will learn how to move, copy, and paste text, as well as insert pictures. And, finally, you will learn how to resize and format pictures and graphics.

Using Templates and Applying Themes

You can enhance your documents by using a template or applying a theme. A *template* is a predesigned file that incorporates formatting elements, such as a theme and layouts, and may include content that can be modified. A *theme* is a collection of design choices that includes colors, fonts, and special effects used to give a consistent look to a document, workbook, or presentation. Microsoft provides high quality templates and themes, designed by professional designers to make it faster and easier to create high-quality documents. Even if you use a theme to apply colors, fonts, and special effects, they can later be changed individually or to a completely different theme.

STEP 1

Open a Template

➤ You can access a template in any of the Office applications (see Figure 22). Even if you know only a little bit about the software, you could then make a few changes so that the file would accurately represent your specific needs. The document also would be prepared much more quickly than if you designed it yourself from a blank file. For example, you might want to prepare a home budget using an Excel template, such as the Family monthly budget planner template, that is available by typing *Budget* in the *Suggested searches* template list.

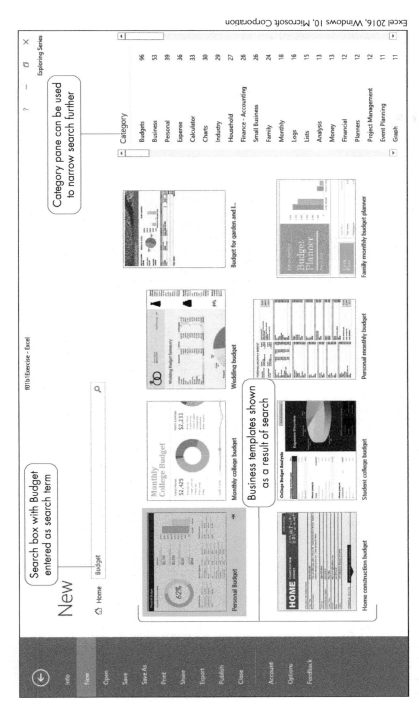

FIGURE 22 Templates in Excel

The Templates list is comprised of template groups available within each Office application. The search box enables you to locate other templates that are available online. When you click one of the Suggested searches, additional choices are displayed. Once you select a template, you can view more information about the template including author information, a general overview about the template, and additional views (if applicable).

To search for and use a template, complete the following steps:

1. Open the Microsoft application with which you will be working.
2. Type a search term in the *Search for online templates box*, or click one of the Suggested search terms.
3. Scroll through the template options or use the pane at the right to narrow your search further.
4. Select a template, and review its information in the window that opens.
5. Click Create to open the template in the application.

A Help window may display along with the worksheet template. Read it for more information about the template, or close it to continue working.

Apply a Theme

Applying a theme enables you to visually coordinate various page elements. Themes are a bit different for each of the Office applications. In Word, a theme is a set of coordinating fonts, colors, and special effects, such as shadowing or glows that are combined into a package to provide a stylish appearance (see Figure 23). In PowerPoint, a theme is a file that includes the formatting elements like a background, a color scheme, and slide layouts that position content placeholders. Themes in Excel are similar to those in Word in that they are a set of coordinating fonts, colors, and special effects. Themes in Excel will not only change the color of the fill in a cell, but will also affect any SmartArt or charts in the workbook. Access also has a set of themes that coordinate the appearance of fonts and colors for objects such as Forms and Reports. In Word and PowerPoint, themes can be accessed from the Design tab. In Excel they can be accessed from the Page Layout tab. In Access, themes can be applied to forms and reports. To apply a theme, click the Themes arrow, and select a theme from the Themes gallery.

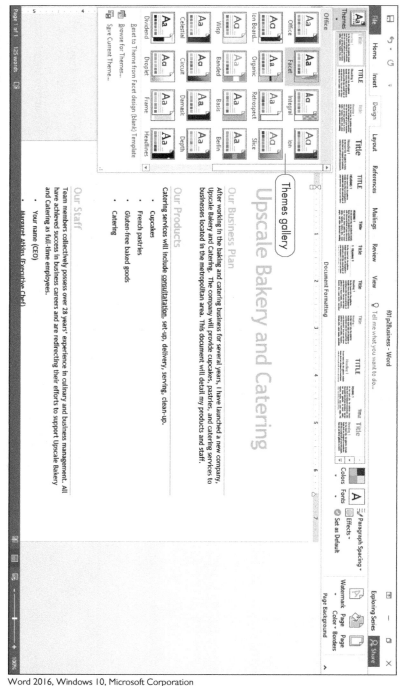

FIGURE 23 Themes in Word

Word 2016, Windows 10, Microsoft Corporation

Modifying Text

Formatting and modifying text in documents, worksheets, or presentations is an essential function when using Office applications. Centering a title, formatting cells, or changing the font color or size are tasks that occur frequently. In all Office applications, the Home tab provides tools for editing selected text. You can also use the Mini toolbar for making quick changes to selected text.

Select Text

Before making any changes to existing text or numbers, you must first select the characters. A general rule that you should commit to memory is "Select, then do." A foolproof way to select text or numbers is to place the pointer before the first character of the text you want to select, and then drag to highlight the intended selection. Before you drag, be sure that the pointer takes on the shape of the letter *I*, called the *I-beam* T. Although other methods for selecting exist, if you remember only one way, it should be the click-and-drag method. If your attempted selection falls short of highlighting the intended area, or perhaps highlights too much, click outside the selection and try again.

Sometimes it can be difficult to precisely select a small amount of text, such as a single word or sentence. Other times, the task can be overwhelming large, such as when selecting an entire 550-page document. In either case there are shortcuts to select-ing text. The shortcuts shown in Table 2 are primarily applicable to text in Word and PowerPoint. When working with Excel, you will more often need to select multiple cells. To select multiple cells, drag the intended selection when the pointer displays as a large white plus sign ⊕.

TABLE 2 Shortcut Selection in Word and PowerPoint

Item Selected	Action
One word	Double-click the word.
One line of text	Place the pointer at the left of the line, in the margin area. When the pointer changes to a right-pointing arrow, click to select the line.
One sentence	Press and hold Ctrl, and click in the sentence to select it.
One paragraph	Triple-click in the paragraph.
One character to the left of the insertion point	Press and hold Shift, and press the left arrow on the keyboard.
One character to the right of the insertion point	Press and hold Shift, and press the right arrow on the keyboard.
Entire document	Press and hold Ctrl, and press A on the keyboard.

Once you have selected the desired text, besides applying formatting, you can delete or simply type over to replace the text.

Edit Text

At times, you will want to make the font size larger or smaller, change the font color, or apply other font attributes. For example, if you are creating a handout for a gallery show opening, you may want to apply a different font to emphasize key information such as dates and times. Because such changes are commonplace, Office places those formatting commands in many convenient places within each Office application.

You can find the most common formatting commands in the Font group on the Home tab. As noted earlier, Word, Excel, and PowerPoint all share very similar Font groups that provide access to tasks related to changing the character font. Remember that you can place the pointer over any command icon to view a summary of the icon's purpose, so although the icons might at first appear cryptic, you can use the pointer to quickly deter-mine the purpose and applicability to your desired text change.

The way characters display onscreen or print in documents, including qualities such as size, spacing, and shape, is determined by the font. Office applications have a default font, Calibri, which is the font that will be in effect unless you change it. Other font attri-butes include bold, italic, and font color, all of which can be applied to selected text. Some formatting commands, such as Bold and Italic, are called *toggle commands*. They act somewhat like light switches that you can turn on and off. Once you have applied bold formatting to text, the Bold command is highlighted on the Ribbon when that text is selected again. To undo bold formatting, click Bold again.

If you want to apply a different font to a section of your project for added emphasis or interest, you can make the change by selecting a font from within the Font group on the Home tab. You can also change the font by selecting from the Mini toolbar.

If the font change that you plan to make is not included as a choice on either the Home tab or the Mini toolbar, you can find what you are looking for in the Font dialog box. Click the Dialog Box Launcher in the bottom-right corner of the Font group. Figure 24 shows a sample Font dialog box. Because the Font dialog box provides many formatting choices in one window, you can make several changes at once. Depending on the application, the contents of the Font dialog box vary slightly, but the purpose is consistent—providing access to choices related to modifying characters.

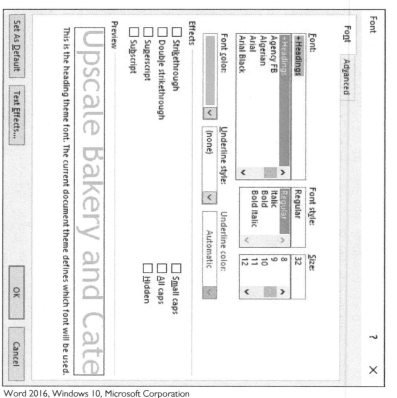

FIGURE 24 The Font Dialog Box

Word 2016, Windows 10, Microsoft Corporation

Use the Mini Toolbar

You have learned that you can always use commands on the Home tab of the Ribbon to change selected text within a document, worksheet, or presentation. Although using the Ribbon to select commands is simple enough, the **Mini toolbar** provides an even faster way to accomplish some of the same formatting changes. When you select any amount of text within a worksheet, document, or presentation, move the pointer slightly within the selection to display the Mini toolbar (see Figure 25). The Mini toolbar provides access to the most common formatting selections, such as bold or italic, or font type or color. Unlike the Quick Access Toolbar, the Mini toolbar is not customizable, which means that you cannot add or remove options from the toolbar.

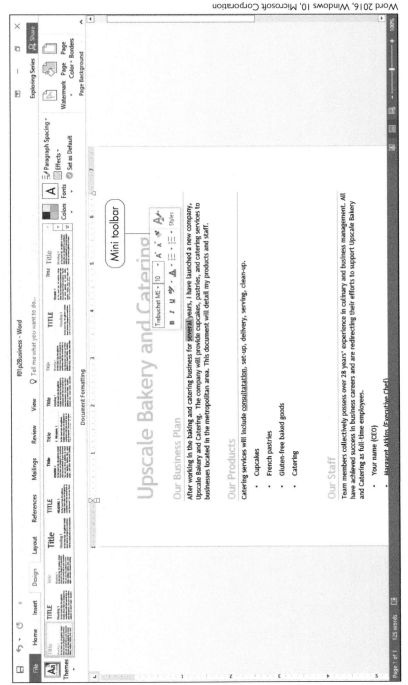

FIGURE 25 The Mini Toolbar

The Mini toolbar is displayed only when text is selected. The closer the pointer is to the Mini toolbar, the darker the toolbar becomes. As you move the pointer away from the selected text, the Mini toolbar eventually fades away. If the Mini toolbar is no longer displayed, you can right-click the selection to make the Mini toolbar appear again. To make selections from the Mini toolbar, click a command on the toolbar. To temporarily remove the Mini toolbar from view, press Esc.

To permanently disable the Mini toolbar so that it does not display in any open file when text is selected, complete the following steps:

1. Click the File tab and click Options.

2. Click General.

3. Click the *Show Mini toolbar on selection* check box to deselect it.

4. Click OK.

Copy Formats with Format Painter

STEP 3 Using *Format Painter*, you can copy all formatting from one area to another in Word, PowerPoint, and Excel (see Figure 26). If, for example, a heading in Word includes multiple formatting features, you will save time by copying the entire set of formatting options to the other headings. In so doing, you will ensure the consistency of formatting for all headings because they will appear exactly alike.

FIGURE 26 Format Painter

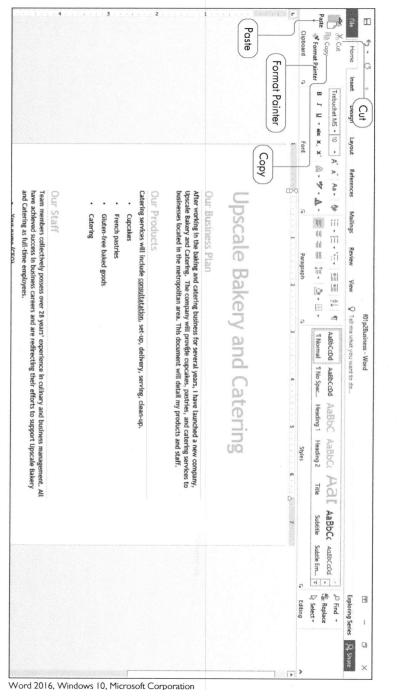

Word 2016, Windows 10, Microsoft Corporation

To copy a format, complete the following steps:

1. Select the text containing the desired format.
2. Single-click Format Painter if you want to copy the format to only one other selection. If, however, you plan to copy the same format to multiple locations, continue selecting text in various locations to apply the format. Then, to turn off Format Painter, click Format Painter again or press Esc.
3. Select the area to which the copied format should be applied.

If you single-clicked Format Painter to copy the format to one other selection, Format Painter turns off once the formatting has been applied. If you double-clicked Format Painter to copy the format to multiple locations, continue selecting text in various locations to apply the format. Then, to turn off Format Painter, click Format Painter again or press Esc.

Relocating Text

On occasion, you will want to relocate a section of text from one area to another. Suppose that you have included text on a PowerPoint slide that you believe would be more appropriate on a different slide. Or perhaps an Excel formula should be copied from one cell to another because both cells should be totaled in the same manner. You can move the slide text or copy the Excel formula by using the cut, copy, and paste features found in the Clipboard group on the Home tab. The Office *Clipboard* is an area of memory reserved to temporarily hold selections that have been cut or copied and allows you to paste the selections. When the computer is shut down or loses power, the contents of the Clipboard are erased, so it is important to finalize the paste procedure during the current session.

Cut, Copy, and Paste Text

STEP 4 ⟫⟫ To *cut* means to remove a selection from the original location and place it in the Office Clipboard. To *copy* means to duplicate a selection from the original location and place a copy in the Office Clipboard. Although the Clipboard can hold up to 24 items at one time, the usual procedure is to paste the cut or copied selection to its final destination fairly quickly. To *paste* means to place a cut or copied selection into another location. In addition to using the Clipboard group icons, you can also cut, copy, and paste in any of the ways listed in Table 3.

TABLE 3	Cut, Copy, and Paste Options
Command	**Actions**
Cut	• Click Cut in Clipboard group.
	• Right-click selection and select Cut.
	• Press Ctrl+X.
Copy	• Click Copy in Clipboard group.
	• Right-click selection and select Copy.
	• Press Ctrl+C.
Paste	• Click in destination location and select Paste in Clipboard group.
	• Click in destination location and press Ctrl+V.
	• Click Clipboard Dialog Box Launcher to open Clipboard pane. Click in destination location. With Clipboard pane open, click arrow beside intended selection and select Paste.

To cut or copy text, complete the following steps:

1. Select the text you want to cut or copy.
2. Click the appropriate icon in the Clipboard group either to cut or copy the selection. Remember that cut or copied text is actually placed in the Clipboard, remaining there even after you paste it to another location. It is important to note that you can paste the same item multiple times, because it will remain in the Clipboard until you power down your computer or until the Clipboard exceeds 24 items.
3. Click the location where you want the cut or copied text to be placed. The location can be in the current file or in another open file within any Office application.
4. Click Paste in the Clipboard group on the Home tab.

When you paste text you may not want to paste the text with all of its formatting. In some instances, you may want to paste only the text, unformatted, so that it fits in with the formatting of its new location. When pasting text, there are several options available and those options will depend on the program you are using.

Use the Office Clipboard

When you cut or copy selections, they are placed in the Office Clipboard. Regardless of which Office application you are using, you can view the Clipboard by clicking the Clipboard Dialog Box Launcher, as shown in Figure 27.

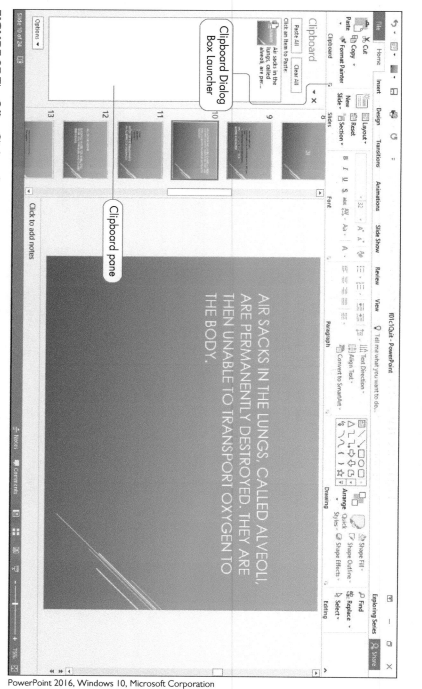

FIGURE 27 The Office Clipboard

PowerPoint 2016, Windows 10, Microsoft Corporation

Unless you specify otherwise when beginning a paste operation, the most recently added Clipboard item is pasted. You can, however, select an item from the Clipboard pane to paste. Click the item in the list to add it to the document. You can also delete items from the Clipboard by clicking the arrow next to the selection in the Clipboard pane and then clicking Delete. You can remove all items from the Clipboard by clicking Clear All. The Options button in the Clipboard pane enables you to control when and where the Clipboard is displayed. Close the Clipboard pane by clicking the Close ☒ button in the top-right corner of the pane or by clicking the arrow in the title bar of the Clipboard pane and selecting Close.

STEP 5

Checking Spelling and Grammar

As you create or edit a file you will want to make sure no spelling or grammatical errors exist. You will also be concerned with wording, being sure to select words or phrases that best represent the purpose of the document, worksheet, or presentation. On occasion, you might even find yourself at a loss for an appropriate word. Word, Excel, and PowerPoint all provide standard tools for proofreading, including a spelling and grammar checker and thesaurus.

Word and PowerPoint check your spelling and grammar as you type. If a word is unrecognized, it is flagged as misspelled or grammatically incorrect. Even though Excel does not check your spelling as you type, it is important to run the spelling checker in Excel. Excel's spelling checker will review charts, pivot tables, and other reports that all need to be spelled correctly. Misspellings are identified with a red wavy underline, grammatical problems are underlined in green, and word usage errors (such as using bear instead of bare) have a blue underline.

To check the spelling for an entire file, complete the following steps:

1. Click the Review tab.
2. Click Spelling and Grammar.

Beginning at the top of the document, each identified error is highlighted in a pane similar to Figure 28. You can then choose how to address the problem by making a selection from the options in the pane.

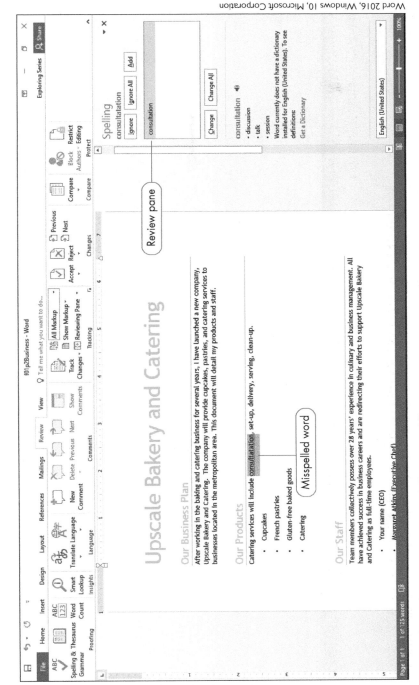

Word 2016, Windows 10, Microsoft Corporation

FIGURE 28 Checking for Spelling and Grammatical Errors

If the word or phrase is truly in error—that is, it is not a person's name or an unusual term that is not in the application's dictionary—you can correct it manually, or you can let the software correct it for you. If you right-click a word or phrase that is identified as a mistake, you will see a shortcut menu similar to that shown in Figure 29. If the Office dictionary makes a suggestion with the correct spelling, you can click to accept the suggestion and make the change. If a grammatical rule is violated, you will have an opportunity to select a correction. However, if the text is actually correct, you can click Ignore or Ignore All (to bypass all occurrences of the flagged error in the current document). Click *Add to Dictionary* if you want the word to be considered correct whenever it appears in any document. Similar selections on a shortcut menu enable you to ignore grammatical mistakes if they are not errors.

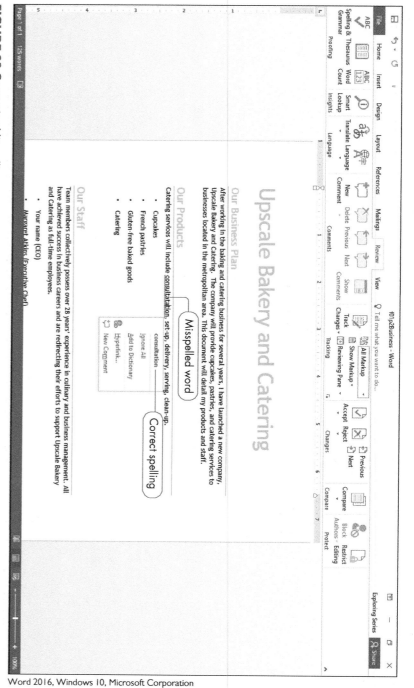

FIGURE 29 Correcting Misspelling

Word 2016, Windows 10, Microsoft Corporation

Working with Pictures and Graphics

Documents, worksheets, and presentations can include much more than just words and numbers. You can add energy and additional description to a project by including pictures and other graphic elements. Although a *picture* is usually just that—a digital photo—it is actually defined as a graphic element.

Insert Pictures and Graphics

STEP 6

You can insert pictures from your own library of digital photos you have saved on your hard drive, OneDrive, or another storage medium, or you can initiate a Bing Image Search for online pictures directly inside the Office program you are using. The Bing search filters are set to use the Creative Commons license system. These are images and drawings that can be used more freely than images from websites. You should read the Creative Commons license for each image you use to avoid copyright infringement. You can also insert a picture from social media sites, such as Facebook, by clicking the Facebook icon at the bottom of the Online Pictures dialog box.

To insert an online picture from a Bing Image Search, complete the following steps:

1. Click in the file where you want the picture to be placed.
2. Click the Insert tab.
3. Click Online Pictures in the Illustrations group.
4. Type a search term in the Bing Image Search box and press Enter.
5. Select your desired image and click Insert (see Figure 30).

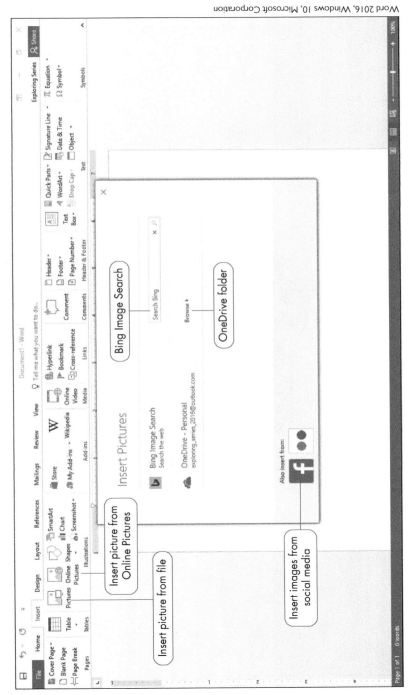

FIGURE 30 Inserting Online Pictures

To insert a picture from a file stored on your computer, complete the following steps:

1. Click in the file where you want the picture to be placed.
2. Click the Insert tab.
3. Click Pictures in the Illustrations group to search for a file located on your computer.
4. Locate the file and select it. Click Insert at the bottom of the dialog box to insert the file into your document.

Resize and Format Pictures and Graphics

You have learned how to add a picture to your document, but quite often, a picture is inserted in a size that is too large or too small for your purposes. To resize a picture, you can drag a corner sizing handle. You should never resize a picture by dragging a center sizing handle, as doing so would skew the picture. You can also resize a picture by adjusting settings in the Size group of the Picture Tools Format tab. When a picture is selected, the Picture Tools Format tab includes options for modifying a picture (see Figure 31). You can apply a picture style or effect, as well as add a picture border, from selections in the Picture Styles group. Click More (see Figure 31) to view a gallery of picture styles. As you point to a style, the style is shown in Live Preview, but the style is not applied until you click it. Options in the Adjust group simplify changing a color scheme, applying creative artistic effects, and even adjusting the brightness, contrast, and sharpness of an image.

FIGURE 31 Formatting a Picture

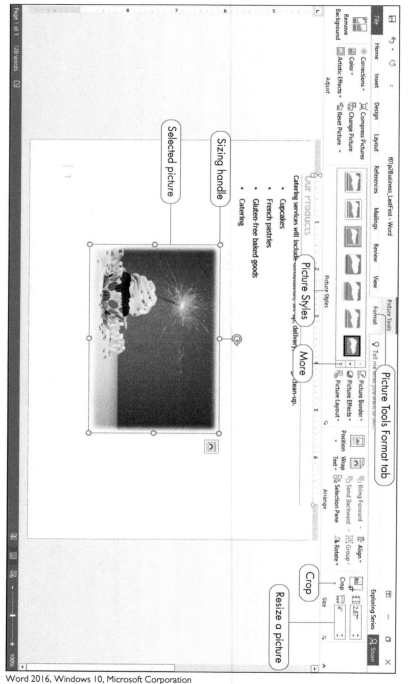

Word 2016, Windows 10, Microsoft Corporation

If a picture contains more detail than is necessary, you can crop it, which is the process of trimming edges that you do not want to display. The Crop tool is located on the Picture Tools Format tab (refer to Figure 31). Even though cropping enables you to adjust the amount of a picture that displays, it does not actually delete the portions that are cropped out unless you actually compress the picture. Therefore, you can later recover parts of the picture, if necessary. Cropping a picture does not reduce the file size of the picture or the document in which it displays.

Quick Concepts

4. What is the difference between a theme and a template?

5. Give an example of when Format Painter could be used.

6. When will an Office application identify a word as misspelled that is not actually misspelled?

Hands-On Exercises

MyITLab®
HOE2 Training

Watch the Video
for this Hands-On
Exercise!

2 Format Document Content

Skills covered: Open a Template • Select Text • Edit Text • Use the Mini Toolbar • Format Painter • Cut, Copy, and Paste Text • Check Spelling and Grammar • Insert a Picture

As the administrative assistant for the Spotted Begonia Art Gallery, you want to create a flyer to announce the *Discover the Artist in You!* kickoff event. You decide to use a template to help you get started more quickly. You will modify the flyer created with the template by adding and editing text and a photo.

STEP 1 ▶▶ OPEN A TEMPLATE

To expedite the process of creating a flyer, you will review the templates that are available in Microsoft Word. You search for flyers and finally choose one that is appropriate for the gallery, knowing that you will be able to replace the photos with your own. Refer to Figure 32 as you complete Step 1.

Word 2016, Windows 10, Microsoft Corporation

FIGURE 32 Use a Template

a. Start Word. In the *Search for online templates* box type the search term **event flyer** to search for event flyer templates Click **Search**.

Your search results in a selection of event flyer templates.

b. Locate the event flyer template in Figure 32 and click to select it. The template appears in a preview. Click **Create** to open the flyer template.

The flyer template that you selected opens in Word.

TROUBLESHOOTING: If you do not find the template in the figure, you may access the template from the student data files — *f01h2Flyer*.

c. Click **Save** on the Quick Access Toolbar. Save the document as **f01h2Flyer_LastFirst.** Because this is the first time to save the flyer file, the Save button on the Quick Access Toolbar opens a dialog box in which you must indicate the location of the file and the file name.

You will replace the template text to create the flyer, adding information such as a title, date, and description. After adding the text to the document, you will modify the organization name in the flyer so it is more like the logo text. Refer to Figure 33 as you complete Step 2.

Step a: Text added

Step c: 26 font size applied

Step b: Eras Bold ITC font applied

MAY 31, 2018
DISCOVER THE ARTIST IN YOU!

Spotted Begonia Art Gallery

A Special Childrens Event

[To replace any tip text with your own, just click it and start typing.
To replace the photo or logo with your own, right-click it and then

[Add Key Event Info Here:]

[Don't Be Shy— Tell Them Why They Can't Miss It!]

[One More Point Here:]

[Add More Great Info Here:]

[You Have Room for Another One Here:]

[COMPANY NAME]

FIGURE 33 Select and Edit Text

Word 2016, Windows 10, Microsoft Corporation

a. Click the [Date] **placeholder** in the main body of the text and type **May 31, 2018** in the placeholder. Click the [Event Title Here] **placeholder** and type **Discover the Artist in You!** in the placeholder. Press **Enter** and continue typing **Spotted Begonia Art Gallery**. Click the [Event Description Heading] **placeholder** and type **A Special Childrens Event**. (Ignore the misspelling at this time.)

You modify the placeholders to customize the flyer for your purposes.

b. Point to the text **Discover the Artist in You!** until the pointer becomes an I-beam. Click and drag to select the text. Click the **Font arrow** on the Mini toolbar. Select **Eras Bold ITC**.

The font is changed.

c. Select the text, **May 31, 2018**. Click the **Font Size arrow** on the Mini toolbar. Select **26** on the Font Size menu.

The font size is changed to 26 pt.

d. Click Save on the Quick Access Toolbar to save the document.

You want the gallery name font to match that of the event description heading in the flyer. You recently learned about using the Format Painter tool to quickly apply font attributes to text. Refer to Figure 34 as you complete Step 3.

FIGURE 34 Use Format Painter

a. Click the **Home tab.** Select the text **A Special Childrens Event**, and click **Format Painter** in the Clipboard group. Drag to select the text **Spotted Begonia Art Gallery**.

The text is now modified to match the font and size of the event description heading.

b. Save the document.

You decide that one of the paragraphs in the flyer would be best near the end of the document. You cut the paragraph and paste it in the new location. Refer to Figure 35 as you complete Step 4.

FIGURE 35 Move Text

a. Point to the text **Spotted Begonia Art Gallery** until the pointer becomes an I-beam. Click and drag to select the text. Press **Ctrl+X.**

The paragraph text is cut from the document and placed in the Office Clipboard.

b. Click before the word *May.* Press **Ctrl+V** to paste the previously cut text.

The text is now moved above the event date.

c. Save the document.

Because this flyer will be seen by the public, it is important to check the spelling and grammar for your document. Refer to Figure 36 as you complete Step 5.

FIGURE 36 Check Spelling and Grammar

a. Press **Ctrl+Home**. Click the **Review tab**, and click **Spelling & Grammar**, in the Proofing group Click **Change** to accept the suggested change to *Children's* in the Spelling pane. Click **OK** to close the dialog box.

The spelling and grammar check is complete.

b. Save the document.

You want to add an image saved on your computer that was taken at a previous children's event held at the gallery. Refer to Figure 37 as you complete Step 6.

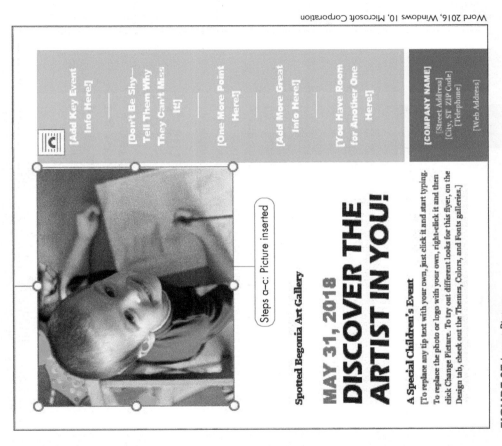

(Steps a–c: Picture inserted)

Spotted Begonia Art Gallery

MAY 31, 2018

DISCOVER THE ARTIST IN YOU!

A Special Children's Event

[To replace any tip text with your own, just click it and start typing. To replace the photo or logo with your own, right-click it and then click Change Picture. To try out different looks for this flyer, on the Design tab, check out the Themes, Colors, and Fonts galleries.]

[Add Key Event Info Here!]

[Don't Be Shy— Tell Them Why They Can't Miss It!]

[One More Point Here!]

[Add More Great Info Here!]

[You Have Room for Another One Here!]

[COMPANY NAME]
[Street Address]
[City, ST ZIP Code]
[Telephone]

[Web Address]

FIGURE 37 Insert Picture

a. Click the **image** to select it. Click the **Insert tab** and then click **Pictures**. Browse to your student data files and locate the *f01h2Art* picture file. Click **Insert**.

The child's image is inserted into the flyer and replaces the template image of the children with ice cream.

b. Save and close the document. You will submit this file to your instructor at the end of the last Hands-On Exercise.

Modify Document Layout and Properties

When working with a document, at some point you must get it ready for distribution and/or printing. Before you send a document or print it, you will want to view the final product to make sure that your margins and page layout are as they should be.

In this section you will learn about Backstage view and explore how to view and edit document properties. You will learn about views and how to change a document view to suit your needs. Additionally, you will learn how to modify the page layout including page orientation and margins as well as how to add headers and footers. Finally, you will explore Print Preview and the various printing options available to you.

Using Backstage View

Backstage view is a component of Office that provides a concise collection of commands related to a file. Using Backstage view, you can view or specify settings related to protection, permissions, versions, and properties. A file's properties include the author, file size, permissions, and date modified. Backstage view also includes options for customizing program settings, signing in to your Office account, and exiting the application. You can create a new document, as well as open, save, print, share, export, and close files using Backstage view. Backstage view also enables you to exit the application.

Click the File tab to see Backstage view (see Figure 38). Backstage view will occupy the entire application window, hiding the file with which you are working. You can return to the application in a couple of ways. Either click the Back arrow in the top-left corner or press Esc on the keyboard.

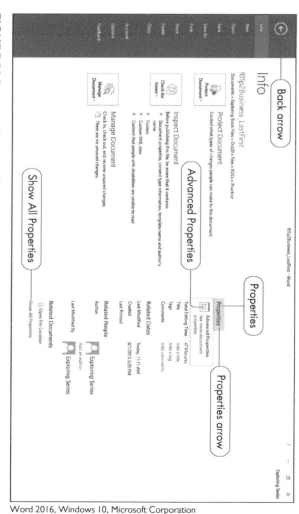

FIGURE 38 Backstage View and Document Properties

Word 2016, Windows 10, Microsoft Corporation

Customize Application Options

General settings in the Office application in which you are working can also be customized (see Figure 39). For example, you can change the AutoRecover settings, a feature that enables Word to recover a previous version of a document, such as the location and save frequency. You can alter how formatting, spelling, and grammar are checked by the application such as ignoring words in all uppercase letters. You can also modify the AutoCorrect feature. Additionally, you can change the language in which the application is displayed or the language for spelling and grammar checking, which may be helpful for a language course.

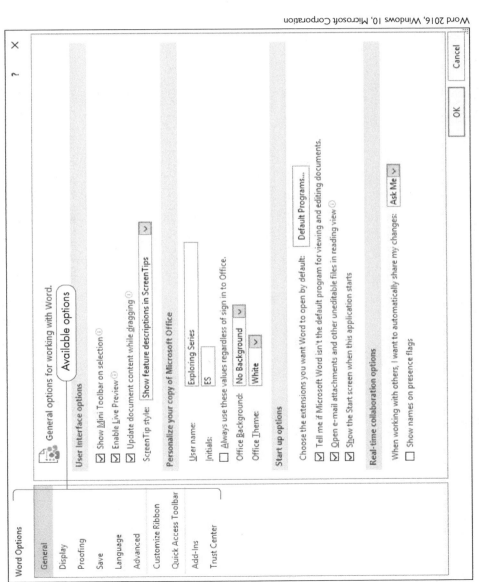

Word 2016, Windows 10, Microsoft Corporation

FIGURE 39 Application Options in Word

To customize an Office application, complete the following steps:

1. Click the File tab.
2. Click Options and select the option of your choice.
3. Click OK.

View and Edit Document Properties

STEP 1 >> It is good to include information that identifies a document, such as the author, document purpose, intended audience, or general comments. Those data elements, or metadata, are saved with the document, but do not appear in the document as it displays onscreen or is printed. You can use the Document Properties, located in Backstage view, to display descriptive information. You can even search for a file based on metadata you assign a document. For example, suppose you apply a tag of *Picasso* to all documents you create that are associated with that particular artist. Later, you can use that keyword as a search term, locating all associated documents. Statistical information related to the current document such as file size, number of pages, and total words are located on the Info page of Backstage view. You can modify some document information, such as adding a title or comments, but for more possibilities, display the Advanced Properties (refer to Figure 38).

Changing the Document View

As you prepare a document, you may find that you want to change the way you view it. A section of your document may be easier to view when you can see it magnified, for example. Alternatively, some applications have different views to make working on your project easier.

The **status bar**, located at the bottom of the program window, contains information relative to the open file and is unique to each specific application. When you work with Word, the status bar informs you of the number of pages and words in an open document. The Excel status bar displays summary information, such as average and sum, of selected cells. The PowerPoint status bar shows the slide number and total number of slides in the presentation. It also provides access to Notes and Comments.

The status bar also includes commonly used tools for changing the **view**—the way a file appears onscreen—and for changing the zoom size of onscreen file contents. The view buttons (see Figure 40) on the status bar of each application enable you to change the view of the open file. For instance, you can use Slide Sorter view to look at a PowerPoint slide presentation with multiple slides displayed or use Normal view to show only one slide in large size.

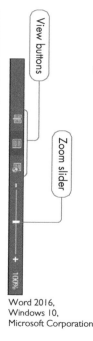

FIGURE 40 The Status Bar

View buttons

Zoom slider

Word 2016,
Windows 10,
Microsoft Corporation

Additional views for all Office applications are available on the View tab. Word's Print Layout view is useful when you want to see both the document text and such features as margins and page breaks. Web Layout view is useful to see what the page would look like on the Internet. Read Mode view provides a clean look that displays just the content without the Ribbon or margins. It is ideal for use on a tablet where the screen may be smaller than on a laptop or computer. PowerPoint, Excel, and Access also provide other unique view options. As you learn more about Office applications, you will become aware of the views that are specific to each application.

The **Zoom slider** is a horizontal bar on the bottom-right side of the status bar that enables you to increase or decrease the size of the document onscreen. You can drag the slider along the slider in either direction to increase or decrease the magnification of the file (refer to Figure 40). Be aware, however, that changing the size of text onscreen does not change the font size when the file is printed or saved.

Changing the Page Layout

When you prepare a document or worksheet, you are concerned with the way the project appears onscreen and possibly in print. The Layout tab in Word and the Page Layout tab in Excel provide access to a full range of options such as margin settings and page orientation. PowerPoint does not have a Page Layout tab, since its primary purpose is displaying contents onscreen rather than in print.

Because a document or workbook is most often designed to be printed, you may need to adjust margins and change the page orientation for the best display. In addition, perhaps the document or spreadsheet should be centered on the page vertically or the text should be aligned in columns. You will find these and other common page settings in the Page Setup group on the Layout (or Page Layout) tab. For less common settings, such as determining whether headers should print on odd or even pages, you use the Page Setup dialog box.

Change Margins

STEP 3 A *margin* is the area of blank space that displays to the left, right, top, and bottom of a document or worksheet. Margins display when you are in Print Layout or Page Layout view, or in Backstage view previewing a document to print. As shown in Figure 41, you can change the margins by clicking Margins in the Page Setup group. You can also change margins in the Print area on Backstage view.

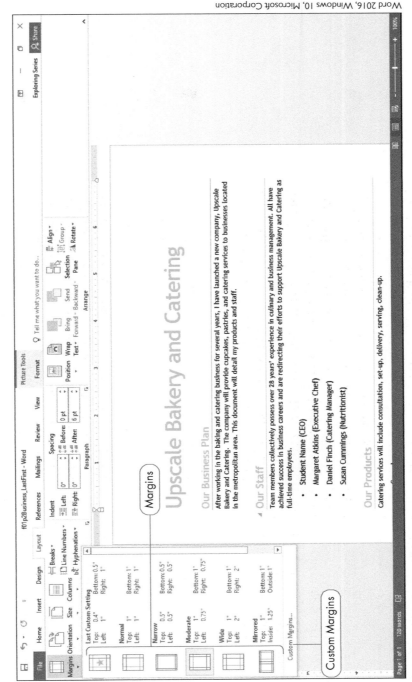

FIGURE 41 Page Margins in Word

Modify Document Layout and Properties • Common Features 2016

To change margins in Word and Excel, complete the following steps:

1. Click the Layout (or Page Layout) tab.
2. Click Margins in the Page Setup group.
3. Select a preset margin option or click Custom Margins (refer to Figure 41) to display the Page Setup dialog box where you can apply custom margin settings.
4. Click OK to accept the settings and close the dialog box.

Change Page Orientation

Documents and worksheets can be displayed in different page orientations. A page displayed or printed in *portrait orientation* is taller than it is wide. A page in *landscape orientation* is wider than it is tall. Word documents are usually more attractive displayed in portrait orientation, whereas Excel worksheets are often more suited to landscape orientation.

To change the page orientation, complete the following steps:

1. Click the Layout (or Page Layout) tab.
2. Click Orientation in the Page Setup group.
3. Select Portrait or Landscape.

Orientation is also an option in the Print area of Backstage view.

Use the Page Setup Dialog Box

The Page Setup group contains the most commonly used page options in the particular Office application. Some are unique to Excel, and others are more applicable to Word. Other less common settings are available in the Page Setup dialog box only, displayed when you click the Page Setup Dialog Box Launcher. The Page Setup dialog box includes options for customizing margins, selecting page orientation, centering horizontally or vertically, printing gridlines, and creating headers and footers. Figure 42 shows both the Excel and Word Page Setup dialog boxes.

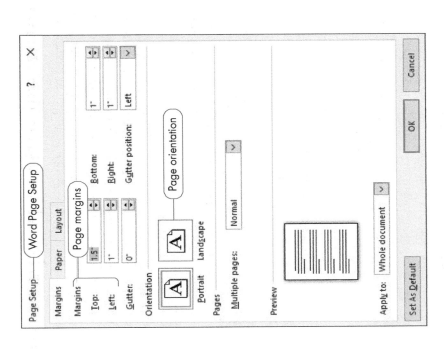

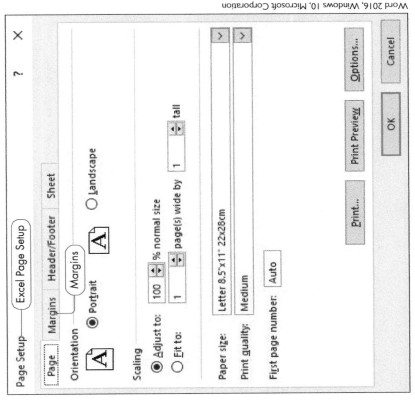

FIGURE 42 Page Setup Dialog Boxes in Word and Excel

Modify Document Layout and Properties • Common Features 2016

Inserting a Header and Footer

The purpose of including a header or footer in a document is to better identify the document and give it a professional appearance. A **header** consists of one or more lines at the top of each page. A **footer** displays at the bottom of each page. One advantage of using headers and footers is that you specify the content only once, after which it displays automatically on all pages. Although you can type the text yourself at the top or bottom of every page, it is time-consuming, and the possibility of making a mistake is great. As a header, you might include an organization name or a class number so that each page identifies the document's origin or purpose. A page number is a typical footer, although it could just as easily be included in a header.

To apply a header or footer, complete one of the following steps (based on the application):

- Select a header or footer in Word by clicking the Insert tab and then clicking Header or Footer (see Figure 43). Choose from a predefined list, or click Edit Header (or Edit Footer) to create an unformatted header or footer.

- Select a header or footer in Excel by clicking the Insert tab and clicking Header and Footer. Select the left, center, or right section and type your own footer or use a predefined field code such as date or file name.

- Select a header or footer for PowerPoint by clicking the Insert tab, clicking Header and Footer, and then checking the footer option for slides. In PowerPoint, a footer's location will depend on the theme applied to the presentation. For some themes, the footer will appear on the side of the slide rather than at the bottom. Headers and footers are available for Notes and Handouts as well.

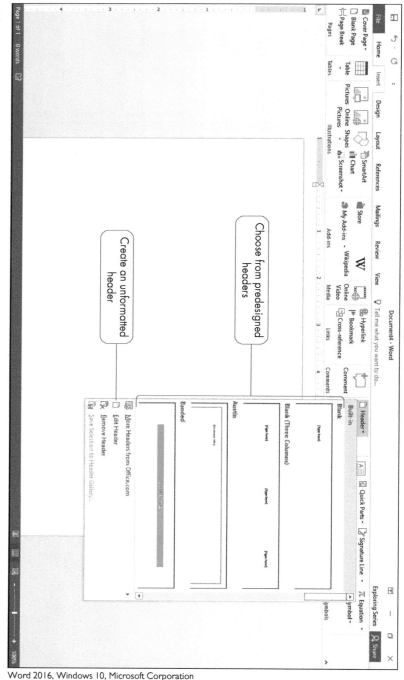

Create an unformatted header

Choose from predesigned headers

FIGURE 43 Insert Header in Word

After typing a header or footer, it can be formatted like any other text. It can be formatted in any font or font size. In Word or Excel, when you want to leave the header and footer area and return to the document, click Close Header and Footer (see Figure 44).

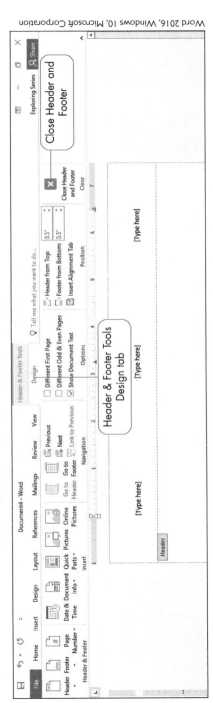

FIGURE 44 Close Header and Footer

Previewing and Printing a File

>> When you want to print an Office file, you can select from various print options, including the number of copies and the specific pages to print. It is a good idea to take a look at how your document or worksheet will appear before you print it. The Print Preview feature of Office enables you to do just that. In the Print Preview pane, you will see all items, including any headers, footers, graphics, and special formatting.

STEP 5

> **To view a file before printing, complete the following steps:**
>
> 1. Click the File tab.
> 2. Click Print.

The subsequent Backstage view shows the file preview on the right, with print settings located in the center of the Backstage screen. Figure 45 shows a typical Backstage Print view. If you know that the page setup is correct and that there are no unique print settings to select, you can simply print without adjusting any print settings.

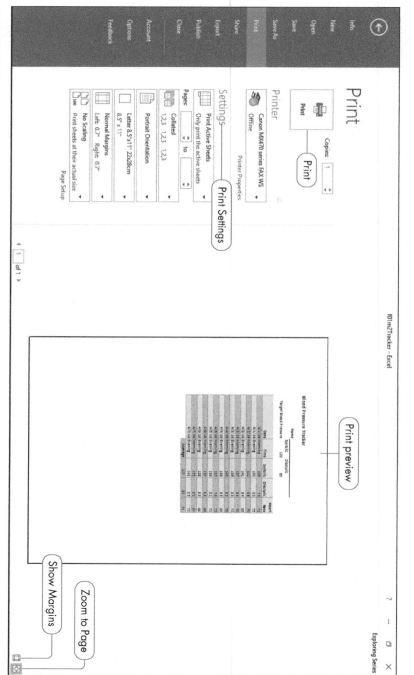

Excel 2016, Windows 10, Microsoft Corporation

FIGURE 45 Backstage Print View in Excel

Options to show the margins (*Show Margins*) and to increase the size of the print preview (*Zoom to Page*) are found on the bottom-right corner of the preview (refer to Figure 45). Remember that increasing the font size by adjusting the zoom applies to the current display only; it does not actually increase the font size when the file is printed or saved. To return the preview to its original view, click *Zoom to Page* once more.

Other options in the Backstage Print view vary depending on the application in which you are working. For example, PowerPoint's Backstage Print view includes options for printing slides and handouts in various configurations and colors, whereas Excel's focuses on worksheet selections and Word's includes document options. Regardless of the Office application, you will be able to access Settings options from Backstage view, including page orientation (landscape or portrait), margins, and paper size. To print a file, click the Print button (refer to Figure 45).

Quick Concepts

7. What functions and features are included in Backstage view?

8. Why would you need to change the view of a document?

9. What is the purpose of a header or footer?

▲ Watch the Video for this Hands-On Exercise!

Hands-On Exercises

3 Modify Document Layout and Properties

Skills covered: Enter Document Properties • Change the Document View • Change Margins • Insert a Footer • Preview a File • Change Page Orientation

You continue to work on the thank-you letter you previously started. As the administrative assistant for the Spotted Begonia Art Gallery, you must be able to search for and find documents previously created. You know that by adding tags to your letter you will more easily be able to find it at a later time. You will review and add document properties, and prepare the document to print and distribute by changing the page setup. Additionally, you will add a footer with Spotted Begonia's information. Finally, you will explore printing options, and save the letter.

STEP 1 ▶▶ ENTER DOCUMENT PROPERTIES

You will add document properties, which will help you locate the file when performing a search of your hard drive. Refer to Figure 46 as you complete Step 1.

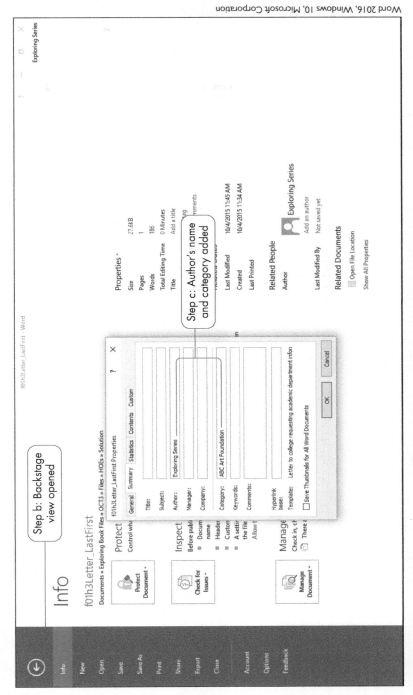

FIGURE 46 Backstage View

a. Open *f01h1Letter_LastFirst* if you closed it at the end of Hands-On Exercise 1, and save it as **f01h3Letter_LastFirst**, changing h1 to h3.

The letter is now open in Word.

b. Click the **File tab** and click **Properties** at the top-right of Backstage view. Click **Advanced Properties**.

The Properties dialog box opens so you can make changes.

Hands-On Exercise 3   115

c. Select the **Author box** and type your first and last name. Select the **Category box** and type **ABC Art Foundation**. Click **OK**.

You added the Author and Category properties to your document.

d. Save the document.

STEP 2 ⟫ CHANGE THE DOCUMENT VIEW

To get a better perspective on your letter, you want to explore the various document views available in Word. Refer to Figure 47 as you complete Step 2.

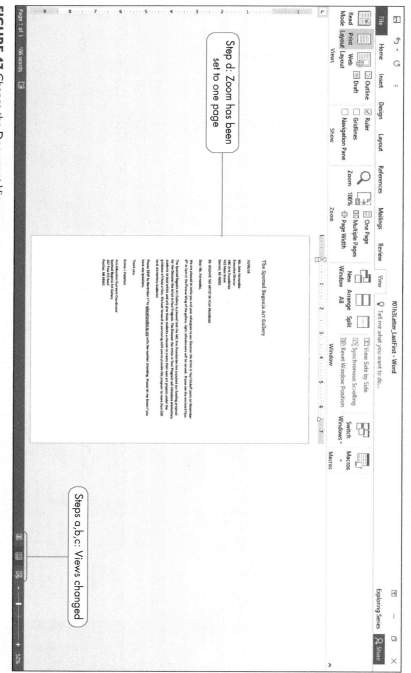

Step d: Zoom has been set to one page

Steps a,b,c: Views changed

FIGURE 47 Change the Document View

Word 2016, Windows 10, Microsoft Corporation

a. Click **Read Mode** on the status bar. Observe the changes to the Ribbon.

The view is changed to Read Mode, which is a full-screen view.

b. Click **Web Layout** on the status bar. Observe the changes to the view.

The view is changed to Web Layout and simulates how the document would appear on the Web.

c. Click **Print Layout** on the status bar. Observe the changes to the view.

The document has returned to Print Layout view.

d. Click the **View tab** and click **Zoom** in the Zoom group. Click the **One Page option**. Click **OK**.

The entire letter is displayed.

While the letter was displayed in One Page zoom, you observed that the margins were too large. You will change the margins so they are narrower. Refer to Figure 48 as you complete Step 3.

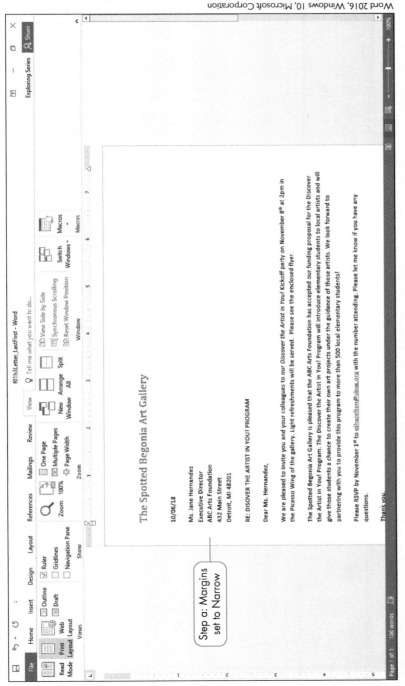

Step a: Margins set to Narrow

FIGURE 48 Change Margins

a. Click the **Layout tab** and click **Margins** in the Page Setup group. Select **Narrow**. Observe the changes.

   The document margins were changed to Narrow.

b. Click the **View tab** and click **100%** in the Zoom group.

   The document returns to its previous view.

c. Save the document.

Additional information such as a phone number and website need to be added to the letter. You decide to add these to the letter as a footer. Refer to Figure 49 as you complete Step 4.

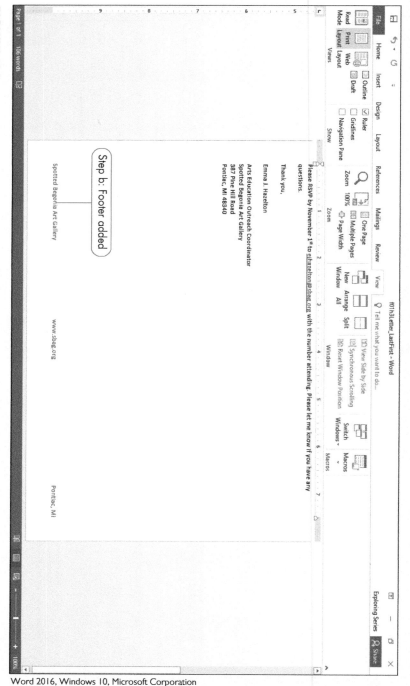

FIGURE 49 Footer

Step b: Footer added

Spotted Begonia Art Gallery   www.sbag.org   Pontiac, MI

Word 2016, Windows 10, Microsoft Corporation

a. Click the **Insert tab** and click **Footer** in the Header & Footer group. Click the **Blank (three columns)** footer.

The document opens in Header and Footer view. You select a footer with little formatting.

b. Click **[Type here]** on the far left of the footer. Type **Spotted Begonia Art Gallery** in that placeholder. Click **[Type here]** in the center of the footer. Type **www.sbag.org** in that placeholder. Click **[Type here]** on the far right of the footer. Type **Pontiac, MI** in that placeholder. On the Header & Footer Tools Design tab, click **Close Header and Footer** in the Close group.

The footer information is entered.

c. Save the document.

STEP 5 ≫ PREVIEW A FILE AND CHANGE PAGE ORIENTATION

You have reviewed and finalized the letter, so you will print the document so it can be sent to its recipient. You will first preview the document as it will appear when printed. Refer to Figure 50 as you complete Step 5.

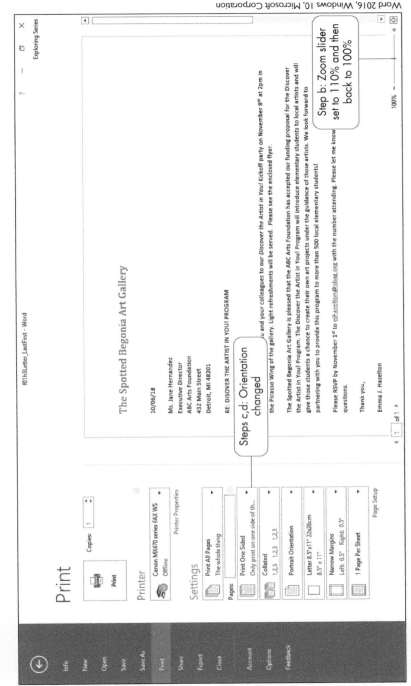

FIGURE 50 Backstage Print View

a. Click the **File tab** and click **Print**.

It is always a good idea to check the way a file will look when printed before actually printing it.

b. Drag the **Zoom slider on the status bar** to increase the document view to 110%. Click **Zoom to Page** (located at the far right of the status bar).

Your print preview returns to the original size.

c. Click **Portrait Orientation** in the Settings area. Click **Landscape Orientation**.

The letter appears in a wider and shorter view.

d. Return to Portrait Orientation to see the original view.

You decide that the flyer is more attractive in portrait orientation, so you return to that setting.

e. Save and close the file. Based on your instructor's directions, submit the following:

f01h2Flyer_LastFirst
f01h3Letter_LastFirst

Chapter Objectives Review

After reading this chapter, you have accomplished the following objectives:

1. Start an Office application.

- Your Microsoft account connects you to all of Microsoft's Internet-based resources.
- Change a Microsoft account: If you share your computer with another user, each user can have access to his own Microsoft account; you can easily switch between accounts so you can access your own files.

2. Work with files.

- Create a new file: You can create a document as a blank document or with a template.
- Open a file: You can open an existing file using the Open dialog box. Previously saved files can be accessed using the Recent documents list.
- Save a file: Saving a file enables you to open it later for additional updates or reference. Files are saved to a storage medium such as a hard drive, CD, flash drive, or to the cloud on OneDrive.

3. Use common interface components.

- Use the Ribbon: The Ribbon, the long bar located just beneath the title bar containing tabs, groups, and commands, is the command center of Office applications.
- Use a shortcut menu: A shortcut menu provides choices related to the object, selection, or area of the document on which you right-click.
- Use keyboard shortcuts: Keyboard shortcuts are keyboard equivalents for software commands. Universal keyboard shortcuts in Office include Ctrl+C (Copy), Ctrl+X (Cut), Ctrl+V (Paste), and Ctrl+Z (Undo).
- Customize the Ribbon: You can personalize the Ribbon in your Office applications, giving you easier access to a frequently used set of commands that are unique to you or your business.
- Use the Quick Access Toolbar: The Quick Access Toolbar, located at the top-left corner of any Office application window, provides one-click access to commonly executed tasks such as saving a file or undoing recent actions.
- Customize the Quick Access Toolbar: You use certain actions in an Office application often, and for more convenient access, you can add a button for each action to the Quick Access Toolbar.

4. Get help.

- Use the *Tell me what you want to do* box: The *Tell me what you want to do* box not only links to online resources and technical support but also provides quick access to functions.
- Use Enhanced ScreenTips: An Enhanced ScreenTip describes a command and provides a keyboard shortcut, if applicable.

5. Install add-ins.

- Add-ins are custom programs or additional commands that extend the functionality of a Microsoft Office program.

6. Use templates and apply themes.

- Open a template: Templates are a convenient way to save time when designing a document.
- Apply a theme: Themes are a collection of design choices that include colors, fonts, and special effects used to give a consistent look to a document, workbook, or presentation.

7. Modify text.

- Select text: To select text or numbers, place the pointer before the first character or digit you want to select, and then drag to highlight the intended selection. Before you drag, be sure that the pointer takes on the shape of the letter I, called the I-beam.
- Edit text: You can edit the font, font color, size, and many other attributes.
- Use the Mini toolbar: The Mini toolbar provides instant access to common formatting commands after text is selected.
- Copy formats with the Format Painter: Easily apply formatting from one selection to another by using Format Painter.

8. Relocate text.

- Cut, copy, and paste text: To cut means to remove a selection from the original location and place it in the Office Clipboard. To copy means to duplicate a selection from the original location and place a copy in the Office Clipboard. To paste means to place a cut or copied selection into another location.
- Use the Office Clipboard: When you cut or copy selections, they are placed in the Office Clipboard. You can paste the same item multiple times; it will remain in the Clipboard until you power down your computer or until the Clipboard exceeds 24 items.

9. Check spelling and grammar.

- Office applications check and mark spelling and grammar errors as you type for later correction. The Thesaurus enables you to search for synonyms.

10. Work with pictures and Graphics.

- Insert pictures and graphics: You can insert pictures from your own library of digital photos you have saved on your hard drive, OneDrive, or another storage medium, or you can initiate a Bing search for online pictures directly inside the Office program you are using.
- Resize and format pictures and graphics: To resize a picture, drag a corner sizing handle; never resize a picture by dragging a center sizing handle. You can apply

a picture style or effect, as well as add a picture border, from selections in the Picture Styles group.

11. Use Backstage view.

- *Customize application options:* You can customize general settings in the Office application in which you are working, such as AutoRecover settings and location and save frequency.
- *View and edit document properties:* Information that identifies a document, such as the author, document purpose, intended audience, or general comments can be added to the document's properties. Those data elements are saved with the document, but do not appear in the document as it displays onscreen or is printed.

12. Change the document view.

- The status bar provides information relative to the open file and quick access to View and Zoom level options. Each application has a set of views specific to the application.

13. Change the page layout.

- *Change margins:* A margin is the area of blank space that displays to the left, right, top, and bottom of a document or worksheet.

- *Change page orientation:* Documents and worksheets can be displayed in different page orientations. Portrait orientation is taller than it is wide; landscape orientation is wider than it is tall.
- *Use the Page Setup dialog box:* The Page Setup dialog box includes options for customizing margins, selecting page orientation, centering horizontally or vertically, printing gridlines, and creating headers and footers.

14. Insert a header and footer.

- A footer displays at the bottom of each page.
- A header consists of one or more lines at the top of each page.

15. Preview and print a file.

- It is important to review your file before printing.
- Print options can be set in Backstage view and include page orientation, the number of copies, and the specific pages to print.

Key Terms Matching

Match the key terms with their definitions. Write the key term letter by the appropriate numbered definition.

a. Access
b. Add-in
c. Clipboard
d. Backstage view
e. Cloud storage
f. Format Painter
g. Footer
h. Group
i. Header
j. Margin

k. Microsoft Office
l. Mini toolbar
m. OneDrive
n. Quick Access Toolbar
o. Ribbon
p. Status bar
q. Tab
r. Tell me what you want to do box
s. Template
t. Theme

1. _____ A tool that copies all formatting from one area to another.

2. _____ Stores up to 24 cut or copied selections for use later on in your computing session.

3. _____ A task-oriented section of the Ribbon that contains related commands.

4. _____ An online app used to store, access, and share files and folders.

5. _____ Custom programs or additional commands that extend the functionality of a Microsoft Office program.

6. _____ A component of Office that provides a concise collection of commands related to an open file and includes save and print options.

7. _____ A tool that displays near selected text that contains formatting commands.

8. _____ Relational database software used to store data and convert it into information.

9. _____ Consists of one or more lines at the bottom of each page.

10. _____ A predesigned file that incorporates formatting elements, such as a theme and layouts, and may include content that can be modified.

11. _____ A collection of design choices that includes colors, fonts, and special effects used to give a consistent look to a document, workbook, or presentation.

12. _____ A component of the Ribbon that is designed to appear much like a tab on a file folder.

13. _____ Provides handy access to commonly executed tasks such as saving a file and undoing recent actions.

14. _____ The long bar at the bottom of the screen that houses the Zoom slider and various View buttons.

15. _____ A productivity software suite including a set of software applications, each one specializing in a particular type of output.

16. _____ Allows you to search for help and information about a command or task you want to perform, and will also present you with a shortcut directly to that command.

17. _____ The long bar located just beneath the title bar containing tabs, groups, and commands.

18. _____ The area of blank space that displays to the left, right, top, and bottom of a document or worksheet.

19. _____ A technology used to store files and to work with programs that are stored in a central location on the Internet.

20. _____ Consists of one or more lines at the top of each page.

Multiple Choice

1. The Recent documents list shows documents that have been previously:

 (a) Printed.
 (b) Opened.
 (c) Saved in an earlier software version.
 (d) Deleted.

2. In Word or PowerPoint a quick way to select an entire paragraph is to:

 (a) Place the pointer at the left of the line, in the margin area, and click.
 (b) Triple-click inside the paragraph.
 (c) Double-click at the beginning of the paragraph.
 (d) Press Ctrl+C inside the paragraph.

3. When you want to copy the format of a selection but not the content, you should:

 (a) Double-click Copy in the Clipboard group.
 (b) Right-click the selection and click Copy.
 (c) Click Copy Format in the Clipboard group.
 (d) Click Format Painter in the Clipboard group.

4. Which of the following is *not* a benefit of using OneDrive?

 (a) Save your folders and files to the cloud.
 (b) Share your files and folders with others.
 (c) Hold video conferences with others.
 (d) Simultaneously work on the same document with others.

5. What does a red wavy underline in a document, spreadsheet, or presentation mean?

 (a) A word is misspelled or not recognized by the Office dictionary.
 (b) A grammatical mistake exists.
 (c) An apparent word usage mistake exists.
 (d) A word has been replaced with a synonym.

6. Which of the following is *true* about headers and footers?

 (a) They can be inserted from the Design tab.
 (b) Headers and footers only appear on the last page of a document.
 (c) Headers appear at the top of a document.
 (d) Only page numbers can be included in a header or footer.

7. Live Preview:

 (a) Opens a predesigned document or spreadsheet that is relevant to your task.
 (b) Provides a preview of the results of a choice you are considering before you make a final selection.
 (c) Provides a preview of an upcoming Office version.
 (d) Enlarges the font onscreen.

8. You can get help when working with an Office application in which one of the following areas?

 (a) The *Tell me what you want to do* box
 (b) Status bar
 (c) Backstage view
 (d) Quick Access Toolbar

9. In PowerPoint, a file that includes formatting elements such as a background, a color scheme, and slide layout is a:

 (a) Theme.
 (b) Template.
 (c) Scheme.
 (d) Variant.

10. A document or worksheet printed in landscape orientation is:

 (a) Taller than it is wide.
 (b) Wider than it is tall.
 (c) A document with 2" left and right margins.
 (d) A document with 2" top and bottom margins.

Practice Exercises

1 Designing Webpages

You have been asked to make a presentation to the local business association. With the mayor's renewed emphasis on growing the local economy, many businesses are interested in establishing a Web presence. The business owners would like to know a little bit more about how webpages are designed. In preparation for the presentation, you will proofread and edit your PowerPoint file. You decide to insert an image to enhance your presentation. Refer to Figure 51 as you complete this exercise.

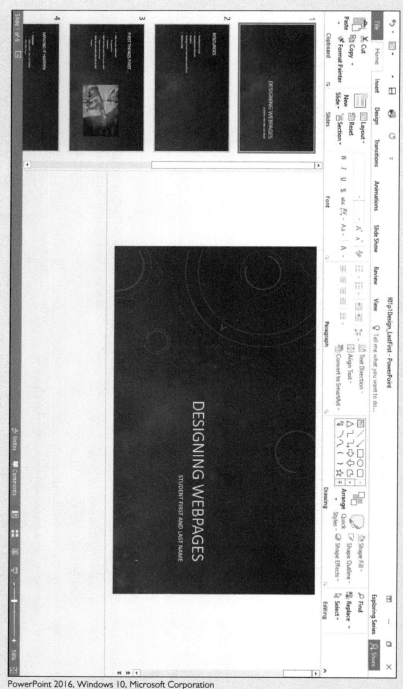

FIGURE 51 Designing Webpages Presentation

PowerPoint 2016, Windows 10, Microsoft Corporation

a. Open *f01p1Design*. Click the **File** tab, click **Save As**, and save the file as **f01p1Design_LastFirst**.

b. Ensure that Slide 1 is visible, select the text *Firstname Lastname*, and type your own first and last names. Click an empty area of the slide to cancel the selection.

c. Click the **Design** tab, then click the **Celestial theme** in the Themes group to apply it to all slides.

d. Click the **Review tab** and click **Spelling** in the Proofing group. In the Spelling pane, click **Change** or **Ignore** to make changes as needed. Most identified misspellings should be changed. The words *KompoZer* and *Nvu* are not misspelled, so you should ignore them when they are flagged. Click **OK** when you have finished checking spelling.

e. Click the **Slide Show tab**. Click **From Beginning** in the Start Slide Show group. Click each slide to view the show and press **Esc** when you reach the last slide, slide 6.

f. Click **Slide 2** in the Slides pane on the left. Triple-click to select the **Other tools** text on the slide and press **Backspace** on the keyboard to delete the text.

g. Click **Slide 4** in the Slides pane. Triple-click to select the **FrontPage.Nvu** text and press **Backspace** to delete the text.

h. Click the **Insert tab**. Click **Header & Footer** in the Text group. Click the **Slide number check box** to select it and click **Apply to All**.

i. Press **Ctrl+End** to place the insertion point at the end of *Templates* on Slide 4 and press **Enter**. Type **Database Connectivity** to create a new bulleted item.

j. Click **Slide 3** in the Slides pane. Click the **Insert tab** and click **Pictures** in the Images group. Browse to the student data files, locate and select *f01p1website*, and then click **Insert.**

k. Click the **Shape height box** in the Size group on the Picture Tools Format tab. Type **4** and then press Enter.

l. Click **Slide 6** in the Slides pane. Click the **Insert tab**, and then click **Store** in the Add-ins group. In the search box, type **multiple response poll**. Press **Enter**. The add-in will resize if the window or resolution is small.

m. Click the **Multiple Response Poll** and then click **Trust It** to insert it into the slide.

n. Click the **Insert question here text box** in the poll window, and type **Do you have a website?**

o. Click the first **Insert option here text box** and type **Yes.** Click the second **Insert option here text box** and type **No.** Click **Preview** in the poll window.

p. Click the **File tab** and click **Print.** Click the **Full Page Slides arrow** and click **6 Slides Horizontal** to see a preview of all of the slides as a handout. Click the **Back arrow**.

q. Click **Slide 1** in the Slides pane to move to the beginning of the presentation.

r. Drag the **Zoom slider** on the status bar to the right to **130%** to magnify the text. Use the **Zoom slider** to move to **60%.**

s. Save and close the file. Based on your instructor's directions, submit f01p1Design_LastFirst.

You have always been interested in baking and have worked in the field for several years. You now have an opportunity to devote yourself full time to your career as the CEO of a company dedicated to baking cupcakes and pastries, and to catering. One of the first steps in getting the business off the ground is developing a business plan so that you can request financial support. You will use Word to develop your business plan. Refer to Figure 52 as you complete this exercise.

a. Open *f01p2Business*. Click the **File tab**, click **Save As**, and save the file as **f01p2Business_LastFirst**.

b. Click the **Review tab** and click **Spelling & Grammar** in the Proofing group. Click **Change** for all suggestions and then click OK.

c. Select the paragraphs beginning with *Our Staff* and ending with (*Nutritionist*). Click the **Home tab** and click **Cut** in the Clipboard group. Click to the left of *Our Products* and click **Paste**.

Upscale Bakery and Catering

Our Business Plan

After working in the baking and catering business for several years, I have launched a new company, Upscale Bakery and Catering. The company will provide cupcakes, pastries, and catering services to businesses located in the metropolitan area. This document will detail my products and staff.

Our Staff

Team members collectively possess over 28 years' experience in culinary and business management. All have achieved success in business careers and are redirecting their efforts to support Upscale Bakery and Catering as full-time employees.

- Student Name (CEO)
- Margaret Atkins (Executive Chef)
- Daniel Finch (Catering Manager)
- Susan Cummings (Nutritionist)

Our Products

Catering services will include consultation, set-up, delivery, serving, clean-up.

- Cupcakes
- French pastries
- Gluten-free baked goods
- Catering

FIGURE 52 Upscale Bakery Business Plan

d. Select the text **Your name** in the first bullet in the *Our Staff* section and replace it with your first and last names. Select the entire bullet list, click the **Font Size arrow** and then click **11**.

e. Double-click **Format Painter** in the Clipboard group on the Home tab. Drag the Format Painter pointer to change the other *Our Staff* bullets' font size to **11 pt**. Drag across all four *Our Products* bullets. Click Format Painter to deselect it.

f. Click the *Tell me what you want to do* box, and type **Footer**. Click **Add a Footer** scroll to locate the **Sideline footer**, click to add it to the page. Click **Close Header and Footer** on the Header & Footer Tools Design tab.

g. Select the last line in the document, which says *Insert and position picture here*, and press **Delete**. Click the **Insert tab** and click **Online Pictures** in the Illustrations group.

- Click in the **Bing Image Search box**, type **Cupcakes**, and then press **Enter**.
- Select any cupcake image and click **Insert**. Do not deselect the image.

TROUBLESHOOTING: If you are unable to find a cupcake image in the Bing Image Search then you can use f01p2Cupcake from the student data files.

- Ensure the **Picture Tools Format tab** is active, and in the Picture Styles group, click the **Soft Edge Rectangle**.
- Click the **Shape width box** in the Size group and change the width to **4**.
- Click outside the picture.

h. Click the **File tab**. In the Properties section, add the tag **Business Plan**. Add your first and last name to the Author property.

i. Click **Print** in Backstage view. Change Normal Margins to **Moderate Margins**. Click the **Back arrow**.

j. Click the **picture** and click **Center** in the Paragraph group on the Home tab.

k. Save and close the file. Based on your instructor's directions, submit f01p2Business_LastFirst.

Mid-Level Exercises

1 Reference Letter

You are an instructor at a local community college. A student asked you to provide her with a letter of reference for a job application. You have used Word to prepare the letter, but now you want to make a few changes before it is finalized.

a. Open *f01m1Refletter* and save it as **f01m1Refletter_LastFirst.**

b. Select the date and point to several font sizes on the Mini toolbar. Use Live Preview to compare them. Click **11.**

c. Change the rest of the letter (below the date) to font size 11.

d. Apply bold to the student's name, *Stacy VanPatten*, in the first sentence.

e. Customize the Quick Access Toolbar so that a Spelling and Grammar button is added.

f. Use the button you just added to correct all errors using Spelling and Grammar. Stacy's last name is spelled correctly.

g. Select the word *intelligent* in the second paragraph, and use the Thesaurus to find a synonym. Replace *intelligent* with **gifted.** Change the word *an* to **a** just before the new word. Close the Thesaurus.

h. Add the tag **reference letter** to the Properties for the file in Backstage view.

i. Move the last paragraph—beginning with *In my opinion*—to position it before the second paragraph—beginning with *Stacy is a gifted.*

j. Move the insertion point to the beginning of the document.

k. Change the margins to **Narrow.**

l. Preview the document as it will appear when printed.

m. Save and close the file. Based on your instructor's directions, submit f01m1Refletter_LastFirst.

2 Medical Monitoring

You are enrolled in a Health Informatics program of study in which you learn to manage databases related to health fields. For a class project, your instructor requires that you monitor your blood pressure, recording your findings in an Excel worksheet. You have recorded the week's data and will now make a few changes before printing the worksheet for submission.

a. Open *f01m2Tracker* and save it as **f01m2Tracker_LastFirst.**

b. Preview the worksheet as it will appear when printed. Change the orientation of the worksheet to **Landscape.** Close the Preview.

c. Click in the cell to the right of *Name* and type your first and last names. Press **Enter.**

d. Change the font of the text in **cell C1** to **Verdana.** Use Live Preview to try some font sizes. Change the font size to **20.**

e. Add the Spelling and Grammar feature to the Quick Access Toolbar, and then check the spelling for the worksheet to ensure that there are no errors.

f. Get help on showing decimal places. You want to increase the decimal places for the values in **cells E22, F22,** and **G22** so that each value shows one place to the right of the decimal. Select the cells and then use the *Tell me what you want to do* box to immediately apply the changes. You might use **Increase Decimals** as a search term. When you find the answer, increase the decimal places to **1.**

DISCOVER ⊞

g. Click **cell A1** and insert an Online Picture of your choice related to blood pressure. Resize and position the picture so that it displays in an attractive manner. Apply the **Soft Edges** picture effect to the image and set to **5 pt.**

h. Change the page margins to **Wide.**

i. Insert a footer with the page number in the center of the spreadsheet footer area. Click on any cell in the worksheet.

j. Change the View to **Normal.**

k. Open Backstage view and adjust print settings to print two copies. You will not actually print two copies unless directed by your instructor.

l. Save and close the file. Based on your instructor's directions, submit f01m2Tracker_LastFirst.

3 Today's Musical Artists

CREATIVE
CASE

COLLABORATION
CASE

With a few of your classmates, you will use PowerPoint to create a single presentation on your favorite musical artists. Each student must create at least one slide and then all of the slides will be added to the presentation. Because everyone's schedule is varied, you will use your OneDrive to pass the presentation file among the group.

a. Designate one student to create a new presentation and save it as **f01m3Music_GroupName**.

b. Add your group member names to the Author Properties in Backstage view.

c. Add a theme to the presentation.

d. Add one slide that contains the name of an artist, the genre, and two or three interesting facts about the artist.

e. Insert a picture of the artist or clip art that represents the artist.

f. Put your name on the slide that you created. Save the presentation.

g. Pass the presentation to the next student so that he or she can perform the same tasks in Steps d–f and save the presentation before passing it on to the next student. Continue until all group members have created a slide in the presentation.

h. Save and close the file. Based on your instructor's directions, submit f01m3Music_GroupName.

Fitness Planner

GENERAL CASE

You will use Microsoft Excel to develop a fitness planner. Open *f01b1Exercise* and save it as **f01b1Exercise_LastFirst**. Because the fitness planner is a template, the exercise categories are listed, but without actual data. You will personalize the planner. Change the orientation to **Landscape**. Move the contents of **cell A2** (*Exercise Planner*) to **cell A1**. Click **cell A8** and use Format Painter to copy the format of that selection to **cells A5 and A6**. Increase the font size of **cell A1 to A18**. Use the *Tell me what you want to do* box to learn how to insert a header and put your name in the header. Begin the fitness planner, entering at least one activity in each category (warm-up, aerobics, strength, and cooldown). Insert a picture from a Bing Image Search that is appropriate for the planner. You may want to use **exercise** as your search term. Check the spelling in the workbook. Add the tag **Exercise Planner** to the Properties in Backstage view. Review the document in Print Preview. Ensure that the tracker fits on a single sheet of paper when printed. Resize the image if necessary to fit on the page. Save and close the file. Based on your instructor's directions, submit f01b1Exercise_LastFirst.

Household Records

DISASTER RECOVERY

FROM SCRATCH

Use Microsoft Excel to create a detailed (fictional) record of valuables in your household. In case of burglary or disaster, an insurance claim is expedited if you are able to itemize what was lost along with identifying information such as serial numbers. You will then make a copy of the record on another storage device for safekeeping outside your home (in case your home is destroyed by a fire or weather-related catastrophe). Design a worksheet listing at least five fictional appliances and pieces of electronic equipment along with the serial number of each. Change the orientation to **Landscape**. Use the *Tell me what you want to do* box to learn how to insert a header and put your name in the header. Return to Normal view. Insert a picture from a Bing Image Search that is appropriate for the record. You may want to use **appliances** as your search term. Review the document in Print Preview. Ensure that the records fit on a single sheet of paper when printed. Move and resize the image as necessary so that it fits on the page when printed. Check the spelling in the workbook. Add the tag **Disaster Recovery** to the Properties in Backstage view. Save the workbook as **f01b2Household_LastFirst**. Save and close the file. Based on your instructor's directions, submit f01b2Household_LastFirst.

You are a member of the Student Government Association (SGA) at your college. As a community project, the SGA is sponsoring a Stop Smoking drive designed to provide information on the health risks posed by smoking cigarettes and to offer solutions to those who want to quit. The SGA has partnered with the local branch of the American Cancer Society as well as the outreach program of the local hospital to sponsor free educational awareness seminars. As the secretary for the SGA, you will help prepare a PowerPoint presentation that will be displayed on screens around campus and used in student seminars. The PowerPoint presentation has come back from the reviewers with only one comment: A reviewer suggested that you spell out Centers for Disease Control and Prevention, instead of abbreviating it. You will use Microsoft Office to help with those tasks.

Open and Save Files

You will open, review, and save a PowerPoint presentation.

a. Open *f01c1Quit* and save it as **f01c1Quit_LastFirst.**

Select Text, Move Text, and Format Text

A reviewer commented that you should modify the text on slide 12. The last sentence in the paragraph should be first since it is the answer to the question on the previous slide. You also add emphasis to the sentence.

a. Click **Slide 12**, and select the text **Just one cigarette – for some people.**

b. Cut the selected text and then paste it at the beginning of the paragraph.

c. Use the Mini toolbar to apply **Italics** to the text *Just one cigarette – for some people.*

Apply a Theme and Change the View

There is a blank theme for the slides, so you apply a different theme to the presentation.

a. Apply the **Metropolitan** theme to the presentation.

b. Change the View to Slide Sorter. Click **Slide 2** and drag to move Slide 2 to the end of the presentation. It will become the last slide (Slide 22).

c. Return to Normal view.

Insert and Modify a Picture

You will add a picture to the first slide and then resize it and position it.

a. Click **Slide 1**, and insert an online picture appropriate for the topic of **smoking.**

b. Resize the picture and reposition it.

c. Click outside the picture to deselect it.

Use the *Tell me what you want to do* Box

A reviewer suggested that you spell out Centers for Disease Control and Prevention, instead of abbreviating it. You know that there is a find and replace option to do this but you cannot remember where it is. You use the *Tell me what you want to do box* to help you with this function. You then replace the text.

a. Use the *Tell me what you want to do box* to search for **replace.**

b. Use the results from your search to find a function that will find and then replace the single occurrence of *CDC* with **Centers for Disease Control and Prevention.**

Customize the Quick Access Toolbar

You often preview and print your presentations and find it would be easier to have a button on the Quick Access Toolbar to do so. You customize the toolbar by adding this shortcut.

a. Add the Print Preview button to the Quick Access Toolbar.

b. Add the Print button to the Quick Access Toolbar.

Use Print Preview, Change Print Layout, and Print

To get an idea of how the presentation will look when printed, you will preview the presentation. You decide to print the slides so that two slides will appear on one page.

a. Preview the document as it will appear when printed.

b. Change the Print Layout to **2 Slides** (under the Handouts section).

c. Preview the document as it will appear when printed.

d. Adjust the print settings to print two copies. You will not actually print two copies unless directed by your instructor.

Check Spelling and Change View

Before you call the presentation complete, you will correct any spelling errors and view the presentation as a slide show.

a. Check the spelling. The word *hairlike* is not misspelled, so it should not be corrected.

b. View the slide show. Click after reviewing the last slide to return to the presentation.

c. Save and close the file. Based on your instructor's directions, submit f01c1Quit_LastFirst.

Access A relational database management system in which you can record and link data, query databases, and create forms and reports.

Add-in A custom program or additional command that extends the functionality of a Microsoft Office program.

Backstage view A component of Office that provides a concise collection of commands related to an open file.

Clipboard An area of memory reserved to temporarily hold selections that have been cut or copied and allows you to paste the selections.

Cloud storage A technology used to store files and to work with programs that are stored in a central location on the Internet.

Command A button or area within a group that you click to perform tasks.

Contextual tab A tab that contains a group of commands related to the selected object.

Copy A command used to duplicate a selection from the original location and place a copy in the Office Clipboard.

Cut A command used to remove a selection from the original location and place it in the Office Clipboard.

Dialog box A box that provides access to more precise, but less frequently used, commands.

Dialog Box Launcher A button that when clicked opens a corresponding dialog box.

Enhanced ScreenTip A small message box that displays when you place the pointer over a command button. The purpose of the command, short descriptive text, or a keyboard shortcut if applicable will display in the box.

Excel An application that makes it easy to organize records, financial transactions, and business information in the form of worksheets.

Footer One or more lines at the bottom of each page.

Format Painter A feature that enables you to quickly and easily copy all formatting from one area to another in Word, PowerPoint, and Excel.

Gallery An area in Word which provides additional text styles. In Excel, the gallery provides a choice of chart styles, and in PowerPoint, the gallery provides transitions.

Group A subset of a tab that organizes similar tasks together.

Header An area with one or more lines of information at the top of each page.

Landscape orientation A document layout when a page is wider than it is tall.

Live Preview A feature that displays a preview of the results of a selection.

Margin The area of blank space that displays to the left, right, top, and bottom of a document or worksheet.

Microsoft Office A productivity software suite including a set of software applications, each one specializing in a particular type of output.

Mini toolbar A toolbar that provides access to the most common formatting selections, such as adding bold or italic, or changing font type or color. Unlike the Quick Access Toolbar, the Mini toolbar is not customizable.

OneDrive An app used to store, access, and share files and folders.

Paste A command used to place a cut or copied selection into another location.

Picture A digital photo, defined as a graphic element retrieved from storage media such as a hard drive or a CD.

Portrait orientation A document layout when a page is taller than it is wide.

PowerPoint An application that enables you to create dynamic presentations to inform groups and persuade audiences.

Quick Access Toolbar A toolbar located at the top-left corner of any Office application window, this provides fast access to commonly executed tasks such as saving a file and undoing recent actions.

Ribbon The command center of Office applications. It is the long bar located just beneath the title bar, containing tabs, groups, and commands.

Shortcut menu A menu that provides choices related to the selection or area at which you right-click.

Smart Lookup A feature that provides information about tasks or commands in Office, and can also be used to search for general information on a topic such as *President George Washington*.

Status bar A bar located at the bottom of the program window that contains information relative to the open file. It also includes tools for changing the view of the file and for changing the zoom size of onscreen file contents.

Tab Located on the Ribbon, each tab is designed to appear much like a tab on a file folder, with the active tab highlighted.

Tell me what you want to do box Located to the right of the last tab, this box enables you to search for help and information about a command or task you want to perform and also presents you with a shortcut directly to that command.

Template A predesigned file that incorporates formatting elements, such as a theme and layouts, and may include content that can be modified.

Theme A collection of design choices that includes colors, fonts, and special effects used to give a consistent look to a document, workbook, presentation, or database form or report.

Toggle commands A button that acts somewhat like light switches that you can turn on and off. You select the command to turn it on, then select it again to turn it off.

Title bar Located just above the Ribbon, this bar identifies the current file name and the application in which you are working.

View The various ways a file can appear on the screen.

Word An application that can produce all sorts of documents, including memos, newsletters, forms, tables, and brochures.

Zoom slider A feature that displays at the far right side of the status bar. It is used to increase or decrease the magnification of the file.

Introduction to Excel

Introduction to Excel

LEARNING OUTCOME

You will create and format a basic Excel worksheet.

OBJECTIVES & SKILLS: After you read this chapter, you will be able to:

Introduction to Spreadsheets

OBJECTIVE 1: EXPLORE THE EXCEL WINDOW
Identify Excel Window Elements; Identify Columns, Rows, and Cells; Navigate in and Among Worksheets

OBJECTIVE 2: ENTER AND EDIT CELL DATA
Enter Text, Use Auto Fill to Complete a Sequence, Enter Values, Enter a Date, Clear Cell Contents

HANDS-ON EXERCISE 1:
Introduction to Spreadsheets

Mathematical Operations and Formulas

OBJECTIVE 3: CREATE FORMULAS
Use Cell References in Formulas, Apply the Order of Operations, Use Semi-Selection to Create a Formula, Copy Formulas

OBJECTIVE 4: DISPLAY CELL FORMULAS
Display Cell Formulas

HANDS-ON EXERCISE 2:
Mathematics and Formulas

Worksheet Structure and Clipboard Tasks

OBJECTIVE 5: MANAGE COLUMNS AND ROWS
Insert Cells, Columns, and Rows; Delete Cells, Columns, and Rows; Hide a Column or Row; Adjust Column Width; Adjust Row Height

OBJECTIVE 6: SELECT, MOVE, COPY, AND PASTE DATA
Select a Range, Move a Range, Copy and Paste a Range, Use Paste Options and Paste Special

HANDS-ON EXERCISE 3:
Worksheet Structure and Clipboard Tasks

Worksheet Formatting

OBJECTIVE 7: APPLY CELL STYLES, ALIGNMENT, AND FONT OPTIONS
Apply a Cell Style, Merge and Center Data, Change Cell Alignment, Wrap Text, Increase Indent, Apply a Border, Apply Fill Color

OBJECTIVE 8: APPLY NUMBER FORMATS
Apply Number Formats, Increase and Decrease Decimal Places

HANDS-ON EXERCISE 4:
Worksheet Formatting

Worksheets, Page Setup, and Printing

OBJECTIVE 9: MANAGE WORKSHEETS
Insert a Worksheet, Delete a Worksheet, Copy or Move a Worksheet, Rename a Worksheet, Group Worksheets

OBJECTIVE 10: SELECT PAGE SETUP OPTIONS
Set Page Orientation, Select Scaling Options, Set Margin Options, Create a Header or Footer, Select Sheet Options

OBJECTIVE 11: PREVIEW AND PRINT A WORKSHEET
View in Print Preview, Set Print Options, Print a Worksheet

HANDS-ON EXERCISE 5:
Worksheets, Page Setup, and Printing

CASE STUDY | OK Office Systems

Alesha Bennett, the general manager at Ok Office Systems (OKOS), asked you to calculate the retail price, sale price, and profit analysis for selected items on sale this month. Using markup rates provided by Alesha, you will calculate the retail price, the amount OKOS charges its customers for the products. You will calculate sale prices based on discount rates between 10% and 30%. Finally, you will calculate the profit margin to determine the percentage of the final sale price over the cost.

After you create the initial pricing spreadsheet, you will be able to change values and see that the formulas update the results automatically. In addition, you will insert data for additional sale items or delete an item based on the manager's decision. After inserting formulas, you will format the data in the worksheet to have a professional appearance.

Creating and Formatting a Worksheet

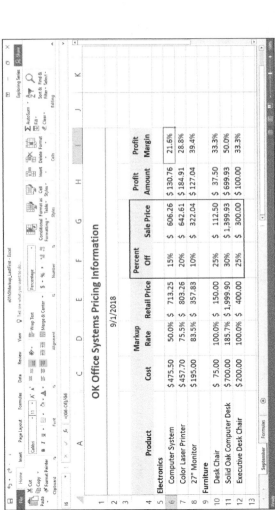

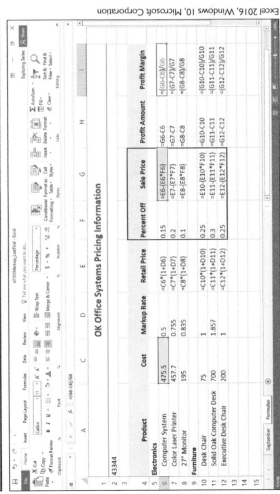

Excel 2016, Windows 10, Microsoft Corporation

FIGURE 1 Completed OKOS Worksheet

CASE STUDY | OK Office Systems

Starting File	File to be Submitted
e01h1Markup	e01h5Markup_LastFirst

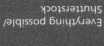

Introduction to Excel • Excel 2016

Introduction to Spreadsheets

Organizing, calculating, and evaluating quantitative data are important skills needed today for personal and managerial decision making. You track expenses for your household budget, maintain a savings plan, and determine what amount you can afford for a house or car payment. Retail managers create and analyze their organizations' annual budgets, sales projections, and inventory records. Charitable organizations track the donations they receive, the distribution of those donations, and overhead expenditures.

You should use a spreadsheet to maintain data and perform calculations. A *spreadsheet* is an electronic file that contains a grid of columns and rows used to organize related data and to display results of calculations, enabling interpretation of quantitative data for decision making.

Performing calculations using a calculator and entering the results into a ledger can lead to inaccurate values. If an input value is incorrect or needs to be updated, you have to recalculate the results manually, which is time-consuming and can lead to inaccuracies. A spreadsheet makes data entry changes easy. If the formulas are correctly constructed, the results recalculate automatically and accurately, saving time and reducing room for error.

In this section, you will learn how to design spreadsheets. In addition, you will explore the Excel window and learn the name of each window element. Then, you will enter text, values, and dates in a spreadsheet.

Exploring the Excel Window

In Excel, a *worksheet* is a single spreadsheet that typically contains descriptive labels, numeric values, formulas, functions, and graphical representations of data. A *workbook* is a collection of one or more related worksheets contained within a single file. By default, new workbooks contain one worksheet. Storing multiple worksheets within one workbook helps organize related data together in one file and enables you to perform calculations among the worksheets within the workbook. For example, you might want to create a budget workbook of 13 worksheets, one for each month to store your personal income and expenses and a final worksheet to calculate totals across the entire year.

Identify Excel Window Elements

Like other Microsoft Office programs, the Excel window contains the Quick Access Toolbar, the title bar, sizing buttons, and the Ribbon. In addition, Excel contains unique elements. Figure 2 identifies elements specific to the Excel window, and Table 1 lists and describes the Excel window elements.

FIGURE 2 Excel Window

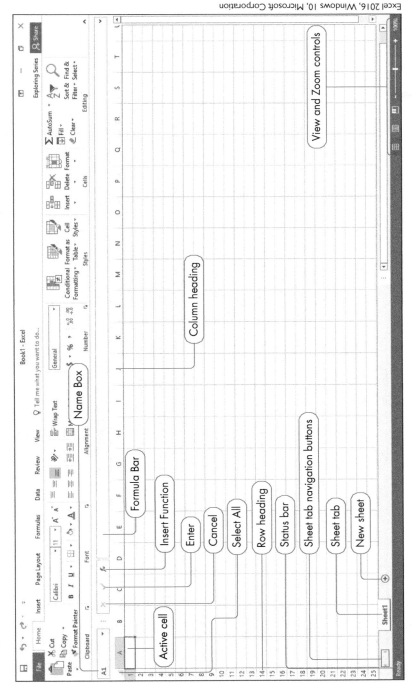

137

TABLE 1 Excel Elements

Element	Description
Name Box	An element located below the Ribbon and displays the address of the active cell. Use the Name Box to go to a cell, assign a name to one or more cells, or select a function.
Cancel ☒	When you enter or edit data, click Cancel to cancel the data entry or edit, and revert back to the previous data in the cell, if any. Cancel changes from gray to red when you position the pointer over it.
Enter ☑	When you enter or edit data, click Enter to accept data typed in the active cell and keep the current cell active. Enter changes from gray to blue when you position the pointer over it.
Insert Function *fx*	Click to display the Insert Function dialog box to search for and select a function to insert into the active cell. The Insert Function icon changes from gray to green when you position the pointer over it.
Formula Bar	An element located below the Ribbon and to the right of the Insert Function command. Shows the contents of the active cell. You enter or edit cell contents here or directly in the active cell. Drag the bottom border of the Formula Bar down to increase the height of the Formula Bar to display large amounts of data or a long formula contained in the active cell.
Select All ▢	The triangle at the intersection of the row and column headings in the top-left corner of the worksheet. Click it to select everything contained in the active worksheet.
Column headings	The letters above the columns. For example, B is the letter above the second column.
Row headings	The numbers to the left of the rows, such as 1, 2, 3, and so on. For example, 3 is the row heading for the third row.
Active cell	The current cell, which is indicated by a dark green border.
Sheet tab	A visual label that looks like a file folder tab. A sheet tab shows the name of a worksheet contained in the workbook. When you create a new Excel workbook, the default worksheet is named Sheet1.
New sheet ⊕	Click to insert a new worksheet to the right of the current worksheet.
Sheet tab navigation	If your workbook contains several worksheets, Excel may not show all the sheet tabs at the same time. Use the buttons to display the first, previous, next, or last worksheet.
Status bar	The row at the bottom of the Excel window. It displays information about a selected command or operation in progress. For example, it displays *Select destination and press ENTER or choose Paste* after you use the Copy command.
View controls	Icons on the right side of the status bar that control how the worksheet is displayed. Click a view control to display the worksheet in Normal, Page Layout, or Page Break Preview. ***Normal view*** displays the worksheet without showing margins, headers, footers, and page breaks. ***Page Layout view*** shows the margins, header and footer area, and a ruler. ***Page Break Preview*** indicates where the worksheet will be divided into pages.
Zoom control	Drag the zoom control to increase the size of the worksheet onscreen to see more or less of the worksheet data.

Introduction to Spreadsheets • Excel 2016

Identify Columns, Rows, and Cells

A worksheet contains columns and rows, with each column and row assigned a heading. Columns are assigned alphabetical headings from columns A to Z, continuing from AA to AZ, and then from BA to BZ until XFD, which is the last of the possible 16,384 columns. Rows have numeric headings ranging from 1 to 1,048,576. Depending on your screen resolution, you may see more or fewer columns and rows than what are shown in the figures in this text.

The intersection of a column and a row is a *cell*; a total of more than 17 billion cells are available in a worksheet. Each cell has a unique *cell address*, identified by first its column letter and then its row number. For example, the cell at the intersection of column C and row 6 is cell C6 (see Figure 3). The active cell is the current cell. Excel displays a dark green border around the active cell in the worksheet, and the Name Box shows the location of the active cell, which is C6 in Figure 3. The contents of the active cell, or the formula used to calculate the results of the active cell, appear in the Formula Bar. Cell references are useful when referencing data in formulas, or in navigation.

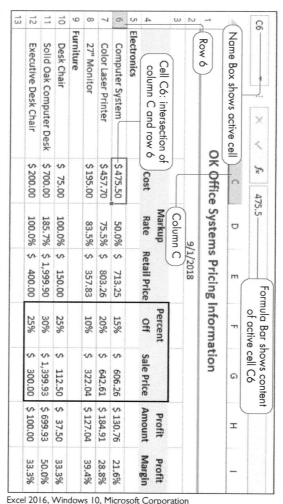

FIGURE 3 Columns, Rows, and Cells

Excel 2016, Windows 10, Microsoft Corporation

Navigate in and Among Worksheets

To navigate to a new cell, click it or use the arrow keys on the keyboard. When you press Enter, the next cell down in the same column becomes the active cell. If you work in a large worksheet, use the vertical and horizontal scroll bars to display another area of the worksheet and click in the desired cell to make it the active cell. The keyboard contains several keys that can be used in isolation or in combination with other keys to navigate in a worksheet. Table 2 lists the keyboard navigation methods. The Go To command is helpful for navigating to a cell that is not visible onscreen.

TABLE 2 Keystrokes and Actions

Keystroke	Used to
←	Move up one cell in the same column.
→	Move down one cell in the same column.
↓	Move left one cell in the same row.
↑	Move right one cell in the same row.
Tab	Move right one cell in the same row.
Page Up	Move the active cell up one screen.
Page Down	Move the active cell down one screen.
Home	Move the active cell to column A of the current row.
Ctrl+Home	Make cell A1 the active cell.
Ctrl+End	Make the rightmost, lowermost active corner of the worksheet—the intersection of the last column and row that contains data. Does not move to cell XFD1048576 unless that cell contains data.
F5 or Ctrl+G	Display the Go To dialog box to enter any cell address.

To display the contents of another worksheet within the workbook, click the sheet tab at the bottom of the workbook window, above the status bar. After you click a sheet tab, you can then navigate within that worksheet.

Entering and Editing Cell Data

You should plan the structure of a worksheet before you start entering data. Using the OKOS case presented at the beginning of the chapter as an example, use the following steps to plan the worksheet design, enter and format data, and complete the workbook. Refer to Figure 1 for the completed workbook.

Plan the Worksheet Design

1. **State the purpose of the worksheet.** The purpose of the OKOS worksheet is to store data about products on sale and to calculate important details, such as the retail price based on markup, the sales price based on a discount rate, and the profit margin.

2. **Decide what outputs are needed to achieve the purpose of the worksheet.** Outputs are the results you need to calculate. For the OKOS worksheet, the outputs include columns to calculate the retail price (i.e., the selling price to your customers), the sale price, and the profit margin. In some worksheets, you might want to create an *output area*, the region in the worksheet to contain formulas dependent on the values in the input area.

3. **Decide what input values are needed to achieve the desired output.** Input values are the initial values, such as variables and assumptions. You may change these values to see what type of effects different values have on the end results. For the OKOS worksheet, the input values include the costs OKOS pays the manufacturers, the markup rates, and the proposed discount rates for the sale. In some worksheets, you should create an *input area*, a specific region in the worksheet to store and change the variables used in calculations. For example, if you applied the same Markup Rate and same Percent Off for all products, it would be easier to create an input area at the top of the worksheet to change the values in one location rather than in several locations.

Enter and Format the Data

4. **Enter the labels, values, and formulas in Excel.** Use the design plan (steps 2–3) as you enter labels, input values, and formulas to calculate the output. In the OKOS worksheet, descriptive labels (the product names) appear in the first column to indicate that the values on a specific row pertain to a specific product. Descriptive labels appear at the top of each column, such as Cost and Retail Price, to describe the values in the respective column. Change the input values to test that your formulas produce correct results. If necessary, correct any errors in the formulas to produce correct results. For the OKOS worksheet, change some of the original costs and markup rates to ensure the calculated retail price, selling price, and profit margin percentage results update correctly.

5. **Format the numerical values in the worksheet.** Align decimal points in columns of numbers and add number formats and styles. In the OKOS worksheet, you will use Accounting Number Format and the Percent Style to format the numerical data. Adjust the number of decimal places as needed.

6. **Format the descriptive titles and labels.** Add bold and color to headings so that they stand out and are attractive. Apply other formatting to headings and descriptive labels. In the OKOS worksheet, you will center the main title over all the columns, bold and center column labels over the columns, and apply other formatting to the headings.

Complete the Workbook

7. **Document the workbook as thoroughly as possible.** Include the current date, your name as the workbook author, assumptions, and purpose of the workbook. Some people provide this documentation in a separate worksheet within the workbook. You can also add some documentation in the Properties section when you click the File tab.

8. **Save and share the completed workbook.** Preview and prepare printouts for distribution in meetings, send an electronic copy of the workbook to those who need it, or upload the workbook on a shared network drive or in the cloud.

STEP 1

Enter Text

Text is any combination of letters, numbers, symbols, and spaces not used in calculations. Excel treats phone numbers, such as 555-1234, and Social Security numbers, such as 123-45-6789, as text entries. You enter text for a worksheet title to describe the contents of the worksheet, as row and column labels to describe data, and as cell data. In Figure 4, the cells in column A contain text, such as Class. Text aligns at the left cell margin by default.

To enter text in a cell, complete the following steps:

1. Make sure the cell is active where you want to enter text.

2. Type the text. If you want to enter a numeric value as text, such as a class section number, type an apostrophe and the number, such as '002.

3. Make another cell the active cell after entering data by completing one of the following steps:

   - Press Enter on the keyboard.
   - Press an arrow key on the keyboard.
   - Press Tab on the keyboard.

   Keep the current cell active after entering data by completing one of the following steps:

   - Press Ctrl+Enter on the keyboard.
   - Click Enter (the check mark between the Name Box and the Formula Bar).

As soon as you begin typing a label into a cell, the **AutoComplete** feature searches for and automatically displays any other label in the same column that matches the letters you type. The top half of Figure 4 shows Spreadsheet Apps is typed in cell A3. When you start to type *Sp* in cell A4, AutoComplete displays Spreadsheet Apps because a text entry in the same column already starts with *Sp*. AutoComplete displays Spreadsheet Apps because a text entry continue typing to enter a different label, such as Spanish II. The bottom half of Figure 4 shows that '002 was entered in cell B4 to start the text with a 0. Otherwise, Excel would have eliminated the zeros in the class section number. Ignore the error message that displays when you intentionally use an apostrophe to enter a number which is not actually a value.

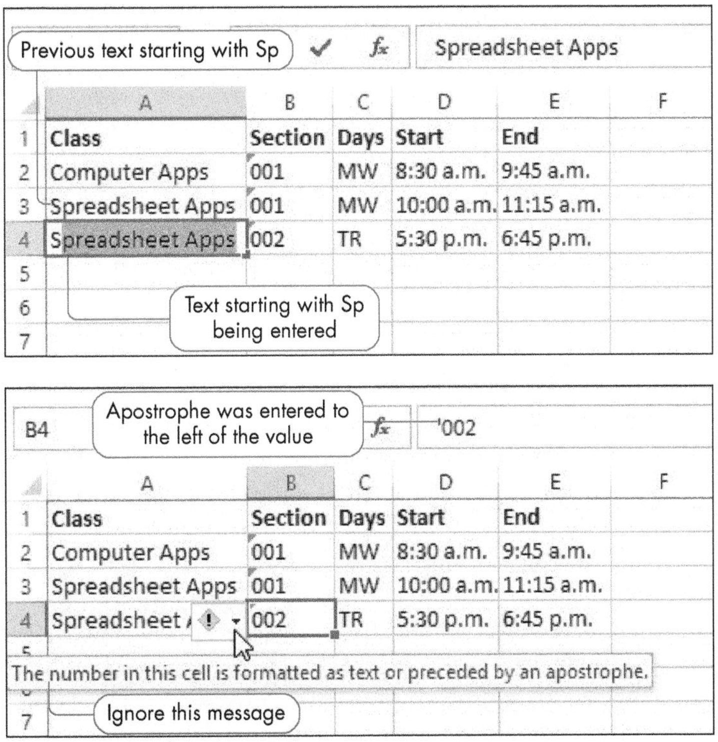

FIGURE 4 Entering Text

Use Auto Fill to Complete a Sequence

>> While AutoComplete helps to complete a label that is identical to another label in the same column, **Auto Fill** is a feature that helps you complete a sequence of words or values. For example, if you enter January in a cell, use Auto Fill to fill in the rest of the months in adjacent cells so that you do not have to type the rest of the month names. Auto Fill can help you complete other sequences, such as quarters (Qtr 1, etc.), weekdays, and weekday abbreviations after you type the first item in the sequence. Figure 5 shows the results of filling in months, abbreviated months, quarters, weekdays, abbreviated weekdays, and increments of 5.

FIGURE 5 Auto Fill Examples

	A	B	C	D	E	F	G	H	I
1	January	Jan	Qtr 1	Monday	Mon	1	5		
2	February	Feb	Qtr 2	Tuesday	Tue	2	10		
3	March	Mar	Qtr 3	Wednesday	Wed	3	15		
4	April	Apr	Qtr 4	Thursday	Thu	4	20		
5	May	May	Qtr 1	Friday	Fri	5	25		
6	June	Jun		Saturday	Sat	6	30		
7	July	Jul		Sunday	Sun	7	35		
8	August								
9	September	Sep							
10	October	Oct							
11	November	Nov							
12	December	Dec							
13									
14									
15									

Incremented values filled in

Fill options

Auto Fill Options

- ○ Copy Cells
- ◉ Fill Series
- ○ Fill Formatting Only
- ○ Fill Without Formatting
- ○ Flash Fill

Excel 2016, Windows 10, Microsoft Corporation

To use Auto Fill to complete a series of text (such as month names), complete the following steps:

1. Type the first label (e.g., January) in the starting cell (e.g., cell A1) and press Ctrl+Enter to keep that cell the active cell.

2. Point to the *fill handle* (a small green square in the bottom-right corner of the active cell) until the pointer changes to a thin black plus sign.

3. Drag the fill handle to repeat the content in other cells (e.g., through cell A12).

Immediately after you use Auto Fill, Excel displays Auto Fill Options in the bottom-right corner of the filled data (refer to Figure 5). Click Auto Fill Options to display several fill options: Copy Cells, Fill Series, Fill Formatting Only, Fill Without Formatting, or Flash Fill. The menu will also include other options, depending on the cell content: Fill Months for completing months; Fill Weekdays for completing weekdays; and Fill Days, Fill Weekdays, Fill Months, Fill Years to complete dates. Select Fill Formatting Only when you want to copy the formats but not complete a sequence. Select Fill Without Formatting when you want to complete the sequence but do not want to format the rest of the sequence.

To use Auto Fill to fill a sequence of consecutive numbers (such as 1, 2, 3, etc.), complete the following steps:

1. Type the first number in the starting cell (e.g., cell F1) and press Ctrl+Enter to keep that cell the active cell.

2. Drag the fill handle to fill the content in other cells. Excel will copy the same number for the rest of the cells.

3. Click Auto Fill Options and select Fill Series. Excel will change the numbers to be in sequential order, starting with the original value you typed.

For non-consecutive numeric sequences, you must specify the first two values in sequence. For example, if you want to fill in 5, 10, 15, and so on, you must enter 5 and 10 in two adjacent cells before using Auto Fill so that Excel knows to increment by 5.

To use Auto Fill to fill a sequence of number patterns (such as 5, 10, 15, 20 shown in the range G1:G7 in Figure 5), complete the following steps:

1. Type the first two numbers of the sequence in adjoining cells.
2. Select those two cells containing the starting two values.
3. Drag the fill handle to fill in the rest of the sequence.

TIP: FLASH FILL

Flash Fill is a similar feature to Auto Fill in that it can quickly fill in data for you; however, *Flash Fill* uses data in previous columns as you type in a new label in an adjoining column to determine what to fill in. For example, assume that column A contains a list of first and last names (such as Penny Sumpter in cell A5), but you want to have a column of just first names. To do this, type Penny's name in cell B5, click Fill in the Editing group on the Home tab and select Flash Fill to fill in the rest of column B with people's first names based on the data entered in column A.

Enter Values

STEP 3 ⟩⟩ *Values* are numbers that represent a quantity or a measurable amount. Excel usually distinguishes between text and value data based on what you enter. The primary difference between text and value entries is that value entries can be the basis of calculations, whereas text cannot. In Figure 3, the data below the Cost, Markup Rates, and Percent Off labels are values. Values align at the right cell margin by default. After entering values, align decimal places and apply formatting by adding characters, such as $ or %. Entering values is the same process as entering text: Type the value in a cell and click Enter or press Enter.

TIP: ENTERING VALUES WITH TRAILING ZEROS OR PERCENTAGES

You do not need to type the last 0 in 475.50 shown in cell C6 in Figure 3. Excel will remove or add the trailing 0 depending on the decimal place formatting. Similarly, you do not have to type the leading 0 in a percentage before the decimal point. Type a percent in the decimal format, such as .5 for 50%. You will later format the value.

Enter Dates and Times

STEP 4 ⟩⟩ You can enter dates and times in a variety of formats. You should enter a static date to document when you create or modify a workbook or to document the specific point in time when the data were accurate, such as on a balance sheet or income statement. Later, you will learn how to use formulas to enter dates that update to the current date. In Figure 6, the data in column A contains the date 9/1/2018 in different formats. Dates are values, so they align at the right side of a cell. The data in column C contains the time 2:30 PM but in different formats.

▲	A	B	C	D
1	9/1/2018		2:30:00 PM	
2	Saturday, September 1, 2018		14:30	
3	9/1		2:30 PM	
4	9/1/18		14:30:00	
5	09/01/18		2:30:00 PM	
6	1-Sep			
7	1-Sep-18			
8	September 1, 2018			
9				

Excel 2016, Windows 10, Microsoft Corporation

FIGURE 6 Date and Time Examples

Excel displays dates differently from the way it stores dates. For example, the displayed date 9/1/2018 represents the first day in September in the year 2018. Excel stores dates as serial numbers starting at 1 with January 1, 1900, so that you can create formulas, such as to calculate how many days exist between two dates. For example, 9/1/2018 is stored as 43344.

Edit and Clear Cell Contents

After entering data in a cell, you may need to change it. For example, you may want to edit a label to make it more descriptive, such as changing a label from OKC Office Systems Information to OKC Office Systems Pricing Information. Furthermore, you might realize a digit is missing from a value and need to change 500 to 5000.

To edit the contents of a cell, compete the following steps:

1. Click the cell.
2. Click in the Formula Bar or press F2 to put the cell in edit mode. The insertion point displays on the right side of the data in the cell when you press F2.
3. Make the changes to the content in the cell.
4. Click or press Enter.

You may want to clear or delete the contents in a cell if you no longer need data in a cell.

To clear the contents of a cell, complete the following steps:

1. Click the cell.
2. Press Delete or click the cell, click Clear in the Editing group on the Home tab, and select the desired option (see Figure 7).

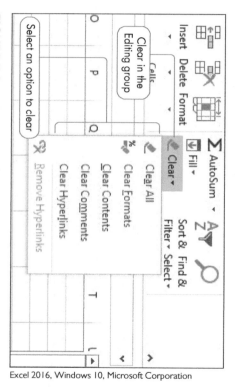

FIGURE 7 Clear Options

Excel 2016, Windows 10, Microsoft Corporation

1. What are two major advantages of using an electronic spreadsheet instead of a paper-based ledger?
2. What are the visual indicators that a cell is the active cell?
3. What steps should you perform before entering data into a worksheet?
4. What three types of content can you enter into a cell? Give an example for each type.

Hands-On Exercises

1 Introduction to Spreadsheets

Skills covered: Enter Text • Use Auto Fill to Complete a Sequence • Enter Values • Enter a Date • Clear Cell Contents

As the assistant manager of OKOS, you will create a worksheet that shows the cost (the amount OKOS pays its suppliers), the markup percentage (the amount by which the cost is increased), and the retail selling price. You also will list the discount percentage (such as 25% off) for each product, the sale price, and the profit margin percentage.

STEP 1 >> ENTER TEXT

Now that you have planned the OKOS worksheet, you are ready to enter labels for the title, column labels, and row labels. You will type a title in cell A1, product labels in the first column, and row labels in the fourth row. Refer to Figure 8 as you complete Step 1.

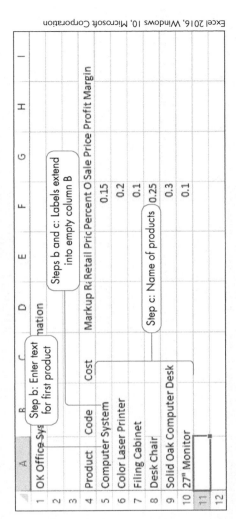

FIGURE 8 Text Entered in Cells

Excel 2016, Windows 10, Microsoft Corporation

a. Open *e01h1Markup* and save it as **e01h1Markup_LastFirst**.

When you save files, use your last and first names. For example, as the Excel author, I would save my workbook as *e01h1Markup_MulberyKeith*.

TROUBLESHOOTING: If you make any major mistakes in this exercise, you can close the file, open *e01h1Markup* again, and then start this exercise over.

b. Click **cell A5**, type **Computer System**, and then press **Enter**.

When you press Enter, the next cell down—cell A6 in this case—becomes the active cell. The text does not completely fit in cell A5, and some of the text appears in cell B5. If you make cell B5 the active cell, the Formula Bar is empty, indicating that nothing is stored in that cell.

c. Type **Color Laser Printer** in cell **A6** and press **Enter**.

When you start typing C in cell A6, AutoComplete displays a ScreenTip suggesting a previous text entry starting with C—*Computer System*—but keep typing to enter Color Laser Printer instead.

d. Continue typing the rest of the text in **cells A7** through **A10** as shown in Figure 8. Text in column A appears to flow into column B.

You just entered the product labels to describe the data in each row.

e. Click **Save** on the Quick Access Toolbar to save the changes you made to the workbook.

> You should develop a habit of saving periodically. That way if your system unexpectedly shuts down, you will not lose everything you worked on.

STEP 2 » USE AUTO FILL TO COMPLETE A SEQUENCE

You want to assign a product code for each product on sale. You will assign consecutive numbers 101 to 106. After typing the first code number, you will use Auto Fill to complete the rest of the series. Refer to Figures 9 and 10 as you complete Step 2.

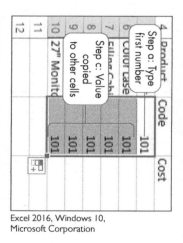

Excel 2016, Windows 10,
Microsoft Corporation

FIGURE 9 Auto Fill Copied Original Value

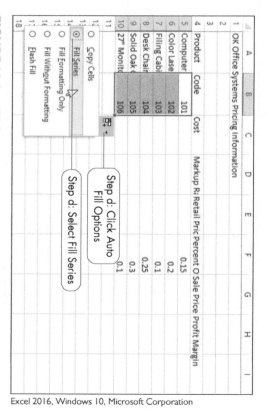

Excel 2016, Windows 10, Microsoft Corporation

FIGURE 10 Auto Fill Sequence

a. Click **cell B5**, type **101**, and then press **Ctrl+Enter**.

> The product name Computer System no longer overlaps into column B after you enter data into cell B5. The data in cell A5 is not deleted; the rest of the label is hidden until you increase the column width later.

b. Position the pointer on the fill handle in the bottom-right corner of **cell B5**.

> The pointer looks like a black plus sign when you point to a fill handle.

Hands-On Exercise 1

146

c. Double-click the **cell B6 fill handle**.

Excel copies 101 as the item number for the rest of the products. Excel stops inserting item numbers in column B when it detects the last label in cell A10 (refer to Figure 9).

d. Click **Auto Fill Options** and select **Fill Series**. Save the workbook.

Excel changes the duplicate values to continue sequentially in a series of numbers.

Now that you have entered the descriptive labels and item numbers, you will enter the cost and markup rate for each product. Refer to Figure 11 as you complete Step 3.

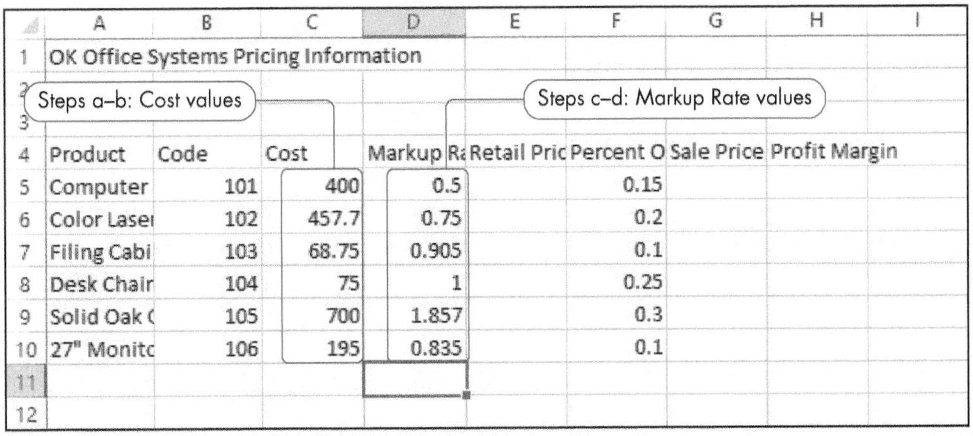

	A	B	C	D	E	F	G	H	I
1	OK Office Systems Pricing Information								
2									
3					Steps c–d: Markup Rate values				
4	Product	Code	Cost	Markup R:	Retail Pric	Percent O	Sale Price	Profit Margin	
5	Computer	101	400	0.5		0.15			
6	Color Laser	102	457.7	0.75		0.2			
7	Filing Cabi	103	68.75	0.905		0.1			
8	Desk Chair	104	75	1		0.25			
9	Solid Oak (	105	700	1.857		0.3			
10	27" Monitc	106	195	0.835		0.1			
11									
12									

Steps a–b: Cost values

FIGURE 11 Values Entered in Cells

a. Click **cell C5**, type **400**, and then press **Enter**.

b. Type the remaining costs in **cells C6** through **C10** shown in Figure 11.

To improve your productivity, use the number keypad (if available) on the right side of your keyboard. It is much faster to type values and press Enter on the number keypad rather than to use the numbers on the keyboard. Make sure Num Lock is active before using the number keypad to enter values.

c. Click **cell D5**, type **0.5**, and then press **Enter**.

You entered the markup rate as a decimal instead of a percentage. You will apply Percent Style later, but now you will concentrate on data entry.

d. Type the remaining values in **cells D6** through **D10** as shown in Figure 11. Save the workbook.

As you review the worksheet, you realize you need to provide a date to indicate when the sale starts. Refer to Figure 12 as you complete Step 4.

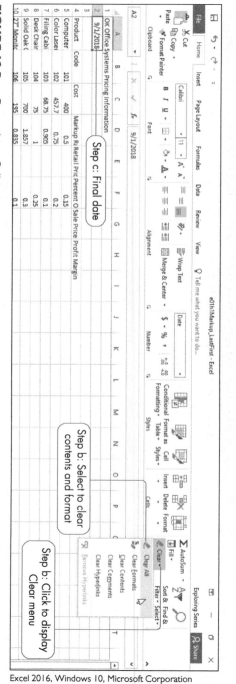

FIGURE 12 Date Entered in a Cell

a. Click **cell A2**, type **9/1**, and then press **Enter**.

The date aligns on the right cell margin by default. Excel displays 1-Sep instead of 9/1.

b. Click **cell A2**, click **Clear** in the Editing group on the Home tab, and then select **Clear All**.

The Clear All command clears both cell contents and formatting in the selected cell(s).

c. Type **9/1/2018 in cell A2** and press **Ctrl+Enter**.

> **TROUBLESHOOTING:** If you did not use Clear All and typed 9/1/2018 in cell A2, Excel would have retained the previous date format and displayed 1-Sep again.

When you type the month, day, and year such as 9/1/2018, Excel enters the date in that format (unless it has a different date format applied).

d. Save the workbook. Keep the workbook open if you plan to continue with the next Hands-On Exercise. If not, close the workbook, and exit Excel.

Excel 2016, Windows 10, Microsoft Corporation

Mathematical Operations and Formulas

A *formula* combines cell references, arithmetic operations, values, and/or functions used in a calculation. Formulas transform static numbers into meaningful results that update as values change. For example, a payroll manager can build formulas to calculate the gross pay, deductions, and net pay for an organization's employees, or a doctoral student can create formulas to perform various statistical calculations to interpret his or her research data.

In this section, you will learn how to use mathematical operations in Excel formulas. You will refresh your memory of the mathematical order of operations and learn how to construct formulas using cell addresses so that when the value of an input cell changes, the result of the formula changes without you having to modify the formula.

Creating Formulas

Use formulas to help you analyze how results will change as the input data changes. You can change the value of your assumptions or inputs and explore the results quickly and accurately. For example, if your rent increases, how does that affect your personal budget? Analyzing different input values in Excel is easy after you build formulas. Simply change an input value and observe the change in the formula results. In the OKOS product sales worksheet, the results for the Retail Price, Sale Price, and Profit Margin labels were calculated by using formulas (refer to Figure 1).

Use Cell References in Formulas

STEP 1 >> You should use cell references instead of values in formulas where possible. You may include values in an input area—such as dates, salary, or costs—that you will need to reference in formulas. Referencing these cells in your formulas, instead of typing the value of the cell to which you are referring, keeps your formulas accurate if you change values to perform a what-if analysis.

Figure 13 shows a worksheet containing input values and results of formulas. The figure also displays the actual formulas used to generate the calculated results. For example, cell E2 contains the formula =B2+B3. Excel uses the value stored in cell B2 (10) and adds it to the value stored in cell B3 (2). The result (12) appears in cell E2 instead of the actual formula. The Formula Bar displays the formula entered into the active cell.

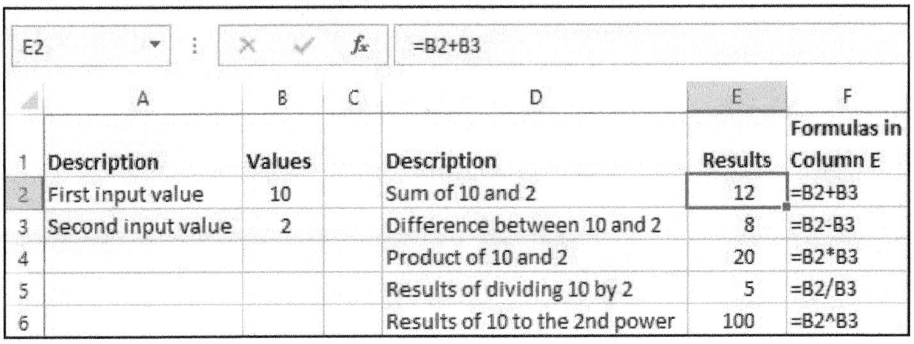

E2	▾	:	×	✓	f_x	=B2+B3	

▲	A	B	C	D	E	F
						Formulas in
1	Description	Values		Description	Results	Column E
2	First input value	10		Sum of 10 and 2	12	=B2+B3
3	Second input value	2		Difference between 10 and 2	8	=B2-B3
4				Product of 10 and 2	20	=B2*B3
5				Results of dividing 10 by 2	5	=B2/B3
6				Results of 10 to the 2nd power	100	=B2^B3

Excel 2016, Windows 10, Microsoft Corporation

FIGURE 13 Formula Results

To enter a formula, complete the following steps:

1. Click the cell.
2. Type an equal sign (=), followed by the arithmetic expression, using cell references instead of values. Do not include any spaces in the formula.
3. Click Enter or press Enter.

TIP: EQUAL SIGN NEEDED

If you type B2+B3 without the equal sign, Excel does not recognize that you entered a formula and stores the "formula" as text.

TIP: UPPER OR LOWERCASE

When you create a formula, type the cell references in uppercase, such as =B2+B3, or lowercase, such as =b2+b3. Excel changes cell references to uppercase automatically.

In Figure 13, cell B2 contains 10, and cell B3 contains 2. Cell E2 contains =B2+B3 but shows the result 12. If you change the value of cell B3 to 5, cell E2 displays the new result, which is 15. However, if you had typed actual values in the formula, =10+2, you would have to edit the formula to =10+5, even though the value in cell B3 was changed to 5. Using values in formulas can cause problems as you might forget to edit the formula or you might have a typographical error if you edit the formula. Always design work-sheets in such a way as to be able to place those values that might need to change as input values. Referencing cells with input values in formulas instead of using the values themselves will avoid having to modify your formulas if an input value changes later.

TIP: WHEN TO USE A VALUE IN A FORMULA

Use cell references instead of actual values in formulas, unless the value will never change. For example, if you want to calculate how many total months are in a specified number of years, enter a formula such as =B5*12, where B5 contains the number of years. You might want to change the number of years, so you type that value in cell B5. However, every year always has 12 months, so you can use the value 12 in the formula.

Apply the Order of Operations

The *order of operations* (also called order of precedence) are rules that controls the sequence in which arithmetic operations are performed, which affects the result of the calculation. Excel performs mathematical calculations left to right in this order: **Parentheses**, **Exponentiation**, **Multiplication** or **Division**, and finally **Addition** or **Subtraction**. Some people remember the order of operations with the phrase *Please Excuse My Dear Aunt Sally.*

Table 3 lists the primary order of operations. Use Help to learn about the complete order of precedence.

TABLE 3 Order of Operations

Order	Description	Symbols
1	Parentheses	( )
2	Exponentiation	^
3	Multiplication and Division	* and / (respectively)
4	Addition and Subtraction	+ and − (respectively)

Pearson Education, Inc.

Figure 14 shows formulas, the sequence in which calculations occur, calculations, the description, and the results of each order of operations. The highlighted results are the final formula results. This figure illustrates the importance of symbols and use of parentheses.

	A Input	B/C Formula	D Sequence	E Description	F Result
1	Input	Formula	Sequence	Description	Result
2	2	=A2+A3*A4+A5	1	3 (cell A3) * 4 (cell A4)	12
3	3		2	2 (cell A2) + 12 (order 1)	14
4	4		3	14 (order 2) + 5 (cell A5)	19
5	5				
6		=(A2+A3)*(A4+A5)	1	2 (cell A2) + 3 (cell A3)	5
7			2	4 (cell A4) + 5 (cell A5)	9
8			3	5 (order 1) * 9 (order 2)	45
9					
10		=A2/A3+A4*A5	1	2 (cell A2) / 3 (cell A3)	0.666667
11			2	4 (cell A4) * 5 (cell A5)	20
12			3	0.666667 (order 1) + 20 (order 2)	20.66667
13					
14		=A2/(A3+A4)*A5	1	3 (cell A3) + 4 (cell A4)	7
15			2	2 (cell A2) / 7 (order 1)	0.285714
16			3	0.285714 (order 2) * 5 (cell A5)	1.428571
17					
18		=A2^2+A3*A4%	1	4 (cell A4) is converted to percentage	0.04
19			2	2 (cell A2) to the power of 2	4
20			3	3 (cell A3) * 0.04 (order 1)	0.12
21			4	4 (order 2) + 0.12 (order 3)	4.12

Excel 2016, Windows 10, Microsoft Corporation

FIGURE 14 Formula Results Based on Order of Operations

Use Semi-Selection to Create a Formula

STEP 2 ›› To decrease typing time and ensure accuracy, use **semi-selection**, a process of selecting a cell or range of cells for entering cell references as you create formulas. Semi-selection is often called **pointing** because you use the pointer to select cells as you build the formula. Some people prefer using the semi-selection method instead of typing a formula so that they can make sure they use the correct cell references as they build the formula.

To use the semi-selection technique to create a formula, complete the following steps:

1. Click the cell where you want to create the formula.
2. Type an equal sign (=) to start a formula.
3. Click the cell that contains the value to use in the formula. A moving marquee appears around the cell or range you select, and Excel displays the cell or range reference in the formula.
4. Type a mathematical operator.
5. Continue clicking cells, selecting ranges, and typing operators to finish the formula. Use the scroll bars if the cell is in a remote location in the worksheet, or click a worksheet tab to see a cell in another worksheet.
6. Press Enter to complete the formula.

Copy Formulas

After you enter a formula in a cell, you duplicate the formula without retyping the formula for other cells that need a similar formula. Previously, you learned about the Auto Fill feature that enables you to use the fill handle to fill in a series of values, months, quarters, and weekdays. You can also use the fill handle to copy the formula in the active cell to adjacent cells down a column or across a row, depending on how the data are organized. Cell references in copied formulas adjust based on their relative locations to the original formula.

To copy a formula to other cells using the fill handle, complete the following steps:

1. Click the cell with the content you want to copy to make it the active cell.
2. Point to the fill handle in the bottom-right corner of the cell until the pointer changes to the fill pointer (a thin black plus sign).
3. Drag the fill handle to copy the formula.

Displaying Cell Formulas

Excel shows the result of the formula in the cell (see the top half of Figure 15); however, you might want to display the formulas instead of the calculated results in the cells (see the bottom half of Figure 15). Displaying the cell formulas may help you double-check all your formulas at one time or troubleshoot a problem with a formula instead of clicking in each cell containing a formula and looking at just the Formula Bar.

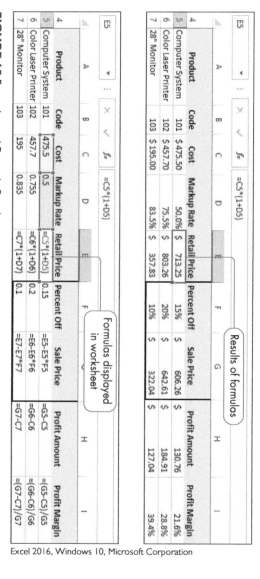

Results of formulas

E5	:	×	✓	fx	=C5*(1+D5)			
▲	A	B	C	D	E	F	G	H
4	Product	Code	Cost	Markup Rate	Retail Price	Percent Off	Sale Price	Profit Amount	Profit Margin
5	Computer System	101	$ 475.50	50.0%	$ 713.25	15%	$ 606.26	$ 130.76	21.6%
6	Color Laser Printer	102	$ 457.70	75.5%	$ 803.26	20%	$ 642.61	$ 184.91	28.8%
7	28" Monitor	103	$ 195.00	83.5%	$ 357.83	10%	$ 322.04	$ 127.04	39.4%

Formulas displayed in worksheet

E5	▼	:	×	✓	fx	=C5*(1+D5)		
▲	A	B	C	D	E	F	G	H	I
4	Product	Code	Cost	Markup Rate	Retail Price	Percent Off	Sale Price	Profit Amount	Profit Margin
5	Computer System	101	475.5	0.5	=C5*(1+D5)	0.15	=E5-E5*F5	=G5-C5	=(G5-C5)/G5
6	Color Laser Printer	102	457.7	0.755	=C6*(1+D6)	0.2	=E6-E6*F6	=G6-C6	=(G6-C6)/G6
7	28" Monitor	103	195	0.835	=C7*(1+D7)	0.1	=E7-E7*F7	=G7-C7	=(G7-C7)/G7

FIGURE 15 Formulas and Formula Results

Excel 2016, Windows 10, Microsoft Corporation

To display cell formulas in the worksheet, complete one of the following steps:

- Press Ctrl and the grave accent (`) key, sometimes referred to as the tilde key, in the top-left corner of the keyboard, below the Esc key.
- Click Show Formulas in the Formula Auditing group on the Formulas tab.

To hide the formulas and display the formula results again, repeat the preceding process.

5. What is the order of operations? Provide and explain two examples that use four different operators: one with parentheses and one without.

6. Why should you use cell references instead of typing values in formulas?

7. When would it be useful to display formulas instead of formula results in a worksheet?

Hands-On Exercises

2 Mathematical Operations and Formulas

In Hands-On Exercise 1, you created the basic worksheet for OKOS by entering text, values, and a date for items on sale. Now you will insert formulas to calculate the missing results—specifically, the retail (before sale) price, sale price, and profit margin. You will use cell addresses in your formulas, so when you change a referenced value, the formula results will update automatically.

Skills covered: Use Cell References in Formulas • Apply the Order of Operations • Use Semi-Selection to Create a Formula • Copy Formulas • Display Cell Formulas

STEP 1 » USE CELL REFERENCES IN A FORMULA AND APPLY THE ORDER OF OPERATIONS

The first formula you create will calculate the retail price. The retail price is the price you originally charge. It is based on a percentage of the original cost so that you earn a profit. Refer to Figure 16 as you complete Step 1.

a. Open *e01h1Markup_LastFirst* if you closed it at the end of Hands-On Exercise 1 and save it as **e01h2Markup_LastFirst**, changing h1 to h2.

b. Click **cell E5.**

Cell E5 is the cell where you will enter the formula to calculate the retail selling price of the first item.

c. Type **=C5*(1+D5)** and view the formula and the colored cells and borders on the screen.

As you build or edit a formula, each cell address in the formula displays in a specific color, and while you type or edit the formula, the cells referenced in the formula have a temporary colored border. For example, in the formula =C5*(1+D5), C5 appears in blue, and D5 appears in red. Cell C5 has a temporarily blue border and light blue shading, and cell D5 has a temporarily red border with light red shading to help you identify cells as you construct your formulas (refer to Figure 16).

You enclosed 1+D5 in parentheses to control the order of operations so that 1 is added to the value in cell D5 (0.5). The result is 1.5, which represents 150% of the cost. That result is then multiplied by the value in C5 (400). If you did not use the parentheses, Excel would multiply the value in C5 by 1 (which would be 400) and add that result to the value in D5 (0.5) for a final result of 400.5, which would have given you incorrect results.

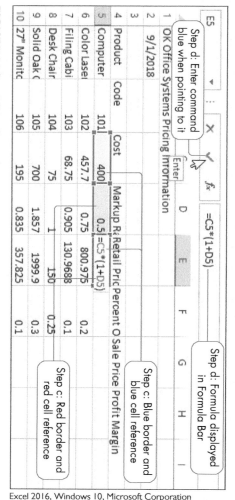

FIGURE 16 Retail Price Formula

			=C5*(1+D5)				
E5		✕ ✓	fₓ =C5*(1+D5)				

Step d: Enter command blue when pointing to it — Enter

Step d: Formula displayed in Formula Bar

	A	B	C	D	E	F	G	H
1	OK Office Systems Pricing Information							
2	9/1/2018							
3								
4	Product	Code	Cost	Markup R	Retail Pric	Percent O	Sale Price	Profit Margin
5	Computer	101	400	0.5	=C5*(1+D5)	0.2		
6	Color Laser	102	457.7	0.75	800.975	0.1		
7	Filing Cabi	103	68.75	0.905	130.9688	0.1		
8	Desk Chair	104	75	1	150	0.25		
9	Solid Oak C	105	700	1.857	1999.9	0.3		
10	27" Monitc	106	195	0.835	357.825	0.1		

Step c: Blue border and blue cell reference

Step c: Red border and red cell reference

An alternative formula also calculates the correct retail price: =C5*D5+C5 or =C5+C5*D5. In this formula, 400 (cell C5) is multiplied by 0.5 (cell D5); that result (200) represents the dollar value of the markup. Excel adds the value 200 to the original cost of 400 to obtain 600, the retail price. You were instructed to enter =C5*(1+D5) to demonstrate the order of operations.

d. Click **Enter** ☑ (between the Name Box and the Formula Bar) and view the formula in the Formula Bar to check it for accuracy.

The result of the formula, 600, appears in cell E5, and the formula displays in the Formula Bar. This formula first adds 1 (the decimal equivalent of 100%) to 0.5 (the value stored in cell D5). Excel multiplies that sum of 1.5 by 400 (the value stored in cell C5). This calculation reflects a retail price is 150% of the original cost.

TROUBLESHOOTING: If the result is not correct, click the cell and look at the formula in the Formula Bar. Click in the Formula Bar, edit the formula to match the formula shown in Step c, and click Enter (the check mark between the Name Box and the Formula Bar). Make sure you start the formula with an equal sign.

e. Position the pointer on the **cell E5 fill handle**. When the pointer changes from a white plus sign to a thin black plus sign, double-click the **fill handle**.

Excel copies the retail price formula for the remaining products in your worksheet. Excel detects when to stop copying the formula when it detects the last label in the dataset.

f. Click **cell E6**, the cell containing the first copied retail price formula, look at the Formula Bar, and then save the workbook.

The formula in cell E6 is =C6*(1+D6). It was copied from the formula in cell E5, which is =C5*(1+D5). Excel adjusts the row references in this formula as you copied the formula down a column so that the results are based on each row's data.

TROUBLESHOOTING: The result in cell E7 may show more decimal places than shown in Figure 16. Do not worry about this slight difference.

STEP 2 ≫ USE SEMI-SELECTION AND APPLY THE ORDER OF OPERATIONS TO CREATE A FORMULA

Now that you have calculated the retail price, you will calculate a sale price. This week, the computer is on sale for 15% off the retail price. Refer to Figure 17 as you complete Step 2.

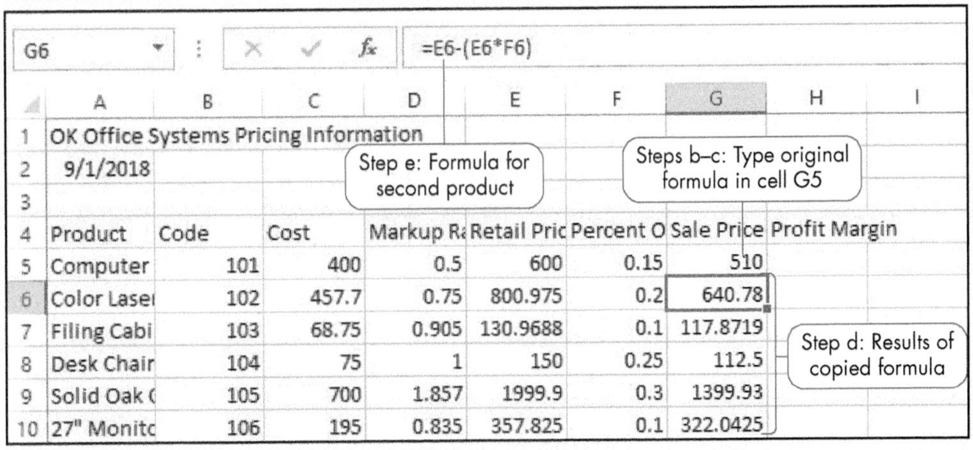

FIGURE 17 Sale Price Formula

a. Click **cell G5**, the cell where you will enter the formula to calculate the sale price.

b. Type **=**, click **cell E5**, type **-**, click **cell E5**, type *****, and then click **cell F5**. Notice the color-coding in the cell addresses. Press **Ctrl+Enter** to keep the current cell the active cell.

You used the semi-selection method to enter a formula. The result is 510. Looking at the formula, you might think E5–E5 equals zero; remember that because of the order of operations, multiplication is calculated before subtraction. The product of 600 (cell E5) and 0.15 (cell F5) equals 90, which is then subtracted from 600 (cell E5), so the sale price is 510.

c. Click **cell G5**, type **=E5-(E5*F5)**, and then click **Enter**.

Although the parentheses are not needed because the multiplication occurs before the subtraction, it may be helpful to add parentheses to make the formula easier to interpret.

d. Double-click the **cell G5 fill handle** to copy the formula down column G.

e. Click **cell G6**, the cell containing the first copied sale price formula, view the Formula Bar, and save the workbook.

The original formula was =E5-(E5*F5). The copied formula in cell G6 is adjusted to =E6-(E6*F6) so that it calculates the sales price based on the data in row 6.

STEP 3 ⟩⟩ **USE CELL REFERENCES IN A FORMULA AND APPLY THE ORDER OF OPERATIONS**

After calculating the sale price, you want to know the profit margin OKOS will earn. OKOS will sell it for $510. The profit of $110 is then divided by the $400 cost, which gives OKOS a profit margin of 0.215686, which will be formatted later as a percent 21.6%. Refer to Figure 18 as you complete Step 3.

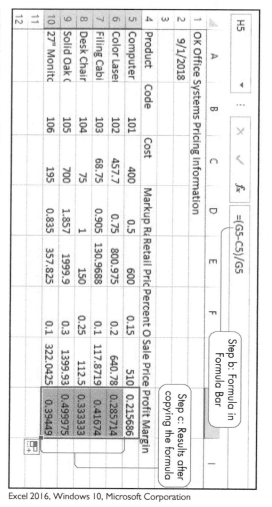

	A	B	C	D	E	F	G
	H5		▼	:	×	✓	fx	=(G5-C5)/G5
1	OK Office Systems Pricing Information						
2	9/1/2018						
3							
4	Product	Code	Cost	Markup R	Retail Pric	Percent O	Sale Price	Profit Margin
5	Computer	101	400	0.5	600	0.15	510	0.215686
6	Color Laser	102	457.7	0.75	800.975	0.2	640.78	0.285714
7	Filing Cabi	103	68.75	0.905	130.9688	0.1	117.8719	0.41674
8	Desk Chair	104	75	1	150	0.25	112.5	0.333333
9	Solid Oak C	105	700	1.857	1999.9	0.3	1399.93	0.499975
10	27" Monito	106	195	0.835	357.825	0.1	322.0425	0.39449
11							
12							

Step b: Formula in Formula Bar

Step c: Results after copying the formula

FIGURE 18 Profit Margin Formula

a. Click **cell H5**, the cell where you will enter the formula to calculate the profit margin.

   The profit margin is the profit (difference in sales price and cost) percentage of the sale price.

b. Type **=(G5-C5)/G5** and notice the color-coding in the cell addresses. Press **Ctrl+Enter**.

   The formula must first calculate the profit, which is the difference between the sale price (510) and the original cost (400). The difference (110) is then divided by the sale price (510) to determine the profit margin of 0.215686, or 21.6%.

c. Double-click the **cell H5 fill handle** to copy the formula down the column.

d. Click **cell H6**, the cell containing the first copied profit margin formula, look at the Formula Bar, and then save the workbook.

   The original formula was =(G5-C5)/G5, and the copied formula in cell H6 is =(G6-C6)/G6.

STEP 4 >> DISPLAY CELL FORMULAS

You want to see how the prices and profit margins are affected when you change some of the original cost values. For example, the supplier might notify you that the cost to you will increase. In addition, you want to see the formulas displayed in the cells temporarily. Refer to Figures 19 and 20 as you complete Step 4.

	A	B	C	D	E	F	G	H	I
1	OK Office Systems Pricing Informatio								
2									
3									
4	Product	Code	Cost	Markup R;	Retail Pric	Percent O	Sale Price	Profit Margin	
5	Computer	101	475.5	0.5	713.25	0.15	606.2625	0.215686	
6	Color Laser	102	457.7	0.755	803.2635	0.2	642.6108	0.287749	
7	Filling Cabi	103	68.75	0.905	130.9688	0.05	124.4203	0.447437	
8	Desk Chair	104	75	1	150	0.25	112.5	0.333333	
9	Solid Oak	105	700	1.857	1999.9	0.3	1399.93	0.499975	
10	27" M			0.835	357.825	0.1	322.0425	0.39449	
11									

Step a: New value in cell C5

Step b: New value in cell D6

Step a: Updated results in cells E5, G5, and H5

Step c: Updated results in cells G7 and H7

Step c: New value in cell F7

Excel 2016, Windows 10, Microsoft Corporation

FIGURE 19 Results of Changed Values

	A	B	C	D	E	F	G	H
1	OK Office Systems Pri							
2	43344							
3								
4	Product	Code	Cost	Markup Rate	Retail Price	Percent Off	Sale Price	Profit Margin
5	Computer System	101	475.5	0.5	=C5*(1+D5)	0.15	=E5-(E5*F5)	=(G5-C5)/G5
6	Color Laser Printer	102	457.7	0.755	=C6*(1+D6)	0.2	=E6-(E6*F6)	=(G6-C6)/G6
7	Filing Cabinet	103	68.75	0.905	=C7*(1+D7)	0.05	=E7-(E7*F7)	=(G7-C7)/G7
8	Desk Chair	104	75	1	=C8*(1+D8)	0.25	=E8-(E8*F8)	=(G8-C8)/G8
9	Solid Oak Computer D	105	700	1.857	=C9*(1+D9)	0.3	=E9-(E9*F9)	=(G9-C9)/G9
10	27" Monitor	106	195	0.835	=C10*(1+D10)	0.1	=E10-(E10*F10)	=(G10-C10)/G10

Step d: Date displays as a serial number

Step d: Values appear left aligned

Step d: Formulas displayed instead of results

Excel 2016, Windows 10, Microsoft Corporation

FIGURE 20 Formulas Displayed in the Worksheet

a. Click **cell C5**, type **475.5**, and then press **Enter**.

   The results of the retail price, sale price, and profit margin formulas change based on the new cost.

b. Click **cell D6**, type **0.755**, and then press **Enter**.

   The results of the retail price, sale price, and profit margin formulas change based on the new markup rate.

c. Click **cell F7**, type **0.05**, and then press **Ctrl+Enter**.

The results of the sale price and profit margin formulas change based on the new markdown rate. Note that the retail price did not change because that formula is not based on the markup rate.

d. Press **Ctrl+`** (the grave accent mark).

The workbook now displays the formulas rather than the formula results (refer to Figure 20). This is helpful when you want to review several formulas at one time. Numbers are left-aligned, and the date displays as a serial number when you display formulas.

e. Press **Ctrl+`** (the grave accent mark).

The workbook now displays the formula results in the cells again.

f. Save the workbook. Keep the workbook open if you plan to continue with the next Hands-On Exercise. If not, close the workbook, and exit Excel.

Worksheet Structure and Clipboard Tasks

Although you plan worksheets before entering data, you might need to insert a new row to accommodate new data, delete a column that you no longer need, hide a column of confidential data before printing worksheets for distribution, or adjust the size of columns and rows so that the data fit better. Furthermore, you may decide to move data to a different location in the same worksheet or even to a different worksheet. Instead of deleting the original data and typing it in the new location, select and move data from one cell to another. In some instances, you might want to create a copy of data entered so that you can explore different values and compare the results of the original data set and the copied and edited data set.

In this section, you will learn how to make changes to columns and rows. Furthermore, you will also learn how to select ranges, move data to another location, copy data to another range, and use the Paste Special feature.

Managing Columns and Rows

As you enter and edit worksheet data, you might need to adjust the row and column structure to accommodate new data or remove unnecessary data. You can add rows and columns to add new data and delete data, columns, and rows that you no longer need. Adjusting the height and width of rows and columns, respectively, can often present the data better.

Insert Cells, Columns, and Rows

STEP 1 ▶▶ After you construct a worksheet, you might need to insert cells, columns, or rows to accommodate new data. For example, you might want to insert a new column to perform calculations or insert a new row to list a new product.

> **To insert a new column or row, complete the following set of steps:**
>
> 1. Click in the column or row.
> 2. Click the Insert arrow in the Cells group on the Home tab (see Figure 21).
> 3. Select Insert Sheet Columns or Insert Sheet Rows.

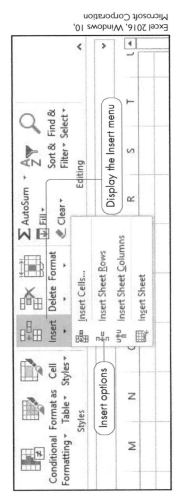

FIGURE 21 Insert Menu

Alternatively, you can use a shortcut menu. Right-click the column (letter) or row (number) heading. Then select Insert from the shortcut menu.

Excel inserts new columns to the left of the current column and new rows above the active row. If the current column is column C and you insert a new column, the new column becomes column C, and the original column C data are now in column D. Likewise, if the current row is 5 and you insert a new row, the new row is row 5, and the original row 5 data are now in row 6. When you insert cells, rows, and columns, cell addresses in formulas adjust automatically.

Inserting a cell is helpful when you realize that you left out an entry after you have entered all of the data. Instead of inserting a new row or column, you just want to move the existing content down or over to enter the missing value. You can insert a single cell in a particular row or column.

To insert one or more cells, complete the following steps:

1. Click in the cell where you want the new cell.
2. Click the Insert arrow in the Cells group on the Home tab.
3. Select Insert Cells.
4. Select an option from the Insert dialog box (see Figure 22) to position the new cell and click OK.

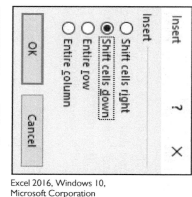

FIGURE 22 Insert Dialog Box

Excel 2016, Windows 10,
Microsoft Corporation

Alternatively, click Insert in the Cells group. The default action of clicking Insert is to insert a cell at the current location, which moves existing data down in that column only.

Delete Cells, Columns, and Rows

STEP 2

If you no longer need a cell, column, or row, you should delete it. For example, you might want to delete a row containing a product you no longer carry. In these situations, you are deleting the entire cell, column, or row, not just the contents of the cell to leave empty cells. As with inserting new cells, columns, or rows, any affected formulas adjust the cell references automatically.

To delete a column or row, complete the following sets of steps:

1. Click the column or row heading for the column or row you want to delete.
2. Click Delete in the Cells group on the Home tab.

Alternatively, click in any cell within the column or row you want to delete, click the Delete arrow in the Cells group on the Home tab (see Figure 23), and then select Select Delete Sheet Columns or Delete Sheet Rows. Another alternative is to right-click the column letter or row number for the column or row you want to delete and then select Delete from the shortcut menu.

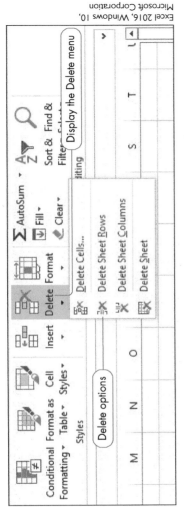

FIGURE 23 Delete Menu

To delete a cell or cells, complete the following steps:

1. Select the cell(s).
2. Click the Delete arrow in the Cells group.
3. Select Delete Cells to display the Delete dialog box (see Figure 24).
4. Click the appropriate option to shift cells left or up and click OK.

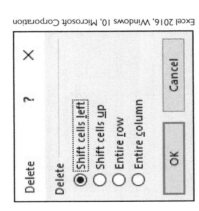

FIGURE 24 Delete Dialog Box

Alternatively, click Delete in the Cells group. The default action of clicking Delete is to delete the active cell, which moves existing data up in that column only.

Hide and Unhide Columns and Rows

If your worksheet contains information you do not want to display, hide some columns and/or rows before you print a copy for public distribution. However, the column or row is not deleted. If you hide column B, you will see columns A and C side by side. If you hide row 3, you will see rows 2 and 4 together. Figure 25 shows that column B and row 3 are hidden. Excel displays a double line between column headings (such as between A and C), indicating one or more columns are hidden, and a double line between row headings (such as between 2 and 4), indicating one or more rows are hidden.

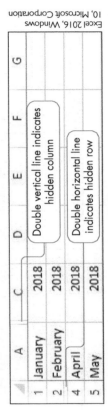

FIGURE 25 Hidden Columns and Rows

To hide a column or row, complete one of the following sets of steps:

1. Select a cell or cells in the column or row you want to hide.
2. Click Format in the Cells group on the Home tab (refer to Figure 26).
3. Point to Hide & Unhide.
4. Select Hide Columns or Hide Rows, depending on what you want to hide.

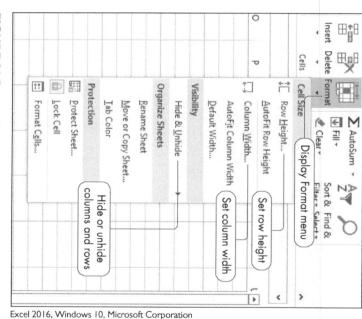

FIGURE 26 Format Menu

Excel 2016, Windows 10, Microsoft Corporation

Alternatively, you can right-click the color or row heading(s) you want to hide. Then select Hide.

You can hide multiple columns and rows at the same time. To select adjacent columns (such as columns B through E) or adjacent rows (such as rows 2 through 4), drag across the adjacent column or row headings and use the Hide command.

To hide nonadjacent columns or rows, complete the following steps:

1. Press and hold Ctrl while you click the desired column or row headings.
2. Use any acceptable method to hide the selected columns or rows.

To unhide a column or row, complete the following steps:

1. Select the columns or rows on both sides of the hidden column or row. For example, if column B is hidden, drag across column letters A and C.
2. Click Format in the Cells group on the Home tab (refer to Figure 26), point to Hide & Unhide, and select Unhide Columns or Unhide Rows, depending on what you want to display again.

TIP: UNHIDING COLUMN A, ROW 1, AND ALL HIDDEN ROWS/COLUMNS

Unhiding column A or row 1 is different because you cannot select the row or column on either side. To unhide column A or row 1, type A1 in the Name Box and press Enter. Click Format in the Cells group on the Home tab, point to Hide & Unhide, and select Unhide Columns or Unhide Rows to display column A or row 1, respectively. If you want to unhide all columns and rows, click Select All (the triangle above the row 1 heading and to the left of the column A heading) and use the Hide & Unhide submenu.

Adjust Column Width

STEP 3 »» After you enter data in a column, you often need to adjust the *column width*—the horizontal measurement of a column in a table or a worksheet. In Excel, column width is measured by the number of characters or pixels. For example, in the worksheet you created in Hands-On Exercises 1 and 2, the labels in column A displayed into column B when those adjacent cells were empty. However, after you typed values in column B, the labels in column A appeared cut off. You will need to widen column A to show the full name of all of your products.

TIP: POUND SIGNS DISPLAYED

Numbers and dates appear as a series of pound signs (#######) when the cell is too narrow to display the complete value, and text appears to be truncated.

To widen a column to accommodate the longest label or value in a column, complete one of the following sets of steps:

- Point to the right vertical border of the column heading. When the pointer displays as a two-headed arrow, double-click the border. For example, if column B is too narrow to display the content in that column, double-click the right vertical border of the column B heading.

- Click Format in the Cells group on the Home tab (refer to Figure 26) and select AutoFit Column Width.

To adjust the width of a column to an exact width, complete the following sets of steps:

- Drag the vertical border to the left to decrease the column width or to the right to increase the column width. As you drag the vertical border, Excel displays a ScreenTip specifying the width (see Figure 27) from 0 to 255 characters and in pixels.

- Click Format in the Cells group on the Home tab (refer to Figure 26), select Column Width, type a value that represents the maximum number of characters to display in the Column width box in the Column Width dialog box, and then click OK.

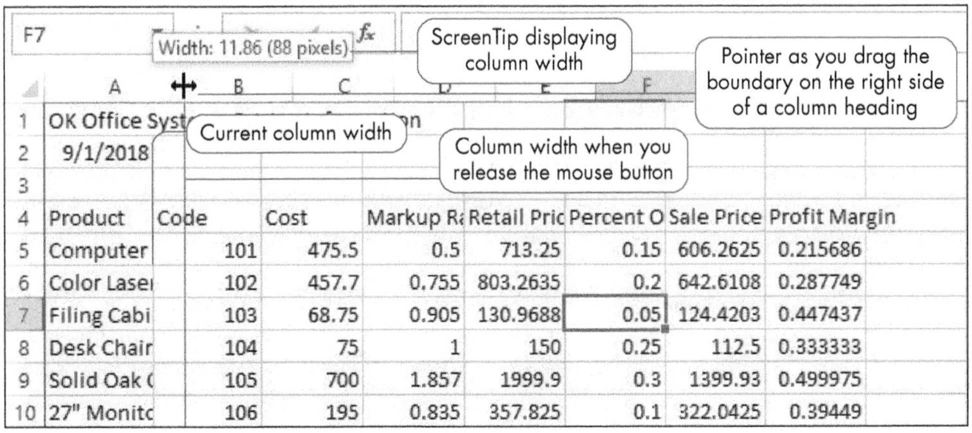

FIGURE 27 Increasing Column Width

Adjust Row Height

You can adjust the **row height**—the vertical measurement of the row—in a way similar to how you change column width by double-clicking the border between row numbers or by selecting Row Height or AutoFit Row Height from the Format menu (refer to Figure 26). In Excel, row height is a value between 0 and 409 based on point size (abbreviated as pt) and pixels. Whether you are measuring font sizes or row heights, one point size is equal to 1/72 of an inch. Your row height should be taller than your font size. For example, with an 11-pt font size, the default row height is 15.

TIP: MULTIPLE COLUMN WIDTHS AND ROW HEIGHTS

You can set the size for more than one column or row at a time to make the selected columns or rows the same size. Drag across the column or row headings for the area you want to format, and set the size using any method.

Selecting, Moving, Copying, and Pasting Data

You may already know the basics of selecting, cutting, copying, and pasting data in other programs, such as Microsoft Word. These tasks are somewhat different when working in Excel.

Select a Range

A **range** refers to a group of adjacent or contiguous cells in a worksheet. A range may be as small as a single cell or as large as the entire worksheet. It may consist of a row or part of a row, a column or part of a column, or multiple rows or columns, but will always be a rectangular shape, as you must select the same number of cells in each row or column for the entire range. A range is specified by indicating the top-left and bottom-right cells in the selection. For example, in Figure 28, the date is a single-cell range in cell A2, the Color Laser Printer data are stored in the range A6:H6, the cost values are stored in the range C5:C10, and the sales prices and profit margins are stored in range G5:H10. A **nonadjacent range** contains multiple ranges, such as D5:D10 and F5:F10. At times, you will select nonadjacent ranges so that you can apply the same formatting at the same time, such as formatting the nonadjacent range D5:D10 and F5:F10 with Percent Style.

⯅	A	B	C	D	E	F	G	H	I
1	OK Office Systems Pricing Information								
2		9/1/2018							
3									
4	Product	Code	Cost	Markup Ra	Retail Pric	Percent O	Sale Price	Profit Margin	
5	Computer System	101	475.5	0.5	713.25	0.15	606.2625	0.215686	
6	Color Laser Printer	102	457.7	0.755	803.2635	0.2	642.6108	0.287749	
7	Filing Cabine	103	68.75	0.905	130.9688	0.05	124.4203	0.447437	
8	Desk Chair	104	75	1	150	0.25	112.5	0.333333	
9	Solid Oak Computer Desk	105	700	1.857	1999.9	0.3	1399.93	0.499975	
10	27" Monitor	106	195	0.835	357.825	0.1	322.0425	0.39449	
11									

Range in a row — Single-cell range — Range in a column — Rectangular range of cells

FIGURE 28 Sample Ranges

Excel 2016, Windows 10, Microsoft Corporation

Table 4 lists methods to select ranges, including nonadjacent ranges.

TABLE 4	Selecting Ranges
To Select:	**Do This:**
A range	Drag until you select the entire range. Alternatively, click the first cell in the range, press and hold Shift, and click the last cell in the range.
An entire column	Click the column heading.
An entire row	Click the row heading.
Current range containing data, including headings	Click in the range of data and press Ctrl+A.
All cells in a worksheet	Click Select All or press Ctrl+A twice.
Nonadjacent range	Select the first range, press and hold Ctrl, and select additional range(s).

A green border appears around a selected range. Any command you execute will affect the entire range. The range remains selected until you select another range or click in any cell in the worksheet.

TIP: NAME BOX

Use the Name Box to select a range by clicking in the Name Box, typing a range address such as B15:D25, and pressing Enter.

Move a Range

You can move cell contents from one range to another. For example, you might want to move an input area from the right side of the worksheet to above the output range. When you move a range containing text and values, the text and values do not change. However, any formulas that refer to cells in that range will update to reflect the new cell addresses.

To move a range, complete the following steps:

1. Select the range.
2. Click Cut in the Clipboard group to copy the range to the Clipboard (see Figure 29). Unlike cutting data in other Microsoft Office applications, the data you cut in Excel remain in their locations until you paste them elsewhere. A moving dashed green border surrounds the selected range and the status bar displays *Select destination and press ENTER or choose Paste.*
3. Ensure the destination range—the range where you want to move the data—is the same size or greater than the size of the cut range.
4. Click in the top-left corner of the destination range, and use the Paste command (see Figure 29). If any cells within the destination range contain data, Excel overwrites that data when you use the Paste command.

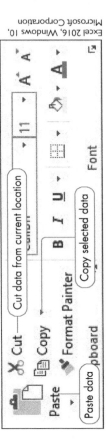

Excel 2016, Windows 10,
Microsoft Corporation

FIGURE 29 Cut, Copy, Paste

Copy and Paste a Range

You may want to copy cell contents from one range to another. When you copy a range, the original data remain in their original locations. For example, you might copy your January budget to another worksheet to use as a model for creating your February budget. Cell references in copied formulas adjust based on their relative locations to the original data. Furthermore, you want to copy formulas from one range to another range. In this situation where you cannot use the fill handle, you will use the Copy and Paste functions to copy the formula.

To copy a range, complete the following steps:

1. Select the range.

2. Click Copy in the Clipboard group (refer to Figure 29) to copy the contents of the selected range to the Clipboard. A moving dashed green border surrounds the selected range and the status bar displays *Select destination and press ENTER or choose Paste*.

3. Ensure the destination range—the range where you want to copy the data—is the same size or greater than the size of the copied range.

4. Click in the top-left corner of the destination range where you want the duplicate data, and click Paste (refer to Figure 29). If any cells within the destination range contain data, Excel overwrites that data when you use the Paste command. The original range still has the moving dashed green border, and the pasted copied range is selected with a solid green border. Figure 30 shows a selected range (A4:H10) and a copy of the range (J4:Q10). Immediately after you click Paste, the ***Paste Options button*** displays in the bottom-right corner of the pasted data. Click the arrow to select a different result for the pasted data.

5. Press Esc to turn off the moving dashed border around the originally selected range.

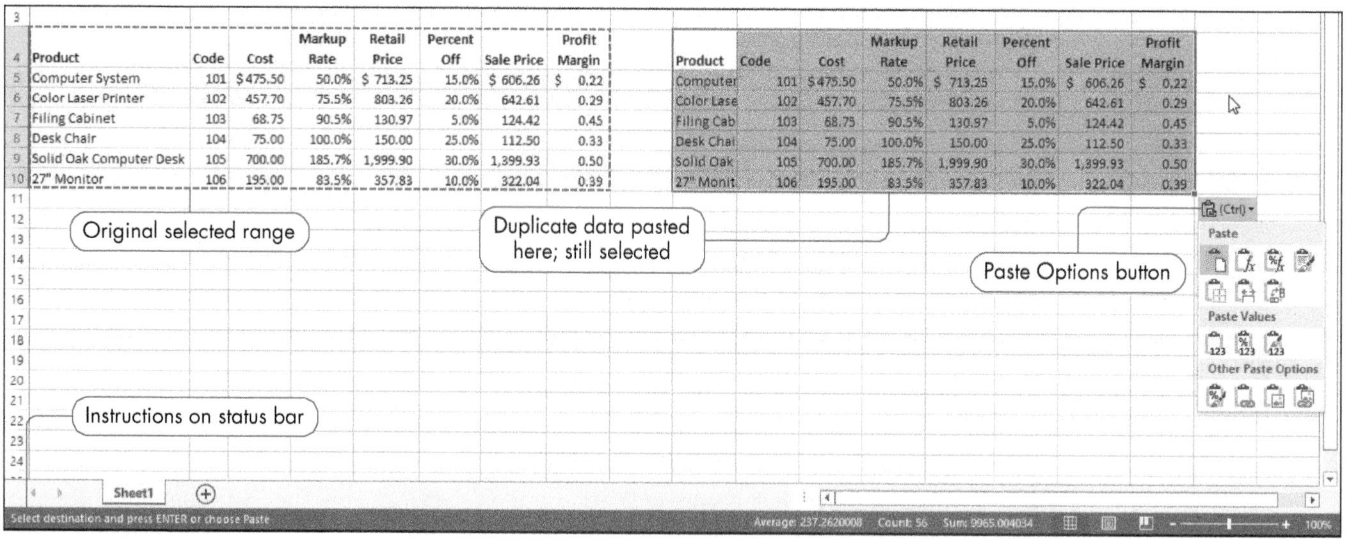

STEP 5 ❯❯

Original selected range

Instructions on status bar

Duplicate data pasted here; still selected

Paste Options button

FIGURE 30 Copied and Pasted Range

Excel 2016, Windows 10, Microsoft Corporation

TIP: COPY AS PICTURE

Instead of clicking Copy, if you click the Copy arrow in the Clipboard group, you can select Copy (the default option) or Copy as Picture. When you select Copy as Picture, you copy an image of the selected data. Then paste the image elsewhere in the workbook or in a Word document or PowerPoint presentation. However, when you copy the data as an image, you cannot edit individual cell data after you paste the image.

Use Paste Options and Paste Special

STEP 6 »» Sometimes you might want to paste data in a different format than they are in the Clipboard. For example, you might want to preserve the results of calculations before changing the original data. To do this, you can paste the data as values. If you want to copy data from Excel and paste them into a Word document, you can paste the Excel data as a worksheet object, as unformatted text, or in another format.

To paste data from the Clipboard into a different format, complete the following steps:

1. Click the Paste arrow in the Clipboard group (see Figure 31).
2. Point to command to see a ScreenTip and a preview of how the pasted data will look.
3. Click the option you want to apply.

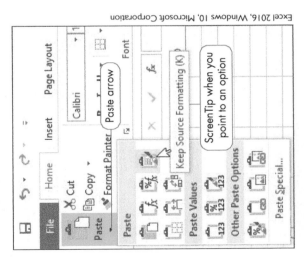

Excel 2016, Windows 10, Microsoft Corporation

FIGURE 31 Paste Options

Table 5 lists and describes some of the options in the Paste gallery that opens when you click the Paste arrow in the Clipboard or the Paste Options button that displays immediately after you use Paste. Paste options enable you to paste content or attributes, such as a formula or format.

TABLE 5 Paste Options

Icon	Option Name	Paste Description
	Paste	Cell contents and all formatting from copied cells
	Formulas	Formulas, but no formatting, from copied cells
	Formulas & Number Formatting	Formulas and number formatting, such as Currency, but no font formatting, such as font color, fill color, or borders
	Keep Source Formatting	Cell contents and formatting from copied cells
	No Borders	Cell contents, number formatting, and text formatting except borders
	Keep Source Column Widths	Cell contents, number and text formatting, and the column width of the source data when pasting in another column
	Transpose	Transposes data from rows to columns and columns to rows
	Values	Unformatted values that are the results of formulas, not the actual formulas
	Values & Number Formatting	Values that are the results of formulas, not the actual formulas; preserves number formatting but not text formatting
	Values & Source Formatting	Values that are the results of formulas, not the actual formulas; preserves number and text formatting
	Formatting	Number and text formatting only from the copied cells; no cell contents
	Paste Link	Creates a reference to the source cells (such as =$G$15), not the cell contents; preserves number formatting but not text formatting
	Picture	Creates a picture image of the copied data; pasted data is not editable
	Linked Picture	Creates a picture with a reference to the copied cells; if the original cell content changes, so does the picture
	Paste Special	Opens the Paste Special dialog box (see Figure 32)

FIGURE 32 Paste Special Dialog Box

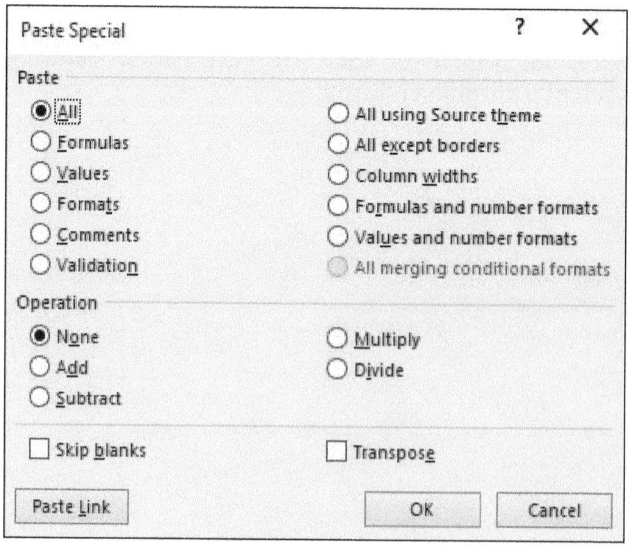

Excel 2016, Windows 10, Microsoft Corporation

TIP: TRANSPOSING COLUMNS AND ROWS

After entering data into a worksheet, you might want to transpose the columns and rows so that the data in the first column appear as column labels across the first row, or the column labels in the first row appear in the first column. Figure 33 shows the original data with the months in column A and the utility costs in columns B, C, and D. In the transposed data, the months are shown in the first row, and each row contains utility information. The original formats (bold and right-aligned) are copied in the transposed data.

	A	B	C	D
1	Month	Gas	Electric	Water
2	January	$275	$120	$35
3	February	$265	$114	$35
4	March	$200	$118	$35
5				
6				

	F	G	H	I	J
1	Month	January	February	March	
2	Gas	$275	$265	$200	
3	Electric	$120	$114	$118	
4	Water	$35	$35	$35	

(Ctrl) ▸

Excel 2016, Windows 10,
Microsoft Corporation

FIGURE 33 Transposed Data

Copy Excel Data to Other Programs

You can copy Excel data and use it in other applications, such as in a Word document or in a PowerPoint slide show. For example, you might perform statistical analyses in Excel and copy the data into a research paper in Word. Or, you might want to create a budget in Excel and copy the data into a PowerPoint slide show for a meeting.

After selecting and copying a range in Excel, you must decide how you want the data to appear in the destination application. Click the Paste arrow in the destination application to see a gallery of options or to select the Paste Special option.

Quick Concepts

8. Give an example of when you would delete a column versus when you would hide a column.

9. When should you adjust column widths instead of using the default width?

10. Why would you use the Paste Special options in Excel?

3 Worksheet Structure and Clipboard Tasks

Skills covered: Insert Columns and Rows • Delete a Row • Hide a Column • Adjust Column Width • Adjust Row Height • Select a Range • Move a Range • Copy and Paste a Range • Use Paste Special

You want to insert a column to calculate the amount of markup and delete a row containing data you no longer need. You also want to adjust column widths to display the labels in the columns. In addition, your supervisor asked you to enter data for a new product. Because it is almost identical to an existing product, you will copy the original data and edit the copied data to save time. You also want to experiment with the Paste Special option to see the results of using it in the OKOS workbook.

STEP 1 ▶▶ INSERT A COLUMN AND ROWS

You decide to add a column to display the amount of profit. Because profit is a dollar amount, you want to keep the profit column close to another column of dollar amounts. Therefore, you will insert the profit column before the profit margin (percentage) column. You will insert new rows for product information and category names. Refer to Figure 34 as you complete Step 1.

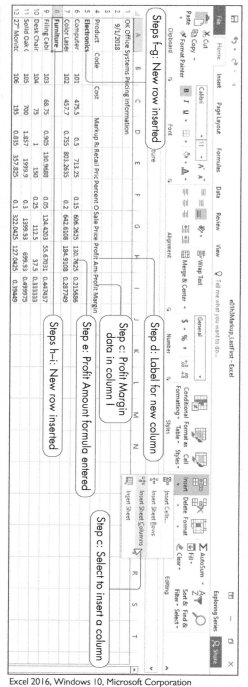

FIGURE 34 Column and Rows Inserted

Excel 2016, Windows 10, Microsoft Corporation

a. Open *e01h2Markup_LastFirst* if you closed it at the end of Hands-On Exercise 2 and save it as **e01h3Markup_LastFirst**, changing h2 to h3.

b. Click **cell H5** (or any cell in column H).

You want to insert a column between the Sale Price and Profit Margin columns so that you can calculate the profit amount in dollars.

c. Click the **Insert arrow** in the Cells group and select **Insert Sheet Columns**.

You inserted a new blank column H. The data in the original column H are now in column I.

d. Click **cell H4**, type **Profit Amount**, and then press **Enter**.

e. Ensure the active cell is **cell H5**. Type **=G5-C5** and click **Enter**. Double-click the **cell H5 fill handle**.

You calculated the profit amount by subtracting the original cost from the sale price and then copied the formula down the column.

f. Right-click the **row 5 heading** and select **Insert** from the shortcut menu.

You inserted a new blank row 5, which is selected. The original rows of data move down a row each.

g. Click **cell A5**. Type **Electronics** and press **Ctrl+Enter**. Click **Bold** in the Font group on the Home tab.

You typed and applied bold formatting to the category name Electronics above the list of electronic products.

h. Right-click the **row 8 heading** and select **Insert** from the shortcut menu.

You inserted a new blank row 8. The data that was originally on row 8 is now on row 9.

i. Click **cell A8**. Type **Furniture** and press **Ctrl+Enter**. Click **Bold** in the Font group on the Home tab and save the workbook.

You typed and applied bold formatting to the category name Furniture above the list of furniture products.

STEP 2 ≫ DELETE A ROW AND HIDE A COLUMN

You just realized that you do not have enough filing cabinets in stock to offer on sale, so you need to delete the Filing Cabinet row. The item numbers are meaningful to you, but the numbers are not necessary for the other employees. Before distributing the worksheet to the employees, you want to hide column B. Because you might need to see that data later, you will hide it rather than delete it. Refer to Figure 35 as you complete Step 2.

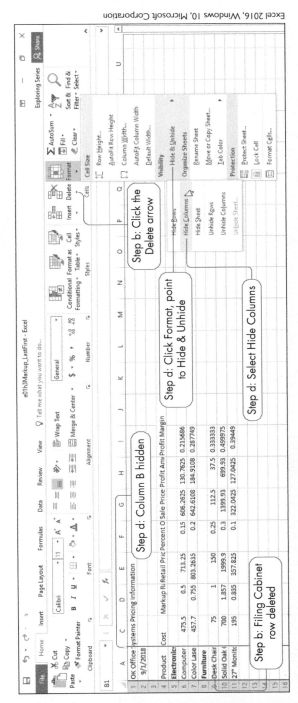

Excel 2016, Windows 10, Microsoft Corporation

FIGURE 35 Row Deleted and Column Hidden

a. Click **cell A9** (or any cell on row 9), the row that contains the Filing Cabinet data.

b. Click the **Delete arrow** in the Cells group and select **Delete Sheet Rows**.

The Filing Cabinet row is deleted, and the remaining rows move up one row.

> **TROUBLESHOOTING:** If you accidentally delete the wrong row or accidentally selected Delete Sheet Columns instead of Delete Sheet Rows, click Undo on the Quick Access Toolbar to restore the deleted row or column.

c. Click the **column B heading**.

d. Click **Format** in the Cells group, point to **Hide & Unhide**, and then select **Hide Columns**.

Excel hides column B. You see a gap in column heading letters A and C, indicating column B is hidden instead of deleted.

e. Save the workbook.

STEP 3 » ADJUST COLUMN WIDTH AND ROW HEIGHT

As you review your worksheet, you notice that the labels in column A appear cut off. You will increase the width of that column to display the entire product names. In addition, you want to make row 1 taller. Refer to Figure 36 as you complete Step 3.

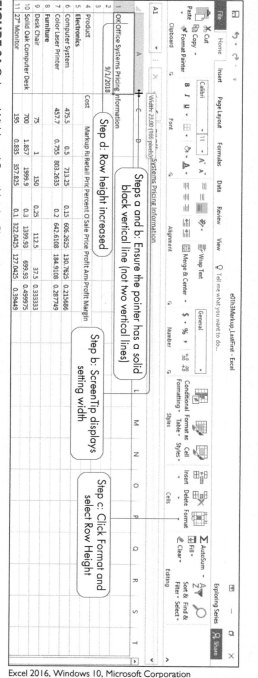

FIGURE 36 Column Width and Row Height Changed

Excel 2016, Windows 10, Microsoft Corporation

a. Point to the right border of column A. When the pointer looks like a double-headed arrow with a solid black vertical line, double-click the border.

When you double-click the border between two columns, Excel adjusts the width of the column on the left side of the border to fit the contents of that column. Excel increased the width of column A based on the cell containing the longest content (the title in cell A1). You decide to adjust the column width to the longest product name instead.

b. Point to the right border of column A until the double-headed arrow appears. Drag the border to the left until the ScreenTip displays **Width: 23.00 (166 pixels)**. Release the mouse button.

You decreased the column width to 23 for column A. The longest product name is visible. You will not adjust the other column widths until after you apply formats to the column headings in Hands-On Exercise 4.

c. Click **cell A1**. Click **Format** in the Cells group and select **Row Height**.

The Row Height dialog box opens so that you can adjust the height of the current row.

d. Type **30** in the **Row height box** and click **OK**. Save the workbook.

You increased the height of the row that contains the worksheet title so that it is more prominent.

You want to move the 27" Monitor product to be immediately after the Color Laser Printer product. Before moving the 27" Monitor row, you will insert a blank row between the Color Laser Printer and Furniture rows. Refer to Figure 37 as you complete Step 4.

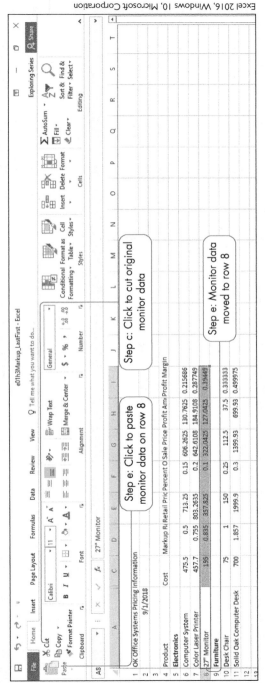

FIGURE 37 Row Moved to New Location

a. Right-click the **row 8 heading** and select **Insert** from the menu.

You will insert a blank row so that you can move the 27" Computer Monitor data to be between the Color Laser Printer and Furniture rows.

b. Select the **range A12:I12**.

You selected the range of cells containing the 27" Monitor data.

c. Click **Cut** in the Clipboard group.

A moving dashed green border outlines the selected range. The status bar displays the message *Select destination and press ENTER or choose Paste.*

d. Click **cell A8.**

This is the first cell in the destination range. If you cut and paste a row without inserting a new row first, Excel will overwrite the original row of data, which is why you inserted a new row in step a.

e. Click **Paste** in the Clipboard group and save the workbook.

The 27" Monitor product data is now located on row 8.

STEP 5 » COPY AND PASTE A RANGE

Alesha told you that a new chair is on its way. She asked you to enter the data for the Executive Desk Chair. Because most of the data is the same as the Desk Chair data, you will copy the original Desk Chair data, edit the product name, and change the cost to reflect the cost of the second chair. Refer to Figure 38 as you complete Step 5.

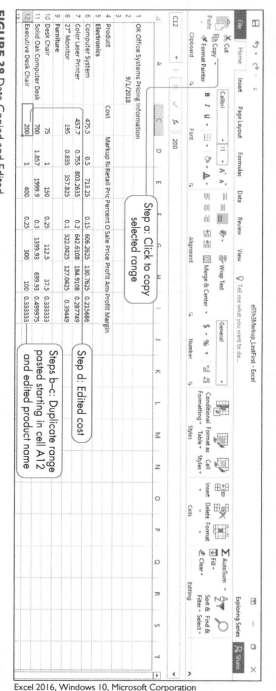

FIGURE 38 Data Copied and Edited

a. Select the **range A10:I10** and click **Copy** in the Clipboard group.

You copied the row containing the Desk Chair product data to the Clipboard.

b. Click **cell A12**, click **Paste** in the Clipboard group, and then press **Esc**.

The pasted range is selected in row 12.

c. Click **cell A12**, press **F2** to activate Edit Mode, press **Home**, type **Executive**, press **Spacebar**, and then press **Enter**.

You edited the product name to display Executive Desk Chair.

d. Change the value in **cell C12** to **200**. Save the workbook.

The formulas calculate the results based on the new cost of 200 for the Executive Desk Chair.

STEP 6 » USE PASTE SPECIAL

During your lunch break, you want to experiment with some of the Paste Special options. Particularly, you are interested in pasting Formulas and Value & Source Formatting. First, you will apply bold and a font color to the title to help you test these Paste Special options. Refer to Figure 39 as you complete Step 6.

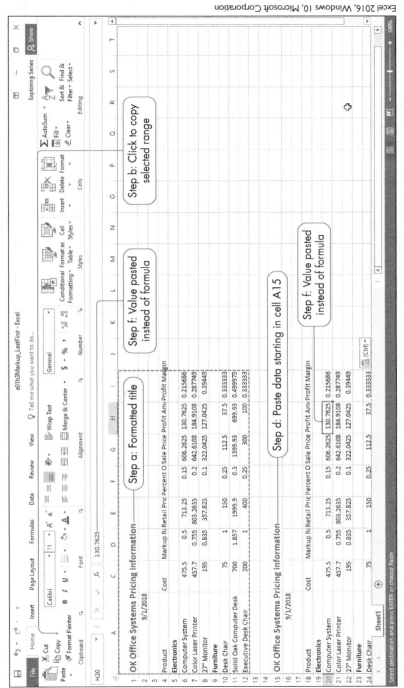

FIGURE 39 Paste Special Results

Excel 2016, Windows 10, Microsoft Corporation

a. Click **cell A1**. Change the font size to **14**, click **Bold**, click the **Font Color arrow** in the Font group and then select **Gold, Accent 4, Darker 50%**.

You will format text to see the effects of using different Paste Special options.

b. Select the **range A1:I12** and click **Copy** in the Clipboard group.

c. Click **cell A15**, the top-left corner of the destination range.

d. Click the **Paste arrow** in the Clipboard group and point to **Formulas**, the second icon from the left in the Paste group.

Without clicking the command, Excel shows you a preview of what that option would do. The pasted copy would not contain the font formatting you applied to the title or the bold on the two category names. In addition, the pasted date would appear as a serial number. The formulas would be maintained.

e. Position the pointer over **Values & Source Formatting**, the first icon from the right in the Paste Values group.

This option would preserve the formatting, but it would convert the formulas into the current value results.

f. Click **Values & Source Formatting**, click **cell H6** to see a formula, and then click **cell H20**. Press **Esc** to turn off the border.

Cell H6 contains a formula, but in the pasted version, the equivalent cell H20 has converted the formula result into an actual value. If you were to change the original cost on row 20, the contents of cell H20 would not change. In a working environment, this is useful only if you want to capture the exact value in a point in time before making changes to the original data.

g. Save the workbook. Keep the workbook open if you plan to continue with the next Hands-On Exercise. If not, close the workbook and exit Excel.

Hands-On Exercise 3

Worksheet Formatting

After entering data and formulas, you should format the worksheet. A professionally formatted worksheet—through adding appropriate symbols, aligning decimals, and using fonts and colors to make data stand out—makes finding and analyzing data easy. You apply different formats to accentuate meaningful details or to draw attention to specific ranges in a worksheet.

In this section, you will learn to apply a cell style, different alignment options, including horizontal and vertical alignment, text wrapping, and indent options. In addition, you will learn how to format different types of values.

Applying Cell Styles, Alignment, and Font Options

Different areas of a worksheet should have different formatting. For example, the title may be centered in 16-pt size; column labels may be bold, centered, and Dark Blue font; and input cells may be formatted differently from output cells. You can apply different formats individually, or you can apply a group of formats by selecting a cell style. A *cell style* is a collection of format settings to provide a consistent appearance within a worksheet and among similar workbooks. A cell style controls the following formats: font, font color and font size, borders and fill colors, alignment, and number formatting.

To apply a cell style to a cell or a range of cells, complete the following steps:

1. Click Cell Styles in the Styles group on the Home tab to display the Cell Styles gallery (see Figure 40).

2. Position the pointer over a style name to see a Live Preview of how the style will affect your worksheet data. The gallery provides a variety of built-in styles to apply to the selected cell or range.

3. Click a style to apply it to the selected cell or range.

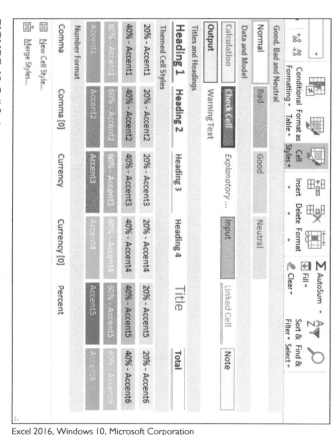

FIGURE 40 Cell Styles

Excel 2016, Windows 10, Microsoft Corporation

Alignment refers to how data are positioned in the boundaries of a cell. Each type of data has a default alignment. Text aligns at the left cell margin, and dates and values align at the right cell margin. You should change the alignment of cell contents to improve the appearance of data within the cells. The Alignment group (see Figure 41) on the Home tab contains several commands to help you align and format data.

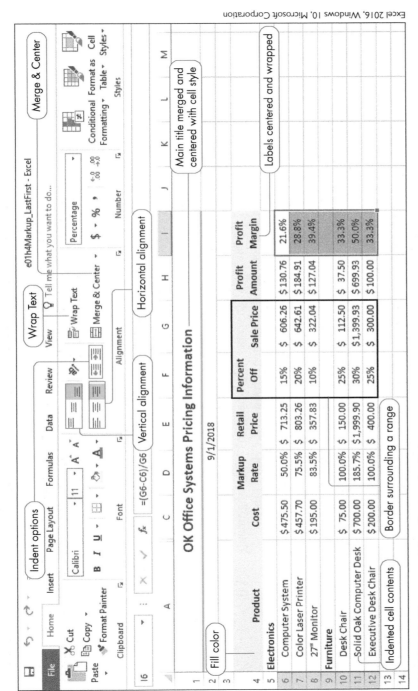

Excel 2016, Windows 10, Microsoft Corporation

FIGURE 41 Alignment and Font Settings Applied

TIP: ALIGNMENT OPTIONS
The Format Cells dialog box contains additional alignment options. To open the Format Cells dialog box, click the Dialog Box Launcher in the Alignment group on the Home tab. The Alignment tab in the dialog box contains the options for aligning data.

Merge and Center Labels

» You may want to place a title at the top of a worksheet and center it over the columns of data in the worksheet. You can center main titles over all columns in the worksheet, and you can center category titles over groups of related columns. You can also merge cells on adjacent rows.

To merge and center cells, complete the following steps:

1. Enter the text in the top left cell of the range.
2. Select the range of cells across which you want to center the label.
3. Click Merge & Center in the Alignment group on the Home tab.

Only data in the far left cell (or top-right cell) are merged. Any other data in the merged cells are deleted. Excel merges the selected cells together into one cell, and the merged cell address is that of the original cell on the left. The data are centered within the merged cell. If you want to split a merged cell into multiple cells, click the merged cell and click Merge & Center. Unmerging places the data in the top-left cell.

For additional options, click the Merge & Center arrow. Table 6 lists the four merge options.

TABLE 6 Merge Options

Option	Results
Merge & Center	Merges selected cells and centers data into one cell.
Merge Across	Merges the selected cells but keeps text left aligned or values right aligned.
Merge Cells	Merges a range of cells on multiple rows as well as in multiple columns.
Unmerge Cells	Separates a merged cell into multiple cells again.

Pearson Education, Inc.

Change Horizontal and Vertical Cell Alignment

Horizontal alignment specifies the position of data between the left and right cell margins, and *vertical alignment* specifies the position of data between the top and bottom cell margins. Bottom Align is the default vertical alignment (as indicated by the light green background on the Ribbon), and Align Left is the default horizontal alignment for text. In Figure 41, the labels on row 4 have Center horizontal alignment and the title in row 1 has Middle Align vertical alignment. To change alignments, click the desired alignment setting(s) in the Alignment group on the Home tab.

TIP: ROTATE CELL DATA

People sometimes rotate headings in cells. To rotate data in a cell, click Orientation in the Alignment group and select an option, such as Angle Clockwise.

Wrap Text

Sometimes you have to maintain specific column widths, but the data do not fit entirely. Use *wrap text* to make data appear on multiple lines by adjusting the row height to fit the cell contents within the column width. Excel wraps the text on two or more lines within the cell. In Figure 41, the Markup Rate and Percent Off labels on row 4 are examples of wrapped text.

To wrap text within a cell, complete the following steps:

1. Click the cells or select the range of cells that contain labels that need to be wrapped.
2. Click Wrap Text in the Alignment group.

TIP: LINE BREAK IN A CELL

If a long text label does not fit well in a cell even after you have applied wrap text, you might want to insert a line break to display the text label on multiple lines within the cell. To insert a line break while you are typing a label, press Alt+Enter where you want to start the next line of text within the cell.

Increase and Decrease Indent

Cell content is left-aligned or right-aligned based on the default data type. However, you can *indent* the cell contents to offset the data from its current alignment. For example, text is left-aligned, but you can indent it to offset it from the left side. Indenting helps others see the hierarchical structure of data. Accountants often indent the word Totals in financial statements so that it stands out from a list of items above the total row. Values are right-aligned by default, but you can indent a value to offset it from the right side of the cell. In Figure 41, Computer System and Desk Chair are indented.

To increase or decrease the indent of data in a cell, complete the following steps:

1. Click the cell that contains data.
2. Click Increase Indent or Decrease Indent in the Alignment group.

TIP: INDENTING VALUES

Values are right aligned by default. You should align the decimal places in a column of values. If the column label is wide, the values below it appear too far on the right. To preserve the values aligning at the decimal places, use the Align Right horizontal alignment and click Increase Indent to shift the values over to the left a little for better placement.

Apply Borders and Fill Color

STEP 4 You can apply a border or fill color to accentuate data in a worksheet. A *border* is a line that surrounds a cell or a range of cells. Use borders to offset some data from the rest of the worksheet data. To apply a border, select the cell or range that you want to have a border, click the Borders arrow in the Font group, and select the desired border type. In Figure 41, a border surrounds the range F4:G12. To remove a border, select No Border from the Borders menu.

Add some color to your worksheets to emphasize data or headers by applying a fill color. *Fill color* is a background color that displays behind the data in a cell so that the data stand out. You should choose a fill color that contrasts with the font color. For example, if the font color is Black, Text 1, you might choose Yellow fill color. If the font color is White, Background 1, you might apply Blue or Dark Blue fill color. The color palette contains two sections: Theme Colors and Standard Colors. The Theme Colors section displays variations of colors that match the current theme applied in the worksheet. For example, it contains shades of blue, such as Blue, Accent 5, Lighter 80%. The Standard Colors section contains basic colors, such as Dark Red and Red.

To apply a fill color, complete the following steps:

1. Select the cell or range that you want to have a fill color.
2. Click the Fill Color arrow on the Home tab to display the color palette.
3. Select the color choice from the Fill Color palette. In Figure 41, the column labels in row 4 contain the Blue, Accent 1, Lighter 80% fill color. If you want to remove a fill color, select No Fill from the bottom of the palette. Select More Colors to open the Colors dialog box, click the Standard tab or Custom tab, and then click a color.

For additional border and fill color options, complete the following steps:

1. Click the Dialog Box Launcher in the Font group to display the Format Cells dialog box.
2. Click the Border tab to select border options, including the border line style and color.
3. Click the Fill tab to set the background color, fill effects, and patterns.

Applying Number Formats

Values have no special formatting when you enter data. However, you should apply *number formats*, settings that control how a value is displayed in a cell. For example, you might want to apply either the Accounting or Currency number format to monetary values. Changing the number format changes the way the number displays in a cell, but the format does not change the stored value. If, for example, you enter 123.456 into a cell and format the cell with the Currency number type, the value shows as $123.46 onscreen, but the actual value 123.456 is used for calculations. When you apply a number format, specify the number of decimal places to display onscreen.

STEP 5

Apply a Number Format

The default number format is General, which displays values as you originally enter them. General number format does not align decimal points in a column or include symbols, such as dollar signs, percent signs, or commas. Table 7 lists and describes the primary number formats in Excel.

TABLE 7 Number Formats

Format Style	Display
General	A number as it was originally entered. Numbers are shown as integers (e.g., 12345), decimal fractions (e.g., 1234.5), or in scientific notation (e.g., 1.23E+10) if the number exceeds 11 digits.
Number	A number with or without the 1,000 separator and with any number of decimal places. Negative numbers can be displayed with parentheses and/or red.
Currency	A number with the 1,000 separator and an optional dollar sign (which is placed immediately to the left of the number). Negative values are preceded by a minus sign or are displayed with parentheses or in red. Two decimal places display by default.
Accounting Number Format	A number that contains the $ on the left side of the cell and formats the value with a comma for every three digits on the left side of the decimal point and displays two digits to the right of the decimal point. Negative values display in parentheses, and zero values display as hyphens.
Comma Style	A number is formatted with a comma for every three digits on the left side of the decimal point and displays two digits to the right of the decimal point. Used in conjunction with Accounting Number Format to align commas and decimal places.
Date	The date in different ways, such as Long Date (March 14, 2016) or Short Date (3/14/16 or 14-Mar-16).
Time	The time in different formats, such as 10:50 PM or 22:50 (military time).
Percent Style	The value as it would be multiplied by 100 (for display purpose), with the percent symbol. The default number of decimal places is zero if you click Percent Style in the Number group or two decimal places if you use the Format Cells dialog box. However, you should typically increase the number of decimal points to show greater accuracy.
Fraction	A number as a fraction; use when no exact decimal equivalent exists. A fraction is entered into a cell as a formula such as =1/3. If the cell is not formatted as a fraction, the formula results display.
Scientific	A number as a decimal fraction followed by a whole number exponent of 10; for example, the number 12345 would appear as 1.23E+04. The exponent, +04 in the example, is the number of places the decimal point is moved to the left (or right if the exponent is negative). Very small numbers have negative exponents.
Text	The data left aligned; is useful for numerical values that have leading zeros and should be treated as text, such as postal codes or phone numbers. Apply Text format before typing a leading zero so that the zero displays in the cell.
Special	A number with editing characters, such as hyphens in a Social Security number.
Custom	Predefined customized number formats or special symbols to create your own customized number format.

The Number group on the Home tab contains commands for applying **Accounting Number Format**, **Percent Style**, and **Comma Style** numbering formats. You can click the Accounting Number Format arrow and select other denominations, such as English pounds or euros. For other number formats, click the Number Format arrow and select the numbering format you want to use. For more specific numbering formats than those provided, select More Number Formats from the Number Format menu or click the Number Dialog Box Launcher to open the Format Cells dialog box with the Number tab options readily available. Figure 42 shows different number formats applied to values.

	A	B
1	General	1234.567
2	Number	1234.57
3	Currency	$1,234.57
4	Accounting	$ 1,234.57
5	Comma	1,234.57
6	Percent	12%
7	Short Date	3/1/2018
8	Long Date	Thursday, March 1, 2018

Excel 2016, Windows 10,
Microsoft Corporation

FIGURE 42 Number Formats

Increase and Decrease Decimal Places

STEP 5 ▶▶ After applying a number format, you may need to adjust the number of decimal places that display. For example, if you have an entire column of monetary values formatted in Accounting Number Format, Excel displays two decimal places by default. If the entire column of values contains whole dollar values and no cents, displaying .00 down the column looks cluttered. Decrease the number of decimal places to show whole numbers only.

To change the number of decimal places displayed, complete the following steps:

1. Click the cell or select a range of cells containing values that need to have fewer or more decimal places.

2. Click Increase Decimal in the Number group on the Home tab to display more decimal places for greater precision or Decrease Decimal to display fewer or no decimal places.

11. What is the importance of formatting a worksheet?

12. Describe five alignment and font formatting techniques used to format labels that are discussed in this section.

13. What are the main differences between Accounting Number Format and Currency format? Which format has its own command on the Ribbon?

4 Worksheet Formatting

Skills covered: Apply a Cell
Style • Merge and Center Data •
Change Cell Alignment • Wrap Text
• Increase Indent • Apply a Border
• Apply Fill Color • Apply Number
Formats • Increase and Decrease
Decimal Places

In the first three Hands-On Exercises, you entered data about products on sale, created formulas to
calculate markup and profit, and inserted new rows and columns to accommodate the labels Electronics
and Furniture to identify the specific products. You are ready to format the worksheet. Specifically, you
will center the title, align text, format values, and apply other formatting to enhance the readability of the
worksheet.

STEP 1 ▶▶ APPLY A CELL STYLE AND MERGE AND CENTER THE TITLE

To make the title stand out, you want to apply a cell style and center it over all the data columns. You will use the Merge & Center
command to merge cells and center the title at the same time. Refer to Figure 43 as you complete Step 1.

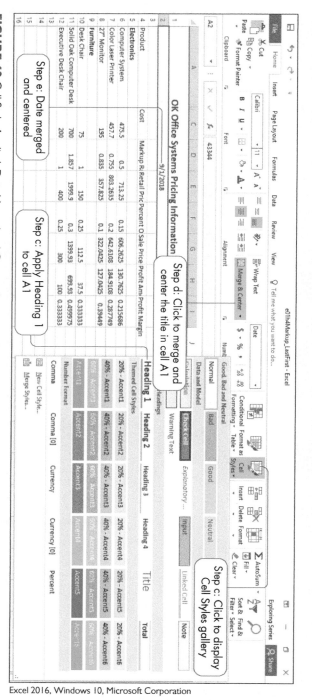

FIGURE 43 Cell Style Applied; Data Merged and Centered

a. Open *e01h3Markup_LastFirst* if you closed it at the end of Hands-On Exercise 3 and save
it as **e01h4Markup_LastFirst**, changing h3 to h4.

b. Select the **range A15:I26** and press **Delete**.

You maintained a copy of your Paste Special results in the *e01h3Markup_LastFirst*
workbook, but you do not need it to continue.

c. Select the **range A1:I1**, click **Cell Styles** in the Styles group on the Home tab, and then
click **Heading 1**.

You applied the Heading 1 style to the range A1:I1. This style formats the contents with
15-pt font size, Blue-Gray, Text 2 font color, and a thick blue bottom border.

d. Click **Merge & Center** in the Alignment group.

Excel merges cells in the range A1:I1 into one cell and centers the title horizontally
within the merged cell, which is cell A1.

TROUBLESHOOTING: If you merge too many or not enough cells, unmerge the cells and start again. To unmerge cells, click in the merged cell. The Merge & Center command is shaded in green when the active cell is merged. Click Merge & Center to unmerge the cell. Then select the correct range to merge and use Merge & Center again.

e. Select the **range A2:I2**. Click **Merge & Center** in the Alignment group. Save the workbook.

TROUBLESHOOTING: If you try to merge and center data in the range A1:I2, Excel will keep the top-left data only and delete the date. To merge separate data on separate rows, you must merge and center data separately.

You will wrap the text in the column headings to avoid columns that are too wide for the data, but which will display the entire text of the column labels. In addition, you will horizontally center column labels between the left and right cell margins. Refer to Figure 44 as you complete Step 2.

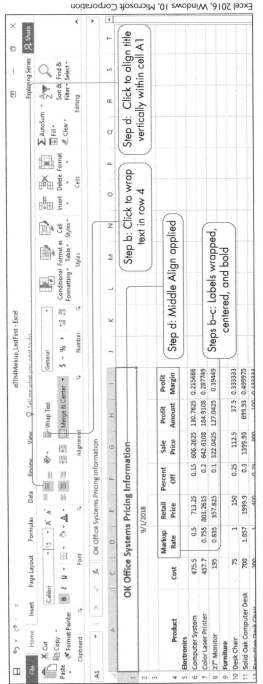

FIGURE 44 Formatted Column Labels

a. Select the **range A4:I4** to select the column labels.

b. Click **Wrap Text** in the Alignment group.

The multiple-word column headings are now visible on two lines within each cell.

c. Click **Center** in the Alignment group and click **Bold** in the Font group to format the selected column headings.

The column headings are centered horizontally between the left and right edges of each cell.

d. Click **cell A1**, which contains the title, click **Middle Align** in the Alignment group, and then save the workbook.

Middle Align vertically centers data between the top and bottom edges of the cell.

As you review the first column, you notice that the category names, Electronics and Furniture, do not stand out. You decide to indent the labels within each category to better display which products are in each category. Refer to Figure 45 as you complete Step 3.

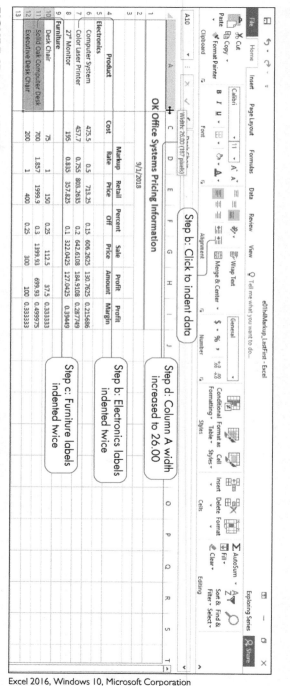

FIGURE 45 Indented Cell Contents

Excel 2016, Windows 10, Microsoft Corporation

a. Select the **range A6:A8**, the cells containing Electronic products labels.

b. Click **Increase Indent** in the Alignment group twice.

The three selected product names are indented below the Electronics heading.

c. Select the **range A10:A12**, the cells containing furniture products, and click **Increase Indent** twice.

The three selected product names are indented below the Furniture heading. Notice that the one product name appears cut off.

d. Increase the column A width to **26.00**. Save the workbook.

You want to apply a light blue fill color to highlight the column headings. In addition, you want to emphasize the percent off and sale prices. You will do this by applying a border around that range. Refer to Figure 46 as you complete Step 4.

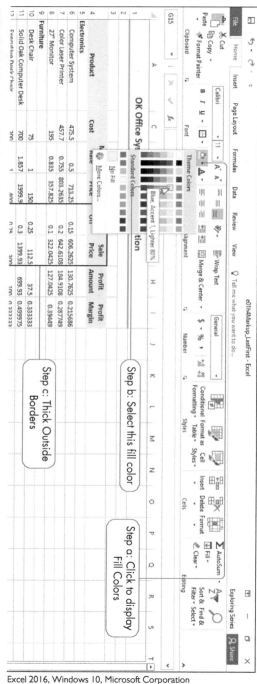

FIGURE 46 Border and Fill Color Applied

Excel 2016, Windows 10, Microsoft Corporation

a. Select the **range A4:I4** and click the **Fill Color arrow** in the Font group.

b. Click **Blue, Accent 1, Lighter 80%** in the Theme Colors section (second row, fifth column).

You applied a fill color to the selected cells to draw attention to these cells.

c. Select the **range F4:G12**, click the **Border arrow** in the Font group, and then select **Thick Outside Borders**.

You applied a border around the selected cells.

d. Click in an empty cell below the columns of data to deselect the cells. Save the workbook.

STEP 5 ⟫ APPLY NUMBER FORMATS AND INCREASE AND DECREASE DECIMAL PLACES

You need to format the values to increase readability and look more professional. You will apply number formats and adjust the number of decimal points displayed. Refer to Figure 47 as you complete Step 5.

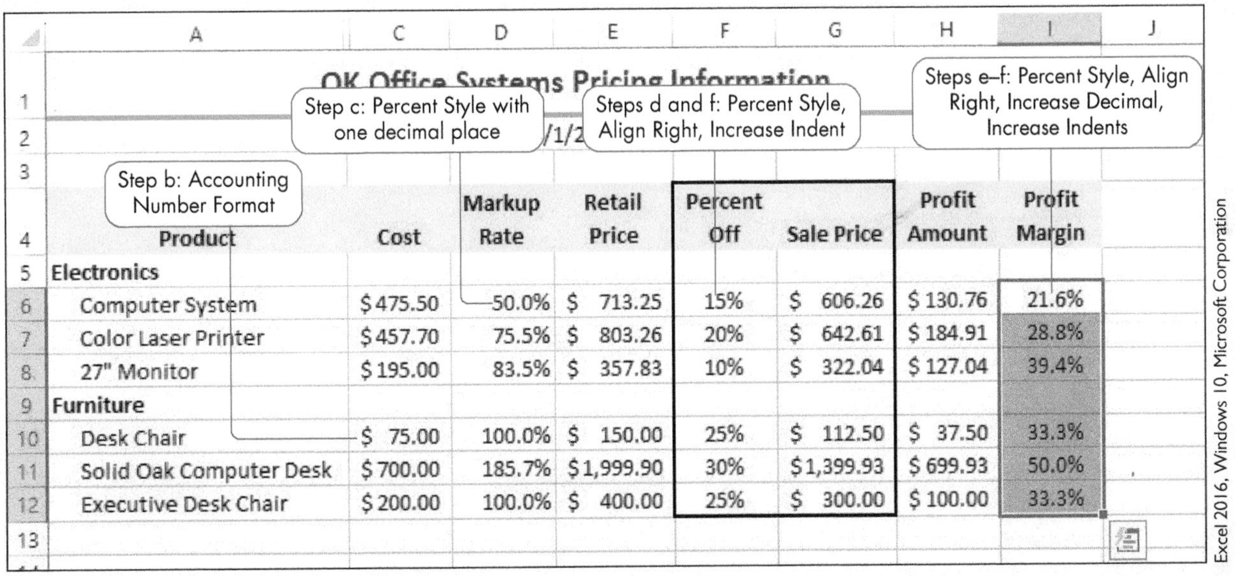

OK Office Systems Pricing Information

Product	Cost	Markup Rate	Retail Price	Percent Off	Sale Price	Profit Amount	Profit Margin
Electronics							
Computer System	$475.50	50.0%	$ 713.25	15%	$ 606.26	$ 130.76	21.6%
Color Laser Printer	$457.70	75.5%	$ 803.26	20%	$ 642.61	$ 184.91	28.8%
27" Monitor	$195.00	83.5%	$ 357.83	10%	$ 322.04	$ 127.04	39.4%
Furniture							
Desk Chair	$ 75.00	100.0%	$ 150.00	25%	$ 112.50	$ 37.50	33.3%
Solid Oak Computer Desk	$700.00	185.7%	$1,999.90	30%	$1,399.93	$ 699.93	50.0%
Executive Desk Chair	$200.00	100.0%	$ 400.00	25%	$ 300.00	$ 100.00	33.3%

Step b: Accounting Number Format

Step c: Percent Style with one decimal place

Steps d and f: Percent Style, Align Right, Increase Indent

Steps e–f: Percent Style, Align Right, Increase Decimal, Increase Indents

Excel 2016, Windows 10, Microsoft Corporation

FIGURE 47 Number Formats and Decimal Places

a. Select the **range C6:C12**. Press and hold **Ctrl** as you select the **ranges E6:E12 and G6:H12**.

Because you want to apply the same format to nonadjacent ranges, you hold down Ctrl while selecting each range.

b. Click **Accounting Number Format** in the Number group. If some cells display pound signs, increase the column widths as needed.

You formatted the selected nonadjacent ranges with the Accounting Number Format. The dollar signs align on the left cell margins and the decimals align.

c. Select the **range D6:D12**, click **Percent Style** in the Number group, and then click **Increase Decimal** in the Number group.

You formatted the values in the selected range with Percent Style and increased the decimal to show one decimal place to avoid misleading your readers by displaying the values as whole percentages.

d. Apply **Percent Style** to the **range F6:F12**.

e. Select the **range I6:I12**, apply **Percent Style**, and then click **Increase Decimal**.

f. Select the **range F6:F12**, click **Align Right**, and then click **Increase Indent** twice. Select the **range I6:I12**, click **Align Right**, and then click **Increase Indent**.

With values, you want to keep the decimal points aligned, but you can then use Increase Indent to adjust the indent so that the values appear more centered below the column labels.

g. Save the workbook. Keep the workbook open if you plan to continue with the next Hands-On Exercise. If not, close the workbook and exit Excel.

Worksheets, Page Setup, and Printing

When you start a new blank workbook in Excel, the workbook contains one worksheet named Sheet1. However, you can add additional worksheets. The text, values, dates, and formulas you enter into the individual worksheets are saved under one workbook file name. Having multiple worksheets in one workbook is helpful to keep related items together.

Although you might distribute workbooks electronically as email attachments or you might upload workbooks to a corporate server, you should prepare the worksheets in case you need to print them or in case others who receive an electronic copy of your workbook want to print the worksheets.

In this section, you will copy, move, and rename worksheets. You will also select options on the Page Layout tab. Specifically, you will use the Page Setup, Scale to Fit, and Sheet Options groups. After selecting page setup options, you will learn how to print your worksheet.

Managing Worksheets

Creating a multiple-worksheet workbook takes some planning and maintenance. Worksheet tab names should reflect the contents of the respective worksheets. In addition, you can insert, copy, move, and delete worksheets within the workbook. You can even apply background color to the worksheet tabs so that they stand out onscreen. Figure 48 shows a workbook in which the sheet tabs have been renamed, colors have been applied to worksheet tabs, and a worksheet tab has been right-clicked so that the shortcut menu appears.

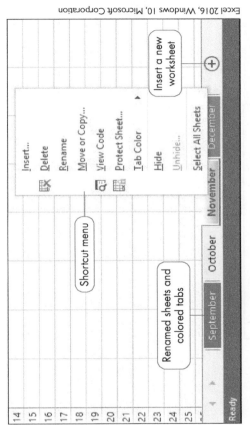

FIGURE 48 Worksheet Tabs

The active sheet tab has a green horizontal bar below the sheet name, and the sheet name is bold and green. If a color (such as Red) has been applied to the sheet tab, the tab shows in the full color when it is not active. When that sheet is active, the sheet tab color is a gradient of the selected color.

Insert and Delete a Worksheet

Sometimes you need more than one worksheet in the workbook. For example, you might want one worksheet for each month to track your monthly income and expenses for one year. When tax time comes around, you have all your data stored in one workbook file. You can insert additional, rename, copy, and move worksheets. Adding worksheets within one workbook enables to you save related sheets of data together.

To insert a new worksheet, complete one of the following sets of steps:

- Click New sheet to the right of the last worksheet tab.
- Click the Insert arrow (either to the right or below Insert) in the Cells group on the Home tab and select Insert Sheet.
- Right-click any sheet tab, select Insert from the shortcut menu (refer to Figure 48), click Worksheet in the Insert dialog box, and click OK.
- Press Shift+F11.

If you no longer need the data in a worksheet, delete the worksheet. Doing so will eliminate extra data in a file and reduce file size.

To delete a worksheet in a workbook, complete one of the following sets of steps:

- Click the Delete arrow (either to the right or below Delete) in the Cells group on the Home tab and select Delete Sheet.
- Right-click any sheet tab and select Delete from the shortcut menu (refer to Figure 48).

If the sheet you are trying to delete contains data, Excel will display a warning: *Microsoft Excel will permanently delete this sheet. Do you want to continue?* Click Delete to delete the worksheet, or click Cancel to keep the worksheet. If you try to delete a blank worksheet, Excel will not display a warning; it will immediately delete the sheet.

Copy or Move a Worksheet

After creating a worksheet, you may want to copy it to use as a template or starting point for similar data. For example, if you create a worksheet for your September budget, you might want to copy the worksheet and easily edit the data on the copied worksheet to enter data for your October budget. Copying the entire worksheet saves you a lot of valuable time in entering and formatting the new worksheet, and it preserves the column widths and row heights. The process for copying a worksheet is similar to moving a sheet.

To copy a worksheet, complete one of the following sets of steps:

- Press and hold Ctrl as you drag the worksheet tab.
- Right-click the sheet tab, select Move or Copy to display the Move or Copy dialog box, select the *To book* and *Before sheet* options (refer to Figure 49), click the *Create a copy* check box, and then click OK.

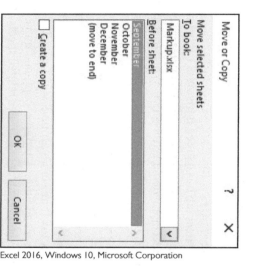

FIGURE 49 Move or Copy Dialog Box

Excel 2016, Windows 10, Microsoft Corporation

You can arrange the worksheet tabs in a different sequence. For example, if the December worksheet is to the left of the October and November worksheets, move the December worksheet to be in chronological order.

To move a worksheet, complete one of the following sets of steps:

- Drag a worksheet tab to the desired location. As you drag a sheet tab, the pointer resembles a piece of paper. A down-pointing triangle appears between sheet tabs to indicate where the sheet will be placed when you release the mouse button.
- Click Format in the Cells group on the Home tab (refer to Figure 35) and select Move or Copy Sheet.
- Right-click the sheet tab you want to move and select Move or Copy to display the Move or Copy dialog box. You can move the worksheet within the current workbook or to a different workbook. In the *Before sheet* list, select the worksheet you want to come after the moved worksheet and click OK.

Rename a Worksheet

The default worksheet name Sheet1 does not describe the contents of the worksheet. You should rename worksheet tabs to reflect the sheet contents. For example, if your budget workbook contains monthly worksheets, name the worksheets September, October, etc. Although you can have spaces in worksheet names, keep worksheet names relatively short. The longer the worksheet names, the fewer sheet tabs you will see at the bottom of the workbook window without scrolling.

To rename a worksheet, complete one of the following sets of steps:

- Double-click a sheet tab, type the new name, and then press Enter.
- Click the sheet tab for the sheet you want to rename, click Format in the Cells group on the Home tab (refer to Figure 35), select Rename Sheet, type the new sheet name, and then press Enter.
- Right-click the sheet tab, select Rename from the shortcut menu (refer to Figure 48), type the new sheet name, and then press Enter.

TIP: CHANGE TAB COLOR

You can change the color of each worksheet tab to emphasize the difference among the sheets. For example, you might apply red to the September tab and yellow to the October tab. Right-click a sheet tab, select Tab Color, and select a color from the color palette.

Selecting Page Setup Options

The Page Setup group on the Page Layout tab contains options to set the margins, select orientation, specify page size, select the print area, and apply other options (see Figure 50). The Scale to Fit group contains options for adjusting the scaling of the spreadsheet on the printed page. When possible, use the commands in these groups to apply page settings. Table 8 lists and describes the commands in the Page Setup group.

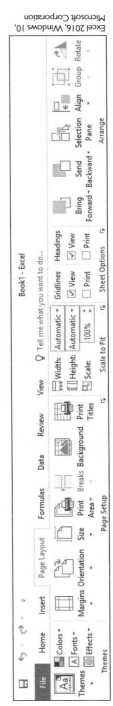

Excel 2016, Windows 10, Microsoft Corporation

FIGURE 50 Page Layout Tab

TABLE 8   Page Setup Commands

Command	Description
Margins	Displays a menu to select predefined margin settings. The default margins are 0.75" top and bottom and 0.7" left and right. You will often change these margin settings to balance the worksheet data better on the printed page. If you need different margins, select Custom Margins.
Orientation	Displays orientation options. The default page orientation is portrait, which is appropriate for worksheets that contain more rows than columns. Select landscape orientation when worksheets contain more columns than can fit in portrait orientation. For example, the OKOS worksheet might appear better balanced in landscape orientation because it has eight columns.
Size	Displays a list of standard paper sizes. The default size is 8 ½" by 11". If you have a different paper size, such as legal paper, select it from the list.
Print Area	Displays a list to set or clear the print area. When you have very large worksheets, you might want to print only a portion of that worksheet. To do so, select the range you want to print, click Print Area in the Page Setup group, and select Set Print Area. When you use the Print commands, only the range you specified will be printed. To clear the print area, click Print Area and select Clear Print Area.
Breaks	Displays a menu to insert or remove page breaks.
Background	Enables you to select an image to appear as the background behind the worksheet data when viewed onscreen (backgrounds do not appear when the worksheet is printed).
Print Titles	Enables you to select column headings and row labels to repeat on multiple-page printouts.

TIP: APPLYING PAGE SETUP OPTIONS TO MULTIPLE WORKSHEETS

When you apply Page Setup Options, those settings apply to the current worksheet only. However, you can apply page setup options, such as margins or a header, to multiple worksheets at the same time. To select adjacent sheets, click the first sheet tab, press and hold Shift, and click the last sheet tab. To select nonadjacent sheets, press and hold Ctrl as you click each sheet tab. Then choose the Page Setup options to apply to the selected sheets. When you are done, right-click a sheet tab and select Ungroup Sheets.

Specify Page Options

STEP 2

To apply several page setup options at once or to access options not found on the Ribbon, click the Page Setup Dialog Box Launcher. The Page Setup dialog box organizes options into four tabs: Page, Margins, Header/Footer, and Sheet. All tabs contain Print and Print Preview buttons. Figure 51 shows the Page tab.

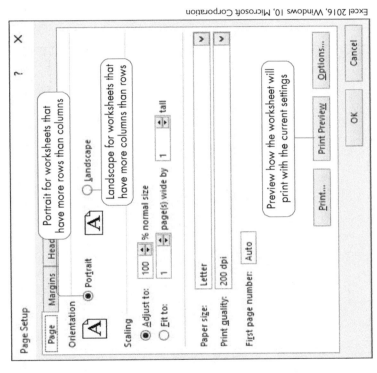

FIGURE 51 Page Setup Dialog Box: Page Tab

The Page tab contains options to select the orientation and paper size. In addition, it contains scaling options that are similar to the options in the Scale to Fit group on the Page Layout tab. You use scaling options to increase or decrease the size of characters on a printed page, similar to using a zoom setting on a photocopy machine. You might want to use the *Fit to* option to force the data to print on a specified number of pages.

Set Margin Options

The Margins tab (see Figure 52) contains options for setting the specific margins. In addition, it contains options to center the worksheet data horizontally or vertically on the page, which are used to balance worksheet data equally between the left and right margins or top and bottom margins, respectively.

Page Setup

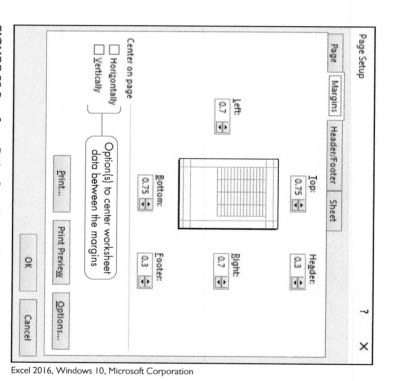

FIGURE 52 Page Setup Dialog Box: Margins Tab

Excel 2016, Windows 10, Microsoft Corporation

STEP 3

Create Headers and Footers

» The Header/Footer tab (see Figure 53) lets you create a header and/or footer that appears at the top and/or bottom of every printed page. Click the arrows to choose from several preformatted entries, or alternatively, click Custom Header or Custom Footer, insert text and other objects, and click the appropriate formatting button to customize the headers and footers. Use headers and footers to provide additional information about the worksheet. You can include your name, the date the worksheet was prepared, and page numbers, for example.

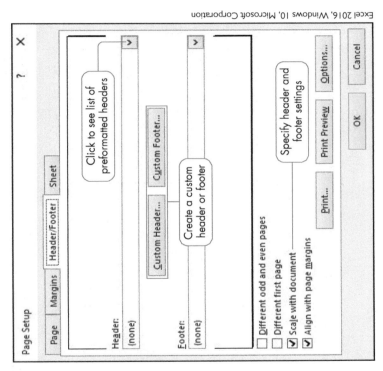

Excel 2016, Windows 10, Microsoft Corporation

FIGURE 53 Page Setup Dialog Box: Header/Footer Tab

You can create different headers or footers on different pages, such as one header with the file name on odd-numbered pages and a header containing the date on even-numbered pages. Click the *Different odd and even pages* check box to select it in the Page Setup dialog box (see Figure 53).

You might want the first page to have a different header or footer from the rest of the printed pages, or you might not want a header or footer to show up on the first page but want the header or footer to display on the remaining pages. Click the *Different first page* check box to select it in the Page Setup dialog box to specify a different first page header or footer.

Instead of creating headers and footers using the Page Setup dialog box, you can click the Insert tab and click Header & Footer in the Text group. Excel displays the worksheet in Page Layout view with the insertion point in the center area of the header. Click inside the left, center, or right section of a header or footer. When you click inside a section within the header or footer, Excel displays the Header & Footer Tools Design contextual tab (see Figure 54). Enter text or insert data from the Header & Footer Elements group on the tab. Table 9 lists and describes the options in the Header & Footer Elements group. To get back to Normal view, click any cell in the worksheet and click Normal in the Workbook Views group on the View tab.

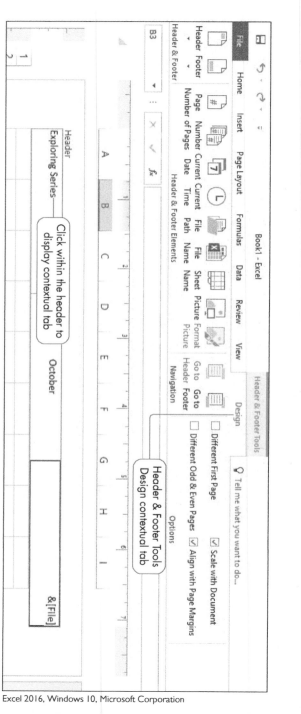

FIGURE 54 Headers & Footer Tools Design Contextual Tab

Excel 2016, Windows 10, Microsoft Corporation

TABLE 9 Header & Footer Elements Options

Option Name	Result
Page Number	Inserts the code &[Page] to display the current page number.
Number of Pages	Inserts the code &[Pages] to display the total number of pages that will print.
Current Date	Inserts the code &[Date] to display the current date, such as 5/19/2018. The date is updated to the current date when you open or print the worksheet.
Current Time	Inserts the code &[Time] to display the current time, such as 5:15 PM. The time is updated to the current time when you open or print the worksheet.
File Path	Inserts the code &[Path]&[File] to display the path and file name, such as C:\Users\Keith\Documents\e01h4Markup. This information changes if you save the workbook with a different name or in a different location.
File Name	Inserts the code &[File] to display the file name, such as e01h4Markup. This information changes if you save the workbook with a different name.
Sheet Name	Inserts the code &[Tab] to display the worksheet name, such as September. This information changes if you rename the worksheet.
Picture	Inserts the code &[Picture] to display and print an image as a background behind the data, not just the worksheet.
Format Picture	Enables you to adjust the brightness, contrast, and size of an image after you use the Picture option.

Pearson Education, Inc.

TIP: VIEW TAB

If you click the View tab and click Page Layout, Excel displays an area *Click to add header* at the top of the worksheet.

Select Sheet Options

The Sheet tab (see Figure 55) contains options for setting the print area, print titles, print options, and page order. Some of these options are also located in the Sheet Options group on the Page Layout tab.

By default, Excel displays gridlines onscreen to show you each cell's margins, but the gridlines do not print unless you specifically select the Gridlines check box in the Page Setup dialog box or the Print Gridlines check box in the Sheet Options group on the Page Layout tab. In addition, Excel displays row (1, 2, 3, etc.) and column (A, B, C, etc.) headings onscreen. However, these headings do not print unless you click the *Row and column headings* check box in the Page Setup dialog box or click the Print Headings check box in the Sheet Options group on the Page Layout tab. For most worksheets, you do not need to print gridlines and row/column headings. However, when you want to display and print cell formulas instead of formula results, you might want to print the gridlines and row/column headings. Doing so will help you analyze your formulas. The gridlines help you see the cell boundaries, and the headings help you identify what data are in each cell. At times, you might want to display gridlines to separate data on a regular printout to increase readability.

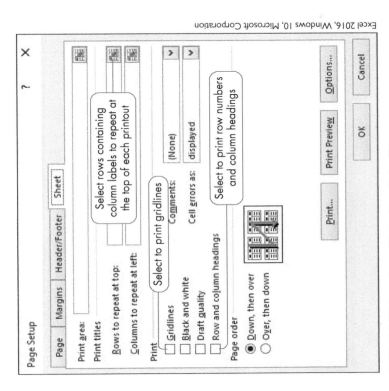

Excel 2016, Windows 10, Microsoft Corporation

FIGURE 55 Page Setup Dialog Box: Sheet Tab

TIP: REPEATING ROWS AND COLUMNS

If you have spreadsheet data that would take more than one printed page, open the Page Setup dialog box, click the Sheet tab, click in the *Rows to repeat at top* box, and then select the row(s) containing column labels. That way, when the pages print, the rows containing the descriptive column labels will repeat at the top of each printed page so that you can easily know what data is in each column. Likewise, if the spreadsheet has too many columns to print on one page, you can click in the *Columns to repeat at left* box on the Sheet tab within the Page Setup dialog box and select the column(s) so that the row labels will display on the left side of each printed page.

Previewing and Printing a Worksheet

STEP 4 » Microsoft Office Backstage view displays print options and displays the worksheet in print preview mode. Print preview helps you see before printing if the data are balanced on the page or if data will print on multiple pages.

You can specify the number of copies to print and which printer to use to print the worksheet. The first option in the Settings area specifies what to print. The default option is Print
Active Sheets. You might want to choose other options, such as Print Entire Workbook or
Print Selection, or specify which pages to print. If you are connected to a printer capable of
duplex printing, you can print on only one side or print on both sides. You can also collate,
change the orientation, specify the paper size, adjust the margins, and adjust the scaling.

The bottom of the Print window indicates how many pages will print. If you do not
like how the worksheet will print, click Page Setup at the bottom of the print settings to
open the Page Setup dialog box so that you can adjust margins, scaling, column widths,
and so on until the worksheet data appear the way you want them to print.

TIP: PRINTING MULTIPLE WORKSHEETS

To print more than one worksheet at a time, select the sheets you want to print. To select adjacent
sheets, click the first sheet tab, press and hold Shift, and click the last sheet tab. To select nonadjacent
sheets, press and hold Ctrl as you click each sheet tab. When you display the Print options in Microsoft
Office Backstage view, Print Active Sheets is one of the default settings. If you want to print all of the
worksheets within the workbook, change the setting to Print Entire Workbook.

Quick Concepts

14. Why would you insert several worksheets of data in one workbook instead of creating
    a separate workbook for each worksheet?

15. Why would you select a *Center on page* option in the Margins tab within the Page Setup
    dialog box if you have already set the margins?

16. List at least five elements you can insert in a header or footer.

17. Why would you want to print gridlines and row and column headings?

5 Worksheets, Page Setup, and Printing

Skills covered: Copy or Move a Worksheet • Rename a Worksheet • Group Worksheets • Set Page Orientation • Select Scaling Options • Set Margin Options • Create a Header or Footer • View in Print Preview • Print a Worksheet

You are ready to complete the OKOS worksheet. You want to copy the existing worksheet so that you display the results on the original sheet and display formulas on the duplicate sheet. Before printing the worksheet for your supervisor, you want to make sure the data will appear professional when printed. You will adjust some page setup options to put the finishing touches on the worksheet.

STEP 1 ›› COPY, MOVE, AND RENAME A WORKSHEET

You want to copy the worksheet, move it to the right side of the original worksheet, and rename the duplicate worksheet so that you can show formulas on the duplicate sheet. Refer to Figure 56 as you complete Step 1.

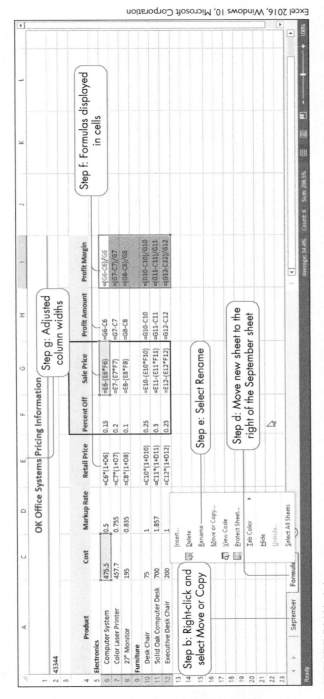

FIGURE 56 Worksheets

Excel 2016, Windows 10, Microsoft Corporation

a. Open *e01h4Markup_LastFirst* if you closed it at the end of Hands-On Exercise 4 and save it as **e01h5Markup_LastFirst**, changing h4 to h5.

b. Right-click the **Sheet1 tab** at the bottom of the worksheet and select **Move or Copy**.

 The Move or Copy dialog box opens so that you can move the existing worksheet or make a copy of it.

c. Click the **Create a copy check box** to select it and click **OK**.

 The duplicate worksheet is named Sheet1 (2) and is placed to the left of the original worksheet.

d. Drag the **Sheet1 (2) worksheet tab** to the right of the Sheet1 worksheet tab.

 The duplicate worksheet is now on the right side of the original worksheet.

e. Right-click the **Sheet1 sheet tab**, select **Rename**, type **September**, and then press **Enter**. Rename Sheet1 (2) as **Formulas**.

 You renamed the original worksheet as September to reflect the September sales data, and you renamed the duplicate worksheet as Formulas to indicate that you will keep the formulas displayed on that sheet.

Hands-On Exercise 5   197

Because the worksheet has several columns, you decide to print it in landscape orientation. You want to set a 1" top margin and center the data between the left and right margins. Furthermore, you want to make sure the data fits on one page on each sheet. Currently, if you were to print the Formulas worksheet, the data would print on two pages. Refer to Figure 57 as you complete Step 2.

STEP 2 ≫ SET PAGE ORIENTATION, SCALING, AND MARGIN OPTIONS

f. Press **Ctrl+`** to display the formulas in the Formulas worksheet.

g. Change these column widths in the Formulas sheet:

- Column A (**13.00**)
- Columns C and D (**6.00**)
- Columns E, G, H, and I (**7.00**)
- Column F (**5.00**)

You reduced the column widths so that the data will fit on a printout better.

h. Save the workbook.

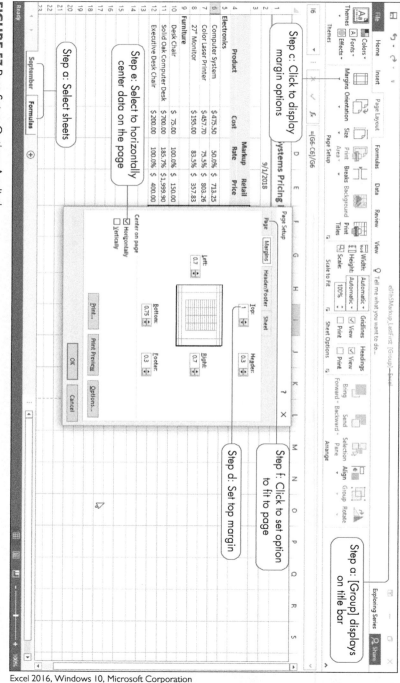

FIGURE 57 Page Setup Options Applied

Step c: Click to display margin options

Step e: Select to horizontally center data on the page

Step a: Select sheets

Step d: Set top margin

Step f: Click to set option to fit to page

Step a: [Group] displays on title bar

Excel 2016, Windows 10, Microsoft Corporation

a. Click the **September sheet tab**, press and hold down **Ctrl**, and then click the **Formulas sheet tab**.

Both worksheets are grouped together as indicated by [Group] after the file name on the title bar. Anything you do on one sheet affects both sheets.

b. Click the **Page Layout tab**, click **Orientation** in the Page Setup group, and then select **Landscape** from the list.

Because both worksheets are grouped, both worksheets are formatted in landscape orientation.

c. Click **Margins** in the Page Setup group on the Page Layout tab and select **Custom Margins**. The Page Setup dialog box opens with the Margins tab options displayed.

d. Click the **Top spin arrow** to display **1**.

Because both worksheets are grouped, the 1" top margin is set for both worksheets.

Hands-On Exercise 5

198

e. Click the **Horizontally check box** to select it in the Center on page section.

Because both worksheets are grouped, the data on each worksheet are centered between the left and right margins.

f. Click the **Page tab** within the Page Setup dialog box, click **Fit to** in the Scaling section, and then click **OK**. Save the workbook.

The Fit to option ensures that each sheet fits on one page.

STEP 3 ›› **CREATE A HEADER**

To document the grouped worksheets, you want to include your name, the sheet name, and the file name in a header. Refer to Figure 58 as you complete Step 3.

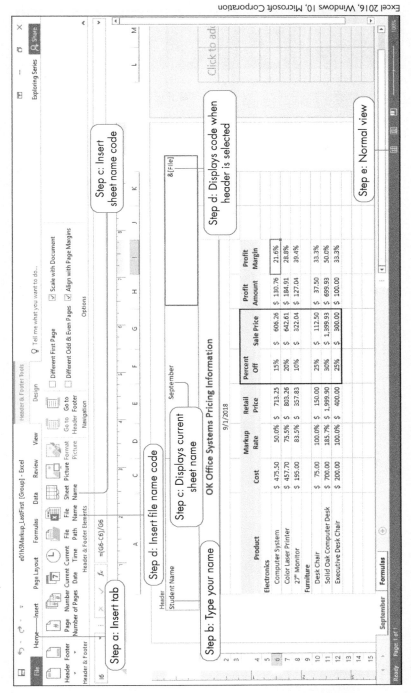

FIGURE 58 Header

a. Ensure the worksheets are still grouped, click the **Insert tab**, and then click **Header & Footer** in the Text group.

Excel displays the Header & Footer Tools Design contextual tab and the worksheet displays in Page Layout view, which displays the header area, margin space, and ruler. The insertion point blinks inside the center section of the header.

b. Click in the left section of the header and type your name.

c. Click in the center section of the header and click **Sheet Name** in the Header & Footer Elements group on the Design tab.

Excel inserts the code &[Tab]. This code displays the name of the worksheet. If you change the worksheet tab name, the header will reflect the new sheet name.

d. Click in the right section of the header and click **File Name** in the Header & Footer Elements group on the Design tab.

Excel inserts the code &[File]. This code displays the name of the file. Because the worksheets were grouped when you created the header, a header will appear on both worksheets. The file name will be the same; however, the sheet names will be different.

Hands-On Exercise 5

Excel 2016, Windows 10, Microsoft Corporation

e. Click in any cell in the worksheet, click **Normal** on the status bar, and then save the workbook.

Normal view displays the worksheet, but does not display the header or margins.

f. Click the **Review tab** and click **Spelling** in the Proofing group. Correct all errors, if any, and click **OK** when prompted with the message, *Spell check complete. You're good to go!* Save the workbook.

You should always spell-check a workbook before publishing it.

STEP 4 >> VIEW IN PRINT PREVIEW AND PRINT

Before printing the worksheets, you should preview it. Doing so helps you detect margin problems and other issues, such as a single row or column of data flowing onto a new page. Refer to Figure 59 as you complete Step 4.

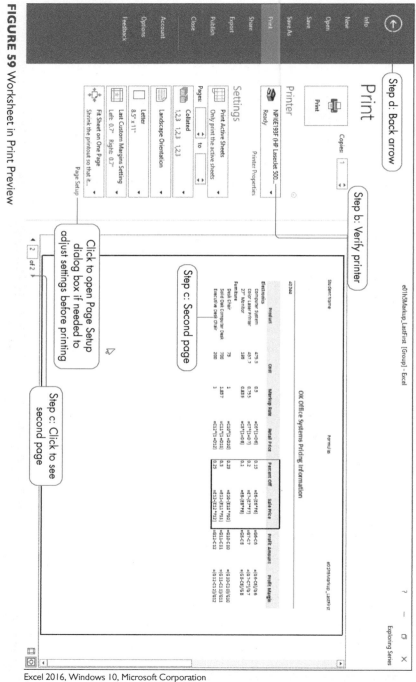

FIGURE 59 Worksheet in Print Preview

Excel 2016, Windows 10, Microsoft Corporation

a. Click the **File tab** and click **Print**.

The Microsoft Office Backstage view displays print options and a preview of the worksheet.

b. Verify the Printer box displays the printer that you want to use to print your worksheet, and verify the last Settings option displays Fit Sheet on One Page.

The bottom of Backstage shows 1 of 2, indicating two pages will print.

c. Click **Next Page** to see the second page, which is the data on the Formulas worksheet, and verify the last Settings option displays Fit Sheet on One Page.

Check the Print Preview window to make sure the data are formatted correctly and would print correctly.

d. Click the **Back arrow** and save the workbook.

Although you did not print the worksheets, all the print options are saved.

e. Save and close the file. Based on your instructor's directions, submit e01h5Markup_ LastFirst. Once the file is closed, the Formulas sheet may not display the formulas when you open the workbook again. If that happens, press **Ctrl+`** again.

Chapter Objectives Review

After reading this chapter, you have accomplished the following objectives:

1. Explore the Excel window.

- A worksheet is a single spreadsheet containing data. A workbook is a collection of one or more related worksheets contained in a single file.
- Identify Excel window elements: The Name Box displays the name of the current cell. The Formula Bar displays the contents of the current cell. The active cell is the current cell. A sheet tab shows the name of the worksheet.
- Identify columns, rows, and cells: Columns have alphabetical headings, such as A, B, C. Rows have numbers, such as 1, 2, 3. A cell is the intersection of a column and row and is indicated with a column letter and a row number.
- Navigate in and among worksheets: Use the arrow keys to navigate within a sheet, or use the Go To command to go to a specific cell. Click a sheet tab to display the contents on another worksheet.

2. Enter and edit cell data.

- You should plan the worksheet design by stating the purpose, deciding what output you need, and then identifying what input values are needed. Next, you enter and format data in a worksheet. Finally, you document, save, and then share a workbook.
- Enter text: Text may contain letters, numbers, symbols, and spaces. Text aligns at the left side of a cell.
- Use Auto Fill to complete a sequence. Auto Fill can automatically fill in sequences, such as month names or values, after you enter the first label or value. Double-click the fill handle to fill in the sequence.
- Enter values: Values are numbers that represent a quantity. Values align at the right side of a cell by default.
- Enter dates and times: Excel stores dates and times as serial numbers so that you can calculate the number of days between dates or times.
- Edit and clear contents: You might want to edit the contents of a cell to correct errors or to make labels more descriptive. Use the Clear option to clear the cell contents and/or formats.

3. Create formulas.

- A formula is used to perform a calculation. The formula results display in the cell.
- Use cell references in formulas: Use references, such as =B5+B6, instead of values within formulas.
- Apply the order of operations: The most commonly used operators are performed in this sequence: Parentheses, exponentiation, multiplication, division, addition, and subtraction.

- Use semi-selection to create a formula: When building a formula, click a cell containing a value to enter that cell reference in the formula.
- Copy formulas with the fill handle: Double-click the fill handle to copy a formula down a column.

4. Display cell formulas.

- By default, the results of formulas appear in cells.
- Display formulas by pressing Ctrl+`.

5. Manage columns and rows.

- Insert cells, columns, and rows: Insert a cell to move the remaining cells down or to the right. Insert a new column or row for data.
- Delete cells, columns, and rows: You should delete cells, columns, and rows you no longer need.
- Hide and unhide columns and rows: Hiding rows and columns protects confidential data from being displayed.
- Adjust column width: Double-click between the column headings to widen a column based on the longest item in that column, or drag the border between column headings to increase or decrease a column width.
- Adjust row height: Drag the border between row headings to increase or decrease the height of a row.

6. Select, move, copy, and paste data.

- Select a range: A range may be a single cell or a rectangular block of cells.
- Move a range to another location: After selecting a range, cut it from its location. Then select the top-left corner of the destination range to make it the active cell and paste the range there.
- Copy and paste a range: After selecting a range, click Copy, click the top-left corner of the destination range, and then click Paste to make a copy of the original range.
- Use Paste Options and Paste Special: The Paste Special option enables you to specify how the data are pasted into the worksheet.
- Copy Excel data to other programs: You can copy Excel data and paste it in other programs, such as in Word or PowerPoint.

7. Apply cell styles, alignment, and font options.

- Cell styles contain a collection of formatting, such as font, font color, font size, fill, and borders. You can apply an Excel cell style to save formatting time.
- Merge and center labels: Type a label in the left cell, select a range including the data you typed, and then click Merge & Center to merge cells and center the label within the newly merged cell.

- Change horizontal and vertical cell alignment: The default horizontal alignment depends on the data entered, and the default vertical alignment is Bottom Align.

- Wrap text: Use the Wrap Text option to present text on multiple lines in order to avoid having extra-wide columns.

- Increase and decrease indent: To indicate hierarchy of data or to offset a label, increase or decrease how much the data are indented in a cell.

- Apply borders and fill colors: Borders and fill colors help improve readability of worksheets.

8. Apply number formats.

- Apply a number format: The default number format is General, which does not apply any particular format to values. Apply appropriate formats to values to present the data with the correct symbols and decimal alignment. For example, Accounting Number Format is a common number format for monetary values.

- Increase and decrease decimal places: After applying a number format, you might want to increase or decrease the number of decimal places displayed.

9. Manage worksheets.

- Insert and delete a worksheet: You can insert new worksheets to include related data within one workbook, or you can delete extra worksheets you do not need.

- Copy or move a worksheet: Drag a sheet tab to rearrange the worksheets. You can copy a worksheet within a workbook or to another workbook.

- Rename a worksheet: The default worksheet tab name is Sheet1, but you should change the name to describe the contents of the worksheet.

10. Select page setup options.

- The Page Layout tab on the Ribbon contains options for setting margins, selecting orientation, specifying page size, selecting the print area, and applying other settings.

- Specify page options: Page options include orientation, paper size, and scaling.

- Set margin options: You can set the left, right, top, and bottom margins. In addition, you can center worksheet data horizontally and vertically on a page.

- Create headers and footers: Insert a header or footer to display documentation, such as your name, date, time, and worksheet tab name.

- Select sheet options: Sheet options control the print area, print titles, print options, and page order.

11. Preview and print a worksheet.

- Before printing a worksheet, you should display a preview to ensure the data will print correctly. The Print Preview helps you see if margins are correct or if isolated rows or columns will print on separate pages.

- After making appropriate adjustments, you can print the worksheet.

Key Terms Matching

Match the key terms with their definitions. Write the key term letter by the appropriate numbered definition.

a. Alignment
b. Auto Fill
c. Cell
d. Column width
e. Fill color
f. Fill handle
g. Formula
h. Formula Bar
i. Input area
j. Name Box

k. Order of operations
l. Output area
m. Range
n. Row height
o. Sheet tab
p. Text
q. Value
r. Workbook
s. Worksheet
t. Wrap text

1. _____ A spreadsheet that contains formulas, functions, values, text, and visual aids.

2. _____ A file containing related worksheets.

3. _____ A range of cells containing values for variables used in formulas.

4. _____ A range of cells containing results based on manipulating the variables.

5. _____ Identifies the address of the current cell.

6. _____ Displays the content (text, value, date, or formula) in the active cell.

7. _____ Displays the name of a worksheet within a workbook.

8. _____ The intersection of a column and row.

9. _____ Includes letters, numbers, symbols, and spaces.

10. _____ A number that represents a quantity or an amount.

11. _____ Rules that control the sequence in which Excel performs arithmetic operations.

12. _____ Enables you to copy the contents of a cell or cell range or to continue a sequence by dragging the fill handle over an adjacent cell or range of cells.

13. _____ A small green square at the bottom-right corner of a cell.

14. _____ The horizontal measurement of a column.

15. _____ The vertical measurement of a row.

16. _____ A rectangular group of cells.

17. _____ The position of data between the cell margins.

18. _____ Formatting that enables a label to appear on multiple lines within the current cell.

19. _____ The background color appearing behind data in a cell.

20. _____ A combination of cell references, operators, values, and/or functions used to perform a calculation.

Multiple Choice

1. Which step is *not* part of planning a worksheet design?
   (a) Decide what input values are needed.
   (b) State the purpose of the worksheet.
   (c) Decide what outputs are needed to achieve the purpose.
   (d) Enter labels, values, and formulas.

2. You just copied a range of data containing formulas. However, you want to preserve the formula results and the original number and text formatting in the pasted range. Which paste option would you select?
   (a) Formulas
   (b) Keep Source Formatting
   (c) Values & Source Formatting
   (d) Values & Number Formatting

3. Given the formula =B1*B2+B3/B4^2, what operation is calculated first?
   (a) B1*B2
   (b) B2+B3
   (c) B3/B4
   (d) B4^2

4. How can you display formulas within the cells instead of the cell results?
   (a) Press Ctrl+G.
   (b) Press Ctrl+`.
   (c) Click Cell References on the Home tab.
   (d) Press Ctrl+C.

5. What is a fast way to apply several formats at one time?
   (a) Click each one individually.
   (b) Apply a cell style.
   (c) Use Auto Fill.
   (d) Use Copy and Paste options.

6. Which of the following is *not* an alignment option?
   (a) Increase Indent
   (b) Merge & Center
   (c) Fill Color
   (d) Wrap Text

7. Which of the following characteristics is *not* applicable to the Accounting Number Format?
   (a) Dollar sign immediately on the left side of the value
   (b) Commas to separate thousands
   (c) Two decimal places
   (d) Zero values displayed as hyphens

8. You selected and copied worksheet data containing formulas. However, you want the pasted copy to contain the current formula results rather than formulas. What do you do?
   (a) Click Paste in the Clipboard group on the Home tab.
   (b) Click the Paste arrow in the Clipboard group and select Formulas.
   (c) Click the Paste arrow in the Clipboard group and select Values & Source Formatting.
   (d) Display the Paste Special dialog box and select Formulas & Number Formatting.

9. Assume that the data on a worksheet consume a whole printed page and a couple of columns on a second page. You can do all of the following *except* what to force the data to print all on one page?
   (a) Decrease the Scale value.
   (b) Increase the left and right margins.
   (c) Decrease column widths if possible.
   (d) Select a smaller range as the print area.

10. What should you do if you see pound signs (###) instead of values or results of formulas?
    (a) Increase the zoom percentage.
    (b) Delete the column.
    (c) Adjust the row height.
    (d) Increase the column width.

Practice Exercises

1 Mathematics Review

You want to brush up on your math skills to test your logic by creating formulas in Excel. You realize that you should avoid values in formulas most of the time. Therefore, you created an input area that contains values you will use in your formulas. To test your knowledge of formulas, you will create an output area that will contain a variety of formulas using cell references from the input area. You will include a formatted title, the date prepared, and your name. After creating and verifying formula results, you will change input values and observe changes in the formula results. You want to display cell formulas, so you will create a picture copy of the formulas view. Refer to Figure 60 as you complete this exercise.

	A	B	C	D	E
1			Excel Formulas and Order of Precedence		
2	Date Created:	42614	Student Name		
3					
4	Input Area:		Output Area:		
5	First Value	2	Sum of 1st and 2nd values		=B5+B6
6	Second Value	4	Difference between 4th and 1st values		=B8-B5
7	Third Value	6	Product of 2nd and 3rd values		=B6*B7
8	Fourth Value	8	Quotient of 3rd and 1st values		=B7/B5
9			2nd value to the power of 3rd value		=B6^B7
10			1st value added to product of 2nd and 4th values and difference between sum and 3rd value		=B5+B6*B8-B7
11			Product of sum of 1st and 2nd and difference between 4th and 3rd values		=(B5+B6)*(B8-B7)
12			Product of 1st and 2nd added to product of 3rd and 4th values		=(B5*B6)+(B7*B8)

Excel 2016, Windows 10, Microsoft Corporation

FIGURE 60 Formula Practice

a. Open *e01p1Math* and save it as **e01p1Math_LastFirst.**

b. Type the current date in **cell B2** in this format: 9/1/2018. Type your first and last names in **cell D2.**

c. Adjust the column widths by doing the following:

- Click in any cell in column A and click **Format** in the Cells group.
- Select **Column Width**, type **12.57** in the Column width box, and then click **OK.**
- Click in any cell in column B and set the width to **11.**
- Click in any cell in column D and set the width to **35.57.**

d. Select the **range A1:E1**, click **Merge & Center** in the Alignment group, click **Bold** in the Font group, and then change the font size to **14.**

e. Select the **range B5:B8** and click **Center** in the Alignment group.

f. Select the **range D10:D12** and click **Wrap Text** in the Alignment group.

g. Enter the following formulas in column E:

- Click **cell E5.** Type **=B5+B6** and press **Enter.** Excel adds the value stored in cell B5 (1) to the value stored in cell B6 (2). The result (3) appears in cell E5, as described in cell D5.
- Enter appropriate formulas in **cells E6:E8**, pressing **Enter** after entering each formula. Subtract to calculate a difference, multiply to calculate a product, and divide to calculate a quotient.
- Type **=B6^B7** in **cell E9** and press **Enter.** Calculate the answer: 2*2*2 = 8.
- Enter **=B5+B6*B8-B7** in **cell E10** and press **Enter.** Calculate the answer: 2*4 = 8; 1+8 = 9; 9-3 = 6. Multiplication occurs first, followed by addition, and finally subtraction.
- Enter **=(B5+B6)*(B8-B7)** in **cell E11** and press **Enter.** Calculate the answer: 1+2 = 3; 4-3 = 1; 3*1 = 3. This formula is almost identical to the previous formula; however, calculations in parentheses occur before the multiplication.
- Enter **=B5*B6+B7*B8** in **cell E12** and press **Enter.** Calculate the answer: 1*2 = 2; 3*4 = 12; 2+12 = 14.

h. Edit a formula and the input values:

- Click **cell E12** and click in the Formula Bar to edit the formula. Add parentheses as shown: **=(B5*B6)+(B7*B8)** and click **Enter** to the left side of the Formula Bar. The answer is still 14. The parentheses do not affect order of operations because multiplication occurred before the addition. The parentheses help improve the readability of the formula.

- Type **2** in **cell B5**, **4** in **cell B6**, **6** in **cell B7**, and **8** in **cell B8**.

- Double-check the results of the formulas using a calculator or your head. The new results in cells E5:E12 should be 6, 6, 24, 3, 4096, 28, 12, and 56, respectively.

i. Double-click the **Sheet1 tab**, type **Results**, and then press **Enter**. Right-click the **Results sheet tab**, select **Move or Copy**, click **(move to end)** in the *Before sheet* section, click the **Create a copy check box** to select it, and click **OK**. Double-click the **Results (2) sheet tab**, type **Formulas**, and then press **Enter**.

j. Ensure that the Formulas sheet tab is active, click the **Formulas sheet tab** and click **Show Formulas** in the Formula Auditing group. Double-click between the column A and column B headings to adjust the column A width. Double-click between the column B and column C headings to adjust the column B width. Set **24.00 width** for column D.

k. Ensure that the Formulas worksheet is active, click the **Page Layout tab**, and do the following:

- Click the **Gridlines Print check box** to select it in the Sheet Options group.
- Click the **Headings Print check box** to select it in the Sheet Options group.

l. Click the **Results sheet tab**, press and hold **Ctrl**, and click the **Formulas sheet tab** to select both worksheets. Do the following:

- Click **Orientation** in the Page Setup group and select **Landscape**.
- Click the **Insert tab**, click **Header & Footer** in the Text group. Click **Go to Footer** in the Navigation group.
- Type your name on the left side of the footer.
- Click in the center section of the footer and click **Sheet Name** in the Header & Footer Elements group.
- Click in the right section of the footer and click **File Name** in the Header & Footer elements group.

m. Click in the worksheet, press **Ctrl+Home**, and click **Normal View** on the status bar.

n. Click the **File tab** and click **Print**. Verify that each worksheet will print on one page. Press **Esc** to close the Print Preview, and right-click the worksheet tab and click **Ungroup Sheets.**

o. Save and close the file. Based on your instructor's directions, submit e01p1Math_LastFirst.

2 Calendar Formatting

FROM SCRATCH

You want to create a calendar for July 2018. The calendar will enable you to practice alignment settings, including center, merge and center, and indents. In addition, you will need to adjust column widths and increase row height to create cells large enough to enter important information, such as birthdays, in your calendar. You will create a formula and use Auto Fill to complete the days of the week and the days within each week. To improve the appearance of the calendar, you will add fill colors, font colors, and borders to create a red, white, and blue effect to celebrate Independence Day. Refer to Figure 61 as you complete this exercise.

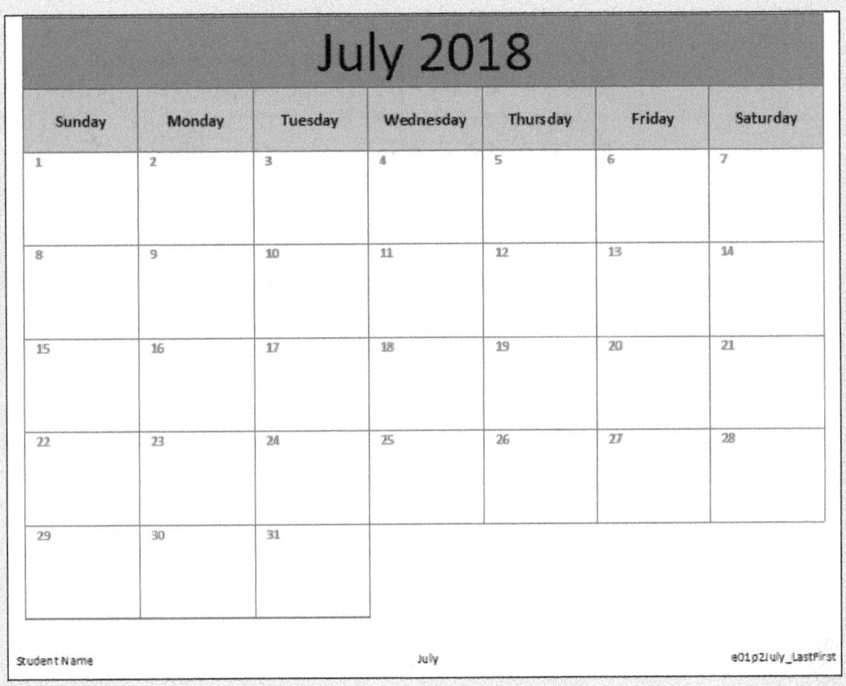

Excel 2016, Windows 10, Microsoft Corporation

July 2018

Sunday	Monday	Tuesday	Wednesday	Thursday	Friday	Saturday
1	2	3	4	5	6	7
8	9	10	11	12	13	14
15	16	17	18	19	20	21
22	23	24	25	26	27	28
29	30	31				

Student Name   July   e01p2July_LastFirst

FIGURE 6 I Calendar

a. Click the **File tab**, select **New**, and click **Blank workbook**. Save the workbook as **e01p2July_LastFirst**.

b. Type **'July 2018** in **cell A1** and click **Enter** on the left side of the Formula Bar.

> **TROUBLESHOOTING:** If you do not type the apostrophe before July 2018, the cell will display July-18 instead of July 2018.

c. Format the title:

- Select the **range A1:G1** and click **Merge & Center** in the Alignment group.
- Change the font size to **48**.
- Click the **Fill Color arrow** and click **Blue** in the Standard Colors section of the color palette.
- Click **Middle Align** in the Alignment group.

d. Complete the days of the week:

- Type **Sunday** in **cell A2** and click **Enter** to the left side of the Formula Bar.
- Drag the **cell A2 fill handle** across the row through **cell G2** to use Auto Fill to complete the rest of the weekdays.
- Ensure that the **range A2:G2** is selected. Click the **Fill Color arrow** and select **Blue, Accent 1, Lighter 40%** in the Theme Colors section of the color palette.
- Apply bold and change the font size to **14 size** to the selected range.
- Click **Middle Align** and click **Center** in the Alignment group to format the selected range.

e. Complete the days of the month:

- Type **1** in **cell A3** and press **Ctrl+Enter**. Drag the **cell A3 fill handle** across the row through **cell G3**.
- Click **Auto Fill Options** in the bottom-right corner of the copied data and select **Fill Series** to change the numbers to 1 through 7.
- Type **=A3+7** in **cell A4** and press **Ctrl+Enter**. Usually you avoid numbers in formulas, but the number of days in a week is always 7. Drag the **cell A4 fill handle** down through **cell A7** to get the date for each Sunday in July.

- Keep the **range A4:A7** selected and drag the fill handle across through **cell G7**. This action copies the formulas to fill in the days in the month.
- Select the **range D7:G7** and press **Delete** to delete the extra days 32 through 35 because July has only 31 days.

f. Format the columns and rows:

- Select **columns A:G**. Click **Format** in the Cells group, select **Column Width**, type **16** in the Column width box, and then click **OK**.
- Select **row 2**. Click **Format** in the Cells group, select **Row Height**, type **54**, and then click **OK**.
- Select **rows 3:7**. Set the row height to **80**.

g. Apply borders around the cells:

- Select the **range A1:G7**. Click the **Borders arrow** in the Font group and select **More Borders** to display the Format Cells dialog box with the Border tab selected.
- Click the **Color arrow** and select **Red**.
- Click **Outline** and **Inside** in the Presets section. Click **OK**. This action applies a red border inside and outside the selected range.

h. Clear the border formatting around cells that do not have days:

- Select the **range D7:G7**.
- Click **Clear** in the Editing group and select **Clear All**. This action removes the red borders around the cells after the last day of the month.

i. Format the days in the month:

- Select the **range A3:G7**. Click **Top Align** and **Align Left** in the Alignment group.
- Click **Increase Indent** in the Alignment group to offset the days from the border.
- Click **Bold** in the Font group, click the **Font Color arrow** and select **Blue**, and click the **Font Size arrow**, and then select **12**.

j. Double-click the **Sheet1 tab**, type **July**, and then press **Enter**.

k. Deselect the range and click the **Page Layout tab** and do the following:

- Click **Orientation** in the Page Setup group and select **Landscape**.
- Click **Margins** in the Page Setup group and select **Custom Margins**. Click the **Horizontally check box** to select it in the *Center on page* section and click **OK**.

l. Click the **Insert tab** and click **Header & Footer** in the Text group and do the following:

- Click **Go to Footer** in the Navigation group.
- Click in the left side of the footer and type your name.
- Click in the center of the footer and click **Sheet Name** in the Header & Footer Elements group on the Design tab.
- Click in the right side of the footer and click **File Name** in the Header & Footer Elements group on the Design tab.
- Click in any cell in the workbook, press **Ctrl+Home**, and then click **Normal** on the status bar.

m. Save and close the file. Based on your instructor's directions, submit e01p2July_LastFirst.

You are the assistant manager at Downtown Theatre, where touring Broadway plays and musicals are performed. You will analyze ticket sales by completing a worksheet that focuses on seating charts for each performance. The spreadsheet will identify the seating sections, total seats in each section, and the number of seats sold for a performance. You will then calculate the percentage of seats sold and unsold. Refer to Figure 62 as you complete this exercise.

	A	B	C	D	E	F
1		Downtown Theatre				
2		Ticket Sales by Seating Section				
3		3/31/2018				
4						
		Available Seats	Seats Sold	Percentage Sold	Percentage Unsold	
5	Section					
6	Box Seats	25	12	48.0%	52.0%	
7	Front Floor	120	114	95.0%	5.0%	
8	Back Floor	132	108	81.8%	18.2%	
9	Tier 1	40	40	100.0%	0.0%	
10	Mezzanine	144	138	95.8%	4.2%	
11	Balcony	106	84	79.2%	20.8%	

Excel 2016, Windows 10, Microsoft Corporation

FIGURE 62 Theatre Seating Data

a. Open *e01p3TicketSales* and save it as **e01p3TicketSales_LastFirst**.
b. Double-click the **Sheet1 sheet tab**, type **Seating**, and press **Enter**.
c. Type **3/31/2018** in cell **A3** and press **Enter**.
d. Format the title:
 • Select the **range A1:E1** and click **Merge & Center** in the Alignment group.
 • Click **Cell Styles** in the Styles group and select **Title** in the Titles and Headings section.
 • Click **Bold** in the Font group.
e. Format the subtitle and date:
 • Use the Merge & Center command to merge the **range A2:E2** and center the subtitle.
 • Use the Merge & Center command to merge the **range A3:E3** and center the date.
f. Select the **range A5:E5**, click **Wrap Text**, click **Center**, and click **Bold** to format the column labels.
g. Right-click the **row 9 heading** and select **Insert** from the shortcut menu to insert a new row. Type the following data in the new row: **Back Floor**, **132**, **108**.
h. Move the Balcony row to be the last row by doing the following:
 • Click the **row 6 heading** and click **Cut** in the Clipboard group on the Home tab.
 • Right-click the **row 12 heading** and select **Insert Cut Cells** from the menu.
i. Adjust column widths by doing the following:
 • Double-click between the column A and column B headings.
 • Select columns **B** and **C headings** to select the columns, click **Format** in the Cells group, select **Column Width**, type **9** in the **Column width box**, and then click **OK**. Because columns B and C contain similar data, you set the same width for these columns.
 • Set the width of columns D and E to **12**.
j. Select the **range B6:C11**, click **Align Right** in the Alignment group, and then click **Increase Indent** twice in the Alignment group.

k. Click **cell D6** and use semi-selection to calculate and format the percentage of sold and unsold seats by doing the following:

- Type =, click **cell C6**, type /, and then click **cell B6** to enter =C6/B6.
- Press **Tab** to enter the formula and make cell E6 the active cell. This formula divides the number of seats sold by the total number of Box Seats.
- Type **=(B6-C6)/B6** and click **Enter** on the left side of the Formula Bar to enter the formula and keep cell E6 the active cell. This formula must first subtract the number of sold seats from the available seats to calculate the number of unsold seats. The difference is divided by the total number of available seats to determine the percentage of unsold seats.
- Select the **range D6:E6**, click **Percent Style** in the Number group, and then click **Increase Decimal** in the Number group. Keep the range selected.
- Double-click the **cell E6 fill handle** to copy the selected formulas down their respective columns. Keep the range selected.
- Click **Align Right** in the Alignment group and click **Increase Indent** twice in the Alignment group. These actions will help center the data below the column labels. Do not click Center; doing so will center each value and cause the decimal points not to align. Deselect the range.

l. Display and preserve a screenshot of the formulas by doing the following:

- Click **New sheet**, double-click the **Sheet1 sheet tab**, type **Formulas**, and then press **Enter.**
- Click the **View tab** and click **Gridlines** in the Show group to hide the gridlines on the Formulas worksheet. This action will prevent the cell gridlines from bleeding through the screenshot you are about to embed.
- Click the **Seating sheet tab**, click the **Formulas tab** on the Ribbon, and then click **Show Formulas** in the Formula Auditing group to display cell formulas.
- Click **cell A1** and drag down to **cell E11** to select the range of data.
- Click the **Home tab**, click **Copy arrow** in the Clipboard group, select **Copy as Picture,** and then click **OK** in the Copy Picture dialog box.
- Click the **Formulas sheet tab**, click **cell A1**, and then click **Paste.**
- Click the **Page Layout tab**, click **Orientation** in the Page Setup group, and then select **Landscape** to change the orientation for the Formulas sheet.
- Click the **Seating sheet tab**, click the **Formulas tab**, and then click **Show Formulas** in the Formula Auditing group to hide the cell formulas.

m. Click the **Seating sheet tab**, press **Ctrl** and click the **Formulas sheet tab** to group the two sheets. Click the **Page Layout tab**, click **Margins** in the Page Setup group, and then select **Custom Margins.** Click the **Horizontally check box** to select it and click **Print Preview.** Excel centers the data horizontally based on the widest item in each worksheet. Verify that the worksheets each print on one page. If not, go back into the Page Setup dialog box for each worksheet and reapply settings if needed. Press **Esc** to leave the Print Preview mode.

n. Click the **Page Setup Dialog Box Launcher**, click the **Header/Footer tab** in the Page Setup dialog box, click **Custom Footer**, click in the center section of the header and type your name, click in the center section of the header, click **Insert File Name**, and then click **OK** to close the Footer dialog box. Click **of the header**, click **Insert Sheet Name**, click in the **right section of the header**, click **Insert File Name**, and then click **OK** to close the Footer dialog box. Click **OK** to close the Page Setup dialog box.

o. Right-click the **Seating sheet tab** and select **Ungroup Sheets.**

p. Save and close the file. Based on your instructor's directions, submit e01p3TicketSales_LastFirst.

Mid-Level Exercises

Guest House Rental Rates

ANALYSIS CASE

You manage a beach guest house in Ft. Lauderdale containing three types of rental units. Prices are based on peak and off-peak times of the year. You want to calculate the maximum daily revenue for each rental type, assuming all units are rented. In addition, you will calculate the discount rate for off-peak rental times. Finally, you will improve the appearance of the worksheet by applying font, alignment, and number formats.

a. Open *e01m1Rentals* and save it as **e01m1Rentals_LastFirst**.

b. Apply the **Heading 1** cell style to the **range A1:G1** and the **20% - Accent1** cell style to the **range A2:G2**.

c. Merge and center Peak Rentals in the **range C4:D4**, over the two columns of peak rental data. Apply **Dark Red fill color** and **White, Background 1 font color**.

d. Merge and center Off-Peak Rentals in the **range E4:G4** over the three columns of off-peak rental data. Apply **Blue fill color** and **White, Background 1 font color**.

e. Center and wrap the headings on row 5. Adjust the width of columns D and E, if needed. Center the data in the **range B6:B8**.

f. Create and copy the following formulas:

- Calculate the Peak Rentals Maximum Revenue by multiplying the number of units by the peak rental price per day.

- Calculate the Off-Peak Rentals Maximum Revenue by multiplying the number of units by the off-peak rental price per day.

- Calculate the Discount rate for the Off-Peak rental price per day. For example, using the peak and off-peak per day values, the studio apartment rents for 75% of its peak rental rate. However, you need to calculate and display the off-peak discount rate, which is .20 for the Studio Apartment. To calculate the discount rate, divide the off-peak per day rate by the peak per day rate. Subtract that result from 1, which represents 100%.

g. Format the monetary values with **Accounting Number Format**. Format the Discount Rate formula results in **Percent Style** with one decimal place. Adjust column widths if necessary to display the data.

h. Apply **Blue, Accent 1, Lighter 80% fill color** to the **range E5:G8**.

i. Select the **range C5:D8** and apply a custom color with **Red 242, Green 220**, and **Blue 219**.

j.  Answer the four questions below the worksheet data. If you change any values to answer the questions, change the values back to the original values.

k. Create a copy of the Rental Rates worksheet, place the new sheet to the right side of the original worksheet, and rename the new sheet **Formulas**. Display cell formulas on the Formulas sheet.

l. Group the worksheets and do the following:

- Select landscape orientation.
- Set **1"** top, bottom, left, and right margins. Center the data horizontally on the page.
- Insert a footer with your name on the left side, the sheet name code in the center, and the file name code on the right side.
- Apply the setting to fit to one page.

m. Click the **Formulas sheet tab** and set options to print gridlines and headings. Adjust column widths.

n. Save and close the file. Based on your instructor's directions, submit e01m1Rentals_LastFirst.

2 Real Estate Sales Report

You are a small real estate agent in Indianapolis. You track the real estate properties you list for clients. You want to analyze sales for selected properties. Yesterday, you prepared a workbook with a worksheet for recent sales data and another worksheet listing several properties you listed. You want to calculate the number of days that the houses were on the market and their sales percentage of the list price. In one situation, the house was involved in a bidding war between two families that really wanted the house. Therefore, the sale price exceeded the list price.

a. Open *e01m2Sales* and save it as **e01m2Sales_LastFirst.**

b. Delete the row that has incomplete sales data. The owners took their house off the market.

c. Type **2018-001** in **cell A5** and use Auto Fill to complete the series to assign a property ID to each property.

d. Calculate the number of days each house was on the market in column C. Copy the formula down that column.

e. Format list prices and sold prices with **Accounting Number Format** with zero decimal places.

f. Calculate the sales price percentage of the list price in cell H5. The second house was listed for $500,250, but it sold for only $400,125. Therefore, the sale percentage of the list price is 79.99%. Format the percentages with two decimal places.

g. Wrap the headings on row 4.

h. Insert a new column between the Date Sold and List Price columns. Do the following:
   - Move the Days on Market range C4:C13 to the new column.
   - Delete the empty column C.

i. Edit the list date of the 41 Chestnut Circle house to be **4/22/2018.** Edit the list price of the house on Amsterdam Drive to be **$355,000.**

j. Select the property rows and set a **25 row height** and apply **Middle Align.**

k. Apply the **All Borders** border style to the **range A4:H12.** Adjust column widths as necessary.

l. Apply **Align Right** and indent twice the values in the **range E5:E12.**

m. Apply **120% scaling.**

n. Delete the Properties worksheet.

o. Insert a new worksheet and name it **Formulas.**

p. Use the Select All feature to select all data on the Houses Sold worksheet and copy it to the Formulas worksheet.

q. Complete the following steps on the Formulas worksheet:
   - Hide the Date Listed and Date Sold columns.
   - Display cell formulas.
   - Set options to print gridlines and row and column headings.
   - Adjust column widths.

r. Group the worksheets and do the following:
   - Set landscape orientation.
   - Center the page horizontally and vertically between the margins.
   - Insert a footer with your name on the left side, the sheet tab code in the center, and the file name code on the right side.

s. Save and close the file. Based on your instructor's directions, submit e01m2Sales_LastFirst.

3 Problem Solving with Classmates

COLLABORATION CASE

Your instructor wants all students in the class to practice their problem-solving skills. Pair up with a classmate so that you can create errors in a workbook and then see how many errors your classmate can find in your worksheet and how many errors you can find in your classmate's worksheet.

a. Create a folder named **Exploring** on your OneDrive and give access to that drive to a classmate and your instructor.

b. Open *e01h5Markup_LastFirst*, which you created in the Hands-On Exercises, and save it as **e01m3Markup_LastFirst**, changing h5 to m3.

c. Edit each main formula to have a deliberate error (such as a value or incorrect cell reference) in it and then copy the formulas down the columns.

d. Save the workbook to your shared folder on your OneDrive.

e. Open the workbook your classmate saved on his or her OneDrive and save the workbook with your name after theirs, such as *e01m3Markup_MulberyKeith_KrebsCynthia*.

f. Find the errors in your classmate's workbook, insert comments to describe the errors, and then correct the errors.

g. Save the workbook back to your classmate's OneDrive and close the file. Based on your instructor's directions, submit e01m3Markup_LastFirst_LastFirst.

Tip Distribution

GENERAL CASE

You are a server at a restaurant in Portland. You must tip the bartender 13% of each customer's drink sales and the server assistant 1.75% of the food sales plus 2% of the drink sales. You want to complete a worksheet that shows the sales, tips, and your net tip. Open *e01b1Server* and save it as **e01b1Server_LastFirst**.

Insert a column between the Drinks and Tip Left columns. Type the label **Subtotal** in cell D6. Calculate the food and drinks subtotal for the first customer and copy the formula down the column. In column F, enter a formula to calculate the amount of the tip as a percentage of the subtotal for the first customer's sales. Format the results with Percent Style with one decimal place. Type **13%** in cell G7, type **1.75%** in cell H7, and type **2%** in cell I7. Copy these percentage values down these three columns. Horizontally center the data in the three percentage columns.

In cell I7, calculate the bartender's tip for the first customer, using the rule specified in the first paragraph. In cell K7, calculate the assistant's tip for the first customer, using the rule specified in the first paragraph. In cell L7, calculate your net tip after giving the bartender and server their share of the tips. Copy the formulas from the range J7:L7 down their respective columns. Merge and center **Customer Subtotal and Tip** in the range B5:E5. **Tip Rates** in the range F5:I5, and **Tip Amounts** in the range J5:L5. Apply Currency format to the monetary values. Apply borders around the Customer Subtotal and Tip Amounts sections similar to the existing border around the Customer Subtotal and Tip section. For the range A6:L6, apply **Orange, Accent 2, Lighter 40%** fill color, center horizontal alignment, and wrap text. Apply **Orange, Accent 2, Lighter 80%** fill color to the values in the Tip Left column and the My Net Tip column.

Set 0.2" left and right margins, select Landscape orientation, and set the scaling to fit to one page. Include a footer with your name on the left footer, the sheet name code in the center, and file name code on the right side. Copy the worksheet and place the copied worksheet on the right side of the original worksheet. Rename the copied worksheet as **Tip Formulas**. On the Tip Formulas worksheet, display cell formulas, print gridlines, print headings, and adjust the column widths. Change the Tips sheet tab color to **Orange, Accent 2,** and change the Tip Formulas sheet tab color to **Orange, Accent 2, Darker 25%**. Save and close the file. Based on your instructor's directions, submit e01b1Server_LastFirst.

Net Proceeds from House Sale

DISASTER RECOVERY

Daryl Patterson is a real estate agent. He wants his clients to have a realistic expectation of how much money they will receive when they sell their houses. Sellers know they have to pay a commission to the agent and pay off their existing mortgages; however, many sellers forget to consider they might have to pay some of the buyer's closing costs, title insurance, and prorated property taxes. The realtor commission and estimated closing costs are based on the selling price and the respective rates. The estimated property taxes are prorated based on the annual property taxes and percentage of the year. For example, if a house sells three months into the year, the seller pays 25% of the property taxes. Daryl created a worksheet to enter values in an input area to calculate the estimated deductions at closing and calculate the estimated net proceeds the seller will receive. However, the worksheet contains errors. Open *e01b2Proceeds* and save it as **e01b2Proceeds_LastFirst**. Review the font formatting and alignment for consistency. Use Help to learn how to insert comments into cells. As you identify the errors, insert comments in the respective cells to explain the errors. Correct the errors, including formatting errors. Apply Landscape orientation, 115% scaling, 1.5" top margin, and center horizontally. Insert your name on the left side of the header, the sheet name code in the center, and the file name code on the right side. Save and close the file. Based on your instructor's directions, submit e01b2Proceeds_LastFirst.

Capstone Exercise

You are a division manager for a regional hearing-aid company in Cheyenne, Wyoming. Your sales managers travel frequently to some of the offices in the western region. You need to create a travel expense report for your managers to use to record their budgeted and actual expenses for their travel reports. The draft report contains a title, input areas, and a detailed expense area.

Format the Title and Complete the Input Areas

Your first tasks are to format the title and complete the input area. The input area contains two sections: Standard Inputs that are identical for all travelers and Traveler Inputs that the traveler enters based on his or her trip.

a. Open *e01c1Travel* and save it as **e01c1Travel_LastFirst**.

b. Merge and center the title over the **range A1:E1** and set the row height for the first row to **40**.

c. Apply the **Input cell style** to the ranges **B3:B6, E3:E4**, and **E6:E7**, and then apply the **Calculation cell style** to **cell E5**. Part of the borders are removed when you apply these styles.

d. Select the **ranges A3:B6** and **D3:E7**. Apply **Thick Outside Borders**.

e. Enter **6/1/2018** in **cell E3** for the departure date, **6/5/2018** in **cell E4** for the return date, **149** in **cell E6** for the hotel rate per night, and **18%** in **cell E7** for the hotel tax rate.

f. Enter a formula in **cell E5** to calculate the number of days between the return date and the departure date.

Insert Formulas

The Detailed Expenses section contains the amount budgeted for the trip, the actual expenses reported by the traveler, percentage of the budget spent on each item, and the amount the actual expense went over or under budget. You will insert formulas for this section. Some budgeted amounts are calculated based on the inputs. Other budgeted amounts, such as airfare, are estimates.

a. Enter the amount budgeted for Mileage to/from Airport in **cell B12**. The amount is based on the mileage rate and roundtrip to the airport from the Standard Inputs section.

b. Enter the amount budgeted for Airport Parking in **cell B13**. This amount is based on the airport parking daily rate and the number of total days traveling (the number of nights + 1) to include both the departure and return dates. For example, if a person departs on June 1 and returns on June 5, the total number of nights at a hotel is 4, but the total number of days the vehicle is parked at the airport is 5.

c. Enter the amount budgeted for Hotel Accommodations in **cell B16**. This amount is based on the number of nights, the hotel rate, and the hotel tax rate.

d. Enter the amount budgeted for Meals in **cell B17**. This amount is based on the daily meal allowance and the total travel days (# of hotel nights + 1).

e. Enter the % of Budget in **cell D12**. This percentage indicates the percentage of actual expenses to budgeted expenses. Copy the formula to the **range D13:D18**.

f. Enter the difference between the actual and budgeted expenses in **cell E12**. Copy the formula to the **range E13:E18**. If the actual expenses exceeded the budgeted expenses, the result should be positive. If the actual expenses were less than the budgeted expense, the result should be negative, indicating under budget.

Add Rows, Indent Labels, and Move Data

The Detailed Expenses section includes a heading Travel to/from Destination. You want to include two more headings to organize the expenses. Then you will indent the items within each category. Furthermore, you want the monetary columns together, so you will insert cells and move the Over or Under column to the right of the Actual column.

a. Insert a new row 15. Type **Destination Expenses** in **cell A15**. Bold the label.

b. Insert a new row 19. Type **Other** in **cell A19**. Bold the label.

c. Indent twice the labels in the **ranges A12:A14, A16:A18**, and **A20**.

d. Select the **range D10:D21** and insert cells to shift the selected cells to the right.

e. Cut the **range F10:F21** and paste it in the **range D10:D21** to move the Over or Under data in the new cells you inserted.

Format the Detailed Expenses Section

You are ready to format the values to improve readability. You will apply Accounting Number Format to the monetary values on the first and total rows, Comma Style to the monetary values in the middle rows, and Percent Style for the percentages.

a. Apply **Accounting Number Format** to the **ranges B12:D12** and **B21:D21**.

b. Apply **Comma Style** to the **range B13:D20**.

c. Apply **Percent Style** with one decimal place to the **range E12:E20**.

d. Underline the **range: B20:D20**. Do not use the border feature.

e. Apply the cell style **Bad** to **cell D21** because the traveler went over budget.

f. Select the **range A10:E21** and apply **Thick Outside Borders**.

g. Select the **range A10:E10**, apply **Blue-Gray, Text 2, Lighter 80% fill color**, apply **Center** alignment, and apply **Wrap Text**.

Manage the Workbook

You will apply page setup options, insert a footer, and, then duplicate the Expenses statement worksheet.

a. Spell-check the workbook and make appropriate corrections.

b. Set a **1.5"** top margin and select the margin setting to center the data horizontally on the page.

c. Insert a footer with your name on the left side, the sheet name code in the center, and the file name code on the right side.

d. Copy the Expenses worksheet, move the new worksheet to the end, and rename it **Formulas**.

e. Display the cell formulas on the Formulas worksheet, change to landscape orientation, and adjust column widths. Use the Page Setup dialog box or the Page Layout tab to print gridlines and row and column headings.

f. Save and close the file. Based on your instructor's directions, submit e01c1Travel_LastFirst.

Glossary

Accounting Number Format A number format that displays $ on the left side of a cell, formats a value with a comma for every three digits on the left side of the decimal point, and displays two digits to the right of the decimal point.

Active cell The current cell in a worksheet. It is indicated by a dark green border, and the Name Box shows the location of the active cell.

Alignment The placement of data within the boundaries of a cell. By default, text aligns on the left side, and values align on the right side of a cell.

AutoComplete A feature that searches for and automatically displays any other label in that column that matches the letters you type.

Auto Fill A feature that helps you complete a sequence of months, abbreviated months, quarters, weekdays, weekday abbreviations, or values. Auto Fill also can be used to fill or copy a formula down a column or across a row.

Border A line that surrounds a cell or a range of cells to offset particular data from the rest of the data in a worksheet.

Cancel An icon between the Name Box and Formula Bar. When you enter or edit data, click Cancel to cancel the data entry or edit, and revert back to the previous data in the cell, if any. Cancel changes from gray to red when you position the pointer over it.

Cell The intersection of a column and row in a table, such as the intersection of column B and row 5.

Cell address The unique identifier of a cell, starting with the column letter and then the row number, such as C6.

Cell style A set of formatting applied to a cell to produce a consistent appearance for similar cells within a worksheet.

Column heading The alphabetical letter above a column in a worksheet. For example, B is the column heading for the second column.

Column width The horizontal measurement of a column in a table or a worksheet. In Excel, it is measured by the number of characters or pixels.

Comma Style A number format that formats a value with a comma for every three digits on the left side of the decimal point and displays two digits to the right of the decimal point.

Enter An icon between the Name Box and Formula Bar. When you enter or edit data, click Enter to accept data typed in the active cell and keep the current cell active. Enter changes from gray to blue when you position the pointer over it.

Fill color The background color that displays behind the data in a cell so that the data stands out.

Fill handle A small green square at the bottom-right corner of the active cell. You can position the pointer on the fill handle and drag it to repeat the contents of the cell to other cells or to copy a formula in the active cell to adjacent cells down the column or across the row.

Flash Fill A feature that fills in data or values automatically based on one or two examples you enter using another part of data entered in a previous column in the dataset.

Formula A combination of cell references, operators, values, and/ or functions used to perform a calculation.

Formula Bar An element located below the Ribbon and to the right of the Insert Function command. It shows the contents of the active cell. You enter or edit cell contents in the Formula Bar for the active cell.

Horizontal alignment The placement of cell data between the left and right cell margins. By default, text is left-aligned, and values are right-aligned.

Indent A format that offsets data from its default alignment within the margins or cell. For example, if text is left-aligned, the text may be indented or offset from the left side to stand out. If a value is right-aligned, it can be indented or offset from the right side of the cell.

Input area A range of cells in a worksheet used to store and change the variables used in calculations.

Insert Function An icon between the Name Box and Formula Bar. Click Insert Function to open the Insertion Function dialog box to search for and insert a particular function.

Name Box An element located below the Ribbon, which displays the address of the active cell.

New sheet An icon that, when clicked, inserts a new worksheet in the workbook.

Nonadjacent range A collection of multiple ranges (such as D5:D10 and F5:F10) that are not positioned in a contiguous cluster in an Excel worksheet.

Normal view The default view of a worksheet that shows worksheet data but not margins, headers, footers, or page breaks.

Number format A setting that controls how a value appears in a cell.

Order of operations A rule that controls the sequence in which arithmetic operations are performed. Also called the *order of precedence.*

Output area The range of cells in an Excel worksheet that contain formulas dependent on the values in the input area.

Page Break Preview A view setting that displays the worksheet data and page breaks within the worksheet.

Page Layout view A view setting that displays the worksheet data, margins, headers, and footers.

Paste Options button An icon that displays in the bottom-right corner immediately after using the Paste command. It enables the user to apply different paste options.

Percent Style A number format that displays a value as if it was multiplied by 100 and with the % symbol. The default number of decimal places is zero if you click Percent Style in the Number group or two decimal places if you use the Format Cells dialog box.

Pointing The process of using the pointer to select cells while building a formula. Also known as *semi-selection*.

Range A group of adjacent or contiguous cells in a worksheet. A range can be adjacent cells in a column (such as C5:C10), in a row (such as A6:H6), or a rectangular group of cells (such as G5:H10).

Row heading A number to the left side of a row in a worksheet. For example, 3 is the row heading for the third row.

Row height The vertical measurement of the row in a worksheet.

Select All The triangle at the intersection of the row and column headings in the top-left corner of the worksheet. Click it to select everything contained in the active worksheet.

Semi-selection The process of using the pointer to select cells while building a formula. Also known as *pointing*.

Sheet tab A visual label that looks like a file folder tab. In Excel, a sheet tab shows the name of a worksheet contained in the workbook.

Sheet tab navigation Visual elements that help you navigate to the first, previous, next, or last sheet within a workbook.

Spreadsheet An electronic file that contains a grid of columns and rows used to organize related data and to display results of calculations, enabling interpretation of quantitative data for decision making.

Status bar The row at the bottom of the Excel window that displays instructions and other details about the status of a worksheet.

Text Any combination of letters, numbers, symbols, and spaces not used in Excel calculations.

Value A number that represents a quantity or a measurable amount.

Vertical alignment The placement of cell data between the top and bottom cell margins.

View controls Icons on the right side of the status bar that enable you to change to Normal, Page Layout, or Page Break view to display the worksheet.

Workbook A collection of one or more related worksheets contained within a single file.

Worksheet A single spreadsheet that typically contains descriptive labels, numeric values, formulas, functions, and graphical representations of data.

Wrap text An Excel feature that makes data appear on multiple lines by adjusting the row height to fit the cell contents with the column width.

Zoom control A control that enables you to increase or decrease the size of the worksheet data onscreen.

Formulas and Functions

Formulas and Functions

OBJECTIVES & SKILLS: After you read this chapter, you will be able to:

Formula Basics

OBJECTIVE 1: USE RELATIVE, ABSOLUTE, AND MIXED CELL REFERENCES IN FORMULAS
Use a Relative Cell Reference, Use an Absolute Cell Reference, Use a Mixed Cell Reference

HANDS-ON EXERCISE 1:
Formula Basics

Function Basics

OBJECTIVE 2: INSERT A FUNCTION
Insert a Function, Insert a Function Using Formula AutoComplete, Use the Insert Function Dialog Box

OBJECTIVE 3: INSERT BASIC MATH AND STATISTICS FUNCTIONS
Use the SUM Function, Use the AVERAGE and MEDIAN Functions, Use the MIN and MAX Functions, Use the COUNT Functions, Perform Calculations with Quick Analysis Tools

OBJECTIVE 4: USE DATE FUNCTIONS
Use the TODAY Function, Use the NOW Function

HANDS-ON EXERCISE 2:
Function Basics

Logical, Lookup, and Financial Functions

OBJECTIVE 5: DETERMINE RESULTS WITH THE IF FUNCTION
Use the IF Function

OBJECTIVE 6: USE LOOKUP FUNCTIONS
Use the VLOOKUP Function, Create the Lookup Table, Use the HLOOKUP Function

OBJECTIVE 7: CALCULATE PAYMENTS WITH THE PMT FUNCTION
Use the PMT Function

HANDS-ON EXERCISE 3:
Logical, Lookup, and Financial Functions

LEARNING OUTCOME

You will apply formulas and functions to calculate and analyze data.

CASE STUDY | Townsend Mortgage Company

You are an assistant to Erica Matheson, a mortgage broker at the Townsend Mortgage Company. Erica spends her days reviewing mortgage rates and trends, meeting with clients, and preparing paperwork. She relies on your expertise in using Excel to help analyze mortgage data.

Today, Erica provided you with sample mortgage data: loan number, house cost, down payment, mortgage rate, and the length of the loan in years. She asked you to perform some basic calculations so that she can check the output provided by her system to verify if it is calculating results correctly. She wants you to calculate the amount financed, the periodic interest rate, the total number of payment periods, the percent of the house cost that is financed, and the payoff year for each loan. In addition, you will calculate totals, averages, and other basic statistics.

Furthermore, she has asked you to complete another worksheet that uses functions to look up interest rates from a separate table, calculate the monthly payments, and determine how much (if any) the borrower will have to pay for private mortgage insurance (PMI).

Performing Quantitative Analysis

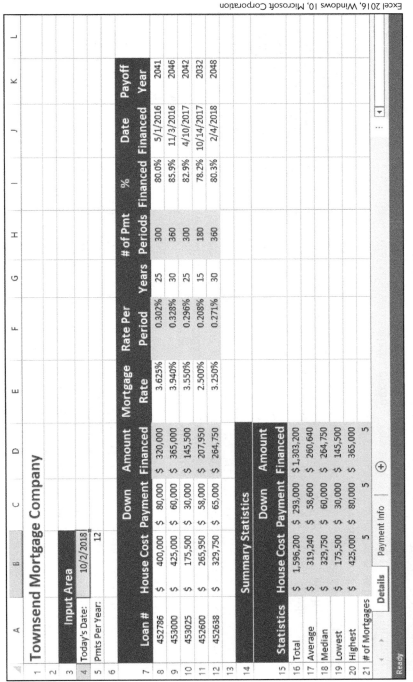

Townsend Mortgage Company

	Input Area										
Today's Date:	10/2/2018										
Pmts Per Year:	12										

Loan #	House Cost	Down Payment	Amount Financed	Mortgage Rate	Rate Per Period	Years	# of Pmt Periods	% Financed	Date Financed	Payoff Year
452786	$ 400,000	$ 80,000	$ 320,000	3.625%	0.302%	25	300	80.0%	5/1/2016	2041
453000	$ 425,000	$ 60,000	$ 365,000	3.940%	0.328%	30	360	85.9%	11/3/2016	2046
453025	$ 175,500	$ 30,000	$ 145,500	3.550%	0.296%	25	300	82.9%	4/10/2017	2042
452600	$ 265,950	$ 58,000	$ 207,950	2.500%	0.208%	15	180	78.2%	10/14/2017	2032
452638	$ 329,750	$ 65,000	$ 264,750	3.250%	0.271%	30	360	80.3%	2/4/2018	2048

Summary Statistics

Statistics	House Cost	Down Payment	Amount Financed
Total	$ 1,596,200	$ 293,000	$ 1,303,200
Average	$ 319,240	$ 58,600	$ 260,640
Median	$ 329,750	$ 60,000	$ 264,750
Lowest	$ 175,500	$ 30,000	$ 145,500
Highest	$ 425,000	$ 80,000	$ 365,000
# of Mortgages	5	5	5

Details | Payment Info

Ready

Excel 2016, Windows 10, Microsoft Corporation

FIGURE I Townsend Mortgage Company Worksheet

CASE STUDY | Townsend Mortgage Company

Starting File	File to be Submitted
e02h1Loans	e02h3Loans_LastFirst

Formulas and Functions • Excel 2016

Formula Basics

When you increase your understanding of formulas, you can build robust workbooks that perform a variety of calculations for quantitative analysis. Your ability to build sophisticated workbooks and to interpret the results increases your value to any organization. By now, you should be able to build simple formulas using cell references and mathematical operators and use the order of operations to control the sequence of calculations in formulas.

In this section, you will create formulas in which cell addresses change or remain fixed when you copy them.

Using Relative, Absolute, and Mixed Cell References in Formulas

When you copy a formula, Excel either adjusts or preserves the cell references in the copied formula based on how the cell references appear in the original formula. Excel uses three different ways to reference a cell in a formula: relative, absolute, and mixed. Relative references change when a formula is copied. For example, if a formula containing the cell A1 is copied down one row in the column, the reference would become A2. In contrast, absolute references remain constant, no matter where they are copied. Mixed references are a combination of both absolute and relative, where part will change and part will remain constant.

When you create a formula that you will copy to other cells, ask yourself the following question: Do the cell references contain constant or variable values? In other words, should the cell references be adjusted or always refer to the same cell location, regardless of where the copied formula is located?

STEP 1

Use a Relative Cell Reference

A *relative cell reference* is the default method of referencing in Excel. It indicates a cell's relative location, such as five rows up and one column to the left, from the original cell containing the formula. When you copy a formula containing a relative cell reference, the cells referenced in the copied formula change relative to the position of the copied formula. Regardless of where you paste the formula, the cell references in the copied formula maintain the same relative distance from the cell containing the copied formula, as the cell references the relative location to the original formula cell.

In Figure 2, the formulas in column F contain relative cell references. When you copy the original formula =D2-E2 from cell F2 down one row to cell F3, the copied formula changes to =D3-E3. Because you copy the formula *down* the column to cell F3, the column letters in the formula stay the same, but the row numbers change to reflect the row to which you copied the formula. Using relative referencing is an effective time-saving tool. For example, using relative cell addresses to calculate the amount financed ensures that each borrower's down payment is subtracted from his or her respective house cost.

Use an Absolute Cell Reference

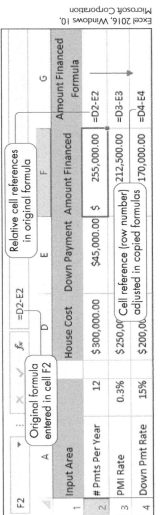

FIGURE 2 Relative Cell References

Excel 2016, Windows 10,
Microsoft Corporation

STEP 2 In many calculations there are times in which a value should remain constant, such as an interest rate or payoff date. In these situations absolute cell references are utilized. An *absolute cell reference* provides a constant reference to a specific cell. When you copy a formula containing an absolute cell reference, the cell reference in the copied formula does not change, regardless of where you copy the formula. An absolute cell reference appears with a dollar sign before both the column letter and row number, such as $B$4.

In Figure 3, the down payment is calculated by multiplying the house cost by the down payment rate (15%). Each down payment calculation uses a different purchase price and constant down payment rate, therefore an absolute reference is required. Cell E2 contains =D2*$B$4 ($300,000*15.0%) to calculate the first borrower's down payment ($45,000). When you copy the formula down to the next row, the copied formula in cell E3 is =D3*$B$4. The relative cell reference D2 changes to D3 (for the next house cost) and the absolute cell reference $B$4 remains the same to refer to the constant 15.0% down payment rate. This formula ensures that the cell reference to the house cost changes for each row but that the house cost is always multiplied by the rate in cell B4.

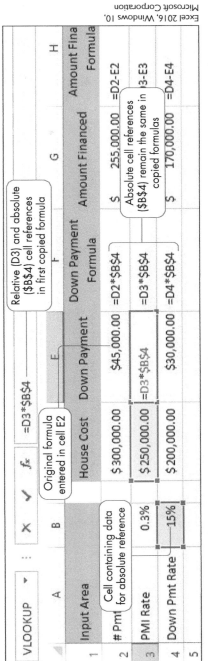

FIGURE 3 Relative and Absolute Cell References

Excel 2016, Windows 10,
Microsoft Corporation

TIP: INPUT AREA AND ABSOLUTE CELL REFERENCES

To illustrate the effect of modifying an assumption (e.g., the down payment rate changes from 15% to 20%), it is efficient to enter the new input value in only one cell (e.g., B4) rather than including the same value in a string of formulas. In Figure 3, values that can be modified, such as the down payment rate, are put in an input area. Generally, formulas use absolute references to the cells in the input area. For example, B4 is an absolute cell reference in all the down payment calculations. If the value in B4 is modified, Excel recalculates the amount of down payment for all the down payment formulas. By using cell references from an input area, you can perform what-if analyses very easily.

When utilizing the fill option to copy a formula, if an error or unexpected result occurs, a good starting point for troubleshooting is checking input values to determine if an absolute or mixed reference is needed. Figure 4 shows what happens if the down payment formula used a relative reference to cell B4. If the original formula in cell E2 is =D2*B4, the copied formula becomes =D3*B5 in cell E3. The relative cell reference to B4 changes to B5 when you copy the formula down. Because cell B5 is empty, the $350,000 house cost in cell D3 is multiplied by 0, giving a $0 down payment, which is not a valid down payment amount.

| VLOOKUP | ▼ | : | × | ✓ | fx | =D3*B5 | |

	A	B	C	D	E	F
1	Input Area			House Cost	Down Payment	
2	When formula is copied from cell E2 to E3, the relative reference becomes B5				Down Payment Formula	
3	PMI Rate	0.3%		$250,000.00 =D3*B5	$45,000.00 =D2*B4	Relative cell reference (B5) is not correct
4	Down Pmt Rate	15%		$200,000.00	$0.00 =D3*B5	
5					=D4*B6	

FIGURE 4 Error in Formula

Excel 2016, Windows 10,
Microsoft Corporation

STEP 3

Use a Mixed Cell Reference

A *mixed cell reference* combines an absolute cell reference with a relative cell reference. When you copy a formula containing a mixed cell reference, either the column letter or the row number that has the absolute reference remains fixed while the other part of the cell reference that is relative changes in the copied formula. $B4 and B$4 are examples of mixed cell references. In the reference $B4, the column B is absolute, and the row number is relative; when you copy the formula, the column letter B does not change, but the row number will change. In the reference B$4, the column letter B changes, but the row number, 4, does not change. To create a mixed reference, type the dollar sign to the left of the part of the cell reference you want to be absolute.

In the down payment formula, you can change the formula in cell E2 to be =D2*B$4. Because you are copying down the same column, only the row reference 4 must be absolute; the column letter stays the same. Figure 5 shows the copied formula =D3*B$4 in cell E3. In situations where you can use either absolute or mixed references, consider using mixed references to shorten the length of the formula.

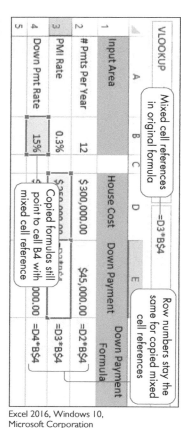

VLOOKUP					
	A	B	C	D	E
1	Input Area			House Cost	Down Payment
2	# Pmts Per Year	12		$300,000.00	$45,000.00 =D2*B$4
3	PMI Rate	0.3%		$250,000.00	=D3*B$4
4	Down Pmt Rate	15%		$200,000.00	=D4*B$4
5					

Mixed cell references in original formula =D3*B$4

Copied formulas still point to cell B4 with mixed cell reference

Row numbers stay the same for copied mixed cell references

FIGURE 5 Relative and Mixed Cell References

Excel 2016, Windows 10,
Microsoft Corporation

TIP: THE F4 KEY

The F4 key toggles through relative, absolute, and mixed references. Click a cell reference within a formula on the Formula Bar and press F4 to change it. For example, click in B4 in the formula =D2*B4. Press F4 and the relative cell reference (B4) changes to an absolute cell reference ($B$4). Press F4 again and $B$4 becomes a mixed reference (B$4); press F4 again and it becomes another mixed reference ($B4). Press F4 a fourth time and the cell reference returns to the original relative reference (B4).

Quick Concepts

1. What happens when you copy a formula containing a relative cell reference one column to the right?

2. Why would you use an absolute reference in a formula?

3. What is the benefit of using a mixed reference?

1 Formula Basics

Erica prepared a workbook containing data for five mortgages financed with the Townsend Mortgage Company. The data include house cost, down payment, mortgage rate, number of years to pay off the mortgage, and the financing date for each mortgage.

STEP 1 » USE A RELATIVE CELL REFERENCE

You will calculate the amount financed by each borrower by creating a formula with relative cell references that calculates the difference between the house cost and the down payment. After verifying the results of the amount financed by the first borrower, you will copy the formula down the Amount Financed column to calculate the other borrowers' amounts financed. Refer to Figure 6 as you complete Step 1.

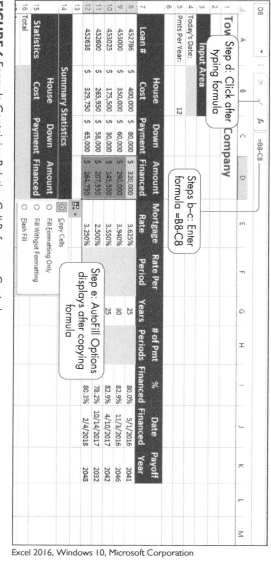

FIGURE 6 Formula Containing Relative Cell Reference Copied

a. Open *e02h1Loans* and save it as **e02h1Loans_LastFirst**.

> **TROUBLESHOOTING:** If you make any major mistakes in this exercise, you can close the file, open *e02h1Loans* again, and then start this exercise over.

The workbook contains two worksheets: Details (for Hands-On Exercises 1 and 2) and Payment Info (for Hands-On Exercise 3). You will enter formulas in the shaded cells.

b. Click **cell D8** in the Details sheet. Type **=** and click **cell B8**, the cell containing the first borrower's house cost.

c. Type **-** and click **cell C8**, the cell containing the down payment by the first borrower.

d. Click **Enter** ✓ (the check mark between the Name Box and Formula Bar) to complete the formula.

The first borrower financed (i.e. borrowed) $320,000, the difference between the cost ($400,000) and the down payment ($80,000).

e. Double-click the **cell D8 fill handle.**

You copied the formula down the Amount Financed column for each mortgage row.

Skills covered: Use a Relative Cell Reference • Use an Absolute Cell Reference • Use a Mixed Cell Reference

The worksheet shown in the figure contains the following data:

Loan #	House Cost	Down Payment	Amount Financed	Mortgage Rate	Rate Per Period	# of Pmt Periods	Years	% Financed	Date Financed	Payoff Year
452786	$ 400,000	$ 80,000	$ 320,000	3.625%			25	80.0%	5/1/2016	2041
453000	$ 350,000	$ 60,000	$ 290,000	3.940%			30	82.9%	11/3/2016	2046
453025	$ 175,500	$ 30,000	$ 145,500	3.550%			25	82.9%	4/10/2017	2042
452600	$ 265,950	$ 58,000	$ 207,950	2.500%				78.2%	10/14/2017	2032
452638	$ 329,750	$ 65,000	$ 264,750	3.250%				80.3%	2/4/2018	2048

	House Cost	Down Payment	Amount Financed
Summary Statistics			
Statistics			
Total			

f. Click **cell D9** and view the formula in the Formula Bar.

The formula in cell D8 is =B8-C8. The formula copied to cell D9 is =B9-C9. Because the original formula contained relative cell references, when you copy the formula down to the next row, the row numbers for the cell references change. Each result represents the amount financed for that particular borrower.

g. Press ↓ and look at the cell references in the Formula Bar to see how the references change for each formula you copied. Save the workbook with the new formula you created.

Column E contains the mortgage rate for each loan. Because the borrowers will make monthly payments, you will modify the given annual interest rate (APR) to a monthly rate by dividing it by 12 (the number of payments in one year) for each borrower. Refer to Figure 7 as you complete Step 2.

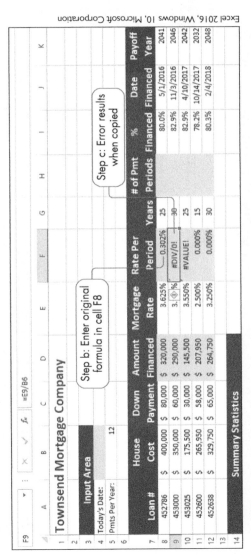

FIGURE 7 Formula Containing Incorrect Relative Cell Reference Copied

Excel 2016, Windows 10, Microsoft Corporation

a. Click **cell F8**.

You will create a formula to calculate the monthly interest rate for the first borrower.

b. Type **=E8/B5** and click **Enter** (the check mark between the Name Box and the Formula Bar).

Typically, you should avoid typing values directly in formulas. Therefore, you use a reference to cell B5, where the number of payments per year is placed in the input area, so that the company can change the payment period to bimonthly (24 payments per year) or quarterly (four payments per year) without adjusting the formula.

c. Double-click the **cell F8 fill handle**, click **cell F9**, and then view the results (see Figure 7).

An error icon displays to the left of cell F9, which displays #DIV/0!, and cell F10 displays #VALUE!. The original formula was =E8/B5. Because you copied the formula =E8/B5 down the column, the first copied formula is =E9/B6, and the second copied formula is =E10/B7. Although you want the mortgage rate cell reference (E8) to change (E9, E10, etc.) from row to row, you do not want the divisor (cell B5) to change. You need all formulas to divide by the value stored in cell B5, so you will edit the formula to make B5 an absolute reference.

d. Click **Undo** in the Quick Access Toolbar to undo the AutoFill process. With F8 as the active cell, click to the right of **B5** in the Formula Bar.

e. Press **F4** and click **Enter** (the check mark between the Name Box and the Formula Bar).

Excel changes the cell reference from B5 to $B$5, making it an absolute cell reference.

The next formula you create will calculate the total number of payment periods for each loan. Refer to Figure 8 as you complete Step 3.

f. Double-click the fill handle to copy the formula down the Rate Per Period column. Click **cell F9** and view the formula in the Formula Bar.

The formula in cell F9 is =E9/$B$5. The reference to E9 is relative and the reference to B5 is absolute. The results of all the calculations in the Rate Per Period column are now correct.

g. Save the workbook.

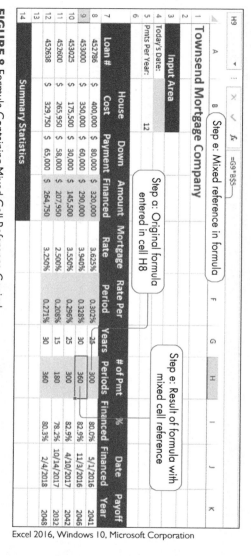

| H9 | ▾ | : | × | ✓ | fx | =G9*B$5 |

Townsend Mortgage Company

	A	B	C	D	E	F	G	H	I	J	K
1	**Input Area**										
2											
3											
4	Today's Date:										
5	Pmts Per Year:	12									
6											
7	Loan #	House Cost	Down Payment	Amount Financed	Mortgage Rate	Rate Per Period	# of Pmt Periods	% Financed	Date Financed	Payoff Year	
8	452786	$ 400,000	$ 80,000	$ 320,000	3.625%	0.302%	25	300	80.0%	5/1/2016	2041
9	453000	$ 350,000	$ 60,000	$ 290,000	3.940%	0.328%	30	360	82.9%	11/3/2016	2046
10	453025	$ 175,500	$ 30,000	$ 145,500	3.550%	0.296%	25	300	82.9%	4/10/2017	2042
11	452600	$ 265,950	$ 58,000	$ 207,950	2.500%	0.208%	15	180	78.2%	10/14/2017	2032
12	452638	$ 329,750	$ 65,000	$ 264,750	3.250%	0.271%	30	360	80.3%	2/4/2018	2048
13											
14	**Summary Statistics**										

Step e: Mixed reference in formula

Step a: Original formula entered in cell H8

Step e: Result of formula with mixed cell reference

Excel 2016, Windows 10, Microsoft Corporation

FIGURE 8 Formula Containing Mixed Cell Reference Copied

a. Click **cell H8** and type **=G8*B5.**

You will multiply the number of years (25) by the number of payment periods in one year (12) using cell references.

b. Press **F4** to make the B5 cell reference absolute and click **Enter.**

You want B5 to be absolute so that the cell reference remains B5 when you copy the formula. The product of 25 years and 12 months is 300 months or payment periods.

c. Copy the formula down the # of Pmt Periods column.

The first copied formula is =G9*$B$5, and the result is 360. You want to see what happens if you change the absolute reference to a mixed reference and copy the formula again. Because you are copying down a column, the column letter B can be relative because it will not change either way, but the row number 5 must be absolute.

d. Ensure that cell H8 is the active cell and click **Undo** on the Quick Access Toolbar to undo the copied formulas.

e. Click within the **$B$5 cell reference** in the Formula Bar. Press **F4** to change the cell reference to a mixed cell reference: B$5. Press **Ctrl+Enter** and copy the formula down the # of Pmt Periods column. Click **cell H9.**

The first copied formula is =G9*B$5 and the result is still 360. In this situation, using either an absolute reference or a mixed reference provides the same results.

f. Save the workbook. Keep the workbook open if you plan to continue with the next Hands-On Exercise. If not, close the workbook and exit Excel.

Function Basics

An Excel *function* is a predefined computation that simplifies creating a formula that performs a complex calculation. Excel contains more than 400 functions, which are organized into 14 categories. Table 1 lists and describes the primary function categories used in this chapter.

TABLE 1 Function Categories and Descriptions	
Category	**Description**
Date & Time	Provides methods for manipulating date and time values.
Financial	Performs financial calculations, such as payments, rates, present value, and future value.
Logical	Performs logical tests and returns the value of the tests. Includes logical operators for combined tests, such as AND, OR, and NOT.
Lookup & Reference	Looks up values, creates links to cells, or provides references to cells in a worksheet.
Math & Trig	Performs standard math and trigonometry calculations.
Statistical	Performs common statistical calculations, such as averages and standard deviations.

When using functions, you must adhere to correct *syntax*, the rules that dictate the structure and components required to perform the necessary calculations. Start a function with an equal sign, followed by the function name, and then its arguments enclosed in parentheses.

- The function name describes the purpose of the function. For example, the function name SUM indicates that the function sums, or adds, values.

- A function's *arguments* specify the inputs—such as cells, values, or arithmetic expressions—that are required to complete the operation. In some cases, a function requires multiple arguments separated by commas.

In this section, you will learn how to insert common functions using the keyboard and the Insert Function and Function Arguments dialog boxes.

Inserting a Function

To insert a function by typing, first type an equal sign, and then begin typing the function name. *Formula AutoComplete* displays a list of functions and defined names that match letters as you type a formula. For example, if you type *=SU*, Formula AutoComplete displays a list of functions and names that start with *SU* (see Figure 9). You can double-click the function name from the list or continue typing the function name. You can even point to a list item and see the ScreenTip describing the function.

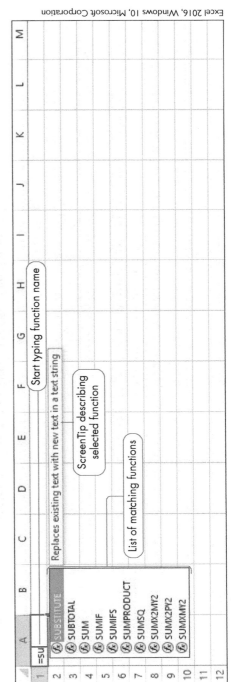

FIGURE 9 Formula AutoComplete

	A	B	C	D	E	F	G	H	I	J
1	=SUM(									
2	SUM(number1, [number2], ...)									
3										

FIGURE 10 Function ScreenTip

Excel 2016, Windows 10,
Microsoft Corporation

After you type the function name and opening parenthesis, Excel displays the *function ScreenTip*, a small pop-up description that displays the function's arguments. The argument you are currently entering is bold in the function ScreenTip (see Figure 10). Square brackets indicate optional arguments. For example, the SUM function requires the number1 argument, but the number2 argument is optional. Click the argument name in the function ScreenTip to select the actual argument in the formula you are creating if you want to make changes to the argument.

You can also use the Insert Function dialog box to search for a function, select a function category, and select a function from the list (see Figure 11). The dialog box is helpful if you want to browse a list of functions, especially if you are not sure of the function you need and want to see descriptions.

To display the Insert Function dialog box, click Insert Function f_x (located between the Name Box and the Formula Bar) or click Insert Function in the Function Library group on the Formulas tab. From within the dialog box, select a function category, such as Most Recently Used, and select a function to display the syntax and a brief description of that function. Click *Help on this function* to display details about the selected function.

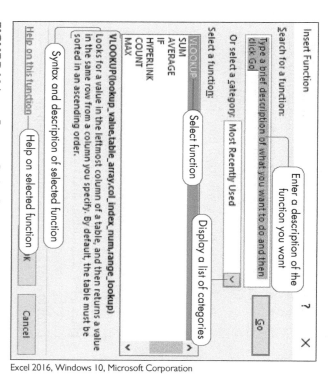

FIGURE 11 Insert Function Dialog Box

Excel 2016, Windows 10, Microsoft Corporation

When you find the function you want, click OK. The Function Arguments dialog box opens so that you can enter the arguments for that specific function (see Figure 12). Argument names in bold (such as number1 in the SUM function) are required. Argument names that are not bold (such as number2 in the SUM function) are optional. The function can operate without the optional argument, which is used when you need additional specifications to calculate a result.

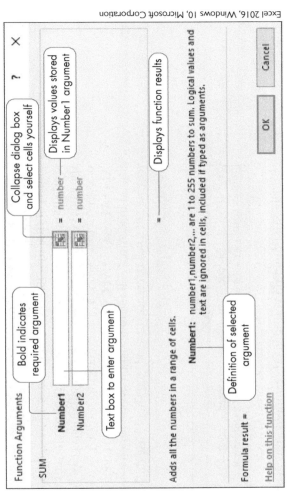

FIGURE 12 Function Arguments Dialog Box

Type the cell references in the argument boxes, or click a collapse button to the right side of an argument box to collapse the dialog box and select the cell or range of cells in the worksheet to designate as that argument. If you click the collapse button to select a range, you need to click the expand button to expand the dialog box again. You also have the ability to manually select the cells for the argument without clicking the collapse button. The collapse button is best used if the desired cells for the arguments view is obstructed. The value, or results, of a formula contained in the argument cell displays on the right side of the argument box (such as 5; 10; 15; 20; 25—the values stored in the range A1:A5 used for the number1 argument). If the argument is not valid, Excel displays an error description on the right side of the argument box.

The bottom of the Function Arguments dialog box displays a description of the function and a description of the argument containing the insertion point. As you enter arguments, the bottom of the dialog box also displays the results of the function, such as 75.

TIP: #NAME?

If you enter a function and #NAME? displays in the cell, you might have mistyped the function name. To avoid this problem, select the function name from the Formula AutoComplete list as you type the function name, or use the Insert Function dialog box. You can type a function name in lowercase letters. If you type the name correctly, Excel converts the name to all capital letters when you press Enter, indicating that you spelled the function name correctly.

Inserting Basic Math and Statistics Functions

Excel includes commonly used math and statistical functions that you can use for a variety of calculations. For example, you can insert functions to calculate the total amount you spend on dining out in a month, the average amount you spend per month purchasing music online, your highest electric bill, and your lowest time to run a mile this week. When using these functions, a change in the values within the ranges referenced will change the results of the function.

Use the SUM Function

The **SUM *function*** totals values in one or more cells and displays the result in the cell containing the function. This function is more efficient to create when you need to add the values contained in three or more contiguous cells. For example, to add the contents of cells A2 through A14, you could enter =A2+A3+A4+A5+A6+A7+A8+A9+A10+ A11+A12+A13+A14, which is time-consuming and increases the probability of enter-ing an inaccurate cell reference, such as entering a cell reference twice or accidentally leaving out a cell reference. Instead, you should use the SUM function, =SUM(A2:A14).

=SUM(number1, [number2],...)

> ### TIP: FUNCTION SYNTAX
> In this text, the function syntax lines are highlighted. Brackets [ ] indicate optional arguments; however, do not actually type the brackets when you enter the argument.

The SUM function contains one required argument (number1) that represents a range of cells to add. The range, such as A2:A14, specifies the first and last of an adja-cent group of cells containing values to SUM. Excel will sum all cells within that range. The number2 optional argument is used when you want to sum values stored in nonad-jacent cells or ranges, such as =SUM(A2:A14,F2:F14). The ellipsis in the function syntax indicates that you can add as many additional ranges as desired, separated by commas.

> ### TIP: AVOIDING FUNCTIONS FOR BASIC FORMULAS
> Do not use a function for a basic mathematical expression. For example, although =SUM(B4/C4) produces the same result as =B4/C4, the SUM function is not needed to perform the basic arithmetic division. Furthermore, someone taking a quick look at that formula might assume it performs addition instead of division. Use the most appropriate, clear-cut formula, =B4/C4.

To insert the SUM function (for example, to sum the values of a range), complete one of the following steps:

- Type =SUM(type the range), and press Enter.
- Type =SUM(drag to select the range, then type the closing) and press Enter.
- Click a cell, click Sum in the Editing group on the Home tab, press Enter to select the suggested range (or drag to select a range), and then press Enter.
- Click in a cell, click AutoSum in the Function Library group on the Formulas tab, either press Enter to select the suggested range or type the range, and then press Enter.
- Click the cell directly underneath the range you would like to SUM and press Alt+=.

Figure 13 shows the result of using the SUM function in cell D2 to total scores (898).

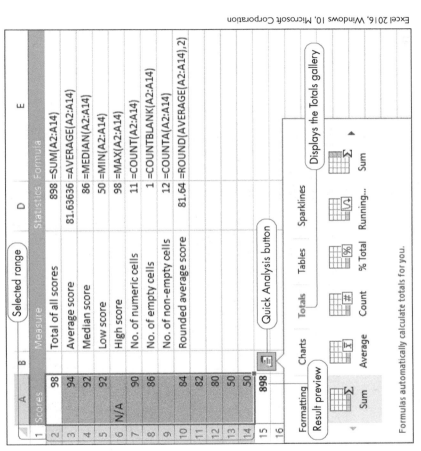

FIGURE 13 Function Results

Excel 2016, Windows 10, Microsoft Corporation

The table in the figure contains the following data:

	A	B	Measure	D Statistics	E Formula
1	Scores				
2	98		Total of all scores	898	=SUM(A2:A14)
3	94		Average score	81.63636	=AVERAGE(A2:A14)
4	92		Median score	86	=MEDIAN(A2:A14)
5	92		Low score	50	=MIN(A2:A14)
6	N/A		High score	98	=MAX(A2:A14)
7	90		No. of numeric cells	11	=COUNT(A2:A14)
8	86		No. of empty cells	1	=COUNTBLANK(A2:A14)
9			No. of non-empty cells	12	=COUNTA(A2:A14)
10	84		Rounded average score	81.64	=ROUND(AVERAGE(A2:A14),2)
11	82				
12	80				
13	50				
14	50				
15	898				
16					

Formulas automatically calculate totals for you.

TIP: SUM ARROW

If you click Sum in the Editing group on the Home tab or in the Function Library group on the Formulas tab, Excel inserts the SUM function. However, if you click the Sum arrow, Excel displays a list of basic functions to select: Sum, Average, Count Numbers, Max, and Min. If you want to insert another function, select More Functions from the list.

TIP: NEST FUNCTIONS AS ARGUMENTS

A *nested function* occurs when one function is embedded as an argument within another function. Each function has its own set of arguments that must be included. For example, cell D10 in Figure 13 contains =ROUND(AVERAGE(A2:A14),2). The ROUND function requires two arguments: number (the number to be rounded) and num_digits (the number of decimals to which the number is to be rounded).

The AVERAGE function is used to create the number to be rounded, and is nested in the number argument of the ROUND function. AVERAGE(A2:A14) returns 81.63636. That value is then rounded to two decimal places, indicated by 2 in the num_digits argument. The result is 81.64. If you change the second argument from 2 to 0, such as =ROUND(AVERAGE (A2:A14),0), the result would be 82.

Use the AVERAGE and MEDIAN Functions

STEP 2 ≫ People often describe data based on central tendency, which means that values tend to cluster around a central value. Excel provides two functions to calculate central tendency: AVERAGE and MEDIAN. The *AVERAGE function* calculates the arithmetic mean, or average, for the values in a range of cells. You can use this function to calculate the class average on a biology test or the average number of points scored per game by a basketball player. In Figure 13, =AVERAGE(A2:A14) in cell D3 returns 81.63636 as the average test score. The AVERAGE function ignores empty cells and cells containing N/A or text.

=AVERAGE (number1,[number2],....)

STEP 3 ≫

The *MEDIAN function* finds the midpoint value, which is the value that one half of the data set is above or below. The median is particularly useful because extreme values often influence arithmetic mean calculated by the AVERAGE function. In Figure 13, the two extreme test scores of 50 distort the average. The rest of the test scores range from 80 to 98. Cell D4 contains =MEDIAN(A2:A14). The median for test scores is 86, which indicates that half the test scores are above 86 and half the test scores are below 86. This statistic is more reflective of the data set than the average. The MEDIAN function ignores empty cells and cells containing N/A or text.

=MEDIAN(number1,[number2],...)

STEP 4 ≫

Use the MIN and MAX Functions

The *MIN function* analyzes an argument list to determine the lowest value, such as the lowest score on a test. Manually inspecting a range of values to identify the lowest value is inefficient, especially in large spreadsheets. In Figure 13, =MIN(A2:A14) in cell D5 identifies that 50 is the lowest test score.

=MIN(number1,[number2],...)

The *MAX function* analyzes an argument list to determine the highest value, such as the highest score on a test. In Figure 13, =MAX(A2:A14) in cell D6 identifies 98 as the highest test score.

=MAX(number1,[number2],...)

TIP: NONADJACENT RANGES

In most basic aggregate functions such as SUM, MIN, MAX, and AVERAGE, you can use multiple ranges as arguments, such as finding the largest number within two nonadjacent (nonconsecutive) ranges. For example, you can find the highest test score where some scores are stored in cells A2:A14 and others are stored in cells K2:K14. Separate each range with a comma in the argument list, so that the formula is =MAX(A2:A14,K2:K14).

Use the COUNT Functions

Excel provides three basic count functions—COUNT, COUNTBLANK, and COUNTA—to count the cells in a range that meet a particular criterion. The *COUNT function* tallies the number of cells in a range that contain values you can use in calculations, such as numerical and date data, but excludes blank cells or text entries from the tally. In Figure 13, the selected range spans 13 cells; however, =COUNT(A2:A14) in cell D7 returns 11, the number of cells that contain numerical data. It does not count the cell containing the text N/A or the blank cell.

The *COUNTBLANK function* tallies the number of cells in a range that are blank. In Figure 13, =COUNTBLANK(A2:A14) in cell D8 identifies that one cell in the range A2:A14 is blank. The *COUNTA function* tallies the number of cells in a range that are not blank, that is, cells that contain data, whether a value, text, or a formula. In Figure 13, =COUNTA(A2:A14) in cell D9 returns 12, indicating that the range A2:A14 contains 12 cells that contain some form of data. It does not count the blank cell; however, it will count cells that contain text such as cell A6.

=COUNT(value1,[value2],...)

=COUNTBLANK(range)

=COUNTA(value1,[value2],...)

Perform Calculations with Quick Analysis Tools

Quick Analysis is a set of analytical tools you can use to apply formatting, create charts or tables, and insert basic functions. When you select a range of data, the Quick Analysis-button displays adjacent to the bottom-right corner of the selected range. Click the Quick Analysis button to display the Quick Analysis gallery and select the analytical tool to meet your needs.

Figure 13 shows the Totals gallery options so that you can sum, average, or count the values in the selected range. Select % Total to display the percentage of the grand total of two or more columns. Select Running Total to provide a cumulative total at the bottom of multiple columns. Additional options can be seen by clicking the right expansion arrow.

Using Date Functions

In order to maximize the use of dates and date functions in Excel, it is important to understand how they are handled in the program. Excel assigns serial numbers to dates. The date January 1, 1900 is the equivalent to the number 1. The number 2 is the equivalent of January 2, 1900 and so on. Basically, Excel adds 1 to every serial number as each day passes. Therefore the newer the date, the bigger the equivalent serial number. For example, assume today is January 1, 2018, and you graduate on May 6, 2018. To determine how many days until graduation, subtract today's date from the graduation date. Excel uses the serial numbers for these dates (43101 and 43226) to calculate the difference of 125 days.

Insert the TODAY Function

STEP 5 >> The *TODAY function* displays the current date in a cell. Excel updates the TODAY function results when you open or print the workbook. The TODAY() function does not require arguments, but you must include the parentheses. If you omit the parentheses, Excel displays #NAME? in the cell with a green triangle in the top-left corner of the cell. When you click the cell, an error icon appears that you can click for more information.

=TODAY()

Insert the NOW Function

The *NOW function* uses the computer's clock to display the current date and military time that you last opened the workbook. (Military time expresses time on a 24-hour period where 1:00 is 1 a.m. and 13:00 is 1 p.m.) The date and time will change every time the workbook is opened. Like the TODAY function, the NOW function does not require arguments, but you must include the parentheses. Omitting the parentheses creates a #NAME? error.

=NOW()

TIP: UPDATE THE DATE AND TIME

Both the TODAY and NOW functions display the date/time the workbook was last opened or last calculated. These functions do not continuously update the date and time while the workbook is open. To update the date and time, press F9 or click the Formulas tab and click *Calculate Now* in the Calculation group.

Quick Concepts

4. What visual features help guide you through typing a function directly in a cell?

5. What type of data do you enter in a Function Arguments dialog box, and what are four things the dialog box tells you?

6. What is the difference between the AVERAGE and MEDIAN functions?

7. What is a nested function, and why would you create one?

Hands-On Exercises

2 Function Basics

Skills covered: Insert a Function • Insert a Function Using Formula AutoComplete • Use the Insert Function Dialog Box • Use the SUM Function • Use the AVERAGE and MEDIAN Functions • Use MIN and MAX Functions • Use the COUNT Functions • Use the TODAY Function

The Townsend Mortgage Company worksheet contains an area in which you will enter summary statistics. In addition, you will include the current date.

STEP 1 >> USE THE SUM FUNCTION

The first summary statistic you calculate is the total value of the houses bought by the borrowers. You will use the SUM function. Refer to Figure 14 as you complete Step 1.

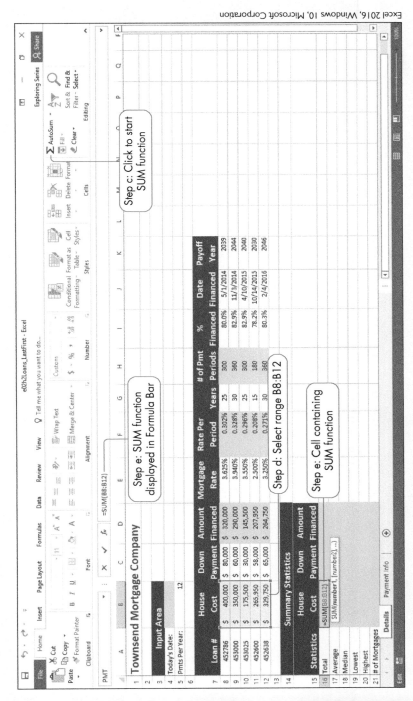

FIGURE 14 SUM Function Calculates Total House Cost

a. Open *e02h1Loans_LastFirst* if you closed it at the end of Hands-On Exercise 1 and save it as **e02h2Loans_LastFirst**, changing h1 to h2.

b. Ensure that the Details worksheet is active and click **cell B16**, the cell where you will enter a formula for the total house cost.

c. Click **AutoSum** Σ AutoSum ▾ in the Editing group on the Home tab.

Excel anticipates the range of cells containing values you want to sum based on where you enter the formula—in this case, A8:D15. This is not the correct range, so you must enter the correct range.

TROUBLESHOOTING: AutoSum, like some other commands in Excel, contains two parts: the main command button and an arrow. Click the main command button when instructed to click Sum to perform the default action. Click the arrow when instructed to click the Sum arrow for additional options. If you accidentally clicked the arrow instead of Sum, press Esc to cancel the SUM function from being completed and try Step c again.

d. Select the **range B8:B12**, the cells containing house costs.

As you use the semi-selection process, Excel enters the range in the SUM function.

TROUBLESHOOTING: If you entered the function without changing the arguments, repeat Steps b–d or edit the arguments in the Formula Bar by deleting the default range, typing B8:B12 between the parentheses and pressing Enter.

e. Click **Enter**.

Cell B16 contains the function = SUM(B8:B12), and the result is $1,521,200.

f. Save the workbook.

STEP 2 》 USE THE AVERAGE FUNCTION

Before copying the functions to calculate the total down payments and amounts financed, you want to calculate. Refer to Figure 15 as you complete Step 2.

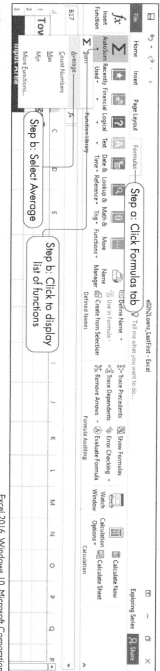

Step a: Click Formulas tab

Step b: Click to display list of functions

Step b: Select Average

FIGURE 15 AVERAGE Function Calculates Average House Cost

Excel 2016, Windows 10, Microsoft Corporation

a. Click the **Formulas tab** and click **cell B17**, the cell where you will display the average cost of the houses.

b. Click the **AutoSum arrow** in the Function Library group and select **Average.**

Excel selects cell B16, which is the total cost of the houses. You need to change the range.

c. Select the **range B8:B12**, the cells containing the house costs.

The function is =AVERAGE(B8:B12).

d. Press **Enter**, making cell B18 the active cell.

The average house cost is $304,240.

e. Save the workbook.

You realize that extreme house costs may distort the average. Therefore, you decide to identify the median house cost to compare it to the average house cost. Refer to Figure 16 as you complete Step 3.

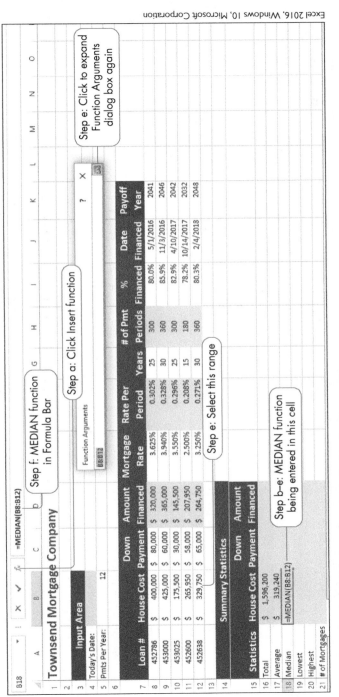

FIGURE 16 MEDIAN Function Calculates the Median House Cost

a. Ensure that cell B18 is the active cell. Click **Insert Function** f_x between the Name Box and the Formula Bar, or in the Function Library group on the Formulas tab.

The Insert Function dialog box opens. Use this dialog box to select the MEDIAN function because it is not available on the Ribbon.

b. Type **median** in the *Search for a function box* and click **Go**.

Excel displays a list of functions in the *Select a function* list. The MEDIAN function is selected at the top of the list; the bottom of the dialog box displays the syntax and the description.

c. Read the MEDIAN function description and click **OK**.

The Function Arguments dialog box opens. It contains one required argument, Number1, representing a range of cells containing values. It has an optional argument, Number2, which you can use if you have nonadjacent ranges that contain values.

d. Click **Collapse Dialog Box** to the right of the Number1 box.

You collapsed the Function Arguments dialog box so that you can select the range.

e. Select the **range B8:B12** and click **Expand Dialog Box** in the Function Arguments dialog box.

The Function Arguments dialog box expands, displaying B8:B12 in the Number1 box.

f. Click **OK** to accept the function arguments and close the dialog box.

Half of the houses purchased cost more than the median, $329,750, and half of the houses cost less than this value. Notice the difference between the median and the average: The average is lower because it is affected by the lowest-priced house, $175,500.

g. Save the workbook.

STEP 4 ›› USE THE MIN, MAX, AND COUNT FUNCTIONS

Erica wants to know the least and most expensive houses so that she can analyze typical customers of the Townsend Mortgage Company. You will use the MIN and MAX functions to obtain these statistics. In addition, you will use the COUNT function to tally the number of mortgages in the sample. Refer to Figure 17 as you complete Step 4.

	A	B	C	D	E	F	G	H	I	J	K
1	**Townsend Mortgage Company**										
2	**Input Area**										
3	Today's Date:										
4											
5	Pmts Per Year:										
6											
7	Loan #	House Cost	Down Payment	Amount Financed	Mortgage Rate	Rate Per Period	Years	# of Pmt Periods	% Financed	Date Financed	Payoff Year
8	452786	$ 400,000	$ 80,000	320,000	3.625%	0.302%	25	300	80.0%	5/1/2016	2041
9	453000	$ 425,000	$ 60,000	365,000	3.940%	0.328%	30	360	85.9%	11/3/2016	2046
10	453025	$ 175,500	$ 30,000	145,500	3.550%	0.296%	25	300	82.9%	4/10/2017	2042
11	457	$	$ 58,000	207,950	2.500%	0.208%	15	180	78.2%	10/14/2017	2032
12	451	$	$ 65,000	264,750	3.250%	0.271%	30	360	80.3%	2/4/2018	2048
13											
14											
15	**Statistics**	House Cost	Down Payment	Amount Financed							
16	Total	$ 1,596,200	$ 293,000	$ 1,303,200							
17	Average	$ 319,240	$ 58,600	$ 260,640							
18	Median	$ 329,750	$ 60,000	$ 264,750							
19	Lowest	$ 175,500	$ 30,000	$ 145,500							
20	Highest	$ 425,000	$ 80,000	$ 365,000							
21	# of Mortgages	5	5	5							

Step g: Value changed in cell B9

Summary Statistics — Down Payment, Amount

Step b: Cell contains MIN function

Step c: Cell contains MAX function

Step d: Cell contains COUNT function

Step f: Formulas copied to these columns

FIGURE 17 MIN, MAX, and COUNT Function Results

a. Click **cell B19**, the cell to display the cost of the lowest-costing house.

b. Click the **AutoSum arrow** in the Function Library group, select **MIN**, select the **range B8:B12**, and then press **Enter**.

The MIN function identifies that the lowest-costing house is $175,500.

c. Click **cell B20**. Click the **AutoSum arrow** in the Function Library group, select **MAX**, select the **range B8:B12**, and then press **Enter**.

The MAX function identifies that the highest-costing house is $400,000.

d. Click **cell B21**. Type **=COUNT(B8:B12)** and press **Enter**.

As you type the letter C, Formula AutoComplete suggests functions starting with C. As you continue typing, the list of functions narrows. After you type the beginning parenthesis, Excel displays the function ScreenTip, indicating the arguments for the function. The range B8:B12 contains five cells.

e. Select the **range B16:B21**.

You want to select the range of original statistics to copy the cells all at one time to the next two columns.

f. Drag the fill handle to the right by two columns to copy to the range C16:D21. Click **cell D21**.

Because you used relative cell references in the functions, the range in the function changes from =COUNT(B8:B12) to =COUNT(D8:D12).

g. Click **cell B9** and, change the cell value to **425000**, and click **Enter**.

The results of all formulas and functions change, including the total, average, and max house costs.

h. Save the workbook.

STEP 5 ⟩⟩ USE THE TODAY FUNCTION

Before finalizing the worksheet you will insert the current date. You will use the TODAY function to display the current date. Refer to Figure 18 as you complete Step 5.

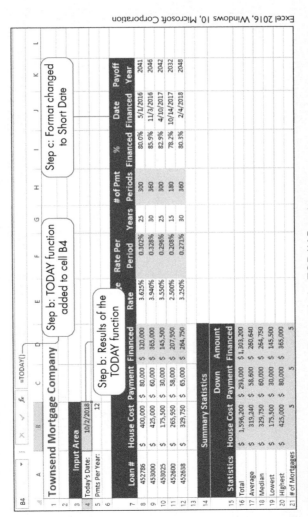

FIGURE 18 Insert the Current Date with the TODAY Function

a. Click **cell B4**, the cell to contain the current date.

b. Click **Date & Time** in the Function Library group, select **TODAY** to display the Function Arguments dialog box, and then click **OK** to close the dialog box.

The Function Arguments dialog box opens, although no arguments are necessary for this function. Excel displays TODAY() in the Edit formula bar, and inserts the current date in Short Date format, such as 6/1/2018, based on the computer system's date.

c. Click the **Format arrow** from the Cells group and select **AutoFit Column Width**.

d. Save the workbook. Keep the workbook open if you plan to continue with the next Hands-On Exercise. If not, close the workbook and exit Excel.

Logical, Lookup, and Financial Functions

As you prepare complex spreadsheets using functions, you will frequently use three function categories: logical, lookup and reference, and finance. Logical functions test the logic of a situation and return a particular result. Lookup and reference functions are useful when you need to look up a value in a list to identify the applicable value. Financial functions are useful to anyone who plans to take out a loan or invest money.

In this section, you will learn how to use the logical, lookup, and financial functions.

Determining Results with the IF Function

The most common logical function is the **IF function**, which tests specified criteria to see if it is true or false, then returns one value when a condition is met, or is true, and returns another value when the condition is not met, or is false. For example, a company gives a $500 bonus to employees who sold *over* $10,000 in merchandise in a week, but no bonus to employees who did not sell over $10,000 in merchandise. Figure 19 shows a worksheet containing the sales data for three representatives and their bonuses, if any.

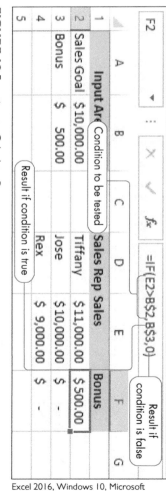

FIGURE 19 Function to Calculate Bonus

Excel 2016, Windows 10, Microsoft Corporation

The IF function has three arguments: (1) a condition that is tested to determine if it is either true or false, (2) the resulting value if the condition is true, and (3) the resulting value if the condition is false.

=IF(logical_test,[value_if_true],[value_if_false])

You might find it helpful to create two flowcharts to illustrate an IF function. First, construct a flowchart that uses words and numbers to illustrate the condition and results. For example, the left flowchart in Figure 20 illustrates the condition to see if sales are greater than $10,000, and the $500 bonus if the condition is true or $0 if the condition is false. Then, create a second flowchart—similar to the one on the right side of Figure 20—that replaces the words and values with actual cell references. Creating these flowcharts can help you construct the IF function that is used in cell F2 in Figure 19.

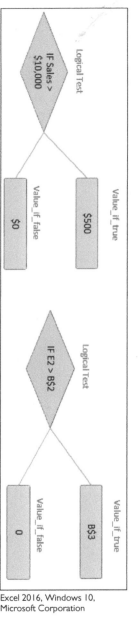

FIGURE 20 Flowcharts Illustrating IF Function

Excel 2016, Windows 10, Microsoft Corporation

Design the Logical Test

The first argument for the IF function is the logical test. The *logical test* contains either a value or an expression that evaluates to true or false. The logical test requires a comparison between at least two variables, such as the values stored in cells E2 and B2. In this example a salesperson receives a bonus IF he or she sells more than the $10,000 quota. The variable of total sales is in cell E2 and the constant of the sales quota is in cell B2. Therefore the logical test IF E2 > B2 translates into the following: if the amount of sales generated is greater than $10,000. Table 2 lists and describes in more detail the logical operators to make the comparison in the logical test.

In Figure 19, cell F2 contains an IF function where the logical test is E2>$B$2 to determine if Tiffany's sales in cell E2 are greater than the sales goal in cell B2. Copying the function down the column will compare each sales representative's sales with the $10,000 value in cell B2.

TABLE 2   Logical Operators

Operator	Description
=	Equal to
<>	Not equal to
<	Less than
>	Greater than
<=	Less than or equal to
>=	Greater than or equal to

Pearson Education, Inc.

Design the Value_If_True and Value_If_False Arguments

The second and third arguments of an IF function are value_if_true and value_if_false. When Excel evaluates the logical test, the result is either true or false. If the logical test is true, the value_if_true argument executes. If the logical test is false, the value_if_false argument executes. Only one of the last two arguments is executed; both arguments cannot be executed, because the logical test is either true or false but not both.

The value_if_true and value_if_false arguments can contain text, cell references, formulas, or constants. In Figure 19, cell F2 contains an IF function in which the value_if_true argument is B$3 and the value_if_false argument is 0. Because the logical test (E2>B$2) is true—that is, Tiffany's sales of $11,000 are greater than the $10,000 goal—the value_if_true argument is executed, and the result displays $500, the value that is stored in cell B3.

Jose's sales of $10,000 are *not* greater than $10,000, and Rex's sales of $9,000 are *not* greater than $10,000. Therefore, the value_if_false argument is executed and returns no bonus in cells F3 and F4.

TIP: AT LEAST TWO POSSIBLE RIGHT ANSWERS

Every IF function can have at least two right solutions to produce the same results. Since the logical test is a comparative expression, it can be written two ways. For example, comparing whether E2 is greater than B2 can be written using greater than (E2>B2) or the reverse can also be compared to see if B2 is less than E2 (B2<E2). Depending on the logical test, the value if true and value if false arguments will switch.

Figure 21 illustrates several IF functions, how they are evaluated, and their results. You can create this worksheet with the input area and IF functions to develop your understanding of how IF functions work.

	A	B	C
1	Input Values		
2	$ 1,000.00		
3	$ 2,000.00		
4	10%		
5	5%		
6	$ 250.00		
7			
8	IF Function	Evaluation	Result
9	=IF(A2=A3,A4,A5)	$1,000 is equal to $2,000: FALSE	5%
10	=IF(A2<A3,A4,A5)	$1,000 is less than $2,000: TRUE	10%
11	=IF(A2<>A3,"Not Equal","Equal")	$1,000 and $2,000 are not equal: TRUE	Not Equal
12	=IF(A2>A3,A2*A4,A2*A5)	$1,000 is greater than $2,000: FALSE	$ 50.00
13	=IF(A2>A3,A2*A4,MAX(A2*A5,A6))	$1,000 is greater than $2,000: FALSE	$ 250.00
14	=IF(A2*A4=A3*A5,A6,0)	$100 (A2*A4) is equal to $100 (A3*A5): TRUE	$ 250.00

FIGURE 21 Sample IF Functions

Excel 2016, Windows 10, Microsoft Corporation

- **Cell A9.** The logical test A2=A3 compares the values in cells A2 and A3 to see if they are equal. Because $1,000 is not equal to $2,000, the logical test is false. The value_if_false argument is executed, which displays 5%, the value stored in cell A5.

- **Cell A10.** The logical test A2<A3 determines if the value in cell A2 is less than the value in A3. Because $1,000 is less than $2,000, the logical test is true. The value_if_true argument is executed, which displays the value stored in cell A4, which is 10%.

- **Cell A11.** The logical test A2<>A3 determines if the values in cells A2 and A3 are not equal. Because $1,000 and $2,000 are not equal, the logical test is true. The value_if_true argument is executed, which displays the text Not Equal.

- **Cell A12.** The logical test A2>A3 is false. The value_if_false argument is executed, which multiplies the value in cell A2 ($1,000) by the value in cell A5 (5%) and displays $50. The parentheses in the value_if_true (A2*A4) and value_if_false (A2*A5) arguments are optional. They are not required but may help you read the function arguments better.

- **Cell A13.** The logical test A2>A3 is false. The value_if_false argument, which contains a nested MAX function, is executed. The MAX function, MAX(A2*A5,A6), multiplies the values in cells A2 ($1,000) and A5 (5%) and returns the higher of the product ($50) and the value stored in cell A6 ($250).

- **Cell A14.** The logical test A2*A4=A3*A5 is true. The contents of cell A2 ($1,000) are multiplied by the contents of cell A4 (10%) for a result of $100. That result is then compared to the result of A3*A5, which is also $100. Because the logical test is true, the function returns the value of cell A6 ($250).

TIP: TEXT AND NESTED FUNCTIONS IN IF FUNCTIONS

You can use text within a formula. For example, you can build a logical test comparing the contents of cell A1 to specific text, such as A1="Input Values". The IF function in cell A11 in Figure 21 uses "Not Equal" and "Equal" in the value_if_true and value_if_false arguments. When you use text in a formula or function, you must enclose the text in quotation marks. However, do not use quotation marks around formulas, cell references, or values. You can also nest functions in the logical test, value_if_true, and value_if_false arguments of the IF function. When you nest functions as arguments, make sure the nested function contains the required arguments for it to work and that you nest the function in the correct argument to calculate accurate results. For example, cell C13 in Figure 21 contains a nested MAX function in the value_if_false argument.

Using Lookup Functions

You can use lookup and reference functions to quickly find data associated with a specified value. For example, when you order merchandise on a website, the webserver looks up the shipping costs based on weight and distance; or at the end of a semester, your professor uses your average, such as 88%, to look up the letter grade to assign, such as B+. There are numerous lookup functions in Excel, including HLOOKUP, INDEX, LOOKUP, MATCH, and VLOOKUP. Each lookup function can be used to identify and return information based, in part, on how the data is organized.

Use the VLOOKUP function

STEP 1 ➤➤ The *VLOOKUP function* accepts a value and looks for the value in the left column of a specified table array and returns another value located in the same row from a specified column. Use VLOOKUP to search for exact matches or for the nearest value that is less than or equal to the search value, such as assigning a B grade for a class average between 80% and 89%. The VLOOKUP function has the following three required arguments and one optional argument: (1) lookup_value, (2) table_array, (3) col_index_num, and (4) range_lookup.

=VLOOKUP(lookup_value,table_array,col_index_num,[range_lookup])

Figure 22 shows a partial grade book that contains a vertical lookup table, as well as the final scores and letter grades. The function in cell F3 is =VLOOKUP(E3,$A$3:$B$7,2).

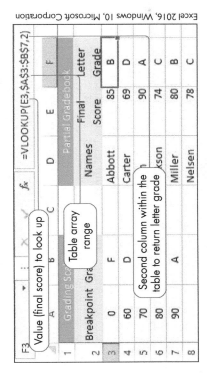

Excel 2016, Windows 10, Microsoft Corporation

FIGURE 22 VLOOKUP Function for Grade Book

The *lookup value* is the cell reference of the cell that contains the value to look up. The lookup value for the first student is cell E3, which contains 85. The *table array* is the range that contains the lookup table: $A$3:$B$7. The table array range must be absolute, the value you want to look up must be located in the first column, and cannot include column labels for the lookup table. The *column index number* is the column number in the lookup table that contains the return values. In this example, the column index number is 2, which corresponds to the letter grades in column B.

TIP: USING VALUES IN FORMULAS

You know to avoid using values in formulas because the input values in a worksheet cell might change. However, as shown in Figure 22, the value 2 is used in the col_index_number argument of the VLOOKUP function. The 2 refers to a particular column within the lookup table and is an acceptable use of a number within a formula.

The last argument in the VLOOKUP function is the optional *range_lookup*. This argument determines how the VLOOKUP function handles lookup values that are not an exact match for the data in the lookup table. By default, the range_lookup is set to TRUE, which is appropriate to look up values in a range. Omitting the optional argument or typing TRUE in it enables the VLOOKUP function to find the nearest value that is less than or equal in the table to the lookup value. For this reason, the first column in a VLOOKUP table array should be sorted from smallest to largest (or A to Z alphabetically) when defaulting to TRUE.

To look up an exact match, enter FALSE in the range_lookup argument. For example, if you are looking up product numbers, you must find an exact match to display the price. The function would look like this: =VLOOKUP(D15,$A$1:$B$50,2,FALSE). The function returns a value for the first lookup value that matches the first column of the lookup table. If no exact match is found, the function returns #N/A. Here is how the VLOOKUP function works:

1. The first argument of the function evaluates the value to be located in the left column of lookup table.

2. Excel searches the first column of the lookup table until it (a) finds an exact match (if possible) or (b) identifies the correct range if an exact match is not required.

3. If Excel finds an exact match, it moves across the table to the column designated by the column index number on that same row, and returns the value stored in that cell. If the last argument is TRUE or omitted, then Excel is looking for an approximate value (NOT an exact value). In this example, if the lookup value is larger than the first number in the first column of the table, it looks to the next value to see if the lookup value is larger and will continue to do so until reaching the largest number in the column. When Excel detects that the lookup value is not greater than the next breakpoint, it stays on that row. It then uses the column index number to identify the column containing the value to return for the lookup value. Because Excel goes sequentially through the breakpoint values, it is mandatory that the first column values are arranged from the lowest value to the highest value for ranges when the range_lookup argument is TRUE or omitted.

In Figure 22, the VLOOKUP function assigns letter grades based on final scores. Excel identifies the lookup value (85 in cell E3) and compares it to the values in the first column of the lookup table (range A3:B7). The last argument is omitted, so Excel tries to find an exact match of 85 or an approximate match; and because the table contains breakpoints rather than every conceivable score and the first column of the lookup table is arranged from the lowest to the highest breakpoints, Excel detects that 85 is greater than 80 but is not greater than 90. Therefore, it stays on the 80 row. Excel looks at the second column (column index number of 2) and returns the letter grade of B. The B grade is then displayed in cell F3.

Create the Lookup Table

A *lookup table* is a range containing a table of values and text from which data can be retrieved. The table should contain at least two rows and two columns, not including headings. Figure 23 illustrates a college directory with three columns. The first column contains professors' names. You look up a professor's name in the first column to see his or her office (second column) and phone extension (third column).

FIGURE 23 College Directory Lookup Table Analogy

Name	Office	Extension
Brazil, Estivan	GT 218b	7243
Fiedler, Zazilia	CS 417	7860
Lam, Kaitlyn	SC 124a	7031
Rodriquez, Lisa	GT 304	7592
Yeung, Braden	CS 414	7314

It is important to plan the table so that it conforms to the way in which Excel can utilize the data in it. Excel cannot interpret the structure of Table 3. If the values you look up are exact values, you can arrange the first column in any logical order. However, to look up an approximate value in a range (such as the range 80–89), you must arrange data from the lowest to the highest value and include only the lowest value in the range (such as 80) instead of the complete range (as demonstrated in Table 3). The lowest value for a category or in a series is the ***breakpoint***. Table 4 shows how to construct the lookup table in Excel. The first column contains the breakpoints—such as 60, 70, 80, and 90—or the lowest values to achieve a particular grade. The lookup table contains one or more additional columns of related data to retrieve.

TABLE 3 Grading Scale

Range	Grade
90–100	A
80–89	B
70–79	C
60–69	D
Below 60	F

TABLE 4 Grades Lookup Table

Range	Grade
0	F
60	D
70	C
80	B
90	A

You can nest functions as arguments inside the VLOOKUP function. For example, Figure 24 illustrates shipping amounts that are based on weight and location (Boston or Chicago). In the VLOOKUP function in cell C3, the lookup_value argument looks up the weight of a package in cell A3. That weight (14 pounds) is compared to the data in the table array argument, which is $E$3:$G$5. To determine which column of the lookup table to use, an IF function is nested as the column_index_number argument. The nested IF function compares the city stored in cell B3 to the text Boston. If cell B3 contains Boston, it returns 2 to use as the column_index_number to identify the shipping value for a package that is going to Boston. If cell B3 does not contain Boston (i.e., the only other city in this example is Chicago), the column_index_number is 3.

C3					f_x	=VLOOKUP(A3,$E$3:$G$5,IF(B3="Boston",2,3))	

▲	A	B	C	D	E	F	G	H
1	Customer Data					Lookup Data		
2	Weight	Location	Shipping		Weight	Boston	Chicago	
3	14	Boston	$ 19.95		0	$ 9.95	$ 12.95	
4	4	Chicago	$ 12.95		5	$ 14.95	$ 16.95	
5	8	Boston	$ 14.95		10	$ 19.95	$ 22.95	

FIGURE 24 IF Function Nested in VLOOKUP Function

Use the HLOOKUP Function

Lookup functions are not limited to only vertical tables. In situations in which data is better organized horizontally, you can design a lookup table where the first row contains the values for the basis of the lookup or the breakpoints, and additional rows contain data to be retrieved. With a horizontal lookup table, use the *HLOOKUP function*. Table 5 shows how quarterly sales data would look in a horizontal lookup table.

TABLE 5 Horizontal Lookup Table

Region	Qtr1	Qtr2	Qtr3	Qtr4
North	3495	4665	4982	5010
South	8044	7692	7812	6252
East	5081	6089	5982	6500
West	4278	4350	4387	7857

The syntax is almost the same as the syntax for the VLOOKUP function, except the third argument is row_index_num instead of col_index_num.

=HLOOKUP(lookup_value,table_array,row_index_num,[range_lookup])

STEP 2

Calculating Payments with the PMT Function

Excel contains several financial functions to help you perform calculations with monetary values. If you take out a loan to purchase a car, you need to know the monthly payment, which depends on the price of the car, the down payment, and the terms of the loan, in order to determine if you can afford the car. The decision is made easier by developing the worksheet in Figure 25 and by changing the various input values as indicated.

B9		▼	:	×	✓	fx	=PMT(B6,B8,−B3)

◢	A	B	C	D
1	Purchase Price	$25,999.00		
2	Down Payment	$ 5,000.00		
3	Amount to Finance	$20,999.00		
4	Payments per Year	12		Periodic interest
5	Interest Rate (APR)	3.500%		rate calculation
6	Periodic Rate (Monthly)	0.292%		
7	Term (Years)	5		Total number of
8	No. of Payment Periods	60		payment periods
9	Monthly Payment	$382.01		
10				

FIGURE 25 Car Loan Worksheet

Creating a loan model helps you evaluate options. You realize that the purchase of a $25,999 car is prohibitive because the monthly payment is $382.01. Purchasing a less expensive car, coming up with a substantial down payment, taking out a longer-term loan, or finding a better interest rate can decrease your monthly payments.

The **PMT function** calculates payments for a loan with a fixed amount at a fixed periodic rate for a fixed time period. The PMT function uses three required arguments and up to two optional arguments: (1) rate, (2) nper, (3) pv, (4) fv, and (5) type.

=PMT(rate,nper,pv,[fv],[type])

The **rate** is the interest rate per payment period. If the annual percentage rate (APR) is 12% and you make monthly payments, the periodic rate is 1% (12%/12 months). With the same APR and quarterly payments, the periodic rate is 3% (12%/4 quarters). Divide the APR by the number of payment periods in one year. However, instead of calculating the periodic interest rate within the PMT function, you can calculate it in a separate cell and refer to that cell in the PMT function, as is done in cell B6 of Figure 25.

The **nper** is the total number of payment periods. The term of a loan is usually stated in years; however, you make several payments per year. For monthly payments, you make 12 payments per year. To calculate the nper, multiply the number of years by the number of payments in one year. You can either calculate the number of payment periods in the PMT function, or calculate the number of payment periods in cell B8 and use that calculated value in the PMT function.

The **pv** is the present value of the loan. The result of the PMT function is a negative value because it represents your debt. However, you can display the result as a positive value by typing a minus sign in front of the present value cell reference in the PMT function.

Quick Concepts

8. Describe the three arguments for an IF function.

9. How should you structure a vertical lookup table if you need to look up values in a range?

10. What are the first three arguments of a PMT function? Why would you divide by or multiply an argument by 12?

Skills covered: Use the VLOOKUP Function • Use the PMT Function • Use the IF Function

3 Logical, Lookup, and Financial Functions

Erica wants you to complete another model that she might use for future mortgage data analysis. As you study the model, you realize you need to incorporate logical, lookup, and financial functions.

STEP 1 ⟩⟩ USE THE VLOOKUP FUNCTION

Rates vary based on the number of years to pay off the loan. Erica created a lookup table for three common mortgage years, and she entered the current APR. The lookup table will provide efficiency later when the rates change. You will use the VLOOKUP function to display the correct rate for each customer based on the number of years of the respective loans. Refer to Figure 26 as you complete Step 1.

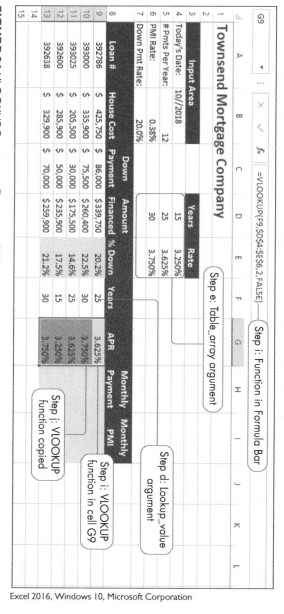

Step i: Function in Formula Bar

Step e: Table_array argument

Step d: Lookup_value argument

Step i: VLOOKUP function argument

Step i: VLOOKUP function in cell G9

Step i: VLOOKUP function copied

Excel 2016, Windows 10, Microsoft Corporation

FIGURE 26 VLOOKUP Function to Determine APR

a. Open *e02h2Loans_LastFirst* if you closed it at the end of Hands-On Exercise 2 and save it as **e02h3Loans_LastFirst**, changing h2 to h3.

b. Click the **Payment Info worksheet tab** to display the worksheet containing the data to complete. Click **cell G9**, the cell that will store the APR for the first customer.

c. Click the **Formulas tab**, click **Lookup & Reference** in the Function Library group, and then select **VLOOKUP**.

The Function Arguments dialog box opens.

d. Ensure that the insertion point is in the Lookup_value box, click the **Collapse Dialog Box**, click **cell F9** to enter F9 in the Lookup_value box, and then click the **Expand Dialog Box** to return to Function Arguments dialog box.

Cell F9 contains the value you need to look up from the table: 25 years.

e. Press **Tab**, click **Collapse Dialog Box** to the right of the Table_array box, select the **range D4:E6**, and then click **Expand Dialog Box** to return to the Function Arguments dialog box.

This is the range that contains that data for the lookup table. The Years values in the table are arranged from lowest to highest. Do *not* select the column labels for the range.

Anticipate what will happen if you copy the formula down the column. What do you need to do to ensure that the cell references always point to the exact location of the table? If your answer is to make the table array cell references absolute, then you answered correctly.

f. Press **F4** to make the range references absolute.

The Table_array box now contains $D$4:$E$6.

g. Press **Tab** and type **2** in the Col_index_num box.

The second column of the lookup table contains the Rates that you want to return and display in the cells containing the formulas.

h. Press **Tab** and type **False** in the Range_lookup box.

To ensure an exact match to look up in the table, you enter *False* in the optional argument.

i. Click **OK**.

The VLOOKUP function uses the first loan's term in years (25) to find an exact match in the first column of the lookup table, and then returns the corresponding rate from the second column, which is 3.625%.

j. Copy the formula down the column.

Spot-check the results to make sure the function returned the correct APR based on the number of years.

k. Save the workbook.

The worksheet now has all the necessary data for you to calculate the monthly payment for each loan: the APR, the number of years for the loan, the number of payment periods in one year, and the initial loan amount. You will use the PMT function to calculate the monthly payment, which includes paying back the principal amount with interest. This calculation does not include escrow amounts, such as property taxes or insurance. Refer to Figure 27 as you complete Step 2.

STEP 2 ≫ USE THE PMT FUNCTION

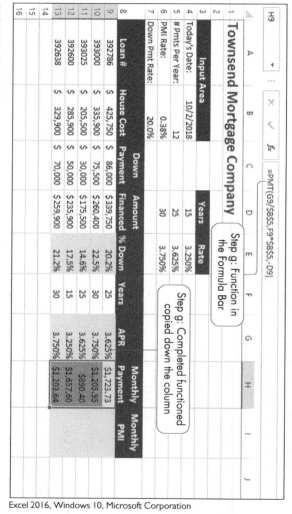

FIGURE 27 PMT Function to Calculate Monthly Payment

Excel 2016, Windows 10, Microsoft Corporation

a. Click **cell H9**, the cell that will store the payment for the first customer.

b. Click **Financial** in the Function Library group, scroll through the list, and then select **PMT**.

The Function Arguments dialog box opens.

TROUBLESHOOTING: Make sure you select PMT, not PPMT. The PPMT function calculates the principal portion of a particular monthly payment, not the total monthly payment itself.

---

c. Type **G9/B5** in the Rate box.

Think about what will happen if you copy the formula. The argument will be G10/B6 for the next customer. Are those cell references correct? G10 does contain the APR for the next customer, but B6 does not contain the correct number of payments in one year. Therefore, you need to make B5 an absolute cell reference because the number of payments per year does not vary.

d. Press **F4** to make the reference to cell B5 absolute.

e. Press **Tab** and type **F9*$B$5** in the Nper box.

You calculate the nper by multiplying the number of years by the number of payments in one year. You must make B5 an absolute cell reference so that it does not change when you copy the formula down the column.

f. Press **Tab** and type **-D9** in the Pv box.

The bottom of the dialog box indicates that the monthly payment is 1723.73008 or $1,723.73.

g. Click **OK**. Copy the formula down the column.

h. Save the workbook.

STEP 3 ≫ USE THE IF FUNCTION

Lenders often want borrowers to have a 20% down payment. If borrowers do not put in 20% of the cost of the house as a down payment, they pay a private mortgage insurance (PMI) fee. PMI serves to protect lenders from absorbing loss if the borrower defaults on the loan, and it enables borrowers with less cash to secure a loan. The PMI fee is about 0.38% of the amount financed. Some borrowers have to pay PMI for a few months or years until the balance owed is less than 80% of the appraised value. The worksheet contains the necessary values in the input area. You use the IF function to determine which borrowers must pay PMI and how much they will pay. Refer to Figure 28 as you complete Step 3.

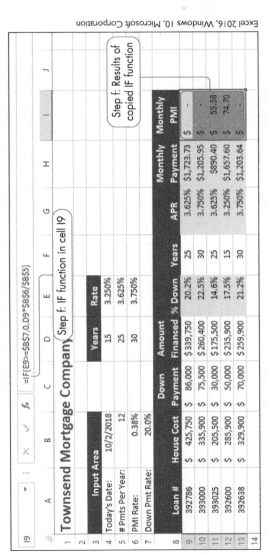

FIGURE 28 IF Function to Calculate Monthly PMI

Excel 2016, Windows 10, Microsoft Corporation

a. Click **cell I9**, the cell that will store the PMI, if any, for the first customer.

b. Click **Logical** in the Function Library group and select **IF**.

The Function Arguments dialog box opens. You will enter the three arguments.

c. Type **E9>=$B$7** in the Logical_test box.

The logical test compares the down payment percentage to see if the customer's down payment is at least 20%, the threshold stored in B7, of the amount financed. The customer's percentage cell reference is relative so that it will change when you copy it down the column; however, cell B7 must be absolute because it contains a value that should remain constant when the formula is copied to other cells.

d. Press **Tab** and type **0** in the Value_if_true box.

If the customer makes a down payment that is at least 20% of the purchase price, the customer does not pay PMI, so a value of 0 will display whenever the logical test is true. The first customer paid 20% of the purchase price, so he or she does not have to pay PMI.

e. Press **Tab** and type **D9*$B$6/$B$5** in the Value_if_false box.

If the logical test is false, the customer must pay PMI, which is calculated by multiplying the amount financed (D9) by the periodic PMI rate (the result of dividing the yearly PMI (B6) by the number of payments per year (B5)).

f. Click **OK** and copy the formula down the column.

The first, second, and fifth customers paid 20% of the purchase price, so they do not have to pay PMI. The third and fourth customers must pay PMI because their respective down payments were less than 20% of the purchase price.

TROUBLESHOOTING: If the results are not as you expected, check the logical operators. People often mistype < and > or forget to type = for >= situations. Correct any errors in the original formula and copy the formula again.

g. Set the worksheets to print on one page. Add a footer with your name on the left, sheet code in the middle, and the file name code on the right.

h. Save and close the file. Based on your instructor's directions, submit e02h3Loans_LastFirst.

Chapter Objectives Review

After reading this chapter, you have accomplished the following objectives:

1. Use relative, absolute, and mixed cell references in formulas.

- Use a relative cell address: A relative reference indicates a cell's location relative to the formula cell. When you copy the formula, the relative cell reference changes.
- Use an absolute cell reference: An absolute reference is a permanent pointer to a particular cell, indicated with $ before the column letter and the row number, such as $B$5. When you copy the formula, the absolute cell reference does not change.
- Use a mixed cell reference: A mixed reference contains part absolute and part relative reference, such as $B5 or B$5. Either the column or the row reference changes, while the other remains constant when you copy the formula.

2. Insert a function.

- A function is a predefined formula that performs a calculation. It contains the function name and arguments. Formula AutoComplete, function ScreenTips, and the Insert Function dialog box help you select and create functions. The Function Arguments dialog box guides you through the entering requirements for each argument.

3. Insert basic math and statistics functions.

- Use the SUM function: The SUM function calculates the total of a range of values. The syntax is =SUM(number1,[number2],...).
- Use the AVERAGE and MEDIAN functions: The AVERAGE function calculates the arithmetic mean of values in a range. The MEDIAN function identifies the midpoint value in a set of values.
- Use the MIN and MAX functions: The MIN function identifies the lowest value in a range, whereas the MAX function identifies the highest value in a range.
- Use the COUNT functions: The COUNT function tallies the number of cells in a range that contain values, whereas the COUNTBLANK function tallies the number of blank cells in a range, and COUNTA tallies the number of cells that are not empty.

- Perform calculations with Quick Analysis tools: With the Quick Analysis tools you can apply formatting, create charts or tables, and insert basic functions.

4. Use date functions.

- Insert the TODAY function: The TODAY function displays the current date.
- Insert the NOW function: The NOW function displays the current date and time.

5. Determine results with the IF function.

- Design the logical test: The IF function is a logical function that evaluates a logical test using logical operators, such as <, >, and =, and returns one value if the condition is true and another value if the condition is false.
- Design the value_if_true and value_if_false arguments: The arguments can contain cell references, text, or calculations. If a logical test is true, Excel executes the value_if_true argument. If a logical test is false, Excel executes the value_if_false argument.
- You can nest or embed other functions inside one or more of the arguments of an IF function to create more complex formulas.

6. Use lookup functions.

- Use the VLOOKUP function: The VLOOKUP function contains the required arguments lookup_value, table_array, and col_index_num and one optional argument, range_lookup.
- Create the lookup table: Design the lookup table using exact values or the breakpoints for ranges. If using breakpoints, the breakpoints must be in ascending order.
- Use the HLOOKUP function: The HLOOKUP function looks up values by row (horizontally) rather than by column (vertically).

7. Calculate payments with the PMT function.

- The PMT function calculates periodic payments for a loan with a fixed interest rate and a fixed term. The PMT function requires the periodic interest rate, the total number of payment periods, and the original value of the loan.

Key Terms Matching

Match the key terms with their definitions. Write the key term letter by the appropriate numbered definition.

a. Absolute cell reference

b. Argument

c. AVERAGE function

d. COUNT function

e. IF function

f. Logical test

g. Lookup table

h. MAX function

i. MEDIAN function

j. MIN function

k. Mixed cell reference

l. NOW function

m. PMT function

n. Relative cell reference

o. SUM function

p. Syntax

q. TODAY function

r. VLOOKUP function

1. _____ A set of rules that governs the structure and components for properly entering a function.

2. _____ Displays the current date.

3. _____ Indicates a cell's specific location; the cell reference does not change when you copy the formula.

4. _____ An input, such as a cell reference or value, needed to complete a function.

5. _____ Identifies the highest value in a range.

6. _____ Tallies the number of cells in a range that contain values.

7. _____ Looks up a value in a vertical lookup table and returns a related result from the lookup table.

8. _____ A range that contains data for the basis of the lookup and data to be retrieved.

9. _____ Calculates the arithmetic mean, or average, of values in a range.

10. _____ Identifies the midpoint value in a set of values.

11. _____ Displays the current date and time.

12. _____ Evaluates a condition and returns one value if the condition is true and a different value if the condition is false.

13. _____ Calculates the total of values contained in two or more cells.

14. _____ Calculates the periodic payment for a loan with a fixed interest rate and fixed term.

15. _____ Indicates a cell's location from the cell containing the formula; the cell reference changes when the formula is copied.

16. _____ Contains both an absolute and a relative cell reference in a formula; the absolute part does not change but the relative part does when you copy the formula.

17. _____ An expression that evaluates to true or false.

18. _____ Displays the lowest value in a range.

Multiple Choice

1. If cell E15 contains the formula =$C$5*$J$15, what type of cell reference is the J$15 in the formula?

(a) Relative reference

(b) Absolute reference

(c) Mixed reference

(d) Syntax

2. What function would most efficiently accomplish the same thing as =(B5+C5+D5+E5+F5)/5?

(a) =SUM(B5:F5)/5

(b) =AVERAGE(B5:F5)

(c) =MEDIAN(B5:F5)

(d) =COUNT(B5:F5)

3. When you start to type =AV, what feature displays a list of functions and defined names?

(a) Function ScreenTip

(b) Formula AutoComplete

(c) Insert Function dialog box

(d) Function Arguments dialog box

4. A formula containing the entry =$B3 is copied to a cell one column to the right and two rows down. How will the entry appear in its new location?

(a) =$B3

(b) =B3

(c) =$C5

(d) =$B5

5. Which of the following functions should be used to insert the current date and time in a cell?

(a) =TODAY()

(b) =CURRENT()

(c) =NOW()

(d) =DATE

6. Which of the following is not an argument of the IF function?

(a) value_if_true

(b) value_if_false

(c) logical_test

(d) lookup_value

7. Which of the following is *not* true about the VLOOKUP function?

(a) The lookup table must be in ascending order.

(b) The lookup table must be in descending order.

(c) The default match type is approximate.

(d) The match type must be false when completing an exact match.

8. The function =PMT(C5,C7,-C3) is stored in cell C15. What must be stored in cell C5?

(a) APR

(b) Periodic interest rate

(c) Loan amount

(d) Number of payment periods

9. Which of the following is *not* an appropriate use of the SUM function?

(a) =SUM(B3:B45)

(b) =SUM(F1:G10)

(c) =SUM(A8:A15,D8:D15)

(d) =SUM(D15-C15)

10. What is the keyboard shortcut to create an absolute reference?

(a) F2

(b) F3

(c) F4

(d) Alt

Hamilton Heights Auto Sales

You are the primary loan manager for Hamilton Heights Auto Sales, an auto sales company located in Missouri. In order to most efficiently manage the auto loans your company finances, you have decided to create a spreadsheet to perform several calculations. You will insert the current date, calculate down payment and interest rates based on credit score, calculate periodic payment amounts, and complete the project with basic summary information. Refer to Figure 29 as you complete this exercise.

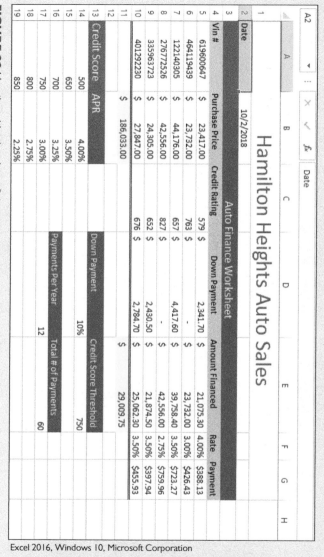

	A	B	C	D	E	F	G	H
1	Date	10/2/2018						
2								
3			Hamilton Heights Auto Sales					
4			Auto Finance Worksheet					
5	Vin #	Purchase Price	Credit Rating	Down Payment	Amount Financed	Rate	Payment	
5	619600647	$ 23,417.00	579	$ 2,341.70	$ 21,075.30	4.00%	$388.13	
6	464119439	$ 23,732.00	763	$ -	$ 23,732.00	3.00%	$426.43	
7	122140305	$ 44,176.00	657	$ 4,417.60	$ 39,758.40	3.50%	$723.27	
8	276772526	$ 42,556.00	827	$ -	$ 42,556.00	2.75%	$759.96	
9	335963723	$ 24,305.00	652	$ 2,430.50	$ 21,874.50	3.50%	$397.94	
10	401292230	$ 27,847.00	676	$ 2,784.70	$ 25,062.30	3.50%	$455.93	
11		$ 186,033.00			$ 29,009.75			
12								
13	Credit Score	APR		Down Payment	Credit Score Threshold			
14	500	4.00%		10%	750			
15	650	3.50%						
16	700	3.25%		Payments Per Year	Total # of Payments			
17	750	3.00%		12	60			
18	800	2.75%						
19	850	2.25%						

FIGURE 29 Hamilton Heights Auto Sales

Excel 2016, Windows 10, Microsoft Corporation

a. Open *e02p1AutoSales* and save it as **e02p1AutoSales_LastFirst**.

b. Click **cell B2**, click the **Formulas tab**, click **Date & Time** in the Function Library group, select **NOW**, and then click **OK** to enter today's date in the cell.

c. Click **cell D5** on the Formulas tab, click **Logical** in the Function Library group, and select **IF**.

d. Type **C5<=$E$14** in the Logical_test box, type **$D$14*B5** in the Value_if_true box, type **0** in the Value_if_false box, and then click **OK**.

This uses the IF function to calculate the required down payment based on credit score. If the customer has a credit score higher than 750 a down payment is not required. All clients with credits scores lower than 750 must pay a required 10% down payment in advance.

e. Use the fill handle to copy the contents of **cell D5** down the column, click **Auto Fill Options** to the lower-right of the copied cells, and then click **Fill Without Formatting** to ensure that the **Bottom Double border** remains applied to cell D10.

f. Calculate the Amount Financed by doing the following:

- Click **cell E5** and type **=B5-D5**.
- Use **cell E5's fill handle** to copy the function down the column.
- Apply **Bottom Double border** to cell E10.

g. Calculate the Rate by doing the following:

- Click **cell F5**. Click **Lookup & Reference** in the Function Library group and select **VLOOKUP**.
- Type **C5** in the Lookup_value box, type **$A$14:$B$19** in the Table_array box, type **2** in the Col_index_num box, and then click **OK**
- Double-click **cell F5's fill handle** to copy the function down the column.
- Click **Auto Fill Options**, and click **Fill Without Formatting**.

h. Calculate the required periodic payment by doing the following:

- Click **cell G5**, click **Financial** in the Function Library Group, and then click **PMT**.
- Type **F5/$D$17** in the Rate box, type **$E$17** in the Nper box, type **−E5** in the Pv box, and then click **OK**.
- Double-click **cell G5's** fill handle to copy the function down the column.
- Click the **Auto Fill Options** button, and click **Fill Without Formatting**.

i. Select the **range B5:B10**, click the **Quick Analysis button**, click **TOTALS**, and select **Sum** from the Quick Analysis Gallery.

j. Click **cell E11** and type **=AVERAGE(E5:E10)** to calculate the average amount financed.

k. Create a footer with your name on the left side, the sheet name code in the center, and the file name on the right side.

l. Save and close the workbook. Based on your instructor's directions, submit e02p1AutoSales_LastFirst.

2 Lockridge Marketing Analytics

As a business analyst for Lockridge Marketing Analytics, you have been tasked with awarding performance bonuses. You prepare a model to calculate employee bonuses based on average customer satisfaction survey results. The survey is based on a scale of 1 to 5 with 5 being the highest rating. Employees with survey results where ratings are between 1 and 2.9 do not receive bonuses, scores between 3 and 3.9 earn a 2% one-time bonus on their monthly salary, and scores of 4 or higher receive a 5% bonus. In addition, you calculate basic summary data for reporting purposes. Refer to Figure 30 as you complete this exercise.

J10		✓	fx		
▲	A	B	C	D	E	F

Lockridge Marketing Analytics

	A	B	C	D	E	F
1						
2						
3	**Inputs and Constants**				**Bonus Data**	
4	Today:	10/2/2018		Rating	1	3
5	Employees Surveyed	6		Bonus	0%	2%
6						
7						
8						
9	**Survey Code**	**Current Salary**	**Monthly Salary**	**Survey Score**	**Rating Bonus**	**Monthly Take Home**
10	38078	$ 50,000	$ 4,166.67	5	$ 208.33	$ 4,375.00
11	41105	$ 75,250	$ 6,270.83	3.5	$ 125.42	$ 6,396.25
12	39752	$ 67,250	$ 5,604.17	4.2	$ 280.21	$ 5,884.38
13	37872	$ 45,980	$ 3,831.67	3	$ 76.63	$ 3,908.30
14	40616	$ 58,750	$ 4,895.83	4.2	$ 244.79	$ 5,140.63
15	40347	$ 61,000	$ 5,083.33	4.5	$ 254.17	$ 5,337.50
16						
17						
18	**Statistics**					
19	Lowest Bonus	$ 76.63				
20	Average Bonus	$ 198.26				
21	Highest Bonus	$ 280.21				

Excel 2016, Windows 10, Microsoft Corporation

FIGURE 30 Lockridge Marketing Analytics

a. Open *e02p2Bonus* and save it as **e02p2Bonus_LastFirst**.

b. Click **cell B4**, click the **Formulas tab**, click **Date & Time** in the Function Library group, select **TODAY**, and then click **OK** to enter today's date in the cell.

c. Click **cell B5**, click the **AutoSum arrow** in the Function Library group, and then select **Count Numbers**. Select the **range A10:A15** and press **Enter**.

d. Click **cell C10**, type **=B10/12**, press **Ctrl+Enter**, and double-click the **fill handle**.

e. Enter the Rating Bonus based on survey average by doing the following:

- Click **cell E10** and type **=C10***.
- Click **Lookup & Reference** in the Function Library group and select **HLOOKUP**.
- Type **D10** in the Lookup_value box, type **E$4:G$5** in the Table_array box, type **2** in the Col_index_num box, and then click **OK**.
- Double-click the **cell E10 fill handle** to copy the formula down the Rating Bonus column.

f. Calculate each employee's monthly take-home by doing the following:

- Click **cell F10** and type **=C10+E10**.
- Double-click the **cell F10 fill handle**.

g. Calculate basic summary statistics by doing the following:

- Click **cell B19**, click the **Formulas tab**, click the **AutoSum arrow**, and then select **MIN**. Select the **range E10:E15** and then press **Enter**.
- In **cell B20**, click the **AutoSum arrow**, select **AVERAGE**, select the **range E10:E15**, and then press **Enter**.
- In **cell B21**, click the **AutoSum arrow**, select **MAX**, select the **range E10:E15**, and then press **Enter**.

h. Create a footer with your name on the left side, the sheet name in the center, and the file name code on the right side.

i. Save and close the workbook. Based on your instructor's directions, submit e02p2Bonus_LastFirst.

Mid-Level Exercises

■ Metropolitan Zoo Gift Shop Weekly Payroll

As manager of the gift shop at the Metropolitan Zoo, you are responsible for managing the weekly payroll. Your assistant developed a partial worksheet, but you need to enter the formulas to calculate the regular pay, overtime pay, gross pay, taxable pay, withholding tax, FICA, and net pay. In addition, you want to include total pay columns and calculate some basic statistics. As you construct formulas, make sure you use absolute and relative cell references correctly in formulas.

a. Open the *e02m1Payroll* workbook and save it as **e02m1Payroll_LastFirst**.

b. Study the worksheet structure and read the business rules in the Notes section.

c. Use IF functions to calculate the regular pay and overtime pay based on a regular 40-hour workweek in **cells E5** and **F5**. Pay overtime only for overtime hours. Calculate the gross pay based on the regular and overtime pay. Abram's regular pay is $398. With 8 overtime hours, Abram's overtime pay is $119.40.

d. Create a formula in **cell H5** to calculate the taxable pay. Multiply the number of dependents by the deduction per dependent and subtract that from the gross pay. With two dependents, Abram's taxable pay is $417.40.

e. Use a VLOOKUP function in **cell I5** to identify and calculate the federal withholding tax. With a taxable pay of $417.40, Abram's tax rate is 25% and the withholding tax is $104.35. The VLOOKUP function returns the applicable tax rate, which you must then multiply by the taxable pay.

f. Calculate FICA in **cell J5** based on gross pay and the FICA rate, and calculate the net pay in cell K5.

g. Copy all formulas down their respective columns.

h. Use Quick Analysis tools to calculate the total regular pay, overtime pay, gross pay, taxable pay, withholding tax, FICA, and net pay on **row 17**.

i. Apply **Accounting Number Format** to the **range C5:C16**. Apply **Accounting Number Format** to the first row of monetary data and to the total row. Apply the **Comma style** to the monetary values for the other employees. Underline the last employee's monetary values and use the Format Cells dialog box to apply Top and Double Bottom borders for the totals.

j. Insert appropriate functions to calculate the average, highest, and lowest values in the Summary Statistics area (the **range I21:K23**) of the worksheet. Format the # of hours calculations as **Number format** with one decimal and the remaining calculations with **Accounting Number Format**.

k. Insert a new sheet named **Overtime**. List the number of overtime hours for the week. Calculate the yearly gross amount spent on overtime assuming the same number of overtime hours per week. Add another row with only half the overtime hours (using a formula). What is your conclusion and recommendation on overtime? Format this worksheet.

l. Insert a footer with your name on the left side, the sheet name in the center, and the file name code on the right side of both worksheets.

m. Save and close the workbook. Based on your instructor's directions, submit e02m1Payroll_LastFirst.

2 Mortgage Calculator

As a financial consultant, you work with a family who plans to purchase a $35,000 car. You want to create a worksheet containing variable data (the price of the car, down payment, date of the first payment, and borrower's credit rating) and constants (sales tax rate, years, and number of payments in one year). Borrowers pay 0.5% sales tax on the purchase price of the vehicle and their credit rating determines the required down payment percentage and APR. Your worksheet needs to perform various calculations.

DISCOVER

a. Start a new Excel workbook, save it as **e02m2Loan_LastFirst**, and then rename Sheet1 **Payment**.

b. Type **Auto Loan Calculator** in cell A1, and then merge and center the title on the first row in the **range A1:F1**. Apply **bold, 18 pt** font size, and **Gold, Accent 4, Darker 25%** font color.

c. Type the labels in the **range A3:A12**. For each label, such as *Negotiated Cost of Vehicle*, merge the cells, such as the **range A4:B4**. Use the Format Painter to copy the formatting to the remaining nine labels. Next type and format the Inputs and Constants values in **column C**.

d. Type **Credit, Down Payment**, and **APR in the range A14:C14**, type the four credit ratings in the first column, the required down payment percentages in the second column, and the respective APRs in the third column. Next format the percentages, and then indent the percentages in the cells as needed.

e. Type labels in the Intermediate Calculations *and* Outputs sections in **column E**.

f. Enter formulas in the Intermediate Calculations and Outputs sections to calculate the following:

- **APR** based on credit rating: Use a Lookup function that references the borrower's credit rating and the table array in range. Include the range_lookup argument to ensure an exact match.

- **Minimum down payment required:** Use a lookup function and calculation. Use the credit rating as the lookup value, and the **table array A15:C18**. Include the range_lookup argument to ensure an exact match. Multiply the function results by the negotiated cost of the house.

- **Sales tax:** Multiply the negotiated cost of the vehicle by the sales tax rate.

- **Total down payment:** The sum of the minimum down payment required and any additional down payment made.

- **Amount of the loan:** The difference between the negotiated cost of the house and the total down payment.

- **Monthly payment:** Principal and interest using the PMT function.

g. Format each section with fill color, bold, underline, number formats, borders, and column widths as needed.

h. Insert a footer with your name on the left side, the sheet name in the center, and the file name code on the right side of both sheets.

i. Save and close the workbook. Based on your instructor's directions, submit e02m2Loan_LastFirst.

3 Facebook and Blackboard

COLLABORATION CASE

FROM SCRATCH

Social media extends past friendships to organizational and product "fan" pages. Organizations such as Lexus, Pepsi, and universities create pages to provide information about their organizations. Some organizations even provide product details, such as for the Lexus ES350. Facebook includes a wealth of information about Microsoft Office products. People share information, pose questions, and reply with their experiences.

a. Log in to your Facebook account. If you do not have a Facebook account, sign up for one and add at least two classmates as friends. Search for Microsoft Excel 2016 and click **Like.**

b. Review postings on the Microsoft Excel wall. Notice that some people post what they like most about Excel or how much it has improved their productivity. Post a note about one of your favorite features about Excel that you have learned so far or how you have used Excel in other classes or on the job.

c. Click the **Discussions link** on the Microsoft Excel Facebook page and find topics that relate to IF or HLOOKUP functions. Post a response to one of the discussions. Take a screenshot of your posting and insert it into a Word document. Save the Word document **as e02m3_LastFirst.**

d. Create a team of three students. Create one discussion that asks people to describe their favorite use of any of the nested functions used in this chapter. Each team member should respond to the posting. Monitor the discussion and, when you have a few responses, capture a screenshot of the dialogue and insert it into your Word document.

e. Go to www.youtube.com and search for one of these Excel topics: absolute references, mixed references, semi-selection, IF function, VLOOKUP function, or PMT function.

f. Watch several video clips and find one of particular interest to you.

g. Post the URL on your Facebook wall. Specify the topic and describe why you like this particular video.

h. Watch videos from the links posted by other students on their Facebook walls. Comment on at least two submissions. Point out what you like about the video or any suggestions you have for improvement.

i. Insert screenshots of your postings in a Word document, if required by your instructor. Save and close the file. Based on your instructor's directions submit e02m3_LastFirst.

Beyond the Classroom

Auto Finance

After graduating from college and obtaining your first job, you have decided to purchase a new vehicle. Before purchasing the car, you want to create a worksheet to estimate the monthly payment based on the purchase price, APR, down payment, and years. Your monthly budget is $500 and you will use conditional logic to automatically determine if you can afford the cars you are evaluating. Open the workbook *e02b1CarLoan* and save it as **e02b1CarLoan_LastFirst**.

Insert a function to automatically enter the current date in cell A4. Starting in cell B12 enter a formula to calculate the down payment for each vehicle price range based on the down payment percentage listed in cell D4. Be sure to use the appropriate absolute or mixed reference and copy the formula to complete range B13:B16. Before calculating the periodic payment for each vehicle, you will need to research the current vehicle interest rates. Conduct an Internet search to determine the current interest rate for a five-year auto loan and enter the value in cell D5. In cell C12 type a function that calculates the periodic payment for the first vehicle based on the input information in range D4:D7. Be sure to use the appropriate absolute or mixed reference and copy the formula to complete range C12:C16. In column D, use an IF function to determine if the first vehicle is financially viable; display either Test Drive or NA based on the criteria in cell D8. Be sure to use the appropriate absolute or mixed reference and copy the formula to complete range D12:D16.

Include a footer with your name on the left side, the date in the center, and the file name on the right side. Save and close the workbook. Based on your instructor's directions, submit e02b1CarLoan_LastFirst.

Park City Condo Rental

You and some friends are planning a Labor Day vacation to Park City, Utah. You have secured a four-day condominium that costs $1,200. Some people will stay all four days; others will stay part of the weekend. One of your friends constructed a worksheet to help calculate each person's cost of the rental. The people who stay Thursday night will split the nightly cost evenly. To keep the costs down, everyone agreed to pay $30 per night per person for Friday, Saturday, and/or Sunday nights. Depending on the number of people who stay each night, the group may owe more money. Kyle, Ian, Isaac, and Daryl agreed to split the difference in the total rental cost and the amount the group members paid. Open the workbook *e02b2ParkCity*, and save it as **e02b2ParkCity_LastFirst**.

Review the worksheet structure, including the assumptions and calculation notes at the bottom of the worksheet. Check the formulas and functions, making necessary corrections. With the existing data, the number of people staying each night is 5, 8, 10, and 7, respectively. The total paid given the above assumptions is $1,110, giving a difference of $90 to be divided evenly among the first four people. Kyle's share should be $172.50. In the cells containing errors, insert comments to describe the error and fix the formulas. Verify the accuracy of formulas by entering an IF function in cell I1 to ensure that the totals match. Nick, James, and Body inform you they cannot stay Sunday night, and Rob wants to stay Friday night. Change the input accordingly. The updated total paid is now $1,200, and the difference is $150. Include a footer with your name on the left side, the date in the center, and the file name on the right side. Save and close the workbook. Based on your instructor's directions, submit e02b2ParkCity_LastFirst.

Capstone Exercise

You are an account manager for Inland Jewelers, a regional company that makes custom class rings for graduating seniors. Your supervisor requested a workbook to report on new accounts created on payment plans. The report should provide details on total costs to the student as well as payment information. Each ring financed has a base price that can fluctuate based on ring personalization.

Insert Current Date

You open the starting workbook you previously created, and insert the current date and time.

a. Open the *e02c1ClassRing* workbook, and then save it as **e02c1ClassRing_LastFirst.**

b. Insert a function in **cell B2** to display the current date and format as a **Long Date.**

c. Set column B's width to **Autofit.**

Calculate Cost

You are ready to calculate the cost of each class ring ordered. The rings are priced based on their base metal as displayed in the range A15:B19.

a. Insert a lookup function in **cell C5** to display the ring cost for the first student.

b. Copy the function from **cell C5** down through **C11** to complete column C.

c. Apply **Accounting Number Format** to **column C.**

Determine the Total Due

You will calculate the total due for each student's order. The total is the base price of the ring plus an additional charge for personalization if applicable.

a. Insert an IF function in **cell E5** to calculate the total due. If the student has chosen to personalize the ring,

there is an additional charge of 5% located in **cell B21** that must be applied; if not, the student pays only the base price. Use appropriate relative and absolute cell references.

b. Copy the function from **cell E5** down through E11 to complete column E.

c. Apply **Accounting Number Format** to **column E.**

Calculate the Monthly Payment

Your next step is to calculate the periodic payment for each student's account. The payments are based on the years financed in column F and the annual interest rate in cell B22. All accounts are paid on a monthly basis.

a. Insert the function in **cell G5** to calculate the first student's monthly payment, using appropriate relative and absolute cell references.

b. Copy the formula down the column.

c. Apply **Accounting Number Format** to **column G.**

Finalize the Workbook

You perform some basic statistical calculations and finalize the workbook with formatting and page setup options.

a. Calculate totals in **cells C12, E12,** and **G12.**

b. Apply **Accounting Number Format** to the **cells C12, E12,** and **G12.**

c. Set **0.3"** left and right margins and ensure that the page prints on only one page.

d. Insert a footer with your name on the left side, the sheet name in the center, and the file name on the right side.

e. Save and close the workbook. Based on your instructor's directions, submit e02c1ClassRing_LastFirst.

Absolute cell reference A designation that indicates a constant reference to a specific cell location; the cell reference does not change when you copy the formula.

Argument An input, such as a cell reference or value, required to complete a function.

AVERAGE function A predefined formula that calculates the arithmetic mean, or average, of values in a range of cells.

Breakpoint The lowest value for a category or in a series.

Formula AutoComplete A feature that displays a list of functions and defined names that match letters as you type a formula.

Function A predefined computation that simplifies creating a formula that performs a complex calculation.

Function ScreenTip A small pop-up description that displays the function's arguments.

Column index number The column number in the lookup table that contains the return values.

COUNT function A predefined formula that tallies the number of cells in a range that contain values you can use in calculations, such as numerical and date data, but excludes blank cells or text entries from the tally.

COUNTA function A predefined formula that tallies the number of cells in a range that are not blank, that is, cells that contain data, whether a value, text, or a formula.

COUNTBLANK function A predefined formula that tallies the number of cells in a range that are blank.

HLOOKUP function A function that looks for a value in the top row of a specified table array and returns another value located in the same column from a specified row.

IF function A predefined formula that evaluates a condition and returns one value if the condition is true and a different value if the condition is false.

Logical test An expression that evaluates to true or false.

Lookup table A range that contains data for the basis of the lookup and data to be retrieved.

Lookup value The cell reference of the cell that contains the value to look up.

MAX function A predefined formula that identifies the highest value in a range.

MEDIAN function A predefined formula that identifies the midpoint value in a set of values.

MIN function A predefined formula that displays the lowest value in a range.

Mixed cell reference A designation that combines an absolute cell reference with a relative cell reference. The absolute part does not change but the relative part does change when you copy the formula.

Nested function A function that contains another function embedded inside one or more of it's arguments.

Nper Total number of payment periods.

NOW function A predefined formula that calculates the current date and military time that you last opened the workbook using the computer's clock.

Pmt function A function that calculates the periodic payment for a loan with a fixed interest rate and a fixed term.

PV A predefined formula that calculates the present value of a loan.

Quick Analysis A set of analytical tools you can use to apply formatting, create charts or tables, and insert basic functions.

Range_lookup An argument that determines how the VLOOKUP and HLOOKUP function handle lookup values that are not an exact match for the data in the lookup table.

Rate The periodic interest rate; the percentage of interest paid for each payment period; the first argument in the PMT function.

Relative cell reference A designation that indicates a cell's relative location from the original cell containing the formula; the cell reference changes when the formula is copied.

SUM function A predefined formula that calculates the total of values contained in one or more cells.

Syntax A set of rules that governs the structure and components for properly entering a function.

Table array The range that contains the lookup table.

TODAY function A predefined formula that displays the current date.

VLOOKUP function A predefined formula that accepts a value, looks the value up in a vertical lookup table with data organized in columns, and returns a result.

Charts

Charts

LEARNING OUTCOME

You will create charts and insert sparklines to represent data visually.

OBJECTIVES & SKILLS: After you read this chapter, you will be able to:

Chart Basics

OBJECTIVE 1: SELECT THE DATA SOURCE
Select an Adjacent Range, Select a Nonadjacent Range

OBJECTIVE 2: CHOOSE A CHART TYPE
Create a Clustered Column Chart, Create a Bar Chart, Change the Chart Type, Create a Line Chart, Create a Pie Chart, Create a Combo Chart, Create an Area Chart, Create a Scatter Chart, Create a Stock Chart

OBJECTIVE 3: MOVE, SIZE, AND PRINT A CHART
Move a Chart to a New Chart Sheet, Move a Chart Within a Worksheet, Size a Chart

HANDS-ON EXERCISE 1:
Chart Basics

Chart Elements

OBJECTIVE 4: ADD, EDIT, AND FORMAT CHART ELEMENTS
Edit and Format Chart Titles; Add and Format Axes Titles; Format Axes; Add, Position, and Format Data

Labels; Format and Position the Legend; Apply a Quick Layout; Format the Chart Area; Format the Plot Area; Format a Data Series; Format the Gridlines; Format a Data Point

HANDS-ON EXERCISE 2:
Chart Elements

Chart Design and Sparklines

OBJECTIVE 5: APPLY A CHART STYLE AND COLORS
Apply a Chart Style, Change Colors

OBJECTIVE 6: MODIFY THE DATA SOURCE
Apply Chart Filters, Switch Row and Column Data

OBJECTIVE 7: CREATE AND CUSTOMIZE SPARKLINES
Insert a Sparkline, Customize Sparklines

HANDS-ON EXERCISE 3:
Chart Design and Sparklines

CASE STUDY | Computer Job Outlook

You are an academic advisor for the School of Computing at a private university in Seattle, Washington. You will visit high schools over the next few weeks to discuss the computing programs at the university and to inform students about the job outlook in the computing industry. Your assistant, Doug Demers, researched growing computer-related jobs in the *Occupational Outlook Handbook* published by the Bureau of Labor Statistics on the U.S. Department of Labor's website. In particular, Doug listed seven jobs, the number of those jobs in 2010, the projected number of jobs by 2020, the growth in percentage increase and number of jobs, and the 2010 median pay. This dataset shows an 18%–31% increase in computer-related jobs in that 10-year time period.

To prepare for your presentation to encourage students to enroll in your School of Computing, you will create several charts that depict the job growth in the computer industry. You know that different charts provide different perspectives on the data. After you complete the charts, you will be able to use them in a variety of formats, such as presentations, fliers, and brochures.

Depicting Data Visually

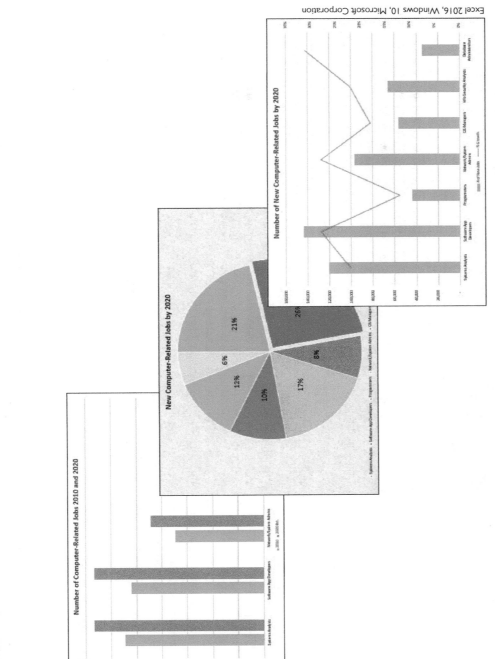

FIGURE 1 Computer Job Outlook Charts

CASE STUDY | Computer Job Outlook

Starting File	File to be Submitted
e03h1Jobs	e03h3Jobs_LastFirst

Chart Basics

A **chart** is a visual representation of numerical data that compares data and reveals trends or patterns to help people make informed decisions. An effective chart depicts data in a clear, easy-to-interpret manner and contains enough data to be useful without overwhelming your audience.

In this section, you will select the data source, choose the best chart type to represent numerical data, and designate the chart's location.

Selecting the Data Source

Look at the structure of the worksheet—the column labels, the row labels, the quantitative data, and the calculated values. Before creating a chart, make sure the worksheet data are organized so that the values in columns and rows use the same value system (such as dollars or units), make sure labels are descriptive, and delete any blank rows or columns that exist in the dataset. Decide what you want to convey to your audience by answering these questions:

- Does the worksheet hold a single set of data, such as average snowfall at one ski resort, or multiple sets of data, such as average snowfall at several ski resorts?

- Do you want to depict data for one specific time period or over several time periods, such as several years or decades?

Figure 2 shows a worksheet containing computer-related job titles, the number of jobs in 2010, the projected number of jobs by 2020, other details, and a chart. Row 3 contains labels merged and centered over individual column labels in row 5. Row 4 is blank and hidden. It is a good practice to insert a blank row between merged labels and individual column labels to enable you to sort the data correctly.

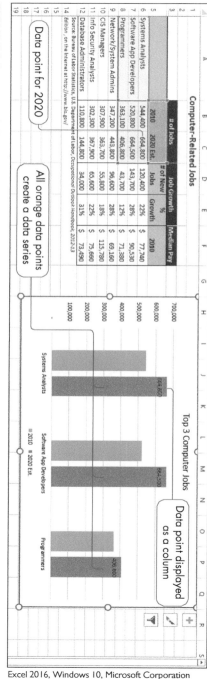

FIGURE 2 Dataset and Chart

Excel 2016, Windows 10, Microsoft Corporation

Each cell containing a value is a **data point**. For example, the value 664,800 in cell C6 is a data point for the estimated number of Systems Analysts in 2020. Each data point in the worksheet creates an individual data point in the chart. A group of related data points that display in row(s) or column(s) in the worksheet create a **data series**. For example, the values 664,800, 664,500, and 406,800 comprise the number of estimated jobs by 2020 data series, which is indicated by the orange columns in the chart.

Identify the data range by selecting values and labels that you want to include in the chart. If the values and labels are not stored in adjacent cells, hold Ctrl while selecting the nonadjacent ranges. Do not select worksheet titles or subtitles; doing so would add unnecessary data to the chart. To create the chart in Figure 2, select the range A5:C8. It is important to select parallel ranges. A parallel range is one that consists of the same starting and end point as another similar range. For example, the range C5:C12 is a parallel range to A5:A12. Including the column headings on row 5 (even though cell A5 is blank) is necessary to include the years in the legend at the bottom of the chart area.

TIP: AVOID USING DATA AGGREGATES AND INDIVIDUAL VALUES

Do not include data aggregates (such as totals or averages) *and* individual values. Including aggregates diminishes the effectiveness of comparing individual data points. It distorts each data point because the columns or bars are too small compared to the total.

TIP: SELECTING COLUMN AND ROW LABELS

When you create a column or bar chart, make sure you include the row labels (such as Systems Analysts) and column headings (such as 2010 and 2020 Est.). If you select only the data, such as the range B6:C12, Excel will display *Series 1* and *Series 2* for the color-coded columns or bars. In that case, you would not know what color represents what year.

Excel transforms the selected data into a chart. A chart may include several chart elements or components. Table 1 lists and describes some of these elements. Figure 3 shows a chart area that contains these elements.

TABLE 1 Chart Elements

Chart Element	Description
Chart area	The container for the entire chart and all of its elements.
Plot area	Region containing the graphical representation of the values in the data series. Two axes form a border around the plot area.
X-axis	The horizontal border that provides a frame of reference for measuring data left to right.
Y-axis	The vertical border that provides a frame of reference for measuring data up and down.
Legend	A key that identifies the color, gradient, picture, texture, or pattern assigned to each data series in a chart. For example, blue might represent values for 2010, and orange might represent values for 2020.

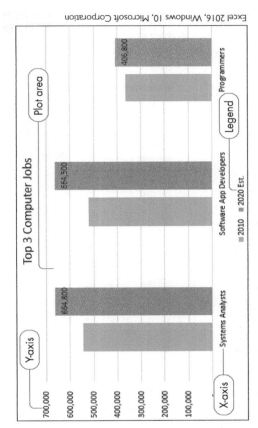

FIGURE 3 Chart Elements

Excel refers to the axes as the category axis and value axis. The *category axis* is the axis that displays descriptive labels for the data points plotted in a chart. The category axis labels are typically text contained in the first column of worksheet data (such as job titles) used to create the chart. The *value axis* is the axis that displays incremental numbers to identify the approximate values (such as number of jobs or revenue) of data points in a chart.

Choosing a Chart Type

You can create different charts from the same dataset; each chart type tells a different story. Select a chart type that appropriately represents the data and tells a story. For example, one chart might compare the number of computer-related jobs between 2010 and 2020, and another chart might indicate the percentage of new jobs by job title. The most commonly used chart types are column, bar, line, pie, and combo (see Table 2). Each chart type is designed to provide a unique perspective to the selected data.

TABLE 2 Common Chart Types

Chart	Chart Type	Description
	Column	Displays values in vertical columns where the height represents the value; the taller the column, the larger the value. Categories display along the horizontal (category) axis.
	Bar	Displays values in horizontal bars where the length represents the value; the longer the bar, the larger the value. Categories display along the vertical (category) axis.
	Line	Displays category data on the horizontal axis and value data on the vertical axis. Appropriate to show continuous data to depict trends over time, such as months, years, or decades.
	Pie	Shows proportion of individual data points to the total or whole of all those data points.
	Combo	Combines two chart types (such as column and line) to plot different data types (such as values and percentages)

Quick Analysis. When you select a range of adjacent cells (such as the range A5:C12) and position the pointer over that selected range, Excel displays Quick Analysis in the bottom-right corner of the selected area. However, Quick Analysis does not display when you select nonadjacent ranges, such as ranges A6:A12 and D6:D12. Quick Analysis displays thumbnails of recommended charts based on the data you selected so that you can create a chart quickly.

To create a chart using Quick Analysis, complete the following steps:

1. Select the data and click Quick Analysis.
2. Click Charts in the Quick Analysis gallery (see Figure 4).
3. Point to each recommended chart thumbnail to see a preview of the type of chart that would be created from the selected data.
4. Click the thumbnail of the chart you want to create.

Computer-Related Jobs

	# of Jobs		Job Growth		Median Pay
	2010	2020 Est.	# of New Jobs	% Growth	2010
Systems Analysts	544,400	664,800	120,400	22%	$ 77,740
Software App Developers	520,800	664,500	143,700	28%	$ 90,530
Programmers	363,100	406,800	43,700	12%	$ 71,380
Network/System Admins	347,200	443,800	96,600	28%	$ 69,160
CIS Managers	307,900	363,700	55,800	18%	$ 115,780
Info Security Analysts	302,300	367,900	65,600	22%	$ 75,660
Database Administrators	110,800	144,800	34,000	31%	$ 73,490

Source: Bureau of Labor Statistics, U.S. Department of Labor, Occupational Outlook Handbook, Edition, on the Internet at http://www.bls.gov/

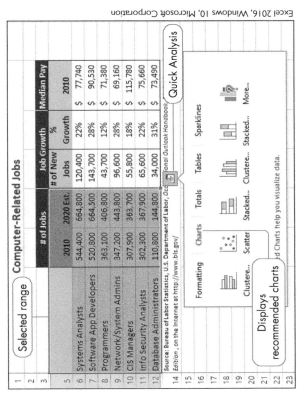

FIGURE 4 Quick Analysis Tool

Insert Tab. The Insert tab contains commands for creating a variety of charts. You must use the Insert tab to create a chart when you select nonadjacent ranges, but you can also use the Insert tab to create a chart when you select adjacent ranges. Clicking a particular chart on the Insert tab displays a gallery of icons representing more specific types of charts.

To create a chart using the Insert tab, complete the following steps:

1. Select the data and click the Insert tab.
2. Complete one of the following steps to select the chart type:
   - Click the chart type (such as Column) in the Charts group and click a chart subtype (such as Clustered Column) from the chart gallery (see Figure 5).
   - Click Recommended Charts in the Charts group to open the Insert Chart dialog box, click a thumbnail of the chart you want in the Recommended Charts tab or click the All Charts tab (see Figure 6) and click a thumbnail, and then click OK.

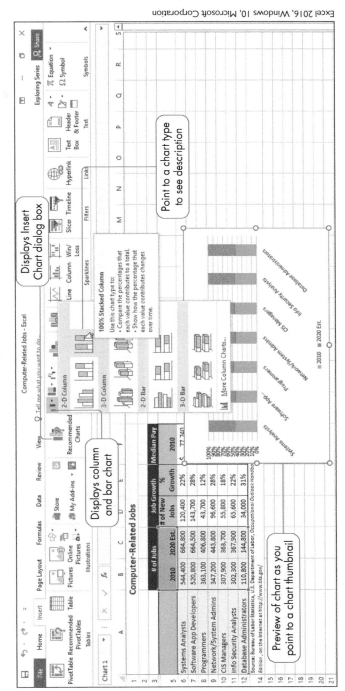

FIGURE 5 Chart Gallery

FIGURE 6 Insert Chart Dialog Box

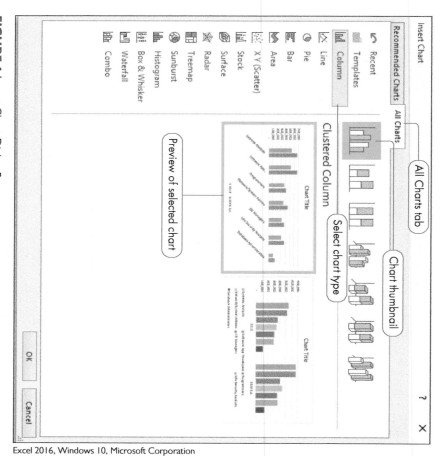

Excel 2016, Windows 10, Microsoft Corporation

Create a Column Chart

> A *column chart* compares values across categories, such as job titles, using vertical columns. The vertical axis displays values, and the horizontal axis displays categories. Column charts are most effective when they are limited to seven or fewer categories. If more categories exist, the columns appear too close together, making it difficult to read the labels.

The column chart in Figure 7 compares the number of projected jobs by job title for 2020 using the non-adjacent ranges A5:A9 and C5:C9 in the dataset shown in Figure 5. The first four job titles stored in the range A6:A9 form the category axis, and the increments of the estimated number of jobs in 2020 in range C6:C9 form the value axis. The height of each column in the chart represents the value of individual data points. For example, the Systems Analysts column is taller than the Programmers column, indicating that more jobs are projected for Systems Analysts than Programmers.

STEP 1

TIP: RECOMMENDED VS. LIST OF ALL CHARTS

If you are unsure which type of chart would be a good choice for the selected data, click Recommended Charts in the Chart group. Excel will analyze the selected data and display thumbnails of recommended charts in the Insert Chart dialog box. Click a thumbnail to see a larger visualization of how your selected data would look in that chart type. The dialog box displays a message indicating the purpose of the selected chart, such as *A clustered bar chart is used to compare values across a few categories. Use it when the chart shows duration or when the category text is long.*

Click the All Charts tab in the Insert Chart dialog box to display a list of all chart types. After you click a type on the left side of the dialog box, the top of the right side displays specific subtypes, such as Clustered Column. When you click a subtype, the dialog box displays an image of that subtype using the selected data.

Charts

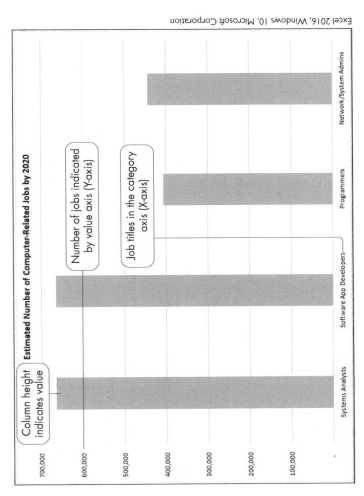

FIGURE 7 Column Chart

A *clustered column chart* compares groups—or clusters—of columns set side by side. The clustered column chart facilitates quick comparisons across data series, and it is effective for comparing several data points among categories. Figure 8 shows a clustered column chart created from the adjacent range A5:C9 in the dataset shown in Figure 5. By default, the job titles in the range A6:A9 appear on the category axis, and the yearly data points appear as columns with the value axis showing incremental numbers. Excel assigns a different color to each yearly data series and includes a legend so that you know what color represents which data series. The 2010 data series is light blue, and the 2020 data series is dark blue. This chart makes it easy to compare the predicted job growth from 2010 to 2020 for each job title and then to compare the trends among job titles.

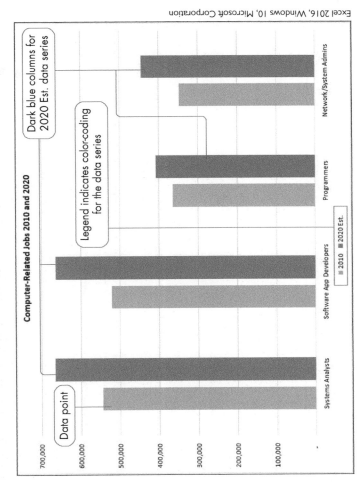

FIGURE 8 Clustered Column Chart

Figure 9 shows a clustered column chart in which the categories and data series are reversed. The years appear on the category axis, and the job titles appear as color-coded data series in the legend. This chart gives a different perspective from that in Figure 8 in that the chart in Figure 9 compares the number of jobs within a given year.

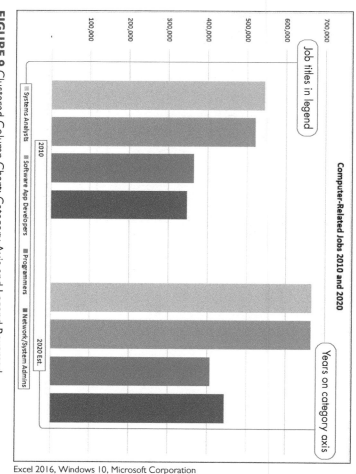

Computer-Related Jobs 2010 and 2020

Job titles in legend

Years on category axis

700,000
600,000
500,000
400,000
300,000
200,000
100,000

2010

2020 Est.

■ Systems Analysts   ■ Software App Developers   ■ Programmers   ■ Network/System Admins

FIGURE 9 Clustered Column Chart: Category Axis and Legend Reversed

A **stacked column chart** shows the relationship of individual data points to the whole category. A stacked column chart displays only one column for each category. Each category within the stacked column is color-coded for one data series. Use the stacked column chart when you want to compare total values across categories, as well as to display the individual category values. Figure 10 shows a stacked column chart in which a single column represents each categorical year, and each column stacks color-coded data-point segments representing the different jobs. The stacked column chart enables you to compare the total number of computer-related jobs for each year. The height of each color-coded data point enables you to identify the relative contribution of each job to the total number of jobs for a particular year. A disadvantage of the stacked column chart is that the segments within each column do not start at the same point, making it more difficult to compare individual segment values across categories.

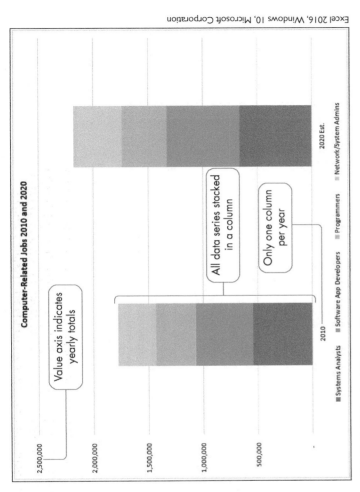

FIGURE 10 Stacked Column Chart

When you create a stacked column chart, make sure data are additive: Each column represents a sum of the data for each segment. Figure 10 correctly uses years as the category axis and the jobs as data series. For each year, Excel adds the number of jobs, and the columns display the total number of jobs. For example, the estimated total number of the four computer-related jobs in 2020 is about 2,180,000. Figure 11 shows a meaningless stacked column chart because the yearly number of jobs by job title is *not* additive. Adding the number of current actual jobs to the number of estimated jobs in the future does not make sense. It is incorrect to state that about 1,200,000 Systems Analysts jobs exist. Be careful when constructing stacked column charts to ensure that they lead to logical interpretation of data.

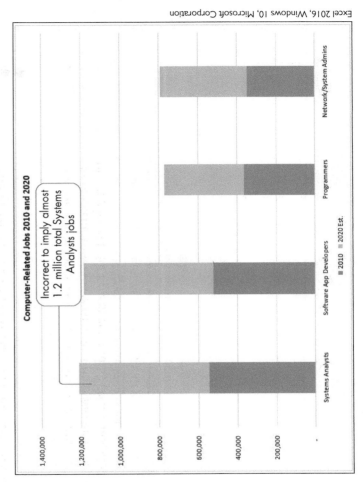

FIGURE 11 Incorrectly Constructed Stacked Column Chart

A ***100% stacked column chart*** converts individual data points (values) into percentages of the total value, similar to a pie chart. Each data series is a different color of the stack, representing a percentage. The total of each column is 100%. This type of chart depicts contributions to the whole. For example, the chart in Figure 12 illustrates that Systems Analysts account for 30% of the computer-related jobs represented by the four job categories in both 2010 and 2020.

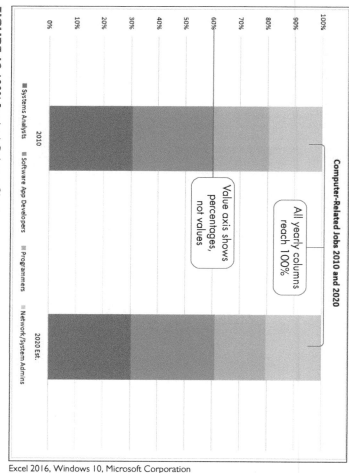

Computer-Related Jobs 2010 and 2020

All yearly columns reach 100%

Value axis shows percentages, not values

■ Systems Analysts ■ Software App Developers ■ Programmers ■ Network/System Admins

2010   2020 Est.

Excel 2016, Windows 10, Microsoft Corporation

FIGURE 12 100% Stacked Column Chart

Create a Bar Chart

STEP 2

A ***bar chart*** compares values across categories using horizontal bars. The horizontal axis displays values, and the vertical axis displays categories (see Figure 13). Bar charts and column charts tell a similar story: they both compare categories of data. A bar chart is preferable when category names are long, such as *Software App Developers*. A bar chart enables category names to appear in an easy-to-read format, whereas a column chart might display category names at an awkward angle or in a smaller font size. The overall decision between a column and a bar chart may come down to the fact that different data may look better with one chart type than the other.

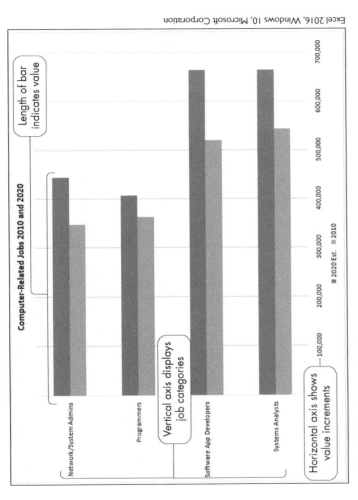

FIGURE 13 Clustered Bar Chart

Change the Chart Type

After you create a chart, you may decide that the data would be better represented by a different type of chart. For example, you might decide a bar chart would display the labels better than a column chart, or you might want to change a clustered bar chart to a stacked bar chart to provide a different perspective for the data. Use the Change Chart Type feature to change a chart to a different type of chart.

To change the type of an existing chart, complete the following steps:

1. Select the chart and click the Design tab.
2. Click Change Chart Type in the Type group to open the Change Chart Type dialog box (which is similar to the Insert Chart dialog box).
3. Click the All Charts tab within the dialog box.
4. Click a chart type on the left side of the dialog box.
5. Click a chart subtype on the right side of the dialog box and click OK.

Create a Line Chart

A *line chart* displays lines connecting data points to show trends over equal time periods. Excel displays each data series with a different line color. The category axis (X-axis) represents time, such as 10-year increments, whereas the value axis (Y-axis) represents a value, such as money or quantity. A line chart enables you to detect trends because the line continues to the next data point. To show each data point, choose the Line with Markers chart type. Figure 14 shows a line chart indicating the number of majors from 2005 to 2020 (estimated) at five-year increments. The number of Arts majors remains relatively constant, but the number of Tech & Computing majors increases significantly over time, especially between the years 2010 and 2020.

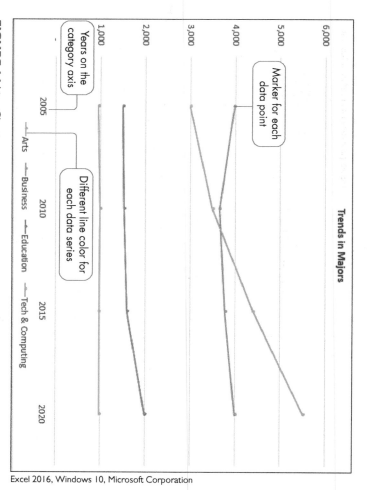

Trends in Majors

FIGURE 14 Line Chart

Excel 2016, Windows 10, Microsoft Corporation

STEP 4

Create a Pie Chart

A **pie chart** shows each data point as a proportion to the whole data series. The pie chart displays as a circle, or "pie," where the entire pie represents the total value of the data series. Each slice represents a single data point. The larger the slice, the larger percentage that data point contributes to the whole. Use a pie chart when you want to convey percentage. Unlike column, bar, and line charts that typically chart multiple data series, pie charts represent a single data series only.

The pie chart in Figure 15 divides the pie representing the estimated number of new jobs into seven slices, one for each job title. The size of each slice is proportional to the percentage of total computer-related jobs depicted in the worksheet for that year. For example, Systems Analysts account for 21% of the estimated total number of new computer-related jobs in 2020. Excel creates a legend to indicate which color represents which pie slice. When you create a pie chart, limit it to about seven data points. Pie charts with too many slices appear too busy to interpret, or shades of the same color scheme become too difficult to distinguish.

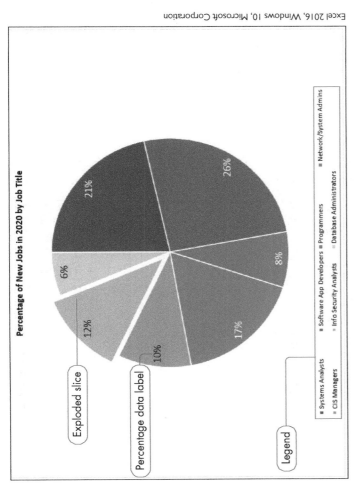

FIGURE 15 Pie Chart

Create a Combo Chart

A *combo chart* is a chart that combines two chart types, such as column and line charts. This type of chart is useful to show two different but related data types. For example, you might want to show the number of new jobs in columns and the percentage growth of new jobs in a line within the same chart (see Figure 16). A combo chart has a primary and a secondary axis. The primary axis displays on the left side of the chart. In this case, the primary axis indicates the number of jobs represented in the columns. The secondary axis displays on the right side of the chart. In this case, the secondary axis indicates the percentage of new jobs created as represented by the line.

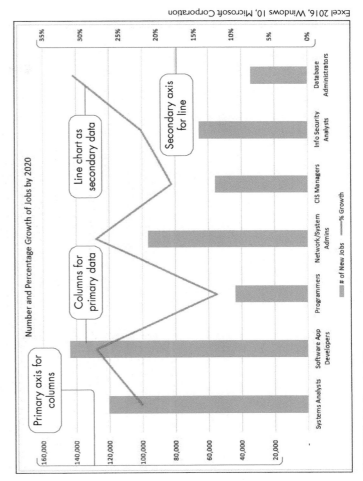

FIGURE 16 Combo Chart

Create Other Chart Types

Excel provides a variety of other types of charts. Two other chart types that are used for specialized analysis are X Y (scatter) charts and stock charts.

An **X Y (scatter) chart** shows a relationship between two numerical variables using their X and Y coordinates. Excel plots one variable on the horizontal X-axis and the other variable on the vertical Y-axis. Scatter charts are often used to represent data in educational, scientific, and medical experiments. Figure 17 shows the relationship between the number of minutes students view a training video and their test scores. The more minutes of a video a student watches, the higher the test score.

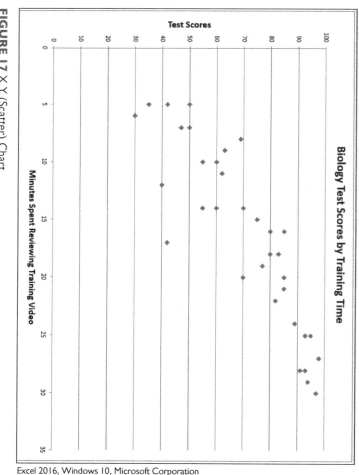

FIGURE 17 X Y (Scatter) Chart

Excel 2016, Windows 10, Microsoft Corporation

A **stock chart** shows fluctuations in stock prices. Excel has four stock subtypes: High-Low-Close, Open-High-Low-Close, Volume-High-Low-Close, and Volume-Open-High-Low-Close. The High-Low-Close stock chart marks a stock's trading range on a given day with a vertical line from the lowest to the highest stock prices. Rectangles mark the opening and closing prices. Figure 18 shows three days of stock prices for a particular company.

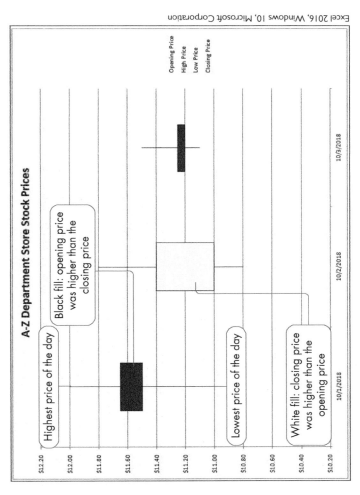

FIGURE 18 Stock Chart

The rectangle represents the difference in the opening and closing prices. If the rectangle has a white fill, the closing price is higher than the opening price. If the rectangle has a black fill, the opening price is higher than the closing price. In Figure 18, on October 1, the opening price was $11.65, and the closing price was $11.50, indicated by the top and bottom of the black rectangle. A line below the rectangle indicates that the lowest trading price is lower than the opening and closing prices. The lowest price was $11.00 on October 1. A line above the rectangle indicates that the highest trading price is higher than the opening and closing prices. The highest price was $12.00 on October 1. If no line exists below the rectangle, the lowest price equals either the opening or closing price, and if no line exists above the rectangle, the highest price equals either the opening or closing price.

TIP: ARRANGE DATA FOR A STOCK CHART

To create an Open-High-Low-Close stock chart, you must arrange data with Opening Price, High Price, Low Price, and Closing Price as column labels in that sequence. If you want to create other variations of stock charts, you must arrange data in a structured sequence required by Excel.

Table 3 lists and describes some of the other types of charts you can create in Excel.

TABLE 3 Other Chart Types

Chart	Chart Type	Description
	Area	Similar to a line chart in that it shows trends over time; however, the area chart displays colors between the lines to help illustrate the magnitude of changes.
	Surface	Represents numeric data and numeric categories. Displays trends using two dimensions on a continuous curve.
	Radar	Uses each category as a spoke radiating from the center point to the outer edges of the chart. Each spoke represents each data series, and lines connect the data points between spokes, similar to a spider web. A radar chart compares aggregate values for several data series. For example, a worksheet could contain the number of specific jobs for 2015, 2016, 2017, and 2018. Each year would be a data series containing the individual data points (number of specific jobs) for that year. The radar chart would aggregate the total number of jobs per year for all four data series.
	Histogram	A histogram is similar to a column chart. The category axis shows bin ranges (intervals) where data is aggregated into bins, and the vertical axis shows frequencies. For example, your professor might want to show the number (frequency) of students who earned a score within each grade interval, such as 60-69, 70-79, 80-89, and 90-100.

Pearson Education, Inc.

STEP 3

Moving, Sizing, and Printing a Chart

Excel inserts the chart as an embedded object in the current worksheet, often to the right of, but sometimes on top of and covering up, the data area. After you insert a chart, you usually need to move it to a different location and adjust its size. If you need to print a chart, decide whether to print the chart only or the chart and its data source.

Move a Chart

When you create a chart, Excel displays the chart in the worksheet, often on top of existing worksheet data. Therefore, you should move the chart so that it does not cover up data. If you leave the chart in the same worksheet, you can print the data and chart on the same page.

To move a chart on an active worksheet, complete the following steps:

1. Point to the chart area to display the Chart Area ScreenTip and the pointer includes the white arrowhead and a four-headed arrow.
2. Drag the chart to the desired location.

You might want to place the chart in a separate worksheet, called a *chart sheet.* A chart sheet contains a single chart only; you cannot enter data and formulas on a chart sheet. If you want to print or view a full-sized chart, move the chart to its own chart sheet.

To move a chart to another sheet or a chart sheet, complete the following steps:

1. Select the chart.

2. Click the Design tab and click Move Chart in the Location group (or right-click the chart and select Move Chart) to open the Move Chart dialog box (see Figure 19).

3. Select one of these options to indicate where you want to move the chart:

   - Click *New sheet* to move the chart to its own sheet. The default chart sheet for the first chart is Chart1, but you can rename it in the Move Chart dialog box or similarly to the way you rename other sheet tabs.

   - Click *Object in*, click the *Object in* arrow, and select the worksheet to which you want to move the chart.

4. Click OK.

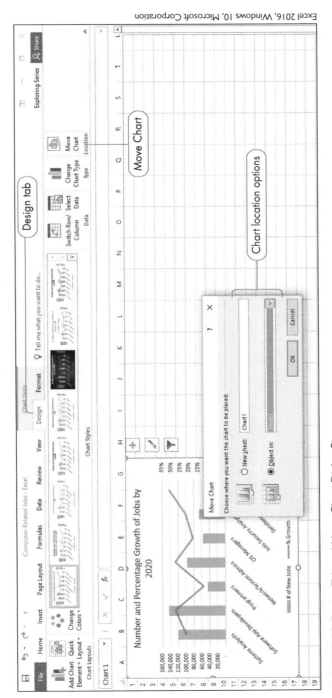

FIGURE 19 Design Tab and Move Chart Dialog Box

Excel 2016, Windows 10, Microsoft Corporation

Size a Chart

If you move a chart to a chart sheet, the chart is enlarged to fill the entire sheet. If you keep a chart embedded within a worksheet, you might want to size the chart to fit in a particular range or to ensure the chart elements are proportional. Use the sizing handles or the Format tab on the Ribbon to change the size of the chart.

To change the chart size with sizing handles, complete the following steps:

1. Select the chart. Excel displays a line border and sizing handles around the chart when you select it. *Sizing handles* are eight circles that display around the four corners and outside middle sections of a chart when you select it.

2. Point to the outer edge of the chart where the sizing handles are located until the pointer changes to a two-headed arrow.

3. Drag the border to adjust the chart's height or width. Drag a corner sizing handle to increase or decrease the height and width of the chart at the same time. Press and hold Shift as you drag a corner sizing handle to change the height and width proportionately.

To change the chart size on the Ribbon, complete the following steps:

1. Select the chart.
2. Click the Format tab.
3. Change the value in the Height and Width boxes in the Size group (see Figure 20).

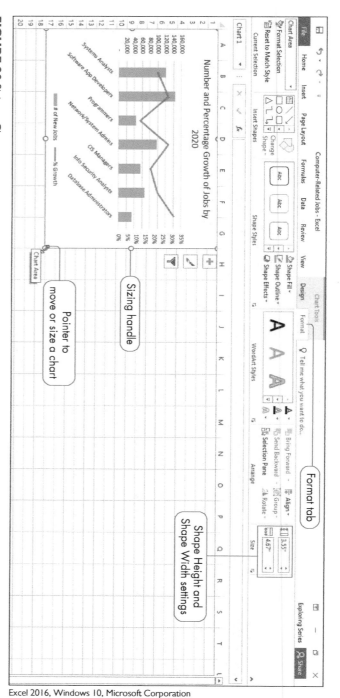

FIGURE 20 Sizing a Chart

Excel 2016, Windows 10, Microsoft Corporation

Print a Chart

After you create a chart, you may want to print it. If you embedded a chart on the same sheet as the data source, you need to decide if you want to print the data only, the data and the chart, or the chart only.

To print the data only, complete the following steps:

1. Select the data.
2. Click the File tab and click Print.
3. Click the first arrow in the Settings section and select Print Selection.
4. Click Print.

To print only the chart as a full page, complete the following steps:

1. Select the chart if it is on a worksheet that also contains data.
2. Click the File tab and click Print.
3. Make sure the default setting is Print Selected Chart.
4. Click Print.

If the data and chart are on the same worksheet, print the worksheet contents to print both, but do not select either the chart or the data before displaying the Print options. The preview shows you what will print. Make sure it displays what you want to print before clicking Print.

If you moved the chart to a chart sheet, the chart is the only item on that worksheet. When you display the print options, the default is Print Active Sheets, and the chart will print as a full-page chart.

Quick Concepts

1. Why should you not include aggregates, such as totals or averages, along with individual data points in a chart?

2. Describe the purpose of each of these chart types: (a) column, (b) bar, (c) line, (d) pie, and (e) combo.

3. How can you use Quick Analysis to create a chart?

4. How do you decide whether to move a chart within the worksheet where you created it or move it to a chart sheet?

1 Chart Basics

Doug Demers, your assistant, gathered data about seven computer-related jobs from the *Occupational Outlook Handbook* online. He organized the data into a structured worksheet that contains the job titles, the number of jobs in 2010, the projected number of jobs by 2020, and other data. Now you are ready to transform the data into visually appealing charts.

Skills covered: Select an Adjacent Range • Create a Clustered Column Chart • Move a Chart to a New Chart Sheet • Select a Nonadjacent Range • Create a Bar Chart • Change the Chart Type • Move a Chart Within a Worksheet • Size a Chart • Create a Pie Chart • Create a Combo Chart

---

STEP 1 》》 CREATE A CLUSTERED COLUMN CHART

You want to compare the number of jobs in 2010 to the projected number of jobs in 2020 for all seven computer-related professions that Doug entered into the worksheet. You decide to create a clustered column chart to depict this data. After you create this chart, you will move it to its own chart sheet. You will format the charts in Hands-On Exercise 2. Refer to Figure 21 as you complete Step 1.

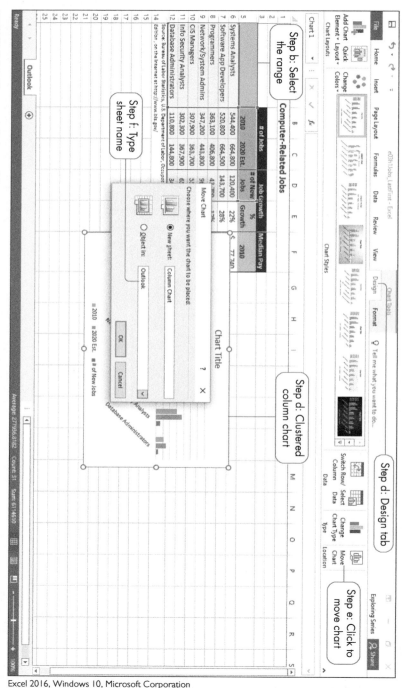

FIGURE 21 Clustered Column Chart

Excel 2016, Windows 10, Microsoft Corporation

a. Open *e03h1Jobs* and save it as **e03h1Jobs_LastFirst.**

TROUBLESHOOTING: If you make any major mistakes in this exercise, you can close the file, open *e03h1Jobs* again, and then start this exercise over.

b. Select the **range A5:D12**.

You selected the job titles, the number of jobs in 2010, the projected number of jobs in 2020, and the number of new jobs. Because you are selecting three data series (three columns of numerical data), you must also select the column headings on row 5.

c. Click **Quick Analysis** at the bottom-right corner of the selected range and click **Charts**.

The Quick Analysis gallery displays recommended charts based on the selected range.

d. Point to **Clustered Column** (the third thumbnail in the Charts gallery) to see a preview of what the chart would look like and click **Clustered Column**.

Excel inserts a clustered column chart based on the selected data. The Design tab displays on the Ribbon while the chart is selected.

e. Click **Move Chart** in the Location group.

The Move Chart dialog box opens for you to specify where to move the chart.

f. Click **New sheet**, type **Column Chart**, and then click **OK**. Save the workbook.

Excel moves the clustered column chart to a new sheet called Column Chart.

STEP 2 ⟩⟩ **CREATE A BAR CHART**

You want to create a bar chart to depict the number of jobs in 2010 and the number of new jobs that will be created by 2020. Finally, you want to change the chart to a stacked bar chart to show the total jobs in 2020 based on the number of jobs in 2010 and the number of new jobs. Refer to Figure 22 as you complete Step 2.

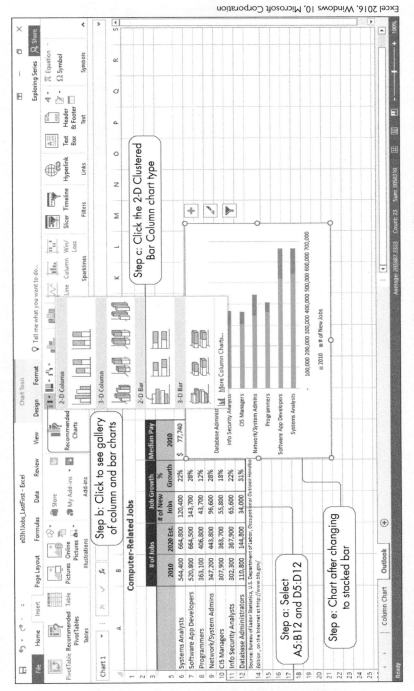

FIGURE 22 Bar Chart

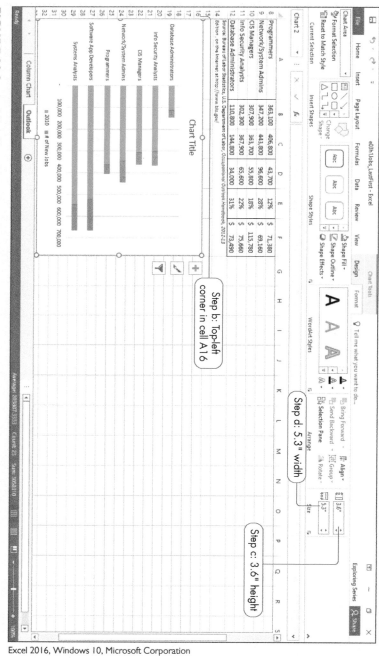

FIGURE 23 Stacked Bar Chart Moved and Sized

Excel 2016, Windows 10, Microsoft Corporation

---

a. Click the **Outlook sheet tab**, select the **range A5:B12**, press and hold **Ctrl**, and then select the **range D5:D12**.

You used Ctrl to select nonadjacent ranges: the job title labels, the number of jobs in 2010, and the number of new jobs.

TIP: PARALLEL RANGES

Nonadjacent ranges should be parallel so that the legend will correctly reflect the data series. This means that each range should contain the same number of related cells. For example, A5:A12, B5:B12, and D5:D12 are parallel ranges. Even though cell A5 is blank, you must select it to have a parallel range with the other two selected ranges that include cells on row 5.

---

b. Click the **Insert tab** and click **Insert Column or Bar Chart** in the Charts group.

The gallery shows both column and bar chart thumbnails.

c. Click **Clustered Bar** in the 2-D Bar section to create a clustered bar chart.

Excel inserts the clustered bar chart in the worksheet.

d. Click **Change Chart Type** in the Type group on the Design tab.

The Change Chart Type dialog box opens. The left side of the dialog box lists all chart types. The top-right side displays thumbnails of various bar charts, and the lower section displays a sample of the selected chart.

e. Click **Stacked Bar** in the top center of the dialog box and click **OK**. Save the workbook.

Excel displays the number of jobs in 2010 in blue and stacks the number of new jobs in orange into one bar per job title. This chart tells the story of how the total projected number of jobs in 2020 is calculated: the number of existing jobs in 2010 (blue) and the number of new jobs (orange).

STEP 3 ▶▶ MOVE AND SIZE A CHART

The bar chart is displayed in the middle of the worksheet. You decide to position it below the job outlook data and adjust its size to make it larger so that it is as wide as the dataset and a little taller for better proportions. Refer to Figure 23 as you complete Step 3.

a. Point to an empty part of the chart area.

The pointer displays a four-headed arrow with the regular white arrowhead, and the Chart Area ScreenTip displays.

TROUBLESHOOTING: Make sure you see the Chart Area ScreenTip as you perform Step b. If you move the pointer to another chart element—such as the legend—you will move or size that element instead of moving the entire chart.

b. Drag the chart so that the top-left corner of the chart appears in **cell A16**.

You positioned the chart below the worksheet data.

c. Click the **Format tab**, select the value in the **Shape Height box**, type **3.6**, and then press **Enter**.

The chart is now 3.6" tall.

d. Select the value in the **Shape Width box**, type **5.3**, and then press **Enter**. Save the workbook.

The chart is now 5.3" wide.

STEP 4 ›› CREATE A PIE CHART

You decide to create a pie chart that depicts the percentage of new jobs by job title calculated from the total number of new jobs created for the seven job titles Doug researched. After creating the pie chart, you will move it to its own sheet. Refer to Figure 24 as you complete Step 4.

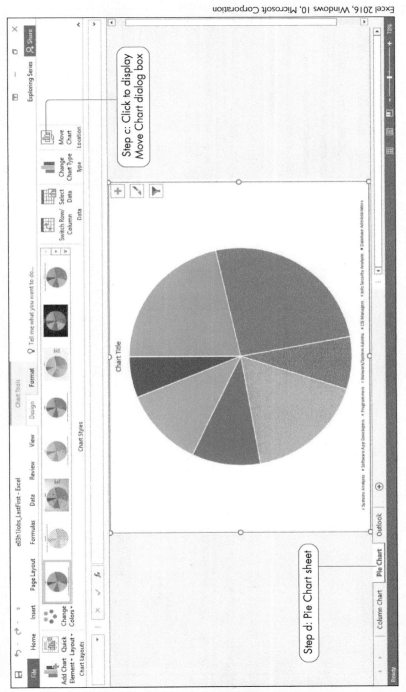

Step c: Click to display Move Chart dialog box

Step d: Pie Chart sheet

FIGURE 24 Pie Chart

a. Select the **range A6:A12**, press and hold **Ctrl**, then select the **range D6:D12**.

> **TROUBLESHOOTING:** Do not select cells A5 and D5 this time because you are creating a pie chart. When creating a chart from a single data series (e.g., # of New Jobs), you do not need to select the column headings.

b. Click the **Insert tab**, click **Insert Pie or Doughnut Chart** in the Charts group, and then select **Pie** in the 2-D Pie group on the gallery.

The pie chart displays in the worksheet.

c. Click **Move Chart** in the Location group on the Design tab.

The Move Chart dialog box opens.

d. Click **New sheet**, type **Pie Chart**, and then click **OK**. Save the workbook.

Excel creates a new sheet called Pie Chart. The pie chart is the only object on that sheet.

STEP 5 ≫ CREATE A COMBO CHART

You want to create a combo chart that shows the number of new jobs in columns and the percentage of new jobs created in a line on the secondary axis. Although the number of new jobs may appear low as represented by the smallest column (such as 34,000 new database administrators), the actual percentage of new jobs created between 2010 and 2020 may be significant as represented by the steep incline of the orange line (such as 31% growth for database administrators). Refer to Figure 25 as you complete Step 5.

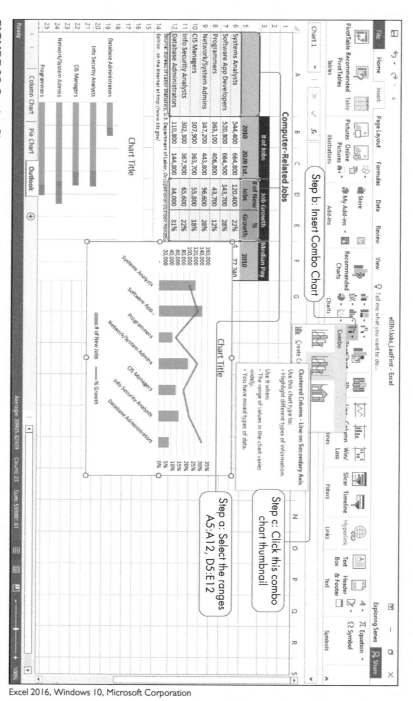

FIGURE 25 Combo Chart

Excel 2016, Windows 10, Microsoft Corporation

a. Click the **Outlook sheet tab**, select the **range A5:A12**, press and hold **Ctrl**, then select the **range D5:E12**.

b. Click the **Insert tab** and click **Insert Combo Chart** in the Charts group.

The Combo Chart gallery of thumbnails displays.

c. Click the **Clustered Column – Line on Secondary Axis thumbnail**, which is the middle thumbnail.

Excel creates a combo chart based on the thumbnail you selected. The number of new jobs displays in blue columns, and the percentage growth displays as an orange line.

d. Click **Move Chart** in the Location group on the Design tab, click **New sheet**, type **Combo Chart**, and then click **OK**.

e. Save the workbook. Keep the workbook open if you plan to continue with the next Hands-On Exercise. If not, close the workbook, and exit Excel.

Chart Elements

After creating a chart, you should add appropriate chart elements. A *chart element* is a component that completes or helps clarify the chart. Some chart elements, such as chart titles, should be included in every chart. Other elements are optional. Table 4 describes the chart elements, and Figure 26 illustrates several chart elements.

TABLE 4 Chart Elements

Element	Description
Axis title	Label that describes the category or value axes. Display axis titles, such as In Millions of Dollars or Top 7 Computer Job Titles, to clarify the axes. Axis titles are not displayed by default.
Chart title	Label that describes the entire chart. It should reflect the purpose of the chart. For example, Houses Sold is too generic, but Houses Sold in Seattle in 2018 indicates the what (Houses), the where (Seattle), and the when (2018). The default text is Chart Title.
Data label	Descriptive label that shows the exact value or name of a data point. Data labels are not displayed by default.
Data table	A grid that contains the data source values and labels. If you embed a chart on the same worksheet as the data source, you might not need to include a data table. Only add a data table with a chart that is on a chart sheet.
Error bars	Visuals that indicate the standard error amount, a percentage, or a standard deviation for a data point or marker. Error bars are not displayed by default.
Gridlines	Horizontal or vertical lines that display in the plot area, designed to help people identify the values plotted by the visual elements, such as a column.
Legend	A key that identifies the color, gradient, picture, texture, or pattern assigned to each data series. The legend is displayed by default for some chart types.
Trendline	A line that depicts trends or helps forecast future data, such as estimating future sales or number of births in a region. Add a trendline to column, bar, line, stock, scatter, and bubble charts. Excel will analyze the current trends and display a line indicating future values based on those trends.

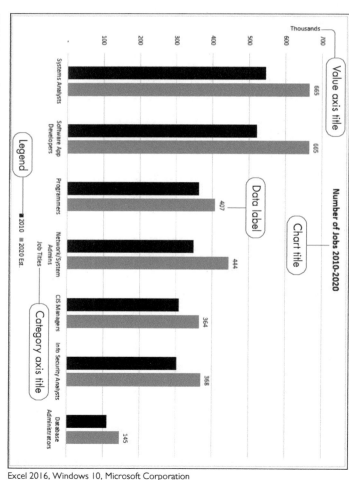

FIGURE 26 Chart Elements

In this section, you will learn how to add, edit, and format chart elements. Specifically, you will learn how to type a chart title, add axis titles, add data labels, and position the legend. Furthermore, you will learn how to format these elements as well as format axes, position the legend, and add gridlines. Finally, you will learn how to format the chart area, plot area, data series, and a data point.

Adding, Editing, and Formatting Chart Elements

After you create a chart, you usually need to add elements to provide labels to describe the chart. Adding descriptive text for labels provides information for the reader to comprehend the chart without knowing or seeing the underlying data. When you create a chart, one or more elements may display by default. For example, when you create the charts in Hands-On Exercise 1, Excel displayed a placeholder for the chart title and displayed a legend so that you know which color represents each data series.

When a chart is selected, three icons display to the right of the chart: Chart Elements, Chart Styles, and Chart Filters. In addition, the Design tab contains the Chart Layouts group that allows you to add and customize chart elements and change the layout of the chart.

When you point to a chart element, Excel displays a ScreenTip with the name of that element. To select a chart element, click it when you see the ScreenTip, or click the Format tab, click the Chart Elements arrow in the Current Selection group, and select the element from the list.

Edit, Format, and Position the Chart Title

> **STEP 1** » Excel includes the placeholder text *Chart Title* above the chart. You should replace that text with a descriptive title. In addition, you might want to format the chart title by applying bold and changing the font, font size, font color, and fill color.

To edit and format the chart title, complete the following steps:

1. Select the chart title.
2. Type the text you want to appear in the title and press Enter.
3. Click the Home tab.
4. Apply the desired font formatting, such as increasing the font size and applying bold.
5. Click the chart to deselect the chart title.

TIP: FONT COLOR

The default font color for the chart title, axes, axes titles, and legend is Black, Text I, Lighter 35%. If you want these elements to stand out, change the color to Black, Text I or another solid color.

By default, the chart title displays centered above the plot area. Although this is a standard location for the chart, you might want to position it elsewhere.

To change the position of the chart title, complete the following steps:

1. Select the chart title and click Chart Elements to the right of the chart.
2. Point to the Chart Title and click the triangle on the right side of the menu option, Chart Title (see Figure 27).
3. Select one of the options:

   • Above Chart: Centers the title above the plot area, decreasing the plot area size to make room for the chart title.

   • Centered Overlay: Centers the chart title horizontally without resizing the plot area: the title displays over the top of the plot area.

   • More Options: Opens the Format Chart Title task pane to apply fill, border, and alignment settings. A *task pane* is a window of options to format and customize chart elements. The task pane name and options change based on the selected chart element. For example, when you double-click the chart title, the Format Chart Title task pane displays.

4. Click Chart Elements to close the menu.

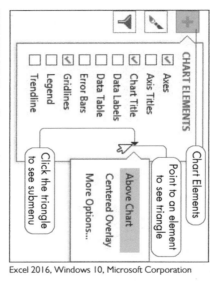

FIGURE 27 Chart Elements List

Excel 2016, Windows 10, Microsoft Corporation

TIP: LINKING A CHART TITLE OR AN AXIS TITLE TO A CELL

Instead of typing text directly in the Chart Title or Axis Title placeholder, you can link the title to a label in a cell. Click the Chart Title or Axis Title placeholder, type = in the Formula Bar, click the cell containing the label you want for the title, and then press Enter. Excel will enter the sheet name and cell reference, such as =Outlook!$A$1, in the Formula Bar. If you change the worksheet label, Excel will also change the title in the chart.

Add, Format, and Position Axis Titles

Axis titles are helpful to provide more clarity about the value or category axis. Axis titles also help you conform to ADA compliance requirements. For example, if the values are abbreviated as 7 instead of 7,000,000 you should indicate the unit of measurement on the value axis as In Millions. You might want to further clarify the labels on the category axis by providing a category axis title, such as Job Titles.

STEP 2

Charts

To add an axis title, complete the following steps:

1. Select the chart and click Chart Elements to the right of the chart.
2. Point to Axis Titles and click the triangle on the right side.
3. Select one or more of these options:
   - **Primary Horizontal:** Displays a title for the primary horizontal axis.
   - **Primary Vertical:** Displays a title for the primary vertical axis.
   - **Secondary Horizontal:** Displays a title for the secondary horizontal axis in a combo chart.
   - **Secondary Vertical:** Displays a title for the secondary vertical axis in a combo chart.
   - **More Options:** Opens the Format Axis Title task pane to apply fill, border, and alignment settings.
4. Click Chart Elements to close the menu.

To use the Design tab to add a chart element, complete the following steps:

1. Click the Design tab.
2. Click Add Chart Element in the Chart Layouts group.
3. Point to an element and select from that element's submenu (see Figure 28).

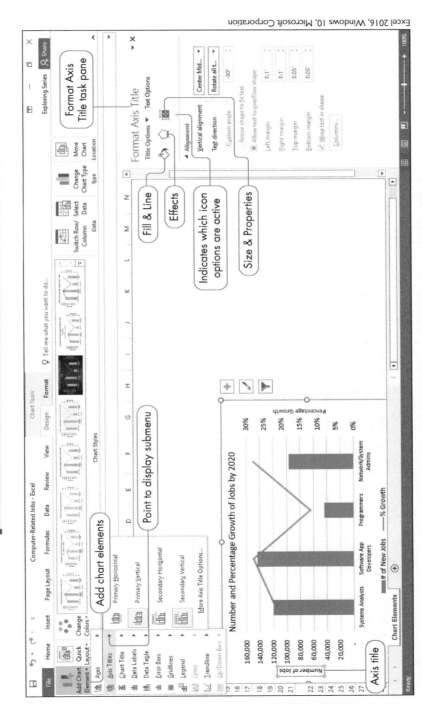

FIGURE 28 Chart Elements Menu and Format Axis Title Task Pane

The horizontal axis title displays below the category labels, and the rotated vertical axis title displays on the left side of the value axis. After including an axis title, click the title, type the text for the title, and then press Enter similarly to editing text for a chart title. You might want to apply font formatting (such as font size and color) to the axis titles similarly to formatting a chart title. Use the Format Axis Title task pane to customize and format the axis title.

To position and format the axis title, complete the following:

1. Double-click the axis title to open the Format Axis Title task pane (refer to Figure 28). Each task pane has categories, such as Title Options and Text Options. Below these categories are icons, such as Fill & Line, Effects, and Size & Properties.

2. Click Title Options and click the Size & Properties icon. The options in the task pane change to display options related to the icon you click. A thin horizontal gray line separates the icons from the options. The line contains a partial triangle that points to the icon that is active to indicate which options are displayed. Figure 28 shows the triangle is pointing to Size & Properties.

3. Change the *Vertical alignment* or *Horizontal alignment* option to the desired position.

4. Click other icons, such as Fill & Line, and select the desired options.

5. Close the Format Axis Title task pane.

6. Click the Home tab and apply font formatting, such as Font Color.

TIP: REMOVE AN ELEMENT

To remove an element, click Chart Elements and click a check box to deselect the check box. Alternatively, click Add Chart Element in the Chart Layouts group on the Chart Tools Design tab, point to the element name, and then select None. You can also select a chart element and press Delete to remove it.

Format the Axes

Based on the data source values and structure, Excel determines the start, incremental, and end values that display on the value axis when you create the chart. However, you might want to adjust the value axis so that the numbers displayed are simplified or fit better on the chart. For example, when working with large values such as 4,567,890, the value axis displays increments, such as 4,000,000 and 5,000,000. You can simplify the value axis by displaying values in millions, so that the values on the axis are 4 and 5 with the word Millions placed by the value axis to indicate the units. Use the Format Axis task pane to specify the bounds, units, display units, labels, and number formatting for an axis.

To format an axis, complete the following steps:

1. Double-click the axis to open the Format Axis task pane (see Figure 29).

2. Click the Axis Options icon, and complete any of the following steps:
   - Change the bounds, units, and display units. The Minimum Bound sets the starting value, and the Maximum Bound sets the ending value on the value axis. The Major Units specifies the intervals of values on the value axis. The Display units converts the values, such as to Millions.
   - Click Tick Marks to change the major and minor tick marks.
   - Click Labels to change the label position.
   - Click Number to change the category, specify the number of decimal places, select how negative numbers display. The Category option specifies the number formatting, such as Currency. Depending on the category, other options may display, such as Decimal places so that you can control the number of decimal places on the value axis.

3. Close the Format Axis task pane.

4. Click the Home tab and apply font formatting, such as Font Color.

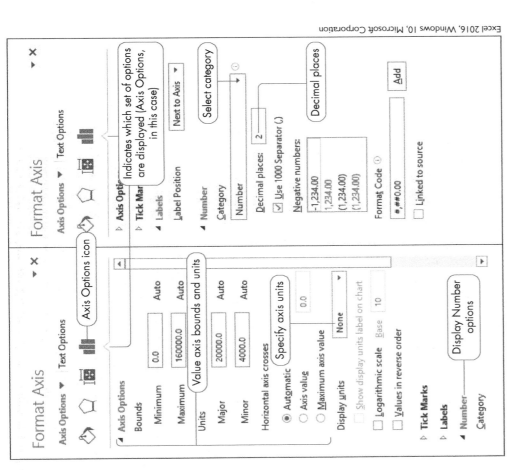

Excel 2016, Windows 10, Microsoft Corporation

FIGURE 29 Format Axis Task Pane

TIP: DISPLAYING OPTIONS WITHIN TASK PANES

A diagonal black triangle next to a category, such as Axis Options, indicates that all of a category's options are displayed (expanded). A triangle with a white fill, such as the one next to Tick Marks, indicates that the category options are not displayed (collapsed).

Add, Position, and Format Data Labels

STEP 3 A data label is descriptive text that shows the exact value or name of a data point. Data labels are useful to indicate specific values for data points you want to emphasize. Typically, you would add data labels only to specific data points, and not all data points. Use either Chart Elements or the Design tab to display data labels.

To add and position data labels, complete the following steps:

1. Select the chart and click Chart Elements to the right of the chart.
2. Click the Data Labels check box to display data labels.
3. Click the arrow to the right of the Data Labels item to select the position, such as Center or Outside End.
4. Click Chart Elements to close the menu.

By default, Excel adds data labels to all data series. If you want to display data labels for only one series, select the data labels for the other data series and press Delete. In Figure 26, data labels are included for the 2020 data series but not the 2010 data series. When you select a data label, Excel selects all data labels in that data series. Use the Format Data Labels task pane to customize and format the data labels. You can also apply font formatting (such as font size and color) to the data labels similarly to formatting a chart title.

To format the data labels, complete the following steps:

1. Double-click a data label to open the Format Data Labels task pane (see Figure 30).

2. Click the Label Options icon.

3. Click Label Options to customize the labels, and complete any of the following steps:

   • Select the Label Contains option. The default is Value, but you might want to display additional label contents, such as Category Name. For example, you might want to add data labels to a pie chart to indicate both Percentage and Category Names.

   • Select the Label Position option, such as Center or Inside End.

4. Click Number and apply number formatting if the numeric data labels are not formatted.

5. Close the Format Data Labels task pane.

6. Click the Home tab and apply font formatting, such as Font Color.

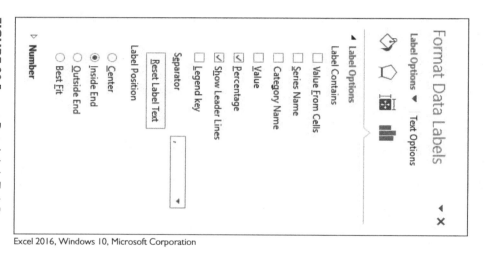

FIGURE 30 Format Data Labels Task Pane

Excel 2016, Windows 10, Microsoft Corporation

Position and Format the Legend

When you create a multiple series chart, the legend displays, providing a key to the color-coded data series. Position the legend to the right, top, bottom, or left of the plot area, similarly to choosing the position for a chart title using Chart Elements. Make sure that the columns, bars, or lines appear proportionate and well balanced after you position the legend. Use the Format Legend task pane to customize and format the legend.

To format the legend, complete the following steps:

1. Double-click the legend to open the Format Legend task pane.
2. Click the Legend Options icon.
3. Select the position of the legend: Top, Bottom, Left, Right, or Top Right.
4. Click the Fill & Line icon, click Border, and set border options if you want to change the border settings for the legend.
5. Close the Format Legend task pane.
6. Click the Home tab and apply font formatting, such as Font Color.

Excel 2016, Windows 10, Microsoft Corporation

FIGURE 31 Quick Layout Gallery

Add and Format Gridlines

Gridlines are horizontal or vertical lines that span across the plot area of the chart to help people identify the values plotted by the visual elements, such as a column. Excel displays horizontal gridlines for column, line, scatter, stock, surface, and bubble charts and vertical gridlines for bar charts. Click either Chart Elements or Add Chart Elements in the Chart Layouts group on the Design tab to add gridlines.

Format gridlines by double-clicking a gridline to open the Format Major Gridlines task pane. You can change the line type, color, and width of the gridlines.

TIP: ALTERNATIVE FOR OPENING FORMAT TASK PANES

Another way to display a task pane is to right-click the chart element and choose Format <element>, where <element> is the specific chart element. If you do not close a task pane after formatting a particular element, such as gridlines, and then click another chart element, the task pane will change so that you can format that particular chart element.

Format the Chart Area, Plot Area, and Data Series

Apply multiple settings, such as fill colors and borders, at once using the Format task pane for an element. To open a chart element's task pane, double-click the chart element. Figure 32 displays the Format Chart Area, Format Plot Area, and Format Data Series task panes with different fill options selected to display the different options that result. All three task panes include the same fill and border elements. For example, you might want to change the fill color of a data series from blue to green. After you select a fill option, such as Gradient fill, the remaining options change in the task pane.

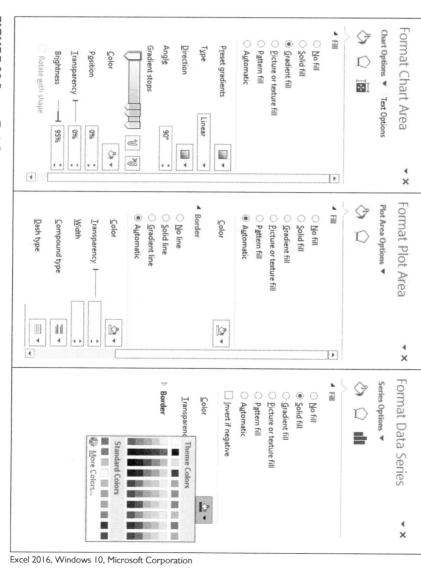

FIGURE 32 Format Task Panes

TIP: USE IMAGES OR TEXTURES

For less formal presentations, you might want to use images or a texture to fill the data series, chart area, or plot area instead of a solid fill color. To use an image or a texture, click the Fill & Line icon at the top of the task pane, click Fill, and then click *Picture or texture fill*. Click File or Online in the *Insert picture from* section and insert an image file or search online to insert an image. The image is stretched by default, but you might want to select the Stack option to avoid distorting the image. To add a texture, click *Picture or texture fill*, click the Texture arrow, and then select a textured background from the gallery of textures. Generally, do not mix images and textures because doing so would create a cluttered appearance.

TIP: ACCESSIBILITY COMPLIANCE

It is a good practice to apply some features that are accessibility compliant for people who have disabilities, such as vision or cognitive impairments, that may prevent them from seeing or comprehending the visual aid. For charts, it is recommended to assign a name to a chart, such as New Jobs, because the default chart name such as Chart 1 is not meaningful. To name a chart, select it and type a name in the Name Box to the left of the Formula Bar.

In addition, you should provide *Alt Text*, which is a title and description that provides an alternative text-based interpretation of the visual, such as a chart. A device can read the title and description to the user. To enter Alt Text for a chart, right-click the chart area to open the Format Chart Area task pane, click Alt Text to display its options, type a brief title in the Title box, and type a descriptive interpretation of the chart in the Description box.

Format a Data Point

STEP 4 ▶▶ Earlier in this chapter, you learned that a data point reflects a value in a single cell in a worksheet. You can select that single data point in a chart and format it differently from the rest of the data series. Select the data point you want to format, display the Format Data Point task pane, and make the changes you want. For example, you might want to focus a person's attention on a particular slice by separating one or more slices from the rest of the chart in an *exploded pie chart* (refer to Figure 15).

To format a pie slice data point, complete the following steps:

1. Click within the pie chart, pause, and then click the particular slice you want to format.

2. Right-click the selected pie slice and select Format Data Point to open the Format Data Point task pane.

3. Click the Fill & Line icon and click the desired option (such as Solid fill) in the Fill category.

4. Click the Color arrow and select a color for a solid fill; select a *Preset gradient*, type, color, and other options for a gradient fill; or insert a picture or select a texture for a picture or texture fill.

5. Click the Series Options icon and drag the Point Explosion to the right to explode the selected pie slice, such as to 12% (see Figure 33).

6. Close the Format Data Point task pane.

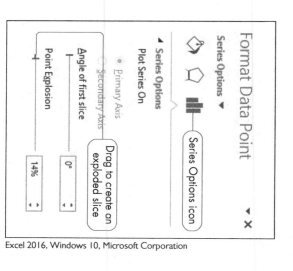

Format Data Point ▼ ✕

Series Options ▼

Series Options icon

▲ Series Options
Plot Series On
● Primary Axis
Secondary Axis

Angle of first slice   0°

Point Explosion   14%

Drag to create an exploded slice

FIGURE 33 Format Data Point Task Pane

Excel 2016, Windows 10, Microsoft Corporation

TIP: DRAG TO EXPLODE A PIE SLICE

Another way to explode a pie slice is to select the specific slice and then drag it away from the pie.

Use the Chart Tools Format Tab

The Format tab contains options to select a chart element, insert shapes, apply shape styles, apply WordArt styles, arrange objects, and specify the size of an object. Table 5 lists and describes the groups on the Format tab.

Group	Description
TABLE 5 Chart Tools Format Tab	
Current Selection	Selects a chart element, displays the task pane to format the selected element, and clears custom formatting of the selected element.
Insert Shapes	Inserts a variety of shapes in a chart.
Shape Styles	Specifies a shape style, fill color, outline color, and shape effect.
WordArt Styles	Adds artistic style, text fill, and text effects to an object.
Arrange	Brings an object forward or backward to layer multiple objects; aligns, groups, and rotates objects.
Size	Adjusts the height and width of the selected object.

Pearson Education, Inc.

Quick Concepts

5. List at least four types of appropriate labels that describe chart elements. What types of things can you do to customize these labels?

6. What is the purpose of exploding a slice on a pie chart?

7. What are some of the fill options you can apply to a chart area or a plot area?

Hands-On Exercises

2 Chart Elements

Skills covered: Edit and Format Chart Titles • Add and Format Axes Titles • Format Axes • Add, Position, and Format Data Labels • Format the Chart Area • Format a Data Point

You want to enhance the computer job column, bar, and pie charts by adding some chart elements. In particular, you will enter a descriptive chart title for each chart, add and format axis titles for the bar chart, add and format data labels for the pie chart, and change fill colors in the pie chart.

STEP 1 ▶ EDIT AND FORMAT CHART TITLES

When you created the column, bar, and pie charts in Hands-On Exercise 1, Excel displayed *Chart Title* at the top of each chart. You will add a title that appropriately describes each chart. In addition, you want to format the chart titles by applying bold and enlarging the font sizes. Refer to Figure 34 as you complete Step 1.

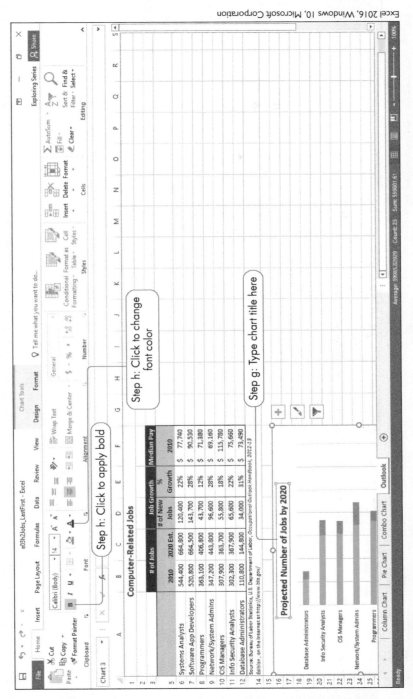

Excel 2016, Windows 10, Microsoft Corporation

FIGURE 34 Formatted Chart Title

a. Open *e03h1Jobs_LastFirst* if you closed it at the end of the Hands-On Exercise 1, and save it as **e03h2Jobs_LastFirst**, changing h1 to h2.

b. Make sure the Combo Chart sheet is the active sheet, select the **Chart Title** placeholder, type **Number of New Computer-Related Jobs by 2020**, and then press **Enter**.

As you type a chart title, Excel displays the text in the Formula Bar. The text does not appear in the chart title until after you press Enter.

TROUBLESHOOTING: If you double-click a title and type directly into the title placeholder, do not press Enter after typing the new title. Doing so will add a blank line.

c. Click the **Home tab**, click **Bold**, click the **Font Color arrow**, and then select **Black, Text 1**.

You applied font formats so that the chart title stands out.

d. Click the **Pie Chart sheet tab**, select the **Chart Title** placeholder, type **New Computer-Related Jobs by 2020**, and then press **Enter**.

Excel displays the text you typed for the chart title.

e. Click the **Home tab**, click **Bold**, click the **Font Size arrow** and select **18**, and then click the **Font Color arrow** and select **Black, Text 1**.

You formatted the pie chart title so that it stands out.

f. Click the **Column Chart sheet tab**, select the **Chart Title** placeholder, type **Number of Computer-Related Jobs 2010 and 2020**, and then press **Enter**. Click **Bold**, click the **Font Size arrow**, and then select **18**. Click the **Font Color arrow** and click **Black, Text 1** font color to the chart title.

g. Click the **Outlook sheet tab**, select the **Chart Title** placeholder, type **Projected Number of Jobs by 2020**, and then press **Enter**.

h. Click **Bold**, click the **Font Size arrow**, and then select **14**. Click the **Font Color arrow** and click **Dark Blue** in the Standard Colors section. Save the workbook.

You formatted the bar chart title to have a similar font color as the worksheet title.

STEP 2)) ADD AND FORMAT AXIS TITLES AND FORMAT AXES

For the bar chart, you want to add and format a title to describe the job titles on the vertical axis. In addition, you want to simplify the horizontal axis values to avoid displaying *,000* for each increment and add the title *Thousands*. Refer to Figure 35 as you complete Step 2.

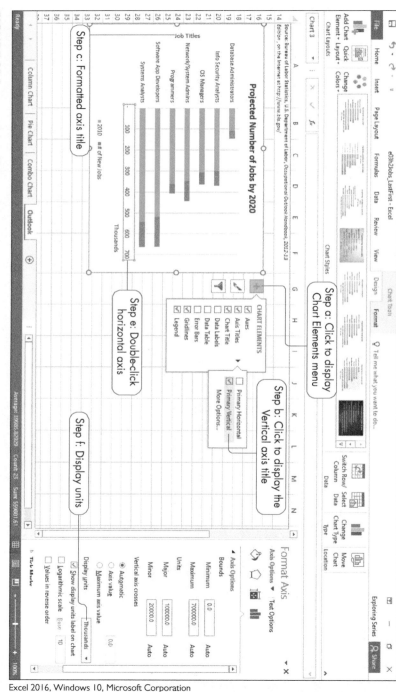

FIGURE 35 Formatted Axis Titles and Axes

Excel 2016, Windows 10, Microsoft Corporation

a. Ensure that the bar chart is selected in the Outlook worksheet and click **Chart Elements** to the right of the chart.

Excel displays the Chart Elements menu.

b. Point to **Axis Titles**, click the **Axis Titles arrow**, and then click the **Primary Vertical check box** to select it. Close the menu.

Excel displays Axis Title on the left side of the vertical axis.

c. Ensure that the Axis Title placeholder is selected, type **Job Titles**, and then press **Enter**.

Excel displays Axis Title on the left side of the vertical axis.

d. Click **Font Color** to apply the default Dark Blue font color to the selected axis title.

e. Point to the **horizontal axis**. When you see the ScreenTip, Horizontal (Value) Axis, double-click the values on the horizontal axis.

The Format Axis task pane opens for you to format the value axis.

f. Click the **Display units arrow** and select **Thousands.**

TROUBLESHOOTING: If the Display units is not shown, click the Axis Options icon, and click Axis Options to display the options.

The axis now displays values such as 700 instead of 700,000. The title Thousands displays in the bottom-right corner of the horizontal axis.

g. Click the **Home tab**, select the title **Thousands**, and then apply **Dark Blue font color** in the Font group. Close the Format Axis task pane. Save the workbook.

ADD AND FORMAT DATA LABELS

The pie chart includes a legend to identify which color represents each computer-related job; however, it does not include numerical labels to help you interpret what percentage of all computer-related jobs will be hired for each position. You want to insert and format percentage value labels. Refer to Figure 36 as you complete Step 3.

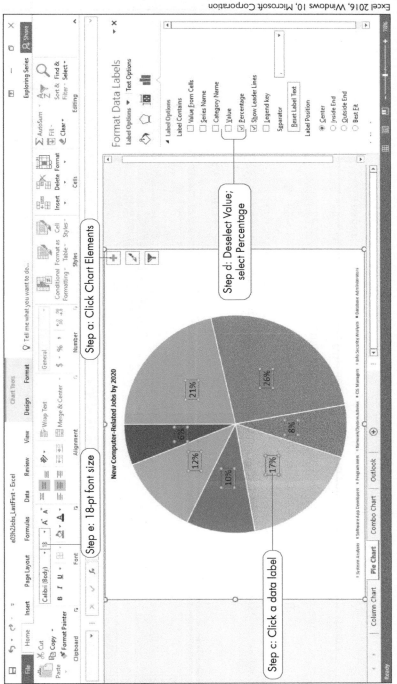

FIGURE 36 Formatted Data Labels

STEP 4 〉〉 FORMAT THE CHART AREA AND A DATA POINT

You want to apply a texture fill to the chart area and change the fill colors for the Software Apps Developers and the Database Administrators slices. Refer to Figure 37 as you complete Step 4.

a. Click the **Pie Chart sheet tab** and click **Chart Elements**.

b. Click the **Data Labels arrow** and select **Center**. Close the Chart Elements menu.

You added data labels to the pie slices. The default data labels show the number of new jobs in the pie slices.

c. Right-click one of the data labels and select **Format Data Labels** to open the Format Data Label task pane.

d. Click **Label Options**, click the **Percentage check box** to select it, and then click the **Value check box** to deselect it. Close the Format Data Labels task pane.

Typically, pie chart data labels show percentages instead of values.

e. Change the font size to **18** to make the data labels larger. Save the workbook.

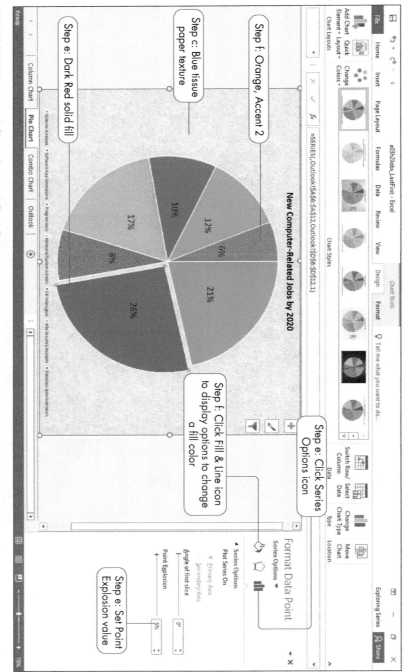

FIGURE 37 Formatted Chart Area and Data Point

Excel 2016, Windows 10, Microsoft Corporation

a. Point to the **chart area** (the white space in the chart) and double-click when you see the Chart Area ScreenTip.

b. Click the **Fill & Line icon** in the Format Chart Area task pane and click **Fill**.

The task pane displays different fill options.

c. Click **Picture or texture fill**, click the **Texture arrow**, and then click **Blue tissue paper**.

The chart area now has the blue tissue paper texture fill.

d. Click the **26% Orange, Accent 2 slice**, pause, and then click the **26% Orange, Accent 2 slice** again to select just that data point (slice).

The first click selects all slices of the pie. The second click selects only the Software App Developers slice so that you can format that data point. Because you did not close the Format Chart Area task pane after Step c, Excel changes to the Format Data Point task pane when you select a data point.

e. Complete the following steps to format the selected data point:

- Click the **Fill & Line icon**, click **Solid fill**, click the **Color arrow**, and then click **Dark Red** in the Standard Colors section.
- Click the **Series Options icon** in the Format Data Point task pane and click the **Point Explosion increment** to **5%**.

You changed the fill color and exploded the slice for the selected data point.

f. Click the **6% Database Administrators slice**, click the **Fill & Line icon** in the Format Data Point task pane, click **Solid fill**, click the **Color arrow**, and then click **Orange, Accent 2**. Close the Format Data Point task pane.

The new color for the Database Administrators slice makes it easier to read the percentage data label.

g. Save the workbook. Keep the workbook open if you plan to continue with the next Hands-On Exercise. If not, close the workbook and exit Excel.

Chart Design and Sparklines

After you add and format chart elements, you might want to experiment with other features to enhance a chart. The Chart Tools Design tab contains two other groups: Chart Styles and Data. These groups enable you to apply a different style or color scheme to a chart or manipulate the data that are used to build a chart. You can also click Chart Styles and Chart Filters to the right of a chart to change the design of a chart.

At times, you might want to insert small visual chart-like images within worksheet cells to illustrate smaller data series rather than a large chart to illustrate several data points. Excel enables you to create small chart-like images in close proximity to individual data points to help you visualize the data.

In this section, you will learn how to apply chart styles and colors, filter chart data, and insert and customize miniature charts (sparklines) within individual cells.

STEP 1

Applying a Chart Style and Colors

A *chart style* is a collection of formatting that controls the color of the chart area, plot area, and data series. Styles, such as flat, 3-D, or beveled, also affect the look of the data series. Figure 38 shows the options when you click Chart Styles to the right of the chart, and Figure 39 shows the Chart Styles gallery that displays when you click Chart Styles on the Design tab. The styles in the Chart Styles gallery reflect what is available for the currently selected chart, such as a pie chart. If you select a different type of chart, the gallery will display styles for that particular type of chart.

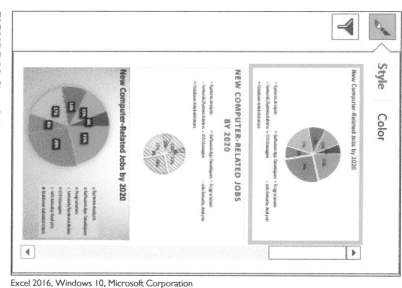

FIGURE 38 Chart Styles

Excel 2016, Windows 10, Microsoft Corporation

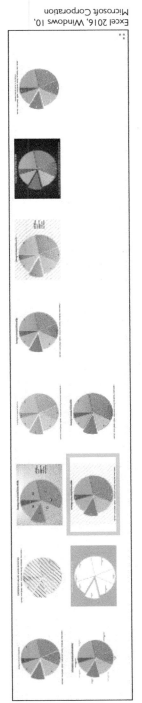

FIGURE 39 Chart Styles Gallery

TIP: CHOOSING APPROPRIATE CHART STYLES

When choosing a chart style, make sure the style complements the chart data and is easy to read. Also, consider whether you will display the chart onscreen in a presentation or print the chart. If you will display the chart in a presentation, consider selecting a style with a black background.

To change the color scheme of the chart, complete the following steps:

1. Click Chart Styles to the right of the chart.
2. Click Color or click Change Colors in the Chart Styles group on the Design tab.
3. Select from the Colorful and Monochromatic sections.

Modifying the Data Source

The data source is the range of worksheet cells that are used to construct a chart. Although you should select the data source carefully before creating a chart, you may decide to alter that data source after you create and format the chart. The Data group on the Design tab is useful for adjusting the data source. Furthermore, you can apply filters to display or hide a data series without adjusting the entire data source.

Apply Chart Filters

>> A *chart filter* controls which data series and categories are visible in a chart. By default, all the data you selected to create the chart are used to construct the data series and categories. However, you can apply a chart filter to focus on particular data. For example, you might want to focus on just one job title at a time. Click Chart Filters to the right of the chart to display the options (see Figure 40). A check mark indicates the data series or categories currently displayed in the chart. Click a check box to deselect or hide a data series or a category.

STEP 2

FIGURE 40 Chart Filter Options

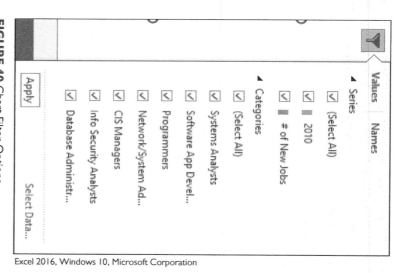

| Values | Names |

▲ Series

☑ (Select All)

☑ 2010

▣ # of New Jobs

▲ Categories

☑ (Select All)

☑ Systems Analysts

☑ Software App Devel...

☑ Programmers

☑ Network/System Ad...

☑ CIS Managers

☑ Info Security Analysts

☑ Database Administr...

Apply   Select Data...

Excel 2016, Windows 10, Microsoft Corporation

Click Select Data in the Data group on the Design tab to open the Select Data Source dialog box (see Figure 41). This dialog box is another way to filter which categories and data series are visible in your chart. Furthermore, this dialog box enables you to change the chart data range, as well as add, edit, or remove data that is being used to create the chart. For example, you might want to add another data series or remove an existing data series from the chart.

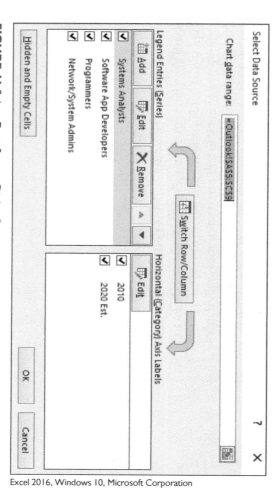

Select Data Source   ?   ×

Chart data range: =Outlook!$A$5:$C$9

⧉ Switch Row/Column ⧉

Legend Entries (Series)   Horizontal (Category) Axis Labels

⊞ Add   ⊞ Edit   ✕ Remove   ▲   ▼   ⊞ Edit

☑ Systems Analysts   ☑ 2010

☑ Software App Developers   ☑ 2020 Est.

☑ Programmers

☑ Network/System Admins

Hidden and Empty Cells   OK   Cancel

FIGURE 41 Select Data Source Dialog Box

Excel 2016, Windows 10, Microsoft Corporation

Switch Row and Column Data

You might want to switch data used to create the horizontal axis and the legend to give a different perspective and to change the focus on the data. For example, you might want to display years as data series to compare different years for categories, and then you might want to switch the data to show years on the category axis to compare job titles within the same year. In Figure 42, the chart on the left uses the job titles to build the data series and legend, and the years display on the horizontal axis. The chart on the right shows the results after switching the data: the job titles build the horizontal axis, and the years build the data series and legend.

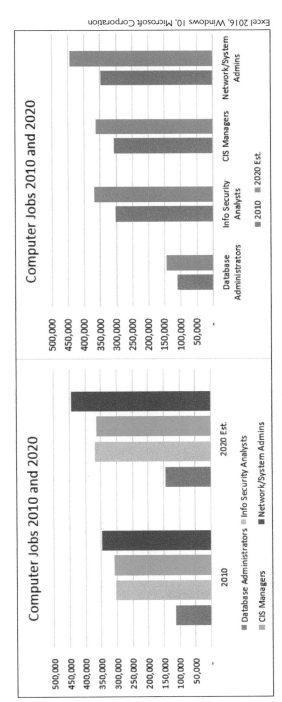

FIGURE 42 Original Chart and Chart with Switched Rows/Columns

---

To switch the row and column data, complete the following steps:

1. Select the chart.
2. Click Switch Row/Column in the Data group on the Design tab.

Creating and Customizing Sparklines

A **sparkline** is a small line, column, or win/loss chart contained in a single cell. The purpose of a sparkline is to present a condensed, simple, succinct visual illustration of data. Unlike a regular chart, a sparkline does not include any of the standard chart labels, such as a chart title, axis label, axis titles, legend, or data labels. Inserting sparklines next to data helps to create a visual "dashboard" to help you understand the data quickly without having to look at a full-scale chart.

Figure 43 shows three sample sparklines: line, column, and win/loss. The line sparkline shows trends over time, such as each student's trends in test scores. The column sparkline compares test averages. The win/loss sparkline depicts how many points a team won or lost each game.

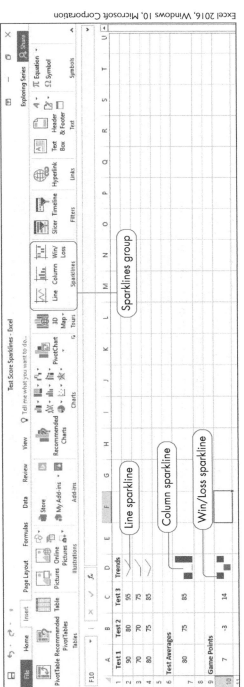

FIGURE 43 Sample Sparklines

Insert a Sparkline

STEP 3

Before creating a sparkline, identify the data range you want to depict (such as A2:C2 for the first person's test score) and where you want to place the sparkline (such as cell D2).

To insert a sparkline, complete the following steps:

1. Click the Insert tab.
2. Click Line, Column, or Win/Loss in the Sparklines group. The Create Sparklines dialog box opens (see Figure 44).
3. Type the cell references containing the values in the Data Range box or select the range.
4. Enter or select the range where you want the sparkline to display in the Location Range box and click OK. The default cell location is the active cell unless you change it.

Create Sparklines

Choose the data that you want

Data Range: A2:C2

Choose where you want the sparklines to be placed

Location Range: D2

OK   Cancel

FIGURE 44 Create Sparklines Dialog Box

Excel 2016, Windows 10, Microsoft Corporation

Customize a Sparkline

After you insert a sparkline, the Sparkline Tools Design tab displays (see Figure 45), with options to customize the sparkline. Table 6 lists and describes the groups on the Sparkline Tools Design tab.

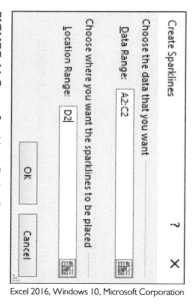

FIGURE 45 Sparkline Tools Design Tab

Excel 2016, Windows 10, Microsoft Corporation

TABLE 6 Sparkline Tools Design Tab

Group	Description
Sparkline	Edits the location and data source for a group or individual data point that generates a group of sparklines or an individual sparkline.
Type	Changes the selected sparkline type (line, column, win/loss).
Show	Displays points, such as the high points, or markers within a sparkline.
Style	Changes the sparkline style, similar to a chart style, changes the sparkline color, or changes the marker color.
Group	Specifies the horizontal and vertical axis settings, groups objects together, ungroups objects, and clears sparklines.

Pearson Education, Inc.

8. What are two ways to change the color scheme of a chart?

9. How can you change a chart so that the data in the legend are on the X-axis and the data on the X-axis are in the legend?

10. What is a sparkline, and why would you insert one?

3 Chart Design and Sparklines

Skills covered: Apply a Chart Style • Apply Chart Filters • Insert a Sparkline • Customize Sparklines

Now that you have completed the pie chart, you want to focus again on the bar chart. You are not satisfied with the overall design and want to try a different chart style. In addition, you would like to include sparklines to show trends for all jobs between 2010 and 2020.

STEP 1 » APPLY A CHART STYLE

You want to give more contrast to the bar chart. Therefore, you will apply the Style 2 chart style. That style changes the category axis labels to all capital letters and displays data labels inside each segment of each bar. Refer to Figure 46 as you complete Step 1.

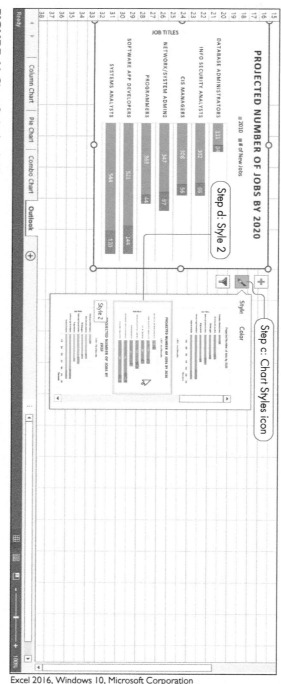

FIGURE 46 Chart Style Applied

a. Open *e03h2Jobs_LastFirst* if you closed it at the end of the Hands-On Exercise 2, and save it as **e03h3Jobs_LastFirst**, changing h2 to h3.

b. Click the **Outlook sheet tab** and click the bar chart to select it.

c. Click **Chart Styles** to the right of the chart.

The gallery of chart styles opens.

d. Point to **Style 2**. When you see the ScreenTip that identifies Style 2, click **Style 2**. Click **Chart Styles** to close the gallery. Save the workbook.

Excel applies the Style 2 chart style to the chart, which displays value data labels in white font color within each stack of the bar chart. The chart title and the category labels display in all capital letters. The legend displays above the plot area.

When you first created the clustered column chart, you included the number of new jobs as well as the number of 2010 jobs and the projected number of 2020 jobs. However, you decide that the number of new jobs is implied by comparing the 2010 to the 2020 jobs. Therefore, you want to set a chart filter to exclude the number of new jobs. Refer to Figure 47 as you complete Step 2.

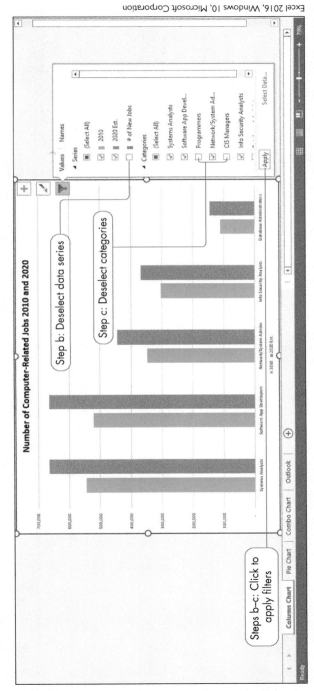

Excel 2016, Windows 10, Microsoft Corporation

FIGURE 47 Chart Filters

a. Click the **Column Chart sheet tab** and click **Chart Filters** on the right of the chart area.

b. Point to the various filter options to see a preview of the filtered data. Click the **# of New Jobs check box** in the Series group to deselect it and click **Apply** at the bottom of the filter window.

The number of new jobs (gray) data series no longer displays in the clustered column chart.

c. Click the **Programmers check box** to deselect the category, click the **CIS Managers check box** to deselect it, and then click **Apply**. Click **Chart Filters** to close the menu. Save the workbook.

The Programmers and CIS Managers categories no longer display in the clustered column chart.

You want to insert sparklines to show the trends between 2010 and 2020. After inserting the sparklines, you want to display the high points to show that all jobs will have major increases by 2020. Refer to Figure 48 as you complete Step 3.

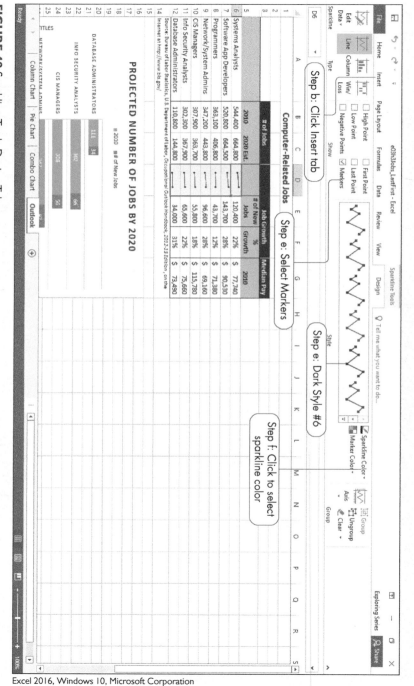

FIGURE 48 Sparkline Tools Design Tab

Excel 2016, Windows 10, Microsoft Corporation

a. Click the **Outlook sheet tab**, select **cell D6**, click the **Insert arrow** in the Cells group, and then select **Insert Sheet Columns**.

You inserted a new column so that you can place the sparklines close to the data you want to visualize.

b. Click the **Insert tab** and click **Line** in the Sparklines group.

c. Select the **range B6:C12** to enter that range in the Data Range box.

You selected multiple rows at one time to create a group of sparklines.

d. Press **Tab** and select the **range D6:D12** to enter that range in the Location Range box. Click **OK**.

Excel inserts sparklines in the range D6:D12 with each sparkline representing data on its respective row. The Sparkline Tools Design tab displays.

e. Click the **Markers check box** in the Show group to select it and click **Sparkline Style Dark #6** in the Style group.

f. Click **Sparkline Color** in the Style group and click **Red** in the Standard Colors section.

g. Click **Axis** in the Group group and click **Same for All Sparklines** in the Vertical Axis Minimum Value Options section. Click **Axis** again and click **Same for All Sparklines** in the Vertical Axis Maximum Value Options section.

Because the sparklines look identical in trends, you changed the axis settings to set the minimum and maximum values as relative to the sparkline values in the entire selected range of rows rather than the default setting that bases the minimum and maximum for each row.

h. Save and close the file. Based on your instructor's directions, submit e03h3jobs_LastFirst.

Chapter Objectives Review

After reading this chapter, you have accomplished the following objectives:

I. Select the data source.

- Decide which data you want to include in a chart. Each value is a data point, and several related data points create a data series in a chart.
- Select the range of data, including appropriate labels. The labels become the legend and the category axis.

2. Choose a chart type.

- After selecting a range, click Quick Analysis and click Charts to display a gallery of recommended chart types.
- Create a column chart: A clustered column chart compares groups of side-by-side columns where the height of the column indicates its value. The taller the column, the larger the value. A stacked column chart shows relationships of individual data points to the whole.
- Create a bar chart: A bar chart compares values across categories using horizontal bars where the width of the bar indicates its value. The wider the bar, the larger the value. A stacked bar chart shows relationships of individual data points to the whole.
- Change the chart type: After creating a chart, you might want to change it to a different type by clicking Change Chart Type in the Type group on the Design tab.
- Create a line chart: A line chart compares trends over time. Values are displayed on the value axis, and time periods are displayed on the category axis.
- Create a pie chart: A pie chart indicates the proportion to the whole for one data series. The size of the slice indicates the size of the value. The larger the pie slice, the larger the value.
- Create a combo chart: A combo chart combines elements of two chart types, such as column and line, to depict different data, such as individual data points compared to averages or percentages.
- Create other chart types: An X Y (scatter) chart shows a relationship between two numerical variables. A stock chart shows fluctuations in prices of stock, such as between the opening and closing prices on a particular day.

3. Move, size, and print a chart.

- Move a chart: The Move Chart dialog box enables you to select a new sheet and name the new chart sheet. To move a chart within a worksheet, click and drag the chart to the desired area.
- Size a chart: Adjust the chart size by dragging a sizing handle or specifying exact measurements in the Size group on the Format tab.

- Print a chart: To print a chart with its data series, the chart needs to be on the same worksheet as the data source. To ensure both the data and the chart print, make sure the chart is not selected. If the chart is on its own sheet or if you select the chart on a worksheet containing other data, the chart will print as a full-sized chart.

4. Add, edit, and format chart elements.

- Click Chart Elements to add elements. Chart elements include a chart title, axis titles, data labels, legend, gridlines, chart area, plot area, data series, and data point.
- Edit, format, and position the chart title: The default chart title is Chart Title, but you should edit it to provide a descriptive title for the chart. Apply font formats, such as bold and font size, to the chart title. Position the chart title above the chart, centered and overlaid, or in other locations.
- Add, format, and position axis titles: Display titles for the value and category axes to help describe the axes better. Apply font formats, such as bold and font size, to the axis titles.
- Format the axes: Change the unit of display for the value axis, such as converting values to In Millions.
- Add, position, and format data labels: Data labels provide exact values for a data series. Select the position of the data labels and the content of the data labels. Apply font formats, such as bold and font size, to the data labels.
- Position and format the legend: Position the legend to the right, top, bottom, or left of the plot area. Change the font size to adjust the label sizes within the legend.
- Add and format gridlines: Gridlines help the reader read across a column chart. Adjust the format of the major and minor gridlines.
- Format the chart area, plot area, and data series: The Format task panes enable you to apply fill colors, select border colors, and apply other settings.
- Format a data point: Format a single data point, such as changing the fill color for a single pie slice or specifying the percentage to explode a slice in a pie chart. Apply font formats, such as bold and font size, to the data points.
- Use the Chart Tools Format tab: Use this tab to select a chart element and insert and format shapes.

5. Apply a chart style and colors.

- Apply a chart style: This feature applies predetermined formatting, such as the background color and the data series color.

6. Modify the data source.

- Add or remove data from the data source to change the data in the chart.

- Apply chart filters: The Select Data Source dialog box enables you to modify the ranges used for the data series. When you deselect a series, Excel removes that series from the chart.

- Switch row and column data: You can switch the way data is used to create a chart by switching data series and categories.

7. Create and customize sparklines.

- Create a sparkline: A sparkline is a miniature chart in a cell representing a single data series.

- Customize a sparkline: Change the data source, location, and style. Display markers and change line or marker colors.

Key Terms Matching

Match the key terms with their definitions. Write the key term letter by the appropriate numbered definition.

a. Axis title
b. Bar chart
c. Category axis
d. Chart area
e. Chart title
f. Clustered column chart
g. Combo chart
h. Data label
i. Data point
j. Data series

k. Gridline
l. Legend
m. Line chart
n. Pie chart
o. Plot area
p. Sizing handle
q. Sparkline
r. Task pane
s. Value axis
t. X Y (scatter) chart

1. _____ Chart that groups columns side by side to compare data points among categories.
2. _____ Miniature chart contained in a single cell.
3. _____ Chart type that shows trends over time in which the value axis indicates quantities and the horizontal axis indicates time.
4. _____ Label that describes the entire chart.
5. _____ Label that describes either the category axis or the value axis.
6. _____ Key that identifies the color, gradient, picture, texture, or pattern fill assigned to each data series in a chart.
7. _____ Chart type that compares categories of data horizontally.
8. _____ Chart that shows each data point in proportion to the whole data series.
9. _____ Numeric value that describes a single value on a chart.
10. _____ Chart that contains two chart types, such as column and line, to depict two types of data, such as individual data points and percentages.
11. _____ A circle that enables you to adjust the height or width of a selected chart.
12. _____ Horizontal or vertical line that extends from the horizontal or vertical axis through the plot area.
13. _____ Chart type that shows the relationship between two variables.
14. _____ Group of related data points that display in row(s) or column(s) in a worksheet.
15. _____ Window of options to format and customize chart elements.
16. _____ Provides descriptive labels for the data points plotted in a chart.
17. _____ Section of a chart that contains graphical representation of the values in a data series.
18. _____ A container for the entire chart and all of its elements.
19. _____ An identifier that shows the exact value of a data point in a chart.
20. _____ Displays incremental numbers to identify approximate values, such as dollars or units, of data points in a chart.

Multiple Choice

1. Which type of chart is the *least* appropriate for depicting yearly rainfall totals for five cities for four years?

   (a) Pie chart

   (b) Line chart

   (c) Column chart

   (d) Bar chart

2. Look at the stacked bar chart in Figure 35. Which of the following is a category on the category axis?

   (a) Thousands

   (b) Job Titles

   (c) CIS Managers

   (d) 700

3. Which of the following is not a type of sparkline?

   (a) Line

   (b) Bar

   (c) Column

   (d) Win-Loss

4. If you want to show exact values for a data series in a bar chart, which chart element should you display?

   (a) Chart title

   (b) Legend

   (c) Value axis title

   (d) Data labels

5. The value axis currently shows increments such as 50,000 and 100,000. What option would you select to display the values in increments of 50 and 100?

   (a) More Primary Vertical Axis Title Options

   (b) Show Axis in Thousands

   (c) Show Axis in Millions

   (d) Show Right to Left Axis

6. You want to create a single chart that shows the proportion of yearly sales for five divisions for each year for five years. Which type of chart can accommodate your needs?

   (a) Pie chart

   (b) Surface chart

   (c) Clustered bar chart

   (d) 100% stacked column chart

7. Currently, a column chart shows values on the value axis, years on the category axis, and state names in the legend. What should you do if you want to organize data with the states on the category axis and the years shown in the legend?

   (a) Change the chart type to a clustered column chart.

   (b) Click Switch Row/Column in the Data group on the Design tab.

   (c) Click Layout 2 in the Chart Layouts group on the Design tab and apply a different chart style.

   (d) Click Legend in the Labels group on the Layout tab and select Show Legend at Bottom.

8. What do you click to remove a data series from a chart so that you can focus on other data series?

   (a) Chart Elements

   (b) Chart Series

   (c) Chart Filters

   (d) Chart Styles

9. Which of the following does not display automatically when you create a clustered column chart?

   (a) Data labels

   (b) Chart title placeholder

   (c) Gridlines

   (d) Legend

10. After you create a line type sparkline, what option should you select to display dots for each data point?

    (a) High Point

    (b) Negative Point

    (c) Sparkline Color

    (d) Markers

Practice Exercises

1 Hulett Family Utility Expenses

Your cousin, Alex Hulett, wants to analyze his family's utility expenses for 2018. He gave you his files for the electric, gas, and water bills for the year. You created a worksheet that lists the individual expenses per month, along with yearly totals per utility type and monthly totals. You will create some charts to depict the data. Refer to Figure 49 as you complete this exercise.

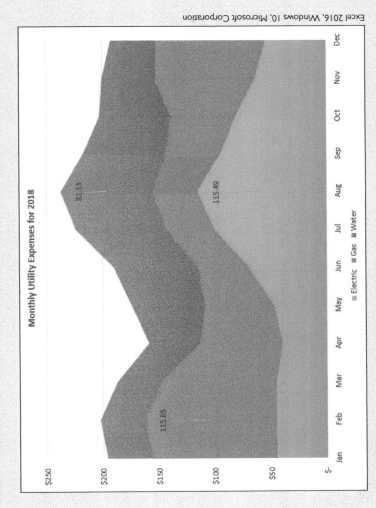

FIGURE 49 Hulett Family Utility Expenses

a. Open *e03p1Utilities* and save it as **e03p1Utilities_LastFirst**.

b. Select the **range A4:E17**, click **Quick Analysis**, click **Charts**, and then click **Clustered Column**.

c. Click **Chart Filters** to the right of the chart and do the following:
   - Deselect the **Monthly Totals check box** in the Series group.
   - Scroll through the Categories group and deselect the **Yearly Totals check box**.
   - Click **Apply** to remove totals from the chart. Click **Chart Filters** to close the menu.

d. Point to the **chart area**. When you see the Chart Area ScreenTip, drag the chart so that the top-left corner of the chart is in **cell A21**.

e. Click the **Format tab** and change the size by doing the following:
   - Click in the **Shape Width box** in the Size group, type **6"**, and then press **Enter**.
   - Click in the **Shape Height box** in the Size group, type **3.5"**, and then press **Enter**.

f. Click the **Design tab**, click **Quick Layout** in the Chart Layouts group, and then click **Layout 3**.

g. Select the **Chart Title placeholder**, type **Monthly Utility Expenses for 2018**, and then press **Enter**.

h. Click the chart, click the **More button** in the Chart Styles group, and then click **Style 6**.

i. Click **Copy** on the Home tab, click **cell A39**, and then click **Paste**. With the second chart selected, do the following:

*   Click the **Design tab**, click **Change Chart Type** in the Type group, click **Line** on the left side of the dialog box, select **Line with Markers** in the top-center section, and then click **OK**.

*   Click the **Electric data series line** to select it and click the highest marker to select only that marker. Click **Chart Elements** and click **Data Labels**.

*   Repeat and adapt the previous bulleted step to add a data label to the highest markers for Gas and Water. Click **Chart Elements** to close the menu.

*   Select the chart, copy it, and then paste it in **cell A57**.

j. Ensure that the third chart is selected and do the following:

*   Click the **Design tab**, click **Change Chart Type** in the Type group, select **Area** on the left side, click **Stacked Area**, and then click **OK**.

*   Click **Move Chart** in the Location group, click **New sheet**, type **Area Chart**, and then click **OK**.

*   Select each data label and change the font size to **12**. Move each data label up closer to the top of the respective shaded area.

*   Select the value axis and change the font size to **12**.

*   Right-click the value axis and select **Format Axis**. Scroll down in the Format Axis task pane, click **Number**, click in the **Decimal places box**, and then type **0**. Close the Format Axis task pane.

*   Change the font size to **12** for the category axis and the legend.

k. Click the **Expenses sheet tab**, select the line chart, and do the following.

*   Click the **Design tab**, click **Move Chart** in the Location group, click **New sheet**, type **Line Chart**, and then click **OK**.

*   Change the font size to **12** for the value axis, category axis, data labels, and legend.

*   Format the vertical axis with zero decimal places.

*   Right-click the **chart area**, select **Format Chart Area**, click **Fill**, click **Gradient fill**, click the **Preset gradients arrow**, and then select **Light Gradient – Accent 1**. Close the Format Chart Area task pane.

l. Click the **Expenses sheet**, select the **range B5:D16** and do the following:

*   Click the **Insert tab**, click **Line** in the Sparkline group, click in the **Location Range box**, type **B18:D18**, and then click **OK**.

*   Click the **High Point check box** to select it and click the **Low Point check box** to select it in the Show group with all three sparklines selected.

m. Create a footer with your name on the left side, the sheet name code in the center, and the file name code on the right of each sheet.

n. Save and close the file. Based on your instructor's directions, submit e03p1Utilities_LastFirst.

2 Trends in Market Value of Houses on Pine Circle

You live in a house on Pine Circle, a quiet cul-de-sac in a suburban area. Recently, you researched the market value and square footage of the five houses on Pine Circle. Now, you want to create charts to visually depict the data to compare values for the houses in the cul-de-sac. Refer to Figure 50 as you complete this exercise.

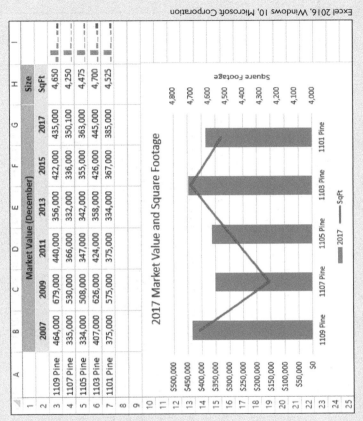

FIGURE 50 Market Values

a. Open *e03p2Pine* and save it as **e03p2Pine_LastFirst**.

b. Select the **range A2:G7**, click **Quick Analysis**, click **Charts**, and then click **Line**.

c. Click **Move Chart** in the Location group, click **New sheet**, type **Line**, and then click **OK**.

d. Select the **Chart Title placeholder** and do the following:

  • Type **Market Value of Pine Circle Houses** and press **Enter**.

  • Apply bold to the chart title, change the font size to **20**, and then select **Olive Green, Accent 3, Darker 50% font color**.

e. Click the **value axis** on the left side of the chart and do the following:

  • Change the font size to 12 and select **Olive Green, Accent 3, Darker 50% font color**.

  • Double-click the value axis to open the Format Axis task pane.

  • Type **300000** in the Minimum Bounds box and press **Enter**. The Maximum Bounds box should change to 700000 automatically.

  • Scroll down in the Format Axis task pane and click **Number** to display those options.

  • Click the **Category arrow** and select **Currency**.

  • Close the Format Axis task pane.

f. Click **Chart Elements**, click the **Axis Titles triangle**, and then click the **Primary Vertical check box** to select it. Type **December Market Values** in the **Axis Title placeholder** and press **Enter**.

g. Make sure the Chart Elements menu is showing, click the **Gridlines triangle**, and then click the **Primary Minor Horizontal check box** to select it.

h. Click the blue **1109 Pine data series line**, click the **Data Labels check box** to select it, and then click **Chart Elements** to close the menu.

i. Click the data labels you just created, click the **Home tab**, click the **Font Color arrow**, and then select **Blue** in the Standard Colors section.

j. Select the category axis, change the font size to **12**, and select **Olive Green, Accent 3, Darker 50% font color**.

k. Right-click the legend and select **Format Legend**. Click **Top** in the Legend Position section of the Format Legend task pane and close the task pane.

l. Click the **Pine Circle sheet tab** and select the **ranges A2:A7** and **G2:H7**.

m. Click the **Insert tab**, click **Insert Combo Chart** in the Charts group, and then click the **Clustered Column – Line on Secondary Axis thumbnail**.

n. Do the following to the chart:

- Move and resize the chart to fill the **range A10:H25**.
- Select the **Chart Title placeholder**, type **2017 Market Value and Square Footage**, and then press **Enter**.
- Double-click the value axis on the left side, scroll down in the Format Axis task pane, click **Number**, click the **Category arrow**, and then select **Currency**.
- Click **Chart Elements**, click the **Axis Titles triangle**, click the **Secondary Vertical check box** to select it, type **Square Footage**, and then press **Enter**. Close the Format Axis Title task pane.

o. Select the **range B3:G7**, click the **Insert tab**, click **Column** in the Sparklines group, make sure B3:G7 displays in the Data Range box, type **I3:I7** in the Location Range box, and then click **OK**.

p. Customize the sparklines by doing the following:

- Click **More** in the Style group and select **Sparkline Style Accent 6, Darker 25%**.
- Click **Last Point** in the Show group.

q. Create a footer with your name on the left side, the sheet name code in the center, and the file name code on the right of both sheets.

r. Save and close the file. Based on your instructor's directions, submit e03p2Pine_LastFirst.

Mid-Level Exercises

1 Airport Passenger Counts

ANALYSIS CASE

As an analyst for the airline industry, you track the number of passengers at the top five major U.S. airports: Atlanta, Chicago, Los Angeles, Dallas/Fort Worth, and Denver. You researched passenger data at http://www.aci-na.org. One worksheet you created lists the number of total yearly passengers at the top five airports for a six-year period. To prepare for an upcoming meeting, you need to create a clustered column chart to compare the number of passengers at each airport. Next, you will create a bar chart to compare the passenger count for the latest year of data available and then emphasize the airport with the largest number of passenger traffic. Finally, you want to insert sparklines to visually represent trends in passengers at each airport over the six-year period. You can then refer to the sparklines and clustered column chart to write a paragraph analyzing the trends to detect.

a. Open *e03m1Airports* and save it as **e03m1Airports_LastFirst**.

b. Create a clustered column chart for the **range A4:G9**. Position and resize the chart to fit in the **range A15:G34**.

c. Customize the chart by doing the following:

- Swap the data on the category axis and in the legend.
- Apply the **Style 6 chart style**.
- Select **Color 12** in the Monochromatic section of the Change Colors gallery.
- Apply the **Light Gradient – Accent 1** preset gradient fill to the chart area.
- Change the fill color of the 2013 data series to **Dark Blue** and change the fill color of the 2008 data series to **Blue, Accent 5, Lighter 60%**.
- Use Help and add a solid **Blue border** around the legend.

d. Type **Passengers by Top U.S. Airports** as the chart title. Change the font color to **Blue**.

e. Adjust the value axis by doing the following:

- Change the display units to **Millions** for the value axis.
- Edit the axis title to display **Millions of Passengers**.

f. Display data labels above the columns for the 2013 data series only.

g. Create a clustered bar chart for the **range A5:A9** and **G5:G9** and then do the following:

- Move the bar chart to a chart sheet named **Bar Chart**.
- Enter **Passengers at Top 5 U.S. Airports in 2013** as the chart title.
- Apply the **Style 3 chart style**.
- Change the font color to **Dark Blue** on the chart title, category axis, and the value axis.
- Format the Atlanta data point with **Dark Blue fill color.**

h. Display the Passenger worksheet and insert **Line sparklines** in the **range H5:H9** to illustrate the data in the **range B5:G9**. This should insert a sparkline to represent yearly data for each airport.

i. Customize the sparklines by doing the following:

- Show the high and low points in each sparkline.
- Apply **Black, Text 1 color** to the high point marker in each sparkline.
- Apply **Dark Red color** to the low point marker in each sparkline.

j. Click **cell A36** and compose a paragraph that analyzes the trends depicted by the airport sparklines. Notice the overall trends in decreased and increased number of passengers and any unusual activity for an airport. Spell-check the worksheet and correct any errors.

k. Set **0.2"** left and right margins and scale to fit to 1 page for the Passenger worksheet.

l. Insert a footer with your name on the left side, the sheet name code in the center, and the file name code on the right on all worksheets.

m. Save and close the file. Based on your instructor's directions, submit e03m1Airports_LastFirst.

2 Grade Analysis

You are a teaching assistant for Dr. Monica Unice's introductory psychology class. You have maintained her grade book all semester, entering three test scores for each student and calculating the final average. You created a section called Final Grade Distribution that contains calculations to identify the number of students who earned an A, B, C, D, or F. Dr. Unice wants you to create a chart that shows the percentage of students who earn each letter grade. Therefore, you decide to create and format a pie chart. You will also create a bar chart to show a sample of the students' test scores. Furthermore, Dr. Unice wants to see if a correlation exists between attendance and students' final grades; therefore, you will create a scatter chart depicting each student's percentage of attendance with his or her respective final grade average.

a. Open *e03m2Psych* and save it as **e03m2Psych_LastFirst.**

b. Create a pie chart from the Final Grade Distribution data located below the student data in the **range F38:G42** and move the pie chart to its own sheet named **Grades Pie.**

c. Customize the pie chart with these specifications:

- Apply the **Style 7 chart style.**
- Type **PSY 2030 Final Grade Distribution - Fall 2018** for the chart title.
- Explode the B grade slice by **10%.**
- Remove the legend.

d. Add centered data labels and customize the labels with these specifications:

- Display these data labels: **Percentage** and **Category Name.** Remove other data labels.
- Change the font size to **20** and apply **Black, Text 1** font color.
- Remove the legend.

e. Create a clustered bar chart using the **range A7:D12** and move the bar chart to its own sheet named **Students Bar Chart.**

f. Customize the bar chart with these specifications:

- Apply the **Style 5 chart style.**
- Type **Sample Student Test Scores** for the chart title.
- Position the legend on the right side.
- Add data labels in the Outside End position for the Final Exam data series.
- Arrange the categories in reverse order so that Atkin is listed at the top and Ethington is listed at the bottom of the bar chart.

g. Create a scatter chart using the **range E7:F33,** the attendance record and final averages from the Grades worksheet. Move the scatter chart to its own sheet named **Scatter Chart.**

h. Apply these label settings to the scatter chart:

- Remove the legend.
- Type **Attendance-Final Average Relationship** for the chart title.
- Add the following primary horizontal axis title: **Percentage of Attendance.**
- Add the following primary vertical axis title: **Student Final Averages.**

DISCOVER

DISCOVER

DISCOVER

i. Use Help to learn how to apply the following axis settings:

- Vertical axis: 40 minimum bound, 100 maximum bound, 10 major units, and a number format with zero decimal places
- Horizontal axis: 40 minimum bound, 100 maximum bound, automatic units

j. Change the font size to **12** on the vertical axis title, vertical axis, horizontal axis title, and horizontal axis. Bold the chart title and the two axes titles.

k. Add the **Parchment texture fill** to the plot area.

l. Insert a linear trendline.

m. Insert Line sparklines in the **range H8:H33** using the three tests score columns. Change the sparkline color to **Purple** and show the low points.

n. Insert a footer with your name on the left, the sheet name code in the center, and the file name code on the right on all the sheets.

o. Save and close the file. Based on your instructor's directions, submit e03m2Psych_LastFirst.

3 Box Office Movies

COLLABORATION CASE

FROM SCRATCH

You and two of your friends like to follow the popularity of new movies at the theater. You will research current movies that have been showing for four weeks and decide which movies on which to report. Work in teams of three for this activity. After obtaining the data, your team will create applicable charts to illustrate the revenue data. Team members will critique each other's charts.

a. Have all three team members log in to a chat client and engage in a dialogue about which movies are currently playing. Each member should research a different theater to see what is playing at that theater. Decide on six movies that have been in theaters for at least four weeks to research. Save a copy of your instant message dialogue and submit based on your instructor's directions.

b. Divide the six movies among the three team members. Each member should research the revenue reported for two movies for the past four weeks. Make sure your team members use the same source to find the data.

Student 1:

c. Create a new Excel workbook and enter appropriate column labels and the four-week data for all six movies. Name Sheet1 **Data**.

d. Format the data appropriately. Save the workbook as **e03m3Movies_GroupName**. Upload the workbook to a shared location, such as OneDrive, invite the other students to share this location, and send a text message to the next student.

Student 2:

e. Create a line chart to show the trends in revenue for the movies for the four-week period.

f. Add a chart title, format the axes appropriately, select a chart style, and then apply other formatting.

g. Move the chart to its own sheet named **Trends**. Save the workbook, upload it to the shared location, and send a text message to the next student.

Student 3:

h. Add a column to the right of the four-week data and total each movie's four-week revenue.

i. Create a pie chart depicting each movie's percentage of the total revenue for your selected movies.

j. Add a chart title, explode one pie slice, add data labels showing percentages and movie names, and then apply other formatting.

k. Move the chart to its own sheet named **Revenue Chart**. Save the workbook, upload it to the shared location, and send a text message to the next student.

Student 1:

l. Critique the charts. Insert a new worksheet named **Chart Critique** that provides an organized critique of each chart. Type notes that list each team member's name and specify what each student's role was in completing this exercise.

m. Save the workbook, upload it to the shared location, and send a text message to the next student.

Student 2:

n. Read the critique of the line chart and make any appropriate changes for the line chart. On the critique worksheet, provide a response to each critique and why you made or did not make the suggested change.

o. Save the workbook, upload it to the shared location, and send a text message to the next student.

Student 3:

p. Read the critique of the pie chart and make any appropriate changes for the pie chart. On the critique worksheet, provide a response to each critique and why you made or did not make the suggested change.

q. Save and close the file. Based on your instructor's directions, submit e03m3Movies_GroupName.

Beyond the Classroom

Historical Stock Prices

You are interested in investing in the stock market. First, you need to research the historical prices for a particular stock. Launch a Web browser, go to finance.yahoo.com, type a company name, such as Apple, and then select the company name from a list of suggested companies. Click the Historical Prices link. Copy the stock data (date, high, low, open, close, volume) for a six-month period and paste it in a new workbook, adjusting the column widths to fit the data. Save the workbook as **e03b1StockData_LastFirst.** Rename Sheet1 **Data.** Display data for only the first date listed for each month; delete rows containing data for other dates. Sort the list from the oldest date to the newest date. Use Help if needed to learn how to sort data and how to create a Volume-Open-High-Low-Close chart. Then rearrange the data columns in the correct sequence. Format the data and column labels.

Insert a row to enter the company name and insert another row to list the company's stock symbol, such as AAPL. Copy the URL from the Web browser and paste it as a source below the list of data and the date you obtained the data. Merge the cells containing the company name and stock symbol through the last column of data and word-wrap the URL.

Create a Volume-Open-High-Low-Close chart on a new chart sheet named **Stock Chart.** Type an appropriate chart title. Set the primary vertical axis (left side) unit measurement to millions and include an axis title **Volume in Millions.** Include a secondary vertical axis (right side) title **Stock Prices.** Apply the Currency number style with 0 decimal places for the secondary axis values. Change the font size to 11 and the font color to Black, Text 1 on the vertical axes and category axis. Hide the legend.

Use Help to research how to insert text boxes. Insert a text box that describes the stock chart: white fill rectangles indicate the closing price was higher than the opening price; black fill rectangles indicate the closing price was lower than the opening price; etc. Create a footer with your name, the sheet name code, and the file name code on both worksheets. Save and close the file. Based on your instructor's directions, submit e03b1StockData_LastFirst.

Harper County Houses Sold

You want to analyze the number of houses sold by type (e.g., rambler, two story, etc.) in each quarter in Harper County. You entered quarterly data for 2018, calculated yearly total number of houses sold by each type, and quarterly total number of houses sold. You asked an intern to create a stacked column chart for the data, but the chart contains a lot of errors.

Open *e03b2Houses* and save it as **e03b2Houses_LastFirst.** Identify the errors and poor design for the chart. Below the chart, list the errors and your corrections in a two-column format. Then correct the problems in the chart. Link the chart title to the cell containing the most appropriate label in the worksheet. Create a footer with your name, the sheet name code, and the file name code. Adjust the margins and scaling to print the worksheet data, including the error list, and the chart on one page. Save and close the file. Based on your instructor's directions, submit e03b2Houses_LastFirst.

Capstone Exercise

You are an analyst for the airline industry. You created a workbook that lists overall airline arrival statistics for several years. In particular, you listed the percentage and number of on-time arrivals, late arrivals, canceled flights, and diverted flights based on information provided by the Bureau of Transportation Statistics. You want to create charts and insert sparklines that show the trends to discuss with airline and airport managers.

Insert and Format Sparklines

The first dataset shows the percentages. You want to insert sparklines that show the trends in the five-year data. The sparklines will help show any trends in on-time arrivals compared to late arrivals, canceled flights, and diverted flights.

a. Open the *e03c1Arrivals* workbook and save it as **e03c1Arrivals_LastFirst.**

b. Insert Line sparklines in the **range G4:G7**, using the data for the five years.

c. Display the high and low points for the sparklines.

d. Change the high point marker color to **Green.**

Create a Pie Chart

You want to focus on the arrival percentages for 2014. Creating a pie chart will help people visualize the breakdown of all operations for that year. After you create the chart, you will move it to its own chart sheet and edit the chart title to reflect 2014 flight arrivals.

a. Select the **range A4:A7** and the **range F4:F7.**

b. Create a pie chart and move it to a chart sheet named **Pie Chart.**

c. Change the chart title to **2014 Flight Arrivals.**

Add and Format Chart Elements

You want to format the chart by applying a different chart style and positioning the legend above the plot area. Furthermore, you need to add data labels so that you will know the percentages for the arrival categories. Finally, you want to emphasize the canceled flights in Dark Red and explode the late arrival pie slice.

a. Apply the **Style 12 chart style** to the pie chart.

b. Format the chart title with **Blue font color.**

c. Position the legend between the chart title and the plot area.

d. Add data labels to the Best Fit position and display.

e. Apply bold to the data labels and change the font size to **12.**

f. Format the Canceled data point with **Dark Red fill color** and format the Late Arrival data point in **Green.**

g. Explode the Late Arrival data point by **5%.**

Create and Size a Column Chart

To provide a different perspective, you will create a clustered column chart using the actual number of flights. The Total Operations row indicates the total number of reported (scheduled) flights. After creating the chart, you will position and size the chart below the source rows.

a. Create a clustered column chart using the **range A10:F15** in the Arrivals sheet.

b. Edit the chart title: **On-Time and Late Flight Arrivals.**

c. Position the clustered column chart so that the top-left corner is in **cell A20.**

d. Change the width to **5.75"** and the height to **3.5".**

Format the Column Chart

Now that you have created the column chart, you realize that some data seems irrelevant. You will filter out the unneeded data, format the value axis to remove digits, insert a vertical axis title, apply a color change, and format the chart area.

a. Apply chart filters to remove the canceled, diverted, and total operations data.

b. Select the value axis, set **500000** for the Major unit, display the axis units **in Millions**, select category **Number** format with 1 decimal place.

c. Add a primary vertical axis title **Number of Flights.**

d. Apply the **Color 2 chart color** to the chart.

e. Apply the **Light Gradient – Accent 3** fill to the chart area.

Finalizing the Workbook

You want to prepare the workbook in case someone wants to print the data and charts. The margins and scaling have already been set. You just need to insert a footer.

a. Create a footer on each worksheet with your name, the sheet name code, and the file name code.

b. Save and close the file. Based on your instructor's direction, submit e03c1Arrivals_LastFirst.

100% stacked column chart A chart type that places data in one column per category, with each column the same height of 100%.

Alt text An accessibility compliance feature where you enter text and a description for an objective, such as a table or a chart. A special reader can read the alt text to a user.

Area chart A chart type that emphasizes magnitude of changes over time by filling in the space between lines with a color.

Axis title A label that describes either the category axis or the value axis. Provides clarity, particularly in describing the value axis.

Bar chart A chart type that compares values across categories using horizontal bars where the length represents the value; the longer the bar, the larger the value. In a bar chart, the horizontal axis displays values and the vertical axis displays categories.

Category axis The chart axis that displays descriptive labels for the data points plotted in a chart. The category axis labels are typically text contained in the first column of worksheet data (such as job titles) used to create the chart.

Chart A visual representation of numerical data.

Chart area A container for the entire chart and all of its elements, including the plot area, titles, legends, and labels.

Chart element A component of a chart that helps complete or clarify the chart.

Chart filter A setting that controls what data series and categories are displayed or hidden in a chart.

Chart sheet A sheet within a workbook that contains a single chart and no spreadsheet data.

Chart style A collection of formatting that controls the color of the chart area, plot area, and data series.

Chart title The label that describes the entire chart. The title is usually placed at the top of the chart area.

Clustered column chart A type of chart that groups, or clusters, columns set side by side to compare several data points among categories.

Column chart A type of chart that compares values vertically in columns where the height represents the value; the taller the column, the larger the value. In a column chart, the vertical axis displays values and the horizontal axis displays categories.

Combo chart A chart that combines two chart types, such as column and line, to plot different types of data, such as quantities and percentages.

Data label An identifier that shows the exact value of a data point in a chart. Appears above or on a data point in a chart. May indicate percentage of a value to the whole on a pie chart.

Data point A numeric value that describes a single value in a chart or worksheet.

Data series A group of related data points that display in row(s) or column(s) in a worksheet.

Data table A grid that contains the data source values and labels to plot data in a chart. A data table may be placed below a chart or hidden from view.

Error bars Visual that indicates the standard error amount, a percentage, or a standard deviation for a data point or marker in a chart.

Exploded pie chart A chart type in which one or more pie slices are separated from the rest of the pie chart for emphasis.

Gridline A horizontal or vertical line that extends from the horizontal or vertical axis through the plot area to guide the reader's eyes across the chart to identify values.

Histogram A chart that is similar to a column chart. The category axis shows bin ranges (intervals) where data is aggregated into bins, and the vertical axis shows frequencies.

Legend A key that identifies the color, gradient, picture, texture, or pattern assigned to each data series in a chart.

Line chart A chart type that displays lines connecting data points to show trends over equal time periods, such as months, quarters, years, or decades.

Pie chart A chart type that shows each data point in proportion to the whole data series as a slice in a circle. A pie chart depicts only one data series.

Plot area The region of a chart containing the graphical representation of the values in one or more data series. Two axes form a border around the plot area.

Radar chart A chart type that compares aggregate values of three or more variables represented on axes starting from the same point.

Sizing handles Eight circles that display on the outside border of a chart—one on each corner and one on each middle side—when the chart is selected; enables the user to adjust the height and width of the chart.

Sparkline A small line, column, or win/loss chart contained in a single cell to provide a simple visual illustrating one data series.

Stacked column chart A chart type that places stacks of data in segments on top of each other in one column, with each category in the data series represented by a different color.

Stock chart A chart type that shows fluctuation in stock prices.

Surface chart A chart type that displays trends using two dimensions on a continuous curve.

k pane A window of options to format and customize chart elements. The task pane name and options change based on the selected chart element.

ndline A line that depicts trends or helps forecast future data in a chart. For example, if the plotted data includes 2005, 2010, and 2015, a trendline can help forecast values for 2020 and beyond.

lue axis The chart axis that displays incremental numbers to identify approximate values, such as dollars or units, of data points in a chart.

X Y (scatter) chart A chart type that shows a relationship between two variables using their X and Y coordinates. Excel plots one coordinate on the horizontal X-axis and the other variable on the vertical Y-axis. Scatter charts are often used to represent data in education, scientific, and medical experiments.

X-axis The horizontal border that provides a frame of reference for measuring data left to right on a chart.

Y-axis The vertical border that provides a frame of reference for measuring data up and down on a chart.

Datasets and Tables

Excel

Datasets and Tables

LEARNING OUTCOME

You will demonstrate how to manage and analyze large sets of data.

OBJECTIVES & SKILLS: After you read this chapter, you will be able to:

CASE STUDY | Reid Furniture Store

Vicki Reid owns Reid Furniture Store in Portland, Oregon. She divided her store into four departments: Living Room, Bedroom, Dining Room, and Appliances. All merchandise is categorized into one of these four departments for inventory records and sales. Vicki has four sales representatives: Chantalle Desmarais, Jade Gallagher, Sebastian Gruenewald, and Ambrose Sardelis. The sales system tracks which sales representative processed each transaction.

The business has grown rapidly, and Vicki hired you to analyze the sales data in order to increase future profits. For example, which department generates the most sales? Who is the leading salesperson? Do most customers purchase or finance? Are sales promotions necessary to promote business, or will customers pay the full price?

You downloaded March 2018 data from the sales system into an Excel workbook. To avoid extraneous data that is not needed in the analysis, you did not include customer names, accounts, or specific product numbers. The downloaded file contains transaction numbers, dates, sales representative names, departments, general merchandise descriptions, payment types, transaction types, and the total price.

Excel 2016, Windows 10, Microsoft Corporation

Reid Furniture Store

Monthly Transactions: March 2018
Down Payment Requirement: 25%

Trans_No	Operator	Sales_First	Sales_Last	Date	Department	Furniture	Pay_Type	Trans_Type	Amount
2018-001	KRM	Sebastian	Gruenewald	3/1/2018	Bedroom	Mattress	Finance	Promotion	2,788
2018-002	RKM	Sebastian	Gruenewald	3/1/2018	Bedroom	Mattress	Finance	Promotion	3,245
2018-003	MAP	Jade	Gallagher	3/1/2018	Living Room	Sofa, Loveseat, Chair Package	Finance	Promotion	10,000
2018-004	MAP	Jade	Gallagher	3/1/2018	Living Room	End Tables	Finance	Promotion	1,000
2018-005	MAP	Jade	Gallagher	3/1/2018	Appliances	Washer and Dryer	Finance	Promotion	2,750
2018-006	COK	Ambrose	Sardelis	3/1/2018	Living Room	Sofa, Loveseat, Chair Package	Finance	Promotion	12,000
2018-007	COK	Ambrose	Sardelis	3/1/2018	Living Room	Sofa, Loveseat, Chair Package	Finance	Promotion	12,000
2018-008	MAP	Jade	Gallagher	3/1/2018	Dining Room	Dining Room Table	Finance	Promotion	3,240
2018-009	COK	Chantalle	Desmarais	3/1/2018	Dining Room	Dining Room Table	Finance	Promotion	4,080
2018-010	KRM	Sebastian	Gruenewald	3/1/2018	Appliances	Washer and Dryer	Finance	Promotion	2,750
2018-011	MAP	Jade	Gallagher	3/2/2018	Dining Room	Dining Room Table and Chairs	Finance	Standard	6,780
2018-012	COK	Chantalle	Desmarais	3/2/2018	Dining Room	Dining Room Table and Chairs	Finance	Standard	10,000
2018-013	KRM	Ambrose	Sardelis	3/2/2018	Appliances	Washer	Paid in Full	Promotion	1,100
2018-014	COK	Chantalle	Desmarais	3/3/2018	Living Room	Recliners	Finance	Standard	2,430
2018-015	COK	Jade	Gallagher	3/3/2018	Dining Room	Dining Room Table and Chairs	Paid in Full	Standard	4,550
2018-016	MAP	Chantalle	Desmarais	3/3/2018	Living Room	Sofa, Loveseat, Chair Package	Paid in Full	Standard	6,784
2018-017	MAP	Jade	Gallagher	3/4/2018	Appliances	Dishwasher	Paid in Full	Standard	640
2018-018	KRM	Sebastian	Gruenewald	3/4/2018	Appliances	Refrigerator, Oven, Microwave Combo	Finance	Promotion	8,490

Tabs: March Totals | March Individual

Reid Furniture

Monthly Transactions: March 2018
Down Payment Requirement: 25%

Trans_No	Date	Sales_First	Sales_Last	Department	Furniture	Pay_Type	Trans_Type	Amount	Down_Pa	Owe
2018-001	3/1/2018	Sebastian	Gruenewald	Bedroom	Mattress	Finance	Promotion	2,788	697.00	2,091.00
2018-002	3/1/2018	Sebastian	Gruenewald	Bedroom	Mattress	Finance	Promotion	3,245	811.25	2,433.75
2018-003	3/1/2018	Jade	Gallagher	Living Room	Sofa, Loveseat, Chair Package	Finance	Promotion	10,000	2,500.00	7,500.00
2018-004	3/1/2018	Jade	Gallagher	Living Room	End Tables	Finance	Promotion	1,000	250.00	750.00
2018-005	3/1/2018	Jade	Gallagher	Appliances	Washer and Dryer	Finance	Promotion	2,750	687.50	2,062.50
2018-006	3/1/2018	Ambrose	Sardelis	Living Room	Sofa, Loveseat, Chair Package	Finance	Promotion	12,000	3,000.00	9,000.00
2018-007	3/1/2018	Ambrose	Sardelis	Dining Room	Dining Room Table	Finance	Promotion	3,240	810.00	2,430.00
2018-008	3/1/2018	Chantalle	Desmarais	Dining Room	Dining Room Table	Finance	Promotion	4,080	1,020.00	3,060.00
2018-009	3/1/2018	Sebastian	Gruenewald	Appliances	Washer and Dryer	Finance	Promotion	2,750	687.50	2,062.50
2018-010	3/2/2018	Jade	Gallagher	Dining Room	Dining Room Table and Chairs	Finance	Standard	6,780	1,695.00	5,085.00
2018-011	3/2/2018	Chantalle	Desmarais	Dining Room	Dining Room Table and Chairs	Finance	Standard	10,000	2,500.00	7,500.00
2018-012	3/2/2018	Ambrose	Sardelis	Appliances	Washer	Paid in Full	Promotion	1,100	1,100.00	-
2018-013	3/3/2018	Chantalle	Gallagher	Living Room	Recliners	Finance	Standard	2,430	607.50	1,822.50
2018-014	3/3/2018	Chantalle	Desmarais	Dining Room	Dining Room Table and Chairs	Paid in Full	Standard	4,550	4,550.00	-
2018-015	3/3/2018	Chantalle	Desmarais	Living Room	Sofa, Loveseat, Chair Package	Finance	Standard	6,784	1,696.00	5,088.00
2018-016	3/4/2018	Jade	Gallagher	Appliances	Dishwasher	Paid in Full	Standard	640	640.00	-
2018-017	3/4/2018	Jade	Gruenewald	Appliances	Refrigerator, Oven, Microwave Combo	Finance	Promotion	8,490	2,122.50	6,367.50
2018-018	3/4/2018	Sebastian	Gruenewald	Appliances	Refrigerator, Oven, Microwave Combo	Finance	Promotion	6,780	1,695.00	5,085.00

Tabs: March Totals | March Individual

FIGURE 1 Reid Furniture Store Datasets

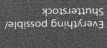

CASE STUDY | Reid Furniture Store

Starting File	File to be Submitted
e04h1Reid	e04h4Reid_LastFirst

Large Datasets

So far you have worked with worksheets that contain small datasets, a collection of structured, related data in a limited number of columns and rows. In reality, you will probably work with large datasets consisting of hundreds or thousands of rows and columns of data. When you work with small datasets, you can usually view most or all of the data without scrolling. When you work with large datasets, you probably will not be able to see the entire dataset onscreen even on a large, widescreen monitor set at high resolution. You might want to keep the column and row labels always in view, even as you scroll throughout the dataset. Figure 2 shows Reid Furniture Store's March 2018 sales transactions. Because it contains a lot of transactions, the entire dataset is not visible. You could decrease the zoom level to display more transactions; however, doing so decreases the text size onscreen, making it hard to read the data.

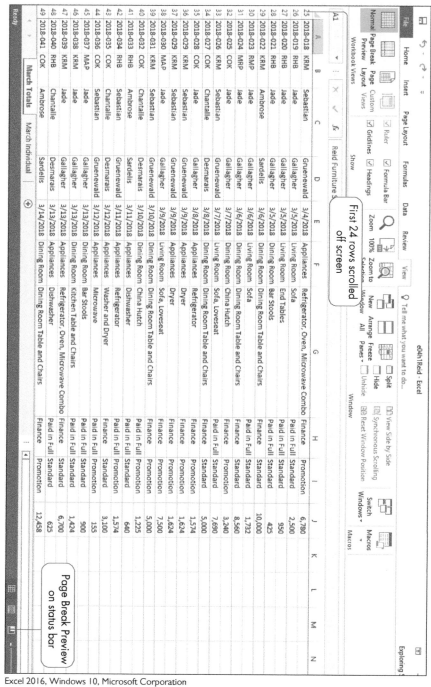

First 24 rows scrolled off screen

Page Break Preview on status bar

FIGURE 2 Large Dataset

Excel 2016, Windows 10, Microsoft Corporation

As you work with larger datasets, realize that the data will not always fit on one page when it is printed. You will need to preview the automatic page breaks and probably insert some manual page breaks in more desirable locations, or you might want to print only a selected range within the large dataset to distribute to others.

In this section, you will learn how to keep labels onscreen as you scroll through a large dataset. In addition, you will learn how to manage page breaks, print only a range instead of an entire worksheet, and print column labels at the top of each page of a large dataset.

Datasets and Tables

TIP: GO TO A SPECIFIC CELL

You can navigate through a large worksheet by using the Go To command. Click Find & Select in the Editing group on the Home tab and select Go To (or press F5 or Ctrl+G) to display the Go To dialog box, enter the cell address in the Reference box, and then press Enter to go to the cell. You can also click in the Name Box, type the cell reference, and then press Enter to go to a specific cell.

Freezing Rows and Columns

STEP 1 When you scroll to parts of a dataset not initially visible, some rows and columns, such as headings, disappear from view. When the row and column labels scroll off the screen, you may not remember what each column or row represents. You can keep labels onscreen by freezing them. *Freezing* is the process of keeping rows and/or columns visible onscreen at all times even when you scroll through a large dataset. Table 1 describes the three freeze options.

TABLE 1	Freeze Options
Option	**Description**
Freeze Panes	Keeps both rows and columns above and to the left of the active cell visible as you scroll through a worksheet.
Freeze Top Row	Keeps only the top row visible as you scroll through a worksheet.
Freeze First Column	Keeps only the first column visible as you scroll through a worksheet.

To freeze one or more rows and columns, use the Freeze Panes option. Before selecting this option, make the active cell one row below and one column to the right of the rows and columns you want to freeze. For example, to freeze the first five rows and the first column, make cell B6 the active cell before clicking the Freeze Panes option. As Figure 3 shows, Excel displays a horizontal line below the last frozen row (row 5) and a vertical line to the right of the last frozen column (column F). Unfrozen rows (such as rows 6–14) and unfrozen columns (such as columns G and H) are no longer visible as you scroll down and to the right, respectively.

	A	B	C	D	E	F	G	H	I	J
1	**Reid Furniture Store**									
2	Monthly Transactions:			March 2018						
3	Down Payment Requirement:			25%						
4			Rows 1–5 and columns A–F frozen							
5	Trans_No	Operator	Sales_First	Sales_Last	Date	Department	Furniture	Pay_Type	Trans_Type	Amount
21	2018-015	MAP	Chantalle	Desmarais	3/3/2018	Living Room	Sofa, Loveseat, Chair Package	Finance	Standard	6,784
22	2018-016	MAP	Jade	Gallagher	3/4/2018	Appliances	Dishwasher	Paid in Full	Standard	640
23	2018-017	MAP	Jade	Gallagher	3/4/2018	Appliances	Refrigerator, Oven, Microwave Combo	Finance	Promotion	8,490
24	2018-018	KRM	Sebastian	Gruenewald	3/4/2018	Appliances	Refrigerator, Oven, Microwave Combo	Finance	Promotion	6,780
25	2018-018	KRM	Sebastian	Gruenewald	3/4/2018	Appliances	Refrigerator, Oven, Microwave Combo	Finance	Promotion	6,780
26	2018-019	RHB	Jade	Gallagher	3/5/2018	Living Room	Sofa	Paid in Full	Standard	2,500
27	2018-020	RHB	Jade	Gallagher	3/5/2018	Living Room	End Tables	Paid in Full	Standard	950
28	2018-021	RHB	Jade	Gallagher	3/5/2018	Dining Room	Bar Stools	Paid in Full	Standard	425
29	2018-022	KRM	Ambrose	Sardelis	3/6/2018	Dining Room	Dining Room Table and Chairs	Finance	Standard	10,000
30	2018-023	RMP	Jade	Gallagher	3/6/2018	Living Room	Sofa	Paid in Full	Standard	1,732
31	2018-024	MRP	Jade	Gallagher	3/6/2018	Dining Room	Dining Room Table and Chairs	Finance	Standard	8,560
32	2018-025	COK	Jade	Gallagher	3/7/2018	Dining Room	China Hutch	Finance	Promotion	3,240
33	2018-026	KRM	Sebastian	Gruenewald	3/7/2018	Living Room	Sofa, Loveseat	Finance	Standard	7,690
34	2018-027	COK	Chantalle	Desmarais	3/8/2018	Dining Room	Dining Room Table and Chairs	Paid in Full	Standard	5,000
35	2018-028	COK	Jade	Gallagher	3/8/2018	Appliances	Refrigerator	Finance	Standard	1,574
36	2018-029	KRM	Sebastian	Gruenewald	3/9/2018	Appliances	Dryer	Finance	Promotion	1,624
37	2018-029	KRM	Sebastian	Gruenewald	3/9/2018	Appliances	Dryer	Finance	Promotion	1,624
38	2018-030	MAP	Jade	Gallagher	3/9/2018	Living Room	Sofa, Loveseat	Finance	Promotion	7,500
39	2018-031	KRM	Sebastian	Gruenewald	3/10/2018	Dining Room	Dining Room Table and Chairs	Finance	Promotion	5,000

Vertical line to the right of last frozen column

Horizontal line below last frozen row

March Totals | March Individual

FIGURE 3 Freeze Panes Set

To unlock the rows and columns from remaining onscreen as you scroll, click Freeze Panes in the Window group and select Unfreeze Panes, which only appears on the menu when you have frozen rows and/or columns. After you unfreeze the panes, the Freeze Panes option appears instead of Unfreeze Panes on the menu again.

When you freeze panes and press Ctrl+Home, the first unfrozen cell is the active cell instead of cell A1. For example, with column F and rows 1 through 5 frozen in Figure 3, pressing Ctrl+Home makes cell G6 the active cell. If you want to edit a cell in the frozen area, click the particular cell to make it active and edit the data.

Printing Large Datasets

For a large dataset, some columns and rows may print on several pages. Analyzing the data on individual printed pages is difficult when each page does not contain column and row labels. To prevent wasting paper, always use Print Preview. Doing so enables you to adjust page settings until you are satisfied with how the data will print.

The Page Layout tab (see Figure 4) contains options to help you prepare large datasets to print. Previously, you changed the page orientation, set different margins, and adjusted the scaling. In addition, you can manage page breaks, set the print area, and print titles.

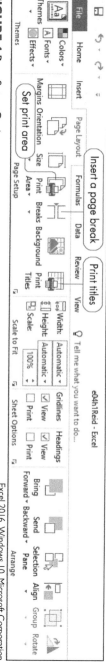

Excel 2016, Windows 10, Microsoft Corporation

FIGURE 4 Page Setup Options

STEP 2

Display and Change Page Breaks

Based on the paper size, orientation, margins, and other settings, Excel identifies how much data can print on a page. Then it displays a *page break*, indicating where data will start on another printed page. To identify where these automatic page breaks will occur, click Page Break Preview on the status bar or in the Workbook Views group on the View tab. In Page Break Preview, Excel displays watermarks, such as Page 1, indicating the area that will print on a specific page. Blue dashed lines indicate where the automatic page breaks occur, and solid blue lines indicate manual page breaks.

If the automatic page breaks occur in an undesirable location, you can insert a manual page break. For example, if you have a worksheet listing sales data by date, the automatic page break might occur within a group of rows for one date, such as between two rows of data for 3/1/2018. To make all rows for that date appear together, you can either insert a page break above the first data row for that date or decrease the margins so that all 3/1/2018 transactions fit at the bottom of the page.

To set a manual break at a specific location, complete the following steps:

1. Click the cell that you want to be the first row and column on a new printed page. For example, if you click cell D50, you create a page for columns A through C, and then column D starts a new page.
2. Click the Page Layout tab.
3. Click Breaks in the Page Setup group and select Insert Page Break. Excel displays a solid blue line in Page Break Preview or a dashed line in Normal view to indicate the manual page breaks you set. Figure 5 shows a worksheet with both automatic and manual page breaks.

To remove a manual page break, complete the following steps:

1. Click a cell below a horizontal page break or a cell to the right of a vertical page break.
2. Click Breaks in the Page Setup group and select Remove Page Break.

To reset all page breaks back to the automatic page breaks, complete the following steps:

1. Click Breaks in the Page Setup group.
2. Select Reset All Page Breaks.

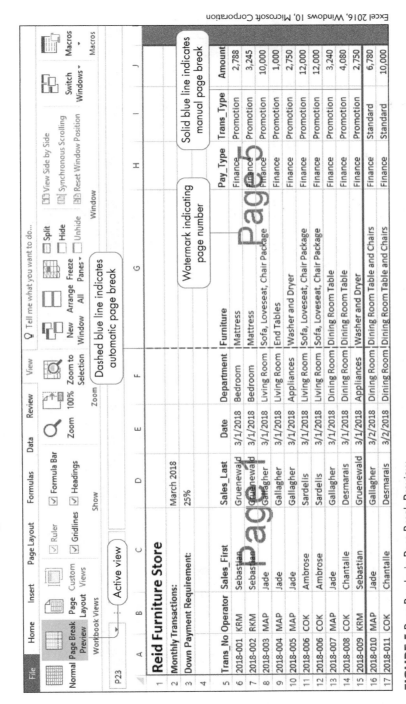

Excel 2016, Windows 10, Microsoft Corporation

FIGURE 5 Page Breaks in Page Break Preview

TIP: USING THE POINTER TO MOVE PAGE BREAKS

To use the pointer to adjust a page break, point to the page break line to see the two-headed arrow and drag the line to the location where you want the page break to occur.

Set and Clear a Print Area

STEP 3 ⟫ The default Print settings send an entire dataset on the active worksheet to the printer. However, you might want to print only part of the worksheet data. If you display the worksheet in Page Break view, you can identify which page(s) you want to print. Then click the File tab and select Print. Under Settings, type the number(s) of the page(s) you want to print. For example, to print page 2 only, type 2 in the Pages text box and in the *to* text box.

You can further restrict what is printed by setting the ***print area***, which is the range of cells that will print. For example, you might want to print only an input area or just the transactions that occurred on a particular date.

To set a print area, complete the following steps:

1. Select the range you want to print.
2. Click the Page Layout tab and click Print Area in the Page Setup group.
3. Select Set Print Area.

In Page Break Preview, the print area has a white background and solid blue border; the rest of the worksheet has a gray background (see Figure 6). In Normal view or Page Layout view, the print area is surrounded by thin gray lines.

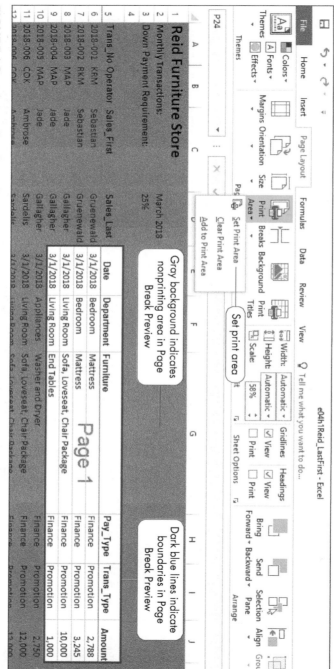

FIGURE 6 Print Area in Page Break Preview

Excel 2016, Windows 10, Microsoft Corporation

To add print areas where each print area will print on a separate page, select the range you want to print, click Print Area, and then select Add to Print Area. To clear the print area, click Print Area in the Page Setup group and select Clear Print Area.

TIP: PRINT A SELECTION

Another way to print part of a worksheet is to select the range you want to print. Click the File tab and click Print. Click the first arrow in the Settings section and select Print Selection. This provides additional flexibility compared to using a defined print area in situations in which you may be required to print materials outside a consistent range of cells.

Print Titles

STEP 4 »

When you print large datasets, it is helpful if every page contains descriptive column and row labels. When you click Print Titles in the Page Setup group on the Page Layout tab, Excel opens the Page Setup dialog box with the Sheet tab active so that you can select which row(s) and/or column(s) to repeat on each page of a printout (see Figure 7).

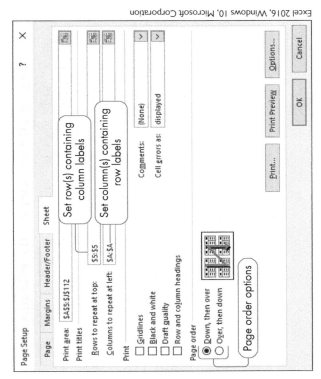

FIGURE 7 Sheet Tab Options

To repeat rows or columns at the top or left of each page when printed, select the row(s) that contain the labels or titles (such as row 5) in the *Rows to repeat at top* box to display $5:$5. To print the row labels at the left side of each page, select the column(s) that contain the labels or titles (such as column A) in the *Columns to repeat at left* box to display AA.

Control Print Page Order

Print order is the sequence in which the pages are printed. By default, the pages print in this order: top-left section, bottom-left section, top-right section, and bottom-right section. However, you might want to print the entire top portion of the worksheet before printing the bottom portion. To change the print order, open the Page Setup dialog box, click the Sheet tab, and then select the desired Page order option (refer to Figure 7).

Quick Concepts

1. What is the purpose of freezing panes in a worksheet?

2. Why would you want to insert page breaks instead of using the automatic page breaks?

3. What steps should you take to ensure that column labels display on each printed page of a large dataset?

Hands-On Exercises

Skills covered: Freeze Rows and Columns • Display and Change Page Breaks • Set and Clear a Print Area • Print Titles

1 Large Datasets

You want to review the large dataset that shows the March 2018 transactions for Reid Furniture Store. You will view the data and adjust some page setup options so that you can print necessary labels on each page.

STEP 1 **)) FREEZE ROWS AND COLUMNS**

Before printing the March 2018 transaction dataset, you want to view the data. The dataset contains more rows than will display onscreen at the same time. You decide to freeze the column and row labels to stay onscreen as you scroll through the transactions. Refer to Figure 8 as you complete Step 1.

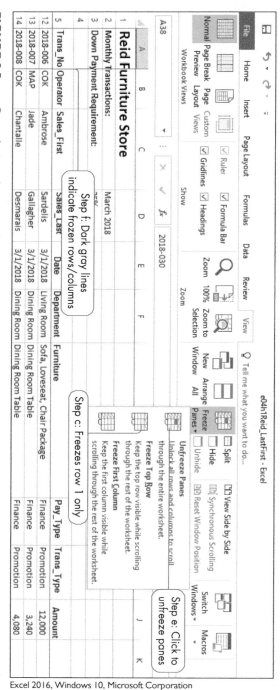

FIGURE 8 Freeze Panes Activated

Excel 2016, Windows 10, Microsoft Corporation

a. Open *e04h1Reid* and save it as **e04h1Reid_LastFirst**.

The workbook contains two worksheets: March Totals (for Hands-On Exercises 1–3) and March Individual (for Hands-On Exercise 4).

b. Press **Page Down** four times to scroll through the dataset. Then press **Ctrl+Home** to go back to the top of the worksheet.

After you press Page Down, the column labels in row 5 scroll off the screen, making it challenging to remember what type of data are in some columns.

c. Click the **View tab**, click **Freeze Panes** in the Window group, and then select **Freeze Top Row**.

A dark gray horizontal line displays between rows 1 and 2.

d. Press **Page Down** to scroll down through the worksheet.

As rows scroll off the top of the Excel window, the first row remains frozen onscreen. The title by itself is not helpful; you need to freeze the column labels as well.

TROUBLESHOOTING: Your screen may differ from Figure 8 due to different Windows resolution settings. If necessary, continue scrolling right and down until you see columns and rows scrolling offscreen.

e. Click **Freeze Panes** in the Window group and select **Unfreeze Panes**.

f. Click **cell B6**, the cell below the row and one column to the right of what you want to freeze. Click **Freeze Panes** in the Window group and select **Freeze Panes**.

Excel displays a vertical line between columns A and B, indicating that column A is frozen, and a horizontal line between rows 5 and 6, indicating the first five rows are frozen.

g. Press **Ctrl+G**, type **Q112** in the Reference box of the Go To dialog box, and then click **OK** to make cell Q112 the active cell.

Rows 6 through 96 and columns B and C are not visible because they scrolled off the screen. Note that the results will vary slightly based on screen resolution.

h. Save the workbook.

You plan to print the dataset so that you and Vicki Reid can discuss the transactions in your weekly meeting. Because the large dataset will not fit on one page, you want to see where the automatic page breaks are and then insert a manual page break. Refer to Figure 9 as you complete Step 2.

STEP 2 » DISPLAY AND CHANGE PAGE BREAKS

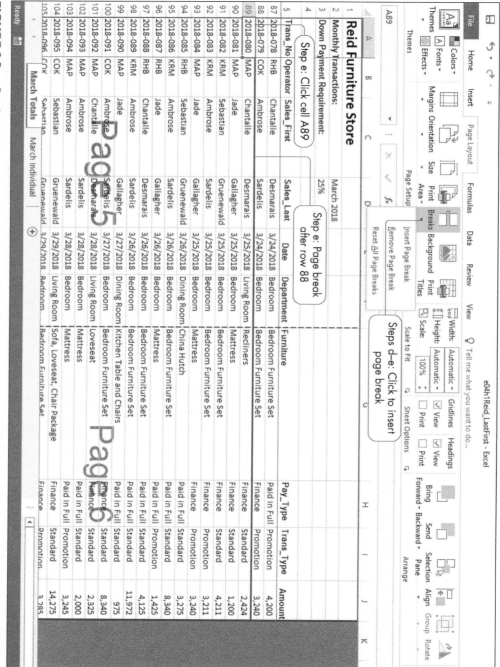

FIGURE 9 Page Breaks

Excel 2016, Windows 10, Microsoft Corporation

a. Press **Ctrl+Home** to move to **cell B6**, the first cell in the unfrozen area. Click the **View tab** and click **Page Break Preview** in the Workbook Views group or on the status bar.

Excel displays blue dashed lines to indicate the automatic page breaks.

b. Scroll down until you see row 44 below the frozen column labels.

The automatic horizontal page break is between rows 46 and 47 (or between rows 45 and 46). You do not want transactions for a particular day to span between printed pages, so you need to move the page break up to keep all 3/13/2018 transactions together.

c. Click **cell A45**, the first cell containing 3/13/2018 data and the cell to start the top of the second page.

d. Click the **Page Layout tab**, click **Breaks** in the Page Setup group, and then select **Insert Page Break**.

You inserted a page break between rows 44 and 45 so that the 3/13/2018 transactions will be on one page.

e. Click **cell A89**, click **Breaks** in the Page Setup group, and then select **Insert Page Break**.

You inserted a page break between rows 88 and 89 to keep the 3/25/2018 transactions on the same page.

f. Save the workbook.

You want to focus on the transactions for only March 1, 2018. To avoid printing more data than you need, you will set the print area to print transactions for only that day. Refer to Figure 10 as you complete Step 3.

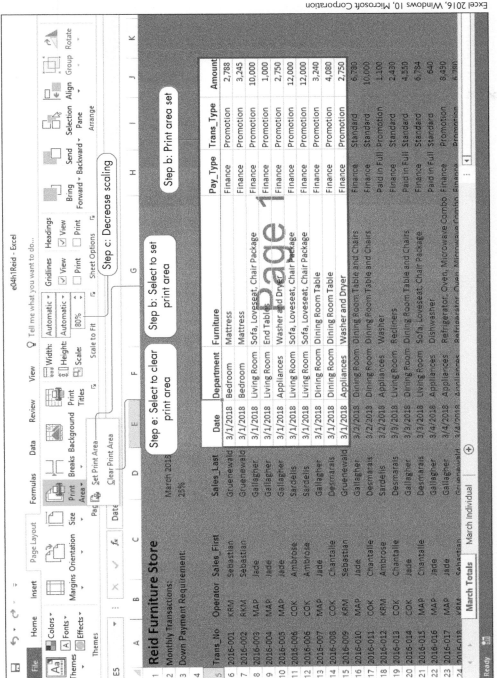

FIGURE 10 Print Area Set

a. Select the **range E5:J15**, the range of data for March 1, 2018.

b. Click the **Page Layout tab**, click **Print Area** in the Page Setup group, and then select **Set Print Area**.

   Excel displays the print area with a border. The rest of the worksheet displays with a gray background.

c. Click **cell E5** and click the **Scale arrow** down four times to display 80% in the Scale to Fit group.

   The selected print area will print on one page.

d. Press **Ctrl+P** to see that only the print area will print. Press **Esc.**

e. Click **Print Area** in the Page Setup group and select **Clear Print Area.**

f. Save the workbook.

Only the first page will print both row and column labels. Pages 2 and 3 will print the remaining row labels, page 4 will print the remaining column labels, and pages 5 and 6 will not print either label. You want to make sure the column and row labels print on all pages. To do this, you will print titles. Refer to Figure 11 as you complete Step 4.

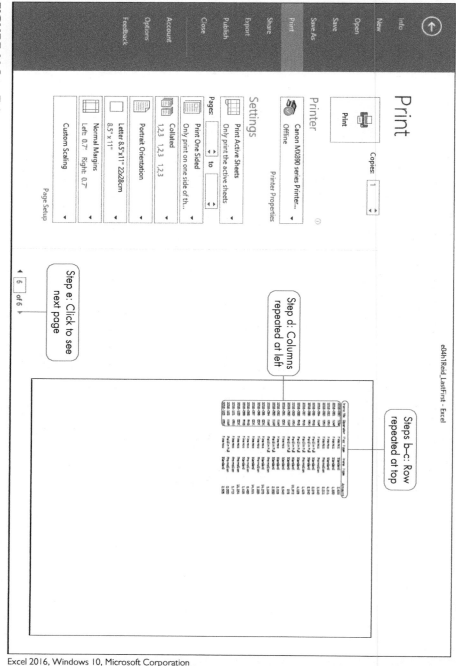

FIGURE 11 Print Titles

Excel 2016, Windows 10, Microsoft Corporation

a. Click **Print Titles** in the Page Setup group.

The Page Setup dialog box opens, displaying the Sheet tab.

b. Click **Collapse Dialog Box** on the right side of the *Rows to repeat at top* box.

Clicking Collapse Dialog Box reduces the dialog box so that you can select a range in the worksheet easily.

c. Click the **row 5 heading** and click **Expand Dialog Box** within the *Page Setup: Rows to repeat at top* dialog box.

You selected the fifth row, which contains the column labels, and expanded the Page Setup dialog box back to its full size.

d. Click in the **Columns to repeat at left box**, type **A:B**, click the **Over, then down** Page order, and then click **Print Preview**.

You have manually entered the columns that contain the heading you want to repeat.

e. Click **Next Page** at the bottom of the Print Preview. Click **Next Page** until the sixth page displays.

Figure 11 shows a preview of the sixth page. The column labels and the first two columns appear on all pages.

f. Click the **Back arrow**.

g. Save the workbook. Keep the workbook open if you plan to continue with the next Hands-On Exercise. If not, close the workbook, and exit Excel.

348   Hands-On Exercise 1

Excel Tables

All organizations maintain lists of data. Businesses maintain inventory lists, educational institutions maintain lists of students and faculty, and governmental entities maintain lists of contracts. Although more complicated related data should be stored in a database management program, such as Access, you can manage basic data structure in Excel tables. A **table** is a structured range that contains related data organized in a method that increases the capability to manage and analyze information.

In this section, you will learn table terminology and rules for structuring data. You will create a table from existing data, manage records and fields, and remove duplicates. You will then apply a table style to format the table.

Understanding the Benefits of Data Tables

When dealing with large datasets it is imperative that documents are strategically organized to maintain data integrity and ease of use. Thus far you have worked with the manipulation of data ranges, and while you can use many tools in Excel to analyze simple data ranges, tables provide many additional analytical and time saving benefits. Using tables in Excel can help create and maintain data structure. **Data structure** is the organization method used to manage multiple data points within a dataset. For example, a dataset of students may include names, grades, contact information, and intended majors of study. The data structure of this dataset would define how the information is stored, organized, and accessed. Although you can manage and analyze data structure as a range in Excel, a table provides many advantages:

- Column headings remain onscreen without having to use Freeze Panes.
- Filter arrows let you sort and filter efficiently.
- Table styles easily format table rows and columns with complementary fill colors.
- Calculated columns let you create and edit formulas that copy down the columns automatically.
- A calculated total row lets you implement a variety of summary functions.
- You can use structured references instead of cell references in formulas.
- You can export table data to a SharePoint list.

Designing and Creating Tables

A table is a group of related data organized in a series of rows and columns that is managed independently from any other data on the worksheet. Once a data range is converted into a table, each column represents a **field**, which is an individual piece of data, such as last names or quantities sold. Each field should represent the smallest possible unit of data. For example, instead of a Name field, separate name data into First Name and Last Name fields. Instead of one large address field, separate address data into Street Address, City, State, and ZIP Code fields. Separating data into the smallest units possible enables you to manipulate the data in a variety of ways for output. Each row in a table represents a **record**, which is a collection of related data about one entity. For example, all data related to one particular transaction form a record in the Reid Furniture Store worksheet. You should plan the structure before creating a table. The more thoroughly you plan, the fewer changes you will have to make to gain information from the data in the table after you create it. To help plan your table, follow these guidelines:

- Enter field (column) names on the top row of the table.
- Keep field names short, descriptive, and unique. No two field names should be identical.

- Format the field names so that they stand out from the data.
- Enter data for each record on a row below the field names.
- Do not leave blank rows between records or between the field names and the first record.

Create a Table

STEP 1

While it is possible to create a table from random unorganized data, it is a best practice first to plan the data structure. When your worksheet data is structured correctly, you can easily create a table. Furthermore, by taking the time to create an organized data structure you will ensure that the data can be used to identify specific information easily, is easy to manage, and is scalable.

- Delete any blank columns between fields in the dataset.
- Make sure each record has something unique, such as a transaction number or ID.
- Insert at least one blank row and one blank column between the table and other data, such as the main titles. When you need multiple tables in one workbook, a best practice is to place each table on a separate worksheet.

To create a table from existing data, complete the following steps:

1. Click within the existing range of data.
2. Click the Insert tab and click Table in the Tables group. The Create Table dialog box opens (see Figure 12), prompting you to enter the range of data.
   - Select the range for the *Where is the data for your table* box if Excel does not correctly predict the range.
   - Select the *My table has headers* check box if the existing range contains column labels.
3. Click OK to create the table.

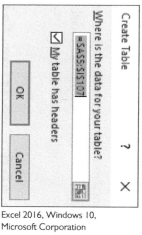

FIGURE 12 Create Table Dialog Box

Excel 2016, Windows 10,
Microsoft Corporation

TIP: QUICK ANALYSIS TABLE CREATION

You can also create a table by selecting a range, clicking the Quick Analysis button, clicking Tables (see Figure 13) in the Quick Analysis gallery, and then clicking Table. While Quick Analysis is efficient for tasks such as creating a chart, it may take more time to create a table because you have to select the entire range first. Some people find that it is faster to create a table on the Insert tab.

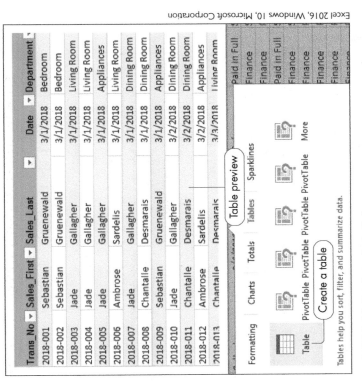

Excel 2016, Windows 10, Microsoft Corporation

FIGURE 13 Quick Analysis Gallery

After you create a table, the Table Tools Design tab displays. Excel applies the default Table Style Medium 2 style to the table, and each cell in the header row has filter arrows (see Figure 14). This text uses the term *filter arrows* for consistency.

TIP: FILTER ARROWS

Click the Filter Button check box in the Table Style Options group on the Design tab to display or hide the filter arrows (see Figure 14). For a range of data instead of a table, click Filter in the Sort & Filter group on the Data tab to display or hide the filter arrows.

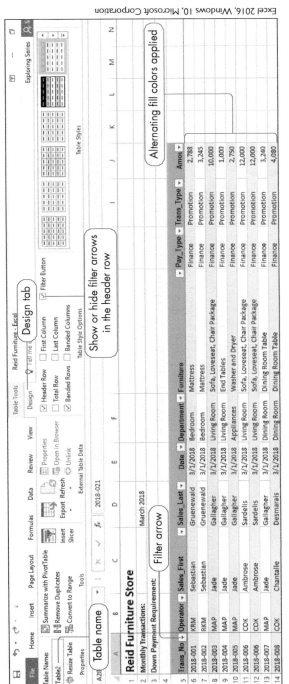

Excel 2016, Windows 10, Microsoft Corporation

FIGURE 14 Excel Table in Default Format

Instead of converting a range to a table, you can create a table structure first and add data to it later. Select an empty range and follow the previously listed steps to create the range for the table. The default column headings are Column1, Column2, and so on. Click each default column heading and type a descriptive label. Then enter the data into each row of the newly created table.

TIP: CONVERTING A TABLE TO A RANGE

To convert a table back to a range, click within the table range, click the Table Tools Design tab, click Convert to Range in the Tools group, and then click Yes in the message box asking, *Do you want to convert the table to a normal range?*

Rename a Table

By default, when a table is created, Excel assigns a name automatically. For example, the first table created in a worksheet will be named Table1. The default nomenclature does not provide descriptive information and, as a best practice, you should change the default name to something more meaningful.

Once a name has been assigned to a table, it can be used when building functions in place of the traditional absolute reference.

To change the table name, complete the following steps:

1. Click the Table Name box in the Properties group of the Table Tools Design tab.
2. Type a new name using the same rules you applied when assigning range names, and press Enter.

Add and Delete Fields

After creating a table, you may need to insert a new field. For example, you might want to add a field for product numbers to the Reid Furniture Store transaction table.

To insert a field, complete the following steps:

1. Click in any data cell (other than the cell containing the field name) in a field that will be to the right of the new field. For example, to insert a new field between the fields in columns A and B, click any cell in column B.
2. Click the Home tab and click the Insert arrow in the Cells group.
3. Select Insert Table Columns to the Left.

If you want to add a field at the end of the right side of a table, click in the cell to the right of the last field name and type a label. Excel will extend the table to include that field and will format the cell as a field name.

You can also delete a field if you no longer need any data for that particular field. Although deleting records and fields is easy, you must make sure not to delete data erroneously. If you accidentally delete data, click Undo immediately.

To delete a field, complete the following steps:

1. Click a cell in the field that you want to delete.
2. Click the Delete arrow in the Cells group on the Home tab.
3. Select Delete Table Columns.

Add, Edit, and Delete Records

STEP 4 ▶▶ After you begin storing data in your newly created table, you might want to add new records, such as adding a new client or a new item to an inventory table. One of the advantages to using tables in Excel is the ability to easily add, edit, or delete records within the dataset.

To add a record to a table, complete the following steps:

1. Click a cell in the record below which you want the new record inserted. If you want to add a new record below the last record, click the row containing the last record.

2. Click the Home tab and click the Insert arrow in the Cells group.

3. Select Insert Table Rows Above to insert a row above the current row, or select Insert Table Row Below if the current row is the last one and you want a row below it.

You can also add a record to the end of a table by clicking in the row immediately below the table and typing. Excel will extend the table to include that row as a record in the table and will apply consistent formatting.

You might need to change data for a record. For example, when a client moves, you need to change the client's address. You edit data in a table the same way you edit data in a regular worksheet cell.

Finally, you can delete records. For example, if you maintain an inventory of artwork in your house and sell a piece of art, delete that record from the table.

To delete a record from the table, complete the following steps:

1. Click a cell in the record that you want to delete.

2. Click the Home tab and click the Delete arrow in the Cells group.

3. Select Delete Table Rows.

Remove Duplicate Rows

STEP 5 ▶▶ A table might contain duplicate records, which can give false results when totaling or performing other calculations on the dataset. For a small table, you might be able to detect duplicate records by scanning the data. For large tables, it is more difficult to iden-tify duplicate records by simply scanning the table with the eye.

To remove duplicate records, complete the following steps:

1. Click within the table and click the Design tab.

2. Click Remove Duplicates in the Tools group to display the Remove Duplicates dialog box (see Figure 15). As an alternate method, you can also click the Data tab and click Remove Duplicates in the Data Tools group to open the Remove Duplicates dialog box.

3. Click Select All to set the criteria to find a duplicate for every field in the record and click OK. If you select individual column(s), Excel looks for duplicates in the specific column(s) only and deletes all but one record of the duplicated data. Excel will display a message box informing you of how many duplicate rows it removed.

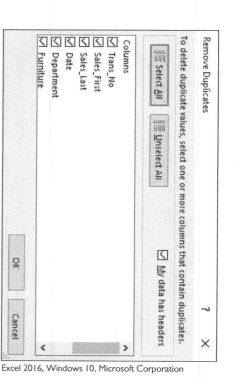

FIGURE 15 Remove Duplicates Dialog Box

Excel 2016, Windows 10, Microsoft Corporation

Applying a Table Style

STEP 6

When you create a table, it is automatically formatted with a table style of alternating colored rows and a bold style for the header row. ***Table styles*** control the fill color of the header row (the row containing field names) and rows of records. In addition, table styles specify bold and border lines. You can change the table style to a color scheme that complements your organization's color scheme or to emphasize data in the header rows or columns. Click the More button in the Table Styles group to display the Table Styles gallery (see Figure 16). To see how a table style will format your table using Live Preview, point to a style in the Table Styles gallery. After you identify a style you want, click it to apply it to the table.

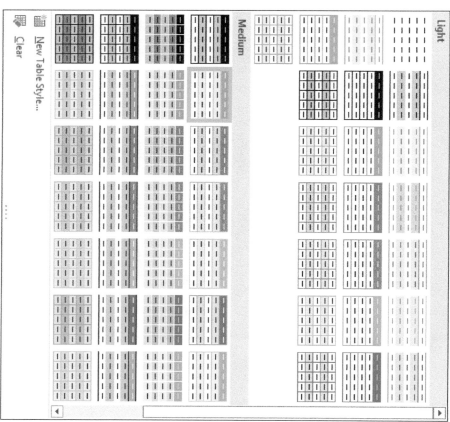

FIGURE 16 Table Styles Gallery

Excel 2016, Windows 10, Microsoft Corporation

After you select a table style, you can control what the style formats. The Table Style Options group contains check boxes to select specific format actions in a table. Table 2 lists the options and the effect of each check box. Avoid overformatting the table. Applying too many formatting effects may obscure the message you want to present with the data.

TABLE 2 Table Style Options

Check Box	Action
Header Row	Displays the header row (field names) when checked; removes field names when not checked. Header Row formatting takes priority over column formats.
Total Row	Displays a total row when selected. Total Row formatting takes priority over column formats.
First Column	Applies a different format to the first column so that the row headings stand out. First Column formatting takes priority over Banded Rows formatting.
Last Column	Applies a different format to the last column so that the last column of data stands out; effective for aggregated data, such as grand totals per row. Last Column formatting takes priority over Banded Rows formatting.
Banded Rows	Displays alternate fill colors for even and odd rows to help distinguish records.
Banded Columns	Displays alternate fill colors for even and odd columns to help distinguish fields.
Filter Button	Displays a filter button on the right side of each heading in the header row.

Quick Concepts

4. List at least four guidelines for planning a table in Excel.

5. Why would you convert a range of data into an Excel table?

6. What are six options you can control after selecting a table style?

Hands-On Exercises

2 Excel Tables

Skills covered: Create a Table • Rename a Table • Add and Delete Fields • Add, Edit, and Delete Records • Remove Duplicate Rows • Apply a Table Style

Although Reid Furniture Store's March transaction data are organized in an Excel worksheet, you know that you will have additional functionality if you convert the range to a table. Refer to Figure 17 as you complete Step 1.

STEP 1 **» CREATE A TABLE**

You want to convert the March Totals data to a table. As you review the table, you will delete the unnecessary Operator field, add two new fields, insert a missing furniture sale transaction, and remove duplicate transactions. Finally, you will enhance the table appearance by applying a table style.

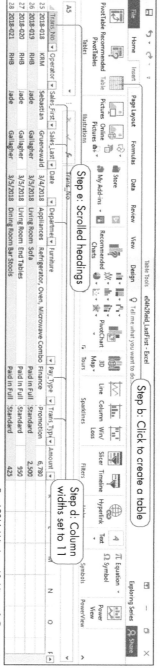

Step e: Scrolled headings

Step b: Click to create a table

Step d: Column widths set to 11

FIGURE 17 Range Converted to a Table

Excel 2016, Windows 10, Microsoft Corporation

a. Open *e04h1Reid_LastFirst* if you closed it at the end of Hands-On Exercise 1, and save it as **e04h2Reid_LastFirst**, changing h1 to h2. Click **Normal** on the status bar.

b. Click in any cell within the transactional data, click the **Insert tab**, and then click **Table** in the Tables group.

The Create Table dialog box opens. The *Where is the data for your table?* box displays =$A$5:$J$112. Keep the *My table has headers* check box selected so that the headings on the fifth row become the field names for the table.

c. Click **OK** and click **cell A5**.

Excel creates a table from the data range and displays the Design tab, filter arrows, and alternating fill colors for the records. The columns widen to fit the field names, although the wrap text option is still applied to those cells.

d. Set the column width to **11** for the Sales_First, Sales_Last, Department, Pay_Type, and Trans_Type fields.

e. Unfreeze the panes and scroll through the table.

With a regular range of data, column labels scroll off the top of the screen if you do not freeze panes. When you scroll within a table, the table's header row remains onscreen by moving up to where the Excel column (letter) headings usually display (see Figure 17). Note that it will not retain the bold formatting when scrolling.

f. Save the workbook.

STEP 2 » RENAME THE TABLE

After creating the table, you will change the name from the default "Table1" to a more descriptive title that meets your business standards. Refer to Figure 18 as you complete Step 2.

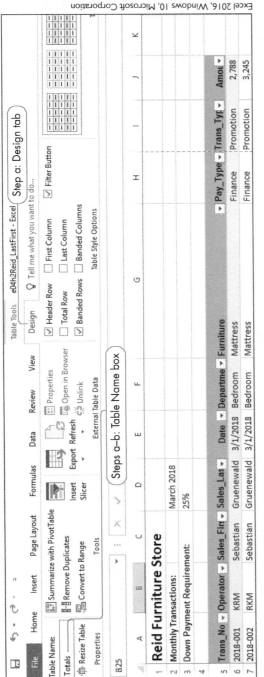

FIGURE 18 Rename the Table

a. Click the **Design tab**, and click the **Table Name box** in the Properties group.

b. Type **Totals** in the Table Name box and press **Enter**.

When a table is created, Excel assigns the default name "table" and a sequential number based on the number of tables in the document. For example, if there were two tables in the document the default name for the second table would be "Table2." In this step you have added a custom name that will be used throughout the rest of the project.

STEP 3 » ADD AND DELETE FIELDS

The original range included a column for the data entry operators' initials. You will delete this column because you do not need it for your analysis. In addition, you want to add a field to display down payment amounts in the future. Refer to Figure 19 as you complete Step 3.

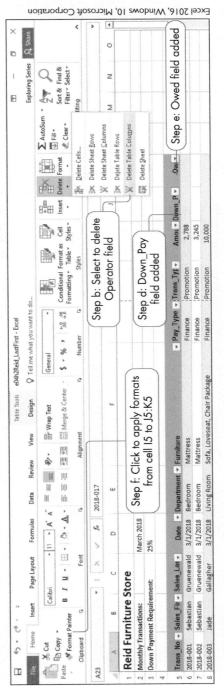

FIGURE 19 Newly Created Fields

a. Click any cell containing a value in the Operator column.

You need to make a cell active in the field you want to remove.

b. Click the **Home tab**, click the **Delete arrow** in the Cells group, and then select **Delete Table Columns.**

Excel deletes the Operator column and may adjust the width of other columns.

Hands-On Exercise 2

c. Set the widths of columns E, F, and G to AutoFit. Click **cell J5**, the first blank cell on the right side of the field names.

d. Type **Down_Pay** and press **Ctrl+Enter**.

Excel extends the table formatting to column J automatically. A filter arrow appears for the newly created field name, and alternating fill colors appear in the rows below the field name. The fill color is the same as the fill color for other field names; however, the font color is White, Background 1, instead of Black Text 1.

e. Click **cell K5**, type **Owed**, and then press **Ctrl+Enter**.

f. Click **cell I5**, click **Format Painter** in the Clipboard group, and then select the **range J5:K5** to copy the format. Save the workbook.

STEP 4 ≫ ADD RECORDS

As you review the March 2018 transaction table, you notice that two transactions are missing: 2018-068 and 2018-104. After finding the paper invoices, you are ready to add records with the missing transaction data. Refer to Figure 20 as you complete Step 4.

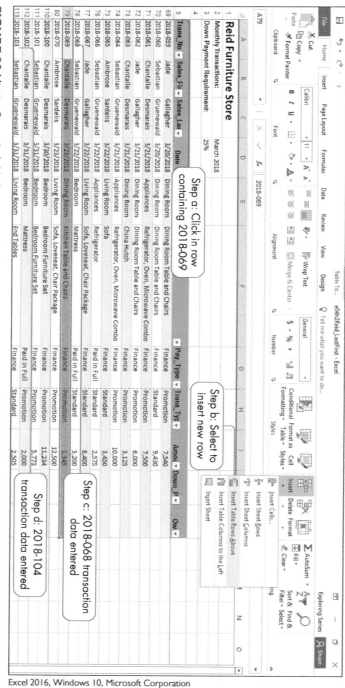

FIGURE 20 Missing Records Added

a. Click **cell A78**.

The missing record 2018-068 needs to be inserted between 2018-067 on row 77 and 2018-069 on row 78.

b. Click the **Home tab**, click the **Insert arrow** in the Cells group, and then select **Insert Table Rows Above**.

Excel inserts a new table row on row 78, between the 2018-067 and 2018-069 transactions.

c. Enter the following data in the respective fields on the newly created row:

2018-068, Sebastian, Gruenewald, 3/22/2018, Bedroom, Mattress, Paid in Full, Standard, 3200

d. Click **cell A114** and enter the following data in the respective fields:

2018-104, Ambrose, Sardelis, 3/31/2018, Appliances, Refrigerator, Paid in Full, Standard, 1500

When you start typing 2018-104 in the row below the last record, Excel immediately includes and formats row 114 as part of the table. Review Figure 20 to ensure that you inserted the records in the correct locations. In the figure, rows 81–109 are hidden to display both new records in one screenshot.

e. Save the workbook.

STEP 5 » **REMOVE DUPLICATE ROWS**

You noticed that the 2018-006 transaction is duplicated on rows 11 and 12 and that the 2018-018 transaction is duplicated on rows 24 and 25. You think the table may contain other duplicate rows. To avoid having to look at the entire table row by row, you will have Excel find and remove the duplicate rows for you. Refer to Figure 21 as you complete Step 5.

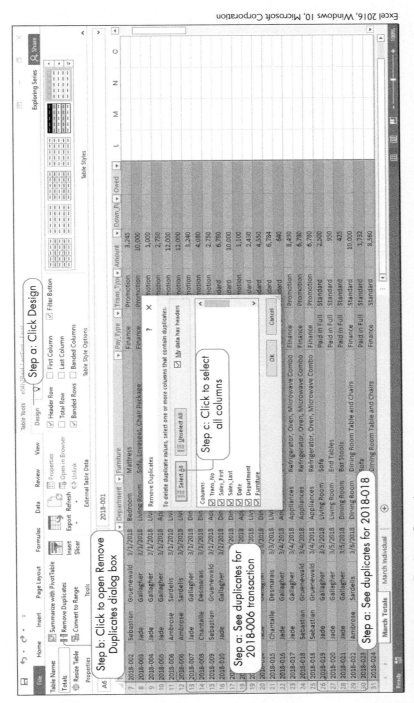

FIGURE 21 Remove Duplicate Records

a. Click a cell in the table. Scroll to see rows 11 and 12. Click the **Design tab**.

The records on rows 11 and 12 are identical. Rows 24 and 25 are also duplicates. You need to remove the extra rows.

b. Click **Remove Duplicates** in the Tools group.

The Remove Duplicates dialog box opens.

c. Click **Select All**, make sure the *My data has headers* check box is selected, and then click **OK**.

Excel displays a message box indicating *5 duplicate records found and removed; 104 unique values remain*.

d. Click **OK** in the message box. Click **cell A109** to view the last record in the table. Save the workbook.

Transaction 2018-104 is located on row 109 after the duplicate records are removed.

STEP 6 》 APPLY A TABLE STYLE

Now that you have finalized the fields and added missing records to the March 2018 transaction table, you want to apply a table style to format the table. Refer to Figure 22 as you complete Step 6.

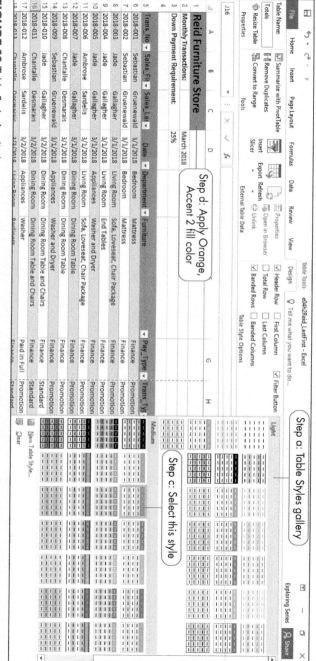

FIGURE 22 Table Style Applied

Excel 2016, Windows 10, Microsoft Corporation

a. Click a cell in the table. Click the **Design tab** and click **More** in the Table Styles group to open the Table Styles gallery.

b. Point to the fourth style on the second row in the Light section.

   Live Preview shows the table with the Table Style Light 10 style but does not apply it.

c. Click **Table Style Medium 3**, the third style on the first row in the Medium section.

   Excel formats the table with the Medium 3 table style, which applies Orange, Accent 2 fill color to the table header row and Orange, Accent 2, Lighter 80% fill color to every other record.

d. Press **Ctrl+Home**. Select the **range A1:C1**, click the **Fill Color arrow** in the Font group on the Home tab, and then click **Orange, Accent 2**.

   You applied a fill color for the title to match the fill color of the field names on the header row in the table.

e. Save the workbook. Keep the workbook open if you plan to continue with the next Hands-On Exercise. If not, close the workbook, and exit Excel.

Table Manipulation

Along with maintaining data structure, tables have a variety of options to enhance and manipulate data, in addition to managing fields, adding records, and applying table styles. You can build formulas and functions, arrange records in different sequences to get different perspectives on the data, and restrict the onscreen appearance of data using filtering. For example, you can arrange the transactions by sales representative. Furthermore, you can display only particular records instead of the entire dataset to focus on a subset of the data. For example, you might want to focus on the financed transactions.

In this section, you will learn how to create structured references, and how to sort records by text, numbers, and dates in a table. In addition, you will learn how to filter data based on conditions you set.

Creating Structured References in Formulas

STEP 1 ▶▶ Your experience in building formulas involves using cell references, such as =SUM(B1:B15) or =H6*$B$3. Cell references in formulas help to identify where the content is on a worksheet, but does not tell the user what the content represents. An advantage to Excel tables is that they use structured references to clearly indicate which type of data is used in the calculations. A *structured reference* is a tag or use of a table element, such as a field heading, as a reference in a formula. As shown in Figure 23, structured references in formulas clearly indicate which type of data is used in the calculations.

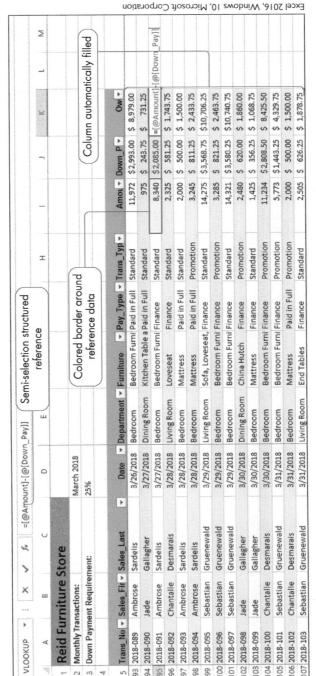

FIGURE 23 Structured Reference

When creating a formula in a table using structured references, field headings are set off by brackets around column headings or field names, such as =[Amount]-[Down_Pay]. The use of field headings without row references in a structured formula is called an *unqualified reference*. After you type the equal sign to begin your formula, type an opening bracket, and then Formula AutoComplete displays a list of field headings. Type or double-click the column name from the list and type the closing bracket. Excel displays a colored border around the referenced column that coordinates with the structured reference in the formula, similar to Excel identifying cell references and their worksheet placement. When you enter a formula using structured references, Excel copies the formula down the rest of the table column automatically, compared to typing references in formulas and using the fill handle to copy the formula down a column.

You can also use the semi-selection process to create a formula. As you click cells to enter a formula in a table, Excel builds a formula like this: =[@Amount]–[@Down_Pay], where the @ indicates the current row. If you use the semi-selection process to create a formula outside the table, the formula includes the table and field names, such as =Table1[@Amount]–Table1[@Down_Pay]. Table1 is the name of the table; Amount and Down_Pay are field names. This structured formula that includes references, such as table name, is called a *fully qualified structured reference*. When you build formulas *within* a table, you can use either unqualified or fully qualified structured references. If you need to use table data in a formula *outside* the table boundaries, you must use fully qualified structured references.

Sorting Data

Sometimes if you rearrange the order of records, new perspective is gained making the information easier to understand. In Figure 2, the March 2018 data are arranged by transaction number. You might want to arrange the transactions so that all of the transactions for a particular sales representative are together. **Sorting** is the process of arranging records by the value of one or more fields within a table. Sorting is not limited to data within tables; normal data ranges can be sorted as well.

Sort One Field

You can sort data in a table or a regular range in a worksheet. For example, you could sort by transaction date or department.

To sort by only one field, complete one of the following steps:

- Click in a cell within the field you want to sort and click Sort & Filter in the Editing group on the Home tab, and select a desired sort option.
- Click in a cell within the field you want to sort and click Sort A to Z, Sort Z to A, or Sort in the Sort & Filter group on the Data tab.
- Right-click the field to sort, point to Sort on the shortcut menu, and then select the type of sort you want.
- Click the filter arrow in the header row and select the desired sort option.

Table 3 lists sort options by data type.

TABLE 3	Sort Options	
Data Type	**Options**	**Explanation**
Text	Sort A to Z	Arranges data in alphabetical order.
	Sort Z to A	Arranges data in reverse alphabetical order.
Dates	Sort Oldest to Newest	Displays data in chronological order; from oldest to newest.
	Sort Newest to Oldest	Displays data in reverse chronological order; from newest to oldest.
Values	Sort Smallest to Largest	Arranges values from the smallest value to the largest.
	Sort Largest to Smallest	Arranges values from the largest value to the smallest.
Color	Sort by Cell Color	Arranges data together for cells containing a particular fill color.
	Sort by Font Color	Arranges data together for cells containing a particular font color.

Sort Multiple Fields

STEP 3 ▶▶ After sorting, if a second sort is applied the original sort will be removed. However, at times, sorting by only one field does not yield the desired outcome. Using multiple level sorts enables like records in the primary sort to be further organized by additional sort levels. For example, you could sort by date of transaction and then by last name. Excel enables you to sort data on 64 different levels.

To perform a multiple level sort, complete the following steps:

1. Click in any cell in the table.
2. Click Sort in the Sort & Filter group on the Data tab to display the Sort dialog box.
3. Select the primary sort level by clicking the Sort by arrow, selecting the field to sort by, and then clicking the Order arrow and selecting the sort order from the list.
4. Click Add Level, select the second sort level by clicking the Then by arrow, select the column to sort by, click the Order arrow, and then select the sort order from the list.
5. Continue to click Add Level and add sort levels until you have entered all sort levels (see Figure 24). Click OK.

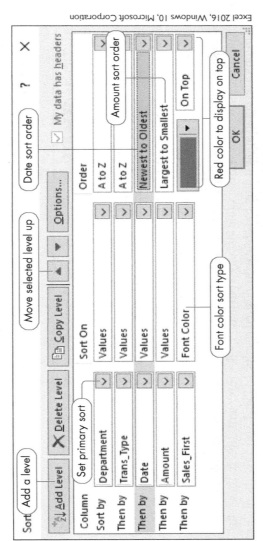

Excel 2016, Windows 10, Microsoft Corporation

FIGURE 24 Sort Dialog Box

Create a Custom Sort

STEP 4 ▶▶ Excel arranges data in alphabetical or numerical order. For example, days of the week are sorted alphabetically: Friday, Monday, Saturday, Sunday, Thursday, Tuesday, and Wednesday. However, you might want to create a custom sort sequence. For example, you can create a custom sort to arrange days of the week in order from Sunday to Saturday.

To create a custom sort sequence, complete the following steps:

1. Click Sort in the Sort & Filter group on the Data tab.
2. Click the Order arrow and select Custom List to display the Custom Lists dialog box (see Figure 25).
3. Select an existing sort sequence in the Custom lists box, or select NEW LIST.
4. Type the entries in the desired sort sequence in the List entries box, pressing Enter between entries.
5. Click Add and click OK.

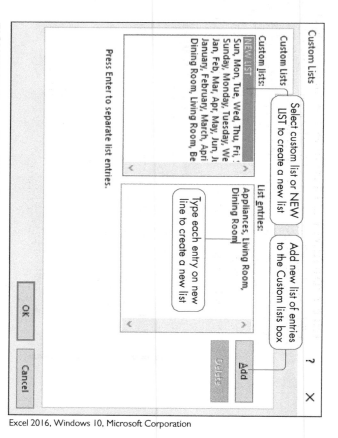

FIGURE 25 Custom Lists Dialog Box

TIP: NAME SORTS

Always check the data to determine how many levels of sorting you need to apply. If your table contains several people with the same last name but different first names, you would first sort by the Last Name field, then sort by First Name field. All the people with the last name Desmarais would be grouped together and further sorted by first name, such as Amanda and then Bradley.

Filtering Data

In some situations you might want to display only a subset of the data available, for example, the data to show transactions for only a particular sales representative. In these situations, you could apply a filter to achieve the desired results. In Excel, you have the ability to filter using various criteria such as date, value, text, and color. *Filtering* is the process of specifying conditions to display only those records that meet certain conditions.

TIP: COPYING BEFORE FILTERING DATA

Often, you need to show different filters applied to the same dataset. You can copy the worksheet and filter the data on the copied worksheet to preserve the original dataset.

Apply Text Filters

When you apply a filter to a text field, the filter menu displays each unique text item. You can select one or more text items from the list to be filtered. Once completed only the selected text will be displayed.

To apply a text filter, complete the following steps:

1. Click any cell in the range of data to be filtered.
2. Click the Data tab and click Filter in the Sort & Filter group to display the filter arrows.
3. Click the filter arrow for the column you will filter.
4. Deselect the (Select All) check mark and click the check boxes for the text you would like to remain visible in the dataset. Click OK.

You can also select Text Filters to see a submenu of additional options, such as Begins With, to select all records for which the name begins with the letter G, for example.

Figure 26 shows the Sales_Last filter menu with two names selected. Excel displays records for these two reps only. The records for the other sales reps are hidden but not deleted. The filter arrow displays a filter icon, indicating which field is filtered. Excel displays the row numbers in blue, indicating that you applied a filter. The missing row numbers indicate hidden rows of data. When you remove the filter, all the records display again.

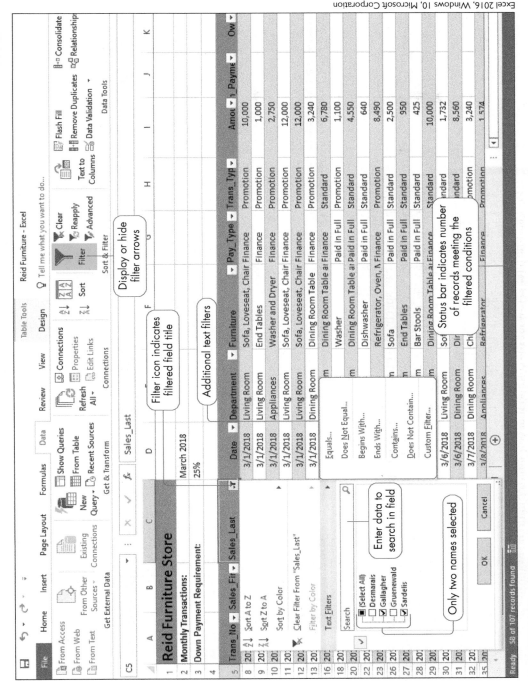

Excel 2016, Windows 10, Microsoft Corporation

FIGURE 26 Filtered Text

Apply Number Filters

STEP 6 >> Excel contains a variety of number filters that enable you to display specific numbers, or a range of numbers such as above average or top 10 values. When you filter a field of numbers, you can select specific numbers. Or, you might want to filter numbers by a range, such as numbers greater than $5,000, or numbers between $4,000 and $5,000. If the field contains a large number of unique entries, you can click in the Search box and enter a value to display all matching records. For example, if you enter $7, the list will display only values that start with $7. The filter submenu enables you to set a variety of number filters. In Figure 27, the amounts are filtered to show only those that are above the average amount. In this situation, Excel calculates the average amount as $4,512. Only records above that amount display.

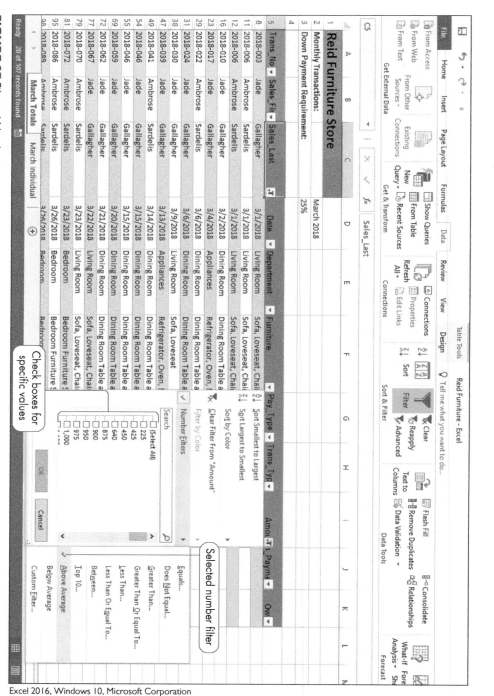

FIGURE 27 Filtered Numbers

Excel 2016, Windows 10, Microsoft Corporation

The Top 10 option enables you to specify the top records. Although the option name is Top 10, you can specify the number or percentage of records to display. For example, you can filter the list to display only the top five or the bottom 7%. Figure 28 shows the Top 10 AutoFilter dialog box.

To filter using the custom Top 10 AutoFilter, complete the following steps:

1. Click anywhere in the range or table, click the Data tab, and click Filter in the Sort & Filter group.
2. Click the filter arrow for the column that contains the data you would like to manipulate, point to Number Filters, and select Top 10.
3. Choose Top or Bottom value, click the last arrow to select either Items or Percent, and click OK.

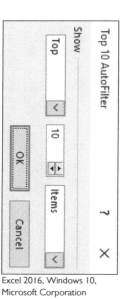

FIGURE 28 Top 10 AutoFilter Dialog Box

Excel 2016, Windows 10, Microsoft Corporation

Datasets and Tables

Apply Date Filters

STEP 7 When you filter a field of dates, you can select specific dates or a date range, such as dates after 3/15/2018 or dates between 3/1/2018 and 3/7/2018. The submenu enables you to set a variety of date filters. For more specific date options, point to Date Filters, point to *All Dates in the Period*, and then select a period, such as Quarter 2 or October. Figure 29 shows the Date Filters menu.

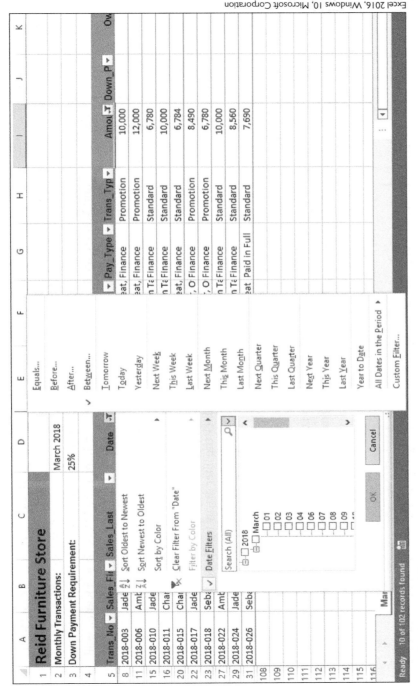

FIGURE 29 Filtered Dates

Apply a Custom Filter

Suppose as the manager of a furniture store, you are only interested in marketing directly to people who spent between $500 and $1,000 in the last month. To quickly identify the required data, you could use a custom AutoFilter. If you select options such as Greater Than or Between, Excel displays the Custom AutoFilter dialog box (see Figure 30). You can also select Custom Filter from the menu to display this dialog box, which is designed for more complex filtering requirements.

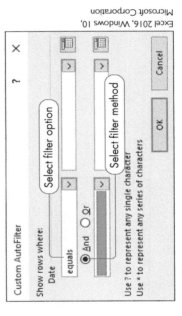

FIGURE 30 Custom AutoFilter Dialog Box

The dialog box indicates the column being filtered. To set the filters, click the arrows to select the comparison type, such as equals or contains. Click the arrow on the right to select a specific text, value, or date entry, or type the data yourself. For ranges of dates or values, click And, and then specify the comparison operator and value or date for the next condition row. For text, click Or. For example, if you want both Gallagher and Desmarais, you must select Or because each data entry contains either Gallagher or Desmarais but not both at the same time.

When filtering, you can use wildcards to help locate information in which there are multiple criteria and no custom filters. For example, to select all states starting with New, type New * in the second box; this will obtain results such as New York or New Mexico. The asterisk (*) is used in exchange for the text after "New" and can represent any number of characters. Therefore this wildcard filter would return states New York, New Mexico, and New Hampshire because they all begin with the word "New." If you want a wildcard for only a single character, type the question mark (?). For example when filtering departments, "R?om" would return any department with room in the name as would "Room*."

Clear Filters

You can remove the filters from one or more fields to expand the dataset again. To remove only one filter and keep the other filters, click the filter arrow for the field from which you wish to clear the filter and select Clear Filter From.

To remove all filters and display all records in a dataset, complete one of the following steps:

- Click Clear in the Sort & Filter group on the Data tab.
- Click Sort & Filter in the Editing group on the Home tab and select Clear.

Quick Concepts

7. What is the purpose of sorting data in a table?

8. What are two ways to arrange (sort) dates?

9. List at least five ways you can filter numbers.

10. Assume you are filtering a list and want to display records for people who live in Boston or New York. What settings do you enter in the Custom AutoFilter dialog box for that field?

Hands-On Exercises

MyITLab®
HOE3 Training

Watch the Video
for this Hands-On
Exercise!

Skills covered: Create a
Structured Reference in a Formula •
Sort One Field • Sort Multiple Fields
• Create a Custom Sort • Apply
Text Filters • Apply a Number Filter
• Apply a Date Filter

3 Table Manipulation

You want to start analyzing the March 2018 transactions for Reid Furniture Store by calculating the totals
owed, then sorting and filtering data in a variety of ways to help you understand the transactions better.

STEP 1 » CREATE A STRUCTURED REFERENCE IN A FORMULA

First, you want to calculate the down payment owed by each customer. You will then calculate the total amount owed by
subtracting the down payment from the total down payment. You will use structured references to complete these tasks. Refer to
Figure 31 as you complete Step 1.

	A	B	C	D		
PMT			✕ ✓ fx	=[Amount]-[Down_Pay]		

Step c: Structured reference

Step d: Comma Style Number
Format applied

Steps b–c: Formula copied down

	A	B	C	D
1	**Reid Furniture Store**			
2	Monthly Transactions:			March 2018
3	Down Payment Requirement:			25%
4				

	A	B	C	E	F	G	H	I	J	K
5	Trans_No ▼	Sales_Fir ▼	Sales_Las ▼	Date ▼	Departme ▼	Furniture ▼	Pay_Type ▼	Trans_Typ ▼	Amou ▼	Down_P ▼	Ow ▼
6	2018-001	Sebastian	Gruenewald	3/1/2018	Bedroom	Mattress		Finance	Promotion	2,788	697.00	=[Amount]-[Do
7	2018-002	Sebastian	Gruenewald	3/1/2018	Bedroom	Mattress		Finance	Promotion	3,245	811.25	2,433.75
8	2018-003	Jade	Gallagher	3/1/2018	Living Room	Sofa, Loveseat, Chair Package		Finance	Promotion	10,000	2,500.00	7,500.00
9	2018-004	Jade	Gallagher	3/1/2018	Living Room	End Tables		Finance	Promotion	1,000	250.00	750.00
10	2018-005	Jade	Gallagher	3/1/2018	Appliances	Washer and Dryer		Finance	Promotion	2,750	687.50	2,062.50
11	2018-006	Ambrose	Sardelis	3/1/2018	Living Room	Sofa, Loveseat, Chair Package		Finance	Promotion	12,000	3,000.00	9,000.00
12	2018-007	Jade	Gallagher	3/1/2018	Dining Room	Dining Room Table		Finance	Promotion	3,240	810.00	2,430.00
13	2018-008	Chantalle	Desmarais	3/1/2018	Dining Room	Dining Room Table		Finance	Promotion	4,080	1,020.00	3,060.00
14	2018-009	Sebastian	Gruenewald	3/1/2018	Appliances	Washer and Dryer		Finance	Promotion	2,750	687.50	2,062.50
15	2018-010	Jade	Gallagher	3/2/2018	Dining Room	Dining Room Table and Chairs		Finance	Standard	6,780	1,695.00	5,085.00
16	2018-011	Chantalle	Desmarais	3/2/2018	Dining Room	Dining Room Table and Chairs		Finance	Standard	10,000	2,500.00	7,500.00
17	2018-012	Ambrose	Sardelis	3/2/2018	Appliances	Washer		Paid in Full	Promotion	1,100	275.00	825.00
18	2018-013	Chantalle	Desmarais	3/3/2018	Living Room	Recliners		Finance	Standard	2,430	607.50	1,822.50

Excel 2016, Windows 10, Microsoft Corporation

FIGURE 31 Create a Structured Reference

a. Open *eO4h2Reid_LastFirst* if you closed it at the end of Hands-On Exercise 2. Save it as
e04h3Reid_LastFirst, changing h2 to h3.

b. Click **cell J6**. Type the formula **=[Amount]*$D$3** and press **Enter**.

The down payment required is 25% of the total purchase price. Structured reference
format is used for Amount to create the formula that calculates the customer's down
payment. Excel copies the formula down the column.

c. Click **cell K6**. Type the formula **=[Amount]-[Down_Pay]** and press **Enter**.

The formula calculates the total value owed to the sales rep and copies the formula down
the column.

d. Select the **range J6:K109** and apply the **Comma Style Number Format**.

e. Save the workbook.

STEP 2 》》 SORT ONE FIELD

You want to compare the number of transactions by sales rep, so you will sort the data by the Sales_Last field. After reviewing the transactions by sales reps, you then want to arrange the transactions to show the one with the largest purchase first and the smallest purchase last. Refer to Figure 32 as you complete Step 2.

	Trans_No ▼	Sales_Fir ▼	Sales_Las ▼	Date ▼	Department ▼	Furniture ▼	Pay_Type ▼	Trans_Typ ▼	Amoun ↓↑	Paymé ▼	Ow ▼
5											
6	2018-073	Chantalle	Desmarais	3/24/2018	Living Room	Sofa, Loveseat, Chair Package	Finance	Standard	17,500	4,375.00	13,125.00
7	2018-097	Sebastian	Gruenewald	3/29/2018	Bedroom	Bedroom Furniture Set	Finance	Standard	14,321	3,580.25	10,740.75
8	2018-095	Sebastian	Gruenewald	3/29/2018	Living Room	Sofa, Loveseat, Chair Package	Finance	Standard	14,275	3,568.75	10,706.25
9	2018-056	Chantalle	Desmarais	3/19/2018	Living Room	Sofa, Loveseat, Chair Package	Finance	Standard	12,500	3,125.00	9,375.00
10	2018-070	Ambrose	Sardelis	3/23/2018	Living Room	Sofa, Loveseat, Chair Package	Finance	Promotion	12,500	3,125.00	9,375.00
11	2018-041	Ambrose	Sardelis	3/14/2018	Dining Room	Dining Room Table and Chairs	Finance	Promotion	12,458	3,114.50	9,343.50
12	2018-072	Ambros				edroom	Bedroom Furniture Set	Finance	Promo	12,50	
13	2018-006	Ambros			ving Room	Sofa, Loveseat, Chair Package	Finance	Promo	00.00	
14	2018-089	Ambrose	Sardelis	3/26/2018	Bedroom	Bedroom Furniture Set	Finance	Standard	11,972	2,993.00	8,979.00
15	2018-100	Chantalle	Desmarais	3/30/2018	Bedroom	Bedroom Furniture Set	Finance	Promotion	11,234	2,808.50	8,425.50
16	2018-011	Chantalle	Desmarais	3/2/2018	Dining Room	Dining Room Table and Chairs	Finance	Standard	10,000	2,500.00	7,500.00
17	2018-003	Jade	Gallagher	3/1/2018	Living Room	Sofa, Loveseat, Chair Package	Finance	Promotion	10,000	2,500.00	7,500.00
18	2018-064	Sebastian	Gruenewald	3/21/2018	Appliances	Refrigerator, Oven, Microwave Combo	Finance	Promotion	10,000	2,500.00	7,500.00
19	2018-022	Ambrose	Sardelis	3/6/2018	Dining Room	Dining Room Table and Chairs	Finance	Standard	10,000	2,500.00	7,500.00

Step a: Click filter arrow and sort A to Z.

Step b: Click filter arrow and sort Largest to Smallest.

FIGURE 32 Sorted Data

Excel 2016, Windows 10, Microsoft Corporation

a. Click the **Sales_Last filter arrow** and select **Sort A to Z**.

Excel arranges the transactions in alphabetical order by last name, starting with Desmarais. Within each sales rep, records display in their original sequence by transaction number. If you scan the records, you can see that Gallagher completed the most sales transactions in March. The up arrow icon on the Sales_Last filter arrow indicates that records are sorted in alphabetical order by that field.

b. Click the **Amount filter arrow** and select **Sort Largest to Smallest**.

The records are no longer sorted by Sales_Last. When you sort by another field, the previous sort is not saved. In this case, Excel arranges the transactions from the one with the largest amount to the smallest amount, indicated by the down arrow icon in the Amount filter arrow.

c. Save the workbook.

STEP 3 » SORT MULTIPLE FIELDS

You want to review the transactions by payment type (financed or paid in full). Within each payment type, you further want to compare the transaction type (promotion or standard). Finally, you want to compare costs within the sorted records by displaying the highest costs first. You will use the Sort dialog box to perform a three-level sort. Refer to Figure 33 as you complete Step 3.

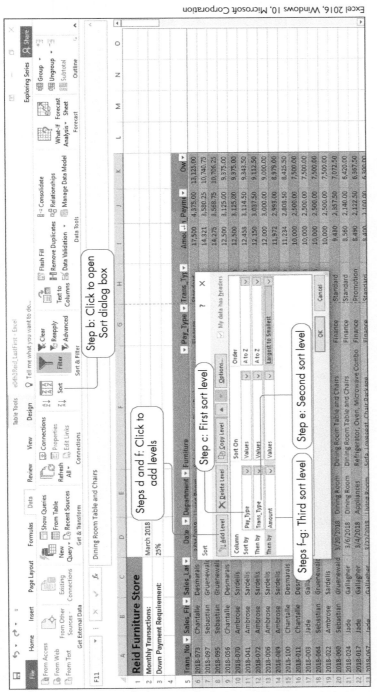

FIGURE 33 Three-Level Sort

a. Click inside the table and click the **Data tab**.

Both the Data and Home tabs contain commands to open the Sort dialog box.

b. Click **Sort** in the Sort & Filter group to open the Sort dialog box.

c. Click the **Sort by arrow** and select **Pay_Type**. Click the **Order arrow** and select **A to Z**.

You start by specifying the column for the primary sort. In this case, you want to sort the records first by the Payment Type column.

d. Click **Add Level**.

The Sort dialog box adds the Then by row, which adds a secondary sort.

e. Click the **Then by arrow** and select **Trans_Type**.

The default order is A to Z, which will sort in alphabetical order by Trans_Type. Excel will first sort the records by the Pay_Type (Finance or Paid in Full). Within each Pay_Type, Excel will further sort records by Trans_Type (Promotion or Standard).

f. Click **Add Level** to add another Then by row. Click the second **Then by arrow** and select **Amount**.

g. Click the **Order arrow** for the Amount sort and select **Largest to Smallest**.

Within the Pay_Type and Trans_Type sorts, this will arrange the records with the largest amount first in descending order to the smallest amount.

h. Click **OK** and scroll through the records. Save the workbook.

Most customers finance their purchases instead of paying in full. For the financed transactions, more than half were promotional sales. For merchandise paid in full, a majority of the transactions were standard sales, indicating that people with money do not necessarily wait for a promotional sale to purchase merchandise.

Hands-On Exercise 3   371

For the month of March you want to closely monitor sales of the Dining Room and Living Room departments. After completing the prior sort, you will add an additional level to create a custom sort of the department's data. Refer to Figure 34 as you complete Step 4.

STEP 4 ⟫ CREATE A CUSTOM SORT

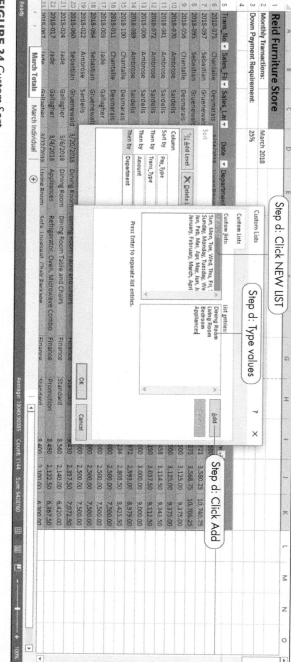

FIGURE 34 Custom Sort

a. Click inside the table and click **Sort** in the Sort & Filter group to open the Sort dialog box.

The Sort dialog box will open with the prior sort criteria displayed.

b. Click the **last level added** in the prior step and click **Add Level**.

c. Select **Department**. Click the **Order arrow** and select **Custom List**.

This will open the Custom Lists dialog box, enabling you to manually specify the sort order.

d. Click **NEW LIST** in the Custom Lists box, click the **List entries box** and type **Dining Room, Living Room, Bedroom, Appliances.** Click **Add**, click **OK**, and click **OK** again to complete to return to the worksheet.

After completing the custom list, the data in column E will be sorted by Dining Room, Living Room, Bedroom, and Appliances as the last step within the custom sort.

e. Save the workbook.

372

Hands-On Exercise 3

STEP 5 ›› APPLY TEXT FILTERS

Now that you know Jade Gallagher had the most transactions for March, you will filter the table to focus on her sales. You notice that she sells more merchandise from the Dining Room department, so you will filter out the other departments. Refer to Figure 35 as you complete Step 5.

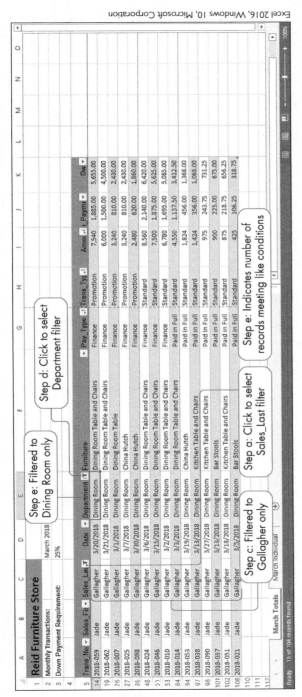

FIGURE 35 Apply Text Filters

a. Click the **Sales_Last filter arrow**.

The (Select All) check box is selected.

b. Click the **(Select All) check box** to deselect all last names.

c. Click the **Gallagher check box** to select it and click **OK**.

The status bar indicates that 33 out of 104 records meet the filtering condition. The Sales_Last filter arrow includes a funnel icon, indicating that this column is filtered.

d. Click the **Department filter arrow**.

e. Click the **(Select All) check box** to deselect all departments, click the **Dining Room check box** to focus on that department, and then click **OK**. Save the workbook.

The remaining 15 records show Gallagher's dining room sales for the month. The Department filter arrow includes a funnel icon, indicating that this column is also filtered.

STEP 6 ›› APPLY A NUMBER FILTER

Vicki is considering giving a bonus to employees who sold high-end dining room furniture during a specific time period (3/16/2018 to 3/31/2018). You want to determine if Jade Gallagher qualifies for this bonus. In particular, you are interested in how much gross revenue she generated for dining room furniture that cost at least $5,000 or more. Refer to Figure 36 as you complete Step 6.

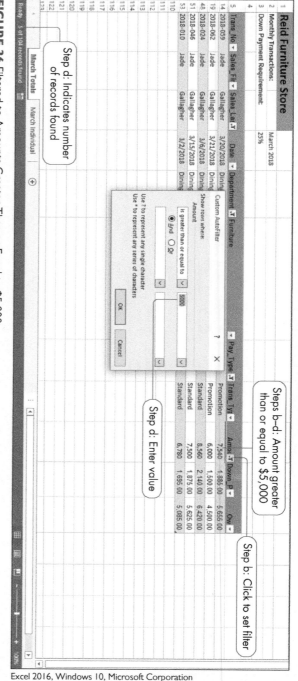

FIGURE 36 Filtered to Amounts Greater Than or Equal to $5,000

a. Select the **range I14:I108** of the filtered list and then view the status bar.

The average transaction amount is $3,754 with 15 transactions (i.e., 15 filtered records).

b. Click the **Amount filter arrow.**

c. Point to **Number Filters** and select **Greater Than Or Equal To.**

The Custom AutoFilter dialog box opens.

d. Type **5000** in the box to the right of *is greater than or equal to* and click **OK.** Save the workbook.

When typing numbers, you can type raw numbers such as 5000 or formatted numbers such as $5,000. Out of Gallagher's original 15 dining room transactions, only 5 transactions (one-third of her sales) were valued at $5,000 or more.

STEP 7 ≫ APPLY A DATE FILTER

Finally, you want to study Jade Gallagher's sales records for the last half of the month. You will add a date filter to identify those sales records. Refer to Figure 37 as you complete Step 7.

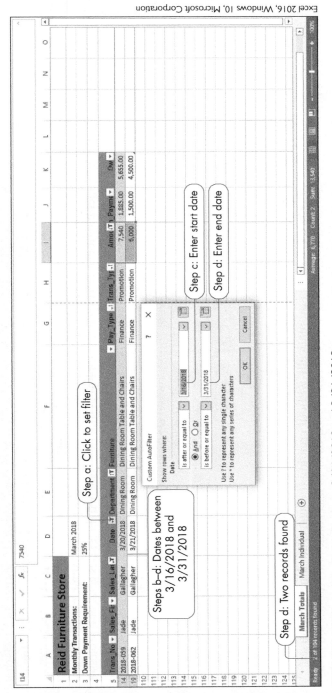

FIGURE 37 Filtered by Dates Between 3/16/2018 and 3/31/2018

a. Click the **Date filter arrow**.

b. Point to **Date Filters** and select **Between**.

The Custom AutoFilter dialog box opens. The default comparisons are *is after or equal to* and *is before or equal to*, ready for you to enter the date specifications.

c. Type **3/16/2018** in the box on the right side of *is after or equal to*.

You specified the starting date of the range of dates to include. You will keep the *And* option selected.

d. Type **3/31/2018** in the box on the right side of *is before or equal to*. Click **OK**.

Gallagher had only two dining room sales greater than $5,000 during the last half of March.

e. Save the workbook. Keep the workbook open if you plan to continue with the next Hands-On Exercise. If not, close the workbook, and exit Excel.

Table Aggregation and Conditional Formatting

In addition to sorting and filtering tables to analyze data, you might want to add fields that provide data aggregation such as Average or Sum of amount purchased. Furthermore, you might want to apply special formatting to cells that contain particular values or text using conditional formatting. *Conditional formatting* applies special formatting to highlight or emphasize cells that meet specific conditions. For example, a sales manager might want to highlight employees that have reached their sales goal, or a professor might want to highlight test scores that fall below the average. You can also apply conditional formatting to point out data for a specific date or duplicate values in a range.

In this section, you will learn how to add a total row to a table along with learning about the five conditional formatting categories and how to apply conditional formatting to a range of values based on a condition you set.

Adding a Total Row

At times, aggregating data provides insightful information. For regular ranges of data, you use basic statistical functions, such as SUM, AVERAGE, MIN, and MAX, to provide summary analysis for a dataset. An Excel table provides the advantage of being able to display a total row automatically without creating the aggregate function yourself. A *total row* displays below the last row of records in an Excel table and enables you to display summary statistics, such as a sum of values displayed in a column.

To display and use the total row, complete the following steps:

1. Click any cell in the table.
2. Click the Design tab.
3. Click Total Row in the Table Style Options group. Excel displays the total row below the last record in the table. Excel displays Total in the first column of the total row.
4. Click a cell in the total row, click that cell's total row arrow, and then select the function result that you desire. Excel calculates the summary statistics for values, but if the field is text, the only summary statistic that can be calculated is Count.
5. Add a summary statistic to another column click in the empty cell for that field in the total row and click the arrow to select the desired function. Select None to remove the function.

Figure 38 shows the active total row with totals applied to the Amount, Down_Pay, and Owed fields. A list of functions displays to change the function for the last field.

FIGURE 38 Total Row

The calculations on the total row use the SUBTOTAL function. The **SUBTOTAL function** calculates an aggregate value, such as totals or averages, for displayed values in a range, table, or database. If you click in a calculated total row cell, the SUBTOTAL function displays in the Formula Bar. The function for the total row looks like this: =SUBTOTAL(function_num,ref1). The function_num argument is a number that represents a function (see Table 4). The ref1 argument indicates the range of values to calculate. The SUBTOTAL function used to total the values in the Owed field would be =SUBTOTAL(109,[Owed]), where the number 109 represents the SUM function, and [Owed] represents the Owed field. A benefit of the SUBTOTAL function is that it subtotals data for filtered records, so you have an accurate total for the visible records.

=SUBTOTAL(function_num,ref1,....)

TABLE 4 Subtotal Function Numbers

Function	Function Number	Table Number
AVERAGE	1	101
COUNT	2	102
COUNTA	3	103
MAX	4	104
MIN	5	105
PRODUCT	6	106
STDEV.S	7	107
STDEV.P	8	108
SUM	9	109
VAR.S	10	110
VAR.P	11	111

TIP: FILTERING DATA AND SUBTOTALS

If you filter the data and display the total row, the SUBTOTAL function's 109 argument ensures that only the displayed data are summed; data for hidden rows are not calculated in the aggregate function.

Table Aggregation and Conditional Formatting • Excel 2016

Applying Conditional Formatting

Conditional formatting helps you and your audience understand a dataset better because it adds a visual element to the cells. The term is called conditional because the formatting only displays when a condition is met. This is similar logic to the IF function you have used. Remember with an IF function, you create a logical test that is evaluated. If the logical or conditional test is true, the function produces one result. If the logical or conditional test is false, the function produces another result. With conditional formatting, if the condition is true, Excel formats the cell automatically based on that condition. If the condition is false, Excel does not format the cell. If you change a value in a conditionally formatted cell, Excel examines the new value to see if it should apply the conditional format.

Apply Conditional Formatting with the Quick Analysis Tool

When you select a range and click the Quick Analysis button, the Formatting options display in the Quick Analysis gallery. Point to a thumbnail to see how it will affect the selected range (see Figure 39). You can also apply conditional formatting by clicking Conditional Formatting in the Styles group on the Home tab.

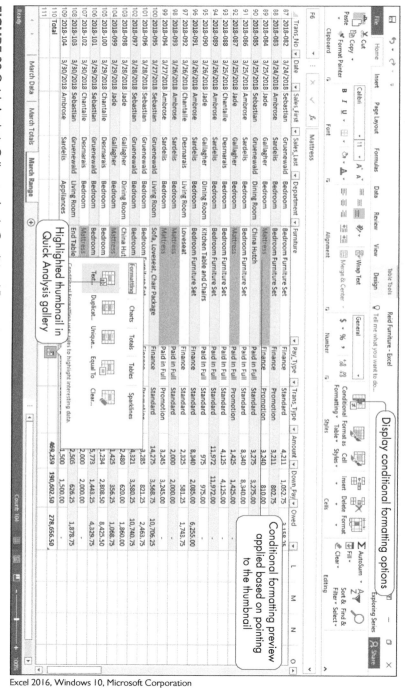

FIGURE 39 Quick Analysis Gallery to Apply Conditional Formatting

Excel 2016, Windows 10, Microsoft Corporation

Datasets and Tables

Table 5 describes the conditional formatting options in the Quick Analysis gallery.

TABLE 5 Conditional Formatting Options in Quick Analysis Gallery

Options	Description
Text Contains	Formats cells that contain the text in the first selected cell. In Figure 39, the first selected cell contains Mattress. If a cell contains Mattress and Springs, Excel would format that cell also because it contains Mattress.
Duplicate Values	Formats cells that are duplicated in the selected range.
Unique Values	Formats cells that are unique; that is, no other cell in the selected range contains the same data.
Equal To	Formats cells that are exactly like the data contained in the first selected cell.
Clear Format	Removes the conditional formatting from the selected range.

Table 6 lists and describes a number of different conditional formats that you can apply if you want more specific rules.

TABLE 6 Conditional Formatting Options

Options	Description
Highlight Cells Rules	Highlights cells with a fill color, font color, or border (such as Light Red Fill with Dark Red Text) if values are greater than, less than, between two values, equal to a value, or duplicate values; text that contains particular characters; or dates when a date meets a particular condition, such as *In the last 7 days*.
Top/Bottom Rules	Formats cells with values in the top 10 items, top 10%, bottom 10 items, bottom 10%, above average, or below average. You can change the exact values to format the top or bottom items or percentages, such as top 5 or bottom 15%.
Data Bars	Applies a gradient or solid fill bar in which the width of the bar represents the current cell's value compared relatively to other cells' values.
Color Scales	Formats different cells with different colors, assigning one color to the lowest group of values and another color to the highest group of values, with gradient colors to other values.
Icon Sets	Inserts an icon from an icon palette in each cell to indicate values compared to each other.

To apply a conditional format, complete the following steps:

1. Select the cells for which you want to apply a conditional format, click the Home tab, and click Conditional Formatting in the Styles group.
2. Select the conditional formatting category you want to apply.

Apply Highlight Cells Rules

STEP 2 ⟫ The Highlight Cells Rules category enables you to apply a highlight to cells that meet a condition, such as cells containing values greater than a particular value. This option contains predefined combinations of fill colors, font colors, and/or borders. For example, suppose you are a sales manager who developed a worksheet containing the sales for each day of a month. You are interested in sales between $5000 and $10,000. You might want to apply a conditional format to cells that contain values within the desired range. To apply this conditional formatting, you would select Highlight Cells Rules and then select Between. In the Between dialog box (see Figure 40), type 5000 in the first value box and 10000 in the second value box, select the type of conditional formatting, such as Light Red Fill with Dark Red Text, and then click OK to apply the formats.

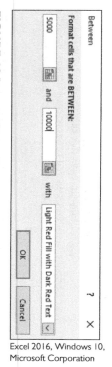

Between	?	×
Format cells that are BETWEEN:		
5000	and	10000	with	Light Red Fill with Dark Red Text
	OK	Cancel

FIGURE 40 Between Dialog Box

Excel 2016, Windows 10, Microsoft Corporation

Figure 41 shows two columns of data that contain conditional formats. The Department column is conditionally formatted to highlight text with a Light Red Fill with Dark Red Text for cells that contain Living Room, and the Amount column is conditionally formatted to highlight values between $5,000 and $10,000 with a Dark Red Border.

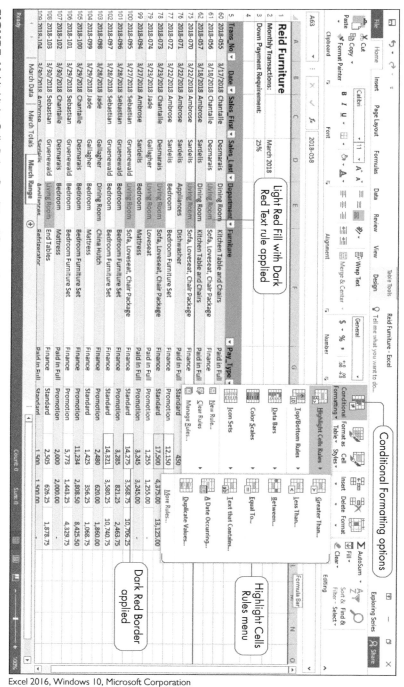

FIGURE 41 Highlight Cells Rules Conditional Formatting

Excel 2016, Windows 10, Microsoft Corporation

 STEP 3

Specify Top/Bottom Rules

You might be interested in identifying the top five sales to reward the sales associates, or want to identify the bottom 15% of of sales for more focused marketing. The Top/Bottom Rules category enables you to specify the top or bottom number, top or bottom percentage, or values that are above or below the average value in a specified range. In Figure 42, the Amount column is conditionally formatted to highlight the top five amounts. (Some rows are hidden so that all top five values display in the figure.) Although the menu option is Top 10 Items, you can specify the exact number of items to format.

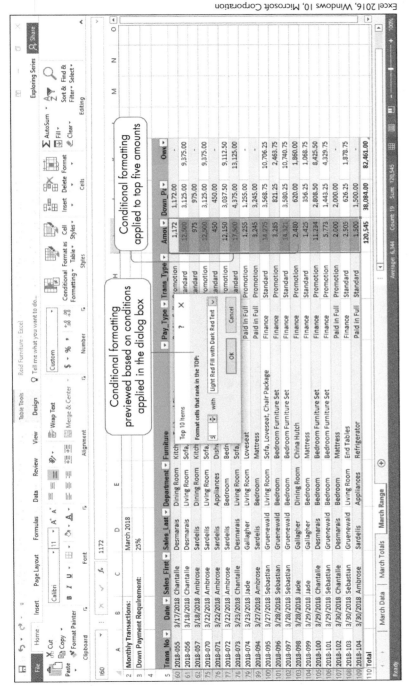

FIGURE 42 Top 10 Items Dialog Box

Display Data Bars, Color Scales, and Icon Sets

STEP 4 ≫ **Data bars** apply a gradient or solid fill bar in which the width of the bar represents the current cell's value compared relatively to other cells' values (see Figure 43). The width of the data bar represents the value in a cell, with a wider bar representing a higher value and a narrower bar a lower value. Excel locates the largest value and displays the widest data bar in that cell. Excel then finds the smallest value and displays the smallest data bar in that cell. Excel sizes the data bars for the remaining cells based on their values relative to the high and low values in the column. If you change the values, Excel updates the data bar widths. Excel uses the same color for each data bar, but each bar differs in size based on the value in the respective cells.

Table Aggregation and Conditional Formatting • Excel 2016

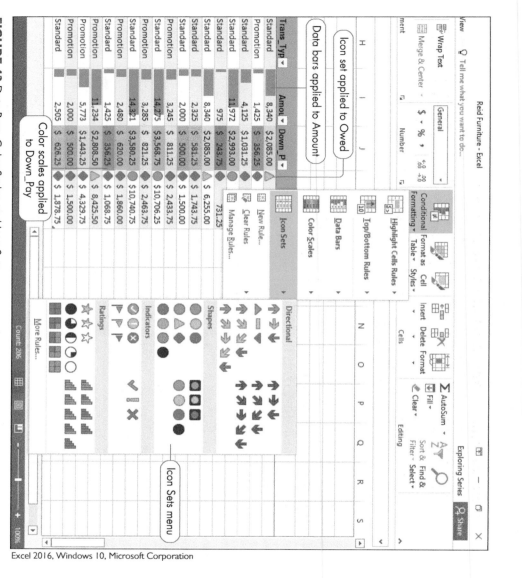

FIGURE 43 Data Bars, Color Scales, and Icon Sets

Excel 2016, Windows 10, Microsoft Corporation

Color scales format cells with different colors based on the relative value of a cell compared to other selected cells. You can apply a two- or three-color scale. This scale assists in comparing a range of cells using gradations of those colors. The shade of the color represents higher or lower values. In Figure 43, for example, the red color scales display for the lowest values, the green color displays for the highest values, and gradients of yellow and orange represent the middle range of values in the Down_Pay column. Use color scales to understand variation in the data to identify trends, for example, to view good stock returns and weak stock returns.

Icon sets are symbols or signs that classify data into three, four, or five categories, based on the values in a range. Excel determines categories of value ranges and assigns an icon to each range. In Figure 43, a three-icon set was applied to the Owed column. Excel divided the range of values between the lowest value of $0 and the highest value of $13,125 into thirds. The red diamond icon displays for the cells containing values in the lowest third ($0 to $4,375), the yellow triangle icon displays for cells containing the values in the middle third ($4,376 to $8,750), and the green circle icon displays for cells containing values in the top third ($8,751 to $13,125). Most purchases fall into the lowest third.

TIP: DON'T OVERDO IT!

Although conditional formatting helps identify trends, you should use this feature wisely and sparingly. Apply conditional formatting only when you want to emphasize important data. When you decide to apply conditional formatting, think about which category is best to highlight the data.

Creating a New Rule

The default conditional formatting categories provide a variety of options. Excel also enables you to create your own rules to specify different fill colors, borders, or other formatting if you do not want the default settings. Excel provides three ways to create a new rule.

To create a new Conditional Formatting rule, complete one of the following steps:

- Click Conditional Formatting in the Styles group and select New Rule.
- Click Conditional Formatting in the Styles group, select Manage Rules to open the Conditional Formatting Rules Manager dialog box, and then click New Rule.
- Click Conditional Formatting in the Styles group, select a rule category such as Highlight Cells Rules, and then select More Rules.

When creating a new rule, the New Formatting Rule dialog box opens (see Figure 44) so that you can define the conditional formatting rule. First, select a rule type, such as *Format all cells based on their values*. The *Edit the Rule Description* section changes, based on the rule type you select. With the default rule type selected, you can specify the format style (2-Color Scale, 3-Color Scale, Data Bar, or Icon Sets). You can then specify the minimum and maximum values, the fill colors for color sets or data bars, or the icons for icon sets. After you edit the rule description, click OK to save your new conditional format.

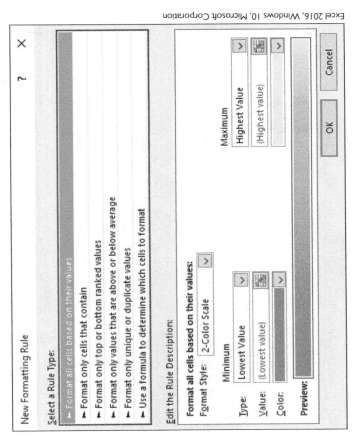

FIGURE 44 New Formatting Rule Dialog Box

Table Aggregation and Conditional Formatting • Excel 2016

If you select any rule type except the *Format all cells based on their values* rule, the dialog box contains a Format button. When you click Format, the Format Cells dialog box opens so that you can specify number, font, border, and fill formats to apply to your rule.

TIP: FORMAT ONLY CELLS THAT CONTAIN

When creating new Conditional Formatting rules, you have the option to format only cells that contain a specific value. This option provides a wide array of things you can format: values, text, dates, blanks, no blanks, errors, or no errors. Formatting blanks is helpful to see where you are missing data, and formatting cells containing errors helps you find those errors quickly. These options can be accessed from the Select a Rule Type box in the New Formatting Rule dialog box when creating a Conditional Formatting rule.

Use Formulas in Conditional Formatting

STEP 5 >> Suppose you want to format merchandise amounts of financed items *and* amounts that are $10,000 or more. You can use a formula to create a conditional formatting rule to complete the task. Figure 45 shows the Edit Formatting Rule dialog box and the corresponding conditional formatting applied to cells.

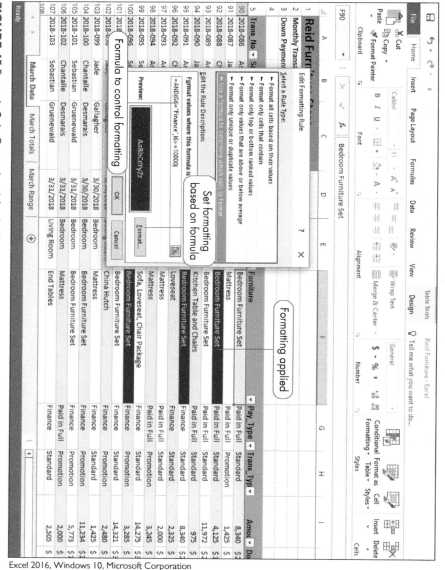

Excel 2016, Windows 10, Microsoft Corporation

FIGURE 45 Formula Rule Created and Applied

To create a formula-based conditional formatting rule, complete the following steps:

1. Select the desired data range.

2. Click the Home tab, click Conditional Formatting in the Styles group, and click New Rule.

3. Select *Use a formula to determine which cells to format* and type the formula, using cell references in the first row, in the *Format values where this formula is true* box.

Once complete, Excel applies the general formula to the selected range, substituting the appropriate cell reference as it makes the comparisons. In the Figure 45 example, =AND(G6="Finance",I6>=10000) requires that the text in the Pay_Type column (column G) contain Finance and the Amount (column I) contain a value that is greater than or equal to $10,000. The AND function requires that both logical tests be met to apply the conditional formatting. A minimum of two logical tests are required; however, you can include additional logical tests. Note that *all* logical tests must be true to apply the conditional formatting.

= AND(logical1,logical2,...)

Manage Rules

Periodically conditional formatting rules may need to be updated, moved, or completely deleted.

To edit or delete conditional formatting rules you create, click Conditional Formatting in the Styles group and select Manage Rules. The Conditional Formatting Rules Manager dialog box opens (see Figure 46). Click the *Show formatting rules for* arrow and select from *current selection, the entire worksheet,* or *this table.* Select the rule, click Edit Rule or Delete Rule, and click OK after making the desired changes. To remove conditional formatting from a range of cells, select the cells. Then click Conditional Formatting, point to Clear Rules, and select Clear Rules from Selected Cells.

To clear all conditional formatting from the entire worksheet, complete the following steps:

1. Click Conditional Formatting in the Styles group on the Home tab.
2. Point to Clear Rules, and then select Clear Rules from Entire Sheet.

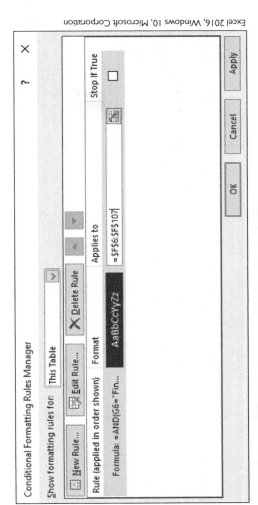

FIGURE 46 Conditional Formatting Rules Manager Dialog Box

Quick Concepts

11. How is conditional formatting similar to an IF function?

12. What conditional formatting would be helpful to identify the three movies with the highest revenue playing at theaters?

13. How is data bar conditional formatting helpful when reviewing a column of data?

Skills covered: Add a Total Row • Apply Highlight Cells Rules • Specify Top/Bottom Rules • Display Data Bars • Use a Formula in Conditional Formatting

4 Table Aggregation and Conditional Formatting

Vicki Reid wants to review the transactions with you. She is interested in Sebastian Gruenewald's sales record and the three highest transaction amounts. In addition, she wants to compare the down payment amounts visually. Finally, she wants you to analyze the amounts owed for sales completed by Sebastian.

STEP 1 >> **ADD A TOTAL ROW**

You want to see the monthly totals for the Amount, Down_Pay, and Owed columns. You will add a total row to calculate the values. Refer to Figure 47 as you complete Step 1.

a. Open *e04h3Reid_LastFirst* if you closed it at the end of Hands-On Exercise 3. Save the workbook as **e04h4Reid_LastFirst**, changing h3 to h4.

b. Select the **March Individual worksheet**, click any cell inside the table, click the **Design tab**, and then click **Total Row** in the Table Style Options group.

Excel displays the total row after the last record. It sums the last field of values automatically. The total amount customers owe is $278,656.50.

c. Click the **Down_Pay cell** in row 110, click the **total arrow**, and then select **Sum**.

You added a total to the Down_Pay field. The total amount of down payment collected is $190,602.50. The formula displays as =SUBTOTAL(109,[Down_Pay]) in the Formula Bar.

d. Click the **Amount cell** in row 110, click the **total arrow**, and then select **Sum**.

You added a total to the Amount column. The total amount of merchandise sales is $469,259. The formula displays as =SUBTOTAL(109,[Amount]) in the Formula Bar.

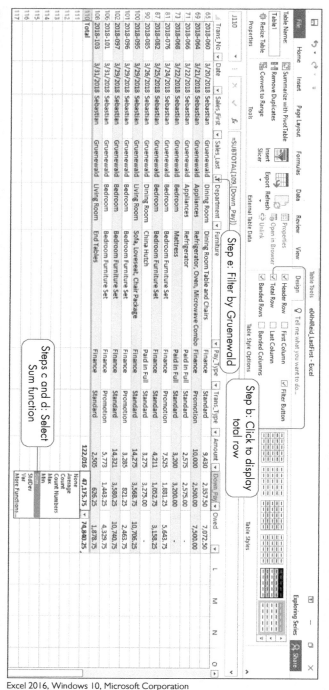

FIGURE 47 Add a Total Row

Excel 2016, Windows 10, Microsoft Corporation

e. Click the **Sales_Last filter arrow**, click the **(Select All) check box**, click the **Gruenewald check box** to select it, and then click **OK**.

The total row values change to display the totals for only Gruenewald: $122,016 (Amount), 47,175.75 (Down_Pay), and 74,840.25 (Owed). This is an advantage of using the total row, which uses the SUBTOTAL function, as opposed to if you had inserted the SUM function manually. The SUM function would provide a total for all data in the column, not just the filtered data.

f. Click the **Data tab** and click **Clear** in the Sort & Filter group to remove all filters.

g. Save the workbook.

STEP 2 >> APPLY HIGHLIGHT CELLS RULES

You want to identify Sebastian's sales for March 2018 without filtering the data. You will set a conditional format to apply a fill and font color so cells that document appliance sales stand out. Refer to Figure 48 as you complete Step 2.

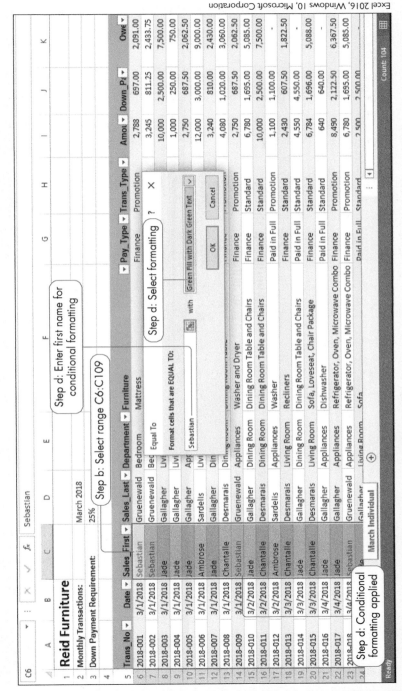

FIGURE 48 Conditional Formatting Rules Manager Dialog Box

a. Select **row headings 6 through 109** in the March Individual worksheet. Click the **Home tab**, click the **Fill Color arrow**, and then select **No Fill**.

You removed the previous table style. This will avoid having too many fill colors when you apply conditional formatting rules.

b. Select the **range C6:C109**.

c. Click **Conditional Formatting** in the Styles group, point to **Highlight Cells Rules**, and then select **Text that Contains**.

The Text that Contains dialog box opens.

d. Type **Sebastian** in the box, click the **with arrow**, and then select **Green Fill with Dark Green Text**. Click **OK**. Deselect the range and save the workbook.

Excel formats only cells that contain Sebastian with the fill and font color.

STEP 3 ❯❯ SPECIFY TOP/BOTTOM RULES

Vicki is now interested in identifying the highest three sales transactions in March. Instead of sorting the records, you will use the Top/Bottom Rules conditional formatting. Refer to Figure 49 as you complete Step 3.

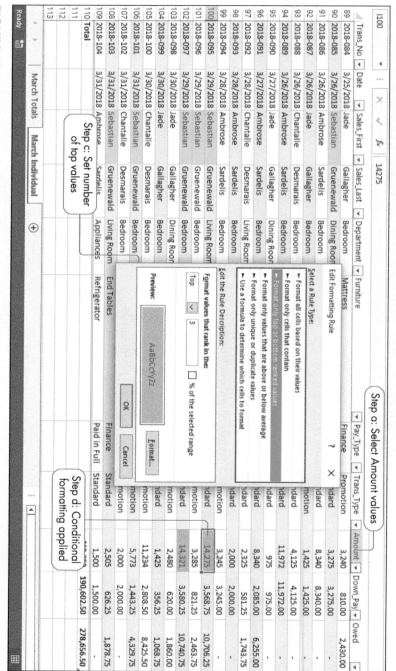

a. Select the **range I6:I109**, the range containing the amounts.

b. Click **Conditional Formatting** in the Styles group, point to **Top/Bottom Rules**, and then select **Top 10 Items.**

   The Top 10 Items dialog box opens.

c. Click the arrow to display **3** and click **OK.**

d. Scroll through the worksheet to see the top three amounts. Save the workbook.

FIGURE 49 Top 3 Amounts Conditionally Formatted

Excel 2016, Windows 10, Microsoft Corporation

STEP 4 ▶▶ DISPLAY DATA BARS

Vicki wants to compare all of the down payments. Data bars would add a nice visual element as she compares down payment amounts. Refer to Figure 50 as you complete Step 4.

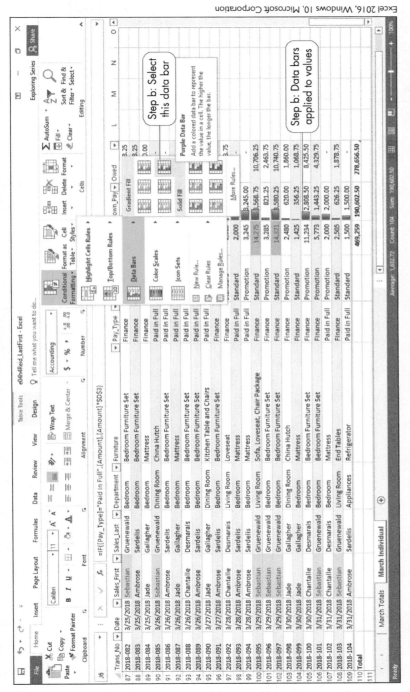

FIGURE 50 Data Bars Conditional Formatting

a. Select the **range J6:J109**, which contains the down payment amounts.

b. Click **Conditional Formatting** in the Styles group, point to **Data Bars**, and then select **Purple Data Bar** in the Gradient Fill section. Scroll through the list and save the workbook.

Excel displays data bars in each cell. The larger bar widths help Vicki quickly identify the largest down payments. However, the largest down payments are identical to the original amounts when the customers pay in full. This result illustrates that you should not accept the results at face value. Doing so would provide you with an inaccurate analysis.

STEP 5 ›› USE A FORMULA IN CONDITIONAL FORMATTING

Vicki's next request is to analyze the amounts owed by Sebastian's customers. In particular, she wants to highlight the merchandise for which more than $5,000 is owed. To do this, you realize you need to create a custom rule that evaluates both the Sales_First column and the Owed column. Refer to Figure 51 as you complete Step 5.

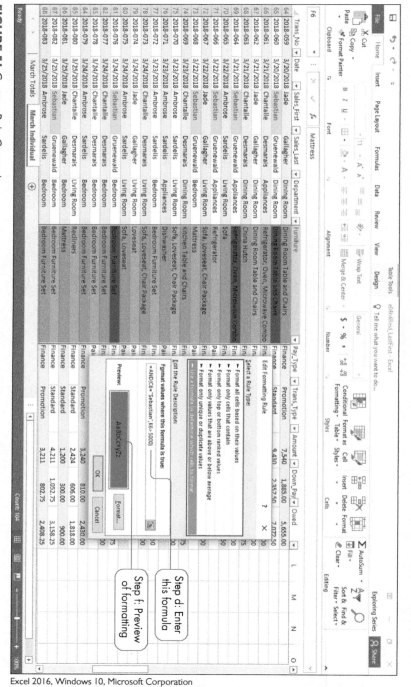

FIGURE 51 Custom Rule Created

Excel 2016, Windows 10, Microsoft Corporation

a. Select the **range F6:F109**, which contains the furniture merchandise.

b. Click **Conditional Formatting** in the Styles group and select **New Rule**.

The New Formatting Rule dialog box opens.

c. Select **Use a formula to determine which cells to format.**

d. Type **=AND(C6="Sebastian",K6>5000)** in the *Format values where this formula is true* box.

Because you are comparing the contents of cell C6 to text, you must enclose the text within quotation marks.

e. Click **Format** to open the Format Cells dialog box.

f. Click the **Font tab**, and click **Bold** in the Font style list. Click the **Border tab**, click the **Color arrow**, select **Blue, Accent 5**, and then click **Outline**. Click the **Fill tab**, click **Blue, Accent 5 background color** (the second color from the right on the first row), and then click **OK**.

Figure 51 shows the Edit Formatting Rule dialog box, but the options are similar to the New Formatting Rule dialog box.

g. Click **OK** in the New Formatting Rule dialog box and scroll through the list to see which amounts owed are greater than $5,000 for Sebastian only.

> **TROUBLESHOOTING:** If the results seem incorrect, click Conditional Formatting and select Manage Rules. Edit the rule you just created and make any corrections to the formula.

h. Save and close the file. Based on your instructor's directions, submit the file e04h4Reid_LastFirst.

Chapter Objectives Review

After reading this chapter, you have accomplished the following objectives:

1. Freeze rows and columns.

- The Freeze Panes setting freezes the row(s) above and the column(s) to the left of the active cell. When you scroll, those rows and columns remain onscreen.
- Use Unfreeze Panes to clear the frozen rows and columns.

2. Print large datasets.

- Display and change page breaks: Display the data in Page Break Preview to see the automatic page breaks. Dashed blue lines indicate automatic page breaks. You can insert manual page breaks, indicated by solid blue lines.
- Set and clear a print area: If you do not want to print an entire worksheet, select a range and set a print area.
- Print titles: Select rows to repeat at top and/or columns to repeat at left to print the column and row labels on every page of a printout of a large dataset.
- Control print page order: You can control the sequence in which the pages will print.

3. Understand the benefits of data tables.

- A table is a structured range that contains related data. Tables have several benefits over regular ranges. The column labels, called field names, display on the first row of a table. Each row is a complete set of data for one record.

4. Design and create tables.

- Plan a table before you create it. Create unique field names on the first row of the table and enter data below the field names, avoiding blank rows.
- Create a table: You can create a table from existing data. Excel applies the Table Style Medium 2 format and assigns a name, such as Table1, to the table. When the active cell is within a table, the Table Tools Design tab displays.
- Rename a table: When a table is created, Excel assigns a generic name and enables you to edit the default to a more suitable name.
- Add and delete fields: You can insert and delete table rows and columns to adjust the structure of a table.
- Add, edit, and delete records: You can add table rows, edit records, and delete table rows.
- Remove duplicate rows: Use the Remove Duplicates dialog box to remove duplicate records in a table. Excel will display a dialog box telling you how many records are deleted.

5. Apply a table style.

- Table styles control the fill color of the header row and records within the table.

6. Create structured references in formulas.

- Structured references use tags as field headings that can be used in formulas in place of cell references.

7. Sort data.

- Sort one field: You can sort text in alphabetical or reverse alphabetical order, values from smallest to largest or largest to smallest, and dates from oldest to newest or

newest to oldest. Click the filter arrow and select the sort method from the list.
- Sort multiple fields: Open the Sort dialog box and add column levels and sort orders.
- Create a custom sort: You can create a custom sort for unique data, such as ensuring that the months sort in sequential order rather than alphabetical order.

8. Filter data.

- Filtering is the process of specifying conditions for displaying records in a table. Only records that meet those conditions display; the other records are hidden.
- Apply text filters: A text filter can find exact text, text that does not equal a condition, text that begins with a particular letter, and so forth.
- Apply number filters: A number filter can find exact values, values that do not equal a particular value, values greater than or equal to a value, and so on.
- Apply date filters: You can set filters to find dates before or after a certain date, between two dates, yesterday, next month, and so forth.
- Apply a custom filter: You can create a custom AutoFilter to filter values by options such as Greater Than, Less Than, or Before.
- Clear filters: If you do not need filters, you can clear the filters.

9. Add a total row.

- You can display a total row after the last record. You can add totals or select a different function, such as Average.

10. Apply conditional formatting.

- Apply conditional formatting with the Quick Analysis Tool: After selecting text, click Formatting in the Quick Analysis gallery to apply a conditional format.
- Apply a highlight cells rule: This rule highlights cell contents with a fill color, font color, and/or border color where the contents match a particular condition.
- Specify a top/bottom rule: This rule enables you to highlight the top or bottom x number of items or percentage of items.
- Display data bars, color scales, and icon sets: Data bars compare values within the selected range. Color scales indicate values that occur within particular ranges. Icon sets display icons representing a number's relative value compared to other numbers in the range.

11. Create a new rule.

- You can create conditional format rules. The New Formatting Rule dialog box enables you to select a rule type.
- Use formulas in conditional formatting: You can create rules based on content in multiple columns.
- Manage rules: Use the Conditional Formatting Rules Manager dialog box to edit and delete rules.

Key Terms Matching

Match the key terms with their definitions. Write the key term letter by the appropriate numbered definition.

a. Color scale
b. Conditional formatting
c. Data bar
d. Field
e. Filtering
f. Freezing
g. Icon set
h. Page break
i. Print area

j. Print order
k. Record
l. Sorting
m. Structured reference
n. SUBTOTAL function
o. Table
p. Table style
q. Total row

1. _____ A conditional format that displays a horizontal gradient or solid fill indicating the cell's relative value compared to other selected cells.

2. _____ The process of listing records or text in a specific sequence, such as alphabetically by last name.

3. _____ The process of specifying conditions to display only those records that meet those conditions.

4. _____ A set of rules that applies specific formatting to highlight or emphasize cells that meet specifications.

5. _____ A group of related fields representing one entity, such as data for one person, place, event, or concept.

6. _____ The rules that control the fill color of the header row, columns, and records in a table.

7. _____ An indication of where data will start on another printed page.

8. _____ A table row that appears below the last row of records in an Excel table and displays summary or aggregate statistics, such as a sum or an average.

9. _____ A conditional format that displays a particular color based on the relative value of the cell contents to the other selected cells.

10. _____ The sequence in which the pages are printed.

11. _____ A tag or use of a table element, such as a field label, as a reference in a formula.

12. _____ Symbols or signs that classify data into three, four, or five categories, based on the values in a range.

13. _____ The range of cells within a worksheet that will print.

14. _____ A predefined formula that calculates an aggregate value, such as totals, for values in a range, a table, or a database.

15. _____ The smallest data element contained in a table, such as first name, last name, address, and phone number.

16. _____ A structure that organizes data in a series of records (rows), with each record made up of a number of fields (columns).

17. _____ The process of keeping rows and/or columns visible onscreen at all times even when you scroll through a large dataset.

Multiple Choice

1. You have a large dataset that will print on several pages. You want to ensure that related records print on the same page with column and row labels visible and that confidential information is not printed. You should apply all of the following page setup options *except* which one to accomplish this task?

(a) Set a print area.
(b) Print titles.
(c) Adjust page breaks.
(d) Change the print page order.

2. You are working with a large worksheet. Your row headings are in column A. Which command(s) should be used to see the row headings and the distant information in columns X, Y, and Z?

(a) Freeze Panes command
(b) Hide Rows command
(c) New Window command and cascade the windows
(d) Split Rows command

3. Which statement is *not* a recommended guideline for designing and creating an Excel table?

(a) Avoid naming two fields with the same name.
(b) Ensure that no blank columns separate data columns within the table.
(c) Leave one blank row between records in the table.
(d) Include field names on the first row of the table.

4. Which of the following characters are wildcards in Excel? (Check all that apply.)

(a) *
(b) #
(c) ?
(d) $

5. What should you do to ensure that records in a table are unique?

(a) Do nothing; a logical reason probably exists to keep identical records.
(b) Use the Remove Duplicates command.
(c) Look at each row yourself and manually delete duplicate records.
(d) Find the duplicate records and change some of the data to be different.

6. Which Conditional Formatting rule is best suited to apply formatting to the top five values in a range of values?

(a) Above Average
(b) Greater Than
(c) Top 10 Items
(d) Between

7. Which date filter option enables you to restrict the view to only dates that occur in March of 2018?

(a) Equals
(b) Before
(c) After
(d) Between

8. Which of the following is an unqualified structured reference?

(a) =[Purchase_Price]-[Down_Payment]
(b) =Sales[Purchase_Price]-Sales[Down_Payment]
(c) =Purchase_Price-Down_Payment
(d) =[Sales]Purchase_Price-[Sales]Down_Payment

9. Which of the following is not an aggregate function that can be applied in a total row?

(a) MAX
(b) AVERAGE
(c) COUNT
(d) VLOOKUP

10. If you would like to set a conditional formatting rule based on the function =AND(G6="Finance", H7<7000), which formatting rule type is needed?

(a) Format all cells based on their values
(b) Format only cells that contain
(c) Use a formula to determine which cells to format
(d) Format only values that are above or below average

Practice Exercises

Collectables and Replacement Values

Marie Maier has collected dinnerware, from a fine china company, since 1986. Between 1986 and 2012, the company produced 30 colors, each with a unique name. Marie created a table in Word that lists the name, number, year introduced, and year retired (if applicable) for each color. She created another table in Word that lists the item number, item, replacement value, and source of information for each item in her collection. Her main sources for replacement values are Homer Laughlin (www.fiestafactorydirect.com), Replacements, Ltd. (www.replacements.com), eBay (www.ebay.com), and two local antique stores. She needs your help to convert the data to Excel tables, apply table formatting, delete duplicate records, insert functions, and sort and filter the data. Refer to Figure 52 as you complete this exercise.

	A	B	C	D	E	F	G	H
1	Color Number	Year Introduced	Year Retired	Status	Color	Item Number	Item	Replacement Value
31	102	2000	2010	Retired	Cinnabar	571	Canister Small	49.99
32	102	2000	2010	Retired	Cinnabar	830	5 Piece Place Setting	35.99
33	102	2000	2010	Retired	Cinnabar	484	Pitcher Large Disc	34.99
34	102	2000	2010	Retired	Cinnabar	467	Chop Plate	25.00
35	102	2000	2010	Retired	Cinnabar	497	Salt and Pepper Set	20.00
36	102	2000	2010	Retired	Cinnabar	465	Luncheon Plate	12.50
37	102	2000	2010	Retired	Cinnabar	439	Spoon Rest	11.99
38	102	2000	2010	Retired	Cinnabar	570	Java Mug	9.99
39	102	2000	2010	Retired	Cinnabar	453	Mug	8.49
40	102	2000	2010	Retired	Cinnabar	446	Tumbler	6.99
41	103	1986	2005	Retired	Rose	494	Covered Coffee Server	75.00
42	103	1986	2005	Retired	Rose	495	Covered Casserole	65.00
43	103	1986	2005	Retired	Rose	489	Pyramid Candleholders	59.99
44	103	1986	2005	Retired	Rose	486	Sauceboat	39.99
45	103	1986	2005	Retired	Rose	830	5 Piece Place Setting	35.00
46	103	1986	2005	Retired	Rose	821	Sugar/Cream Tray Set	29.99
47	103	1986	2005	Retired	Rose	484	Pitcher Large Disc	24.99
48	103	1986	2005	Retired	Rose	478	AD Cup and Saucer	19.99
49	103	1986	2005	Retired	Rose	471	Bowl Large 1 qt	19.99
50	103	1986	2005	Retired	Rose	497	Salt and Pepper Set	18.00
51	103	1986	2005	Retired	Rose	467	Chop Plate	16.95
52	103	1986	2005	Retired	Rose	451	Rim Soup	12.50

FIGURE 52 Fiesta® Collection

Excel 2016, Windows 10, Microsoft Corporation

a. Open **e04p1Collectables** and save it as **e04p1Collectables_LastFirst.**

b. Select the **range A2:D31** on the Colors Data sheet, click in the **Name Box**, type **Colors**, and then press **Enter** to assign the name *Colors* to the selected range.

c. Click **cell A2** on the Items sheet, click the **View tab**, click **Freeze Panes** in the Window group, and then select **Freeze Top Row.**

d. Click the **Insert tab**, click **Table** in the Tables group, and then click **OK** in the Create Table dialog box.

e. Click **More Styles** in the Table Styles group and click **Table Style Medium 5.**

f. Click the **Data tab**, click **Remove Duplicates** in the Data Tools group, and then click **OK** in the Remove Duplicates dialog box. Click **OK** in the message box that informs you that 6 duplicate values were found and removed. 356 unique values remain.

g. Click **cell A2**, click the **Home tab**, click **Sort & Filter** in the Editing group, and then select **Sort Smallest to Largest.**

h. Click **cell B2**, click the **Insert arrow** in the Cells group, and then select **Insert Table Columns to the Left**. Insert two more columns to the left. Do the following to insert functions and customize the results in the three new table columns:

- Type **Year Introduced** in **cell B1**, **Year Retired** in **cell C1**, and **Color** in **cell D1**.
- Click **cell B2**, type =**VLOOKUP([Color Number],colors,3,False)**, and then press **Enter**. Excel copies the function down the Year Introduced column. This function looks up each item's color number using the structured reference *[Color Number]*, looks up that value in the colors table, and then returns the year that color was introduced, which is in the third column of that table.
- Click **cell B2**, click **Copy**, click **cell C2**, and then click **Paste**. Change the 3 to **4** in the col_index_num argument of the pasted function and press **Enter**. Excel copies the function down the Year Retired column. This function looks up each item's color number using the structured reference *[Color Number]*, looks up that value in the colors table, and then returns the year that color was retired, if applicable, which is in the fourth column of that table. The function returns 0 if the retired cell in the lookup table is blank.
- Click the **File tab**, click **Options**, click **Advanced**, scroll down to the Display options for this worksheet section, click the **Show a zero in cells that have zero value check box** to deselect it, and then click **OK**. The zeros disappear. (This option hides zeros in the active worksheet. While this is not desirable if you need to show legitimate zeros, this worksheet is designed to avoid that issue.)
- Click **cell C2**, click **Copy**, click **cell D2**, and then click **Paste**. Change the 4 to **2** in the col_index_num argument of the pasted function and press **Enter**. Excel copies the function down the Color column. This function looks up each item's color number using the structured reference *[Color Number]* to look up that value in the colors table and returns the color name, which is in the second column of that table.

i. Apply wrap text, horizontal centering, and **30.50 row height** to the column labels row. Adjust column widths to AutoFit. Center data horizontally in the Color Number, Year Introduced, Year Retired, and Item Number columns. Apply **Comma Style** to the Replacement Values. Deselect the data.

j. Click **Sort & Filter** in the Editing group and select **Custom Sort** to display the Sort dialog box. Do the following in the Sort dialog box:

- Click the **Sort by arrow** and select **Color**.
- Click **Add Level**, click the **Then by arrow**, and then select **Replacement Value**.
- Click the **Order arrow** and select **Largest to Smallest**.
- Click **Add Level**, click the **Then by arrow**, and select **Source**.
- Click the **Order arrow**, select **Custom List**, and type the following entries: **Ebay Auction, Downtown Antique Store, The Homer Laughlin China Co., Replacements LTD., Keith's Antique Store**. Click **Add** and click **OK**. Click **OK**.

k. Right-click the **Items sheet tab**, select **Move or Copy**, click **(move to end)**, click the **Create a copy check box** to select the option, and then click **OK**. Rename the copied sheet **Retired**.

l. Ensure that Retired is the active sheet. Insert a table column between the Year Retired and Color columns.

- Type **Status** in **cell D1** as the column label.
- Click **cell D2**, type =**IF([Year Retired]=0, "Current", "Retired")**, and then press **Enter**. This function determines that if the cell contains a 0 (which is hidden), it will display the word *Current*. Otherwise, it will display *Retired*.

m. Click the **Status filter arrow**, deselect the **Current check box**, and then click **OK** to filter out the current colors and display only retired colors.

n. Click the **Design tab** and click **Total Row** in the Table Style Options group. Click **cell I358**, click the **Source total cell** (which contains a count of visible items), click the **Source total arrow**, and then select **None**. Click **cell H358**, the Replacement Value total cell, click the **Replacement Value total arrow**, and then select **Sum**.

DISCOVER H

o. Prepare the Retired worksheet for printing by doing the following:

- Set **0.2"** left and right page margins.
- Select the **range E1:I358**, click the **Page Layout tab**, click **Print Area** in the Page Setup group, and then select **Set Print Area**.
- Click **Print Titles** in the Page Setup group, click the **Rows to repeat at top Collapse Dialog Box**, click the **row 1 header**, and then click **Expand Dialog Box**. Click **OK**.
- Click the **View tab** and click **Page Break Preview** in the Workbook Views group. Decrease the top margin to avoid having only one or two records print on the last page.

p. Create a footer with your name on the left side, the sheet name code in the center, and the file name code on the right side of each worksheet.

q. Save and close the file. Based on your instructor's directions, submit e04p1Collectables_LastFirst.

2 Sunny Popcorn, Inc.

You are a financial analyst for Sunny Popcorn, Inc. and have been given the task of compiling a workbook to detail weekly sales information. The current information provided detailed sales rep information, flavors ordered, account type, and volume ordered. The owners are specifically interested in local sales that are generating at least $150.00 a week. To complete the document you will sort, filter, use table tools, and apply conditional formatting. Refer to Figure 53 as you complete this exercise.

▲	A	B	C	D	E	F	G	H
1	Sunny Popcorn Inc							
2	Date	10/6/2018						
3	Deposit	5%						
4								
5								
6	First Name ▼	Last Name ▼	Account type ▼	Flavor ▼	Volume in lbs ▼	Price per lb ▼	Deposit ▼	Amount Due ▼
22	Helen	Sanchez	Local	Regular	58	$2.25	$ 6.53	$ 123.98
23	Yoshio	Guo	Local	Cheese	88	$2.00	$ 8.80	$ 167.20
24	Yong	Lopez	Local	Regular	91	$2.25	$ 10.24	$ 194.51
25	Dalia	Azizi	Local	Regular	33	$2.25	$ 3.71	$ 70.54
26	Kyung	Rodriguez	Local	Carmel	99	$1.50	$ 7.43	$ 141.08
27	Jasmine	Bettar	Local	Cheese	67	$2.00	$ 6.70	$ 127.30
28	Yukio	He	Local	Low Salt	64	$2.25	$ 7.20	$ 136.80
29	Dai	Zhu	Local	Chocolate	62	$2.00	$ 6.20	$ 117.80
30	Nam	Sato	Local	Cheese	66	$2.00	$ 6.60	$ 125.40
31	Ryung	Inoue	Local	Chocolate	17	$2.00	$ 1.70	$ 32.30
32	Raul	Martinez	Local	Crunch	31	$2.25	$ 3.49	$ 66.26
33	Yoshio	Flores	Local	Low Salt	27	$2.25	$ 3.04	$ 57.71
34	Diego	Sun	Local	Low Salt	16	$2.25	$ 1.80	$ 34.20
35	Helen	Cho	Local	Cheese	48	$2.00	$ 4.80	$ 91.20
36	Yoshio	Seo	Local	Chocolate	32	$2.00	$ 3.20	$ 60.80
37	Sang	Allen	Local	Carmel	53	$1.50	$ 3.98	$ 75.53
38	Raj	Hong	Local	Cheese	41	$2.00	$ 4.10	$ 77.90
39	Javier	Hyat	Local	Cheese	100	$2.00	$ 10.00	$ 190.00
40	Brian	Hernandez	Local	Low Salt	16	$2.25	$ 1.80	$ 34.20

Ready   Sales ⊕

FIGURE 53 Sunny Popcorn Inc

Excel 2016, Windows 10, Microsoft Corporation

a. Open *e04p2Popcorn* and save it as **e04p2Popcorn_LastFirst**.

b. Click **cell C7**, click the **Home tab**, click the **Sort & Filter arrow** in the Editing group, and select **Sort A to Z**. This sorts the data by account type in Column C.

c. Click the **Insert tab**, click **Table** in the Tables group, and click **OK** in the Create Table dialog box.

d. Click **Table Style Medium 3** in the Table Styles group on the Design tab.

e. Click **cell G7** and type **=[Price per lb]*[Volume in lbs]*$B$3** and press **Enter**.

f. Click **cell H7** and type **=[Price per lb]*[Volume in lbs]-[Deposit]** and press **Enter**

g. Select the **range G7:H106**, click the **Home tab**, and click **Accounting Number Format** in the Number group.

h. Click the **Design tab** and click **Total Row** in the Table Style Options group.

i. Click the **Deposit Total Row arrow**, and select **Sum**, click the **Volume in lbs Total Row arrow**, and then select **Average**. Apply **Number Style Format** to the results in **cell E107**.

j. Click the **filter arrow** of the Account type column, click the **Select All check box** to deselect it, click **Local**, and click **OK**.

k. Select the **range H22:H51**, click **Quick Analysis**, and then select **Greater Than**. Type **150.00** in the Format cells that are GREATER THAN box, select **Green Fill with Dark Green Text**, and click **OK**.

l. Select the **range E22:E51**, click **Quick Analysis**, and then select **Data Bars**.

m. Click the **Page Layout tab**, click the **Scale box** in the Scale to Fit group, and then type **85%**.

n. Create a footer with your name on the left side, the sheet name code in the center, and the file name code on the right side of each worksheet.

o. Save and close the file. Based on your instructor's directions, submit e04p2Popcorn_LastFirst.

Mid-Level Exercises

1 Crafton's Pet Supplies

You are the inventory manager for Crafton's Pet Supplies. You are currently preforming analysis to determine inventory levels, as well as the total value of inventory on hand. Your last steps will be to check the report for duplicate entries and format for printing.

a. Open *e04m1Inventory* and save it as **e04m1Inventory_LastFirst.**

b. Freeze the panes so that the column labels do not scroll offscreen.

c. Convert the data to a table and name the table **Inventory2018.**

d. Apply **Table Style Medium 3** to the table.

e. Sort the table by Warehouse (A to Z), then Department, and then by Unit Price (smallest to largest). Create a custom sort order for Department so that it appears in this sequence: Food & Health, Collars & Leashes, Toys, Clothes, Training, and Grooming.

f. Remove duplicate records from the table. Excel should find and remove one duplicate record.

g. Create an unqualified structured reference in column G to determine the value of the inventory on hand and apply **Accounting Number Format.** To calculate the inventory on hand multiply the **Unit Price** and the **Amount on Hand.**

h. Apply a **Total Row** to the Inventory2018 table. Set the Inventory Value to Sum, and the Amount on Hand to Average. Format the results to display with two decimal points.

i. Create a new conditional formatting rule that displays any Inventory Value for the **Food & Health** department with a value of $30,000 or more as **Red Accent 2 fill color.** There will be two qualifying entries.

j. Ensure the warehouse information is not broken up between pages when printed. Add a page break to make sure that each warehouse prints on its own consecutive page.

k. Set the worksheet to **Landscape orientation,** and repeat row 1 labels on all pages.

l. Display the Inventory sheet in Page Break Preview.

m. Insert a footer with your name on the left side, the sheet name code in the center, and the file name code on the right side of all four sheets.

n. Save and close the file. Based on your instructor's directions, submit e04m1Inventory_LastFirst.

2 Artwork

You work for a gallery that is an authorized Greenwich Workshop fine art dealer (www.greenwichworkshop.com). Customers in your area are especially fond of James C. Christensen's art. Although customers can visit the website to see images and details about his work, they have requested a list of all his artwork. Your assistant prepared a list of artwork: art, type, edition size, release date, and issue price. In addition, you included a column to identify which pieces are sold out at the publisher, indicating the rare, hard-to-obtain artwork that is available on the secondary market. You now want to convert the data to a table so that you can provide information to your customers.

a. Open *e04m2FineArt* and save it as **e04m2FineArt_LastFirst.**

b. Convert the data to a table and apply **Table Style Medium 5.**

c. Add a row (below the record for *The Yellow Rose*) for this missing piece of art: **The Yellow Rose, Masterwork Canvas Edition, 50** edition size, **May 2009** release date, **$895** issue price. Enter **Yes** to indicate the piece is sold out.

d. Sort the table by Type in alphabetical order and then by Release Date from newest to oldest.

e. Add a total row that shows the largest edition size and the most expensive issue price. Delete the Total label in **cell A205** and **cell H205.** Add a descriptive label in **cell C205** to reflect the content on the total row.

DISCOVER

f. Create a custom conditional format for the Issue Price column with these specifications:

- **4 Traffic Lights** icon set (Black, Red, Yellow, Green)
  - **Red icon** when the number is greater than 1000
  - **Yellow icon** when the number is less than or equal to 1000 and greater than 500
  - **Green icon** when the number is less than or equal to 500 and greater than 250
  - **Black icon** when the number is less than or equal to 250.

g. Filter the table by the **Red Traffic Light** conditional formatting icon.

h. Answer the questions in the range D213:D217 based on the filtered data.

i. Set the print area to print the **range C1:H205**, select the **first row to repeat at the top of each printout**, set **1"** top and bottom margins, set **0.3"** left and right margins, and then select **Landscape orientation**. Set the option to fit the data to 1 page.

j. Wrap text, and horizontally center column labels and adjust column widths and row heights as needed.

k. Create a footer with your name on the left side, the sheet name code in the center, and the file name code on the right side.

l. Save and close the file. Based on your instructor's directions, submit e04m2FineArt_LastFirst.

DISCOVER

Party Music

You are planning a weekend party and want to create a mix of music so that most people will appreciate some of the music you will play at the party. To help you decide what music to play, you have asked five classmates to help you create a song list. The entire class should decide on the general format, capitalization style, and the sequence: Song, Artist, Genre, Released, and approximate song length.

a. Conduct online research to collect data for your favorite 25 songs.

b. Enter the data into a new workbook in the format, capitalization style, and sequence that was decided by the class.

c. Save the workbook as **e04m3PlayList_LastFirst.**

d. Upload the file to a shared folder on OneDrive or Dropbox that everyone in the class can access.

e. Download four workbooks from friends and copy and paste data from their workbooks into yours.

f. Convert the data to a table and apply a table style of your choice.

g. Detect and delete duplicate records. Make a note of the number of duplicate records found and deleted.

h. Sort the data by genre using the custom list: Pop, Rock, R&B, and Jazz, then by artist in alphabetical order, and then by release date with the oldest year first.

i. Set a filter to display songs that were released before 2018.

j. Display the total row and select the function to count the number of songs displayed.

k. Insert comments in the workbook to indicate which student's workbooks you used, the number of duplicate records deleted, and the number of filtered records.

l. Save and close the file. Based on your instructor's directions, submit e04m3PlayList_LastFirst.

Flight Arrival Status

GENERAL CASE

FROM SCRATCH

As an analyst for an airport, you want to study the flight arrivals for a particular day. Select an airport and find its list of flight arrival data. Some airport websites do not list complete details, so search for an airport that does, such as Will Rogers World Airport or San Diego International Airport. Copy the column labels and arrival data (airline, flight number, city, gate, scheduled time, status, etc.) for one day and paste them in a new workbook. The columns may be in a different sequence from what is listed here. However, you should format the data as needed. Leave two blank rows below the last row of data and enter the URL of the webpage from which you got the data, the date, and the time. Save the workbook as **e04b1Flights_LastFirst**. Convert the list to a table and apply a table style.

Sort the table by scheduled time and then by gate number. Apply conditional formatting to the Status column to highlight cells that contain the text Delayed (or similar text). Add a total row to calculate the MODE for the gate number and arrival time. The MODE is the number that appears the most frequently in the dataset. You must select **More Functions** from the list of functions in the total row and search for and select **MODE**. Change the total row label in the first column from Total to **Most Frequent**. Use Help to refresh your memory on how to nest an IF function inside another IF function. Add a calculated column on the right side of the table using a nested IF function and structured references to display **Late** if the actual time was later than the scheduled time, **On Time or Early** if the actual time was earlier than or equal to the scheduled time, or **Incomplete** if the flight has not landed yet.

Name the worksheet **Arrival Time**. Copy the worksheet and name the copied worksheet **Delayed**. Filter the list by delayed flights. Include a footer with your name on the left side, the sheet name code in the center, and the file name code on the right side of both worksheets. Adjust the margins on both worksheets as necessary. Save and close the file. Based on your instructor's directions, submit e04b1Flights_LastFirst.

Dairy Farm

DISASTER RECOVERY

You are the product manager for Schaefer Dairy farm, a local organic farm that produces dairy products. Each month you must run an inventory report to identify and discard expired products before they are sold. Open *e04b2Dairy* and save it as **e04b2Dairy_LastFirst**. Convert the **range A5:E105** to a table, give the table a name, and apply a table style.

Freeze all data above row 6 and create a conditional formatting rule that highlights any package date that is 30 days or older than the manufacture date in B4. Sort the table first by the newly created highlight color then by department. Next, in column E create an IF function using structured referencing to determine the course of action for expired products. The function should display **discard** if the product is expired and nothing if the product is still sellable. Filter the table to display only items that should be discarded, then add a total row that counts the number of items to discard. Format the table so the column headings print at the top of each page and create a footer with your name, the sheet name code, and the file name code. Save and close the file. Based on your instructor's directions, submit e04b2Dairy_LastFirst.

You work for Rockville Auto Sales and have been asked to aid in the development of a spreadsheet to manage sales and inventory information. You will start the task with a prior worksheet that contains vehicle information and sales data for 2018. You need to convert the data to a table. You will manage the large worksheet, prepare the worksheet for printing, sort and filter the table, include calculations, and then format the table.

Prepare the Large Worksheet as a Table

You will freeze the panes so that labels remain onscreen. You also want to convert the data to a table so that you can apply table options.

a. Open the *e04c1AutoSales* workbook and save it as **e04c1AutoSales_LastFirst.**

b. Freeze the first row on the Fleet Information worksheet.

c. Convert the data to a table, name the table **Inventory,** and apply the **Table Style Medium 19.**

d. Remove duplicate records.

Sort and Print the Table

To help the sales agents manage vehicle inventory, you will sort the data. Then you will prepare the large table to print.

a. Sort the table by Make in alphabetical order, add a second level to sort by Year, and a third level to sort by Sticker Price smallest to largest.

b. Repeat the field names on all pages.

c. Change page breaks so each vehicle make is printed on a separate page.

d. Add a footer with your name on the left side, the sheet name code in the center, and the file name code on the right side.

Add Calculated Fields and a Total Row

For tax purposes, the accounting department needs you to calculate the number of vehicles sold, the total value of sticker prices, and actual sales price for vehicles sold in the first quarter.

a. Click the Sales Information worksheet and convert the data to a table, name the table **Sales,** and apply the **Table Style Dark 11.**

b. Create a formula with structured references to calculate the percentage of the Sticker Price in column E.

c. Format the **range E2:E30** with **Percentage Style Number Format.**

d. Add a total row to display the Average of % of Sticker Price and Sum of Sticker Price and Sale Price.

e. Adjust the width of **columns B:E** to show the total values.

Apply Conditional Formatting

You want to help the office manager visualize the differences among the sales. To highlight sales trends, you will apply data bar conditional formatting to the % of Value column.

a. Apply **Data Bars conditional formatting** to the % of Sticker Price data.

b. Create a new conditional format that applies yellow fill and bold font to values that sold for less than 60% of the list price.

c. Edit the conditional format you created so that it formats values 70% or less.

Copy and Filter the Data

In order to isolate first quarter sales, you will filter the data. To keep the original data intact for the sales agents, you will copy the table data to a new sheet and use that sheet to display the filtered data.

a. Copy the Sales Information sheet and place the duplicate sheet to the right of the original sheet tab.

b. Rename the duplicate worksheet **First Quarter Sales.**

c. Rename the table **FirstQuarter.**

d. Display the filter arrows for the data.

e. Filter the data to display January, February, and March sales.

Finalize the Workbook

You are ready to finalize the workbook by adding a footer to the new worksheet and saving the final workbook.

a. Add a footer with your name on the left side, the sheet name code in the center, and the file name code on the right side.

b. Select **Landscape orientation** for all sheets and set appropriate margins so that the data will print on one page.

c. Save and close the file. Based on your instructor's directions, submit e04c1AutoSales_LastFirst.

Glossary

Color scale A conditional format that displays a particular color based on the relative value of the cell contents to the other selected cells.

Conditional formatting A set of rules that applies specific formatting to highlight or emphasize cells that meet specific conditions.

Data bar Data bar formatting applies a gradient or solid fill bar in which the width of the bar represents the current cell's value compared relatively to other cells' values.

Data structure The organization method used to manage multiple data points within a dataset.

Field The smallest data element contained in a table, such as first name, last name, address, and phone number.

Filtering The process of specifying conditions to display only those records that meet those conditions.

Freezing The process of keeping rows and/or columns visible onscreen at all times even when you scroll through a large dataset.

Fully qualified structured reference A structured formula that contains the table name.

Icon set Symbols or signs that classify data into three, four, or five categories, based on values in a range.

Page break An indication of where data will start on another printed page.

Print area The range of cells within a worksheet that will print.

Print order The sequence in which the pages are printed.

Record A group of related fields representing one entity, such as data for one person, place, event, or concept.

Sorting The process of arranging records by the value of one or more fields within a table or data range.

Structured reference A tag or use of a table element, such as a field label, as a reference in a formula. Field labels are enclosed in square brackets, such as [Amount] within the formula.

SUBTOTAL function A predefined formula that calculates an aggregate value, such as totals, for displayed values in a range, a table, or a database.

Table A structured range that contains related data organized in a method that increases the capability to manage and analyze information.

Table style A set of rules that easily format table rows and columns with complementary fill colors.

Total row A table row that appears below the last row of records in an Excel table and displays summary or aggregate statistics, such as a sum or an average.

Unqualified reference The use of field headings without row references in a structured formula.

Subtotals, PivotTables, and PivotCharts

Subtotals, PivotTables, and PivotCharts

LEARNING OUTCOME

You will manage and analyze data by creating subtotals, PivotTables, and PivotCharts.

OBJECTIVES & SKILLS: After you read this chapter, you will be able to:

Subtotals and Outlines

OBJECTIVE 1: SUBTOTAL DATA
Sort Multiple Fields, Subtotal Data, Add a Second Subtotal, Collapse and Expand the Subtotals

OBJECTIVE 2: GROUP AND UNGROUP DATA
Group Data, Ungroup Data

HANDS-ON EXERCISE 1:
Subtotals and Outlines

PivotTable Basics

OBJECTIVE 3: CREATE A PIVOTTABLE
Create a Recommended PivotTable, Create a Blank PivotTable, Rename a PivotTable

OBJECTIVE 4: MODIFY A PIVOTTABLE
Add Rows to a PivotTable, Add Columns to a PivotTable, Remove Fields from a PivotTable, Rearrange Fields in a PivotTable, Change Value Field Settings, Refresh a PivotTable

HANDS-ON EXERCISE 2:
PivotTable Basics

PivotTable Options

OBJECTIVE 5: FILTER AND SLICE A PIVOTTABLE
Set Filters, Insert a Timeline, Insert a Slicer, Customize a Slicer

OBJECTIVE 6: CREATE A CALCULATED FIELD
Create a Calculated Field, Show Values as Calculations

OBJECTIVE 7: CHANGE THE PIVOTTABLE DESIGN
Change the PivotTable Style

HANDS-ON EXERCISE 3:
PivotTable Options

Data Modeling and PivotCharts

OBJECTIVE 8: CREATE A DATA MODEL
Create Relationships, Create a PivotTable from Related Tables

OBJECTIVE 9: CREATE A PIVOTCHART
Create a PivotChart, Modify the PivotChart

HANDS-ON EXERCISE 4:
Data Modeling and PivotCharts

CASE STUDY | Ivory Halls Publishing Company

You are the new vice president of the Sociology Division at Ivory Halls Publishing Company. The sociology domain has many disciplines, such as Family, Introductory, and Race/Class/Gender. Ivory Halls publishes several textbooks in each discipline to appeal to a vast array of university professors and students. Your assistant has prepared a worksheet containing these columns of data for the sociology textbooks:

- Discipline. Textbooks are classified by the overall discipline, such as Family.
- Area. Within each discipline, books are further classified by area. For example, the Family discipline is further classified into two areas: (1) Family Interaction and (2) Marriage and Family.
- Units Sold Wholesale. This column lists the number of books sold to wholesale buyers, such as college bookstores.
- Unit Price Wholesale. This column lists the price per book for wholesale buyers.
- Sales: Wholesale. This is the sales amount resulting by multiplying the Units Sold Wholesale by the Unit Price Wholesale.

Summarizing and Analyzing Data

- Units Sold Retail. This column lists the number of books sold to online customers, such as individual students.
- Unit Price Retail. This column lists the price per book for an online customer.
- Sales: Unit Price. This is the sales amount resulting by multiplying the Units Sold Retail by the Unit Price Retail.
- Total Book Sales: This is the total amount of wholesale and retail sales.

You want to analyze sales for all books published in the Sociology Division. To do this, you will organize data so that you can group data by discipline and then insert subtotal rows. You will also create PivotTables to gain a variety of perspectives of aggregated data, including data from multiple tables. Finally, you will create a PivotChart to depict the aggregated data visually.

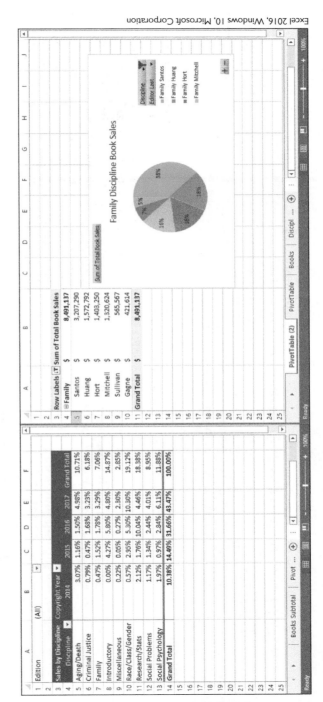

FIGURE 1 Ivory Halls Publishing Company PivotTables

CASE STUDY | Ivory Halls Publishing Company

Starting Files	Files to be Submitted
e05h1Sociology	e05h3Sociology_LastFirst
e05h4Sociology	e05h4Sociology_LastFirst

Subtotals, PivotTables, and PivotCharts • Excel 2016

Subtotals and Outlines

Data alone are meaningless; data translated into meaningful information increase your knowledge so that you can make well-informed decisions. Previously, you used analytical tools such as sorting, filtering, conditional formatting, tables, and charts. These tools help translate raw data into information so that you can identify trends, patterns, and anomalies in a dataset. Now you are ready to explore other functionalities that help you analyze larger amounts of data.

In this section, you will learn how to insert subtotals within a dataset. Then you will learn how to group data to create an outline, collapse and expand groups within the outline, and ungroup data to return them to their original state.

Subtotaling Data

When a dataset is sorted by categories, you can use the Subtotals command to display a total for columns containing values in each category. The Subtotal command inserts a **subtotal row**, which is a row that includes one or more aggregate functions, such as a sum or average, of values within each category within a dataset. This command saves you time so that you do not have to manually insert a blank row for each category and then insert a function on each subtotal row. After you use the Subtotal command, you can then compare the subtotals among categories to analyze the data. Furthermore, when you use the Subtotals command, you can collapse and expand details without having to manually hide and unhide individual rows.

To add subtotals to a dataset, complete the following steps:

1. Sort the dataset using the column that you want to use to group the data. You should select a column that contains multiple occurrences of the same data. For example, the Discipline column contains several books that are classified in the Family discipline. **NOTE: It is important to sort the data into groups first; otherwise the results will be incorrect.**

2. Convert the table to range (if the dataset is a table.) **NOTE: The dataset must be converted to a range, not a table, before you use the Subtotal feature.**

3. Click in the dataset and click the Data tab.

4. Click Subtotal in the Outline group to open the Subtotal dialog box.

5. Click the *At each change in* arrow and select the column by which the data are sorted (see Figure 2). **NOTE: You must select the column by which you sorted data in Step 1.**

6. Click the *Use function* arrow and select the function you want to apply. For columns that contain values, select a function such as Sum, Min, Max, or Count. For text columns, use the Count function to count the number of rows within the group.

7. Select the appropriate column heading check boxes in the *Add subtotal to* list for each field you want to subtotal.

8. Select any other check boxes you want to use and click OK.

For the Ivory Halls Publishing Company, the sociology textbook dataset is sorted by discipline. The Subtotal command inserts a subtotal row, a row within the dataset containing at least one aggregated value when the category you specified in the *At a change in* option changes. For example, when Excel detects a change from the Research/Stats discipline to the Social Problems discipline, a subtotal row is inserted on row 70. Figure 3 shows the subtotal rows highlighted in yellow; however, the Subtotal feature does not add highlighting.

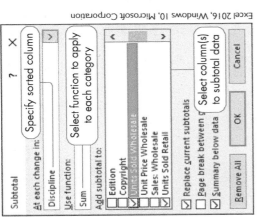

FIGURE 2 Subtotal Dialog Box

Subtotal dialog box:
- At each change in: *(Specify sorted column)* Discipline
- Use function: Sum *(Select function to apply to each category)*
- Add subtotal to:
  - ☐ Edition
  - ☐ Copyright
  - ☑ Units Sold Wholesale
  - ☐ Unit Price Wholesale
  - ☐ Sales: Wholesale
  - ☑ Units Sold Retail
- ☑ Replace current subtotals
- ☐ Page break between groups *(Select column(s) to subtotal data)*
- ☑ Summary below data
- [Remove All] [OK] [Cancel]

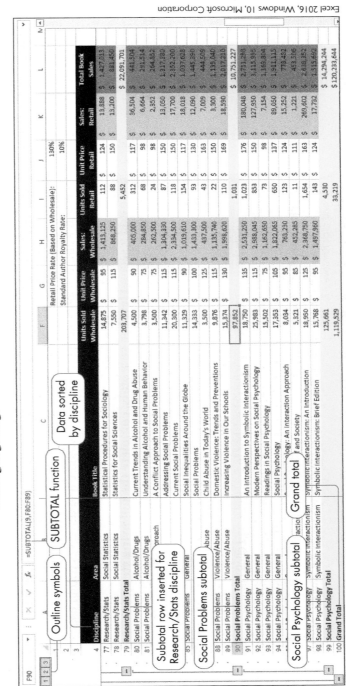

Callouts: Outline symbols · SUBTOTAL function · Data sorted by discipline · Subtotal row inserted for Research/Stats discipline · Social Problems subtotal · Social Psychology subtotal · Grand total

F90 =SUBTOTAL(9,F80:F89)

| | | | | Retail Price Rate (Based on Wholesale): | 130% | | | | | |
| | | | | Standard Author Royalty Rate: | 10% | | | | | |

Row	Discipline	Area	Book Title	Units Sold Wholesale	Unit Price Wholesale	Sales: Wholesale	Units Sold Retail	Unit Price Retail	Sales: Retail	Total Book Sales
77	Research/Stats	Social Statistics	Statistical Procedures for Sociology	14,875	$95	$1,413,125	112	$124	$13,888	$1,427,013
78	Research/Stats	Social Statistics	Statistics for Social Sciences	7,550	$115	$868,250	88	$150	$13,200	$881,450
79	Research/Stats Total			203,707			5,452			$22,091,701
80	Social Problems	Alcohol/Drugs	Current Trends in Alcohol and Drug Abuse	4,500	$90	$405,000	312	$117	$36,504	$441,504
81	Social Problems	Alcohol/Drugs	Understanding Alcohol and Human Behavior	3,798	$75	$284,850	68	$98	$6,664	$291,514
82	Social Problems	Alcohol/Drugs	A Conflict Approach to Social Problems	3,500	$75	$262,500	24	$98	$2,352	$264,852
83	Social Problems	General	Addressing Social Problems	11,342	$115	$1,304,330	87	$150	$13,050	$1,317,380
84	Social Problems	General	Current Social Problems	20,300	$115	$2,334,500	118	$150	$17,700	$2,352,200
85	Social Problems	General	Social Inequalities Around the Globe	11,329	$90	$1,019,610	154	$117	$18,018	$1,037,628
86	Social Problems	Violence/Abuse	Child Abuse in Today's World	14,333	$100	$1,433,300	93	$130	$12,090	$1,445,390
87	Social Problems	Violence/Abuse	Domestic Violence: Trends and Preventions	3,500	$125	$437,500	43	$163	$7,009	$444,509
88	Social Problems		Increasing Violence in Our Schools	9,876	$115	$1,135,740	22	$150	$3,300	$1,139,040
89				15,374	$130	$1,998,620	110	$169	$18,590	$2,017,210
90	Social Problems Total			97,852			1,031			$10,751,227
91	Social Psychology	General	An Introduction to Symbolic Interactionism	18,750	$135	$2,531,250	1,023	$176	$180,048	$2,711,298
92	Social Psychology	General	Modern Perspectives on Social Psychology	25,983	$115	$2,988,045	853	$150	$127,950	$3,115,995
93	Social Psychology	General	Readings in Social Psychology	15,502	$75	$1,162,650	73	$98	$7,154	$1,169,804
94	Social Psychology	General	Social Psychology	17,353	$105	$1,822,065	650	$137	$89,050	$1,911,115
95	Social Psychology	General	Social Psychology: An Interaction Approach	8,034	$95	$763,230	123	$124	$15,252	$778,482
96	Social Psychology	Symbolic Interactionism	Symbolic Interactionism	5,321	$85	$452,285	11	$111	$1,221	$453,506
97	Social Psychology	Symbolic Interactionism	Symbolic Interactionism: An Introduction	18,950	$125	$2,368,750	1,654	$163	$269,602	$2,638,352
98	Social Psychology	Symbolic Interactionism	Symbolic Interactionism: Brief Edition	15,768	$95	$1,497,960	143	$124	$17,732	$1,515,692
99	Social Psychology Total			125,661			4,530			$14,294,244
100	Grand Total			1,119,529			33,219			$120,233,644

FIGURE 3 Subtotaled Data

In Figure 3, the Subtotal command calculates the number of books sold in the Units Sold Wholesale, Units Sold Retail, and the Total Book Sales columns for each discipline. Adding subtotals helps identify which disciplines contribute the highest revenue for the company and which disciplines produce the lowest revenue. You can then analyze the data to determine whether to continue publishing books in high revenue-generating areas or discontinue the publication of books in low-selling areas.

The publisher sold 97,852 wholesale books in the Social Problems discipline compared to 203,707 wholesale books in the Research/Stats discipline, indicating that the number of Research/Stats books sold was more than double the number of Social Problems books sold. A grand total row is inserted at the end of the dataset to indicate that 1,119,529 total wholesale books were sold.

For each subtotal row, Excel inserts a **SUBTOTAL function**, a math & trig function that calculates a subtotal for values contained in a specified range. Cell F90 contains =SUBTOTAL(9,F80:F89) to sum the number of books sold contained in the range F80:F89. The first argument indicates which summary function is used to calculate the subtotal. In this case, the argument 9 sums all values in the range specified in the second argument. Excel inserts the function and its arguments automatically so that you do not have to memorize what the arguments represent. Table 1 lists some of the summary functions and their respective argument values.

TABLE 1	SUBTOTAL Function_Num Argument
Summary Function	**Argument**
AVERAGE	1
COUNT	2
COUNTA	3
MAX	4
MIN	5
SUM	9

Pearson Education, Inc.

Add a Second Level of Subtotals

You can add a second level of subtotals to a dataset. Adding a second level preserves the primary subtotals and adds another level of subtotals for subcategories. For example, you might want to display subtotals for each discipline and the areas within each discipline for the sociology books.

To add a second level of subtotals, complete the following steps:

1. Perform a two-level sort based on primary and secondary categorical data.
2. Click the Data tab and click Subtotal in the Outline group.
3. Click the *At a change in* arrow and specify the column that was used for the secondary sort.
4. Select the function and columns to be subtotaled.
5. Click the *Replace current subtotals* check box to deselect it and click OK.

TIP: REMOVING SUBTOTALS

The subtotal rows are temporary. To remove the rows of subtotals, display the Subtotals dialog box and click Remove All.

Collapse and Expand the Subtotals

The Subtotal command creates an *outline*, a hierarchical structure of data that you can group related data to summarize. When a dataset has been grouped into an outline, you can *collapse* the outlined data to show only main rows, such as subtotals, or expand the outlined data to show all the details. Table 2 explains the outline symbols that appear on the left side of the subtotaled data. Figure 4 shows a dataset that is collapsed to display the discipline subtotals and the grand total after clicking 2. The number of outline symbols depends on the total number of subtotals created. If two subtotal levels are applied, four outline symbols display. Clicking the last number displays the entire list. You can *expand* the dataset to display the detailed rows in the subtotaled or outlined dataset.

TABLE 2 Outline Symbols

Symbol	Description
1	Collapses outline to display the grand total only.
2	Displays subtotals by the main subtotal category and the grand total.
3	Displays the entire list.
+	Expands an outline group to see its details.
–	Collapses an outline group to see its category name only.

Pearson Education, Inc.

Click outline symbol 2 to show category subtotals and grand total

Expand a particular area to show its details

		Discipline	Area	Book Title	Units Sold Wholesale	Unit Price Wholesale	Sales: Wholesale	Units Sold Retail	Unit Price Retail	Sales: Retail	Total Book Sales
14		Aging/Death Total			125,663		$ 12,614,035	1,859		$ 255,643	$ 12,869,678
21		Criminal Justice Total			66,559		$ 6,821,065	4,251		$ 618,750	$ 7,439,815
29		Family Total			76,710		$ 8,049,170	2,849		$ 441,967	$ 8,491,137
42		Introductory Total			179,415		$ 17,221,537	5,259		$ 654,714	$ 17,876,251
48		Miscellaneous Total			37,117		$ 3,179,795	1,838		$ 247,268	$ 3,427,063
63		Race/Class/Gender Total			206,845		$ 22,072,575	6,150		$ 919,953	$ 22,992,528
79		Research/Stats Total			203,707		$ 21,273,970	5,452		$ 817,731	$ 22,091,701
90		Social Problems Total			97,852		$ 10,615,950	1,031		$ 135,277	$ 10,751,227
99		Social Psychology Total			125,661		$ 13,586,235	4,530		$ 708,009	$ 14,294,244
100		Grand Total			1,119,529		$115,434,332	33,219		$ 4,799,312	$120,233,644
101											

Excel 2016, Windows 10, Microsoft Corporation

FIGURE 4 Subtotaled Data Collapsed

Grouping and Ungrouping Data

STEP 4 The Subtotals command outlines data into categories by rows. You can create outlines by columns of related data as well. For Excel to outline by columns, the dataset must contain columns with formulas or aggregate functions. If Excel cannot create the outline, it displays the message box *Cannot create an outline.*

To create an outline by columns, complete the following steps:

1. Click the Data tab.
2. Click the Group arrow in the Outline group.
3. Select Auto Outline.

For more control in creating an outline, you can create groups. *Grouping* is the process of joining rows or columns of related data together into a single entity so that groups can be collapsed or expanded for data analysis. After you create groups in the dataset, you can click a collapse button – to collapse a group to show the outside column or click the expand button + to expand groups of related columns to view the internal columns of data. Grouping enables you to hide raw data while you focus on key calculated results.

To group subtotaled data, complete the following steps:

1. Select the rows or columns you want to group. For column groups, you often select columns containing details but not aggregate columns, such as totals or averages. (Rows are automatically grouped if you use the Subtotals feature.)
2. Click the Data tab.
3. Click Group in the Outline group. If the Group dialog box opens, click *Rows* to group the data by rows or click *Columns* to group the data by columns. Click OK.

In Figure 5, the data is grouped by columns. Because the Units Sold Retail and Unit Price Retail columns are grouped, click – above Sales: Retail to collapse the columns and focus on the Sales: Retail column. Click + above the Sales: Wholesale column to expand (display) the related wholesale columns.

FIGURE 5 Grouped Data

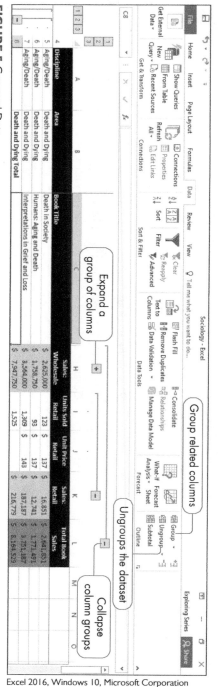

Discipline	Area	Book Title	Sales: Wholesale	Units Sold Retail	Unit Price Retail	Sales: Retail	Total Book Sales
Aging/Death	Death and Dying	Death in Society	$ 2,625,000	123	$ 137	$ 16,851	$ 2,641,851
Aging/Death	Death and Dying	Humans: Aging and Death	$ 1,758,750	93	$ 137	$ 12,741	$ 1,771,491
Aging/Death	Death and Dying	Interpretations in Grief and Loss	$ 3,564,000	1,309	$ 143	$ 187,187	$ 3,751,187
Death and Dying Total			$ 7,947,750	1,525		$ 216,779	$ 8,164,529

Expand a group of columns

Group related columns

Ungroups the dataset

Collapse column groups

Quick Concepts

1. Discuss why a dataset must be sorted by a category before using the Subtotal feature.

2. Describe the two arguments used in the SUBTOTAL function.

3. What is the purpose of grouping and outlining columns in a worksheet?

TIP: REMOVING GROUPS

To remove groups, select all grouped columns or rows and click Ungroup in the Outline group on the Data tab.

Subtotals, PivotTables, and PivotCharts

Hands-On Exercises

Skills covered: Sort Multiple Fields • Subtotal Data • Add a Second Subtotal • Collapse and Expand the Subtotals • Group Data • Ungroup Data

1 Subtotals and Outlines

As vice president of the Sociology Division, you want to analyze your textbook publications. Each textbook falls within a general discipline, and each discipline is divided into several areas. The company tracks units sold, unit prices, and gross sales by two major types of sales: (1) wholesale sales to bookstores and (2) retail sales to individual customers. Your assistant applied Freeze Panes to keep the column headings in row 4 and the disciplines and areas in columns A and B visible regardless of where you scroll.

STEP 1 ≫ SUBTOTAL DATA BASED ON THE PRIMARY SORT

Before you use the Subtotal command, you must sort the data by discipline and then by area. After sorting the data, you will insert subtotals for each discipline. You want to see the totals for the wholesale sales, retail sales, and total book sales. Refer to Figure 6 as you complete Step 1.

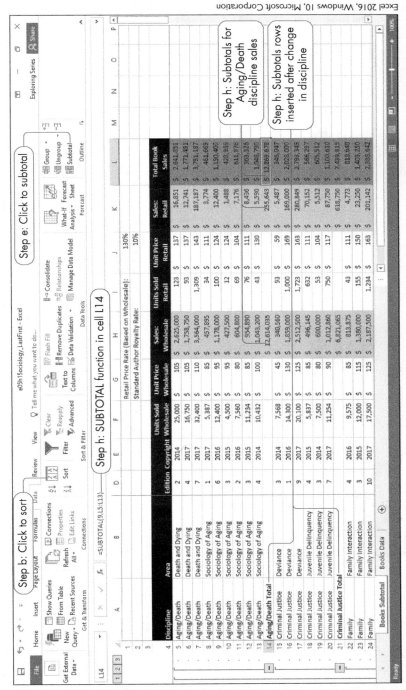

FIGURE 6 Discipline Subtotal Rows

a. Open *e05h1Sociology* and save it as **e05h1Sociology_LastFirst.**

> **TROUBLESHOOTING:** If you make any major mistakes in this exercise, you can close the file, open *e05h1Sociology* again, and then start this exercise over.

The workbook contains two worksheets: Books Subtotal for Hands-On Exercise 1 and Books Data for Hands-On Exercises 2–3.

b. Click the **Data tab** and click **Sort** in the Sort & Filter group.

c. Click the **Sort by arrow** and select **Discipline** in the Sort dialog box.

Hands-On Exercise 1

d. Click **Add Level**, click the **Then by arrow**, and then select **Area**. Click **OK**.

Excel sorts the data by discipline in alphabetical order. Within each discipline, Excel sorts the data further by area. The data are sorted first by disciplines so that you can apply subtotals to each discipline.

e. Click **Subtotal** in the Outline group.

The Subtotal dialog box opens. The default *At each change in* is the Discipline column, and the default *Use function* is Sum. These settings are correct.

f. Click the **Sales: Wholesale check box** to select it in the *Add subtotal to* section.

g. Click the **Sales: Retail check box** to select it in the *Add subtotal to* section.

Excel selected the last column—Total Book Sales—automatically. You selected the other two sales columns to total. Leave the *Replace current subtotals* and *Summary below data* check boxes selected.

h. Click **OK**.

Excel inserts subtotal rows after each discipline category. The subtotal rows include discipline labels and subtotals for the Sales: Wholesale, Sales: Retail, and Total Book Sales columns.

i. Scroll to the right to see the subtotals and click **cell L14**. Save the workbook

Cell L14 contains the SUBTOTAL function for the total book sales for the Aging/Death discipline. The first argument, 9, indicates the SUM function, and L5:L13 is the range of data (all books on Aging/Death) being subtotaled.

> **TROUBLESHOOTING:** If your subtotals do not match the totals in Figure 6, open the Subtotal dialog box, click Remove All, click OK, and repeat steps b through i again.

STEP 2 ❯❯ ADD A SECOND SUBTOTAL

Now you want to add another level to see subtotals for each area within each discipline. You already added subtotals for the primary category (Discipline). Now you will add a subtotal to the second category (Area). When you use the Subtotal dialog box, you will keep the original subtotals intact. Refer to Figure 7 as you complete Step 2.

a. Click **Subtotal** in the Outline group to open the Subtotal dialog box again.

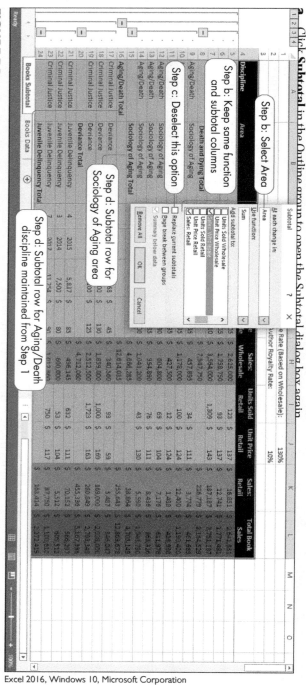

Step b: Select Area

Step b: Keep same function and subtotal columns

Step c: Deselect this option

Step d: Subtotal row for Sociology of Aging area

Step d: Subtotal row for Aging/Death discipline maintained from Step 1

FIGURE 7 Discipline and Area Subtotal Rows

Excel 2016, Windows 10, Microsoft Corporation

b. Click the **At each change in arrow** and select **Area**.

Use function is still Sum, and Excel remembers the last columns you selected in the *Add subtotal to* section—Sales: Wholesale, Sales: Retail, and Total Book Sales.

c. Click the **Replace current subtotals check box** to deselect it.

Deselecting this check box will keep the discipline subtotals.

d. Click **OK** and click cell **L15**. Save the workbook.

Excel inserts subtotal rows after each area. The Formula Bar displays =SUBTOTAL(9,L9:L14). Your data have discipline subtotals and area subtotals within each discipline.

TROUBLESHOOTING: If you subtotal the area first and then the disciplines, Excel adds several discipline subtotals, which repeat the area subtotals. That is why you must subtotal by the primary category first and then subtotal by the secondary category.

STEP 3 **COLLAPSE AND EXPAND THE SUBTOTALS**

You want to compare wholesale, retail, and book sales among the disciplines and then among areas within a discipline. Refer to Figure 8 as you complete Step 3.

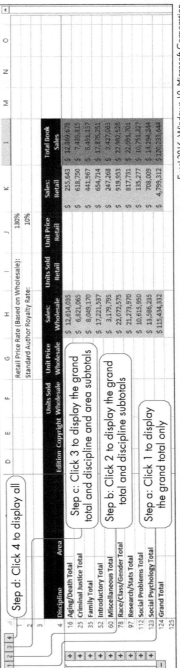

FIGURE 8 Collapsed Subtotals at Level 2

Excel 2016, Windows 10, Microsoft Corporation

a. Click the **1 outline symbol** in the top-left outline area (to the left of the column headings).

You collapsed the outline to show the grand totals only for wholesale, retail, and total book sales.

b. Click the **2 outline symbol** in the top-left outline area (see Figure 8).

You expanded the outline to show the grand and discipline subtotals. Which two disciplines had the highest wholesale and retail sales? Which discipline had the lowest total sales?

c. Click the **3 outline symbol** in the top-left outline area.

You expanded the outline to show the grand, discipline, and area subtotals. Within the Introductory discipline, which area had the lowest sales? How do wholesale and retail sales compare? Are they proportionally the same within each area?

d. Click the **4 outline symbol** in the top-left outline area. Save the workbook.

You expanded the outline to show all details again. If you had not added the second subtotal, the outline would have had three levels instead of four.

Hands-On Exercise 1   413

You want to apply an outline to the columns so that you can collapse or expand the Units Sold and Unit Price columns. Refer to Figure 9 as you complete Step 4.

STEP 4)) GROUP AND UNGROUP DATA

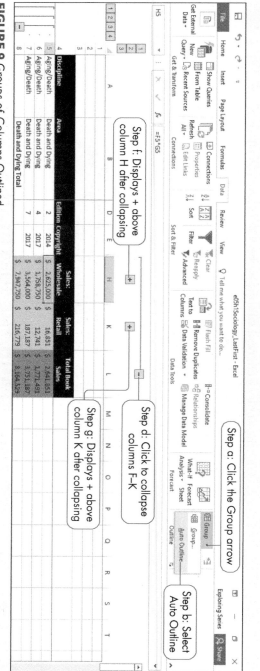

FIGURE 9 Groups of Columns Outlined

Excel 2016, Windows 10, Microsoft Corporation

a. Click the **Group arrow** in the Outline group on the Data tab.

You want to see if Excel can create a column outline for you so that you do not have to select columns and group them individually.

b. Select **Auto Outline.**

Excel displays the message box *Modify existing outline?* because it recognizes that an existing outline exists—the row subtotals outline.

c. Click **OK.**

Excel maintains the outlined subtotal rows and adds outlines the columns. Horizontal lines and collapse buttons appear above the columns that contain formulas (columns H, K, and L). The formula in cell H5 is =F5*G5, so Excel creates an outline to group columns F, G, and H. The formula in cell K5 is =I5*J5, so Excel creates an outline to group columns I, J, and K. It also creates a higher-level outline of columns F through K, because the formula in column L sums the values in columns H and K.

d. Click the **collapse button** above column L.

You collapsed columns F through K to display disciplines, areas, and total sales by title.

e. Click the **expand button** above column L.

You expanded the outline to show columns F through K again.

f. Click the **collapse button** above column H.

You collapsed the outline to hide columns F and G so you can focus on the wholesale sales without the distraction of the Units Sold or Unit Price columns.

g. Click the **collapse button** above column K.

You collapsed the outline to hide columns I and J so you can focus on the retail sales without the distraction of the Units Sold or Unit Price columns.

h. Save the workbook. Keep the workbook open if you plan to continue with the next Hands-On Exercise. If not, save and close the workbook, and exit Excel.

PivotTable Basics

Analyzing large amounts of data is important for making solid business decisions. Entering data is the easy part; retrieving data in a structured, meaningful way is more challenging. *Data mining* is the process of analyzing large volumes of data, using advanced statistical techniques, and identifying trends and patterns in the data. Managers use data-mining techniques to address a variety of questions, such as the following:

- What snack foods do customers purchase most when purchasing Pepsi® products?
- What age group from what geographic region downloads the most top 10 songs from iTunes?
- What hotel chain and rental car combinations are most popular among Delta Air Lines passengers flying into Salt Lake City?

Questions similar to those above help organizations prepare their marketing plans to capitalize on consumer spending patterns. The more you know about your customer demographics, the better you can focus your strategic plans to increase market share.

A *PivotTable report*, commonly referred to as a *PivotTable*, is an interactive table that uses calculations to consolidate and summarize data from a data source into a separate table. PivotTables enable you to analyze data in a dataset without altering the dataset itself. PivotTables are dynamic: You can easily and quickly pivot, or rearrange, data to analyze data from different viewpoints. Looking at data from different perspectives helps identify trends and patterns among the variables that might not be obvious from looking at hundreds or thousands of rows of data yourself.

In this section, you will create a PivotTable. You will learn how to organize and group data into rows and columns, remove and rearrange fields, and change the settings for value fields.

Creating a PivotTable

Before you create a PivotTable, ensure that the data source is well structured by applying the rules for good table design. Use meaningful column labels, ensure data accuracy, and avoid blank rows and columns in the dataset. At least one column must have duplicate values, such as the same discipline or area name for several records, to create categories for organizing and summarizing data. Another column must have numeric values that can be aggregated to produce quantitative summaries, such as averages or sums.

TIP: PIVOTTABLE OR SUBTOTALS?

PivotTables are similar to subtotals because they both produce subtotals, but PivotTables provide more flexibility than subtotals. If you need complex subtotals cross-referenced by two or more categories with filtering and other specifications, create a PivotTable. Furthermore, using the Subtotals command inserts subtotals rows within the dataset, whereas creating a PivotTable does not change the dataset.

Create a Recommended PivotTable

STEP 1 ⟫ You can create a PivotTable from the Quick Analysis gallery or from the Recommended PivotTables command in the Tables group on the Insert tab. One benefit of these methods is that Excel displays previews of recommended PivotTables based on the data in the dataset. Creating a recommended PivotTable is beneficial when you first start using PivotTables so that you can see potential ways to depict the dataset before starting to create PivotTables from scratch.

Subtotals, PivotTables, and PivotCharts

To create a PivotTable using Quick Analysis, complete the following steps:

1. Right-click within a dataset and select Quick Analysis on the shortcut menu.
2. Click Tables in the Quick Analysis gallery.
3. Point to a PivotTable thumbnail to see a preview of the different recommended PivotTables (see Figure 10).
4. Click a PivotTable thumbnail to create the desired PivotTable.

To create a PivotTable from the Recommended PivotTables dialog box, complete the following steps:

1. Click inside the dataset (the range of cells or table).
2. Click the Insert tab and click Recommended PivotTables in the Tables group to open the Recommended PivotTables dialog box (see Figure 11).
3. Point to a thumbnail in the gallery on the left side of the dialog box to display a preview of the PivotTable on the right side.
4. Click a thumbnail to select it and click OK to create the desired PivotTable.

Discipline	Area	Book Title	Edition	Copyright	Units Sold Wholesale	Unit Price Wholesale
Social Psychology	General	Modern Perspectives on Social Psychology	1	2017	25,983	$ 115
Research/Stats	Social Statistics	Statistics for Social Sciences	2	2014	7,550	$ 115
Race/Class/Gender	Race/Ethnicity	America: Diversity in Race and Ethnicity	10			
Research/Stats	Data Analysis	Using SPSS for Research in Sociology	7			
Research/Stats	Social Statistics	Introductory Statistics in Social Research	8	2016	23,575	$ 125
Social Problems	General	Current Social Problems	10	2016	20,300	$ 115
Introductory	Social Sciences	Modern Approach to Social Science: Brief	8	2017	7,340	$ 75
Social Problems	Alcohol/Drugs	Current Trends in Alcohol and Drug Abuse	3	2017	4,500	$ 90
Aging/Death	Sociology of Aging	Human Ages	3	2015	4,500	$ 95
Aging/Death	Death and Dying	Death in Society	2	2014	25,000	$ 105
Aging/Death	Sociology of Aging	The Aging Process	4	2014	10,432	$ 100
Introductory	Conflict Approach	Conflicts in Society: Brief Edition	4	2017	2,750	$ 55
Social Problems	Conflict Approach	A Conflict Approach to Social Problems	3	2014	3,500	$ 75
Introductory	General	Sociology: An Introduction	8	2016	32,123	$ 95
Criminal Justice	Juvenile Delinquency	An Introduction to Juvenile Delinquency	4	2015	5,837	$ 85
Race/Class/Gender	Gender Issues	Social Constructs for Men and Women	8	2016	18,730	$ 120
Race/Class/Gender	Human Sexuality	America: Diversity in Sexuality	2	2015	5,575	$ 75
Miscellaneous	Social Change	Solutions to Our Social Problems	4	2015		
Criminal Justice	Deviance	Deviant Behavior	1	2014	8,500	$ 80
Race/Class/Gender	Human Sexuality	Sexuality Around the Globe	4	2014	5,321	$ 65
Social Psychology	Symbolic Interactionism	Looking at Self and Society	3	2014	8,500	$ 65
Family	Marriage and Family	Diversity and Change in Today's Marriages	7	2016	14,358	$ 90
Miscellaneous	Social Change	Global Concerns of Society	2	2014	4,500	$ 55

Books Subtotal · Books Data · Books

Ready · Average: $124,001.6439 · Count: 1044 · Sum: 2418131314 · 100%

FIGURE 10 Quick Analysis Gallery to Create a Recommended PivotTable

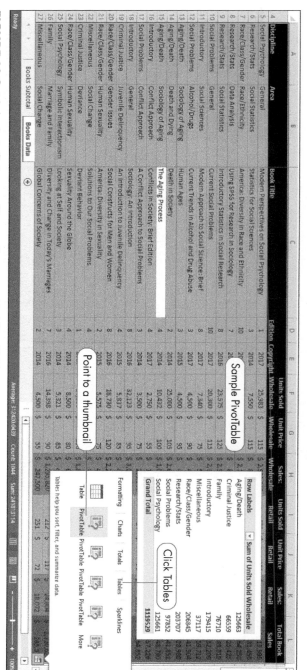

Sample PivotTable

Point to a thumbnail

Click Tables

Excel 2016, Windows 10, Microsoft Corporation

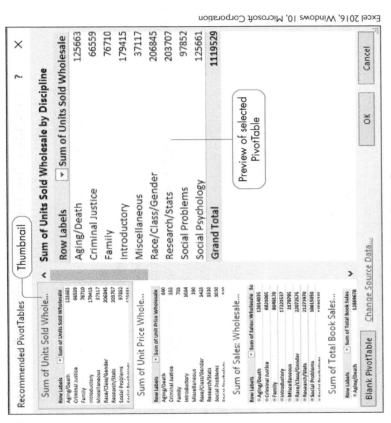

FIGURE 11 Recommended PivotTable Dialog Box

When you select a PivotTable, Excel creates a PivotTable on a new worksheet (see Figure 12) to the left of the worksheet containing the dataset. The **PivotTable Fields List**, a task pane that displays the list of fields in a dataset and areas to place the fields to create the layout to organize data in columns, rows, values, and filters in a PivotTable, displays on the right side of the worksheet. In addition, the Ribbon displays the PivotTable Tools Analyze and Design tabs. If you click outside the PivotTable, the contextual tabs and PivotTable Fields List are no longer displayed. Click within the PivotTable to display these elements again.

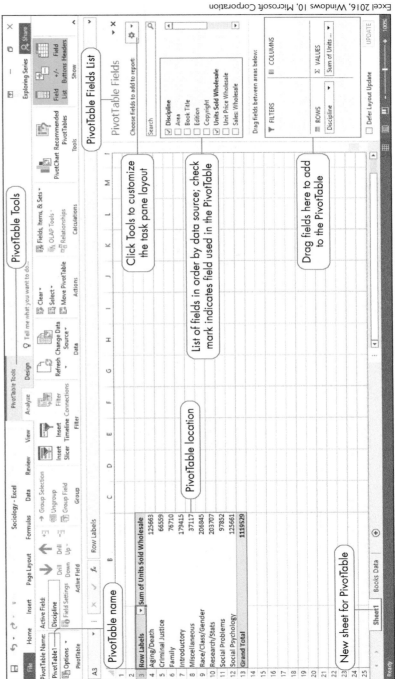

FIGURE 12 Recommended PivotTable

TIP: PIVOTTABLE FIELDS LIST

If the PivotTable Fields List does not appear when you click inside a PivotTable, click Field List in the Show group on the Analyze tab. This command is a toggle, so you can click it to show or hide the PivotTable Fields List.

The PivotTable Fields List contains two sections. The top section contains a list of the fields or column labels contained in the dataset. For example, Figure 12 shows the fields (column labels), such as Discipline, that are contained on row 4 in the Books Data worksheet. The fields are listed in the same order as the original data source; however, you can click Tools and select Sort A to Z to list the fields in alphabetical order in the PivotTable Fields List. If the data source has several fields, scroll through the list or click in the Search box and type a name of a field to find. For example, Figure 12 shows only 7 of the 12 fields from the dataset. You can type Total Book Sales to search for that field.

The bottom section of the PivotTable Fields List contains four areas where you can place fields to organize the layout of the PivotTable. Table 3 describes the four areas of a PivotTable.

TABLE 3 Areas of a PivotTable

Area	Description
FILTERS Area	Displays top-level filters above the PivotTable so that you can set filters to display results based on particular conditions you set. For example, if you drag the Edition field to the FILTERS area, you can then set a filter to display sales for a particular edition, such as for first editions.
COLUMNS Area	Displays columns of summarized data for the selected field(s). For example, if you drag Copyright to the COLUMNS area, the PivotTable displays one column of data for each unique copyright year contained in the dataset.
ROWS Area	Groups the data into categories in the first column based on the selected field(s). For example, the Discipline field is placed in the ROWS area. Each unique discipline label (such as Family) is listed only one time in alphabetical order in the first column regardless how many times the label is present in the original dataset. These labels identify the content on each row.
VALUES Area	Displays summary statistics, such as totals or averages, for the selected field. For example, the Units Sold Wholesale field is selected to calculate the total wholesale units sold for each discipline. The default function is SUM for quantitative fields, such as Units Sold Wholesale. If you select a field containing labels, such as Book Title, the default function is COUNT to count the number of book titles within each discipline.

TIP: NAMING A PIVOTTABLE

A best practice is to assign a name to a PivotTable, such as Wholesale Units Sold by Discipline because the default name such as PivotTable1 is not meaningful. Furthermore, it is a good practice to name a PivotTable so that the workbook is accessibility compliant for people who have disabilities, such as vision or cognitive impairments, that may prevent them from seeing or comprehending the visual aid. To name a PivotTable, click within the PivotTable and type a name in the PivotTable Name box in the PivotTable group on the Analyze tab.

Create a Blank PivotTable

Instead of using a recommended PivotTable, you can create a blank or empty PivotTable so that you can specify the data you want to analyze and where you want the PivotTable to be placed. With this method, you are not restricted to a current dataset within an Excel worksheet; you can specify an external data source such as data on a company's database server or data on a Web page. Furthermore, you can place the PivotTable on a new worksheet or on an existing worksheet.

To create a blank PivotTable, complete the following steps:

1. Click the Insert tab and click PivotTable in the Tables group to open the Create PivotTable dialog box.

2. Select the data that you want to analyze (table or range within the open workbook or a connection to an external dataset).

3. Select where you want to place the PivotTable: New Worksheet or Existing Worksheet. If you click Existing Worksheet, then specify the sheet tab name in the Location box.

4. Click OK to create the PivotTable.

The PivotTable Tools Analyze and Design tabs display, the PivotTable Fields List displays on the right side, and a blank PivotTable is located on the left side (see Figure 13). The PivotTable layout is developed when you drag fields to the areas in the PivotTable Fields List.

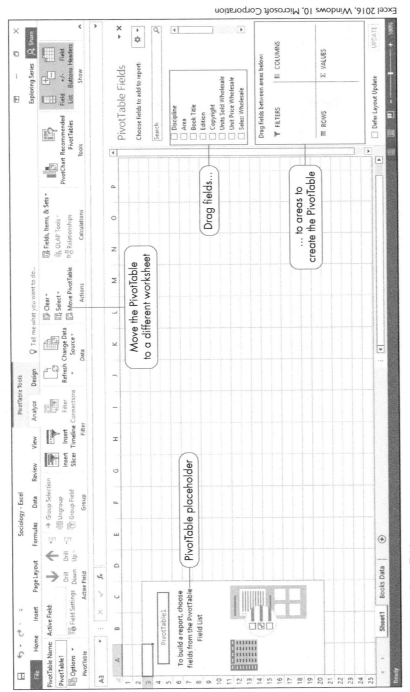

Excel 2016, Windows 10, Microsoft Corporation

FIGURE 13 Blank PivotTable

TIP: MOVE A PIVOTTABLE

After creating a PivotTable, you might want to move it to another worksheet. To move a PivotTable, click within the PivotTable, click Move PivotTable in the Actions group on the Analyze tab to open the Move PivotTable dialog box. Click New Worksheet or click Existing Worksheet and specify the existing sheet name and the cell in the top-left corner to locate the PivotTable, and then click OK.

Modifying a PivotTable

After you create a PivotTable, you might want to modify it to see the data from a different perspective. For example, you might want to add fields to the ROWS, COLUMNS, and VALUES areas in a PivotTable. In addition, you might want to collapse the PivotTable to show fewer details or expand it to show more details.

Add Rows to a PivotTable

You can add one or more fields to the PivotTable to provide a more detailed analysis. The sequence of the fields within the ROWS area dictates the hierarchy. For example, you might want to show the Areas within each Discipline for the Ivory Halls textbook list. To show this hierarchy, list the Discipline field first and Area field second in the ROWS area (see Figure 14).

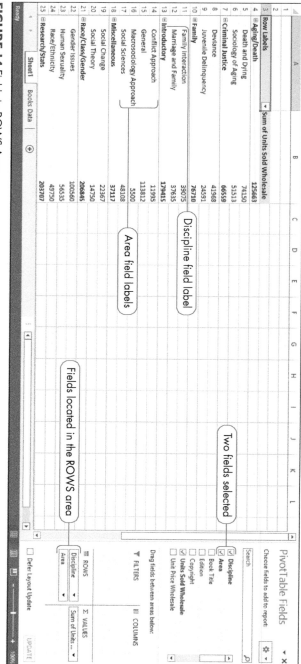

FIGURE 14 Fields in ROWS Area

Excel 2016, Windows 10, Microsoft Corporation

To add a field as a row, complete one of the following steps:

- Click the field's check box to select it in the *Choose fields to add to report* section. Excel adds the field to a PivotTable based on the type of data stored in the field. If the field contains text, Excel usually places that field in the ROWS area.

- Drag the field from the *Choose fields to add to report* section and drop it in the ROWS area.

- Right-click the field name in the *Choose fields to add to report* section and select *Add to Row Labels*.

Add Values in a PivotTable

A PivotTable has meaning when you include quantitative fields, such as quantities and monetary values, to aggregate the data. You can add other quantitative fields. For example, you might want to add the Book Titles and Sales: Wholesale fields (see Figure 15). Excel sums the values for each field listed in the ROWS area. For example, the total number of units sold wholesale for the Family discipline is 76,710, and the total wholesale sales revenue is $8,049,170. If you place a text field, such as Book Title, in the VALUES area, Excel counts the number of records for each group listed in the ROWS area. In this case, Excel counts seven books in the Family discipline.

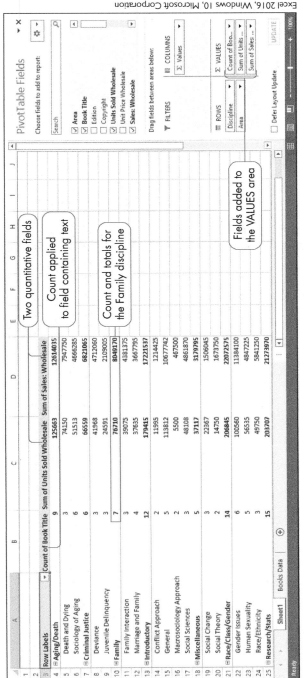

FIGURE 15 Fields in VALUES Area

To add values to the PivotTable, complete one of the following steps:

- Click the field's check box to select it in the *Choose fields to add to report* section. Excel makes the value an aggregate, such as *Sum of Sales*.
- Drag the field from the *Choose fields to add to report* section and drop it in the VALUES area.
- Right-click the field name in the *Choose fields to add to report* section and select *Add to Values*.

Add Columns to a PivotTable

Although you can create subdivisions of data by adding more fields to the ROWS area, you might want to arrange the subdivision categories in columns. Doing so minimizes the redundancy of duplicating subdivision row labels and helps consolidate data. To subdivide data into columns, drag a field from the *Choose fields to add to report* section and drop it in the COLUMNS area. Excel updates the aggregated values by the combination of row and column categories.

Figure 16 shows a PivotTable that uses the Discipline field as rows, the *Sum of Units Sold Wholesale* field as values, and Copyright field as columns. Each discipline label and each copyright year label appears only once in the PivotTable. This added level of detail enables you to see the total sales for each discipline based on its copyright year. The PivotTable includes grand totals for each discipline and grand totals for each year.

Collapse and Expand Items in a PivotTable

If you include two or more fields as ROWS, the PivotTable displays more depth but may be overwhelming. You can hide or collapse the secondary field rows, as needed. For example, if the PivotTable contains both Discipline and Area row labels, you might want to collapse areas for some disciplines. The collapse and expand buttons display to the left of the row labels (see Figure 17). If the buttons do not display, click +/– Buttons in the Show group on the Analyze tab.

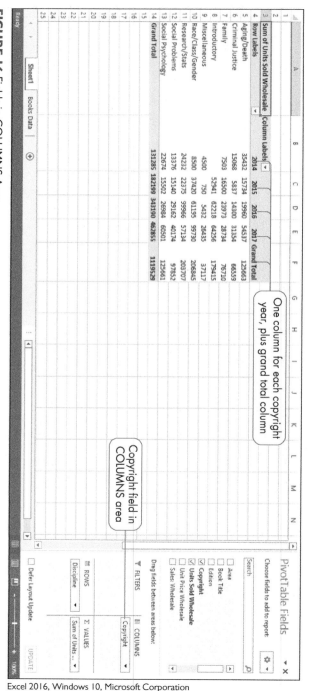

One column for each copyright year, plus grand total column

Copyright field in COLUMNS area

FIGURE 16 Fields in COLUMNS Area

Excel 2016, Windows 10, Microsoft Corporation

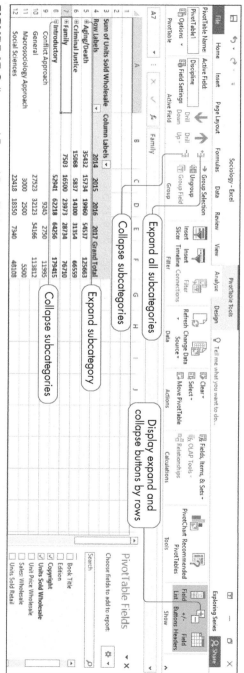

Collapse subcategories

Expand all subcategories

Collapse subcategories

Expand subcategory

Collapse subcategories

Display expand and collapse buttons by rows

FIGURE 17 Collapse and Expand PivotTable

Excel 2016, Windows 10, Microsoft Corporation

To collapse or expand a category, complete one of the following steps:

- Click the collapse button ☐ on the left side of the specific category you want to collapse. Excel hides the subcategories for that particular category and shows only the aggregated totals for the category. Continue collapsing other categories as needed to focus on a particular category's details.
- Click the expand button ☐ on the left side of the category labels to expand the subcategories again.

Remove Fields from a PivotTable

STEP 3

As you continue adding and arranging fields, the PivotTable may contain too much data to be useful or the needs have changed, making it necessary to remove fields. You can remove fields to reduce the amount of data to analyze.

To remove a field from the PivotTable, complete one of the following steps:

- Click the field name in the *Drag fields between areas below* section and select Remove Field.
- Click the check box next to the field name to deselect it in the *Choose fields to add to report* section.
- Drag a field name in the *Drag fields between areas below* section outside the PivotTable Fields List.

Rearrange Fields in a PivotTable

A primary benefit of creating a PivotTable is that you can rearrange (or pivot) fields to view and summarize data from different perspectives. PivotTables provide ease and flexibility in changing the layout and level of depth depicted. As you rearrange the fields within the four areas, you gain a different perspective on the data and provide an easier layout to interpret the data. You might want to pivot the data by moving a field from the COLUMNS area to the ROWS area. As you move fields from one area to another in the PivotTable Fields List, the PivotTable immediately reflects the new layout. For example, your PivotTable might include the Discipline and Copyright fields in the ROWS so that you can view details for each discipline by copyright year. You might want to move the Copyright field to the COLUMNS area to provide a more distinct analysis of revenue for each discipline by copyright year.

To move a field from one PivotTable area to another, complete one of the following steps:

- Drag the field in the *Drag fields between areas below* section.
- Click the field arrow within the area and select Move to Report Filter, Move to Row Labels, Move to Column Labels, or Move to Values.

You can also move a field within its area. Table 4 explains the Move options.

TABLE 4 Move Options

Option	Moves the Field . . .
Move Up	Up one position in the hierarchy within the same area
Move Down	Down one position in the hierarchy within the same area
Move to Beginning	To the beginning of all fields in the same area
Move to End	To the end of all fields in the same area
Move to Report Filter	To the end of the FILTERS area of the PivotTable
Move to Row Labels	To the end of the ROWS area of the PivotTable
Move to Column Labels	To the end of the COLUMNS area of the PivotTable
Move to Values	To the end of the VALUES area of the PivotTable

STEP 4

Change the Values Field Settings

Excel uses the SUM function as the default summary statistic for numerical fields and COUNT as the default statistic for text field. However, you can select a different function for numerical fields. For example, you might want to calculate the average, lowest, or highest value within each group, or identify the lowest sales for each discipline/copyright year combination to see if the older books have decreased sales.

In addition to changing the summary statistic, you might want to change the column label that appears above the summary statistic. By default, words indicate the summary statistic function applied, such as *Sum of Total Sales by Book* or *Average of Total Sales by Book*, depending on the summary statistic applied to the values. Finally, you might need to format the aggregated values.

To modify any of these value settings, complete the following steps:

1. Click a value in the appropriate field in the PivotTable and click Field Settings in the Active Field group on the Analyze tab. Alternatively, click the field's arrow in the VALUES area of the PivotTable Fields List and select Value Field Settings. The Value Field Settings dialog box opens (see Figure 18).

2. Type the name you want to appear as the column label in the Custom Name box. For example, you might want the heading to appear as *Total Sales* instead of *Sum of Total Book Sales*.

3. Select the summary statistical function you want to use to summarize the values in the *Summarize value field by* list.

4. Click Number Format to open an abbreviated version of the Format Cells dialog box. Select a number type, such as Accounting, in the Category list; select other settings, such as number of decimal places in the *Decimal places* box; and then click OK.

5. Click OK in the Value Field Settings dialog box.

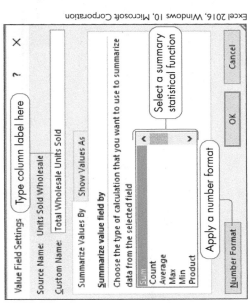

FIGURE 18 Value Field Settings Dialog Box

TIP: MULTIPLE SUMMARY STATISTICS

You can display more than one function for a field. For example, you might want to show both the total book sales and the average book sales. To display multiple summary statistics, drag another copy of the same field to the VALUES area and set each value setting separately.

Refresh a PivotTable

STEP 5 ▶▶ Although PivotTables are powerful, they are not automatically updated if you make any changes to the underlying data in the data source. For example, if you change a sales value or delete a row in the data source, the PivotTable does not reflect the changed data. Unfortunately, this causes PivotTable summary statistics to become outdated with inaccurate results.

To update the PivotTable, complete the following steps:

1. Click in the PivotTable.
2. Click the Analyze tab.
3. Click Refresh in the Data group to refresh the current PivotTable only, or click the Refresh arrow and select Refresh All to refresh all PivotTables in the workbook.

PivotTables should be current when you open a workbook. However, you can specify a setting to ensure that the PivotTables are updated when you open a workbook containing PivotTables.

To ensure PivotTables are up to date when you open a workbook, complete the following steps:

1. Click the Analyze tab.
2. Click the Options in the PivotTable group to open the PivotTable Options dialog box.
3. Click the Data tab, select the *Refresh data when opening the file* check box, and then click OK.

TIP: CHANGE THE DATA SOURCE

To change the data source used to create the PivotTable, click Change Data Source in the Data group on the Analyze tab, select the new range containing the data to pivot, and click OK in the Change Data Source dialog box.

Quick Concepts

4. What are the advantages of using a PivotTable instead of a subtotal?
5. What is the main benefit of creating a PivotTable using Quick Analysis or from the Recommended PivotTables dialog box over creating a blank PivotTable?
6. Describe the four areas of a PivotTable.

Hands-On Exercises

2 PivotTable Basics

After exhausting the possibilities of outlines and subtotals, you want to create a PivotTable to analyze the sociology book sales. You realize you can see the data from different perspectives, enabling you to have a stronger understanding of the sales by various categories.

Skills covered: Create a Recommended PivotTable • Rename a PivotTable • Add Rows to a PivotTable • Add Columns to a PivotTable • Remove Fields from a PivotTable • Rearrange Fields in a PivotTable • Change Value Field Settings • Refresh a PivotTable

---

STEP 1 ≫ CREATE A PIVOTTABLE

Because you want to keep the subtotals you created in the Books Subtotal worksheet, you will create a PivotTable from the Books Data worksheet. Refer to Figures 11 and 19 as you complete Step 1.

a. Open *e05h1Sociology_LastFirst* if you closed it at the end of Hands-On Exercise 1 and save it as **e05h2Sociology_LastFirst**, changing h1 to h2.

b. Click the **Books Data sheet tab**.

Excel does not let you create a PivotTable using subtotaled data. To preserve the subtotals you created in Hands-On Exercise 1, you will use the dataset in the Books Data worksheet.

c. Click **cell A5**, click the **Insert tab**, and then click **Recommended PivotTables** in the Tables group.

The Recommended PivotTables dialog box opens (refer to Figure 11).

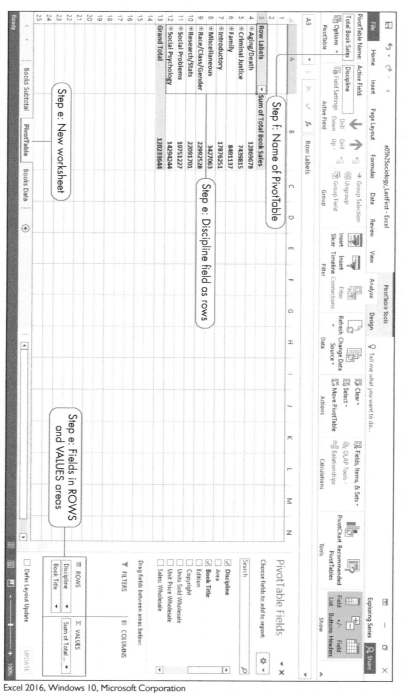

FIGURE 19 PivotTable for Total Book Sales

Excel 2016, Windows 10, Microsoft Corporation

d. Scroll the thumbnails of recommended PivotTables and click the **Sum of Total Book Sales by Discipline thumbnail.** (NOTE: Point to each thumbnail to see the full name.)

You selected this PivotTable to show the overall total book sales for each discipline. The dialog box shows a preview of the selected PivotTable.

e. Click **OK.** Rename Sheet1 as **PivotTable.**

Excel inserts a new Sheet1 worksheet, which you renamed as PivotTable, with the PivotTable on the left side and the PivotTable Fields List on the right side (see Figure 19).

f. Click the **PivotTable Name box** in the PivotTable group on the Analyze tab, type **Total Book Sales,** and then press **Enter.** Save the workbook.

You changed the name of the PivotTable from PivotTable1 to Total Book Sales to comply with accessibility standards and to give meaningful names to the PivotTables within your workbook.

STEP 2 ≫ ADD FIELDS TO ROWS AND COLUMNS

You want to compare sales combinations by discipline, copyright year, and edition. The Discipline field is already in the PivotTable, so you will add the copyright year and edition fields. Refer to Figure 20 as you complete Step 2.

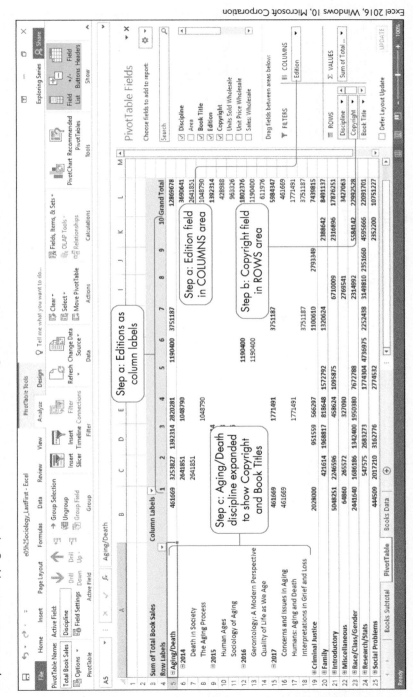

FIGURE 20 Fields Added to Rows and Columns Sales

a. Drag the **Edition field** to the COLUMNS area in the PivotTable Fields List.

Excel displays the total book sales by a combination of discipline and edition. This enables you to compare sales of current editions within each discipline. Blanks appear in the PivotTable when a discipline does not have a specific edition. For example, the Family discipline does not have any first-edition books currently being published.

b. Drag the **Copyright field** between the Discipline and Book Title fields in the ROWS area of the PivotTable Fields List.

The Copyright and Book Titles are not showing in the PivotTable because they are collapsed within the Discipline rows.

Hands-On Exercise 2

c. Click the **Aging/Death expand button** [+]. Save the workbook.

You expanded the Aging/Death discipline to show the copyright years and titles.

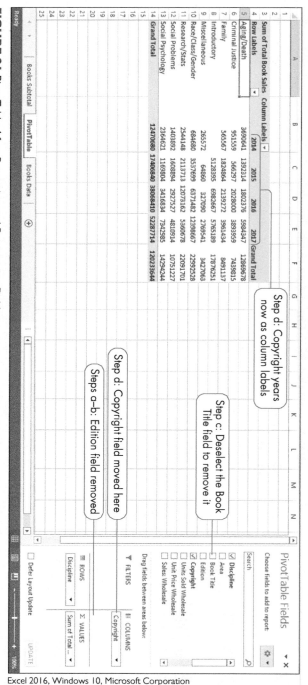

Excel 2016, Windows 10, Microsoft Corporation

STEP 3 ≫ REMOVE AND REARRANGE FIELDS

Although it is informative to compare sales by edition, you think that the PivotTable contains too much detail, so you will remove the Edition field. In addition, the ROWS area contains the Book Titles field, but those data are collapsed; therefore, you will remove it as well. After you remove the fields, you will rearrange other fields to simplify the PivotTable. Refer to Figure 21 as you complete Step 3.

FIGURE 21 PivotTable After Removing and Rearranging Fields

a. Click the **Edition arrow** in the COLUMNS area.

Excel displays a menu of options to apply to this field.

b. Select **Remove Field** on the menu.

You removed the Edition field from the PivotTable. Instead of several sales columns, Excel consolidates the sales into one sales column.

c. Click the **Book Title check box** to deselect it in the *Choose fields to add to report* section of the PivotTable Fields List.

You removed the Book Title field from the PivotTable.

d. Drag the **Copyright field** from the ROWS area to the COLUMNS area. Save the workbook.

You removed the Book Title field from the PivotTable.

This arrangement consolidates the data better. Instead of repeating the copyright years for each discipline, the copyright years are listed only once each at the top of the sales columns.

STEP 4 ▶▶ CHANGE THE VALUES FIELD SETTINGS

After selecting the PivotTable fields, you want to improve the appearance of the sociology textbook PivotTable. You will format the values with the Accounting Number Format and replace the generic Row Labels description with a label that indicates the sociology disciplines. Refer to Figure 22 as you complete Step 4.

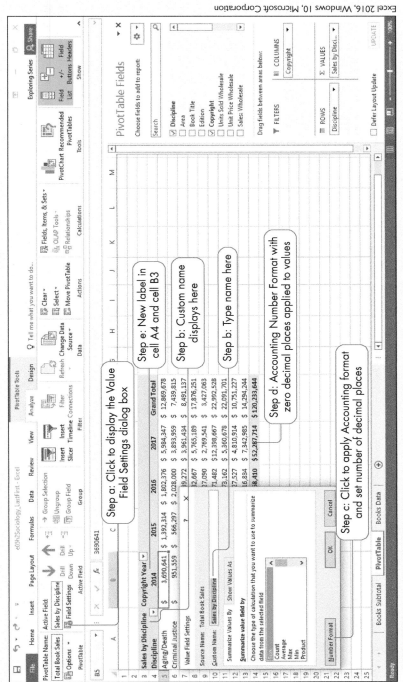

FIGURE 22 Formatted Values and Labels

a. Click **cell B5** and click **Field Settings** in the Active Field group on the Analyze tab.

The Value Field Settings dialog box opens so that you can format the field.

b. Type **Sales by Discipline** in the Custom Name box. Leave Sum as the selected calculation type in the *Summarize value field by* section.

You created a customized name for the calculated field and retained the calculation to sum the values. The Value Field Settings dialog box is still open so that you can format the field.

c. Click **Number Format.**

Excel opens a Format Cells dialog box with only the Number tab.

d. Click **Accounting** in the Category list, change the **Decimal places value** to **0**, click **OK** in the Format Cells dialog box, and then click **OK** in the Value Field Settings dialog box.

You formatted the values with Accounting Number Format with no decimal places, and the heading *Sales by Discipline* displays in cell A3.

e. Type **Discipline** in cell **A4** and type **Copyright Year** in cell **B3**.

You replaced the generic *Row Labels* heading with *Discipline* to describe the contents of the first column, and you replaced the *Column Labels* heading with *Copyright Year*. Although you can create custom names for values, you cannot create custom names for row and column labels. However, you can edit the labels directly in the cells.

f. Select the **range B4:F4** and center the labels horizontally. Save the workbook.

After consulting with the Accounting Department, you realize that the retail prices are incorrect. The unit retail prices are based on a percentage of the wholesale price. The retail unit price is 30% more than the wholesale unit price, but it should be 25%. You will edit the input cell in the original worksheet and refresh the PivotTable to see the corrected results. Refer to Figure 23 as you complete Step 5.

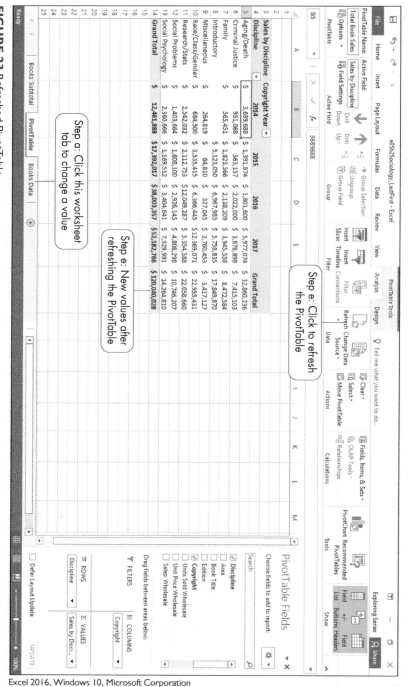

FIGURE 23 Refreshed PivotTable

a. Look at **cell F14**

The current grand total is $120,233,644.

b. Click the **Books Data sheet tab**.

You need to locate and change the retail price percentage.

c. Click **cell J1**, the cell that contains the current retail price percentage.

d. Type **125** and press **Enter**. Save the workbook.

You changed the retail price rate, which changes the results shown in columns J, K, and L in the Books Data worksheet. However, the PivotTable values are not updated yet.

e. Click the **PivotTable sheet tab**.

Notice that the PivotTable aggregate values did not change. The grand total is still $120,233,644. You must refresh the PivotTable.

f. Click the **Analyze tab** and click **Refresh** in the Data group.

Excel updates the PivotTable values based on the change you made in the Books Data worksheet. The grand total is now $120,040,028.

g. Save the workbook. Keep the workbook open if you plan to continue with the next Hands-On Exercise. If not, close the workbook and exit Excel.

Excel 2016, Windows 10, Microsoft Corporation

PivotTable Options

As you have experienced, PivotTables consolidate and aggregate large amounts of data to facilitate data analysis. You can use the Analyze tab to customize the PivotTable for more in-depth analysis. You can add filters, insert slicers, and insert a timeline to include or exclude data from being represented in a PivotTable. In addition, you can perform a variety of calculations and show specific calculation results. Furthermore, you can change the design to control the overall appearance of the PivotTable.

In this section, you will learn how to filter data in a PivotTable. In addition, you will create a calculated field and display subtotals. Finally, you will change the style of the PivotTable.

Filtering and Slicing a PivotTable

PivotTables display aggregated data for each category. However, you may want to set a filter to exclude particular categories or values. You can specify a particular field to filter the PivotTable. In addition, you can include slicers to easily set filters to designate which specific data to include in the PivotTable.

Add Filters

STEP 1 >> You can apply filters to show only a subset of the PivotTable. Similar to applying filters to an Excel table, when you add filters in a PivotTable, the filters only temporarily remove some data from view. The PivotTable displays only data that reflects the filters you enabled. Drag a field to the FILTERS area in the PivotTable Fields List when you want to engage a filter based on a particular field. For example, you might want to filter the PivotTable to show only aggregates for first- and second-edition books. When you drag a field to the FILTERS area, Excel displays the filters above the PivotTable. The first field in the FILTERS area displays in cell A1 with a filter arrow in cell B1. Additional fields added to the FILTERS area display in the subsequent rows.

To set a PivotTable filter, complete the following steps:

1. Drag a field to the FILTERS area in the PivotTable Fields List.
2. Click the filter arrow in cell B1 to open the Filter menu and complete one of the following steps:
   - Select the value in the list to filter the data by that value only.
   - Click the Select Multiple Items check box if you want to select more than one value to filter the PivotTable. Click the check boxes by each value you want to set (see Figure 24).
   - Type a value in the Search box if the list is long and you want to find a value quickly.
3. Click OK.

The PivotTable displays only a subset of the data that meet those conditions and calculates the summary statistics based on the filtered data rather than the complete dataset. The filter arrow displays an icon of a funnel when the PivotTable is being filtered.

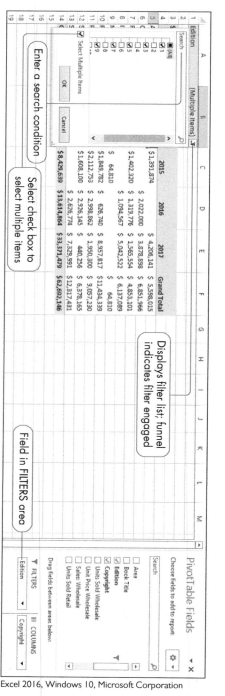

FIGURE 24 Filter Menu

Excel 2016, Windows 10, Microsoft Corporation

Cell B1 displays (All) when no filter is enabled, the value if one filter is enabled, or (Multiple Items) if more than one item is selected. If you no longer need a filter, you can remove it.

To remove a filter from a PivotTable, complete one of the following steps:

- Drag the field from the FILTER area in the PivotTable Fields List to remove the entire filter.
- Click the Filter arrow in cell B1, select (All), and then click OK to remove the filter settings but keep the field in the FILTERS area on the PivotTable Fields List.

You can apply additional filters for rows and columns. For example, you can apply date filters to display summary statistics for data occurring within a particular time frame or apply filters for values within a designated range.

To apply row or column filters in a PivotTable, complete the following steps:

1. Click the Row Labels or Column Labels arrow in the PivotTable (see Figure 25) to open a filter menu.
2. Click the (Select All) check box on the menu to deselect all items.
3. Click the check boxes by the item(s) you want to display and click OK.

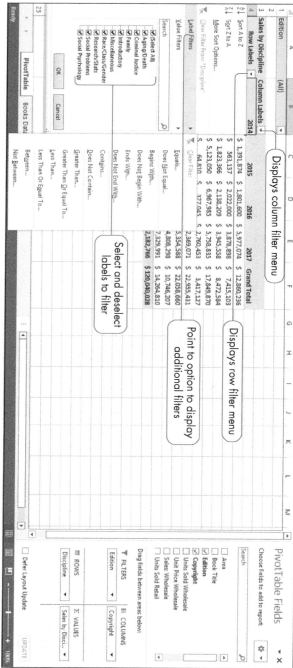

FIGURE 25 Row and Column Filtering

Excel 2016, Windows 10, Microsoft Corporation

Insert a Slicer to Filter a PivotTable

STEP 2 ▸▸ You can insert a *slicer*, a small window containing one button for each unique item in a field so that you can filter the PivotTable quickly. The visual representation is easier to manipulate than adding more fields to the FILTERS area and then setting each field's filter.

To insert a slicer, complete the following steps:

1. Click the Analyze tab.
2. Click Insert Slicer in the Filter group to open the Insert Slicers dialog box (see Figure 26).
3. Click one or more field check boxes to display one or more slicers and click OK.

Insert Slicers ? ×

- [ ] Discipline
- [ ] Area
- [ ] Book Title
- [ ] Edition
- [ ] Copyright
- [ ] Units Sold Wholesale
- [ ] Unit Price Wholesale
- [ ] Sales: Wholesale
- [ ] Units Sold Retail
- [ ] Unit Price Retail
- [ ] Sales: Retail
- [ ] Total Book Sales

OK Cancel

Excel 2016, Windows 10, Microsoft Corporation

FIGURE 26 Insert Slicers Dialog Box

For each field check box you select, Excel inserts a slicer into the worksheet. You can manipulate a slicer by doing one of the following:

- **Move the Slicer.** Drag a slicer to move it in the Excel window to avoid overlapping the slicer and PivotTable.

- **Filter Data by One Value.** Click the slicer button to filter by the value represented by the button. For example, to set a filter to display only 1st editions, click 1 on the Edition filter. Excel displays the slicer buttons in three different colors to indicate selected items, items filtered out, and items that are not applicable due to other filters set. This color coding makes it clear how you filtered the PivotTable.

- **Filter Data by Multiple Values.** Click Multi-Select to be able to click more than one button to filter data for multiple values. For example, to set a filter to display first and second editions, click Multi-Select and click 1 and 2. In Figure 27, the Discipline field is filtered by Family, Introductory, and Social Problems. Although no filter has been enabled for the Edition field, the 6th and 9th edition buttons are unavailable because the three disciplines selected do not have books that are in their sixth or ninth editions.

- **Clear a Filter.** Click Clear Filter in the top-right corner of the slicer to clear the filters for that field.

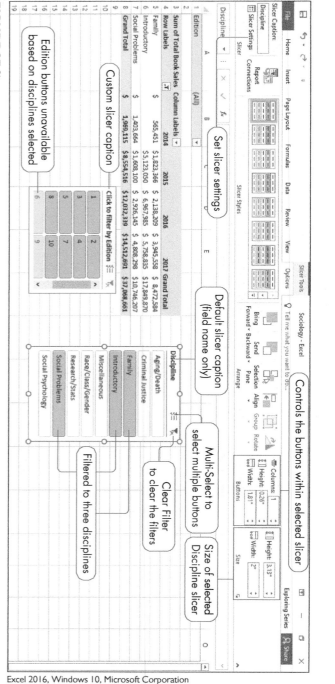

FIGURE 27 Slicers

Excel 2016, Windows 10, Microsoft Corporation

TIP: SLICERS VS. FILTERS AREA

The benefit of using slicers over the FILTERS area is that slicers display color-coded buttons to show which fields are being filtered, whereas using the filter arrows within the PivotTable do not show what fields are currently being filtered.

Customize a Slicer

When you select a slicer, the Slicer Tools Options tab displays so that you can customize a slicer. The default slicer caption displays the field name only. The *slicer caption* is text that displays in the header at the top of the slicer window, similar to a title bar, to identify the data in the field. However, you can customize the slicer by changing its caption. In Figure 27, the caption for the Edition slicer displays an instruction to the user, whereas the caption for the Discipline slicer displays the default field name. Table 5 lists and describes the commands on the Slicer Tools Options tab.

TABLE 5 Slicer Tools Commands

Group	Commands
Slicer	Enables you to change the slicer caption, display the Slicer Settings dialog box for further customization, and manage the PivotTable connected to the slicer. The Edition slicer has been sorted in ascending order. The light blue items 6 and 9 do not apply to the selected disciplines.
Slicer Styles	Applies a style to the slicer by specifying the color of the filtered item in the slicer. For example, given the workbook theme, the default active filters appear in blue and unavailable items appear in light blue.
Arrange	Specifies the slicer's placement in relation to other groups, such as placing a slicer on top of other slicers.
Buttons	Defines how many columns are displayed in the selected slicer and the height and width of each button inside the slicer. For example, the Edition slicer contains two columns, and the Discipline slicer contains one column.
Size	Sets the height and width of the slicer window. For example, the Discipline slicer's height is 3.13".

Pearson Education, Inc.

Insert a Timeline to Filter a PivotTable

When a PivotTable is based on a dataset that contains dates, you might want to filter data to a particular date or range of dates to analyze the data. Insert a **PivotTable timeline** to filter the data based on the date range you want. A PivotTable timeline is a small window that starts with the first date and ends with the last date in the data source. It contains horizontal tiles that you can click to filter data by day, month, quarter, or year.

To insert a timeline and filter data on a timeline in a PivotTable, complete the following steps:

1. Click the Analyze tab.
2. Click Insert Timeline in the Filter group to open the Insert Timelines dialog box, which displays field names of fields that contain date-formatted data.
3. Click a field check box and click OK. Excel displays a timeline in the worksheet, and the Timeline Tools Options tab displays (see Figure 28) so that you can change the timeline caption, apply a style, adjust the size, and show items on the timeline.
4. Click the arrow by the current time level and select a time period: YEARS, QUARTERS, MONTHS, or DAYS. The timeline displays that time period.
5. Click a tile on the timeline to filter data. For example, click March 2018 to filter data in the PivotTable for that particular month. To select multiple time periods, click the tile representing the first time period and drag across the tiles to select consecutive time periods. For non-consecutive time periods (such as the 1st quarter of each year), press and hold Ctrl while you click various time periods on the timeline. To clear the timeline filter, click Clear Filter in the top-right corner of the timeline.

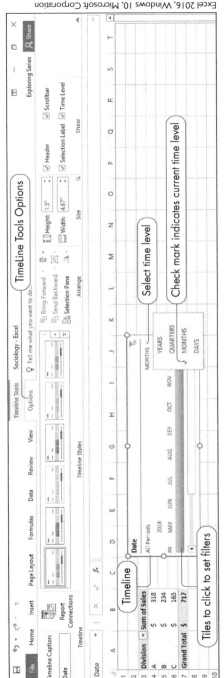

Excel 2016, Windows 10, Microsoft Corporation

FIGURE 28 Timeline

Creating a Calculated Field

STEP 3 ⟫ You can create a **calculated field**, which is a user-defined field that derives its value based on performing calculations in other fields in a PivotTable. The calculated field does not exist in the original dataset. For example, you can create a calculated field that converts totals to percentages for easier relative comparison among categories, or you might want to create a calculated field that determines the number of units sold generated by a 10% increase for the upcoming year.

To create a calculated field, complete the following steps:

1. Select a cell within the PivotTable.

2. Click the Analyze tab.

3. Click Fields, Items, & Sets in the Calculations group and select Calculated Field to display the Insert Calculated Field dialog box (see Figure 29).

4. Type a descriptive label for the calculated field in the Name box.

5. Build a formula starting with the equal sign (=). Instead of using cell references, insert the field names and other operands. For example, = 'Total Book Sales'*.1 calculates a 10% royalty amount on the total book sales.

6. Click OK to insert the calculated field in the PivotTable. Format the numerical values in the calculated field column as needed.

STEP 4

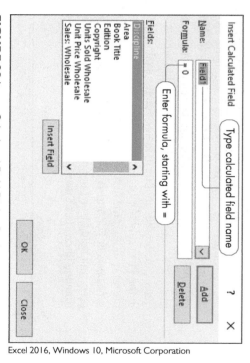

FIGURE 29 Insert Calculated Field Dialog Box

Excel 2016, Windows 10, Microsoft Corporation

Show Values as a Specific Calculation Result

In addition to creating calculated fields, you can apply built-in custom calculations that display relationships between values in rows and columns in the PivotTable. To use a value as a calculation, insert the field in the VALUES area. You might want to repeat the field twice: once for the actual sum and a second time to perform the calculation. For example, you can show each value as a percentage of the grand total or each value's percentage of the row total.

To display values in relation to others, complete the following steps:

1. Click the field in the VALUES area of the PivotTable Fields List and select Value Field Settings (or click within the field in the PivotTable and click Field Settings in the Active Field group on the Analyze tab).

2. Click the Show Values As tab within the Value Field Settings dialog box.

3. Click the *Show values as* arrow and select the desired calculation type. Table 6 lists and describes some of the calculation options.

4. Click Number Format to set number formats, click OK to close the Format Cells dialog box, and then click OK to close the Value Field Settings dialog box.

Pearson Education, Inc.

TABLE 6 Calculation Options

Option	Description
% of Grand Total	Displays each value as a percentage of the grand total.
% of Column Total	Displays each value as a percentage of the respective column total. The values in each column total 100%.
% of Row Total	Displays each value as a percentage of the respective row total. The values in each row total 100%.
% of Parent Row Total	Displays values as: (value for the item) / (value for the parent item on rows). Two fields should be contained in the ROWS area where the first field is a parent of the second field. For example, if Discipline is the first field and Area is the second field, Family would be the parent for the Family Interaction and Marriage and Family areas. The calculation would divide the Family Interaction value by the total value in the Family parent row.
Running Total	Displays values as running totals.
Rank Smallest to Largest	Displays the rank of values in a specific field where 1 represents the smallest value.
Rank Largest to Smallest	Displays the rank of values in a specific field where 1 represents the largest value.

Figure 30 illustrates the use of the Total Sales field inserted three times in the VALUES area: (1) sum of the totals for each discipline and area, (2) % of Parent Row Total, and (3) % of Grand Total. The Discipline and Area fields are the parents to the ROWS area. The Disciplines are the parents to the respective Areas. In the % of Parent Row column, the Death and Dying sales ($3,751,187) are 66.92% of its Aging/Death parent sales of $5,606,170. The Sociology of Aging sales ($1,853,983) are 33.08% of the Aging/Death parent sales. The percentages for the areas within the Aging/Death discipline must add up to 100%. The Aging/Death discipline sales of $5,605,170 is 8.93% of its parent sales, the grand total of $62,796,185.

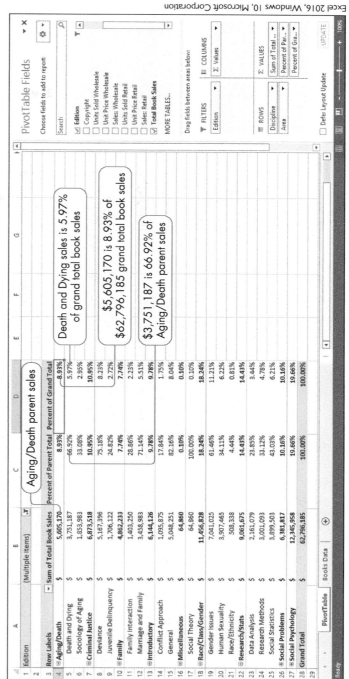

FIGURE 30 PivotTable Tools Design Tab

Excel 2016, Windows 10, Microsoft Corporation

In the Percent of Grand Total column, each parent's sale is the percentage of the grand total, and each area's sales is a percentage of the grand total. The bold discipline (parent) percentages equal 100%, and the area percentages also equal 100% of the total sales.

Changing the PivotTable Design

Excel applies basic formatting to PivotTables. For example, it formats primary row labels in bold to distinguish those categories from the subcategories. In addition, the subtotals are bold to offset these values from the subcategory values. The PivotTable Tools Design tab contains commands for enhancing the format of a PivotTable (see Figure 31).

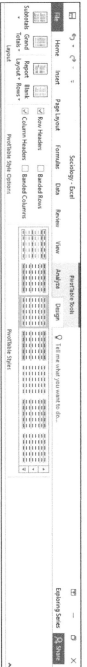

FIGURE 31 PivotTable Tools Design Tab

Excel 2016, Windows 10, Microsoft Corporation

Change the PivotTable Style

STEP 5 A *PivotTable style* controls bold formatting, font colors, shading colors, and border lines. For example, the default Pivot Style Light 16 displays a light blue fill color for the field filters in cells A1 and B1, the column and row labels, and the grand total row.

To change the style, complete the following steps:

1. Click the PivotTable Tools Design tab.
2. Click More in the PivotTable Styles group to display the PivotTable Styles gallery (see Figure 32).
3. Point to a thumbnail on the gallery. Excel shows a preview of how that style will affect the PivotTable.
4. Click a style to apply it to the PivotTable.

Subtotals, PivotTables, and PivotCharts

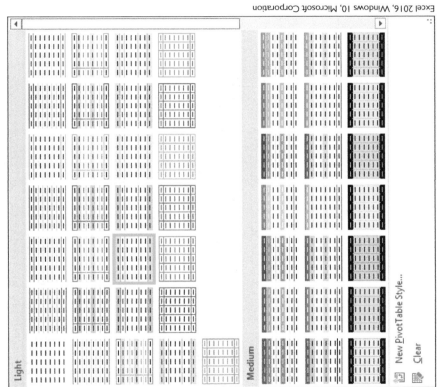

FIGURE 32 PivotTable Styles

Excel 2016, Windows 10, Microsoft Corporation

The PivotTable Style Options group on the Design tab controls which areas of the PivotTable are affected by the style. Click Row Headers to apply special formatting for the first row, Column Headers to apply special formatting to the first column, Banded Rows to format odd and even rows differently, and Banded Columns to format odd and even columns differently.

Change the PivotTable Layout

The Layout group on the Design tab controls the layout of the PivotTable elements. These commands control whether subtotals and grand totals are displayed or hidden. You can customize the location of subtotals by clicking Subtotals in the Layout group on the Design tab. For example, displaying the subtotals at the top of the group draws attention to the totals and enables you to scroll to view all of the supporting data if necessary.

The Report Layout controls the overall format. You can select a compact, outline, or tabular layout. The Report Layout also controls whether item labels are repeated when multiple fields are located in the ROWS area of the PivotTable Fields List. The Blank Rows command enables you to insert blank rows between items or remove blank rows.

Quick Concepts

7. What is the purpose of applying a filter to a PivotTable? What types of filters can you apply?

8. What is a slicer? What is the purpose of a slicer?

9. When would you create a calculated field in a PivotTable?

Skills covered: Set Filters • Insert a Slicer • Customize a Slicer • Create a Calculated Field • Show Values as Calculations • Change the PivotTable Style

3 PivotTable Options

The PivotTable you created has benefited you by allowing you to review sales data by discipline for each copyright year. In addition, you have used the PivotTable to compare grand total sales among disciplines and grand totals by copyright year. Now you want to extend your analysis. You will calculate author royalties from the sales and impose filters to focus your attention on each analysis. Finally, you will apply a different style to the PivotTable.

STEP 1 ›› SET FILTERS

The level of success of the first two editions especially determines the likelihood of approving subsequent revisions and editions. To display aggregated sales for these editions, you will set a filter to remove the other editions so they are not included in the calculated sales data. After you review the first- and second-edition data, you will enable additional filters to review books published in the past two years. Refer to Figure 33 as you complete Step 1.

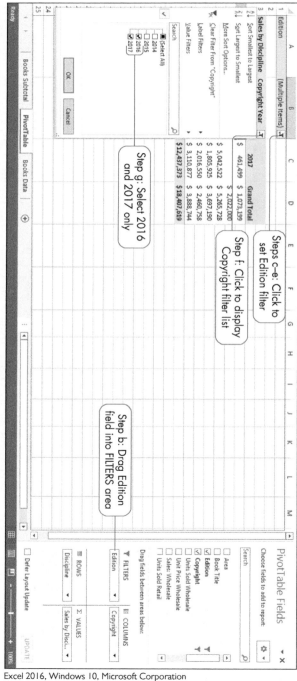

FIGURE 33 Filters Enabled

a. Open *e05h2Sociology_LastFirst* if you closed it at the end of Hands-On Exercise 2 and save it as **e05h3Sociology_LastFirst**, changing h2 to h3.

> **TROUBLESHOOTING:** Click in the PivotTable to display the PivotTable Fields List if necessary.

b. Make sure the PivotTable worksheet tab is active and drag the **Edition field** from the *Choose fields to add to report* section to the FILTERS area.

You can now filter the PivotTable based on the Edition field. Cell A1 displays the field name, and cell B1 displays (All) and the filter arrow.

c. Click the **Edition filter arrow** in **cell B1** and click the **Select Multiple Items check box** to select it.

The list displays a check box for each item.

d. Click the **(All) check box** to deselect it.

e. Click the **1** and **2 check boxes** and click **OK**.

The summary statistics reflect sales data for only first- and second-edition publications. The filter arrow changes to a funnel icon in cell B1. Cell B1 also changes from (All) to (Multiple Items), indicating that multiple items are included in the filter.

f. Click the **Copyright Year filter arrow** in **cell B3** and click the **(Select All) check box** to deselect it.

g. Click the **2016** and **2017 check boxes**, click **OK**, and save the workbook.

Excel filters out data for years that do not meet the condition you set. The filter arrow changes to a funnel icon in cell B3.

STEP 2 ⟫ INSERT AND CUSTOMIZE A SLICER

You might distribute the workbook to colleagues who are not as skilled in Excel as you are. To help them set their own filters, you want to insert slicers. Refer to Figure 34 as you complete Step 2.

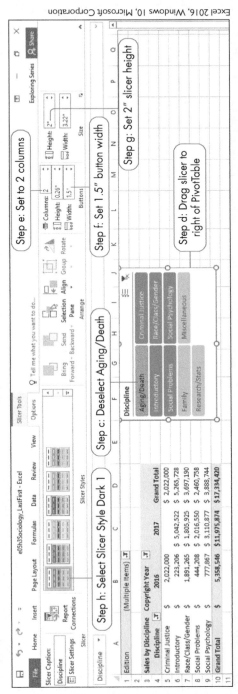

FIGURE 34 Slicer

a. Click **Insert Slicer** in the Filter group on the Analyze tab.

The Insert Slicers dialog box opens, listing each field name.

b. Click **Discipline** and click **OK**.

Excel inserts the Discipline slicer in the worksheet. Six slicer buttons are blue, indicating that those disciplines are selected. The grayed-out buttons at the bottom of the slicer indicate those disciplines are not applicable based on other engaged filters you set (first and second editions and 2016 and 2017 copyright years).

c. Press and hold **Ctrl** as you click **Aging/Death** in the Discipline slicer.

This deselects the Aging/Death discipline.

> **TROUBLESHOOTING:** Because several disciplines are selected, if you click Aging/Death instead of pressing Ctrl as you click it, you set Aging/Death as the only discipline. The others are filtered out. If this happens, immediately click Undo and repeat step c.

d. Drag the slicer to the right of the PivotTable.

You moved the slicer so that it does not cover up data in the PivotTable.

e. Change the **Columns value** to **2** in the Buttons group on the Options tab. Change the button **Width** to **1.5"** in the Buttons group.

The slicer now displays buttons in two columns. You changed the width of the buttons to 1.5" to display the full discipline names within the buttons.

You want to calculate the amount of the sales returned to the authors as royalties. Although the 10% royalty rate is stored in cell J2 in the Books Data worksheet, the value must be used in the calculated field because range names and cell references outside the PivotTable cannot be used. Refer to Figure 35 as you complete Step 3.

STEP 3 ≫ CREATE A CALCULATED FIELD

a. Click within the PivotTable, click the **Analyze tab**, click **Fields, Items, & Sets** in the Calculations group, and then select **Calculated Field**.

The Insert Calculated Field dialog box opens.

b. Type **Author Royalties** in the Name box.

c. Scroll down the Fields list, click **Total Book Sales**, and then click **Insert Field**.

Excel starts to build the formula, which is currently = 'Total Book Sales'.

d. Type ***.1** at the end of the Formula box and click **OK**.

Excel adds Sum of Author Royalties calculated field columns, one for each copyright year category. It calculates the authors' royalties as 10% of the total sales for each copyright year.

e. Click **cell C5**, click **Field Settings** in the Active Field group on the Analyze tab, type **Authors' Royalties** in the Custom Name box in the Value Field Settings dialog box, and then click **OK**.

f. Move the slicer below the PivotTable so that the top-left corner is in **cell A13**.

f. Change the slicer **Height** to **2** in the Size group.

The slicer window is now only 2" tall.

g. Click **More** in the Slicer Styles group and click **Slicer Style Dark 1**. Save the workbook.

Based on the selected workbook theme, Slicer Style Dark 1 applies a dark blue fill color for selected disciplines, dark gray and black font for available but not currently selected disciplines, and light blue fill with medium blue font color for non-applicable disciplines.

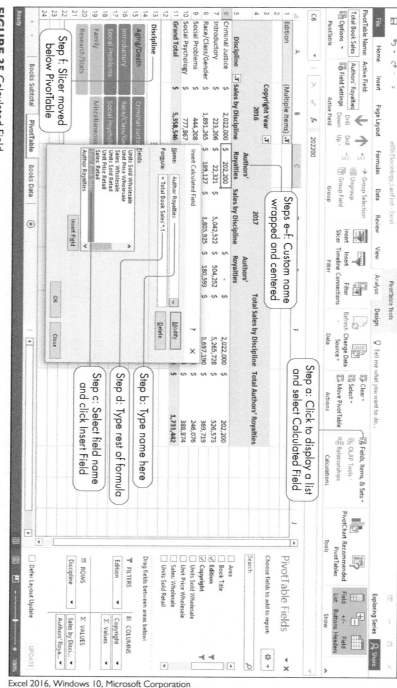

FIGURE 35 Calculated Field

Excel 2016, Windows 10, Microsoft Corporation

g. Select cells **C5** and **E5**, click the **Home tab**, and then click **Center** and **Wrap Text** in the Alignment group. Click **Format** in the Cells group and select **Row Height**, type **30**, and click **OK**. Click **Format**, select **Column Width**, type **12**, and click **OK**.

h. Save the workbook.

STEP 4 ▶▶ SHOW VALUES AS CALCULATIONS

You want to see which copyright year generated the largest sales for each discipline, which discipline contributes the largest percentage of the total sociology sales, and which introductory book has the largest sales contribution within that discipline. Refer to Figure 36 as you complete Step 4.

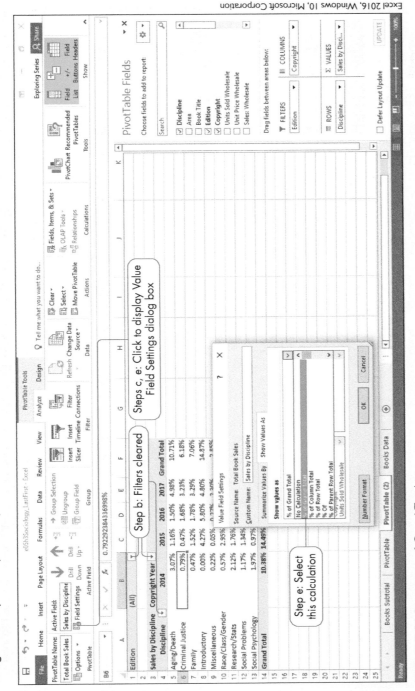

FIGURE 36 Percentage of Grand Total

a. Right-click the **PivotTable sheet tab**, select **Move or Copy**, click **Books Data** in the *Before sheet* list, click the **Create a copy check box** to select it, and then click **OK**.

You copied the PivotTable worksheet to maintain the previous tasks you completed as evidence. You will work with the PivotTable (2) worksheet, which is the active worksheet.

b. Do the following to remove filters, slicer, and Authors' Royalties field:

- Click the **Edition filter** in cell **B1**, click the **(All) check box** to select it, and then click **OK** to clear the Edition filter.
  When you click (All), all edition numbers are selected again, as indicated by the check marks.

- Click the **Discipline filter** in cell **A5** and select **Clear Filter From "Discipline"**.

- Click the **Copyright Year filter** in cell **B3** and select **Clear Filter From "Copyright"**.

- Select the slicer and press **Delete**.

- Click **Authors' Royalties** in the VALUES area of the PivotTable Fields List and select **Remove Field**.

c. Click within any value in the PivotTable, click the **Analyze tab**, and then click **Field Settings** in the Active Field group.

The Value Field Settings dialog box opens.

Hands-On Exercise 3

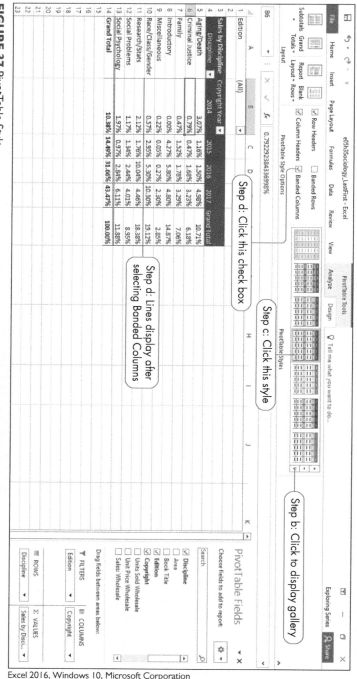

d. Click the **Show Values As tab**, click the **Show values as arrow**, select **% of Row Total**, and then click **OK**.

Excel displays each copyright year's values as percentages for that discipline. All disciplines except Introductory and Research/Stats had the highest percentage of sales for the books with a 2017 copyright. These two disciplines had their highest percentage of sales for books with a 2016 copyright.

e. Click the **Field Settings** in the Active Field group, click the **Show Values As tab** within the dialog box, click the **Show values as arrow**, select **% of Grand Total**, and then click **OK**. Save the workbook.

Refer to Figure 36. Each discipline's yearly value displays as a percentage of the total sales. Which discipline and for what copyright year produces the highest percentage of total sales? Answer: 2017 Race/Class/Gender with 10.30%, followed closely by the 2016 Research/Stats with 10.04%. In general, the Race/Class/Gender discipline contributed the highest percentage of the total sales with 19.12%.

To enhance the readability of the sociology textbook PivotTable, you will change the PivotTable style. Refer to Figure 37 as you complete Step 5.

FIGURE 37 PivotTable Style

a. Make sure the PivotTable (2) sheet tab is active. Click a cell within the PivotTable, click the **Design tab**, and then click **More** in the PivotTable Styles group.

The PivotTable Style gallery displays styles that you can apply.

b. Click **Pivot Style Medium 3** to apply a dark red style to the PivotTable.

c. Click the **Banded Columns check box** to select it in the PivotTable Style Options group to add dark red vertical lines between the columns.

d. Save and close the workbook. You will submit this file to your instructor at the end of the last Hands-On Exercise.

Data Modeling and PivotCharts

When you created a PivotTable earlier in this chapter, you created it from a dataset in a single worksheet. However, the data is often contained in multiple sources, such as multiple worksheets or databases. Excel enables you to use related data to create a PivotTable.

You can create PivotCharts, which like other charts you have created in Excel, provide visual representations of numerical data. Charts help reveal trends or patterns in the data because people can often interpret visual aids easier than reviewing an entire dataset.

In this section, you will select multiple datasets, create a relationship between the datasets, and then create a PivotTable. Finally, you will create and format a PivotChart.

Creating a Data Model

So far, you have been working with data from one table. Often, however, you will want to analyze data contained in multiple tables. A *data model* is a collection of related tables that contain structured data used to create a database. You can create a relationship between two or more Excel tables that have some commonality and relationship, similar to how you can create relationships among common tables in an Access database. You can then perform complex data analysis to make insightful decisions.

Create a Relationship Between Tables

>> A *relationship* is an association or connection between two tables where both tables contain a common field of data. Similar to how a VLOOKUP function looks up data from a range to find matching data in another range, you can create relationships between tables. For example, you want to generate a report that contains sales representatives' names and their respective data, but the data is stored in one table, and the representatives' names are stored in another table. To combine the names and data into one report, you must establish a link (or relationship) between the two tables using the sales representatives' IDs, which is contained in both tables.

STEP 1

To create a relationship between two tables in Excel, complete the following steps:

1. Click the Data tab and click Relationships in the Data Tools group to open the Manage Relationships dialog box.

2. Click New in the dialog box to open the Create Relationship dialog box (see Figure 38).

3. Click the Table arrow and select the name of the primary table. The primary table in this example is SALES.

4. Click the Column (Foreign) arrow and select the name of the column that contains a relationship to the related or lookup table. For example, Rep ID is the column that relates to a column in the other table.

5. Click the Related Table arrow and select the name of the related or lookup table. For example, the related table is REPS.

6. Click the Related Column (Primary) arrow and select the name of the column that is related to the primary table. For example, the ID column in the REPS table relates to the Rep ID column in the SALES table.

7. Click OK in the Create Relationships dialog box and click Close in the Manage Relationships dialog box.

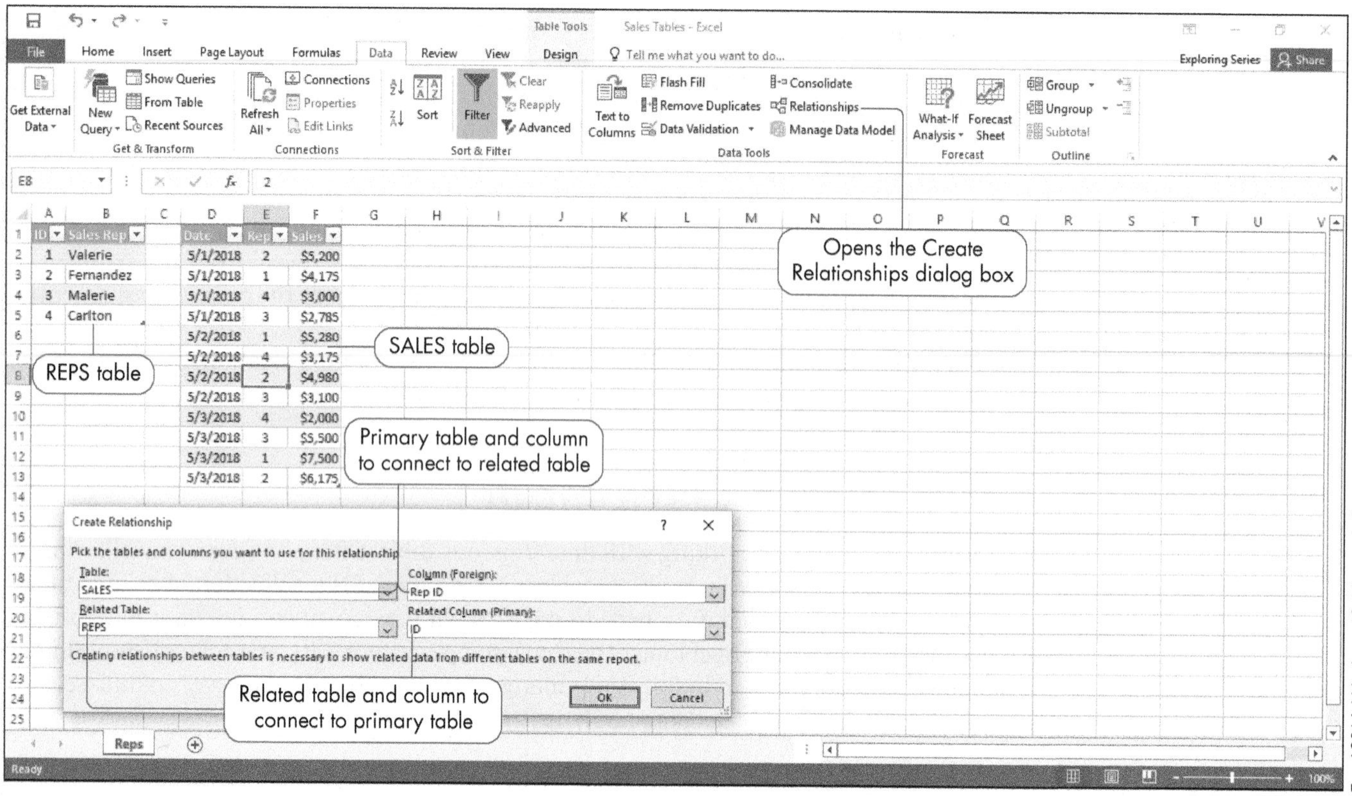
Opens the Create Relationships dialog box
SALES table
REPS table
Primary table and column to connect to related table
Related table and column to connect to primary table
Create Relationship
Pick the tables and columns you want to use for this relationship
Table:
SALES
Column (Foreign):
Rep ID
Related Table:
REPS
Related Column (Primary):
ID
Creating relationships between tables is necessary to show related data from different tables on the same report.
OK
Cancel

Excel 2016, Windows 10, Microsoft Corporation

FIGURE 38 Relating Tables

TIP: CREATING MULTIPLE RELATIONSHIPS

You can create multiple relationships with one table similar to creating relationships among several tables in an Access database. To create multiple relationships, you must create a relationship between two tables at a time. Each combination of tables must have a common field. After creating the first relationship, repeat the process to create a relationship between two other tables.

TIP: EDITING A RELATIONSHIP

If you want to edit the relationship, click Relationships in the Data Tools group to open the Manage Relationships dialog box. Select the relationship you want to edit, click Edit to open the Edit Relationships dialog box (which looks like the Create Relationships dialog box), make the changes, click OK, and then click Close.

Create a PivotTable from Related Tables

STEP 2 After you create a relationship between tables, you can create a PivotTable from both tables. The fields from both tables are available from which to choose, giving you more detailed analysis of the data. When selecting fields, use the common field. For example, if both tables contain sales representatives' IDs, you can use the actual names instead of their IDs for better descriptions in the PivotTable.

To create a PivotTable from the data model, complete the following steps:

1. Click within the primary table.
2. Click the Insert tab and click PivotTable in the Tables group to open the Create PivotTable dialog box (see Figure 39).
3. Make sure the primary table name is displayed in the Table/Range box.
4. Click the *Add this data to the Data Model* check box to select it and click OK.

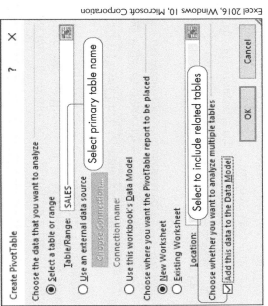

FIGURE 39 Create PivotTable Dialog Box

In the PivotTable Fields List, click ALL to display the names of all related tables. Click the table names to display the field names. You then can arrange the fields in the different area boxes at the bottom of the PivotTable Fields List (see Figure 40).

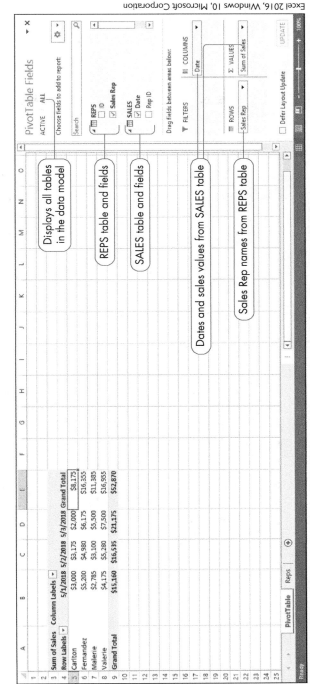

FIGURE 40 PivotTable Created from Related Tables

TIP: POWER PIVOT TABLES

Power Pivot is an add-in that enables you to relate tables and external data from multiple data sources. You can use this add-in to create PivotTables as well as perform other sophisticated analyses. Use the Excel Help feature to look up the topic Power Pivot to learn more about the Power Pivot functionality.

Creating a PivotChart

A **PivotChart** is an interactive graphical representation of the data in a PivotTable. A PivotChart presents the consolidated data visually. When you change the position of a field in either the PivotTable or the PivotChart, the corresponding object changes as well.

STEP 3

To create a PivotChart, complete the following steps:

1. Click inside the PivotTable.
2. Click the Analyze tab and click PivotChart in the Tools group.

Excel creates a PivotChart based on the current PivotTable settings—row labels, column labels, values, and filters. The PivotChart contains elements that enable you to set filters. The ROWS area is replaced with AXIS (CATEGORY), and the COLUMNS area is replaced with LEGEND (SERIES) when you select the PivotChart (see Figure 41). The field used for the FILTERS area remains a field to use to filter data within the PivotChart. The field used for VALUES in a PivotTable remains a field that builds the plot area within the PivotChart.

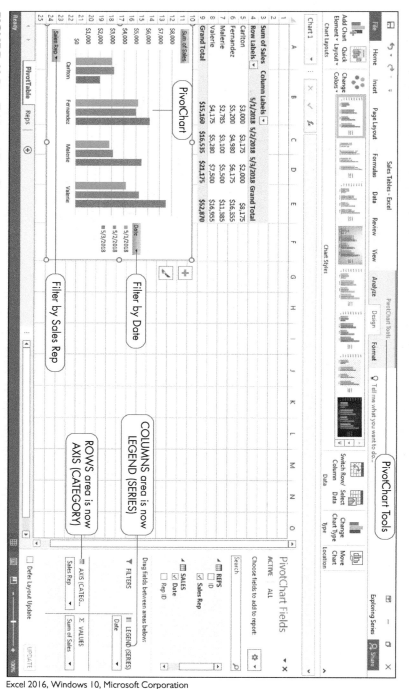

FIGURE 41 PivotTable and PivotChart

Excel 2016, Windows 10, Microsoft Corporation

STEP 4

Modify the PivotChart

Although Excel creates the PivotChart based on the current PivotTable settings, you can change the settings using the PivotChart Fields List. Click the FILTERS arrow and select values to filter the chart. Click the AXIS (CATEGORY) arrows to sort or filter the categories and subcategories in rows. Click the LEGEND (SERIES) to filter the chart based on the values. Changes you make to the PivotChart also affect the corresponding PivotTable. For example, if you apply a filter to the PivotChart, Excel also filters the PivotTable. If you click Switch Rows/Column to change how the data is plotted in the PivotChart, Excel changes the rows and columns in the PivotTable.

Subtotals, PivotTables, and PivotCharts

The PivotChart Tools Analyze tab contains the same options that you used to customize a PivotTable. You can enter a name in the Chart Name box in the PivotChart group, insert slicers and timelines to filter the data depicted in the chart, and refresh the chart after changing the data source. In addition, the Actions group contains the Move Chart option so that you can move a PivotChart to a different worksheet.

The PivotChart Tools Design tab contains the Chart Layouts, Chart Styles, Data, Type, and Location groups, similar to the groups on the Chart Tools Design tab. Table 7 describes the commands in these groups.

TABLE 7	PivotChart Tools Design Tab
Group	**Commands**
Chart Layouts	Add chart elements (such as a chart title and data labels) and apply a layout to the PivotChart.
Chart Styles	Apply a different chart style to the PivotChart and then customize the chart by changing the color scheme.
Data	Switch how rows and columns of data are represented in the PivotChart and change the data source used to create the chart.
Type	Change the chart type, such as changing a column chart to a bar chart.
Location	Move the chart to a different sheet in the workbook.

Pearson Education, Inc.

The Chart Elements and Chart Styles buttons display to the right of a PivotChart when it is selected, similar to these buttons that display when a regular chart is selected. When you click the Chart Elements button, a menu displays to add or remove chart elements, such as the chart title, data labels, and legend. When you click the Chart Styles button, a gallery of chart styles displays so that you can apply a different style to the chart.

When you double-click a chart element, the applicable task pane displays on the right side of the screen so that you can customize that element. For example, if you double-click the chart title, the Format Chart Title task pane displays. If you double-click a slice of a pie in a pie chart, the Format Data Point task pane displays so that you can change the fill color for that slice. Use Excel Help to learn more about customizing PivotCharts.

Quick Concepts

10. When is it beneficial to create a relationship between two tables?

11. What PivotTable areas are used to create the elements in a PivotChart?

12. What happens when you set filters and change fields used in a PivotChart?

4 Data Modeling and PivotCharts

You are converting the data into separate tables to improve the database design of the books data. Your new workbook contains a Books table, an Editor table, and a Discipline table. The Books table uses numbers to code the editor assigned to each book and the discipline for each book. You will build relationships among these tables, create a PivotTable to analyze data by discipline and editor, and then create a PivotChart for the Family discipline.

STEP 1 >> CREATE RELATIONSHIPS

The BOOKS table contains codes instead of discipline categories, and a new column contains editor IDs. You will create relationships between the BOOKS table and the DISCIPLINE and EDITOR tables to build a data model. Refer to Figure 42 as you complete Step 1.

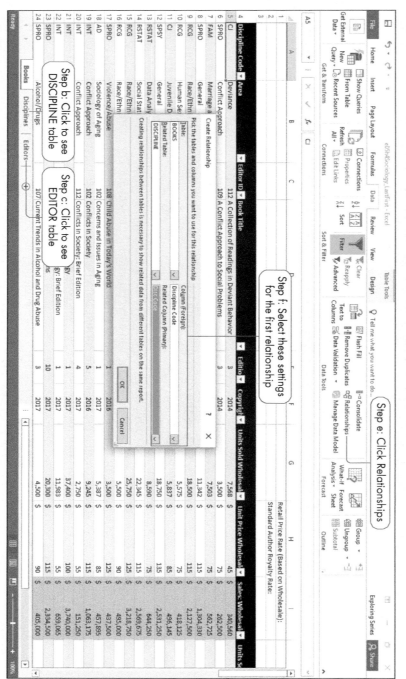

Skills covered: Create Relationships • Create a PivotTable from Related Tables • Create a PivotChart • Modify the PivotChart

FIGURE 42 Relating Tables

Excel 2016, Windows 10, Microsoft Corporation

a. Open *e05h4Sociology* and save it as **e05h4Sociology_LastFirst**.

The Books sheet tab contains the BOOKS table. Notice that the discipline category names have been replaced with discipline codes in the first column. The third column contains codes that represent editor names.

b. Click the **Disciplines sheet tab**.

The Disciplines sheet contains the DISCIPLINE table. Each discipline code and category name is listed only once. For example, FAM is the code for the Family discipline.

c. Click the **Editors sheet tab**.

The Editors sheet contains the EDITOR table. Each editor is listed only once. For example, 101 is Melissa Hort.

d. Click the **Books sheet tab** and click cell **A5**.

e. Click the **Data tab** and click **Relationships** in the Data Tools group.

The Manage Relationships dialog box opens.

f. Click **New** to open the Create Relationship dialog box and do the following:

- Click the **Table arrow** and select **BOOKS**.
- Click the **Column (Foreign) arrow** and select **Discipline Code.**
- Click the **Related Table arrow** and select **DISCIPLINE.**
- Click the **Related Column (Primary) arrow** and select **Disc Code.**
- Click **OK.**

You created a relationship between the BOOKS and DISCIPLINE tables based on the common data, the discipline codes. The Manage Relationships dialog box now displays the relationship you created. You will now add a second relationship before closing the dialog box.

g. Click **New** to open the Create Relationship dialog box and do the following:

- Click the **Table arrow** and select **BOOKS.**
- Click the **Column (Foreign)** and select **Editor ID.**
- Click the **Related Table arrow** and select **EDITOR.**
- Click the **Related Column (Primary)** and select **Editor ID.**
- Click **OK.**

You created a relationship between the BOOKS and EDITOR tables based on the common data, the Editor IDs. The Manage Relationships dialog box now displays the relationship you created.

h. Click **Close** and then save the workbook.

STEP 2 ⟩⟩ **CREATE A PIVOTTABLE FROM RELATED TABLES**

Now that the BOOKS table is related to both the DISCIPLINE and EDITOR tables, you are ready to create a PivotTable using the three tables. Refer to Figure 43 as you complete Step 2.

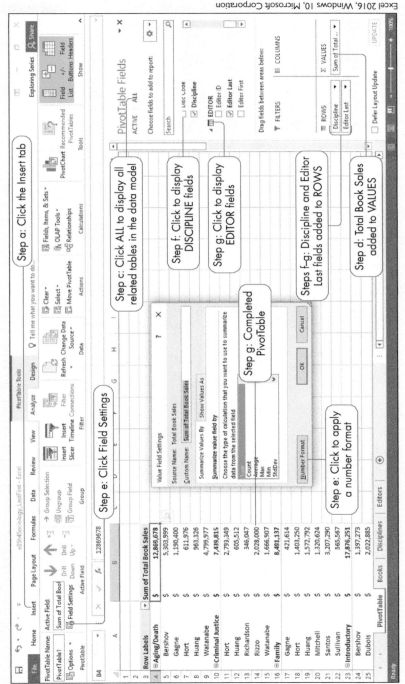

FIGURE 43 PivotTable for Related Tables

a. Click within the dataset on the Books sheet, click the **Insert tab** and click **PivotTable** in the Tables group.

The Create PivotTable dialog box opens with BOOKS as the selected Table/Range.

b. Click the **Add this data to the Data Model check box** to select it and click **OK**.

Excel inserts Sheet1 with a blank PivotTable on the left side.

c. Click **ALL** at the top of the PivotTable Fields List.

The PivotTable Fields List shows BOOKS, DISCIPLINE, and EDITOR table names.

d. Click **BOOKS** to display the fields in the BOOKS table, scroll through the fields, and then click the **Total Book Sales check box** to select it.

The Total Book Sales field is added to the VALUES area.

e. Click **Field Settings** in the Active Field group on the Analyze tab to open the Value Field Settings dialog box and complete the following steps:

- Click **Number Format** to open the Number Format dialog box.
- Click **Accounting** in the Category list.
- Change the **Decimal places to 0.**
- Click **OK** in the Format Cells dialog box.
- Click **OK** in the Value Field Settings dialog box.

The value is formatting with Accounting Number Format with zero decimal places.

f. Click **DISCIPLINE** in the PivotTable Fields List to display the fields in the DISCIPLINE table and click the **Discipline check box** to select it.

The Discipline field is added to the ROWS area.

g. Scroll down and click **EDITOR** to display the fields in the EDITOR table, and then click the **Editor Last check box** to select it.

The Editor Last field is added below the Discipline field in the ROWS area.

h. Double-click the **Sheet1 sheet tab**, type **PivotTable**, and press **Enter**. Save the workbook.

STEP 3 ▶▶ CREATE A PIVOTCHART

You want to create a PivotChart to depict the sales data by editor for the Family discipline. Refer to Figure 44 as you complete Step 3.

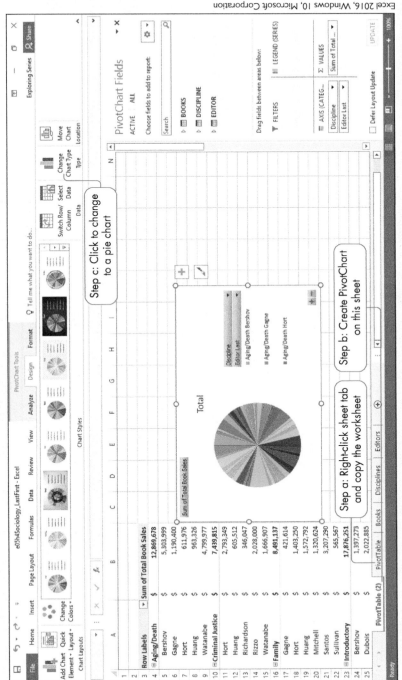

FIGURE 44 PivotChart

a. Right-click the **PivotTable sheet tab**, select **Move or Copy**, click the **Create a copy check box** to select it, and click **OK**.

You created a copy of the PivotTable so that you can preserve that PivotTable settings, modify the duplicate PivotTable, and then create a PivotChart based on the modified PivotTable.

b. Ensure the PivotTable (2) sheet tab is active, click **PivotChart** in the Tools group to open the Insert Chart dialog box, and then click **OK**.

Excel creates a clustered column chart from the PivotTable.

c. Click the **Design tab**.

d. Click **Change Chart Type** in the Type group, click **Pie**, and click **OK**. Save the workbook.

You changed the chart type from a clustered column chart to a pie chart.

The PivotChart depicts too many data points. You will set a filter to display data for the Family discipline only. You will add a descriptive chart title and then display slices from largest to smallest. Finally, you will display percentage data labels. Refer to Figure 45 as you complete Step 4.

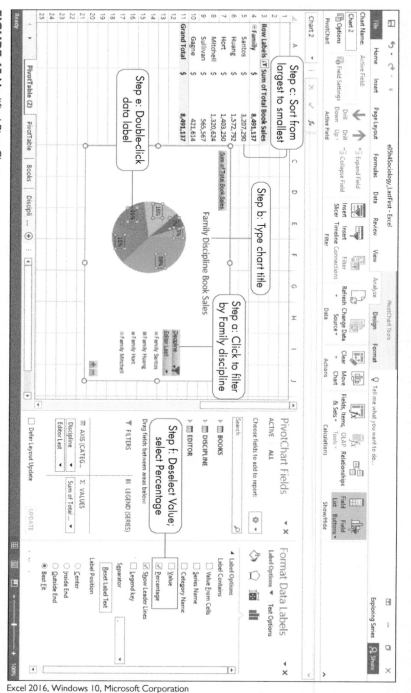

Excel 2016, Windows 10, Microsoft Corporation

FIGURE 45 Modified PivotChart

a. Click the **Discipline arrow** within the PivotChart, click the **(Select All) check box** to deselect all disciplines, click the **Family check box**, and click **OK**.

This action filtered both the PivotChart and the PivotTable to display only Family discipline data.

b. Click **Total** in the chart title, type **Family Discipline Book Sales**, and then press **Enter**.

You changed the chart title to be more descriptive.

c. Click **cell B5** in the PivotTable, click the **Data tab**, and then click **Sort Largest to Smallest** in the Sort & Filter group.

This action sorts the values from largest to smallest in both the PivotTable and in the PivotChart.

d. Click the PivotChart, click **Chart Elements** on the right of the PivotChart and then click the **Data Labels check box** to select it.

You added data labels to the PivotChart.

e. Double-click a data label to display the Format Data Labels task pane.

f. Click the **Value check box** to deselect the values and click the **Percentage check box** to display percentage data labels. Close the Format Data Labels task pane.

g. Save and close the file. Based on your instructor's directions, submit the following:

e05h3Sociology_LastFirst
e05h4Sociology_LastFirst

Chapter Objectives Review

After reading this chapter, you have accomplished the following objectives:

1. Subtotal data.

- The Subtotal dialog box enables you to insert subtotals, such as sums or averages, based on sorted data. This feature detects changes between categories arranged in rows to insert the subtotal rows.

- Add a second level of subtotals: To keep the first level and add a second level, deselect the *Replace current subtotals* check box in the Subtotals dialog box.

- Collapse and expand the subtotals: Click the outline level buttons to collapse the subtotals to the grand total, grand total and subtotals, or entire dataset. Click a particular collapse button to collapse a category, or click an expand button to expand a particular category.

2. Group and ungroup data.

- If the data contain columns of formulas based on other columns and/or row subtotals, use Auto Outline to create an outline based on the data structure. You can then collapse and expand the outline as you review the data. If you no longer need grouped data, select and ungroup the data again.

3. Create a PivotTable.

- Create a Recommended PivotTable: When you use Quick Analysis or Recommended PivotTable, Excel analyzes the dataset to provide recommended PivotTables. The PivotTable displays on a new worksheet, and the PivotTable Fields List displays on the right side of that worksheet. The PivotTable Fields List contains a list of fields in the dataset and areas to control the layout of the PivotTable.

- Create a Blank PivotTable: Use the Ribbon to create a blank PivotTable layout. You can then add fields to design the PivotTable.

4. Modify a PivotTable.

- Add rows to a PivotTable: Add fields to the ROWS area of the PivotTable Fields List to add row categories. The order of the fields within the ROWS area dictates the hierarchy.

- Add values in a PivotTable: Add numerical fields to the VALUES area to display aggregated totals for that field. You can add a field multiple times with a different aggregate for each instance. If you add a field containing text, the default calculation is to provide a count of data.

- Add columns to a PivotTable: Drag fields to the COLUMNS area to add additional columns of details.

- Collapse and expand items in a PivotTable: Click the collapse button to collapse subcategory rows and click the expand button to expand a subcategory of details.

- Remove fields from a PivotTable: Click a field name in the respective area of the PivotTable Fields List and select Remove Field.

- Rearrange fields in a PivotTable: Drag fields from one area to another in the PivotTable Fields List to rearrange fields in the PivotTable.

- Change the value field settings: You can select a different function to calculate the statistics in the PivotTable. You can also apply number formatting, such as Currency, and specify a custom column heading for value columns.

- Refresh a PivotTable: PivotTables do not update automatically if you change the original dataset. You must click Refresh to update the PivotTable.

5. Filter and slice a PivotTable.

- Add filters: Drag a field to the FILTERS area of the PivotTable Fields List and click the Filter arrow above the PivotTable to set the filter conditions. You can also click the row labels arrow in cell A4 to set row filters and click the column arrow in cell B3 to set column filters.

- Insert a slicer to filter a PivotTable: A slicer is a small window containing the values for a particular field. You click buttons in the slicer to set filters for that particular field.

- Customize a slicer: You can specify the slicer's style and size. You can specify how many columns of buttons appear in the slicer and the size of those buttons.

- Insert a timeline to filter a PivotTable: A timeline is a small window that enables you to filter a PivotTable to a particular time period, such as years, quarters, months, or dates.

6. Create a calculated field.

- A calculated field is a user-defined field based on other fields. This field does not exist in the original dataset. You can use basic arithmetic operations, but you cannot use cell references or range names in the calculated field syntax.

- Show values as a specific calculation result: You can apply predefined calculations, such as *% of Grand Total*, for displaying the values in the PivotTable.

7. Change the PivotTable design.

- Change the PivotTable style: A PivotTable style controls bold formatting, font colors, shading colors, and border lines. The PivotTable Styles gallery displays thumbnails of styles from which to choose. When you point to a thumbnail, Excel shows a preview of that style in the PivotTable. Click a style to actually apply it to the PivotTable.

- Change the PivotTable layout: The layout commands control whether subtotals and grand totals are displayed, specifies the location of subtotals, and controls the overall layout.

8. Create a data model.

- Create a relationship between tables: You can create relationships between two or more related tables within one workbook. The relationship is based on a common field, such as IDs, in the tables.

- Create a PivotTable from related tables: After creating the relationships, you can create a PivotTable that uses fields from the related tables. The PivotTable Fields List displays the names of the related tables in the data model.

9. **Create a PivotChart.**

- A PivotChart is similar to a regular chart, except it is based on the categories and structure of the PivotTable, not the original dataset. You can customize a PivotChart with the same methods you use to customize a regular

chart. If you change fields or sort in either the PivotTable or the PivotChart, Excel automatically adjusts the corresponding pivot object.

- Modify the PivotChart: You can modify the PivotChart like a regular chart. You can add a chart title, change the chart type, and add chart elements such as data labels. If you change the fields or set filters for the PivotChart, Excel applies those same changes to the related PivotTable.

Key Terms Matching

Match the key terms with their definitions. Write the key term letter by the appropriate numbered definition.

a. Calculated field
b. COLUMNS area
c. Data mining
d. Data model
e. FILTERS area
f. Grouping
g. Outline
h. PivotChart
i. PivotTable Fields List

j. PivotTable report
k. PivotTable style
l. PivotTable timeline
m. Relationship
n. ROWS area
o. Slicer
p. Slicer caption
q. Subtotal
r. VALUES area

1. _____ An association created between two tables where both tables contain a common field of data.

2. _____ A hierarchical structure of data that you can group related data to summarize.

3. _____ A row that contains at least one aggregate calculation, such as SUM or AVERAGE, that applies for a group of sorted data within a dataset.

4. _____ A process of joining related rows or columns of related data into a single entity so that groups can be collapsed or expanded.

5. _____ The process of analyzing large volumes of data to identify trends and patterns in the data.

6. _____ An interactive table that uses calculations to consolidate and summarize data from a data source into a separate table to enable a person to analyze the data in a dataset without altering the actual data.

7. _____ A user-defined field that performs a calculation based on other fields in a PivotTable.

8. _____ A window listing all unique items in a field so that the user can click button to filter data by that particular item or value.

9. _____ A section within the PivotTable Fields List used to place a field that will display labels to organize data horizontally in a PivotTable.

10. _____ A section within the PivotTable Fields List used to place a field to display summary statistics, such as totals or averages in a PivotTable.

11. _____ A section within the PivotTable Fields List used to place a field so that the user can then filter the data by that field.

12. _____ A section within the PivotTable Fields List used to place a field that will display labels to organize summarized data vertically in a PivotTable.

13. _____ A graphical representation of aggregated data derived from a PivotTable.

14. _____ A task pane that displays the fields in a dataset and enables a user to specify what fields are used to create a layout to organize the data in columns, rows, values, and filters in a PivotTable.

15. _____ The text or field name that appears as a header or title at the top of a slicer to identify the data in that field.

16. _____ A small window that starts with the first date and ends with the last date in the data source. It contains horizontal tiles that you can click to filter data by day, month, quarter, or year..

17. _____ A collection of related tables that contain structured data used to create a database.

18. _____ A set of formatting that controls bold, font colors, shading colors, and border lines.

Multiple Choice

1. A worksheet contains a list of graduates at your university. The worksheet contains these columns in this sequence: Student Last Name, Student First Name, College, Major, and GPA. Data are sorted by College, then by Major, and then by Student Last Name. What is the default *At a change in* setting within the Subtotal dialog box, and what would be a more appropriate setting?

   (a) Student Last Name (default field), GPA (correct field)

   (b) Student First Name (default field), Student Last Name (correct field)

   (c) College (default field), Student Last Name (correct field)

   (d) Student Last Name (default field), College (correct field)

2. You created an outline within a worksheet. What does the − button indicate to the left of a row heading?

   (a) You can click it to collapse the details of that category.

   (b) You can click it to expand the details of that category.

   (c) You can add a new row at that location only.

   (d) One or more columns are hidden.

3. A worksheet contains a PivotTable placeholder and the PivotTable Fields List. No fields have been added to the PivotTable yet. If you click the College Major field check box in the PivotTable Fields List, where does Excel place this field?

   (a) FILTERS area

   (b) COLUMNS area

   (c) ROWS area

   (d) VALUES area

4. You created a PivotTable to summarize commissions earned by employees in each department. What is the default summary statistic for the commissions field when you add it to the PivotTable?

   (a) Average

   (b) Count

   (c) Min

   (d) Sum

5. You have created a PivotTable and made some changes to values in the original dataset from which the PivotTable was created. How does this affect the PivotTable?

   (a) The PivotTable is updated automatically when you make changes to the dataset.

   (b) Changes in the dataset do not affect the PivotTable until you refresh the PivotTable.

6. What settings should you select for a PivotTable if you want to apply a different color scheme and display different fill colors for main category rows and horizontal lines within the PivotTable?

   (a) Banded Rows and Banded Columns check boxes

   (b) Banded Columns check box and a different PivotTable style

   (c) Banded Rows check box and a different PivotTable style

   (d) A different PivotTable style only

7. You have just created a slicer for the State field in a PivotTable. Which of the following does *not* characterize the initial slicer?

   (a) The slicer buttons are set to filter out all records.

   (b) The slicer caption is State.

   (c) The slicer contains one column of state names or abbreviations.

   (d) The slicer may display on top of the PivotTable data.

8. Which PivotTable calculated field is correctly constructed to calculate a 20% tip on a meal at a restaurant?

   (a) =Meal Cost * 20%

   (b) ='Meal Cost'*.2

   (c) ="Meal Cost"*.2

   (d) =B5*1.2

9. You have created a PivotChart showing sales by quarter by sales rep. Before presenting it to management, you notice the name of a rep who has since been fired. How do you remove this rep from the chart without deleting the data?

   (a) Make the employee's data points and axis titles invisible.

   (b) You cannot delete the rep from the chart without first deleting the data.

   (c) Filter the Sales Rep field in the PivotChart and deselect the employee's check box.

   (d) Hide that rep's row(s) in the underlying list, which automatically removes that rep from the chart.

10. Currently, the House Types field is in the ROWS area, the Real Estate Agent field is in the COLUMNS area, and Sum of List Prices is in the VALUES area. How can you modify the PivotTable to display the agent names as subcategories within the house types in the first column?

(a) Drag the Real Estate Agent field from the COLUMNS area and drop it above the House Types field in the ROWS area.

(b) Drag the House Types field from the ROWS area and drop it below the Real Estate Agent field in the COLUMNS area.

(c) Drag the House Types field from the ROWS area to the FILTERS area and drag the Real Estate Agent field from the COLUMNS area to the ROWS area.

(d) Drag the Real Estate Agent field from the COLUMNS area and drop it below the House Types field in the ROWS area.

Practice Exercises

1 January Restaurant Revenue

Your cousin Anthony owns a restaurant in Columbus, Ohio. The restaurant manager tracks daily revenue for the lunch and dinner hours. Anthony wants to analyze revenue by weekday for both the lunch and dinner hours for January. You will add subtotals of revenue by days of the week and by meal time for Anthony. At the end of the year, he wants to analyze data by days of the week and quarters for the whole year. You will create a PivotTable and a PivotChart to organize the data. Refer to Figure 46 as you complete this exercise.

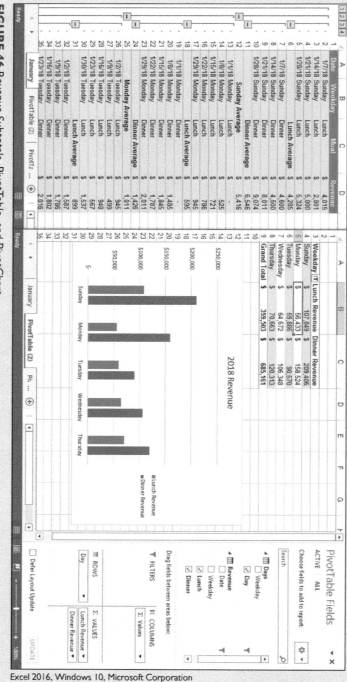

FIGURE 46 Revenue Subtotals, PivotTable, and PivotChart

Excel 2016, Windows 10, Microsoft Corporation

a. Open *e05p1Revenue* and save it as **e05p1Revenue_LastFirst.**

b. Ensure that the January worksheet is active. Complete the following steps to sort the data:

- Click the **Data tab** and click **Sort** in the Sort & Filter group to open the Sort dialog box.
- Click the **Sort by arrow** and select **Weekday.**
- Click the **Order arrow** and select **Custom List** to open the Custom Lists dialog box. Select **Sunday, Monday, Tuesday** in the *Custom lists* section and click **OK.**
- Click **Add Level** in the Sort dialog box, click the **Then by arrow**, and then select **Meal.**
- Click the **Order arrow** for Meal, select **Z to A** to list Lunch before Dinner, and click **OK.**

c. Click **Subtotal** in the Outline group. Complete the following steps in the Subtotal dialog box:

- Click the **At each change in arrow** and select **Weekday.**
- Click the **Use function arrow** and select **Average.**
- Keep the Revenue check box selected and click **OK.**

d. Add a second-level subtotal by meal by completing the following steps:

- Click **Subtotal** in the Outline group.
- Click the **At each change in arrow** and select **Meal.**
- Keep the Average function selected and keep the Revenue check box selected.
- Click the **Replace current subtotals check box** to deselect it. Click **OK.**

e. Click the **2 outline symbol** to collapse the list to see the weekday and grand averages. Which weekday produced the highest revenue? (Saturday) Which weekday produced the lowest revenue? (Monday) Click the **3 outline symbol** to expand the list to see weekday subtotals for lunch and dinner. Increase the width of column C so that the labels fully display.

f. Click the **Yearly Data sheet tab**. The Revenue table lists lunch and dinner revenue for every day in 2018. The Weekday column is coded where 1 = Sunday and 7 = Saturday. Click the **Weekdays sheet tab**. The Days table contains two columns; the Weekday codes with their respective weekday in the Day column. Click the **Yearly Data sheet tab**.

g. Click the **Data tab**, click **Relationships** in the Data Tools group to open the Manage Relationships dialog box, and then and complete the following steps:

- Click **New** to open the Create Relationship dialog box.
- Click the **Table arrow** and select **Revenue** (the main table). Click the **Column (Foreign) arrow** and select **Weekday**.
- Click the **Related Table arrow** and select **Days**. Click the **Related Column (Primary) arrow** and select **Weekday**.
- Click **OK** to close the Create Relationship dialog box. Click **Close** to close the Manage Relationships dialog box.

h. Complete the following steps to create a PivotTable using the related tables:

- Click the **Insert tab** and click **PivotTable** in the Tables group to open the Create PivotTable dialog box.
- Click the **Add this data to the Data Model check box** in the *Choose whether you want to analyze multiple tables* section. Click **OK**. Double-click the **Sheet1 tab**, type **PivotTable**, and then press **Enter**.
- Click **ALL** at the top of the PivotTable Fields List to display all table names.
- Click **Revenue** at the top of the PivotTable Fields List to display the fields for the Revenue table.
- Click the **Lunch** and **Dinner check boxes** in the PivotTable Fields List to display these fields in the VALUES area.
- Click **Days** in the PivotTable Fields List to display the fields for the Days table.
- Click the **Day check box** in the PivotTable Fields List to add this field to the ROWS area.

i. Modify the PivotTable by doing the following:

- Click the **Row Labels arrow** in cell **A3** and select **Sort A to Z**. (Note that this action sorts in sequential order by weekday, not alphabetical order by weekday name.)
- Type **Weekday** in cell **A3** and press **Enter**.
- Click the **Design tab**, click the **More button** in the PivotTable Styles group, and then click **Pivot Style Light 17**.
- Click the **Banded Rows check box** in the PivotTable Style Options group.

j. Format the values by doing the following:

- Click **cell B4**, click the **Analyze tab**, and then click **Field Settings** in the Active Field group.
- Type **Lunch Revenue** in the Custom Name box.
- Click **Number Format**, click **Accounting**, click the **Decimal places arrow** to display **0**, click **OK** in the Format Cells dialog box, and then click **OK** in the Value Field Settings dialog box.
- Click **cell C4** and click **Field Settings** in the Active Field group.
- Type **Dinner Revenue** in the Custom Name box.
- Click **Number Format**, click **Accounting**, click the **Decimal places arrow** to display **0**, click **OK** in the Format Cells dialog box, and then click **OK** in the Value Field Settings dialog box.
- Click the **PivotTable Name box** in the PivotTable group on the Analyze tab, type **Weekday Revenue**, and then press **Enter**.

k. Insert a timeline by completing the following steps:

- Click **Insert Timeline** in the Filter group to open the Insert Timelines dialog box.
- Click the **Date check box** and click **OK** to display the Date timeline. Move the Date timeline so that the top-left corner starts in **cell A13**.
- Click the **MONTHS arrow** in the Date timeline and select **QUARTERS**.
- Click the tile below **Q4** in the timeline to filter the data to reflect weekday totals for the fourth quarter only (October through December).

l. Create a PivotChart from the PivotTable by doing the following.

- Right-click the **PivotTable sheet tab**, select **Move or Copy**, click **PivotTable** in the *Before sheet* list, click the **Create a copy check box** to select it, and then click **OK**.

- Ensure that the PivotTable (2) sheet tab is active. Click the **Date timeline window** and press **Delete**.

- Click the **Analyze tab**, click **PivotChart** in the Tools group, and then click **OK** in the Insert Chart dialog box to create a default clustered column chart.

- Click the **Day arrow** in the bottom-left corner of the PivotChart, click the **Friday** and **Saturday check boxes** to deselect these weekdays so that you can focus on the other days of the week where sales are lower. Click **OK**.

- Click the **Shape Height box** in the Size group on the Format tab, type **3.5**, and then press **Enter**. Click in the **Shape Width box**, type **6**, and then press **Enter**.

- Click **CHART ELEMENTS** on the right of the chart, click the **Chart Title check box**, and click **CHART ELEMENTS** to close the menu.

- Click the **Chart Title placeholder**, type **2018 Revenue**, and then press **Enter**.

- Move the chart so that the top-left corner starts in **cell A12**.

- Click the **Analyze tab**, click the **Field Buttons arrow** in the Show/Hide group, and then select **Hide All** to hide the buttons within the chart area.

m. Create a footer with your name on the left side, the sheet name code in the center, and the file name code on the right side on each worksheet.

n. Save and close the file. Based on your instructor's directions, submit e05p1Revenue_LastFirst.

2 Suburbia Regional Hospital

Alesha Rogers is the Nurse Manager for the Neuro Acute Care Division at Suburbia Regional Hospital. The 12-hour nursing shifts are divided into day and graveyard. Alesha collects data on the number of patients that start each shift, the number of patients admitted, the number of patients discharged, and the number of patients at the end of each shift. She also notes how many nurses worked each shift. Because of your expertise in using Excel to analyze data, she has provided you a basic spreadsheet and asked you to help consolidate the data for her to analyze. She is interested in the number of nurses per daily shift (such as all Sunday graveyard shifts) for the month of April. Refer to Figure 47 as you complete this exercise.

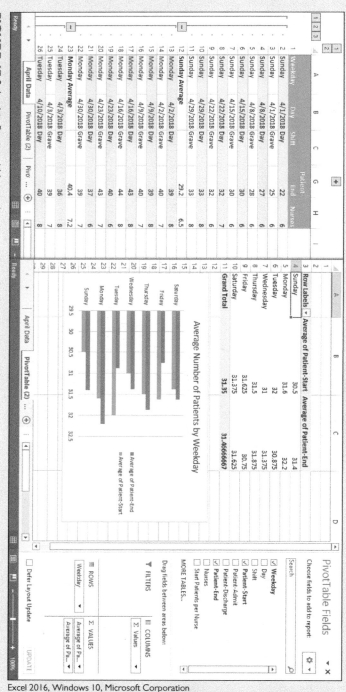

FIGURE 47 Suburbia Regional Hospital

a. Open *e05p2Patients* and save it as **e05p2Patients_LastFirst**.

b. Ensure that the **April Data worksheet** is active. Complete the following steps to sort the data:

- Click the **Data tab** and click **Sort** in the Sort & Filter group.
- Click the **Sort by arrow** and select **Weekday**.
- Click the **Order arrow** and select **Custom List** to open the Custom Lists dialog box. Select **Sunday, Monday, Tuesday** in the *Custom lists* section and click **OK**. Click **OK** in the Sort dialog box.

c. Click **Subtotal** in the Outline group. Complete the following steps in the Subtotal dialog box:

- Click the **At each change in arrow** and select **Weekday**.
- Click the **Use function arrow** and select **Average**.
- Click the **Patient-End check box** to select it, keep the Nurses check box selected, and then click **OK**.

d. Click the **Group arrow** in the Outline group on the Data tab, select **Auto Outline**, and then click **OK**. Click the **collapse button** above column G to collapse the outline.

e. Click the **April Table sheet tab**, click the **Insert tab**, click **Recommended PivotTables** in the Tables group, click the **Sum of Patient-Start by Weekday and Shift thumbnail**, and then click **OK**.

f. Complete the following steps to modify the PivotTable:

- Click the **Day check box** in the PivotTable Fields List to add that field to the ROWS area.
- Move the **Shift field** from the COLUMNS area to the FILTERS area in the PivotTable Fields List.
- Click the **Shift arrow** in **cell B1**, select **Day**, and click **OK** to filter the records to show totals for only the day shifts.
- Click the **PivotTable Name box** in the PivotTable group on the Analyze tab, type **Patients-Nurses**, and then press **Enter**.
- Rename Sheet1 as **PivotTable**.

g. Complete the following steps to create a calculated field:

- Click the **Analyze tab**, click **Fields, Items, & Sets** in the Calculations group, and then select **Calculated Field**.
- Type **Start Patients per Nurse** in the Name box in the Insert Calculated Field dialog box.
- Double-click **Patient-Start** in the Fields list, type **/**, and double-click **Nurses** in the Fields list. Click **OK**.
- Click **cell C3**, click **Field Settings** in the Active Field group, click **Number Format**, click **Number** in the Category list, click the **Decimal places** setting to **0**, click **OK** in the Format Cells dialog box, and then click **OK** in the Value Field Settings dialog box.

h. Click **Insert Slicer** in the Filter group, click the **Weekday check box** in the Insert Slicers dialog box, and then click **OK**.

i. Complete the following steps to customize the filter:

- Move the filter to start in **cell F3**.
- Click **More** in the Slicer Styles group on the Options tab and click **Slicer Style Dark 5**.
- Change the **Width** to **1.5** in the Buttons group on the Options tab.
- Press **Ctrl** and click **Sunday** and **Saturday** in the Weekday slicer to filter out these two days.

j. Copy the PivotTable sheet tab and place the PivotTable (2) sheet tab between the April Data and PivotTable sheet tabs. Ensure that the PivotTable (2) sheet is active and complete the following steps:

- Click the **Shift check box** in the PivotTable Fields List to remove it from the FILTERS area.
- Click the **Day check box** in the PivotTable Fields List to remove it from the ROWS area.
- Click **Multi-Select** in the Weekday slicer window, click **Sunday**, and then click **Saturday** so that all seven days will display.

k. Click in the PivotTable, click the **Analyze tab**, click **PivotChart** in the Tools group, and then complete the following steps:

- Click **Bar** in the Insert Chart dialog box and click **OK**.

- Click the **Sum of Start Patients per Nurse arrow** in the VALUES area of the PivotTable Fields List and select **Remove Field**.

- Click the **Sum of Patients Start arrow** in the VALUES area of the PivotTable Fields List, click **Value Field Settings**, select **Average**, click **Number Format**, select **Number** in the Category list, click **OK** in the Format Cells dialog box, and then click **OK** in the Value Field Settings dialog box.

- Click the **Sum of Patients End arrow** in the VALUES area of the PivotTable Fields List, click **Value Field Settings**, select **Average**, click **Number Format**, select **Number** in the Category list, click **OK** in the Format Cells dialog box, and then click **OK** in the Value Field Settings dialog box.

- Click the **Analyze tab**, click the **Field Buttons arrow** in the Show/Hide group, and then select **Hide All**.

- Click the **Chart Title placeholder**, type **Average Number of Patients by Weekday**, and then press **Enter**.

- Move the chart so that the top-left corner starts in **cell A13**.

l. Create a footer with your name on the left side, the sheet name code in the center, and the file name code on the right side on each worksheet.

m. Save and close the file. Based on your instructor's directions, submit e05p2Patients_LastFirst.

Mid-Level Exercises

1 Mountain View Realty

ANALYSIS CASE

You are a real estate analyst who works for Mountain View Realty in the North Utah County area. You have consolidated a list of houses sold during the past few months and want to analyze the data. For a simple analysis, you will outline the data and use the Subtotal feature. You will then create two PivotTables and a PivotChart to give you a way to perform more in-depth analysis.

a. Open *e05m1RealEstate* and save it as **e05m1RealEstate_LastFirst**.

b. Make sure the Sales Subtotals worksheet is the active sheet and insert the following formulas:

- Insert a formula in **cell G2** to calculate the selling price percentage of the asking price, format it with **Percent Style** with **1** decimal place, and then copy the formula down the column.

- Insert a formula in **cell J2** to calculate the number of days between the listing date and sale date. Copy the formula down the column.

c. Sort the list by city in alphabetical order, then by selling agent in alphabetical order, and finally by listing date in chronological order.

d. Use the Subtotal feature to calculate the average selling price, percentage of asking price, and days on market by city.

e. Apply an automatic outline to the columns and complete the following steps:

- Collapse the outline to hide the listing and sale dates.

- Click the outline symbol to display the grand average and city average rows only. Format the average days on market to zero decimal places.

- Apply wrap text for **cells G1 and J1**.

- Select individually columns G and J and change the column width to **10.00**.

- Change the row height to **24** for the first row.

- Set a print area for the **range C1:J88**.

f. Go to **cell C101** in the Sales Subtotals worksheet. Read the questions and provide the appropriate answers in the respective highlighted cells in the **range G102:G106**. Apply **Accounting Number Format** with **0** decimal places to **cell G102**.

g. Click the **Sales Data sheet tab** and create a blank PivotTable on a new worksheet. Name the new worksheet **PivotTable**. Name the PivotTable **Average City Prices**.

h. Place the **City field** in rows, the **Selling Agent field** in columns, and the **Asking Price** and **Selling Price fields** as values.

i. Modify the PivotTable by completing the following steps:

- Display averages rather than sums with **Accounting Number Format** with **0** decimal places for the two value fields.

- Pivot the data by moving the **City field** below the Values field in the COLUMNS area and moving the **Selling Agents field** to ROWS area.

- Add a filter in **cell B3** to display only Alpine and Cedar Hills.

j. Complete the following steps to change the format of the PivotTable:

- Change the widths of columns A, B, C, D, and E to **11**.

- Change the widths of columns F and G to **14**.

- Wrap text and center horizontally data in **cells B4, D4, F4, and G4**.

- Apply the **Bottom Border** to the **range B4:F4**.

- Change the label in **cell A5** to **Agent**. Change the height of row 4 to **40**.

k. Display the contents on the Sales Data worksheet. You realize that a selling price is incorrect. Change the selling price for Number 40 from *$140,000* to **$1,400,000**. Refresh the PivotTable. Adjust the column widths to match the instructions in step j.

l. Display the contents on the Sales Data worksheet. Create a recommended PivotTable using the **Sum of Selling Price by City** thumbnail. Change the name of the new PivotTable worksheet to **Selling Price**. Make these changes to the new PivotTable:

- Change the value to display averages not sums.

- Apply the **Accounting Number Format** with **0** decimal places to the values.

- Apply **Pivot Style Medium 2** to the PivotTable.

2 Fiesta® Collection

Your Aunt Laura has been collecting Fiesta dinnerware, a popular brand from the Homer Laughlin China Company, since 1986. You help her maintain an inventory. So far, you and Aunt Laura have created a table of color numbers, color names, year introduced, and year retired, if applicable. In a second table, you entered color numbers, item numbers, items, current value, and source. Previously, you helped her research current replacement costs from Homer Laughlin's website (www.hlchina.com), Replacements, Ltd. (www.replacements.com), and eBay (www.ebay.com); however, you believe the retired colors may be worth more now. Laura is especially interested in the values of retired colors so that she can provide this information for her insurance agent. You will build a PivotTable and add slicers to help her with the analysis.

a. Open *e05m2Fiesta* and save it as **e05m2Fiesta_LastFirst**.

b. Create a relationship between the Items table using the Color Number field and the Colors table using the Color Number field.

c. Create a blank PivotTable from within the Items table on the Collection worksheet to analyze multiple tables. Add the data to the data model. Place the PivotTable on a new worksheet and name the worksheet **Retired Colors**. Name the PivotTable **Retired**.

d. Display the names of both tables in the PivotTable Fields List.

e. Display the **Color field** as rows and the sum of the Replacement Value field as values.

f. Add a filter to display aggregates for retired colors only using the **Retired field**. Note that current colors do not have a retirement date, so you must filter out the blanks.

g. Apply the **Pivot Style Medium 7**.

h. Format the values with **Accounting Number Format** with **2** decimal places. Create a custom name **Replacement Value**. Change *Row Labels* in **cell A3** to **Retired Colors**.

i. Add a column to show calculations by completing the following steps:
- Add a second Replacement Value field below the current field in the VALUES area.
- Select the option to display the values as percentages of the grand total.
- Type the custom name **Percent of Total**.

j. Add a slicer for the **Color field**. Select these colors to display: **Apricot, Chartreuse, Lilac, Marigold, Pearl Gray**, and **Sapphire**.

k. Customize the slicer by completing the following steps:
- Apply the **Slicer Style Light 6 style**.
- Display **3** columns within the slicer window.
- Change the button width to **1.5"**. Move the slicer so that the top-left corner starts in **cell E2**.

l. Create a clustered column PivotChart and place it on a new chart sheet named **Retired PivotChart**.

m. Modify the chart by completing these steps:
- Change the chart title to **Replacement Value of Retired Items**.
- Change the Lilac data point fill color to **Purple**.
- Change the value axis font size to **11** and apply **Black, Text 1** font color.

m. Create a column PivotChart from the PivotTable on the Selling Price worksheet. Move the chart to a chart sheet named **Sales Chart**. Complete the following steps for the chart:
- Change the chart title to **Average Selling Price by City** and apply **Dark Blue font color**.
- Remove the legend.
- Apply **Dark Blue fill color** to the data series.

n. Create a footer with your name on the left side, the sheet name code in the center, and the file name code on the right side all worksheets. Adjust page scaling if needed.

o. Save and close the file. Based on your instructor's directions, submit e05m1RealEstate_LastFirst.

- Change the category axis font size to **11** and apply **Black, Text 1** font color.
- Hide the field buttons on the PivotChart.

n. Create a footer with your name on the left side, the sheet name code in the center, and the file name code on the right side of all worksheets.

o. Save and close the file. Based on your instructor's directions, submit e05m2Fiesta_LastFirst.

3 Facebook® Social Phenomenon

Facebook has experienced phenomenal growth since its creation in 2004. What is it that has made Facebook a huge success story, starting a decade after many of the other Web company startups? To understand how people use Facebook, look at its applications. Work with another student to conduct this research, obtain data, and create PivotTables.

a. Open www.checkfacebook.com in a Web browser to read about Facebook's history.

b. Start a new Excel workbook and save it as **e05m3Facebook_LastFirst**.

c. Go to http://statistics.allfacebook.com and use this site to build a worksheet that lists at least 200 application leaders for 10 categories, two of which must be Business and Just For Fun. Each student should find 100 different application leaders. Use collaboration tools to make sure you and your team member use the same format and do not duplicate data.

d. Include data for these columns: Category, Name, Daily Average Use (DAU), Monthly Average Use (MAU), and Daily Growth.

e. Copy your team member's worksheet as a new worksheet in your workbook. Then create a third worksheet to combine the data. Name the sheets appropriately.

f. Format the data and headings appropriately in the combined worksheet.

g. Create a PivotTable based on the data to reflect one perspective of analysis. Format the values and apply desired filters.

h. Have your teammate copy the combined sheet and create his or her own PivotTable with a different perspective, formatting, and desired filters.

i. Discuss your analysis with your team member.

j. Create a footer with your name and your team member's name on the left side, sheet name code in the center, and the file name code on the right side of each worksheet.

k. Save and close the file. Based on your instructor's directions, submit e05m3FaceBook_LastFirst.

Beyond the Classroom

Departing Flights

GENERAL CASE ✓

FROM SCRATCH 🖑

You want to research morning flight departures from Tulsa International Airport (TUL) using data obtained from flightstats.com website. Find the airport's departing flight schedule for yesterday morning and copy the flight information on a worksheet in a new workbook. Name the workbook **e05b1Tulsa_LastFirst**. Clean up the data after copying it. Name the worksheet **Departures**. Copy the worksheet and name the duplicate sheet **Morning Departures**. Sort the data on the Departures sheet by destination and then by airline. Insert subtotals at a change in destination, counting the number of flights. Collapse the subtotals to display the subtotals and grand totals.

Create a blank PivotTable from the Morning Departures sheet. Display the Destination and Airline fields in rows. Display the Status field in columns to display canceled, on-time, and delayed flights. Display the Flight field in the values area and change the field settings to the Count function. Display the Departure Time as a filter and set a filter to include only departure times from 6 to 9 a.m. Name the PivotTable **Morning Departure Status**. Apply **PivotStyle Medium 13 style**. Adjust column widths as needed. Name the worksheet **PivotTable**.

Create a PivotChart from the original dataset. Name the sheet **PivotChart**. Use the Destination field as the axis and the Flight # as the value. Change the value to the Count function. Change the chart type to a bar chart. Set 3.75″ chart height and 5.75″ chart width. Insert a slicer for the Status field and click the slicer button to display only on-time departures. Add a chart title **On-Time Departures**. Create a footer with your name, the sheet name code, and the file name code on each worksheet. Save and close the file. Based on your instructor's directions, submit e05b1Tulsa_LastFirst.

Innovative Game Studio

DISASTER RECOVERY ➕

You work as an assistant to Terry Park, the producer for a video game studio in Phoenix, Arizona. The company produces games for the PlayStation®, Xbox®, and Wii™ consoles. The producer tracks salaries and performance for everyone on a particular team, which consists of artists, animators, programmers, and so forth. Terry tried to create a PivotTable to organize the data by department and then by title within department. He also wants to display total salaries by these categories and filter the data to show aggregates for team members who earned only Excellent and Good performance ratings. In addition, he wants to see what the percentages of total salaries for each job title are of each department's budget. For example, the total salary for Senior Artists is $263,300. That represents 50.27% of the Art Department's salary budget ($523,800) for Excellent-and Good-rated employees. However, the percentages are not displayed correctly. Terry called you in to correct his PivotTable.

Open *e05b2Games* and save it as **e05b2Games_LastFirst**. Identify the errors and make a list of these errors starting on row 41 in the PivotTable worksheet. Correct the errors and improve the format, including a medium PivotStyle, throughout the PivotTable. Create a footer with your name, the sheet name code, and the file name code. Save and close the file. Based on your instructor's directions, submit e05b2Games_LastFirst.

Capstone Exercise

You are an analyst for an authorized Greenwich Workshop® fine art dealer (www.greenwichworkshop.com). Customers are especially fond of James C. Christensen's art. You prepared a list of his artwork: Title (title of each piece of art), Type (the medium, such as Limited Edition Print or Anniversary Edition Canvas), Edition Size (how many copies were produced for purchase), Release Date (the month and year the art was released), Issue Price (the original retail price when the art was released), and Est. Value (the estimated current market value). Studying the data will help you discuss value trends with art collectors.

Sort, Subtotal, and Outline Data

You want to organize data to facilitate using the Subtotal feature to display the average issue price and estimated value by Type.

a. Open *e05c1FineArt* and save it as **e05c1FineArt_LastFirst**.

b. Click the **Subtotals sheet tab**. Sort the data by Type and further sort it by the Title, both in alphabetical order.

c. Use the Subtotal feature to insert subtotal rows by Type to identify the highest Issue Price and Est. Value.

d. Collapse the data by displaying only the subtotals and grand total rows.

e. Set a print area for the **range D1:I247**. Set the scaling to fit to one page.

Create a PivotTable

You want to create a PivotTable to analyze the art by Type, Issue Price, and Est. Value. In addition, you will rename the worksheet and the PivotTable.

a. Click the **Christensen sheet tab** and create a blank PivotTable on a new worksheet.

b. Name the worksheet **Sold Out**.

c. Use the **Type** and **Issue Price fields**, enabling Excel to determine where the fields go.

d. Add the **Est. Value field** to the VALUES area.

e. Name the PivotTable **Average Price by Type.**

Change Value Field Settings and Create a Calculated Field

Excel displays the sum of the values by Type. However, you want to calculate the average values for each art type. In addition, you will calculate the percentage change from the Issue Price to the Est. Value. Finally, you will format the values and enter clear headings in the PivotTable.

a. Modify the value fields to determine the average Issue Price and average Est. Value by type.

b. Customize the value fields by completing the following steps:
- Change the custom names to **Average Issue Price** and **Average Est. Value**, respectively for the two value fields.
- Apply **Currency** number format with **0** decimal places to the two value fields.

c. Insert a calculated field to determine percent change in values between the Est. Value and Issue Price.

d. Customize the calculated field by completing the following steps:
- Change the custom name to **Percent Change in Value**.
- Apply **Percentage** number format with **2** decimal places.

e. Select the **range B3:D3** and apply these formats: wrap text, **Align Right** horizontal alignment, **30** row height, and **10** column widths.

f. Type **Type of Art** in **cell A3** and type **Average of All Art** in **cell A18.**

Filter the PivotTable and Apply a Style

You want to focus on average values for sold-out art because these pieces typically increase in value on the secondary market. The Sold Out column indicates Yes if the art is sold out, blank if the art is still available, or Limited Availability if the art is still available but in limited supply. In addition, you want to narrow the list to particular types. After filtering the data, you will apply a different style to the PivotTable.

a. Set a filter to display only sold-out art (indicated by **Yes**).

b. Set a Type filter to filter out these types Hand Colored Print, Limited Edition Hand Colored Print, Open Edition Canvas, Open Edition Print, and Poster.

c. Apply **Pivot Style Light 23**.

d. Display banded columns.

Insert a Slicer and Timeline

You want to preserve the original PivotTable but create a duplicate so that you can filter data by a timeline and slicer. You will insert a slicer for the Sold Out field and a timeline for the Release Date field. You will then use these elements to filter the data to show only sold-out art for the years 2000 to 2005.

a. Copy the Sold Out worksheet, move the duplicate sheet tab to the left of the Sold Out sheet tab, and rename the new sheet **Types.**

b. Reset the Sold Out filter and then remove the Sold Out field from the FILTERS area.

c. Insert a slicer for the Sold Out field and complete the following steps to customize the slicer:

* Change the slicer height to **1.5"**.
* Apply **Slicer Style Dark 1**.
* Click the **Yes slicer button** to filter the PivotTable to list averages for only sold-out art.

d. Insert a timeline for the Release Date field and complete the following steps:

* Change the time period to **YEARS**.
* Set the timeline to filter to display **2000** to **2005**.
* Change the timeline width to **4"**.

Create a PivotChart

To help interpret the consolidated values of the art, you want to create a PivotChart. You realize that displaying both monetary values and percentages on the same chart is like mixing apples and oranges. If you modify the PivotChart, you will change the PivotTable; therefore, you will copy the Sold Out worksheet and then create a PivotChart from the duplicate worksheet.

a. Copy the Sold Out worksheet, move the duplicate sheet tab to the left of the Types sheet tab, and rename the new sheet **PivotChart.**

b. Create a PivotChart selecting the **Clustered Bar** type.

c. Modify the PivotChart by completing the following steps:

* Move the PivotChart so that the top-left corner starts in **cell A14.**
* Change the chart height to **3.5"** and the width to **6.5".**
* Hide the field buttons in the PivotChart.
* Remove the Percentage Change field.

d. Add a chart title and type **Values for Sold-Out Christensen Art.**

e. Set the upper limit of the value axis to **3000.**

f. Change the chart style to **Style 12.**

g. Select the category labels in the PivotChart and sort the labels from Z to A.

Finalizing Your Workbook

You will finalize your workbook by adding a footer to the worksheets you changed and created.

a. Create a footer on all worksheets (except Christensen) with your name, the sheet name code, and the file name code.

b. Save and close the file. Based on your instructor's directions, submit e05c1FineArt_LastFirst.

Glossary

Calculated field A user-defined field that performs a calculation based on other fields in a PivotTable.

COLUMNS area A section within the PivotTable Fields List used to display columns of summarized data for the selected field(s) that will display labels to organize summarized data vertically in a PivotTable.

Data mining The process of analyzing large volumes of data using advanced statistical techniques to identify trends and patterns in the data.

Data model A collection of related tables that contain structured data used to create a database.

FILTERS area A section within the PivotTable Fields List used to place a field so that the user can then filter the data by that field. Displays top-level filters above the PivotTable so that you can set filters to display results based on particular conditions you set.

Grouping (data) The process of joining rows or columns of related data into a single entity so that groups can be collapsed or expanded for data analysis.

Outline A hierarchical structure of data that you can group related data to summarize. When a dataset has been grouped into an outline, you can collapse the outlined data to show only main rows such as subtotals or expand the outlined data to show all the details.

PivotChart An interactive graphical representation of data in a PivotTable.

PivotTable Fields List A task pane that displays the fields in a dataset and enables a user to specify what fields are used to create a layout to organize the data in columns, rows, values, and filters in a PivotTable.

PivotTable report An interactive table that uses calculations to consolidate and summarize data from a data source into a separate table to enable a person to analyze the data in a dataset without altering the dataset itself. You can rotate or pivot the data in a PivotTable to look at the data from different perspectives. Also referred to simply as a *PivotTable*.

PivotTable style A set of formatting that controls bold, font colors, shading colors, and border lines.

PivotTable timeline A small window that starts with the first date and ends with the last date in the data source. It contains horizontal tiles that you can click to filter data by day, month, quarter, or year.

ROWS area A section within the PivotTable Fields List used to place a field that will display labels to organize data horizontally in a PivotTable. It groups the data into categories in the first column, listing each unique label only once regardless how many times the label is contained in the original dataset.

Slicer A small window containing one button for each unique item in a field so that you can filter the PivotTable quickly.

Slicer caption The text or field name that appears as a header or title at the top of a slicer to identify the data in that field.

VALUES area A section within the PivotTable Fields List used to place a field to display summary statistics, such as totals or averages, in a PivotTable.

Specialized Functions

From Excel Chapter 7 of *Microsoft® Excel 2016, Comprehensive*. Mary Anne Poatsy, Hogan, Lau, and Robert T. Grauer. Copyright © 2017 by Pearson Education, Inc. Published by Pearson Prentice Hall. All Rights Reserved.

Download student resources at http://www.pearsonhighered.com/exploring.

Excel

Specialized Functions

LEARNING OUTCOME:

You will manipulate data using date, logical, lookup, database, and financial functions.

OBJECTIVES & SKILLS: After you read this chapter, you will be able to:

Date, Logical, and Lookup Functions

OBJECTIVE 1. USE DATE FUNCTIONS
Use the YEARFRAC Function; Use the DAYS Function;
Use the DATE, YEAR, and MONTH Functions;
Use Other Date Functions

OBJECTIVE 2. CREATE A NESTED LOGICAL FUNCTION
Create a Nested IF Function, Use the AND Function,
Nest an AND Function, Nest an OR or NOT Function

OBJECTIVE 3. USE ADVANCED LOOKUP FUNCTIONS
Create a Lookup Field, Use the INDEX Function, Use
the MATCH Function

HANDS-ON EXERCISE 1:
Date, Logical, and Lookup Functions

Database Filtering and Functions

OBJECTIVE 4. APPLY ADVANCED FILTERING
Create Criteria and Output Ranges, Apply an
Advanced Filter

OBJECTIVE 5. MANIPULATE DATA WITH DATABASE FUNCTIONS
Use the DSUM Function, Use the DAVERAGE Function,
Use the DMIN Function, Use the DMAX Function, Use
the DCOUNT Function

HANDS-ON EXERCISE 2:
Database Filtering and Functions

Financial Functions

OBJECTIVE 6. USE FINANCIAL FUNCTIONS
Use the PV Function, Use the FV Function, Use the
NPV Function, Use the NPER Function, Use the RATE
Function

OBJECTIVE 7. CREATE A LOAN AMORTIZATION TABLE
Enter Formulas in the Amortization Table, Use the
IPMT Function, Use the PPMT Function, Use the
CUMIPMT Function, Use the CUMPRINC Function

HANDS-ON EXERCISE 3:
Financial Functions

CASE STUDY | Transpayne Filtration

You are an assistant accountant in the Human Resources (HR) Department for Transpayne Filtration, a company that sells water filtration systems to residential customers. Transpayne has locations in Atlanta, Boston, and Chicago, with a manager at each location who oversees several account representatives. You have an Excel workbook that contains names, locations, titles, hire dates, and salaries for the 20 managers and account representatives. To prepare for your upcoming salary analyses, you downloaded salary data from the corporate database into the workbook.

The HR manager wants you to perform several tasks based on locations and job titles. You will use logical functions to calculate annual bonus amounts and database functions to help analyze the data. Finally, you will review financial aspects of automobiles purchased for each manager.

Everything possible/Shutterstock

Using Date, Logical, Lookup, Database, and Financial Functions

---

Logic Lookup worksheet (1-Logic Lookup)

H7 formula: `=IF(E7<$I$2,G7*$J$2,IF(E7<=$I$3,G7*$J$3,G7*$J$4))`

Quick Search Results:	Account Rep			Bonus Amount	Date
Last Day of Year	12/31/2018			Hired before	1/1/2010
Manager Salary Threshold	$ 70,000			Hired on or before	1/1/2015
				Hired after	1/1/2015

Payne Sales Rep Salary Information

Title	Hire Date	Years Employed	Salary	Bonus Amount	Raise Status
Manager	10/14/2007	11.2	$ 68,750	$ 6,188	Due for raise
Account Rep	11/5/2018	0.2	$ 49,575	$ 1,487	NA
Account Rep	6/14/2014	4.5	$ 46,000	$ 2,300	NA
Manager	3/9/2009	9.8	$ 75,800	$ 6,822	NA
Account Rep	12/4/2014	4.1	$ 46,795	$ 2,340	NA
Account Rep	6/5/2014	4.6	$ 43,750	$ 2,188	NA
Account Rep	9/3/2015	3.3	$ 45,250	$ 1,358	NA
Account Rep	7/19/2014	4.5	$ 47,240	$ 2,362	NA

Database worksheet (2-Database)

Criteria Range:

Employee ID	Name	Location	Title	Hire Date	Salary
		Boston	Account Rep		

Output Range:

Employee ID	Name	Location	Title	Hire Date	Salary
2521	Barnes	Boston	Account Rep	6/14/2014	$ 46,000
2848	Gomez	Boston	Account Rep	10/15/2016	$ 46,725
3996	Hartvigsen	Boston	Account Rep	2/18/2015	$ 45,000
4428	Selinger	Boston	Account Rep	11/8/2016	$ 41,525

Tabs: 1-Logic Lookup | 2-Database | 3-Finance

Finance worksheet (3-Finance)

Input Area:

Payment	$ 450.00
APR	5.25%
Years	4
Pmts per Year	12

Basic Output Area:

Loan	$19,444.57
Periodic Rate	0.438%
# of Payments	48

Payment Number	Beginning Balance	Monthly Payment	Interest Paid	Principal Repayment	Ending Balance	Cumulative Interest
1	$19,444.57	$ 450.00	$ 85.07	$ 364.93	$ 19,079.64	$ 85.07
2	$19,079.64	$ 450.00	$ 83.47	$ 366.53	$ 18,713.11	$ 168.54
3	$18,713.11	$ 450.00	$ 81.87	$ 368.13	$ 18,344.98	$ 250.41
4	$18,344.98	$ 450.00	$ 80.26	$ 369.74	$ 17,975.24	$ 330.67
5	$17,975.24	$ 450.00	$ 78.64	$ 371.36	$ 17,603.88	$ 409.31
6	$17,603.88	$ 450.00	$ 77.02	$ 372.98	$ 17,230.90	$ 486.33
7	$17,230.90	$ 450.00	$ 75.39	$ 374.61	$ 16,856.28	$ 561.72
8	$16,856.28	$ 450.00	$ 73.75	$ 376.25	$ 16,480.03	$ 635.46
9	$16,480.03	$ 450.00	$ 72.10	$ 377.90	$ 16,102.13	$ 707.56
10	$16,102.13	$ 450.00	$ 70.45	$ 379.55	$ 15,722.58	$ 778.01
11	$15,722.58	$ 450.00	$ 68.79	$ 381.21	$ 15,341.36	$ 846.80
12	$15,341.36	$ 450.00	$ 67.12	$ 382.88	$ 14,958.48	$ 913.91
13	$14,958.48	$ 450.00	$ 65.44	$ 384.56	$ 14,573.92	$ 979.36
14	$14,573.92	$ 450.00	$ 63.76	$ 386.24	$ 14,187.68	$ 1,043.12
15	$14,187.68	$ 450.00	$ 62.07	$ 387.93	$ 13,799.76	$ 1,105.19
16	$13,799.76	$ 450.00	$ 60.37	$ 389.63	$ 13,410.13	$ 1,165.56
17	$13,410.13	$ 450.00	$ 58.67	$ 391.33	$ 13,018.80	$ 1,224.23
18	$13,018.80	$ 450.00	$ 56.96	$ 393.04	$ 12,625.76	$ 1,281.19
19	$12,625.76	$ 450.00	$ 55.24	$ 394.76	$ 12,230.99	$ 1,336.43
20	$12,230.99	$ 450.00	$ 53.51	$ 396.49	$ 11,834.50	$ 1,389.94
21	$11,834.50	$ 450.00	$ 51.78	$ 398.22	$ 11,436.28	$ 1,441.71

Excel 2016, Windows 10, Microsoft Corporation

FIGURE 1 Transpayne Filtration Workbook

Case Study | Transpayne Filtration

Starting File	File to be Submitted
e07h1Salary	e07h3Salary_LastFirst

Date, Logical, and Lookup Functions

As you have learned, dates are stored as serial numbers. This method of storing dates enables you to perform calculations using cells that contain dates. The Date & Time category in the Function Library contains a variety of functions that work with dates. Previously, you used the TODAY function to return the current date and the NOW function to display the current date and time.

Logical functions enable you to test conditions to determine if a condition is true or false. You have used the IF function, which is the most commonly used logical function. Excel enables you to use two or more functions together to perform complex calculations. For example, people commonly use other functions within an IF function to evaluate complex logical conditions for multiple outcomes.

You have also used lookup and reference functions to look up a value contained elsewhere in a workbook. For example, you are familiar with the VLOOKUP and HLOOKUP functions, which take an identified value, such as the number of months for a certificate of deposit (CD) to mature, look up that value in a vertical or horizontal lookup table, and then obtain a related value, such as the annual percentage rate (APR). Excel contains additional logical functions to perform for more complicated referencing.

In this section, you will learn about some useful date functions and how to include a function as an argument inside another function. In addition, you will learn how to use the MATCH and INDEX lookup functions.

Using Date Functions

The Date & Time category in Excel's Function Library group includes a variety of date and time functions. You can use these functions to calculate when employees are eligible for certain benefits, what the date is six months from now, or what day of the week a particular date falls on.

Calculate Days and Years Between Dates

STEP 1 ▶▶ You might want to calculate the number of days or years between two dates. For example, if you work for a credit card company, you might want to calculate the number of days from a payment due date and the actual payment date. The **DAYS function** calculates the number of days between two dates where the most recent date is entered in the end_date argument and the older date is entered in the start_date argument. For example, if the end date is 9/30/2018 and the start date is 9/1/2018, the DAYS function calculates 29 days between those two dates (see the range A1:B3 in Figure 2). In cell E3, the DAYS function calculates 1,276 days between 1/1/2015 and 6/30/2018.

	A	B	C	D	E	F
1	Start Date	9/1/2018			1/1/2015	
2	End Date	9/30/2018			6/30/2018	
3	DAYS Function	29	=DAYS(B2,B1)		1276	=DAYS(E2,E1)
4	YEARFRAC Function	0.08	=YEARFRAC(B1,B2)		3.50	=YEARFRAC(E1,E2)
5						

FIGURE 2 DAYS and YEARFRAC Functions

Excel 2016, Windows 10, Microsoft Corporation

Instead of calculating the exact number of days between dates, you might want to calculate the fraction of a year or the number of years between two dates. The **YEARFRAC function** calculates the fraction of a year between two dates based on the number of whole days using the start_date and end_date arguments. In Figure 2, the YEARFRAC function in cell B4 calculates 8% of the year exists between 9/1/2018 and 9/30/2018. In cell E4, the YEARFRAC function calculates 3.5 years exist between 1/1/2015 and 6/30/2018. The DAYS and YEARFRAC functions use the same arguments (start_date and end_date) but in reverse order.

=DAYS(end_date,start_date)

=YEARFRAC(start_date,end_date)

Extract Day, Month, and Year

Often, a cell contains an exact date, such as 9/1/2018. However, you might want to extract part of the date, such as just the month, day, or year. For example, if you own a wedding catering business, you might review historical data to identify which month had the most weddings to cater. To do so, you would extract the months from dates when you catered weddings. The **DAY function** displays the day (1–31) within a given date. The **MONTH function** displays the month (1–12), where 1 is January and 12 is December, for a specific date. The **YEAR function** displays the year (such as 2018) for a specific date. Figure 3 illustrates two dates and the results of using the DAY, MONTH, and YEAR functions. The serial_number argument refers to the cell containing a date. If you want to enter a date directly in the argument, you must enclose the date in quotation marks, such as =DAY("6/30/2018").

=DAY(serial_number)

=MONTH(serial_number)

=YEAR(serial_number)

▲	A	B	C	D	E	F
1	Dates	9/1/2018			30-Jun-18	
2						
3	DAY function	1	=DAY(B1)		30	=DAY(E1)
4	MONTH function	9	=MONTH(B1)		6	=MONTH(E1)
5	YEAR function	2018	=YEAR(B1)		2018	=YEAR(E1)

Excel 2016, Windows 10, Microsoft Corporation

FIGURE 3 DAY, MONTH, and YEAR Functions

TIP: EDATE AND EOMONTH FUNCTIONS

Two other date functions are useful. *EDATE* displays a date in the future or past, given a specific number of months. *EOMONTH* displays the last day of a month for a specified number of months from a particular date. For example, =EDATE("9/1/2018",3) displays 12/1/2018, three months from 9/1/2018, whereas =EOMONTH("9/1/2018",3) displays 12/31/2018, the end of the month three months from 9/1/2018.

The default result displays as a serial number, such as 43435 if the cell containing the function is formatted with General number format. To display the actual date, format the cell with Short Date number format.

Creating a Nested Logical Function

Recall from previous experience that the IF function contains three arguments: logical_test, value_if_true, and value_if_false. You can enter formulas within both the value_if_true and value_if_false arguments to perform calculations. For situations with multiple outcomes based on conditions, you can nest IF functions within the value_if_true and value_if_false arguments. A *nested function* is a function that is embedded within an argument of another function. You can nest up to 64 IF functions in the value_if_true and value_if_false arguments.

STEP 2

Nested IF Within an IF Function

When you have three outcomes for a situation, you can test one condition in the logical_test argument, display results if that condition is true in the value_if_true argument, and then test another condition by entering a nested IF function in the value_if_false argument. While the nested IF function can go in either the value_if_true or value_if_false argument, it helps for comprehending a nested IF function to keep the value_if_true argument simple.

For example, assume you want to calculate bonuses for employees based on hire date. You divided the hire dates into three timelines. If an employee was hired before 1/1/2010, the employee receives 9% of her or his salary as a bonus. If an employee was hired between 1/1/2010 and 1/1/2015, the employee earns a 5% bonus. Finally, employees hired after 1/1/2015 receive a 3% bonus (see Figure 4). Because this scenario has three possible outcomes for calculating bonuses, you use logical tests for two of the outcomes. If both logical tests are false, the third outcome is the result.

| E7 | : | × | ✓ | fx | =IF(C7<C$2,D7*D$2,IF(C7<=C$3,D7*D$3,D7*D$4)) |

▲	A	B	C	D	E	F	G
1		Bonus Amount	Date	Percent		Nested IF function	
2	Bonus rate date criteria	Hired before	1/1/2010	9%			
3		Hired on or before	1/1/2015	5%		Bonus percentage based on date criteria	
4		Hired after	1/1/2015	3%			
5							
6	Name	Title	Hire Date	Salary		Bonus Amount	
7	Adams	Manager	10/14/2007	$ 68,750	$ 6,188		
8	Akmatalieva	Account Rep	11/3/2018	$ 49,575	$ 1,487	Dates evaluated by IF functions	
9	Crandell	Manager	3/9/2009	$ 75,800	$ 6,822		
10	Deberard	Account Rep	12/4/2014	$ 46,795	$ 2,340		
11	Hartwigsen	Account Rep	2/18/2015	$ 45,000	$ 1,350		
12	Laing	Manager	1/17/2011	$ 65,500	$ 3,275		
13	Lenz	Account Rep	4/15/2012	$ 49,750	$ 2,488		
14							

FIGURE 4 Nested IF Function Results

Figure 5 illustrates the bonus-calculation process as a flowchart. Diamonds are logical_test arguments, and rectangles are value_if_true and value_if_false arguments. The first logical_test evaluates if the employee was hired before 1/1/2010 (C7<C$2). If that test is TRUE, the salary is multiplied by 9% (D7*D$2). If that test is FALSE, the nested IF function in the value_if_false argument is executed. Figure 6 illustrates the bonus-calculation process with cell references.

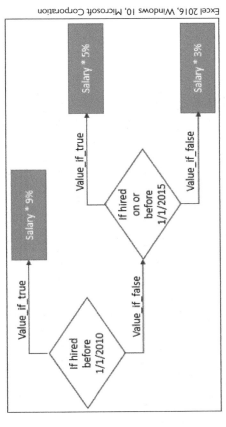

FIGURE 5 Nested IF Function Flowchart

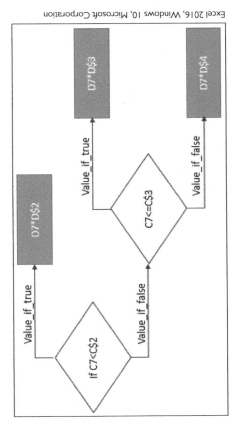

FIGURE 6 Nested IF Function Flowchart with Cell References

Figure 7 shows the nested IF function as the argument in the Value_if_false box in the Function Arguments dialog box. In the Formula Bar, the nested IF statement looks like this:

=IF(C7<C$2,D7*D$2,IF(C7<=C$3,D7*D$3,D7*D$4))

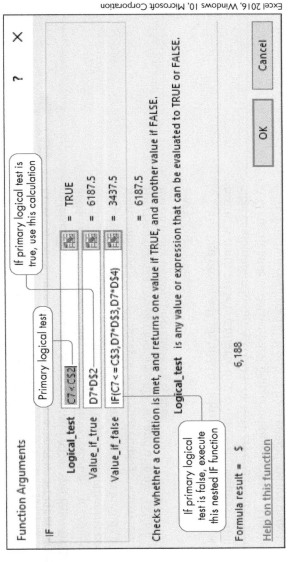

FIGURE 7 Nested IF Function

Date, Logical, and Lookup Functions • Excel 2016

The function uses relative cell references for the hire date (cell C7) so that the cell reference will change to the next hire date when you copy the formula down the column. The formula uses mixed references for the date thresholds (C$2 and C$3) and for the bonus rates (D$2, D$3, and D$4) so that the references will point to the same rows when you copy the formulas down the column.

Because you have three outcomes, you need two logical tests: one for the primary IF function (C7<C$2) and one for the nested IF function (C7<=C$3). The primary logical test evaluates whether the hire date in cell C7 is older than the date in cell C2. If the logical test is true, Excel multiples the salary in cell D7 by the rate in cell D2.

If the primary logical test (C7<C$2) is false, Excel executes the nested IF function in the value_if_false argument. The nested IF function then evaluates whether the hire date in cell C7 is older than or equal to the date in cell C3. If the logical test is true, Excel multiples the salary by the rate in cell D3. If the logical test is false, Excel multiples the salary by the rate in cell D4. You do not need a third logical test to execute the remaining outcome.

The following statements explain how the bonus is calculated for the individual representatives using the nested IF function (refer to Figure 4):

- Adams was hired on 10/14/2007. In this situation, the logical test (C7<C$2) is true. This causes Excel to execute the value_if_true argument D7*D$2, which is $68,750 * 9%.

- Akmatalieva was hired on 11/3/2018. In this situation, the logical test (C8<C$2) is false, as is the secondary logical test (C8<=C$3). This causes Excel to execute the value_if_false argument D8*D$4, which is $49,575 * 3%.

- Deberard was hired on 12/4/2014. In this situation, the logical test (C10<C$2) is false; however, the secondary logical test is true. This causes Excel to execute the value_if_true argument D10*D$3, which is $46,795 * 5%.

STEP 3

Nest AND, OR, and NOT Functions

Excel contains three logical functions to determine whether certain conditions are true or false. These functions are AND, OR, and NOT. You can use these functions to test a logical condition and display either TRUE or FALSE in the cell.

In some situations, you might want to know whether the combination of two conditions is true or false. For example, you might want to include a column to display TRUE if an employee's title is Manager *and if* that employee earns less than $70,000. The **AND** *function* accepts two or more logical tests and displays TRUE if all conditions are true or FALSE if any one of the conditions is false.

=AND(logical1,logical2)

You can create a truth table to help analyze the conditions to determine the overall result. A **truth table** is a matrix that provides the results (TRUE or FALSE) for every possible combination for an AND, OR, or NOT criteria combination. Table 1 illustrates the AND truth table to determine if both conditions are met. The truth table reveals that the AND function displays TRUE only if both conditions are true. If either condition is false, the AND function displays FALSE.

Pearson Education, Inc.

TABLE 1 AND Truth Table

Type of Employee	Current Salary	
	Less than $70,000	$70,000 or more
Manager	TRUE	FALSE
Other Employees	FALSE	FALSE

Figure 8 shows the AND function is used in column E. Adams and Laing are the only managers who earn less than $70,000. Although Crandell is a manager, she earns more than $70,000. Although Lenz earns only $49,750, he is not a manager.

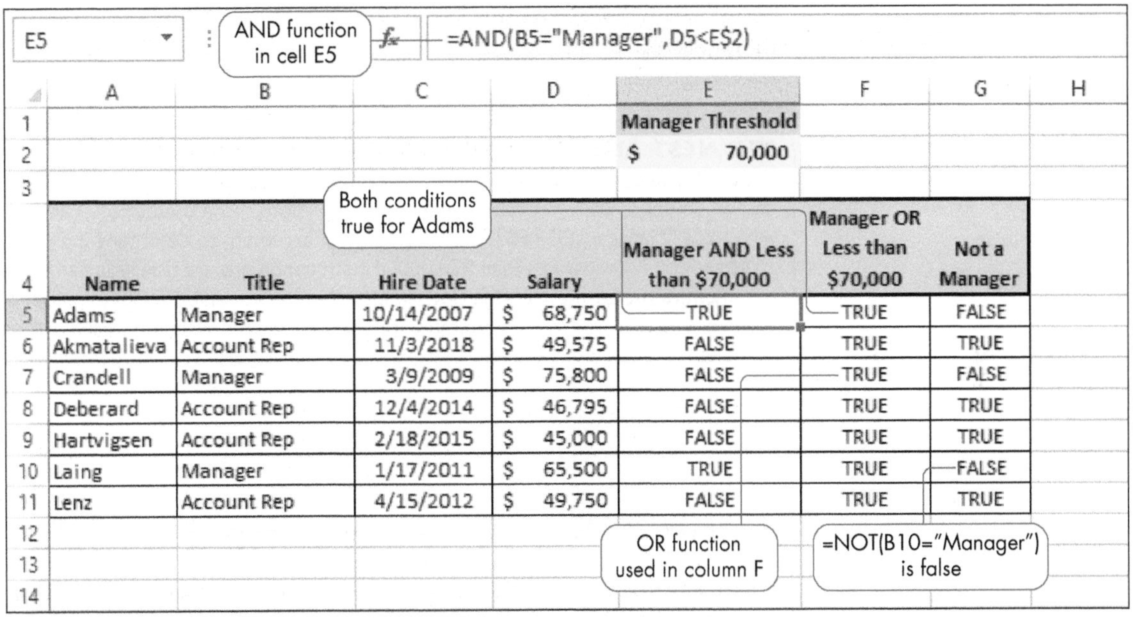

E5	▼	:	fx	=AND(B5="Manager",D5<E$2)				
▲	A	B	C	D	E	F	G	H
1					Manager Threshold			
2					$ 70,000			
3								
						Manager OR		
4	Name	Title	Hire Date	Salary	Manager AND Less than $70,000	Less than $70,000	Not a Manager	
5	Adams	Manager	10/14/2007	$ 68,750	TRUE	TRUE	FALSE	
6	Akmatallieva	Account Rep	11/3/2018	$ 49,575	FALSE	TRUE	TRUE	
7	Crandell	Manager	3/9/2009	$ 75,800	FALSE	TRUE	FALSE	
8	Deberard	Account Rep	12/4/2014	$ 46,795	FALSE	TRUE	TRUE	
9	Hartvigsen	Account Rep	2/18/2015	$ 45,000	FALSE	TRUE	TRUE	
10	Laing	Manager	1/17/2011	$ 65,500	TRUE	TRUE	FALSE	
11	Lenz	Account Rep	4/15/2012	$ 49,750	FALSE	TRUE	TRUE	
12								
13								
14								

Both conditions true for Adams

OR function used in column F

=NOT(B10="Manager") is false

FIGURE 8 AND Function

Unlike the AND function where *all* conditions must be true, the **OR function** evaluates to TRUE if *any* of the conditions are true. It returns FALSE only if all conditions are false. For example, you might want to identify employees who are either managers or who earn less than $70,000.

=OR(logical1,logical2)

Table 2 illustrates the OR truth table to determine if either condition is met. The truth table reveals that the OR function displays TRUE if at least one condition is true. The only time the OR function displays FALSE is if both conditions are false.

TABLE 2 OR Truth Table

Type of Employee	Current Salary	
	Less than $70,000	$70,000 or more
Manager	TRUE	TRUE
Other Employees	TRUE	FALSE

In Figure 8, column F uses the OR function to determine if employees are either managers or earn less than $70,000. The results indicate that either condition is met for all employees. That is, all employees are either managers or earn less than $70,000. Table 3 displays the differences between AND and OR functions.

Pearson Education, Inc.

The **NOT function** evaluates only one logical test and reverses the truth of the logical test. If the logical argument is true, the NOT function returns FALSE, and if the logical argument is false, the NOT function returns TRUE. For example, cell G5 contains =NOT(B5="Manager"). The result is false because Adams is a manager. Cell G6 displays TRUE because it is true that Akmatalieva is not a manager.

=NOT(logical)

TABLE 3 AND vs. OR

	All conditions are true	At least one condition is true	At least one condition is false	All conditions are false
AND	TRUE	FALSE	FALSE	FALSE
OR	TRUE	TRUE	TRUE	FALSE

TIP: NEST AND, OR, AND NOT WITHIN AN IF FUNCTION

Although you can use these functions individually, you can nest these functions within the logical_test argument of an IF function to make these functions more useful. For example, you can nest AND(B5="Manager",D5<E$2) in the logical_test argument to determine if an employee is (1) a manager and (2) earns less than $70,000. If both conditions are true, you can use the value_if_true argument to display the message *Due for raise*. If either condition is false, you can use the value_if_false argument to display N/A. The quotation marks are required when the result should display text. The complete function looks like this:

=IF(AND(B5="Manager",D5<E$2),"Due for raise","N/A")

Using Advanced Lookup Functions

You have used the VLOOKUP and HLOOKUP functions to look up a value, compare it to a lookup table, and then return a result from the lookup table. Two other lookup functions that are helpful are INDEX and MATCH.

Use the Index Function

When you work with a dataset, you might want to display content of a cell in a particular column on a particular row. For example, if a list contains agent names in the first column and their sales in the second column, you might want to know sales amount for the person on the third row. You can use the **INDEX function** to return a value at the intersection of a specified row and column. The following list explains the arguments of the INDEX function.

=INDEX(array,row_num,[column_num])

- **Array.** This argument is one or more ranges. In Figure 9, the array argument in the INDEX function in cell B7 is the range containing the agents and their respective sales: A2:B5.

- **Row_num.** This argument identifies the row number within the array range. In the INDEX function in cell B7 in Figure 9, the row_num is 3 to specify the third row in the array.

- **Column_num.** This argument identifies the column within the reference that contains the value you want. In Figure 9, the column_num is 2 to specify the second column within the range A2:B5.

	A	B	C
1	**Agent**	**Sales**	
2	Judi	$ 10,521	
3	Peyton	$ 14,147	
4	Kenneth	$ 8,454	
5	Cheri	$ 9,254	
6			
7	Value at specific row & column	$ 8,454	=INDEX(A2:B5,3,2)

FIGURE 9 INDEX Function

The INDEX function in cell B7 finds the intersection of the third row and second column in the array. In this case, cell B4 is at that intersection within the range. The INDEX function then returns the data contained in that cell, which is $8,454.

Use the MATCH Function

You might want to look up a particular value, but you do not know where it is located in a dataset. You can use the MATCH function to help look up the position of the data you want. The *MATCH function* searches through a range for a specific value and returns the relative position of that value within the range. Think of the MATCH function like a reverse phone number lookup. Instead of using directory assistance to look up a person's phone number, it would be like using the phone number to look up the person. For example, you can use the MATCH function to identify what row contains the value $8,454. The MATCH function contains three arguments: lookup_value, lookup_array, and match_type. The following list explains the arguments of the MATCH function.

=MATCH(lookup_value,lookup_array,[match_type])

- **Lookup_value.** This argument is the value that you want to find in the array or list. It can be a value, label, logical value, or cell reference that contains one of these items. In Figure 10, cell B8 contains the MATCH function. The lookup_value argument refers to the cell reference (B7) that contains the value to look up. In this case, you want to look up the value $8,454.

- **Lookup_array.** This argument is a range that contains a dataset. In the MATCH function in cell B8 in Figure 10, the lookup_array argument is the range containing the sales values, B2:B5.

- **Match_type.** This argument is 1, 0, or −1 to indicate which value to return. Use 1 to find the largest value that is less than or equal to the lookup_value when the values in the lookup_array are arranged in ascending order. Use −1 to find the smallest value that is greater than or equal to the lookup_value when the values in the lookup_array are in descending order. Use 0 to find the first value that is identical to the lookup_value when the values in the lookup_array have no particular order. In the MATCH function in cell B8 in Figure 10, the match_type is 0 to find an exact match of the highest sales.

	A	B	C
1	**Agent**	**Sales**	
2	Judi	$ 10,521	
3	Peyton	$ 14,147	
4	Kenneth	$ 8,454	
5	Cheri	$ 9,254	
6			
7	Value to look up	$ 8,454	
8	Position of particular value	3	=MATCH(B7,B2:B5,0)

FIGURE 10 MATCH Function

Date, Logical, and Lookup Functions • Excel 2016

The MATCH function in cell B8 looks up the value stored in cell B7 ($8,454), compares it to the range B2:B5, and then finds an exact match on the third row of that range. Therefore, the MATCH function displays 3.

Create a Nested Function

In isolation, the INDEX and MATCH functions seem limited in usage. However, you can use the results (position of a value) from the MATCH function as an argument within the INDEX function to identify data related to that matching value. You can use three separate functions to identify a label related to a value. In Figure 11, cell B8 contains the MAX function to identify the highest sales ($14,147) in the range B2:B5. The MATCH function in cell B9 uses the results from the MAX function to find the position (2) of the highest sales within the range B2:B5. Then the INDEX function in cell B10 uses the position returned from the MATCH function to identify the agent (Peyton) responsible for the highest sales.

	A	B	C
1	**Agent**	**Sales**	
2	Judi	$ 10,521	
3	Peyton	$ 14,147	
4	Kenneth	$ 8,454	
5	Cheri	$ 9,254	
6			
7	**Condition**	**Results**	**Formula**
8	High Sales Amount	$ 14,147	=MAX(B2:B5)
9	Position of High Sales	2	=MATCH(B8,B2:B5,0)
10	Rep w/ Highest Sales	Peyton	=INDEX(A2:B5,B9,1)
11	Rep w/ Highest Sales	Peyton	=INDEX(A2:B5,MATCH(MAX(B2:B5),B2:B5,0),1)

FIGURE 11 MATCH, INDEX, and Nested Functions

To reduce the number of cells containing functions, you can nest the MAX function within the MATCH function, and nest the MATCH function as the second argument in the INDEX function. This nested function will identify the highest sales, identify the position of the highest sales, and then return the name of the agent responsible for those sales. In Figure 11, cell B11 contains the nested function: =INDEX(A2:B5,MATCH(MAX(B2:B5),B2:B5,0),1).

The MAX function is nested within the MATCH function as the lookup_value argument. The MAX function returns $14,147 from the lookup_array range B2:B5. The match_type argument 0 indicates the function is looking for an exact match to the lookup_value. The MATCH function returns 2, the position of $14,147.

The INDEX function uses the entire dataset A2:B5 as the Array. The row_num argument is the position (2) returned from the MATCH function. Once the match is found, the INDEX function returns the contents in the first column, specified by the column_num argument 1. In this dataset, the INDEX function displays Peyton.

You can use the Insert Function and Function Arguments dialog boxes to insert functions as arguments for another function instead of typing the entire nested function directly in the Formula Bar.

To create a nested function using dialog boxes, complete the following steps:

1. Click Insert Function, select the outer function, such as INDEX, in the Insert Function dialog box and then click OK. When you select INDEX, the Select Arguments message box displays to select the argument type. Leave the default option selected and click OK to open the Function Arguments dialog box.

2. Click in the argument box where the nested function is needed, click the Name Box arrow on the Formula Bar, and then select the desired function from the list of recently used functions, or select More Functions from the Name Box list and select the function, such as MATCH, to open the Function Arguments dialog box for the nested function.

3. Enter the arguments for the nested function. Click in the outer function's name, INDEX, in the Formula Bar to display the Function Arguments dialog box for the outer function again.

4. Continue entering or nesting other arguments.

5. Click OK in the outer function's Function Arguments dialog box when the entire function is complete.

Quick Concepts

1. What is the difference between a single IF statement and a nested IF statement?

2. In what situation would you use an AND function instead of a nested IF statement?

3. What is the benefit of nesting the MATCH function inside the INDEX function?

1 Date, Logical, and Lookup Functions

As the Transpayne accounting assistant, you have been asked to identify underpaid account representatives to bring their salaries up to a new minimum standard within the corporation. In addition, you want to calculate annual bonus amounts based on hire date as well as create a quick search lookup field to allow for instant access to individual information.

STEP 1 » **USE THE YEARFRAC FUNCTION**

Your first task is to calculate how long each manager and representative has worked for the company. You will use the YEARFRAC function to calculate the difference between an employee's hire date and December 31, 2018. Refer to Figure 12 as you complete Step 1.

Skills covered: Use the YEARFRAC Function • Create a Nested IF Function • Nest an AND Function • Create a Lookup Field • Use the INDEX Function • Use the MATCH Function

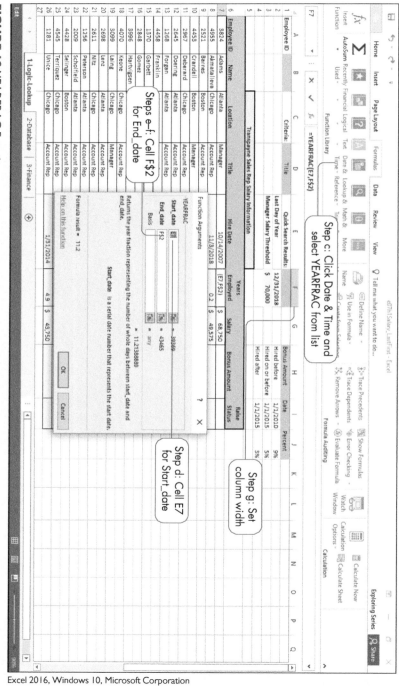

Steps e–f: Cell F$2 for End_date

Step c: Click Date & Time and select YEARFRAC from list

Step d: Cell E7 for Start_date

Step g: Set column width

FIGURE 12 YEARFRAC Function

a. Open *e07h1Salary* and save it as **e07h1Salary_LastFirst**.

TROUBLESHOOTING: If you make any major mistakes in this exercise, you can close the file, open *e07h1Salary* again, and then start this exercise over.

b. Click **cell F7** in the 1-Logic-Lookup worksheet.

c. Click the **Formulas tab**, click **Date & Time** in the Function Library group, scroll through the list of functions, and then select **YEARFRAC**.

The Function Arguments dialog box opens for the YEARFRAC function. The two required arguments are start_date and end_date.

Excel 2016, Windows 10, Microsoft Corporation

d. Click **cell E7** to enter it in the Start_date box.

Cell E7 contains the hire (start) date for Adams. Adams started working for the company on 10/14/2007.

e. Click in the **End_date box** and click **cell F2.**

Cell F2 contains the comparison date of 12/31/2018.

f. Press **F4** twice to change the reference from F2 to F$2.

The mixed reference F$2 keeps the reference to row 2 absolute so that it does not change when you copy the formula down the column.

g. Click **OK.**

The formula indicates that Adams has worked at the company 11.2 years.

h. Click the **Home tab,** click the **Number Format arrow** in the Number group, and then select **Number.** Click **Decrease Decimal** in the Number group one time. Copy the function to the **range F8:F26.** Change the width of column F to **11.43.** Save the workbook.

Because Adams has the earliest hire date, he has worked at the company the longest (indicated by 11.2 years). Akmatalieva was recently hired and has the lowest number in the Years Employed column.

STEP 2 ⟫ CREATE A NESTED IF FUNCTION

Your next task is to calculate the annual bonus amount for each employee. The company uses a tiered bonus system that awards a specific percentage of salary based on hire date. Employees hired before 1/1/2010 receive 9%. Employees hired on or before 1/1/2015 receive 5%, and employees that were hired after 1/1/2015 receive 3%. You will use a nested IF function to calculate each employee's bonus. Refer to Figure 13 as you complete Step 2.

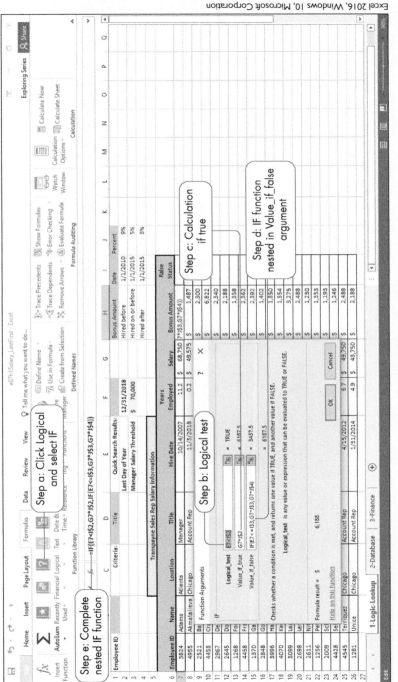

FIGURE 13 Nested IF Function

a. Click **cell H7**, click the **Formulas tab**, click **Logical** in the Function Library group, and then select **IF**.

b. Type **E7<I$2** in the Logical_test box.

The logical test compares the hire date to the first bonus threshold, 1/1/2010. Because you will copy the formula down the column and want to make sure the reference to the employee's hire date changes, use a relative cell reference to the date threshold remains constant, use a mixed cell reference to cell I$2. You could use an absolute reference, but because you are copying the formula down, the column letter I will remain the same. Using a mixed reference keeps the formula shorter and easier to read.

c. Type **G7*J$2** in the Value_if_true box.

This will multiply the salary by the bonus percentage if the logical test provided is true. If the logical test is not true, it will move on to the next argument created in Step d.

d. Click in the **Value_if_false box**, click the **Name Box arrow** above column A, and then select **IF**.

Excel opens another Function Arguments dialog box so that you can enter the arguments for the nested IF function.

e. Type **E7<=I$3** in the Logical_test box, type **G7*J$3** in the Value_if_true box, type **G7*J$4** in the Value_if_false box, and then click **OK**.

The Function Arguments dialog box closes, and Excel enters the nested IF function in cell H7. By entering an IF statement in the main IF function's Value_if_false box, you created a nested function that evaluates the second threshold, 1/1/2015 (cell I3). If the hire date does not fall within the first or second thresholds defined by the primary and secondary logical tests, it will then by default trigger the value_if_false, (G7*J$4). This formula will calculate the bonus based on the lowest bonus amount, 3% (cell J4).

Use relative cell references for the employee's hire date (cell E7), because it should change when you copy the formula down the column. Use a mixed (or an absolute) reference for the threshold date (cell I$3) to ensure it does not change as you copy the formula down the column. Again, using mixed references keeps the formula shorter and easier to read than absolute references, but both produce the same results.

The function returns the value $6,188. This is calculated by multiplying the current salary, $68,750 (cell G7), by the bonus percentage rate of 9% (cell J2).

f. Click the **Home tab**, click **Accounting Number Format** in the Number group, and then click **Decrease Decimal** two times in the Number group.

g. Double-click the **cell H7 fill handle** to copy the function to the **range H8:H26**. Save the workbook.

The Human Resources Director recommends that the company pay managers at least $70,000. You will nest an AND function inside an IF function to determine which managers should receive pay raises based on their current salary level. The salary threshold is located in cell F3 in the 1-Logic-Lookup worksheet. Refer to Figure 14 as you complete Step 3.

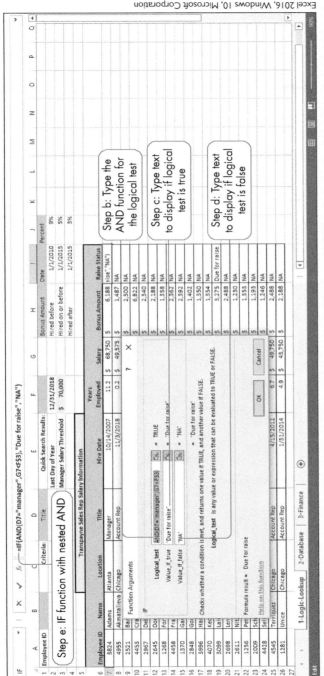

Step e: IF function with nested AND

Step b: Type the AND function for the logical test

Step c: Type text to display if logical test is true

Step d: Type text to display if logical test is false

=IF(AND(D7="manager",G7<F$3),"Due for raise","NA")

FIGURE 14 Nested AND Function Within IF Function

a. Click **cell I7**, click the **Formulas tab**, click **Logical** in the Function Library group, and then select **IF**.

b. Type **AND(D7="manager",G7<F$3)** in the Logical_test box.

Nesting the AND function in the logical test enables you to specify two conditions that must be true: the employee is a manager (D7="manager") and makes less than $70,000 (G7<F$3). You use a mixed reference in cell F3 to ensure that row number 3 does not change when you copy the formula down the column.

TROUBLESHOOTING: Do not make cells D7 or G7 absolute or mixed. If you do, the function will use the incorrect cell references when you copy the function down the column.

c. Type **"Due for raise"** in the Value_if_true box.

If both conditions specified in the AND function are true, the employee is eligible for a raise.

d. Type **"NA"** in the Value_if_false box.

e. Click **OK**, double-click the **cell I7 fill handle** to copy the formula to the **range I8:I26**, change the width of column I to **11.86**, and then save the workbook.

The function now evaluates the employee's title and salary. If both arguments in the AND function are true, then *Due for raise* is displayed; if not, *NA* is displayed.

STEP 4 **》》 CREATE A LOOKUP FIELD USING INDEX AND MATCH FUNCTIONS**

You want to provide a simple search feature so that users can enter an employee number in cell B1 and then display employee title information in cell F1. For example, if Employee ID 4070 is entered in cell B1, cell F1 displays Account Rep. Refer to Figure 15 as you complete Step 4.

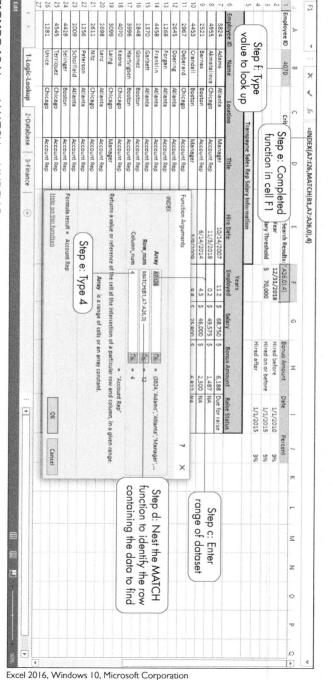

FIGURE 15 Nested MATCH and INDEX Functions

Excel 2016, Windows 10, Microsoft Corporation

a. Click **cell F1**, click **Lookup & Reference** in the Function Library group, and then select **INDEX**.

The Select Arguments message box opens so that you can select the type of arguments to build the function.

b. Select **array,row_num,column_num** and click **OK**.

This argument specifies the array or range to evaluate first, followed by identifying the row number and column number to index. The Function Arguments dialog box opens so that you can enter the required arguments for the INDEX function.

c. Type **A7:I26** in the Array box.

This range defines the location from which Excel will extract information.

d. Type **MATCH(B1,A7:A26,0)** in the Row_num box.

If you nest the MATCH function in the Row_num box of the index function, Excel will look up the position of the employee number in cell B1 within the range A7:A26 and return the relative position, which for employee 4070 is 12.

e. Type **4** in the Column_num box. Click **OK**.

You entered the number 4 in the Column_num box so that the function will return information from the fourth column in the dataset. Currently, the function returns #N/A because cell B1 is blank.

f. Click **cell B1**, type **4070**, and then press **Enter**.

Cell F1 now displays the current position of employee 4070. It does this by matching the Employee ID in column A to the Title in column D.

g. Save the workbook. Keep the workbook open if you plan to continue with the next Hands-On Exercise. If not, close the workbook and exit Excel.

Database Filtering and Functions

Databases store and manipulate data, such as inventory details about automobiles at a particular dealership or financial transaction details for your credit card. While Microsoft Access is more appropriate for relational database modeling, people often use Excel for basic database storage and manipulation. You have some experience in using Excel tables to perform basic database tasks, such as sorting and filtering data. However, you may need to perform more advanced filtering or calculations.

In this section, you will learn how to use advanced filtering techniques and insert database functions. Specifically, you will define a criteria range and extract data that meet certain criteria. Then you will insert the DSUM and DAVERAGE functions to calculate results based on filtered data.

Applying Advanced Filtering

Data become more useful in decision making when you reduce the records to a subset of data that meets specific conditions. For example, a manager might want to identify account reps who earn more than $30,000 in Chicago. The manager can use the filter arrows to filter the table data by job title, salary, and location, and Excel will filter the original dataset by hiding records that do not meet the conditions. Sometimes, however, it may be important to keep the original dataset visible and create a copy of only those records that meet these conditions in another location of the worksheet. To do so, the manager can use advanced filtering techniques.

Define a Criteria Range

>> Before you apply advanced filtering techniques, you must define a criteria range. A *criteria range* is a group of two or more adjacent cells that specifies the conditions used to control the results of a filter. The criteria row is often located below the dataset. A criteria range must contain at least two rows and one column. The first row contains the column labels as they appear in the dataset, and the second row contains the conditions (e.g., values) for filtering the dataset. Figure 16 shows the original dataset, criteria range, and copy of records that meet the conditions.

STEP 1

FIGURE 16 Data, Criteria Range, and Output

	Employee ID	Name	Location	Title	Salary
6	Employee ID	Name	Location	Title	Salary
7	3824	Adams	Atlanta	Manager	$ 68,750
8	4955	Akmatalieva	Chicago	Account Rep	$ 49,575
9	2521	Barnes	Boston	Account Rep	$ 46,000
10	4453	Crandell	Boston	Manager	$ 75,800
11	2967	Deberard	Chicago	Account Rep	$ 46,795
12	2645	Doering	Atlanta	Account Rep	$ 43,750
13	1268	Forgan	Atlanta	Account Rep	$ 45,250
14	4458	Franklin	Atlanta	Account Rep	$ 47,240
15	1370	Garbett	Atlanta	Account Rep	$ 47,835
16	2848	Gomez	Boston	Account Rep	$ 46,725
17	3996	Hartvigsen	Boston	Account Rep	$ 45,000
18	4070	Keone	Chicago	Account Rep	$ 45,125
19	3099	Laing	Chicago	Manager	$ 65,500
20					

Labels on first row of criteria range

Criteria set on second row of criteria range

	Employee ID	Name	Location	Title	Salary
21	Employee ID	Name	Location	Title	Salary
22			Chicago	Account Rep	>30000
23					

	Employee ID	Name	Location	Title	Salary
24					
25	Employee ID	Name	Location	Title	Salary
26	4955	Akmatalieva	Chicago	Account Rep	$ 49,575
27	2967	Deberard	Chicago	Account Rep	$ 46,795
28	4070	Keone	Chicago	Account Rep	$ 45,125
29					
30					
31					
32					
33					
34					

Original data

Output area: copy of records meeting criteria

Excel 2016, Windows 10, Microsoft Corporation

Because you want to display records that meet all three conditions (Location, Title, and Salary), you enter the conditions on the second row of the criteria range, immediately below their respective labels: Chicago below Location, Account Rep below Title, and >3000 below Salary. By default, Excel looks for an exact match. If you want to avoid an exact match for values, enter relational operators. For example, entering >30000 sets the condition for salaries that are greater than $30,000. You can use <, >, <=, >=, and <> relational operators, similar to using relational operators in the logical_test argument of an IF function.

Excel copies only the records that meet all three conditions. Therefore, Adams earning $68,750 from Atlanta is excluded because Adams is a manager, not an account rep, and is not from Chicago. You can set an OR condition in the criteria range. For example, you want to display (a) Chicago account reps who earn more than $30,000 or (b) Atlanta account reps regardless of salary. Figure 17 shows the conditions in the criteria range. Notice that the criteria range contains three rows: column labels on the first row, the first set of conditions on the second row, and the second set of conditions on the third row. Each row of conditions sets an AND condition; that is, each criterion must be met. Each additional row sets an OR condition.

	Employee ID	Name	Location	Title	Salary
6	Employee ID	Name	Location	Title	Salary
7	3824	Adams	Atlanta	Manager	$ 68,750
8	4955	Akmatalieva	Chicago	Account Rep	$ 49,575
9	2521	Barnes	Boston	Account Rep	$ 46,000
10	4453	Crandell	Boston	Manager	$ 75,800
11	2967	Deberard	Chicago	Account Rep	$ 46,795
12	2645	Doering	Atlanta	Account Rep	$ 43,750
13	1268	Forgan	Atlanta	Account Rep	$ 45,250
14	4458	Franklin	Atlanta	Account Rep	$ 47,240
15	1370	Garbett	Atlanta	Account Rep	$ 47,835
16	2848	Gomez	Boston	Account Rep	$ 46,725
17	3996	Hartvigsen	Boston	Account Rep	$ 45,000
18	4070	Keone	Chicago	Account Rep	$ 45,125
19	3099	Laing	Chicago	Manager	$ 65,500
20					
21					

First set of criteria creates AND condition for each item in the row

	Employee ID	Name	Location	Title	Salary
22	Employee ID	Name	Location	Title	Salary
23			Chicago	Account Rep	>30000
24			Atlanta	Account Rep	
25					

Copy of records meeting either condition

Second set of criteria creates OR condition

	Employee ID	Name	Location	Title	Salary
26	Employee ID	Name	Location	Title	Salary
27	4955	Akmatalieva	Chicago	Account Rep	$ 49,575
28	2967	Deberard	Chicago	Account Rep	$ 46,795
29	2645	Doering	Atlanta	Account Rep	$ 43,750
30	1268	Forgan	Atlanta	Account Rep	$ 45,250
31	4458	Franklin	Atlanta	Account Rep	$ 47,240
32	1370	Garbett	Atlanta	Account Rep	$ 47,835
33	4070	Keone	Chicago	Account Rep	$ 45,125
34					
35					

Excel 2016, Windows 10, Microsoft Corporation

FIGURE 17 Criteria Range with AND and OR Conditions

TIP: USING = AND <>

Using equal (=) and unequal (<>) symbols with the criteria values selects records with empty and nonempty fields, respectively. An equal with nothing after it will return all records with no entry in the designated column. An unequal with nothing after it will select all records with an entry in the column. An empty cell in the criteria range returns every record in the list.

Apply the Advanced Filter

STEP 2 » After you create the criteria range, you are ready to apply the advanced filter using the Advanced Filter dialog box. This dialog box enables you to filter the table in place or copy the selected records to another area in the worksheet, specify the list range, specify the criteria range, or display unique records only.

To apply the advanced filter, complete the following steps:

1. Click a cell in the data table.
2. Click the Data tab and click Advanced in the Sort & Filter group.
3. Click the desired action: *Filter the list, in-place* to filter the range by hiding rows that do not match your criteria or *Copy to another location* if you want to copy the rows that match your criteria instead of filtering the original dataset.
4. Ensure the List range displays the range containing the original dataset, including the column headings.
5. Enter the criteria range, including the criteria labels, in the Criteria range box. To perform the advanced filter for the OR condition in Figure 17, you must select all three rows of the criteria range: the column labels, the row containing the criteria for Chicago account reps earning more than $30,000, and the row containing criteria for Atlanta account reps.
6. Specify the Copy to range if you selected *Copy to another location* in Step 3. Enter only the starting row. Excel will copy the column labels and fill in the rows below the heading with the records that meet the conditions you set. Make sure the Copy to range contains sufficient empty rows to accommodate the copied records. If you do not include enough rows, Excel will replace existing data with the copied records. Click OK.

Figure 18 shows the Advanced Filter dialog box with settings to produce the advanced filter shown in Figure 17. The List range box contains $A$6:$E$19 for the dataset. The Criteria range box contains $A$22:$E$24 for the criteria range labels and conditions. The Copy to box contains $A$26:$E$26 for the labels in the output range.

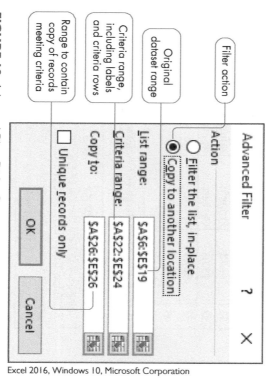

Filter action

Original dataset range

Criteria range, including labels and criteria rows

Range to contain copy of records meeting criteria

Advanced Filter ? ×

Action
○ Filter the list, in-place
● Copy to another location

List range: $A$6:$E$19

Criteria range: $A$22:$E$24

Copy to: $A$26:$E$26

☐ Unique records only

OK   Cancel

FIGURE 18 Advanced Filter Dialog Box

Excel 2016, Windows 10, Microsoft Corporation

TIP: AUTO RANGE NAMES

When you use the Advanced Filter dialog box, Excel assigns the range name Criteria to the criteria range and Extract to the output range.

Manipulating Data with Database Functions

Database functions analyze data for selected records in a dataset. These functions are similar to statistical functions (SUM, AVERAGE, MAX, MIN, COUNT) except that database functions restrict the results to data that meets specific criteria. Data not meeting the specified criteria are filtered out. All database functions use a criteria range that defines the conditions for filtering the data to be used in the calculations. Database functions have three arguments: database, field, and criteria.

- **Database.** The database argument is the entire dataset, including column labels and all data, on which the function operates. The database reference may be represented by a range name. In Figure 19, the database argument is A6:E19.

- **Field.** The field argument is the column that contains the values operated on by the function. You can enter either the name of the column label in quotation marks, such as "Salary" or the number that represents the location of that column within the table. For example, if the Salary column is the fifth column in the table, you can enter a 5 for the field argument. You can also enter a cell reference containing the column label, for example, E6, as shown in Figure 19.

- **Criteria.** The criteria argument defines the conditions to be met by the function. This range must contain at least one column label and a cell below the label that specifies the condition. The criteria argument may include more than one column with conditions for each column label, indicated by a range, such as A22:E23 or a range name. In Figure 19, the criteria range specifies Atlanta as the location and Account Rep as the title.

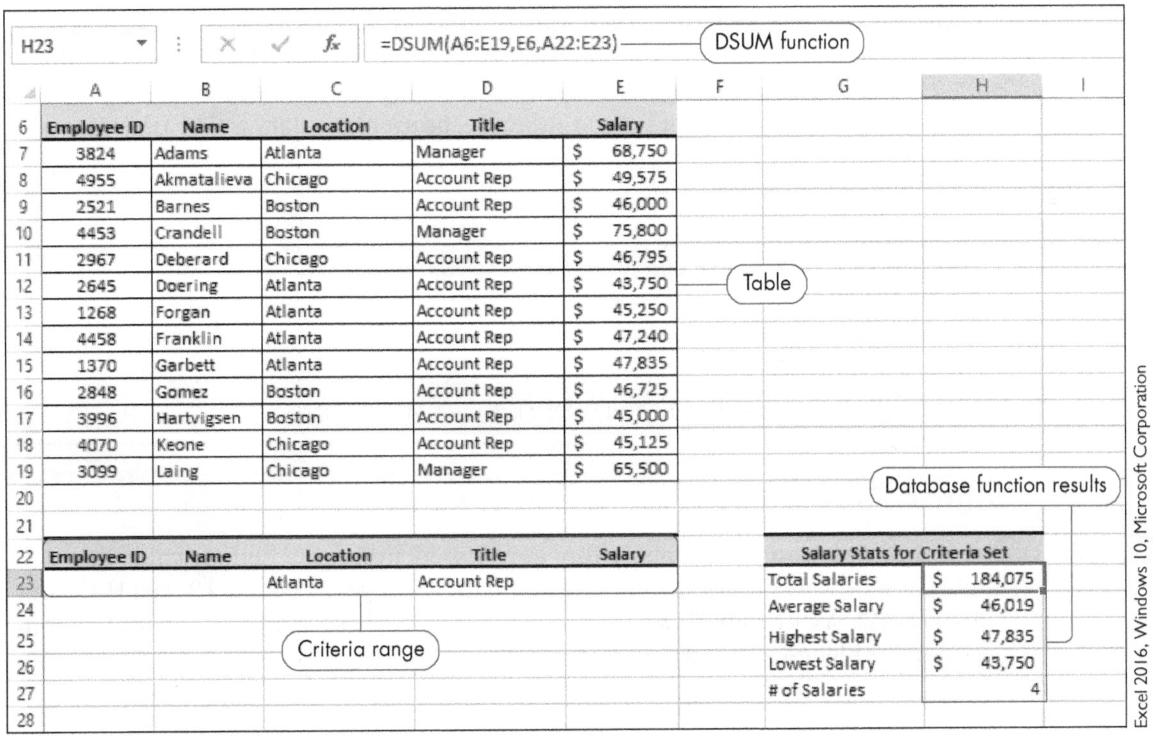

FIGURE 19 Database Functions

To insert a database function, complete the following steps:

1. Click Insert Function in the Function Library group or Insert Function between the Name Box and Formula Bar.
2. Click the Or *select a category* arrow, select Database, and then select the desired database function in the Select a function list.

TIP: USING FORMULA AUTOCOMPLETE

Instead of using the Formulas tab to begin creating a function, you can type = and the first letter of a function. Excel displays the Formula AutoComplete list, showing a list of functions that start with the letter you typed. For example, if you type =D, Excel displays a list of functions that start with the letter D, including most database functions. Select the appropriate function from the list.

STEP 3

Use DSUM and DAVERAGE Functions

The **DSUM function** is a database function that adds the values in a column that match conditions specified in a criteria range. In Figure 19, cell H23 contains =DSUM(A6:E19,E6,A22:E23) to calculate the total salaries for Account Reps in Atlanta. The total salaries paid is $184,075.

=DSUM(database,field,criteria)

The **DAVERAGE function** is a database function that determines the arithmetic mean, or average, of values in a column that match conditions specified in a criteria range. In Figure 19, cell H24 contains =DAVERAGE(A6:E19,E6,A22:E23) to calculate the average salary for Account Reps in Atlanta. The average salary is $46,019.

=DAVERAGE(database,field,criteria)

TIP: USING RANGE NAMES

You can assign range names to the dataset and criteria range to simplify the construction of the arguments in database functions.

TIP: DIVISION BY ZERO—#DIV/0—AND HOW TO AVOID IT

The DAVERAGE function displays a division-by-zero error message if no records meet the specified criteria. You can hide the error message by nesting the DAVERAGE function inside the IFERROR function, which detects the error:

=IFERROR(DAVERAGE(A6:E19,"Salary",A22:E23),"No Records Match the Criteria")

STEP 4

Identify Values with DMAX and DMIN

The **DMAX function** is a database function that identifies the highest value in a column that matches specified conditions in a criteria range. In Figure 19, cell H25 contains =DMAX(A6:E19,E6,A22:E23) to calculate the highest salary for Account Reps in Atlanta. The highest salary is $47,835.

=DMAX(database,field,criteria)

The **DMIN function** is a database function that identifies the lowest value in a column that matches specified conditions in a criteria range. In Figure 19, cell H26 contains =DMIN(A6:E19,E6,A22:E23) to calculate the lowest salary for Account Reps in Atlanta. The lowest salary is $43,750.

=DMIN(database,field,criteria)

Identify the Total Number with DCOUNT

The **DCOUNT function** is a database function that counts the cells that contain numbers in a column that matches specified conditions in a criteria range. In Figure 19, cell H27 contains =DCOUNT(A6:E19,E6,A22:E23) to count the number of Account Reps in Atlanta, which is 4. However, if one of the records is missing a value, DCOUNT excludes that record from being counted. If after completing the DCOUNT, you decide you would like to change the match conditions, you can do so by altering the information entered in the criteria area. To count records containing an empty cell, use DCOUNTA instead.

=DCOUNT(database,field,criteria)

=DCOUNTA(database,field,criteria)

TIP: ADDITIONAL DATABASE FUNCTIONS

Excel contains additional database functions, such as DSTDEV to calculate the sample population standard deviation for values in a column and DVAR to estimate the sample population variance for values in a column when specified conditions are met.

Quick Concepts

4. Why would you use advanced filtering instead of basic filtering?

5. What are the benefits of using database functions?

6. Why would you use a database function instead of advanced filtering?

2 Database Filtering and Functions

Skills covered: Create Criteria and Output Ranges • Apply an Advanced Filter • Use the DAVERAGE Function • Use the DMIN Function • Use the DMAX Function • Use the DCOUNT Function

Other assistant accountants want to be able to enter criteria to see a list of records that meet the conditions they specify. In addition, these assistants then want to calculate summary statistics based on the filtered results.

>> CREATE CRITERIA AND OUTPUT RANGES

You want to set up the workbook with a criteria range and an output range. This will enable other assistant accountants to enter criteria of their choosing to filter the list of salary data. Refer to Figure 20 as you complete Step 1.

a. Open *e07h1Salary_LastFirst* if you closed it at the end of Hands-On Exercise 1, and save it as **e07h2Salary_LastFirst**, changing h1 to h2. Click the **2-Database sheet tab**.

Use this worksheet to preserve the work you did on the first worksheet.

b. Select the **range A2:F2** and click **Copy** in the Clipboard group on the Home tab.

You copied the range containing the column labels.

c. Click **cell A25** and click **Paste** in the Clipboard group on the Home tab.

You pasted the range containing the column labels for the criteria range.

d. Click **cell A30**, paste another copy of the data, and then press **Esc**. Save the workbook.

You pasted another copy of the column labels for the output range in cells A30:F30.

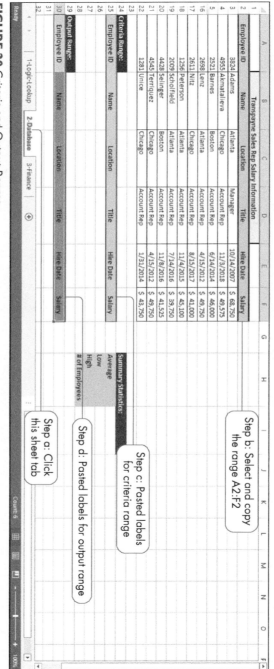

FIGURE 20 Criteria and Output Ranges

You are ready to enter conditions to restrict the output list to Account Reps in Boston. Refer to Figure 21 as you complete Step 2.

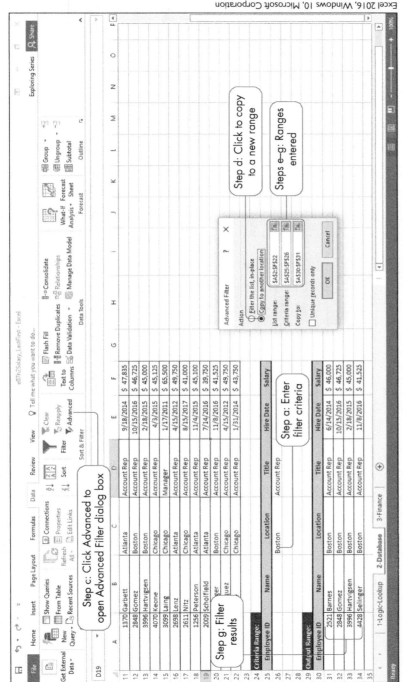

Excel 2016, Windows 10, Microsoft Corporation

FIGURE 21 Conditions and Output

a. Type **Boston** in **cell C26** and type **Account Rep** in **cell D26**.

You entered the conditions on the first row below the labels in the criteria range. Because you entered both conditions on the same row, you created an AND condition. Both conditions must be met in order to display employee data in the output range.

b. Click **cell D19** (or any cell within the dataset).

c. Click the **Data tab** and click **Advanced** in the Sort & Filter group.

The Advanced Filter dialog box opens so that you can specify the desired filter action, the list, the criteria range, and other details.

d. Click **Copy to another location.**

This action will copy the records that meet the conditions to a new location instead of filtering the original dataset.

e. Click in the **List range box** and select the **range A2:F22.**

This range contains the original dataset. The List range box may display the sheet name along with the range, such as '2-Database'!$A$2:$F$22.

f. Click in the **Criteria range box** and select the **range A25:F26.**

You selected the labels and the row containing the conditions for the criteria range. The Criteria range box may display the sheet name along with the range, such as '2-Database'!$A$25:$F$26.

Regardless of the criteria entered in the criteria range A25:F26, you want to calculate the average salary for the records that meet those conditions. You will insert a DAVERAGE function to perform the calculation. Refer to Figure 22 as you complete Step 3.

g. Click in the **Copy to box**, select the **range A30:F30**, and then click **OK**.

Make sure you select only the labels for the output range. The Copy to box may display the sheet name along with the range, such as '2-Database'!$A$30:$F$30. Excel copies the records that meet the condition below the output range labels.

h. Scroll down to see the output records. Save the workbook.

Four employees are Account Reps in Boston.

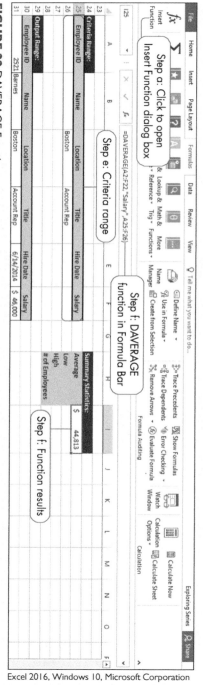

FIGURE 22 DAVERAGE Function

Excel 2016, Windows 10, Microsoft Corporation

a. Click **cell I25**, click the **Formulas tab**, and then click **Insert Function** in the Function Library group.

The Insert Function dialog box opens so that you can select a function category and function.

b. Click the **Or select a category arrow**, select **Database**, select **DAVERAGE** in the *Select a function* list, and then click **OK**.

The Function Arguments dialog box opens so that you can specify the arguments for the DAVERAGE function.

c. Select the **range A2:F22** to enter that range in the Database box.

The Database argument must include the column labels and original dataset.

d. Click in the **Field box**, type **Salary**, and then press **Tab**.

Excel enters the quotation marks around the word Salary for you.

> **TROUBLESHOOTING:** If you type the function instead of using the dialog box, make sure you type the double quotation marks (") around text. Otherwise, Excel will display an error message.

e. Select the **range A25:F26** to enter in the Criteria box.

Excel displays Criteria instead of A25:F26 in the Criteria box because you had previously defined the criteria range in Step 2.

f. Click **OK**. Save the workbook.

The average salary of account reps in Boston is $44,813.

The other accounting assistants would like to see the lowest and highest salaries based on the database conditions. In addition, you want to insert the DCOUNT function to count the number of records that meet the specified conditions. Refer to Figure 23 as you complete Step 4.

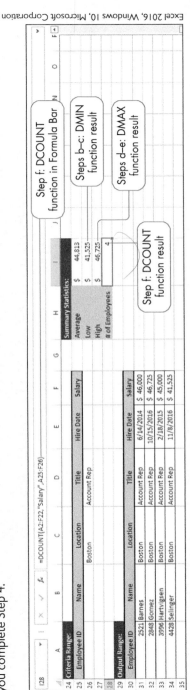

Excel 2016, Windows 10, Microsoft Corporation

FIGURE 23 DMIN, DMAX, DCOUNT Functions

a. Click **cell I26** and click **Insert Function** in the Function Library group.

The Database functions should be listed because that was the last function category you selected.

b. Select **DMIN** in the *Select a function* list and click **OK**.

The Function Arguments dialog box opens so that you can specify the arguments for the DMIN function.

c. Select the **range A2:F22** in the Database box, select the **cell F2** in the Field box, select the range **A25:F26** in the Criteria box, and then click **OK**.

The lowest salary for account reps in Boston is $41,525.

d. Click **cell I27** and click **Insert Function** in the Function Library group. Select **DMAX** in the *Select a function* list and click **OK**.

The Function Arguments dialog box opens so that you can specify the arguments for the DMAX function.

e. Select the **range A2:F22** in the Database box, select the **cell F2** in Field box, select the **range A25:F26** in the Criteria box, and then click **OK**.

The highest salary for account reps in Boston is $46,725.

f. Type **=DCOUNT(A2:F22,"Salary",A25:F26)** in **cell I28** and then press **Enter**.

The company has four account reps in the Boston location.

g. Save the workbook. Keep the workbook open if you plan to continue with the next Hands-On Exercise. If not, close the workbook and exit Excel.

Financial Functions

Excel's financial functions are helpful for business financial analysts and for you in your personal financial management. Knowing what different financial functions can calculate and how to use them will benefit you as you plan retirement savings, identify best rates to obtain your financial goals, and evaluate how future values of different investments compare with today's values.

In this section, you will learn how to prepare a loan amortization table using financial functions. In addition, you will use other financial functions to complete investment analyses.

Using Financial Functions

Previously, you worked with the PMT financial function to calculate the monthly payment of a loan. The Financial category includes a variety of functions to calculate details for investments. For example, you can calculate present or future values, rates, and number of payment periods. Figure 24 illustrates the results of several financial functions. Some of the arguments for the PMT function are similar to the arguments for other financial functions.

1		**Present Value**	
2	Lump Sum	$ 1,000,000.00	
3	Present Value	$ 1,246,221.03	=-PV(B6,B5,B4)
4	Per Year	$ 100,000.00	
5	No. of Years	20	
6	Rate	5%	
7			
8		**Future Value**	
9	Yearly Contribution	$ 3,000.00	
10	No. of Years	40	
11	APR	7%	
12	Future Value	$ 598,905.34	=-FV(B11,B10,B9)
13	Total Contributed	$ 120,000.00	=B9*B10
14	Interest	$ 478,905.34	=B12-B13
15			
16		**Net Present Value**	
17	Invest End of Year	$ 3,000.00	
18	Yearly Income	$ 1,200.00	
19	Rate	3%	
20	Net Present Value	$ 382.85	=NPV(B19,-B17,B18,B18,B18,B18)
21			

FIGURE 24 Financial Functions

Calculate Present and Future Values

>> The **PV function** calculates the total present (current) value of an investment with a fixed rate, specified number of payment periods, and a series of identical payments that will be made in the future. This function illustrates the time value of money in which the value of $1 today is worth more than the value of $1 received at some time in the future, given that you can invest today's $1 to earn interest in the future. For example, you might want to use the PV function to compare a lump-sum payment versus annual payments if you win the lottery to see which is better: receiving $100,000 per year for the next 20 years or $1 million now.

STEP 1

The PV function has three required arguments (rate, nper, and pmt) and two optional arguments (fv and type). The rate, nper, and type arguments have the same definitions as in other financial functions. The pmt argument is the fixed periodic payment. The fv argument represents the future value of the investment. If you do not know the payment, you must enter a value for the fv argument. In Figure 24 cell B3 contains the PV function. The yearly payments of $100,000 invested at 5% yield a higher present value ($1,246,221.03) than the $1 million lump-sum payment.

=PV(rate,nper,pmt,[fv],[type])

The *FV function* calculates the future value of an investment, given a fixed interest rate, term, and identical periodic payments. Use the FV function to determine how much an individual retirement account (IRA) would be worth at a future date. The FV function has three required arguments (rate, nper, and pmt) and two optional arguments (pv and type). If you omit the pmt argument, you must enter a value for the pv argument.

=FV(rate,nper,pmt,[pv],[type])

Assume that you plan to contribute $3,000 a year to an IRA for 40 years and that you expect the IRA to earn 7% interest annually. The future value of that investment—the amount you will have 40 years later—would be $598,905.34. In Figure 24, cell B12 contains the FV function. You would have contributed $120,000 ($3,000 a year for 40 years). The extra $478,905.34 results from compound interest you will earn over the life of your $120,000 investment.

The *NPV function* calculates the net present value of an investment, given a fixed rate (rate of return) and future payments that may be identical or different. It considers periodic future income and payments. The NPV and PV functions are very similar in concept. The difference is that the PV function requires equal payments at the end of a payment period, whereas the NPV function can have unequal but constant payments. The NPV function contains two required arguments (rate and value1) and additional optional arguments (such as value2). If an investment returns a positive net present value, the investment is profitable. If an investment returns a negative net present value, the investment will lose money.

=NPV(rate,value1,value2,)

- **Rate.** The rate argument is the interest rate for one period. It is also called the rate of return or the percentage return on your investment. If an investment pays 12% per year and each period is one month, the rate is 1%.

- **Value1.** The value arguments represent a sequence of payments and income during the investment period. To provide an accurate net present value, the cash flows must occur at equally spaced-out time periods and must occur at the end of each period.

Assume you invest $3,000 at the end of the first year and receive $1,200 during the second, third, and fourth years with a 3% rate. In Figure 24, cell B20 contains the NPV function. The net present value would be $382.85. However, if you pay the $3,000 at the beginning of the first year instead of the end of the first year, you cannot discount the $3,000 since it is already in today's value. You would then subtract it after the function: =NPV(B19,B18,B18,B18)−B17. By investing $3,000 immediately, the net present value is higher at $394.33.

Use NPER and RATE Functions

In some situations, you might have a payment goal and know the stated interest rate, but you need to calculate how many payments you will make. In other situations, you might know the payment and number of payments, but you need to calculate the rate. The NPER and RATE functions are useful in these situations.

The **NPER function** calculates the number of payment periods for an investment or loan given a fixed interest rate, periodic payment, and present value. You can use NPER to calculate the number of monthly payments given a car loan of $30,000, an APR of 5.25%, and a monthly payment of $694.28. In Figure 25, cell B6 contains the NPER function. The NPER would be 48.0001, or about 48 payments. The NPER function contains three required arguments (rate, pmt, and pv) and two optional arguments (fv and type).

=NPER(rate,pmt,pv,[fv],[type])

	Number of Periods	
1		
2	Loan	$ 30,000.00
3	APR	5.25%
4	No. of Payment Periods in Year	12
5	Monthly Payment	$ 694.28
6	Number of Periods	48 =NPER(B3/B4,-B5,B2)
7		
8		Rate
9	Loan	$ 30,000.00
10	Monthly Payment	$ 694.28
11	No. of Periods in Year	12
12	Years	4
13	Periodic Rate	0.44% =RATE(B11*B12,-B10,B9)
14	APR	5.25% =B11*B13
15		
16		
17		

FIGURE 25 NPER and RATE Functions

Excel 2016, Windows 10, Microsoft Corporation

The **RATE function** calculates the periodic rate for an investment or loan given the number of payment periods, a fixed periodic payment, and present value. Use RATE to calculate the periodic rate of a four-year car loan of $30,000 and a monthly payment of $694.28. In Figure 25, cell B13 contains the RATE function. The periodic (monthly) rate would be 0.44%. The APR (5.25%) is found by multiplying the periodic rate by 12. The RATE function contains three required arguments (nper, pmt, and pv) and two optional arguments (fv and type).

=RATE(nper,pmt,pv,[fv],[type])

Creating a Loan Amortization Table

You used the PMT function to calculate the monthly payment for an automobile or house loan with a fixed interest rate (such as 5.75% APR) for a specified period of time (such as 30 years). Although knowing the monthly payment is helpful to analyze a potential loan, you might want to know how much of that payment contains interest and how much goes toward principal (or paying off the loan balance). Recall that a portion of the monthly payment covers the interest you owe and a portion of the monthly payment pays down your principal.

While the monthly payment is constant throughout the life of the loan, the interest and principal portions are not the same every month of the loan. With each payment, you decrease the balance of the loan. The interest is calculated on the balance of the loan, so as you continue making monthly payments, the loan balance continually decreases; therefore, the interest portion decreases and the principal portion increases each month.

To see the interest and principal portions of each monthly payment and the reduction in the loan amount, you can create a *loan amortization table*, which is a schedule that calculates the interest per payment period, principal repayment for each payment, and remaining balance after each payment is made. Figure 26 shows the top and bottom portions of an amortization schedule (rows 18:49 are hidden) for an automobile loan of $30,000 with an APR of 2.74% for a four-year loan with a monthly payment of $660.59, rounded to the nearest penny. The borrower pays a total of $31,708.23 (48 payments of $660.59). These payments equal the principal of $30,000 plus $1,708.23 in interest over the life of the loan.

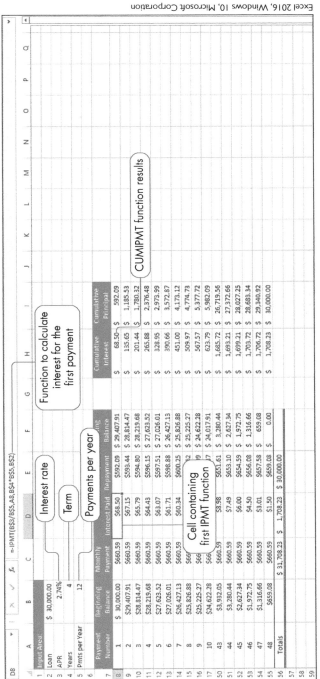

Excel 2016, Windows 10, Microsoft Corporation

FIGURE 26 Loan Amortization Table

Perform Internal Calculations

STEP 2 >> The body of the worksheet reflected in Figure 26 shows how principal and interest comprise each payment. The balance of the loan at the beginning of the first period is $30,000. The monthly payment includes interest and principal repayment. The interest for the first month ($68.50) is calculated by multiplying the beginning loan balance for the period, which is the original loan amount ($30,000) by the monthly interest rate (2.74%/12).

The principal repayment is the amount of the monthly payment that is left over after deducting the monthly interest. For the first payment, the principal repayment is $592.09 ($660.59 − $68.50).

The remaining balance is the difference between the previous remaining balance and the principal repayment. For the first month, subtract the principal repayment from the original loan amount ($30,000 − $592.09).

The interest for the second month ($67.15) is less than interest for the previous period. This is because the balance to start the second period ($29,407.91) is less than the loan balance for the first period ($30,000) because $592.09 was paid in principal with the first payment.

Calculate Interest and Principal Payments with IPMT and PPMT Functions

The financial category contains additional functions to calculate results for loan payments: IPMT and PPMT. You can use these functions in isolation or within the body of a loan amortization table if the table does not allow additional principal payments. If the loan amortization enables you to pay additional principal, these functions will not provide accurate results.

The *IPMT function* calculates the periodic interest for a specified payment period on a loan or an investment given a fixed interest rate, specified term, and identical periodic payments. In Figure 26, the IPMT function calculates the interest payment for each period. For example, the calculation for interest for the first period is: =-IPMT(B$3/B$5,A8,B$4*B$5,B$2). You can type the negative sign after = or before any argument. A benefit of the IPMT function is that it identifies the interest for any given payment without having to create a loan amortization table. The IPMT function has four required arguments and two optional arguments.

=IPMT(rate,per,nper,pv,[fv],[type])

- **Rate.** The rate argument is the periodic interest rate. If the APR is 2.74% (cell B3) and monthly payments are made, the rate is 2.74%/12 (B$3/B$5), or 0.228%.

- **Per.** The per argument is the specific payment or investment period to use to calculate the interest where the first payment period is 1. It is best to include a payment number column as shown in Figure 26. You can use a relative cell reference to avoid having values in the argument.

- **Nper.** This argument represents the total number of payment or investment periods. With a four-year loan consisting of monthly payments, the number of payment periods is 48. You should perform the calculation using the input cells, such as B$4*B$5, in the nper argument instead of typing 48 in case the number of years or number of payments per year changes.

- **Pv.** This argument represents the present value of the loan or investment.

- **Fv.** The optional fv argument represents the future value of the loan or investment. If you omit this argument, Excel defaults to 0. For loan payments, the balance should be zero after you pay off your loan.

- **Type.** The optional type argument represents the timing of the payments. Enter 0 if the payments are made at the end of the period, or enter 1 if the payments are made at the beginning of the period. If you omit this argument, Excel assumes a default of 0.

The *PPMT function* calculates the principal payment for a specified payment period on a loan or an investment given a fixed interest rate, specified term, and identical periodic payments. As shown in Figure 26, you can use the PPMT function to calculate the principal repayment in column E. For example, cell E8 contains =-PPMT(B$3/B$5,A8,B$4*B$5,B$2). You can type the negative sign after = or before any argument. The first month's total payment of $660.59 includes $592.09 principal repayment. The PPMT function has the same four required arguments and two optional arguments as the IPMT function.

=PPMT(rate,per,nper,pv,[fv],[type])

Calculate Cumulative Interest with the CUMIPMT Function

STEP 3

Although the IPMT function calculates the amount of interest paid in one particular loan payment, it does not determine the amount of interest paid over a specific number of payments. You can use the **CUMIPMT function** to calculate the cumulative interest through a specified payment period. This function accumulates the interest paid between selected payments or throughout the entire loan. For the first payment, the cumulative interest is the same as the periodic interest. From that point on, you can calculate the cumulative interest, such as the sum of the interest paid for the first two periods, as shown in cell H9 in Figure 26. If you do not want to calculate a running total for the entire loan, you can specify the interest between two periods, such as between payment periods 13 and 24, to calculate the total interest paid for the second year of the loan. The CUMIPMT contains six arguments.

=CUMIPMT(rate,nper,pv,start_period,end_period,type)

The rate, nper, pv, and type arguments are the same arguments that you use in the IPMT and PPMT functions. The start_period argument specifies the first period you want to start accumulating the interest, and the end_period argument specifies the last payment period you want to include. In Figure 26, the first cumulative interest payment formula in cell H8 uses 1 for both the start_period and end_period arguments. From that point on, the start_period is still 1, but the end_period changes to reflect each payment period, using the payment numbers in column A.

Calculate Cumulative Principal Payments with the CUMPRINC Function

STEP 4

You can use the **CUMPRINC function** to calculate the cumulative principal through a specified payment period. This function accumulates the principal repayment between selected payments or throughout the entire loan. For the first payment, the cumulative principal paid is the same as the first principal repayment. From that point on, you can calculate the cumulative principal payment, such as the sum of the principal repayment paid for the first two periods, as shown in cell I9 in Figure 26. If you do not want to calculate a running total for the entire loan, you can specify the principal repayment between two periods, such as between payment periods 13 and 24, to calculate the total principal repaid for the second year of the loan.

The CUMPRINC contains six arguments. The rate, nper, pv, start_period, end_period, and type arguments are the same arguments that you use in the CUMIPMT function.

=CUMPRINC(rate,nper,pv,start_period,end_period,type)

Quick Concepts

7. What is the difference between PV and NPV calculations?
8. In what situation would you use IPMT and PPMT?
9. What is the difference between IPMT and CUMIPMT?

3 Financial Functions

The location managers want new company cars. Angela Khazen, the chief financial officer, has determined that the company can afford $450 monthly payments based on a 5.25% APR for four-year loans. She wants you to prepare a loan amortization table and running totals for interest and principal repayment.

STEP 1 ≫ CALCULATE THE PRESENT VALUE

Because Angela determined the monthly payment for an automobile, you must use the PV function to calculate the loan amount. Other variables, such as trade-in value of the current vehicle, need to be considered, but you will exclude those variables at the moment. Refer to Figure 27 as you complete Step 1.

FIGURE 27 PV Function

Excel 2016, Windows 10,
Microsoft Corporation

a. Open *e07h2Salary_LastFirst* if you closed it at the end of Hands-On Exercise 2, and save it as **e07h3Salary_LastFirst**, changing h2 to h3. Click the **3-Finance sheet tab.**

You will calculate the periodic interest rate and number of payment periods before you can calculate the present value of the loan.

b. Click **cell E3**, type **=B3/B5**, and then press **Enter**.

The periodic rate, 0.438%, is the result of dividing the APR by the number of payments per year.

c. Type **=B4*B5** in **cell E4** and press **Enter**.

The total number of monthly payments, 48, is the product of the number of years the loan is outstanding and the number of payments per year.

d. Click **cell E2**, click **Financial** in the Function Library group on the Formulas tab, scroll through the list, and then select **PV**.

e. Click **cell E3** to enter that cell reference in the Rate box, click in the **Nper box**, and then click **cell E4**. Click in the **Pmt box**, type **B2**, and then click **OK**.

f. Edit the function by typing **–** between **=** and PV. Press **Enter**. Save the workbook.

The result is $19,444.57 based on four years of $450 monthly payments with an APR of 5.25%. You entered a negative sign after = to display the result as a positive value. If you do not enter a negative sign, Excel will display the loan as a negative value.

Angela wants you to create an amortization table. The column labels and payment numbers have already been entered into the worksheet. Now you will enter formulas to show the beginning loan balance for each payment, the monthly payment, interest paid, and principal repayment. Refer to Figure 28 as you complete Step 2.

Formula bar: **D8** =-IPMT(E$3,A8,E$4,E$2) ← Step c: IPMT function

	A	B	C	D	E	F
1	Input Area:			Basic Output Area:		
2	Payment	$ 450.00		Loan	$19,444.57	
3	APR	5.25%		Periodic Rate	0.438%	
4	Years	4		# of Payments	48	
5	Pmts per Year	12				
6						
7	Payment Number	Beginning Balance	Monthly Payment	Interest Paid	Principal Repayment	Ending Balance
8	1	$19,444.57	$ 450.00	$ 85.07	$ 364.93	$ 19,079.64
9	2	$19,079.64	$ 450.00	$ 83.47	$ 366.53	$ 18,713.11
10	3	$18,713.11	$ 450.00	$ 81.87	$ 368.13	$ 18,344.98
48	41	$3,095.59	$ 450.00	$ 15.44	$ 434.56	$ 3,095.59
49	42	$2,659.13	$ 450.00	$ 13.54	$ 436.46	$ 2,659.13
50	43	$2,220.77	$ 450.00	$ 11.63	$ 438.37	$ 2,220.77
51	44	$1,780.48	$ 450.00	$ 9.72	$ 440.28	$ 1,780.48
52	45	$1,338.27	$ 450.00	$ 7.79	$ 442.21	$ 1,338.27
53	46	$894.13	$ 450.00	$ 5.85	$ 444.15	$ 894.13
54	47	$448.04	$ 450.00	$ 3.91	$ 446.09	$ 448.04
55	48		$ 450.00	$ 1.96	$ 448.04	$ (0.00)
56	Totals		$ 21,600.00	$ 2,155.43	$ 19,444.57	
57						

Annotations:
- Step e: =B8-E8 formula
- Step d: PPMT function
- Step a: Reference to original loan amount
- Step f: =F8 formula (0.15)
- Step i: Total paid
- Step i: Total interest
- Step i: Total principal repaid

Excel 2016, Windows 10, Microsoft Corporation

FIGURE 28 Loan Amortization Table

a. Click **cell B8**, type **=E2**, and then press **Tab**.

You entered a reference to the original loan amount because that is the beginning balance to start the first payment period. Referencing the original cell is recommended instead of typing the value directly in the cell due to internal rounding. Furthermore, if you change the original input values, the calculated loan amount will change in both cells B8 and E2.

b. Type **=B$2** in **cell C8** and press **Ctrl+Enter**. Drag the **cell C8 fill handle** to copy the payment to the **range C9:C55**.

The monthly payment is $450.00. You entered a reference to the original monthly payment so that if you change it in cell B2, Excel will update the values in the Monthly Payment column automatically. The cell reference must be a mixed (B$2) or absolute ($B$2) reference to prevent the row number from changing when you copy the formula down the column later.

c. Click **cell D8**, click **Financial** in the Function Library, select **IPMT** to open the Function Arguments dialog box, type **E$3** in the Rate box, type **A8** in the Per box, type **E$4** in the Nper box, type **E$2** in the PV box, and then click **OK**. Edit the function by typing – between = and IPMT to convert the results to a positive value. Press **Ctrl+Enter**. Drag the **cell D8 fill handle** to copy the **IPMT** function to the **range D9:D55**.

The IPMT function calculates the interest of a specific payment based on the starting balance of $19,444.57 with a periodic interest of .438% over 48 payments. By not making cell A8 absolute, the function is able to adjust the period to match the specific period of evaluation.

d. Click **cell E8**, click **Financial** in the Function Library, select **PPMT** to open the Function Arguments dialog box, type **E$3** in the Rate box, type **A8** in the Per box, type **E$4** in the Nper box, type **E$2** in the PV box, and then click **OK**. Edit the function by typing – between = and PPMT to convert the results to a positive value. Press **Ctrl+Enter**. Drag the **cell E8 fill handle** to copy the PPMT function to the **range E9:E55**.

To calculate the principal repayment, subtract the interest of the first payment $85.07 from the monthly payment of $450. The remaining portion of the payment $364.93 goes toward paying down the principal owed. Using the PPMT function automatically completed these calculations.

e. Click in **cell F8** and type **=B8-E8**.

This calculates the ending balance after the first payment is made. The ending balance of $19,079.64 is calculated by subtracting the amount of principal in the payment $364.93 from the balance currently owed $19,444.57.

f. Click in **cell B9**, type **=F8**, and then press **Ctrl+Enter**.

The beginning balance of the second payment is also the ending balance of the first payment. The easiest method to populate the column is by referencing the ending balance from the prior month (cell F8). However, this can also be calculated by subtracting the previous principal repayment value (such as $364.93) from the previous month's beginning balance (such as $19,444.57).

g. Drag the **cell B9 fill handle** to copy the cell reference to the **range B10:B55**.

h. Drag the **cell F8 fill handle** to copy the formula to the **range F9:F55**.

The ending balance in cell F55 should be $0, indicating that the loan has been completely paid off.

i. Type SUM functions in **cells C56, D56**, and **E56**. Select the **range A56:F56** and apply the **Top and Double Bottom Border**. Save the workbook.

You calculated totals for the appropriate columns, noting that column B is a running balance and cannot be logically totaled. Figure 28 shows the top and bottom portions of the amortization table with rows 11 through 47 hidden.

The loan amortization table shows how much of each payment is interest and how much pays down the principal. However, Angela wants you to include a column to show the cumulative interest after each payment. Refer to Figure 29 as you complete Step 3.

H8	:	×	✓	ƒx	=CUMIPMT(E$3,E$4,E$2,A$8,A8,0)							
⯅	A	B	C	D	E	F		J	K	L	M	
1	Input Area:			Basic Output Area:								
2	Payment	$ 450.00		Loan	$19,444.57							
3	APR	5.25%		Periodic Rate	0.438%							
4	Years	4		# of Payments	48							
5	Pmts per Year	12										
6												
7	Payment Number	Beginning Balance	Monthly Payment	Interest Paid	Principal Repayment	Ending Balance	Cumulative Interest	Cumulative Principal				
8	1	$19,444.57	$ 450.00	$ 85.07	$ 364.93	$19,079.64	$ 85.07					
9	2	$19,079.64	$ 450.00	$ 83.47	$ 366.53	$18,713.11	$ 168.54					
10	3	$18,713.11	$ 450.00	$ 81.87	$ 368.13	$18,344.98	$ 250.41					
48	41	$3,530.15	$ 450.00	$ 15.44	$ 434.56	$ 3,095.59	$ 2,101.02					
49	42	$3,095.59	$ 450.00	$ 13.54	$ 436.46	$ 2,659.13	$ 2,114.57					
50	43	$2,659.13	$ 450.00	$ 11.63	$ 438.37	$ 2,220.77	$ 2,126.20					
51	44	$2,220.77	$ 450.00	$ 9.72	$ 440.28	$ 1,780.48	$ 2,135.92					
52	45	$1,780.48	$ 450.00	$ 7.79	$ 442.21	$ 1,338.27	$ 2,143.71					
53	46	$1,338.27	$ 450.00	$ 5.85	$ 444.15	$ 894.13	$ 2,149.56					
54	47	$894.13	$ 450.00	$ 3.91	$ 446.09	$ 448.04	$ 2,153.47					
55	48	$448.04	$ 450.00	$ 1.96	$ 448.04	$ (0.00)	$ 2,155.43					
56	Totals		$ 21,600.00	$ 2,155.43	$ 19,444.57							
57												

Steps a–e: CUMIPMT function

Step f: Last result should match cell D56 total

Excel 2016, Windows 10, Microsoft Corporation

FIGURE 29 Cumulative Interest

a. Click **cell H8**, click **Financial** in the Function Library group on the Formulas tab, and then select **CUMIPMT**.

The Function Arguments dialog box displays so that you can enter the arguments for the CUMIPMT function.

b. Type the following arguments: **E$3** in the Rate box, **E$4** in the Nper box, **E$2** in the Pv box, and **A$8** in the Start_period box.

Make sure the cell references you enter in Rate, Nper, Pv, and Start_period boxes are mixed as shown to prevent the row number from changing as you copy the formula down the column.

TIP: MIXED OR ABSOLUTE REFERENCES

You can also use absolute references; however, the entire formula is easier to read (and is shorter) in the Formula Bar when you use mixed instead of absolute references.

---

c. Type **A8** in the End_period box.

This reference should be relative so that it reflects the current month's payment number as you copy the formula down the column.

d. Press **Tab**, type **0** in the Type box, and then click **OK**.

The cumulative interest for the first payment is the same as the first payment's interest. However, the formula displays a negative result, as indicated by the parentheses.

e. Edit the function by typing - between = and CUMIPMT to convert the results to a positive value. Press **Enter**.

The cumulative interest at the end of the first payment is identical to the interest on the first payment.

f. Copy the formula through **cell H55**. Save the workbook.

The cumulative interest in cell H55 should match the total interest paid calculated in cell D56: $2,155.43.

Angela wants to see the cumulative principal paid after making each loan payment. You will use the CUMPRINC function to calculate the cumulative principal paid. Refer to Figure 30 as you complete Step 4.

STEP 4 ⟩⟩ CALCULATE CUMULATIVE PRINCIPAL PAID

I8   fx   =CUMPRINC(E$3,E$4,E$2,A$8,A8,0)

	A	B	C	D	E	F	G	H	I
1	Input Area:				Basic Output Area:				
2	Payment	$	450.00		Loan	$19,444.57			
3	APR		5.25%		Periodic Rate	0.438%			
4	Years		4		# of Payments	48			
5	Pmts per Year		12						
6									
7	Payment Number	Beginning Balance	Monthly Payment	Interest Paid	Principal Repayment	Ending Balance		Cumulative Interest	Cumulative Principal
8	1	$19,444.57	$ 450.00	$ 85.07	$ 364.93	$ 19,079.64		$ 85.07	$ 364.93
9	2	$19,079.64	$ 450.00	$ 83.47	$ 366.53	$ 18,713.11		$ 168.54	$ 731.46
10	3	$18,713.11	$ 450.00	$ 81.87	$ 368.13	$ 18,344.98		$ 250.41	$ 1,099.59
48	41	$3,530.15	$ 450.00	$ 15.44	$ 434.56	$ 3,095.59		$ 2,101.02	$ 16,348.98
49	42	$3,095.59	$ 450.00	$ 13.54	$ 436.46	$ 2,659.13		$ 2,114.57	$ 16,785.43
50	43	$2,659.13	$ 450.00	$ 11.63	$ 438.37	$ 2,220.77		$ 2,126.20	$ 17,223.80
51	44	$2,220.77	$ 450.00	$ 9.72	$ 440.28	$ 1,780.48		$ 2,135.92	$ 17,664.08
52	45	$1,780.48	$ 450.00	$ 7.79	$ 442.21	$ 1,338.27		$ 2,143.71	$ 18,106.29
53	46	$1,338.27	$ 450.00	$ 5.85	$ 444.15	$ 894.13		$ 2,149.56	$ 18,550.44
54	47	$894.13	$ 450.00	$ 3.91	$ 446.09	$ 448.04		$ 2,153.47	$ 18,996.53
55	48	$448.04	$ 450.00	$ 1.96	$ 448.04	$ (0.00)		$ 2,155.43	$ 19,444.57
56	Totals		$ 21,600.00	$ 2,155.43	$ 19,444.57				
57									

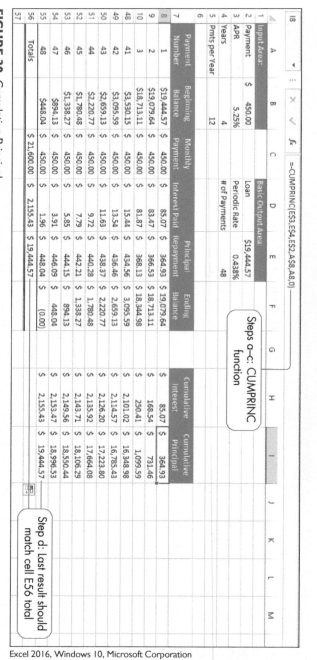

Steps a–c: CUMPRINC function

Step d: Last result should match cell E56 total

FIGURE 30 Cumulative Principal

Excel 2016, Windows 10, Microsoft Corporation

a. Click **cell I8**, click **Financial** in the Function Library group, and then select **CUMPRINC**.

The Function Arguments dialog box displays so that you can enter the arguments for the CUMPRINC function.

b. Type the following arguments: **E$3** in the Rate box, **E$4** in the Nper box, **E$2** in the Pv box, **A$8** in the Start_period box, **A8** in the End_period box, and **0** in the Type box.

c. Click **OK** and edit the function by typing **-** between **=** and CUMPRINC. Press **Ctrl+Enter**.

d. Copy the formula from **cell I8** to the **range I9:I55**.

The cumulative principal in cell I55 should match the total principal repayment calculated in cell E56: $19,444.57.

e. Save and close the file. Based on your instructor's directions, submit e07h3Salary_LastFirst.

Chapter Objectives Review

After reading this chapter, you have accomplished the following objectives:

1. Use date functions.

- Calculate days and years between dates: The DAYS function calculates the number of days between two dates, and the YEARFRAC function calculates the fraction of a year between two dates.

- Extract day, month, and year: The DAY function displays the day (1–31) within a month. The MONTH function displays the month (1–12) where 1 is January and 12 is December for a date. The YEAR function displays the year such as 2018 for a specific date.

2. Create a nested logical function.

- A nested IF function is one that contains one or more additional IF functions nested inside one or more arguments. This type of nested function helps derive calculations for complex situations with multiple outcomes.

- Nested IF within an IF function: When more than two outcomes are possible, you can nest an additional IF function within the value_if_true argument and/or value_if_false argument of an IF function.

- Nest AND, OR, and NOT functions: Nested AND, OR, and NOT statements give you the ability to evaluate multiple conditions at the same time. The AND function returns TRUE if all conditions are true. The OR function returns TRUE if any condition is true. The NOT function returns TRUE if the statement is false and FALSE if the statement is true.

3. Use advanced lookup functions.

- Use the INDEX function: The INDEX function returns a value or the reference to a value within a range.

- Use the MATCH function: The MATCH function returns the position of a value in a list.

- Create a nested function: Nest the MATCH function inside the INDEX function to identify a location and then return related data.

4. Apply advanced filtering.

- Define a criteria range: Before you apply advanced filtering, you must define the criteria range that is separate from the table or list, contains column labels, and lists the conditions on the row(s) immediately below the column labels in the criteria range. Conditions listed on the same row form an AND condition. Conditions on multiple rows form an OR condition.

- Apply the Advanced Filter: Once applied, the Advanced Filter only displays information that meets predefined criteria. The output can filter the original table or copy records that meet the conditions in the output area.

5. Manipulate data with database functions.

- Use DSUM and DAVERAGE functions: The DSUM function adds the values in a database column based on specified conditions. The DAVERAGE function averages the values in a numeric database based on specified conditions.

- Identify values with DMAX and DMIN: The DMAX function returns the highest value in a database column that matches specified criteria. In contrast, the DMIN function returns the lowest value in a database column that matches specified criteria.

- Identify the total number with DCOUNT: The DCOUNT function counts the cells that contain numbers in a database column that match specified criteria.

6. Use financial functions.

- Calculate present and future values: The FV function calculates the future value of an investment. The PV function calculates the present value of an investment. These functions require a fixed rate, specified term, and identical periodic payments. The NPV function calculates net present value for an investment with a fixed rate where future payments may be identical or different.

- Use NPER and RATE functions: The NPER function calculates the number of payment periods for a loan or an investment with a fixed rate, present value, and identical periodic payments. The RATE function calculates the periodic interest rate for an investment or loan with a given number of payment periods, a fixed period payment, and present value.

7. Create a loan amortization table.

- A loan amortization table is a schedule of monthly payments, interest per period, principal repayment per period, and balances.

- Perform internal calculations: Use basic arithmetic operations to manually calculate interest and principal payments.

- Calculate interest and principal payments with IPMT and PPMT functions: The IPMT function calculates the periodic interest for a specified payment period on a loan or investment. The PPMT function calculates the principal payment for a specified payment period on a loan or investment.

- Calculate cumulative interest with CUMIPMT function: The CUMIPMT function calculates the cumulative interest for a specific period on a loan or investment.

- Calculate cumulative principal payments with the CUMPRINC function: The CUMPRINC function calculates the cumulative principal for a specific payment period.

Match the key terms with their definitions. Write the key term letter by the appropriate numbered definition.

a. AND function

b. CUMIPMT function

c. CUMPRINC function

d. DAVERAGE function

e. DCOUNT function

f. DMAX function

g. DMIN function

h. DSUM function

i. FV function

j. INDEX function

k. IPMT function

l. Loan amortization table

m. MATCH function

n. NOT function

o. NPER function

p. NPV function

q. OR function

r. PPMT function

s. PV function

t. YEARFRAC function

1. _____ Calculates the number of periods for an investment or loan given a fixed rate, period payment, and present value.

2. _____ Calculates the future value of an investment given a fixed rate, a term, and identical periodic payments.

3. _____ Calculates the net present value of an investment with a fixed rate and periodic payments that may be identical or different.

4. _____ Calculates cumulative principal for a specified payment period.

5. _____ Calculates the present value of an investment with a fixed rate, specified number of periods, and identical periodic payments that will be made in the future.

6. _____ Calculates cumulative interest for a specified payment period.

7. _____ A schedule showing monthly payments, interest per payment, amount toward paying off the loan, and the remaining balance for each payment.

8. _____ Calculates the principal payment for a specified payment period on a loan or an investment given a fixed rate, a specified term, and identical periodic payments.

9. _____ Calculates periodic interest for a specific payment period on a loan or investment with a fixed rate, a specified term, and identical periodic payments.

10. _____ Counts the cells that contain a number in a database column that matches specified conditions.

11. _____ Identifies the highest value in a database column that matches specified conditions.

12. _____ Identifies the lowest value in a database column that matches specified conditions.

13. _____ Averages values in a database column that match specified conditions.

14. _____ Adds values in a database column that match specified conditions.

15. _____ Calculates the fraction of a year between two dates based on the number of whole days.

16. _____ Returns a value or reference to a value within a range based on the intersection of a specific row and column.

17. _____ Identifies the position of a value in a list based on a lookup value, a lookup array, and a match type.

18. _____ Returns TRUE if the argument is false and FALSE if the argument is true.

19. _____ Returns TRUE if any argument is true and returns FALSE if all arguments are false.

20. _____ Returns TRUE when all arguments are true and FALSE when at least one argument is false.

Multiple Choice

1. Today's date (February 12, 2018) is stored in cell B1. The last day of the semester (May 4, 2018) is stored in cell B2. You want to know how many days until the end of the semester? Which function should you use?

   (a) =DAYS(B1,B2)
   (b) =DAYS(B2,B1)
   (c) =YEARFRAC(B1,B2)
   (d) =DAY(B1)

2. The date 5/12/2018 is stored in cell C1. What function should you use to extract just 12?

   (a) =YEAR(C1)
   (b) =MONTH(C1)
   (c) =DAYS(B1,C1)
   (d) =DAY(C1)

3. Your workbook contains a list of artwork. Column B lists Sold Out if the piece is sold out, Available if it is still readily available, or Limited if only a few pieces are available. In the third column, you want to display TRUE if the art is not sold out. What function would produce the same results as =OR(B1="Available",B1="Limited")?

   (a) =AND(B1="Available",B1="Limited")
   (b) =IF(B1="Sold Out","TRUE","FALSE")
   (c) =NOT(B1="Sold Out")
   (d) =TRUE(B1<>"Sold Out")

4. A workbook contains a list of members in the Computer Club. You want to identify the number of students who are freshmen who are Information Systems majors. Without filtering the dataset, what function should you use?

   (a) DCOUNT
   (b) COUNTA
   (c) DSUM
   (d) COUNT

5. A worksheet contains the times in which runners completed a race, with the times organized from fastest to slowest. You will use the MATCH function to identify what place a runner came in given a time of 4:05 (four minutes and five seconds). Which argument should contain the specific runner's time?

   (a) Lookup_array
   (b) Lookup_value
   (c) Match_type
   (d) Row_num

6. What function would you use to calculate the total interest paid for the first year of a mortgage?

   (a) CUMIPMT
   (b) IPMT
   (c) PPMT
   (d) CUMPRINC

7. When you are performing an advanced filter, where do you enter the range for the dataset?

   (a) Criteria range
   (b) Output range
   (c) List range
   (d) Copy to range

8. The original mortgage loan was for $300,000 with a 5% APR for 30 years. You want to calculate the interest on the last monthly payment at the end of the 15th year. What value should be referenced for the per argument in the IPMT function?

   (a) 15
   (b) 180
   (c) 30
   (d) 0.05/12

9. A local police office wants to create a rule that if an officer pulls over a person for exceeding the speed limit by at least five miles per hour or if that person has two or more speeding violations on record, the officer will fine the speeder the higher of $200 or $50 for each mile over the speed limit. Otherwise, the fine is $45. The speed limit is entered in cell B5, the person's speed is entered in cell B10, and the person's number of previous tickets is entered in cell B11. What function derives the correct answer?

   (a) =IF(AND(B10>B5,B11>=2),200,45)
   (b) =IF(AND(B10-B5>=5,B11<2),MAX(200, (B10-B5)*50),45)
   (c) =IF(OR(B10-B5>=5,B11>=2),MAX(200, (B10-B5)*50),45)
   (d) =IF(OR(B10>B5,B11>=2),MAX(200,50),45)

10. What function would you use to calculate the total number of periods in a loan or investment?

   (a) NPER
   (b) RATE
   (c) PV
   (d) FV

Practice Exercises

1 Furniture Sales

As the manager of Reid's Furniture Store, you track sales transactions by sales person, department, amount, and payment type. Customers either finance their purchase through your store or pay in full at the time of purchase. You will calculate down payments and balances for all transactions. If a transaction is paid in full, the balance is zero. Customers who finance their transactions must pay off the balance within four years from the transaction date. You want to review paid-in-full transactions above $4,000, identify the highest cash transaction, and identify which sales person was responsible for that sale. Refer to Figure 31 as you complete this exercise.

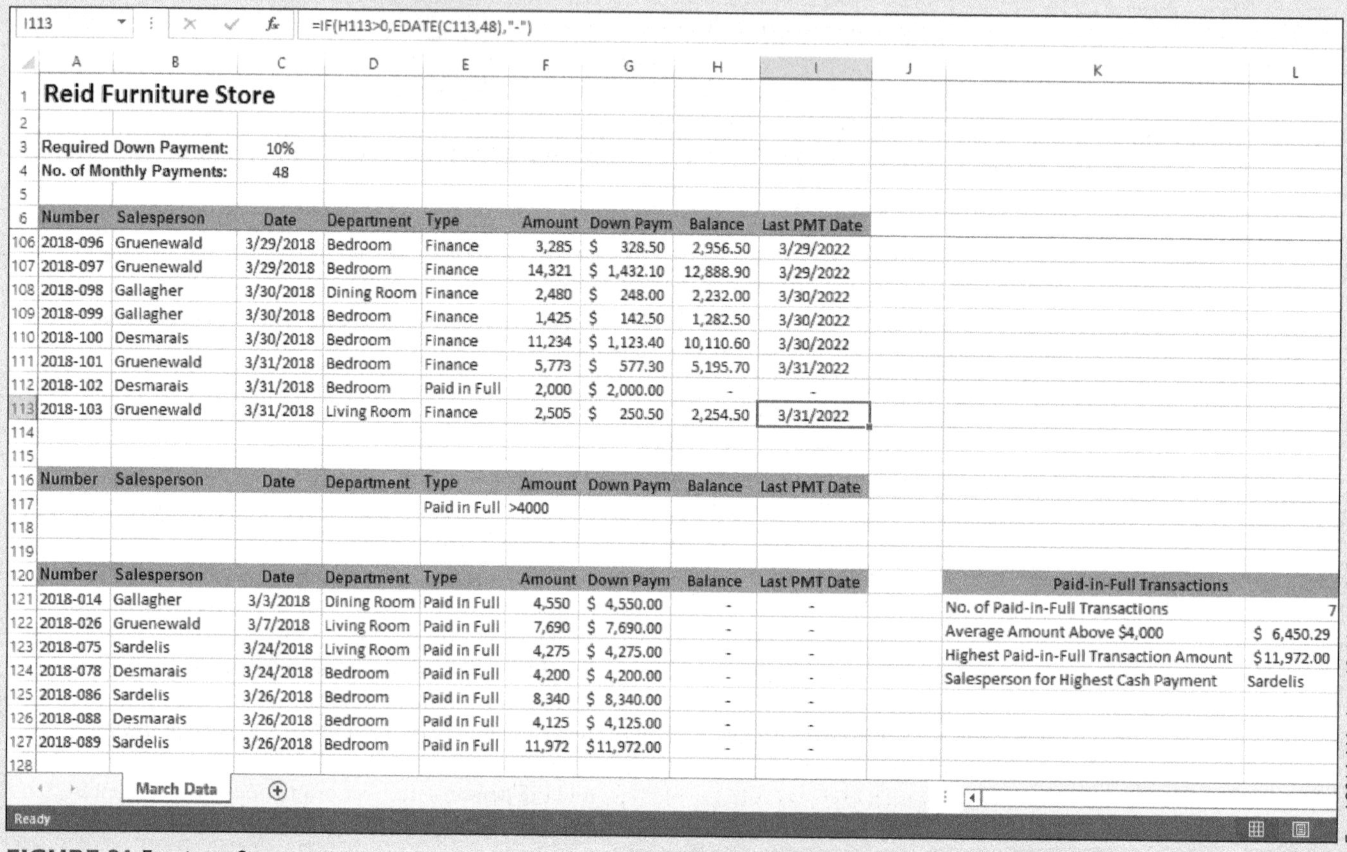

	A	B	C	D	E	F	G	H	I	J	K	L
I113			f_x	=IF(H113>0,EDATE(C113,48),"-")								
1	**Reid Furniture Store**											
2												
3	Required Down Payment:	10%										
4	No. of Monthly Payments:	48										
5												
6	Number	Salesperson	Date	Department	Type	Amount	Down Paym	Balance	Last PMT Date			
106	2018-096	Gruenewald	3/29/2018	Bedroom	Finance	3,285	$ 328.50	2,956.50	3/29/2022			
107	2018-097	Gruenewald	3/29/2018	Bedroom	Finance	14,321	$ 1,432.10	12,888.90	3/29/2022			
108	2018-098	Gallagher	3/30/2018	Dining Room	Finance	2,480	$ 248.00	2,232.00	3/30/2022			
109	2018-099	Gallagher	3/30/2018	Bedroom	Finance	1,425	$ 142.50	1,282.50	3/30/2022			
110	2018-100	Desmarais	3/30/2018	Bedroom	Finance	11,234	$ 1,123.40	10,110.60	3/30/2022			
111	2018-101	Gruenewald	3/31/2018	Bedroom	Finance	5,773	$ 577.30	5,195.70	3/31/2022			
112	2018-102	Desmarais	3/31/2018	Bedroom	Paid in Full	2,000	$ 2,000.00	-				
113	2018-103	Gruenewald	3/31/2018	Living Room	Finance	2,505	$ 250.50	2,254.50	3/31/2022			
114												
115												
116	Number	Salesperson	Date	Department	Type	Amount	Down Paym	Balance	Last PMT Date			
117					Paid in Full >4000							
118												
119												
120	Number	Salesperson	Date	Department	Type	Amount	Down Paym	Balance	Last PMT Date			
121	2018-014	Gallagher	3/3/2018	Dining Room	Paid in Full	4,550	$ 4,550.00	-		No. of Paid-in-Full Transactions	7	
122	2018-026	Gruenewald	3/7/2018	Living Room	Paid in Full	7,690	$ 7,690.00	-		Average Amount Above $4,000	$ 6,450.29	
123	2018-075	Sardelis	3/24/2018	Living Room	Paid in Full	4,275	$ 4,275.00	-		Highest Paid-in-Full Transaction Amount	$11,972.00	
124	2018-078	Desmarais	3/24/2018	Bedroom	Paid in Full	4,200	$ 4,200.00	-		Salesperson for Highest Cash Payment	Sardelis	
125	2018-086	Sardelis	3/26/2018	Bedroom	Paid in Full	8,340	$ 8,340.00	-				
126	2018-088	Desmarais	3/26/2018	Bedroom	Paid in Full	4,125	$ 4,125.00	-				
127	2018-089	Sardelis	3/26/2018	Bedroom	Paid in Full	11,972	$11,972.00	-				
128												

Paid-in-Full Transactions

March Data

Ready

FIGURE 31 Furniture Store

a. Open *e07p1Furniture* and save it as **e07p1Furniture_LastFirst**.

b. Calculate the down payment for all sales. If a transaction is not financed, the down payment is identical to the amount. If the transaction is financed, the down payment is 10% of the amount purchased. Complete the following steps:

- Click **cell G7**.
- Click the **Formulas tab**, click **Logical** in the Function Library, and then select **IF**.
- Type **NOT(E7="Finance")** in the Logical_test box in the Function Arguments dialog box.
- Press **Tab** and type **F7** in the Value_if_true box.
- Press **Tab** and type **F7*C$3** to multiply the amount purchased by the down payment percentage rate in cell C3. Click **OK**.
- Double-click the **cell G7 fill handle** to copy the formula to the **range G8:G113**.

c. Click **cell H7**, type **=F7-G7**, and press **Ctrl+Enter**. Copy the formula to the **range H8:H113**. Notice that paid-in-full transactions show a negative sign (–) instead of a value.

d. Click **cell I7** and calculate the date the payment is due by completing the following steps:

- Click **Logical** in the Function Library and select **IF**.
- Type **H7>0** in the Logical_test box in the Function Arguments dialog box.
- Click in the **Value_if_true box**, click the **Name Box arrow**, select **More Functions**, type **EDATE**, click **Go**, and then click **OK**.
- Type **C7** in the Start_date box.
- Click in the **Months box**, type **C$4**, and then click **OK**.
- Edit the function to look like this: **=IF(H7>0,EDATE(C7,48),"-")**
- Double-click the **cell I7 fill handle** to copy the formula to the **range I8:I113**.

e. Create a criteria range that specifies Paid in Full transaction types and amounts greater than $4,000 by completing the following steps:

- Select the **range A6:I6** and click **Copy** in the Clipboard group on the Home tab.
- Click **cell A116** and click **Paste** in the Clipboard group on the Home tab to create the header for the criteria range.
- Click **cell A120** and click **Paste** in the Clipboard group on the Home tab to create the header for the output range. Press **Esc.**
- Click **cell E117** and type **Paid in Full.**
- Click **cell F117** and type **>4000.**

f. Apply an advanced filter by completing the following steps:

- Click **cell F113**, click the **Data tab**, and click **Advanced** in the Sort & Filter group.
- Click **Copy to another location.**
- Click in the **List range box** and select the **range A6:I113**.
- Click in the **Criteria range box** and select the **range A116:I117**.
- Click in the **Copy to box** and select the **range A120:I120**. Click **OK.**

g. Calculate the number of paid-in-full transactions by completing the following steps:

- Click **cell L121**, click **Insert Function**, select **Database**, select **DCOUNT**, and then click **OK.**
- Type **A6:I113** in the Database box.
- Click in the **Field box** and type **"Amount"**.
- Click in the **Criteria box** and type **A116:I117**. Click **OK.**

h. Calculate the average amount for paid-in-full transactions over $4,000 by completing the following steps:

- Click **cell L122**, click **Insert Function**, select **DAVERAGE**, and then click **OK.**
- Type **A6:I113** in the Database box.
- Click in the **Field box** and type **"Amount"**.
- Click in the **Criteria box** and type **A116:I117**. Click **OK.**

i. Calculate the largest amount for paid-in-full transactions over $4,000 by completing the following steps:

- Click **cell L123**, click **Insert Function**, select **DMAX**, and then click **OK.**
- Type **A6:I113** in the Database box.
- Click in the **Field box** and type **"Amount"**.
- Click in the **Criteria box** and type **A116:I117**. Click **OK.**

j. Identify the sales person who completed the largest paid-in-full transaction by completing the following steps:

- Click **cell L124**, click the **Formulas tab**, click **Lookup & Reference** in the Function Library, select **INDEX**, and then click **OK**. Select **array,row_num,colum_num**. Click **OK.**
- Type **A6:I113** in the Array box.
- Click in the **Row_num box** and type **MATCH(L123,F6:F113,0)** to identify the row that contains the largest cash amount.
- Click in the **Col_num box**, type **2** to specify that the second column of the dataset contains the salespeople's names, and then click **OK**. The completed function looks like this: **=INDEX(A6:I113,MATCH(L123,F6:F113,0),2)**. Sardelis is the salesperson who completed the largest paid-in-full transaction.

2 Detailed Loan Amortization

Detailed Loan Amortization

You are planning to buy a house soon, so you want to set up a detailed loan amortization table. So far, you have designed a worksheet with a loan parameters area (i.e., input area), a summary area, and amortization table column labels. You want to build in mechanisms to prevent formula errors if input data are missing and to hide zeros from displaying if you take out a shorter-term loan or pay it off early. However, you must keep formulas in place for a traditional 30-year loan. In addition, you will notice overpayments on the last payment if you pay extra toward the principal each month. To make the amortization table as flexible as possible and to avoid errors, you will create several nested IF functions. Refer to Figure 32 as you complete this exercise.

k. Create a footer with your name on the left side, the sheet name code in the center, and the file name code on the right side.

l. Save and close the file. Based on your instructor's directions, submit e07p1Furniture_LastFirst.

Cell H9: `=CUMIPMT(A5,A7*A8,A4,A13,H5,0)`

Loan Parameters

$400,000	Principal
6.25%	Annual Interest Rate
3/1/2018	Date of First Payment
20	Term of Loan (Years)
12	Number of Payments Per Year
TRUE	

Amortization Schedule

Payment Number	Date	Beginning Balance	Regular Payment	Interest	Principal	Cumulative Principal	Ending Balance
1	3/1/2018	$400,000.00	$2,923.71	$2,083.33	$840.38	$840.38	$399,159.62
2	4/1/2018	$399,159.62	$2,923.71	$2,078.96	$844.76	$1,685.14	$398,314.86
3	5/1/2018	$398,314.86	$2,923.71	$2,074.56	$849.16	$2,534.29	$397,465.71
4	6/1/2018	$397,465.71	$2,923.71	$2,070.13	$853.58	$3,387.87	$396,612.13
5	7/1/2018	$396,612.13	$2,923.71	$2,065.69	$858.02	$4,245.90	$395,754.10
6	8/1/2018	$395,754.10	$2,923.71	$2,061.22	$862.49	$5,108.39	$394,891.61
7	9/1/2018	$394,891.61	$2,923.71	$2,056.73	$866.99	$5,975.37	$394,024.63
8	10/1/2018	$394,024.63	$2,923.71	$2,052.21	$871.50	$6,846.88	$393,153.12
9	11/1/2018	$393,153.12	$2,923.71	$2,047.67	$876.04	$7,722.92	$392,277.08
10	12/1/2018	$392,277.08	$2,923.71	$2,043.11	$880.60	$8,603.52	$391,396.48
11	1/1/2019	$391,396.48	$2,923.71	$2,038.52	$885.19	$9,488.71	$390,511.29
12	2/1/2019	$390,511.29	$2,923.71	$2,033.91	$889.80	$10,378.51	$389,621.49
13	3/1/2019	$389,621.49	$2,923.71	$2,029.28	$894.43	$11,272.94	$388,727.06
14	4/1/2019	$388,727.06	$2,923.71	$2,024.62	$899.09	$12,172.04	$387,827.96
15	5/1/2019	$387,827.96	$2,923.71	$2,019.94	$903.78	$13,075.81	$386,924.19
16	6/1/2019	$386,924.19	$2,923.71	$2,015.23	$908.48	$13,984.29	$386,015.71
17	7/1/2019	$386,015.71	$2,923.71	$2,010.50	$913.21	$14,897.51	$385,102.49
18	8/1/2019	$385,102.49	$2,923.71	$2,005.74	$917.97	$15,815.48	$384,184.52
19	9/1/2019	$384,184.52	$2,923.71	$2,000.96	$922.75	$16,738.23	$383,261.77
20	10/1/2019	$383,261.77	$2,923.71	$1,996.16	$927.56	$17,665.79	$382,334.21

Loan Summary Information

Monthly Payment (P&I Only)	$2,923.71
Scheduled Number of Payments	240
Normal Payoff Date	2/1/2038
Actual Number of Payments	240
Actual Payoff Date	2/1/2038
Total of All Interest Payments	$301,691.07

Payment Number / Date / Ending Balance (<=100000)

Payment Number	Date	Ending Balance
203	1/1/2035	$98,160.95
204	2/1/2035	$95,748.49
205	3/1/2035	$93,323.47
206	4/1/2035	$90,885.81
207	5/1/2035	$88,435.46
208	6/1/2035	$85,972.35
209	7/1/2035	$83,496.41
210	8/1/2035	$81,007.58
211	9/1/2035	$78,505.78
212	10/1/2035	$75,990.95
213	11/1/2035	$73,463.02
214	12/1/2035	$70,921.93
215	1/1/2036	$68,367.60
216	2/1/2036	$65,799.97
217	3/1/2036	$63,218.97
218	4/1/2036	$60,624.52
219	5/1/2036	$58,016.56
220	6/1/2036	$55,395.02
221	7/1/2036	$52,759.82
222	8/1/2036	$50,110.90

FIGURE 32 Detailed Amortization Table

Excel 2016, Windows 10, Microsoft Corporation

a. Open e07p2House and save it as **e07p2House_LastFirst.**

b. Click in each cell in the **range B13:F13** to look at the formulas in the Formula Bar. Delete the contents of **cell A7** and look at the #NUM! errors.

c. Click **cell A9**, click the **Formulas tab**, click **Logical**, and then select **AND**. In the Function Arguments dialog box, complete the following steps:

- Type **A4>0** in the Logical1 box.
- Type **A5>0** in the Logical2 box.
- Type **A6>0** in the Logical3 box.
- Type **A7>0** in the Logical4 box.
- Type **A8>0** in the Logical5 box and click **OK**.

The arguments ensure that if any required input value is missing, the AND function returns FALSE. You will use cell A10's results to avoid error messages in calculated cells. Currently, the result is FALSE because you deleted the contents of cell A7.

d. Assign the range name **DataEntered** to **cell A9** so that you can use a range name in formulas that refer to this cell.

e. Enter the following replacement functions on row 13 to test if data have been entered or if cell A13 contains a value greater than zero. If data have been entered, calculations occur. If not, the functions return zeros:

- **Cell A13: =IF(DataEntered,1,0)**

If DataEntered (cell A9) is TRUE, Excel will display 1 for first payment number. If DataEntered is FALSE, Excel will display 0 for first payment number.

- **Cell B13: =IF(A13>0,A6,"")**

If cell A13 is greater than 0, Excel will display date of first payment entered in cell A6. If cell A13 contains a value of 0, Excel displays an empty cell.

- **Cell C13: =IF(A13>0,A4,0)**
- **Cell D13: =IF(A13>0,H$4,0)**
- **Cell E13: =IF(A13>0,IPMT(A$5/A$8,A13,H$5,-A$4),0)**
- **Cell F13: =IF(A13>0,PPMT(A$5/A$8,A13,H$5,-A$4),0)**
- **Cell G13: =IF(A13>0,-CUMPRINC(A$5/A$8,H$5,A$4,A$13,A13,0),0)**
- **Cell H13: =C13-F13**

f. Edit the formula in **cell H4** to be **=IF(DataEntered,PMT(A5/A8,H5,-A4),0)**. Edit the formula in **cell H5** to be **=IF(DataEntered,A7*A8,0)**.

All error messages should be gone now.

g. Type **30** in **cell A7** to see calculated results appear.

Because all required input values are entered, the AND function in cell A10 indicates TRUE, which is then used in several IF functions that display calculated results if all required inputs are entered.

h. Type the following formulas on row 14 to calculate values for the second payment:

- **Cell A14: =IF(H13>1,A13+1,0)**

This function calculates the next payment number only if the previous ending balance is greater than one. (The ending balance in cell H13 may display $0, but due to rounding, the actual value may be one or two cents. This is why the logical argument is H13>1).

- **Cell B14: =IF(A14>0,DATE(YEAR(B13),MONTH(B13)+1,DAY(B13)),0)**

The date functions identify the specific year, month, and day and add 1 to increase each due date to the next month. The result is 43191 because it is a serial date so far. You will format it soon.

- **Cell C14: =IF(A14>0,H13,0)**

The beginning balance is equal to the ending balance from the previous period.

i. Format **cell B14** as **Short Date** and format **range C13:H14** as **Currency** (not Accounting Number Format).

j. Select the **range D13:H13** and drag the fill handle down to copy the formulas to row 14. Select the **range A14:H14** and drag the fill handle down to copy the formulas to row 373—one row after the end of the 360th payment in which the 30-year loan is paid off.

k. Click **cell A7** and change the value to **20** years. Scroll down the amortization table to row 252—the end of the 240th payment in which the 20-year loan is paid off. Notice that rows 253 through 372 contain zeros because the loan is paid off.

l. Click the **File tab**, click **Options**, and then click **Advanced** to see Advanced Options for working with Excel.

m. Scroll through the options to see *Display options for this worksheet: Payments*, click the **Show a zero in cells that have zero value check box** to deselect it, and then click **OK**. Deselecting this option hides the zeros in rows 253 through 372, but Excel keeps the formulas intact in case the results change. If you change the term to 30 years again, the results will display in the otherwise empty cells.

n. Click **cell D13** and type **=IF(A13>0,IF(C13>$H$4,$H$4,C13*A$5/A$8+C13),0)**. If cell A13 is 0, then the result shows zero. If the logical_test is true, the nested IF statement checks the current balance against the regular monthly payment. If the balance is greater, you pay the monthly payment. If the monthly payment is higher, you pay the balance plus the interest on the balance only to avoid overpayment. Double-click the **cell D13 fill handle** to copy the formula down the column through **cell D373**.

o. Click **cell H6**, type **=IF(DataEntered,DATE(YEAR(A6),MONTH(A6)+(A7-1)*A8+11,DAY(A6)),0)**, and then format it as **Short Date** to determine the normal payoff date if you do not make any extra payments.

p. Click **cell H7** and type **=IF(DataEntered,MATCH(0,BeginningBalance,0)-1,0)**. The MATCH function searches the existing range name BeginningBalance for the smallest value that is greater than or equal to zero. The balance never goes exactly to zero because of a rounding error. Thus, the row above the match corresponds to the number of actual payments.

q. Click **cell H8** and type **=IF(DataEntered,INDEX(AmortizationTable,H7,2),0)**. Apply the **Short Date format** to **cell H8**. The INDEX function returns the date from column 2 of the row within the table that was returned by the MATCH function in the above step.

r. Click **cell H9**, type **=-CUMIPMT(A5/A8,A7*A8,A4,A13,H5,0)**, and then format it as **Currency**.

s. Complete the criteria range by typing **<=100000** in **cell L13**. You want to locate the payments where the ending balance is less than $100,000.

t. Perform an advanced filter by completing the following steps:
- Click **cell H13**, click the **Data tab**, and then click **Advanced**.
- Click **Copy to another location**.
- Make sure the **List range** is $A$12:$H$373.
- Click in the **Criteria range box** and select the **range J12:L13**.
- Click in the **Copy to box** and select the **range N12:P12**. Click OK.

u. Create a footer with your name on the left side, the sheet name code in the center, and the file name code on the right side.

v. Save and close the file. Based on your instructor's directions, submit e07p2House_LastFirst.

3 Financial Investments

Some of your friends are in a business finance class. They are studying for their first test and will have to use financial calculators. They are practicing for the test, they want to make sure they are calculating investment variables correctly. You volunteered to set up an investment model in which they enter the input variables to check their answers against formula calculations you will enter. Refer to Figure 33 as you complete this exercise.

E11	▼	:	×	✓	fx	=-FV(E7,E9,E10,E5)		
▲	A	B	C	D	E	F
1	**Instructions:**	Enter input values in cells with light blue.				
2						
3	**Investment Variable**	PMT/FV	FV	NPER/FV	RATE/FV	
4	Payments Per Year	12	12	12	12	
5	Present Value	$ 100,000.00	$ 100,000.00	$ 100,000.00	$ 100,000.00	
6	APR	10.00%	10.00%	10.00%	10.00%	
7	Rate	0.83%	0.83%	0.83%	0.83%	
8	Term	20	20	20	20	
9	No. of Payments	240	240	240	240	
10	Periodic Payment	$ 965.02	$ 965.02	$ 965.02	$ 965.02	
11	Future Value	$ 1,465,614.73	$ 1,465,614.73	$ 1,465,614.73	$ 1,465,614.73	
12						

Excel 2016, Windows 10, Microsoft Corporation

FIGURE 33 Financial Functions

a. Open *e07p3Finance* and save it as **e07p3Finance_LastFirst.**

b. Calculate the periodic rate, number of periods, periodic payment, and future value in column B by completing the following steps:

- Click **cell B7** and type **=B6/B4** to calculate the periodic rate.
- Click **cell B9** and type **=B8*B4** to calculate the number of payment periods.
- Click **cell B10**, click the **Formulas tab**, click **Financial** in the Function Library group, scroll down, and then select **PMT**. Type **B7** in the Rate box, type **B9** in the Nper box, and then type **-B5** in the PV box. Click **OK** to calculate the monthly payment.
- Click **cell B11**, click **Financial** in the Function Library group, and then select **FV**. Type **B7** in the Rate box, type **B9** in the Nper box, type **B10** in the Pmt box, and then type **B5** in the Pv box. Click **OK** and edit the formula by typing - on the right side of =.

c. Calculate the number of payments, periodic rate, and present value in column C by completing the following steps:

- Click **cell C9** and type **=C8*C4** to calculate the number of payment periods.
- Click **cell C7** and type **=C6/C4** to calculate the periodic rate.
- Click **cell C5**, click **Financial** in the Function Library group, and then select **PV**. Type **C7** in the Rate box, type **C9** in the Nper box, and then type **C10** in the Pmt box. Click **OK** and edit the formula by typing - on the right side of =.

d. Calculate the rate, number of payment periods, term, and future value in column D by completing the following steps:

- Click **cell D7** and type **=D6/D4** to calculate the periodic rate.
- Click **cell D9**, click **Financial** in the Function Library group, and then select **NPER**. Type **D7** in the Rate box, type **D10** in the Pmt box, type **-D5** in the Pv box, and then click **OK**.
- Click **cell D8** and type **=D9/D4** to calculate the term (i.e., number of years).
- Click **cell D11** and type **=-FV(D7,D9,D10,D5)** to calculate the future value.

e. Calculate the number of payment periods, rate, APR, and future value in column E by completing the following steps:

- Click **cell E9** and type **=E8*E4** to calculate the number of payment periods.
- Click **cell E7**, click **Financial** in the Function Library group, and then select **RATE**. Type **E9** in the Nper box, type **-E10** in the Pmt box, type **E5** in the Pv box, and then click **OK**.
- Click **cell E6** and type **=E7*E4** to calculate the APR.
- Click **cell E11** and type **=-FV(E7,E9,E10,E5)** to calculate the future value.

f. Create a footer with your name on the left side, the sheet name code in the center, and the file name code on the right side.

g. Save and close the file. Based on your instructor's directions, submit e07p3Finance_LastFirst.

Mid-Level Exercises

■ West Coast University Admissions Office

You work in the Admissions Office for West Coast University, a mid-sized regional university in California. Your assistant entered a list of college applicants for the Fall 2018 semester. You determine if a student qualifies for early admission or early rejection based on SAT and GPA. After determining the immediate admissions and rejections, you calculate a total score based on SAT and GPA to determine regular admissions and rejections.

a. Open *e07m1Admissions* and save it as **e07m1Admissions_LastFirst**.

b. Enter a date function in **cell E14** that calculates the number of days between the Initial Deadline and the Date Received. Copy the function to the **range E15:E513**. A negative value indicates the application was received after the initial deadline.

c. Enter a nested logical function in **cell H14** to display either Yes or No in the Admit Early column. The university admits a student early if that student meets both the Early Admission criteria for the SAT (cell B6) and GPA (cell B7). That is, the student's SAT score must be 2000 or higher, and the GPA must be 3.80 or higher. Use relative and mixed references to the cells in the Admission Criteria range. Based on the requirements, the first student, Frank Aaron, will not be admitted early. Copy the function to the **range H15:H513**.

d. Enter a nested logical function in **cell I14** to display either Yes or No in the Reject Early column. The university rejects a student early if that student has either an SAT score less than 1000 (cell C6) or a GPA below 1.80 (C7). Use relative and mixed references to the cells in the Admission Criteria range. Copy the function to the **range I15:I513**.

e. Enter a formula in **cell J14** to calculate an applicant's Score. Apply the multiplier (found in the Miscellaneous Standards & Filter range) to the student's GPA and add that score to the SAT. Frank Aaron's score is 3496. Copy the function to the **range J15:J513**.

f. Enter a nested IF function inside a main IF function in **cell K14** (the Final Decision column). The decision text should be one of the following: Early Admission, Early Rejection, Admit, or Reject. Hint: Two logical tests are based on the Yes/No displayed in the Admit Early and Reject Early columns. For regular admission, a student must have a combined admission score that is 2900 or higher. A student is rejected if his or her score is lower than the threshold. Use a mixed reference to the cell in the Miscellaneous Standards & Filter range. Copy the function, select the **range K15:K513**, click **Paste** on the Home tab, and then click **Formulas** to copy just the formulas. If you use a regular Paste option, the double bottom borders will copy with the formulas.

g. Type the criteria in Criteria Range 1:

- **>=2900** in **cell L6**
- **Early Admission** in **cell M6**

h. Enter a database function in **cell H6** to count the total number of early admissions with >= the threshold score. Use the **range L5:M6** for the criteria range.

i. Enter a database function in **cell I6** to calculate the average SAT score for early admissions with >= threshold score. Use the **range L5:M6** for the criteria range.

j. Enter a database function in **cell J6** to calculate the average GPA for early admissions with >= threshold score. Use the **range L5:M6** for the criteria range.

k. Type the criteria in Criteria Range 2:

- **In State** in **cell L10**
- **Early Admission** in **cell M10**

l. Enter a database function in **cell H7** to count the total number of in-state early admissions. Use the **range L9:M10** for the criteria range.

m. Enter a database function in **cell I7** to calculate the average SAT for early in-state admissions. Use the **range L9:M10** for the criteria range.

n. Enter a database function in **cell J7** to calculate the average GPA for all in-state early admissions. Use the **range L9:M10** for the criteria range.

MyITLab®
Grader

o. Enter a database function in **cell H9** to calculate the highest score for all in-state early admissions. Use the **range L9:L10** for the criteria range.

p. Enter an INDEX function with a nested MATCH function in **cell H10** to identify the last name of the person who had the highest overall score for in-state early admissions. The function should display Alevy.

q. Create a footer with your name on the left side, Page 1 of 28 codes in the middle, and the file name code on the right side.

r. Save and close the file. Based on your instructor's directions, submit e07m1Admissions_LastFirst.

2 Artwork Database

You are an analyst for an art gallery that is an authorized Greenwich Workshop fine art dealer (www.greenwichworkshop.com). Customers in your area are especially fond of James C. Christensen's art. You prepared a list of artwork: art, type, edition size, release date, issue price, and estimated market value. You want to identify highly sought-after pieces based on age, percentage of value increase, and sold-out status. In addition, you want to apply an advanced filter and identify specific details from the filtered data.

DISCOVER H

a. Open *e07m2Art* and save it as **e07m2Art_LastFirst.**

b. Make sure the Valuable worksheet is active and enter the YEARFRAC function in **cell G2** to calculate the number of years from the release date and the date in **cell Q2.** Use relative and mixed references correctly. Format the value with **Comma Style** with one decimal place. Copy the function to the **range G3:G165.**

c. Enter a nested logical function in **cell L2** to display **Highly Valuable** if either condition is met:

- The release date is on or before December 31, 1989, or
- The sold-out status is Yes *and* the percentage increase in value is at least 500% *and* the Edition Size was less than 400.

Enter an empty text string if the conditions are not met. Hint: You will need to nest two logical functions within the logical test argument. Use cell references to the two conditions.

d. Copy the function from **cell L2** to the **range L3:L165.**

e. Click **cell O10** and enter the database function to count the number of art pieces where the comment is Highly Valuable. The criteria range is located in the range N6:N7.

f. Click **cell O11** and enter the database function to calculate the average of art pieces where the comment is Highly Valuable. The criteria range is located in the range N6:N7.

g. Click **cell O12** and enter the database function to calculate the total estimated value of art pieces where the comment is Highly Valuable. The criteria range is located in the range N6:N7.

h. Display the Database worksheet. Assign a range name called **database** to the **range A14:J178.** Assign a range name called **Criteria** to the **range A7:J9.**

i. Create column labels for the criteria range and replace the Edition Size with a second Release Date column label. Set the following conditions in the criteria range:

- Sold-out limited-edition canvases released after 1/1/2000 and before 12/31/2003
- Sold-out limited-edition prints released after 1/1/2000 and before 12/31/2003

j. Create an advanced filter using the database list and criteria range. Filter the records in place.

k. Enter the appropriate database function in **cell C2** in the Summary Statistics area to calculate the highest estimated value of the filtered records. Apply **Currency** format and left-align the value.

DISCOVER H

l. Enter a nested function using INDEX and MATCH to display the title (in cell C3) and the release date (in cell C4) for highest estimated valued filtered artwork. Left-align and format the date.

m. Create a footer with your name on the left side, the sheet name code in the center, and the file name code on the right side on each worksheet.

n. Save and close the file. Based on your instructor's directions, submit e07m2Art_LastFirst.

ANALYSIS CASE

COLLABORATION CASE

An out-of-state family member asked for your assistance with financial planning. First, he is considering purchasing a house and would like you to create a detailed amortization table and calculate cumulative principal paid, as well as cumulative interest throughout the loan, total amount of interest, and interest for selected years. In addition, he is considering a five-year investment in which you invest $75 per month. He would like you to calculate the interest earned per month and the ending values. Once you have completed the work, you will upload your file to OneDrive to allow for review.

Student 1:

a. Open *e07m3Personal* and save it as **e07m3Personal_LastFirst**.

b. Enter formulas on the Loan worksheet to complete the Calculations area, which is **range E2:E5**.

c. Enter values **1** through **360** in the Payment Number column, starting in **cell A10**.

d. Calculate values for the first payment on row 10 using appropriate relative, mixed, and absolute references:

- Beginning Balance: Create a reference to the calculated monthly payment.
- Monthly Payment: Enter a reference to the calculated monthly payment.
- Interest Paid: Use the appropriate financial function to calculate the interest payment for the given period.
- Principal Repayment: Use the appropriate financial function to calculate the principal repayment for the given period.
- Ending Balance: Enter the formula to calculate the ending balance after you make the first payment.

e. Type a reference to display the beginning balance for the second period. Copy formulas down their respective columns to row 369. Apply **Accounting Number Format** to the monetary values.

f. Calculate the following cumulative values:

- Total Interest: Enter the appropriate financial function to calculate the total interest for the entire loan in **cell I6**.
- Cumulative Interest: Use the appropriate financial function to calculate the cumulative interest for each period, starting in **cell H10**. The final value in cell H369 should be identical to the value calculated in cell I6.
- Cumulative Principal: Use the appropriate financial function to calculate the cumulative principal for each period, starting in **cell I10**. The final value in cell I369 should match the loan amount in cell E3.
- Interest Paid Summary: Enter individual financial functions to calculate total interest paid during specific years in the **range I2:I5**. The first function calculates total interest for the fifth year only, which is $13,441.15.

g. Format monetary values with **Accounting Number Format.**

h. Set appropriate margins and page scaling to fit one page so that if you decide to print the Loan worksheet, all columns fit across each page. Repeat the headings on row 9 on all pages. Create a footer with your name and the worksheet tab code on the right side of the Loan worksheet.

i. Save the file to OneDrive to share with student 2.

Student 2:

j. Open *e07m3Personal_LastFirst* and save it as **e07m3Personal_LastFirst_LastFirst**, using your name after the first student's name.

k. Display the Investment worksheet and in **cell A12**, enter a reference to the original start of the first investment period date. In **cell A13**, enter the DATE function with nested YEAR, MONTH, and DAY functions with appropriate arguments. Ensure that the month number represents the next month. Copy the formula down the column and apply different but complementary shading, such as starting with **Dark Blue, Text 2, Lighter 80%** for the first 12 months, applying

Dark Blue, Text 2, Lighter 60% to the next 12 months, and continuing to apply darker shades for to each 12-month period of dates. Apply right horizontal alignment and increase the indent three times for the dates in column A.

l. Enter formulas for the first period:

- Beginning Value: Type **0**.
- Interest Earned: Enter a formula to calculate the interest for the first period. Use relative and mixed references only.
- End-of-Period Invest: Enter a reference to the Deposit per Period found in the Input Area.
- Ending Value: Calculate the Ending Value, which includes the Beginning Value, Interest Earned, and End-of-Period Invest.

m. Calculate the second period's Beginning Value by referencing the previous period's Ending Value. Copy formulas down the columns.

n. Enter the appropriate financial function in **cell E75** to calculate the final value of the invest-ment. This value should be identical to the value shown in cell E71.

o. Format monetary values with **Accounting Number Format.**

p. Adjust margins and insert a page break so that the first three years of investment display on page 1. Center the worksheet data between the left and right margins, and repeat the column headings at the top of page 2. Create a footer with your name on the left side, the sheet name code in the center, and the file name code on the right side of all worksheets.

q. Click the Loan worksheet and change the value in **cell B2** to **$350,000.**

r. Click the Investment worksheet and change **cell B5** to **$125.00**.

s. Answer the questions on the Q&A worksheet.

t. Save and close the file. Based on your instructor's directions, submit e07m3Personal_LastFirst_LastFirst.

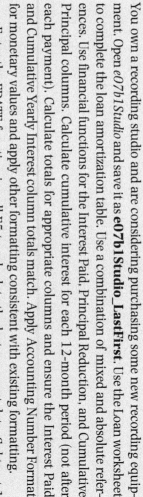

Beyond the Classroom

Studio Recording Equipment

GENERAL CASE ✓

You own a recording studio and are considering purchasing some new recording equipment. Open *e07b1Studio* and save it as **e07b1Studio_LastFirst**. Use the Loan worksheet to complete the loan amortization table. Use a combination of mixed and absolute references. Use financial functions for the Interest Paid, Principal Reduction, and Cumulative Principal columns. Calculate cumulative interest for each 12-month period (not after each payment). Calculate totals for appropriate columns and ensure the Interest Paid and Cumulative Yearly Interest column totals match. Apply Accounting Number Format for monetary values and apply other formatting consistent with existing formatting.

Enter the EDATE function in cell F5 to calculate the last payment date. Subtract 1 from the EDATE result in cell F5 to display the correct final payment date. Enter the MATCH function in cell F7 to determine which payment number results in a cumulative principal of at least $5,000. Add one to the function result to get the correct payment number.

Create a criteria range in the **range A77:H78**. Enter **>0** for the Cumulative Yearly Interest criterion. Create an output range in the **range A81:H81**. Apply an advanced filter using the dataset, criteria range, and output range. The filter should display only five payment rows plus the total row.

Use the PV and NPV worksheet to complete a yearly analysis assuming you pay for the equipment upfront (instead of taking out a loan) and want to compare estimated income and expenses related to the equipment for a five-year period. Calculate the net yearly benefit, the present value of net income, the present value of upfront cost, and the present value of recurring costs. Total the Present Value column. In cell I15, use the NPV function to calculate the net present value of all income and costs. Use Help to find an example of upfront costs combined with yearly income and expenses. The NPV result should be identical to the total of the Present Value column. Adjust margins, column widths, and page setup options as needed. Create a footer with your name, the sheet name code, and the file name code on each worksheet. Save and close the file. Based on your instructor's directions, submit e07b1Studio_LastFirst.

Cruises

DISASTER RECOVERY ✚

You just started working for a travel agency that specializes in working with cruise companies departing from Miami and traveling to the Caribbean and Mexico/Central America. Carter, your predecessor, created a database in Excel that lists details about each cruise, such as number of days of the cruise, departure date, destination, cruise line, ship name, and posted rates by cabin type. In addition, Carter calculated 10% discounts on Outside and Balcony cabins and discounts for Interior and Deluxe cabins based on these rules:

- 15% discount on Deluxe/Suite cabins for either 4- OR 5-day cruises
- 20% discount on Interior cabins with both (a) 7 or more day cruise AND (b) 4 rating
- 25% discount on Interior cabins with both (a) 7 or more day cruise AND (b) 3.5 rating

Open *e07b2Cruises* and save it as **e07b2Cruises_LastFirst**. Insert a date function in column A to replace the days that are currently entered as values. Correct the errors with the discount formula in the Adj-Suite column and in the Adj-Interior column. Insert comments in **cells L10 and O10** describing the errors and what you did to correct the errors. Carter also created a criteria range to be able to filter records for seven-day cruises to the Caribbean that depart before May 1, 2018, with a rating of either 4 or 5. Correct and document errors in this range and apply the advanced filter again, copying the results in the output range. Carter created an Adjusted Rate Statistics area using database functions to identify the lowest, highest, and average adjusted rates for the four cabin types that meet the conditions in the criteria range. In addition, he calculated the number of cruises meeting the criteria. Correct and document errors in this section. Create a footer with your name, the sheet name, and the file name. Adjust the scaling so that the worksheet data fit on seven pages. Save and close the file. Based on your instructor's directions, submit e07b2Cruises_LastFirst.

Capstone Exercise

You own five apartment complexes in Colorado. You created a dataset listing the apartment numbers, apartment complex names, number of bedrooms, rental price, whether the apartment is occupied or not, and the date the apartment was last remodeled. You want to insert some functions to perform calculations to help you decide which apartments need to be remodeled.

To focus on the apartments that need to be remodeled, you will use advanced filtering and database functions for your analysis. Finally, you are considering purchasing a sixth apartment complex. You will perform some financial calculations and analyses to help you decide if you will purchase the complex.

Perform Calculations

You want to calculate the number of years ago before 1/1/2018 that each apartment was last remodeled. In addition, you will update the pet deposit based on how long ago the apartment was remodeled. Recently remodeled apartments with two or more bedrooms will require a $275 deposit, whereas apartments remodeled over 10 years ago will require only a $200 deposit. Finally, you will display a comment *Need to Remodel* if an apartment is not occupied and was last remodeled over 10 years ago. The Constants for Formulas range contains values to use in formulas.

a. Open *e07c1Apartment* and save it as **e07c1Apartment_LastFirst.**

b. Make sure the Summary worksheet is active.

c. Insert a date function in **cell G8** to calculate the number of years between the current date (1/1/2018) and the last remodel date in the Last Remodel column. Use relative and mixed references correctly. Copy the function to the **range G9:G57.** Unit 101 was last remodeled 13.75 years ago.

d. Insert a nested logical function in **cell H8** to display the required pet deposit for each unit. If the unit has two or more bedrooms and was remodeled within the past 10 years from 1/1/2018, the deposit is $275; if not, it is $200. The pet deposit for Unit 101 is $200.

e. Enter a nested logical function in **cell I8** to display **Need to Remodel** if the apartment is unoccupied and was last remodeled more than 10 years ago from the 1/1/2018 date. For all other apartments, display **No Change.** Although Unit 101 was last remodeled over 10 years, the recommendation is No Change because the unit is occupied.

f. Copy the functions in the **range H8:I8** to the range **H9:I57.**

Create a Search Area

You want to be able to perform a simple search to enter an apartment unit number and display the rent for that apartment.

a. Type **101** in **cell B2**; this is the cell where you enter an apartment unit #.

b. Insert a nested MATCH function within an INDEX function in **cell B3** that will look up the rental price in column D using the apartment number referenced in cell B2. With 101 entered in cell B2, the lookup function displays $950.00.

Manage a Database List

The Database worksheet contains an identical list of apartments. You want to know how many two- and three-bedroom apartments should be remodeled, the value of lost rent, and the year of the oldest remodel on those units. You need to apply an advanced filter and enter some database functions to address the owner's concerns.

a. Click the *Database* **sheet tab.**

b. Enter conditions in the criteria range for unoccupied two- and three-bedroom apartments that need to be remodeled.

c. Apply an advanced filter based on the criteria range. Filter the existing database in place.

d. Enter a database function in **cell C8** to calculate the number of apartments that need to be remodeled based on the advanced filter you created.

e. Enter a database function in **cell C9** to calculate the total value of monthly rent lost for the apartments that need to be remodeled based on the advanced filter you created.

f. Enter a database function in **cell C10** to calculate the date of the apartment that had the oldest remodel date based on the filtered data.

Loan Amortization

You are considering purchasing a sixth apartment complex for $1,850,000 with a down payment of $750,000 for 30 years at 4.75%, with the first payment due on March 20, 2018. You will perform internal calculations and build a loan amortization table.

a. Click the **Loan sheet tab.**

b. Enter the loan parameters in the Input Area and insert formulas to perform calculations in the Summary Calculations. Format the monetary values with **Accounting Number Format.**

c. Complete the loan amortization table. In **cell C11**, enter a formula to reference the date stored in cell B7. Insert a nested date function in **cell C12** to calculate the date for the next payment. Copy the function to the **range C13:C370**.

d. Enter a formula in **cell D11** to reference the value stored in cell E2. Insert a formula in **cell D12** that references the ending balance for the previous payment row. Copy the formula to the **range D13:D370**.

e. Enter a financial function in **cell E11** to calculate the interest paid. Copy the formula to the **range E12:E370**.

f. Enter a financial function in **cell F11** to calculate the principal payment. Copy the function to the **range F12:F370**.

g. Enter a formula in **cell G11** to calculate the ending balance. Copy the formula to the **range G12:G370**. The last ending balance should be $0. Adjust the width of column G, if needed, to display the values.

h. Select the **range D11:G370** and apply **Accounting Number Format**.

Finance Function

You want to calculate the present value of potential monthly rent of $2,000 for 8 apartments for 30 years.

a. Enter the monthly rent per unit in **cell I2** and number of units in **cell I3**.

b. Click **cell I4** and insert a financial function to calculate the present value of the total monthly rent you will collect for the 8 units for 30 years. Use the number of periods and monthly rate from the Summary Calculations section.

c. Select **cells I2 and I4** and apply **Accounting Number Format**.

Workbook Completion

You are ready to complete the workbook by adding a footer with identifying information.

a. Create a footer with your name on the left side, the sheet name code in the center, and the file name code on the right side of each worksheet.

b. Set **0.4"** left and right margins for the Database sheet.

c. Set **0.5"** left and right margins and repeat row 10 on all pages in the Loan sheet.

d. Save and close the file. Based on your instructor's directions, submit e07c1Apartment_LastFirst.

Glossary

AND function A logical function that returns TRUE when all arguments are true and FALSE when at least one argument is false.

Criteria range A group of two or more adjacent cells that specifies the conditions used to control the results of a filter.

CUMIPMT function A financial function that calculates the cumulative interest through a specified payment period.

CUMPRINC function A financial function that calculates the cumulative principal through a specified payment period.

Database function A function that analyzes data for selected records in a dataset.

DAVERAGE function A database function that calculates the arithmetic mean, or average, of values in a column that match specified conditions in a criteria range.

DAY function A date function that displays the day (1-31) within a given date.

DAYS function A date function that calculates the number of days between two dates where the most recent date is entered in the end_date argument and the older date is entered in the start_date argument.

DCOUNT function A database function that counts the cells that contain numbers in a column that matches specified conditions in a criteria range.

DMAX function A database function that identifies the highest value in a column that matches specified conditions in a criteria range.

DMIN function A database function that identifies the lowest value in a column that matches specified conditions in a criteria range.

DSUM function A database function that adds the values in a column that match specified conditions in a criteria range.

FV function A financial function that calculates the future value of an investment, given a fixed interest rate, term, and identical periodic payments.

INDEX function A lookup and reference function that returns a value at the intersection of a specified row and column.

IPMT function A financial function that calculates the periodic interest for a specified payment period on a loan or an investment given a fixed interest rate, specified term, and identical periodic payments.

Loan amortization table A schedule showing monthly payments, interest per payment, amount toward paying off the loan, and the remaining balance after each payment for a loan.

MATCH function A lookup and reference function that searches for a specific value and returns the relative position of a value within a range.

MONTH function A date function that displays the month (1–12) where 1 is January and 12 is December for a specific date.

NOT function A logical function that returns TRUE if the argument is false and FALSE if the argument is true.

NPER function A financial function that calculates the number of payment periods for an investment or loan given a fixed interest rate, periodic payment, and present value.

NPV function A financial function that calculates the net present value of an investment, given a fixed discount rate (rate of return) and future payments that may be identical or different.

OR function A logical function that returns TRUE if any argument is true and returns FALSE if all arguments are false.

PPMT function A financial function that calculates the principal payment for a specified payment period on a loan or an investment given a fixed interest rate, specified term, and identical periodic payments.

PV function A financial function that calculates the total present (current) value of an investment with a fixed rate, specified number of payment periods, and a series of identical payments that will be made in the future.

RATE function A financial function that calculates the periodic rate for an investment or loan given the number of payment periods, a fixed periodic payment, and present value.

Truth table A matrix that provides the results (TRUE or FALSE) for every possible combination for an AND, OR, or NOT criteria combination.

YEAR function A date function that displays the year (such as 2018) for a specific date

YEARFRAC function A date function that calculates the fraction of a year between two dates based on the number of whole days using the start_date and end_date arguments.

Microsoft Office 2016 Specialist Excel Core

Online Appendix materials can be found in the Student Resources located at www.pearsonhighered.com/exploring.

MOS Obj Number	Objective Text	Exploring Chapter	Exploring Section
1.0	**Create and Manage Worksheets and Workbooks**		
1.1	**Create Worksheets and Workbooks**		
1.1.1	create a workbook	Introduction to Excel	Entering and Editing Cell Data
1.1.2	import data from a delimited text file	Managing Data	Importing Data from External Sources
1.1.3	add a worksheet to an existing workbook	Introduction to Excel	Managing Worksheets
1.1.4	copy and move a worksheet	Introduction to Excel	Managing Worksheets
1.2	**Navigate in Worksheets and Workbooks**		
1.2.1	search for data within a workbook	Office 2016 Common Features	Working with Files
1.2.2	navigate to a named cell, range, or workbook element	Introduction to Excel	Exploring the Excel Window
1.2.3	insert and remove hyperlinks	Multiple-Sheet Workbook Management	Inserting Hyperlinks
1.3	**Format Worksheets and Workbooks**		
1.3.1	change worksheet tab color	Introduction to Excel	Managing Worksheets
1.3.2	rename a worksheet	Introduction to Excel	Managing Worksheets
1.3.3	change worksheet order	Introduction to Excel	Managing Worksheets
1.3.4	modify page setup	Introduction to Excel	Selecting Page Setup Options
1.3.5	insert and delete columns or rows	Introduction to Excel	Managing Columns and Rows
1.3.6	change workbook themes	Introduction to Excel	Applying Cell Styles, Alignment, and Font Options
1.3.7	adjust row height and column width	Introduction to Excel	Managing Columns and Rows
1.3.8	insert headers and footers	Introduction to Excel	Selecting Page Setup Options
1.4	**Customize Options and Views for Worksheets and Workbooks**		
1.4.1	hide or unhide worksheets	Multiple-Sheet Workbook Management	Managing Windows
1.4.2	hide or unhide columns and rows	Introduction to Excel	Managing Columns and Rows
1.4.3	customize the Quick Access toolbar	Office 2016 Common Features	Getting Started with Office Applications
1.4.4	change workbook views	Introduction to Excel	Selecting Page Setup Options

From MOS Appendix of *Microsoft® Excel 2016, Comprehensive*. Mary Anne Poatsy, Hogan, Lau, and Robert T. Grauer. Copyright © 2017 by Pearson Education, Inc. Published by Pearson Prentice Hall. All Rights Reserved. Download student resources at http://www.pearsonhighered.com/exploring.

MOS Obj Number	Objective Text	Exploring Chapter	Exploring Section
1.4.5	change window views	Office 2016 Common Features	Modifying Document Layout and Properties
1.4.6	modify document properties	Office 2016 Common Features	Modifying Document Layout and Properties
1.4.7	change magnification by using zoom tools	Office 2016 Common Features	Modifying Document Layout and Properties
1.4.8	display formulas	Introduction to Excel	Displaying Cell Formulas
1.5 Configure Worksheets and Workbooks for Distribution			
1.5.1	set a print area	Introduction to Excel	Selecting Page Setup Options
1.5.2	save workbooks in alternative file formats	Collaboration and Workbook Distribution	Saving a Workbook in Different Formats
1.5.3	print all or part of a workbook	Introduction to Excel	Selecting Page Setup Options, Previewing and Printing a Worksheet
1.5.4	set print scaling	Introduction to Excel	Selecting Page Setup Options
1.5.5	display repeating row and column titles on multipage worksheets	Introduction to Excel	Selecting Page Setup Options
1.5.6	inspect a workbook for hidden properties or personal information	Collaboration and Workbook Distribution	Using the Document Inspector
1.5.8	inspect a workbook for compatibility issues	Collaboration and Workbook Distribution	Checking Compatibility
2.0 Manage Data Cells and Ranges			
2.1 Insert Data in Cells and Ranges			
2.1.1	replace data	Charts	Adding, Editing, and Formatting Chart Elements
2.1.2	cut, copy, or paste data	Introduction to Excel	Selecting, Moving, Copying, and Pasting Data
2.1.3	paste data by using special paste options	Introduction to Excel	Selecting, Moving, Copying, and Pasting Data
2.1.4	fill cells by using Auto Fill	Introduction to Excel	Entering and Editing Cell Data
2.1.5	insert and delete cells	Introduction to Excel	Managing Columns and Rows
2.2 Format Cells and Ranges			
2.2.1	merge cells	Introduction to Excel	Applying Cell Styles, Alignment, and Font Options
2.2.2	modify cell alignment and indentation	Introduction to Excel	Applying Cell Styles, Alignment, and Font Options
2.2.3	format cells by using Format Painter	Office 2016 Common Features	Modifying Text
2.2.4	wrap text within cells	Introduction to Excel	Applying Cell Styles, Alignment, and Font Options
2.2.5	apply number formats	Introduction to Excel	Applying a Number Format
2.2.6	apply cell formats	Introduction to Excel Templates, Styles, and Macros	Applying Cell Styles, Alignment, and Font Options
2.2.7	apply cell styles	Introduction to Excel	Applying Cell Styles, Alignment, and Font Options

MOS Obj Number	Objective Text	Exploring Chapter	Exploring Section
2.3	**Summarize and Organize Data**		
2.3.1	insert sparklines	Charts	Creating and Customizing Sparklines
2.3.2	outline data	Summarizing And Analyzing Data	Subtotaling Data, Grouping and Ungrouping Data
2.3.4	apply conditional formatting	Datasets and Tables	Applying Conditional Formatting
3.0	**Create Tables**		
3.1	**Create and Manage Tables**		
3.1.1	create an Excel table from a cell range	Datasets and Tables	Designing and Creating Tables
3.1.2	convert a table to a cell range	Datasets and Tables	Designing and Creating Tables
3.1.3	add or remove table rows and columns	Datasets and Tables	Designing and Creating Tables
3.2	**Manage Table Styles and Options**		
3.2.1	apply styles to tables	Datasets and Tables	Applying a Table Style
3.2.2	configure table style options	Datasets and Tables	Applying a Table Style
3.2.3	insert total rows	Datasets and Tables	Adding a Total Row
3.3	**Filter and Sort a Table**		
3.3.1	filter records	Datasets and Tables	Filtering Data
3.3.2	sort data by multiple columns	Datasets and Tables	Sorting Data
3.3.3	change sort order	Datasets and Tables	Sorting Data
3.3.4	remove duplicate records	Datasets and Tables	Designing and Creating Tables
4.0	**Perform Operations with Formulas and Functions**		
4.1	**Summarize Data by using Functions**		
4.1.1	insert references	Formulas and Functions	Using Relative, Absolute, and Mixed Cell References in Formulas
4.1.2	perform calculations by using the SUM function	Formulas and Functions	Inserting Basic Math and Statistics Functions
4.1.3	perform calculations by using MIN and MAX functions	Formulas and Functions	Inserting Basic Math and Statistics Functions
4.1.4	perform calculations by using the COUNT function	Formulas and Functions	Inserting Basic Math and Statistics Functions
4.1.5	perform calculations by using the AVERAGE function	Formulas and Functions	Inserting Basic Math and Statistics Functions
4.2	**Perform Conditional Operations by using Functions**		
4.2.1	perform logical operations by using the IF function	Formulas and Functions	Determining Results with the IF Function
4.2.2	perform logical operations by using the SUMIF function	Statistical Functions	Using Conditional Math and Statistical Functions

MOS Obj Number		Objective Text	Exploring Chapter	Exploring Section
4.2.3		perform logical operations by using the AVERAGEIF function	Statistical Functions	Using Conditional Math and Statistical Functions
4.2.4		perform statistical operations by using the COUNTIF function	Statistical Functions	Using Conditional Math and Statistical Functions
4.3	**Format and Modify Text by using Functions**			
4.3.1		format text by using RIGHT, LEFT, and MID functions	Managing Data	Manipulating Text with Functions
4.3.2		format text by using UPPER, LOWER, and PROPER functions	Managing Data	Manipulating Text with Functions
4.3.3		format text by using the CONCATENATE function	Managing Data	Manipulating Text with Functions
5.0	**Create Charts and Objects**			
5.1	**Create Charts**			
5.1.1		create a new chart	Charts	Choosing a Chart Type
5.1.2		add additional data series	Charts	Modifying the Data Source
5.1.3		switch between rows and columns in source data	Introduction to Excel	Selecting, Moving, Copying, and Pasting Data
5.1.4		analyze data by using Quick Analysis	Charts	Choosing a Chart Type
5.2	**Format Charts**			
5.2.1		resize charts	Charts	Moving, Sizing, and Printing a Chart
5.2.2		add and modify chart elements	Charts	Adding, Editing, and Formatting Chart Elements
5.2.3		apply chart layouts and styles	Charts	Adding, Editing, and Formatting Chart Elements
5.2.4		move charts to a chart sheet	Charts	Moving, Sizing, and Printing a Chart
5.3	**Insert and Format Objects**			
5.3.1		insert text boxes and shapes	Charts	Beyond the Classroom
5.3.2		insert images	Office 2016 Common Features	Working with Pictures and Graphics
5.3.3		modify object properties	Charts Office 2016 Common Features	Adding, Editing, and Formatting Chart Elements Working with Pictures and Graphics
5.3.4		add alternative text to objects for accessibility	Charts	Adding, Editing, and Formatting Chart Elements

Microsoft Office 2016 Specialist Excel Expert

MOS Obj Number	Objective Text	Exploring Chapter	Exploring Section
1.0	**Manage Workbook Options and Settings**		
1.1	**Manage Workbooks**		
1.1.1	save a workbook as a template	Standardizing Workbooks	Creating and Using a Template
1.1.2	copy macros between workbooks	Online Appendix	Online Appendix
1.1.3	reference data in another workbook	Multiple-Sheet Workbook Management	Inserting Hyperlinks, Linking Workbooks
1.1.4	reference data by using structured references	Datasets and Tables	Creating Structured References in Formulas
1.1.5	enable macros in a workbook	Standardizing Workbooks	Setting Macro Security
1.1.6	display hidden ribbon tabs	Online Appendix	Online Appendix
1.2	**Manage Workbook Review**		
1.2.1	restrict editing	Standardizing Workbooks	Protecting a Cell, a Worksheet, and a Workbook
1.2.2	protect a worksheet	Standardizing Workbooks	Protecting a Cell, a Worksheet, and a Workbook
1.2.3	configure formula calculation options	Online Appendix	Online Appendix
1.2.4	protect workbook structure	Standardizing Workbooks	Protecting a Cell, a Worksheet, and a Workbook
1.2.5	manage workbook versions	Online Appendix	Online Appendix
1.2.6	encrypt a workbook with a password	Standardizing Workbooks	Protecting a Cell, a Worksheet, and a Workbook
2.0	**Apply Custom Data Formats and Layouts**		
2.1	**Apply Custom Data Formats and Validation**		
2.1.1	create custom number formats	Online Appendix	Online Appendix
2.1.2	populate cells by using advanced Fill Series options	What-If Analysis Online Appendix	Creating a One-Variable Data Table Online Appendix
2.1.3	configure data validation	Multiple-Sheet Workbook Management	Validating Data
2.2	**Apply Advanced Conditional Formatting and Filtering**		
2.2.1	create custom conditional formatting rules	Datasets and Tables	Applying Conditional Formatting, Creating a New Rule
2.2.2	create conditional formatting rules that use formulas	Datasets and Tables	Creating a New Rule
2.2.3	manage conditional formatting rules	Datasets and Tables	Applying Conditional Formatting, Creating a New Rule

MOS Obj Number		Objective Text	Exploring Chapter	Exploring Section
2.3	**Create and Modify Custom Workbook Elements**			
2.3.1		create custom color formats	Online Appendix	Online Appendix
2.3.2		create and modify cell styles	Standardizing Workbooks	Applying Cell Styles
2.3.3		create and modify custom themes	Standardizing Workbooks	Applying Themes and Backgrounds
2.3.4		create and modify simple macros	Standardizing Workbooks	Creating a Macro
2.3.5		insert and configure form controls	Standardizing Workbooks	Creating Macro Buttons
2.4	**Prepare a Workbook for Internationalization**		Online Appendix	Online Appendix
2.4.1		display data in multiple international formats	Online Appendix	Online Appendix
2.4.2		apply international currency formats	Online Appendix	Online Appendix
2.4.3		manage multiple options for +Body and +Heading fonts	Online Appendix	Online Appendix
3.0	**Create Advanced Formulas**			
3.1	**Apply Functions in Formulas**			
3.1.1		perform logical operations by using AND, OR, and NOT functions	Using Date, Logical, Lookup, Database, and Financial Functions	Creating a Nested Logical Function
3.1.2		perform logical operations by using nested functions	Using Date, Logical, Lookup, Database, and Financial Functions	Creating a Nested Logical Function
			Online Appendix	Online Appendix
3.1.3		perform statistical operations by using SUMIFS, AVERAGEIFS, and COUNTIFS functions	Statistical Functions	Using Conditional Math and Statistical Functions
3.2	**Look Up Data by using Functions**			
3.2.1		look up data by using the VLOOKUP function	Formulas and Functions	Using Lookup Functions
3.2.2		look up data by using the HLOOKUP function	Formulas and Functions	Using Lookup Functions
3.2.3		look up data by using the MATCH function	Using Date, Logical, Lookup, Database, and Financial Functions	Using Advanced Lookup Functions
3.2.4		look up data by using the INDEX function	Using Date, Logical, Lookup, Database, and Financial Functions	Using Advanced Lookup Functions
3.3	**Apply Advanced Date and Time Functions**			
3.3.1		reference the date and time by using the NOW and TODAY functions	Formulas and Functions	Using Date Functions
3.3.2		serialize numbers by using date and time functions	Using Date, Logical, Lookup, Database, and Financial Functions	Using Date Functions

MOS Obj Number	Objective Text	Exploring Chapter	Exploring Section
3.4	**Perform Data Analysis and Business Intelligence**		
3.4.1	import, transform, combine, display, and connect to data	Managing Data	Importing Data from External Sources
3.4.2	consolidate data	Online Appendix	Online Appendix
3.4.3	perform what-if analysis by using Goal Seek and Scenario Manager	What-If Analysis	Determining Optimal Input Values Using Goal Seek, Using Scenario Manager
3.4.4	use cube functions to get data out of the Excel data model	Online Appendix	Online Appendix
3.4.5	calculate data by using financial functions	Formulas and Functions Using Date, Logical, Lookup, Database, and Financial Functions	Calculating Payments with the PMT Function, Using Financial Functions
3.5	**Troubleshoot Formulas**		
3.5.1	trace precedence and dependence	Multiple-Sheet Workbook Management	Auditing Formulas
3.5.2	monitor cells and formulas by using the Watch Window	Multiple-Sheet Workbook Management	Setting Up a Watch Window
3.5.3	validate formulas by using error checking rules	Multiple-Sheet Workbook Management	Auditing Formulas, Validating Data
3.5.4	evaluate formulas	Multiple-Sheet Workbook Management	Auditing Formulas
3.6	**Define Named Ranges and Objects**		
3.6.1	name cells	What-If Analysis	Creating and Maintaining Range Names
3.6.2	name data ranges	What-If Analysis	Creating and Maintaining Range Names
3.6.3	name tables	Datasets and Tables	Rename a Table
3.6.4	manage named ranges and objects	What-If Analysis	Creating and Maintaining Range Names
4.0	**Create Advanced Charts and Tables**		
4.1	**Create Advanced Charts**		
4.1.1	add trendlines to charts	Online Appendix	Online Appendix
4.1.2	create dual-axis charts	Charts	Choosing a Chart Type
4.1.3	save a chart as a template	Online Appendix	Online Appendix
4.2	**Create and Manage PivotTables**		
4.2.1	create PivotTables	Summarizing and Analyzing Data	Creating a PivotTable
4.2.2	modify field selections and options	Summarizing and Analyzing Data	Modifying a PivotTable
4.2.3	create slicers	Summarizing and Analyzing Data	Filtering and Slicing a PivotTable
4.2.4	group PivotTable data	Summarizing and Analyzing Data	Creating a PivotTable, Modifying a PivotTable

MOS Obj Number	Objective Text	Exploring Chapter	Exploring Section
4.2.5	reference data in a PivotTable by using the GETPIVOTDATA function	Online Appendix	Online Appendix
4.2.6	add calculated fields	Summarizing and Analyzing Data	Creating a Calculated Field
4.2.7	format data	Summarizing and Analyzing Data	Modifying a PivotTable, Changing the PivotTable Design
4.3	**Create and Manage Pivot Charts**		
4.3.1	create PivotCharts	Summarizing and Analyzing Data	Creating a PivotChart
4.3.2	manipulate options in existing PivotCharts	Summarizing and Analyzing Data	Creating a PivotChart
4.3.3	apply styles to PivotCharts	Summarizing and Analyzing Data	Creating a PivotChart
4.3.4	drill down into PivotChart details	Summarizing and Analyzing Data	Creating a PivotChart

Introduction to Access

Introduction to Access

LEARNING
OUTCOME   You will demonstrate understanding of relational database concepts.

OBJECTIVES & SKILLS: After you read this chapter, you will be able to:

Databases Are Everywhere

OBJECTIVE 1: OPEN, SAVE, AND ENABLE CONTENT IN A DATABASE
Open a Database, Save a Database with a New Name, Enable Content in a Database

OBJECTIVE 2: RECOGNIZE DATABASE OBJECT TYPES
Examine the Access Interface, Explore Table Datasheet View, Navigate Through Records, Explore Table Datasheet View, Rename and Describe Tables, Understand Relationships Between Tables

OBJECTIVE 3: MODIFY DATA IN TABLE DATASHEET VIEW
Understand the Difference Between Working in Storage and Memory, Change Data in Table Datasheet View

OBJECTIVE 4: ADD RECORDS TO A TABLE
Add Records to a Table

OBJECTIVE 5: DELETE RECORDS FROM A TABLE
Delete Records from a Table

OBJECTIVE 6: USE DATABASE UTILITIES
Back Up a Database, Compact and Repair a Database, Encrypt a Database, Print Information

HANDS-ON EXERCISE 1:
Databases Are Everywhere!

Filters and Sorts

OBJECTIVE 7: WORK WITH FILTERS
Use a Selection Filter to Find Exact Matches, Use a Selection Filter to Find Records Containing a Value, Use Filter By Form

OBJECTIVE 8: PERFORM SORTS
Sort Table Data

HANDS-ON EXERCISE 2:
Filters, Sorts, Relationships, and Sort Table Data

Access Database Creation

OBJECTIVE 9: CREATE A DATABASE
Create a Blank Desktop Database, Create a Desktop Database Using a Template, Add Records to a Downloaded Desktop Database, Explore the Database Objects in a Downloaded Desktop Database Template, Create a Table Using an Application Part, Create a Web App Using a Template

HANDS-ON EXERCISE 3:
Access Database Creation

CASE STUDY | Managing a Business in the Global Economy

Northwind Traders is an international gourmet food distributor that imports and exports specialty foods from around the world. Keeping track of customers, vendors, orders, and inventory is a critical task. The owners of Northwind have just purchased an order-processing database created with Microsoft Access 2016 to help manage their customers, suppliers, products, and orders.

You have been hired to learn, use, and manage the database. Northwind's owners are willing to provide training about their business and Access. They expect the learning process to take about three months. After three months, your job will be to support the order-processing team as well as to provide detail and summary reports to the sales force as needed. Your new job at Northwind Traders will be a challenge, but it is also a good opportunity to make a great contribution to a global company. Are you up to the task?

Finding Your Way Through an Access Database

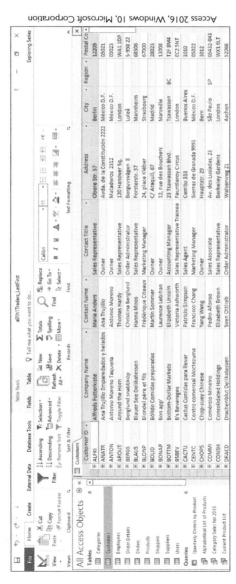

FIGURE 1 Northwind Traders Database

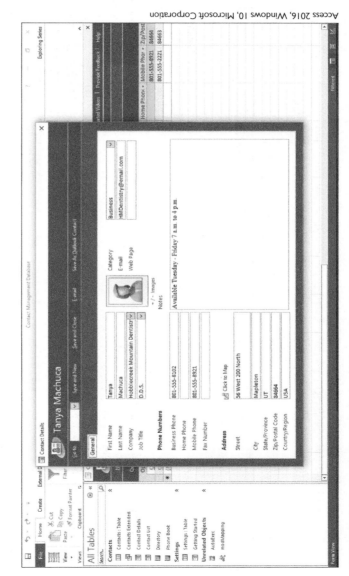

FIGURE 2 Northwind Traders Contacts Database

CASE STUDY | Managing a Business in the Global Economy

Starting File	Files to be Submitted
a01h1Traders	a01h1Traders_LastFirst_*CurrentDate* a01h2Traders_LastFirst a01h3Contacts_LastFirst

Databases Are Everywhere!

A **database** is a collection of data organized as meaningful information that can be accessed, managed, stored, queried, sorted, and reported. You probably participate in data collection and are exposed to databases on a regular basis. Your college or university stores your personal and registration data. When you registered for this course, your data was entered into a database. If you have a bank account, have a Social Security card, have a medical history, or have booked a flight with an airline, your information is stored in a database.

You use databases online without realizing it, such as when you shop or check your bank statement. Even when you type a search phrase into Google and click Search, you are using Google's massive database with all of its stored webpage references and keywords. Look for something on Amazon, and you are searching Amazon's database to find a product that you might want to buy. Figure 3 shows the results of searching for a term on Pearson's website. The search has accessed the Pearson database, and the results are displayed in a webpage.

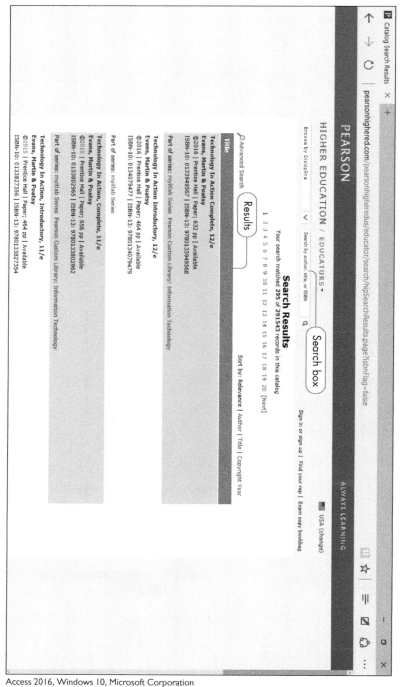

FIGURE 3 Pearson Website Search

Access 2016, Windows 10, Microsoft Corporation

A **database management system (DBMS)** is a software system that provides the tools needed to create, maintain, and use a database. Database management systems make it possible to access and control data and display the information in a variety of formats. **Access** is the database management system included in professional editions of the Office 2016 suite. Access is a valuable decision-making tool used by many organizations. More advanced DBMS packages include Microsoft SQL Server, MySQL, and Oracle.

Organizations from all industries rely on data to conduct daily operations. Businesses maintain and analyze data about their students, customers, employees, orders, volunteers, activities, and facilities. Data and information are two terms that are often used interchangeably. However, when it comes to databases, the two terms mean different things. Data is what is entered into a database. Information is the finished product that is produced by the database. Data is converted to information by selecting, performing calculations, and sorting. Decisions in an organization are usually based on information produced by a database, rather than raw data. For example, the number 55 is just data, because it could mean anything. Only when a label is attached to it (for example, as someone's age) does it take on meaning and become information.

In this section, you will learn the fundamentals of organizing data in a database, explore Access database objects and the purpose of each object, and examine the Access interface.

Opening, Saving, and Enabling Content in a Database

STEP 1 ▶▶ As you work through the material in this text, you will frequently be asked to open a database, save it with a new name, and enable content. You can also start by creating a new database if appropriate.

If you have been provided a database, open the file to get started. When you open any database for the first time, you will be presented with a warning that it might contain harmful code. By enabling the content, the database file will be trusted on the computer you are working on. All content from this publisher and associated with this text can be trusted.

To open an existing Access database and enable content, complete the following steps:

1. Start Access 2016. Backstage view displays. (Note: If Access is already open, click the File tab to display Backstage view).
2. Click Open Other Files.
3. Click Browse ▢ to open the Open dialog box.
4. Locate and select the database and click Open.
5. Click Enable Content on the message bar (see Figure 4). Access will close and reopen the database, and the security warning disappears and will not appear again for this database.

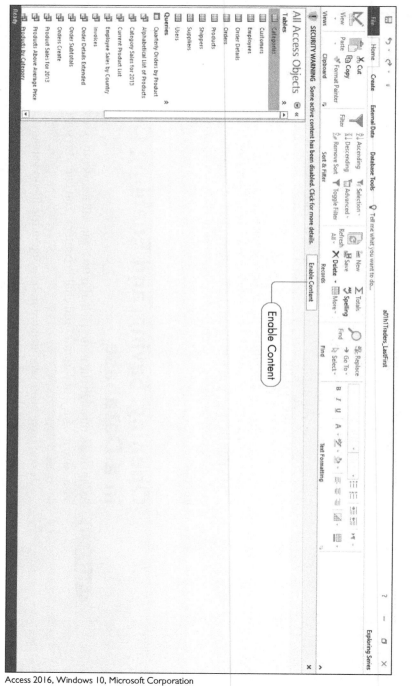

FIGURE 4 Access Security Warning

Access 2016, Windows 10, Microsoft Corporation

Backstage view gives you access to the Save As command. Most assignments will have you save the starting database file with a new name.

To save the database with a new name, complete the following steps:

1. Click the File tab.
2. Select Save As.
3. Ensure Save Database As is selected (see Figure 5).
4. Click Save As.
5. Type the new name for your database, and click Save.

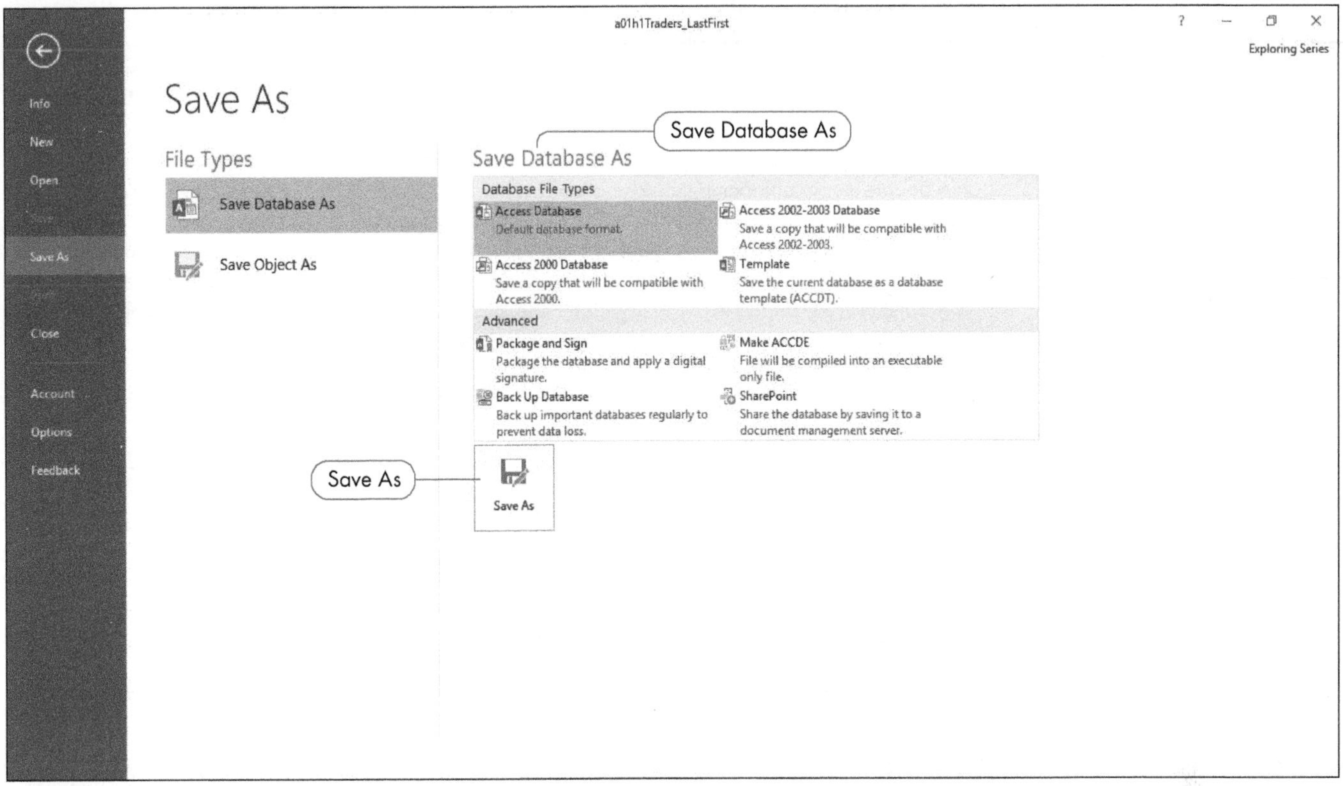

FIGURE 5 Access Save As Options

TIP: ALTERNATIVE SAVE FORMAT: ACCESS DATABASE EXECUTABLE

Creating an Access Database Executable (ACCDE) file allows users to enter data, but not add, modify, or delete objects. In other words, the only task they can do is data entry. This file format protects against users changing designs or deleting objects.

To create an Access Database Executable, click the File tab, click Save As, and double-click Make ACCDE. Click Save to save as an Access Database Executable.

Recognizing Database Object Types

STEP 2 » Databases must be carefully managed to keep information accurate. Data need to be changed, added, and deleted. Managing a database also requires that you understand when data is saved and when you need to use the Save commands.

In Access, each component created and used to make the database function is known as an *object*. Objects include tables, queries, forms, and reports, and can be found in the *Navigation Pane*. The Navigation Pane is an Access interface element that organizes and lists the objects in an Access database. The Navigation Pane appears on the left side of the screen, and displays all objects. You can open any object by double-clicking the object's name in the list.

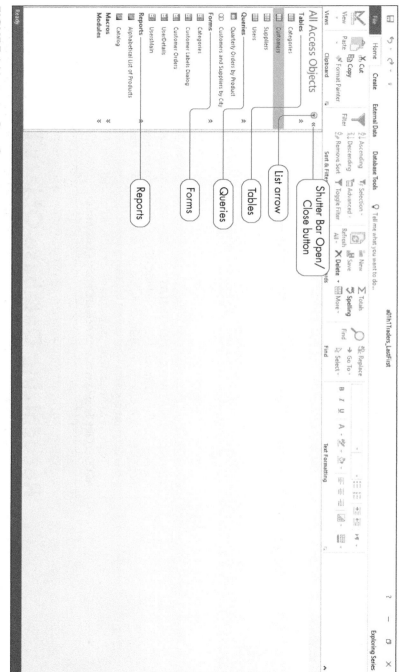

FIGURE 6 Navigation Pane Features

Access 2016, Windows 10, Microsoft Corporation

Labels in figure: Shutter Bar Open/Close button, List arrow, Tables, Queries, Forms, Reports

---

TIP: NAVIGATION PANE DISPLAY

You can toggle the display of the Navigation Pane by clicking the Shutter Bar Open/Close button at the top-right corner of the pane. The Shutter Bar Open/Close button appears as a double arrow. If the Navigation Pane is shown, the button will appear as a double arrow pointing left « and it will hide the Navigation Pane when clicked. If the Navigation Pane is hidden, the button appears as a double arrow pointing right » and it will show the Navigation Pane when clicked. You can collapse the contents of an object group by clicking the group heading or the double arrows to the right of the group heading. To expand the contents of an object group that has been hidden, click the heading again or click the double arrows to the right of the group heading again. To change the way objects are grouped in the Navigation Pane, click the list arrow on the Navigation Pane title bar and select your preferred configuration of the available options. Refer to Figure 6 to see the features of the Navigation Pane.

Most databases contain multiple tables. By default, the objects display in groups by object type in the Navigation Pane. In other words, you will see a list of tables, followed by queries, followed by forms, followed by reports. The purpose of each of these objects is described below.

- A **table** is where all data is stored in your database, and thus can be said to be the foundation of each database. Tables organize data into columns and rows. Each column represents a **field**, a category of information we store in a table. For example, in the Northwind database, a table containing customer information would include fields such as Customer ID, Company Name, and City. Each row in a table contains a **record**, a complete set of all the fields about one person, place, event, or concept. A customer record, for example, would contain all of the fields about a single customer, including the Customer ID, the Company Name, Contact Name, Contact Title, Address, City, etc. Figure 7 shows both fields and records. The **primary key** is a field (or combination of fields) that uniquely identifies each record in a table. Common primary keys are driver's license number, government

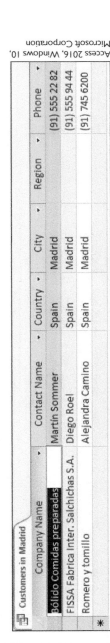

ID number (such as a Social Security number), passport number, and student ID. Many of these primary keys are generated by a database. Your college or university's database likely assigns a unique identifier to a student as soon as they apply, for example.

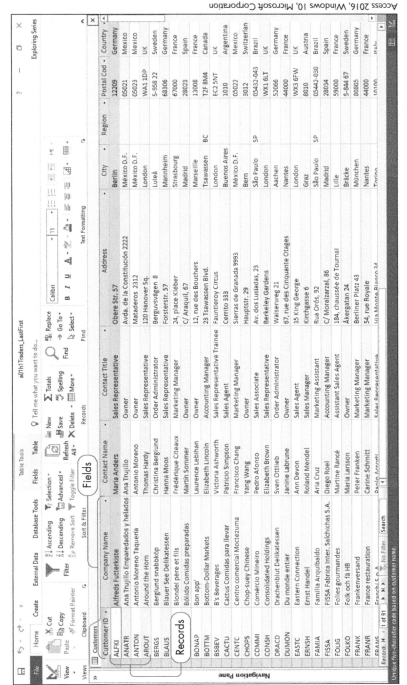

FIGURE 7 An Access Table

- A *query* (or queries, plural) is a question you ask about the data in your database. Notice the word query is similar to the word inquiry, which means question. It produces a subset of data that provides information about the question you have asked. For example, a query may display a list of which customers live in a specific town, or a list of children registered for a specific after-school program. You can double-click a query in the Navigation Pane and you will notice the interface is similar to that of a table, as shown in Figure 8.

FIGURE 8 An Access Query

- A *form* allows simplified entry and modification of data. Much like entering data on a paper form, a database form enables you to add, modify, and delete table data. Most forms display one record at a time, which helps prevent data entry errors. Forms are typically utilized by the users of the database, while the database designer creates and edits the form structure. Figure 9 shows a form. Notice a single record is displayed.

Databases Are Everywhere! • Access 2016

- A **report** contains professional-looking formatted information from underlying tables or queries. Much like a report you would prepare for a class, a report enables you to perform research and put the results into a readable format. The report can then be viewed on-screen, saved to a file, or printed. Figure 10 shows a report in Print Preview mode.

FIGURE 9 An Access Form

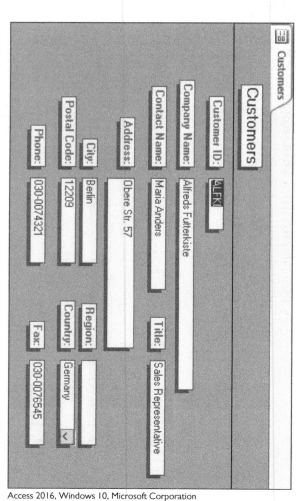

Access 2016, Windows 10, Microsoft Corporation

FIGURE 10 An Access Report

Customer Contacts

Contact Name	Company Name	Contact Title	Phone	City	Region	Country
Alejandra Camino	Romero y tomillo	Accounting Manager	(91) 745 6200	Madrid		Spain
Alexander Feuer	Morgenstern Gesundkost	Marketing Assistant	0342-023176	Leipzig		Germany
Ana Trujillo	Ana Trujillo Emparedados y helados	Owner	(5) 555-4729	México D.F.		Mexico
Anabela Domingues	Tradição Hipermercados	Sales Representative	(11) 555-2167	São Paulo	SP	Brazil
André Fonseca	Gourmet Lanchonetes	Sales Associate	(11) 555-9482	Campinas	SP	Brazil
Ann Devon	Eastern Connection	Sales Agent	(171) 555-0297	London		UK
Annette Roulet	La maison d'Asie	Sales Manager	61.77.61.10	Toulouse		France
Antonio Moreno	Antonio Moreno Taqueria	Owner	(5) 555-3932	México D.F.		Mexico
Aria Cruz	Familia Arquibaldo	Marketing Assistant	(11) 555-9857	São Paulo	SP	Brazil
Art Braunschweiger	Split Rail Beer & Ale	Sales Manager	(307) 555-4680	Lander	WY	USA
Bernardo Batista	Que Delicia	Accounting Manager	(21) 555-4252	Rio de Janeiro	RJ	Brazil
Carine Schmitt	France restauration	Marketing Manager	40.32.21.21	Nantes		France
Carlos González	LILA-Supermercado	Accounting Manager	(9) 331-6954	Barquisimeto	Lara	Venezuela
Carlos Hernández	HILARIÓN-Abastos	Sales Representative	(5) 555-1340	San Cristóbal	Táchira	Venezuela
Catherine Dewey	Maison Dewey	Sales Agent	(02) 201 24 67	Bruxelles		Belgium
Christina Berglund	Berglund snabbköp	Order Administrator	0921-12 34 65	Luleå		Sweden
Daniel Tonini	La corne d'abondance	Sales Representative	30.59.84.10	Versailles		France

Page: ◄ ◄ 1 ► ►| ►* ✕ No Filter ◄ ▲

Access 2016, Windows 10, Microsoft Corporation

Figure 11 displays the different object types in Access with the foundation object—the table—in the center of the illustration. The purpose each object serves is explained underneath the object name. The flow of information between objects is indicated by single-arrowhead arrows if the flow is one direction only. Two-arrowhead arrows indicate that the flow goes both directions. For example, you can use forms to view, add, delete, or modify data from tables.

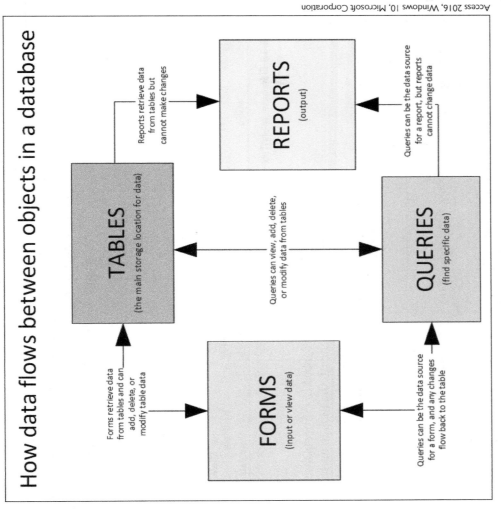

How data flows between objects in a database

Access 2016, Windows 10, Microsoft Corporation

FIGURE 11 Flow of Information Between Object Types

Two other object types, macros and modules, are rarely used by beginning Access users. A **macro** object is a stored series of commands that carry out an action. Macros are often used to automate tasks. A **module** is an advanced object written using the VBA (Visual Basic® for Applications) programming language. Modules provide more functionality than macros, but are not generally required for even intermediate users.

Examine the Access Interface

While Access includes the standard elements of the Microsoft Office applications interface such as the title bar, the Ribbon, the Home tab, Backstage view, and scroll bars, it also includes elements unique to Access.

The Access Ribbon has five tabs that always display, as well as tabs that appear only when particular objects are open. The two tabs that are unique to Access are:

- External Data tab: Contains all of the operations used to facilitate data import and export. See Figure 12.

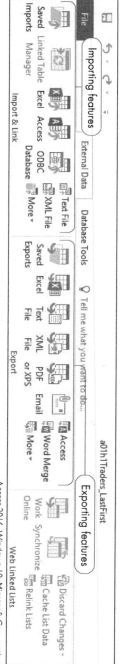

FIGURE 12 External Data Tab

a01h1Traders_LastFirst

Importing features

Imports
Saved Linked Table Excel Access ODBC
Manager Database

Exporting features

Access 2016, Windows 10, Microsoft Corporation

- Database Tools tab: Contains the feature that enables users to create relationships between tables and enables use of more advanced features of Access. Figure 13 shows the Database Tools tab.

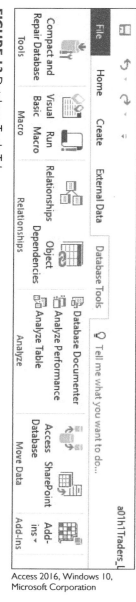

FIGURE 13 Database Tools Tab

a01h1Traders_L

Access 2016, Windows 10, Microsoft Corporation

By default, Access uses a Tabbed Documents interface. That means that each object that is open has its own tab beneath the Ribbon and to the right of the Navigation Pane. You can switch between open objects by clicking a tab to make that object active, similar to the way an Excel worksheet has tabs at the bottom of the screen. Figure 14 shows the Access interface with multiple objects open.

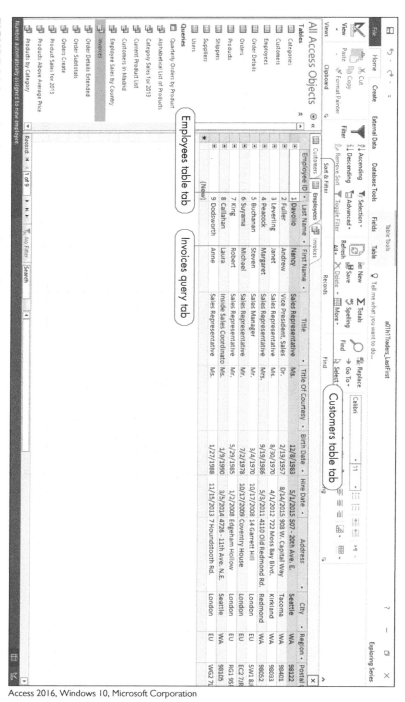

FIGURE 14 Access Database with Multiple Objects Open

Access 2016, Windows 10, Microsoft Corporation

Explore Table Datasheet View

Access provides two different ways to view a table: Datasheet view and Design view. When you double-click a table, Datasheet view displays by default. **Datasheet view** is a grid containing fields (columns) and records (rows). You can view, add, edit, and delete records in Datasheet view. Figure 15 shows the Customers table in Datasheet view. Each row contains a record for a specific customer. Click the record selector, or row heading, at the beginning of a row to select the record. Each column represents a field, or one attribute about a customer. Click the field selector, or column heading, to select a field.

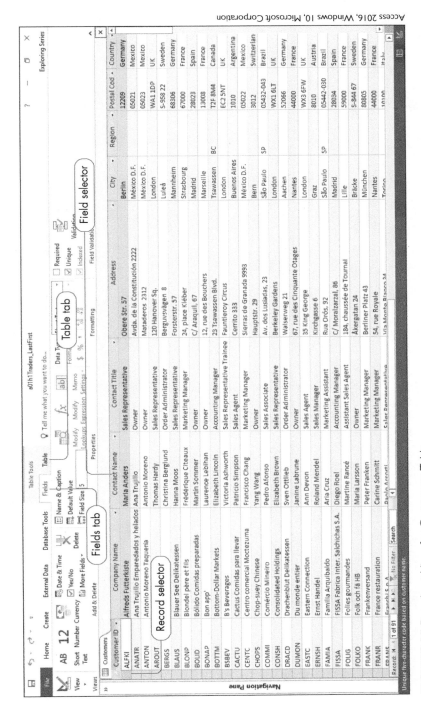

FIGURE 15 Datasheet View for Customers Table

Notice the Customers table shows records for 91 employees. The customer records contain multiple fields about each customer, including the Company Name, Contact Name, and so on. Occasionally a field does not contain a value for a particular record. For example, many customers do not have a Region assigned. Access shows a blank cell when data is missing.

Navigate Through Records

The navigation bar at the bottom of Figure 16 shows that the Customers table has 91 records and that record number 18 is the current record. The pencil symbol to the left of record 18 indicates that the data in that record is being edited and that changes have not yet been saved. The pencil icon disappears when you move to another record. Access saves data automatically as soon as you move from one record to another. This may seem counterintuitive at first because other Office applications, such as Word and Excel, do not save changes and additions automatically. The navigation arrows enable you to go to the first record, the previous record, the next record, or the last record. Click the right arrow with a yellow asterisk to add a new (blank) record.

FIGURE 16 Navigation Arrows in a Table

Customer ID	Company Name	Contact Name	Contact Title	Address	City	Region	Postal Cod...	Country
ALFKI	Alfreds Futterkiste	Maria Anders	Sales Representative	Obere Str. 57	Berlin		12209	Germany
ANATR	Ana Trujillo Emparedados y helados	Ana Trujillo	Owner	Avda. de la Constitución 2222	México D.F.		05021	Mexico
ANTON	Antonio Moreno Taquería	Antonio Moreno	Owner	Mataderos 2312	México D.F.		05023	Mexico
AROUT	Around the Horn	Thomas Hardy	Sales Representative	120 Hanover Sq.	London		WA1 1DP	UK
BERGS	Berglunds snabbköp	Christina Berglund	Order Administrator	Berguvsvägen 8	Luleå		S-958 22	Sweden
BLAUS	Blauer See Delikatessen	Hanna Moos	Sales Representative	Forsterstr. 57	Mannheim		68306	Germany
BLONP	Blondel père et fils	Frédérique Citeaux	Marketing Manager	24, place Kléber	Strasbourg		67000	France
BOLID	Bólido Comidas preparadas		Owner	C/ Araquil, 67	Madrid		28023	Spain
BONAP	Bon app'		Owner	12, rue des Bouchers	Marseille		13008	France
BOTTM	Bottom-Dollar Markets	Elizabeth Lincoln	Accounting Manager	23 Tsawassen Blvd.	Tsawassen	BC	T2F 8M4	Canada
BSBEV	B's Beverages		Sales Representative Trainee	Fauntleroy Circus	London		EC2 5NT	UK
CACTU	Cactus Comidas para llevar		Sales Agent	Cerrito 333	Buenos Aires		1010	Argentina
CENTC	Centro comercial Moctezuma	Francisco Chang	Marketing Manager	Sierras de Granada 9993	México D.F.		05022	Mexico
CHOPS	Chop-suey Chinese		Owner	Hauptstr. 29	Bern		3012	Switzerland
COMMI	Comércio Mineiro	Pedro Afonso	Sales Associate	Av. dos Lusíadas, 23	São Paulo	SP	05432-043	Brazil
CONSH	Consolidated Holdings	Elizabeth Brown	Sales Representative	Berkeley Gardens	London		WX1 6LT	UK
DRACD	Drachenblut Delikatessen		Order Administrator	Walserweg 21	Aachen		52066	Germany
DUMON	Du monde entier	Janine Labrune	Owner	67, rue des Cinquante Otages	Nantes		44000	France
EASTC	Eastern Connection	Ann Devon	Sales Agent	35 King George	London		WX3 6FW	UK
ERNSH	Ernst Handel		Sales Manager	Kirchgasse 6	Graz		8010	Austria
FAMIA	Familia Arquibaldo		Marketing Assistant	Rua Orós, 92	São Paulo	SP	05442-030	Brazil
FISSA	FISSA Fabrica Inter. Salchichas S.A.	Diego Roel	Accounting Manager	C/ Moralzarzal, 86	Madrid		28034	Spain
FOLIG	Folies gourmandes		Assistant Sales Agent	184, chaussée de Tournai	Lille		59000	France
FOLKO	Folk och fä HB		Owner	Åkergatan 24	Bräcke		S-844 67	Sweden
FRANK	Frankenversand	Peter Franken	Marketing Manager	Berliner Platz 43	München		80805	Germany
FRANR	France restauration	Carine Schmitt	Marketing Manager	54, rue Royale	Nantes		44000	France
FRANS		Paolo Accorti	Sales Representative	Via Monte Bianco 34	Torino		10100	Italy

Record: 18 of 91

Navigation works for more than just tables. Navigation arrows are also available in queries and forms. Figure 17 shows the same navigation arrows appearing in forms.

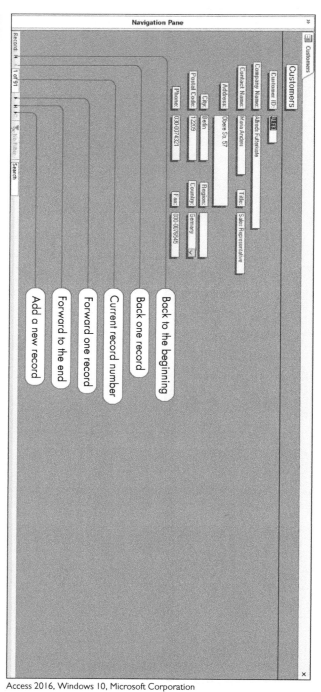

FIGURE 17 Navigation Arrows in a Form

Add a new record
Forward to the end
Forward one record
Current record number
Back one record
Back to the beginning

In addition to navigating, you also have access to the Find command. The Find command is located in the Find group on the Home tab, and can be used to locate specific records. You can search for a single field or the entire record, match all or part of the selected field(s), move forward or back in a table, or specify a case-sensitive search.

To find a record using the Find command, complete the following steps:

1. Open the table that contains the data you are searching for. Note that if you want to search a query, form, or report, you can follow the same steps, except open the appropriate object instead of the table.

2. Click any cell within the field you want to search. For example, if you want to search the City field in the Customers table, as shown in Figure 18, click any City value.

3. Ensure the Home tab is selected.

4. Click Find in the Find group.

5. Type the value you are searching for in the Find What box. Note that the entry is not case sensitive.

6. Click Find Next to find the next matching value.

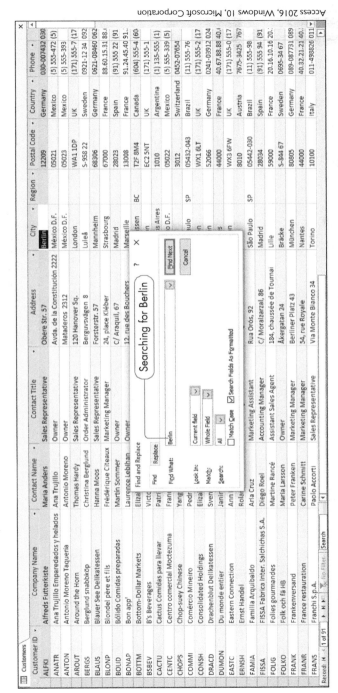

FIGURE 18 Find Command

Explore Table Design View

Design view gives you a detailed view of the table's structure and is used to create and modify a table's design by specifying the fields it will contain, the fields' data types, and their associated properties. When you double-click a table in the Navigation Pane, it will open in Datasheet view, as the design of a table typically does not change frequently.

To switch between Datasheet and Design view, complete the following steps:

1. Click the Home tab.

2. Click View in the Views group to toggle between the current view and the previous view. See Figure 19.

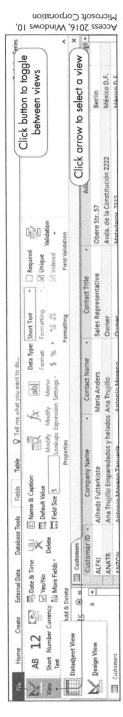

FIGURE 19 View Button

Also notice the arrow that allows you to select either Design or Datasheet view. Either way of performing this task is correct.

Data types define the type of data that will be stored in a field, such as short text, numeric, currency, date/time, etc. For example, if you need to store the hire date of an employee, you would input a field name and select the Date/Time data type. A *field property* defines the characteristics of a field in more detail. For example, for the field OrderDate, you could set add validation (the OrderDate must be today's date or later), or choose whether the field is required or not. Though some changes can be made to the field properties in Datasheet view, Design view gives you access to more properties.

Figure 20 shows Design view for the Orders table. In the top portion, each row contains the field name the data type, and an optional description for each field in the table. In the bottom portion, the Field Properties pane contains the properties (details) for a field. Click a field, and the properties for that field display in the Field Properties section of Design view window. Depending on a field's data type, the available properties will change.

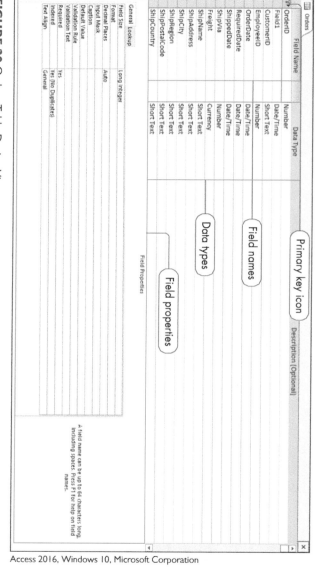

Orders		
Field Name	Data Type	Description (Optional)
OrderID	Number	
Field1	Date/Time	
CustomerID	Short Text	
EmployeeID	Number	
OrderDate	Date/Time	
RequiredDate	Date/Time	
ShippedDate	Date/Time	
ShipVia	Number	
Freight	Currency	
ShipName	Short Text	
ShipAddress	Short Text	
ShipCity	Short Text	
ShipRegion	Short Text	
ShipPostalCode	Short Text	
ShipCountry	Short Text	

Primary key icon

Field names

Data types

General | Lookup
Field Size	Long Integer
Format	
Decimal Places	Auto
Input Mask	
Caption	
Default Value	
Validation Rule	
Validation Text	
Required	Yes
Indexed	Yes (No Duplicates)
Text Align	General

Field properties

Field Properties

A field name can be up to 64 characters long, including spaces. Press F1 for help on field names.

FIGURE 20 Orders Table Design View

Access 2016, Windows 10, Microsoft Corporation

Notice the key icon next to the OrderID field; this denotes this field is the primary key in the Orders table; it ensures that each record in the table is unique and can be distinguished from every other record. You may have multiple orders from the same customer, but you can tell they are different because there are two separate OrderIDs. This is why many companies ask for you to include your account number when you pay a bill. The account number, similar to an OrderID, uniquely identifies you and helps ensure that the payment is not applied to the wrong customer.

In Figure 20, the OrderID field has an AutoNumber data type—a number that is generated by Access and is automatically incremented each time a record is added. Each field's data type determines the type of input accepted.

Rename and Describe Tables

To make a table easy to use, Access includes a few properties you can modify. Tables default to a name of Table1 (or Table2, etc.) if you do not specify otherwise. As you can imagine, this would be very difficult to navigate.

To rename a table, complete the following steps:

1. Verify that the table is closed. If it is not closed, right-click the table tab and select Close. A table cannot be renamed while it is open.
2. Right-click the table name in the Navigation Pane.
3. Select Rename on the shortcut menu.
4. Type the new name over the selected text and press Enter.

Tables also include a description, which can be useful to provide documentation about the contents of a table. For example, most tables in the Northwind database are straightforward. However, just in case, the database comes with predefined descriptions for most tables. This can provide a user with additional clarification regarding the purpose of a table if they know where to look. By default, descriptions are not shown unless you right-click the table and select Table Properties. If you are working with a complex database, adding descriptions can be extremely helpful for new users. Figure 21 shows a table description.

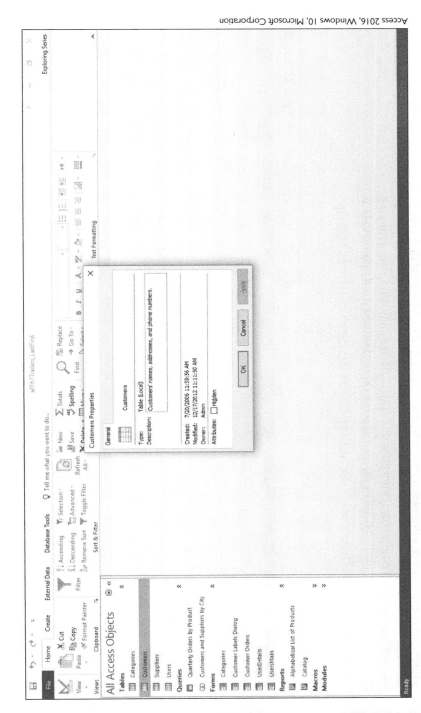

FIGURE 21 Previewing a Table Description

To enter a table description, complete the following steps:

1. Right-click the table name in the Navigation Pane.
2. Select Table Properties on the shortcut menu.
3. Type the description in the Table Properties dialog box and click OK.

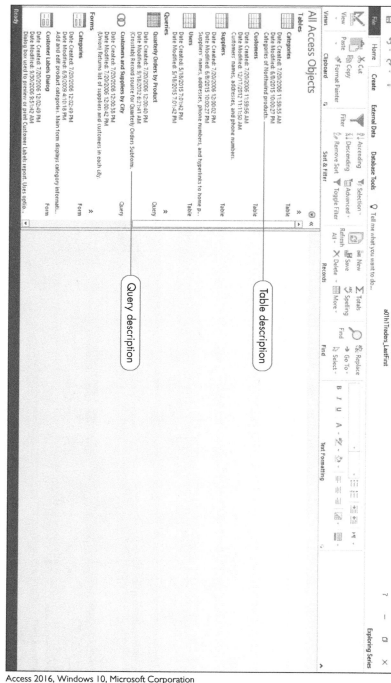

FIGURE 22 Detail View of Objects

Understand Relationships Between Tables

A *relationship* is a connection between two tables using a common field. The benefit of a relationship is the ability to efficiently combine data from related tables for the purpose of creating queries, forms, and reports. If you are using an existing database, relationships are likely created already. The design of the Northwind database, which contains multiple tables, is illustrated in Figure 23. The tables have been created, the field names have been added, and the data types have been set. The diagram shows the relationships that were created between tables using join lines. Join lines enable you to create a relationship between two tables using a common field. For example, the Suppliers table is joined to the Products table using the common field SupplierID. These table connections enable you to query the database for information stored in multiple tables. This feature gives the manager the ability to ask questions like "What products are produced by the supplier Exotic Liquids?" In this case, the name of the supplier (Exotic Liquids) is stored in the Supplier table, but the products are stored in the Products table. Notice in Figure 24, you can tell there is a table related to the Supplier table, because a plus sign ⊞ appears to the left of each Supplier. If you click the plus sign, you will see a list of products produced by this company.

556

Introduction to Access

Access 2016, Windows 10, Microsoft Corporation

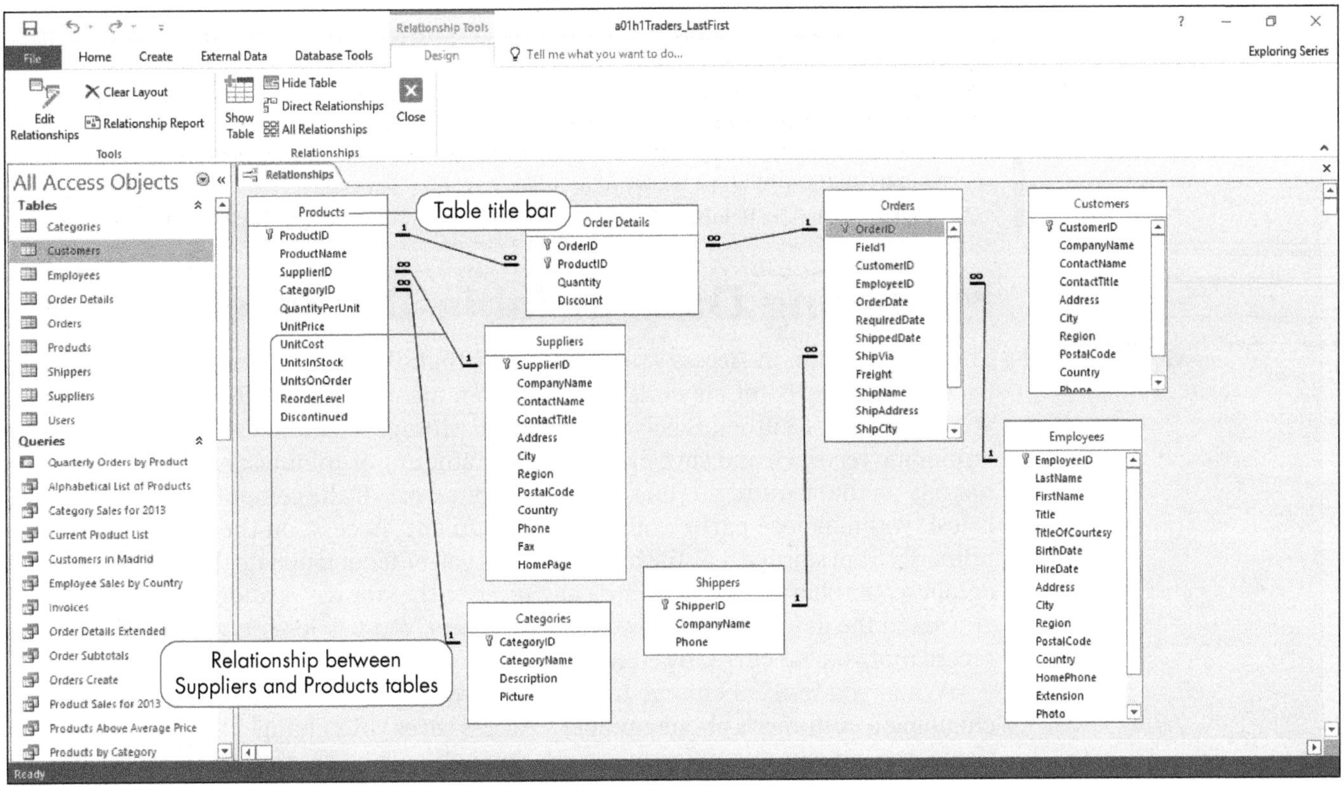

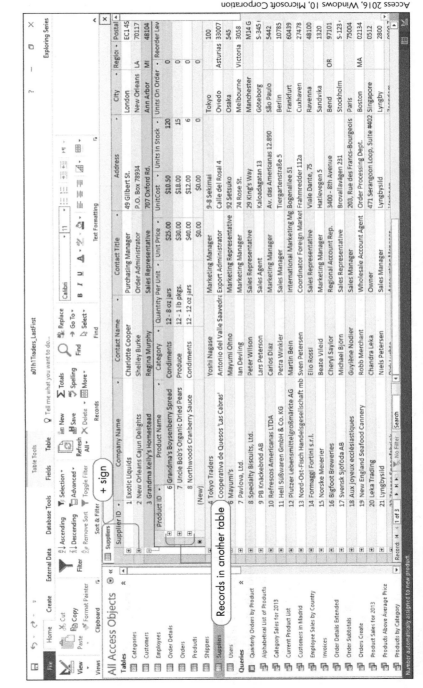

FIGURE 23 Northwind Database Relationships

Access 2016, Windows 10, Microsoft Corporation

FIGURE 24 Related Tables

However, you can view the existing relationships in any database to familiarize yourself with the way tables work together.

To view existing database relationships, complete the following steps:

1. Click Relationships in the Relationships group on the Database Tools tab.

2. Reposition tables by dragging the table's title bar (as shown above in Figure 23) to a new location so all relationships are visible. This is not required, but doing so may make the relationships easier to follow.

3. Click Close in the Relationships group of the Design tab to close the Relationships window.

STEP 3

Modifying Data in Table Datasheet View

The Save function in Access works differently than the other Office applications. Word, Excel, and PowerPoint all work primarily from memory (RAM). In those applications, your work is not automatically saved to your storage location. Office may perform an automatic recovery and save every specified amount of minutes; however, you should not rely on that feature, so you should save your work. If the computer crashes or power is lost, you may lose part or all of your document. Access, on the other hand, works primarily from storage (i.e., the hard drive). As you enter and update the data in an Access database, the changes are automatically saved to the storage location you specified when you saved the database. If a power failure occurs, you will lose only the changes to the record that you are currently editing.

When you make a change to a record's content in an Access table (for example, changing a customer's phone number), Access saves your changes as soon as you move the insertion point to a different record. You will only be prompted to save if you make changes to the design of the table (such as changing the font or background color). Editing data is done similarly in queries and forms. Recall that reports cannot change data, so changes to data cannot be done there.

To edit a record, tab to the field you want to modify and type the new data. When you start typing, you erase all existing data in the field because the entire field is selected.

TIP: UNDO WORKS DIFFERENTLY

You can click Undo to reverse the most recent change (the phone number you just modified, for example) to a single record immediately after making changes to that record. However, unlike other Office programs that enable multiple Undo steps, you cannot use Undo to reverse multiple edits in Access. Undo (and Redo) are found on the Quick Access Toolbar.

STEP 4

Adding Records to a Table

Data in a database will be constantly changing. You should expect new data to be added. If you are working with a Customer database, you would expect new customers to be added constantly. If you are dealing with a Restaurant database, new menu items could be added daily.

To add a new record to a table, complete the following steps:

1. Open the table in Datasheet view (if it is not already open) by double-clicking it in the Navigation Pane.

2. Click New in the Records group on the Home tab.

3. Begin typing. If you are unable to type, you have probably selected a field with a data type of AutoNumber, which Access assigns for you. If this is the case, click in a different field and begin typing. The asterisk record indicator changes to a pencil symbol to show that you are in editing mode (see Figure 25). Note: you can follow the same process to add a record in a form (shown in Figure 26) or query.

4. Press Tab to move to the following field and enter data, and repeat this step until you have input all required data for this record.

5. Move to another record by clicking elsewhere or pressing Tab in the last field in a record. As soon as you move to another record, Access automatically saves the changes to the record you created or changed.

FIGURE 25 Adding a Record Using a Table

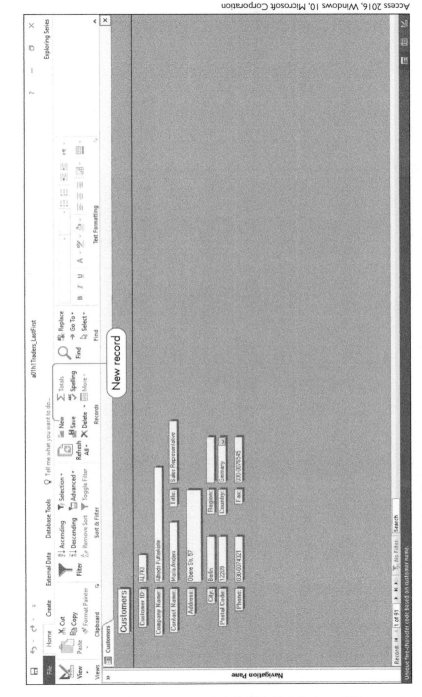

FIGURE 26 Adding a Record Using a Form

As with most of Office, there are a number of ways to perform the same task. Data entry is the same. See Table 1 for a list of some shortcuts you can use when performing data entry.

TABLE 1 Keyboard Shortcuts for Entering Data

Keystroke	Result
Up arrow (↑)	Moves insertion point up one row.
Down arrow (↓)	Moves insertion point down one row.
Left arrow (←)	Moves insertion point left one field in the same row.
Right arrow (→)	Moves insertion point right one field in the same row.
Tab or Enter	Moves insertion point right one field in the same row.
Shift+Tab	Moves insertion point left one field in the same row.
Home	Moves insertion point to the first field in the current row.
End	Moves insertion point to the last field in the current row.
Esc	Cancels any changes made in the current field while in Edit mode.
Ctrl+Z	Reverses the last unsaved edit.

Pearson Education, Inc.

STEP 5

Deleting Records from a Table

Deciding to delete records is not a simple decision. Many times, deleting records is a bad idea. Say you are working in the database for an animal shelter. Once an animal has been adopted, you may be tempted to delete the animal from the database. However, you would then lose any record of the animal ever existing, and if the owner calls asking if the animal has had its shots, or how old the animal is, you would no longer be able to provide that information. Often, instead of deleting information, you would create a yes/no field indicating that a record is no longer relevant. For example, the shelter database might have a check box for adopted. If the adopted box is checked yes, the animal is no longer at the shelter, but the information is still available. That said, sometimes you will certainly find it appropriate to delete a record.

To delete a record from a table, complete the following steps:

1. Click the record selector for the record you want to delete (see Figure 27).
2. Click Delete in the Records group on the Home tab. Click Yes in the warning dialog box.

Note that you can take similar steps in queries and forms.

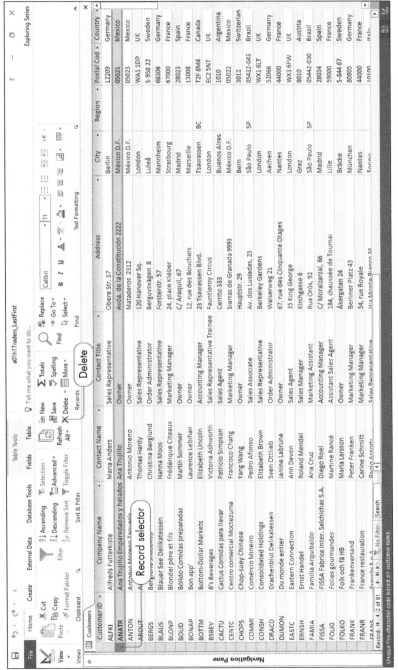

FIGURE 27 Deleting a Record

If you attempt to delete a record, you may get an error message. For example, if you try to delete a customer who has adopted pets, you may get a message stating *You cannot delete this record because another table has related records.* Even though the customer may have moved, they cannot be deleted because related records exist in another table, in this case, animals the customer has adopted.

Using Database Utilities

Database administrators spend a lot of time maintaining databases. Software utility programs make this process simpler. As Access is a database management utility, there are a number of tools that can be used to protect, maintain, and improve performance of a database.

Back Up a Database

STEP 6 >> ***Back Up Database*** is a utility that creates a duplicate copy of the entire database to protect from loss or damage. Imagine what would happen to a firm that loses track of orders placed, a charity that loses the list of donor contributions, or a hospital that loses the digital records of its patients. Making backups is especially important when you have multiple users working with the database. When you use the Back Up Database utility, Access provides a file name for the backup that uses the same file name as the database you are backing up, an underscore, and the current date. This makes it easy for you to keep track of databases by the date they were created.

Keep in mind, backing up a database on the same storage device as the original database can leave you with no protection in the event of hardware failure. Backups are typically stored on a separate device, such as an external hard drive or network drive.

To back up a database, complete the following steps:

1. Click the File tab.
2. Click Save As.
3. Click Back Up Database under the Advanced group (see Figure 28).
4. Click Save As. Revise the location and file name if you want to change either and click Save.

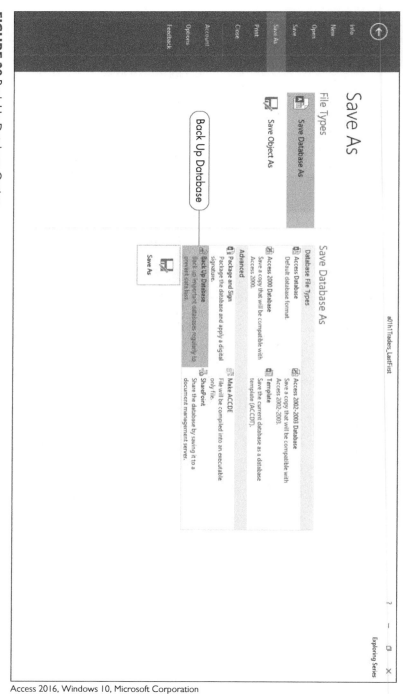

FIGURE 28 Back Up Database Option

Access 2016, Windows 10, Microsoft Corporation

Compact and Repair a Database

Databases have a tendency to expand with everyday use and may become corrupt, so Access provides the *Compact and Repair Database* utility. Compact and Repair Database reduces the size of a database and fixes any errors that may exist in the file.

To compact and repair an open database, complete the following steps:

1. Click the File tab.
2. Click Compact and Repair Database in the Info options. If you have any unsaved design changes, you will be prompted to save before the compact and repair can complete.

Alternately, you can have Access perform a Compact and Repair automatically.

To have Access compact and repair a database each time you close the database, complete the following steps:

1. Click the File tab.
2. Click Options.
3. Click Current Database.
4. Click the Compact on Close check box under Application Options in the Options for the current database pane.
5. Click OK.

TIP: SPLIT DATABASES

Another utility built into Access is the *Database Splitter* tool, which puts the tables in one file (the back-end database), and the queries, forms, and reports in a second file (the front-end database). This way, each user can create their own queries, forms, and reports without potentially changing an object someone else needs.

To split a database, click the Database Tools tab and click Access Database in the Move Data group. Click Split Database and click OK.

Encrypt a Database

To protect a database from unauthorized access, you can encrypt the database, which enables you to password-protect the stored information. Adding a password requires that the database be opened in exclusive mode. Open Exclusive mode guarantees that you are the only one currently using the database.

To open a database in exclusive mode, complete the following steps:

1. Ensure that the database is closed. You cannot open a database with exclusive access unless it is currently closed.
2. Click the File tab.
3. Click Open.
4. Click Browse to display the Open dialog box.
5. Locate and click the database you want to open, and click the Open arrow at the bottom of the dialog box. Make sure you click the arrow next to the word Open, and not the Open button.
6. Select Open Exclusive from the list. The database opens in exclusive mode.

To add a password once the database has been opened in exclusive mode, complete the following steps:

1. Click the File tab.
2. Click Encrypt with Password. The Set Database Password dialog box opens.
3. Type a password, and re-enter the password in the Verify box. Click OK.

Print Information

Though Access is primarily designed to store data electronically, you may want to produce a print copy of your data.

To print information from any object (table, query, form, report) in your database, complete the following steps:

1. Click the File tab.
2. Click Print. The right panel display changes to enable you to choose a print option.
3. Click Print.
4. Change any settings that may need changing (for example, the print range or number of copies).
5. Click OK.

It is good practice to preview your work before printing a document. This way, if you notice an error, you can fix it and not waste paper.

To preview your work before printing, complete the following steps:

1. Click the File tab.
2. Click Print.
3. Click Print Preview.
4. Click Close Print Preview on the Print Preview tab to exit without printing, or click Print to open the Print dialog box (see Figure 29).

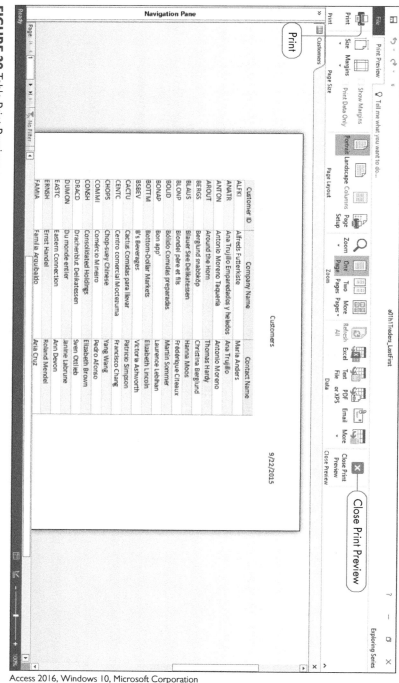

FIGURE 29 Table Print Preview

Access 2016, Windows 10, Microsoft Corporation

Quick Concepts

1. Name the four main types of objects in an Access database and briefly describe the purpose of each.
2. What is the difference between Datasheet view and Design view in a table?
3. How does Access handle saving differently than other Office programs such as Excel?
4. How do relationships benefit a database user?

Hands-On Exercises

MyITLab®
HOE1 Training

▶ Watch the Video
for this Hands-On
Exercise!

Skills covered: Open a Database • Save a Database with a New Name • Enable Content in a Database • Examine the Access Interface • Explore Table Datasheet View • Navigate Through Records • Explore Table Design View • Rename and Describe Tables • Understand Relationships Between Tables • Understand the Difference Between Working in Storage And Memory • Change Data in Table Datasheet View • Add Records to a Table • Delete Records from A Table • Back Up a Database • Compact and Repair a Database • Encrypt a Database • Print Information

1 Databases Are Everywhere!

Northwind purchases food items from suppliers around the world and sells them to restaurants and specialty food shops. Northwind depends on the data stored in its Access database to process orders and make daily decisions. You will open the Northwind database, examine the Access interface, review the existing objects in the database, and explore Access views. You will add, edit, and delete records using both tables and forms. Finally, you will back up the database.

STEP 1 ⟫ **OPEN, SAVE, AND ENABLE CONTENT IN A DATABASE**

As you begin your job, you first will become familiar with the Northwind database. This database will help you learn the fundamentals of working with database files. Refer to Figure 30 as you complete Step 1.

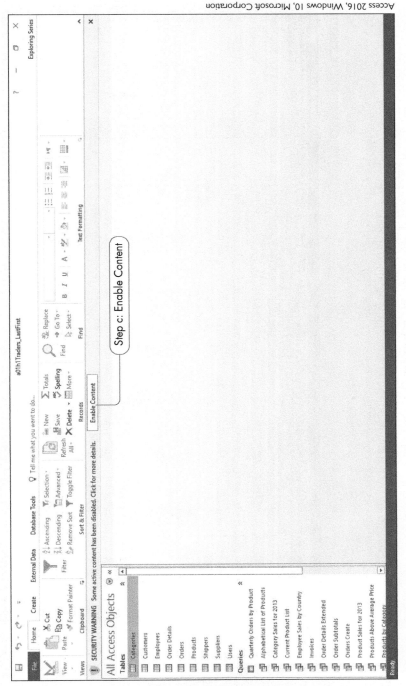

FIGURE 30 Northwind Database

Hands-On Exercise 1

Access 2016, Windows 10, Microsoft Corporation

565

a. Open Access, click **Open Other Files**, and click **Browse** 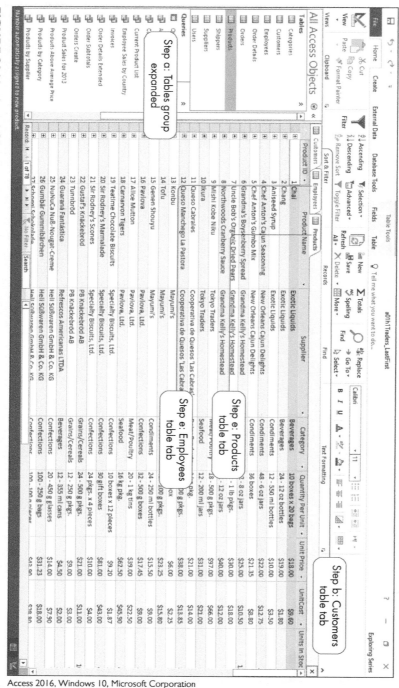. Navigate to the folder location designated by your instructor. Click *a01h1Traders* and click **Open**.

b. Click the **File tab** and click **Save As**. Click **Save As** and save the file as **a01h1Traders_LastFirst**.

When you save files, use your last and first names. For example, as the Access author, I would save my database as "a01h1Traders_CameronEric."

The Security Warning message bar appears below the Ribbon, indicating that some database content is disabled.

c. Click **Enable Content** on the Security Warning message bar.

When you open an Access file, you should enable the content.

STEP 2 ›› RECOGNIZE DATABASE OBJECT TYPES

Now that you have opened the Northwind database, you examine the Navigation Pane, objects, and views to become familiar with these fundamental Access features. Refer to Figure 31 as you complete Step 2.

FIGURE 31 Northwind Objects

a. Scroll through the Navigation Pane and notice the Access objects listed under each expanded group.

The Tables group and the Forms group are expanded, displaying all of the table and form objects. The Queries, Reports, Macros, and Modules groups are collapsed so that the objects in those groups are not displayed.

b. Double-click the **Customers table** in the Navigation Pane.

Access 2016, Windows 10, Microsoft Corporation

The Customers table opens in Datasheet view, showing the data contained in the table. The Customers tab displays below the Ribbon indicating the table object is open. Each customer's record displays on a table row. The columns of the table display the fields that comprise the records.

c. Click **View** in the Views group on the Home tab.

The view of the Customers table switches to Design view. The top portion of Design view displays each field that comprises a customer record, the field's data type, and an optional description of what the field should contain. The bottom portion of Design view displays the field properties (details) for the selected field.

d. Click **View** in the Views group on the Home tab again.

Because the View button is a toggle, your view returns to Datasheet view, which shows the data stored in the table.

e. Double-click **Employees** in the Tables group of the Navigation Pane. Double-click **Products** in the same location.

The Employees and Products tables open. The tabs for three table objects display below the Ribbon: Customers, Employees, and Products.

f. Click **Shutter Bar Open/Close** [«] on the title bar of the Navigation Pane to hide the Navigation Pane. Click again to [»] show the Navigation Pane.

Shutter Bar Open/Close toggles to allow you to view more in the open object window, or to enable you to view your database objects.

g. Scroll down in the Navigation Pane and click **Reports**.

The Reports group expands, and all report objects display.

h. Scroll up until you can see Forms. Click **Forms** in the Navigation Pane.

The Forms group collapses and individual form objects no longer display.

You want to learn to edit the data in the Northwind database, because data can change. For example, employees will change their address and phone numbers when they move, and customers will change their order data from time to time. Refer to Figure 32 as you complete Step 3.

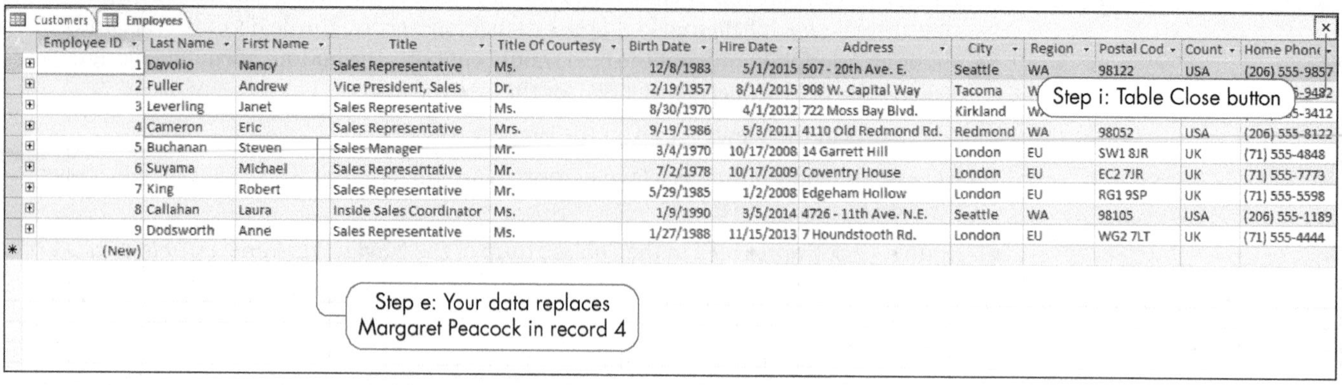

Step e: Your data replaces Margaret Peacock in record 4

Step i: Table Close button

FIGURE 32 Northwind Employees Table

Access 2016, Windows 10, Microsoft Corporation

a. Click the **Employees tab** to view the Employees table.

b. Double-click **Peacock** (the value of the Last Name field in the fourth row); the entire name highlights. Type your last name to replace Peacock.

The pencil symbol in the record selector box indicates that the record is being edited but has not yet been saved.

c. Press **Tab** to move to the next field in the fourth row. Replace Margaret with your first name and press **Tab.**

You have made changes to two fields in the same record.

d. Click **Undo** on the Quick Access Toolbar.

Your first and last names revert back to Margaret Peacock because you have not yet left the record.

e. Type your first and last names again to replace Margaret Peacock. Press **Tab.**

You should now be in the title field and the title, Sales Representative, is selected. The record has not been saved, as indicated by the pencil symbol in the record selector box.

f. Click anywhere in the third row where Janet Leverling's data is stored.

The pencil symbol disappears, indicating that your changes have been saved.

g. Click the **Address field** in the first row, Nancy Davolio's record. Select the entire address and then type **4004 East Morningside Dr.** Click anywhere on the second record, Andrew Fuller's record.

h. Click **Undo.**

Nancy Davolio's address reverts back to 507 - 20th Ave. E. However, the Undo command is now faded. You can no longer undo the change that you made replacing Margaret Peacock's name with your own.

i. Click **Close** ☒ at the top of the table to close the Employees table.

The Employees table closes. You are not prompted to save your changes; they have already been saved for you because Access works in storage, not memory. If you reopen the Employees table, you will see your name in place of Margaret Peacock's name.

STEP 4 » ADD RECORDS TO A TABLE

You have been asked to add new information about a new line of products to the Northwind database. Refer to Figure 33 as you complete Step 4.

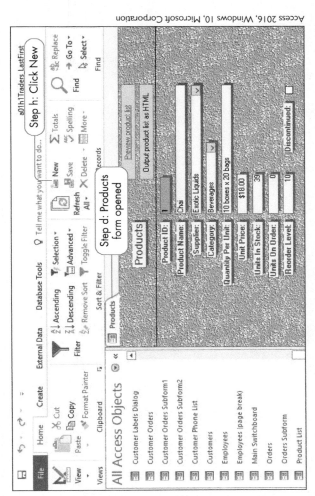

Access 2016, Windows 10, Microsoft Corporation

FIGURE 33 Adding Data Using Products Form

a. Right-click the **Customers tab** and click **Close All**.

b. Click the **Tables group** in the Navigation Pane to collapse it. Click the **Reports group** in the Navigation Pane to collapse it as well.

c. Click the **Forms group** in the Navigation Pane to expand the list of available forms.

d. Double-click the **Products form** to open it.

e. Click the **Next record** arrow. Click **Last record**, click **Previous record**, and then click **First record**.

f. Click **Find** in the Find group on the Home tab, type **Grandma** in the **Find box**, click the **Match arrow**, and then select **Any Part of Field**. Click **Find Next**.

   You should see the data for Grandma's Boysenberry Spread. Selecting the Any Part of Field option will return a match even if it is contained in the middle of a word.

g. Close the Find dialog box.

h. Click **New** in the Records group of the Home tab.

i. Type the following information for a new product. Click, or press **Tab**, to move into the next cell. Notice as soon as you begin typing, Access will assign a ProductID to this product.

Field Name	Value to Type
Product Name	*Your names* **Pecan Pie** (replacing Your name with your last name)
Supplier	**Grandma Kelly's Homestead** (click the arrow to select from the list of Suppliers)
Category	**Confections** (click the arrow to select from the list of Categories)
Quantity Per Unit	**1**
Unit Price	**15.00**
Units in Stock	**18**
Units on Order	**50**
Reorder Level	**20**
Discontinued	**No** (leave the check box unchecked)

Hands-On Exercise 1

j. Click anywhere on the Pecan Pie record you just typed. Click the **File tab**, click **Print**, and then click **Print Preview**.

The first four records display in the Print Preview.

k. Click **Last Page** in the navigation bar and click **Previous Page** to show the new record you entered.

The beginning of the Pecan Pie record is now visible. The record continues on the next page.

l. Click **Close Print Preview** in the Close Preview group.

m. Close the Products form.

STEP 5 ›› **DELETE RECORDS FROM A TABLE**

To help you understand how Access stores data, you verify that the new product is in the Products table. You also attempt to delete a record. Refer to Figure 34 as you complete Step 5.

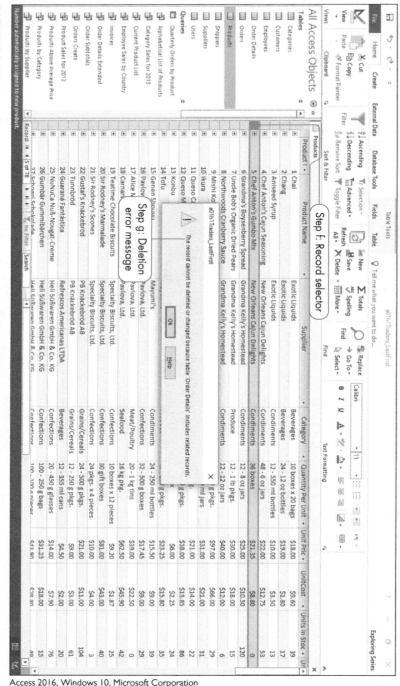

FIGURE 34 Deleting Data

Access 2016, Windows 10, Microsoft Corporation

a. Click the **Forms group** in the Navigation Pane to collapse it. Expand the **Tables group**.

b. Double-click the **Products table** to open it.

c. Click **Last record** in the navigation bar.

The Pecan Pie record you entered in the Products form is listed as the last record in the Products table. The Products form was created from the Products table. Your newly created record, Pecan Pie, is stored in the Products table even though you added it using the form.

d. Navigate to the fifth record in the table, Chef Anton's Gumbo Mix.

e. Use the horizontal scroll bar to scroll right until you see the Discontinued field.

The check mark in the Discontinued check box tells you that this product has been discontinued.

f. Click the **record selector** to the left of the fifth record.

A border surrounds the record and the record is shaded, indicating it is selected.

g. Click **Delete** in the Records group and read the error message.

The error message that displays tells you that you cannot delete this record because the table 'Order Details' has related records. (Customers ordered this product in the past.) Even though the product is now discontinued and no stock remains, it cannot be deleted from the Products table because related records exist in the Order Details table.

h. Click **OK**.

i. Navigate to the last record and click the **record selector** to highlight the entire row.

The Pecan Pie record you added earlier is displayed.

j. Click **Delete** in the Records group. Read the warning.

The warning box that displays tells you that this action cannot be undone. Although this product can be deleted because it was just entered and no orders were created for it, you do not want to delete the record.

k. Click **No**. You do not want to delete this record. Close the Products table.

> **TROUBLESHOOTING:** If you clicked Yes and deleted the record, return to Step 4d. Re-open the form and re-enter the information for this record. This will be important later in this lesson.

STEP 6 ⟫ USE DATABASE UTILITIES

You will protect the Northwind database by using the Back Up Database utility. Refer to Figure 35 as you complete Step 6.

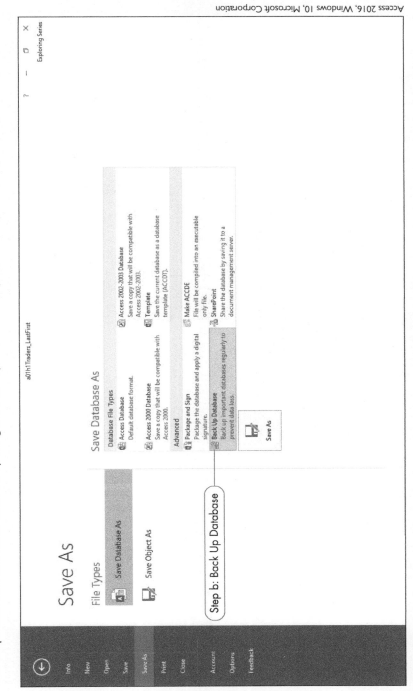

FIGURE 35 Backing Up a Database

a. Click the **File tab** and click **Save As.**

b. Double-click **Back Up Database** under the Advanced section to open the Save As dialog box.

The backup utility assigns the default name by adding a date to your file name.

c. Verify that the Save in folder displays the location where you want your file saved and click **Save.**

You just created a backup of the database after completing Hands-On Exercise 1. The original database file remains onscreen.

d. Keep the database open if you plan to continue with Hands-On Exercise 2. If not, close the database and exit Access.

Filters and Sorts

Access provides you with many tools that you can use to change the order of information and to identify and extract only the data needed at the moment. You may want to find specific information, such as which suppliers are located in Denton, TX, or which customers have placed orders in the last seven days. There may be other times you simply want to sort information rather than extract information.

In this section, you will learn how to sort information and to isolate records in a table based on criteria.

Working with Filters

Suppose you wanted to see a list of the products in the Confections category in the Northwind database. To obtain this list, you would open the Products table in Datasheet view and create a filter. A *filter* allows you to specify conditions to display only those records that meet those conditions. These conditions are known as criteria (or criterion, singular), and are a number, a text phrase, or an expression (such as >50) used to select records from a table. Therefore, to view a list of all Confections, you would filter the Products table, displaying only records with a Category value of Confections. In this case, Category being equal to Confections is the criterion.

You can use filters to analyze data quickly. Applying a filter does not delete any records; filters only hide records that do not match the criteria. Two types of filters are discussed in this section: Selection filter and Filter By Form.

Use a Selection Filter to Find Exact Matches

STEP 1 ⟩⟩ A *Selection filter* displays only the records that match a criterion you select. You can use a Selection filter to find records that equal a criterion. For example, if you filter a name field and you select "equals Eric", you would only find customers who have a name of Eric (but not any other variation). Selection filters are not case sensitive, so any variation of capitalization (ERIC, eric) would also appear in the search results.

To use a Selection filter to find an exact match, complete the following steps:
1. Click in any field that contains the criterion on which you want to filter.
2. Click Selection in the Sort & Filter group on the Home tab.
3. Select Equals "criterion" from the list of options (*criterion* will be replaced by the value of the field).

Figure 36 displays a Customers table with 91 records. The records in the table are displayed in sequence according to the CustomerID. The navigation bar at the bottom indicates that the active record is the second row in the table. Owner in the Job Title field is selected.

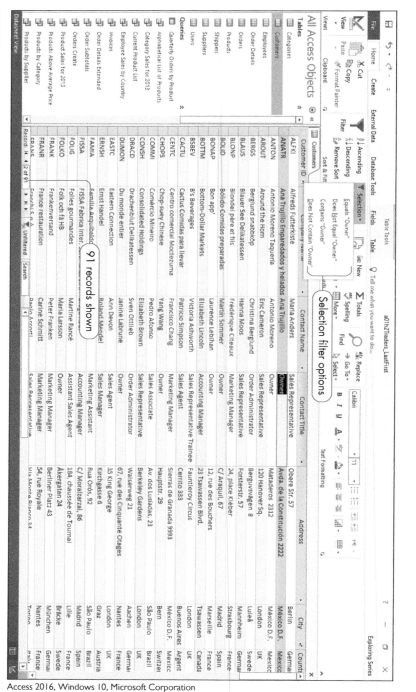

FIGURE 36 Unfiltered Customers Table

Access 2016, Windows 10, Microsoft Corporation

Figure 37 displays a filtered view of the Customers table, showing records with the job title Owner. The navigation bar shows that this is a filtered list containing 17 records matching the criterion. The Customers table still contains the original 91 records, but only 17 records are visible with the filter applied.

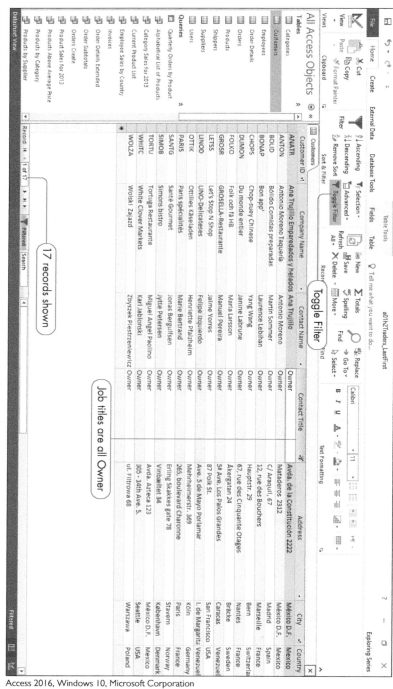

FIGURE 37 Filtered Customers Table

Access 2016, Windows 10, Microsoft Corporation

Introduction to Access

You can click Toggle Filter (refer to Figure 37) at any time to remove all filters and display all the records in the table. Filters are a temporary method for examining table data. If you close the filtered table and reopen it, the filter will be removed and all of the records will be visible again. You can at any point click Toggle Filter to display the results of the last saved filter.

Use a Selection Filter to Find Records Containing a Value

STEP 2 ≫ You can also use a Selection filter to find records that contain a criterion. For example, if you filter a name field and you select "contains Eric", it would find Eric, as well as names containing Eric (such as Erica, Erich, Erick, and even Broderick, Frederick, and Frederica). As with the exact match, this is not case sensitive, as shown in the results in Figure 38.

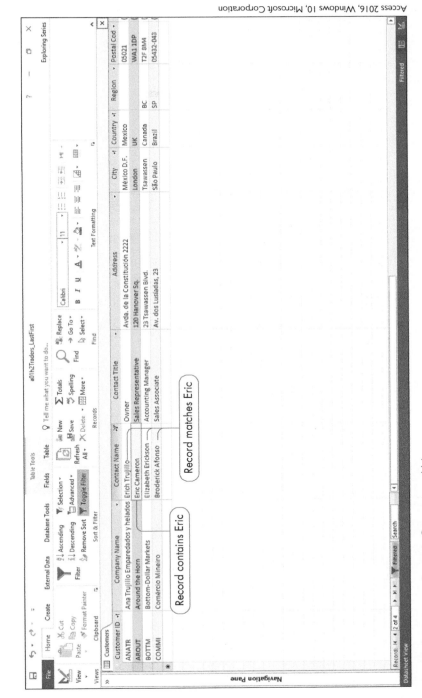

FIGURE 38 Finding Records Containing a Value

To use a Selection filter to find all values containing certain text, complete the following steps:

1. Click in any field that contains the criterion on which you want to filter.
2. Click Selection in the Sort & Filter group on the Home tab.
3. Select Contains "criterion" from the list of options (*criterion* will be replaced by the value of the field).

Your results will show all records containing a partial or full match.

Use Filter By Form

STEP 3 ≫ *Filter By Form* is a more versatile method of selecting data because it enables you to display records based on multiple criteria. When you use Filter By Form, all of the records are hidden and Access creates a blank form in a design grid. You see only field names with an arrow in the first field. Figure 39 shows Filter By Form in Datasheet view, and Figure 40 shows Filter By Form in a form view.

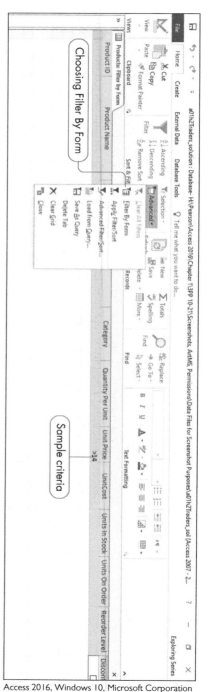

FIGURE 39 Filter By Form in a Table

Access 2016, Windows 10, Microsoft Corporation

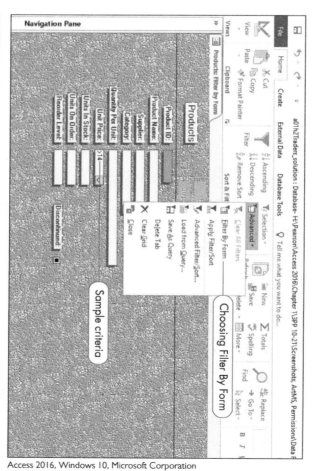

FIGURE 40 Filter By Form in a Form

Access 2016, Windows 10, Microsoft Corporation

An advantage of using this filter method is that you can specify AND and OR logical operators. If you use the AND operator, a record is included in the results if all the criteria are true. If you use the OR operator, a record is included if at least one criterion is true. Another advantage of Filter By Form is that you can use a comparison operator such as equal (=), not equal (<>), greater than (>), less than (<), greater than or equal to (>=), and less than or equal to (<=).

To use Filter By Form, complete the following steps:

1. Click Advanced in the Sort & Filter group on the Home tab.
2. Click Filter By Form.
3. Click in the field you want to use as a criterion. Click the arrow to select the criterion from existing data.
4. Add additional criterion and comparison operators as required.
5. Click Toggle Filter in the Sort & Filter group on the Home tab to apply the filter.

Performing Sorts

You can change the order of information by sorting one or more fields. A *sort* lists records in a specific sequence, such as alphabetically by last name or by ascending EmployeeID.

Sort Table Data

STEP 4 ▶▶ Ascending sorts a list of text data in alphabetical order or a numeric list in lowest to highest order. Descending sorts a list of text data in reverse alphabetical order or a numeric list in highest to lowest order. You can equate this to these terms outside of a database. When you are coming down from a high place (such as the top of a ladder), you are said to be descending, and when you are climbing a ladder, you are ascending. Figure 41 shows the Customers table sorted in ascending order by city name.

FIGURE 41 Sorted Customers Table

To sort a table on one criterion, complete the following steps:

1. Click in the field that you want to use to sort the records.
2. Click Ascending or Descending in the Sort & Filter group on the Home tab.

Access can sort records by more than one field. When sorting by multiple criteria, Access first sorts by the field located on the left. It is important to understand that in order to sort by multiple fields, you must arrange your columns in this order. This may lead to moving a field to the left so it is sorted first.

To move a field, complete the following steps:

1. Click the column heading and hold down the left mouse button. A thick line appears to the left of the column.

2. Drag the field to the appropriate position.

Once the column has been moved, you can perform a sort by selecting the field to the left, sorting, and then doing the same for the secondary sort column.

Quick Concepts

5. What is the purpose of creating a filter?

6. What is the difference between a Selection filter and a Filter By Form?

7. What is a comparison operator and how is it used in a filter?

8. What are the benefits of sorting records in a table?

Skills covered: Use a Selection Filter to Find Exact Matches • Use a Selection Filter to Find Records Containing a Value • Use Filter By Form • Sort Table Data

2 Filters and Sorts

The sales manager at Northwind Traders wants quick answers to her questions about customer orders. You use the Access database to filter tables to answer these questions, then sort the records based on the manager's requirements.

STEP 1 ❯❯ USE A SELECTION FILTER TO FIND EXACT MATCHES

The sales manager asks for a list of customers who live in London. You use a Selection filter with an equal condition to locate these customers. Refer to Figure 42 as you complete Step 1.

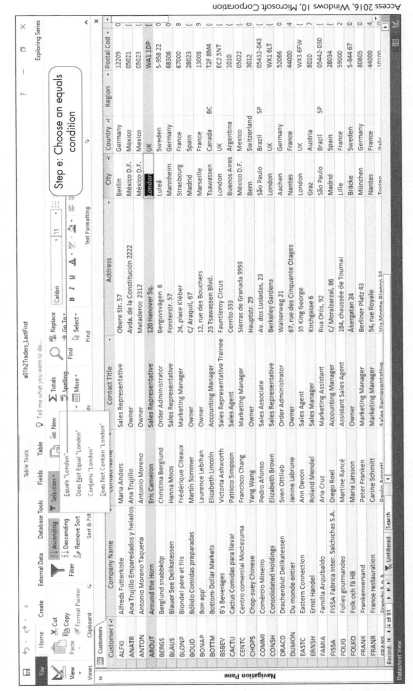

Step e: Choose an equals condition

Access 2016, Windows 10, Microsoft Corporation

FIGURE 42 Filtering the Customers Table

a. Open the *a01h1Traders_LastFirst* database if you closed it after the last Hands-On Exercise and save it as **a01h2Traders_LastFirst**, changing h1 to h2. Click **Enable Content**.

b. Double-click the **Customers table** in the Navigation Pane, navigate to record 4, and then replace Thomas Hardy with your name in the Contact Name field.

c. Scroll right until the City field is visible. The fourth record has a value of London in the City field. Click the field to select it.

d. Click **Selection** in the Sort & Filter group on the Home tab.

e. Select **Equals "London"** from the menu. Six records are displayed.

The navigation bar display shows that six records that meet the London criterion are available. The other records in the Customers table are hidden. The Filtered icon also displays on the navigation bar and column heading, indicating that the Customers table has been filtered.

f. Click **Toggle Filter** in the Sort & Filter group to remove the filter.

g. Click **Toggle Filter** again to reset the filter.

STEP 2)) USE A SELECTION FILTER TO FIND RECORDS CONTAINING A VALUE

The sales manager asks you to narrow the list of London customers so that it displays only Sales Representatives. To accomplish this task, you add a second layer of filtering using a Selection filter. Refer to Figure 43 as you complete Step 2.

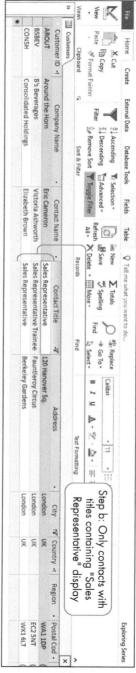

Step b: Only contacts with titles containing "Sales Representative" display

FIGURE 43 Filtered Customers

Access 2016, Windows 10, Microsoft Corporation

a. Click in any field value in the Contact Title field that contains the value **Sales Representative.**

b. Click **Selection** in the Sort & Filter group, click **Contains "Sales Representative"**, and compare your results to those shown in Figure 43.

Three records match the criteria you set. You have applied a second layer of filtering to the customers in London. The second layer further restricts the display to only those customers who have the words Sales Representative contained in their titles. Because you chose Contains as your filter, any representatives with the phrase Sales Representative appear. This includes Victoria Ashworth, who is a Sales Representative Trainee.

> **TROUBLESHOOTING:** If you do not see the record for Victoria Ashworth, you selected Equals "Sales Representative" instead of Contains "Sales Representative". Repeat Steps a and b, making sure you select Contains "Sales Representative".

c. Close the Customers table. Click **Yes** when prompted to save the design changes to the Customers table.

You are asked to provide a list of records that do not match just one set of criteria. You will provide a list of all extended prices less than $50 for a specific sales representative. Use Filter By Form to provide the information when two or more criteria are necessary. You also preview the results in Print Preview to see how the list would print. Refer to Figure 44 as you complete Step 3.

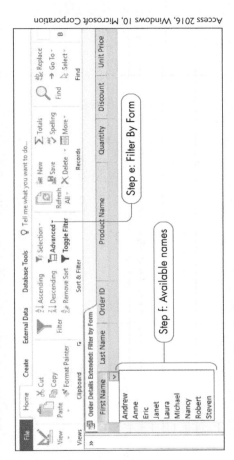

Access 2016, Windows 10, Microsoft Corporation

FIGURE 44 Using Filter By Form

a. Click the **Tables group** in the Navigation Pane to collapse the listed tables.

b. Click the **Queries group** in the Navigation Pane to expand the list of available queries.

c. Locate and double-click **Order Details Extended** to open it.

This query contains information about orders. It has fields containing information about the sales person, the Order ID, the product name, the unit price, quantity ordered, the discount given, and an extended price. The extended price is a field used to total order information.

d. Click **Advanced** in the Sort & Filter group and select **Filter By Form** from the list. The first field, First Name, is active by default.

All of the records are now hidden, and you see only field names and an arrow in the first field. Although you are applying Filter By Form to a query, you can use the same process as applying Filter By Form to a table. You are able to input more than one criterion using Filter By Form.

e. Click the **First Name arrow**.

A list of all available first names appears. Your name should be on the list. Figure 44 shows *Eric Cameron*, which replaced Margaret Peacock in Hands-On Exercise 1.

TROUBLESHOOTING: If you do not see your name and you do see Margaret on the list, you probably skipped steps in Hands-On Exercise 1. Close the query without saving changes, return to the first Hands-On Exercise, and then rework it, making sure not to omit any steps. Then you can return to this location and work the remainder of this Hands-On Exercise.

f. Select your first name from the list.

g. Click in the first row under the Last Name field to reveal the arrow. Locate and select your last name by clicking it.

h. Scroll right until you see the Extended Price field. Click in the first row under the Extended Price field and type **<50**.

This will select all of the items that you ordered where the total was less than 50.

i. Click **Toggle Filter** in the Sort & Filter group.

You have specified which records to include and have executed the filtering by clicking Toggle Filter.

j. Click the **File tab**, click **Print**, and then click **Print Preview**.

You instructed Access to preview the filtered query results. The preview displays the query title as a heading. The current filter is applied, as well as page numbers.

k. Click **Close Print Preview** in the Close Preview group.

l. Close the Order Details Extended query. Click **Yes** when prompted to save your changes.

STEP 4 ≫ SORT TABLE DATA

The Sales Manager is pleased with your work; however, she would like some of the information to appear in a different order. You will now sort the records in the Customers table using the manager's new criteria. Refer to Figure 45 as you complete Step 4.

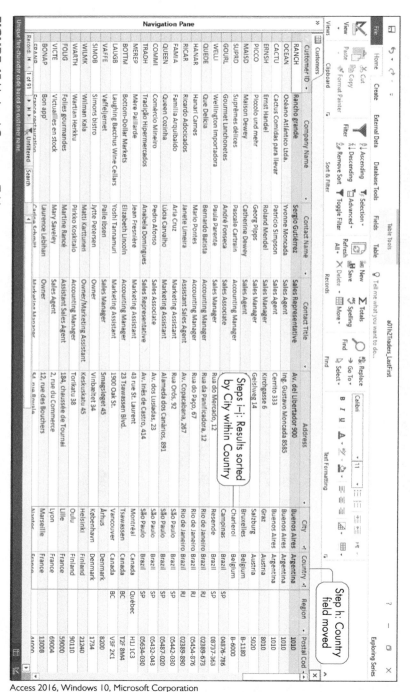

FIGURE 45 Updated Customers Table

a. Click the **Queries group** in the Navigation Pane to collapse the listed queries.

b. Click the **Tables group** in the Navigation Pane to expand the list of available tables and double-click the **Customers table** to open it.

This table contains information about customers. The table is sorted in alphabetical order by Company Name.

Access 2016, Windows 10, Microsoft Corporation

c. Click **Shutter Bar Open/Close** in the Navigation Pane to hide the Navigation Pane.

It will be easier to locate fields in the Customer table if the Navigation Pane is hidden.

d. Click any entry in the Customer ID field. Click **Descending** in the Sort & Filter group on the Home tab.

Sorting in descending order on a text field produces a reverse alphabetical order.

e. Scroll right until you can see both the Country and City fields.

f. Click the **Country column heading.**

The entire field is selected.

g. Click the **Country column heading** again and hold down the **left mouse button.**

A thick line displays on the left edge of the Country field.

h. Check to make sure that you see the thick line. Drag the **Country field** to the left until the thick line moves between the City and Region fields. Release the mouse button and the Country field position moves to the right of the City field.

You moved the Country field next to the City field so that you can easily sort the table based on both fields.

i. Click any city name in the City field and click **Ascending** in the Sort & Filter group.

The City field displays the cities in alphabetical order.

j. Click any country name in the Country field and click **Ascending.**

The countries are sorted in alphabetical order. The cities within each country also are sorted alphabetically. For example, the customer in Graz, Austria, is listed before the customer in Salzburg, Austria.

k. Close the Customers table. Click **Yes** to save the changes to the design of the table.

l. Click **Shutter Bar Open/Close** in the Navigation Pane to show the Navigation Pane.

STEP 5 ≫ **VIEW RELATIONSHIPS**

To further familiarize yourself with the database, you examine the connections between the tables in the Northwind database. Refer to Figure 46 as you complete Step 5.

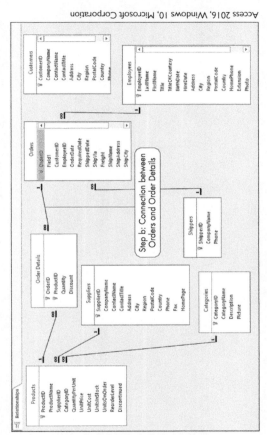

Access 2016, Windows 10, Microsoft Corporation

FIGURE 46 Northwind Relationships

a. Click the **Database Tools tab** and click **Relationships** in the Relationships group.

b. Examine the join lines showing the relationships that connect the various tables. For example, the Orders table is connected to the Order Details table using the OrderID field as the common field.

c. Close the Relationships.

d. Close the database. You will submit this file to your instructor at the end of the last Hands-On Exercise.

Access Database Creation

Now that you have examined the fundamentals of an Access database and explored the power of databases, it is time to create one! In this section, you explore the benefits of creating a database using each of the methods discussed in the next section.

Creating a Database

When you first start Access, Backstage view opens and provides you with three methods for creating a new database. These methods are:

- Create a blank desktop database
- Create a database from a template (note: there will be many templates shown)
- Create a custom web app

Creating a blank desktop database lets you create a database specific to your requirements. Rather than starting from scratch by creating a blank desktop database, you may want to use a template to create a new database. An Access *template* is a predefined database that includes professionally designed tables, forms, reports, and other objects that you can use to jumpstart the creation of your database. Creating a *custom web app* enables you to create a database that you can build and then use and share with others through the Web.

Figure 47 shows the options for creating a custom web app, a blank desktop database, and multiple templates from which you can select the method for which you want to create a database.

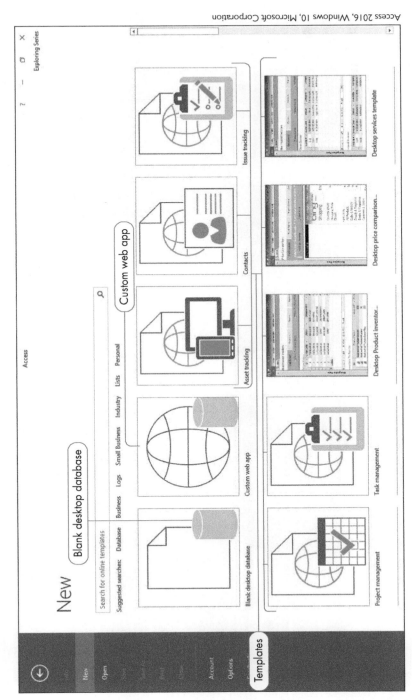

FIGURE 47 Options for Creating a New Database

Create a Blank Desktop Database

Often, if you are migrating from Excel to Access, you would start by creating a blank desktop database. At that point, you could import your existing structure and data into a new table. Another time you might use a blank desktop database is when you are starting a project and want to design your own tables.

When you create a blank desktop database, Access opens to a blank table in Datasheet view where you can add fields or data. You can also refine the table in Design view. You would then create additional tables and objects as necessary. Obviously, this task requires some level of Access knowledge, so unless you have requirements to follow, you may be better served using a template.

To create a blank desktop database, complete the following steps:

1. Open Access. (If Access is already open, click the File tab to open Backstage view and click New.)
2. Click the Blank desktop database tile.
3. Type the file name for the file in the text box, click Browse to navigate to the folder where you want to store the database file, and then click OK.
4. Click Create (see Figure 48).
5. Type data in the empty table that displays.

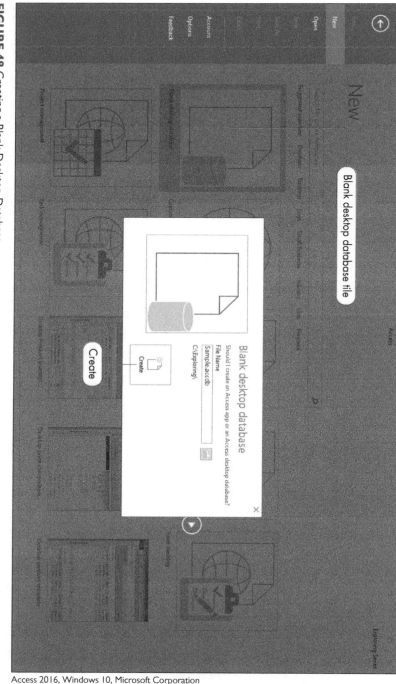

FIGURE 48 Creating a Blank Desktop Database

Access 2016, Windows 10, Microsoft Corporation

Create a Desktop Database Using a Template

 **STEP 1** Using a template to start a database saves you a great deal of creation time. Working with a template can also help a new Access user become familiar with database design. Templates are available from Backstage view, where you can select from a variety of templates or search online for more templates.

Access also provides templates for desktop use.

To create a desktop database from a template, complete the following steps:

1. Open Access. (If Access is already open, click the File tab to open Backstage view and click New.)

2. Click the desktop database template you want to use, or use the search box at the top of the page. Figure 49 shows some examples of templates.

3. Type the file name for the file in the text box, click Browse to navigate to the folder where you want to store the database file, and then click OK.

4. Click Create to download the template.

   The database will be created and will open.

5. Click Enable Content in the Security Warning message bar.

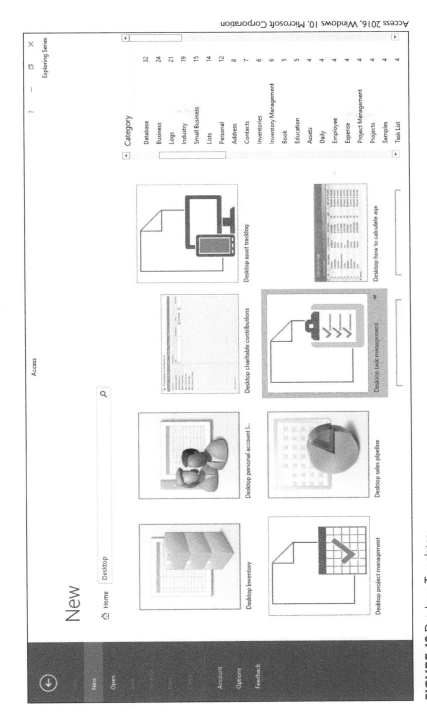

FIGURE 49 Database Templates

Once the database is open, you may see a Getting Started page that includes links you can use to learn more about the database. When finished reviewing the learning materials, close the Getting Started page to view the database. Figure 50 displays the Getting Started page included with the Desktop task management template. Notice the hyperlink to import contacts from Microsoft Outlook. If you use Outlook, this is a nice feature. Close the Getting Started page to return to the database. Because you downloaded a template, some objects will have already been created. You can work with these objects just as you did in the first three sections of this chapter. Edit any object to meet your requirements.

Introduction to Access

FIGURE 50 Getting Started Page for a Template

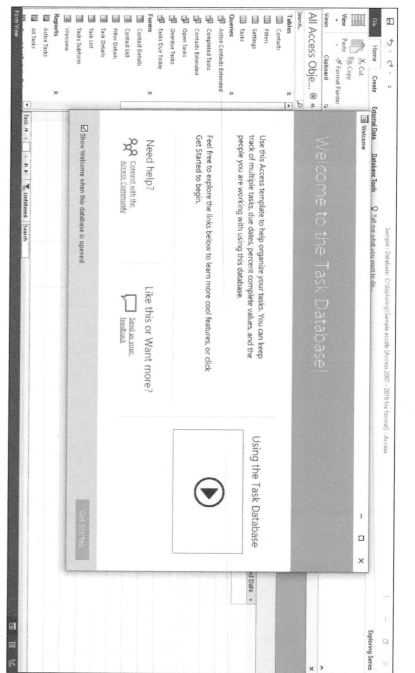

Access 2016, Windows 10, Microsoft Corporation

TIP: CREATE A TEMPLATE FROM A DATABASE

If you have a database you may want to reuse in the future, you can save it as a template. Doing so will enable you to create new databases with the same tables, queries, forms, and reports as the one you have created. You can also reuse parts of the database as application parts.

To create a template from an existing database, click the File tab, click Save As, and then double-click Template. Set options such as the name and description and click OK.

If you check the option for Application Part, this template will also be available under User Templates on the Application Parts menu on the Create tab.

Add Records to a Downloaded Desktop Database

STEP 2 ▶▶ Once a desktop database template has been downloaded, you can use it as you would use any Access database. Figure 51 shows the Desktop Task Management template. Review the objects listed in the Navigation Pane. Once you are familiar with the database design, you can enter your data using a table or form.

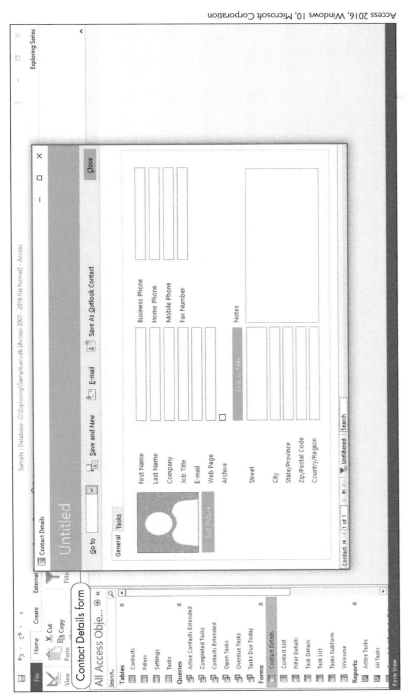

FIGURE 51 Desktop Task Management Database

Explore the Database Objects in a Downloaded Desktop Database Template

One of the reasons to use a template is so you do not have to create any of the objects. Therefore, you will notice each template comes with a varying amount of predefined queries, forms, and reports. Familiarize yourself with the unique features of a template; as they are professionally designed, they are typically well thought out.

Create a Table Using an Application Part

An *application part* enables you to add a set of common Access components to an existing database, such as a table, a form, and a report for a related task. These are provided by Microsoft and offer components (for example, a Contacts table) you can add to an existing database, rather than creating an entirely new database, as shown in Figure 52.

To add an application part to a database, complete the following steps:

1. Click Application Parts in the Templates group on the Create tab.
2. Select one of the options from the list.
3. Respond to the dialog boxes. For example, if you insert an Issues application part, you may be prompted to create a relationship between Issues and an existing table (such as Customers). Setting up a relationship is not required, but may be appropriate.
4. Check the Navigation Pane to verify that the new components were created.

FIGURE 52 Adding an Application Part

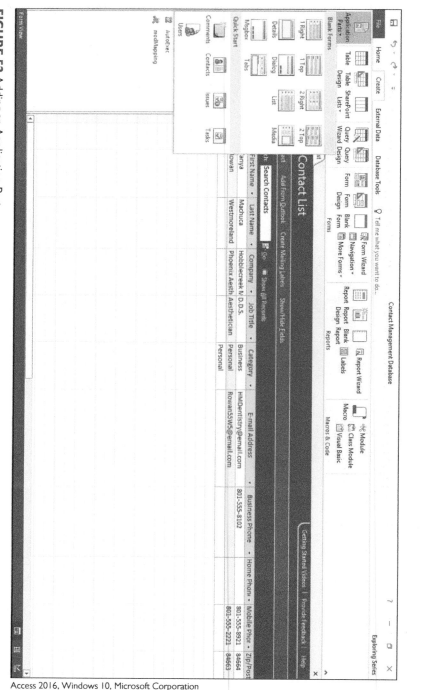

Access 2016, Windows 10, Microsoft Corporation

Create a Web App Using a Template

An Access Web app (or application) is a type of database that lets you build a browser-based database app. You can create a database in the cloud that you and others can access and use simultaneously. This requires that you use a host server such as SharePoint (a Web app platform developed by Microsoft) or Office 365 (a cloud service edition of SharePoint).

Before creating a Web app, ensure that you have access to a host server. In a business environment, this would likely be set up and maintained by your Information Technology department. Your college or university may not give students access to this server. If they do, your professor can give you the information you will need.

To create a Web app using SharePoint, complete the following steps:

1. Click the File tab.
2. Click New.
3. Click Custom web app.
4. Type an App Name.
5. Input the web location (which will be provided by your company's technology professionals or by your professor, if available).
6. Click Create.
7. Create tables. This can be done manually, from a template, or from an existing data source.

In a business environment (and on the Microsoft Office Specialist examination for Access) you may need to migrate the database you have created to a SharePoint server. Doing so is similar to the Save operation covered earlier in the chapter.

To migrate an existing database to a SharePoint server, complete the following steps:

1. Click the File tab.
2. Click Save As.
3. Click SharePoint.
4. Click Save As.
5. Select the location on the SharePoint server where you wish to save your database, and click Save.

As mentioned earlier, SharePoint is typically used more in a corporate environment, so you may not have a SharePoint server available at your college or university.

Quick Concepts

9. What is a custom web app, and what is required to build a custom web app?

10. What are two benefits of using a template to create a database?

11. If you want to add a component to an existing database (such as a Contacts table), what would you use?

Hands-On Exercises

3 Access Database Creation

Skills covered: Create a
Database Using a Template • Add
Records to a Downloaded Desktop
Database • Explore the Database
Objects in a Downloaded Desktop
Database Template

After working with the Northwind database on the job, you decide to use Access to create a personal contact database. Rather than start from a blank table, you use an Access Contact Manager desktop template to make your database creation simpler.

STEP 1 >> CREATE A DATABASE USING A TEMPLATE

You locate an Access desktop template that you can use to create your personal contact database. This template not only allows you to store names, addresses, telephone numbers, and other information, but also lets you categorize your contacts, send email messages, and create maps of addresses. You download and save the template. Refer to Figure 53 as you complete Step 1.

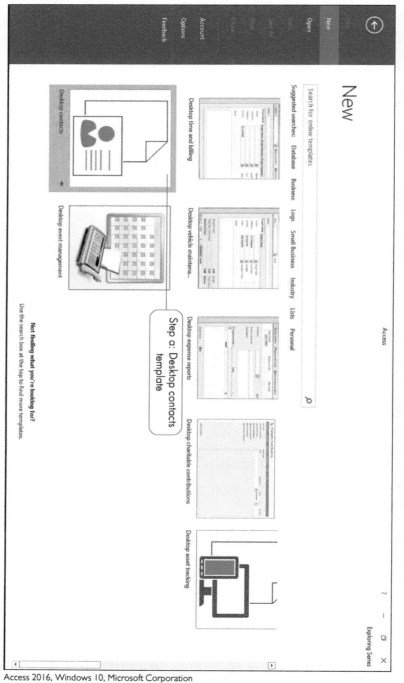

FIGURE 53 Database Templates

Access 2016, Windows 10, Microsoft Corporation

a. Open Access. Scroll down and click the **Desktop contacts** template tile.

> **TROUBLESHOOTING:** If the Desktop contacts template is not visible, you can use the search box at the top of the screen.

b. Click **Browse** to navigate to the folder where you are saving your files, type **a01h3Contacts_LastFirst** as the file name, and then click **OK**.

c. Click **Create** to download the template.

d. Click the *Show Getting Started when this database is opened* check box to deselect it, and close the Getting Started with Contacts page.

The database displays the Contact List form.

e. Click **Enable Content** on the Security Warning message bar.

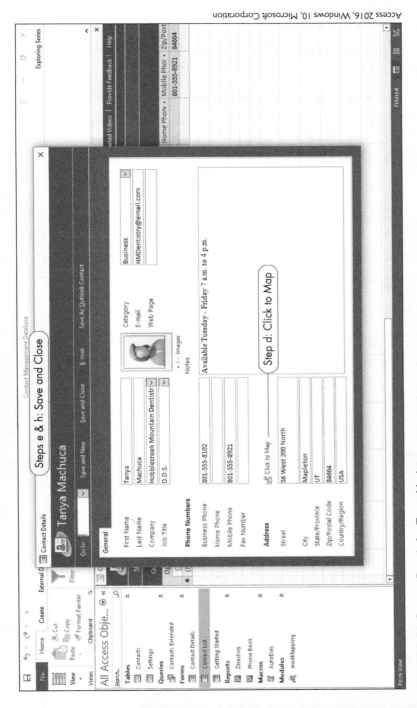

FIGURE 54 Contact Details for Tanya Machuca

Because the database opens in the Contact List form, you decide to begin by entering a contact in the form. Refer to Figure 54 as you complete Step 2.

a. Click in the First Name field of the first record. Type the following information, pressing **Tab** between each entry. Do not press Tab after entering the ZIP/Postal Code.

Field Name	Value to Type
First Name	**Tanya**
Last Name	**Machuca**
Company	**Hobblecreek Mountain Dentistry**
Job Title	**D.D.S.**
Category	**Business** (select from list)
E-mail	**HMDentistry@email.com**
Business Phone	**801-555-8102**
Home Phone	(leave blank)
Mobile Phone	**801-555-8921**
Zip/Postal Code	**84664**

b. Click **Open** in the first field of Dr. Machuca's record.

Open is a hyperlink to a different form in the database. The Contact Details form opens, displaying Dr. Machuca's information. More fields are available for you to use to store information. (Note that this form could also be opened from the Navigation Pane.)

Hands-On Exercise 3

593

c. Type the following additional information to the record:

Field Name	Value to Type
Street	**56 West 200 North**
City	**Mapleton**
State/Province	**UT**
Country/Region	**USA**
Notes	**Available Tuesday - Friday 7 a.m. to 4 p.m.**

d. Click the **Click to Map** hyperlink to view a map to Dr. Machuca's office.

Bing displays a map to the address in the record. You can get directions, locate nearby businesses, and use many other options.

TROUBLESHOOTING: You may be prompted to choose an application. Select any Web browser such as Microsoft Edge from the list.

---

e. Close the map. Click **Save and Close** in the top center of the form to close the Contact Details form.

The record is saved.

f. Click **New Contact** beneath the Contact List title bar.

The Contact Details form opens to a blank record.

g. Type the following information for a new record, pressing **Tab** to move between fields. Some fields will be blank.

Field Name	Value to Type
First Name	**Rowan**
Last Name	**Westmoreland**
Company	**Phoenix Aesthetics**
Job Title	**Aesthetician**
Mobile Phone	**801-555-2221**
Street	**425 North Main Street**
City	**Springville**
State/Province	**UT**
Zip/Postal Code	**84663**
Category	**Personal**
E-mail	**Rowan55W5@email.com**
Notes	**Recommended by Michelle**

h. Click **Save and Close.**

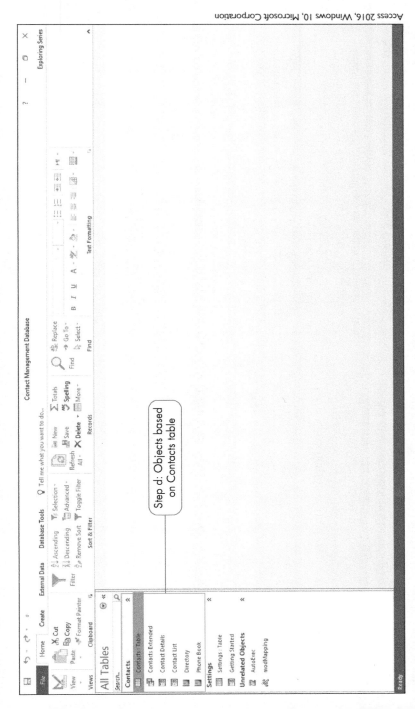

FIGURE 55 Tables and Related Views

STEP 3 ≫ EXPLORE THE DATABASE OBJECTS IN A DOWNLOADED DESKTOP DATABASE TEMPLATE

You explore the objects created by the template so that you understand the organization of the database. Refer to Figure 55 as you complete Step 3.

a. Double-click the **Contacts table** in the Navigation Pane.

The information you entered using the Contact List form and the Contact Details form displays in the Contacts table.

b. Double-click the **Phone Book report** in the Navigation Pane.

The Phone Book report opens displaying the contact name and phone information organized by category.

c. Double-click the **Directory report** in the Navigation Pane.

The Directory report opens, displaying a full alphabetical contact list. The Directory report was designed to display more fields than the Phone Book, but it is not organized by category.

d. Click **All Access Objects** on the Navigation Pane and select **Tables and Related Views**.

You can now see the objects that are based on the Contacts table.

e. Right-click the **Directory report tab** and select **Close All**.

f. Close the database and exit Access. Based on your instructor's directions, submit the following:

a01h1Traders_LastFirst_*CurrentDate*

a01h2Traders_LastFirst

a01h3Contacts_LastFirst

Step d: Objects based on Contacts table

Hands-On Exercise 3

595

Chapter Objectives Review

After reading this chapter, you have accomplished the following objectives:

1. Open, save, and enable content in a database.

- A database is a collection of data organized as meaningful information that can be accessed, managed, stored, queried, sorted, and reported.
- A database management system (DBMS) is a software system that provides the tools to create, maintain, and use a database. Access is the database management system found in business versions of Microsoft Office.
- When a database is first opened, Access displays a message bar with a security warning. Click Enable Content if you trust the database's source.

2. Recognize database object types.

- An Access database is a structured collection of four major types of objects—tables, forms, queries, and reports.
- The foundation of a database is its tables, the objects in which data is stored. Each table in the database has a collection of fields (a piece of information stored in a database, such as a name), which are displayed as columns. Each row is referred to as a record, which is a set of all fields about an entry in the table.
- The primary key in a table is the field (or combination of fields) that uniquely identifies a record in a table (such as a driver's license number).
- A query is a question you ask about the data in your database.
- A form enables simplified entry and modification of data.
- A report contains professional-looking formatted information from underlying tables or queries.
- Examine the Access interface: Objects are organized and listed in the Navigation Pane. Access also uses a Tabbed Documents interface in which each object that is open has its own tab.
- Explore table Datasheet view: Datasheet view is a grid containing fields (columns) and records (rows).
- Navigate through records: Navigation arrows enable you to move through records, with arrows for the first, previous, next, and last records, as well as one to add a new record.
- Explore table Design view: Design view gives you a detailed view of the table's structure and is used to create and modify a table's design by specifying the fields it will contain, the fields' data types, and their associated properties.
- Rename and describe tables: Tables can be renamed as necessary and a description can be added. The description gives the user more information about what an object does.

3. Modify data in table Datasheet view.

- Access works primarily from storage. Records can be added, modified, or deleted in the database, and as the information is entered, it is automatically saved. Undo cannot reverse edits made to multiple records.

4. Add records to a table.

- A pencil symbol displays in the record selector box to indicate when you are in editing mode. Moving to another record saves the changes.

5. Delete records from a table.

- To delete a record, click the record selector and click Delete in the Records group on the Home tab.

6. Use database utilities.

- Back up a database: The Back Up Database utility creates a duplicate copy of the database. This may enable users to recover from failure.
- The Compact and Repair utility reduces the size of a database and fixes any errors that may exist in the file.
- Encrypt a database: Encrypting databases enables you to add a password to a database.
- Print information: Access can create a print copy of your data. Previewing before printing is a good practice to avoid wasting paper.

7. Work with filters.

- A filter displays records based on a set of criteria that is applied to a table to display a subset of records in that table.
- Use a selection filter to find exact matches: A selection filter can be used to find exact matches.
- Use a selection filter to find records containing a value: A selection filter can find partial matches, for example, find values containing a certain phrase.
- Use filter by form: Filter By Form displays records based on multiple criteria and enables the user to apply logical operators and use comparison operators.

8. Perform sorts.

- Sort table data: Sorting changes the order of information, and information may be sorted by one or more fields.
- Data can be sorted ascending (low to high) or descending (high to low).

9. Create a database.

- Creating a blank desktop database: Creating a blank desktop database enables you to create a database specific to your requirements.
- Create a desktop database using a template: A template is a predefined database that includes professionally designed tables, forms, reports, and other objects that you can use to jumpstart the creation of your database.
- Add records to a downloaded desktop database: Once a database has been created, it can be used as any other database is.
- Explore the database objects in a downloaded database template: Once you create a database using a template, explore it and become familiar with the contents.
- Create a table using an application part: If you require a certain type of table (such as Contacts) you can add them using an application part.
- Create a Web app using a template: Creating a custom web app using a template enables you to create a database that you can build and use and share with others through the Web.

Key Terms Matching

Match the key terms with their definitions. Write the key term letter by the appropriate numbered definition.

a. Application part
b. Database
c. Database Management System (DBMS)
d. Datasheet view
e. Design view
f. Field
g. Filter
h. Filter By Form
i. Form
j. Navigation Pane

k. Object
l. Primary key
m. Query
n. Record
o. Relationship
p. Report
q. Selection filter
r. Sort
s. Table
t. Template

1. _____ A filtering method that displays only records that match selected criteria.

2. _____ A filtering method that displays records based on multiple criteria.

3. _____ A main component that is created and used to make a database function, such as a table or form.

4. _____ A method of listing records in a specific sequence (such as alphabetically).

5. _____ A predefined database that includes professionally designed tables, forms, reports, and other objects.

6. _____ A question you ask about the data in your database.

7. _____ An Access interface element that organizes and lists database objects in a database.

8. _____ An Access object that simplifies entering, modifying, and deleting table data.

9. _____ A set of common Access components that can be added to an existing database.

10. _____ An object that contains professional-looking formatted information from underlying tables or queries.

11. _____ An object used to store data, organizing data into columns and rows.

12. _____ Complete set of all the fields about one person, place, event, or concept.

13. _____ The field (or combination of fields) that uniquely identifies each record in a table.

14. _____ View that enables you to create and modify a table design.

15. _____ A collection of data organized as meaningful information that can be accessed, managed, stored, queried, sorted, and reported.

16. _____ A connection between two tables using a common field.

17. _____ A grid that enables you to add, edit, and delete the records of a table.

18. _____ A piece of information stored in a table, such as a company name or city.

19. _____ A software system that provides the tools needed to create, maintain, and use a database.

20. _____ Enables you to specify conditions to display only those records that meet certain conditions.

Multiple Choice

1. Which of the following is an example of an Access object?

   (a) Database
   (b) Field
   (c) Form
   (d) Record

2. Where is data in a database stored?

   (a) Form
   (b) Query
   (c) Report
   (d) Table

3. You edit several records in an Access table. When should you execute the Save command?

   (a) Immediately after you edit a record
   (b) Once at the end of the session
   (c) Records are saved automatically; the save command is not required
   (d) When you close the table

4. Which of the following is *not* true of an Access database?

   (a) Each field has a data type that establishes the kind of data that can be entered.
   (b) Every record in a table has the same fields as every other record.
   (c) Every table in a database contains the same number of records as every other table.
   (d) A primary key uniquely identifies a record.

5. Which of the following is true regarding table views?

   (a) You can add, edit, and delete records using Design view.
   (b) Datasheet view shows a detailed view of the table design.
   (c) Datasheet view provides access to more field properties than Design view.
   (d) Changes made in Datasheet view are automatically saved when you move the insertion point to a different record.

6. Which of the following utilities is used to recover in the event of loss or damage?

   (a) Back Up Database
   (b) Compact and Repair Database
   (c) Database Splitter
   (d) Encrypt Database

7. Which of the following would be matched if you use a Selection filter's exact match option for the name Ann?

   (a) Ann, ANN, and ann
   (b) Danny, Ann, and Anny
   (c) Ann (but not ANN)
   (d) Both a and b

8. Which of the following conditions is available through a Selection filter?

   (a) Equal condition
   (b) Delete condition
   (c) AND condition
   (d) OR condition

9. All of the following statements are true about creating a database *except*:

   (a) Creating a custom web app requires that you use a server (such as SharePoint).
   (b) When creating a blank desktop database, Access opens to a blank table in Datasheet view.
   (c) Using a template to create a database saves time because it includes predefined objects.
   (d) The objects provided in a template cannot be modified.

10. To add a predefined table to an existing database, you should use which of the following?

    (a) Application part
    (b) Blank desktop database
    (c) Custom web app
    (d) Database template

Practice Exercises

■ Replacement Parts

As a recent hire at Replacement Parts, you are tasked with performing updates to the customer database. You have been asked to open the company's database, save it with a new name, and then modify, add, and delete records. You will then back up the database, apply filters and sorts, and use an application part to add a new table that will be used to track customer shipping and receiving complaints. Refer to Figure 56 as you complete the exercise.

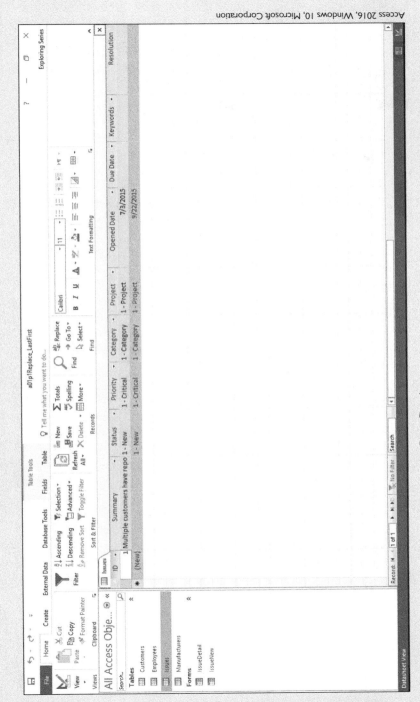

FIGURE 56 Issues Table Added to Replacement Parts Database

a. Open the *a01p1Replace* file. Save the database as **a01p1Replace_LastFirst**. Click **Enable Content** on the message bar.

b. Double-click the **Manufacturers table** to open the table in Datasheet view. Locate record 800552 (Haas). Change the name to **Haas International** and the CountyOfOrigin to **Austria**.

c. Type the following new records:

MfgID	ManufacturerName	CountryOfOrigin	EmployeeID
801411	Bolshoy Fine China	Russia	817080
801422	Tejada and Sons	Dominican Republic	816680
801433	Lubitz UK	England	817580

d. Delete record **800661** (John Bradshaw).

e. Close the Manufacturers table.

f. Click the **File tab**, click **Save As**, and then double-click **Back Up Database**. Accept the default backup file name and click **Save**.

g. Double-click the **Customers table** to open the table in Datasheet view.

h. Click the **State field** for the first record (Diego Martinez). Click **Selection** in the Sort & Filter group, and then click **Equals "OR"** to display the two customers in Oregon. Close the table, selecting **Save** when prompted.

i. Double-click the **Employees table** to open the table in Datasheet view.

j. Click the **plus sign** ⊞ next to Alfonso Torres. Notice he is assigned as the representative for the manufacturer Antarah.

This information is available due to the relationship already created in the database between Employees and Manufacturers.

k. Click **Advanced** in the Sort & Filter group on the Home tab, and select **Filter By Form**. Click in the Salary field. Type **>60000** and click **Toggle Filter** in the Sort & Filter group on the Home tab to apply the filter. Six employees are displayed. Close the table, selecting **Save** when prompted.

l. Double-click the **Manufacturers table** to open the table in Datasheet view.

m. Click any value in the Manufacturer Name field. Click **Ascending** in the Sort & Filter group to sort the table by the name of the manufacturer. Close the table, selecting **Save** when prompted.

n. Click **Application Parts** in the Templates group on the Create tab. Select **Issues**. Select the option for "There is no relationship." Click **Create**.

o. Double-click the **Issues table** to open the table in Datasheet view.

p. Add a new record, typing **Multiple customers have reported damaged goods received in Denton, Texas,** in the Summary field. Leave all other fields as the default values. Compare your results to Figure 56.

q. Close the database and exit Access. Based on your instructor's directions, submit the following:
a01p1Replace_LastFirst
a01p1Replace_LastFirst_CurrentDate

2 Custom Coffee

The Custom Coffee Company provides coffee, tea, and snacks to offices in Miami. Custom Coffee also provides and maintains the equipment for brewing the beverages. To improve customer service, the owner recently had an Access database created to keep track of customers, orders, and products. This database will replace the Excel spreadsheets currently maintained by the office manager. The company hired you to verify and input all the Excel data into the Access database. Refer to Figure 57 as you complete the exercise.

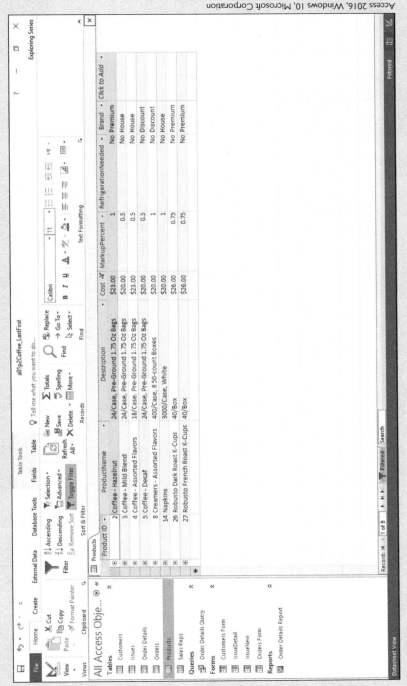

Access 2016, Windows 10, Microsoft Corporation

FIGURE 57 Filtered Products Table

a. Open the *a01p2Coffee* file and save the database as **a01p2Coffee_LastFirst**. Click **Enable Content** on the message bar.

b. Click the **Database Tools tab** and click **Relationships** in the Relationships group. Review the table relationships. Notice the join line between the Customers and Orders tables.

c. Click **Close** in the Relationships group.

d. Double-click the **Sales Reps table** to open it in Datasheet view. For rep number 2, replace **YourFirstName** and **YourLastName** with your first and last names. For example, as the Access author, I would type *Eric* in place of YourFirstName and *Cameron* in place of YourLastName. Close the table by clicking **Close** on the right side of the Sales Reps window.

e. Double-click the **Customers table** to open it in Datasheet view. Click **New** in the Records group. Add a new record by typing the following information; press **Tab** after each field:

Customer Name:	**Bavaro Driving School**
Contact:	**Ricky Watters**
Address1:	**1 Clausen Way**
Address2:	**Floor 2**
City:	**South Bend**

State: IN
Zip Code: 46614
Phone: (857) 519-6661
Credit Rating: A
Sales Rep ID: 2

Notice the pencil symbol in the record selector for the new record. This symbol indicates the new record has not been saved. Press **Tab**. The pencil symbol disappears, and the new customer is automatically saved to the table.

f. Click the **City field** for the second record (South Bend). Click **Selection** in the Sort & Filter group, and select **Equals "South Bend"** to display the four customers located in the town of South Bend.

g. Save and close the table by clicking **Close** on the right side of the Customers window, and clicking **Yes** when asked if you want to save the changes.

h. Double-click the **Products** table to open it in Datasheet view. Click **New** in the Records group. Add a new record by typing the following information:

Product ID: **26**
ProductName: **Robusto Dark Roast K-Cups**
Description: **40/Box**
Cost: **26**
MarkupPercent: **.75**
RefrigerationNeeded   **No**
Brand   **Premium**

i. Add a second product using the following information:

Product ID: **27**
ProductName: **Robusto French Roast K-Cups**
Description: **40/Box**
Cost: **26**
MarkupPercent: **.75**
RefrigerationNeeded   **No**
Brand   **Premium**

j. Click **Advanced** in the Sort & Filter group and select **Filter By Form**. Type **>=20** in the Cost field and click **Toggle Filter** in the Sort & Filter group. All products costing $20 or more (there will be 8) display. See Figure 57.

k. Save and close the table by clicking **Close** on the right side of the Products window, and clicking Yes when asked if you want to save the changes.

l. Click the **File tab**, click **Save As**, and then double-click **Back Up Database**. Accept the default backup file name and click **Save**.

m. Click **Application Parts** in the Templates group of the Create tab. Select **Issues**. Click **Next** to accept the default relationship. Select **CustomerName** as the Field from 'Customers', select **Sort Ascending** from Sort this field, and then type **Customer** as the name for the lookup column. Click Create.

n. Double-click the **Issues table** to open it in Datasheet view.

o. Select **Advantage Sales** for the Customer and type **Customer reports hazelnut coffee delivered instead of decaf** in the Summary field. Leave all other fields as the default values.

p. Close the database and exit Access. Based on your instructor's directions, submit the following: a01p2Coffee_LastFirst a01p2Coffee_LastFirst_CurrentDate

3 Healthy Living

FROM SCRATCH

You and two friends from your gym have decided to use Access to help you reach your weight goals. You decide to use the Access Nutrition template to help you get organized. Refer to Figure 58 as you complete this exercise.

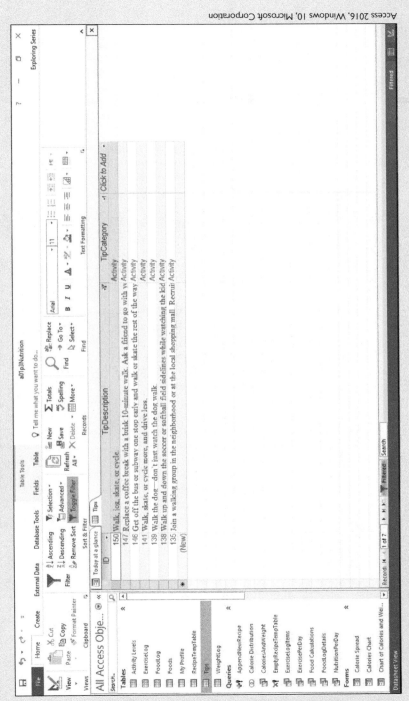

FIGURE 58 Filtered Tips Table

a. Open Access and click the **Desktop Nutrition tracking** template in Backstage view.

b. Type **a01p3Nutrition_LastFirst** in the File name box. Click **Browse**. Navigate to the location where you are saving your files in the File New Database dialog box, click **OK** to close the dialog box, and then click **Create** to create the new database.

c. Click **Enable Content** on the message bar. Double-click the **My Profile** table in the Navigation Pane to open it in Datasheet view.

d. Delete the existing record.

e. Type the following information in as a new record, pressing **Tab** between each field:

Sex:	**Male**
Height:	**64**
Weight:	**190**
Age:	**48**
Lifestyle:	**Lightly Active**
Goal:	**Lose weight**

f. Click **New** in the Records group. Type the following information, pressing **Tab** between each field:

Sex:	**Male**
Height:	**69**
Weight:	**140**
Age:	**45**
Lifestyle:	**Moderately Active**
Goal:	**Gain weight**

g. Click **New** in the Records group. Type the following information, pressing **Tab** between each field:

Sex:	**Female**
Height:	**66**
Weight:	**140**
Age:	**40**
Lifestyle:	**Moderately Active**
Goal:	**Maintain my weight**

h. Close the table by clicking **Close** on the right side of the My Profile window.

i. Double-click the **Foods table.** Click **Advanced** in the Records group and then select **Filter By Form.**

j. Click the **Calories field** for the first record. Type **<200** in the Calories field and **>=15** in the Fiber [grams] field. Click **Toggle Filter** in the Sort & Filter group.

You will have a list of all high = fiber, low = calorie foods in the database (there are three).

k. Save and close the table by clicking **Close** on the right side of the Foods window, and clicking **Yes** when asked if you want to save the changes.

l. Double-click the **Tips table** to open it in Datasheet view.

m. Click in the first **TipCategory.** Click **Ascending** in the Sort & Filter group to sort the tips in alphabetical order.

n. Highlight the word **Walk** in the fifth record (ID #138). Make sure you do not highlight the space after the word Walk when you highlight. Click **Selection** in the Sort & Filter group, and select **Contains "Walk".**

Seven tips appear that contain the word walk. See Figure 58.

o. Save and close the table by clicking **Close** on the right side of the Tips window, and clicking **Yes** when asked if you want to save the changes.

p. Click the **File tab,** click **Save As,** and then double-click **Back Up Database.** Use the default backup file name.

q. Close the database and exit Access. Based on your instructor's directions, submit the following:

a01p3Nutrition_LastFirst
a01p3Nutrition_LastFirst
a01p3Nutrition_LastFirst_*CurrentDate*

Mid-Level Exercises

■ Sunshine Mental Health Services

Sunshine Mental Health Services provides counseling and medication services. They have recently expanded their database to include patients in addition to the staff. You were hired to replace their former Information Technology support staff member. You will work to update the data in the database, familiarize yourself with the table relationships, filter and sort a table, and add a table to keep track of user accounts.

a. Open the *a01m1Sunshine* file and save the database as **a01m1Sunshine_LastFirst**. Click **Enable Content** on the Security Warning message bar.

b. Open the **Staff table** in Datasheet view.

c. Locate the record for Kovit Ang (StaffID 80073). Replace his Address with **11 Market Street**, replace his City with **Harrison**, and his ZIPCode with **04040**. Leave all other fields with their current values.

d. Add yourself as a new staff member. Type a StaffID of **99999** and type your name in the FullName field. Type **1 Clinton Terrace** for your Address, **Harrison** as your City, **ME** as your State, and **04040** as your ZIP. Type a JobCode of **300**, a Salary of **48500**, and a 401k contribution of **0.02**. Click the box in the Active field so a check box appears in the box.

e. Delete record **80399** (Stan Marsh).

f. Sort the table by Salary in descending order. Save and close the table.

g. Click **Relationships** in the Relationships group on the Database Tools tab and notice the relationship between the Position table and the Staff table, and the relationship between the Staff table and Patients table. Each position has staff associated with it, and staff members have patients associated with them. Close the Relationships window.

h. Rename the **Pos table** to **Position**. Add a description to the table stating **This table contains a list of all available job titles at the company.** Click **OK**.

i. Open the **Position table** in Datasheet view. Click the **plus sign** next to JobCode 100 (Social Worker). Notice seven social workers are employed by the company. Click the **plus sign** next to JobCode 300 (IT Support). Only your name should appear. Close the table.

j. Open the **Patients table** in Datasheet view. Use a Selection filter to show all patients associated with StaffID **80073**. Save and close the table.

k. Open the **Staff table** in Datasheet view. Use Filter By Form to display all staff members who earn a salary of more than **80000**. Toggle the filter to verify the results. Save and close the table.

l. Back up the database. Accept the default file name.

m. Add a **Users application part** to the database. Change the relationship so there is One 'Staff' to many 'Users' by clicking the arrow next to Patients and selecting **Staff**. Click **Next**. Select the **FullName** field from 'Staff', choose the **Sort Ascending** option, and name the lookup column **User**. Click **Create**.

n. Open the **Users table** in Datasheet view.

o. Select **Adolfo Ortiz** in the User field. Type **aortiz@sunshinementalhealth.org** for Email and **aortiz** for Login. Leave the FullName blank. Close the table.

p. Create a form based on the Patients table using the Form button in the Forms group of the Create tab. Save the form as **Patient Data Entry**.

q. Switch to Form view of the form. Delete the phone number for PatientID **1** (Minoru Kobayashi). Close the form.

r. Close the database and exit Access. Based on your instructor's directions, submit the following:
a01m1Sunshine_LastFirst
a01m1Sunshine_LastFirst_CurrentDate

2 National Conference

ANALYSIS CASE

The Association of Higher Education will host its National Conference on your campus next year. To facilitate the conference, the Information Technology department has replaced last year's Excel spreadsheets with an Access database containing information on the rooms, speakers, and sessions. Your assignment is to create a room itinerary that will list all of the sessions, dates, and times for each room. The list will be posted on the door of each room for the duration of the conference.

a. Open the *a01m2NatConf* file and save the database as **a01m2NatConf_LastFirst**. Click **Enable Content** on the Security Warning message bar.

b. Open **Relationships**.

c. Review the objects and relationships in the database. Notice that there is a relationship between Speakers and SessionSpeaker. Close the relationships.

d. Open the **SessionSpeaker table**. Scroll to the first blank record at the bottom of the table and type a new record using SpeakerID **99** and SessionID **09**. (Note: Speaker 99 does not exist.) How does Access respond? Press **Escape** twice to cancel your change.

e. Open the **Speakers table**. Replace *YourFirstName* with your first name and *YourLastName* with your last name. Close the Speakers table.

f. Open the **Sessions table** and use a Selection filter to identify the sessions that take place in room 101.

g. Sort the filtered results in ascending order by the **SessionTitle** field. Save and close the table.

h. Open the **Master List - Sessions and Speakers** report. Right-click the **Master List - Sessions and Speakers** tab and select **Report View**.

i. Apply a filter that limits the report to sessions in **Room 101** only. The process will be similar to applying a filter to a table.

j. View the report in Print Preview. Close Print Preview and close the report.

k. Back up the database. Use the default backup file name.

l. Open the *a01m2Analysis* document in Word and save as **a01m2Analysis_LastFirst**. Use the database objects you created to answer the questions. Save and close the document.

m. Close the database and exit Access. Based on your instructor's directions, submit the following:
a01m2NatConf_LastFirst
a01m2NatConf_LastFirst_CurrentDate
a01m2Analysis_LastFirst

DISCOVER ★ ⊞

3 New Castle County Technical Services

RUNNING CASE

New Castle County Technical Services (NCCTS) provides technical support for a number of companies in the greater New Castle County, Delaware, area. They are working to move their record keeping to an Access database. You will add, update, and delete some records, add filters, and create a backup.

This project is a running case.

a. Open the database *a01m3NCCTS* and save the database as **a01m3NCCTS_LastFirst**. Click **Enable Content** on the Security Warning message bar.

b. Open the **Call Types table** in Datasheet view. Type the following rates for the HourlyRate field and then close the table:

Description	HourlyRate
Hardware Support	30
Software Support	25
Network Troubleshooting	40
Network Installation	40
Training	50

Description	HourlyRate
Security Camera Maintenance	40
Virus Removal	25
Disaster Recovery	60
VoIP Service	45
Other	35

c. Open the **Reps table** in Datasheet view. Add a new record, filling in the value **8** for the RepID field, your last name as the rep's last name, and your first name as the rep's first name.

d. Sort the Reps table by **LastName** in ascending order. Close the table.

e. Open the **Customers table** in Datasheet view. Locate the record for **Edwin VanCleef** (PC030). Delete the entire record.

f. Click in the **City field** for SVC Pharmacy. Use the Selection filter to only show customers who are located in the city of **Newark**. Save and close the table.

g. Open the **Calls table** in Datasheet view. Use **Filter By Form** to filter the HoursLogged field so only calls with 10 or more hours logged on the call (**>=10**) are displayed. Save and close the table.

h. Back up the database, using the default name.

i. Close the database and exit Access. Based on your instructor's directions, submit the following:

a01m3NCCTS_LastFirst

a01m3NCCTS_LastFirst_CurrentDate

Beyond the Classroom

Creating a Student Database

GENERAL CASE

FROM SCRATCH

Create a new blank desktop database, name the file **a01b1Students_LastFirst**, and then save the database in the location where you are saving your files. Create a new table using the Contacts application part. Delete the Company, JobTitle, BusinessPhone, HomePhone, FaxNumber, Country/Region, WebPage, Attachments, ContactName, and FileAs fields from the Company table. Save the table, then switch to Datasheet view. Enter the information about at least five students, fictional or real, including your own information. Enter their major in the Notes field. Sort the table by last name in ascending order. Create a filter to display students with your major. Delete all queries, forms, and reports. Close the database and exit Access. Based on your instructor's directions, submit a01b1Students_LastFirst.

Lugo Web Hosting

DISASTER RECOVERY

Your Access database has become corrupted and you are in the process of restoring it from a backup from two weeks ago. In the last two weeks, there have been only a few changes. All users who previously had a 900 GB quota have had their quotas increased to 1 TB. In addition, all users who were previously on the server named Aerelon have been moved to another server, Caprica. You have determined you can use filters to help fix the data in the Users table. Open the *a01b2Lugo_Backup* file and save the database as **a01b2Lugo_LastFirst**. Apply filters to show users who meet the conditions above and then manually change the data for each user. Sort the table by the server in ascending order. Close the database and exit Access. Based on your instructor's directions, submit a01b2Lugo_LastFirst.

Capstone Exercise

You are employed as a technical supervisor at a chain of book-stores. One of the store managers has expressed confusion about Access. You have offered to train her on the basics of Access. To avoid mistakes in the main database, you will save the file with a new name. You will then train her on the basics of the data-base system, including making data modifications, sorting and filtering, adding an application part, and creating a backup.

Modify Data in a Table

You will open an original database file and save the database with a new name. You will then demonstrate adding, updating, and deleting information.

a. Open the *a01c1Books* file and save the database as **a01c1Books_LastFirst.**

b. Open the **Publishers table** in Datasheet view. Notice that some of the publisher city and state information is missing. Update the database with the information below and close the table.

PubID	PubName	PubCity	PubState
DC	DC Comics	New York	NY
SM	St. Martin	Boston	MA
TB	Triumph Books	Chicago	IL
TL	Time Life	Pueblo	CO

c. Change the PubCity for Pearson to **Hoboken.**

d. Close the Publishers table.

e. Open the **Author table** in Datasheet view.

f. Navigate to the last record (Author ID of XXXX01) and replace **YourFirstName** with your first name and **YourLastName** with your last name. Close the table.

g. Open the **Author table** again and notice the changes you made have been stored.

h. Click the **plus sign** next to your name. Notice the book Social Media: A Student's View is listed. Close the table again.

i. Open the **Books table** in Datasheet view. Notice the book with ISBN 9780809400775 (American Cooking: The Northwest) has no items in stock. Delete this record.

j. Close the table.

Sort a Table and Apply a Selection Filter

You will sort the publisher's table by name and then apply a filter to display only publishers located in New York.

a. Open the **Publishers table** in Datasheet view. Notice Time Life appears after Triumph Books. This is because the table is sorted by the PubID field.

b. Click in any record in the PubName field and sort the field in ascending order.

c. Apply a Selection filter to display only publishers with a PubCity equal to **New York.**

d. Close the table and save the changes.

Use Filter By Form

You will obtain a list of all books with more than 50 units in stock. This will help the management decide on what books to put on sale. You will use Filter By Form to accomplish this. You will also demonstrate how filters are saved.

a. Open the **Books table** in Datasheet view.

b. Use Filter By Form to display books with more than 50 units in stock. Save and close the table.

c. Open the **Books table** in Datasheet view. Click **Toggle Filter** in the Sort & Filter group to demonstrate that the filter is saved.

Back Up a Database and Add an Application Part

You will demonstrate adding an application part to the manager to show how tables are created. You will first back the database up to reinforce the importance of backing up the data.

a. Create a backup copy of your database, accepting the default file name.

b. Add a Comments application part, selecting the option **One 'Books' to many 'Comments'.** Select the **Title field** for the Field from Books and **Sort Ascending** for Sort this field. Name the lookup column **Book.**

c. Open the **Comments table** in Datasheet view. Add a new comment. Select **Social Media: A Student's View** for the Book. Use the current date and add **A fun and insightful book!** for the Comment field.

d. Close the database and exit Access. Based on your instructor's directions, submit the following:

a01c1Books_LastFirst
a01c1Books_LastFirst_*CurrentDate*

Glossary

Access The database management system included in the Office suite.

Application part A feature that enables you to add a set of common Access components to an existing database, such as a table, a form, and a report for a related task.

Back Up Database A utility that creates a duplicate copy of the entire database to protect from loss or damage.

Compact and Repair Database A utility that reduces the size of a database and fixes any errors that may exist in the file.

Custom Web app A feature which enables users to create a database that you can build and then use and share with others through the Web.

Database A collection of data organized as meaningful information that can be accessed, managed, stored, queried, sorted, and reported.

Database Management System (DBMS) A software system that provides the tools needed to create, maintain, and use a database.

Database Splitter A utility that puts the tables in one file (the back-end database), and the queries, forms, and reports in a second file (the front-end database).

Datasheet view A grid containing fields (columns) and records (rows) used to view, add, edit, and delete records.

Design view A view which gives users a detailed view of the table's structure and is used to create and modify a table's design by specifying the fields it will contain, the fields' data types, and their associated properties.

Field A category of information stored in a table (such as Customer ID or Company Name).

Field Property A feature which defines the characteristics of a field in more detail.

Filter A feature which allows users to specify conditions to display only those records that meet those conditions.

Filter By Form A more versatile method of selecting data, enabling users to display records based on multiple criteria.

Form An object which simplified entry and modification of data.

Macro A stored series of commands that carry out an action; often used to automate simple tasks.

Module An advanced object written using the VBA (Visual Basic for Applications) programming language.

Navigation Pane An Access interface element that organizes and lists the objects in an Access database.

Object A component created and used to make the database function (such as a table, query, form, or report).

Primary key The field (or combination of fields) that uniquely identifies each record in a table.

Query A question users ask about the data in a database.

Record A complete set of all the fields about one person, place, event, or concept.

Relationship A connection between two tables using a common field.

Report An object which contains professional-looking formatted information from underlying tables or queries.

Selection Filter A method of selecting that displays only the records that match a criterion you select.

Sort A feature which lists records in a specific sequence.

Table The location where all data is stored in a database; organizes data into columns and rows.

Template A predefined database that includes professionally designed tables, forms, reports, and other objects that you can use to jumpstart the creation of your database.

Tables and Queries in Relational Databases

From Access Chapter 2 of *Microsoft® Office 2016, Volume 1*. Mary Anne Poatsy, Mulbery, Krebs, Hogan, Cameron, Davidson. Lau, Lawson, Williams, and Robert T. Grauer. Copyright © 2017 by Pearson Education, Inc. Published by Pearson Prentice Hall. All Rights Reserved.

Download student resources at http://www.pearsonhighered.com/exploring.

Tables and Queries in Relational Databases

LEARNING OUTCOMES

- You will create and modify tables for data input and organization.
- You will develop queries to extract and present data.

OBJECTIVES & SKILLS: After you read this chapter, you will be able to:

Table Design, Creation, and Modification

OBJECTIVE 1: DESIGN A TABLE

OBJECTIVE 2: CREATE AND MODIFY TABLES AND WORK WITH DATA

Create a Table in Datasheet View, Delete a Field, Set a Table's Primary Key, Work with Field Properties, Create a New Field in Design View, Modify the Table in Datasheet View

HANDS-ON EXERCISE 1:

Table Design, Creation, and Modification

Multiple-Table Databases

OBJECTIVE 3: SHARE DATA

Import Excel Data, Import Data from an Access Database, Modify an Imported Table's Design, Add Data to an Imported Table

OBJECTIVE 4: ESTABLISH TABLE RELATIONSHIPS

Establish Table Relationships, Enforce Referential Integrity

HANDS-ON EXERCISE 2:

Multiple-Table Databases

Single-Table Queries

OBJECTIVE 5: CREATE A SINGLE-TABLE QUERY

Create a Single-Table Query

OBJECTIVE 6: USE THE QUERY WIZARD

Use the Query Wizard

OBJECTIVE 7: SPECIFY QUERY CRITERIA FOR DIFFERENT DATA TYPES

Specify Query Criteria

OBJECTIVE 8: UNDERSTAND QUERY SORT ORDER

Specify Query Sort Order

OBJECTIVE 9: RUN, COPY, AND MODIFY A QUERY

Run, Copy, and Modify a Query; Change Query Data

HANDS-ON EXERCISE 3:

Single-Table Queries

Multitable Queries

OBJECTIVE 10: CREATE A MULTITABLE QUERY

Add Additional Tables to a Query, Create a Multitable Query

OBJECTIVE 11: MODIFY A MULTITABLE QUERY

Modify a Multitable Query, Summarize Data Using a Multitable Query

HANDS-ON EXERCISE 4:

Multitable Queries

CASE STUDY | Bank Audit

During a year-end review, a bank auditor uncovers mishandled funds at Commonwealth Federal Bank in Wilmington, Delaware. In order to analyze the data in more detail, the auditor asks you to create an Access database so he can review the affected customers, the compromised accounts, and the branches involved.

As you begin, you realize that some of the data are contained in external Excel and Access files that you decide to import directly into the new database. Importing from Excel and Access is fairly common, and will help to avoid errors that are associated with data entry. Once the data have been imported, you will use queries to determine exactly which records are relevant to the investigation.

This chapter introduces the Bank database case study to present the basic principles of table and query design. Once the new database is created and all the data are entered, you will help the auditor answer questions by creating and running queries. The value of that information depends entirely on the quality of the underlying data—the tables.

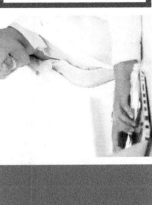

Syda Productions/
Shutterstock

Designing Databases and Extracting Data

Number of Customer Accounts

Customer ID	Number of Accounts
30001	5
30002	1
30003	4
30004	4
30005	4
30006	1
30007	2
30009	2
30010	2
30011	3

Customers
- CustomerID
- FirstName
- LastName
- Street
- City
- State
- Zip
- Phone

Accounts
- AccountID
- CustomerID
- BranchID
- Balance
- OpenDate

Branch
- BranchID
- Manager
- Location
- StartDate

FIGURE 1 Bank Audit Database

CASE STUDY | Bank Audit

Starting Files	File to be Submitted
Blank desktop database a02h2Accounts a02h2Customers	**a02h4Bank_LastFirst**

Tables and Queries in Relational Databases • Access 2016

Table Design, Creation, and Modification

Good database design begins with the tables. Tables provide the framework for all of the activities you perform in a database. If the framework is poorly designed, the database will not function as expected. Whether you are experienced in designing tables or are a new database designer, the process should not be done haphazardly. You should follow a systematic approach when creating tables for a database.

In this section, you will learn the essentials of good table design. After developing and analyzing the table design on paper, you will implement that design in Access. In this chapter you will learn to refine them by changing the properties of various fields.

Designing a Table

Recall that a table is a collection of records, with each record made up of a number of fields. During the table design process, consider the specific fields you will need in each table; list the proposed fields with the correct tables, and determine what type of data each field will store (numbers, dates, pictures, etc.) The order of the fields within the table and the specific field names are not significant at this stage as they can be changed later. What is important is that the tables contain all necessary fields so that the database can produce the required information later.

For example, consider the design process necessary to create a database for a bank. Most likely you have a bank account and know that the bank maintains data about you. Your bank has your name, address, phone number, and Social Security number. It also knows which accounts you have (checking, savings, money market), if you have a credit card with that bank, and what its balance is. Additionally, your bank keeps information about its branches around the city or state. If you think about the data your bank maintains, you can make a list of the categories of data needed to store that information. These categories for the bank—customers, accounts, branches—become the tables in the bank's database. A bank's customer list is an example of a table; it contains a record for each bank customer.

After the tables have been identified, add the necessary fields using these six guidelines, which are discussed in detail in the following paragraphs:

- Include the necessary data.
- Design for now and for the future.
- Store data in their smallest parts.
- Determine primary keys.
- Link tables using common fields.
- Design to accommodate calculations.

Figure 2 shows a customer table and two other tables found in a sample Bank database. It also lists fields that would be needed in each table.

Customers Table

| CustomerID |
| FirstName |
| LastName |
| Street |
| City |
| State |
| Zip |
| Phone |

Accounts Table

| AccountID |
| CustomerID |
| BranchID |
| OpenDate |

Branch Table

| BranchID |
| Manager |
| Location |
| StartDate |

FIGURE 2 Rough Draft of Tables and Fields in a Sample Bank Database

Include Necessary Data

A good way to determine what data are necessary in tables is to consider the output you will need from your database. You will probably need to create professional-looking reports for others, so begin by creating a rough draft of the reports you will need. Then design tables that contain the fields necessary to create those reports. In other words, ask yourself what information will be expected from the database (output) and determine the data required (input) to produce that information. Consider, for example, the tables and fields in Figure 2. Is there required information that could not be generated from those tables?

- You will be able to determine how long a customer has banked with the branch because the date he or she opened the account is stored in the Accounts table, which will connect to the Customers and Branch tables.

- You will be able to determine which branch a customer uses because the Accounts table includes both the CustomerID and the BranchID. The Accounts table will eventually connect to both the Customers and Branch tables, making it possible to gather this information.

- You will not be able to generate the monthly bank statement. In order to generate a customer bank statement (showing all deposits and withdrawals for the month), you would need to add an additional table—to track activity for each account.

- You will not be able to email a customer because the Customers table does not contain an email field at this time.

If you discover a missing field, such as the email field, you can add it during the initial design process or later.

Design for Now and for the Future

As the information requirements of an organization evolve over time, the database systems that hold the data must change as well. When designing a database, try to anticipate the future needs of the system and build in the flexibility to satisfy those demands. For example, you may also decide to create additional fields for future use (such as an

Table Design, Creation, and Modification • Access 2016

615

email or customer photo field). However, additional fields will also require more storage space, which you will need to calculate, especially when working with larger databases. Good database design must balance the data collection needs of the company with the cost associated with collection and storage. Plans must also include the frequency and cost necessary to modify and update the database.

In the Bank database, for example, you would store each customer's name, address, and home phone number. You would also want to store additional phone numbers for many customers—a cell phone number, and perhaps a work number. As a database designer, you will design the tables to accommodate multiple entries for similar data.

Store Data in Their Smallest Parts

The table design in Figure 2 divides a customer's name into two fields (FirstName and LastName) to store each value individually. You might think it easier to use a single field consisting of both the first and last name, but that approach is too limiting. Consider a list of customer names stored as a single field:

- Sue Grater
- Rick Grater
- Nancy Gallagher
- Harry Weigner
- Barb Shank
- Pete Shank

The first problem in this approach is the lack of flexibility: You could not easily create a salutation for a letter using the form *Dear Sue* or *Dear Ms. Gallagher* because the first and last names are not accessible individually.

A second difficulty is that the list of customers cannot be easily displayed in alphabetical order by last name because the last name begins in the middle of the field. The most common way to sort names is by the last name, which you can do more efficiently if the last name is stored as a separate field.

Think of how an address might be used. The city, state, and postal code should always be stored as separate fields. You may need to select records from a particular state or postal code, which will be easier if you store the data as separate fields.

Determine Primary Keys

When designing your database tables, it is important to determine the primary key, the field that will uniquely identify each record in a table. For example, in Figure 2, the CustomerID field will uniquely identify each customer in the database.

Plan for Common Fields Between Tables

As you create the tables and fields for the database, keep in mind that some tables will be joined in relationships using common fields. Creating relationships will help you to extract data from more than one table when creating queries, forms, and reports. For example, you will be able to determine which customers have which accounts by joining the Customers and Accounts tables. For now, you should name the common fields the same (although that is not a firm requirement in Access). For example, CustomerID in the Customers table will join to the CustomerID field in the Accounts table. Draw a line between common fields to indicate the joins, as shown in Figure 3. These join lines will be created in Access when you learn to create table relationships later in the chapter.

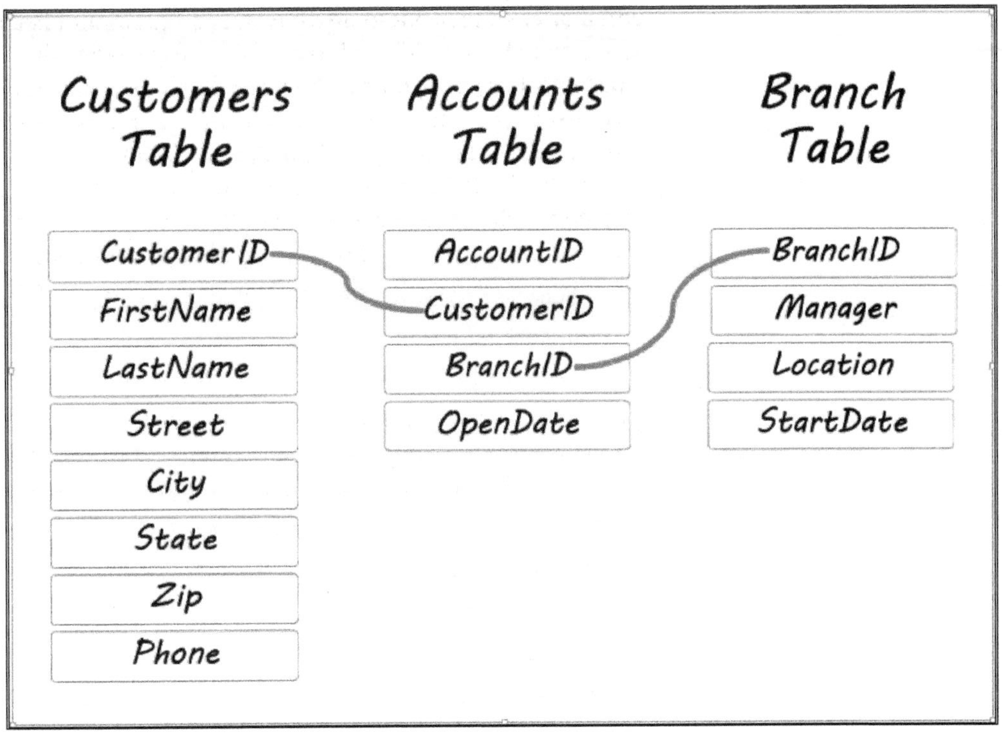

Customers Table

- CustomerID
- FirstName
- LastName
- Street
- City
- State
- Zip
- Phone

Accounts Table

- AccountID
- CustomerID
- BranchID
- OpenDate

Branch Table

- BranchID
- Manager
- Location
- StartDate

FIGURE 3 Determine Relationships Using Common Fields

Avoid *data redundancy*, which is the unnecessary storing of duplicate data in two or more tables. Having redundant or duplicate data in multiple tables can lead to serious errors. Suppose the customer address data were stored in both the Customers and Accounts tables. If a customer moved to a new address, it is possible that the address would be updated in only one of the two tables. The result would be inconsistent and unreliable information. Depending on which table you would use to check an address, either the new or the old one might be given to someone requesting the information. Storing the address in only one table is more reliable; if it changes, it only needs to be updated one time (in the Customers table) and can be referenced again and again from that table.

TIP: ADD CALCULATED FIELDS TO A TABLE

A calculated field produces a value from an expression or function that references one or more existing fields. Access enables you to store calculated fields in a table using the calculated data type, and to include those fields in queries, forms, and reports. However, many Access users prefer to create calculated fields in their query designs rather than in the tables themselves.

Design to Accommodate Calculations

Calculated fields are frequently created in database objects with numeric data, such as a monthly interest field that multiplies the balance in a customer's account by 1% each month (Balance*.01). You can also create calculated fields using date/time data. For example, if you want to store the length of time a customer has had an account, you can create a calculated field that subtracts the opening date from today's date. The result will be the number of days each customer has been an account holder.

A person's age is another example of a calculated field using date arithmetic—the date of birth is subtracted from today's date and the result is divided by 365 (or 365.25 to account for leap years). It might seem easier to store a person's age as a number rather than the birth date and avoid the calculated field, but that would be a mistake because age changes over time and the field would need to be updated each time it changes. You can use date arithmetic to subtract one date from another to find out the number of days, months, or years that have elapsed between them.

Table Design, Creation, and Modification • Access 2016

617

Creating and Modifying Tables and Working with Data

STEP 1 >>> Tables can be created in a new blank database or in an existing database.

To create a table, complete one of the following steps:

- Enter field names and table data directly in Datasheet view.
- Type field names in rows in Design view and then enter the data in Datasheet view.
- Import data from another database or application, such as Excel.
- Use a template.

Regardless of how a table is first created, you can always modify it later to include a new field or modify an existing field. Figure 4 shows a table created by entering fields in Design view.

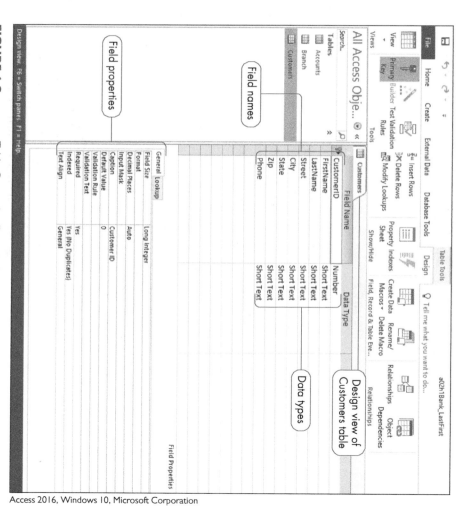

FIGURE 4 Customers Table Created in Design View

Access 2016, Windows 10, Microsoft Corporation

When you add a new field to a table, the field must be given an appropriate name to identify the data it holds. The field name should be descriptive of the data and can be up to 64 characters in length, including letters, numbers, and spaces. Field names cannot begin with a leading blank space. Database developers sometimes use Pascal Case notation for field names. Instead of spaces in multiword field names, you can use uppercase letters to distinguish the first letter of each new word, for example, ProductCost or LastName (sometimes developers use Camel Case, which is similar to Pascal Case, where the first letter of the first word is lowercase). It is sometimes preferable to avoid spaces in field names, because spaces can cause naming conflicts with other applications that may use these fields, such as Microsoft Visual Basic for Applications.

Fields can be added, deleted, or renamed either in Design view or Datasheet view. To delete a field in Datasheet view, select the field and press Delete. Click Yes in the message box.

To delete a field in Design view, complete the following steps:

1. Click the record selector of the field you want to delete to select it.
2. Click Delete Rows in the Tools group on the Design tab.
3. Click Yes in the message box that displays to confirm that you want to permanently delete the field and the data in it. Click No if you do not want to delete the field.
4. Click Yes in the second message box that displays if the selected field you are deleting is a primary key. Click No if you do not want to delete the primary key.

To rename a field, double-click the field name you want to change, type the new field name, press Enter, and then save the table.

TIP: HIDE FIELDS IN AN ACCESS DATASHEET

To hide a field in a datasheet, right-click the column selector that displays the field name and from the shortcut menu, select Hide Fields. To make the field visible again, right-click any column selector, select Unhide Fields, and select the appropriate column's check box.

Determine Data Type

Every field has an assigned *data type* that determines the type of data that can be entered and the operations that can be performed on that data. Access recognizes 12 data types. Table 1 lists these data types, their uses, and examples of each. You can change a data type after you have entered data into your table, but do so with caution. Be aware of messages from Access indicating that you may lose data when you save your changes. In some cases, changing data types is inconsequential; for example, you may want to convert a number to a currency value. This type of change would only affect the formatting displayed with the values, but not the underlying values themselves. In any case, when designing tables, choose the initial data type carefully, and be sure to back up your database before changing data types.

TABLE 1 Data Types and Uses		
Data Type	**Description**	**Example**
Short Text	Stores alphanumeric data, such as a customer's name or address. It can contain alphabetic characters, numbers, and/or special characters (e.g., an apostrophe in O'Malley). Social Security numbers, telephone numbers, and postal codes should be designated as text fields because they are not used in calculations and often contain special characters such as hyphens and parentheses. A short text field can hold up to 255 characters.	2184 Walnut Street
Long Text	Lengthy text or combinations of text and numbers, such as several sentences or paragraphs; used to hold descriptive data. Long text controls can display up to 64,000 characters.	A description of product packaging
Number	Contains a value that can be used in a calculation, such as the number of credits a course is worth. The contents are restricted to numbers, a decimal point, and a plus or minus sign.	12
Date/Time	Stores dates or times that can be used in date or time arithmetic.	10/31/2018 1:30:00 AM
Currency	Used for fields that contain monetary values.	$1,200

Table Design, Creation, and Modification • Access 2016

TABLE 1 Continued

Data Type	Description	Example
AutoNumber	A special data type used to assign the next consecutive number each time you add a record. The value of an AutoNumber field is unique for each record in the table.	1, 2, 3
Yes/No	Only one of two values can be stored, such as Yes or No, True or False, or On or Off (also known as a Boolean). For example, is a student on the Dean's list: Yes or No.	Yes
OLE Object	Contains an object created by another application. OLE objects include pictures and sounds.	JPG image
Hyperlink	Stores a Web address (URL) or the path to a folder or file. Hyperlink fields can be clicked to retrieve a webpage or to launch a file stored locally.	http://www.irs.gov
Attachment	Used to store multiple images, spreadsheet files, Word documents, and other types of supported files.	An Excel workbook
Calculated	The results of an expression that references one or more existing fields.	[Price]*.05
Lookup Wizard	Creates a field that enables you to choose a value from another table or from a list of values by using a list box or a combo box.	Accounts table with a CustomerID field that looks up the customer from the records in the Customers table

Pearson Education, Inc.

STEP 2

Set a Table's Primary Key

The primary key is the field (or possibly a combination of fields) that uniquely identifies each record in a table. Access does not require that each table have a primary key. However, a good database design usually includes a primary key in each table. You should select unique and infrequently changing data for the primary key. For example, a credit card number may seem to be unique, but would not make a good primary key because it is subject to change when a new card is issued due to fraudulent activity.

You probably would not use a person's name as the primary key, because several people could have the same name. A value like CustomerID, as shown in the Customers table in Figure 5, is unique and is a better choice for the primary key. When no field seems to stand out as a primary key naturally, you can create a primary key field with the AutoNumber data type. The **AutoNumber** data type is a number that automatically increments each time a record is added.

Figure 6 depicts a Speakers table, where no unique field can be identified from the data itself. In this case, you can identify the SpeakerID field with an AutoNumber data type. Access automatically numbers each speaker record sequentially with a unique ID as each record is added.

Customers

Customer ID	FirstName	LastName	Street	City	State	Zip	Phone	Click to Add
30001	Allison	Millward	2732 Baker Blvd.	Greensboro	NC	27492	(555) 334-5678	
30002	Bernett	Fox	12 Orchestra Terrace	High Point	NC	27494	(555) 358-5554	
30003	Clay	Hayes	P.O. Box 555	Greensboro	NC	27492	(555) 998-4457	
30004	Cordle	Collins	2743 Bering St.	Winston-Salem	NC	27492	(555) 447-2283	
30005	Eaton	Wagner	2743 Bering St.	Greensboro	NC	27492	(555) 988-3346	
30006	Kwasi	Williams	89 Jefferson Way	High Point	NC	27494	(555) 447-5565	
30007	Natasha	Simpson	187 Suffolk Ln.	Greensboro	NC	27493	(555) 775-3389	
30008	Joy	Jones	305 - 14th Ave. S.	Winston-Salem	NC	27493	(555) 258-7655	
30009	John	Nunn	89 Chiaroscuro Rd.	Greensboro	NC	27494	(555) 998-5557	
30010	Laura	Peterson	120 Hanover Sq.	Winston-Salem	NC	27492	(555) 334-6654	
30011	YourName	YourName	800 University Ave.	High Point	NC	27494	(555) 447-1235	
0								

SpeakerID	First Name	Last Name	Address	City	Sta	Zip Co	Phone Numl	Email	AreaOfExpertise	Click to Add
1	Jerri	Williams	10000 SW 59 Court	Miami	FL	33146	(305) 777-8888	cahsley@um.edu	Student Life	
2	Warren	Brasington	9470 SW 25 Street	Philadelphia	PA	19104	(215) 888-7654	wbrasington@up.edu	Residence Halls	
3	James	Shindell	14088 Malaga Avenue	Miami	FL	33146	(305) 773-4343	jshindell@um.edu	Administration	
		od	400 Roderigo Avenue	Gainesville	FL	32611	(352) 555-5555	ewood@uf.edu	Student Life	
		amson	9290 NW 59 Steet	Athens	GA	30602	(706) 777-1111	kpark@ug.edu	Student Life	
7	Holly	Davis	108 Los Pinos Place	Tuscaloosa	AL	35487	(205) 888-4554	wwilliamson@ua.edu	Deans' Office	
8	David	Tannen	8009 Riviera Drive	Gainesville	FL	32611	(352) 388-7676	hdavis.uf.edu	Residence Halls	
9	Jeffrey	Jacobsen	50 Main Street	Philadelphia	PA	19104	(215) 777-2211	dtannen@up.edu	Student Life	
10	Jerry	Masters	490 Bell Drive	Athens	GA	30602	(706) 388-9999	jjacobsen@ug.edu	Wellness	
11	Kevin	Kline	2000 Main Highway	Miami	FL	33146	(305) 777-8998	jmasters@um.edy	Wellness	
			2980 SW 89 Street	Gainesville	FL	32611	(352) 877-8900	kkline@uf.edu	Student Life	
			110 Center Highway	Athens	GA	30602	(706) 893-8872	jwithers@ug.edu	Wellness	
			2987 SW 14 Avenue	Philadelphia	PA	19104	(215) 558-7748	ballman@up.edu	Counseling Center	
			1008 West Marine Road	Miami	FL	33146	(305) 877-4993	mmiller@um.edu	Student Life	
15	Nancy	Vance	1878 W. 6 Street	Gainesville	FL	32611	(352) 885-4330	nvance@uf.edu	Counseling Center	
16	George	Jensen	42-15 81 Street	Elmhurst	NY	11373	(718) 555-6666	gjensen@school.edu	Residence Halls	
(New)										

SpeakerID (AutoNumber data type) is the primary key

Next record will be assigned SpeakerID 17

FIGURE 6 Speakers Table with an AutoNumber Primary Key

Explore a Foreign Key

In order to share data between two tables, the tables must share a common field. The common field will generally be the primary key in one table; the same field in the adjoining table is denoted as the *foreign key*. The CustomerID is the primary key (identified with a primary key icon) in the Customers table and uniquely identifies each customer in the database. It also displays as a foreign key in the related Accounts table. The Accounts table contains the CustomerID field to establish which customer owns the account. A CustomerID can be entered only one time in the Customers table, but it may be entered multiple times in the Accounts table because one customer may own several accounts (checking, savings, credit card, etc.). Therefore, the CustomerID is the primary key in the Customers table and a foreign key in the Accounts table, as shown in Figure 7.

CustomerID	FirstName	LastName	Street	City	State	Zip	Phone	Click to Add
30001	Allison	Millward	2732 Baker Blvd.	Greensboro	NC	27492	(555) 334-5678	
30002	Bennett	Fox	12 Orchestra Terrace	High Point	NC	27494	(555) 358-5554	
30003	Clay	Hayes	P.O. Box 555	Greensboro	NC	27492	(555) 998-4457	
30004	Cordie	Collins	2743 Bering St.	Winston-Salem	NC	27492	(555) 447-2283	
		Wagner	2743 Bering St.	Greensboro	NC	27492	(555) 988-3346	
		Williams	89 Jefferson Way	High Point	NC	27494	(555) 447-5565	
		Simpson	187 Suffolk Ln.	Greensboro	NC	27493	(555) 775-3389	
30008	Joy	Jones	305 - 14th Ave. S.	Winston-Salem	NC	27493	(555) 258-7655	
30009	John	Nunn	89 Chiarosauro Rd.	Greensboro	NC	27494	(555) 998-5557	
30010	Laura	Peterson	120 Hanover Sq.	Winston-Salem	NC	27492	(555) 334-6654	
30011	YourName	YourName	800 University Ave.	High Point	NC	27494	(555) 447-1235	

Primary Key in Customers table

Account ID	Customer ID	Branch ID	Balance	Open Date	Click to Add
1001	30010	B50	$5,600.00	4/28/2012	
1002	30001	B10	$1,200.00	4/13/2010	
1003	30004	B20	$15,490.00	5/28/2009	
	30001	B10	$630.00	9/21/2008	
			$1,300.00	7/22/2010	
			$550.00	7/3/2008	
1008	30004	B40	$1,620.00	6/7/2011	
1009	30005	B50	$2,100.00	9/30/2012	
1010	30001	B20	$1,500.00	2/7/2011	
1011	30005	B10	$3,000.00	3/18/2015	
1012	30002	B30	$290.00	10/16/2016	
			$1,900.00	3/14/2012	

Foreign Key in Accounts table

FIGURE 7 Two Tables Illustrating Primary and Foreign Keys

TIP: BEST FIT COLUMNS

If a field name is cut off in Datasheet view, you can adjust the column width by positioning the pointer on the vertical border on the right side of the column. When the pointer displays as a two-headed arrow, double-click the border. You can also click More in the Records group on the Home tab, select Field Width, and then click Best Fit in the Column Width dialog box.

Work with Field Properties

STEP 3 ≫ While a field's data type determines the type of data that can be entered and the operations that can be performed on that data, its *field properties* determine how the field looks and behaves. The field properties are set to default values according to the data type, but you can modify them if necessary. Field properties are commonly set in Design view, as shown in Figure 4; however, certain properties can be set in Datasheet view, on the Table Tools Fields tab. Common property types are defined in Table 2.

Field Size is a commonly changed field property. The field size determines the amount of space a field uses in the database. A field with a Short Text data type can store up to 255 characters; however, you can limit the characters by reducing the field size property. For example, you might limit the State field to only two characters because all state abbreviations are two letters. When setting field sizes, you may want to anticipate any future requirements of the database that might necessitate larger values to be stored.

You can set the *Caption property* to create a label that is more understandable than a field name. While Pascal Case is often preferred for field names, adding a space between words is often more readable. When a caption is set, it displays at the top of a table or query column in Datasheet view (instead of the field name), and when the field is used in a report or form. For example, a field named CustomerID could have the caption *Customer Number*.

Set the Validation Rule property to restrict data entry in a field to ensure that correct data are entered. The validation rule checks the data entered when the user exits the field. If the data entered violate the validation rule, an error message displays and prevents the invalid data from being entered into the field. For example, if you have set a rule on a date field that the date entered must be on or after today, and a date in the past is entered in the field, an error message will display. You can customize the error message (validation text) when you set the validation rule.

The Input Mask property simplifies data entry by providing literal characters that are typed for every entry, such as hyphens in a Social Security number (- -), or dashes in a phone number. Input masks ensure that data in fields such as these are consistently entered and formatted.

TABLE 2	Common Access Table Property Types and Descriptions
Property Type	**Description**
Field Size	Determines the maximum number of characters of a text field or the format of a number field.
Format	Changes the way a field is displayed or printed but does not affect the stored value.
Input Mask	Simplifies data entry by providing literal characters that are typed for every entry, such as hyphens in a Social Security number (- -) or slashes in a date. It also imposes data validation by ensuring that data entered conform to the mask.
Caption	Enables an alternate (or more readable) name to be displayed other than the field name; alternate name displays in datasheets, forms, and reports.
Default Value	Enters automatically a predetermined value for a field each time a new record is added to the table. For example, if most customers live in Los Angeles, the default value for the City field could be set to Los Angeles to save data entry time and promote accurate data entry.
Validation Rule	Requires data entered to conform to a specified rule.
Validation Text	Specifies the error message that is displayed when the validation rule is violated.
Required	Indicates that a value for this field must be entered. Primary key fields always require data entry.
Allow Zero Length	Allows entry of zero length text strings ("") in a Hyperlink, or Short or Long Text fields.
Indexed	Increases the efficiency of a search on the designated field.
Expression	Used for calculated fields only. Specifies the expression you want Access to evaluate and store.
Result Type	Used for calculated fields only. Specifies the format for the calculated field results.

Create a New Field in Design View

STEP 4 >> At times, it may be necessary to add table fields that were not included in the original design process. While it is possible to add fields in Datasheet view (using the Click to Add arrow at the top of an empty column), Design view, as shown in Figure 4, offers more flexibility in setting field properties.

To add a new field in Design view, complete the following steps:

1. Click in the first empty field row in the top pane of the table's Design view.
2. Enter the Field Name, Data Type, and Description (optional), and then set the Field Properties.
3. Click the row selector, and then click and drag the new field to place it in a different position in the table.
4. Click Save on the Quick Access Toolbar, and then switch to Datasheet view to enter or modify data.

Modify the Table in Datasheet View

STEP 5 >> Whereas Design view is commonly used to create and modify the table structure by enabling you to add and edit fields and set field properties, Datasheet view is used to add, edit, and delete records. Datasheet view of an Access table displays data in a grid format—rows represent records and columns represent fields. You can select a record by clicking the record selector on the left side of each record. Use the new blank record (marked with an asterisk) at the end of the table to add a new record, or click the New (blank) record button on the navigation bar at the bottom of the table.

Quick Concepts

1. What is meant by "Store data in its smallest parts" when designing database tables?
2. What is the difference between a primary key and a foreign key?
3. Which field property creates a more readable label that displays in the top row in Datasheet view and in forms and reports?

1 Table Design, Creation, and Modification

Creating a database for the bank auditor at Commonwealth Federal Bank as he investigates the mishandled funds will be a great opportunity for you to showcase your database design and Access skills.

STEP 1 >> CREATE A TABLE IN DATASHEET VIEW

You create a new desktop database to store information about the mishandled funds. You enter the data for the first record (BranchID, Manager, and Location). Refer to Figure 8 as you complete Step 1.

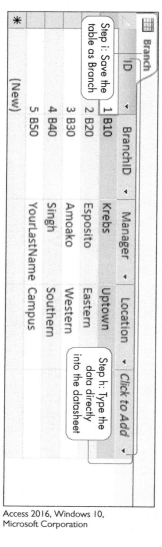

FIGURE 8 Create the Branch Table in Datasheet View

Access 2016, Windows 10,
Microsoft Corporation

a. Start Microsoft Office Access 2016 and click **Blank desktop database.**

b. Type **a02h1Bank_LastFirst** into the File Name box.

c. Click **Browse** to find the folder location where you will store the database and click **OK.** Click **Create** to create the new database.

Access will create the new database named a02h1Bank_LastFirst and a new table will automatically open in Datasheet view. There is already an ID field in the table by default.

d. Click **Click to Add** and select **Short Text** as the Data type.

Click to Add changes to Field1. Field1 is selected to make it easier to change the field name.

e. Type **BranchID** and press **Tab.**

A list of data types for the third column opens so that you can select the data type for the third column.

f. Select Short Text in the Click to Add window, type **Manager,** and then press **Tab.**

g. Select Short Text in the Click to Add window, and then type **Location.**

h. Click in the first column (the ID field) next to the New Record asterisk, press **Tab,** and then type the data for the new table as shown in Figure 8, letting Access assign the ID field for each new record (using the AutoNumber data type). Replace *YourLastName* with your own last name.

i. Click **Save** on the Quick Access Toolbar. Type **Branch** in the Save As dialog box and click **OK.**

Entering field names, data types, and data directly in Datasheet view provides a simplified way to create the table initially.

STEP 2 ›› DELETE A FIELD AND SET A TABLE'S PRIMARY KEY

It is possible to modify tables even after data have been entered; however, be alert to potential messages from Access after you make design changes that may affect your data. In this step, you will modify the Branch table. You examine the design of the table and realize that the BranchID field is a unique identifier, making the ID field redundant. You delete the ID field and make the BranchID field the primary key field. Refer to Figure 9 as you complete Step 2.

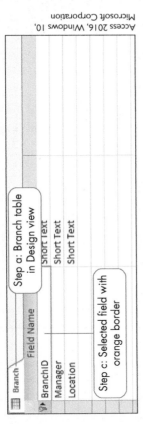

Access 2016, Windows 10,
Microsoft Corporation

FIGURE 9 Branch Table in Design View

a. Click **View** in the Views group on the Home tab to switch to Design view of the Branch table.

The field name for each of the four fields displays along with the data type.

b. Ensure that the ID field selected, click **Delete Rows** in the Tools group on the Design tab. Click **Yes** to both warning messages.

Access responds with a warning that you are about to permanently delete a field and a second warning that the field is the primary key. You delete the field because you will set the BranchID field as the primary key.

c. Ensure that the BranchID field is selected, as shown in Figure 9.

d. Click **Primary Key** in the Tools group on the Design tab.

You set BranchID as the primary key. The Indexed property in the Field Properties section at the bottom of the design window displays Yes (No Duplicates).

e. Click **Save** on the Quick Access Toolbar to save the table.

TIP: SHORTCUT MENU

You can right-click a row selector to display a shortcut menu to copy a field, set the primary key, insert or delete rows, or access table properties. Use the shortcut menu to make these specific changes to the design of a table.

Hands-On Exercise 1

You will modify the table design further to comply with the bank auditor's specifications. Refer to Figure 10 as you complete Step 3.

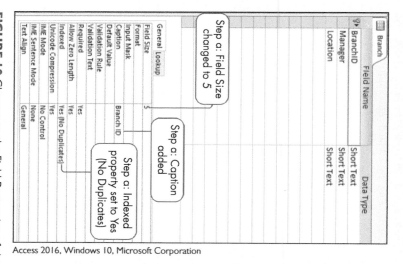

FIGURE 10 Changes to the Field Properties of the Branch Table in Design View

Access 2016, Windows 10, Microsoft Corporation

a. Click in the **BranchID field name**; modify the BranchID field properties by completing the following steps:

- Click in the **Field Size box** and change 255 to **5.**
- Click in the **Caption box** and type **Branch ID**. Make sure Branch and ID have a space between them.

  A caption provides a more descriptive field name. It will display as the column heading in Datasheet view.

- Check the Indexed property; confirm it is Yes (No Duplicates).

b. Click the **Manager field name**; modify the Manager field properties by completing the following steps:

- Click in the **Field Size box** in the Field Properties pane, and change 255 to **30.**
- Click in the **Caption box** in the Field Properties pane, and type **Manager's Name.**

c. Click the **Location field name** and modify the following Location field properties by completing the following steps:

- Click in the **Field Size box** and change 255 to **30.**
- Click in the **Caption box** and type **Branch Location.**

TIP: F6 FUNCTION KEY TO SWITCH TO FIELD PROPERTIES

With a field name selected in the top pane of the Design window, you can press the F6 function key to toggle to the field properties for the selected field. Continue to press F6 to cycle through the additional elements of the Access screen.

You notify the auditor that a date field is missing in your new table. Modify the table to add the new field. Refer to Figure 11 as you complete Step 4.

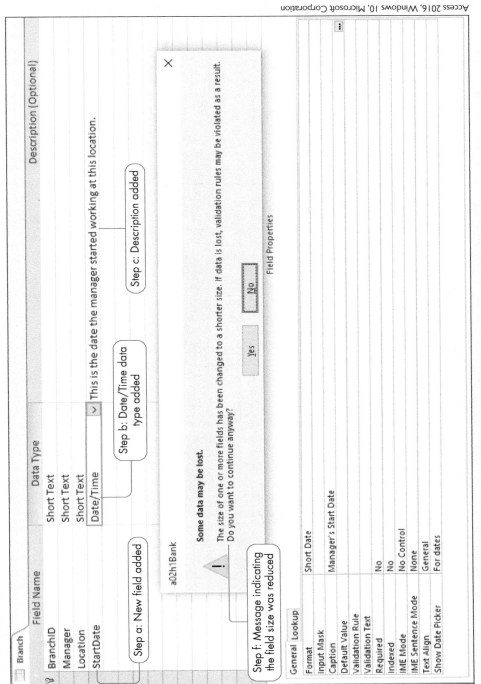

Step a: New field added

Step b: Date/Time data type added

Step c: Description added

Step f: Message indicating the field size was reduced

Some data may be lost.

The size of one or more fields has been changed to a shorter size. If data is lost, validation rules may be violated as a result. Do you want to continue anyway?

This is the date the manager started working at this location.

Field Properties

Access 2016, Windows 10, Microsoft Corporation

FIGURE 11 Adding a New Field to the Branch Table in Design View

a. Click in the first blank field row below the Location field name and type **StartDate**.

You added a new field to the table.

b. Press **Tab** to move to the Data Type column. Click the **Data Type arrow** and select **Date/Time**.

TIP: KEYBOARD SHORTCUT FOR DATA TYPES

You also can type the first letter of the data type, such as d for Date/Time, s for Short Text, or n for Number. To use the keyboard shortcut, click in the field name and press Tab to advance to the Data Type column. Next, type the first letter of the data type.

c. Press **Tab** to move to the Description column and type **This is the date the manager started working at this location.**

d. Click in the **Format box** in the Field properties pane, click the **arrow**, and then select **Short Date** from the list of date formats.

e. Click in the **Caption box** and type **Manager's Start Date.**

f. Click **Save** on the Quick Access Toolbar.

A warning dialog box opens to indicate that "Some data may be lost" because the size of the BranchID, Manager, and Location field properties were shortened (in the previous step). It asks if you want to continue anyway. Always read the Access warning! In this case, you can click Yes to continue because you know that the existing and anticipated data are no longer than the new field sizes.

g. Click **Yes** in the warning box.

STEP 5 » MODIFY THE TABLE IN DATASHEET VIEW

As you work with the auditor, you will modify tables in the Bank database from time to time and add and modify records. Refer to Figure 12 as you complete Step 5.

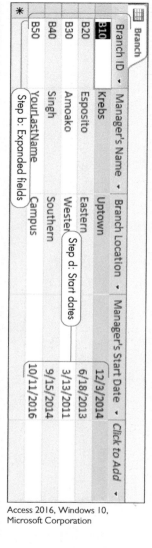

Branch ID	Manager's Name	Branch Location	Manager's Start Date	Click to Add
B10	Krebs	Uptown	12/3/2014	
B20	Esposito	Eastern	6/18/2013	
B30	Amoako	Western	3/13/2011	
B40	Singh	Southern	9/15/2014	
B50	YourLastName	Campus	10/11/2016	

FIGURE 12 Start Dates Added to the Branch Table

Access 2016, Windows 10, Microsoft Corporation

a. Right-click the **Branch tab** and click **Datasheet View** from the shortcut menu.

The table displays in Datasheet view. The field captions display at the top of the columns, but they are cut off.

b. Position the pointer over the border between Branch ID and Manager's Name so that it becomes a double-headed arrow, and double-click the border. Repeat the process for the border between Manager's Name and Branch Location, the border between Branch Location and Manager's Start Date, and the border after Manager's Start Date.

The columns contract or expand to display the best fit for each field name.

c. Click inside the **Manager's Start Date** in the first record and click the **Date Picker** [icon] next to the date field. Use the navigation arrows to find and select **December 3, 2014** from the calendar.

You can also enter the dates by typing them directly into the StartDate field.

d. Type the start date directly in each field for the rest of the managers, as shown in Figure 12.

e. Click the **Close** ⊠ at the top-right corner of the datasheet, below the Ribbon. Click **Yes** to save the changes.

f. Double-click the **Branch table** in the Navigation Pane to open the table. Check the start dates.

g. Click the **File tab**, click **Print**, and then click **Print Preview**.

Occasionally, users will print an Access table. However, database developers usually create reports to print table data.

h. Click **Close Print Preview** and close the Branch table.

i. Keep the database open if you plan to continue with the Hands-On Exercise. If not, close the database and exit Access.

TROUBLESHOOTING: If you accidentally click Close on top of the Ribbon, you will exit Access completely. To start again, launch Access and click the first file in the Recent list.

Multiple-Table Databases

In Figure 2, the sample Bank database contains three tables—Customers, Accounts, and Branch. You created one table, the Branch table, in the previous section using Datasheet view and modified the table fields in Design view. You will create the two remaining tables using different methods—by importing data from external sources.

In this section, you will learn how to import data from Excel and Access, modify tables, create indexes, create relationships between tables, and enforce referential integrity.

Sharing Data

Most companies and organizations store some type of data in Excel spreadsheets. Often, the data stored in those spreadsheets can be more efficiently managed in an Access database. At other times, importing data from Excel and other applications can reduce the data entry effort for your database.

Import Excel Data

 Access provides you with a wizard that guides you through the process of importing data from Excel.

To import an Excel spreadsheet to Access, complete the following steps:

1. Click the External Data tab.
2. Click Excel in the Import & Link group. The Get External Data – Excel Spreadsheet dialog box opens, as shown in Figure 13.

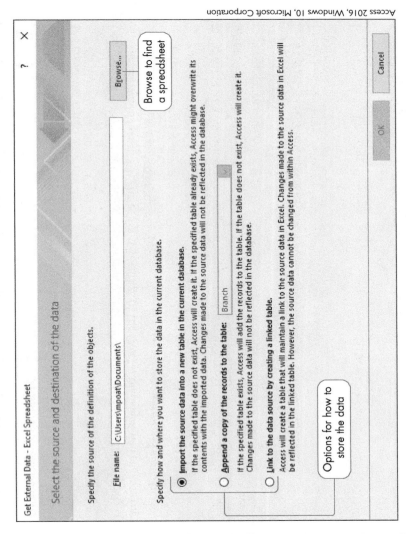

Access 2016, Windows 10, Microsoft Corporation

FIGURE 13 Import Excel Data

3. Click Browse to locate the Excel file you want to import, click the file to select it, and then click Open to specify this file as the source of the data.

4. Ensure the *Import the source data* option is selected, and click OK. The Import Spreadsheet Wizard launches.

5. Select the worksheet from the list of worksheets shown at the top of the dialog box, as shown in Figure 14 and then click Next.

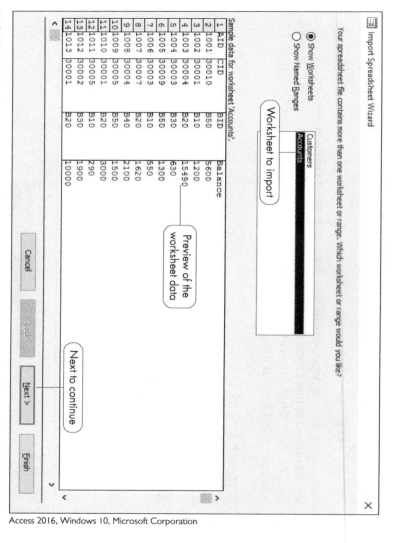

FIGURE 14 Available Worksheets and Preview of Data

6. Ensure the *First Row Contains Column Headings* check box is selected, and click Next, as shown in Figure 15. The column headings of the Excel spreadsheet will become the field names in the Access table.

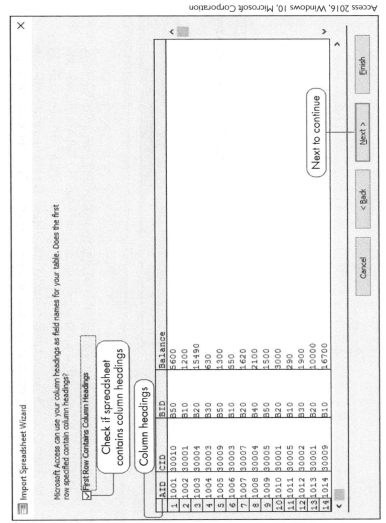

FIGURE 15 Excel Column Headings Become Access Field Names

7. Change the field options for the imported data, as shown in Figure 16, and then click Next.

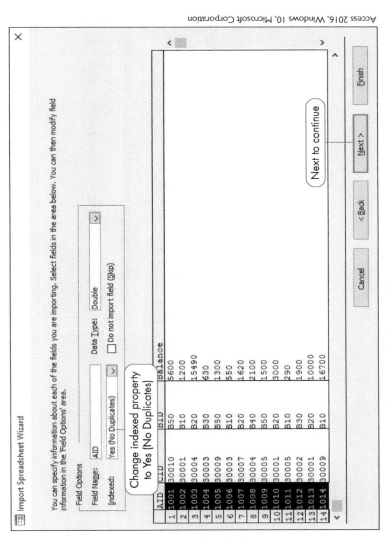

FIGURE 16 Change Field Options for Imported Data

Multiple-Table Databases • Access 2016

8. Click the *Choose my own primary key* option if the imported data has a field that is acceptable as a primary key, as shown in Figure 17, and then click Next. Access will set the value in the first column of the spreadsheet (for example, AID) as the primary key field of the table. You can also allow Access to set the primary key if there is no value that is eligible to be a key field, or to set no primary key at all.

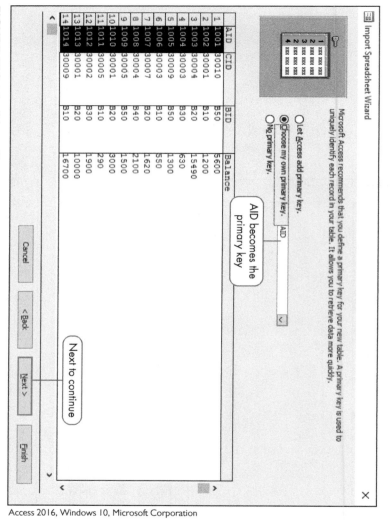

FIGURE 17 Set the Primary Key

Access 2016, Windows 10, Microsoft Corporation

9. Type the new table name in the Import to Table box, as shown in Figure 18, and then click Finish.

10. Click Close when prompted to Save Import Steps.

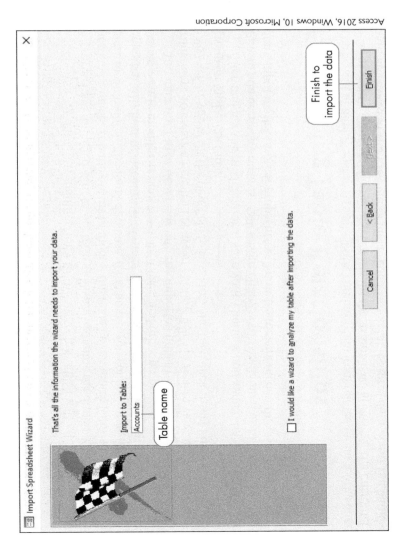

FIGURE 18 Enter a Table Name

TIP: LINKING TO EXTERNAL DATA

At times you might need to include a table in your database that already exists in another database. Instead of importing the data from this external source, you can create a link to it from within your database, and the table remains in the original database. You will be able to use the linked data as usual, without being able to modify the original table's design. You can also link to existing spreadsheets from your database without having to copy a large amount of data into your file.

Import Access Data

STEP 2 A wizard can also guide you as you import data from Access databases. You can import tables, queries, forms, reports, pages, macros, and modules from other databases. You can also modify the design of objects that are imported into your database.

To import an Access table into an existing database, complete the following steps:

1. Click the External Data tab.

2. Click Access in the Import & Link group. The Get External Data – Access Database dialog box opens.

3. Ensure that the *Import tables, queries, forms, reports, macros, and modules into the current database* option is selected.

4. Click Browse to locate the Access database you want to import.

5. Click the file to select it, and then click Open to specify this file as the source of the data.

6. Select the table you want to import, and then click OK. (Click Select All if the database contains multiple tables and you want to import all of them, and then click OK.)

Modify an Imported Table's Design and Add Data

STEP 3

Importing data from other applications saves typing and prevents errors that may occur while entering data, but modifications to the imported tables will often be required. After you have imported a table, open the table and examine the design to see if changes need to be made. You may want to modify the table by renaming fields so that they are more meaningful. In the Bank database, for example, you could change the name of the imported AID field to AccountID to make it more readable and meaningful. Switch to Design view to modify the data types, field sizes, and other properties.

You may want to fit new fields into the imported tables or delete unnecessary fields from them. To create a new field between existing fields in Design view, click in the row below where you want the new field to be added, and then click Insert Rows in the Tools group on the Design tab.

After making the modifications, save your changes and switch back to Datasheet view to add or modify records. Any design changes you made such as to field sizes, captions, input masks, or other properties will now be implemented in the datasheet.

STEP 4

Establishing Table Relationships

STEP 5

The benefit of a relationship is to efficiently combine data from related tables for the purpose of creating queries, forms, and reports. In the example we are using, the customer data are stored in the Customers table. The Branch table stores data about the bank's branches, management, and locations. The Accounts table stores data about account ownership and balances.

The common fields that were determined in the design phase of the tables can now be used to establish relationships between them.

To create the relationship between the common fields of two tables, complete the following steps:

1. Click the Database Tools tab.
2. Click Relationships in the Relationships group.
3. Drag the primary key field name from one table to the foreign key field name of the related table (for example, CustomerID in the Customers table to CustomerID in the Accounts table).
4. Set the desired options in the Edit Relationships dialog box, and click OK. Figure 19 shows the Bank database with relationships created by joining common fields.

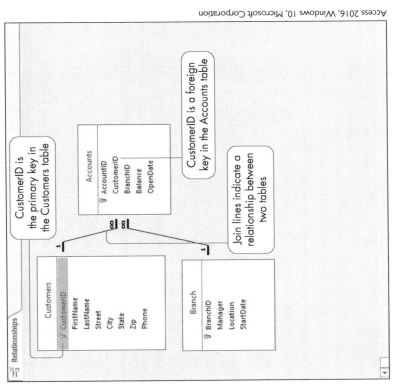

FIGURE 19 Relationships in the Bank Database

Access 2016, Windows 10, Microsoft Corporation

Labels in figure:
- CustomerID is the primary key in the Customers table
- CustomerID is a foreign key in the Accounts table
- Join lines indicate a relationship between two tables
- Customers: CustomerID, FirstName, LastName, Street, City, State, Zip, Phone
- Accounts: AccountID, CustomerID, BranchID, Balance, OpenDate
- Branch: BranchID, Manager, Location, StartDate

TIP: RETRIEVE DATA QUICKLY WITH INDEXING

When you set the primary key in Access, the Indexed property is automatically set to Yes (No Duplicates). The indexed property setting enables quick sorting in primary key order and quick retrieval based on the primary key. For non-primary key fields, it may be beneficial to set the Indexed property to Yes (Duplicates OK). Again, Access uses indexing to sort and retrieve data quickly based on the indexed field.

The primary key of a table plays a significant role when setting relationships. You cannot join two tables unless a primary key has been set in the primary table, which is one side of the relationship's join line. The other side of the relationship join line is most often the foreign key of the related table. A foreign key is a field in one table that is also the primary key and common field of another table. In the Bank database, CustomerID has been set as the primary key in the Customers table and also exists in the Accounts table. Therefore, a relationship can be set between the Customers table and the Accounts table, where CustomerID is the foreign key. Similarly, the Branch table can be joined to the Accounts table because BranchID has been set as the primary key in the Branch table, and BranchID is the foreign key in the Accounts table.

Enforce Referential Integrity

STEP 6 When you begin to create a relationship in Access, the Edit Relationships dialog box displays. The first check box, Enforce Referential Integrity, should be checked in most cases. *Referential integrity* enforces rules in a database that are used to preserve relationships between tables when records are changed.

When referential integrity is enforced, you cannot enter a foreign key value in a related table unless the primary key value exists in the primary table. In the case of the Bank database, the customer information is first entered into the Customers table before a customer's account information (which also includes CustomerID) can be entered into the Accounts table. If you attempt to enter an account prior to entering the customer information, an error will display, as shown in Figure 20. When referential integrity is enforced, usually you cannot delete a record in one table if it has related records in another table. For example, you cannot delete a record in one table if it has related records in another table. For example, you may not want to delete a customer from the Customers table if he or she has active accounts in the Accounts table.

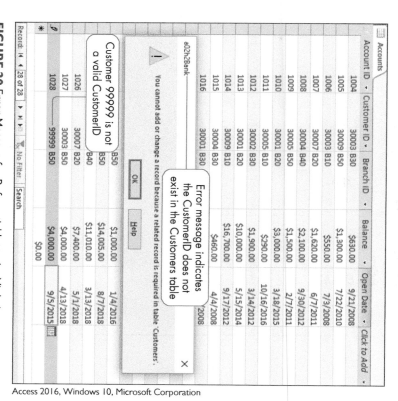

FIGURE 20 Error Message for Referential Integrity Violation

Access 2016, Windows 10, Microsoft Corporation

Set Cascade Options

When you create a relationship in Access and click the Enforce Referential Integrity check box, Access presents two additional options: Cascade Update Related Fields and Cascade Delete Related Records (see Figure 21). Check the *Cascade Update Related Fields* option so that when the primary key value is modified in a primary table, Access will automatically update all foreign key values in a related table. If a CustomerID is updated for some reason, all of the matching CustomerID values in the Accounts table will update automatically.

Check the *Cascade Delete Related Records* option so that when a record containing a primary key value is deleted in a primary table, Access will automatically delete all records in related tables that match the primary key. If one branch of a bank closes and its record is deleted from the Branch table, any account that is associated with this branch would then be deleted. Access will give a warning first to enable you to avoid the action of deleting records inadvertently.

Setting the Cascade Update and Cascade Delete options really depends on the business rules of an organization, and they should be set with caution. For example, if a branch of a bank closes, do you really want the accounts at that branch to be deleted? Another option might be to assign them to a different branch of the bank.

Establish a One-to-Many Relationship

Figure 21 also shows that the relationship that will be created will be a one-to-many relationship. Access provides three different relationships for joining tables: one-to-one, one-to-many, and many-to-many. The most common type by far is the one-to-many relationship. A *one-to-many relationship* is established when the primary key value in the primary table can match many of the foreign key values in the related table.

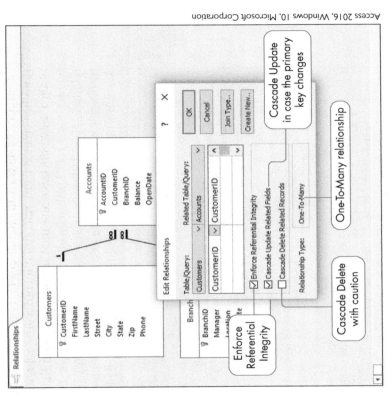

FIGURE 21 Cascade Update and Delete Options

For example, a bank customer will be entered into the Customers table one time only. The primary key value, which is the CustomerID number, might be 1585. That same customer could set up a checking, savings, and credit card account. With each account, the CustomerID (1585) is required and therefore will occur three times in the Accounts table. The value is entered one time in the Customers table and three times in the Accounts table. Therefore, the relationship between Customers and Accounts is described as one-to-many. Table 3 lists and describes all three types of relationships you can create between Access tables.

TABLE 3 Relationship Types	
Relationship Type	**Description**
One-to-Many	The primary key table must have only one occurrence of each value. For example, each customer must have a unique identification number in the Customers table. The foreign key field in the related table may have repeating values. For example, one customer may have many different account numbers.
One-to-One	Two different tables use the same primary key. Exactly one record exists in the second table for each record in the first table. Sometimes security issues require a single table to be split into two related tables. For example, in an organization's database anyone in the company might be able to access the Employee table and find the employee's office number, department assignment, or telephone extension. However, only a few people need to have access to the employee's network login password, salary, Social Security number, performance review, or marital status, which would be stored in a second table. Tables containing this information would use the same unique identifier to identify each employee.
Many-to-Many	This is an artificially constructed relationship allowing many matching records in each direction between tables. It requires construction of a third table called a junction table. For example, a database might have a table for employees and one for projects. Several employees might be assigned to one project, but one employee might also be assigned to many different projects.

Figure 22 displays the Relationships window for the Bank database and all the relationships created using referential integrity. The join line between the CustomerID field in the Customers table and the CustomerID field in the Accounts table indicates that a one-to-many relationship has been set. The number 1 displays on the one side of the relationship and the infinity symbol displays the many side. You can switch the positions of the Branch and Accounts tables in the Relationships window without changing the relationship itself.

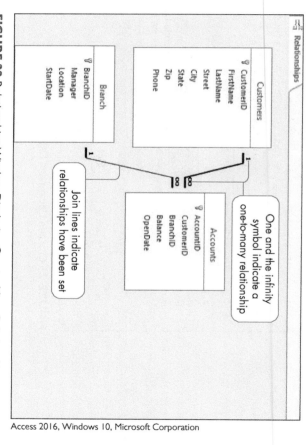

FIGURE 22 Relationships Window Displaying One-to-Many Relationships

Access 2016, Windows 10, Microsoft Corporation

TIP: NAVIGATING BETWEEN THE RELATIONSHIPS WINDOW AND A TABLE'S DESIGN

When you right-click a table's title bar in the Relationships window, the shortcut menu offers you the option to open the table in Design view. This is a convenient feature because if you want to link one table to another table, the joined fields must have the same data type. This shortcut enables you to check the fields and revise them if a table contains a field with the wrong data type.

Quick Concepts

4. Describe a scenario that may require you to import Excel data into Access.

5. What is the purpose of setting a relationship between two tables?

6. Why would you decide to use the Cascade Delete option (or not) when setting a relationship?

7. Specify two database tables that you might design that would contain a one-to-many relationship. Describe the relationship.

Hands-On Exercises

Skills covered: Import Excel Data • Import Data from an Access Database • Modify an Imported Table's Design • Add Data to an Imported Table • Establish Table Relationships • Enforce Referential Integrity

2 Multiple-Table Databases

You created a new Bank database, and a new Branch table. Now you are ready to import additional tables—one from an Excel spreadsheet and one from an Access database. Assume that the data are formatted correctly and are structured properly so that you can begin the import process.

STEP 1 ▶▶ IMPORT EXCEL DATA

You and the auditor have discovered several of Commonwealth's files that contain customer data. These files need to be analyzed, so you decide to import the data into Access. In this step, you import an Excel spreadsheet into the Bank database. Refer to Figure 23 as you complete Step 1.

All Access Obje... ⊙ «

Search...

Tables

Branch

Customers

Step e: Imported column headings

CID	FirstName	LastName	Street	City	State	Zip	Phone	Click to Add
30001	Allison	Millward	2732 Baker Blvd.	Greensboro	NC	27492	5553345678	
30002	Bernett	Fox	12 Orchestra Terrace	High Point	NC	27494	5553585554	
30003	Clay	Hayes	P.O. Box 555	Greensboro	NC	27492	5559984457	
30004	Cordle	Collins	2743 Bering St.	Winston-Salem	NC	27492	5554472283	
30005	Eaton	Wagner	2743 Bering St.	Greensboro	NC	27492	5559883346	
30006	Kwasi	Williams	89 Jefferson Way	High Point	NC	27494	5554475565	
30007	Natasha	Simpson	187 Suffolk Ln.	Greensboro	NC	27493	5557753389	
30008	Joy	Jones	305 - 14th Ave. S.	Winston-Salem	NC	27493	5552587655	
30009	John	Nunn	89 Chiaroscuro Rd.	Greensboro	NC	27494	5559985557	
30010	Laura	Peterson	120 Hanover Sq.	Winston-Salem	NC	27492	5553346654	

Access 2016, Windows 10, Microsoft Corporation

FIGURE 23 Imported Customers Table

a. Open *a02h1Bank_LastFirst* if you closed it at the end of Hands-On Exercise 1, and save it as **a02h2Bank_LastFirst**, changing h1 to h2.

b. Click **Enable Content** below the Ribbon to indicate that you trust the contents of the database.

c. Click the **External Data tab** and click **Excel** in the Import & Link group to launch the Get External Data – Excel Spreadsheet feature. Ensure that the *Import the source data into a new table in the current database* option is selected.

> **TROUBLESHOOTING:** Ensure that you click Excel in the Import & Link group to import the spreadsheet and not the Excel command in the Export group.

d. Click **Browse** and navigate to your student data files. Select the *a02h2Customers* workbook. Click **Open** and click **OK** to open the Import Spreadsheet Wizard.

e. Ensure that the *First Row Contains Column Headings* check box is checked to indicate to Access that column headings exist in the Excel file.

The field names CID, FirstName, LastName, Street, City, State, ZIP, and Phone will import from Excel along with the data stored in the rows in the worksheet. You will modify the field names later in Access.

f. Click **Next.**

g. Ensure that CID is displayed in the Field Name box in Field Options. Click the **Indexed arrow** and select **Yes (No Duplicates).** Click **Next.**

The CID (CustomerID) will become the primary key in this table. It needs to be a unique identifier, so you must change the property to No Duplicates.

h. Click the **Choose my own primary key option.** Make sure that the CID field is selected. Click **Next.**

The final screen of the Import Spreadsheet Wizard asks you to name your table. The name of the Excel worksheet is Customers, and Access defaults to the worksheet name. It is an acceptable name.

i. Click **Finish** to accept Customers as the table name.

A dialog box opens prompting you to save the steps of this import to use again. If this is data that is to be collected in Excel and updated to the database on a regular basis, saving the import steps would save time. You do not need to save the import steps in this example.

j. Click **Close.**

The new table displays in the Navigation Pane of the Bank database.

k. Open the imported Customers table in Datasheet view and double-click the border between each of the field names to adjust the columns to Best Fit. Compare your table to Figure 23.

l. Save and close the table.

The auditor asks you to import an Access database table that contains account information related to the accounts you are analyzing. You use the Import Wizard to import the database table. Refer to Figure 24 as you complete Step 2.

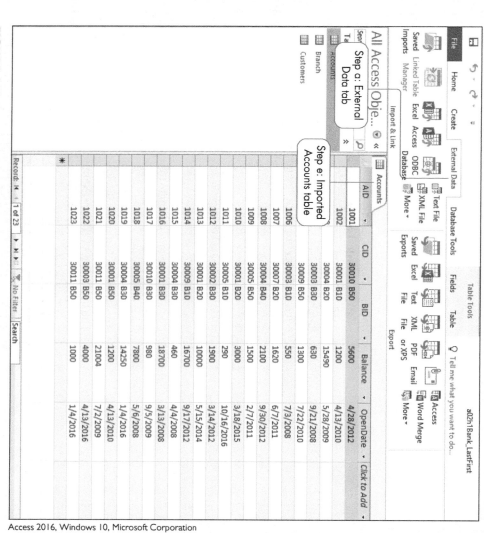

FIGURE 24 Imported Accounts Table

a. Click the **External Data tab** and click **Access** in the Import & Link group to launch the Get External Data – Access Database feature. Ensure that the *Import tables, queries, forms, reports, macros, and modules into the current database* option is selected.

b. Click **Browse** and navigate to your student data files. Select the *a02h2Accounts* database. Click **Open** and click **OK** to open the Import Objects dialog box.

c. Click the **Accounts table** for importing and click **OK.**

d. Click **Close** in the Save Import Steps dialog box.

The Navigation Pane now contains three tables: Accounts, Branch, and Customers.

e. Open the imported Accounts table in Datasheet view and compare it to Figure 24.

f. Close the table.

STEP 3 ≫ MODIFY AN IMPORTED TABLE'S DESIGN

When importing tables from either Excel or Access, the fields may have different data types and property settings than required to create table relationships. You will modify the tables so that each field has the correct data type and field size. Refer to Figure 25 as you complete Step 3.

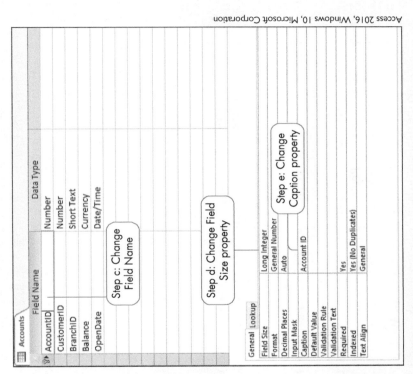

Access 2016, Windows 10, Microsoft Corporation

FIGURE 25 Modified Accounts Table Design

a. Right-click the **Accounts table** in the Navigation Pane.

b. Select Design view from the shortcut menu to open the table in Design view.

The Accounts table displays with the primary key AID selected.

c. Change the AID field name to **AccountID.**

d. Change the Field Size property to **Long Integer.**

Long Integer ensures that there will be enough numbers as the number of customers grows over time and may exceed 32,768 (the upper limit for Integer values).

Hands-On Exercise 2

641

e. Type **Account ID** in the Caption box for the AccountID field. The caption contains a space between Account and ID.

f. Click the **CID** field. Change the CID field name to **CustomerID**.

g. Change the Field Size property to **Long Integer**.

You can select the Field Size option using the arrow, or you can type the first letter of the option you want. For example, type l for Long Integer or s for Single. Make sure the current option is completely selected before you type the letter.

h. Type **Customer ID** in the Caption box for the CustomerID field. The caption contains a space between Customer and ID.

i. Click the **BID field**. Change the BID field name to **BranchID**.

j. Type **5** in the Field Size property box in the Field Properties.

k. Type **Branch ID** in the Caption property box for the Branch ID field.

l. Change the Data Type of the Balance field to **Currency**.

The Currency data type is used for fields that contain monetary values. In this case, changing the data type is not consequential; formatting the imported Balance field as Currency will not change the original data values.

m. Change the Data Type of the OpenDate field to **Date/Time** and set **Short Date** in the Format field property. Type **Open Date** in the Caption property box.

The OpenDate field stores the date that each account was opened.

n. Click **View** in the Views group to switch to Datasheet view. Read the messages and click **Yes** to each one.

In this case, it is OK to click Yes because the shortened fields will not cut off any data. Leave the table open.

o. Right-click the **Customers table** in the Navigation Pane and from the shortcut menu, select **Design View**.

p. Change the CID field name to **CustomerID**. Change the Field Size property of the CustomerID field to **Long Integer** and add a caption, **Customer ID**. Take note of the intentional space between Customer and ID.

The Accounts table and the Customers table will be joined using the CustomerID field. Both fields must have the same data type.

q. Change the Field Size property to **20** for the FirstName, LastName, Street, and City fields. Change the Field Size for State to **2**.

r. Change the data type for ZIP and Phone to **Short Text**. Change the Field Size property to **15** for both fields. Remove the @ symbol from the Format property where it exists for all fields in the Customers table.

s. Click the **Phone field name** and click **Input Mask** in Field Properties. Click the **ellipsis** on the right side to launch the Input Mask Wizard. Click **Yes** to save the table and click **Yes** to the *Some data may be lost* warning. Click **Finish** to apply the default phone number input mask.

The phone number input mask enables users to enter 6105551212 in the datasheet, and Access will display it as (610) 555-1212.

t. Click **Save** to save the design changes to the Customers table.

Now that you have created the Access tables, you discover that you need to add another customer and his account records to them. Refer to Figure 26 as you complete Step 4.

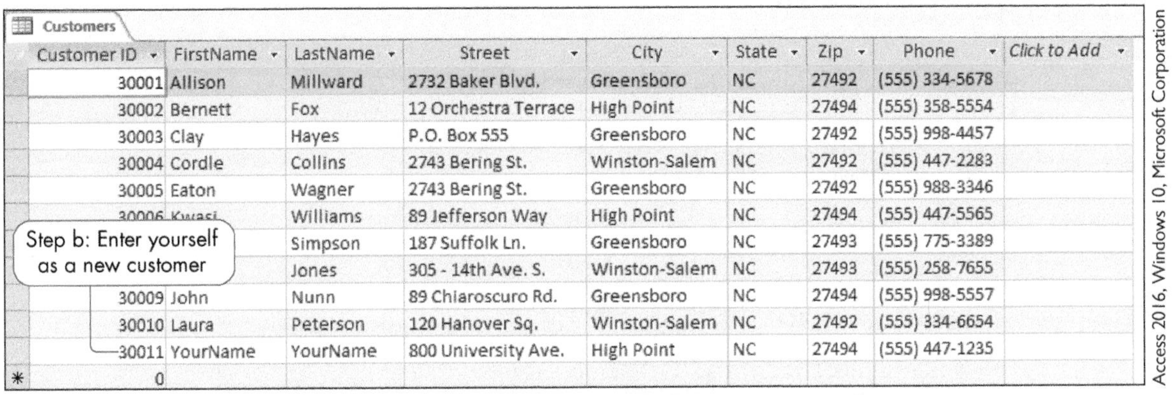

Customer ID	FirstName	LastName	Street	City	State	Zip	Phone	Click to Add
30001	Allison	Millward	2732 Baker Blvd.	Greensboro	NC	27492	(555) 334-5678	
30002	Bernett	Fox	12 Orchestra Terrace	High Point	NC	27494	(555) 358-5554	
30003	Clay	Hayes	P.O. Box 555	Greensboro	NC	27492	(555) 998-4457	
30004	Cordle	Collins	2743 Bering St.	Winston-Salem	NC	27492	(555) 447-2283	
30005	Eaton	Wagner	2743 Bering St.	Greensboro	NC	27492	(555) 988-3346	
30006	Kwasi	Williams	89 Jefferson Way	High Point	NC	27494	(555) 447-5565	
	Simpson		187 Suffolk Ln.	Greensboro	NC	27493	(555) 775-3389	
	Jones		305 - 14th Ave. S.	Winston-Salem	NC	27493	(555) 258-7655	
30009	John	Nunn	89 Chiaroscuro Rd.	Greensboro	NC	27494	(555) 998-5557	
30010	Laura	Peterson	120 Hanover Sq.	Winston-Salem	NC	27492	(555) 334-6654	
30011	YourName	YourName	800 University Ave.	High Point	NC	27494	(555) 447-1235	

Step b: Enter yourself as a new customer

Access 2016, Windows 10, Microsoft Corporation

FIGURE 26 Customers Table Displaying the Added Customer ID 30011

a. Click **View** in the Views group to display the Customers table in Datasheet view.

The asterisk at the bottom of the table data in the row selector area is the indicator of a place to enter a new record.

b. Click next to the * in the **Customer ID field** in the new record row below 30010. Type **30011**. Fill in the rest of the data using your personal information as the customer. You may use a fictitious address and phone number.

Note the phone number format. The input mask you set formats the phone number.

c. Close the Customers table. The Accounts table tab is open.

TROUBLESHOOTING: If the Accounts table is not open, double-click Accounts in the Navigation Pane.

d. Click next to the * in the **Account ID field** in the new record row. Type **1024**. Type **30011** as the Customer ID and **B50** as the Branch ID. Type **14005** for the Balance field value. Type **8/7/2018** for the Open Date.

e. Add the following records to the Accounts table:

Account ID	Customer ID	Branch ID	Balance	Open Date
1025	30006	B40	$11,010	3/13/2018
1026	30007	B20	$7,400	5/1/2018

f. Close the Accounts table, but keep the database open.

The tables for the bank investigation have been designed and populated. Now you will establish connections between the tables. Look at the primary and foreign keys as a guide. Refer to Figure 27 as you complete Step 5.

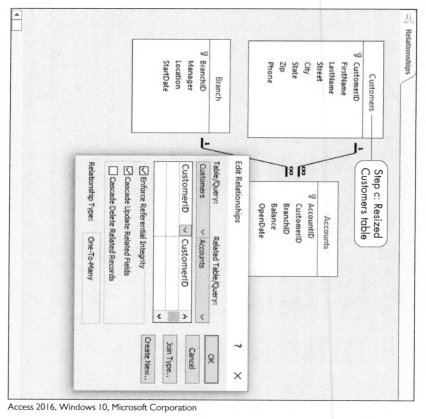

Access 2016, Windows 10, Microsoft Corporation

FIGURE 27 Relationships Between Tables

a. Click the **Database Tools tab** and click **Relationships** in the Relationships group.

The Relationships window opens and the Show Table dialog box displays.

> **TROUBLESHOOTING:** If the Show Table dialog box does not open, click Show Table in the Relationships group on the Relationship Tools Design tab.

b. Double-click each of the three tables displayed in the Show Table dialog box to add them to the Relationships window. Click **Close** in the Show Table dialog box.

> **TROUBLESHOOTING:** If you have a duplicate table, click the title bar of the duplicated table and press Delete.

c. Click and drag the border of the Customers table field list to resize it so that all of the fields are visible. Arrange the tables as shown in Figure 27.

d. Drag the **BranchID field** (the primary key) in the Branch table onto the BranchID field (the foreign key) in the Accounts table. The Edit Relationships dialog box opens. Click the **Enforce Referential Integrity** and **Cascade Update Related Fields check boxes** to select them. Click **Create**.

A black line displays, joining the two tables. It has a 1 at the end near the Branch table and an infinity symbol on the end next to the Accounts table. You have established a one-to-many relationship between the Branch and Accounts tables. Each single branch is connected with many accounts.

e. Drag the **CustomerID field** (the primary key) in the Customers table onto the CustomerID field (the foreign key) in the Accounts table. The Edit Relationships dialog box opens. Click the **Enforce Referential Integrity** and **Cascade Update Related Fields check boxes** to select them. Click **Create.**

You have established a one-to-many relationship between the Customers and Accounts tables. A customer will have only a single CustomerID number. The same customer may have many different accounts: Savings, Checking, Credit Card, and so forth.

TROUBLESHOOTING: If you get an error message when you click Create, verify that the data types of the joined fields are the same. To check the data types from the Relationships window, right-click the title bar of a table and select Table Design from the shortcut menu. Modify the data type of the join fields, if necessary. Customer ID should be Number and Branch ID should be Short Text in both tables.

f. Click **Save** on the Quick Access Toolbar to save the changes to the relationships. Close the Relationships window.

STEP 6 ≫ ENFORCE REFERENTIAL INTEGRITY

The design of the Bank database must be 100% correct; otherwise, data entry may be compromised. Even though you are confident that the table relationships are set correctly, you decide to test them by entering some invalid data. If referential integrity is enforced, the invalid data will be rejected by Access. Refer to Figure 28 as you complete Step 6.

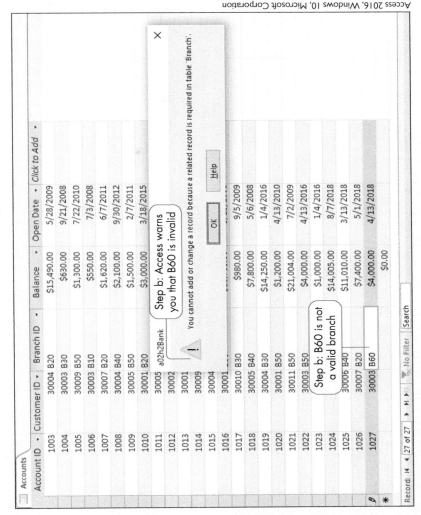

FIGURE 28 Referential Integrity Enforces Accurate Data Entry

a. Double-click the **Accounts table** to open it in Datasheet view.

b. Add a new record, pressing **Tab** after each field: Account ID: **1027**, Customer ID: **30003**, Branch: **B60**, Balance: **4000**, Open Date: **4/13/2018**. Press **Enter**.

You attempted to enter a nonexistent BranchID (B60) and were not allowed to make that error. A warning message is telling you that a related record in the Branch table is required, because the Accounts table and the Branch table are connected by a relationship with Enforce Referential Integrity checked.

c. Click **OK**. Double-click the **Branch table** in the Navigation Pane and examine the data in the BranchID field. Notice the Branch table has no B60 record. Close the Branch table.

d. Replace B60 with **B50** in the new Accounts record and press **Tab** three times. As soon as the focus moves to the next record, the pencil symbol disappears and your data are saved.

You successfully identified a BranchID that Access recognizes. Because referential integrity between the Accounts and Branch tables has been enforced, Access looks at each data entry item in a foreign key and matches it to a corresponding value in the table where it is the primary key. In Step b, you attempted to enter a nonexistent BranchID and were not allowed to make that error. In Step d, you entered a valid BranchID. Access examined the index for the BranchID in the Branch table and found a corresponding value for B50.

e. Close the Accounts table.

f. Close any open tables.

g. Keep the database open if you plan to continue with the Hands-On Exercise. If not, close the database and exit Access.

Single-Table Queries

A *query* enables you to ask questions about the data stored in a database and then provides the answers to the questions by creating subsets or summaries of data in a datasheet. If you wanted to see which customers currently have an account with a balance over $5,000, you could find the answer by creating an Access query.

In this section, you will use the Simple Query Wizard and Query Design view to create single-table queries that display only data that you select. Multitable queries will be covered in the next section.

Creating a Single-Table Query

Because data are stored in tables in a database, you always begin a query by determining which table (or tables) contain the data that you need. For the question about account balances over $5,000, you would use the Accounts table. You can create a single-table query in two ways—by using the Simple Query Wizard or the Query Design tool in the Queries group on the Create tab. While the Simple Query Wizard offers a step-by-step guide to creating a query, the Query Design tool allows for more flexibility and customization, and is often the preferred method for creating queries.

After you design a query, you run it to display the results in a datasheet. A query's datasheet looks like a table's datasheet, except that it is usually a subset of the fields and records found in the table on which it is based. The subset shows only the records that match the criteria that were added in the query design. The subset may contain different sorting of the records than the sorting in the underlying table. You can enter new records in a query, modify existing records, or delete records in Datasheet view. Any changes made in Datasheet view are reflected in the underlying table on which the query is based.

Create a Single-Table Select Query

Select queries are a type of query that displays only the fields and records that match criteria entered in the query design process.

To create a select query using the Query Design tool, complete the following steps:

1. Click the Create tab.
2. Click Query Design in the Queries group on the Design tab.
3. Select the table you want for your query from the Show Table dialog box.
4. Click Add to add the table to the top pane of the query design and close the Show Table dialog box.
5. Drag the fields needed from the table's field list to the query design grid (or alternatively, double-click the field names); then add criteria and sorting options.
6. Click Run in the Results group on the Design tab to show the results in Datasheet view.

Use Query Design View

Query Design view is divided into two sections: The top pane displays the tables from which the data will be retrieved, and the bottom pane (known as the query design grid) displays the fields and the criteria that you set. In the query design grid, you select only the fields that contain the data you want in the query and arrange them in the order that you want them displayed in the query results. You add criteria to further limit (or filter) the records to display only those that you require in the results. The design grid also enables you to sort the records based on one or more fields. You can create calculated fields to display data based on expressions that use the fields in the underlying table. For example, you could calculate the monthly interest earned on each bank account by multiplying the Balance by an interest rate. If a query contains more than one table, the join lines between tables display as they were created in the Relationships window.

The query design grid (the bottom pane) contains columns and rows. Each field in the query has its own column and contains multiple rows. The rows allow you to control the query results.

- The Field row displays the field name.
- The Table row displays the data source (in some cases, a field occurs in more than one table, for example, when it is a join field; therefore, it is often beneficial to display the table name in the query design grid).
- The Sort row enables you to sort in ascending or descending order (or neither).
- The Show row controls whether the field will be displayed or hidden in the query results.
- The *Criteria row* is used to set the rules that determine which records will be selected, such as customers with account balances greater than $5,000.

Figure 29 displays the query design grid with the Show Table dialog box open. The Accounts table has been added from the Show Table dialog box. Figure 30 shows Design view of a sample query with four fields, with a criterion set for one field and sorting set on another. The results of the query display in Datasheet view, as shown in Figure 31.

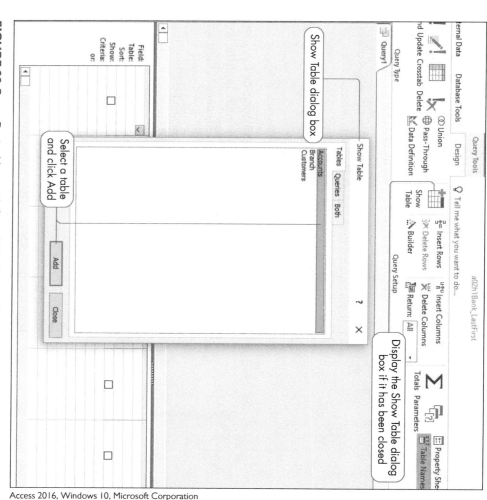

FIGURE 29 Query Design View with Show Table Dialog Box

Access 2016, Windows 10, Microsoft Corporation

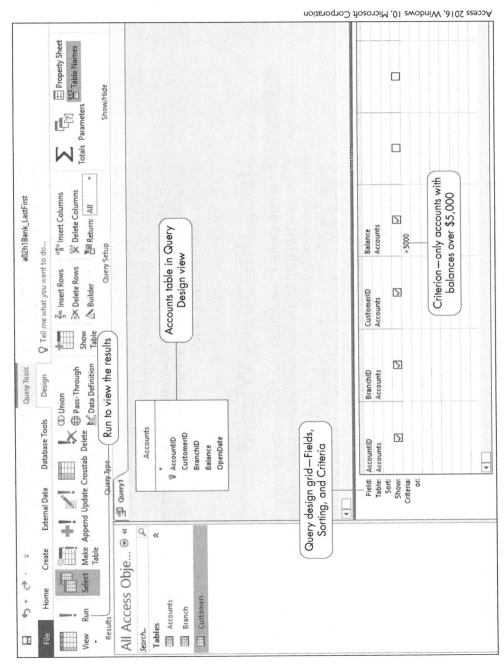

FIGURE 30 Query Design View with Sample Criterion

Run to view the results

Accounts table in Query Design view

Criterion—only accounts with balances over $5,000

Query design grid—Fields, Sorting, and Criteria

Access 2016, Windows 10, Microsoft Corporation

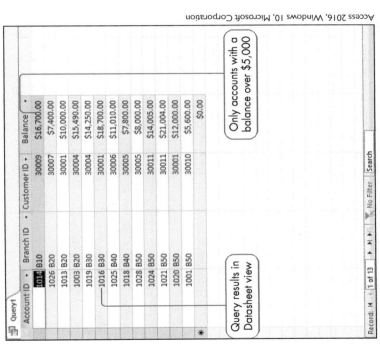

Only accounts with a balance over $5,000

Query results in Datasheet View

Access 2016, Windows 10, Microsoft Corporation

FIGURE 31 Query Results in Datasheet View

Each time you need to fine-tune the query, switch back to Design view, make a change, and then run the query again to view the results. After you are satisfied with the results, you may want to save the query so it becomes a permanent part of the database and can be used later. Each time you run a query, the results will update based on the current data in the underlying table(s).

Using the Query Wizard

STEP 1

The **Simple Query Wizard** guides you through query design with a step-by-step process. The wizard is helpful for creating basic queries that do not require criteria. However, even if you initially design the query with a wizard, you are able to modify it later in Design view. After the wizard completes, you can switch to Design view and add criteria as needed. You can also add additional tables and fields to an existing query when conditions change. To launch the Query Wizard, click the Create tab and click Query Wizard in the Queries group (see Figure 32).

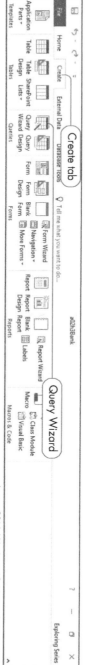

Access 2016, Windows 10, Microsoft Corporation

FIGURE 32 Launching the Query Wizard

Select Simple Query Wizard in the New Query dialog box, as shown in Figure 33.

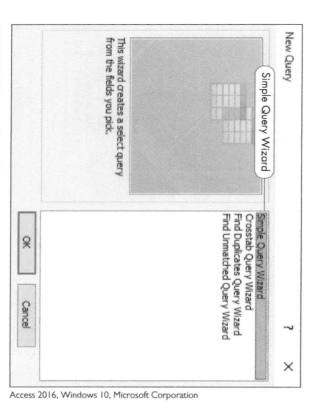

Access 2016, Windows 10, Microsoft Corporation

FIGURE 33 Simple Query Wizard

In the first step of the Simple Query Wizard dialog box, you specify the tables or queries and fields required in your query. When you select a table from the Tables/Queries arrow (queries can also be based on other queries), a list of the table's fields displays in the Available Fields list box (see Figures 34 and 35).

Tables and Queries in Relational Databases

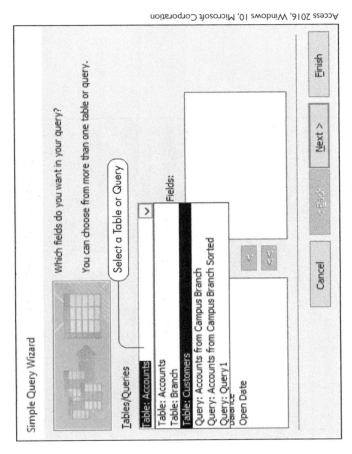

FIGURE 34 Specify Which Tables or Queries to Use

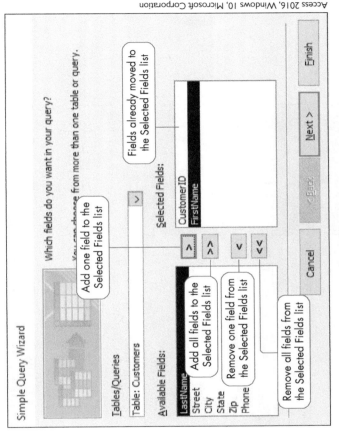

FIGURE 35 Specify the Fields for the Query

Select the necessary fields and add them to the Selected Fields list box using the directional arrows shown in Figure 35. In the next screen (shown in Figure 36), you choose between a detail and a summary query. The detail query shows every field of every record in the result. The summary query enables you to group data and view only summary records. For example, if you were interested in the total funds deposited at each of the bank branches, you would set the query to Summary, click Summary Options, and then click Sum on the Balance field. Access would then sum the balances of all accounts for each branch.

Simple Query Wizard

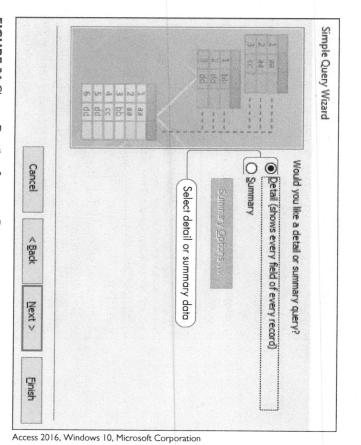

FIGURE 36 Choose Detail or Summary Data

Access 2016, Windows 10, Microsoft Corporation

The final dialog box of the Simple Query Wizard prompts for the name of the query. Assign descriptive names to your queries so that you can easily identify what each one does (see Figure 37).

Simple Query Wizard

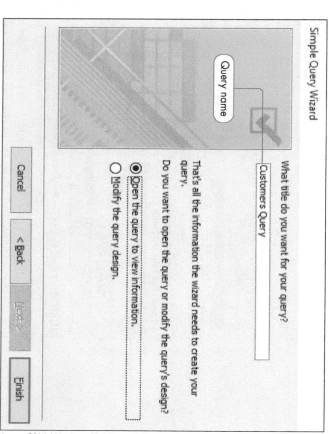

FIGURE 37 Name the Query

Access 2016, Windows 10, Microsoft Corporation

Specifying Query Criteria for Different Data Types

You set criteria to limit the records to display only those that you require in the query results. When specifying a criterion for a query, you may need to include a delimiter— a special character that surrounds a criterion's value. The delimiter required is determined by the field data type. Text fields require quotation marks before and after the text; for example, "Campus" could be used to display customers from the Campus branch in the Bank database. Access automatically adds the quotation marks around text, but to ensure that the correct delimiter is used, you may want to include the delimiters yourself.

When the criterion is in a date field, you enclose the criterion in pound signs, such as #10/14/2018#. Access automatically adds the pound signs around dates, but to ensure that the correct delimiter is used, you may want to include the delimiters yourself. A date value can be entered using any allowed format, such as February 2, 2018, 2/2/2018, or 2-Feb-18. Use plain digits (no delimiter) for the criteria of a numeric field, currency, or AutoNumber. You can enter numeric criteria with or without a decimal point and with or without a minus sign. Commas and dollar signs are not allowed. You enter criteria for a Yes/No field as Yes or No. See Table 4 for query criteria and examples.

TABLE 4 Query Criteria

Data Type	Criteria	Example
Text	"Harry"	For a FirstName field, displays only text that matches Harry exactly. The quotation marks can be typed, or Access will add them automatically.
Numeric	5000	For a Quantity field, displays only numbers that match 5000 exactly (do not specify commas, currency symbols, etc.).
Date	#2/2/2018#	For a ShippedDate field, shows orders shipped on February 2, 2018.
Yes/No	Yes	For a Discontinued field, returns records where the check box is selected, denoting Yes.

Pearson Education, Inc.

Use Wildcards

Wildcards are special characters that can represent one or more characters in a text value. Suppose you want to use a criterion to search for the last name of a customer, but you are not sure how to spell the name; however, you know that the name starts with the letters *Sm*. You can use a wildcard with a text value (such as Sm*) to search for the name.

You enter wildcard characters in text values in the Criteria row of a query. Therefore, if you want to search for names that start with the letters *Sm*, specify the criterion in the LastName field as *Sm**. All last names that begin with *Sm* would display in the results. Wildcard characters can be placed in the beginning, middle, or end of a text string. Table 5 shows more query criterion examples that use wildcards.

TABLE 5 Query Criteria Using Wildcards

Character	Description	Example	Result
*	Matches any number of characters in the same position as the asterisk	Sm*	Small, Smiley, Smith, Smithson
?	Matches a single character in the same position as the question mark	H?ll	Hall, Hill, Hull
[ ]	Matches any single character within the brackets	F[ae]ll	Fall and Fell, but not Fill or Full
[!]	Matches any character not in the brackets	F[!ae]ll	Fill and Full, but not Fall or Fell

Pearson Education, Inc.

Use Comparison Operators in Queries

Comparison operators, such as equal (=), not equal (<>), greater than (>), less than (<), greater than or equal to (>=), and less than or equal to (<=), can be used in query criteria. Comparison operators enable you to limit the query results to only those records that meet the criteria. For example, if you only want to see accounts that have a balance greater than $5,000, you would type >5000 in the Criteria row of the Balance field. Table 6 shows more comparison operator examples.

TABLE 6 Comparison Operators in Queries

Expression	Example
=10	Equals 10
<>10	Not equal to 10
>10	Greater than 10
>=10	Greater than or equal to 10
<10	Less than 10
<=10	Less than or equal to 10

Pearson Education, Inc.

Work with Null

Sometimes finding null values is an important part of making a decision. For example, if you need to know which orders have been completed but not shipped, you would create a query to find the orders with a null (missing) ShipDate. The term that Access uses for a blank field is ***null***. Table 7 provides two examples of when to use the null criterion in a query.

TABLE 7 Establishing Null Criteria Expressions

Expression	Description	Example
Is Null	Use to find blank fields	For a SalesRepID field in the Customers table when the customer has not been assigned to a sales representative.
Is Not Null	Used to find fields with data	For a ShipDate field: a value has been entered to indicate that the order was shipped to the customer.

Pearson Education, Inc.

Establish AND, OR, and NOT Criteria

Remember the earlier question, "Which customers currently have an account with a balance over $5,000?" This question was answered by creating a query with a single criterion. At times, questions are more focused and require queries with multiple criteria. For example, you may need to know "Which customers from the Eastern branch currently have an account with a balance over $5,000?" To answer this question, you specify two criteria in different fields using the ***AND condition***. This means that the query results will display only records that match *all* criteria. When the criteria are in the same row of the query design grid, Access interprets this as an AND condition. You can also use the AND logical operator to test two criteria in the same field, as shown in Table 8.

When you have multiple criteria and you need to satisfy only one, not all of the criteria, use the ***OR condition***. The query results will display records that match any of the specified criteria. You can use the OR logical operator, and type the expression into the Criteria row, separating the criteria with the OR keyword. Table 8 shows an example of an OR condition created using this method. You can also type the first criterion into the Criteria row and then type the next criterion by using the Or row in the same field or a different field in the design grid (see Figure 38).

The NOT logical operator returns all records except the specified criteria. For example, "Not Eastern" would return all accounts except those opened at the Eastern branch.

TABLE 8 AND, OR, and NOT Queries

Logical Operator	Example	Result
AND	>5000 AND <10000	For a Balance field, returns all accounts with a balance greater than $5,000 and less than $10,000.
OR	"Eastern" OR "Campus"	For a Location field, returns all accounts that are at the Eastern or the Campus branch.
NOT	Not "Campus"	For a Location field, returns all records except those in the Campus branch.

Pearson Education, Inc.

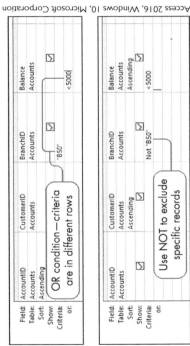

AND condition—criteria are in the same row

OR condition—criteria are in different rows

Use NOT to exclude specific records

Access 2016, Windows 10, Microsoft Corporation

FIGURE 38 Query Design Views Showing the AND, OR, and NOT Operators

TIP: FINDING VALUES IN A DATE RANGE

To find the values contained within a date range, use the greater than (>) and less than (<) operators. For example, to find the values of dates on or after January 1, 2018, and on or before December 31, 2018, use the criterion >=1/1/2018 and <=12/31/2018. You can also use the BETWEEN operator to find the same inclusive dates, for example, BETWEEN 1/1/2018 and 12/31/2018.

Understanding Query Sort Order

The query sort order determines the order of records in a query's Datasheet view. You can change the order of records by specifying the sort order in Design view. When you want to sort using more than one field, the sort order is determined from left to right. The order of columns should be considered when first creating the query. For example, a query sorted by LastName and then by FirstName must have those two fields in the correct order in the design grid. When modifying sort order, it is sometimes necessary to rearrange fields, or add and delete columns in the query design grid.

To change order, add, or delete fields in the query design grid, complete one of the following steps:

- Change the order of a field: select the column you want to move by clicking the column selector. Click again and drag the selected field to its new location.
- Insert an additional column in the design grid: select a column and click Insert Columns in the Query Setup group on the Design tab. The additional column will insert to the left of the selected column.
- Delete a column: click the column selector to select the column and click Delete Columns in the Query Setup group, or press Delete on the keyboard.

Running, Copying, and Modifying a Query

Once your query is designed and saved, you run it to view the results. After you create a query, you may want to create a duplicate copy to use as the basis for creating a similar query. Duplicating a query saves time when you need the same tables and fields but with slightly different criteria.

Run a Query

There are several ways to run a query. One method is from within Design view: click Run in the Results group on the Design tab. Another method is to locate the query in the Navigation Pane and double-click it (or select the query in the Navigation Pane and press Enter). The results will display in a datasheet as a tab in the main window.

Copy and Modify a Query

Sometimes you want a number of queries in which each query is similar to another that you have created. To avoid having to recreate each query from scratch, you can create a copy of an existing query and then modify it to accommodate the new criteria. For example, you need a list of accounts in each branch. In a case like this, you create a query for one branch and then save a copy of the query and give it a new name. Finally, you would change the criteria to specify the next branch.

To create a query based on an existing query, complete the following steps:

1. Open the query you want to copy.
2. Click the File tab and click Save As.
3. Click Save Object As in the File Types section.
4. Ensure that Save Object As is selected in the Database File Types section and click Save As.
5. Type the name you want to use for the new query in the Save As dialog box and click OK (see Figure 39).
6. Switch to Design view of the copied query and modify the query criteria, as necessary.
7. Save and run the modified query.

TIP: COPYING THE QUERY IN THE NAVIGATION PANE

You can also right-click the original query in the Navigation Pane and from the shortcut menu, select Copy. Right-click in the empty space of the Navigation Pane again and then select Paste. Type a name for the new query in the Paste As dialog box and click OK.

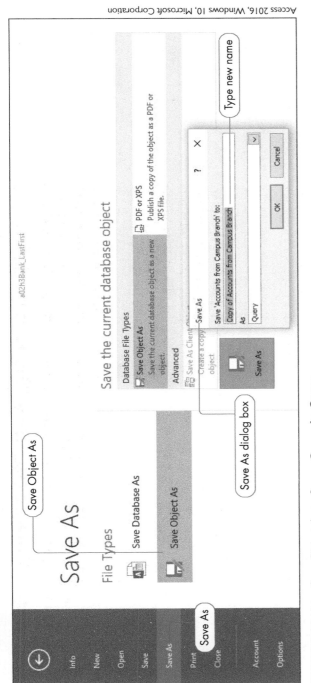

a02h3Bank_LastFirst

Save As

File Types

Save Database As

Save Object As

Save Object As

Save the current database object

Database File Types

Save Object As
Save the current database object as a new object.

Advanced

PDF or XPS
Publish a copy of the object as a PDF or XPS file.

Save As Client Object
Create a copy of the object

Save As

Save 'Accounts from Campus Branch' to:

Copy of Accounts from Campus Branch

As

Query

OK   Cancel

Type new name

Save As dialog box

FIGURE 39 Using Save Object As to Save a Copy of a Query

Change Query Data

>> Be aware that query results in the datasheet display the actual records that are stored in the underlying table(s). Being able to correct an error immediately while it is displayed in the query datasheet is an advantage. You can save time by not having to close the query, open the table, find the error, fix it, and then run the query again. However, use caution when editing records in query results since you will be changing the original table data.

STEP 3

Quick Concepts

8. Define a single-table query. Give an example.

9. Give an example of how to use the Criteria row to find certain records in a table.

10. Why would you use an OR condition in a query?

11. Why would you want to copy an existing query?

3 Single-Table Queries

The tables and table relationships have been created, and some data have been entered in the Bank database. Now, you begin the process of analyzing the bank data for the auditor. You will do so using queries. You decide to begin with the Accounts table.

Skills covered: Use the Query Wizard • Specify Query Criteria • Specify Query Sort Order • Change Query Data • Run, Copy, and Modify a Query

---

STEP 1 **>> USE THE QUERY WIZARD**

You decide to start with the Query Wizard, knowing you can always alter the design of the query later in Design view. You will show the results to the auditor using Datasheet view. Refer to Figure 40 as you complete Step 1.

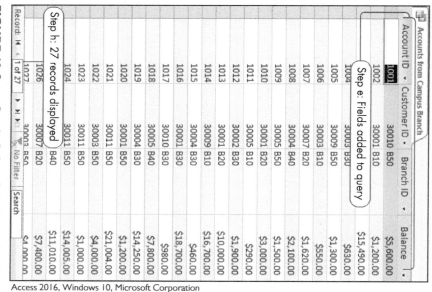

Accounts from Campus Branch

Account ID	Customer ID	Branch ID	Balance
1001	30010 B50		$5,600.00
1002	30001 B10		$1,200.00
1003	30003 B50		$15,490.00
1004	30003 B50		$630.00
1005	30009 B50		$1,300.00
1006	30003 B10		$550.00
1007	30007 B20		$1,620.00
1008	30004 B40		$2,100.00
1009	30005 B50		$1,500.00
1010	30005 B50		$3,000.00
1011	30001 B20		$290.00
1012	30002 B30		$1,900.00
1013	30001 B20		$10,000.00
1014	30009 B10		$16,700.00
1015	30004 B30		$460.00
1016	30001 B30		$18,700.00
1017	30010 B30		$980.00
1018	30005 B40		$7,800.00
1019	30004 B50		$14,250.00
1020	30001 B50		$1,200.00
1021	30011 B50		$21,004.00
1022	30003 B50		$4,000.00
1023	30011 B50		$1,000.00
1024	30001 B50		$14,005.00
1025	30011 B50		$11,010.00
1026	30007 B20		$7,400.00
1027	30003 B50		$4,000.00

Step e: Fields added to query

Step h: 27 records displayed

Record: 1 of 27 ► No Filter Search

FIGURE 40 Query Results Before Criteria Are Applied

Access 2016, Windows 10, Microsoft Corporation

---

a. Open *a02h2Bank_LastFirst* if you closed it at the end of Hands-On Exercise 2, and save it as **a02h3Bank_LastFirst**, changing h2 to h3.

b. Click the **Create tab** and click **Query Wizard** in the Queries group.

The New Query dialog box opens. Simple Query Wizard is selected by default.

c. Click **OK**.

d. Verify that Table: Accounts is selected in the Tables/Queries box.

e. Click **AccountID** in the Available Fields list, then click **Add One Field** [>] to move it to the Selected Fields list. Repeat the process with **CustomerID, BranchID**, and **Balance**.

The four fields should now display in the Selected Fields list box.

f. Click **Next**.

g. Confirm that Detail (shows every field of every record) is selected and click **Next**.

h. Name the query **Accounts from Campus Branch**. Click **Finish**.

This query name describes the data in the query results. Your query should have four fields: AccountID, CustomerID, BranchID, and Balance. The Navigation bar indicates that 27 records meet the query criteria.

STEP 2 ⟫ SPECIFY QUERY CRITERIA AND SORT ORDER

The auditor indicated that the problem seems to be confined to the Campus branch. You use this knowledge to revise the query to display only Campus accounts. Refer to Figure 41 as you complete Step 2.

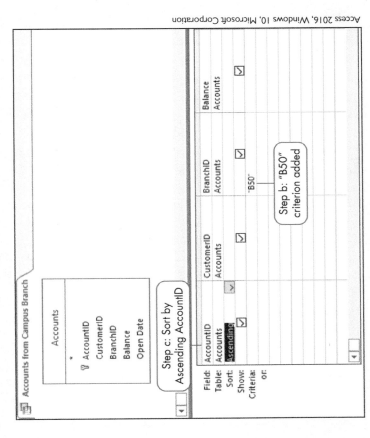

FIGURE 41 Enter Criteria and Add Sort Order

a. Click the **Home tab** and click **View** in the Views group.

The Accounts from Campus Branch query opens in Design view. You have created this query to view only those accounts at the Campus branch. However, other branches' accounts also display. You need to limit the query results to only the records of interest.

b. Click in the **Criteria row** (fifth row) in the BranchID column, type **B50**, and press **Enter**.

B50 is the BranchID for the Campus branch. Access queries are not case sensitive; therefore, b50 and B50 will produce the same results. Access adds quotation marks around text criteria after you press Enter, or you can type them yourself.

c. Click in the **Sort row** (third row) in the AccountID column and select **Ascending**.

d. Click **Run** in the Results group.

You should see nine records in the query results, all from Branch B50, sorted in ascending order by Account ID.

STEP 3 » CHANGE QUERY DATA AND RUN, COPY, AND MODIFY A QUERY

When the query results are on the screen, the auditor notices that some of the data are incorrect, and one of the accounts is missing. From your experience with Access, you explain to the auditor that the data can be changed directly in a query rather than switching back to the table. Refer to Figure 42 as you complete Step 3.

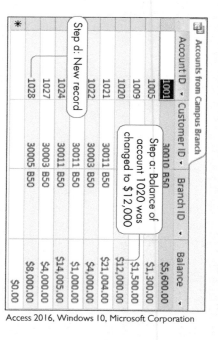

FIGURE 42 Changes Made in the Query Datasheet

Access 2016, Windows 10, Microsoft Corporation

a. Click in the **Balance field** in the record for account 1020. Change $1,200 to **$12,000**. Press **Enter.** Save and close the query.

You modified the record directly in the query results.

b. Double-click the **Accounts table** in the Navigation Pane

Only one account shows a $12,000 balance. The Account ID is 1020 and the Customer ID is 30001. The change you made in the Accounts table from the Campus Branch query datasheet automatically changed the data stored in the underlying table.

c. Open the Customers table. Notice the name of the customer whose CustomerID is 30001, Allison Millward. Close the Customers table.

d. Add a new record to the Accounts table with the following data: **1028** (Account ID), **30005** (Customer ID), **B50** (Branch ID), **8000** (Balance), and **8/4/2018** (Open Date). Press **Tab.**

> **TROUBLESHOOTING:** If the Accounts table is not open, double-click Accounts in the Navigation Pane.

The new record is added to the Accounts table.

e. Double-click the **Accounts from Campus Branch query** in the Navigation Pane.

Customer 30005 now shows two accounts: one with a balance of $1,500 and one with a balance of $8,000.

f. Click the **File tab,** click **Save As,** click **Save Object As,** and then click **Save As.** Type **Accounts from Campus Branch Sorted** as the query name. Click **OK.**

g. Click **View** in the Views group to return to Design view of the copied query.

h. Click in the **Sort row** of the AccountID field and select **(not sorted)**. Click in the **Sort row** of the CustomerID field and select **Ascending**. Click in the **Sort row** of the BalanceID field and select **Ascending**.

i. Click **Run** in the Results group.

Customer 30005 now shows two accounts with the two balances sorted in ascending order. Likewise, all other customers with more than one account are listed in ascending order by balance.

j. Save the query. Close the Accounts from Campus Branch Sorted query and close the Accounts table.

k. Keep the database open if you plan to continue with the Hands-On Exercise. If not, close the database and exit Access.

Multitable Queries

Multitable queries contain two or more tables, and enable you to take advantage of the relationships that have been set in your database. When you extract information from a database with a query, often you will need to pull data from multiple tables. One table may contain the core information that you want, while another table may contain the related data that make the query provide the complete results.

For example, the sample Bank database contains three tables: Customers, Accounts, and Branch. You connected the tables through relationships in order to store data efficiently and to enforce consistent data entry between them. The Customers table provides the information for the owners of the accounts. However, the Accounts table includes the balances of each account—the key financial information. Therefore, both the Customers and Accounts tables are needed to provide the information that you want: which Customers own which Accounts.

Creating a Multitable Query

There are several ways to create multitable queries. The simplistic method is to add tables to an existing query, or to copy an existing query and then add to it. You can also create a multitable query from scratch either using the Query Wizard or the Query Design tool.

Add Additional Tables to a Query

One way to create a multitable query is to add tables and fields to an existing query, for example to add branch or customer data to a query that includes account information.

To add tables to a saved query, complete the following steps:

1. Open the existing query in Design view.
2. Add additional tables to a query by dragging tables from the Navigation Pane directly into the top pane of the query design window.
3. Add fields, criteria, and sorting options in the query design grid.
4. Run and save the query.

For example, the Branch and Customers tables were added to the query, as shown in Figure 43. The join lines between tables indicate that relationships were previously set in the Relationships window. With the additional tables and fields available, you can now add the customer's name (from Customers) and the branch location name (from Branch) rather than using CustomerID and BranchID in your results. The datasheet will contain more readily identifiable information than ID numbers for customers and locations.

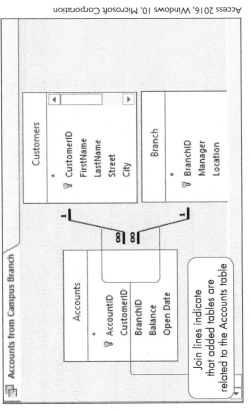

FIGURE 43 Two Additional Tables Added to a Query

Create a Multitable Query

Creating a multitable query from scratch is similar to creating a single-table query; however, choosing the right tables and managing the relationships in the query might require some additional skills. First, you should only use related tables in a multitable query. Related tables are tables that are joined in a relationship using a common field. Generally, related tables should already be joined in the Relationships window when you begin to create a multitable query. Using Figure 43 as a guide, creating a query with the Accounts and Branch tables would be acceptable, as would using Accounts and Customers tables, or Accounts, Branch, and Customers tables. All three scenarios include related tables. However, creating a query with only the Branch and Customers tables would not be acceptable because these tables are not directly related to one another (in other words, they do not have a common field).

To create a multitable query, complete the following steps:

1. Click the Create tab.
2. Click Query Design in the Queries group.
3. Add the tables you want in your query from the Show Table dialog box. Close the Show Table dialog box.
4. Drag the fields you want to display from the tables to the query design grid (or alternatively, double-click the field names); then add criteria and sorting options.
5. Click Run in the Results group on the Design tab to show the results in Datasheet view.

TIP: PRINT THE RELATIONSHIP REPORT TO HELP CREATE A MULTITABLE QUERY

When you create a multitable query, you only include related tables. As a guide, when the Relationships window is open, you can print the Relationship Report. Click the Database Tools tab, then click Relationship Report in the Tools group on the Relationship Tools Design tab. This report will provide a diagram that displays the tables, fields, and relationships in your database. The report is exportable to other formats such as Word if you want to share it with colleagues.

Modifying a Multitable Query

After creating a multitable query, you may find that you did not include all of the fields you needed, or you may find that you included fields that are unnecessary to the results. To modify multitable queries, use the same techniques you learned for single-table queries.

- To add tables, use the Show Table dialog box in the Query Setup group on the Query Tools Design tab (or drag the tables into the top pane of the query design from the Navigation Pane).

- To remove tables, click the unwanted tables and press Delete.

- To add fields, double-click the fields you want to include.

- To remove fields, click the column selector of each field and press Delete.

Join lines between related tables should display automatically in a query if the relationships were previously established, as shown in Figure 43.

TIP: MULTITABLE QUERIES INHERIT RELATIONSHIPS

When you add two or more related tables to a query, join lines display automatically. You can delete a join line in a query with no impact on the relationship set in the database. Deleting a join line only affects the relationship in the individual query. The next time you create a query with the same tables, the relationships will be inherited from the database. And, if you open the Relationships window, you will find the join lines intact.

Add and Delete Fields in a Multitable Query

In Figure 44, three tables, as well as the join lines between the tables, display in the top pane of Design view. All the fields from each of the tables are now available for use in the query design grid. Figure 44 shows that Location (from the Branch table) replaced BranchID and LastName (from the Customers table) replaced CustomerID to make the results more useful. BranchID was deleted from the query; therefore, the "B50" criterion was removed as well. "Campus" was added to the Location field's Criteria row in order to extract the names of the branches rather than their BranchID numbers. Because criteria values are not case sensitive, typing "campus" is the same as typing "Campus" and both will return the same results. The results of the revised query are shown in Figure 45.

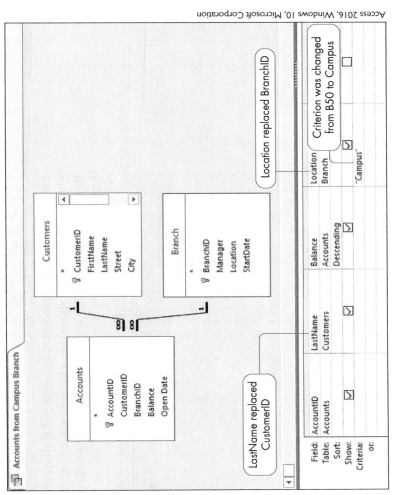

LastName replaced CustomerID

Location replaced BranchID

Criterion was changed from B50 to Campus

FIGURE 44 Modify the Query Design

Account ID	LastName	Balance	Branch Location
1021	YourName	$21,004.00	Campus
1024	YourName	$14,005.00	Campus
1020	M		Campus
1028	W	Accounts are from the Campus branch	Campus
1001	Peterson	$5,600.00	Campus
1027	Hayes	$4,000.00	Campus
1022	Hayes	$4,000.00	Campus
1009	Wagner	$1,500.00	Campus
1005	Nunn	$1,300.00	Campus
1023	YourName	$1,000.00	Campus

FIGURE 45 Datasheet View of a Multitable Query

Add Join Lines in a Multitable Query

In Figure 46, two tables are added to the query design, but no join line connects them. The results of the query will be unpredictable and will display more records than expected. The Customers table contains 11 records, and the Branch table contains 5 records. Because Access does not know how to interpret the unrelated tables, the results will show 55 records—every possible combination of customer and branch (11 × 5). See Figure 47.

To fix this problem, you can create join lines using existing tables if the tables contain a common field with the same data type. In this example, in which there is no common field, you can add an additional table that provides join lines between all three tables. You can add the Accounts table, which provides join lines between the two existing tables, Customers and Branch, and the added Accounts table. As soon as the third table is added to the query design, the join lines display automatically.

Over time, your databases may grow, and additional tables will be added. Occasionally, new tables are added to the database but not to the Relationships window. When queries are created with the new tables, join lines will not be established. When this happens, add join lines to create relationships with the new tables. Or you can create temporary join lines in the query design window. These join lines will provide a temporary relationship between tables (for that query only) and enable Access to interpret the query properly.

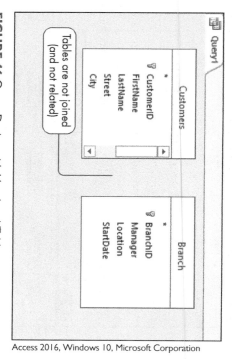

Tables are not joined (and not related)

FIGURE 46 Query Design with Unrelated Tables

Access 2016, Windows 10, Microsoft Corporation

LastName	Branch ID	Branch Location	Manager's Start Date
Millward	B10	Uptown	12/3/2014
Millward	B20	Eastern	6/18/2013
Millward	B30	Western	3/13/2011
Millward	B40	Southern	9/15/2014
Millward	B50	Campus	10/11/2016
Fox	B10	Uptown	2014
Fox	B20	Eastern	013
Fox	B30	Western	011
Fox	B40	Southern	014
Fox	B50	Campus	10/11/2016
Hayes	B10	Uptown	12/3/2014
Hayes	B20	Eastern	6/18/2013
Hayes	B30	Western	3/13/2011
Hayes	B40	Southern	9/15/2014
Hayes	B50	Campus	10/11/2016
Collins	B10	Uptown	12/3/2014
Collins	B20	Eastern	6/18/2013
Collins	B30	Western	3/13/2011
Collins	B40	Southern	9/15/2014
Collins	B50	Campus	10/11/2016
Wagner	B10	Uptown	12/3/2014
Wagner	B20	Eastern	6/18/2013
Wagner	B30	Western	3/13/2011
Wagner	B40	Southern	9/15/2014
Wagner	B50	Campus	10/11/2016
Williams	B10	Uptown	12/3/2014
Williams	B20	Eastern	6/18/2013

Result shows 55 records

Access shows one record for every Branch for each Customer

Record: 14 1 of 55 ▶ ▶I ▶* No Filter Search

FIGURE 47 Query Results Using Unrelated Tables

Access 2016, Windows 10, Microsoft Corporation

Tables and Queries in Relational Databases

Summarize Data Using a Multitable Query

STEP 4 ≫ You can get valuable information from your database using a multitable query. For example, if you want to know how many accounts each customer has, you would create a new query and add both the Customers and Accounts tables to Design view. After you verify that the join lines are correct, you add the CustomerID field from the Customers table and the AccountID field from the Accounts table to the query design grid. When you initially run the query, the results show duplicates in the CustomerID column because some customers have multiple accounts.

To summarize this information (how many accounts each customer has), complete the following steps:

1. Switch to Design view and click Totals in the Show/Hide group on the Query Tools Design tab. The Total row displays. Both fields show the Group By option in the Total row. The Total row enables you to summarize records by using functions such as Sum, Average, Count, etc.

2. Click in the Total row of the AccountID field, select Count from the list of functions, and run the query again. This time the results show one row for each customer and the number of accounts for each customer.

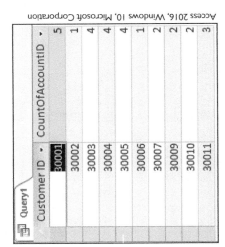

Customer ID	CountOfAccountID
30001	5
30002	1
30003	4
30004	4
30005	4
30006	1
30007	2
30009	2
30010	2
30011	3

Access 2016, Windows 10, Microsoft Corporation

FIGURE 48 Datasheet Results with the Count of Accounts per Customer

12. What is the advantage of creating a multitable query?

13. What is the benefit of summarizing data in a multitable query?

14. What is the result of creating a query with two unrelated tables?

Hands-On Exercises

4 Multitable Queries

Skills covered: Add Additional Tables to a Query • Create a Multitable Query • Modify a Multitable Query • Summarize Data Using a Multitable Query

Based on the auditor's request, you will evaluate the data further. This requires creating queries that are based on multiple tables rather than on a single table. You decide to open an existing query, add additional tables, and then save the query with a new name.

» ADD ADDITIONAL TABLES TO A QUERY

The previous query was based on the Accounts table, but now you need to add information to the query from the Branch and Customers tables. You will add the Branch and Customers tables to the query. Refer to Figure 49 as you complete Step 1.

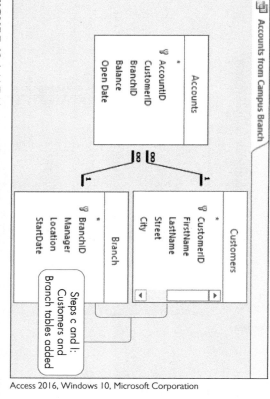

FIGURE 49 Add Tables to an Existing Query

Access 2016, Windows 10, Microsoft Corporation

a. Open *a02h3Bank_LastFirst* if you closed it at the end of Hands-On Exercise 3, and save it as **a02h4Bank_LastFirst**, changing h3 to h4.

b. Right-click the **Accounts from Campus Branch query** in the Navigation Pane and select **Design View** from the shortcut menu.

c. Drag the **Branch table** from the Navigation Pane to the top pane of the query design grid to the right of the Accounts table.

A join line connects the Branch table to the Accounts table. The tables in the query inherit the relationship created earlier in the Relationships window.

d. Drag the **Location field** from the Branch table to the first empty column in the design grid.

The Location field should be positioned to the right of the Balance field.

e. Click the **Show check box** below the BranchID field to clear the check box and hide this field from the results.

The BranchID field is no longer needed in the results because the Location field provides the branch name instead. Because you deselected the BranchID Show check box, the BranchID field will not display the next time the query is run.

f. Delete the B50 criterion in the BranchID field.

g. Type **Campus** as a criterion in the Location field and press **Enter**.

Access adds quotation marks around Campus for you because Campus is a text criterion. You are substituting the Location criterion (*Campus*) in place of the BranchID criterion (B50).

h. Click in the AccountID field **Sort row**, click the arrow, and then click **(not sorted)**. Click in the **Sort row** of the Balance field. Click the arrow and select **Descending**.

i. Click **Run** in the Results group.

The BranchID field does not display in Datasheet view because you hid the field in Step e. Only Campus accounts display in the datasheet (10 records). Next, you will add the Customers LastName field to and delete the CustomerID field from the query.

j. Save the changes to the query design.

k. Click **View** in the Views group to return to Design view. Point over the column selector at the top of the BranchID field, and when a downward arrow displays, click to select it. Press **Delete**.

The BranchID field has been removed from the grid.

l. Drag the **Customers table** from the Navigation Pane to the top pane of the query design grid and reposition the tables so that the join lines are not blocked (see Figure 49).

The join lines automatically connect the Customers table to the Accounts table (similar to Step c above).

m. Drag the **LastName field** in the Customers table to the second column in the design grid.

The LastName field should be positioned to the right of the AccountID field.

n. Click the **column selector** in the CustomerID field to select it. Press **Delete**.

The CustomerID field is no longer needed in the results because we added the LastName field instead.

o. Click **Run** in the Results group.

The last names of the customers now display in the results.

p. Save and close the query.

STEP 2 》》 CREATE A MULTITABLE QUERY

After discussing the query results with the auditor, you realize that another query is needed to show those customers with account balances of $1,000 or less. You create the query and view the results in Datasheet view. Refer to Figure 50 as you complete Step 2.

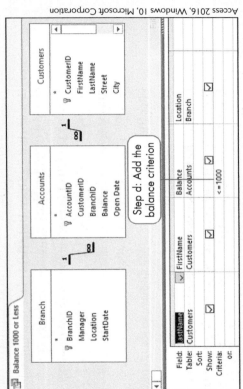

Access 2016, Windows 10, Microsoft Corporation

FIGURE 50 Create a Multitable Query

a. Click the **Create tab** and click **Query Design** in the Queries group.

b. Double-click the **Branch table name** in the Show Table dialog box. Double-click **Accounts** and **Customers** so that all three are added to Design view. Click **Close** in the Show Table dialog box.

Three tables are added to the query.

c. Double-click the following fields to add them to the query design grid: **LastName, FirstName, Balance, and Location.**

d. Type **<=1000** in the Criteria row of the Balance column.

e. Click **Run** in the Results group to see the query results.

Six records that have a balance of $1,000 or less display.

f. Click **Save** on the Quick Access Toolbar and type **Balance 1000 or Less** as the Query Name in the Save As dialog box. Click **OK**.

STEP 3 » MODIFY A MULTITABLE QUERY

The auditor requests additional changes to the Balance 1000 or Less query you just created. You will modify the criteria to display the accounts that were opened on or after January 1, 2011, with balances of $2,000 or less. Refer to Figure 51 as you complete Step 3.

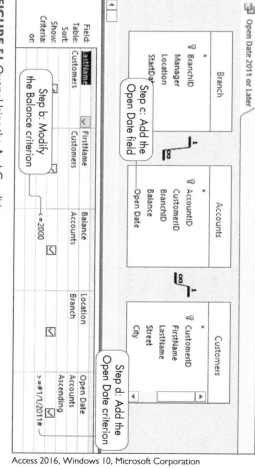

FIGURE 51 Query Using the And Condition

a. Click **View** in the Views group to switch the Balance 1000 or Less query to Design view.

b. Type **<=2000** in place of <=1000 in the Criteria row of the Balance field and press **Enter**.

c. Double-click the **Open Date field** in the Accounts table in the top pane of Design view to add it to the first blank column in the design grid.

d. Type **>=1/1/2011** in the Criteria row of the Open Date field and press **Enter** to extract only accounts that have been opened since January 1, 2011.

After you type the expression and then move to a different column, Access will add the # symbols around the date automatically.

e. Click **Run** in the Results group to display the results of the query.

Five records display in the query results.

f. Click the **File tab**, click **Save As**, and then click **Save Object As**. Type **Open Date 2011 or Later** as the query name. Click **OK**.

g. Click **View** in the Views group to return to Design view of the copied query.

h. Click in the **Sort row** of the Open Date field and select **Ascending**.

i. Click **Run** in the Results group.

The records are sorted from the earliest open date on or after January 1, 2011, to the most recent open date.

j. Save and close the query.

STEP 4 **>> SUMMARIZE DATA USING A MULTITABLE QUERY**

The auditor wants to know the number of accounts each customer has opened. You create a query using a Total row to obtain these data. Refer to Figure 52 as you complete Step 4.

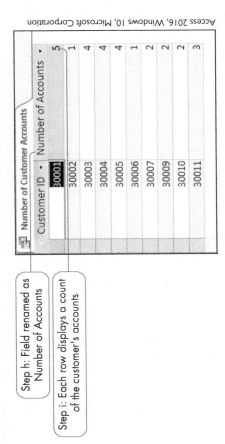

Step h: Field renamed as Number of Accounts

Step i: Each row displays a count of the customer's accounts

Access 2016, Windows 10, Microsoft Corporation

FIGURE 52 Number of Accounts per Customer

a. Click the **Create tab** and click **Query Design** in the Queries group.

b. Add the **Accounts table** and the **Customers table** to the top section of Design view. Click **Close** in the Show Table dialog box.

c. Double-click the **CustomerID** in the Customers table in the top section of Design view to add it to the first blank column in the design grid, and double-click the **AccountID** in the Accounts table to add it to the second column.

d. Click **Run** in the Results group.

The results show there are 28 records. Every account a customer has opened is displayed. The auditor wants only the total number of accounts a customer has, so you modify the query.

e. Click **View** in the Views group to return to Design view of the query.

f. Click **Totals** in the Show/Hide group.

Both columns show the Group By option in the Total row.

g. Click **Group By** in the Total row of the AccountID field and select **Count**.

h. Modify the AccountID field to read **Number of Accounts: AccountID**.

You typed a new field name followed by a colon that will display Number of Accounts in the datasheet when you run the query.

i. Click **Run** in the Results group. Resize the columns of the datasheet to fully display the results.

The results show one row for each customer and the number of accounts each customer has opened since the database was created.

j. Click **Save** on the Quick Access Toolbar and type **Number of Customer Accounts** as the query name. Close the query.

k. Close the database and exit Access. Based on your instructor's directions, submit a02h4Bank_LastFirst.

Hands-On Exercise 4

Chapter Objectives Review

After reading this chapter, you have accomplished the following objectives:

1. Design a table.

- Include necessary data: Consider the output requirements when creating table structure. Determine the data required to produce the expected information.
- Design for now and for the future: When designing a database, anticipate the future needs of the system and build in the flexibility to satisfy those demands.
- Store data in their smallest parts: Store data in their smallest parts for more flexibility. Storing a full name in a Name field is more limiting than storing a first name in a separate FirstName field and a last name in a separate LastName field.
- Determine primary keys: When designing your database tables, it is important to determine which field will uniquely identify each record in a table.
- Plan for common fields between tables: Tables are joined in relationships using common fields. Name the common fields with the same name and make sure they have the same data type.
- Design to accommodate calculations: Calculated fields are frequently created with numeric data. You can use date arithmetic to subtract one date from another to find the number of days, months, or years that have elapsed between them.

2. Create and modify tables and work with data.

- You can create tables in Datasheet view or Design view. Alternatively, you can import data from another database or an application such as Excel to create tables in an Access database.
- Determine data type: Data type properties determine the type of data that can be entered and the operations that can be performed on that data. Access recognizes 12 data types.
- Set a table's primary key: The primary key is the field that uniquely identifies each record in a table.
- Explore a foreign key: A foreign key is a field in one table that is also the primary key of another table.
- Work with field properties: Field properties determine how the field looks and behaves. Examples of field properties are the Field Size property and the Caption property.
- Create a new field in Design view: It may be necessary to add table fields that were not included in the original design process. While it is possible to add fields in Datasheet view, Design view offers more flexibility.
- Modify the table in Datasheet view: Datasheet view is used to add, edit, and delete records. Design view is used to create and modify the table structure by enabling you to add and edit fields and set field properties.

3. Share data.

- Import Excel data: You can import data from other applications such as an Excel spreadsheet.

- Import Access data: You can import data from another database by using the Import Wizard.
- Modify an imported table's design and data: After importing a table, examine the design and make necessary modifications. Modifications may include changing a field name, adding new fields, or deleting unnecessary fields.

4. Establish table relationships.

- Use Show Table to add tables to the Relationships window. Drag a field name from one table to the corresponding field name in another table to join the tables.
- Enforce referential integrity: Referential integrity enforces rules in a database that are used to preserve relationships between tables when records are changed.
- Set cascade options: The Cascade Update Related Fields option ensures that when the primary key is modified in a primary table, Access will automatically update all foreign key values in a related table. The Cascade Delete Related Records option ensures that when the primary key is deleted in a primary table, Access will automatically delete all records in related tables that reference the primary key.
- Establish a one-to-many relationship: A one-to-many relationship is established when the primary key value in the primary table can match many of the foreign key values in the related table. One-to-one and many-to-many are also relationship possibilities, but one-to-many relationships are the most common.

5. Create a single-table query.

- Create a single-table select query: A single-table select query uses fields from one table to display only those records that match certain criteria.
- Use Query Design view: Use Query Design view to create and modify a query. The top portion of the view contains tables with their respective field names and displays the join lines between tables. The bottom portion, known as the query design grid, contains columns and rows that you use to control the query results.

6. Use the Query Wizard.

- The Query Wizard is an alternative method for creating queries. It enables you to select tables and fields from lists. The last step of the wizard prompts you to save the query.

7. Specify query criteria for different data types.

- Different data types require different syntax. Date fields are enclosed in pound signs (#) and text fields in quotations (""). Numeric and currency fields require no delimiters.
- Use wildcards: Wildcards are special characters that can represent one or more characters in a text value. A question mark (?) is a wildcard that stands for a

single character in the same position as the question mark, while an asterisk (*) is a wildcard that stands for any number of characters in the same position as the asterisk.

- Use comparison operators in queries: Comparison operators such as equal (=), not equal (<>), greater than (>), less than (<), greater than or equal to (>=), and less than or equal to (<=) can be used in the criteria of a query to limit the query results to only those records that meet the criteria.

- Work with null: Access uses the term null for a blank field. Null criteria can be used to find missing information.

- Establish AND, OR, and NOT criteria: The AND, OR, and NOT conditions are used when queries require logical criteria. The AND condition returns only records that meet all criteria. The OR condition returns records meeting any of the specified criteria. The NOT logical operator returns all records except the specified criteria.

8. Understand query sort order.

- The query sort order determines the order of records in a query's Datasheet view. You can change the order of records by specifying the sort order in Design view.

- The sort order is determined from the order of the fields from left to right. Move the field columns to position them in left to right sort order.

9. Run, copy, and modify a query.

- Run a query: To obtain the results for a query, you must run the query. To run the query, click Run in the Results group in Design view. Another method is to locate the

query in the Navigation Pane and double-click it. A similar method is to select the query and press Enter.

- Copy and modify a query: To save time, after specifying tables, fields, and conditions for one query, copy the query, rename it, and then modify the fields and criteria in the second query.

- Change query data: You can correct an error immediately while editing records in the query datasheet. Use caution when editing records in query results because you will be changing the original table data.

10. Create a multitable query.

- Add additional tables to a query: Open the Navigation Pane and drag the tables from the Navigation Pane directly into the top section of Query Design view.

- Create a multitable query: Multitable queries contain two or more tables enabling you to take advantage of the relationships that have been set in your database.

11. Modify a multitable query.

- Add and delete fields in a multitable query: Multitable queries may need to be modified. Add fields by double-clicking the field name in the table you want; remove fields by clicking the column selector and pressing Delete.

- Add join lines in a multitable query: If the tables have a common field, create join lines by dragging the field name of one common field onto the field name of the other table. Or you can add an additional table that will provide a join between all three tables.

- Summarize data using a multitable query: Use the total row options of a field such as Count to get answers.

Key Terms Matching

Match the key terms with their definitions. Write the key term letter by the appropriate numbered definition.

a. AND condition

b. AutoNumber

c. Caption property

d. Cascade Delete Related Records

e. Cascade Update Related Fields

f. Comparison Operator

g. Criteria row

h. Data redundancy

i. Data type

j. Field property

k. Foreign key

l. Multitable query

m. Null

n. One-to-many relationship

o. OR condition

p. Query

q. Referential Integrity

r. Simple Query Wizard

s. Wildcard

1. _____ Special character that can represent one or more characters in the criterion of a query.

2. _____ Characteristic of a field that determines how it looks and behaves.

3. _____ Returns only records that meet all criteria.

4. _____ A row in the Query Design view that determines which records will be selected.

5. _____ Determines the type of data that can be entered and the operations that can be performed on that data.

6. _____ Used to create a more understandable label than a field name label that displays in the top row in Datasheet view and in forms and reports.

7. _____ Enables you to ask questions about the data stored in a database and provides answers to the questions in a datasheet.

8. _____ The term Access uses to describe a blank field.

9. _____ A number that automatically increments each time a record is added.

10. _____ The unnecessary storing of duplicate data in two or more tables.

11. _____ When the primary key value in the primary table can match many of the foreign key values in the related table.

12. _____ A field in one table that is also the primary key of another table.

13. _____ An option that directs Access to automatically update all foreign key values in a related table when the primary key value is modified in a primary table.

14. _____ Rules in a database that are used to preserve relationships between tables when records are changed.

15. _____ Contains two or more tables, enabling you to take advantage of the relationships that have been set in your database.

16. _____ Returns records meeting any of the specified criteria.

17. _____ Provides a step-by-step guide to help you through the query design process.

18. _____ When the primary key value is deleted in a primary table, Access will automatically delete all foreign key values in a related table.

19. _____ Uses greater than (>), less than (<), greater than or equal to (>=), and less than or equal to (<=), etc. to limit query results that meet these criteria.

Multiple Choice

1. All of the following are suggested guidelines for table design *except*:

(a) Include all necessary data.
(b) Store data in its smallest parts.
(c) Avoid date arithmetic.
(d) Link tables using common fields.

2. Which of the following determines how the field names can be made more readable in table and query datasheets?

(a) Field size
(b) Data type
(c) Caption property
(d) Normalization

3. When entering, deleting, or editing input masks:

(a) The table must be in Design view.
(b) The table must be in Datasheet view.
(c) The table may be in either Datasheet or Design view.
(d) Data may only be entered in a form.

4. With respect to importing data into Access, which of the following statements is *true*?

(a) The Import Wizard works only for Excel files.
(b) The Import Wizard is found on the Create tab.
(c) You can assign a primary key while you are importing Excel data.
(d) Imported table designs cannot be modified in Access.

5. The main reason to set a field size in Access is to:

(a) Limit the length of values in a table.
(b) Make it possible to delete records.
(c) Keep your database safe from unauthorized users.
(d) Keep misspelled data from being entered into a table.

6. An illustration of a one-to-many relationship would be:

(a) An employee listed in the Employees table earns a raise so the Salaries table must be updated.
(b) A customer may have more than one account in an accounts table.
(c) Each employee in an Employees table has a matching entry in the Salaries table.
(d) An employee leaves the company so that when he is deleted from the Employees table, his salary data will be deleted from the Salaries table.

7. A query's specifications as to which tables to include must be entered on the:

(a) Table row of the query design grid.
(b) Show row of the query design grid.
(c) Sort row of the query design grid.
(d) Criteria row of the query design grid.

8. When adding date criteria to the Query Design view, the dates you enter must be delimited by:

(a) Parentheses ().
(b) Pound signs (#).
(c) Quotes (" ").
(d) At signs (@).

9. It is more efficient to make a copy of an existing query rather than to create a new query when which of the following is *true*?

(a) The existing query contains only one table.
(b) The existing query and the new query use the same tables and fields.
(c) The existing query and the new query have the exact same criteria.
(d) The original query is no longer being used.

10. Which of the following is *true* for the Query Wizard?

(a) No criteria can be added as you step through the Wizard.
(b) You can only select related tables as a source.
(c) Fields with different data types are not allowed.
(d) You are required to summarize the data.

Practice Exercises

Philadelphia Bookstore

FROM SCRATCH

Tom and Erin Mullaney own and operate a bookstore in Philadelphia, Pennsylvania. Erin asked you to help her create an Access database to store the publishers and the books that they sell. The data for the publishers and books is currently stored in Excel worksheets that you decide to import into a new database. You determine that a third table—for authors—is also required. Your task is to create and populate the three tables, set the table relationships, and enforce referential integrity. You will then create queries to extract information from the tables. Refer to Figure 53 as you complete this exercise.

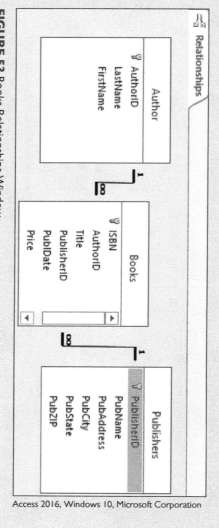

Access 2016, Windows 10, Microsoft Corporation

FIGURE 53 Books Relationships Window

a. Open Access and click **Blank desktop database**. Type **a02p1Books_LastFirst** in the **File Name box**. Click **Browse** to navigate to the location where you are saving your files in the File New Database dialog box, click **OK** to close the dialog box, and then click **Create** to create the new database.

b. Type **11** in the Click to Add column and click **Click to Add**. The field name becomes Field1, and *Click to Add* now displays as the third column. In the third column, type **Beschloss**, and then press **Tab**. Repeat the process for the fourth column; type **Michael R.** and press **Tab** two times. The insertion point returns to the first column where (New) is selected.

c. Press **Tab**. Type the rest of the data using the following table. These data will become the records of the Author table.

ID	Field1	Field2	Field3
1	11	Beschloss	Michael R.
(New)	12	Turow	Scott
	13	Rice	Anne
	14	King	Stephen
	15	Connelly	Michael
	16	Rice	Luanne
	17	*your last name*	*your first name*

d. Click **Save** on the Quick Access Toolbar. Type **Author** in the Save As dialog box and click **OK**.

e. Click **View** in the Views group to switch to Design view of the Author table.

f. Select **Field1**—in the second row—in the top portion of the table design and type **AuthorID** to rename the field. In the Field Properties section in the lower pane of the table design, type **Author ID** in the Caption box and verify that Long Integer displays for the Field Size property.

---

676   Practice Exercises

g. Select **Field2** and type **LastName** to rename the field. In the Field Properties section in the bottom portion of Design view, type **Author's Last Name** in the Caption box and type **20** as the field size.

h. Select **Field3** and type **FirstName** to rename the field. In the Field Properties section in the bottom portion of the table design, type **Author's First Name** as the caption and type **15** as the field size.

i. Click the **ID field row selector** (which displays the primary key) to select the row, and then click **Delete Rows** in the Tools group. Click **Yes** two times to confirm both messages.

j. Click the **AuthorID row selector**, and then click **Primary Key** in the Tools group to set the primary key.

k. Click **Save** on the Quick Access Toolbar to save the design changes. Click **Yes** to the *Some data may be lost* message. Close the table.

l. Click the **External Data tab** and click **Excel** in the Import & Link group to launch the Get External Data – Excel Spreadsheet feature. Verify that the *Import the source data into a new table in the current database* option is selected. click **Browse**, and then navigate to your student data folder. Select the *a02p1Books* workbook, click **Open**, and then click **OK**. This workbook contains two worksheets. Follow the steps below:

- Select the **Publishers worksheet** and click **Next**.
- Click the **First Row Contains Column Headings check box** to select it and click **Next**.
- Ensure that the PubID field is selected, click the **Indexed arrow**, select **Yes (No Duplicates)**, and then click **Next**.
- Click the **Choose my own primary key arrow**, ensure that PubID is selected, and then click **Next**.
- Accept the name Publishers for the table name, click **Finish**, and then click **Close** without saving the import steps.

m. Use the Import Wizard again to import the Books worksheet from the *a02p1Books* workbook into the Access database. Follow the steps below:

- Ensure that the Books worksheet is selected and click **Next**.
- Click the **First Row Contains Column Headings check box** to select it, and click **Next**.
- Click the **ISBN column**, click the down arrow, set the Indexed property box to **Yes (No Duplicates)**, and then click **Next**.
- Click the **Choose my own primary key arrow**, select **ISBN** as the primary key field, and then click **Next**.
- Accept the name Books as the table name. Click **Finish** and click **Close** without saving the import steps.

n. Right-click the **Books table** in the Navigation Pane and select **Design View**. Make the following changes:

- Click the **PubID field** and change the name to **PublisherID**.
- Set the caption property to **Publisher ID**.
- Change the PublisherID Field Size property to **2**.
- Click the **ISBN field** and change the Field Size property to **13**.
- Change the AuthorCode field name to **AuthorID**.
- Change the AuthorID Field Size property to **Long Integer**.
- Click the **ISBN field row selector** (which displays the primary key) to select the row. Click and drag to move the row up to the first position in the table design.
- Click **Save** on the Quick Access Toolbar to save the design changes to the Books table. Click **Yes** to the *Some data may be lost* warning.
- Close the table.

o. Right-click the **Publishers table** in the Navigation Pane and select **Design View**. Make the following changes:

- Click the **PubID field** and change the name to **PublisherID**.
- Change the PublisherID Field Size property to **2**.
- Change the Caption property to **Publisher's ID**.
- Change the Field Size property to **50** for the PubName and PubAddress fields.

- Change the Pub Address field name to **PubAddress** (remove the space).
- Change the PubCity Field Size property to **30.**
- Change the PubState Field Size property to **2.**
- Change the Pub ZIP field name to **PubZIP** (remove the space).
- Click **Save** on the Quick Access Toolbar to save the design changes to the Publishers table. Click **Yes** to the *Some data may be lost* warning. Close all open tables.

p. Click the **Database Tools tab** and click **Relationships** in the Relationships group. Click **Show Table.** If the Show Table dialog box does not open automatically, follow the steps below:

- Double-click each table name in the Show Table dialog box to add it to the Relationships window and close the Show Table dialog box.
- Drag the **AuthorID field** from the Author table onto the AuthorID field in the Books table.
- Click the **Enforce Referential Integrity** and **Cascade Update Related Fields check boxes** in the Edit Relationships dialog box to select them. Click **Create** to create a one-to-many relationship between the Author and Books tables.
- Drag the **PublisherID field** from the Publishers table onto the PublisherID field in the Books table.
- Click the **Enforce Referential Integrity** and **Cascade Update Related Fields check boxes** in the Edit Relationships dialog box to select them. Click **Create** to create a one-to-many relationship between the Publishers and Books tables.
- Click **Save** on the Quick Access Toolbar to save the changes to the Relationships window, then in the Relationships group, click **Close.**

q. Click the **Create tab,** and then click **Query Wizard** in the Queries group. With Simple Query Wizard selected, click **OK.**

- Select the Publishers table, double-click to add **PubName, PubCity,** and **PubState** to the Selected Fields list. Click **Next,** and then click **Finish.** In Datasheet view, double-click the border to the right of each column to set the column widths to Best Fit. Click **Save** on the Quick Access Toolbar.

r. Click the **File tab,** click **Save As,** and then double-click **Save Object As.** Modify the copied query name to **New York Publishers Query,** and then click **OK.**

- Click **View** in the Views group on the Home tab to switch to Design view of the query. Click and drag the **Books table** from the Navigation Pane into the top pane of the query design window.
- Select the Books table, double-click **Title** and **PublDate** to add the fields to the query design grid.
- Click in the Criteria row of the PubState field, and type **NY.** Click the **Sort** cell of the PublDate field, click the arrow, and then click **Descending.**
- Click **Run** in the Results group (12 records display in the Datasheet sorted by PublDate in descending order). Double-click the border to the right of each column to set the column widths to Best Fit.
- Save and close the query.

s. Close the database and exit Access. Based on your instructor's directions, submit a02p1Books_LastFirst.

2 Employee Salary Analysis

The Morgan Insurance Company offers a full range of insurance services. They store all of the firm's employee data in an Access database. This file contains each employee's name and address, job performance, salary, and title, but needs to be imported into a different existing database. A database file containing two of the tables (Location and Titles) already exists; your job is to import the employee data from Access to create the third table. Once imported, you will modify field properties and set new relationships. The owner of the company, Victor Reed, is concerned that some of the Atlanta and Boston salaries may be below the guidelines published by the national office. He asks that you investigate the salaries of the two offices and create a separate query for each city. Refer to Figure 54 as you complete this exercise.

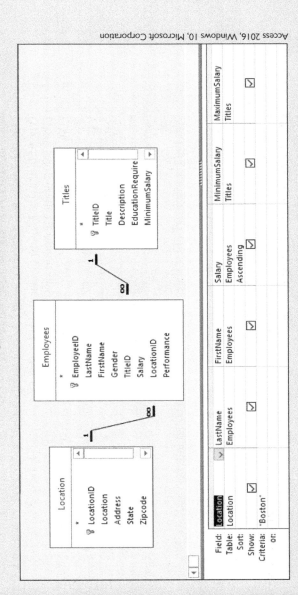

Access 2016, Windows 10, Microsoft Corporation

FIGURE 54 Boston Salaries Query Design

a. Open *a02p2Insurance* and save it as **a02p2Insurance_LastFirst**. Double-click the **Location table** and review the data to become familiar with the field names and the type of information stored in the table. Review the Titles table. Close both tables.

b. Click the **External Data tab**, click **Access** in the Import & Link group, and then complete the following steps:

- Click **Browse** and navigate to the *a02p2Employees* database in the location of your student data files. Select the file, click **Open**.
- Click **OK** in the Get External Data – Access Database dialog box.
- Select the **Employees table**, and then click **OK**.
- Click **Close** without saving the import steps.

c. Double-click the **Employees table** in the Navigation Pane, then click **View** in the Views group on the Home tab to switch to Design view of the Employees table. Make the following changes:

- Ensure that the EmployeeID field is selected, and then click **Primary Key** in the Tools group.
- Click the **LastName field** and change the Field Size property to **20**.
- Change the Caption property to **Last Name**.
- Click the **FirstName field** and change the Field Size property to **20**.
- Change the Caption property to **First Name**.
- Click the **LocationID field** and change the Field Size property to **3**.
- Change the Caption property to **Location ID**.
- Click the **TitleID field** and change the Field Size property to **3**.
- Change the Caption property to **Title ID**.
- Change the Salary field data type to **Currency** and change General Number in the Format property in field properties to **Currency**.
- Save the design changes. Click **Yes** to the *Some data may be lost* warning.

d. Click **View** in the Views group to view the Employees table in Datasheet view and examine the data. Click any record in the Title ID and then click **Ascending** in the Sort & Filter group on the Home tab. Multiple employees are associated with the T01, T02, T03, and T04 titles.

e. Double-click the **Titles table** in the Navigation Pane to open it in Datasheet view. Notice that the T04 title is not in the list.

f. Add a new record in the first blank record at the bottom of the Titles table. Use the following data:

- Type **T04** in the TitleID field.
- Type **Senior Account Rep** in the Title field.
- Type **A marketing position requiring a technical background and at least three years of experience** in the Description field.
- Type **Four year degree** in the Education Requirements field.
- Type **45000** in the Minimum Salary field.
- Type **75000** in the Maximum Salary field.

g. Close all tables. Click **Yes** if you are prompted to save changes to the Employees table.

h. Click the **Database Tools tab** and click **Relationships** in the Relationships group, and then Click **Show Table**. Follow the steps below:

- Double-click each of the three table names in the Show Table dialog box to add it to the Relationships window and close the Show Table dialog box.
- Drag the **LocationID field** in the Location table onto the LocationID field in the Employees table.
- Click the **Enforce Referential Integrity** and **Cascade Update Related Fields check boxes** in the Edit Relationships dialog box to select them. Click **Create** to create a one-to-many relationship between the Location and Employees tables.
- Drag the **TitleID field** in the Titles table onto the TitleID field in the Employees table (move the field lists by clicking and dragging their title bars as needed so that they do not overlap).
- Click the **Enforce Referential Integrity** and **Cascade Update Related Fields check boxes** in the Edit Relationships dialog box to select it. Click **Create** to create a one-to-many relationship between the Titles and Employees tables.
- Click **Save** on the Quick Access Toolbar to save the changes to the Relationships window and close the Relationships window.

i. Click the **Create tab** and click the **Query Wizard** in the Queries group. Follow the steps below:

- Select **Simple Query Wizard** and click **OK**.
- Select **Table: Employees** in the Tables/Queries box.
- Double-click **LastName** in the Available Fields list to move it to the Selected Fields list.
- Double-click **FirstName** in the Available Fields list to move it to the Selected Fields list.
- Double-click **LocationID** in the Available Fields list to move it to the Selected Fields list.
- Click **Next**.
- Type **Employees Location** as the query title and click **Finish**.
- Click **View** in the Views group on the Home tab to switch to Design view of the query. Click and drag the **Titles** table from the Navigation Pane into the top pane of the query design window.
- Double-click **Title** in the Titles table to add the field to the query design grid.
- Click the **Sort** cell of the LocationID field, click the arrow, and then click **Ascending**.
- Click **Run** in the Results group (311 records display in the Datasheet sorted by LocationID in ascending order). Double-click the border to the right of each column to set the column widths to Best Fit.
- Save and close the query.

j. Click the **Create tab** and click the **Query Wizard** in the Queries group. Follow the steps below:

- Select **Simple Query Wizard** and click **OK**.
- Select **Table: Location** in the Tables/Queries box.
- Double-click **Location** in the Available Fields list to move it to the Selected Fields list.
- Select **Table: Employees** in the Tables/Queries box.

- Double-click **LastName**, **FirstName**, and **Salary**.
- Select **Table: Titles** in the Tables/Queries box.
- Double-click **MinimumSalary** and **MaximumSalary**. Click **Next**.
- Ensure that the *Detail (shows every field of every record)* option is selected, and click **Next**.
- Type **Atlanta Salaries** as the query title and click **Finish**.

k. Click **View** in the Views group on the Home tab to switch to Design view of the Atlanta Salaries query.

- Click in the Criteria row of the Location field, and type **Atlanta**. Click the **Sort cell** of the Salary field, click the arrow, and then click **Ascending.**
- Click **Run** in the Results group. Review the data to determine if any of the Atlanta employees have a salary less than the minimum or greater than the maximum when compared to the published salary range. These salaries will be updated later.
- Save and close the query.

l. Right-click the **Atlanta Salaries query** in the Navigation Pane and from the shortcut menu, select **Copy**. Right-click a blank area in the Navigation Pane and select **Paste**. In the Paste As dialog box, type **Boston Salaries** for the query name. Click **OK.**

m. Right-click the **Boston Salaries query** in the Navigation Pane and select **Design View**. In the Criteria row of the Location field, replace Atlanta with **Boston.**

- Click **Run** in the Results group. Review the data to determine if any of the Boston employees have a salary less than the minimum or greater than the maximum when compared to the published salary range.
- Modify some data that have been incorrectly entered. In the query results, for the first employee, Frank Cusack, change the salary to **$48,700.00**; for Brian Beamer, **$45,900.00**; for Lorna Weber, **$45,700.00**; for Penny Pfleger, **$45,800.00**.
- Save and close the query.

n. Close the database and exit Access. Based on your instructor's directions, submit a02p2Insurance_LastFirst.

Mid-Level Exercises

My Game Collection

ANALYSIS CASE

Over the years, you have collected quite a few video games, so you have cataloged them in an Access database. In the Games table. After opening the database, you will create two more tables—one to identify the game system (System) that runs your game and the other to identify the category or genre of the game (Category). Then, you will join each table in a relationship so that you can query the database.

a. Open *a02m1Games* and save the database as **a02m1Games_LastFirst**. Open the Games table and review the fields containing the game information. Close the table.

b. Click the **Create tab** and click **Table Design** in the Tables group.

c. Type **SystemID** for the first Field Name and select **AutoNumber** as the Data Type.

d. Type **SystemName** for the second Field Name and accept **Short Text** as the Data Type.

e. Set **SystemID** as the primary key. Add the caption **System ID**.

f. Change the SystemName Field Size property to **15**. Add the caption **System Name**, making sure there is a space between System and Name. Save the table as **System**. Switch to Datasheet view.

g. Add the system names to the System table as shown below, letting Access use AutoNumber to create the SystemID values. Close the table when finished.

System ID	System Name
1	XBOX 360
2	PS3
3	Wii
4	NES
5	PC Game
6	Nintendo 3DS

h. Click the **Create tab** and click **Table Design** in the Tables group. Type **CategoryID** for the first Field Name and select **AutoNumber** as the Data Type. Set the CategoryID as the primary key.

i. Type **CategoryDescription** for the second Field Name and accept **Short Text** as the Data Type. Change the Field Size property to **25**. Add the caption **Category Description**, making sure there is a space between Category and Description. Save the table as **Category**, saving the changes to the table design. Switch to Datasheet view.

j. Add the category descriptions to the Category table as shown below, letting Access use AutoNumber to create the CategoryID values. Close the table when finished.

CategoryID	Category Description
1	Action
2	Adventure
3	Arcade
4	Racing
5	Rhythm
6	Role-playing
7	Simulation
8	Sports

k. Click the **Database Tools tab** and click **Relationships** in the Relationships group. Display all three tables in the Relationships window and close the Show Table dialog box. Create a one-to-many relationship between CategoryID in the Category table and CategoryID in the Games table. Enforce referential integrity and cascade update related fields.

l. Create a one-to-many relationship between SystemID in the System table and SystemID in the Games table. Enforce referential integrity and cascade update related fields. Close the Relationships window, saving the changes.

m. Use the Query Wizard to create a simple query using the Games table. Add the following fields in the query (in this order): GameName, Rating. Save the query as **Ratings Query**.

n. Switch to Design view. Sort the Rating field in ascending order and run the query. Close the query, saving the changes.

o. Create a multitable query in Design view using all three tables. Add the following fields (in this order): GameName, CategoryDescription, Rating, SystemName, and DateAcquired.

p. Sort the query in ascending order by GameName and run the query. Save the query as **Game List Query** and close the query.

q. Copy the **Game List Query** and paste it into the Navigation Pane using the name **PS3 Games.** Modify the query in Design view by using **PS3** as the criterion for SystemName. Remove the sort by GameName and sort in ascending order by Rating. The query results should include 7 records.

r. Close the PS3 Games query, saving the changes. Assume you are going home for Thanksgiving and you want to take your **Wii** gaming system and games home with you—but you only want to take home games with a rating of **Everyone.**

s. Create a query named **Thanksgiving Games** that shows the name of the game, its rating, the category description of the game, and the system name for each. Run the query. The results of the query will tell you which games to pack. Close the query.

t. Close the database and exit Access. Based on your instructor's directions, submit a02m1Games_LastFirst.

DISCOVER 🅷

2 The Prestige Hotel

The Prestige Hotel chain caters to upscale business travelers and provides state-of-the-art conference, meeting, and reception facilities. It prides itself on its international, four-star cuisine. Last year, it began a member reward club to help the marketing department track the purchasing patterns of its most loyal customers. All of the hotel transactions are stored in the database. Your task is to help the managers of the Prestige Hotels in Denver and Chicago identify their customers who stayed in a room last year and who had three persons in their party.

a. Open *a02m2Hotel* and save the file as **a02m2Hotel_LastFirst.** Review the data contained in the three tables. Specifically, study the tables and fields containing the data you need to analyze: dates of stays in Denver and Chicago suites, the members' names, and the numbers in the parties.

b. Import the location data from the Excel file *a02m2Location* into your database as a new table. The first row of the worksheet contains column headings. Set the LocationID Indexed property to **Yes (No Duplicates)** and set the Data Type to **Long Integer.** Select the **LocationID field** as the primary key. Name the table **Location.** Do not save the import steps.

c. Open the Relationships window and create a relationship between the Location table and the Orders table using the LocationID field. Enforce referential integrity and cascade update related fields. Create a relationship between the Orders and Members tables using the MemNumber field, ensuring that you enforce referential integrity and cascade update related fields. Create a relationship between the Orders and Service tables using the ServiceID field, ensuring that you enforce referential integrity and cascade update related fields. Save and close the Relationships window.

d. Open the Members table and use the Find command to locate Bryan Gray's name. Replace his name with your own first and last names. Locate Nicole Lee's name and replace it with your name. Close the table.

e. Create a query using the following fields: ServiceDate (Orders table), City (Location table), NoInParty (Orders table), ServiceName (Service table), FirstName (Members table), and LastName (Members table). Set the criteria to show services only from **7/1/2017** to **6/30/2018.** Use the Between operator to limit the output to **Denver.** Use the NoInParty criterion to **3.** Sort the results in ascending order by the ServiceDate.

f. Run the query and examine the number of records in the status bar at the bottom of the query. It should display 155. If your number of records is different, examine the criteria and make corrections.

g. Change the order of the query fields so that they display as FirstName, LastName, ServiceDate, City, NoInParty, and ServiceName. Save the query as **Denver Rooms 3 Guests**. Close the query.

h. Copy the **Denver Rooms 3 Guests** query and paste it, renaming the new query **Chicago Rooms 3 Guests**.

i. Open the Chicago Rooms 3 Guests query in Design view and change the criterion for City to **Chicago**. Run the query and save the changes. It should display 179 results. Close the query.

j. Review the criteria of the two previous queries and then create a third query named **Denver and Chicago Rooms 3 Guests**. Use the criteria from the two individual queries as a basis to create a combination AND–OR condition. The results will display guests in **Denver** or **Chicago** with 3 guests and service dates between **7/1/2013** and **6/30/2018**. The records returned in the results should equal the sum of the records in the two individual queries (334 records). Run, save, and close the query.

k. Close the database and exit Access. Based on your instructor's directions, submit a02m2Hotel_LastFirst.

3 New Castle County Technical Services

RUNNING CASE

New Castle County Technical Services (NCCTS) provides technical support for a number of companies in the greater New Castle County, Delaware area. Once you have completed the changes to the database tables and set the appropriate relationships, you will be ready to extract information by creating queries.

a. Open the database *a01m3NCCTS_LastFirst* and save it as a02m3NCCTS_LastFirst changing 01 to 02.

b. Open the Call Types table in Design view. Before you create your queries, you want to modify some of the table properties:

- Set the caption of the HourlyRate field to **Hourly Rate.**
- View the table in Datasheet view, and save the changes when prompted.

c. Close the table.

d. Make the following additional changes to the tables:

- Open the Calls table in Design view. Change the data type of the CallTypeID field to **Number.**
  - Set the caption of the HoursLogged field to **Hours Logged.**
  - Set the caption of the OpenedDate field to **Opened Date** and set the format to **Short Date.**
  - Set the caption of the ClosedDate field to **Closed Date** and set the format to **Short Date.**
  - Set the caption of the CustomerSatisfaction field to **Customer Satisfaction.**
  - View the table in Datasheet view, and save the changes when prompted. You will not lose any data by making this change, so click **Yes** in the message box when prompted. Close the table.

- Open the Customers table in Design view. Set the field size of CompanyName to **50** and the caption to **Company Name.** View the table in Datasheet view, and save the changes when prompted. You will not lose any data by making this change, so click **Yes** in the message box when prompted. Close the table.

- Open the Reps table in Design view. Set the caption of the RepFirst field to **Rep First Name.** Set the caption of the RepLast field to **Rep Last Name.** View the table in Datasheet view, and save the changes when prompted. Close the table.

e. Open the Relationships window. Create a join line between the Call Types and Calls tables, ensuring that you enforce referential integrity and cascade update related fields. Set a relationship between Reps and Calls and between Customers and Calls using the same options. Save and close the Relationships window.

f. Create a multitable query, following the steps below:

• Add the following fields (in this order): **CallID** (from Calls), **Description** (from Call Types), **CompanyName** (from Customers), and **RepFirst** and **RepLast** (from Reps).

• Run the query, and then modify it to add **HoursLogged** (from Calls).

• Sort the query by HoursLogged in ascending order. Set the criteria of the HoursLogged field to **Is Not Null** and run the query again.

• Modify the criteria of the HoursLogged field to **>=5** and **<=10**, the description to **Disaster Recovery**, and the rep to **Barbara**.

• Save the query as **Complex Disaster Recovery Calls_Barbara**. Run and then close the query.

g. Create a copy of the **Complex Disaster Recovery Calls_Barbara** query, and modify it following the steps below:

• Save the copy of the query as **Complex Network Installation Calls_Barbara**.

• Modify the query so that the description displays Barbara's network installation calls that logged between 5 and 10 hours.

• Save, run, and then close the query.

h. Close the database and exit Access. Based on your instructor's directions, submit a02m3NCCTS_LastFirst.

Database Administrator Position

Create a database to keep track of candidates for open positions at Secure Systems, Inc., database management experts. Use the Internet to search for information about database management positions. One useful site is published by the federal government's Bureau of Labor Statistics. It compiles an Occupational Outlook Handbook describing various positions, the type of working environment, the education required, salary information, and the projected growth. The website is http://www.bls.gov/ooh. Research the necessary information in order to create the database using these requirements:

a. Create a new database named **a02b1Admin_LastFirst**.

b. Create three tables including the field names as follows, and in the specified orders:

- **Candidates (CandidateID, FirstName, LastName, Phone, Email)**,

- **JobOpenings (JobOpeningID, JobName, RequiredSkill, HourlyPayRate, DataPosted, Supervisor)**,

- **Interviews (InterviewSequenceID, CandidateID, JobOpeningID, InterviewedBy, DateOfInterview, Rank)**.

c. Set the data types, field properties, and a primary key for each table.

d. Set table relationships, and be sure to enforce referential integrity between them. Cascade update related fields

e. Add 10 candidates to the Candidates table.

f. Add a **Database Administrator** job and four other sample jobs to the JobOpenings table.

g. Add eight sample interviews—four for the Database Administrator position and four for others. Rank each candidate on a scale of 1 to 5 (with 5 as the highest).

h. Create a query that lists the LastName, FirstName, JobOpeningID, InterviewedBy, DateOfInterview, and Rank fields. Display only Database Administrator interviews with a ranking of 3 or lower. Sort by LastName and then by FirstName. Run and save the query as **Database Admin Low Rank**. Close the query

i. Close the database and exit Access. Based on your instructor's directions, submit a02b1Admin_LastFirst.

May Beverage Sales

A coworker explained that he was having difficulty with queries that were not returning correct results, and asked you to help diagnose the problem. Open *a02b2Traders* and save it as **a02b2Traders_LastFirst**. It contains two queries, *May 2018 Orders of Beverages and Confections* and *2018 Beverage Sales by Ship Country*. The May 2018 Orders of Beverages and Confections query is supposed to contain only information for orders shipped in May 2018. You find other shipped dates included in the results. Change the criteria to exclude the other dates. Run and save the query. Close the query.

The 2018 Beverage Sales by Ship Country query returns no results. Check the criteria in all fields and modify so that the correct results are returned. Run and save the query. Close the query.

Close the database and exit Access. Based on your instructor's directions, submit a02b2Traders_LastFirst.

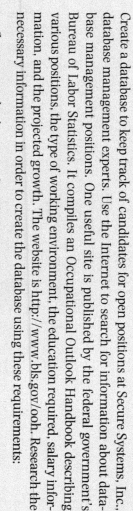

Capstone Exercise

The Morris Arboretum in Chestnut Hill, Pennsylvania tracks donors in Excel. They also use Excel to store a list of plants in stock. As donors contribute funds to the Arboretum, they can elect to receive a plant gift from the Arboretum. These plants are both rare plants and hard-to-find old favorites, and they are part of the annual appeal and membership drive to benefit the Arboretum's programs. The organization has grown, and the files are too large and inefficient to handle in Excel. You will begin by importing the files from Excel into a new Access database. Then you will create a table to track donations, create a relationship between the two tables, and create some baseline queries.

Create a New Database

You will examine the data in the Excel worksheets to determine which fields will become the primary keys in each table and which fields will become the foreign keys.

a. Open the *a02c1Donors* Excel workbook, examine the data, and close the workbook.

b. Open the *a02c1Plants* Excel workbook, examine the data, and close the workbook.

c. Create a new, blank database named **a02c1Arbor_LastFirst**. Close the new blank table created automatically by Access without saving it.

Import Data from Excel

You will import two Excel workbooks into the database.

a. Click the **External Data tab** and click **Excel** in the Import & Link group.

b. Navigate to and select the *a02c1Donors* workbook to be imported.

c. Select the **First Row Contains Column Headings** option.

d. Set the DonorID field Indexed option to **Yes (No Duplicates)**.

e. Choose **DonorID** as the primary key when prompted and accept the table name Donors.

f. Import the *a02c1Plants* workbook, set the **ID field** as the primary key, and then change the indexing option to **Yes (No Duplicates)**.

g. Accept the table name Plants.

h. Change the ID field name in the Plants table to **PlantID**.

i. Open each table in Datasheet view to examine the data. Close the tables.

Create a New Table

You will create a new table to track the donations as they are received from the donors.

a. You will create a new table in Design view and save the table as **Donations**.

b. Add the following fields in Design view and set the properties as specified:

- Add the primary key field as **DonationID** with the **Number Data Type** and a field size of **Long Integer**.
- Add **DonorID** (a foreign key) with the **Number Data Type** and a field size of **Long Integer**.
- Add **PlantID** (a foreign key) as a **Number** and a field size of **Long Integer**.
- Add **DateOfDonation** as a **Date/Time** field.
- Add **AmountOfDonation** as a **Currency** field.

c. Switch to Datasheet view, and save the table when prompted. You will enter data into the table in a later step. Close the table.

Create Relationships

You will create the relationships between the tables using the Relationships window.

a. Open the Donors table in Design view and change the Field Size property for DonorID to **Long Integer** so it matches the Field Size property of DonorID in the Donations table. Save and close the table.

b. Open the Plants table in Design view and change the Field Size property for PlantID to **Long Integer** so it matches the Field Size property for PlantID in the Donations table. Save and close the table.

c. Identify the primary key fields in the Donors table and the Plants table and join them with their foreign key counterparts in the related Donations table. Enforce referential integrity and cascade and update related fields. Save and close the Relationships window.

Add Sample Data to the Donations Table

You will add 10 records to the Donations table.

a. Add the following records to the Donations table:

Donation ID	Donor ID	Plant ID	Date of Donation	Amount of Donation
10	8228	611	3/1/2018	$150
18	5448	190	3/1/2018	$ 55
6	4091	457	3/12/2018	$125
7	11976	205	3/14/2018	$100
1	1000	25	3/17/2018	$120
12	1444	38	3/19/2018	$ 50
2	1444	38	4/3/2018	$ 50
4	10520	49	4/12/2018	$ 60
5	3072	102	4/19/2018	$ 50
21	1204	25	4/22/2018	$120

b. Sort the Donations table by the AmountOfDonation field in descending order. Close the table.

Use the Query Wizard

You will create a query of all donations greater than $100 in the Donations table.

a. Add the DonorID and AmountOfDonation fields from Donations table.

b. Save the query as **Donations Over 100**.

c. Add criteria to include only donations of more than $100.

d. Sort the query results in ascending order by AmountOfDonation.

e. Run the query.

f. Save and close the query.

Create a Query in Design View

You will create a query that identifies donors and donations.

a. Create a query that identifies the people who made a donation after April 1, 2018. This list will be given to the Arboretum staff so they can notify the donors that a plant is ready for pickup. The query should list the date of the donation, donor's full name (LastName,

FirstName), phone number, the amount of the donation, and name of the plant they want (in that order). Add the tables and fields necessary to produce the query.

b. Sort the query by date of donation in descending order, then by donor last name in ascending order.

c. Run, close, and save the query as **Plant Pickup List**.

Copy and Modify a Query in Design View

You will copy a query and modify it to add and sort by a different field.

a. Copy the Plant Pickup List query and paste it using **ENewsletter** as the query name.

b. Open the ENewsletter query in Design view and delete the DateofDonation column.

c. Add the ENewsletter field to the first column of the design grid and set it to sort in ascending order, so that the query sorts first by ENewsletter and then by LastName.

d. Run, save, and close the query. Close the database and exit Access. Based on your instructor's directions, submit a02c1Arbor_LastFirst.

Glossary

AND condition In a query, returns only records that meet all criteria.

AutoNumber A number that automatically increments each time a record is added.

Caption property Used to create a more readable label that displays in the top row in Datasheet view and in forms and reports.

Cascade Delete Related Records When the primary key value is deleted in a primary table, Access will automatically delete all foreign key values in a related table.

Cascade Update Related Fields An option that directs Access to automatically change all foreign key values in a related table when the primary key value is modified in a primary table.

Comparison Operators Use greater than (>), less than (<), greater than or equal to (>=), and less than or equal to (<=), etc. to limit query results that meet these criteria.

Criteria row A row in Query Design view that determines which records will be selected.

Data redundancy The unnecessary storing of duplicate data in two or more tables.

Data type Determines the type of data that can be entered and the operations that can be performed on that data.

Field properties Characteristics of fields that determine how they look and behave.

Foreign key A field in a related table that is the primary key of another table.

Multitable queries Results contain fields from two or more tables, enabling you to take advantage of the relationships that have been set in your database.

Null The term Access uses to describe a blank field value.

One-to-many relationship When the primary key value in the primary table can match many of the foreign key values in the related table.

OR condition In a query, returns records meeting any of the specified criteria.

Query A question about the data stored in a database answers provided in a datasheet.

Referential Integrity Rules in a database that are used to preserve relationships between tables when records are changed.

Simple Query Wizard Provides a step-by-step guide to help you through the query design process.

Wildcards Special characters that can represent one or more characters in the criterion of a query.

Using Queries to Make Decisions

Using Queries to Make Decisions

LEARNING OUTCOME

You will create queries to perform calculations and summarize data.

OBJECTIVES & SKILLS: After you read this chapter, you will be able to:

Calculations and Expressions

OBJECTIVE 1: CREATE A QUERY WITH A CALCULATED FIELD
Understand the Order of Operations, Build Expressions

OBJECTIVE 2: FORMAT CALCULATED RESULTS
Format Fields

OBJECTIVE 3: RECOVER FROM COMMON ERRORS
Recognize and Correct Common Errors

OBJECTIVE 4: VERIFY CALCULATED RESULTS
Evaluate Results

HANDS-ON EXERCISE 1:
Calculations and Expressions

The Expression Builder and Functions

OBJECTIVE 5: CREATE EXPRESSIONS USING THE EXPRESSION BUILDER
Use the Expression Builder

OBJECTIVE 6: USE BUILT-IN FUNCTIONS
Calculate a Loan Payment with the Pmt Function

HANDS-ON EXERCISE 2:
The Expression Builder and Functions

Aggregate Functions

OBJECTIVE 7: ADD AGGREGATE FUNCTIONS TO DATASHEETS
Display a Total Row for a Query

OBJECTIVE 8: CREATE QUERIES WITH AGGREGATE FUNCTIONS
Create a Totals Query, Add Grouping to a Totals Query, Add Conditions to a Totals Query, Add a Calculated Field to a Totals Query

HANDS-ON EXERCISE 3:
Aggregate Functions

CASE STUDY | Real Estate Investors

After completing their degrees in Business at Passaic County Community College (PCCC) and a weekend seminar in real estate investing, Donald Carter and Matthew Nevoso were ready to test their skills in the marketplace. Don and Matt had a simple strategy—buy distressed properties at a significant discount, then resell the properties for a profit. Based on their seminar, they knew to gather key information such as the asking price, the number of bedrooms, square feet, and days on the market. Because they are just starting out, they decided to consider less expensive houses.

Based on a tip from the real estate seminar, they decide to create a database using Access, using data from a variety of home listing services. They approached you to help them find houses that meet their criteria. This new database approach should hopefully help them acquire their first investment property.

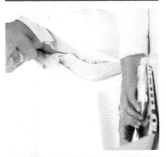

Perform Calculations and Summarize Data Using Queries

First Name	Last Name	List Price	Square Feet	Listing	Sold	Price Per Sq Ft	Payment
Philip	DeFranco	$109,140.00	1133	10004	No	$96.33	$416.84
Chardae	Myles	$129,780.00	1132	10028	No	$114.65	$495.67
Makarem	Abdeljawad	$136,680.00	1375	10008	No	$99.40	$522.02
Meera	Shah	$138,990.00	1276	10016	No	$108.93	$530.85
StudentLast	StudentFirst	$140,693.00	1490	10069	No	$94.42	$537.35
Makarem	Abdeljawad	$140,904.00	1301	10061	No	$108.30	$538.16
Makarem	Abdeljawad	$142,380.00	1373	11028	No	$103.70	$543.80
Chardae	Myles	$163,737.00	1476	10910	No	$110.93	$625.36
Jaynish	Mody	$164,436.00	1850	10117	No	$88.88	$628.03
Jaynish	Mody	$166,320.00	1437	10082	No	$115.74	$635.23
Chardae	Myles	$166,552.00	1623	10851	No	$102.62	$636.12
Chardae	Myles	$166,800.00	1598	10014	No	$104.38	$637.06
Philip	DeFranco	$168,000.00	1680	10002	No	$100.00	$641.65
Chardae	Myles	$168,354.00	1651	10885	No	$101.97	$643.00
Philip	DeFranco	$174,230.00	1771	10104	No	$98.38	$665.44
StudentFirst	StudentLast	$174,720.00	1610	10921	No	$108.52	$667.31
Meera	Shah	$174,720.00	1694	11035	No	$103.14	$667.31
Chardae	Myles	$175,336.00	1855	10868	No	$94.52	$669.66
StudentFirst	StudentLast	$175,560.00	1562	11036	No	$112.39	$670.52
Meera	Shah	$176,176.00	1761	10025	No	$100.04	$672.87
Jaynish	Mody	$177,984.00	1707	10066	No	$104.27	$679.78
Chardae	Myles	$179,088.00	1837	10010	No	$97.49	$683.99
Chardae	Myles	$179,100.00	1946	11079	No	$92.03	$684.04
Chardae	Myles	$179,712.00	1854	10102	No	$96.93	$686.38
Chardae	Myles	$180,180.00	1896	10019	No	$95.03	$688.17
Total		**$167,100.47**				**$102.10**	

Record: 1 of 32

FIGURE 1 Real Estate Investors Property Database – Mortgage Payments Query

NameOfList	AvgOfSalePrice	NumberSold	DaysOnMarket
Algernon Listings	$324,697.22	18	23.50
FastHouse	$288,314.50	6	22.33
Houses 4 Sale	$218,039.00	2	23.50
Local Listings	$341,085.67	9	23.56
Major Houses	$235,757.88	8	24.75
Trullo	$236,885.21	19	26.05
Wholesaler	$276,654.92	26	26.12
Total		**88**	

FIGURE 2 Real Estate Investors Property Database – Results by Realtor Revised Query

CASE STUDY | Real Estate Investors

Starting File	Files to be Submitted
a03h1Property	a03h1PropertyCheck_LastFirst
	a03h3Property_LastFirst

Using Queries to Make Decisions • Access 2016

Calculations and Expressions

There are going to be times, when manipulating data in an Access database, that you will want to perform calculations. A field storing the number of hours worked multiplied by a field storing the hourly pay rate will calculate the gross pay, for example. Unfortunately, calculations may not always be that easy. If you have received a paycheck, you realize your gross pay is not the same as the amount as your paycheck. Your net pay will be lower, due to common deductions such as Social Security, Medicare, federal and state income taxes, unemployment insurance, and union dues. Some deductions may be a flat rate, and others may be calculated based on the paycheck amount, so even what appears to be a simple calculation can be complex.

At first glance, you may not see an obvious location for you to enter a calculation in Access. However, Access includes many built-in calculations and functions. Calculations appear commonly in queries, but can also be added to tables, forms, and reports.

In this section, you will learn how to create a calculated field in a query. You will also format the calculations to enhance readability.

Creating a Query with a Calculated Field

Rather than performing a calculation outside of the database and then inputting the result into your database, you should instead store the components of the calculation in the database. Calculating values rather than inputting values will reduce errors and inconsistencies. If your database stored the hours worked and paycheck amount, both fields would have to be updated if there was a change in the hours the employee worked. However, if you store only the hours worked and calculate the paycheck amount, you do not have to worry about updating multiple fields. The next time the paycheck is calculated, the results will be updated and corrected.

As another example, a table might contain the times when employees clock in and out of work. You could create a calculation in a query to determine how many hours each employee worked by subtracting the ClockIn field from the ClockOut field. A combination of elements that produce a value is known as an *expression*. A *calculated field* is a field that displays the result of an expression rather than data stored in a field. You may find one or more of the following elements in a calculated field:

- Arithmetic operator (for example, ., *, /, +, or −)

- *Constant*, a value that does not change (such as −20 or 3.14)

- Function (built-in calculations like Pmt)

- Identifier (the names of fields, controls, or properties)

Understand the Order of Operations

The *order of operations* determines the sequence by which operations are calculated in a mathematical expression. Evaluate expressions in parentheses first, then exponents, then multiplication and division, and, finally, addition and subtraction. You may remember PEMDAS (or the mnemonic device, "Please Excuse My Dear Aunt Sally") from a math class. Table 1 shows some examples of the order of operations. Access uses the following symbols:

- Parentheses ( )
- Exponentiation ^
- Multiplication *
- Division /
- Addition +
- Subtraction −

TABLE 1 Examples of Order of Operations

Expression	Order to Perform Calculations	Output
=2+3*3	Multiply first and then add.	11
=(2+3)*3	Add the values inside the parentheses first and then multiply.	15
=2+2^3	Evaluate the exponent first, $2^3 = 2*2*2$ (or 8). Then add.	10
=10/2+3	Divide first and then add.	8
=10/(2+3)	Add first to simplify the parenthetical expression and then divide.	2
=10*2–3*2	Multiply first and then subtract.	14

Build Expressions

STEP 1 >> As mentioned earlier, expressions can contain a number of different elements. Expressions can be typed manually or inserted using Access tools.

The challenging part is typically creating the expression. Consider the following scenario. Your company plans on allowing customers to pay off their balance in 12 monthly payments. The balance is stored in your Access database in a field named Balance. To divide this into equal payments, you would type Balance/12 in the Field row of a blank column. For example, if the Balance field was $1,200, you divide by 12. You are left with a monthly payment of $100. See Figure 3 for an example of the Balance field added to a query.

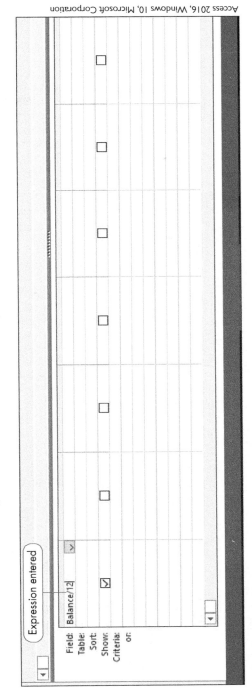

FIGURE 3 Balance Field in a Query

Access 2016, Windows 10, Microsoft Corporation

However, many companies will apply some sort of surcharge or add interest when customers pay balances off in installments. From your perspective as someone creating a query, this makes the calculation more complex. Your company may decide to add a surcharge of 20% (or, .20) of the balance. In this case, you will need to include a multiplication step in the above calculation. You will multiply the results by 1.20. Why multiply by 1.20 rather than .20? If you multiplied by .20 and divided by 12, you would only see the surcharge amount and not the total amount due for each payment. If the Balance field was $1,200, the monthly payment needs to be more than the $100 in the previous example.

If you multiply $1,200 by .20, you get a result of $20. The $20 does not represent the amount due, it represents the surcharge. Therefore, multiplying by 1.20 will give you the balance plus the surcharge. Dividing that by 12 gives you a monthly payment of $120. Note that there are multiple ways to implement this calculation, so this is not the only solution.

To create a calculated field within a query, complete the following steps:

1. Open the query in Design view.
2. Click the Field row (top row) of a blank column. Recall that the Field row is found in the bottom pane of the design.
3. Type the desired expression. See Figure 4 for an example of a query with an expression.
4. Click Run in the Results group to display the results in Datasheet view.

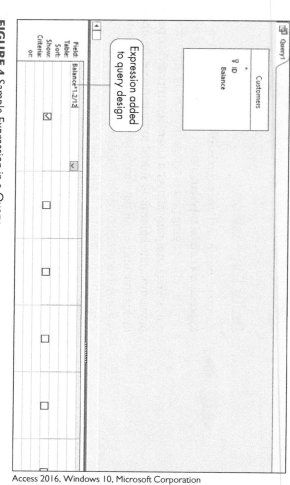

FIGURE 4 Sample Expression in a Query

Access 2016, Windows 10, Microsoft Corporation

When you type the preceding expression into the Field row and click another field, Access adds a few things to the expression. As shown in Figure 5, Access adds brackets [ ] around Balance, which Access uses to indicate a field name. In addition, you see that Access has added Expr1: to the start of the expression. This is how Access assigns a column heading to this field.

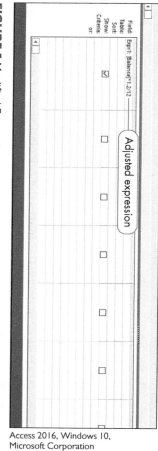

FIGURE 5 Modified Expression

Access 2016, Windows 10,
Microsoft Corporation

If you were to run the query, the column heading would be *Expr1*. If you wanted to name this column MonthlySurcharge, you would start the expression with the name, followed by a colon, followed by the expression (or, if Expr1: already appears, replace Expr1 with the name and leave the colon in place). The column is renamed MonthlySurcharge in Figure 6.

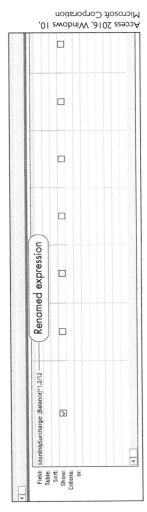

FIGURE 6 Expression Renamed

The query results, as shown in Figure 7, display a decimal number in the MonthlySurcharge column. Notice that the results are not easy to read and should be formatted.

FIGURE 7 Unformatted Results

To see the entire calculated field expression in Design view, right-click the Field row and select Zoom. A new window (the Zoom window) will open to enable you to easily see and edit the entire contents of the cell, as shown in Figure 8. Once you are done modifying a field, click Close in the top-right corner of the Zoom window.

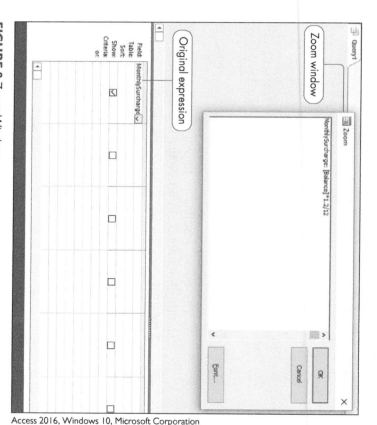

FIGURE 8 Zoom Window

STEP 2

Formatting Calculated Results

When using calculated fields in queries, you may want to format the results. Spending a few moments formatting your output will make your query results more readable. For example, if you are calculating a net pay, you likely do not care about anything after two decimal places. It makes more sense to say you are making $980.15 a week than to say you are making $980.1498343432743.

To format a field in a query, use the **Property Sheet**. The Property Sheet enables you to change the way a field appears. For example, a numeric field has settings such as number format and number of decimal places, while other data types will have settings specific to that type. The Property Sheet is in many ways similar to the Field Properties in a table.

To format a field, complete the following steps:

1. Open the query in Design view.
2. Click the Field row of the field you want to format.
3. Click Property Sheet in the Show/Hide group on the Design tab.
4. Click the appropriate option and choose the setting desired. You can change the format by clicking the Format property arrow and selecting your desired format (such as Currency for numeric fields). For numeric fields, the Decimal Places property will allow you to choose the number of decimal places that display. To change the caption (which appears as the name of the column), click the text box next to the Caption property and type your desired column heading. Figure 9 shows the Property Sheet options related to a numeric field.
5. Close the Property Sheet, if desired, by clicking Close as shown in Figure 9. After using the Property Sheet, it will be displayed in the future when the query is opened in Design view, unless you close it. However, as most of your users will not be viewing the query in Design view, it should not matter either way if the Property Sheet is closed or not.

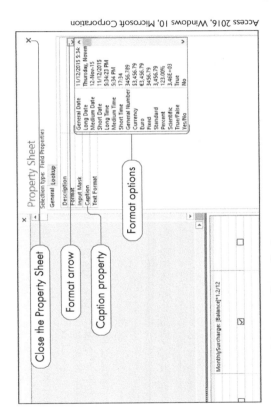

FIGURE 9 Property Sheet Options

Recovering from Common Errors

STEP 3 When creating calculated fields, there are a number of common errors that can occur. Learning how to recognize errors and recover from issues is important. Some common types of errors are shown below:

- Forgetting the colon between the column title and the formula

  A correct formula would look like this:

  MonthlySurcharge: [Balance]*1.2/12

  If you forget the colon, the formula looks like this instead:

  MonthlySurcharge [Balance]*1.2/12

  and you will get an invalid syntax error, indicating something is wrong with the way the formula is written, as shown in Figure 10.

FIGURE 10 Syntax Error Warning

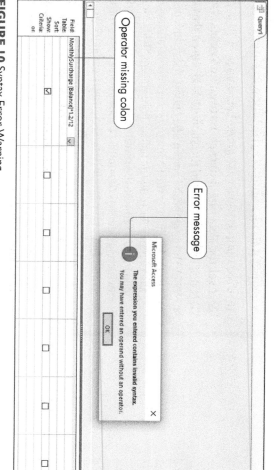

Access 2016, Windows 10, Microsoft Corporation

- Spelling a field name incorrectly

  If a field's name is Balance and you mistype it, you will get an error when you run the query. You may end up with a formula that looks like this:

  MonthlySurcharge: [Baalnce]*1.2/12

  When you run the query, you will be prompted by Access to give a value for Baalnce, as shown in Figure 11. This happens because Access does not know what Baalnce is.

FIGURE 11 Result of Spelling Error in Field Name

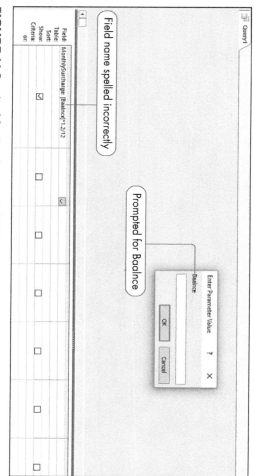

Access 2016, Windows 10, Microsoft Corporation

- Forgetting the order of operations

  If you do not check your formulas, you may get bad values. For example, the following would not produce the expected output:

  NewMonthlyBalance: [Balance] + 100/12

  If you want addition to be done before division, you must remember the parentheses:

  NewMonthlyBalance: ([Balance] + 100)/12

Verifying Calculated Results

STEP 4 » After your query runs, look at the field values in Datasheet view and look at the calculated values. You may find that the results do not make sense. In a real-world scenario, you will not be given step-by-step directions, and instead will apply critical thinking skills to your work. Access will calculate exactly what you tell it to calculate, even if you make logical errors in the calculation.

When you run a query, you need to analyze the results and ask yourself if the results make sense. Assume you are calculating a car payment for a $10,000 car, with monthly payments for 5 years. If your formula is incorrect, you may end up with a monthly payment result like $1,000. If you look at your results, you should say to yourself, "Does it make sense for me to pay $1,000 every month for five years to finance a $10,000 car?"

You can verify results with a calculator or by copying and pasting data into Excel. Recreate the calculations in Excel and compare the answers to the query results in Access. The Access calculated field, the calculator, and the Excel calculations should all return identical results.

Quick Concepts

1. What are the four types of elements that can appear as part of an expression in Access?

2. Briefly describe the order of operations. Give an example of how the order of operations makes a difference in a calculation.

3. How does Access respond when you spell a field name incorrectly in a query?

4. How can the Property Sheet make query results more readable?

Hands-On Exercises

1 Calculations and Expressions

Skills covered: Build Expressions • Format Fields • Recognize and Correct Common Errors • Evaluate Results

Using the data from the homes for sale lists that Don and Matt acquired, you are able to help them target properties that meet their criteria. As you examine the data, you discover other ways to analyze the properties. You create several queries and present your results to the two investors for their comments.

STEP 1 》》 BUILD EXPRESSIONS

You begin your analysis by creating a query using the Properties and Agents tables from the Property database. The Properties table contains all the properties the investors will evaluate; the Agents table contains a list of real estate agents who represent the properties' sellers. In this exercise, you will add requested fields and only show properties that have not been sold. You will then build an expression to calculate the price per square foot for each property. Refer to Figure 12 as you complete Step 1.

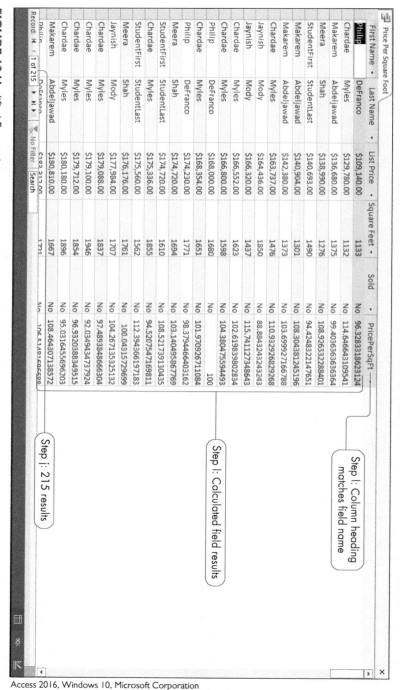

FIGURE 12 Modified Expression

a. Open *a03h1Property*. Save the database as **a03h1Property_LastFirst**.

> **TROUBLESHOOTING:** Throughout the remainder of this chapter, click Enable Content whenever you are working with student files.

> **TROUBLESHOOTING:** If you make any major mistakes in this exercise, you can close the file, open *a03h1Property* again, and then start this exercise over.

b. Open the Agents table and replace the name *Dilson Herrera* with your name. Close the table.

c. Click the **Create tab** and click **Query Design** in the Queries group to create a new query.

The Show Table dialog box opens so you can specify the table(s) and/or queries to include in the query design.

d. Select the **Agents table** and click **Add**. Select the **Properties table** and click **Add**. Click **Close** to close the Show Table dialog box.

e. Double-click the **FirstName** and **LastName fields** in the Agents table to add them to the query.

f. Double-click the **ListPrice**, **SqFeet**, and **Sold fields** in the Properties table to add them to the query.

g. Click **Run** in the Results group to display the results in Datasheet view.

A total of 303 properties appear in the results.

h. Switch to Design view. Type **No** in the Criteria row of the Sold field.

i. Click the **Sort row** in the ListPrice field. Click the **arrow** and select **Ascending**.

j. Click **Run** to see the results.

The 215 unsold properties appear in the datasheet, with the least expensive houses displayed first.

k. Click **Save** on the Quick Access Toolbar and type **Price Per Square Foot** as the Query Name in the Save As dialog box. Click **OK**.

l. Switch to Design view. Click the **Field row** of the first blank column of the query design grid. Right-click and select **Zoom** to show the Zoom window. Type **PricePerSqFt: ListPrice/SqFeet** and click **OK**.

Access inserts square brackets around the fields for you. The new field divides the values in the ListPrice field by the values in the SqFeet field.

m. Click **Run** in the Results group to view the results. Adjust column widths as necessary.

The new calculated field, PricePerSqFt, is displayed. Compare your results to those shown in Figure 12.

TROUBLESHOOTING: If you see pound signs (#####) in an Access column, double-click the vertical line between column headings to increase the width.

TROUBLESHOOTING: If, when you run the query, you are prompted for a value, cancel and return to Design view. Ensure that you have entered the formula from Step l in the first row of a blank column, not the criteria line.

n. Save the changes to the query and close the query.

STEP 2 » FORMAT FIELDS

Don and Matt would like the field formatted with two decimal places. You will change the format to Currency and add a caption to the calculated field. Refer to Figure 13 as you complete Step 2.

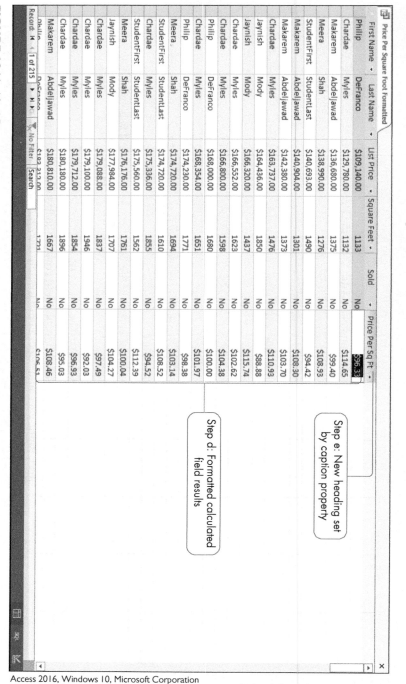

FIGURE 13 Modified Expression

a. Right-click the **Price Per Square Foot query** in the Navigation Pane and click **Copy**. Right-click in the Navigation Pane again and click **Paste**. Type **Price Per Square Foot Formatted** in the Paste As dialog box and click **OK**.

b. Open the Price Per Square Foot Formatted query in Design View.

c. Click the **PricePerSqFt calculated field cell.** Click **Property Sheet** in the Show/Hide group on the Design tab.

The Property Sheet displays.

d. Click the **Format property**. Click the **Format property arrow** and select **Currency**.

e. Click the **Caption property** and type **Price Per Sq Ft**. Press **Enter**. Close the Property Sheet.

f. Click **Run** to view your changes.

The calculated field values are formatted as Currency, and the column heading displays Price Per Sq Ft instead of PricePerSqFt.

g. Compare your result to Figure 13. Save the changes to the query.

A few errors arise as you test the new calculated fields. You check the spelling of the field names in the calculated fields because that is a common mistake. Refer to Figure 14 as you complete Step 3.

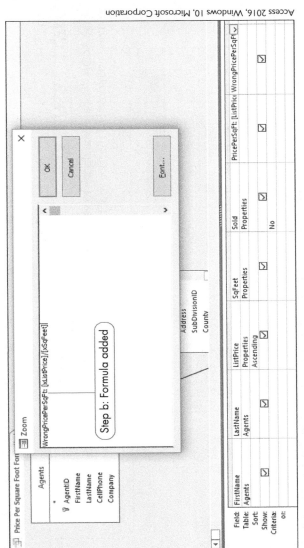

Access 2016, Windows 10, Microsoft Corporation

FIGURE 14 Incorrect Expression

a. Switch to Design view of the Price Per Square Foot Formatted query. Scroll to the first blank column of the query design grid and click the Field row.

b. Right-click and select **Zoom** to display the Zoom window. Type **WrongPricePerSqFt: xListPrice/xSqFeet**. Your formula should match Figure 14. Click OK in the Zoom window.

   Be sure that you added the extra x's to the field names. You are intentionally misspelling the field names to see how Access will respond.

c. Click **Property Sheet** in the Show/Hide group of the Design tab. Click the **Format property**. From the menu, select **Currency**. Click the **Caption box** and type **Wrong Price Per Sq Ft**. Close the Property Sheet.

d. Click **Run** in the Results group.

   You should see the Enter Parameter Value dialog box. Access does not recognize xListPrice in the tables defined for this query in the first record. When Access does not recognize a field name, it will ask you to supply a value.

e. Type **100000** in the first parameter box. Press **Enter** or click **OK**.

   Another Enter Parameter Value dialog box displays, asking that you supply a value for xSqFeet. Again, this error occurs because the tables defined for this query do not contain an xSqFeet field.

f. Type **1000** in the second parameter box and press **Enter**.

   The query has the necessary information to run and returns the results in Datasheet view.

g. Examine the results of the calculation for Wrong Price Per Sq Ft.

   All of the records show 100 because you entered the values 100000 and 1000, respectively, into the parameter boxes. The two values are treated as constants and give the same results for all records.

h. Return to Design view. Display the Zoom window. Correct the errors in the WrongPricePerSqFt field by changing the formula to **WrongPricePerSqFt: [ListPrice]/[SqFeet]**. Click **OK**.

i. Run and save the query. Close the query.

The calculated values in the last two columns should be the same.

STEP 4 >> EVALUATE RESULTS

Because you are in charge of the Access database, you decide to verify your data prior to showing it to the investors. You use two methods to check your calculations: estimation and checking your results using Excel. Refer to Figure 15 as you complete Step 4.

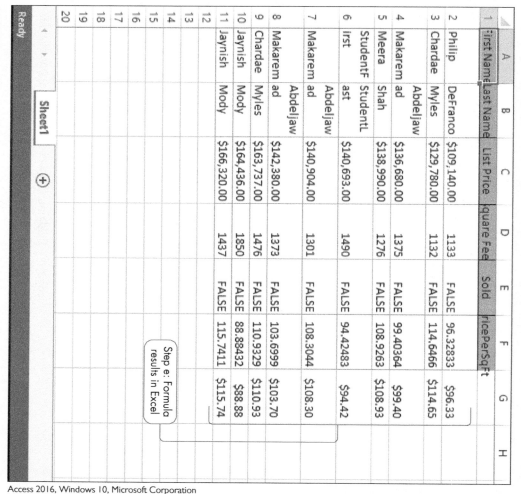

	A	B	C	D	E	F	G	H
1	First Name	Last Name	List Price	Square Fee	Sold	PricePerSqFt		
2	Philip	DeFranco	$109,140.00	1133	FALSE	96.32833	$96.33	
3	Chardae	Myles	$129,780.00	1132	FALSE	114.6466	$114.65	
4	Makarem	Abdeljaw ad	$136,680.00	1375	FALSE	99.40364	$99.40	
5	Meera	Shah	$138,990.00	1276	FALSE	108.9263	$108.93	
6	StudentF irst	StudentL ast	$140,693.00	1490	FALSE	94.42483	$94.42	
7	Makarem	Abdeljaw ad	$140,904.00	1301	FALSE	108.3044	$108.30	
8	Makarem	Abdeljaw ad	$142,380.00	1373	FALSE	103.6999	$103.70	
9	Chardae	Myles	$163,737.00	1476	FALSE	110.9329	$110.93	
10	Jaynish	Mody	$164,436.00	1850	FALSE	88.88432	$88.88	
11	Jaynish	Mody	$166,320.00	1437	FALSE	115.7411	$115.74	
12								
13								
14								
15								
16								
17								
18								
19								
20								

Step e: Formula results in Excel

Ready   Sheet1 +

FIGURE 15 Calculation Copied to Excel

a. Open the Price Per Square Foot query in Datasheet view. Examine the PricePerSqFt field.

One of the ways to verify the accuracy of the calculated data is to ask yourself if the numbers make sense.

b. Locate the 13th record with Philip DeFranco as the listing agent, an asking price of $168,000, and square footage of 1680. The result ($100.00) makes sense, since 168,000/1680 = 100.

TROUBLESHOOTING: If the 13th record is not the one listed above, ensure that you have sorted the query by the List Price in ascending order, as specified in Step 1i.

c. Open a new, blank workbook in Excel and then switch to Access. Select the first 10 records. Click **Copy** in the Clipboard group on the Home tab.

You will verify the calculation in the first 10 records by pasting the results in Excel.

d. Switch to Excel and click the **Paste** button in the Clipboard group on the Home tab.

The field names display in the first row, and the 10 records display in the next 10 rows. The fields are located in columns A–F. The calculated field results are pasted in column F as values rather than as a formula.

TROUBLESHOOTING: If you see pound signs (#####) in an Excel column, double-click the vertical line between column headings to increase the width.

e. Click **cell G2**. Type **=C2/D2** and press **Enter**. Click **cell G2**, and click **Copy** in the Clipboard group. Select the **range G3:G11** and click **Paste** in the Clipboard group. Compare your results to Figure 15.

The formula divides the list price by the square feet. Compare the results in columns F and G. The numbers should be the same, except for the number of decimal places.

f. Save the Excel workbook as **a03h1PropertyCheck_LastFirst**. Close the file, and exit Excel. You will submit this file to your instructor at the end of the last Hands-On Exercise.

g. Keep the database open if you plan to continue with the next Hands-On Exercise. If not, close the database and exit Access.

The Expression Builder and Functions

In the last Hands-On Exercise, you calculated the price per square foot for real estate properties to help evaluate properties on the investment list. You were able to type the expression manually.

When you encounter more complex expressions, the *Expression Builder* tool can help you create more complicated expressions. The Expression Builder's size enables you to easily see complex formulas and functions in their entirety. In addition, it provides easy access to objects, operators, and functions.

In this section, you will learn how to create expressions with the Expression Builder. You also will learn how to use built-in functions.

Creating Expressions Using the Expression Builder

The Expression Builder helps you create expressions by supplying you with access to fields, operators, and functions. When you use the Expression Builder to help create expressions, you can eliminate spelling errors in field names. Another advantage is that when you insert a function, placeholders tell you which values belong where. Experienced users may have functions memorized, but new users have the Expression Builder to provide support.

Once you open the Expression Builder, the Expression Builder dialog box displays. The top portion is an empty rectangular box known as the expression box. The left column of the Expression Builder dialog box contains Expression Elements (see Figure 16), which include the built-in functions, objects from the current database (including tables), and common expressions.

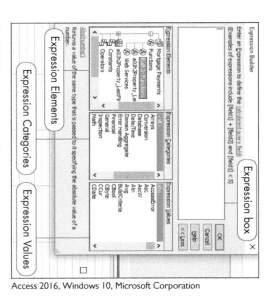

FIGURE 16 Expression Builder

Access 2016, Windows 10, Microsoft Corporation

The middle column displays the Expression Categories based on the item selected in the Expression Elements box (see Figure 16 above). For example, when the Built-In Functions item is selected in the Expression Elements box, the available built-in function categories, such as the Math category, are displayed in the Expression Categories box.

The right column displays the Expression Values, if any, for the categories that you selected in the Expression Categories box (see Figure 16 above). For example, if you click Built-In Functions in the Expression Elements box and click Date/Time in the Expression Categories box, the Expression Values box lists all of the built-in functions in the Date/Time category.

You can create an expression by manually typing text in the expression box or by double-clicking the elements from the bottom section in the Expression Builder dialog box.

To create an expression with the Expression Builder, complete the following steps:

1. Open a query in Design view (or create a new query).

2. Click the Field row of a blank column.

3. Click Builder in the Query Setup group of the Design tab to launch the Expression Builder.

4. Type the calculated field name and type a colon if you want to name the column. Although this is not required, as mentioned earlier in this chapter, this will change the title of the column in Datasheet view.

5. Type the name of a field (surrounded in [ ] brackets). Alternately, you can click the source table or query listed in the Expression Elements section and double-click the field you want. Using the second method will insert a field in a format resembling [Properties]![Beds] as shown in Figure 17. In this example, the table name Properties appears in brackets, followed by an exclamation point, followed by the field name Beds in brackets. As long as you do not have multiple fields with the same name, you can safely delete the table name and exclamation point (leaving you with [Beds] in this example). If you want to use operators (such as +) you can type those manually.

6. Repeat the previous step for each field you want to add to the calculation, remembering to take the order of operations into account. See Figure 17 as an example formula created in the Expression Builder.

7. Click OK to close the Expression Builder window.

8. Click Run in the Results group to view the results in Datasheet view.

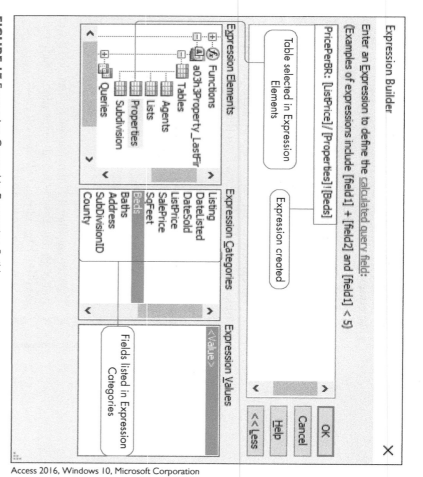

FIGURE 17 Expression Created in Expression Builder

Access 2016, Windows 10, Microsoft Corporation

Using Built-In Functions

A *function* is a predefined computation that performs a complex calculation. There are around 150 functions built into Access. If you are familiar with Excel, many of these will be familiar to you. Functions produce results based on inputs. Each input (such as a field name or a number) used to produce output for a function is known as an *argument*. Some functions have optional arguments, which are not required but may be necessary for your task.

Many of the tasks that are built-in would otherwise be difficult to perform. Figuring out the payment of a loan or determining the year portion of a date without functions would not be easy.

Once you identify what functionality is required, you can check the Built-In Functions in the Expression Builder to see if the function exists, or use search engines or Access Help. If the function exists, add the function to the expression box and replace «placeholder text» with the argument values. See Figure 18 for an example function inserted using the Expression Builder.

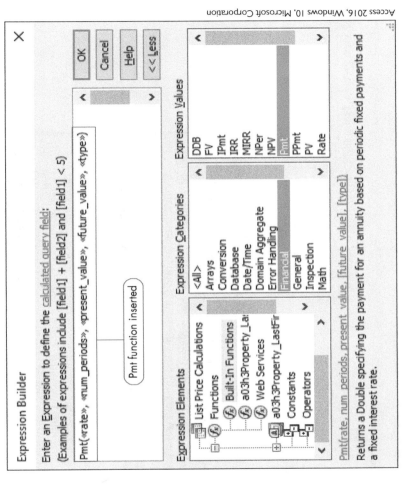

FIGURE 18 Function Inserted Using the Expression Builder

Functions work the same in Access, Excel, and programming languages (such as C#, Java, or Python). This chapter will demonstrate one function.

To create an expression containing a function with the Expression Builder, complete the following steps:

1. Open a query in Design view (or create a new query).

2. Click the Field row of a blank column.

3. Click Builder in the Query Setup group of the Design tab to launch the Expression Builder.

4. Type the calculated field name and type a colon if you want to name the column. Although this is not required, as mentioned earlier in this chapter, this will change the title of the column in Datasheet view.

5. Double-click Functions in the Expression Elements section of the window (see Figure 19). Click Built-In Functions. The list of available functions will appear in the Expression Categories box.

6. Locate and click the function category in the Expression Categories section, as shown in Figure 19. If you are unsure of the category, you can use Help or search through the category labeled <All>. .

7. Double-click the function name in the Expression Values section to add it. Most functions include one or more placeholder text fields, text surrounded by «» symbols. These provide you guidance as to what data should be entered in each location. Notice an example of placeholder text in Figure 19.

8. Click a placeholder text element to select it, unless your function does not have placeholder text.

9. Type the number, field name, or calculation you want to replace the placeholder (for example, in Figure 19, the first placeholder text was replaced by .05/12). Note that you can also add a field by clicking the desired table or query listed in the Expression Elements section and double-clicking the field you want. In Figure 19, notice that [Properties]![ListPrice] has replaced the third placeholder. As discussed earlier, the table name and exclamation point can often be removed safely.

10. Click OK to close the Expression Builder window.

11. Click Run in the Results group to view the results in Datasheet view.

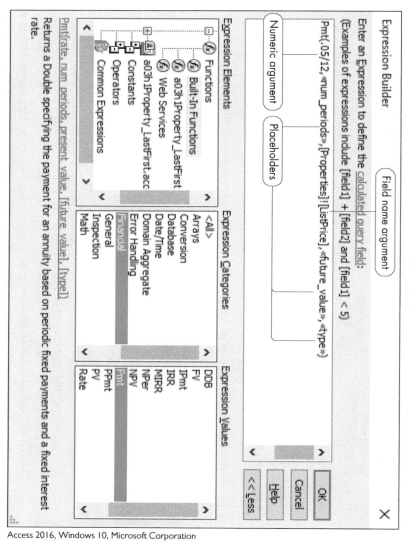

Expression Builder

Enter an Expression to define the calculated query field:
(Examples of expressions include [field1] + [field2] and [field1] < 5)

Pmt(.05/12, «num_periods», [Properties]![ListPrice], «future_value», «type»)

Numeric argument   Placeholders   Field name argument

Expression Elements

- Functions
  - Built-In Functions
  - a03h 1Property_LastFirst
  - Web Services
  - a03h 1Property_LastFirst.acc
- Constants
- Operators
- Common Expressions

Expression Categories

<All>
Arrays
Conversion
Database
Date/Time
Domain Aggregate
Error Handling
Financial
General
Inspection
Math

Expression Values

DDB
FV
IPmt
IRR
MIRR
NPer
NPV
Pmt
PPmt
Pv
Rate

OK   Cancel   Help   << Less

Pmt(rate, num_periods, present_value, [future_value], [type])

Returns a Double specifying the payment for an annuity based on periodic fixed payments and a fixed interest rate.

FIGURE 19 Expression with Some Arguments Filled In

STEP 2

Calculate a Loan Payment with the Pmt Function

» The *Pmt function* calculates the loan payment given the rate, number of periods (also known as term), and the present value of the loan (the principal). If necessary, two other arguments (future value and type) can be used, but they are not necessary for many calculations. The Pmt function uses the following syntax:

Pmt(rate, num_periods, present_value, future_value, type)

After inserting the function using the Expression Builder, you will supply at least the rate, num_periods, and present_value arguments. The arguments are as follows:

- **rate:** Interest rates are usually stated as yearly rates, so the rate must be converted to the rate per period. If a loan is paid monthly, divide the yearly rate by 12. Typically this is entered as a decimal followed by the division (for example, .05/12). It is also acceptable to enter this as a percentage (5%/12).

- **num_periods:** Multiply the number of years of the loan by the number of payments per year. The total number of payments for a monthly payment would be calculated as the number of years multiplied by 12.
- **present_value:** The amount of the loan.
- **future_value** and **type:** The last two arguments—future value and type—are both optional, so they are usually left blank or filled in with zero.

The following example shows how to use the Pmt function to calculate the payment for a loan with a 5% interest rate, paid 12 times a year. This loan will be paid for four years and has a present value of $12,500. Figure 20 shows how it appears in the Expression Builder.

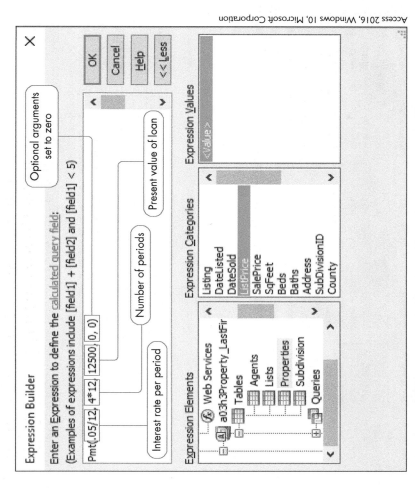

Access 2016, Windows 10, Microsoft Corporation

FIGURE 20 Pmt Function with Arguments Filled In

The Pmt function will return a negative value, as a loan payment is considered a debit. In this case, it returns −287.87. If you would like to display this as a positive number, place a negative sign in front of the loan amount.

Pmt(.05/12, 4*12, −12500, 0, 0)

By default, the column heading will display Expr1 for any calculated field, as shown in the first Hands-On Exercise. To change this, you can replace Expr1 with the desired column heading, followed by a colon (:), to the left of the calculation.

MonthlyPmt: Pmt(.05/12, 4*12, −12500, 0, 0)

Quick Concepts

5. List two benefits of using the Expression Builder to create expressions.

6. What is an example argument in the Pmt function? What does this argument do?

7. Given the following function: Pmt(.05/12, 5*12, 50000, 0, 0), how many years is the loan for and how much is the initial amount of the loan?

Hands-On Exercises

Skills covered: Use the Expression Builder • Calculate a Loan Payment with the Pmt Function

2 The Expression Builder and Functions

When Don and Matt ask you to calculate the price per bedroom and the price per room for each property, you use the Expression Builder to make the task easier. You also create an additional calculated field showing the estimated mortgage for each property.

STEP 1 》 USE THE EXPRESSION BUILDER

You will create a copy of the Price Per Square Foot Formatted query from the previous Hands-On Exercise and paste it using a new name. You will add a few more calculated fields to the new query. You will create one calculation to determine the price per bedroom for each house. You will create a second field to calculate the price per room. For this calculation, you will assume that each property has a kitchen, a living room, a dining room, and the listed bedrooms and bathrooms. The calculations you will create are shown in Figure 21. Your expected output is shown in Figure 22.

List Price Calculations

Field:	FirstName	LastName	ListPrice	SqFeet	Sold	PricePerBR: [ListPrice]/[Beds]	PricePerRoom: [ListPrice]/([Beds]+[Baths]+3)
Table:	Agents	Agents	Properties	Properties	Properties		
Sort:	Ascending						
Show:	☑	☑	☑	☑	☑	☑	☑
Criteria:							
or:							

Step i: PricePerBR calculation

Step s: PricePerRoom calculation

FIGURE 21 Expanded Calculations

Access 2016, Windows 10, Microsoft Corporation

Mortgage Payments | **List Price Calculations**

First Name	Last Name	List Price	Square Feet	Sold	Price Per Bedroom	Price Per Room
Philip	DeFranco	$109,140.00	1133	No	$54,570.00	$18,190.00
Chardae	Myles	$129,780.00	1132	No	$64,890.00	$21,630.00
Makarem	Abdeljawad	$136,680.00	1375	No	$68,340.00	$22,780.00
Meera	Shah	$138,990.00	1276	No	$69,495.00	$23,165.00
StudentFirst	StudentLast	$140,693.00	1490	No	$70,346.50	$23,448.83
Makarem	Abdeljawad	$140,904.00	1301	No	$70,452.00	$23,484.00
Makarem	Abdeljawad	$142,380.00	1373	No	$71,190.00	$20,340.00
Chardae	Myles	$163,737.00	1476	No	$81,868.50	$27,289.50
Jaynish	Mody	$164,436.00	1850	No	$82,218.00	$23,490.86
Jaynish	Mody	$166,320.00	1437	No	$83,160.00	$27,720.00
Chardae	Myles	$166,552.00	1623	No	$83,276.00	$23,793.14
Chardae	Myles	$166,800.00	1598	No	$83,400.00	$27,800.00
Philip	DeFranco	$168,000.00	1680	No	$84,000.00	$25,846.15
Chardae	Myles	$168,354.00	1651	No	$84,177.00	$28,059.00
Philip	DeFranco	$174,230.00	1771	No	$87,115.00	$29,038.33
Meera	Shah	$174,720.00	1694	No	$87,360.00	$29,120.00
StudentFirst	StudentLast	$174,720.00	1610	No	$87,360.00	$26,880.00
Chardae	Myles	$175,336.00	1855	No	$87,668.00	$29,222.67
StudentFirst	StudentLast	$175,560.00	1562	No	$87,780.00	$29,260.00
Meera	Shah	$176,176.00	1761	No	$88,088.00	$25,168.00
Jaynish	Mody	$177,984.00	1707	No	$88,992.00	$27,382.15
Chardae	Myles	$179,088.00	1837	No	$89,544.00	$29,848.00
Chardae	Myles	$179,100.00	1946	No	$89,550.00	$25,585.71
Chardae	Myles	$179,712.00	1854	No	$89,856.00	$27,648.00
Chardae	Myles	$180,180.00	1896	No	$90,090.00	$30,030.00
Makarem	Abdeljawad	$180,810.00	1667	No	$90,405.00	$30,135.00
Philip	DeFranco	$192,312.00	1751	No	$91,656.00	$20,552.00

Record: 2 of 215

Step k: Caption set for first calculation

Step t: Caption set for second calculation

FIGURE 22 Payment Calculation

a. Open *aO3h1Property_LastFirst* if you closed it at the end of Hands-On Exercise 1, and save it as **aO3h2Property_LastFirst**, changing h1 to h2.

b. Create a copy of the Price Per Square Foot Formatted query with the name **List Price Calculations**.

c. Open the List Price Calculations query in Design view. Click the **WrongPricePerSqFt field**. Click **Delete Columns** in the Query Setup group on the Design tab.

d. Click the **Field row** in the PricePerSqFt column and click **Builder** in the Query Setup group.

The Expression Builder dialog box opens, displaying the current formula.

e. Double-click the **PricePerSqFt field name** and type **PricePerBR**.

f. Double-click the **[SqFeet] field** in the expression and press **Delete**.

g. Click the **plus sign** ⊞ next to the aO3h2Property_LastFirst database in the Expression Elements box to expand the list. Click the **plus sign** next to Tables and select the **Properties table**.

The fields from the Properties table are now listed in the middle column (Expression Categories).

h. Double-click the **Beds field** to add it to the expression box.

The expression now reads PricePerBR: [ListPrice]/[Properties]![Beds].

i. Highlight the **[Properties]! prefix** in front of *Beds* and press **Delete**.

The expression now reads PricePerBR: [ListPrice]/[Beds]. As the Beds field name is unique within our query, the table name is not necessary. Removing this makes the query easier to read. If a field named Beds appeared in more than one table in our query, removing the table name would cause problems.

j. Click **OK** and click **Run** to view the query results.

Notice that the column heading still reads Price Per Sq Ft. Also notice that the column's contents are formatted as Currency. These settings were copied when the query was copied.

k. Switch to Design view and ensure that the PricePerBR field is selected. Click **Property Sheet** in the Show/Hide group and change the **Caption** to **Price Per Bedroom**. Close the Property Sheet. Run the query and examine the changes.

The PricePerBR column now has an appropriate caption.

l. Switch to Design view. Select the entire **PricePerBR expression**, right-click the selected expression, and then select **Copy**. Right-click the **Field row** of the next blank column and select **Paste**.

You will edit the copied expression so that it reflects the price per room, assuming that the kitchen, living room, dining room, and the bedrooms and bathrooms will make up the number of rooms.

m. Click **Builder** in the Query Setup group.

n. Change the PricePerBR field name to **PricePerRoom**.

o. Add **an opening parenthesis** before the [Beds] portion of the formula. Type a **plus sign** after [Beds].

As you want the addition to be done first, enclose the addition in parentheses. The expression box should read PricePerRoom: [ListPrice]/([Beds]+

p. Click the **plus sign** next to the aO3h2Property_LastFirst database in the Expression Elements box to expand the list. Click the **plus sign** next to Tables and select the **Properties table**.

The fields from the Properties table are now listed in the Expression Categories box.

q. Double-click the **Baths field** to add it to the expression box.

r. Type another plus sign after [Baths] and type **3** followed by a right parenthesis. In other words, you will type **+3)** in the expression box.

s. Delete the [Properties]! portion of the expression and click **OK** to close the Expression Builder.

The expression now reads PricePerRoom: [ListPrice]/([Beds]+[Baths]+3). Your final formula is the list price divided by the total number of rooms. The total number of rooms is the number of bedrooms (in the Beds field), plus the number of bathrooms (found in the Baths field), plus 3 (a constant representing the kitchen, living room, and dining room).

t. Click **Property Sheet** in the Show/Hide group. Type **Price Per Room** in the Caption box. Click the Format box, click the drop-down menu, and select **Currency**. Close the Property Sheet.

Compare your formulas to Figure 21. This figure has expanded the column widths for readability.

u. Run the query. Adjust column widths as necessary. Compare your results to Figure 22.

v. Save and close the query.

Don and Matt feel like they are close to making an offer on a house. They would like to restrict the query to houses that cost $190,000 or less. They would also like to calculate the estimated mortgage payment for each house. You create this calculation using the Pmt function. You make the following assumptions: 80% of the sale price to be financed, a 30-year term, monthly payments, and a fixed 4.0% annual interest rate. Refer to Figures 23 and 24 as you complete Step 2.

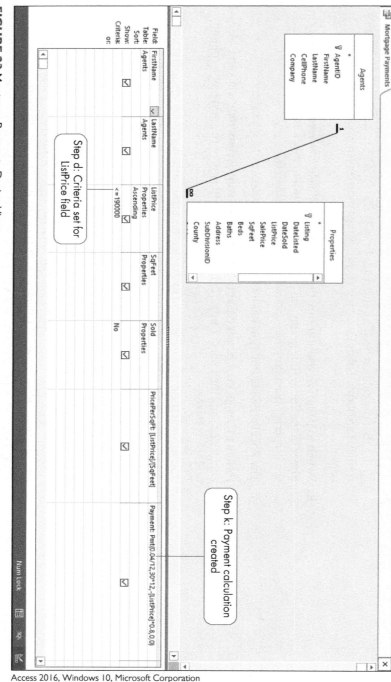

FIGURE 23 Mortgage Payments Design View

Field:	FirstName	LastName	ListPrice	SqFeet	Sold	PricePerSqFt: [ListPrice]/[SqFeet]	Payment: Pmt(0.04/12,30*12,-[ListPrice]*0.8,0,0)
Table:	Agents	Agents	Properties	Properties	Properties		
Sort:			Ascending				
Show:	☑	☑	☑	☑	☑	☑	☑
Criteria:			<=190000		No		
or:							

Step d: Criteria set for ListPrice field

Step k: Payment calculation created

Agents
* AgentID
FirstName
LastName
CellPhone
Company

Properties
* Listing
DateListed
DateSold
ListPrice
SalePrice
SqFeet
Beds
Baths
Address
SubDivisionID
County

Mortgage Payments

Num Lock

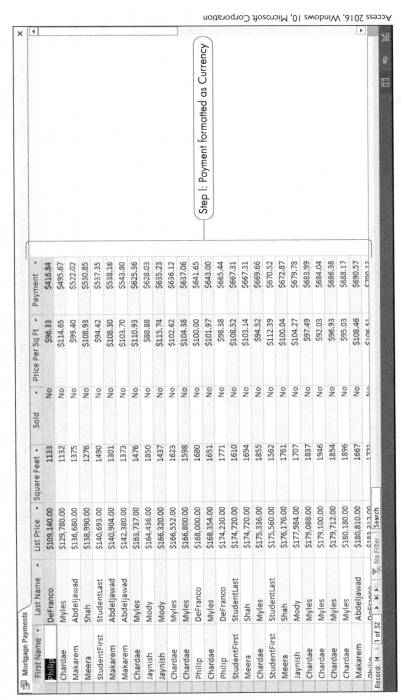

First Name	Last Name	List Price	Square Feet	Sold	Price Per Sq Ft	Payment
Phillip	DeFranco	$109,140.00	1133	No	$96.33	$416.84
Chardae	Myles	$129,780.00	1132	No	$114.65	$495.67
Makarem	Abdeljawad	$136,680.00	1375	No	$99.40	$522.02
Meera	Shah	$138,990.00	1276	No	$108.93	$530.85
StudentFirst	StudentLast	$140,693.00	1490	No	$94.42	$537.35
Makarem	Abdeljawad	$140,904.00	1301	No	$108.30	$538.16
Makarem	Abdeljawad	$142,380.00	1373	No	$103.70	$543.80
Chardae	Myles	$163,737.00	1476	No	$110.93	$625.36
Jaynish	Mody	$166,436.00	1850	No	$88.88	$628.03
Jaynish	Mody	$166,320.00	1437	No	$115.74	$635.23
Chardae	Myles	$166,552.00	1623	No	$102.62	$636.12
Chardae	Myles	$166,800.00	1598	No	$104.38	$637.06
Phillip	DeFranco	$168,000.00	1680	No	$100.00	$641.65
Chardae	Myles	$168,354.00	1651	No	$101.97	$643.00
Phillip	DeFranco	$174,230.00	1771	No	$98.38	$665.44
StudentFirst	StudentLast	$174,720.00	1610	No	$108.52	$667.31
Meera	Shah	$174,720.00	1694	No	$103.14	$667.31
Chardae	Myles	$175,336.00	1855	No	$94.52	$669.66
StudentFirst	StudentLast	$175,560.00	1562	No	$112.39	$670.52
Meera	Shah	$176,176.00	1761	No	$100.04	$672.87
Jaynish	Mody	$177,984.00	1707	No	$104.27	$679.78
Chardae	Myles	$179,088.00	1837	No	$97.49	$683.99
Chardae	Myles	$179,100.00	1946	No	$92.03	$684.04
Chardae	Myles	$179,712.00	1854	No	$96.93	$686.38
Chardae	Myles	$180,180.00	1896	No	$95.03	$688.17
Makarem	Abdeljawad	$180,810.00	1667	No	$108.46	$690.57
Philip	DeFranco	$181,313.00	1731	No	$106.51	$700.13

Record: ◀ ◀ 1 of 32 ▶ ▶▶ ▶✱ No Filter Search

Step I: Payment formatted as Currency

FIGURE 24 Mortgage Payments Results

a. Create a copy of the Price Per Square Foot Formatted query named **Mortgage Payments.**

b. Right-click **Mortgage Payments** and select **Design View.**

c. Delete the WrongPricePerSqFt field.

TROUBLESHOOTING: If you do not see the WrongPricePerSqFt field, ensure that you copied the correct query.

d. Type **<=190000** in the Criteria row of the ListPrice column. Press **Enter.**

The query, when it is run, will show only the houses that cost $190,000 or less.

e. Click the **Field row** of the first blank column. Click **Builder** in the Query Setup group to open the Expression Builder dialog box.

f. Double-click **Functions** in the Expression Elements box and select **Built-In Functions.**

g. Select **Financial** in the Expression Categories box.

h. Double-click **Pmt** in the Expression Values box.

The expression box displays:

Pmt(«rate», «num_periods», «present_value», «future_value», «type»)

i. Position the insertion point before the Pmt function. Type **Payment:** to the left of the Pmt function, with a space after the colon. The expression box now displays:

Payment: Pmt(«rate», «num_periods», «present_value», «future_value», «type»)

Hands-On Exercise 2

717

j. Click each argument to select it and substitute the appropriate information. Make sure there is a comma between each argument.

Argument	Replacement Value
«rate»	.04/12
«num_periods»	30*12
«present_value»	[ListPrice]*.8
«future_value»	0
«type»	0

Note that the loan is a 30-year loan with 12 payments per year, hence the calculation for the number of payments. Also note, Don and Matt plan on financing 80% of the cost, putting 20% down. Therefore, you will multiply the list price by .8 (80%).

k. Click **OK**. Examine Figure 23 to make sure that you have entered the correct arguments.

l. Open the Property Sheet for the Payment field and change the format to **Currency**. Close the Property Sheet. Run the query.

Notice that the payment amounts are negative numbers (displayed in parentheses). You will edit the formula to change the negative payment values to positive.

m. Right-click the **Mortgage Payments tab** and select **Design View**. Click **Builder**. Add a **minus sign (−)** to the left of [ListPrice] and click **OK**.

By adding the negative sign in front of the ListPrice field, you ensure that the value is displayed as a positive number. The expression now reads:

Payment: Pmt(.04/12,30*12, −[ListPrice]*.8,0,0)

n. Run the query and examine the results. Adjust column widths as necessary.

The query displays a column containing the calculated monthly mortgage payment, formatted as currency, as shown in Figure 24.

o. Save and close the query. Keep the database open if you plan to continue with the next Hands-On Exercise. If not, close the database and exit Access.

Aggregate Functions

An *aggregate function* performs a calculation on an entire column of data and returns a single value. One example of an aggregate function is Sum.

Access refers to aggregate functions as Totals. Totals can be added to Datasheet view of a query, or they can be added to a query's Design view. Based on the data type, different aggregate functions will be available. Numeric fields are eligible for all of the functions, whereas Short Text fields are not. A list of common aggregate functions is shown in Table 2.

In the Property database, the average home price per county could be presented in a query or a report. This would give prospective buyers a good idea of home prices in their target counties. Almost every company or organization that uses a database will require some type of aggregate data.

TABLE 2	Common Aggregate Functions
Function	**Description**
Avg (Average)	Calculates the average value for a column.
Count	Counts the number of values in a column.
Max (Maximum)	Returns the item with the highest value.
Min (Minimum)	Returns the item with the lowest value.
Sum	Totals the items in a column.

In this section, you will learn how to create and work with aggregate functions. Specifically, you will learn how to use the Total row and create a totals query.

Adding Aggregate Functions to Datasheets

STEP 1 » Aggregate data helps users evaluate the values in a single record to the aggregate of all the records. If you are considering buying a property in Story County, Iowa, for $150,000, and the average price of a property in that county is $450,000, you know you are getting a good deal (or buying a bad property).

Access provides two methods of adding aggregate functions—a *Total row*, which displays the results of the aggregate function as the last row in Datasheet view of a table or query, and a totals query created in Query Design view. The totals query will be defined shortly.

The Total row method is quick and easy and has the advantage of showing the totals while still showing the individual records. Adding a Total row to a query or table can be accomplished by most users, even those who are not familiar with designing a query. Figure 25 shows the Total row added to Datasheet view of a query. In this image, the average of the List Price is displayed. The available aggregate functions are shown in the Price Per Sq Ft column. You can choose any of the aggregate functions that apply to numeric fields.

FIGURE 25 Total Row in Datasheet View

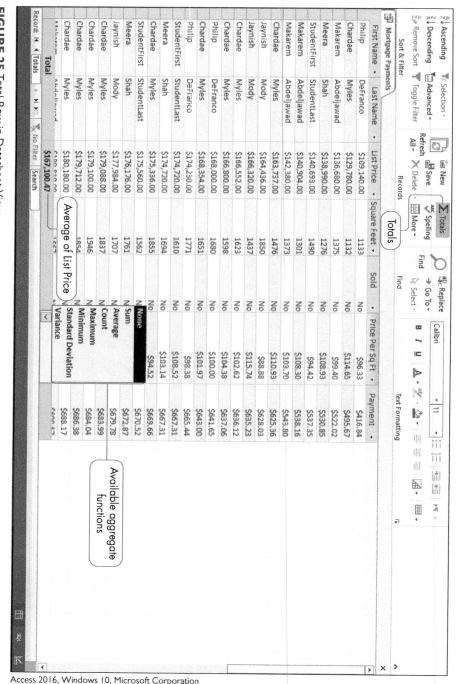

Access 2016, Windows 10, Microsoft Corporation

To add a Total row to the Datasheet view of a query or table, complete the following steps:

1. View the query or table in Datasheet view.

2. Click Totals in the Records group on the Home tab. The Total row is added at the bottom of the datasheet, below the new record row.

3. Select one of the aggregate functions (such as Average, Count, or Sum) in the new Total row by clicking in the cell and clicking the arrow.

Creating Queries with Aggregate Functions

The total row, though useful, is limited. Many times, you may require in-depth statistics. Instead of wanting to see the average sale price for houses, you may want to see the average sale price by city. Instead of seeing the average price for every item your store sells, you may want to see the average price for each category. Using the total row in the previous example, this is not feasible. Another limitation of using the total row is that you might want to see the average sale price, minimum sale price, and maximum sale price. Using the previous method, this is difficult to do.

Another way to display aggregate functions requires changes to the query design. A **totals query** contains an additional row in the query design grid and is used to display aggregate data when the query is run. This provides two distinct advantages over the total row. The first allows you to show only the results of the aggregate functions (and not the detail), and the second enables you to see statistics by category.

Create a Totals Query

>> Instead of showing detail, the overall statistics for the entire table or query may be displayed using a totals query. For example, if you want to see the number of listings, average value, and the average size in square feet for all properties in your table, you can use a totals query to get that data and not see details. Instead of having hundreds of rows of data with a summary row at the bottom (which could be missed), a totals query can display only the aggregate function results. Figure 26 shows a totals query in Design view, and Figure 27 shows the results.

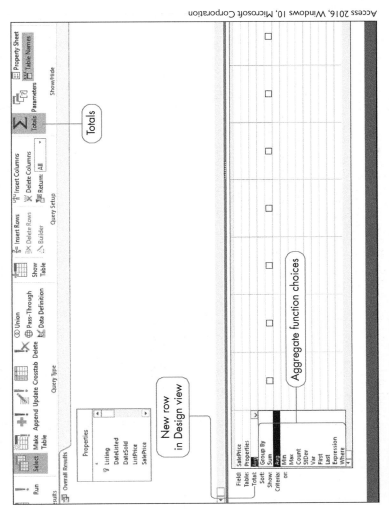

Access 2016, Windows 10, Microsoft Corporation

FIGURE 26 Totals Query Design View

Access 2016, Windows 10, Microsoft Corporation

FIGURE 27 Totals Query Results

To create a totals query, complete the following steps:

1. Create a query in Design view and add the fields for which you want to get statistics.
2. Click Totals in the Show/Hide group on the Design tab. A new Total row displays in the query design grid between the Table and Sort rows. Notice that it defaults to Group By.
3. Click Group By and select the aggregate function you want applied for each field.
4. Display the Property Sheet (as done earlier in this chapter) and adjust settings to meet your requirements.
5. Click Run in the Results group to see the results.

If you want to see the results of multiple aggregate functions for a single field, you can add the same field multiple times to a query. Display the Total row and select a different aggregate function for each column. When you run the query, you will see the results of each aggregate function in each column. For example, if you wanted to see the average, count, and sum of a field, you would add it three times to the query design, display the Total row, select the appropriate aggregate function for each column, and run the query.

Add Grouping to a Totals Query

Grouping a query allows you to summarize your data by the values of a field. For example, instead of seeing overall averages, you may want to see the results for each county. In this case, add County as a grouping level to see statistics by County.

To group an existing totals query, complete the following steps:

1. Add the field you want to group by to the query in Design view. For readability, the field should appear as the first field in the query.

2. Verify that the Total row displays Group By for the added field (see Figure 28), and run the query.

If you want to see the results by county, add the County field to the query and leave the Total row with the default of Group By. You may want to move this column to the beginning, as it will make your query easier to read.

Figure 28 shows Design view of a totals query with five columns, one of which is the grouping field. Figure 29 shows the results of this query. Notice that the resulting query shows one row for each county.

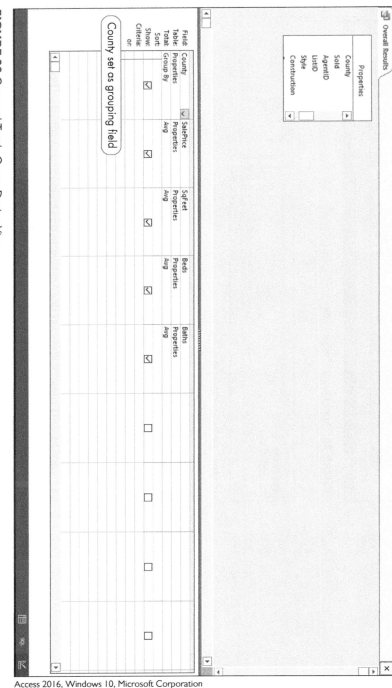

County set as grouping field

FIGURE 28 Grouped Totals Query Design View

Access 2016, Windows 10, Microsoft Corporation

Overall Results

County	AvgOfSalePrice	AvgOfSqFeet	AvgOfBeds	AvgOfBaths
Bergen	$220,431.12	2218.08163265306	3.12244897959184	1.63265306122449
Essex	$284,091.38	2844.50574712644	3.90804597701149	1.86206896551724
Hudson	$243,285.50	2645.23529411765	3.41176470588235	1.64705882352941
Mercer	$341,085.67	3242.675	4.45	2
Morris	$322,404.05	3105.6875	4.140625	1.890625
Passaic	Results shown for each county	2049.03846153846	2.80769230769231	1.75
Sussex		2968	4.5	2.1

FIGURE 29 Grouped Totals Query Results

Add Conditions to a Totals Query

Totals queries can provide even better information if you add criteria. For example, if you wanted to see the number of houses, average price, and average square feet for only the sold properties, grouped by county, you can add the Sold field to the query. Set the criteria to Yes to indicate that the Sold field is yes.

To add conditions to an existing totals query, complete the following steps:

1. Double-click the field you want to limit by to add it to the design grid. The location of this field is not important, as it will not be displayed.
2. Select Where from the menu in the Total row.
3. Enter the condition.
4. Run the query.

Figure 30 shows a query with a condition added, and Figure 31 shows the results. Compare this to Figure 29 to see the change in results.

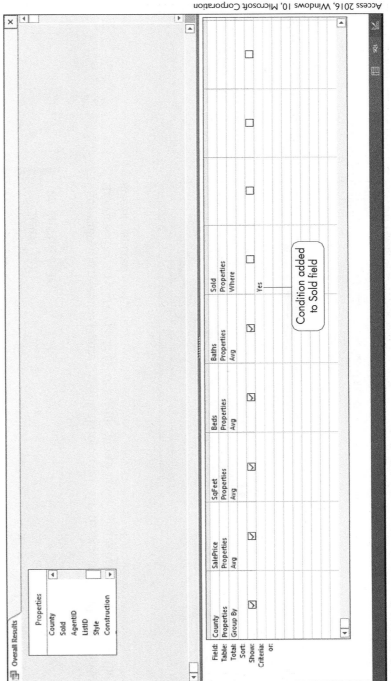

Overall Results

Properties

- County
- Sold
- AgentID
- ListID
- Style
- Construction

Field:	County	SalePrice	SqFeet	Beds	Baths	Sold
Table:	Properties	Properties	Properties	Properties	Properties	Properties
Total:	Group By	Avg	Avg	Avg	Avg	Where
Sort:						
Show:	☑	☑	☑	☑	☑	☐
Criteria:						Yes
or:						

Condition added to Sold field

FIGURE 30 Totals Query with Condition Design View

FIGURE 31 Totals Query with Condition Results

Overall Results					
County	AvgOfSalePrice	AvgOfSqFeet	AvgOfBeds	AvgOfBaths	
Bergen	$220,431.12	2223.11764705882	3.29411764705882	1.73529411764706	
Essex	$284,091.38	2829.53846153846	3.96153846153846	1.94230769230769	
Hudson	$243,285.50	2432.25	3	1.75	
Mercer	$341,085.67	3440.55555555556	4.55555555555556	2	
Morris	$322,404.05	3233.42857142857	4.33333333333333	1.9047619047619	
Passaic	$219,325.20	2171.4	2.8	1.8	
Sussex	$269,411.17	2610	3.83333333333333	2	

Access 2016, Windows 10,
Microsoft Corporation

TIP: MULTIPLE GROUPING LEVELS

At times, you may want to add multiple grouping fields. For example, instead of grouping by state, you might want to group by city. However, if you group by city, customers with the same city name in different states would be grouped together. For example, all 50 states have a location named Greenville. If you grouped by city, all customers with a city of Greenville, regardless of state, would appear as a group. This is probably not your intention. Instead, you probably would want to see results by city and state, and thus would want to add both fields to a query and select Group By.

Add a Calculated Field to a Totals Query

Calculated fields can also have aggregate functions applied to them. For example, you may want to calculate mortgage payments, and see the average of your calculation.

STEP 3

To apply an aggregate function to a totals query, complete the following steps:

1. Create the calculation you want to summarize, using any of the methods discussed earlier in this chapter.

2. Select the appropriate aggregate function from the menu in the Total row (see Figure 32).

3. Run the query.

The results will resemble Figure 33. Note that you can also use any of the other methods shown earlier, so you can add grouping (as shown in the figures below) and format the field as required.

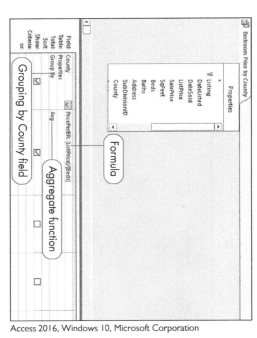

Access 2016, Windows 10, Microsoft Corporation

FIGURE 32 Adding Calculated Field to a Totals Query

Bedroom Price by County

County	PricePerBR
Bergen	$73,946.82
Essex	$76,025.00
Hudson	$81,793.61
Mercer	$74,941.35
Morris	$77,588.72
Passaic	$75,387.97
Sussex	$69,097.29

PricePerBR results for each County

Results grouped by County name

FIGURE 33 Calculated Field Results

Quick Concepts

8. What are the benefits of aggregate functions? List three examples of aggregate functions.

9. How does a Total row change the display of the query's Datasheet view?

10. What is a totals query?

11. What would it mean if a query is "grouped by" state?

Skills covered: Display a Total Row for a Query • Create a Totals Query • Add Grouping to a Totals Query • Add Conditions to a Totals Query • Add a Calculated Field to a Totals Query

3 Aggregate Functions

The investors decide it would be helpful to analyze the property lists they purchased. Some of the lists do not have homes that match their target criteria. The investors will either purchase new lists or alter their criteria. You create several totals queries to evaluate the property lists.

STEP 1 ⟫ DISPLAY A TOTAL ROW FOR A QUERY

You begin your property list analysis by creating a total row in Datasheet view of the Mortgage Payments query. This will give you a variety of aggregate information for important columns. Refer to Figure 34 as you complete Step 1.

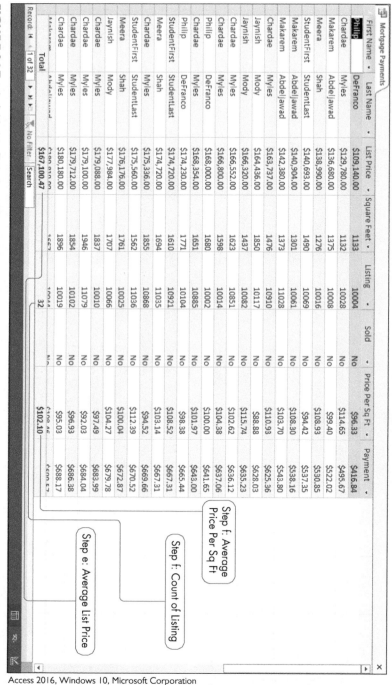

First Name	Last Name	List Price	Square Feet	Listing	Sold	Price Per Sq Ft	Payment
Philip	DeFranco	$109,140.00	1133	10004	No	$96.33	$416.84
Chardae	Myles	$129,780.00	1132	10028	No	$114.65	$495.67
Makarem	AbdelJawad	$136,680.00	1375	10008	No	$99.40	$522.02
Meera	Shah	$138,990.00	1276	10016	No	$108.93	$530.85
StudentFirst	StudentLast	$140,693.00	1490	10069	No	$94.42	$537.35
Makarem	AbdelJawad	$140,904.00	1301	10061	No	$108.30	$538.16
Makarem	AbdelJawad	$142,380.00	1373	11028	No	$103.70	$543.80
Chardae	Myles	$163,737.00	1476	10910	No	$110.93	$625.36
Jaynish	Mody	$164,436.00	1850	10117	No	$88.88	$628.03
Jaynish	Mody	$166,320.00	1437	10082	No	$115.74	$635.23
Chardae	Myles	$166,552.00	1623	10851	No	$102.62	$636.12
Chardae	Myles	$166,800.00	1598	10014	No	$104.38	$637.06
Philip	DeFranco	$168,000.00	1680	10002	No	$100.00	$641.65
Chardae	Myles	$168,354.00	1651	10885	No	$101.97	$643.00
Philip	DeFranco	$174,230.00	1771	10104	No	$98.38	$665.44
StudentFirst	StudentLast	$174,720.00	1610	10921	No	$108.52	$667.31
Meera	Shah	$174,720.00	1694	11035	No	$103.14	$667.31
Chardae	Myles	$175,336.00	1855	10868	No	$94.52	$669.66
StudentFirst	StudentLast	$175,560.00	1562	11036	No	$112.39	$670.52
Meera	Shah	$176,176.00	1761	10025	No	$100.04	$672.87
Jaynish	Mody	$177,984.00	1707	10066	No	$104.27	$679.78
Chardae	Myles	$179,088.00	1837	10010	No	$97.49	$683.99
Chardae	Myles	$179,100.00	1946	11079	No	$92.03	$684.04
Chardae	Myles	$179,712.00	1854	10102	No	$96.93	$686.38
Chardae	Myles	$180,180.00	1896	10019	No	$95.03	$688.17
Makarem	AbdelJawad		1663	10044	No	$108.46	$690.57
Total		**$167,100.47**		**32**		**$102.10**	

Record: 14 ◀ 1 of 32 ▶ ▶I ▶* No Filter Search

FIGURE 34 Totals Added to Datasheet View

Step f: Average Price Per Sq Ft

Step f: Count of Listing

Step e: Average List Price

a. Open *a03h2Property_LastFirst* if you closed it at the end of Hands-On Exercise 2 and save it as **a03h3Property_LastFirst**, changing h2 to h3.

b. Open the **Mortgage Payments query** in Design view. Drag the **Listing field** from the Properties table to the fifth column.

The Listing field is now in the fifth column, between the SqFeet and Sold fields. The other columns shift to the right.

> **TROUBLESHOOTING:** If you drag the Listing field to the wrong position, you can drag it again to the correct location.

c. Switch to Datasheet view. Click **Totals** in the Records group on the Home tab.

Access 2016, Windows 10, Microsoft Corporation

d. Click the **cell** that intersects the Total row and the List Price column.

e. Click the **arrow** and select **Average** to display the average value of all the properties that have not sold. Adjust column widths as necessary to ensure that all values are displayed.

The average list price of all properties is $167,100.47.

f. Click the **arrow** in the Total row in the Listing column and select **Count** from the list.

The count of properties in this datasheet is 32.

g. Click the **arrow** in the Total row in the Price Per Sq Ft column and select **Average** from the list.

The average price per square foot is $102.10.

h. Compare your results to Figure 34. Save and close the query.

STEP 2 » **CREATE A TOTALS QUERY AND ADD GROUPING AND CONDITIONS**

You create a totals query to help Don and Matt evaluate the properties in groups. Refer to Figure 35 and Figure 36 as you complete Step 2.

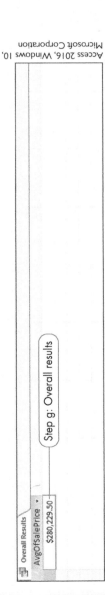

FIGURE 35 Overall Results Query Output

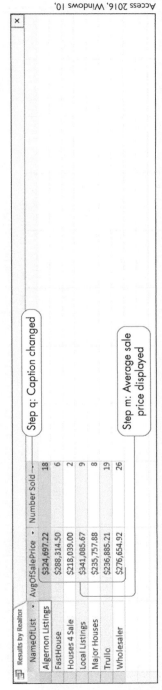

FIGURE 36 Results by Realtor Query Output

a. Click **Query Design** in the Queries group of the Create tab.

You create a new query in Query Design; the Show Table dialog box opens.

b. Click the **Properties table** in the Show Table dialog box and click **Add**. Close the Show Table dialog box.

c. Double-click the **SalePrice** and **Sold** fields to add them to the query.

d. Click **Totals** in the Show/Hide group of the Design tab to show the Total row.

A new row labeled Totals displays in the query design grid, between the Table and Sort rows. Each field has Group By listed in the new row by default.

e. Click the **Group By arrow** in the SalePrice column Total row and select **Avg.**

f. Click the **Group By arrow** in the Sold column Total row and select **Where**. Type **Yes** in the Criteria row.

This criterion will limit the results to sold houses only.

g. Click the **SalePrice field** and click **Property Sheet** in the Show/Hide group. Change the SalePrice format to **Currency**. Close the Property Sheet. Run the query and adjust the column width if necessary. Compare your results to Figure 35.

The results show an overall average of $280,229.50 for the sold properties in the database.

h. Click **Save** on the Quick Access Toolbar and type **Overall Results** in the Save As dialog box. Click **OK**. Close the query.

i. Click **Query Design** in the Query group of the Create tab to create a new query.

j. Add the Properties table and the Lists table from the Show Table dialog box. Close the Show Table dialog box.

k. Add the NameOfList field from the Lists table and the SalePrice, Listing, and Sold fields from the Properties table to the query.

l. Click **Totals** in the Show/Hide group to show the Total row.

A new row labeled Total appears between the Table and Sort rows.

m. Change the Total row for SalePrice to **Avg**.

n. Change the Total row for Listing to **Count**.

o. Change the Total row for Sold to **Where**. Type **Yes** in the Criteria row.

This criterion will limit the results to sold houses only.

p. Click the **SalePrice field** and click **Property Sheet** in the Show/Hide group. Change the SalePrice format to **Currency**.

q. Click the **Listing field** and change the caption to **Number Sold**. Close the Property Sheet. Run the query and widen the columns as shown in Figure 36.

Notice that Houses 4 Sale has the lowest average sale price. As Don and Matt are hoping to focus on inexpensive properties, they can focus on properties offered by this source. Notice also that the query results show the number of properties sold in each source, in addition to the average sale price. This will help determine which sources have been more effective.

r. Click **Save** on the Quick Access Toolbar and type **Results By Realtor** in the Save As dialog box. Click **OK**. Keep the query open for the next step.

The previous query shows the average value of the properties by realtor. However, Don and Matt learned at the seminar they attended that the longer a property has been on the market, the better your chances of negotiating a better price. You will revise the query to show, on average, how long each realtor takes to sell a house. Refer to Figure 37 as you complete Step 3.

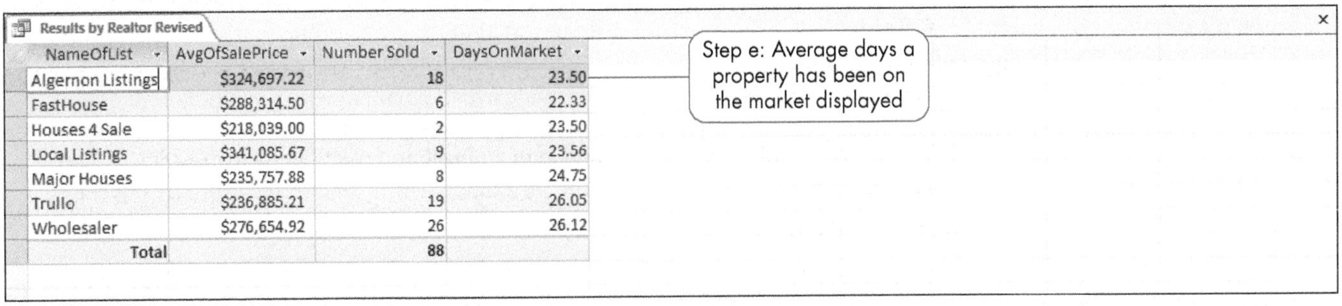

Results by Realtor Revised				
NameOfList ▾	AvgOfSalePrice ▾	Number Sold ▾	DaysOnMarket ▾	
Algernon Listings	$324,697.22	18	23.50	Step e: Average days a property has been on the market displayed
FastHouse	$288,314.50	6	22.33	
Houses 4 Sale	$218,039.00	2	23.50	
Local Listings	$341,085.67	9	23.56	
Major Houses	$235,757.88	8	24.75	
Trullo	$236,885.21	19	26.05	
Wholesaler	$276,654.92	26	26.12	
Total		88		

Access 2016, Windows 10, Microsoft Corporation

FIGURE 37 Results by Realtor Revised Query Output

a. Click the **File tab**, select **Save As**, and click **Save Object As**. Click **Save As** and type **Results By Realtor Revised**. Click **OK**.

b. Click **Totals** in the Records group of the Home tab. Click in the Total row for the **NumberSold** column, click the arrow and select **Sum**.

The total number of houses sold (88) now displays at the bottom of the Number Sold column.

c. Switch to Design view. In the field row of the first blank column, type **DaysOnMarket: [DateSold]-[DateListed]** to create a new calculated field. Change the Total row from Group By to **Avg**.

The DaysOnMarket field will show the average number of days on the market for each sold listing.

d. Display the Property Sheet for the DaysOnMarket field and change the Format property to **Fixed**. Close the Property Sheet.

e. Run the query and examine the DaysOnMarket field. Adjust column widths as necessary. Compare your results to Figure 37.

Houses 4 Sale listings have an average of 23.50 days on the market. Since this is in-line with their competitors, it lets you know they are neither fast nor slow with sales.

f. Save and close the query.

g. Close the database and exit Access. Based on your instructor's directions, submit the following files:

a03h1PropertyCheck_LastFirst

a03h3Property_LastFirst

Chapter Objectives Review

After reading this chapter, you have accomplished the following objectives:

1. Create a query with a calculated field.

- Expressions can contain a combination of arithmetic operators, constants, functions, and identifiers.
- Understand the order of operations: Calculated fields follow the same order of operations as mathematical equations—parentheses, then exponentiation, then multiplication and division, and finally addition and subtraction.
- Build expressions: Expressions must be written in a certain way. Rules govern the way you give instructions to Access.

2. Format calculated results.

- Calculated results may not have the format you want; change the properties of a calculated field using the Property Sheet.

3. Recover from common errors.

- Common errors include forgetting the colon in the appropriate location, spelling errors, and misuse of the order of operations.

4. Verify calculated results.

- Always check the results of your equation: Access will check for errors in the way something is written, but not logic errors.

5. Create expressions using the Expression Builder.

- The Expression Builder will help you create complex expressions by enabling you to choose fields and built-in functions easily.
- Click the Builder icon to open the tool.

6. Use built-in functions.

- Access includes 150 built-in functions, or predefined computations that perform complex calculations.

- Some functions require arguments, which are inputs (often fields or constants) given to a function.
- Calculate a loan payment with the Pmt function: The Pmt function accepts the rate, number of payments, and loan amount and calculates a loan payment. Two other arguments, future value and type, are typically left as zero.

7. Add aggregate functions to datasheets.

- Aggregate functions, including functions such as Sum, Avg, and Count, perform calculations on an entire column of data and return a single value.
- The total row displays at the bottom of a query or table; it can perform any aggregate function on each column.

8. Create queries with aggregate functions.

- Create a totals query: Create a query as usual and click the Totals button in Design view.
- Add grouping to a totals query: Grouping enables you to summarize your data by the values of a field. For example, instead of showing overall averages, add County as a grouping field and see averages for each county.
- Add conditions to a totals query: Similar to other queries, conditions can be added to totals queries, such as only showing listings with the Sold field equal to No.
- Add a calculated field to a totals query: You can apply an aggregate function to the results of a calculation: for example, subtract one date from another, and calculate the overall average of the difference between those dates.

Key Terms Matching

Match the key terms with their definitions. Write the key term letter by the appropriate numbered definition.

a. Aggregate function

b. Argument

c. Calculated field

d. Constant

e. Expression

f. Expression Builder

g. Function

h. Grouping

i. Order of operations

j. Pmt function

k. Property Sheet

l. Total row

m. Totals query

1. _____ A combination of elements that produce a value.

2. _____ A field that displays the result of an expression rather than data stored in a field.

3. _____ A predefined computation that performs a complex calculation.

4. _____ A value that does not change.

5. _____ A method of summarizing data by the values of a field.

6. _____ An Access tool that helps you create more complicated expressions.

7. _____ Calculates the loan payment given the rate, number of periods (also known as term), and the present value of the loan (the principal).

8. _____ A way to display aggregate data when a query is run.

9. _____ The sequence by which operations are performed in a mathematical expression.

10. _____ A method to display aggregate function results as the last row in Datasheet view of a table or query.

11. _____ The location where you change settings such as number format and number of decimal places.

12. _____ The input used to produce output for a function.

13. _____ A calculation performed on an entire column of data that returns a single value. Includes functions such as Sum, Avg, and Count.

Multiple Choice

1. Which of the following *cannot* be used in a calculated field?

(a) The number 12

(b) An asterisk (*)

(c) [HoursWorked] (a field in the current database)

(d) All of these can be used in a calculated field

2. When creating a calculation, which of the following would be identified as an error by Access?

(a) A field name spelled wrong in a calculation.

(b) An incorrect formula (for example, adding two numbers instead of subtracting).

(c) An order of operations error (for example, [HourlyPay] + 2 * [HoursWorked]).

(d) A missing colon in the expression (for example: TotalHours [OTHours]+[RegHours]).

3. What is the result of the following expression?

2 * 5 + 8 - 6 / 2

(a) 6

(b) 15

(c) 20

(d) 23

4. Which of the following *cannot* be adjusted in the Property Sheet?

(a) Caption

(b) Mathematical expression

(c) Number format (for example, displaying numbers as Currency)

(d) Number of decimal places

5. Which of the following could *not* be done using an aggregate function?

(a) Averaging a series of numbers

(b) Calculating the payment amount of a loan

(c) Counting the number of values that exist

(d) Finding the smallest value

6. Which of the following can be added to a totals query?

(a) Conditions

(b) Grouping fields

(c) Aggregate functions

(d) All of the above can be added to a totals query.

7. Which statement about a totals query is true?

(a) A totals query is created in Datasheet view.

(b) A totals query may contain several grouping fields but only one aggregate field.

(c) A totals query is limited to only two fields, one grouping field and one aggregate field.

(d) A totals query may contain several grouping fields and several aggregate fields.

8. Which of the following statements is true?

(a) A total order cost is an example of a common field to group by.

(b) A last name is an example of a common field to group by.

(c) For best results, add as many "group by" fields as possible.

(d) None of the above statements is true.

9. If you want to calculate aggregate statistics about graduation rates for students in a college database, which of the following would provide the *least* useful information if you were to group by it?

(a) Gender

(b) High School

(c) Race

(d) Social Security Number

10. Which of the following about the Total row in Query design is *false*?

(a) The Total row enables you to apply aggregate functions to the fields.

(b) The Total row is hidden by default in all new queries.

(c) The Total row is located between the Table and Sort rows.

(d) The Total row applies only to non-numeric fields.

Practice Exercises

Conforto Insurance

The Conforto Insurance Agency is a mid-sized company with offices located across the country. Each employee receives an annual performance review. The review determines employee eligibility for salary increases and the annual performance bonus. The employee data is stored in an Access database, which is used to monitor and maintain employee records. Your task is to calculate the salary increase for each employee; you will also calculate the average salary for each position. Refer to Figure 38 as you complete this exercise.

FIGURE 38 Average Salary by Position Results

a. Open *a03p1Insurance*. Save the database as **a03p1Insurance_LastFirst**.

b. Click the **Create tab** and click **Query Design** in the Queries group to create a new query. Select the **Employees table** and click **Add**. Select the **Titles table** and click **Add**. Click **Close** to close the Show Table dialog box.

c. Double-click the **LastName, FirstName, Performance**, and **Salary** fields from the Employees table to add them to the query. Double-click the **Increase** field from the Titles table to add it to the query.

d. Click the Field row of the first blank column in the query design grid and type **NewSalary: [Salary]+[Salary]*[Increase]** to create a calculated field that adds the existing salary to the increase.

e. Click **Run** in the Results group to run the query.

f. Switch to Design view. Ensure the NewSalary calculated field is selected. Click **Property Sheet** in the Show/Hide group to display the Property Sheet. Click the **Format property** in the Property Sheet. Click the **Format property arrow** and select **Currency**. Type **New Salary** in the Caption box.

g. Click **Run** in the Results group to view the results. Adjust column widths as necessary. Save the query as **Updated Salaries**. Close the query.

h. Click the **Create tab** and click **Query Design** in the Queries group to create a new query. Select the **Employees table** and click **Add**. Select the **Titles table** and click **Add**. Click **Close** to close the Show Table dialog box.

i. Double-click the **TitleName field** from the Titles table. Double-click the **Salary field** from the Employees table.

j. Click **Totals** in the Show/Hide group to display the Total row. Change the Total row for Salary to **Avg**. Leave the TitleName field set to Group By.

k. Click the **Salary field**. Click the **Format property** in the Property Sheet. Click the **Format property arrow** and select **Currency**.

l. Click **Run** in the Results group to view the results. Adjust column widths as necessary. Save the query as **Average Salary By Position** and compare your results to Figure 38. Close the query.

m. Close the database and exit Access. Based on your instructor's directions, submit a03p1Insurance_LastFirst.

2 South Bend Yachts

South Bend Luxury Motor Yachts, a local boat seller, hired a new Chief Financial Officer (CFO). The new CFO, Rosta Marinova, asked the financing department to provide her with some summaries. She would like to determine how much financing the company is currently offering, offer financing with interest to customers, and see aggregate purchase statistics for local cities. Refer to Figure 39 as you complete this exercise.

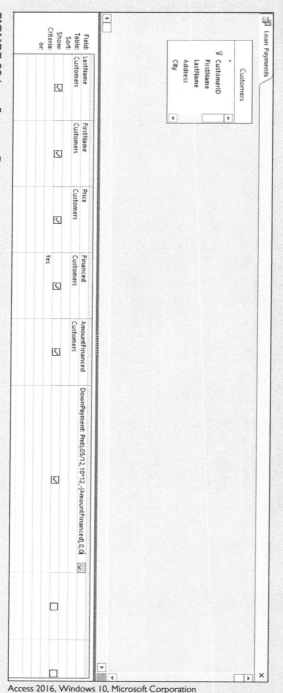

Access 2016, Windows 10, Microsoft Corporation

FIGURE 39 Loan Payments Design

a. Open *a03p2Boats* and save the database as **a03p2Boats_LastFirst**.

b. Click the **Create tab** and click **Query Design** in the Queries group to create a new query. Select the **Customers table** and click **Add. Click Close** to close the Show Table dialog box.

c. Double-click the **LastName, FirstName, Price, Financed,** and **AmountFinanced** fields.

d. Click the **Field row** of the first blank column and type **DownPayment: [Price]-[AmountFinanced].**

e. Click **Run** in the Results group to run the query. Examine the results. Adjust column widths as necessary.

f. Click **Save** on the Quick Access Toolbar and type **Down Payment Amounts** as the Query Name in the Save As dialog box. Click **OK.**

g. Switch to Design view. Click the **Criteria row** for the Financed field and type **Yes.** This will limit the results to financed boats. Boats that were not financed were paid for in full when purchased.

h. Click the **checkbox** on the Show row of the Financed field so it does not display when the query is run.

i. Sort the query by DownPayment in descending order by clicking the **Sort row** for the DownPayment field and selecting **Descending.**

j. Click **Property Sheet** in the Show/Hide group. In the Caption box, type **Down Payment.**

k. Click **Run** in the Results group to view the results. Adjust column widths as necessary. Notice that the column heading for the DownPayment field appears with a space in the name.

l. Save and close the query.

m. Click the **Create tab** and click **Query Design** in the Queries group to create a new query. Select the **Customers table** and click **Add. Click Close** to close the Show Table dialog box.

n. Double-click the fields **LastName, FirstName, Price, Financed,** and **AmountFinanced** to add them to the query.

o. Click the Field row of the first blank column. Click **Builder** in the Query Setup group to open the Expression Builder. Double-click **Functions**. Double-click **Functions**, and select **Built-In Functions**. Select **Financial**, and double-click **Pmt** in the Expression Values box.

p. Position the insertion point before the Pmt function. Type **DownPayment:** to the left of the function (including the colon).

q. Click each argument to select it, and substitute the appropriate information below. Once you have entered the information, click **OK**.

- **.05/12** for rate (5% interest, paid monthly).
- **10*12** for num_periods (10 year loan, 12 payments per year).
- Use **[AmountFinanced]** for the present_value.
- Use **0** in place of future_value and type.

r. Click **Property Sheet** in the Show/Hide group. In the Caption box, type **Monthly Payment**. Select **Currency** as the format.

s. Click the **Criteria row** for the Financed field and type **Yes**.

t. Click **Run** in the Results group to examine the results.

u. Click **Totals** in the Show/Hide group on the Design tab. Click Group By in the Monthly Payment column, click the drop-down menu, and select **Avg**.

v. Switch to Design view. Add a **minus sign** in front of [AmountFinanced] in the DownPayment calculation to display the results as positive numbers. Compare your design to Figure 39.

w. Click **Run** in the Results group to examine the results. Adjust column widths as necessary. Save the query as **Loan Payments** and close the query.

x. Close the database and exit Access. Based on your instructor's directions, submit a03p2Boats_LastFirst.

I. Small Business Loans

 ANALYSIS CASE

 **FROM SCRATCH**

You are the manager of a regional business loan department for the U.S. Small Business Administration office. You have decided to evaluate whether Access could be used in place of the Excel worksheet you are currently using. You will create a blank desktop database, add a table, add some sample customers, and import some recent data from an Excel spreadsheet. You will also calculate the payments for the loans that are currently on the books by creating a query using the Pmt function. You will also summarize loans by the type of loan (M = Mortgage, C = Car, and O = Other).

a. Open Access and create a new blank desktop database named **a03m1Loans_LastFirst**.

b. Switch to Design view. Type **Customers** in the **Save As dialog box** and click **OK**.

c. Change the first Field Name to **CustomerID** and accept AutoNumber as the Data Type. Type **Company** in the second row and press **Tab**. Accept Short Text as the Data Type. Type **FirstName** in the third row and press **Tab**. Accept Short Text as the Data Type.

d. Type the remainder of the fields, selecting Short Text for the data type:

LastName	Short Text
City	Short Text
State	Short Text
Zip	Short Text

e. Verify that the first field is set as the primary key.

f. Switch to Datasheet view. Click **Yes** to save the table. Add the records as shown in the following table. Note that Access will assign an ID. Once you have typed the records, close the Customers table.

Company	FirstName	LastName	City	State	Zip
Jones and Co	Robert	Paterson	Greensboro	NC	27401
Elements, Inc.	Merve	Kana	Paterson	NJ	07505
Godshall Meats, LLC	Francisco	De La Cruz	Beverly Hills	CA	90210

g. Click the **External Data tab** and click **Excel** in the Import & Link group. Click **Browse** to locate the *a03m1Loans* spreadsheet. Select the workbook and click **Open** at the bottom of the dialog box.

h. Ensure that *Import the source data into a new table in the current database.* is selected and click **OK**. Click **Next** three times, accepting the defaults, until you are asked to add a primary key. Click the *Choose my own Primary Key* option, and ensure **LoanID** is selected. Click **Next** once more and click **Finish**, accepting Loans as the table name. Click **Close** in the Get External Data dialog box.

i. Open the Loans table in Design view. Select the **InterestRate field** and change the format to **Percent**. Change the field size for the CustomerID field to **Long Integer**. Save and close the table, selecting **Yes** when prompted that some data may be lost.

j. Click the **Database Tools tab** and click **Relationships** in the Relationships group. Add both tables to the Relationships window and close the Show Table dialog box.

k. Drag the **CustomerID field** from the Customers table and drop it onto the **CustomerID field** in the Loans table. Check the **Enforce Referential Integrity** checkbox in the Edit Relationships dialog box and click **Create**. Save and close the Relationships window.

l. Create a query in Design view using the two tables. Add the **Company** field from the Customers table and the **LoanID, Amount, InterestRate, Term,** and **LoanClass fields** from the Loans table. Sort the query by LoanID in ascending order. Save the query as **Loan Payments.**

m. Add a calculated field named **Payment** in the first blank column to calculate the loan payment for each loan, using the Expression Builder. Use the Pmt function. Insert the appropriate field names in place of the placeholder arguments. Assume that the loans have monthly payments (12 payments per year). Ensure that the payment displays as a positive number. Run the query. The first loan should have a value of 243.1544965429B (the extra decimal places will be removed shortly).

  DISCOVER H

n. Switch to Design view and change the format for the Payment field to **Currency**. Run the query again to verify your change.

o. Click **Totals** in the Records group on the Home tab. Change the value for the Total row for the Amount column to **Sum** and the values for the InterestRate and Term to **Average**. Adjust column widths as necessary. Save and close the query.

p. Create a copy of Loan Payments. Save the new query as **Loan Payments Summary**.

q. Open the Loan Payments Summary query in Design view and rearrange the columns as follows: LoanClass, LoanID, Amount, and InterestRate. Delete columns Company, Term, and Payment. Click **Totals** in the Show/Hide group. Change the Total row for LoanID to **Count**, for the Amount field to **Sum**, and for the InterestRate field to Avg. Run the query.

r. Switch to Design view and display the Property Sheet. For the LoanID field, change the caption to **Loans**. For the Amount field, change the caption to **Total Amount** and change the format to **Currency**. For the InterestRate field, change the caption to **Avg Interest Rate** and change the format to **Percent**. Run the query. Adjust column widths as necessary. Save and close the query.

s. Close the database and exit Access. Based on your instructor's directions, submit a03m1Loans_LastFirst.

2 Investment Properties

You are in charge of Dysan Investment's database, which contains all of the information on the properties your firm has listed and sold. Your task is to determine the length of time each property was on the market before it sold. You also have been tasked with calculating the sales commission from each property sold. Two agents will receive commission on each transaction: the listing agent and the selling agent. You also will summarize the sales data by employee and calculate the average number of days each employee's sales were on the market prior to selling and the total commission earned by the employees.

a. Open *a03m2Homes*. Save the database as **a03m2Homes_LastFirst**.

b. Create a new query, add the Agents, Properties, and SubDivision tables, and then add the following fields: from the Agents table, add the LastName field; from the Properties table, the DateListed, DateSold, SalePrice, SellingAgent, and ListingAgent fields; and from the SubDivision table, the Subdivision field.

c. Add criteria to the table to ensure that the DateSold field is not empty (in other words, properties that have not been sold). You will need to use a function named IsNull to accomplish this. Format the SalePrice field as **Currency**. Save the query as **Sales Report**.

d. Create a calculated field using the Expression Builder named **DaysOnMarket** by subtracting DateListed from DateSold. This will calculate the number of days each sold property was on the market when it sold. Add a caption of **Days on Market**.

e. Calculate the commissions for the selling and listing agents using two calculated fields. The listing commission rate is 3.5% of the sale price, and the selling commission rate is 2.5% of the sale price. You can type these in directly or use the Expression Builder. Name the newly created fields **ListComm** and **SellComm**. Add captions of **Listing Commission** and **Selling Commission** and format the fields as **Currency**.

f. Run the query. Adjust column widths as necessary. Display the Total row. Calculate the average number of days on the market and the sum for the SalePrice and the two commission fields. Adjust column widths so all values are visible, and save and close the query.

g. Create a copy of the Sales Report query named **Sales Summary by Last Name**. Remove the DateListed, SellingAgent, ListingAgent, and Subdivision fields.

DISCOVER

DISCOVER

h. Display the Total row. Group by LastName and change the DateSold field Total row to **Where,** so the condition carries over. Show the sum of SalePrice, the average of DaysOnMarket, and the sum for both ListComm and SellComm. Change the caption for the SalePrice field to **Total Sales** and format the DaysOnMarket field as **Fixed.** Run the query. Adjust column widths as necessary.

i. Adjust the Total row in Datasheet view so it shows the sum of TotalSales. Adjust column widths as necessary. Save and close the query.

j. Create a copy of the Sales Summary by Last Name query named **Sales Summary by Subdivision** and open the query in Design view. Remove the LastName field. Add the Subdivision field to the query and ensure the Total row is set to Group By. Sort the query results on the DaysOnMarket field in Ascending order. Limit the results to only return the top five values (hint: look in the Query Setup group of the Design tab).

k. Run the query and ensure only the top 5 values display. Save and close the query.

l. Close the database and exit Access. Based on your instructor's directions, submit a03m2Homes_LastFirst.

3 **New Castle County Technical Services**

RUNNING
CASE

New Castle County Technical Services (NCCTS) provides technical support for a number of local companies. Part of their customer service evaluation involves logging how calls are closed and a quick, one-question survey given to customers at the end of a call, asking them to rate their experience from 1 (poor) to 5 (excellent). To evaluate the effectiveness of their operation, they asked you to create some queries to help evaluate the performance of the company.

a. Open the database that already you finished *a02m3NCCTS_LastFirst* and save the database as **a03m3NCCTS_LastFirst.**

b. Create a new query in Design view. Select the rep first and last names from the Reps table, and the CallID and CustomerSatisfaction fields from the Calls table.

c. Group by the RepFirst and RepLast fields. Display the count of the CallID field and average for the CustomerSatisfaction field.

d. Change the caption for the CallID field to **Num Calls.**

e. Format the CustomerSatisfaction average in Standard format and change the caption to **Avg Rating.**

f. Add a new calculated field named **AvgResponse.** Subtract the OpenedDate from the ClosedDate. Format the field as **Fixed.** Display the average for this field.

g. Run the query. Adjust column widths to ensure all data is displayed. Save the query as **Tech Ratings** and close the query.

h. Create a new query in Design view. Select the Description field from the Call Types table, and the CallID and CustomerSatisfaction field from the Calls table.

i. Group by the Description field. Display the count of the CallID field and average for the CustomerSatisfaction field.

j. Change the caption for the CallID field to **Num Calls.**

k. Format the CustomerSatisfaction average in Standard format and change the caption to **Avg Rating.**

l. Run the query. Adjust column widths as necessary. Save the query as **Call Type Effectiveness** and close the query.

m. Create a new query in Design view. Select the CompanyName field from the Customers table, and the CallID and CustomerSatisfaction field from the Calls table.

n. Group by the CompanyName field. Display the count of the CallID field and average for the CustomerSatisfaction field.

o. Format the CustomerSatisfaction average in Standard format and change the caption to **Avg Rating.**

p. Change the caption for the CallID field to **Num Calls.**

q. Run the query. Display the Total row. Show the sum of the Num Calls column. Adjust column widths as necessary.

r. Save the query as **Customer Happiness** and close the query.

s. Close the database and exit Access. Based on your instructor's directions, submit a03m3NCCTS_LastFirst.

Beyond the Classroom

Denton Credit Union

GENERAL CASE

Open *a03b1Denton*, which contains data from a local credit union. Save the database as **a03b1Denton_LastFirst**. Replace Your Name in the Branch table with your first and last name.

Create a query to calculate how long each manager has worked for the credit union: Display the manager and start date, and create a calculated field named **YearsWithCompany** to determine the number of years each manager has been in his or her position. Hint: Find a built-in Date/Time function to use the current date, subtract the start date, and divide the result by 365.25 (Note: the .25 at the end accounts for leap years). Display the calculated field in Fixed format, and add a caption to the field to display Years With Company as the column heading. Adjust column widths in Datasheet view as necessary. Save the query as Longevity.

Create a totals query to summarize each customer's account balances. List the customer's last name and first name from the Customer table, and the sum of all account balances (found in the Account table), grouping by both the last and first name. Format the total of the balances as Currency and add a caption of **Total Balance**. Display the sum of the total balances in Datasheet view ($141,074), adjust column widths as necessary, and save the query as **Customer Balances**.

Create a totals query to show each city (found in the Customer table) and total account balances for each city. For example, the total amount for customers in Denton is $61,510. Format the sum of the Balance field as currency with a caption of **Total Balance**. Adjust column widths as necessary in Datasheet view. Save the query as **Balances by City**.

Close the database and exit Access. Based on your instructor's directions, submit a03b1Denton_LastFirst.

Too Many Digits

DISASTER RECOVERY

This chapter introduced you to calculated fields. Open the database *a03b2Interest* and save the database as **a03b2Interest_LastFirst**. Open the Monthly Interest Payments query in Datasheet view. Notice the multiple digits to the right of the decimal in the MonthlyInterest column; there should only be two digits. Search the Internet or Access Help to find a function that will resolve this rounding problem. You only want to display two digits to the right of the decimal. Display the Total row in Datasheet view and display the total of the MonthlyInterest field. Adjust column widths as necessary. Save and close the query. Close the database and exit Access. Based on your instructor's directions, submit a03b2Interest_LastFirst.

Capstone Exercise

Northwind Traders, an international gourmet food distributor, hired a new CEO. She asked for your assistance in providing summaries of data that took place before she started with the company. To help her with her strategic planning, you will create queries to perform data analysis. Based on your meeting, you plan on creating four queries. One query will find orders with major delays. Another query will summarize the cost impact of customer discounts. A third query will be used to help evaluate financing. The final query will calculate the total sales by country.

Database File Setup

You will open the Northwind Traders food database, use Save As to make a copy of the database, and then use the new database to complete this capstone exercise. You will add yourself to the employee database.

a. Locate and open *a03c1Food* and save the database as **a03c1Food_LastFirst**.

b. Open the Employees table. Add yourself as an employee. Fill in all information, with the hire date as the current date. Set your Title to **Technical Aide**, extension to **1144**, and the Reports To field to **Buchanan, Steven**. Leave the Photo and Notes fields blank.

c. Close the Employees table.

Shipping Efficiency Query

You will create a query to calculate the number of days between the date an order was placed and the date the order was shipped for each order. The result of your work will be a list of orders that took more than 30 days to ship. The salespeople will be required to review the records and report the source of the delay for each order. The CEO feels there may be issues with one of the shipping companies, and would like data to back that up.

a. Create a query using Query Design. From the Customers table, include the fields CompanyName, ContactName, ContactTitle, and Phone. From the Orders table, include the fields OrderID, OrderDate, and ShippedDate.

b. Run the query and examine the records. Save the query as **Shipping Efficiency**.

c. Add a calculated field named **DaysToShip** to calculate the number of days taken to fill each order. (Hint: The expression will include the OrderDate and the ShippedDate; the results will not contain negative numbers.)

d. Run the query and examine the results. Does the data in the DaysToShip field look accurate? Save the query.

e. Add criteria to limit the query results to include only orders that took more than 30 days to ship.

f. Add the Quantity field from the Order Details table and the ProductName field from the Products table to the query. Sort the query by ascending OrderID. When the sales reps contact these customers, these two fields will provide useful information about the orders.

g. Add the caption **Days to Ship** to the DaysToShip field. Switch to Datasheet view to view the results. Adjust column widths as necessary.

h. Save and close the query.

Order Summary Query

The CEO is considering the financial impact of discounts. She asked for a query showing the employee name, number of orders they have taken, and the total discount amount they have given customers. She hopes to see if there is a correlation between the discount offered and the number of sales.

a. Create a query using Query Design and add the Orders, Order Details, Products, and Customers tables. Add the fields OrderID and OrderDate from the Orders table. Set both fields' Total row to **Group By**.

b. Add a calculated field in the third column. Name the field **ExtendedAmount**. This field should multiply the quantity ordered (from the Order Details table) by the unit price for that item (from the Products table). This will calculate the total amount for each order. Format the calculated field as **Currency** and change the caption to **Total Dollars**. Change the Total row to **Sum**.

c. Add a calculated field in the fourth column. Name the field **DiscountAmount**. The field should multiply the quantity ordered, the unit price for that item, and the discount field (from the Customers table). This will calculate the total discount for each order. Format the calculated field as **Currency** and add a caption of **Discount Amt.** Change the Total row to **Sum.**

d. Run the query. Examine the results. Most customers should have a discount of 10% of the total dollars, but some customers will have no discount. Save the query as **Order Summary**. Return to Design view.

e. Add criteria to the OrderDate field so only orders made between 1/1/2016 and 12/31/2016 are displayed. Change the Total row to **Where**. This expression will display only orders that were placed in 2016.

f. Run the query and view the results. Adjust column widths as necessary. Save and close the query.

Order Financing Query

The CEO would like the salespeople to discuss financing with customers. In order to do so, she would like you to create a query showing the impact on price for prior orders. This way, the reps can give customers a comparison with an order they have already placed. For the moment, she is considering a 5% interest rate, paid over 12 months. She would like you to leave the results as negative numbers.

a. Create a copy of the Order Summary query named **Order Financing**.

b. Open the Order Financing query in Design view and remove the DiscountAmount field.

c. Add a new field using the Expression Builder named **SamplePayment**. Insert the Pmt function with the following parameters:

- Use **.05/12** for the rate argument (5% interest, paid monthly).
- Use the number **12** for the num_periods argument (12 months).
- Use the calculated field **[ExtendedAmount]** for the present_value.
- Use the value **0** for both future_value and type.

d. Change the Total row to **Expression** for the SamplePayment field.

e. Change the Format for the SamplePayment field to **Currency**.

f. Run the query and examine the results. Adjust column widths as necessary. The results appear as negative numbers, as requested. Save and close the query.

Order Summary by Country Query

The company is planning on opening up some shipping centers internationally. The previous CEO had been considering Brazil, Denmark, and Germany as potential shipping center locations, but he was working from older data. You will provide a list of total shipment value by country for the year before the current CEO started to best inform her decision making.

a. Create a copy of the Order Summary query named **Order Summary by Country**.

b. Open the query in Design view. Replace the OrderID field with the Country field from the Customers table.

c. Run the query and examine the summary records; there should be 21 countries listed.

d. Switch to Design view and change the sort order so that the country with the highest ExtendedAmount is first and the country with the lowest ExtendedAmount is last.

e. Run the query and verify the results. Note the ExtendedAmount field has a caption of Total Dollars, so this is the field the query will be sorted by.

f. Save and close the query.

g. Close the database and exit Access. Based on your instructor's directions, submit a03c1Food_LastFirst.

Glossary

Aggregate function A calculation performed on an entire column of data which returns a single value. Includes functions such as Sum, Avg, and Count.

Argument Input used to produce output for a function.

Calculated field A field that displays the result of an expression rather than data stored in a field.

Constant A value that does not change.

Expression A combination of elements that produce a value.

Expression Builder An Access tool that helps you create more complicated expressions.

Function A predefined computation that performs a complex calculation.

Grouping A method of summarizing data by the values of a field.

Order of operations The sequence by which operations are performed in a mathematical expression.

Pmt function A function that calculates the periodic loan payment given a fixed rate, number of periods (also known as term), and the present value of the loan (the principal).

Property Sheet The location you change settings such as number format and number of decimal places.

Total row A method to display aggregate function results as the last row in Datasheet view of a table.

Totals query An additional row in the query design grid used to display aggregate data when the query is run.

Creating and Using Professional Forms and Reports

Creating and Using Professional Forms and Reports

LEARNING OUTCOMES

- You will develop and modify forms to input and manage data.
- You will create and modify reports to display and present information.

OBJECTIVES & SKILLS: After you read this chapter, you will be able to:

Form Basics

OBJECTIVE 1: CREATE FORMS USING FORM TOOLS
Create a Form Using the Form Tool, Create a Split Form, Create a Multiple Items Form

OBJECTIVE 2: MODIFY FORMS
Edit Data in Form View, Delete a Field, Add a Field, Format Controls, Add a Theme

OBJECTIVE 3: WORK WITH A FORM LAYOUT
Modify a Form Layout

OBJECTIVE 4: SORT RECORDS IN A FORM
Sort Records in a Form

HANDS-ON EXERCISE 1:
Form Basics

Report Basics

OBJECTIVE 5: CREATE REPORTS USING REPORT TOOLS
Use the Report Tool, Use the Report Wizard

OBJECTIVE 6: USE REPORT VIEWS
Use Print Preview, Publish to PDF

OBJECTIVE 7: MODIFY A REPORT
Add a Field, Remove a Field, Change Orientation, Apply a Theme

OBJECTIVE 8: SORT RECORDS IN A REPORT
Sort Records in a Report

HANDS-ON EXERCISE 2:
Report Basics

CASE STUDY | Coffee Shop Starts New Business

Coffee shop owner Ryung Park decided to use her knowledge of the coffee and retail industry to sell her specialty products to businesses around the country. She created an Access database to help track her customer, product, and order information.

Ryung created a database with tables to store data for customers, products, sales reps, and orders. She is currently using these tables to enter data and retrieve information. Ryung realizes that forms have an advantage over tables because they can be designed to display one record at a time—this can reduce potential data-entry errors. Ryung would like to create several reports so she can stay on top of her business by reviewing them each week. You have been hired to help Ryung create the new forms and reports that she needs.

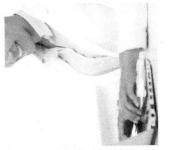

Moving Beyond Tables and Queries

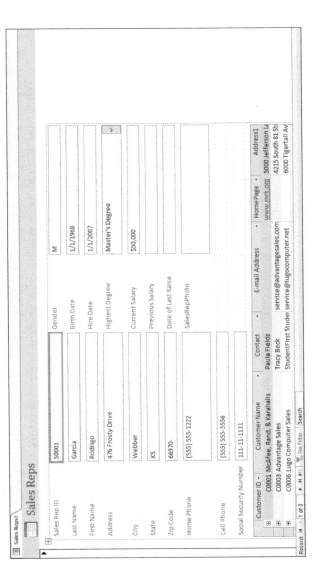

Sales Reps

Sales Rep ID	S0001
Last Name	Garcia
First Name	Rodrigo
Address	476 Frosty Drive
City	Webber
State	KS
Zip Code	66970-
Home Phone	(555) 555-1222
Cell Phone	(555) 555-5556
Social Security Number	111-11-1111
Gender	M
Birth Date	1/1/1968
Hire Date	1/1/2007
Highest Degree	Master's Degree
Current Salary	$50,000
Previous Salary	
Date of Last Raise	
SalesRepPhoto	

Customer ID	Customer Name	Contact	E-mail Address	HomePage	Address1
C0001	McAfee, Rand, & Karahalis	Paula Fields		www.mrk.org	5000 Jefferson L
C0003	Advantage Sales	Tracy Beck	service@advantagesales.com		4215 South 81 St
C0006	Lugo Computer Sales	StudentFirst Studei	service@lugocomputer.net		6000 Tigerfall Av

Record: I◄ ◄ 1 of 3 ► ►I ►❚ 🏷 No Filter | Search

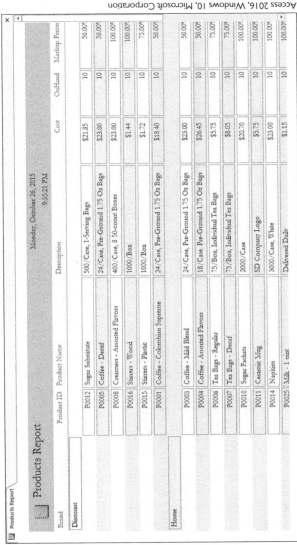

Products Report

Monday, October 26, 2015
9:35:21 PM

Product ID	Product Name	Description	Cost	OnHand	Markup Perce
Brand					
Discount					
P0012	Sugar Substitute	500/Case, 1-Serving Bags	$21.85	10	50.009
P0005	Coffee - Decaf	24/Case, Pre-Ground 1.75 Oz Bags	$23.00	10	50.009
P0008	Creamers - Assorted Flavors	400/Case, 8 50-count Boxes	$23.00	10	100.009
P0016	Stirrers - Wood	1000/Box	$1.44	10	100.009
P0015	Stirrers - Plastic	1000/Box	$1.72	10	75.009
P0001	Coffee - Colombian Supreme	24/Case, Pre-Ground 1.75 Oz Bags	$18.40	10	50.009
House					
P0003	Coffee - Mild Blend	24/Case, Pre-Ground 1.75 Oz Bags	$23.00	10	50.009
P0004	Coffee - Assorted Flavors	18/Case, Pre-Ground 1.75 Oz Bags	$26.45	10	50.009
P0006	Tea Bags - Regular	75/Box, Individual Tea Bags	$5.75	10	75.009
P0007	Tea Bags - Decaf	75/Box, Individual Tea Bags	$8.05	10	75.009
P0010	Sugar Packets	2000/Case	$20.70	10	100.009
P0011	Ceramic Mug	SD Company Logo	$5.75	10	100.009
P0014	Napkins	3000/Case, White	$23.00	10	100.009
P0025	Milk - 1 cent	Delivered Daily	$1.15	10	100.009

FIGURE 1 Coffee Shop Starts New Business Database

CASE STUDY | Coffee Shop Starts New Business

Starting File	Files to be Submitted
a04h1Coffee	a04h2Coffee_LastFirst
	a04h2Products_LastFirst

Form Basics

Most Access database applications use forms rather than tables for data entry and for finding information. A **form** is a database object used to add data to or edit data in a table. Three main reasons exist for using forms rather than tables for adding, updating, and deleting data:

- You are less likely to edit the wrong record by mistake.
- You can create a form that shows data from more than one table simultaneously.
- You can create Access forms to resemble the paper (or other types of) forms that users employ in their data entry processes.

When you are adding or editing data using a table with many records, you may navigate to the wrong record accidentally. A form is less likely to allow this type of error because most forms restrict entry to one record at a time.

Many forms require two tables as their record sources. For example, you may want to view a customer's details (name, address, email, phone, etc.) as well as all of the orders he or she has placed at the same time. This would require using data from both the Customers and the Orders tables in one form. Such a form enables a user to view two record sources at the same time and make changes—additions, edits, or deletions—to one or both sources of data. When a change is made in the form, the data in the underlying table (or tables) are affected. A form is really a mirror image of the data in the tables and simply presents a user-friendly interface for users of the database.

Access forms can be designed to emulate the paper documents already used by an organization. When paper forms are currently used to collect data, it is a good idea to design the electronic forms to resemble the paper forms. This will make the data entry process more efficient and ease the transition from paper form to electronic form.

In this section, you will learn the basics of form design. You will discover multiple methods to create and modify Access forms.

Creating Forms Using Form Tools

Access provides a variety of options for creating forms. You will eventually develop a preference for one or two types of form layouts, but keep in mind that you have a good variety of options, if needed. You will want your forms to balance ease of use with the power to be effective.

Access provides 14 different tools for creating forms. You can find these options in the Forms group on the Create tab. The Forms group contains four of the most common form tools (Form, Form Design, Blank Form, and Form Wizard), a list of Navigation forms, and More Forms. The Navigation list provides six templates to create a user interface for a database; the More Forms list provides four additional form tools (Multiple Items, Datasheet, Split Form, and Modal Dialog). Select a table or query in the Navigation Pane, click one of the tools, and Access will create a form based on the selected table or query. The most common of these tools, the **Form tool**, is used to create data entry forms for customers, employees, products, and other types of tables. You can also find Application Parts, which are predefined building blocks that you can use to build database objects, in the Templates group on the Create tab.

A list of the Form tools available in Access is found in Table 1. Several of the tools will be covered in this chapter. Some tools will not be covered in detail, because they are not commonly used or because they are beyond the scope of this chapter (e.g., Form Design, Blank Form, Navigation forms, and Modal Dialog Form). Use Microsoft Access Help to find more information about Form tools not covered in this chapter.

TABLE 1 Form Tools in Access

Form Tool	Use
Form	Creates a form with a stacked layout that displays all of the fields in the record source.
Form Design	Creates a new blank form in Design view.
Blank Form	Creates a new blank form in Layout view.
Form Wizard	Creates a custom form based on your answers to a series of step-by-step questions.
Navigation	Creates user-interface forms that can also be used on the Internet. Six different Navigation form layouts are available from the list.
Split Form	Creates a two-part form with a stacked layout in one section and a tabular layout in the other.
Multiple Items	Creates a tabular layout form that includes all of the fields from the record source.
Datasheet	Creates a form that resembles the datasheet of a table or query.
Modal Dialog	Creates a custom dialog box that requires user input that is needed for a database object.

TIP: USABILITY TESTING

After a database object (such as a form) is finalized, it should be tested by both the database designer and the end users. The designer should be certain that the form meets any requirements the users have given him or her. The designer should also browse through the records to make sure the values in all records (and not just the first record) display correctly. After testing is completed by both designer and end users, the form should be modified and tested again before it is deployed with the database.

Ideally, a form should simplify data entry. Creating a form is a collaborative process between the database designer and the end users. This process continues throughout the life of the form, because the data needs of an organization may change over time. Forms designed long ago to collect data for a new customer account may not include an email or a website field; both the customer table and its associated form would have to be modified to include these fields. The designer needs to strike a balance between collecting the data required for use by the database and cluttering the form with extraneous fields. The database users generally offer good opinions about which fields should be on a form and how the form should behave. If you listen to their suggestions, your forms will function more effectively, the users' work will be easier, and the data will contain fewer data-entry errors.

After discussing the form with the users, it will help you to create the form in Access if you sketch the form first. After sketching the form, you will have a better idea of which form tool to use to create the form. After the form is created, use the sketch to determine which fields are required and what the order of the fields should be.

Identify a Record Source

Before you create a form, you must identify the record source. A *record source* (or data source) is the table or query that supplies the records for a form or report. Use a table if you want to include all the records from a single table. Create a query as the record source first if you need to filter the records in the source table, combine records from two or more related tables, or if you do not want to display all fields from the table(s) on your form. For example, if a sales rep wants to create a form that displays customers from a single state only—where his customers reside—he or she should base the form on a query.

Use the Form Tool

STEP 1 ➤ As noted earlier, the Form tool is the most common tool for creating forms. A usable form can be created with a single click.

To use the Form tool, complete the following steps:

1. Select a table or query in the Navigation Pane.
2. Click Form in the Forms group on the Create tab.

Based on the table or query selected, Access automatically creates a new form. You may need to modify the form slightly, but you can create a stacked layout form with just one click. A *stacked layout* displays fields in a vertical column for one record at a time, as shown in Figure 2. The other type of layout you can use is a *tabular layout*, which displays data horizontally across the page.

Products

Product ID	P0001
Product Name	Coffee - Colombian Supreme
Description	24/Case, Pre-Ground 1.75 Oz Bags
Cost	$18.40
Markup Percent	50.00%
Refrigeration Needed	☐
Brand	Discount
Year Introduced	2018

FIGURE 2 Form with a Stacked Layout

Access 2016, Windows 10, Microsoft Corporation

Understand Controls

Controls are the text boxes, buttons, labels, and other tools you use to add, edit, and display the data in a form or report. Notice in Figure 3 that each field has a label on the left and a text box on the right, both of which are referred to as controls. The form controls that display values are generally text box controls, and the boxes describing those values are label controls. In Figure 3, Product ID, Product Name, Description, etc. are label controls. The boxes containing the values for each field (P0001, Coffee–Colombian Supreme, etc.) are text box controls.

A *layout control* provides guides to help keep controls aligned horizontally and vertically and give your form a neat appearance, as shown in Figure 3.

There may be times when you will select controls in order to format, delete, or move them during your design process. To select an individual control, click the text box or the label as needed.

To select multiple controls to work with them simultaneously, complete one of the following steps:

- Click the first control, press and hold Ctrl, and then click the additional controls you want to include in the selection.
- Press Ctrl+A to select all of the controls on a form at one time.

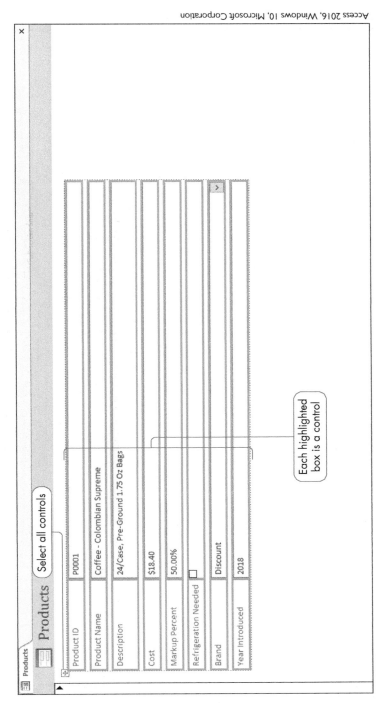

FIGURE 3 Form with Label and Text Box Controls

Work with Form Views

There are three different views of a form available. The first, *Form view*, is the user interface primarily used for data entry and modification. You cannot make changes to the form layout or design in Form view. Figure 4 shows a form in Form view. Notice that forms can be designed to include time-saving features such as drop-down lists and check boxes.

The second view, *Layout view*, enables you to make changes to the layout while simultaneously viewing the data in the form. Layout view is useful for testing the functionality of the form and adjusting the sizes of controls (text boxes and labels) as needed while viewing the data. When you create a form using the Form tool, Access opens the form in Layout view, ready for this type of customization, as shown in Figure 5.

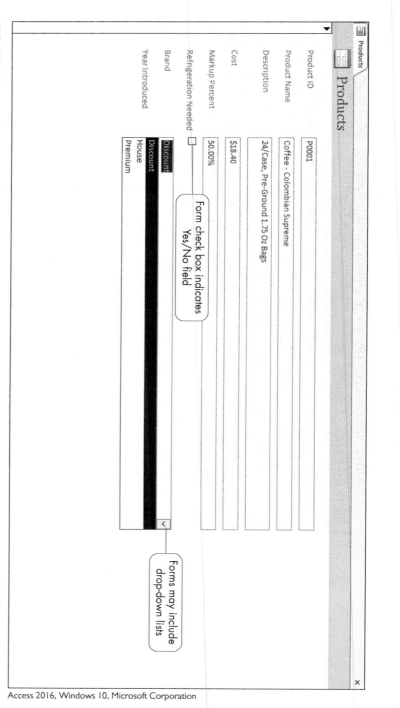

FIGURE 4 Form in Form View

Products

Product ID   P0001
Product Name   Coffee - Colombian Supreme
Description   24/Case, Pre-Ground 1.75 Oz Bags
Cost $18.40
Markup Percent   50.00%
Refrigeration Needed
Brand   Discount
                         House
                         Premium
Year Introduced

Form check box indicates Yes/No field

Forms may include drop-down lists

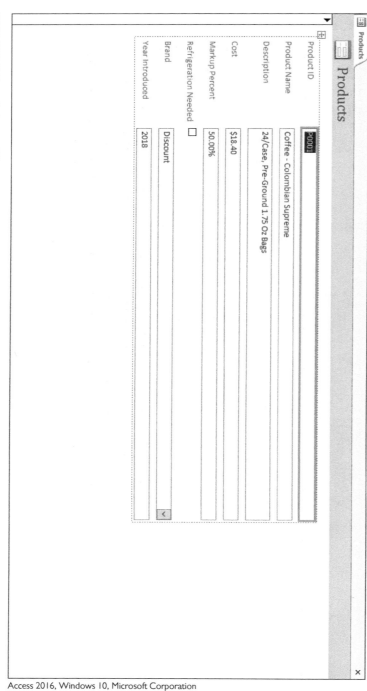

FIGURE 5 Form in Layout View

Products

Products

Product ID   P0001
Product Name   Coffee - Colombian Supreme
Description   24/Case, Pre-Ground 1.75 Oz Bags
Cost $18.40
Markup Percent   50.00%
Refrigeration Needed
Brand   Discount
Year Introduced   2018

The third view, **Design view**, enables you to change advanced design settings that are not available in Layout view, such as removing a layout control, and gives you even more control over form design. Many forms can be made by toggling back and forth between Layout view for modifications and Form view for usability testing; however, Design view offers possibilities for more advanced adjustments. Figure 6 shows a form in Design view. Form views will be described in more detail later in this chapter.

To switch between the Form views, with the form open, click the View arrow in the Views group on the Home tab, and then select Form View, Layout View, or Design View. Alternatively, click the View buttons on the status bar at the bottom of the Access window, or right-click the form's window tab and select an option from the shortcut menu.

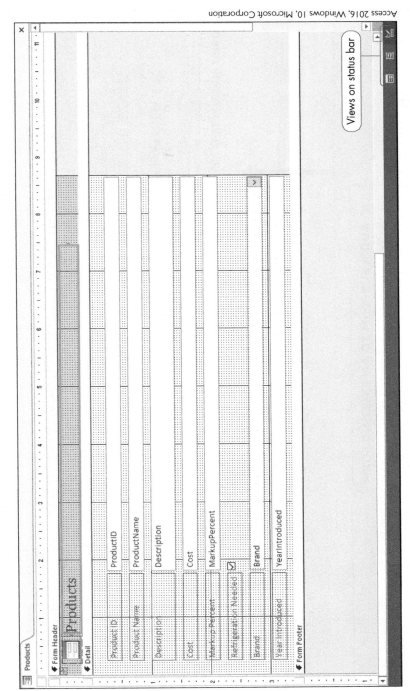

FIGURE 6 Form in Design View.

Work with a Subform

When you use the Form tool to create a form, Access analyzes the table relationships in the database. If the table that the main form is based upon is related to another table, Access automatically adds a subform to the main form. The subform displays records in the related table, generally laid out in a datasheet format. For example, assume you have sales representatives stored in a Sales Reps table and related customer information stored in a Customers table. In this example, if you create a new form based on the Sales Reps table using the Form tool, Access will add a Customers subform to the bottom of the main form, displaying all customers assigned to each sales representative (see Figure 7). At times, you may want the subform as part of your form; at other times, you may want to remove it if it is not relevant to the requirements of the form design.

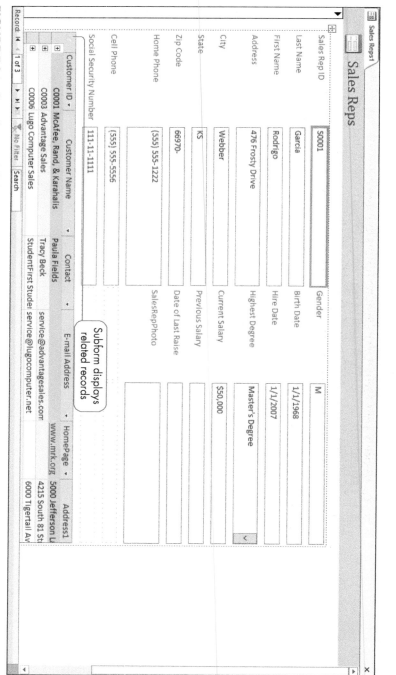

Access 2016, Windows 10, Microsoft Corporation

FIGURE 7 Sales Reps Form with Related Customers Subform

To remove a subform from a form, complete the following steps:

1. Click the View arrow in the Views group on the Home tab, and select Design View.
2. Click anywhere in the subform control and press Delete.
3. Save the form.

TIP: ADD A SUBFORM TO AN EXISTING FORM

It is possible to add a subform to an existing form by using the SubForm Wizard. In Design view of the form, in the Controls group, click the Subform/Subreport tool, and then click in the form where you want the subform to display. The wizard will prompt you for the record source and through the steps for creating the subform.

Create a Split Form

A *split form* combines two views of the same record source—by default: the top section is displayed in a stacked layout (Form view) and the bottom section is displayed in a tabular layout (Datasheet view). If you select a record in the top section of the form, the same record will be selected in the bottom section of the form and vice versa. For example, if you create a split form based on an Orders table, you can select an Order in the bottom (datasheet) section and then enter or edit the order's information in the top (Form view) section (see Figure 8). This gives you the option to navigate between orders more quickly in the bottom section, and then when you locate the one you need, you can move to the top section to work with the record in Form view; however, you can add, edit, or delete records in either section. The splitter bar divides the form into two halves. You can adjust the splitter bar up or down (unless this option is disabled).

To create a split form, complete the following steps:

1. Select a table or query in the Navigation Pane.
2. Click More Forms, and click Split Form in the Forms group on the Create tab.

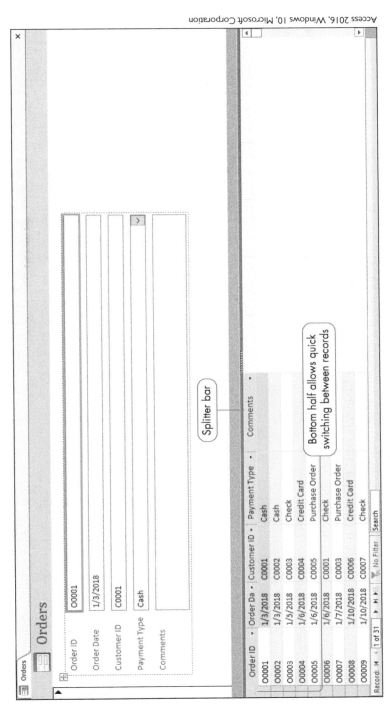

FIGURE 8 Split Form

Create a Multiple Items Form

A *multiple items form* displays multiple records in a tabular layout similar to a table's Datasheet view. However, a multiple items form provides you with more customization options than a datasheet, such as the ability to add graphical elements, buttons, and other controls. Figure 9 shows a multiple items form created from the Sales Rep table.

To create a multiple items form, complete the following steps:

1. Select a table or query in the Navigation Pane.
2. Click More Forms, and click Multiple Items in the Forms group on the Create tab.

Sales Reps

Sales Rep ID	Last Name	First Name	Address	City	State	Zip Code	Home Phone
S0001	Garcia	Rodrigo	476 Frosty Drive	Webber	KS	66970-	(555) 555-1222
S0002	Xu	Huan	371 Rodeo Circle	Mine Hill	NJ	07803-	(555) 555-1222
S0003	Mukopadhyay	Priyanka	842 Purcell Road	Mount Vernon	NY	10557-	(555) 555-1222
(New)							

Record: I◄ I of 3 ►H► No Filter Search

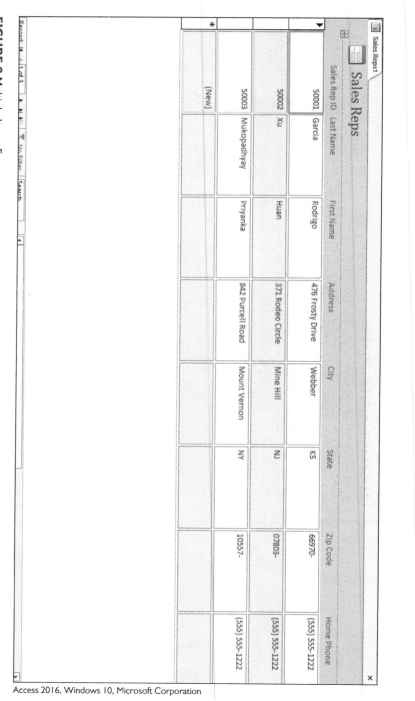

FIGURE 9 Multiple Items Form

Access 2016, Windows 10, Microsoft Corporation

Create Forms Using the Other Form Tools

A datasheet form is a replica of a table or query's Datasheet view except that it allows form properties to be set to control the behavior of the form. For example, you can create a datasheet form to display data in a table-like format but change the form's property so as not to allow a record to be deleted. This protects the data from accidental deletions while still providing users with the familiar Datasheet view.

TIP: FORM PROPERTIES

A form's Property Sheet enables you to control the behavior and formatting of controls in your forms. To access the Property Sheet, from Layout view or Design view, click Property Sheet in the Tools group on the Design tab. At the top of the Property Sheet, use the list arrow to select a control; you will see multiple tabs containing many individual attributes of the selected control that you can change. For example, the Format tab contains options for changing the styling of a control.

The Form Design tool and the Blank Form tools can be used to create forms manually from scratch in Design view or Layout view, respectively. Use these form types if you want to have complete control over your form's design. In either case, after opening a completely blank form, click Add Existing Fields in the Tools group on the Design tab, and then add the necessary fields by dragging and dropping them onto the blank form from the Field List pane.

The Navigation commands in the Forms group enable you to create user interfaces that have the look and feel of Web-based forms and enable users to open and close the objects of a database. For example, you can create a form that enables users to click buttons for the various forms, reports, and other objects that you want them to view in the database. This is an excellent way to simplify the database navigation for data-entry personnel who may not be that familiar with navigating in Access. These forms are also useful for setting up an Access database on the Internet.

The Modal Dialog Form tool can be used to create a dialog box. This feature is useful when you need to gather information from the user or provide information to the user, such as a message. Dialog boxes are common in all Microsoft Office applications.

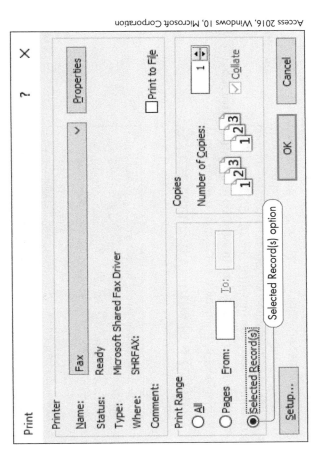

Access 2016, Windows 10, Microsoft Corporation

FIGURE 10 Print Selected Records Using a Form

Modifying Forms

As previously mentioned, Access provides different views for a form; most forms display Layout, Form, and Design views. As you work with the form tools to create and modify forms, you will need to switch between the three form views in Access. Much of your design work can be done in Layout view; sometimes, you will need to switch to Design view to use a more advanced feature, such as changing the order of the fields as you press Tab to move from one to the next, or to use an option that is otherwise unavailable. Users of the form will typically only work in Form view; there is little reason for a user to switch to Layout or Design view, and these views can be disabled by the database designer to protect the integrity of the form. Modifications to the form should ideally be done only by a designated designer.

Use Form View to Edit Data

STEP 2 Use Form view to add, edit, and delete data in a form; the layout and design of the form cannot be changed in this view. The Navigation bar at the bottom of the form provides buttons to move between records, and you can click the New (blank) record button to add a new record. You can move from one field to another field by pressing the Tab key or clicking the desired field with your mouse.

Use Layout View to Modify Form Design

Use Layout view to alter the form design while viewing the data. The data is not editable in this view. You use Layout view to add or delete fields in a form, change the order of fields, modify field or form properties (such as which views are available), change the control widths, and enhance a form by adding a theme or styling. Reviewing the data in

Layout view makes it easier to size controls, and to ensure that all data is visible in Form view. It is good practice to toggle back and forth between Layout view and Form view when making changes to the form's design.

TIP: USE THE FORM LAYOUT TOOLS TABS

Forms have a number of options that you can use in your design process. In Layout view, you have access to three contextual tabs on the Ribbon that provide a number of tools for modifying forms as follows:

- Design tab: Use this tab to make changes to the design of the form, such as applying themes, inserting headers and footers, and additional controls.
- Arrange tab: Use this tab to change the layout of a form, to move fields up or down, or to control margins.
- Format tab: Use this tab to work with fonts, font size, and colors, to add or remove bolding, italics, or underlining, adjust text alignment, or add a background image.

Similarly, in Design view, the Form Design Tools tabs are available (Design, Arrange, and Format) with many of the same options you will find in Layout view.

Adjust Column Widths in a Form

When column widths are adjusted in a form with a stacked layout, all field sizes will increase and decrease in size together. Therefore, it is best to make sure that the columns are wide enough to accommodate the widest value in each field. For example, if a form contains information such as a customer's first name, last name, address, city, state, ZIP, phone, and email address, you will need to make sure the longest address and the longest email address are completely visible (because those fields are likely to contain the longest data values).

To increase or decrease column widths in a form with a stacked layout, complete the following steps:

1. Display the form in (Stacked) Layout view, and click the text box control of the first field to select it.
2. Point to the right border of the control until the pointer turns into a double-headed arrow. Drag the right edge of the control to the left or right until you arrive at the desired width.

You will notice that all field sizes change as you change the width of the first field. All fields that are included in the layout will have a standard width. If you want to resize one specific field, you will remove that field from the layout control. Select the field and the label to be removed, right-click, and then from the shortcut menu, click Layout, and select Remove Layout. If you remove a field from the layout control, it stays on the form but can be moved and resized more freely.

STEP 3 ▶▶

Add and Delete Form Fields

▶ There will be instances when you will want to add or delete form fields. At times, new fields may be added to tables and then need to be incorporated into forms. At other times, you may decide that while a field is present in a table, it is not necessary to display it to users in a form.

To add a field to a form, complete the following steps:

1. Display the form in (Stacked) Layout view, and click Add Existing Fields in the Tools group on the Design tab.

   A Field List pane displays at the right of the form. For a single-table form, you will see a list of fields from the table (record source). For a multiple-table form, click the plus sign (+) to the left of the appropriate table to expand it, and locate the desired field(s).

2. Click and drag the desired field to the precise location on the form, using the shaded line as a guide for positioning the new field. Alternatively, you can double-click a field to add it to the form; the field will be added below the selected field. The other fields will automatically adjust to make room for the new field, as shown in Figure 11.

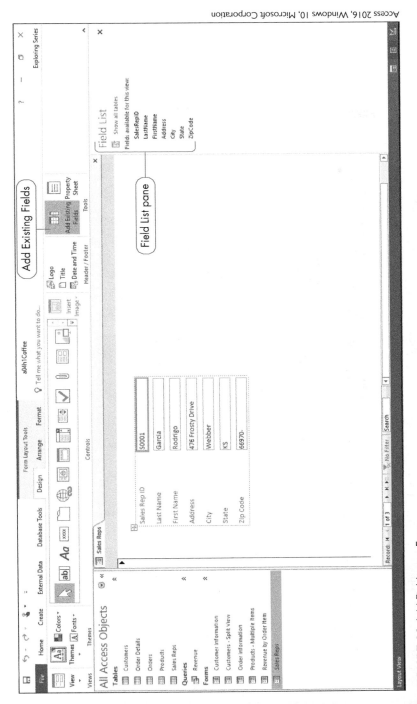

FIGURE 11 Add Fields to a Form

To delete a field from a form, complete the following steps:

1. Display the form in (Stacked) Layout view, and click the text box control of the field to be deleted (note the shaded border around the control).

2. Click Select Row in the Rows & Columns group on the Arrange tab in order to select the text box and its associated label. Alternatively, click the text box control, press and hold Ctrl, and then click the associated label control to select them both.

3. Press Delete.

   The other fields will automatically adjust to close the gap around the deleted field.

Add a Theme to a Form

You can apply a theme to a form in order to give the form a more professional appearance. A ***theme*** is a defined set of colors, fonts, and graphics that can be applied to forms (or reports). In Layout or Design view, click Themes in the Themes group on the Design tab, point to a theme to see its name in the ScreenTip and a Live Preview of the theme in the form, and then click to select it. By default, the theme will be applied to all objects in your database.

Right-click a theme in the gallery to apply it to the current form only or to all the forms in your database that share a common theme. You can create customized themes and save them on your system so that they can be used again. Apply your custom settings, and then click the Save Current Theme command, as shown in Figure 12.

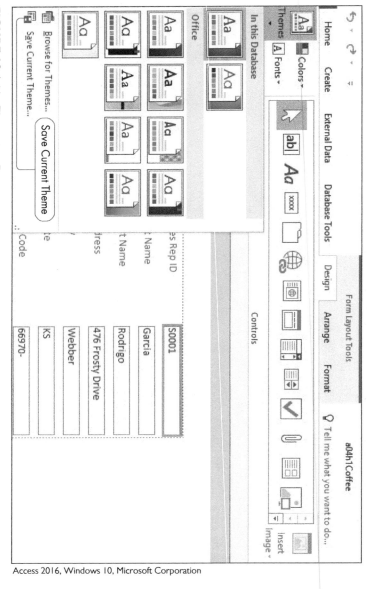

FIGURE 12 Add a Theme to a Form

Access 2016, Windows 10, Microsoft Corporation

Modify Form Controls

When you view a form in Layout view, the Form Layout Tools tab displays the Design, Arrange, and Format tabs. The Format tab contains a series of commands that enable you to change the font, display, and alignment of the controls on a form. At times, you may want to change the formatting of one or more controls. For example, if you have a form that shows the information about the sale of vehicles, you might want to emphasize the net profit of each transaction by changing the font or background color of the control.

From the Form Layout Tools Format tab, you can change a number of control attributes. Table 2 illustrates some of commands you would likely use.

TABLE 2   Common Formats for Form Controls

Font size	Click the Font Size arrow in the Font group.
Font emphasis	Click Bold, Italic, or Underline in the Font group.
Alignment	Click Align Left, Center, or Align Right in the Font group.
Background color	Click the Background Color arrow in the Font group.
Font color	Click the Font Color arrow in the Font group.
Number format	Use the tools in the Number group to select number formats such as Currency, Percent, Comma formatting, or to increase or decrease decimal places.

TIP: STYLING A FORM

Modifying the font sizes, changing the font colors, and adding background colors to controls can enhance a form and make it more user-friendly. Select familiar fonts, such as Arial or Calibri, for both the form label and text box controls. Apply bold to the labels in order to help the user distinguish labels from the text boxes. Consider right-aligning the labels and left-aligning the text box controls to reduce distance between the labels and fields, as illustrated in Figure 13. You may also want to separate the primary key field from the rest of the form by providing a sufficient visual boundary. One note of caution: using too many fonts, font sizes, colors, and other effects can detract from your design.

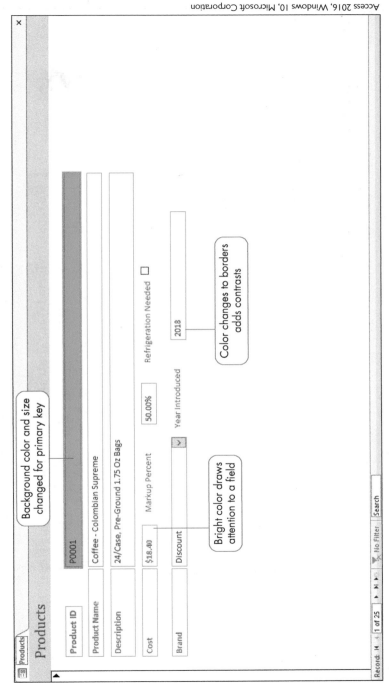

FIGURE 13 A Well-Designed Form with Styling

Working with a Form Layout

When you use one of the form tools to create a new form, Access adds a layout control to help align the fields. The layout control helps keep controls aligned in order to give your form a neat appearance. The layout control provides structure for the fields, but is somewhat restrictive. If you want to have more control over the location of your fields, you can remove the layout control and position the controls manually on the form.

To remove a control from a layout and reposition it, complete the following steps:

1. Select the field and the label to be removed, right-click, and from the shortcut menu, point to Layout and then select Remove Layout.
2. Drag and drop the control(s) as desired to a different location on the form.

Modify a Form Layout

STEP 4 You can use the tools on the Arrange tab to change the layout of a form, to move fields up and down, and to control margins. The Arrange tab displays in both Layout view and Design view.

The Table group of the Arrange tab contains commands that enable you to add gridlines to a form's layout, change the layout from stacked to tabular (and vice versa), or remove the layout (the Remove Layout command is available only in Design view).

To apply or change the layout of a form, complete the following steps:

1. Open the form in Layout or Design view.

2. Select multiple controls by clicking the first control, pressing and holding Ctrl, and then clicking the additional controls you want to include in the layout. To select all of the controls on a form, press Ctrl+A. If the controls already have a layout applied, click any control that is part of the layout, and click Select Layout in the Rows & Columns group on the Arrange tab.

3. Click Tabular or Stacked in the Table group on the Arrange tab.

To remove a form layout control, complete the following steps:

1. Switch to Design view (the Remove Layout option on the Ribbon is only available in Design view), and click any one of the controls that is currently part of the layout.

2. Click Select Layout in the Rows & Columns group on the Arrange tab.

3. Click Remove Layout in the Table group.

4. Switch to Layout view. Drag and drop the control(s) as desired to a different location on the form.

The Rows & Columns group also contains commands that enable you to insert rows and columns in a form's layout. In a form with a stacked layout, you may want to separate some controls from the rest of the fields, or create some empty space so that fields can be added or repositioned. For example, you can select a control (or multiple controls) and click Insert Below. This will create an empty row (or space) below the selected controls. This group also contains the Select Layout, Select Column, and Select Row commands, which you can use to select the entire layout, or a single column or row in a layout. In Figure 14, three empty rows have been inserted above the Cost field.

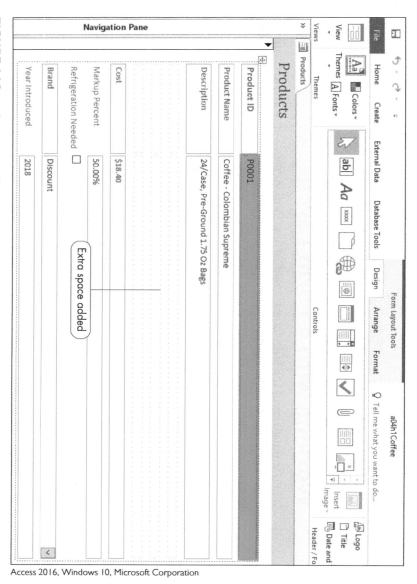

FIGURE 14 Rows Inserted in a Form Layout

Access 2016, Windows 10, Microsoft Corporation

Sorting Records in a Form

When a form is created using a Form tool, the sort order of the records in the form is initially dependent on the sort order of the record source—the underlying table or query. Tables are usually sorted by the primary key, whereas queries are generally sorted in a variety of ways. No matter how the records are initially sorted, you can modify the sort order in a form. Adding and removing sorts are shown in Figure 15.

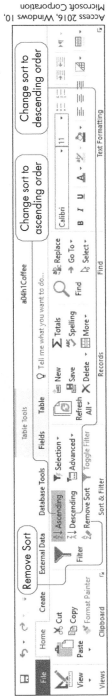

Access 2016, Windows 10,
Microsoft Corporation

FIGURE 15 Adding and Removing Sort Order

Sort by a Single Field

You can easily sort on a single field, in ascending or descending order. The sort order in a form can be different from the sort order of an underlying table or query.

To sort by a single field, complete the following steps:

1. Open the form in Form view, and select the field by which you want to sort.
2. Click Ascending or Descending in the Sort & Filter group on the Home tab.

If you want to sort on multiple fields, you can create a query with a more advanced sort order, and then base the form on the query. Open the query in Design view, add the sort settings you want, save the query, and then use the query as the record source of the form. To remove the sort order in a form, open the form in Form view, then click Remove Sort in the Sort & Filter group on the Home tab.

Quick
Concepts

1. How does a form simplify data entry (when compared to entering data into a table)?

2. What is the record source of a form?

3. What is the advantage of creating a form with a subform?

4. Why is using a layout control to keep your form fields in a neat arrangement sometimes a disadvantage?

Hands-On Exercises

1 Form Basics

After talking with Ryung about her data-entry needs, you decide to create several sample forms using different formats. You will show each form to Ryung to get feedback and see if she has any preferences.

Skills covered: Create a Form Using the Form Tool • Create a Split Form • Create a Multiple Items Form • Edit Data in Form View • Delete a Field • Add a Field • Format Controls • Add a Theme • Modify a Form Layout • Sort Records in a Form

STEP 1 »» **CREATE FORMS USING FORM TOOLS**

You will create a number of forms using different layouts. Refer to Figure 16 as you complete Step 1.

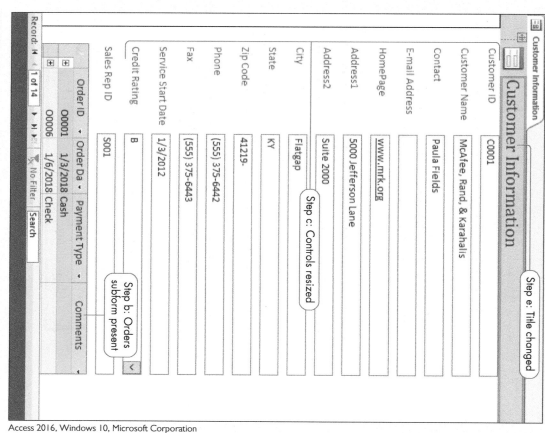

Step e: Title changed

Customer Information

Customer Information

Customer ID	C0001
Customer Name	McAfee, Rand, & Karahalls
Contact	Paula Fields
E-mail Address	
HomePage	www.mrk.org
Address1	5000 Jefferson Lane
Address2	Suite 2000
City	Flatgap
State	KY
Zip Code	41219-
Phone	(555) 375-6442
Fax	(555) 375-6443
Service Start Date	1/3/2012
Credit Rating	B
Sales Rep ID	S001

Step c: Controls resized

Step b: Orders subform present

Order ID	Order Da	Payment Type	Comments
O0001	1/3/2018	Cash	
O0006	1/6/2018	Check	

Record: I◄ ◄ 1 of 14 ► ►I ►✱ 🗙 No Filter Search

FIGURE 16 Customer Information Form

Access 2016, Windows 10, Microsoft Corporation

764

a. Open *a04h1Coffee* and save it as **a04h1Coffee_LastFirst**.

b. Click the **Customers table** in the Navigation Pane to select the table but not to open it. Click the **Create tab**, and then click **Form** in the Forms group.

   Access creates a new form with two record sources—Customers (with stacked layout, on top) and Orders (with datasheet layout, below). Access detected a one-to-many relationship between the Customers and Orders tables, and so it created a main form with its associated subform below it. The form opens in Layout view.

c. Ensure that the top text box containing *C0001* is selected. The text box is outlined with a shaded border. Move the pointer to the right edge of the shaded border until the pointer changes to a double-headed arrow. Drag the right edge to the left until the text box is approximately half of its original size.

   All of the text boxes and the subform at the bottom adjust in size when you adjust the top text box. This is a characteristic of Layout view—enabling you to modify all controls at once.

d. Ensure that the labels to the left of the text boxes display without being cut off. If they are cut off, adjust the size of the labels as you did in Step c.

e. Click **Save** on the Quick Access Toolbar, and then type **Customer Information** as the form name in the **Save As dialog box**. Click **OK**.

f. Click the **Customers title** at the top of the form to select it, click the title again, and then change the title to **Customer Information**. Press **Enter** to accept the change. Your form should now look like Figure 16. Save and close the form.

g. Verify that the Customers table is selected in the Navigation Pane. Click the **Create tab**, click **More Forms** in the Forms group, and then select **Split Form**.

   Access creates a new form with a split view, one view in stacked layout and one view laid out like a datasheet.

h. Scroll down and click anywhere in the *Coulter Office Supplies* customer record in the bottom pane (datasheet) of the form (record 14).

   The top pane shows all the information for this customer in a stacked layout view.

i. Click the **Customers title** at the top of the form to select it, click **Customers** again, and then change the title to **Customers - Split View**. Press **Enter** to accept the change.

j. Click **Save** on the Quick Access Toolbar and type **Customers - Split View** in the Form Name box Click **OK**. Close the form.

k. Click the **Products table** in the Navigation Pane. Click the **Create tab**, click **More Forms** in the Forms group, and then select **Multiple Items**.

Access creates a new multiple-item form based on the Products table. The form resembles a table's Datasheet view.

l. Click the **Products title** at the top of the form to select it, click **Products** again, and then change the title to **Products - Multiple Items**. Press **Enter** to accept the change.

m. Save the form as **Products - Multiple Items** and close the form.

n. Click the **Orders table** in the Navigation Pane. Click **Form** in the Forms group on the Create tab.

A form with a subform showing each line of the order is created.

o. Click the **Home tab**. Click the **View arrow** in the Views group, and select **Design View**. Click anywhere inside the subform and press **Delete**.

The subform is removed.

p. Switch to Form view to observe the change. Save the form as **Order Information**. Close all open objects.

STEP 2 ≫ **USE FORM VIEW TO EDIT DATA**

Now that you have created several forms, you will show Ryung how to test the forms for usability Refer to Figure 17 as you complete Step 2.

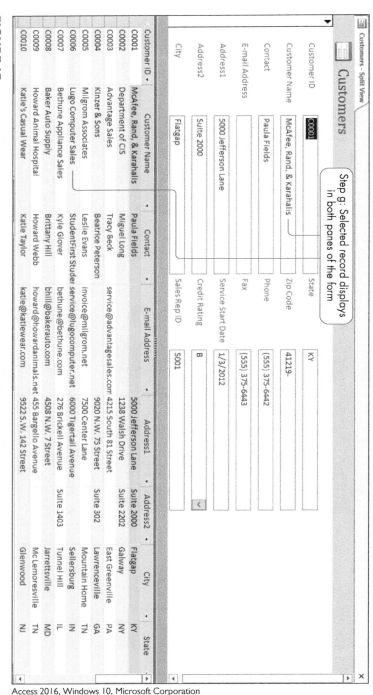

Step g: Selected record displays in both panes of the form

FIGURE 17

a. Right-click the **Customer Information form** in the Navigation Pane, and from the shortcut menu, select **Open**. Advance to the sixth customer, *Lugo Computer Sales,* using **Next record** on the Navigation bar at the bottom of the form.

TROUBLESHOOTING: Two Navigation bars exist, the inside one for the subform and the bottom-most one for the main form. Make sure you use the bottom-most one that displays the record count of 14.

b. Double-click the **Customers table** in the Navigation Pane.

Two tabs now display in the main window. You will compare the table data and the form data while you make changes to both.

c. Verify that the sixth record of the Customers table is *Lugo Computer Sales*, which corresponds to the sixth record in the Customer Information form. Click the tabs to switch between the table and the form.

d. Click the **Customer Information tab** and replace *Adam Sanchez*, the contact for Lugo Computer Sales, with your name. Advance to the next record to save the changes. Click the **Customers tab** to see that the contact name changed in the table as well.

Changes to the Contact field and the other fields in the Customer Information form automatically change the data in the underlying table. Likewise, if you change data in the table, it will update automatically in the form.

TROUBLESHOOTING: If the change from *Adam Sanchez* to your name does not display in the Customers table, check the Customer Information form to see if the pencil 🖉 displays in the left margin of the record. If it does, save the record by advancing to the next customer in the form and recheck to see if the name has changed in the underlying table.

---

e. Close the Customer Information form and the Customers table.

f. Open the Customers – Split View form. In the bottom pane of the split form, click **Lugo Computer Sales**, the sixth record. Notice that the top pane now displays the information for Lugo Computer Sales in a stacked layout. Notice also that there is an error in the email address—*service* is misspelled. In the top pane of the form, change the email address to **service@lugocomputer.net**.

g. Click another record in the bottom pane and then click back on **Lugo Computer Sales**, as shown in Figure 17.

The pencil disappears from the record selector box and the changes are saved to the table.

STEP 3 ›› USE LAYOUT VIEW TO MODIFY A FORM DESIGN

You will make some changes to the layouts based on feedback Ryung gave you after seeing the forms in action. You will also add a missing field to the main table and then add it to the form. Refer to Figure 18 as you complete Step 3.

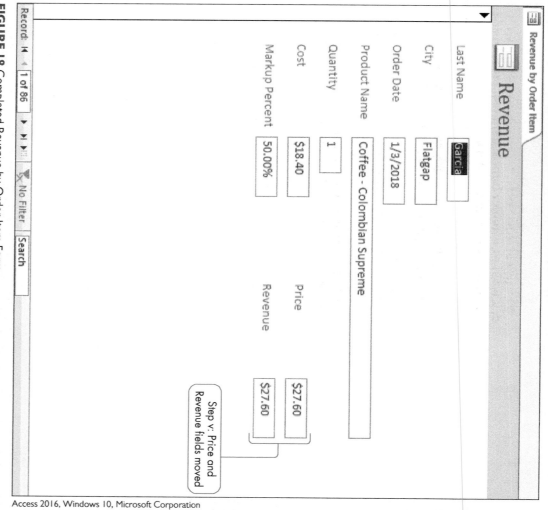

FIGURE 18 Completed Revenue by Order Item Form

Access 2016, Windows 10, Microsoft Corporation

a. Switch to Layout view with the Customers – Split View form open. Point to the **splitter bar**, the border between the top and bottom pane of the window. When the pointer shape changes to a double-headed arrow, drag the **splitter bar** until it almost touches the Sales Rep ID field. Save and close the form.

b. Open the Products – Multiple Items form in Layout view. Point to the bottom edge of **Product ID P0001** until the pointer shape changes to a double-headed arrow. Drag the bottom edge up to reduce the height of the rows so they are as tall as they need to be to accommodate the information.

Changing the height of one row affects the height of all the rows in the form.

c. Click anywhere in the **Cost column** and click **Select Column** in the Rows & Columns group on the Arrange tab. Press **Delete** to remove the column (alternatively, right-click in the column, and from the shortcut menu, select **Delete Column**). Delete the **MarkupPercent** column.

d. Click the **Refrigeration Needed label** to select it. Change the label to the abbreviation **Refrig?** Resize the column so it is wide enough to display the label text. Save and close the form.

e. Open the Customer Information form in Layout view.

f. Click the **Design tab**. Click **Themes** in the Themes group. Right-click the **Slice theme** and select **Apply Theme to This Object Only**.

The fonts and color scheme that are built into the theme are applied.

TROUBLESHOOTING: You can determine which theme is named Slice by pointing to a theme in the gallery and waiting for a ScreenTip to display. The Office theme is displayed first and the others are displayed in alphabetical order after it.

g. Click the **Format tab**. Click **Shape Fill** in the Control Formatting group. Select **Light Turquoise, Background 2** under Theme Colors.

The background color of the CustomerID field changes to light turquoise. The theme colors in the palette are those built into the Slice theme.

TROUBLESHOOTING: If you do not see Light Turquoise, Background 2 in the theme colors, ensure that you have selected the Slice theme.

TROUBLESHOOTING: If the entire form background changes to turquoise, click Undo and ensure that only the Customer ID text box containing *C0001* is selected.

h. Select the **Customer Name field** (which should be *McAfee, Rand, & Karahalis*). Change the font size to **16**.

The customer name appears in a larger font, setting it apart from the other fields.

i. Save and close the form.

j. Right-click the **Customers table** in the Navigation Pane, and select **Design View**.

You will add the HomePage hyperlink field to the Customers table.

k. Click the **Address1 field** and click **Insert Rows** in the Tools group on the Design tab.

A new row is inserted above the Address1 field.

l. Type **HomePage** in the blank **Field Name box** and select **Hyperlink** as the Data Type.

m. Save and close the Customers table.

n. Right-click the **Customer Information form** in the Navigation Pane, and select **Layout View**.

You will add the HomePage field to the Customer Information form.

o. Click **Add Existing Fields** in the Tools group on the Design tab to display the Field List pane.

p. Click the **HomePage field**. Drag the field from the Field List pane to the form, below the E-mail Address field, until a shaded line displays between *E-mail Address and Address1* and then drop it. Close the Field List pane.

Access displays a shaded line to help you place the field in the correct location.

TROUBLESHOOTING: If the placement of the field is incorrect, you can click Undo and try again. Alternatively, select the label and text box controls and use the Move Up or Move Down commands in the Arrange group.

q. Switch to Form view. Press **Tab** until you reach the HomePage field, type **www.mrk.org**, and then press **Tab**.

Because HomePage is a hyperlink field, Access formats it automatically in the form.

Save and close the form.

r. Click the **Revenue query** in the Navigation Pane. Click **Form** in the Forms group on the Create tab to create a new form based on this query.

The Revenue query is the record source for the form.

s. Switch to Design view. Click the first label, **Last Name**, press and hold **Ctrl**, and then click each of the other controls (alternatively, press Ctrl+A).

You have selected all label and text box field controls (from *Last Name* down to *Revenue*).

t. Click **Remove Layout** in the Table group on the Arrange tab. Switch back to Layout view.

TROUBLESHOOTING: Recall that the Remove Layout option only displays on the Ribbon in Design view, so if you do not see the button, ensure that you are in Design view.

u. Resize the controls individually so they are approximately the same sizes as shown in Figure 18.

v. Click the **Price control**. Press and hold **Ctrl** and click the **Revenue control**, the **Price label**, and the **Revenue label**. Drag the fields to the locations shown in Figure 18. Switch to Form view.

w. Save the form as **Revenue by Order Item**. Close the form.

STEP 4 >> USE A LAYOUT CONTROL AND SORT RECORDS IN A FORM

Ryung has an old Sales Reps form that she hopes you can make easier to read but keep in the vertical format. She tested the Customer Information form and likes the way it is working; however, she asks you to change the sort order to make it easier to find customers alphabetically by their names. Refer to Figure 19 as you complete Step 4.

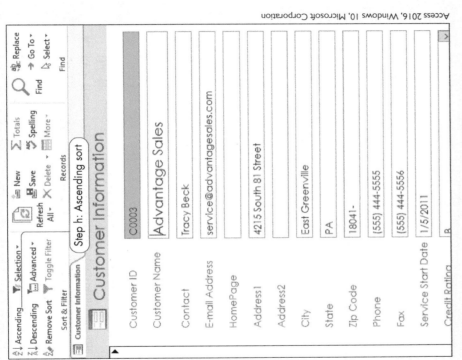

Access 2016, Windows 10, Microsoft Corporation

FIGURE 19

a. Open the Sales Reps form in Layout view. Notice that the form is not attractively laid out.

b. Click **Select All** in the Selection group on the Format tab.

All 14 controls are selected in the form.

c. Click **Tabular** in the Table group on the Arrange tab.

The controls are lined up horizontally across the top of the form.

d. Click **Stacked** in the Table group on the Arrange tab. Switch to Form view.

The controls are lined up vertically and the form is much easier to read.

e. Save and close the form.

f. Open the Customer Information form in Form view. Click **Next record** in the Navigation bar at the bottom several times to advance through the records.

Note that the customers are in Customer ID order.

g. Click **First record** in the Navigation bar to return to customer *McAfee, Rand, & Karahalis*.

h. Click in the **Customer Name text box**, and click **Ascending** in the Sort & Filter group on the Home tab.

Advantage Sales displays (Customer ID C0003), as it is the first customer name in alphabetical order, as shown in Figure 19.

i. Click **Next record** in the Navigation bar at the bottom of the form to advance through the records.

The records are now in Customer Name order.

j. Save and close the Customer Information form.

k. Keep the database open if you plan to continue with the Hands-On Exercise. If not, close the database, and exit Access.

Report Basics

By now, you know how to plan a database, create tables, establish relationships between tables, enter data into tables, and extract data using queries. In the previous section of this chapter, you learned how to create and modify several types of data-entry forms. In this section, you will learn how to create professional reports using the report-generating tools in Access.

A *report* is a document that displays information from a database in a format that outputs meaningful information to its readers. Access reports can be printed, viewed onscreen, or even saved as files, such as Word documents. You cannot use reports to change data in your database; a report is designed for output of information only based on data from tables or queries in your database (record sources).

The following are all examples of reports that might be created in Access:

- A telephone directory sorted by last name
- A customer report grouped by orders pending for each customer
- An employee list grouped by department
- A monthly statement from a bank
- A bill or invoice
- A set of mailing labels

Reports are used to help the reader understand and analyze information. For example, in a report you can group the customers together for each sales rep and highlight the customers who have not placed an order in six months. This is an example of using a list of customers from the Customers table together with other data in the database as an effective business analysis tool. To increase business, the sales reps could contact their customers who have not ordered in the past six months and review the findings with the sales manager. A sales report could then be run each month to see if the strategy has helped to produce any new business.

In this section, you will create reports in Access by first identifying a record source, then designing the report, and finally choosing a Report tool. You will learn how to modify a report by adding and deleting fields, resizing columns, and adding a theme. You will also learn about the report sections, the report views, and controls on reports.

Creating Reports Using Report Tools

Access provides five different report tools for creating reports. The report tools are located on the Create tab in the Reports group, as shown in Figure 20. The most common of the tools, the Report tool, is used to instantly create a tabular report based on a selected table or query. The Report Design tool is used to create a new blank report in Design view. This tool is used by advanced users who want to create a report from scratch with no help from Access. The Blank Report tool is used to create a new report in Layout view by inserting fields and controls manually to design the report. The Report Wizard tool will prompt you through a series of step-by-step screens and help you create a report based on your selections. The Labels tool is used to create printable labels using one of the preformatted templates provided by Access. Table 3 provides a summary of the five report tools and their usages. Once you create a report using one of the report tools, you can perform modifications in either Layout view or Design view.

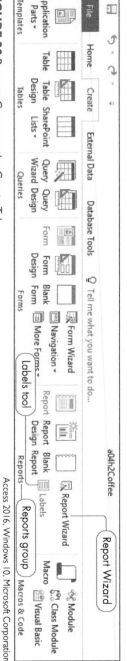

FIGURE 20 Reports Group on the Create Tab

Access 2016, Windows 10, Microsoft Corporation

TABLE 3 Report Tools and Their Usages

Report Tool	Usage
Report	Create a tabular report showing all of the fields in the record source.
Report Design	Create a new blank report in Design view. Add fields and controls manually.
Blank Report	Create a new blank report in Layout view. Drag and drop to add fields and controls manually.
Report Wizard	Answer a series of step-by-step questions and Access will design a custom report for you.
Labels	Select a preformatted label template and create printable labels.

Pearson Education, Inc.

Before you create a report in Access, you should consider the following questions:

- What is the purpose of the report?
- Who will use the report?
- Which tables, queries, and fields are needed for the report?
- How will the report be distributed? Will users view the report directly from the Access database, or will they receive it through email, fax, or the Internet?
- Will the results be converted to Word, Excel, HTML, or another format?

In the Forms section of this chapter, you learned that it is helpful to talk to users and design a form before you launch Access. The same applies to creating an Access report. Users can give you solid input, and creating a design will help you determine which report tool to use to create the report.

The first step in planning your report is to identify the record source. You may use one or more tables, queries, or a combination of tables and queries as the report's record source. Sometimes, a single table contains all of the records you need for the report. Other times, you will incorporate several tables. When data from multiple related tables are needed to create a report, you can first create a single query (with criteria, if necessary) and then base the report on that query. Multiple tables used in a query must be related, as indicated with join lines.

Reports can contain text and numeric data as well as formatting, calculated fields, graphics, and so forth. For example, you can add a company logo to the report header. Be sure that you have appropriate permission to use any company logo, graphic, or photo in your reports in order to avoid inappropriate or illegal use of an asset.

Use the Report Tool

STEP 1

The easiest way to create a report is with the Report tool. The *Report tool* is used to create a tabular report based on the selected table or query.

To create a report using the Report tool, complete the following steps:

1. Select a table or query in the Navigation Pane.
2. Click Report in the Reports group on the Create tab.

Sales Reps

Sales Reps

Tuesday, November 3, 2015
12:00:36 AM

Sales Rep ID	Last Name	First Name	Address	City	State	Zip Code	Home Phone	Cell Phone	Social Security Number	Gender
S0001	Garcia	Rodrigo	476 Frosty Drive	Webber	KS	66970-	(555) 555-1222	(555) 555-5556	111-11-1111	M
S0002	Xu	Huan	371 Rodeo Circle	Mine Hill	NJ	07803-	(555) 555-1222	(555) 555-5556	111-22-3333	F
S0003	Mukopadh yay	Priyanka	842 Purcell Road	Mount Vernon	NY	10557-	(555) 555-1222	(555) 555-5556	111-33-5555	F

1

Access 2016, Windows 10,
Microsoft Corporation

FIGURE 21 Tabular Report Created with the Report Tool

Access creates a tabular layout report instantly. Notice that this type of report displays data horizontally in columns across the page, as shown in Figure 21.

If you prefer, you can display a report using a stacked layout, which displays fields in a vertical column. This type of report is less common, as it would result in longer printouts. The number of pages depends on the number of records in the record source.

Use the Report Wizard

The **Report Wizard** prompts you for input in a series of steps to generate a customized report. The wizard enables you to make certain customizations quickly and easily without having to be an expert in report design.

To create a report using the Report Wizard, complete the following steps:

1. Select the report's record source (table or query) in the Navigation Pane, and click Report Wizard in the Reports group on the Create tab. The wizard opens with the selected table or query (the record source) displayed in the first dialog box. Although you chose the record source before you started, the first dialog box enables you to select fields from the selected source or additional tables or queries.

2. Click the Tables/Queries list arrow to display a list of available tables or queries, if you want to choose a different record source. Select the fields you want to include in the report. You can select an available field and then click $>$ to add a single field to the Selected Fields list, $>>$ to select all fields, $<$ to remove a field, $<<$ and to remove all fields from the report. See Figure 22. Set the desired fields and click Next.

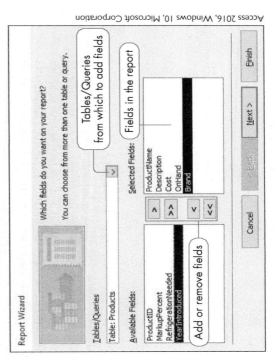

Access 2016, Windows 10, Microsoft Corporation

FIGURE 22 Selecting Fields in the Report Wizard

Creating and Using Professional Forms and Reports

3. Apply the desired grouping in the next dialog box, shown in Figure 23. Grouping enables you to organize and summarize your data in a report, based on values in a field. For example, you can group products by their brand name and average the cost of products in each group. To group records in a report, select the field you want to group by and click Add One Field ⌄ to add the new group. If you need a second or third grouping level, add those field names in order. The order in which you select the groups dictates the order of display in the report. In Figure 23, the products are grouped by the Brand field. Once you have selected the appropriate options, click Next. For a basic report, you would not select any grouping fields, and instead just click Next.

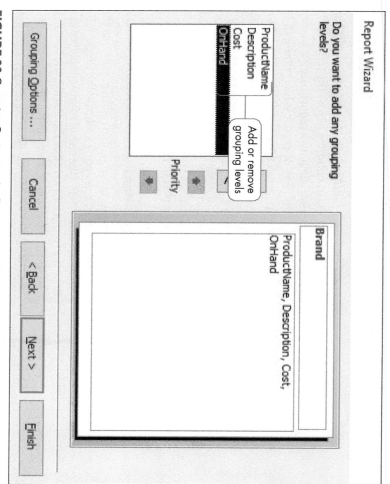

FIGURE 23 Grouping Options in the Report Wizard

Access 2016, Windows 10, Microsoft Corporation

4. Apply the desired sorting and summary options in the next dialog box. Figure 24 displays the sort options for a grouped report. You can click Summary Options if you want to add aggregate functions (e.g., sum, average, minimum, and maximum) and to specify whether you want to see detailed records on the report or only the aggregate results (see Figure 25). You can also choose to calculate values as percentages of totals in your report results. If no grouping is specified in your report, the summary options are not available. In Figure 25, no summary options are selected. Click OK to return to the Report Wizard. The sort options are the same as before. Set the appropriate options and click Next.

Report Wizard

What sort order and summary information do you want for detail records?

You can sort records by up to four fields, in either ascending or descending order.

1	ProductName	>	Ascending
2		>	Ascending
3		>	Ascending
4		>	Ascending

Summary Options ...

Summary Options (only available when grouping is present)

Cancel   < Back   Next >   Finish

FIGURE 24 Sort and Summarize Grouped Data in the Report Wizard

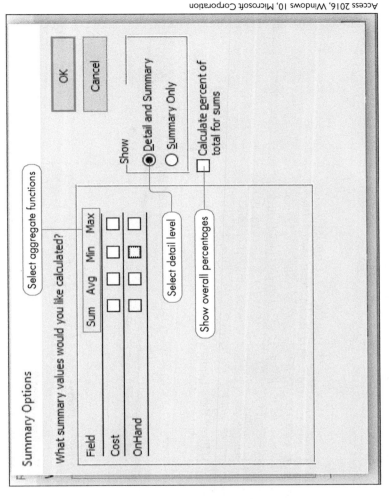

Summary Options

Select aggregate functions

What summary values would you like calculated?

Field	Sum	Avg	Min	Max
Cost	☐	☐	☐	☐
OnHand	☐	☐	☐	☐

Select detail level

Show overall percentages

Show
 ● Detail and Summary
 ○ Summary Only
 ☐ Calculate percent of total for sums

OK

Cancel

FIGURE 25 Summary Options Dialog Box

5. Select the layout in the next dialog box, shown in Figure 26, to determine the report's appearance. In a grouped report, you will be prompted to select the layout from three options:

- Stepped Layout will display column headings at the top of the page and keep the grouping field(s) in their own row.
- Block Layout will include the grouping field(s) in line with the data, saving some space when printing. It has one set of column headings at the top of each page.
- Outline Layout will display the grouping field(s) on their own separate rows and has column headings inside each group. This leads to a longer report when printing but may help make the report easier to read.

Clicking any of these layouts will give you a general preview in the preview area. In a report without grouping, the layouts are Columnar, Tabular, and Justified. You can determine how the data fits on a page by selecting Portrait or Landscape. Click Next.

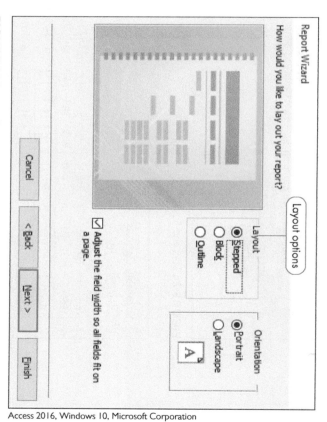

FIGURE 26 Layout Options for Grouped Data in the Report Wizard

6. Enter a report name and click Finish. Your grouped report will resemble Figure 27.

FIGURE 27 Grouped Report

Products		
Brand		
Discount		
Product Name	**Description**	**Cost Ind**
Coffee - Colombian Supren	24/Case, Pre-Ground 1.75 Oz Bags	$18.40 10
Coffee - Decaf	24/Case, Pre-Ground 1.75 Oz Bags	$23.00 10
Creamers - Assorted Flavor	400/Case, 8 50-count Boxes	$23.00 10
Stirrers - Plastic	1000/Box	$1.72 10
Stirrers - Wood	1000/Box	$1.44 10
Sugar Substitute	500/Case, 1-Serving Bags	$21.85 10
House		
Ceramic Mug	SD Company Logo	$5.75 10
Coffee - Assorted Flavors	18/Case, Pre-Ground 1.75 Oz Bags	$26.45 10
Coffee - Mild Blend	24/Case, Pre-Ground 1.75 Oz Bags	$23.00 10
Coffee Filters	500/Case, Fits 10-12 Cup Coffee Maker	$3.45 10
Milk - 1 pint	Delivered Daily	$1.15 10
Milk - 1 quart	Delivered Daily	$2.30 10
Napkins	3000/Case, White	$23.00 10
Popcorn - Buttered	36/Case, 3.75 Oz Microwave Bags	$10.92 10
Popcorn - Plain	36/Case, 3.75 Oz Microwave Bags	$9.78 10

Grouping field displays as its own column

Access 2016, Windows 10, Microsoft Corporation

Use the Label Wizard

The **Label Wizard** enables you to easily create mailing labels, name tags, and other specialized tags. A mailing label report is a specialized report that you can create and print with name-brand labels, such as Avery and many others. If you purchase a store brand label from an office supply store, it will generally state the comparable manufacturer and product number; the wizard provides a long list of both manufacturers and label sizes.

To use the Label Wizard, complete the following steps:

1. Select the table or query that you will use as the record source for the report.
2. Click Labels in the Reports group on the Create tab.
3. Select the manufacturer, product number, unit of measure, label type, and then click Next.
4. Select the font and color options, and then click Next.
5. Add the fields to the prototype label, as shown in Figure 28. You add the fields exactly as you would like them to display, including adding commas, spacing, and pressing Enter to move to the next line, where applicable.

Label Wizard

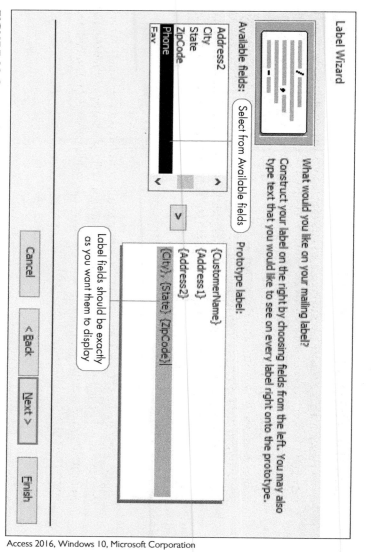

What would you like on your mailing label?

Construct your label on the right by choosing fields from the left. You may also type text that you would like to see on every label right onto the prototype.

Available fields:

Select from Available fields

Address2
City
State
ZipCode
Phone
Fax

Prototype label:

{CustomerName}
{Address1}
{Address2}
{City}, {State} {ZipCode}

Label fields should be exactly as you want them to display

Cancel   < Back   Next >   Finish

FIGURE 28 Create a Customers Prototype Label

Access 2016, Windows 10, Microsoft Corporation

6. Add sort fields; for example, you may want to sort by state or zip code, and then click Next.

7. Name the report and then click Finish to generate your label report. The results using the Customers table are shown in Figure 29.

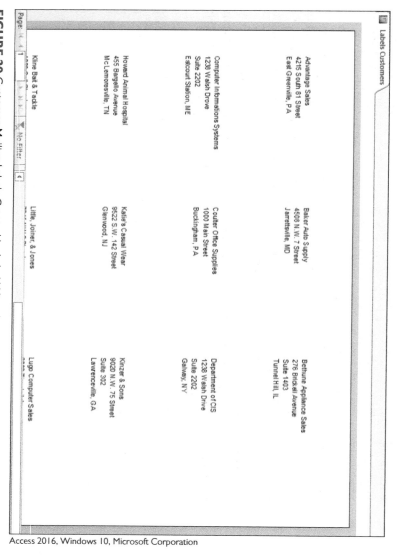

Labels Customers

Advantage Sales
4215 South 81 Street
East Greenville, PA

Baker Auto Supply
4508 N.W. 7 Street
Jarrettsville, MD

Bethune Appliance Sales
276 Brickell Avenue
Suite 1403
Tunnel Hill, IL

Computer Informations Systems
1238 Walsh Drive
Suite 2202
Estcourt Station, ME

Coulter Office Supplies
1000 Main Street
Buckingham, PA

Department of CIS
1238 Walsh Drive
Suite 2202
Galway, NY

Howard Animal Hospital
455 Bargello Avenue
McLemoresville, TN

Katie's Casual Wear
9522 S.W. 142 Street
Glenwood, NJ

Kinzer & Sons
9020 N.W. 75 Street
Suite 302
Lawrenceville, GA

Kline Bait & Tackle

Little, Joiner, & Jones

Lugo Computer Sales

Page: 1   ▶ ▶ ▶   No Filter   ◀

FIGURE 29 Customer Mailing Labels Created by Label Wizard

Access 2016, Windows 10, Microsoft Corporation

Using Report Views

As you work with the report tools to create and modify reports, you might need to switch between the four report views in Access—Report, Layout, Design, and Print Preview. Report view and Print Preview are generally used only for viewing or printing the report. To make modifications to a report, use Layout view and Design view. Most of the design work can be done in Layout view, but sometimes Design view is necessary to apply a more advanced feature, such as setting the tab order of the controls. To switch between the four views, click the View arrow in the Views group, and then select the desired view (alternatively, right-click the report tab, and from the shortcut menu, select the desired view).

View a Report in Report View

Report view enables you to view a report onscreen in a continuous page layout. However, because the data cannot be changed in Report view, it is simply a way of viewing the information without having to worry about accidentally moving a control. You can also use Report view to filter data, if necessary.

Print or Save a Report in Print Preview

STEP 2 ⟫ *Print Preview* enables you to see exactly what the report will look like when it is printed. You cannot modify the design of the report or the data in Print Preview. By default, Print Preview will display all the pages in the report. Figure 29 displays the mailing labels report in Print Preview.

From Print Preview, you have the option to export and save the report to a different file type, such as Word. This is a useful option if you plan to share a report electronically but do not want to distribute the entire database. In the Data group, on the Print Preview tab, you will find a number of eligible file types, as shown in Figure 30. Select the option in the Data group, and then follow the onscreen prompts to export your report. Commonly used formats include Excel, Word, and Portable Document Format (PDF).

Portable Document Format (PDF) is a file type that was created for exchanging documents independently of software applications and operating system environments. In other words, you can email a report in PDF format to users running various operating systems, and they can open it even if they do not have Microsoft Access installed. PDF files open in Adobe Reader, a free downloadable program; recent versions of Windows have a built-in Reader program that displays PDF files as well.

Because databases contain a great deal of information, Access reports can become very long, requiring many pages to print. At times, reports can be formatted incorrectly, or blank pages might print in between each page of information. Be sure to troubleshoot your reports before sending them to the printer, or to recipients via email.

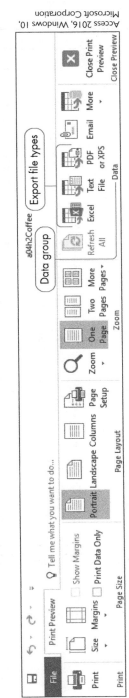

FIGURE 30 Data Group on Print Preview Tab

Alter a Report in Layout View

Use Layout view to alter the report design while still viewing the data. You should use Layout view to add or delete fields in the report, modify field properties, change the column widths, group, sort, and summarize data. The Page Setup tab presents options for setting the page size, orientation, and margins. Although you will be able to view your modifications along with the data in Layout view, you will still need to check the report in Print Preview to evaluate all the changes before printing it.

Modifying a Report

After you create a report by using one of the report tools, you may want to modify it. Some of the common changes you make in reports are adding and deleting controls, changing the arrangement, widths, and formatting of controls, and modifying the title. From either Layout or Design view, there are four tabs available for report modification:

- **Design:** Use this tab to make changes to the design of the report, such as adding fields, grouping and sorting records, changing themes, and inserting additional controls.

- **Arrange:** Use this tab to change the layout of a report, to move fields up and down, and to control margins and spacing.

- **Format:** Use this tab to work with fonts, font size, and colors, add or remove bolding, italics, or underlining, adjust text alignment, or add a background image or color.

- **Page Setup:** Use this tab to change paper size, margins, or page orientation, or to format reports into multiple columns.

STEP 3

Modify the Layout of a Report

The Arrange tab displays in both Layout view and Design view. Some key commands on the Arrange tab from Layout view are highlighted in Figure 31.

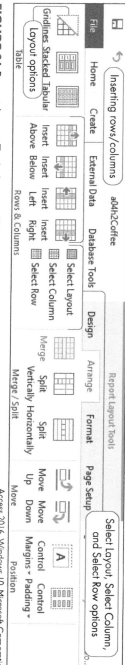

FIGURE 31 Report Layout Tools Arrange Tab

Access 2016, Windows 10, Microsoft Corporation

The Table group contains commands that enable you to add gridlines to a report's layout, and to change a report's layout from stacked to tabular (and vice versa). The Remove Layout command is available in Design view only. For example, if a report was created with a tabular layout, you could change it to a stacked layout.

To change a report's layout from tabular to stacked, complete the following steps:

1. Open the report in Layout view and click the Arrange tab.
2. Click any text box in the Detail section of the report.
3. Click Select Layout in the Rows & Columns group.
4. Click Stacked in the Table group.

The Rows & Columns group contains commands that enable you to insert rows and columns inside a report's layout. In a report with a stacked layout, you may want to separate some controls from the rest of the fields, or create some empty space so that fields can be added or repositioned. For example, you can select a control (or multiple controls) and click Insert Below. This will create an empty row (or space) below the selected controls. This group also contains the Select Layout, Select Column, and Select Row commands, which you can use to select the entire layout, or a single column or row in a layout.

The Merge/Split group contains commands that enable you to merge and split the controls on a report. There are times when you might want to deviate from the basic row and column formats that the report tools create. For example, you can make a label such as *Product Name* display in two controls (Product and Name), with one positioned below the other, rather than in one single control.

The Move group contains commands to move a field up or down in a stacked layout. Moving controls up or down in a report may cause unexpected results; you can always click Undo if you need to reverse your changes.

The Position group contains commands to control the margins and the padding (the spacing between controls) in a report. The preset margin settings are convenient to use; ensure that if you change the margins, you preview the report to view the result.

Modify Report Controls

The Format tab contains a series of commands that enable you to change the font, display, and alignment of the controls on a report, as shown in Figure 32. The formatting tools in Access are similar to those in other Microsoft Office applications.

To format report controls, complete the following steps:

1. Open the report in Layout view (or Design view), then select the control(s) you want to format.
2. Click the Format tab, and click the formatting tools as desired.

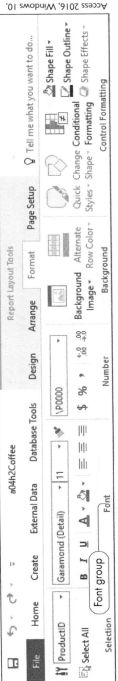

Access 2016, Windows 10, Microsoft Corporation

FIGURE 32 Report Layout Tools Format Tab

TIP: INSERT A LOGO IN A REPORT

To insert a logo in a report, open the report in Layout (or Design) view, and then click Logo in the Header / Footer group on the Design tab. In the Insert Picture dialog box, locate the image, click the file, and then click Open. The picture will display in the Report Header section; use the Property Sheet to modify the size and other attributes, if necessary.

Add a Field to a Report

At times, new fields may be added to tables and then need to be incorporated into reports. Alternatively, you might be creating a customized report and want to add fields individually. Adding a field to a report with a stacked or tabular layout is similar to adding a field to a form.

To add a field to a report, complete the following steps:

1. Open the report in Layout view, then click Add Existing Fields in the Tools group on the Design tab.

   The Field List pane displays at the right of the report. For a single-table report, you will be presented with a list of fields from the table (record source). For a multiple-table report, click the + (plus sign) to the left of the appropriate table to expand it, and locate the desired field(s).

2. Click and drag the desired field to the precise location on the report, using the shaded line as a guide for positioning the new field. Alternatively, you can double-click a field to add it to the report; the field will be added below the selected field. The other fields will automatically adjust to make room for the new field.

Delete a Field from a Report

You may decide that even though a field was available in a table or in a query that was used as the record source, it is not necessary to display it to users in a report. Not all fields in a database are necessarily relevant to reports that you create.

To delete a field from the Detail section of a report, complete the following steps:

1. Open the report in Layout view, and click the text box control of the field to be deleted (note the shaded border around the control).

2. Click Select Row in the Rows & Columns group on the Arrange tab in order to select the text box and its associated label. Alternatively, click the text box control, press and hold Ctrl, and then click the associated label control to select them both.

3. Press Delete.

The other fields will automatically adjust to close the gap around the deleted field.

Adjust Column Widths in a Report

You can adjust the width of each column in a tabular report individually so that each column is wide enough to accommodate the widest value in the field. For example, if a report contains first name, last name, address and city, and email address, you will need to make sure the longest value in each field is completely visible. Scroll through the records to ensure that all values can be viewed by report users.

To modify column widths in a tabular report, complete the following steps:

1. Open the report in Layout view, and click the text box control of the field you want to resize.

2. Point to the right border of the control until the pointer turns into a double-headed arrow. Drag the right edge of the control to the left or right until you arrive at the desired width.

Change Margins and Orientation

At times, you will want to print a report in Landscape orientation as opposed to Portrait; that decision will depend upon how many columns you want to display across the page, the widths of the fields, and other formatting considerations. The Page Setup tab presents options similar to those you may have used in Word. In the Page Size group, you can change the margins, and in the Page Layout group, you can work with Page Setup options, including setting the orientation of your report, as shown in Figure 33.

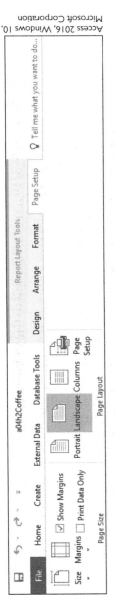

FIGURE 33 Report Layout Tools Page Setup Tab

Access 2016, Windows 10,
Microsoft Corporation

Add a Theme to the Report

You can enhance the report's appearance by applying one of the built-in Access themes.

To apply a theme, complete the following steps:

1. Open the report in Layout or Design view, and select Themes in the Themes group on the Design tab.

2. Point to a theme to see its name in the ScreenTip and a Live Preview of the theme in the report, and click to select it. By default, the theme will be applied to all objects in your database. Right-click a theme in the gallery to apply it to the current report only, or to all the reports in your database that share a common theme.

Work with a Report Layout Control

When you use one of the report tools to create a new report, Access will add a layout control to help align the fields. Layout controls in reports work similarly to layout controls in forms. The layout control provides guides to help keep controls aligned horizontally and vertically, and give your report a neat appearance. If you want to have more control over the location of your fields, you can remove the layout control and position the controls manually on the report.

To remove the layout control from a report, complete the following steps:

1. Open the report in Design view (the option is not available on the Ribbon in Layout view), and click anywhere in the layout control you want to remove.

2. Click Select Layout in the Rows & Columns group on the Arrange tab.

3. Click Remove Layout in the Table group. All of the controls are still available in the report, but can now be managed individually.

You can add a layout control to a report by first selecting all the controls you want to include in the layout. To select multiple controls, click the first control, press and hold Ctrl, and then click the additional controls you want to include. To select all of the controls on a form, press Ctrl+A. Click Tabular or Stacked in the Table group.

Sorting Records in a Report

STEP 4 ▶▶ When a report is created using the Report tool, the sort order of the records in the report is initially dependent on the sort order of the record source—similar to the way records are sorted in a form. The primary key of the record source usually controls the sort order. However, a report has an additional feature for sorting. While in Layout view or Design view, click Group & Sort in the Grouping & Totals group on the Design tab. The Group, Sort, and Total pane displays at the bottom of the report. This pane enables you to group records together and to override the sort order in the report's record source. Note that if you do not use the Report Wizard, this is generally how you would add grouping and totals to a report.

Change the Sorting in a Report

Sorting is important because sorting by a primary key may not be intuitive. For example, sorting by a field like LastName might be a better choice as opposed to CustomerID, so users can locate the records in alphabetical order by LastName.

To change the sorting in a report, complete the following steps:

1. Open the report in Layout or Design view, and click Group & Sort in the Grouping & Totals group on the Design tab.

2. Click *Add a sort* and select the field by which you want to sort. The default sort order is ascending.

3. Add another sort by clicking *Add a sort* again. For example, you could sort first by Brand and then by ProductName, as shown in Figure 34.

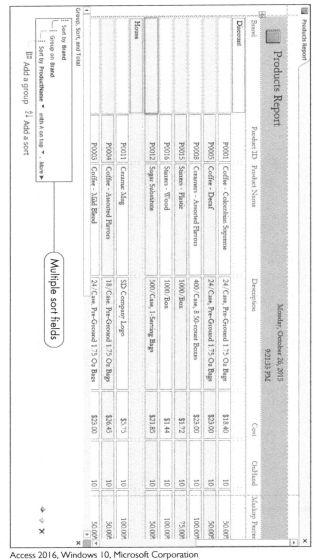

Access 2016, Windows 10, Microsoft Corporation

FIGURE 34 Report in Layout View with Two Sort Fields

Quick Concepts

5. What is the difference between Report view and Layout view?

6. What is the benefit of saving a report as another type of file?

7. Why is it important to view your reports in Print Preview?

8. Why would you decide to remove a report layout control when modifying a report?

9. Why is sorting the records in a report important?

Hands-On Exercises

MylTLab®
HOE2 Training

Watch the Video
for this Hands-On
Exercise!

2 Report Basics

Skills covered: Use the Report Tool • Use the Report Wizard • Use Print Preview • Publish to PDF • Add a Field • Remove a Field • Change Orientation • Apply a Theme • Sort Records in a Report

You create a products report using the Access Report tool to help Ryung manage her product information. You will modify the column widths so that they all fit across one page. You will also use the Report Wizard to create additional reports that Ryung requires.

STEP 1 >> CREATING REPORTS USING REPORT TOOLS

You use the Report tool to create an Access report to help Ryung manage her product information. This report is especially useful for determining which products she needs to order to fill upcoming orders. You also use the Report Wizard to determine sales by city. Refer to Figure 35 as you complete Step 1.

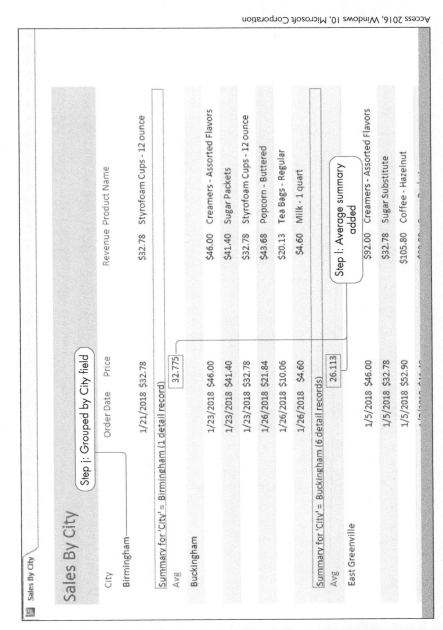

Access 2016, Windows 10, Microsoft Corporation

FIGURE 35 Sales by City Report

a. Open *a04h1Coffee_LastFirst* if you closed it at the end of Hands-On Exercise 1 and save it as **a04h2Coffee_LastFirst**, changing h1 to h2.

b. Select the **Products table** in the Navigation Pane. Click the **Create tab** and click **Report** in the Reports group.

   Access creates a new tabular layout report based on the Products table. The report opens in Layout view ready for editing.

c. Click the **Products title** at the top of the report to select it, click again on **Products**, and then change the title to **Products Report**. Press **Enter** to accept the change.

d. Right-click the **Products report tab** and select **Print Preview.**

The report is too wide for the page; you will close Print Preview and change the orientation to Landscape.

e. Click **Close Print Preview** in the Close Preview group to return to Layout view.

f. Click the **Page Setup tab** and click **Landscape** in the Page Layout group.

The report changes to Landscape orientation. Most of the columns now fit across one page. You will make further revisions to the report later so that it fits on one page.

g. Save the report as **Products Report.** Close the report.

h. Select the **Revenue query** in the Navigation Pane. Click the **Create tab** and click **Report Wizard** in the Reports group.

The Report Wizard launches.

i. Click the **City field** and click **Add One Field** ⌄ to add the City field to the report. Repeat the same process for the **OrderDate, Price, Revenue,** and **ProductName fields.** Click **Next.**

j. Ensure that **City** is selected, click **Add One Field** ⌄ to add grouping by city. Click **Next.**

k. Click the **arrow** in the first sort box, and select **OrderDate.** Accept the default sort order as Ascending. Click **Summary Options.**

l. Click the **Avg check box** in the Price row to summarize the Price field. Click **OK.**

m. Click **Next.** Click **Next** again to accept the default layout.

n. Type **Sales by City** for the title of the report. Click **Finish.**

The report is displayed in Print Preview mode.

o. Click **Close Print Preview.**

p. Save and close the report.

STEP 2 » USING REPORT VIEWS

The Products Report you created looks good, according to Ryung. However, she does not have Access installed on her home computer, and would like to have a copy of the report saved in PDF format so she can review it outside of the office. You will save a copy of the report for her Refer to Figure 36 as you complete Step 2.

Step a: Report in PDF format

Products Report

Sunday, November 4, 2015
9:24:45 PM

Product ID	Product Name	Description	Cost	Markup Percent	Refrigeration Needed	Brand
P0001	Coffee - Colombian Supreme	24/Case, Pre-Ground 1.75 Oz Bags	$18.40	50.00%	☐	Discount
P0002	Coffee - Hazelnut	24/Case, Pre-Ground 1.75 Oz Bags	$26.45	100.00%	☐	Premium
P0003	Coffee - Mild Blend	24/Case, Pre-Ground 1.75 Oz Bags	$23.00	50.00%	☐	House
P0004	Coffee - Assorted Flavors	18/Case, Pre-Ground 1.75 Oz Bags	$26.45	50.00%	☐	House
P0005	Coffee - Decaf	24/Case, Pre-Ground 1.75 Oz Bags	$23.00	50.00%	☐	Discount
P0006	Tea Bags - Regular	75/Box, Individual Tea Bags	$5.75	75.00%	☐	House
P0007	Tea Bags - Decaf	75/Box, Individual Tea Bags	$8.05	75.00%	☐	House
P0008	Creamers - Assorted Flavors	400/Case, 8 50-count Boxes	$23.00	100.00%	☐	Discount
P0009	Creamers - Liquid	200/Case, Individual Creamers	$17.25	100.00%	☑	Premium
P0010	Sugar Packets	2000/Case	$20.70	100.00%	☐	House
P0011	Ceramic Mug	SD Company Logo	$5.75	100.00%	☐	House
P0012	Sugar Substitute	500/Case, 1-Serving Bags	$21.85	50.00%	☐	Discount
P0013	Coffee Filters	500/Case, Fits 10-12 Cup Coffee Maker	$3.45	50.00%	☐	House
P0014	Napkins	3000/Case, White	$23.00	100.00%	☐	House
P0015	Stirrers - Plastic	1000/Box	$1.72	75.00%	☐	Discount
P0016	Stirrers - Wood	1000/Box	$1.44	100.00%	☐	Discount
P0017	Spoons	500/Box, White Plastic	$17.25	100.00%	☐	House
P0018	Popcorn - Plain	36/Case, 3.75 Oz Microwave Bags	$9.78	100.00%	☐	House
P0019	Popcorn - Buttered	36/Case, 3.75 Oz Microwave Bags	$10.92	100.00%	☐	House
P0020	Soup - Chicken	50 Envelopes	$11.50	100.00%	☐	Premium
P0021	Soup - Variety Pak	50 Envelopes	$13.80	100.00%	☐	Premium
P0022	Styrofoam Cups - 10 ounce	1000/Case	$19.55	50.00%	☐	House

Access 2016, Windows 10, Microsoft Corporation

FIGURE 36 Products Report Saved in PDF Format

a. Open the Products Report and on the **File** tab, click **Print**, and select **Print Preview**. Click **PDF or XPS** in the Data group on the Print Preview tab. Navigate to where you are saving your files, type the file name **a04h2Products_LastFirst**, ensure that *Open file after publishing* is selected, and then click **Publish**.

Windows will open the report in your system's default PDF viewer, which may be Adobe Reader or the Windows Reader app. Close the reader window. You will submit this file to your instructor at the end of the last hands-on exercise.

b. Ensure that you return to the Access window, and in the Export – PDF dialog box, click **Close** when prompted to save the export steps.

c. Click **Close Print Preview** and close the report.

STEP 3 >> MODIFYING A REPORT

Products Retrospect

Step 1: Retrospect theme applied

Products Report

Tuesday, November 3, 2015
9:32:32 AM

Product ID	Product Name	Description	Cost	OnHand	Markup Percent	Refrig?	Brand
P0001	Coffee - Colombian Supreme	24/Case, Pre-Ground 1.75 Oz Bags	$18.40	10	50.00%	☐	Discount
P0002	Coffee - Hazelnut	24/Case, Pre-Ground 1.75 Oz Bags	$26.45	10	100.00%	☐	Premium
P0003	Coffee - Mild Blend	24/Case, Pre-Ground 1.75 Oz Bags	$23.00	10	50.00%	☐	House
P0004	Coffee - Assorted Flavors	18/Case, Pre-Ground 1.75 Oz Bags	$26.45	10	50.00%	☐	House
P0005	Coffee - Decaf	24/Case, Pre-Ground 1.75 Oz Bags	$23.00	10	50.00%	☐	Discount
P0006	Tea Bags - Regular	75/Box, Individual Tea Bags	$5.75	10	75.00%	☑	House
P0007	Tea Bags - Decaf	75/Box, Individual Tea Bags	$8.05	10	75.00%	☐	House
P0008	Creamers - Assorted Flavors	400/Case, 8 50-count Boxes	$23.00	10	100.00%	☐	Discount
P0009	Creamers - Liquid	200/Case, Individual Creamers	$17.25	10	100.00%	☐	Premium
P0010	Sugar Packets	2000/Case	$20.70	10	100.00%	☐	House
P0011	Ceramic Mug	SD Company Logo	$5.75	10	100.00%	☐	House
P0012	Sugar Substitute	500/Case, 1-Serving Bags	$21.85	10	50.00%	☐	Discount
P0013	Coffee Filters	500/Case, Fits 10-12 Cup Coffee Maker	$3.45	10	50.00%	☐	House
P0014	Napkins	3000/Case, White	$23.00	10	100.00%	☐	House
P0015	Stirrers - Plastic	1000/Box	$1.72	10	75.00%	☐	Discount

FIGURE 37 Products Retrospect Report

a. Right-click the **Products table** and select **Design View**.

You need to add the OnHand field to the Products table.

b. Click in the **MarkupPercent field**, and then click **Insert Rows** in the Tools group on the Design tab.

A new blank row displays above the MarkupPercent field.

c. Type **OnHand** in the Field Name box and select **Number** as the Data Type.

d. Save the table. Click **View** in the Views group to switch to Datasheet view.

The new OnHand column contains no data. Next, you will add some sample data to the new field for testing purposes only.

e. Type the number **10** for each item's OnHand value.

f. Close the Products table.

g. Right-click **Products Report** in the Navigation Pane, and select **Layout View**.

h. Click **Add Existing Fields** in the Tools group on the Design tab to open the Field List pane.

i. Drag the **OnHand field** from the Field List pane between the Cost and MarkupPercent fields. Close the Field List pane.

Because of the tabular layout control, Access adjusts all the columns to make room for the new OnHand field.

j. Display the report in Print Preview.

The report is still too wide for a single page.

k. Click **Close Print Preview**. Ensure that you are in Layout view.

l. Scroll to and then click anywhere in the **Year Introduced column**. Click the **Arrange tab** and click **Select Column** in the Rows & Columns group. Press **Delete** to remove the column.

The Year Introduced column is removed from the report.

m. Scroll to and then click the **ProductID column heading** and drag the right border to the left until the Product ID heading still fits, but any extra white space is removed.

n. Scroll to and then click the **Refrigeration Needed column heading** and rename the column **Refrig?**. Adjust the width of the *Refrig?* column heading so that any extra white space is removed.

o. Click **Themes** in the Themes group on the Design tab.

The available predefined themes display.

p. Right-click the **Organic theme** and select **Apply Theme to This Object Only**. Display the report in Print Preview.

Access reformats the report using the Organic theme. The report is still too wide for a single page. You will make further adjustments in the next steps.

q. Click **Close Print Preview** and save the report. Click the **File tab**, select **Save As**, select **Save Object As**, and then click **Save As**. Type **Products Organic** as the report name and click **OK**.

You saved the report with one theme. Now, you will apply a second theme to the report and save it with a different name.

r. Ensure that the report is in Layout view. You notice that the Brand column is extending over the dashed page break to its right and needs to be resized to fit on the page. Drag the right border of the Brand column to the left so that it fits inside the page break. Scroll down the report to ensure that all of the values in the column are visible. Narrow columns as required to ensure that all columns are fitting inside the dashed page break. Save the report.

s. Click **Themes** in the Themes group to apply a different theme. Right-click the **Retrospect theme** and select **Apply Theme to This Object Only**. Display the report in Print Preview.

If you do not apply the theme to this object only, all database objects will adopt the Retrospect theme.

t. Click **Close Print Preview**. Click the **File tab**, select **Save As**, select **Save Object As**, and then click **Save As**. Type **Products Retrospect** as the report name and click **OK**. Close the report.

You will be able to show Ryung two product reports with different themes applied.

Ryung would like the Products Report records to be sorted and grouped by Brand. You will change the sort order, group the records, and preview the report to see the results Refer to Figure 38 as you complete Step 4.

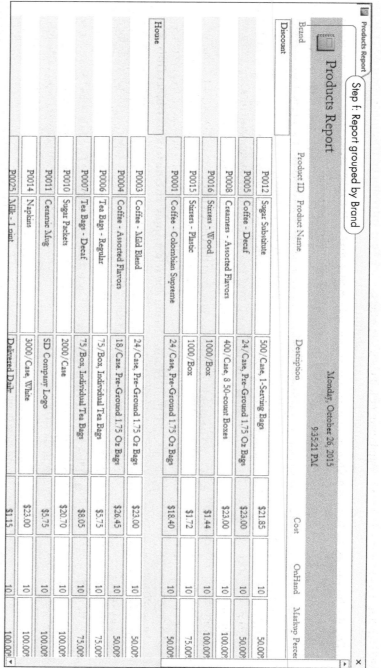

FIGURE 38 Products Report Grouped by Brand

a. Open **Products Report** in Layout view.

b. Click **Group & Sort** in the Grouping & Totals group on the Design tab.

The *Add a group* and *Add a sort* options display at the bottom of the report.

c. Click **Add a sort**.

A new Sort bar displays at the bottom of the report.

d. Select **Brand** from the list.

The report is now sorted by Brand in ascending order (with Discount at the top).

e. Click **Add a group**.

f. Select **Brand** from the list.

The report is now grouped by Brand.

> **TROUBLESHOOTING:** If the options do not display, the Group, Sort, and Total pane may have been open. If the pane is closed after selecting the command, try clicking Group & Sort again.

g. View the report in Report view. Save and close the report.

h. Close the database and exit Access. Based on your instructor's directions, submit the following:

a04h2Coffee_LastFirst

a04h2Products_LastFirst

Chapter Objectives Review

After reading this chapter, you have accomplished the following objectives:

1. Create forms using form tools.

- Identify a record source: A record source is the table or query that supplies the records for the form.
- Use the Form tool: The Form tool creates a basic form that opens in Layout view.
- Understand controls: Controls are the text boxes, buttons, labels, and other tools you use to add, edit, and display data in a form or report.
- Work with form views: Form view is a simplified interface used for data entry, but it allows no design changes. Layout view enables users to make changes to the layout while viewing the data in the form. Design view enables you to change advanced design settings that are not available in Layout view.
- Work with a subform: A subform displays data from a related table for each record in the main table.
- Create a split form: A split form combines two views of the same record source—one section is displayed in a stacked layout and the other section is displayed in a tabular layout.
- Create a multiple items form: This form displays multiple records in a tabular layout similar to a table's Datasheet view, with more customization options.
- Create forms using the other form tools: A datasheet form is a replica of a table or query's Datasheet view except that it still retains form properties. The Form Design tool and the Blank Form tools can be used to create a form manually. The Navigation option in the Forms group enables you to create user interface forms that have the look and feel of Web-based forms and enable users to open and close the objects of a database. The Modal Dialog Form tool can be used to create a dialog box.

2. Modify forms.

- Use Form view to edit data: Most users will work in Form view. This enables changes to data but not to design elements.
- Use Layout view to modify form design: Layout view enables you to change the design of a form while viewing data.
- Adjust column widths in a form: Column widths often need to be adjusted. Size the columns to accommodate the widest entry in a field.
- Add and delete form fields: Fields can be added to an existing form using the Field List. Fields can be removed by selecting the text box and the label controls and pressing Delete.
- Add a theme to a form: Themes can be applied to a single form or to all objects in the database.
- Modify form controls: The Format tab enables changes to the font, including bold, italic, underlining, font size, font color, font background, and alignment.

3. Work with a form layout.

- Modify a form layout: The Arrange tab displays in both Layout view and Design view, and enables you to change form layout, field order, and spacing options.

4. Sort records in form.

- Sort by a single field: Forms can be sorted by a single field in either ascending or descending order.

5. Create reports using report tools.

- Use the Report tool: Access has five report tools. The Report tool instantly creates a tabular report based on a table or query. The Report Design tool creates a new blank report in Design view. The Blank Report tool creates a new blank report so that you can insert controls and design the report manually in Layout view. The Report Wizard tool steps you through the process to create a report. The Labels tool creates a page of mailing labels using a template.
- Use the Report Wizard to create a report: The Report Wizard will guide you step by step through creating a report, prompting you for input and generating output. The wizard enables you to group records of a common type and summarize data in your reports.
- Use the Label Wizard: The Label Wizard can produce printable labels. Access includes predefined standard formats for common labels.

6. Use report views.

- View a report in Report view: Report view is ideal for viewing data onscreen. Neither data nor the design can be changed in this view.
- Print or save a report in Print Preview: Print Preview shows how the report will display when printed. It also enables you to save the report as a file in a number of formats, such as Word and PDF.
- Alter a report in Layout view: Layout view enables you to change the design of a report while viewing data.

7. Modify a report.

- Modify the layout of a report: The Arrange tab displays in both Layout view and Design view. The tools on the Arrange tab enable you to work with the layout of a report to give it a more uniform appearance.
- Modify report controls: The Format tab enables changes to the font, including bold, italic, underlining, font size, font color, font background, and alignment.
- Add a field to a report: Fields can be added to an existing report using the Field List.
- Delete a field from a report: Fields can be deleted either in Layout or Design view.
- Adjust column widths in a report: Column widths often need to be adjusted. Be sure to make the column wide enough to display the widest value in a field.

- Change margins and orientation: You can display the report in portrait or landscape mode and increase or decrease margin sizes.

- Add a theme to the report: Themes can be applied to a single report or to all objects in the database.

- Work with a Report Layout control: The Layout control keeps the fields neatly spaced, making it harder to move fields independently but keeping a standard format.

8. Sort records in a report.

- Change the sorting in a report: You can sort report records by a single or multiple fields.

Key Terms Matching

Match the key terms with their definitions. Write the key term letter by the appropriate numbered definition.

a. Control
b. Design view
c. Form
d. Form tool
e. Form view
f. Label Wizard
g. Layout control
h. Layout view
i. Multiple Items form
j. Portable Document Format (PDF)
k. Print Preview
l. Record source
m. Report
n. Report tool
o. Report view
p. Report Wizard
q. Split form
r. Stacked layout
s. Tabular layout
t. Theme

1. _____ A database object that is used to add data into or edit data in a table.

2. _____ Used to create data entry forms for customers, employees, products, and other tables.

3. _____ The table or query that supplies the records for a form or report.

4. _____ Displays fields in a vertical column.

5. _____ Displays fields horizontally.

6. _____ A text box, button, label, or other tool you use to add, edit, and display the data in a form or report.

7. _____ Provides guides to help keep controls aligned horizontally and vertically and give your form a uniform appearance.

8. _____ A simplified user interface primarily used for data entry; does not allow you to make changes to the layout.

9. _____ Enables users to make changes to a layout while viewing the data in the form or report.

10. _____ Enables you to change advanced design settings you cannot see in Layout view, such as removing a layout control.

11. _____ Combines two views of the same record source—one section is displayed in a stacked layout and the other section is displayed in a tabular layout.

12. _____ Displays multiple records in a tabular layout similar to a table's Datasheet view, with more customization options.

13. _____ A defined set of colors, fonts, and graphics that can be applied to a form or report.

14. _____ A database document that outputs meaningful information to its readers.

15. _____ Used to instantly create a tabular report based on the table or query currently selected.

16. _____ Prompts you for input and then uses your answers to generate a customized report.

17. _____ Enables you to easily create mailing labels, name tags, and other specialized tags.

18. _____ Enables you to determine what a printed report will look like in a continuous page layout.

19. _____ Enables you to see exactly what the report will look like when it is printed.

20. _____ A file type that was created for exchanging documents independent of software applications and operating system environment.

Multiple Choice

1. A report can be made from one or more tables or a query. The object(s) that a report is based on is known as the:

   (a) Control.

   (b) Record Source.

   (c) Theme.

   (d) Tabular Layout.

2. Which of the following statements is *false?*

   (a) Both forms and reports can use tabular and stacked layouts.

   (b) A stacked layout displays data in a vertical column.

   (c) A tabular layout displays data horizontally.

   (d) Stacked layouts are more common for reports because they use less paper when printed.

3. In order to summarize data in a report and override the sort order of the record source you would use:

   (a) A text box.

   (b) A button on a report.

   (c) The Group, Sort, and Total Pane.

   (d) A label on a report.

4. The simplest view you can use to modify control widths in a form is:

   (a) Layout view.

   (b) Form view.

   (c) Design view.

   (d) Print Preview.

5. Which of the following views provides you with the most flexibility in modifying forms and reports?

   (a) Design view

   (b) Layout view

   (c) Form view/Report view

   (d) Print Preview

6. Which of the following statements about reports is *false?*

   (a) Reports can be saved to a file (such as a Word document) on your computer.

   (b) Reports are primarily used to modify data.

   (c) Reports can produce output in a number of ways, including mailing labels.

   (d) Reports can be created simply by using the Report tool.

7. Use the _____ to see exactly what the printed report will look like before printing.

   (a) Report tool

   (b) Report Wizard

   (c) Report view

   (d) Print Preview

8. If you need to send a report to a user who does not have Microsoft Office available, which of the following file formats would be the best choice to ensure it can be opened?

   (a) Word

   (b) Excel

   (c) Reader

   (d) Portable Document Format (PDF)

9. Which of the following statements is *false?*

   (a) Reports are generally used for printing, emailing, or viewing data on the screen.

   (b) Layouts for forms and reports are the predefined sets of colors, fonts, and graphics.

   (c) Forms are often used for inputting data.

   (d) Forms and reports both include controls, such as text boxes, that can be resized.

10. Which of the following statements is *true?*

   (a) You can group records to show a list of properties by state.

   (b) You can sort records in reports but not in forms.

   (c) A sort can only be set on one field at a time.

   (d) You can either group or sort records (but not both).

1 Financial Management Prospects

You are working as a customer service representative for a financial management firm. Your task is to contact a list of prospective customers and introduce yourself and the services of your company. You will create a form to view, add, and update data for one customer at a time. After creating the form, you will customize it and add sorting. You will also create a report to display all of the information on one screen, for viewing purposes. Refer to Figure 39 as you complete this exercise.

Access 2016, Windows 10, Microsoft Corporation

FIGURE 39 Grouped and Sorted Leads Report

a. Open *a04p1Prospects*. Save the database as **a04p1Prospects_LastFirst**.

b. Click the **Leads table** in the Navigation Pane. Click the **Create tab**, and click **Form** in the Forms group.

A new form based on the Leads table opens in Layout view.

c. Select the **ID text box** of record 1 and drag the right border to the left to resize the column to approximately half of its original width.

The other text boxes will resize as well.

d. Change the title of the form to **New Leads**.

e. Click **Themes** in the Themes group of the Design tab. Apply the **Integral theme** to this form only.

f. Change the font size of the NetWorth text box control to **14** and change the Background Color to **Turquoise, Accent 3**.

g. Click **Select Row** in the Rows & Columns group on the Arrange tab. Click **Move Up** in the Move group until NetWorth displays above First.

> **TROUBLESHOOTING:** If the text box and the label do not move together, click Undo, ensure that both controls are selected, and then follow the instructions in Step g.

h. Save the form as **Leads Form**. Switch to Form view.

i. Navigate to Record 63. Enter your first and last names in the appropriate fields. Leave the Email field blank.

j. Click in the **Last field** and then click **Ascending** in the Sort & Filter group of the Home tab. Farrah Aaron should be the first record displayed unless your last name appears before hers alphabetically.

k. Save and close the form.

l. Click the **Leads table** in the Navigation Pane. Click the **Create tab**, click **More Forms** in the Forms group, and then select **Split Form**.

m. Modify the form title to read **Leads-Split Form**. Save the form as **Leads-Split Form** and close the form.

n. Click the **Leads table**. Click **Report** in the Reports group on the Create tab. A new report is created based on the Leads table.

o. Make the fields as narrow as possible to remove extra white space. Change the report's orientation to **Landscape**.

p. Delete the **ID**, **Address**, and **City** columns from the report.

q. Ensure that **Group & Sort** is selected in the Grouping & Totals group on the Design tab. Group the records by **State** and sort them by **LastName** in ascending order. Close the Group, Sort, and Total pane.

r. Save the report as **Leads Report**. Close the report.

s. Close the database and exit Access. Based on your instructor's directions, submit a04p1Prospects_LastFirst.

The Human Resources department of the Comfort Insurance Agency has initiated its annual employee performance reviews. You will create a form for them to perform data entry using the Form tool and a multiple items form. You will create a report to display locations, and a report displaying employee salary increases by location. Additionally, you will save the salary increases report as a PDF file. Refer to Figure 40 as you complete this exercise.

Employee Compensation

Employee Compensation

Location	YearHired	LastName	FirstName	Salary	2018Increase	2018Raise
L01						
	2012	Abrams	Wendy	$47,500.00	3.00%	1425
	2008	Anderson	Vicki	$47,900.00	4.00%	1916
	2012	Bichette	Susan	$61,500.00	4.00%	2460
	2010	Block	Leonard	$26,200.00	3.00%	786
	2011	Brown	Patricia	$20,100.00	5.00%	1005
	2009	Brumbaugh	Paige	$49,300.00	3.00%	1479
	2011	Daniels	Phil	$42,600.00	3.00%	1278
	2010	Davis	Martha	$51,900.00	4.00%	2076
	2009	Drubin	Lolly	$37,000.00	3.00%	1110
	2011	Fantis	Laurie	$28,000.00	3.00%	840
	2009	Fleming	Karen	$41,100.00	3.00%	1233
	2008	Gander	John	$38,400.00	3.00%	1152
	2010	Grippando	Joan	$26,100.00	3.00%	783
	2012	Harrison	Jenifer	$44,800.00	3.00%	1344
	2011	Imber	Elise	$63,700.00	4.00%	2548
	2012	Johnshon	Billy	$21,800.00	5.00%	1090
	2012	Johnson	Debbie	$39,700.00	3.00%	1191

FIGURE 40 Employee Compensation Report

a. Open *a04p2Insurance*. Save the database as **a04p2Insurance_LastFirst**.

b. Click the **Locations table** in the Navigation Pane. Click the **Create tab**, and click **Form** in the Forms group.

c. Click the **View arrow** in the Views group on the Home tab, and select **Design View**. Click anywhere in the subform control, and press **Delete**. Switch to Layout view.

d. Ensure that the **LocationID text box** containing *L01* in Record 1 is selected. Drag the right border to the left to resize the column to approximately half of its original width. The other text boxes will resize as well.

e. Click **Themes** in the Themes group on the Design tab. Right-click the **Wisp theme**, and select **Apply Theme to This Object Only**.

f. Change the font size of the Location text box control (containing *Atlanta*) to **14**, and change the Background Color to **Green, Accent 6, Lighter 60%**.

g. Click **Select Row** in the Rows & Columns group on the Arrange tab. Click **Move Up** in the Move group until Location displays above LocationID.

h. Save the form as **Locations Data Entry**.

i. Click **Layout view**, and delete the **LocationID field**. Delete the **Office Phone label**. Move the **Office Phone field** to the row immediately below the Location field.

j. Add **LocationID** back to the form from the Field List, immediately below the Address field. Close the Field List pane.

k. Switch to Form view, and then save and close the form.

l. Click the **Locations table** in the Navigation Pane. Click the **Create tab**, and click **Report** in the Reports group.

m. Click the **LocationID label**, and drag the right border of the label to the left to reduce the size of the control to approximately half of its original size.

n. Repeat the sizing process with the **Zipcode label** and the **OfficePhone label**. Adjust the other column widths until there are no controls on the right side of the vertical dashed line (page break). Drag the control containing the page number to the left so that it is inside the page break.

o. Display the report in Report view. Verify that the report is only one page wide in Report view. Save the report as **Locations** and close the report.

p. Click the **Employees Query** in the Navigation Pane. Click the **Create tab**, and click **Report Wizard** in the Reports group. Respond to the prompts as follows:

  • Add all the fields to the Selected Fields list. Click **HireDate**, and remove the field from the Selected Fields. Remove **YearHired** from the Selected Fields. Click **Next**.

  • Accept grouping by Location. Click **Next**.

  • Select **LastName** for the first sort order, and **FirstName** for the second (ascending order for both). Click **Summary Options**.

  • Click **Sum** for Salary, **Avg** for 2018Increase, and **Avg** for YearsWorked. Click **OK**. Click **Next**.

  • Accept the Stepped layout. Change Orientation to **Landscape**. Click **Next**.

  • Type **Employee Compensation** for the title of the report. Click **Finish**.

q. Click **Close Print Preview**. Switch to Layout view.

r. Adjust the column widths so that all of the data values are visible and the columns all fit within the vertical dashed border (page break). Some of the text boxes and labels will need to be relocated; select the control to be moved and click and drag it to a new location.

s. Click **Themes** in the Themes group on the Design tab. Right-click the **Slice theme** and select **Apply Theme to This Object Only**. Adjust the label widths and report title so that they are fully visible. Scroll to the bottom of the report and move any text boxes, such as the page number control, so that they are inside the page break. Resize all text boxes and labels so that their values are fully visible.

t. Delete the **YearsWorked field** and **label**.

u. Click and drag **YearHired** from the Field List into the report layout. Drag and drop the column into the space immediately to the right of the Location column. Close the Field List. Display the report in Print Preview. Compare your report to Figure 40. Make adjustments as required.

v. Save the report as a PDF file named **a04p2Employee_Compensation_LastFirst**. Close the reader window.

w. Save and close the Employee Compensation report.

x. Create a Multiple Items form based on the Titles table. Resize the fields so that they are all visible onscreen without scrolling. Save the form as **Job Titles**. Close the form.

y. Close the database and exit Access. Based on your instructor's directions, submit the following:

   a04p2Insurance_LastFirst
   a04p2Employee Compensation_LastFirst

Hotel Chain

ANALYSIS CASE

You are the general manager of a large hotel chain. You track revenue by categories, such as conference room rentals and weddings. You want to create a report that shows which locations are earning the most revenue in each category. You will also create a report to show you details of your three newest areas: St. Paul, St. Louis, and Seattle.

a. Open *a04m1Rewards*. Save the database as **a04m1Rewards_LastFirst**.

b. Select the **Members table**, and create a Multiple Items form. Save the form as **Maintain Members**.

c. Modify the form in Layout view as follows:
   - Change the MemNumber label to **MemID**, and reduce the MemNumber column width.
   - Adjust the column widths to eliminate extra white space.
   - Delete the form icon (the picture next to the title of the form) in the Form Header.

d. Change the sorting on the MemberSince control so that the members who joined most recently are displayed first.

e. Click the **LastName field**. Change the Control Padding to **Wide**. (Hint: Search **Control Padding** in the *Tell me what you want to do...* box).

f. Save and close the form.

g. Select the **Revenue query**, and create a report using the Report Wizard. Answer the wizard prompts as follows:
   - Include all fields in the report.
   - Add grouping first by **City** and then by **ServiceName**.
   - Add a Sum to the Revenue field, and click the **Summary Only option**.
   - Select **Outline Layout**.
   - Name the report **Revenue by City and Service**.

h. Scroll through all the pages to check the layout of the report while in Print Preview mode.

i. Close Print Preview. Switch to Layout view, and delete the **NumInParty** and **PerPersonCharge** controls.

j. Change the font size, font color, and background color of the Sum control (found at the bottom of the report) so the control stands out from the other controls.

k. Change the font size, font color, and background color of the Grand Total control (found at the end of the report) so the control stands out as well.

l. Change the sort on the report, so that it sorts by city in descending order—that is, so that the last city alphabetically (St. Paul) is displayed first.

m. Examine the data in the report to determine and note which city (St. Paul, St. Louis, or Seattle) has the highest Sum of event revenue. You will use this information to modify a query. Save and close the report.

n. Modify the Totals by Service query so that the criteria for the City field is the city you determined had the highest sum of event revenue (St. Paul, St. Louis, or Seattle). Run, save, and close the query.

o. Create a report using the Report tool based on the Totals by Service query. Name the report **Targeted City**.

p. Close the report.

q. Close the database and exit Access. Based on your instructor's directions, submit a04m1Rewards_LastFirst.

2 Benefit Auction

You are helping to organize a benefit auction to raise money for families who lost their homes in a natural disaster. The information for the auction is currently stored in an Excel spreadsheet, but you have volunteered to import it into Access. You will create a form to manage the data-entry process. You also create two reports: one that lists the items collected in each category and one for labels so you can send the donors a thank-you letter after the auction.

a. Open Access, and create a new database named **a04m2Auction_LastFirst**.

A new table displays with an ID column.

b. Switch to Design view. Type **Items** in the **Save As dialog box**, and click **OK**.

c. Change the ID Field Name to **ItemID**. Type **Description** in the second row, and press **Tab**. Set **Short Text** as the Data Type. Type **50** in the **Field Size property** in Field Properties.

d. Type the remainder of the fields and adjust the data types as shown:

Field Name	Data Type
DateOfDonation	Date/Time
Category	Short Text
Price	Currency
DonorName	Short Text
DonorAddress1	Short Text
DonorAddress2	Short Text

e. Open Excel. Open the *a04m2Items* file. Examine the length of the Category, Donor Name, Donor Address 1, and Donor Address 2 columns. Determine how many characters are needed for each field based on the longest value in each column, and round that value up to the nearest 5. For example, if a field needs 23 characters, you would round up to 25. You will use this to change field sizes in the table.

f. Change the field sizes for Category, DonorName, DonorAddress1, and DonorAddress2 to the sizes you chose in Step e. Save the table.

g. Copy and paste the 26 rows from the Excel spreadsheet into the Items table. To paste the rows, locate the * to the left of the first blank row, click the Record Selector, right-click the Record Selector, and then from the shortcut menu, select Paste. Resize the columns so all data is visible. Close the table.

> **TROUBLESHOOTING:** Once you have pasted the data, ensure that your chosen field sizes did not cause you to lose data. If so, update the field sizes, delete the records you pasted to the table, and then repeat Step g.

h. Verify that the Items table is selected in the Navigation Pane. Create a new form using the **Form** tool.

i. Change the layout of the form to **Tabular Layout**. Resize field widths to reduce extra space. It is acceptable for field values in the text boxes to display on two lines.

j. Change the title of the form to **Items for Auction**.

k. Add conditional formatting so that each Price that is greater than 90 has a text color of **Green** (seventh column, first row below Standard Colors).

l. Save the form as **Auction Items Form**.

m. Switch to Form view. Create a new record with the following data. Note that the form will automatically assign an ItemID for you.

Description	DateOfDonation	Category	Price	DonorName	DonorAddress1	DonorAddress2
iPad	12/31/2018	House	$400	Staples	500 Market St.	Brick, NJ 0872

n. Add a sort to the form, so that the lowest priced items display first. Save and close the form.

o. Select the **Items table** in the Navigation Pane, and create a report using the Report Wizard. Include all fields except the two donor address fields, group by Category, include the Sum of Price as a Summary Option, accept the default layout, and then save the report as **Auction Items by Category.**

p. Switch to Layout view, and adjust the controls so that all data is visible. Adjust the widths of the controls until there are no controls extending over the right side of the vertical dashed line (page break). Preview the report to verify that the column widths are correct.

q. Sort the report so the least expensive item is displayed first in each group. Save and close the report.

r. Create mailing labels based on the Avery 5660 template. Place the donor name on the first line, address (**DonorAddress1**) on the second, and city, state, and ZIP (**DonorAddress2**) on the third line. Sort the labels by **DonorName**. Name the report **Donor Labels**. After you create the labels, display them in Print Preview mode to verify that all values will fit onto the label template. Close the label report.

s. Close the database and exit Access. Based on your instructor's directions, submit a04m2Auction_LastFirst.

DISCOVER

3 New Castle County Technical Services

RUNNING CASE

New Castle County Technical Services (NCCTS) provides technical support for a number of companies in the greater New Castle County, Delaware, area. Now that you have completed the database tables, set the appropriate relationships, and created queries, you are ready to create a form and a report.

a. Open the database a03m3NCCTS_LastFirst and save it as **a04m3NCCTS_LastFirst.**

b. Create a split form based on the Calls table.

c. Apply the **Integral theme** to this form only.

d. Add the **Description field** by dragging and dropping it immediately below the CallTypeID (Hint: Click **Show all tables** in the Field List pane, and locate the field by expanding the **Call Types table**). Close the Field List pane. Switch to Form view and ensure that the records are sorted by CallID in ascending order.

e. Save the form as **Calls Data Entry**, and close the form.

f. Use the Report tool to create a basic report based on the Customer Happiness query.

g. Sort the records by the **Avg Rating field** in ascending order.

h. Apply the **Integral theme** to this report only.

i. Change the title of the report to **Customer Satisfaction Ratings**, and format the background color of the control to **Medium Gray** (under Standard Colors).

j. Set the font color of the title control to **Blue, Accent 2**, the font size to **20**, and the alignment to **Center.** Click the default logo in the report header and press **Delete.**

k. Switch to Report view. Save the report as **Customer Satisfaction Survey**, and close the report.

l. Close the database and exit Access. Based on your instructor's directions, submit a04m3NCCTS_LastFirst.

Create a Split Form

GENERAL CASE ✓

FROM SCRATCH 🖎

This chapter introduced you to Access forms, including the split form. It is possible to convert an existing form into a split form if you know how to modify form properties. First, create a new database and name the file **a04b1BooksImport_LastFirst**. Next, import only the Books table and Books form from the *a04b1BooksImport* database. To import the objects, click the **External Data tab** and click **Access** in the Import & Link group. Perform an Internet search to find the steps to convert a form to a split form. Use the information from the Internet to convert the Books form into a split form. Make sure the datasheet is in the bottom pane of the form. Delete the AuthorCode text box and label from the top pane of the form. Change the form so that it sorts by Title in ascending order. Increase the font size of the Title control to **14**, and change its background color to **Medium Gray** (under Standard Colors). Apply the **Integral** theme to this form only. Save the form as **Split Form Books.** Switch to Form view, and then close the form. Close the database and exit Access. Based on your instructor's directions, submit a04b1Split_LastFirst.

Properties by City

DISASTER RECOVERY

A co-worker is having difficulty with an Access report and asked you for your assistance. He was trying to fix the report and seems to have made things worse. Open the *a04b2Sales* database and save the file as **a04b2Sales_LastFirst.** Open the Properties Report in Report view. The report columns do not fit across one page. In addition, there is a big gap between two fields, and he moved the Beds and Baths fields so they are basically on top of one another. Add all of the fields to a tabular layout. Group the records first by City, and then by Beds in descending order. Within each group, sort the report by ListPrice in descending order. Change the report to Landscape orientation and adjust the column widths so they all fit across one page (inside the dashed vertical page break). Apply the Organic theme to this report only, and switch to Report view. Save the new report as **Properties by City,** close the report, and then delete the original **Properties Report** from the database (right-click the report in the Navigation Pane, and from the shortcut menu, select **Delete**). Close the database and exit Access. Based on your instructor's directions, submit a04b2Sales_LastFirst.

Capstone Exercise

Your boss asked you to prepare a schedule for each speaker for the national conference being hosted next year on your campus. She wants to mail the schedules to the speakers so that they can provide feedback on the schedule prior to its publication. You assure her that you can accomplish this task with Access.

Database File Setup

You need to copy an original database file, rename the copied file, and then open the copied database to complete this Capstone exercise. After you open the copied database, you replace an existing employee's name with your name.

a. Open the *a04c1_NatConf* database, and save it as **a04c1NatConf_LastFirst.**

b. Open the Speakers table.

c. Find and replace *YourName* with your own first and last name. Close the table.

Create and Customize a Form

You want to create a form to add and update the Speakers table. Use the Form tool to create the form and modify the form as required. You will also add a layout to an existing form.

a. Select the **Speakers table** in the Navigation Pane as the record source for the form.

b. Use the **Form tool** to create a new form with a stacked layout.

c. Change the form's title to **Enter/Edit Speakers.**

d. Reduce the width of the text box controls to approximately half of their original size.

e. Delete the **Sessions subform** control from the form.

f. View the form and the data in Form view. Sort the records by **LastName** in ascending order.

g. Save the form as **Edit Speakers.** Close the form.

h. Open the Room Information form in Layout view. Select all controls in the form, and apply the **Stacked Layout.**

i. Switch to Form view, and then save and close the form.

Create a Report

You will create a report based on the Speaker and Room Schedule query. You decide to use the Report Wizard to accomplish this task. You will also email the schedule to the presenters, so you will save the report as a PDF file.

a. Select the **Speaker and Room Schedule query** in the Navigation Pane as the record source for the report.

b. Activate the **Report Wizard,** and use the following options as you proceed through the wizard steps:

- Select all of the available fields for the report.
- View the data by Speakers.
- Accept LastName and FirstName as the grouping levels.
- Use **Date** as the primary sort field in ascending order.
- Accept the Stepped and Portrait options.

- Save the report as **Speaker Schedule.**
- Switch to Layout view, and apply the **Organic theme** to this report only.

c. Switch to Report view to determine whether all of the columns fit across the page. Switch to Layout view, and ensure that the column widths are adjusted accordingly.

d. Switch to Print Preview, and save the report as a PDF named **a04c1Speaker_LastFirst.**

e. Close the reader program that displays the PDF report, and return to Access. Close Print Preview. Save and close the report.

Add an Additional Field to the Query and the Report

You realize that the session start times were not included in the query. You add the field to the query and then create a new report with the Report Wizard to include the missing field.

a. Open the Speaker and Room Schedule query in Design view.

b. Add the **StartingTime field** from the Sessions table to the design grid, after the Date field. Run the query.

c. Save and close the query.

d. Click the **Speaker and Room Schedule query.** Activate the Report Wizard again and use the following options:

- Select all of the available fields for the report.
- View the data by Speakers.
- Use the LastName and FirstName fields as the grouping levels.
- Use **Date** as the primary sort field in ascending order.
- Use **StartingTime** as the secondary sort field in ascending order.
- Select the **Stepped** and **Portrait options.**
- Name the report **Speaker Schedule Revised.**
- Switch to Layout view and apply the **Facet theme** to this report only.

e. Adjust the widths of the columns and other controls so that all the data is visible and fits across the page. Switch to Report view to ensure that the adjustments were appropriate. Return to Layout view, and make any required changes.

f. Add spaces to the column heading labels so that all values display as two words where appropriate, for example, the label *LastName* should read **Last Name.** *RoomID* as **Room ID**, etc.

g. Save and close the report.

h. Close the database and exit Access. Based on your instructor's directions, submit the following:

a04c1NatConf_LastFirst

a04c1Speaker_LastFirst

Glossary

Control A text box, button, label, or other tool you use to add, edit, and display the data in a form or report.

Design view Enables you to change advanced design settings you cannot see in Layout view, such as removing a layout control.

Form A database object that is used to add data into or edit data in a table.

Form tool Used to create data entry forms for customers, employees, products, and other primary tables.

Form view A simplified interface primarily used for data entry; does not allow you to make changes to the layout.

Label Wizard Enables you to easily create mailing labels, name tags, and other specialized tags.

Layout control Provides guides to help keep controls aligned horizontally and vertically and give your form a uniform appearance.

Layout view Enables users to make changes to a layout while viewing the data in the form or report.

Multiple Items form Displays multiple records in a tabular layout similar to a table's Datasheet view, with more customization options.

Portable Document Format (PDF) A file type that was created for exchanging documents independent of software applications and operating system environment.

Print Preview Enables you to see exactly what the report will look like when it is printed.

Record source The table or query that supplies the records for a form or report.

Report A database document that outputs meaningful, professional-looking, formatted information from underlying tables or queries.

Report tool Used to instantly create a tabular report based on the table or query currently selected.

Report view Enables you to determine what a printed report will look like in a continuous page layout.

Report Wizard Prompts you for input and then uses your answers to generate a customized report.

Split form Combines two views of the same record source—one section is displayed in a stacked layout and the other section is displayed in a tabular layout.

Stacked layout Displays fields in a vertical column.

Tabular layout Displays fields horizontally.

Theme A defined set of colors, fonts, and graphics that can be applied to a form or report.

Appendix: Microsoft Office 2016 Specialist Access

Online Appendix materials can be found in the Student Resources located at www.pearsonhighered.com/exploring.

MOS Obj Number	Objective Text	Exploring Chapter	Exploring Section
1.0	**Create and Manage a Database**		
1.1	**Create and Modify Databases**		
1.1.1	create a blank desktop database	Introduction to Access	Creating a Database
1.1.2	create a database from a template	Introduction to Access	Creating a Database
1.1.3	create a database by using import objects or data from other sources	Tables and Queries in Relational Databases	Sharing Data
1.1.4	delete database objects	Creating and Using Professional Forms and Reports	Form Basics, Hands-On Exercise
1.2	**Manage Relationships and Keys**		
1.2.1	create and modify relationships	Tables and Queries in Relational Databases	Establishing Table Relationships
1.2.2	set the primary key	Tables and Queries in Relational Databases	Creating and Modifying Tables and Working with Data
1.2.3	enforce referential integrity	Tables and Queries in Relational Databases	Establishing Table Relationships
1.2.4	set foreign keys	Tables and Queries in Relational Databases	Establishing Table Relationships
1.2.5	view relationships	Tables and Queries in Relational Databases	Establishing Table Relationships
1.3	**Navigate through a Database**		
1.3.1	navigate specific records	Introduction to Access	Recognize Database Object Types
1.3.2	create and modify a navigation form	Creating and Using Professional Forms and Reports	Creating Forms Using Form Tools
1.3.3	set a form as the startup option	Analyzing and Improving Database Performance	Controlling Navigation
1.3.4	display objects in the Navigation Pane	Introduction to Access	Recognizing Database Object Types
1.3.5	change views of objects	Introduction to Access	Recognizing Database Object Types
1.4	**Protect and Maintain Databases**		
1.4.1	compact a database	Introduction to Access	Using Database Utilities
1.4.2	repair a database	Introduction to Access	Using Database Utilities
1.4.3	back up a database	Introduction to Access	Using Database Utilities
1.4.4	split a database	Introduction to Access	Using Database Utilities
1.4.5	encrypt a database with a password	Introduction to Access	Using Database Utilities
1.4.6	recover data from backup	Online Appendix	Online Appendix

MOS Obj Number	Objective Text	Exploring Chapter	Exploring Section
1.5 Print and Export Data			
1.5.1	print reports	Creating and Using Professional Forms and Reports	Using Report Views
1.5.2	print records	Creating and Using Professional Forms and Reports	Creating Forms Using Form Tools
1.5.3	save a databases as a template	Introduction to Access	Creating a Database
1.5.4	export objects to alternative formats	Exchanging Data Between Access and Other Applications	Exporting Data to Excel
2.0 Build Tables			
2.1 Create Tables			
2.1.1	create a table	Tables and Queries in Relational Databases	Creating and Modifying Tables, Working with Data
2.1.2	import data into tables	Tables and Queries in Relational Databases	Sharing Data
2.1.3	create linked tables from external sources	Tables and Queries in Relational Databases	Sharing Data
2.1.4	import tables from other databases	Tables and Queries in Relational Databases	Sharing Data
2.1.5	create a table from a template with application parts	Tables and Queries in Relational Databases	Creating a Database
2.2 Manage Tables			
2.2.4	rename tables	Introduction to Access	Recognizing Database Object Types
2.2.3	add table descriptions	Introduction to Access	Recognizing Database Object Types
2.2.2	add total rows	Tables and Queries in Relational Databases	Designing a Table
2.2.1	hide fields in tables	Tables and Queries in Relational Databases	Creating and Modifying Tables and Working with Data
2.3 Manage Records in Tables			
2.3.1	update records	Introduction to Access	Modifying Data in Table Datasheet View
2.3.2	add records	Introduction to Access	Adding Records to a Table
2.3.3	delete records	Introduction to Access	Deleting Records from a Table
2.3.4	append records from external data	Exchanging Data Between Access and Other Applications	Importing an Excel Spreadsheet
2.3.5	find and replace data	Introduction to Access	Working with Filters
2.3.6	sort records	Introduction to Access	Performing Sorts
2.3.7	filter records	Introduction to Access	Working with Filters
2.4 Create and Modify Fields			
2.4.1	add fields to tables	Tables and Queries in Relational Databases	Creating and Modifying Tables and Working with Data
2.4.2	add validation rules to fields	Tables and Queries in Relational Databases	Creating and Modifying Tables and Working with Data
2.4.3	change field captions	Tables and Queries in Relational Databases	Creating and Modifying Tables and Working with Data
2.4.4	change field sizes	Tables and Queries in Relational Databases	Creating and Modifying Tables and Working with Data

MOS Obj Number	Objective Text	Exploring Chapter	Exploring Section
2.4.5	change field data types	Tables and Queries in Relational Databases	Creating and Modifying Tables and Working with Data
2.4.6	configure fields to auto-increment	Tables and Queries in Relational Databases	Creating and Modifying Tables and Working with Data
2.4.7	set default values	Tables and Queries in Relational Databases	Creating and Modifying Tables and Working with Data
2.4.8	using input masks	Tables and Queries in Relational Databases	Creating and Modifying Tables and Working with Data
2.4.9	delete fields	Tables and Queries in Relational Databases	Creating and Modifying Tables and Working with Data

3.0 Create Queries

3.1 Create a Query

MOS Obj Number	Objective Text	Exploring Chapter	Exploring Section
3.1.1	run a query	Tables and Queries in Relational Databases	Running, Copying, and Modifying a Query
3.1.2	create a crosstab query	Moving Beyond the Select Query	Summarizing Data with a Crosstab Query
3.1.3	create a parameter query	Reducing Errors and Extracting Better Information	Customizing Output Based on User Input
3.1.4	create an action query	Moving Beyond the Select Query	Determining When to Use an Action Query
3.1.5	create a multi-table query	Tables and Queries in Relational Databases	Creating a Multitable Query
3.1.6	save a query	Tables and Queries in Relational Databases	Creating a Multitable Query

3.2 Modify a Query

MOS Obj Number	Objective Text	Exploring Chapter	Exploring Section
3.2.1	rename a query	Tables and Queries in Relational Databases	Running, Copying, and Modifying a Query
3.2.2	add fields	Tables and Queries in Relational Databases	Creating and Modifying Tables and Working with Data
3.2.3	remove fields	Tables and Queries in Relational Databases	Creating and Modifying Tables and Working with Data
3.2.4	hide fields	Tables and Queries in Relational Databases	Creating and Modifying Tables and Working with Data
3.2.5	sort data within queries	Tables and Queries in Relational Databases	Understanding Query Sort Order
3.2.6	format fields within queries	Tables and Queries in Relational Databases	Creating and Modifying Tables and Working with Data

3.3 Create Calculated Fields and Grouping within Queries

MOS Obj Number	Objective Text	Exploring Chapter	Exploring Section
3.3.1	add calculated fields	Tables and Queries in Relational Databases	Modifying a Multitable Query
3.3.2	set filtering criteria	Tables and Queries in Relational Databases	Specifying Query Criteria for Different Data Types
3.3.3	group and summarize data	Tables and Queries in Relational Databases	Specifying Query Criteria for Different Data Types
3.3.4	group data by using comparison operators	Tables and Queries in Relational Databases	Specifying Query Criteria for Different Data Types
3.3.5	group data by using arithmetic and logical operators	Tables and Queries in Relational Databases	Specifying Query Criteria for Different Data Types

4.0 Create Forms

4.1 Create a Form

MOS Obj Number	Objective Text	Exploring Chapter	Exploring Section
4.1.1	create a form	Creating and Using Professional Forms and Reports	Creating Forms Using Form Tools
4.1.2	create a form from a template with application parts	Creating and Using Professional Forms and Reports	Creating Forms Using Form Tools
4.1.3	save a form	Creating and Using Professional Forms and Reports	Creating Forms Using Form Tools
4.2	**Configure Form Controls**		
4.2.1	move form controls	Creating and Using Professional Forms and Reports	Form Basics, Hands-On Exercise
4.2.2	add form controls	Creating and Using Professional Forms and Reports	Modifying Forms
4.2.3	modify data sources	Creating and Using Professional Forms and Reports	Creating Forms Using Form Tools
4.2.4	remove form controls	Creating and Using Professional Forms and Reports	Creating Forms Using Form Tools
4.2.5	set form control properties	Creating and Using Professional Forms and Reports	Creating Forms Using Form Tools
4.2.6	manage labels	Creating and Using Professional Forms and Reports	Modifying Forms
4.2.7	add sub-forms	Creating and Using Professional Forms and Reports	Creating Forms Using Form Tools
4.3	**Format a Form**		
4.3.1	modify tab order	Advanced Forms and Reports	Setting the Tab Order
4.3.2	configure print settings	Creating and Using Professional Forms and Reports	Creating Forms Using Form Tools
4.3.3	sort records by form field	Creating and Using Professional Forms and Reports	Sorting Records in a Form
4.3.4	apply a theme	Creating and Using Professional Forms and Reports	Modifying Forms
4.3.5	control form positioning	Online Appendix	Online Appendix
4.3.6	insert backgrounds	Creating and Using Professional Forms and Reports	Working with a Form Layout
4.3.7	insert headers and footers	Creating and Using Professional Forms and Reports	Modifying Forms
4.3.8	insert images	Creating and Using Professional Forms and Reports	Working with a Form Layout
5.0	**Create Reports**		
5.1	**Create a Report**		
5.1.1	create a report based on the query or table	Creating and Using Professional Forms and Reports	Creating Reports Using Report Tools
5.1.2	create a report in Design view	Creating and Using Professional Forms and Reports	Creating Reports Using Report Tools
5.1.3	create a report by using a wizard	Creating and Using Professional Forms and Reports	Creating Reports Using Report Tools
5.2	**Configure Report Controls**		
5.2.1	group and sort fields	Creating and Using Professional Forms and Reports	Creating Reports Using Report Tools

MOS Obj Number	Objective Text	Exploring Chapter	Exploring Section
5.2.2	modify data sources	Advanced Techniques	Using an SQL SELECT Statement as a Record Source
5.2.3	add report controls	Creating and Using Professional Forms and Reports	Modifying a Report
5.2.4	add and modify labels	Creating and Using Professional Forms and Reports	Modifying a Report
5.3 Format a Report			
5.3.1	format a report into multiple columns	Creating and Using Professional Forms and Reports	Modifying a Report
5.3.2	add calculated fields	Creating and Using Professional Forms and Reports	Creating Reports Using Report Tools
5.3.3	control report positioning	Creating and Using Professional Forms and Reports	Modifying a Report
5.3.4	format report elements	Creating and Using Professional Forms and Reports	Modifying a Report
5.3.5	change report orientation	Creating and Using Professional Forms and Reports	Modifying a Report
5.3.6	insert header and footer information	Creating and Using Professional Forms and Reports	Modifying a Report
5.3.7	insert images	Creating and Using Professional Forms and Reports	Modifying a Report
5.3.8	apply a theme	Creating and Using Professional Forms and Reports	Modifying a Report

Index